THE OXFOR

# EUROPEAN ISLAM

# THE OXFORD HANDBOOK OF
# EUROPEAN ISLAM

*Edited by*
JOCELYNE CESARI

# OXFORD
UNIVERSITY PRESS

Great Clarendon Street, Oxford, OX2 6DP,
United Kingdom

Oxford University Press is a department of the University of Oxford.
It furthers the University's objective of excellence in research, scholarship,
and education by publishing worldwide. Oxford is a registered trade mark of
Oxford University Press in the UK and in certain other countries

© Oxford University Press 2015

The moral rights of the authors have been asserted

First published 2015
First published in paperback 2016

All rights reserved. No part of this publication may be reproduced, stored in
a retrieval system, or transmitted, in any form or by any means, without the
prior permission in writing of Oxford University Press, or as expressly permitted
by law, by licence or under terms agreed with the appropriate reprographics
rights organization. Enquiries concerning reproduction outside the scope of the
above should be sent to the Rights Department, Oxford University Press, at the
address above

You must not circulate this work in any other form
and you must impose this same condition on any acquirer

Published in the United States of America by Oxford University Press
198 Madison Avenue, New York, NY 10016, United States of America

British Library Cataloguing in Publication Data
Data available

Library of Congress Cataloging in Publication Data
Data available

ISBN 978-0-19-960797-6 (Hbk.)
ISBN 978-0-19-877932-2 (Pbk.)

Links to third party websites are provided by Oxford in good faith and
for information only. Oxford disclaims any responsibility for the materials
contained in any third party website referenced in this work.

# Acknowledgements

This book is the outcome of several convergent efforts. First and foremost, I am grateful to all the authors who have worked relentlessly with me to create more than a juxtaposition of case studies, i.e. a consistent critical analysis of the knowledge on Islam and Muslims in Western and Eastern Europe. I also would like to thank Amanda Garrett and Aline Longstale who assisted me in the editorial work with great competence and patience.

# CONTENTS

*List of Figures* xi
*List of Tables* xiii
*List of Maps* xv
*List of Contributors* xvii

Introduction 1
JOCELYNE CESARI

## PART I  ISLAM AS A POSTCOLONIAL, POST-SECOND WORLD WAR RELIGION IN EUROPE

1. France 23
   JENNIFER A. SELBY

2. The United Kingdom 64
   SOPHIE GILLIAT-RAY

3. Germany 104
   RIEM SPIELHAUS

4. The Netherlands 158
   MAURITS S. BERGER

5. Belgium 222
   NADIA FADIL, FARID EL ASRI, AND SARAH BRACKE

## PART II  THE ARRIVAL OF ISLAM AS POST-1974 MIGRATION

6. Italy 265
   CHANTAL SAINT-BLANCAT

7. Spain  311
ANA I. PLANET CONTRERAS

8. Greece  350
VENETIA EVERGETI, PANOS HATZIPROKOPIOU, AND NICOLAS PREVELAKIS

9. Scandinavian Countries  391
GARBI SCHMIDT AND JONAS OTTERBECK

# PART III  THE OLD EUROPEAN LAND OF ISLAM

10. Bosnia and Herzegovina  429
AHMET ALIBAŠIĆ

11. Albanians' Islam(s)  475
ISA BLUMI AND GËZIM KRASNIQI

12. Russia  517
STÉPHANE A. DUDOIGNON

13. Bulgaria  565
ANTONINA ZHELYAZKOVA

# PART IV  ISLAM AND EUROPEAN SECULARISM

14. The Institutionalization of Islam in Europe  619
SILVIO FERRARI AND ROSSELLA BOTTONI

15. Shariah in Europe  656
MATHIAS ROHE

16. Hijab  701
JENNIFER A. SELBY

# PART V  ISLAM AND EUROPEAN POLITICS

17. Islamophobia 745
    AYHAN KAYA

18. Radicalization 770
    DANIELA PISOIU

    Conclusion: Is There a European Islam? 802
    JOCELYNE CESARI

*Names Index* 807
*Subject Index* 815

# List of Figures

| | | |
|---|---|---|
| 1.1 | Immigration in France by country, 2008 | 26 |
| 8.1 | Apprehensions of undocumented aliens in Greece, 2002–11 | 365 |
| 9.1 | Number of Muslims in Sweden: estimation | 396 |
| 11.1 | Importance of religion among Albanians in the Balkans | 493 |
| 11.2 | Attended religious service among Albanians in the Balkans | 493 |
| 13.1 | Organizational structure of the Muslim confession in Bulgaria | 591 |
| 16.1 | Poster of the SVP with woman wearing niqab, 2009. © Schweizerzeit Verlags AG | 727 |

# List of Tables

| | | |
|---|---|---|
| 1.1 | Unemployment in France based on nationality | 28 |
| 1.2 | Shifts in the education levels of immigrants and non-immigrants | 30 |
| 3.1 | Persons in Germany from Muslim majority countries according to religion and region of origin (%) | 111 |
| 3.2 | Religious affiliation of individuals with a *Migrationshintergrund* (migrant background) in Germany according to their country of origin (%) | 113 |
| 3.3 | Muslims in Germany according to denomination (%) | 115 |
| 6.1 | Foreign citizens in Italy from Muslim majority countries | 269 |
| 7.1 | Immigration to Spain from Muslim countries | 316 |
| 7.2 | Employees in Spain of Muslim origin | 316 |
| 7.3 | Religious definition in Spain | 337 |
| 8.1 | Key features of the five most numerous nationalities of Muslim migrants in Greece, 2001 | 367 |
| 9.1 | Foreign citizens in Denmark 1965–75 | 394 |
| 9.2 | Foreign citizens and descendants in Denmark 1980–2005 | 395 |
| 9.3 | Immigration of some size to Sweden from Muslim majority countries (absolute numbers) | 397 |
| 9.4 | Total number of immigrants to Norway (selected countries) | 398 |
| 9.5 | Employment rates among immigrants and the Danish majority population 2009 | 404 |
| 13.1 | Population according to denomination and census years (1910–2011) | 570 |
| 13.2 | Educational structure of larger ethnic communities in Bulgaria—persons over 20 (in %) | 573 |
| 13.3 | Number and percentage of Bulgaria's minority populations 1992/2001/2011 | 574 |
| 14.1 | Comparative table on the institutionalization of Islam in Europe | 644 |
| 17.1 | Anti-Muslim statements (agreement in %) | 752 |

## List of Maps

| | | |
|---|---|---|
| 6.1 | Muslim places of worship in Italy by region | 278 |
| 6.2 | Places of worship in Italy affiliated to the Union of Islamic Organizations and Communities in Italy | 286 |
| 6.3 | Places of worship in Italy affiliated to the Islamic Confederation of Italy | 287 |
| 7.1 | Islamic communities in Spain registered with the Ministry of Justice | 320 |

# List of Contributors

**Ahmet Alibašić** is Assistant Professor at the Faculty of Islamic Studies at the University of Sarajevo and director of the Center for Advanced Studies, Sarajevo.

**Farid El Asri** is an Anthropologist (UCL), Assistant Professor, Sciences-Po Rabat, International University of Rabat, and Researcher and Coordinator of the Interdisciplinary Centre for the Study of Islam in the Contemporary World (CISMOC), Université Catholique de Louvain, Belgium.

**Maurits S. Berger** holds the chair of Islam in the Contemporary West at the Center for Religious Studies at Leiden University, and is a senior research associate with the Clingendael Institute for International Relations in The Hague.

**Isa Blumi** is Associate Professor of Middle East and Global History, Georgia State University, and Visiting Professor of International History, Graduate Institute, Geneva.

**Rossella Bottoni** is a Researcher in History and Systems of Church–State Relations, Catholic University, Milan.

**Sarah Bracke** is Associate Research Professor of Sociology at Ghent University, Belgium. In 2014–15 she worked on a project entitled *Gender and Sexuality in Western Europe's 'Muslim Question'* at the Minda de Gunzburg Center for European Studies, Harvard University.

**Jocelyne Cesari** is Director of the Islam in the West program at Harvard University and Senior Research Fellow at the Berkley Center for Religion, Peace and World Politics at Georgetown University, USA. Her most recent books are *The Awakening of Muslim Democracy: Religion, Modernity and the State* (Cambridge University Press, 2014) *and Why the West Fears Islam, Exploration of Muslims in Liberal Democracies* (Palgrave Macmillan, 2013).

**Stéphane A. Dudoignon** is a Senior Research Fellow at the National Centre for Scientific Research and a Lecturer at the School of Advanced Studies in Social Sciences in Paris, France.

**Venetia Evergeti** is a Visiting Research Fellow at the University of Surrey, UK.

**Nadia Fadil** is Assistant Professor at the Katholieke Universiteit Leuven, Belgium.

**Silvio Ferrari** is a Professor of Canon Law at the University of Milan, Italy.

**Sophie Gilliat-Ray** is Professor in Religious and Theological Studies at Cardiff University and Director for the Centre for the Study of Islam in the UK.

**Panos Hatziprokopiou** is Assistant Professor at Aristotle University of Thessaloniki, Greece.

**Ayhan Kaya** is Professor of Politics, and Jean Monnet Chair of European Politics of Interculturalism, at the Department of International Relations, Istanbul Bilgi University, Turkey.

**Gëzim Krasniqi** is a Ph.D. candidate and research assistant at the University of Edinburgh, Scotland.

**Jonas Otterbeck** is an Associate Professor of Islamic Studies, Lund University, Sweden.

**Daniela Pisoiu** is a Researcher at the Institute for Peace Research and Security Policy at the University of Hamburg, Germany.

**Ana I. Planet Contreras** is Professor of Arabic and Islamic Studies, at Universidad Autónoma de Madrid, Spain.

**Nicolas Prevelakis** is Assistant Director of Curricular Development at the Center for Hellenic Studies and Lecturer on Social Studies, Harvard University, USA.

**Mathias Rohe** is Director of the Erlangen Centre for Islam & Law in Europe, Friedrich-Alexander Universität Erlangen-Nuernberg, Germany.

**Chantal Saint-Blancat** is Associate Professor of Sociology at the University of Padova, Italy.

**Garbi Schmidt** is a Professor of Intercultural Studies at University of Roskilde, Denmark.

**Jennifer A. Selby** is an Associate Professor of Religious Studies at Memorial University of Newfoundland, Canada.

**Riem Spielhaus** is a Researcher at the Erlangen Centre for Islam & Law in Europe, Friedrich-Alexander Universität Erlangen-Nürnberg, Germany.

**Antonina Zhelyazkova** is Chairperson of the Board of Directors at the International Centre for Minority Studies and Intercultural Relations, Sofia, Bulgaria.

# INTRODUCTION

## JOCELYNE CESARI

For centuries, Muslim countries and Europe have engaged one another through theological dialogues, diplomatic missions, political rivalries, and power struggles. In the last thirty years, however, due in large part to globalization and migration, what was previously an engagement *across* national and cultural boundaries has increasingly become an internalized encounter *within* Europe itself. The debate is no longer one of distant and isolated communities, but rather one of endogenous, face-to-face cultural and religious interactions. Questions of the hijab in schools, freedom of expression in the wake of the Danish cartoon crisis, and the role of shariah have come to the forefront of contemporary European discourse. The recurrent question nowadays is: Are Islamic religious principles compatible with liberal secular European values?

## WHY A HANDBOOK?

Over the last two decades, the amount of literature exploring the issues of Islam in Europe has grown exponentially. A substantial number of publications from fields as diverse as history, sociology, economics, and anthropology have emerged in an attempt to make sense of this ever-evolving and politically emotive debate.

There has also been a corresponding growth in the number of edited volumes produced on the subject. Most of these volumes have been limited in scope, however, and tend to be either collections of essays or the proceedings of academic conferences.[1]

Edited volumes or single-authored books address multiple subjects such as continuity and change in the making of Muslim identities, the development of mosques and

---

[1] Abumalham 1995; Antes and Hewer 1994; Anwar 1983, 1984, 1985; Bistolfi and Zabbal 1995; Garaudy and Zughayb 1984; Gerholm and Lithman 1988; van Koningsveld 1995; Lewis and Schnapper 1994; Maréchal 2002; Metcalfe 1996; Nielsen 1987, 1992; Nielsen and Centre for Research in Ethnic Relations 1999; Nonneman et al. 1996; Renaerts 1994; Shadid and van Koningsveld 1991, 1995, 1996; Speelman et al. 1991; Vertovec and Peach 1997.

Muslim associations, the struggle to establish Muslim schools in the European context (Doomernik 1991), and social responses to the establishment of Muslim institutions (Rath 1996, 2001, 2005; Sunier and Meyer 1996; Waardenburg 1991, 2001; Esch and Roovers 1986). Others have focused on specific social or institutional aspects of Islam in Europe, such as issues of Muslim youth (Vertovec et al. 1998), political participation (Shadid and van Koningsveld 1996; Klausen 2005; Cesari 2013), legal questions and secularism (Borras et al. 1998; Ferrari 1996; Ferrari and Bradney 2000; Foblets 1996; Nielsen 1979, 1987; Rohe 2007; Cesari et al. 2005), conversion (Allievi 1999), the hijab as a cultural and political phenomenon (Coppes 1994), and radicalization of Muslims (Pargeter 2008; Colsaert 2008). Despite these publications, an examination of the current literature reveals a dearth of fully fledged international comparisons that empirically investigate these issues across national borders on the basis of a single research design. This Handbook has the ambition to fill this gap by presenting a systematic and cross-national analysis.

For this reason, the different contributions in this volume present a comprehensive approach to the multiple and changing ways Islam has been studied across European countries. Instead of being another collection of essays on different countries or another book with a specific focus, like women or radicalization, the Handbook aims to be extensive and analytical. In the first part, it addresses the state of knowledge of Islam and Muslims within a selection of European countries, while presenting a critical review of the most up-to-date data and survey findings specific to each country. In the second part, it analyses issues of secularism, radicalization, Islamophobia, shariah, and hijab across European countries.

Each national chapter provides a review of the contemporary literature on Islam and Muslims in the country, focusing on the most common topics emerging from this literature, i.e. immigration issues, socio-economic status, religion and secularism, political participation, and international constraints. The selected countries are representative of the three main locations of Muslims in Europe: the countries with postcolonial migration like France or the UK, the new immigration countries like Italy and Spain, and the historical lands of Muslims in Europe where they are either minorities (Bulgaria, Russia) or constitute the majority (Albania and Bosnia). The thematic chapters address secularism, radicalization, shariah, hijab, and Islamophobia with the goal of synthesizing different national discussions into a more comparative theoretical framework.

On one hand, the originality of the Handbook lies in the analytical review of the knowledge amassed on Islam and Muslims per country and across countries; and on the other hand, in bringing together the analyses of all these issues in one comprehensive publication. The challenge for all contributors, either per country or per thematic issue, was to ensure that the material in the Handbook would be relevant beyond the specific information or facts it conveys. In other words, each chapter is an attempt to balance cutting-edge assessment with the knowledge that the content itself will eventually be superseded by events. That is why all the contributors have produced interpretations with the hope that they will still be relevant to understanding Islam in Europe in the near future. The following trends emerged from our collective effort: the opposite evolution of the research agendas in Western and Eastern Europe, the persistent influence of immigration and socio-economic status on the status of Islam in Europe, the relevance of the public culture on religion specific to each country, and the importance of the international context. Finally, the most challenging common point is conceptual and methodological and relates to the ways of approaching Islam in different national contexts.

## The Inverted Trajectories of the Research Agendas in Western and Eastern Europe

The different contributions highlight opposite and convergent moves within the scholarly discourse regarding Muslims in Europe. In the postcolonial countries, Muslims have been investigated in the 1960s and 1970s through the lens of immigration studies. Similarly, for countries of recent immigration like Spain or Italy since the 1980s, immigration studies dominate the current research agenda. For the older immigration countries, like France or the UK, the cultural and religious dimensions of the research became predominant in the 1980s. After 9/11, both immigration and cultural studies have been redefined by security concerns and the influence of international constraints.

For this reason, all chapters on Muslims in Western Europe start with an analysis of the immigration cycles and studies on the statistics, numbers, and immigration policies related to the presence of Muslims. They all show that the research on Islam is influenced by the diverse political agendas of integration. In other words, most of the academic production in Western Europe has followed the integration cycles of Muslim immigrants in an attempt to provide data that can be helpful to policy-makers. This has been done to the point that in some countries, like Germany, the state has become the major agent of the production of knowledge on Islam and Muslims. Even when the influence is not so direct, or the research is not sponsored by public institutions, it nevertheless addresses political questions such as: Is Islam compatible with democracy and secularism? What are the causes of radicalization among Muslims in Europe?

Interestingly, the research motivated by more 'scholarly' interests—like comparing the religiosity of Muslims across ethnic or immigrant backgrounds to other religious groups in Europe—is much more sparse. So, despite the ongoing debate on the visibility of Islamic activities in public spaces, there is still very little information on the daily practices of Muslims in ways similar to the information that exists for other religious groups. In this regard, sociology of religion, a specifically European social science, still remains marginal when it comes to Muslims and production of data that can be compared to those existing for Protestants, Catholics, or Jews. At the same time, ethnographies of Muslim communities in multiple localities have mushroomed but do not provide a clear picture of the most significant trends in terms of acculturation or social practices of Muslims.

In Eastern Europe, the opposite shift from religious to immigration studies is observable. Due to the historical legacy of the Ottoman Empire in the Balkans, Islam was included in religious studies or orientalism and/or as part of ethnic studies or folklore under communist regimes. As in Western Europe, the ideological influence on research agendas is strong but manifests itself differently. During the communist era, 'legitimate' domains of studies were not connected to any sociological investigation of Islam since Muslim groups were treated as 'ethnic' minorities under the rubric of folklore. Therefore, Islam as a religion was studied in philosophy or history departments while the reality of Muslims was documented under 'ethnic studies'. The influx of immigrants from Muslim countries into Eastern Europe has led to new fields of investigation on immigration, primarily dominated by political science and external research agencies. The chapter on Bulgaria shows, for example, the increasing role of the European Union in defining new research agendas on the questions of immigration and cultural diversity. More generally a gap has emerged between studies on Islam and ethnic minorities on one hand, and studies on new immigrants on the other. The research on Islam presented in the chapter on Greece is a paradigmatic case of this gap.

## Immigration, Integration, and Social Status

Issues such as discrimination, postcolonial identity, adaptation, and assimilation have dominated the research agenda in Western Europe. The immigration policies of the post-Second World War era brought the first wave of Muslims to Europe, but there have been many phases of Muslim immigration to Europe ever since, each one characterized by its own unique and diverse set of political and social challenges. Today, we see this diversity embodied in the newest wave of Muslim refugees from Bosnia, Iraq, and Somalia to Western Europe, as well as in the increasing immigration to countries that had previously never received large numbers of Muslim immigrants, such as Greece, Spain, and Italy, and also to Eastern European countries that all have significant Muslim minorities or are Muslim-majority countries themselves, like Bosnia, Albania, and Russia.

Most Muslim immigrants have come to Western Europe from former colonies of European countries as a source of low-skilled labour. As such, they have often lacked the resources and education necessary for success in mainstream European society. Such disparities, combined with racial and religious discrimination in the workplace, have consistently placed Muslims on the bottom rung of the European economic and social ladder. Adding to the problem, Western economies have changed their policies in the past few decades and now offer fewer entry-level or working-class jobs, especially to new immigrants. All chapters examine the economic disparities between European Muslims and non-Muslims and shed light on the ways in which this inequality has affected current political debates on national identity and immigration in the various countries covered by the Handbook.

By investigating socio-economic status over a broader range than simply Muslim groups, the authors of the different national chapters have compared Muslims with other immigrant groups of non-European extraction who face similar challenges of integration. For this reason, one common theme across the chapters indirectly sheds light on what might be described as a 'Muslim underclass'. This controversial term refers to less social mobility and the persistence of discrimination, even when the level of education or resources of Muslims are comparable to other immigrant groups. In other words, discrimination seems to exist for immigrants or citizens from a Muslim background. In this regard, one of the outcomes of the Handbook investigation is to show that the concept of 'underclass' needs clarification and deserves a more systematic and comparative research across European countries.

In the same vein, the different chapters on Islam in Western Europe show an increasing culturalization of immigration and citizenship politics. The 'Islamic Problem' as phrased by media and politicians weighs heavily on the design of immigration and integration policies. Or, to say it differently, since September 2001 'the radicalized, "non-Western" disenfranchised, held politically responsible for the systemic changes of neoliberal globalization to European labor markets in the 1990s, have been fused with suspect Muslim individuals or groups. Culturally unassimilated, ideologically inassimilable, and transnationally implicated as disloyal, the "racial politics of the War on Terror" has produced "intolerable subjects".'[2]

The rise of the Islamic Problem is with no doubt due to the fact that Muslims stand at the core of three major social 'problems'—immigration; class and economic integration; ethnicity and multiculturalism. Therefore, all chapters on Western Europe show how the categories of 'immigrant' and 'Muslim' overlap.[3]

In the eastern part of Europe, the 'Islamic Problem' is not related (yet) to immigration but to the memory of Ottoman domination and to the specifics of the communist era. Muslim groups are considered the illegitimate 'heirs' or remnants of Ottoman domination which until now is very negatively depicted in the various national narratives. For this reason, Islam has been under-studied in history and philosophy departments. Under communist regimes, Muslims were apprehended as ethnic minorities or 'folkorized', while the acquisition of demographics or socio-economic data was systematically neglected or biased.

## Religion in Public Space

All contributors explore the reality of Islam in Europe in the broader context of the status of religion in each European country. It is these very precepts and attitudes towards

---

[2] Alana Lentin and Gavin Titley, 'The Crisis of "Multiculturalism" in Europe: Mediated Minarets, Intolerable Subjects', *European Journal of Cultural Studies* 15(2) (April 2012): 124.

[3] In the USA, 'the prototypical immigrant is a low-skilled Mexican or Central American worker rather than a conservative Muslim. Of the 15.5 million legal immigrants who entered the USA between 1989 and 2004, only 1.2 million were from predominantly Muslim countries. There was a sharp drop from more than 100,000 per year prior to 2002 down to approximately 60,000 in 2003, but this recovered somewhat to 90,000 in 2004. Immigration in the USA is thus a topic in which the issues of Islam and terrorism are at best marginal issues.' US Office of Immigration Statistics, *2004 Yearbook of Immigration Statistics*, January 2006: 13, <http://www.dhs.gov/xlibrary/assets/statistics/yearbook/2004/Yearbook2004.pdf>, accessed 27 October 2012. Jocelyne Cesari, 'Securitization and Religious Divides in Europe: Muslims in Western Europe After 9/11', GSRL-Paris and Harvard University, 1 June 2006.

religion overall (and not just Islam) that have often been the greatest obstacle to the integration and assimilation of Muslims in Europe.

European secularism has traditionally dictated that state interactions with religious institutions display neutrality. There has been much diversity in how this principle has been applied, from the official establishment of religion in England to the radical separation of church and state in France. The first principle of secularity, differentiation of religion and politics, does not equate to the separation of church and state. If this were the case, France would be the only secular country in Europe. Rather, it refers to differentiation *and* cooperation between church and state.

As analysed by Silvio Ferrari and Rossella Botoni in Chapter 14, differentiation takes three main forms across Europe. The first form includes the existence of a state religion as well as the extension of rights to other religious groups, as is the case for the UK and Scandinavian countries. The second form entails formal agreements of cooperation between state and religious institutions, as is the case in Belgium, Germany, Spain, Italy, and the Netherlands. The third form is the separation between state and religious institutions, as is the case for France.

Cooperation between the state and religious institutions is also implemented in different ways: either the state provides for the teaching of religion in public schools, grants religious organizations free access to public-owned media, or gives direct/indirect funding to religious institutions.[4] Usually, religious organizations must comply with specific state requirements in order to receive this conditional support. For example, religious groups must organize local and national representative bodies to serve as counterparts to state institutions. In countries where a denominational teaching of religion is offered in public schools, as is the case in Germany and Spain, the religious community is required to design a central religious authority that serves as an interlocutor with the state. This authority gives credentials to teachers of religion in public schools, cooperates with state agencies to train the teachers, and approves curricula. For groups with strong religious infrastructure, like the Catholic Church, such requirements are easy to fulfil. But for others, like Muslims, these institutions have often been built from scratch.

Due to these particular circumstances, facilitating the cooperation between the state and Muslim groups has been a common concern of European governments and has led to the creation of Muslim representative bodies in Belgium, Spain, and France. For state agents, these bodies are aimed at reducing the gap between the political and legal status enjoyed by other religious groups and Muslims. They also are seen as a way to assuage feelings of discrimination that could potentially fuel Islamic radicalism and, ultimately, to ensure that the leadership of Muslim organizations falls into the hands of 'moderates'.[5]

---

[4] Gerhard Robbers, 'State and Church in the European Union', in Gerhard Robbers (ed.), *State and Church in the European Union* (Baden-Baden: Nomos, 2005).

[5] Joel S. Fetzer and J. Christopher Soper, 'Explaining and Accommodation of Muslim Religious Practices in France, Britain and Germany', paper presented at the Muslims in Western Europe Politics Conference, Bloomington, Indiana, 22–4 September 2005; Jonathan Laurence (ed.), *The Emancipation of Europe's Muslims: The State's Role in Minority Integration* (Princeton: Princeton University Press, 2012).

Interestingly, this institutional integration of Islam within the dominant framework of European secularism shows the willingness—even the eagerness in some cases—of major Muslim organizations to cooperate with the state. However, such cooperation is rarely presented in the public discourse as a positive sign of Muslim integration within secular cultures, and the dominant rhetoric continues to describe Islam in opposition to secularism.

At a deeper and even less explored level, the state has become an active agent in reshaping Islam by creating new Islamic institutions and leaders. Those leaders are state-appointed or bureaucratic leaders who often compete or conflict with other authorities that derive their authority from other sources, such as scholarly expertise or transnational networks.

Yet, despite the differing legal definitions of the status of religion in society, a common feature of modern European life has been the increasing illegitimacy of the role of religion in the public space. This trend has often found itself at odds with Islamic immigration and Muslims, who have come to Europe with their own understanding of church–state relations and the role of religion. Several symbolic issues, from the hijab and the burqini to minarets (see Chapter 16 on 'Hijab' by Jennifer Selby), positions on homosexuality, and various family issues, have led to controversial and heated debates within the various European nations examined in this Handbook. For this reason, the hijab and other contested issues, like Islamic law, have been addressed in greater length in thematic chapters.

The recognition of Islamic law within existing legal systems, alongside the concern that specific subcultures can stifle individual rights, is another example of the tension between political orders and Muslim communities. The debate was set in motion in February 2008 by the declaration of the Archbishop of Canterbury approving the inclusion of shariah principles within European legislations.[6] Like the term Muslim, shariah has become a construct used in political debates to oppose Islam to Western democratic principles. The construct operates on the historical and political decontextualization of shariah as a fixed medieval set of laws. It also projects the situation of some Muslim-majority countries into Europe.

In most Muslim-majority countries, shariah is confined to family law, although there has recently been an expansion of shariah to areas of criminal law (*hudud*)—including stoning to death and harsh corporal punishments—in countries such as Mauritania or Afghanistan.[7]

The concern about the intolerant use of shariah in some Muslim states is transferred to Europe without taking into account the completely different context in which references

---

[6] 'Shari'a law "could have UK role"', *BBC News*, 4 July 2008 <http://news.bbc.co.uk/2/hi/uk_news/7488790.stm>, accessed 24 July 2012.

[7] It is worth mentioning that the claim by some political actors in Muslim-majority countries that divine law is comprehensive and therefore a source of constitutional law diverges from the traditional perception of politics in the Islamic tradition, which is based on the distinction of shariah from *siyasah* (politics). See Cesari, Jocelyne, *The Awakening of Muslim Democracy: Religion, Modernity and the State* (Cambridge: Cambridge University Press, 2014).

to shariah operate. Where there is democratic constitutionalism, the debate does not stem from constitutional issues. Contrary to the widespread belief that Muslims in the West seek the inclusion of shariah in the constitutions of European countries, most of the surveys discussed in the Handbook show that Muslims are quite satisfied with the secular nature of European political regimes. When Muslims agitate for change, they engage in politics and the democratic process, utilizing mainstream parties and institutions.[8] This does not mean, however, that they renounce Islamic principles and legal rules as a guide or structure for their daily lives.[9] If the fear of *hudud* or (Islamic criminal law) is not well-founded, there are still questions regarding the compatibility of shariah with legal pluralism.

It is within this changing framework of the pluralization of family law, and the growing importance of contract and arbitration, that Islamic norms may find a place within European legal references. Additionally, the right to cultural identity, which is a part of European legislation,[10] can be used to justify and promulgate the recognition of Islamic norms within European legal frameworks. There is, however, a restrictive condition on the possible recognition of shariah within legal pluralism, which is that Islamic norms should not contradict the basic principles of equality between individuals. These clashes have surfaced in countries where arbitration procedures are permitted. It is therefore not surprising that these procedures have become the focus of political concern about shariah misuse.

Mathias Rohe has closely examined the literature and jurisprudence of several key European countries in order to ascertain the arguments used by the courts and by Muslims when conflicts arise between the two.[11] The plethora of national laws in Europe and the diversity among Muslim groups make comparison difficult, but he found a general trend of recognizing foreign law. This means that legal systems distinguish between national and foreign jurisprudence, therefore giving the possibility to residents to utilize their national laws. In these situations, the country of residence applies foreign law even if it is discriminatory. It is worth noting that Islamic laws on marriage, divorce, and custody of children that are applied in the European context differ greatly according to the status of Islam in the legal system of the country of origin.[12]

---

[8] Zsolt Nyiri, 'Muslims in Europe: Basis for Greater Understanding Already Exists', *Gallup Polling 2007*. <http://www.gallup.com/corporate/115/About-Gallup.aspx>, accessed 12 January 2011.

[9] Jocelyne Cesari, *Muslims in the West After 9/11: Religion, Law and Politics* (New York: Routledge, 2010).

[10] Cesari, *Muslims in the West After 9/11*, 13. The right to freedom of thought, as promulgated in the European Convention on Human Rights, relates to convictions and modes of behaviour which are central to personal identity.

[11] Mary E. Hess, '2010 Presidential Address: Learning Religion and Religiously Learning Amid Global Cultural Flows', *Religious Education* 106(4) (2011): 360–77.

[12] In the Sunni tradition, four schools of jurisprudence have codified Islamic law: Shafi'i, Hanafi, Hanbali, and Maleki. With the emergence of nation-states at the end of the Ottoman Empire, each new country has, most of the time, adopted the school of jurisprudence of the majority Muslim population as the source for civil law while continuously reforming it. See Knut S. Vikor, *Between God and the Sultan: A History of Islamic Law* (New York: Oxford University Press, 2005).

## International Constraints

The attacks of 9/11 in the USA—and the Madrid and London bombings of 2004 and 2005 in particular—have raised questions about the potential links between Western Muslims, radical Islam, and terrorism. In recent years, scholars and journalists have begun to explore the ways in which international, politicized Islam has influenced (or has been perceived to have influenced) Muslims in Europe (see Chapter 18 by Daniele Pisoiu).

Others, however, have tried to explore the anti-Islamic backlash, often known as Islamophobia, which has taken hold in many quarters of Europe. It should be noted that the term 'Islamophobia' emerged as early as 1997 during the discussions in Britain on the topic of anti-Muslim discrimination. Its use has since then spread all over Europe and has intensified after 9/11 and the Madrid and London bombings (see Chapter 18 by Daniele Pisoiu).

Ayhan Kaya used a comparative perspective to analyse Islamophobia[13] in the broader context of European neo-liberalism after 1989 and the Soviet collapse. In this regard, further research could be comparing the social milieux that have encouraged the rise of right-wing movements in Europe to those that have fostered the rise of Muslim radicalism in other parts of the world. One might also relate the diffuse rise in Muslim religiosity both in Europe and beyond to the rising social conservatism and apoliticism in Europe itself and also to the correlative trend towards moralization and personalization in the global political sphere.

The role of state multiculturalist policies brings us to our next point of interest, namely that of state responses to Muslim radicalism and Muslim communitarianism. It is especially important to focus on these matters in light of recent moves to create Muslim 'representative' organizations in Europe and the slow shift away from state patronage of multiculturalist and communalist tendencies in educational systems, legal systems, and society at large. Until very recently, in fact, a variety of European states gave asylum, support, and considerable freedom of movement to an appreciable number of Muslim radicals exiled from Arab countries.

# How to Approach Islam

A challenge for all the authors of the Handbook has been the thorny issue of defining Islam and the Islamic conception of religion. They wished to avoid the risk of employing an essentialist or a normative approach to the definition of either Islam or religion itself. That is why, in any chapter, there is neither a definition of Islam *a priori* nor an attempt to arbitrarily link predefined Islamic features to a definition of religion, but rather an analysis of Muslim involvement with and relation to the various issues discussed above.

---

[13] Runnymede Trust, *Islamophobia: A Challenge for Us All* (London: Runnymede Trust, 1997).

That is why the question of Islam surfaces in multiple and various domains from immigration and education to international relations.

All the chapters highlight the fact that the concept of Islam as an identifying force has entered the public discussion only in the last quarter-century. Prior to that, there were, and still are, nationalist associations of Algerians, Pakistanis, Yemenis, Turks, Arabs, and so forth who were not necessarily defined by Islam. The fact that all these identities, with their various locations and socio-economic and cultural profiles, have come to be broadly designated as 'Muslim communities' is a matter that requires deliberate attention and a willingness to look beyond assumptions of stable, tangible, and readily identifiable indices of Islam.

Clearly, the changes in the definition of a Muslim and of what constitutes a Muslim community are the result of a major change in European societies in the recent past. This is firstly a change in the way in which Muslims, or rather specific persons and collectives of Muslim extraction, organize and view themselves. But it is also a change in the European social perception of Muslims in light of increased terrorism and more frequent incidents of veiling as well as the succession of dramatic events from the Rushdie Affair to the assassination of Theo Van Gogh and the Danish cartoons crisis.

It is therefore crucial to avoid using or perceiving Islam as a primary unifying signifier that can only serve as a stark contrast to the 'West'. In this regard, Talal Asad's[14] insistence on deconstructing the Christian assumption of the Western approach to religion and the increasing disconnection between beliefs and practices certainly helps in understanding the debates over some Islamic claims in the public sphere.

The Handbook plans to propose a clearer identification and delimitation of what constitutes the category 'Islam', family extraction notwithstanding, in terms of three major categories: a multilayered approach to individual religiosity, the influence of transnational movements on the redefinition of Islamic orthodoxy in Europe, and the influence of social media on both the praxis and the doxa.

## Believing, Behaving, and Belonging

The first concerns the distinctions arising from the continuum of beliefs and practices of Muslims. At one end of this continuum are the ones who might be called 'sociologically Muslim', namely those who demonstrate a complete indifference to Islam, or even abandon it. And indeed, incipient movements of 'former Muslims' have emerged in Germany and France. On the other end of the continuum, Muslims are characterized by a strict observance of Islamic precepts, usually linked to extraterritorial identity and various manners of dress and behaviour. In between these two extremes, lie minimally believing and/or minimally practising Muslims, pious Muslims unconcerned with public affairs,

---

[14] Talal Asad, *Genealogies of Religion: Discipline and Reasons of Power in Christianity and Islam* (Baltimore: Johns Hopkins University Press, 1993).

culturally sentimentalist Muslims or persons who have become 'defensively' Muslim, and much more.

Overall, the data across chapters show that Muslims in Western Europe declare themselves as more religious than the general public. But what does this mean? Unlike the common expectation, it does not automatically reflect more intense religious practices. Recent empirical work has highlighted an increasing disjunction between believing, behaving, and belonging[15] among followers of all denominations, which is useful to understand the religiosity of Muslims in Europe. These three dimensions have historically been systematically linked or associated in the definition of a person's religiosity. However, sociological analyses shed light on the disjunction of these three dimensions and apprehend this disjunction as modern forms of religiosity.[16] Thus, a person can believe without automatically behaving and belonging; can belong without believing or behaving; or can behave without believing or belonging. For example, surveys have shown that many Christians maintain private, individual religious beliefs but do not practise on a regular basis (i.e. believing without behaving), or in some cases, Christian identity has taken on more cultural than spiritual meanings.

The studies discussed in the different chapters show that, for Muslims, the behaving is more challenging than belonging or believing. In other words, belonging is often strongly asserted even in the case of weakness or lack in beliefs. A line emerges between being a 'practising Muslim' and just 'being Muslim'. This difference indicates that 'being Muslim' is an identity with no clear relation to a set of practices or even beliefs. So when people say that they are very much Muslims, it does not mean that they are pious.

A widespread notion of 'Muslim culture' with no fixed content seems to override the more circumscribed definition of 'being Muslim' that is usually measured in polls. In consequence, the analytical reviews provided by the Handbook's chapters draw a complex and rich web of meanings and behaviours both on what it is to be a Muslim *and* a citizen. It is not possible from the existing data to conclude that Islamic religiosity impinges on cultural or political integration. Most interestingly, the data reveal that Islam is not *per se* the main factor in the building of Muslims' social identities or in their political participation. Instead, other elements—ethnicity, class, and residential distribution among them—have an effect that requires further investigation. The second relevant category of investigation refers to the influence of transnational Muslim organizations (Jamaat at Tabligh, Muslim Brothers) on the identification and mobilization of Muslims in Europe.

---

[15] For a systematic use of this approach to religion on Muslim groups in Europe and the USA, see Jocelyne Cesari, *Why the West Fears Islam: Exploration of Muslims in Liberal Democracies* (New York: Palgrave Macmillan, 2013).

[16] G. Davie, *Religion in Britain since 1945: Believing Without Belonging* (Oxford: Blackwell, 1994); D. Hervieu-Léger, 'Religion und sozialer Zusammenhalt in Europa', *Transit* 26 (2003): 101–19.

## Growing Influence of Global Salafism

The proliferation of religious authorities and the shrinking realm of their legitimacy is by no means a new phenomenon and has been the subject of many studies.[17] Both mass education and new forms of communication have contributed to the increase of actors who claim the right to talk on behalf of Islam in both authoritative and normative ways. Therefore, established religious figures, such as the sheikhs of Al-Azhar or Medina, are increasingly challenged by the engineer, the student, the businessman, and the autodidact, who mobilize the masses and speak for Islam in sports stadiums, on the blogosphere, and over airwaves worldwide. This trend predates the internet and is related to public education programmes and the increased availability of new technological communicative media, such as magazines, cassette tapes, and CDs.[18] However, the internet has added a new element to this proliferation of religious voices: the greater influence of globalized authority figures who have an audience beyond their particular cultural background. This transnationalization of religious voices can be defined as 'neo' pan-Islamism. Although there are multiple forms of this contemporary pan-Islam, contemporary Salafism has become the most widespread.

Today, the conditions for communication and the circulation of people and ideas make the *ummah* (community of Muslim believers) all the more effective as a concept, especially considering the fact that nationalist ideologies have been waning. The imagined *ummah* has a variety of forms, the most influential of which emphasizes direct access to the Qur'an and Muslim unity that transcends national and cultural diversity. In this sense, those extolling this modern trend can be called pan-Islamists even though the restoration of the caliphate is no longer their priority.[19] It is worth noting that not all these movements are reactionary or defensive. For this reason, a distinction must be drawn between the Wahhabi/Salafi and Tablighi movements on one hand and the Muslim Brotherhood on the other. Both trends dominate global

---

[17] Dale Eickelman, 'Mainstreaming Islam: Taking Charge of the Faith', *Encounters* 2 (2010): 185–203.

[18] Traditionally, authority was conferred according to one's theological knowledge and mastery of the methodologies used to interpret this knowledge. Only those who possessed knowledge that had been passed down through a chain of authorities or a line of recognized masters could claim legitimacy as religious leaders. Though formal education was an important component throughout much of the Muslim world, the transmission of knowledge did not always rely on formal education, especially if the knowledge being passed down was esoteric in nature (as was the case of the Sufi masters).

[19] The Hizb ut-Tahrir party is one of the most significant contemporary pan-Islamist movements that still advocates for the restoration of the caliphate. Founded in Jerusalem in 1953, it claims branches in the Muslim world as well as Europe and the USA. In Great Britain, the party is known under the name Muhajirrun, and has been active in the public sphere, particularly before 11 September 2001. Suha Taji-Farouki, *A Fundamental Quest: Hizb al-Tahrir and the Search for the Islamic Caliphate* (London: Grey Seal, 1996).

interpretations of Islam across Europe but have very different positions vis-à-vis modernity.

Wahhabism as a specific interpretation of the Islamic tradition that emerged in the eighteenth century in the Arabian Peninsula with the teachings of Muhammad Ibn Abdel Wahab (1703–92), whose literalist interpretations of the Qur'an became the official doctrine of the Saudi Kingdom upon its creation in 1932. Wahhabism is characterized by a rejection of critical approaches to the Islamic tradition. Mystical approaches and historical interpretations alike are held in contempt. Orthodox practice can be defined as a direct relation to the revealed Text, with no recourse to the historical contributions of the various juridical schools (*madhab*). In this literalist interpretation of Islam, nothing must come between the believer and the Text: customs, culture, and Sufism must all be done away with.

The heirs of this rigorist and puritanical line of thought, also known as Salafi, make up the existing Saudi religious establishment. Adherents of Wahhabism have rejected all ideas and concepts that are deemed Western, maintaining a strictly revivalist agenda. They contend that the Qur'an and Hadith, when interpreted according to the precedents of the Pious Forefathers (*al-salaf al-salih*), offer the most superior form of guidance to Muslims. As a stringently revivalist movement, Wahhabism seeks the 'Islamization of societies',[20] which entails formulating contemporary ways of life in relation to the conditions of seventh-century Arabia by 'returning to the sources' whose 'true meaning', Wahhabis argue, was lost over the centuries following Prophet Muhammad's death.[21] In their resistance to European expansionism and globalization, Wahhabis have remained true to their literalist, anti-historical, and anti-traditionalist origins by rejecting the teachings and methods of the traditional schools of jurisprudence.[22] In sum, the

---

[20] 'Movements that were conceived as movements of "renewal" were in fact more a part of the ongoing processes of Islamization of societies on the frontiers of the Islamic world. They were, in effect, part of the "formation" of the Islamic societies rather than the "reformation" of existing ones' (John Obert Voll, 'Foundations for Renewal and Reform: Islamic Movements in the Eighteenth and Nineteenth Centuries', in John L. Esposito (ed.), *The Oxford History of Islam* (Oxford: Oxford University Press, 1999), 516–17).

[21] John L. Esposito, *Islam: The Straight Path* (New York: Oxford University Press, 1998), 117–18.

[22] The modernist and pro-Western reformism of early Salafism has been marginalized in postcolonial Muslim countries. Most Islamic reformist movements became anti-Western for two reasons, one readily apparent and the other more subtle. First, Western policies during colonial and postcolonial periods have supported secular, authoritarian regimes, from the Shah in Iran to Sadat and Mubarak in Egypt, while simultaneously unquestioningly backing Israel. This has resulted in Muslims associating the West with despotic, anti-Islam regimes. The second, less obvious explanation is tied to domestic developments in Muslim nations, in which state actions have reduced the influence of Islam in social life and disempowered Muslim clerics and religious authorities. States began to absorb and cast their influence on traditional Islamic authorities and co-opt Islamic organizations. Therefore, these religious leaders who put their Islamic expertise to the service of oppressive regimes were delegitimized in the eyes of their populations. In some ways, the Muslim Brotherhood is still carrying the message of the original *salafiyya* movement by maintaining a contextualized and modernist interpretation of Islam.

Wahhabi interpretation can be defined as a revivalist movement premised upon the return to the 'unadulterated' Islam of the Pious Forefathers.

The most significant difference between the global Salafi Islam of today and the original Wahhabi period is a difference in audience: in other words, Salafi decisions and interpretations are no longer limited to the Saudi Kingdom but are now followed by Muslims around the world. The fatwas of Sheikh Abdul Aziz Ibn Baaz (d. 1999), Grand Mufti of the Saudi Kingdom, and of Sheikh Al-Albani (d. 1999) are the shared points of reference for their followers in Europe and the USA, and more generally throughout the Muslim world. The movement has succeeded in imposing its beliefs not as one interpretation among many but as the global orthodox doctrine of Sunni Islam.

The considerable financial resources of the Saudi state have certainly also helped to create this situation of religious monopoly. In the 1970s, Saudi Arabia began investing internationally in a number of organizations that 'widely distributed Wahhabi literature in all the major languages of the world, gave out awards and grants, and provided funding for a massive network of publishers, schools, mosques, organizations, and individuals'.[23] In the West, this *dawa* (proselytization) resulted in the construction of new Islamic centres in Malaga, Madrid, Milan, Mantes-la-Jolie, Edinburgh, Brussels, Lisbon, Zagreb, Washington, Chicago, and Toronto, to name just a few; the financing of Islamic Studies chairs in American universities; and the proliferation of multilingual internet sites. In March 2002, the official Saudi magazine *Ain al-Yaqin* estimated that the Saudi royal family has 'wholly or partly financed' approximately 210 Islamic centres, 1,500 mosques, 202 colleges, and 2,000 Islamic schools in Muslim-minority countries.[24] It is important to note that these estimates do not include the number of institutions funded by the Saudi government in its entirety or other sources within Saudi Arabia that finance Wahhabi proselytizing.[25] According to some estimates, the Saudi Kingdom spent over $80 billion on various Islam-related causes in Muslim-minority countries between 1973 and 2002.[26] King Fahd alone invested over $75 billion in the construction of schools, mosques, and Islamic institutions outside of the Kingdom in the 1970s and 1980s.[27,28]

---

[23] Abou El Fadl, *The Great Theft: Wrestling Islam from the Extremists* (San Francisco: Harper, 2005), 73–4.

[24] 'Inside the Kingdom', *Time*, 15 September 2003. <http://www.time.com/time/magazine/article/0,9171,1005663,00.html>, accessed 25 July 2012.

[25] 'Inside the Kingdom'.

[26] Alexander Alexiev, 'Wahhabism: State-Sponsored Extremism Worldwide', testimony before the U.S. Senate Subcommittee on Terrorism, Technology and Homeland Security, 26 June 2003. <http://kyl.senate.gov/legis_center/subdocs/sc062603_alexiev.pdf>, accessed 25 July 2012.

[27] Rachel Bronson, *Thicker than Oil: America's Uneasy Partnership with Saudi Arabia* (New York: Oxford University Press, 2006), 10.

[28] According to its website, the King Fahd Foundation has wholly or partially funded thirty such projects in Africa, six in South America, twenty-three in Asia, six in Australia and Oceania, twelve in Europe, and twenty-two in North America (the website is <http://www.kingfahdbinabdulaziz.com/main/m400.htm>).

This massive effort of propagation has contributed to the promotion of Wahhabism as the sole legitimate guardian of Islamic thought.[29]

The construction of mosques, schools, and other Islamic institutions is only one strategy of the Saudis to circulate the Wahhabi ideology. They also rely heavily on media to promote and spread their message, whether through the circulation of handouts, the creation of websites, or the airing of satellite television shows. For example, in 1984, the Kingdom of Saudi Arabia opened the King Fahd Complex for Printing the Holy Qur'an in Medina. According the website of the now-deceased King Fahd bin Abdul 'Aziz, the Complex produces between 10 and 30 million copies of the Qur'an each year. Copies of the Qur'an are also available in Braille, as are video and audio recordings of Qur'anic recitations. By 2000, the Complex had produced 138 million copies of the Qur'an translated into twenty languages.[30]

It is extremely difficult to gauge the precise influence exerted by Wahhabism on Muslim religious practice. In the case of European Muslims, the influence cannot simply be measured by statistics. In a minority culture lacking both institutions for religious education and the means by which to produce new forms of knowledge, the easy access to theology that Salafism offers is one of the main reasons for its popularity. The widespread diffusion of Salafi teachings means that even non-Salafi Muslims evaluate their Islamic practice by Wahhabite standards. In other words, even if most Muslims do not follow Wahhabite dress codes—white tunic, head covering, beard for men, niqab[31] for women—the Salafi norm often becomes the standard image of what a good Muslim ought to be.[32]

---

[29] In addition to funds coming straight from the Saudi government, the Kingdom also supports proxy organizations that spread Wahhabism. A notable organization that depends on Saudi funding is the Muslim World League (MWL, Rabitat al-'Alam al-Islami). Today, the Muslim World League oversees a number of non-governmental organizations such as the International Islamic Relief Organization (IIRO), the World Assembly of Muslim Youth (WAMY), the Holy Qur'an Memorization International Organization, the International Islamic Organization for Education, Makkah Al-Mukarramah Charity Foundation for Orphans, the Commission on Scientific Signs in the Qur'an and Sunnah, The World Supreme Council for Mosques, and The Fiqh (Islamic Jurisprudence) Council. Although to the outside world they strongly emphasize their strong humanitarian aims (providing relief, assisting orphans, etc.), these organizations are often focused on propagating a Salafist interpretation of Islam. Many, including the IIRO and the WAMY, concentrate on setting up and supporting mosque centres with an orthodox persuasion, as well as hiring, training, and subsidizing imams with Salafi/Wahhabi orientation, and publishing and disseminating Salafist literature.

[30] The main website is <http://www.kingfahdbinabdulaziz.com/main/m600.htm>.

[31] A cloth covering the face according to Wahhabi law.

[32] Another group, albeit with much fewer financial resources, that takes a traditionalist and legalistic approach to Islam is the Tabligh, sometimes referred to as the Jehovah's Witnesses of Islam. The Tabligh is usually described as a pious and proselytizing movement whose primary aim is to promote Islamic education. The essential principle of this sect within the Deobandi movement—founded in 1927 in India—is that every Muslim is responsible for spreading the values and practices of Islam. In the last two decades, this movement has gained a wide following, especially in Europe and the USA. In these conditions, competition rages in the West between Tablighis and Salafis, and anathemas rain down on both sides.

Despite the strong presence of many different interpretations at the grassroots level,[33] the Salafi revivalist interpretation of Islam dominates the internet Dawa. For this reason, the third category or point of interest in further research on Islam is the explosion of electronic media, following an earlier period marked by the use of educational and other infrastructures, which in fact are still in existence to this day. This rise in new media leads to new forms of homogenized global Islam, which some seek to subscribe to or revive, but which are at variance with most of the social practices of Muslims in the West. Very little work has been done to shed light on this 'online' religiosity and how it influences the practices of Muslims in different cultural and national contexts.

In sum, the Handbook highlights black holes in the abundant literature on Islam and Muslims in Europe. First, there is a need to analyse in more depth the mechanisms of social and economic mobility of Muslim groups, especially as many preconceived ideas of who is integrated (and how) influence policy-making and political rhetoric on Islam. Second, there is a dearth of information on Islamic religiosity within and across countries, as well as of in-depth analysis of the ongoing redefinition of Islamic practices under the influence of transnational influences and local acculturations. For this reason, the localization of transnational processes appears as a key domain of future research to make sense of the variations across national and political contexts.

## Select Bibliography

Abbas, Tahir (ed.) (2007). *Islamic Political Radicalism: A European Perspective*. Edinburgh: Edinburgh University Press.

Abumalham Mas, Montserrat and Simposio Internacional sobre Comunidades Islámicas en Europa y en España (1995). *Comunidades Islámicas En Europa*. Colección Estructuras y Procesos. Serie Ciencias Sociales. Madrid: Editorial Trotta.

Akbarzadeh, Shahram and Fethi Mansouri (eds.) (2007). *Islam and Political Violence: Muslim Diaspora and Radicalism in the West*. Library of International Relations 34. London and New York: Tauris Academic Studies.

Allievi, Stefano (1999). *Les Convertis à l'Islam: Les Nouveaux Musulmans d'Europe*. Paris: L'Harmattan.

---

[33] There are Muslim Brotherhood groups that are very active at the grassroots level and in creating Muslim organizations to cooperate with political institutions (see Brigitte Maréchal, *Les Frères Musulmans en Europe: Racines et Discours* [*Muslim Brothers in Europe: Roots and Discourses*] (Leuven: Brill, 2008)). There are religious authorities related to some Muslim countries (Morocco, Algeria, and Turkey) who propagate a traditional interpretation of Islam. Finally, there is a proliferation of independent authorities: scholars (Tariq Ramadan, Professor of Islamic Studies at Oxford University, and known for his reformist thinking), social activists (Hamza Yusuf, Director of the Zeytuna Institute in San Francisco), and more traditional authorities (Cheikh Qaradawi, who became global with his show on Al Jazeera called *Al Sharia wal Hayat* [Sharia and Life]). For a typology of the different religious leaders operating in Europe and in the USA, see Jocelyne Cesari, *When Islam and Democracy Meet* (New York: Palgrave Macmillan, 2004).

Allievi, Stefano and Jørgen S. Nielsen (eds.) (2003). *Muslim Minorities*, vol. 1: *Muslim Networks and Transnational Communities in and across Europe*. Leiden and Boston: Brill.
Antes, Peter and Chris Hewer (1994). 'Islam in Europe', in S. Gill, G. D'Costa, and U. King (eds.), *Religion in Europe: Contemporary Perspectives*. Kampen: Kok Pharos, 46–67.
Anwar, Muhammad (1983). 'Employment Patterns of Muslims in Western Europe', *Journal of the Institute of Muslim Minority Affairs* 5(1): 99–122.
Asad, Talal (1993). *Genealogies of Religion: Discipline and Reasons of Power in Christianity and Islam*. Baltimore: Johns Hopkins University Press.
—— (2003). *Formations of the Secular: Christianity, Islam, Modernity*. Stanford: Stanford University Press.
'Azmah, 'Azīz and Effie Fokas (eds.) (2007). *Islam in Europe: Diversity, Identity and Influence*. Cambridge: Cambridge University Press.
Bistolfi, Robert and François Zabbal (1995). *Islams d'Europe: Intégration Ou Insertion Communautaire?* Collection Monde en Cours. La Tour d'Aigues: Editions de l'Aube.
Borrás Rodríguez, Alegría, Salima Mernissi, and R. Babadji (1998). *El Islam Jurídico y Europa: Derecho, Religión, y Política*. Antrazyt 110. Barcelona: Icaria.
Bronson, Rachel (2006). *Thicker than Oil: America's Uneasy Partnership with Saudi Arabia*. New York: Oxford University Press.
Cesari, Jocelyne (2014). *The Awakening of Muslim Democracy: Religion, Modernity and the State*. New York, Cambridge University Press.
Cesari, Jocelyne (2004). *When Islam and Democracy Meet: Muslims in Europe and in the United States*. New York: Palgrave Macmillan.
—— (2006). 'Securitization and Religious Divides in Europe: Muslims in Western Europe after 9/11', GSRL-Paris and Harvard University, 1 June.
—— (ed.) (2010). *Muslims in the West After 9/11: Religion, Law and Politics*. New York: Routledge.
—— (2013). *Why the West Fears Islam: Exploration of Muslims in Liberal Democracies*. New York: Palgrave Macmillan.
Cesari, Jocelyne, Seán McLoughlin, and Network of Comparative Research on Islam and Muslims in Europe (eds.) (2005). *European Muslims and the Secular State*. Aldershot and Burlington, VT: Ashgate.
Coolsaet, R. (ed.) (2008). *Jihadi Terrorism and the Radicalisation Challenge in Europe*. Aldershot and Burlington, VT: Ashgate.
Coppes, R. (1994). 'Niet zomaar een stukje stof. Hoofddoekjes-affaires in Frankrijk, Nederland en Groot-Brittannië', *Sociologische Gids* 41: 130–43.
Davie, Grace (1994). *Religion in Britain since 1945: Believing Without Belonging*. Oxford: Blackwell.
de Changy, J., Felice Dassetto, and Brigitte Maréchal (2007). *Relations et Co-Inclusion, Islam en Belgique*. Compétences Interculturelles. Paris: Harmattan.
Doomernik, Jeroen (1991). *Turkse Moskeeën En Maatschappelijke Participatie: De Institutionalisering Van De Turkse Islam in Nederland En De Duitse Bondsrepubliek*. Nederlandse Geografische Studies 129. Amsterdam: Koninklijk Nederlands Aardrijkskundig Genootschap; Instituut voor Sociale Geografie, Faculteit Ruimtelijke Wetenschappen, Universiteit van Amsterdam.
Eickelman, Dale (2010). 'Mainstreaming Islam: Taking Charge of the Faith', *Encounters* 2: 185–203.
El Fadl, Abou (2005). *The Great Theft: Wrestling Islam from the Extremists*. San Francisco: HarperCollins.

Esch, W. van and M. Roovers (1987). *Islamitisch Godsdienstonderwijs in Nederland, België, Engeland en West-Duitsland.* Nijmegen: Instituut voor Toegepaste Sociologie (ITS).
Esposito, John L. (1998). *Islam: The Straight Path.* New York: Oxford University Press.
Ferrari, Silvio (1996). *L'Islam in Europa: Lo Statuto Giuridico Delle Comunità Musulmane.* Bologna: Il Mulino.
Ferrari, Silvio and Anthony Bradney (eds.) (2000). *Islam and European Legal Systems.* Aldershot and Burlington, VT: Ashgate.
Fetzer, Joel S. and Christopher Soper (2005). 'Explaining the Accommodation of Muslim Religious Practices in France, Britain and Germany', paper presented at the Muslims in Western Europe Politics Conference, Bloomington, Indiana, 22–4 September.
Foblets, Marie-Claire (1996). *Familles, Islam, Europe: Le Droit Confronté au Changement.* Musulmans d'Europe. Paris: L'Harmattan.
Garaudy, Roger and Mahdī Zughayb (1984). *Promesses de l'Islam.* Arabic: *Wuʿūd Al-Islām.* al-Ṭabʿah. Bayrūt: al-Dār al-ʿĀlamīyah.
Gerholm, Tomas, Yngve Georg Lithman, Stockholm University, Centrum för invandringsforskning, and Kungl. Vitterhets, historie och antikvitets akademien (eds.) (1988). *The New Islamic Presence in Western Europe.* London and New York: Mansell.
Goody, Jack (2004). *Islam in Europe.* Cambridge: Polity Press.
Hervieu-Léger, D. (2003). 'Religion und sozialer Zusammenhalt in Europa', *Transit* 26: 101–19.
Hess, Mary E. (2011). '2010 Presidential Address: Learning Religion and Religiously Learning Amid Global Cultural Flows', *Religious Education* 106(4): 360–77.
Hunter, Shireen (ed.) (2002). *Islam, Europe's Second Religion: The New Social, Cultural, and Political Landscape.* Westport, CT: Praeger.
Jenkins, Philip (2007). *God's Continent: Christianity, Islam, and Europe's Religious Crisis.* Future of Christianity Trilogy. Oxford and New York: Oxford University Press.
Jonker Gerdien and Valerie Amiraux (eds.) (2006). *Politics of Visibility: Young Muslims in European Public Spaces.* Bielefeld: Transcript Verlag.
Kepel, Gilles (2004). *The War for Muslim Minds: Islam and the West.* Cambridge, MA: Belknap Press of Harvard University Press.
Klausen, Jytte (2005). *The Islamic Challenge: Politics and Religion in Western Europe.* Oxford and New York: Oxford University Press.
—— (2009). *The Cartoons that Shook the World.* New Haven: Yale University Press.
Laurence, Jonathan (ed.) (2012). *The Emancipation of Europe's Muslims: The State's Role in Minority Integration.* Princeton: Princeton University Press.
Lentin, Alana and Gavin Titley (2012). 'The Crisis of "Multiculturalism" in Europe: Mediated Minarets, Intolerable Subjects', *European Journal of Cultural Studies* 15(2): 123–38.
Lewis, Bernard and Dominique Schnapper (eds.) (1994). *Musulmans en Europe.* English: *Muslims in Europe.* Social Change in Western Europe. London: Pinter and New York: St. Martin's Press.
Maréchal, Brigitte (2002). *L'Islam et les Musulmans dans l'Europe Élargie: Radioscopie.* English: *Guidebook on Islam and Muslims in the Wide Contemporary Europe.* Louvain-la-Neuve: Bruylant-Academia.
—— (2008). *Les Frères Musulmans en Europe: Racines et Discours* [*Muslim Brothers in Europe: Roots and Discourses*]. Leuven: Brill.
Maussen, Marcel (2006). *Ruimte Voor De Islam? Stedelijk Beleid, Voorzieningen, Organisaties.* Apeldoorn: Het Spinhuis.

Metcalf, Barbara Daly (ed.) (1996). *Making Muslim Space in North America and Europe.* Comparative Studies on Muslim Societies 22. Berkeley: University of California Press.

Nielsen, Jørgen S. (1979). *Forms and Problems of Legal Recognition for Muslims in Europe.* Research Paper No. 2. Birmingham: Centre for the Study of Islam and Christian–Muslim Relations, Selly Oak Colleges.

—— (1987). *Islam and Religious Education in England: Introduction.* Research Papers: Muslims in Europe No. 33. Birmingham: Centre for the Study of Islam and Christian–Muslim Relations, Selly Oak Colleges.

—— (1992). *Muslims in Western Europe.* Islamic Surveys 20. Edinburgh: Edinburgh University Press.

—— (2004). *Muslims in Western Europe,* 3rd edn. New Edinburgh Islamic Surveys. Edinburgh: Edinburgh University Press.

Nielsen, Jørgen S. and Centre for Research in Ethnic Relations (1999). *Towards a European Islam.* Migration, Minorities, and Citizenship. New York: St. Martin's Press.

Nonneman, Gerd, Tim Niblock, and Bogdan Szajkowski (eds.) (1996). *Muslim Communities in the New Europe.* Reading: Ithaca Press.

Pargeter, Alison (2008). *The New Frontiers of Jihad: Radical Islam in Europe.* Philadelphia: University of Pennsylvania Press.

Rath, Jan (1996). *Nederland En Zijn Islam: Een Ontzuilende Samenleving Reageert Op Het Ontstaan Van Een Geloofsgemeenschap.* Migratie-En Etnische Studies. Amsterdam: Het Spinhuis.

—— (2001). *Nederland En Zijn Islam.* English: *Western Europe and its Islam.* International Comparative Social Studies, vol. 2. Leiden and Boston: Brill.

—— (2005). 'Mijn Hemel, Daar Komen De Moslims!' *MO Samenlevingsopbouw,* vol. 23: 4–7 <http://dare.uva.nl/record/279527>.

Renaerts, Monique (1994). *Islam and Europe: The Millennium Conference 1994.* Brussels: King Baudouin Foundation, Forward Studies Programme.

Robbers, Gerhard (2005). 'State and Church in the European Union', in Gerhard Robbers (ed.), *State and Church in the European Union.* Baden-Baden: Nomos, 577–89.

Rohe, Mathias (2007). *Muslim Minorities and the Law in Europe: Chances and Challenges.* New Delhi, India: Global Media Publications.

Roy, Olivier (2004). *Globalized Islam: The Search for a New Ummah.* CERI Series in Comparative Politics and International Studies. New York: Columbia University Press.

Runnymede Trust (1997). *Islamophobia: A Challenge for Us All.* London: Runnymede Trust.

Samad, Yunas and Kasturi Sen (eds.) (2007). *Islam in the European Union: Transnationalism, Youth and the War on Terror.* Karachi: Oxford University Press.

Seufert, Günter and Jean Jacques Waardenburg (eds.) (1999). *Turkish Islam and Europe/ Türkischer Islam Und Europa.* Beiruter Texte Und Studien Bd. 82. Türkischer Islam und Europa/Europe and Christianity as Reflected in Turkish Muslim Discourse & Turkish Muslim Life in the Diaspora: Papers of the Istanbul Workshop October 1996. Istanbul: In Kommission bei Franz-Steiner-Verlag Stuttgart.

Shadid, W. A. R. (1995). *Religious Freedom and the Position of Islam in Western Europe: Opportunities and Obstacles in the Acquisition of Equal Rights (with an Extensive Bibliography).* Kampen, the Netherlands: Kok Pharos.

Shadid, W. A. R. and P. Sj van Koningsveld (1991). *The Integration of Islam and Hinduism in Western Europe.* Kampen, the Netherlands: Kok Pharos.

—— (eds.) (1995). *Religious Freedom and the Position of Islam in Western Europe: Opportunities and Obstacles in the Acquisition of Equal Rights*. Kampen, the Netherlands: Kok Pharos.

—— (eds.) (1996). *Muslims in the Margin: Political Responses to the Presence of Islam in Western Europe*. Kampen, the Netherlands: Kok Pharos.

Speelman, G. M. and Centre for the Study of Islam and Christian–Muslim Relations (1991). *Religion and State in Europe: Two Seminar Reports*. CSIC Papers. Europe, no. 4. Birmingham: Centre for the Study of Islam and Christian–Muslim Relations, Selly Oak Colleges.

Sunier, Thijl (1996). *Islam in Beweging: Turkse Jongeren En Islamitische Organisaties*. Migratie-En Etnische Studies. Amsterdam: Het Spinhuis.

Sunier, Thijl and Astrid Meyer (1996). 'Religion', in Hans Vermeulen (ed.), *Immigrant Policy for a Multicultural Society. A Comparative Study of Integration, Language and Religious Policy in Five Western European Countries*. Brussels: Migration Policy Group, 101–30.

Taji-Farouki, Suha (1996). *A Fundamental Quest: Hizb al-Tahrir and the Search for the Islamic Caliphate*. London: Grey Seal.

van Koningsveld, Pieter (1995). 'Islam in Europe', in John L. Esposito (ed.), *The Oxford Encyclopedia of the Modern Islamic World*, vol. 2. Oxford: Oxford University Press, 290–6.

Vertovec, Steven and Ceri Peach (eds.) (1997). *Islam in Europe: The Politics of Religion and Community*. Migration, Minorities, and Citizenship Series. Basingstoke: Macmillan and New York: St. Martin's Press.

Vertovec, Steven, Alisdair Rogers, and Dansk Center for Migration Og Etniske Studier (eds.) (1998). *Muslim European Youth: Reproducing Ethnicity, Religion, Culture*. Research in Ethnic Relations Series. Aldershot and Brookfield, VT: Ashgate.

Vikor, Knut S. (2005). *Between God and the Sultan: A History of Islamic Law*. New York: Oxford University Press.

Voll, John Obert (1999). 'Foundations for Renewal and Reform: Islamic Movements in the Eighteenth and Nineteenth Centuries', in John L. Esposito (ed.), *The Oxford History of Islam*. Oxford: Oxford University Press, 509–48.

Waardenburg, Jean-Jacques (1991). 'Muslim Associations and Official Bodies in Some European Countries', in Wasif Shadid and Pieter van Koningsveld (eds.), *The Integration of Islam and Hinduism in Western Europe*. Kampen, the Netherlands: Kok Pharos, 24–42.

—— (2001). *Institutionale Vormgevingen van de Islam in Nederland gezien in Europees Perspectief*. Werkdocumenten W 118. The Hague: Scientific Council for the Government Policy (WRR).

—— (2002). *Islam: Historical, Social and Political Perspectives*. Religion and Reason 40. Berlin and New York: Walter de Gruyter.

—— (2003). *Muslims and Others: Relations in Context*. Religion and Reason 41. Berlin and New York: Walter de Gruyter.

—— (2007). *Muslims as Actors: Islamic Meanings and Muslim Interpretations in the Perspective of the Study of Religions*. Religion and Reason 46. Berlin and New York: Walter de Gruyter.

Wiktorowicz, Quintan (2005). *Radical Islam Rising: Muslim Extremism in the West*. Lanham, MD: Rowman & Littlefield.

# PART I

## ISLAM AS A POSTCOLONIAL, POST-SECOND WORLD WAR RELIGION IN EUROPE

CHAPTER 1

# FRANCE

JENNIFER A. SELBY

THE experiences and representations of Muslims in France are significant benchmarks with which to gauge the broader socio-politics of Islam in the West. France is home to the largest Muslim population in Western Europe. This factor as well as its unique Republican citizenship model and *laïque* (French secular) separation of religion and politics significantly shape the lives of French Muslims. As we will see, assimilationist policies have had differing effects. On the one hand, in contrast to other European nation-states described in this volume, France is relatively open to granting citizenship rights to new immigrants, of whom many are Muslim. On the other hand, the French Republic applies sharp legal regulations to visible forms of religiosity in the public sphere that often pejoratively affect Muslims amid highly mediatized debates. This chapter considers some of the ways this complex and dynamic context impacts French Muslims through socio-historical analysis and by situating academic research within five broad topics: (i) the history and politics of immigration and of "counting" Muslims; (ii) how the nation's separation of religion and politics renders visible religious signs like hijabs problematic; (iii) political participation trends; (iv) French institutionalization of Islam; and lastly, (v) contemporary figures and studies of Islamic movements, radicalism, and Islamophobia. These are politics that have defined and been shaped by scholarship on the subject; woven into this overview is consideration of how academic study has examined and contributed to characterizations of French Muslims. Despite the long-standing presence of Muslims, a shift from a broad-based sociology of immigration with little attention to Islam in the 1960s–1970s to a central focus beginning with the "headscarf affair" at the end of the 1980s is noted.

## IMMIGRATION AND STATISTICAL STUDIES

Muslims have lived in France since the Moor invasion from Spain in the eighth century and continue to migrate thirteen centuries later. Sociological perspectives and French statistical agencies have shaped knowledge production on Islam in France, initially through the study of immigration. French demographic agencies were among the first in France to formally count French Muslims (Tribalat 1995, 1996; Alba and Silberman 2002), and, in so doing, influenced the way its communities are oftentimes perceived as immigrants. This chapter's first section identifies key migration trends and how they have shaped the origins of most Muslims in France, from the first waves of male North African temporary workers, to an increase of women and Muslims of sub-Saharan, Turkish, and Middle Eastern origins. This overview also considers the role of research in reinforcing the perception of Muslims as immigrants in the 1960s and 1970s, and with the 1983 *Marche des Beurs* reflecting a shift to scholarly emphases on the group's socio-economic statuses.

With the exception of long-standing residents and a small number of *Français-de-Souche* (so-called native French) converts, many French Muslims immigrated to France in the twentieth century in two principal periods: following the First World War, when a devastating number of casualties and the rise of industrialization meant that temporary workers from nearby North African colonies were encouraged to work in factories; and in the era surrounding the Algerian War (1954–62) as male migrants sought employment opportunities, facilitated because Algeria was a French department. With the end of the First World War, more organized programs of immigration sponsored by government and industry replaced the more spontaneous largely North African immigration before 1914 (Ogden 1989: 44). Of course, Muslims of Algerian origin who were part of this wave were French nationals (Cesari 2009: 195). The Paris Mosque with its 33-meter minaret in the city's 5th district was inaugurated in 1926 as a gesture of recognition to the more than 100,000 Algerian soldiers who died during the war.

Aforementioned, the majority of these migrants were young single men of Maghrebian origin. Their projects in France typically had two objectives: to send remittances to their families and to gain greater social status in their countries of origin (Zehraoui 1994: 16). Most settled in the outskirts of northern and eastern cities like Paris, Marseille, Lyon, and Lille because of their concentration of metallurgical factories (Stora 1992; Silverstein 2004). This migration wave impacted the social and physical geographies of these suburban regions. Initially many built shacks and lived in shantytowns close to the factories where they worked. Beginning in the early 1960s, these shantytowns were replaced by high-rise apartment social housing projects or *habitations à loyer modéré* (HLMs) by the French government in an effort to improve conditions (Kepel 2012; Moran 2012). These sites became significant in the 2000s when the accidental deaths of two adolescents ignited social tensions leading to three weeks of riots (this period is considered in greater detail in the subsection "Policing and the *banlieues*").

Following the independence of Algeria in 1962, immigration to French suburban regions widened to include other African workers, particularly from West Africa. Paris's *banlieues* thus welcomed increasingly culturally heterogeneous numbers of Muslims. Following the "Franco flight" in the 1970s when French non-Muslims began leaving suburban regions, its residents were increasingly of Muslim and of immigrant origin.

An "ethnic penalty" became clear (Santelli 2007). Immigrant Muslim families gained access to government-sponsored housing at the very moment when it was no longer a symbol of progress (Cesari 2005). Today approximately 3 million people live in social low-income housing in the outskirts of Paris alone (Kepel 1987; Begag and Delorme 1994; Fausto 1992). While the precise numbers are not known, many of these residents are Muslims. In the 1970s and 1980s, there was little academic interest in the religious dimensions of this immigration.

Sociologically, two notable changes beginning in the 1960s and 1970s in this primarily North African migration to the peripheries of industrialized French cities shifted the discourses of Islam in France: industrialization and roboticization, and a new family reunification immigration policy. The country's immigration policies began tightening in the 1970s in response to rising unemployment. President Valéry Giscard d'Estaing's government (1974–81) unsuccessfully sought to repatriate 500,000 North Africans and offered lump sum payments to encourage workers to leave (Killian 2006: 17). In the early 1980s, in the midst of this recession, the far right grew under the leadership of Jean-Marie Le Pen's *Front National* (FN, the National Front party) (Bréchon and Mitra 1992: 63; Wieviorka 1993: 55). Ethnic minorities who lived in the outskirts of these industrialized cities were greatly affected by this change in industry and Muslims became both the symbols and targets of FN's anti-immigration rhetoric with exclusionary nationalist campaign slogans like, *On n'est plus chez nous* ("We are no longer at home").

One response to this xenophobic rhetoric was the *Première marche pour l'égalité et contre le racisme* (the "First March for Equality and Against Racism") also called the *Marche des Beurs*,[1] organized by a number of second-generation immigrants to draw attention to the problem. The mediatized *Marche des Beurs* from Marseille to Paris and subsequent demonstrations reflected the second generation's differing politics and claim for rights from their parents. The FN's anti-Islam position arguably also led many second-generation youth, troubled by unemployment and racism, to look to their religious beliefs and practices as sources of identity. Scholarly attention primarily examined the *Beurs* movement and the creation of organizations like *SOS Racisme* as reflecting ethnic-based social movements, and not ones centered on religious affiliations (see Jazouli 1992; Rey 1996; Leveau and Wihtol de Wenden 2001; Beaud and Pialoux 2003). As Fetzer and Soper note (2005: 6), so-called religious elements were largely ignored by social scientists because religion was not seen as an influential factor: "one reason for this silence on religious questions has been the perception among social scientists [...] that Western Europe is essentially secular and that issues of church and state are no longer relevant to public policy."

---

[1] *Verlan*, which comes from *à l'envers* or reverse, refers to spoken words whose sounds are reversed to create a new "code" with the same meaning as the original word, like *keufs* for *flics* (cops). Some *verlan* is straightforward, like *ouf* that signifies *fou* (crazy). Often pointed to with the *Marche des Beurs* in 1982, "Arabes" became known as the *Beurs*. More than twenty-five years later, *Beurs* are sometimes now known as the *Rebeu* (Bachman and Besier 1984; Lefkowitz 1991; Merle 1997).

By the 1990s, the foreign workforce in France had been reduced by half (Hargreaves 2007: 53). These factors led North African immigrants to occupy "the lowest ranking in the country's ethnic hierarchy" (Hargreaves 2007: 146). Women were equally vulnerable to this economic downturn, as they often found themselves in positions of economic and social dependence on their husbands and male relatives. Contrasting the 1950s with the 1990s underscores how the country's changing economic climate has impacted both socio-economic opportunities and the ways in which Muslims have been perceived in France.

Most of this early immigration stemmed from the former colonies of the Maghreb, Algeria, Tunisia, and Morocco. Contemporarily, Muslim populations in France include converts as well as immigrants from the Middle East, Turkey, Iran, and sub-Saharan Africa (see Figure 1.1). Like the immigration data, statistics on religious affiliation are shaped by French politics. A number of studies suggest a broad Muslim population range, between 5 and 18% of the total French population. These estimates vary because of a lack of concrete data. In its calculations of demographic indicators based on vital records and census data, the national statistical agency INSEE (*Institut national de la statistique et des études économiques*) does not gather data on religion. The smaller INED (*Institut national d'études démographiques*) examines both national and international demographics to generate its estimates, including data from the Ministry of the Interior and from the *Bureau des migrations internationales* on immigrant flows (INED 2010, 2011). A 2010 report from the French Minister of the Interior suggested there were 5–6 million Muslims living in France (Agence France-Presse 2010b).

As neither of these institutes asks directly about religious affiliation, the resulting lacuna has led demographers to create their own statistics (see Tribalat 1996; Couvreur 1998; Boyer 1998; Borrel and Simon 2005; Gourévitch 2008). A 2003 report suggested that France contains 3.5–5 million Muslims, of whom 1–1.6 million are of Algerian

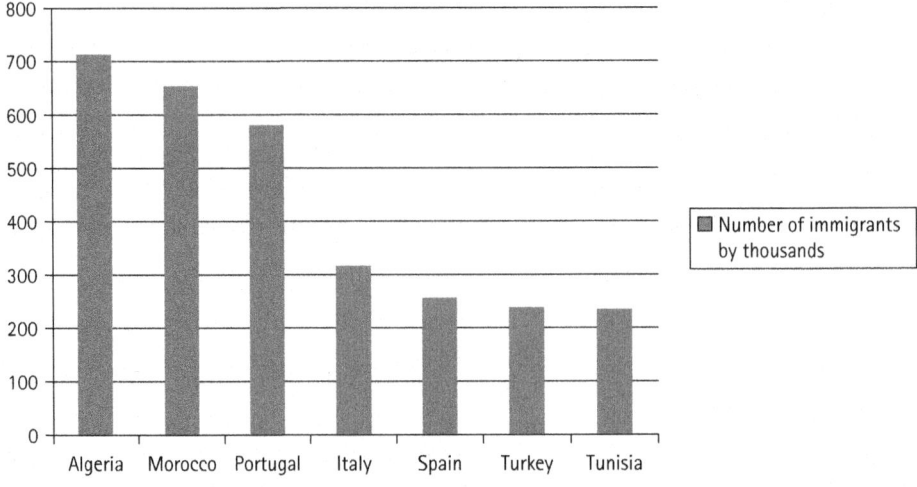

FIGURE 1.1 Immigration in France by country, 2008

origin; 800,000–1 million are Moroccan; 400,000–500,000 are from the "Orient" (especially Turkey); 250,000–500,000 are of West African origin; 300–400 are clandestine Muslims; and several thousand are converts (see Dargent 2003: 3). A range of data also exists from private agencies and international groups. For instance, a 2010 Pew study estimated 4.7 million Muslims (Pew Forum 2011).

Other statistical studies can be pieced together to tell us something about the make-up of French Muslim communities. A 2011 IFOP (*Institut Français d'Opinion Publique*) study published in *La Croix* claimed that most Muslims in France continue to live primarily in the Ile-de-France Parisian region and in the northern and eastern sections of the country. This IFOP study also suggests that the bulk of the Muslim population is young: 31% of the Muslim population falls between the ages of 18 and 24 compared to 12% of the non-Muslim population.

The absence of accurate quantitative data can be explained by a "religion-blind" approach. The religious or ethnic origins of residents are not collected by government statistical agencies or the nationwide census every nine years. This decision stems from a *laïque*-based cultivation of sameness in the public sphere and can be read as in keeping with France's common anti-multiculturalist position. Indeed, from a Republican perspective, fostering a multicultural ethos through the collection of data on religion serves to further stratify cultural, racial, and linguistic differences rather than to unite citizens (Le Monde 2009; Schnapper 1994; Stasi Report 2003; Harris Interactive 2006). A more culturally homogeneous public sphere acts to erase difference to ensure "equality through invisibility" (Simon 2008: 8; for other critiques of this demographic collection see Silverman 1992: 37; Hargreaves 2007: 11).[2] With this lack of concrete demographic information, the closest approximation of the ethnic origins and religious affiliations of the French population is approximated through data published about the nationality of residents. Sectarian differences among Muslims are also estimated. Of course, these approximations are problematic in that they falsely correlate immigration from some countries with Muslimness and discount, among other factors, the numerous Muslims who have lived in France for more than three generations or who may not be of immigrant origin. The French assimilationist position has thus impacted the collection of demographic information about religious affiliation and, quantitatively, what is known about French Muslims.

## Socio-economics

A number of studies have charted how Muslims in France are characterized by socio-economic marginality and are more likely to be unemployed than the remainder

---

[2] Fear of a multicultural ethos is also articulated as concern for "communalism" (*communautarisme*), the idea that one will identify more with one's ethnic or cultural group than with society as a whole (Chevalérias 2008).

of the French population (Hargreaves 2007; Santelli 2007; Laitkin 2009; Adida, Laitin and Valfort 2010: 58). A 2007 INSEE study shows that the unemployment rate for immigrants is more than double that of French nationals (Perrin-Hayes 2008); of course, Muslims fall into both of these groups. Foreign women are particularly affected (see Table 1.1). Three recent studies further exemplify this point.

The first, based on 2005 INSEE data, claims that unemployment among people of French origin was 9.2%, while it was 14% among those with foreign backgrounds. Of course, one's place of birth does not determine one's religious identity or engagement. Because of a lack of quantitative data, "foreigner" is awkwardly correlated with "Muslimness." The published statistic of 14% is also inaccurate for it does not account for the high rate of unemployment among illegal immigrants, non-working individuals who are no longer seeking employment, the number of men and women who do not have the necessary French-language or literacy skills to search for legal work, or the European economic crisis in the 2010s. The percentage of unemployed is therefore likely higher than 14%.

A second statistical study published in Le Monde reveals that young people of North African origin born in France, even with equal or better qualifications compared with a *Français de Souche* candidate, have less success in obtaining employment than other applicants (Hargreaves 2007: 58). This study used blind CVs to conclude that an equally qualified young man with a "Muslim" sounding first and last name would receive less interest and fewer call-backs. As Jocelyne Cesari (2009: 217) notes, there are a number of factors that work in tandem to create this unbalanced situation, most predominantly, "residential segregation, creating the political problem of the *banlieues*." For young qualified Muslim applicants, a suburban address or postal code acts as a hindrance (Amrani and Beaud 2004; Selby 2012: 186n2). A 2005 DARES study further underscores how living in the suburbs appears to affect one's employability (http://www.epsilon.insee.fr/jspui/bitstream/1/3927/1/2005.04-17.3.pdf). Beyond charted discrimination in employment, high unemployment rates in these suburban areas enforce a widespread assumption of a causal link between Islam and poverty.

Table 1.1 Unemployment in France based on nationality

|  | French nationals | Foreigners total | EU nationals | Foreigners outside the European Union |
| --- | --- | --- | --- | --- |
| Men | 7% | 14.80% | 7.30% | 19.60% |
| Women | 8.00% | 18.30% | 8.90% | 26.10% |
| Total | 7.50% | 16.30% | 8.10% | 22.20% |

Source: "Situation des immigrés et des non-immigrés sur le marché du travail."
Enquêtes Emploi du 1er au 4e trimestre, 2007.
Retrieved June 20, 2012 from <http://www.insee.fr/fr/themes/document.asp?ref_id=ip1212>.

A third report produced in 2010 by David Laitin, Claire Adida, and Marie-Anne Valfort, "Les Français musulmans sont-ils discriminés dans leur propre pays? Une étude expérimentale sur le marché du travail" (Are French Muslims Discriminated Against in Their Country? An Experimental Study of the Labour Force), suggests similar results. It offers conclusive evidence of religious discrimination in the French labor market suggested in the aforementioned *Le Monde* study. Laitin et al. conclude that their results are "unambiguous in finding significant religious discrimination against Muslims" (2010). The study similarly involved creating employment CVs for three fictional job-seekers with differing religious and national backgrounds: one French secular individual, one French-Senegalese with a Christian first name, and one French-Senegalese with a Muslim first name. It found that the Christian job applicant was more than twice as likely as the Muslim applicant to receive a call-back. As we will see in the Islamophobia section, employees who wear hijabs report a higher degree of discrimination.

## The *Beurgeoisie*

Thus far I have characterized the majority of French Muslims as economically disfavored and living in stratified *banlieue* regions, but this situation does not reflect the group as a whole. Sometimes called the *beurgeoisie*, or upwardly mobile Muslims, these more socio-economically advantaged individuals make up an elite and powerful group not accounted for with the previous demographic snapshot. Generally, they have accessed more central urban neighborhoods and experienced socio-economic prosperity in France. Since 1982, first-generation immigrants (again, awkwardly correlated with Muslims) have become increasingly educated, with more than five times as many holding at least the equivalent of a bachelor's degree (see Table 1.2).

This growth might also reflect how Muslims in France have gained social mobility. A play on words combining *beur* (*verlan* for Arab; cf. footnote 2) and *bourgeois*, the *beurgeoisie* refers largely to second-generation immigrants, the children of working-class, *banlieue*-living immigrants, mostly from the Maghreb, who have found economic and professional success in France (Hargreaves 1998; Leveau and Wihtol de Wenden 2000). The children of upper-class immigrants who hold high-status positions such as lawyers, doctors, and businesspeople are not usually considered *beurs*. The *beurgeoisie* today are generally more integrated into French society than their parents were and have higher rates of professional and economic successes. They are a small but noteworthy group that have had an impact on Islam-related commerce, notably the availability of high-end halal products in France (Wihtol de Wenden 2011).

Largely due to economic factors, the make-up of the Muslim population in the Republic has thus shifted since the end of the Algerian War in the 1960s. While Muslim communities were once predominantly immigrant-based, of North African origins, and residing in the suburban areas of large French cities, they now increasingly comprise a young and French-born population. So too the threads of scholarship have changed, from studies charting immigration, to those mapping ethnic and urban studies and

Table 1.2 Shifts in the education levels of immigrants and non-immigrants

| Year | No diploma, CEP | BECP, CAP, BEP | Bachelor's degree | Greater than a bachelor's degree |
| --- | --- | --- | --- | --- |
| French nationals | | | | |
| 1982 | ~45% | ~25–30% | ~10–15% | ~10–15% |
| 1999 | ~20% | ~40% | ~15% | ~20–25% |
| 2004–2005 | ~18% | ~30–40% | ~15% | ~20–30% |
| Immigrants to France | | | | |
| 1982 | ~80% | ~10% | ~5% | ~5% |
| 1999 | ~40% | ~20–30% | ~10–15% | ~20% |
| 2004–2005 | ~40% | ~20% | ~10% | ~20–25% |

Source: Évolution de la structure des diplômes des immigrés et des non-immigrés (Institut national de la statistique et des études économiques (INSEE)).
Recensements de 1982 et 1999, enquêtes annuelles de recensement de 2004 et 2005.
Retrieved June 20, 2012 from <http://www.insee.fr/fr/themes/document.asp?ref_id=ip1098&reg_id=0&page=graph#graphique1>.

social movements in the analysis of the *Beur* movement, to demographic concerns. Socio-economic disparities have charted Muslimness through countries of origin and through self-reporting within associations like *SOS Racisme* and the *Collectif Contre l'Islamophobie en France* (CCIF, Collective Against Islamophobia in France). These academic foci are in part attributable to shifts in the broad economic make-up of the community: from unskilled industrialization, to increased unemployment and socio-political marginalization, to immigration policies that have favored family reunification and have "feminized" public debates about Islam. It is to this emphasis on Islam through gender studies that I now turn.

## HEADSCARF AFFAIRS

This section examines the impact of immigration policy and the country's conceptualization of secularity related to what have become known as "headscarf affairs." Recall the "masculine" industrial immigration following the First and Second World Wars. Under the presidency of Valéry Giscard d'Estaing, this gendered migration was replaced in the 1970s with a more "feminized" family reunification immigration policy. The country's more recent immigrant population effectively moved public discourse about Islam in France from male workers (and unrest in the suburbs) toward a greater hijab focus (Koven 1992: 26; Amiraux 2003b, 2007). As single male North African worker migration fell, the visibility of Muslim women and children, particularly those wearing visible religious signs, grew. A greater number of female migrants in the French territory meant that children of North African origin—many of whom were from practicing Muslim families—were born, educated in public schools, and socialized in France. As we shall see, beginning in the 1980s, the visibility of Muslim girls in public schools and women in the public sphere inspired a variety of new policies, politics, and scholarship. Research has examined first-generation (Killian 2006, 2003; Selby 2012) and, to a greater extent, second-generation female Muslim immigrants (Lacoste-Dujardin 1991, 1992, 1994; Khosrokhavar 1997; Cesari 1998; Venel 1999; Tetreault 2000, 2001; Guénif-Souilamas 2000; Fernando 2010). This gendered immigration policy shift therefore impacted the politics, public perception, and examinations of Islam in France.

While many Muslims' experiences in France are shaped by this common immigration history, arguably all French Muslims are impacted by the country's conceptualization of secularity, which some theorists have claimed privileges a "Christian secularism," or what French historian Jean Baubérot (2003) terms *catholaïcité*. Articulations of French secularism or *laïcité* significantly shape debates and controversies about religiosity, particularly related to the public visibility of many Muslim women. Concerns with the power and presence of religion emerged with the French Revolution in the eighteenth century and initially centered on Catholicism. A law formally separating church and state passed in 1905—the *Loi du 9 décembre 1905 concernant la séparation des Églises et de l'État*—so that religious signs and beliefs were formally assigned to the private sphere (see Assemblée Nationale 1905). Jean Baubérot (1998) notes that Catholicism therein lost its social vocation. Notably, the Republic no longer officially funded religious education (there remain exceptions; see Bowen 2009: 445–6), and public institutions were to be independent of religious interests (Favell 1998: 75). In 1946, likely in an effort to reassert French identity following German occupation in the Second World War (Baubérot 1998: 186), the principle of *laïcité* was enshrined in the French constitution (Brulard 1997: 177).

Three political and legal shifts in 1989, 2004, and 2011 have shaped the visibility and rights of French Muslims and have generated a great deal of academic interest. Questions of diversity related to regionalisms, religiosity, or ethnicity are generally managed by the French state through the inculcation of a common language and culture within the national school system (Keaton 2006: 31; see also Brulard 1997: 175; Gauchet 1998: 52; Stasi Report 2003: 17, 23). Schools have been key spaces for disputes related to religiosity and difference (McGoldrick 2006; Agence France-Presse 2011a).

Following an immigration shift to favor women's migration, controversy relating to Islam and *laïcité* in France emerged in a suburban public school in October 1989 with a "headscarf affair." The case was eventually brought to the French Supreme Court that ruled that hijabs and other religious symbols in schools were permissible so long as they were not "conspicuous" or "militant." The court left the interpretation of these terms to individual schools (Brulard 1997: 179). This 1989 case marked a shift in French secular debates with its focus on the visibility of hijabs (Bloul 1996; Brulard 1997; Venel 1999; Dayan-Herzbrun 2000; Bowen 2004a; Killian 2006; see also Chapter 16, this volume) and emphasis on Islam and gender studies in studies of French Muslims. Scholars began considering the politics of Islam in the public sphere as well as reasons why young women veil in contemporary France.

The ruling from the *Court de cassation* appeared to quell the initial issue, but the "headscarf affair" reemerged with gusto five years later in 1994 as local school administrators sought clearer nationally implemented guidelines to determine the acceptability of head-coverings worn by Muslim girls. The government responded with the *Bayrou Circulaire* (or Bayrou Decree) issued by Education Minister François Bayrou. The *Circulaire* sought to distinguish between "discrete" (preferred) and "ostentatious" (i.e. proselytizing and discriminating) religious signs (Joppke 2007: 323) to make their interpretation less ambiguous for teachers and administrators. Following its publication, from 1994 to 2003, a number of hijab-related expulsions, student protests, and judicial decisions of headscarf-wearing girls from the ages of 9 to 18 both confirmed and overturned its proposals (Winter 2006). Continued concern in public schools and dissatisfaction over the subjectivity of this classification led in part to the July 2003 Jacques Chirac-mandated consultative commission to investigate the acceptability of visible religious signs in public schools and make more formal nationally-based recommendations.

After six months of public forums and round tables, this highly mediatized 2003 commission led to a legal change that restricted the visibility of "conspicuous" religious signs in schools. Directed by Bernard Stasi and a group of nineteen scholars, government officials, and experts, and interviewing 140 individuals about the acceptability of religious signs in public schools, the "Stasi Commission" (*Commission de réflexion sur l'application du principe de laïcité dans la République*) made twenty-six recommendations related to the protection of *laïcité* in schools (Weil 2009; Laurence and Vaisse 2006: 166). A number of scholars have argued that, despite its supposed attention to a number of religious signs, it is difficult to deny the commission's targeting of the Muslim headscarf and associated Islamic cultural tenets treating the status and actions of women (Silverstein 2004; Bowen 2007: 42; Scott 2007; Selby 2011b: 446). One of its twenty-six recommendations regarding religious signs was adopted meaningfully. Lawmakers voted on the bill (Law 2004 - 228) to ban conspicuous religious signs in public schools and government offices on February 10, 2004. The law effectively banned symbols and forms of dress that obviously denote the religious identity of students, notably the Muslim veil, the Jewish *kippa*, and large Christian crosses carried on the back. It received strong support and passed, almost unanimously (494 votes in favor, 36 against, and 31 abstentions) on March 15, 2004 (Lyon and Spini 2004; Weil 2009: 2701). The report deems more discrete signs acceptable, like medallions, small crosses, Stars of David, hands of Fatima, or little Qur'ans (Stasi Report 2003: 23). It was instituted with relatively little controversy or rejection from the broader Muslim community (Ministère de l'éducation nationale de l'enseignement supérieur et de la recherché 2005; Winter 2008: 224; Selby 2011a).[3]

In the years since the 2004 law banning conspicuous religious signs in public schools, following a broader European trend (see Chapter 16, this volume), public debates have

---

[3] Former inspector general of the Education Ministry Hanifa Chérifi's June 2005 report claimed that the majority of students removed their religious signs; only forty-seven students refused to conform to the law and the remaining ninety-six students who objected transferred to private schools (Ministère de l'intérieur et de l'aménagement du territoire 2005: 41).

shifted to emphasize the public visibility of face veils (the niqab and *burqa*) in the public sphere. In early 2009, a communist member of the National Assembly and former mayor of Vénissieux, André Gerin, noted an "alarming" rise in the number of women donning the *voile intégral* (full-face-covering hijab) in his constituency near Lyon. Gerin was not alone in expressing concern. Former President Nicolas Sarkozy echoed that, "the burqa is not welcome in the French Republican territory" (Gabizon 2009).[4] With a great deal of public support,[5] Sarkozy commissioned a 2010 "Fact-finding mission on the practice of wearing the full veil on the national territory" (*Rapport d'information fait en application de l'article 145 du règlement au nom de la mission d'information sur la pratique du port du voile intégral sur le territoire national*) or the "Gerin Report" (named after its commissioner). A 658-page report was presented to the National Assembly on January 26, 2010.

Unlike previous commissions that have treated religion in the public sphere, the Gerin Report solely examined niqabs and *burqas*. After considering factors related to the equality of the sexes, women's freedom and dignity, a rise in dangerous Islamism, and security and neighborliness, it concluded that face-covering veils are impediments to women's sexual equality and reflected signs of growing Islamism that must be curtailed. In response to these concerns, the French were the first to legally restrict these face-covering garments in Europe, on April 11, 2011 (Reuters 2010b). The legal restriction entails €150 fines or citizenship classes (or both) for a woman caught covering her face (Radio Free Europe 2011). It carries far greater penalties for husbands, fathers, or brothers convicted of "forcing" the veil on a woman. For men, a €30,000 fine and a year in prison would be doubled if the victim is a minor (*Le Monde* 2010). In sum, culminating with this 2011 law, the visibility of hijabs has drawn significant attention in France, a point echoed in the scholarship examining these garments. Also, on a juridical level, this focus has translated into two laws, in 2004 and 2011, which restrict hijabs in public schools and face-covering hijabs in the public sphere. Even if focused on the public visibility of some Muslim women, the introduction of these laws to enforce French secularism impacts the lives of all French Muslims. In his testimony before the Gerin

---

[4] These issues coincide with April 2011 conversations and televised political debates ostensibly about national identity that appeared to solely discuss Islam in France and its effect on French secularism. Polemic began on a French television program, *Paroles de Français*, when President Sarkozy explained that the Muslim population of France should be able to practice their religion, but he did not want it to become a large part of the French identity (see Pouchard 2011; Cabana 2011; Galaud 2011). The proposal for the debate caused a division within the party, with some members believing it would cause the stigmatization of Muslims. Some French Muslim leaders like Dalil Boubakeur similarly deemed the debate Islamophobic (Libération 2011).

More than the full-face veil ban, this debate has led to an important decline in Sarkozy's popularity among French Muslims.

[5] Polling data suggest that most French citizens agreed with the restriction on face veils with fines in the public sphere. An opinion poll conducted by Taylor Nelson Sofres for *Europe 1* in April 2010 suggested that 63% of the French population fully supported an outright ban (Étude TNS Sofres-Logica 2010). A similar February 2010 survey conducted by the *Financial Times* indicated that 70% of French citizens supported a ban (Blitz 2010).

Commission, CFCM president Mohammed Moussaoui noted the stigmatizing effect of apparatuses like it (Assemblée Nationale 2010: 373).

## INSTITUTIONALIZATION

Despite this formalized Republican separation of church and state that seeks to privatize religiosity, the French state has historically and contemporarily sought to institutionalize and centralize religious authorities. As we saw in the previous section, Islam in France has been monitored and shaped through the creation of government commissions designed to scrutinize affairs affecting Republican politics. This section examines institutionalization of the tradition through the struggling place of private Islamic schools, the creation of the French Council of the Muslim Faith (CFCM) and its work on the reception and qualifications of imams, as well as the instauration of a number of institutes, prayer spaces, cemeteries, and halal regulation. Attention to the institutionalization of Islam in France has generated notable research (Bowen 2007, 2011; Caeiro 2005a; Fetzer and Sopher 2005; Frégosi 1996, 1998, 2011; Laurence and Vaisse 2006).

Scholarly attention to this institutionalization arguably stems in part from common shifts in the challenges facing Muslim communities. As Laurence and Vaisse note (2006), the first generation of Muslim immigrants focused their attention on securing better rights for foreign workers; the second generation fought against racism and discrimination through left-leaning non-religiously focused activism, like the *Beur* movement; and the most recent generation increasingly identifies with a more pan-Islamic globalized Islam as a way to assert identities in a public sphere shaped by *laïque* debates.

## Islamic Schools

The 2004 law restricting conspicuous religious signs largely concerned Muslim girls not only because of its implicit headscarf focus but also because, unlike the Catholic, Protestant, and Jewish populations, the French Muslim population has only a handful of private Islamic schools where headscarves are permitted (Innovative Minds 2004). Most young women who wear hijabs attend public schools where the law is in effect. Here I mention six private Islamic institutions; three are situated outside Paris, one in Lille, and one outside of Lyon. Another exists in La Réunion, a French overseas territory. In theory, under the 1959 Debré Law, provided that they follow the set state school curriculum and submit to inspections, faith-based private schools are eligible for government grants that pay the wages of state-accredited teachers (Bowen 2009: 447). Only one private Muslim school has thus far succeeded in securing funding, the Lycée Averroès in Lille. Inspiration for its creation grew after the aforementioned 1994 Bayou Decree when nineteen headscarf-wearing students from the Lycée Faidherbe were expelled when their head-coverings were deemed as conspicuous. Surviving initially on donations and becoming an association in November 2001, the school began receiving some financial support from the state in July 2003 (Innovative Minds 2004). In the 2010–11 school year it had 150 students enrolled, up from fifteen in 2003–4 (see Lycée Averroès n.d.). It has received support from national Muslim organizations. For instance, the *Union des organizations islamiques de France* (UOIF) was involved in its launch (along with the *Collège Al-Kindi*; see Mazawi 2010: 184).

For the remaining schools, funding has been a significant issue. For some critics, private Muslim schools threaten the cohesiveness of the Republic (Mazawi 2010: 177). Some feel their focus is counter-productive to the integration of Muslim immigrants (see Bowen 2009). At the same time, given its claims that it adheres to the National Education pedagogical curriculum program, others have suggested that state funding rejections have been Islamophobic in nature (*Le Nouvel Observateur* 2008; Bowen 2009). The private Muslim school Collège Lycée Al-Kindi in a suburb of Lyon admitted its first twenty-two pupils in March 2007 after an eight-month financial struggle (Heneghan 2007). Even if most girl pupils wear them, headscarves are not obligatory at Al-Kindi and its religion class is optional. In March 2008, *Éducation et Savoir* ("Education and Knowledge") opened in the Parisian suburb of Vitry-sur-Seine (Val-de-Marne). Like other private Muslim schools, their biggest challenge has not been obtaining an operation license, but in securing funding. It has so far been funded by a medley of private donors and associations in France (Islam Online 2008).

Like the Al-Kindi high school in a suburb of Lyon, the *Collège Lycée Réussite* ("Success") in the northern Parisian suburb of Aubervilliers (Seine-Saint-Denis) and *Éducation et Savoir* in Villeneuve-Saint-Georges (Val-de-Marne) have not been successful in securing funding. *La Réussite* began as an association in 1992 and opened in October 2001. Its website emphasizes the scholastic achievement of its 100 students and notes that students of all religious backgrounds are welcome (see *Collège Lycée Réussite* 2011 and overview of this school in Bowen 2011: 110–24). It is regularly on the precipice of bankruptcy and relies primarily on charitable donations; in 2008, *La Réussite*'s teachers worked for several months without pay and it continues to have financial issues (Nixey 2009; Thomas 2010). At the time of writing, the *Éducative* school had opened. It has a different model in that it charges €4,500 annually and is otherwise funded by Turkish foreign sources (*Le Monde* 2009). In sum, while there is clearly a clientele for these schools, reliable funding has not yet been established. The institutionalization of private Islamic schools is far from ecure.

## The CFCM and Other Groups

In 2003 the tradition was governmentalized[6] when then-Interior Minister Nicolas Sarkozy inaugurated the *Conseil Français du Culte Musulman* (CFCM or French Council of the Muslim Faith) as a centralized representative body for French Muslims. In keeping with the official representatives in place in France for French Catholics, Jews,

---

[6] Sarah Bracke and Nadia Fadil (2012: 42) usefully define governmentality as "the ways in which governments try to produce 'the citizen' and all the organized practices and techniques through which subjects are governed."

and Protestants, beginning in the 1980s, discussions began to formalize a similar group for Muslims. These efforts coalesced alongside post-9/11 securitization initiatives. The CFCM acts at the national level while Regional Councils of the Muslim Faith (CRCM) were established and elected at the local level. Even if common in the French state, Vincent Geisser notes that comparatively this kind of government top-down intervention is rare in Europe (2010: 42).

Created under the auspices of offering greater representation, the state's involvement in the CFCM has drawn criticisms about state interference. These remarks were sharpest with the initial appointment of Dalil Boubakeur as the first council president by Sarkozy and with complaints that the organization follows a Protestant model of representation and does not adequately represent the diverse make-up of French Muslims (see Caeiro 2005a: 71–84; Amiraux 2003a: 24–5; Winter 2008: 85–7). Critiques regarding a lack of representiveness were central to divisions in elections for the organization in 2011, which reelected Mohammed Moussaoui as the organization's president. The GMP (Mosque of Paris) and the UOIF boycotted, alleging voting rules favored Moroccan-based groups (*Le Monde* 2011a).

In part due to its perceived lack of legitimacy among French Muslims, a number of other organizations have grown. The largest parallel group is the UOIF, an umbrella organization of more than 200 mosques and local Islamic associations founded in 1983 (Caeiro 2005b). The UOIF organizes a large annual gathering in Le Bourget that attracts thousands of Muslims from across the country; in 2011, more than 53,000 people attended the weekend-long gathering (Euro-Islam 2009b). Their ideological stance has sometimes been depicted as reformist Islam inspired by the Muslim Brotherhood movement (Caeiro 2003); the UOIF follows similar principles of education and civic engagement, and does not hold allegiance to a specific school of jurisprudence (*madhab*). For these reasons, even if the UOIF is recognized as a legitimate member of the CFCM with its president sitting on the CFCM executive, the organization has been considered as suspect by public authorities.

A number of scholars have charted the place of the Muslim Brotherhood in France (Kepel 2004; Maréchal 2008; Ternisien 2011). Members of the pan-Islamic Muslim Brotherhood (founded in Egypt in 1928) began migrating from Arab countries at the end of the 1950s. In comparing the group's presence in the UK and France, Brigitte Maréchal notes that in the latter, "where government policies are focused on the integration of individuals and not collective groups, the claims are usually less explicit and provocative as they seem to be limited to the social sphere" (2008: 37). The Swiss-born grandson of Hassan al-Banna (1906–48), the group's founder, remains a controversial figure in French political and academic circles. Tariq Ramadan (b. 1962), a scholar of Contemporary Islamic Studies at Oxford University, was strongly critiqued by Nicholas Sarkozy on the French television debate program, *100 minutes pour convaincre*, on November 20, 2003, and by French essayist Caroline Fourest (2004; see also Frégosi 1998: 117 and 2004: 138 on Ramadan's theological message).

Other important Muslim organizations include the National Federation of French Muslims (FNMF, the *Federation nationale des musulmans de France*), controlled by counterparts in Morocco, and the Paris Mosque (GMP, *Grande Mosquée de Paris*), led by former CFCM president Dalil Boubakeur and financed by the Algerian government. The *Parti des musulmans de France* (PMF, Muslim Party of France), created in Strasbourg in 1997 by Mohamed Ennacer Latrèche, seeks to reflect the political interests of French Muslims. Its influence has been largely restricted to the Alsatian region (http://fr.wikipedia.org/wiki/Parti_des_musulmans_de_France). It has not won any elections.

Salafism, stemming from Saudi Arabian religious doctrine and associated with literalist conservatism, has been charted by scholars as a growing movement in France since the 1990s. Women who wear niqabs are often characterized as members of this group (like "Mme. M." who was the first person whose citizenship request in 2008 was refused based primarily on her alleged allegiance to this group; see Prada-Bordenave 2008; Mullally 2010), which is why the 2010 Gerin Report that preceded the 2011 law banning full-face veils in the public sphere spends some time qualifying their presence. The Gerin Report suggests that there are between 12,000 and 15,000 Salafis in France (2010: 59). The report characterizes the group pejoratively as radical, ghettoizing (*communautariste*), and anti-woman (Assemblée Nationale 2010: 31). While he does not condemn the practice entirely, CFCM president Mohammed Moussaoui testified before the commission that the niqab is "an extreme practice that the CFCM does not wish to see become established in the national territory" (Assemblée Nationale: 36; see also Selby 2011b: 387). Samir Amghar's *Le salafisme d'aujourd'hui: mouvements sectaires en occident* (2011) echoes that the group's popularity has grown in France, particularly among second-generation Muslim youth (see also Kepel 2004). Contextualizing the group's growth, Amghar distinguishes between pietist, political, and revolutionary Salafism and suggests that 95% of French Salafis fall into the pietist category (Gauthier 2012).

Similarly, the Jamaat at-Tabligh, founded in India in 1927, is a revivalist movement targeting the return of Muslims to the "right path." It became global after the Second World War and established itself in France in the late 1960s (Amghar 2009: 32). There are very few scholarly surveys of this group and its followers in the French context, likely due to their secrecy and separatist posture vis-à-vis mainstream society. For these reasons and because they preach a conservative interpretation of Islam, they are often associated with radical activism (see the next section).

## "Home-grown" Imams

Related to this concern for an institutionalized *Islam de France*, there has been a push for "home-grown" imams. Indeed, the training of imams was amongst the first tasks delegated to the CFCM, as the training and low salaries of imams were identified in three reports as contributing to an extremist subculture among Muslims in France. The *Haut Commissariat à l'Intégration* (High Commission on Integration) released "L'Islam dans la République" in 2000 that discussed the question of imam training. It suggested that training for Muslim leaders was not sufficiently developed and recommended that such training take place through a university setting. The 2005 Machelon Report (see *Ministère de l'intérieur et de l'aménagement du territoire* 2005) was commissioned by the French Prime Minister to examine some of the legal issues concerning the relations between the state and religious denominations. The Machelon Report suggests the creation of a state-funded institute of Islamic theology in Strasbourg. More quantitatively, according to the 2003 King Baudoin Foundation survey, of approximately 1,000 imams in France, just over half were permanent residents, fewer than half received regular salaries, and one-third speak little or no French. Attempts to create French-run training centers to rectify these issues have been unsuccessful. From 1994 to 2000, the Mosque of Paris housed a training institute for imams that closed due to lack of subsidies. The *Institut d'Études Islamiques de Paris* (Paris Institute of Islamic Studies) suffered a similar fate. Since these closures a number of other organizations have offered a variety of Islamic studies programs, including the *Centre de Recherche sur l'Islam* (CERSI, Centre of Research on Islam), the *Institut Français des Études et Sciences Islamiques* (IFESI, French Institute of Islamic Studies and Sciences), and the *Institut Européen des Sciences Humaines* (IESH, European Institute of Human Sciences) (King Baudouin Foundation 2003: 17). These institutes have been unable to continue operating. Their primary roadblock has been budgetary.

## Prayer Spaces and Mosques

There is not an abundance of congregational prayer space for Muslims in France, whether in public or private settings. Controversy has emerged surrounding the use of public street space for congregational prayer, with particular attention placed on two streets in Paris's Goutte d'Or in the 18th district. In response to the visibility of Friday prayer on these streets, in June 2010, anti-Muslim far right groups organized a sausage and wine *apéro géant* (giant appetizer event) to critique halal sensibilities in the multi-ethnic area of Paris; others emerged in Nice and Lyon. Organizers sought to denounce what they deemed the Islamization of France but were later banned due to their anti-Islam message. In response, 800 protesters gathered, singing the Marseillaise, brandishing salami and wearing berets while denouncing "the arrogance of Muslims" (RFI 2010). Far right National Front leader Marine Le Pen compared the Parisian street prayers to German Nazi occupation, a position with which 39% of French citizens allegedly agreed (Reuters 2010a; IFOP 2010). In response to the debate and the spatial issue of outdoor prayer which he deemed "unacceptable," then French Interior Minister Claude Guéant announced that a former barracks in the same *arrondissement* would be used to better accommodate the large prayer-attending community. An unused barracks owned by the Ministry of Defense near Porte des Poissonniers in the periphery of the city will be turned into a makeshift mosque to accommodate the overflow of people (RFI 2011).

This repurposing reflects the lack of space available in mosques and legal issues with their financing and construction. While there is a long history of mosque construction dating to the eighth century, with the exception of the Mosque of Paris built in the 1920s in the city's 5th district, more concerted construction began with the wave of Muslim immigrants after the Second World War. Many of these prayer spaces were built ad hoc and served male factory workers. Following a 1981 law under Mitterrand that facilitated the creation of social and cultural associations by non-citizens, many more Muslim associative spaces with affiliations to Algeria, Morocco, and Turkey were created (Bowen 2010: 30). These Islamic centers facilitated marriage rites, funerals, classes, and recreational activities (Cesari 2009: 215). Often these mosques and associations were converted from private homes, apartments, and warehouses and offered Arabic classes and after-school tutoring. The possibility of creating associations meant there was a substantial climb, from 500 mosques in 1985 to 1,279 mosques by 1992 (see Bowen 2010: 30–1). Frégosi (1998: 118) notes the disparity of religious sites per capita for Muslims in contrast with Catholics, Protestants, and Jews, pointing to a lack of land-holdings and prejudice as obstacles to this end. However, recent reports suggest mosque creation continues to rise. A 2011 report by CFCM president Mohammed Moussaoui suggests that there were between 100 and 150 mosques under construction across France (*Le Figaro* 2011c; Le Bars 2012a; see also Institut Français d'Opinion Publique 2009). In addition, should it be completed—at the time of writing its building permit has been revoked and construction on the 2,500 m$^2$ building has stalled—the Mosque of Marseille could be France's largest mosque (Euro-Islam 2009a; La Croix 2013).

Despite land acquisition and the proliferation of buildings, resentment toward Muslim prayer space remains notable, as the outdoor prayer controversies and *apéro* responses suggest. While reflecting growth, the CFCM announcement of increased mosque construction does not account for two factors: the considerable internal disputes that take place in their construction and the growing number of non-Muslim French who are reluctant to see mosques and minarets in their environs. In the wake of the minaret ban in Switzerland, a 2009 IFOP poll suggested that a growing number of French people do not want a mosque in their backyards. The study concludes that 41% of French people are opposed to new construction of mosques, up from 22% in 2001 (IFOP 2009). In 1989, resistance to the presence of mosques was also high: 38% of the French did not want to see a mosque near their residence. Arguably, therefore, anti-mosque sentiments peak in moments when other controversies related to Islam (in both 1989 and 2009 related to hijabs) are in the public eye.

## Cemeteries

Another practical issue that has received far less media and scholarly attention compared to hijab debates is that of Islamically-appropriate cemetery plots.[7] Burial grounds have been places of contention in the French landscape given that *laïque* laws dictate

---

[7] A separate issue has been the desecrations of cemeteries across the country (*Le Figaro* 2010). Brice Hortefeux, the Minister of the Interior announced in a report that between January 1 and September 30, 2010, 485 cemeteries and religious sites were vandalized, 410 of which were Christian sites, forty of

that there should be no separate or specially marked plot areas to allow the deceased to face Mecca. A 2009 report published in *Le Parisien* suggests that, with the exception of the cemetery in Bobigny (Seine-Saint-Denis), there are eighty confessional plots available in France (*Le Parisien* 2009). In an effort to respond to the needs of the families of deceased Muslims, papers were signed in October 2009 to create the first Muslim cemetery in the eastern city of Strasbourg, possible given the province of Alsace's exclusion from the 1905 law on secularism (Belghiti 2009). There remain few available Muslim plots in the rest of the country. Given these issues of availability as well as cultural and familial ties, many Muslims of immigrant origin opt to be buried in their or their parents' country of origin.

## Halal Regulation

A last institutional arm has centered upon halal food regulation through supermarkets, butcheries, and abattoirs. Even if fewer than 50% of French Muslims consider themselves as practicing, the halal food industry in France is thriving. Halal food products deemed permissible according to Islamic law first appeared in French commercial spaces in the 1970s, and were sold mainly in immigrant-owned butcheries. Since then, their demand and sales have increased dramatically so that by 2011, the sector amassed €7.6 billion in annual sales (Crumley 2011a). Distribution has expanded: at first, the market was supplied mainly by international companies serving the Middle East and North Africa; more recently, multinational companies, such as Nestlé and Pazani, have begun producing a wide variety of halal products across Europe (Crumley 2011a).

In a 2009 IFOP study for *Le Figaro*, 59% of Muslims claimed to purchase halal foods regularly, including meats, but also a wide variety of other foods. Ninety-two percent of halal product consumers regularly buy their goods in a halal butcher shop and 34% find halal products in supermarkets like Casino (IFOP 2011). Halal-certified foods are becoming increasingly solicited. In eight of their 362 branches, popular French fast-food chain Quick has begun selling halal-certified meat with success. This availability in regions with larger Muslim populations has brought media attention and has been well received by many French Muslims (Blackler 2010; Brochen 2010). At the same time, as the market has grown, controversy about the sale and the authenticity of halal products in France has also emerged. The *Débat Halal* website (http://www.debat-halal.fr) is an example of a consumer-driven internet resource that publishes information about popular halal-certified products and their legitimacy for French consumers (Crumley 2011a). Currently, there are no unified standards by which the production and sale of halal products are governed in France.

---

which were Muslim (of which thirty-four were mosques or prayer rooms and six were cemeteries) and thirty-five of which were Jewish (*Agence France-Presse* 2010a).

The availability of religiously sanctioned products is further reflected in concerns around the accessibility of halal-based abattoirs for everyday consumers, particularly with annual Eid al-Adha celebrations at the end of the hajj. While most French Muslims obtain halal meats through their neighborhood halal butcher, when the community seeks to find greater quantities or desires a closer relationship with the sacrificial animal for the Feast of Sacrifice, availability and access to abattoirs become an issue (Bowen 2009: 449). Animal rights activists like actress Brigitte Bardot have voiced discontent against ritual halal slaughter practices in France; critics of her campaign have commented how "it was more about targeting minorities than animal welfare" (Biedermann 2011).

In sum, the French government has been involved in the institutionalization of Islam through a number of means. Firstly, while it has not tended to facilitate partial state funding for Islamic private schools, it has created a state interlocutor—the CFCM—which itself has inspired the creation of a number of counter-representative institutions like the UOIF. Secondly, the regulation of imams has reflected a French state seeking to shape Muslim institutions through language, securitization, and limiting immigration should they be found to have suspicious ties. In addition, a number of institutes such as the *Institut du Monde Arab* and the *Institut des Cultures d'Islam*, as well as a dedicated wing on the celebrated *Musée du Louvre*, have sought to showcase the cultural contributions of Muslims. Prayer and burial spaces in cemeteries remain key issues for the viability of Islam in France. Lastly, halal products have come under some regulation as demand has increased substantially since the 1980s.

## French Muslim Religiosity

As aforementioned, noteworthy qualitative research has outlined the everyday experiences of Muslims with a recent focus on second-generation women (Bowen 2007; Cesari 1998, 2001; Fernando 2010; Gaspard and Khosrokhavar 1995; Guénif-Souilamas 2000; Keaton 2006; Killian 2006; Lacoste-Dujardin 1992; Moran 2012; Parvez 2011; Tetreault 2001; Venel 1999; Weibel 2000). Generally these studies have sought to add nuance and complexity to depictions that have stereotyped religiously practicing women. Findings have highlighted the individualization of practice: that for most women religious dress is not intended to promote a political project, and that with important exceptions, many male and female Muslims practice their faith in accordance with the French distinction of private and public spheres. These depictions counter common monolithic portrayals of passive women railing against assimilation and the French state.

Indeed, in light of the aforementioned mediatized controversies regarding religious practice in the public sphere, it is worth considering whether these issues *actually* reflect the concerns of mainstream French Muslims. A number of quantitative studies suggest that few French Muslims find these issues of pressing concern. Two recent polls suggest that a relatively small percentage of French Muslims consider themselves as *pratiquants* (practicing Muslims) and that a far greater number see themselves as *croyants* (believing Muslims), an understanding of belief which does not appear to trespass the desired *laïque* public sphere delineated in recent laws. In both studies, the definitional distinction between *pratiquants* and *croyants* lies in whether one prays five times per day and attends *jumu'ah* midday prayer on Fridays like the *pratiquants* (Bowen 2004 also uses these categories). Strikingly, while they receive a great deal of attention from the press and through academic investigation, data suggest that the majority of the French Muslim population does not deem these three issues as significant in their quotidian lives.

The first poll, a 2011 INED study (*Institut national d'études démographiques*) conducted between September 2008 and February 2009 with 21,000 respondents, suggests that 33% of Muslims in France consider themselves as "practicing and believing" and that a higher percentage of Muslims born in France, 43%, say they are *croyants* but not *pratiquants*. This study claims that only 10% of the French Muslim population participates in midday congregational prayer on Fridays, which has been a controversial issue in one district of Paris because of an overflow of congregants into the street. A far higher percentage of French Muslims—80%—say they observe the fast of Ramadan and that they attend mosque regularly during this month. This 2011 INED study also maintains that the religious practices of Muslims born in France differ from first-generation immigrants. This point is notable as more time passes from the initial large waves of immigration in the mid-twentieth century (see also Lagrange 2013).

A second study similarly complicates the representativeness of these controversies as common concerns among French Muslims. In it results from a 2011 IFOP poll are paired with longitudinal data from 1989 (IFOP 2011). It suggests that 41% of French Muslims consider themselves as "believers" of Islam, 22% as having "Muslim origins," and 2% as without religion, suggesting that these respondents deem "Muslim" as a cultural rather than as a religious category. Again, the month of Ramadan appears to be an exception in terms of religious practice: 80% of those surveyed in this IFOP study said they fast, whether completely or partially, during this month. Also notable is that, in comparison with 1989 findings, this IFOP study suggests that the number of Muslims who deem themselves as "believing and practicing" (or *pratiquants*) has risen slightly. Compared with 37% of the French Muslim population who categorized themselves under this category in 1989, in 2011, 41% saw themselves as *pratiquants*. In addition, the 2011 results suggest a significant shift among young people. Compared to 1989 findings where 7% of Muslims under 25 claimed to attend mosque once a week, in 2011, 23% of young people attested to attending *jumu'ah* prayer. While not as dramatic, a similar climb in mosque attendance is found among all ages and both genders (generally up to 25% from 16% in 1989). Female respondents claimed Islam to be more important in their lives than men (INED 2010: 126), but most of the 25% of French Muslim Friday prayer attendees are men.

The trend reported in these two studies of fewer *pratiquants* and more *croyants* is replicated among the percentage of women reporting to wear hijabs. In other words, while the number of books, commissions, and laws treating headscarves might give the impression that there are many practicing Muslims in France, the data suggest otherwise. The IFOP quantitative study proposes a minority percentage—26% of women of those who call themselves *pratiquantes*—regularly wear the hijab while only 8% of all women who self-define as Muslim and are under 35 wear hijabs on a daily basis. This percentage appears to grow with age: 30% of self-defined Muslim women who are 50 years or older wear head-coverings. This statistic does not distinguish between niqabs and hijabs. Even should we reference the higher measurement of 30%, the number of women wearing hijabs is likely less than we might expect based on the intensity and fervor of public debate. The challenge then is to gauge their importance in the face of disparate accounts (Parvez 2011; Open Society Foundations 2011). For instance, the 2010 Gerin Report that preceded the law enacting fines for women who wear niqabs and *burqas* suggests two figures: the first of 367 fully-veiled women across the country from a study undertaken by the DCRI (*Direction centrale du renseignement intérieur* for *Le Figaro*; see *Le Figaro* 2009) and the second, which is given more weight in the Gerin Report, from the Minister of the Interior, that estimates 1,900 full-face veil wearing women, of which one quarter are converts and one half live in the Ile-de-France region (Assemblée Nationale 2010: 24–9). These polling data distinguishing between *pratiquants* and *croyants* suggest that the number of Muslims who are affected by these debates as everyday practitioners may be more limited than we might expect according to media accounts, government reports, and academic analyses. The data therefore remind us that responses to the debates chronicled in this chapter may affect fewer French Muslims than first appears.

## Political Representation

Not a great deal is known about the political participation and representation of Muslims in France. As we will see, scholarly publications present differing accounts. On the one hand, Rahsaan Maxwell's (2010, 2012) work analyzing voting rates among minority migrant groups correlates ethnic background (i.e. Maghrebian origins) with religiosity. Maxwell shows that non-participation in the 2004 national French elections cannot be explained by religious affiliation, but rather the neighborhoods in which voters lived. Comparing immigrants of Maghrebian and Caribbean origin with native French, Maxwell concludes that "migrant/native turnout difference is no longer statistically significant once a series of geographic variable are included in the analysis" (2010: 426). His findings suggest that more significant than religious affiliation is to appreciate how socio-economically disadvantaged areas have a lower voter turnout than more "advantaged" regions. Residence in underprivileged neighborhoods also remains an important predictor of minority unemployment (Richard 2007; Maxwell 2010). Another factor is captured by Laurence and Vaisse (2006: 199) who qualify that only half of the French Muslim population are eligible to vote, given that many are not citizens or are underage.

On the other hand, the Centre for Political Research at *Sciences Politiques*' (CEVIPOF) 2011 report on the "Muslim Vote" concludes differently. The report suggests that, with the exception of the second round of voting in the 2002 victory of Jacques Chirac, since 1965, Muslim voters have played decisive roles in presidential results because these elections have been won by only a few points. Recall the *Beur* movement of the 1980s that reflected a significant moment of change in the perception of voice and power within the Muslim community. By the late 1980s, Leveau and Wihtol de Wenden (2001) chart an increased political and scholarly interest of an "ethnic vote." Indeed, during the 1989 presidential elections, second-generation Maghrebis were said to be encouraged to vote collectively, as the group was perceived to have significant political power: 84% of the so-called Maghrebi population voted for François Mitterrand (Hargreaves 1998).

Politically, French Muslim voters appear to vote more to the left. For instance, CEVIPOF reports that 95% of the community voted for Ségolène Royal in 2007 and only 5% for Nicolas Sarkozy (2011: 2). This suggestion was echoed in 2012. Reports claim that 2 million Muslims voted in the 2012 presidential elections, of whom 93% voted for François Hollande (Heiser 2012; Jacques 2012). Given that Hollande defeated Sarkozy by 1.1 million votes in the election, these reports suggest that the "Muslim vote" was a significant factor. Prior to the elections, media outlets chronicled imams and French Islamic associations calling upon Muslims to "do their duty as citizens and go to the polls" (Ganley 2012b: 1; Crumley 2012). In his analysis, Nick Hewlett (2012) notes that Socialist leader François Hollande's 2012 presidential victory appears to have uncharacteristically mobilized the traditional working class, which might include Muslim voters (Barzegar 2012).[8] Following Hollande's 2012 victory, photographs posted on the inflammatory French website *Observatoire de l'Islamisation* showed Muslims "waving the flags of their native countries and jubilant over the defeat of Sarkozy" (Barillas 2012). Together these studies, reports, and news stories suggest that being Muslim shapes voting tendencies.

Despite these studies that differently interpret the role of religiosity in voting habits and preferences, there is a paucity of work that examines Muslim political representatives (Jytte Klausen's 2005 comparative work is a notable exception). At the time of writing, there are currently no elected Muslim members in the national legislature.[9] However, even if not elected, there has been an important rise in the number of

---

[8] Following the national elections in May 2012, President Hollande appointed Yamina Benguigui (b. 1957) (whose parents are of Algerian origin) as junior minister for French Living Abroad (*Le Nouvel Observateur* 2012). Previously, in the March 2008 French municipal elections, she had been elected in the XXe arrondissement to the *Conseil de Paris* and is known for her films on gender issues in the North African immigrant community in France. Hollande also appointed Algerian-born Kader Arif (b. 1959) as junior minister for Veteran Affairs (*Le Monde* 2012). These publicly visible members of government arguably reflect a shift in French politics and recognition of the lack of representation of visible minorities and women as political representatives. In 2012 there was gender parity in the cabinet for the first time in French history.

[9] So-called Muslim cabinet ministers have been more prominent. Equal Opportunities Minister Azouz Begag (b. 1957) was selected by then-Prime Minister Dominique de Villepin in June 2005; he resigned in 2007 to participate in the unsuccessful presidential campaign of François Bayrou. Nicolas

candidates who have presented themselves for elections. The 2007 national elections saw a significant increase in the number of candidates of Muslim backgrounds when compared to the national parliamentary elections in 2002. Of the approximately 7,500 candidates in each election, fewer than twelve candidates in 2002 came from minority backgrounds; the number grew to just under 250 in the 2007 election. In 2002, no minority candidates succeeded to the second round of voting, whereas eight minority candidates made the second round in 2007 (Euro-Islam n.d.). In 2011, Kenza (Kendra) Drider became the first woman wearing the *voile intégral* (full-face hijab) to announce her candidacy for presidency (Allen 2011; *Daily Mail* 2011; Nikolas 2011).

## ISLAMOPHOBIA AND RADICALISM

Islamophobia, "an outlook or world-view involving an unfounded dread and dislike of Muslims" (Runnymede Trust 1997; see also Cesari 2006; Allen 2010: 3; Shryock 2010), was coined in the late 1990s to express an irrational fear of Islam. It differs from racism and xenophobia because of its religion focus. Following Said (1978) and like Mamdani (2004), Orsi (2003: 171) has further recognized a commonplace post-9/11 distinction between "good Islam—which we recognized as like ourselves—and a bad distorted something else that existed in Middle Eastern lands but had nothing to do with Islam and was our enemy." This section briefly considers scholarship examining Islamophobia in France and concludes by turning to public opinion polls. Benn and Jawad (2004) argue that the sentiment can be traced back to the 1989 Rushdie Affair and 9/11-related discrimination; however, religion-based discrimination in France can be traced to before this time. As we saw in the first section, the contemporary unemployment and socio-economic discrimination that affected first-generation Muslim male workers has at times been explained by racism and xenophobia (Lainé et al. 2005). Racism has often been cited as a chief cause of police discrimination, as reflected in the incidents which spurred suburban riots in 2005 and 2007 (Mohammed and Mucchielli 2006; Dufresne 2007). Of course, as Cesari notes, this discrimination is the culmination of "issues of poverty, ethnicity, and Islam [that] tend to be conflated, both in current political discourse and in political practice" (Cesari 2005).

---

Sarkozy introduced three members of Muslim background. In 2007 he appointed Algerian-Moroccan Rachida Dati (b. 1965) to the position of Justice Minister until, following some controversy, she resigned in 2009 and became mayor of Paris's 7th district (Euro-Islam 2007). In the same year he appointed Fadela Amara (b. 1964), former leader of the suburban activist organization *Ni Putes Ni Soumises* (Neither Whores Nor Submissives) as Secretary of State for Urban Policies. Amara has called herself an atheist. She left this government office in 2010 and in January 2011 was named Minister for Social Affairs (*Le Monde* 2011b). Also noteworthy is Nagat Vallaud-Belkacem (b. 1977) who was adviser to Ségolène Royal's 2007 presidential campaign and since 2008 has been the sixth deputy mayor of Lyon, responsible for major events, youth, and community life.

One of the most complete sources on Islamophobic incidents in France is compiled by the *Collectif Contre l'Islamophobie en France* (CCIF, Collective Against Islamophobia in France). The CCIF was founded in October 2003 "in reaction to the essentialist presentation of a monolithic Islam in the French public sphere" (see: http://www.islamophobie.net/presentation.php). It releases annual data on Islamophobic incidents in France. The CCIF expects there are many more incidents than those reported because of the stigma or feelings of powerlessness among victims and because the organization has not yet gained widespread attention. Based on the statistics accumulated for anti-Islamic acts against individuals, the CCIF distinguishes between three types of Islamophobic actors: within public services (mainly administration, education, and public enterprises); by private companies (mostly in the medical, commercial, and leisure sectors); and by individuals. Its 2010 report notes a continued rise in Islamophobic occurrences with 152 acts reported in 2010. Of these incidents, two figures are noteworthy: 75.6% of Islamophobic acts in the preceding year (2009) were directed toward individuals (and not institutions) and 92% were directed against women (in total, 115 of 152 acts were toward women).

This finding supports sociologist Vincent Geisser's (2010) suggestion that Islamophobia has been no more pronounced in France than in other Western European countries post-9/11. Rather, he posits that the greater impact in the post-9/11 period has been what he calls "hijabophobia," or the rejection of the hijab (2010: 43–4). Geisser's argument about a rise in hijabophobia is evidenced in the number of government-mandated commissions examining these issues and in the 2004 and 2011 laws that have come into practice that formally restrict hijabs in public schools and government offices and face-covering hijabs in the public sphere.[10]

A second more latent example of Islamophobia was apparent in the response by some French politicians following the 2005 suburban riots. Rather than considering factors of discrimination and socio-economic disenfranchisement, *polygamy* among the majority-Muslim population of African origin emerged in the press and in the responses of some politicians as the root cause of the tensions (Selby 2013).[11] While the aforementioned long-standing tensions around immigration, unemployment, and ethnic and religious difference are likely sources to qualify the suburban unrest, in 2005 members of the leading center-right UMP party (Union for a Popular Movement—*Union pour un Mouvement Populaire*) as well as public intellectuals argued that the riots stemmed from a lack of parental control by polygamous families of African origin. During the curfew period, then-President Jacques Chirac similarly pointed his finger at "disintegrating"

---

[10] Jocelyne Cesari suggests that a great deal of scholarship on Islam published in France reflects attempts to combat Islamophobia. In this discussion she explicitly cites Geisser and Lorcerie's *La Nouvelle Islamophobie* (2003) (see Cesari 2009: 200).

[11] Polygamy was unofficially accepted until the 1993 Pasqua law introduced a ban on residence permits for more than one spouse (Freedman 2004: 114; Costa-Lascoux 1994: 29). The estimated number of polygamists in France varies with reports ranging from 8,000–40,000 polygamous families or between 150,000 and 400,000 individuals (Institut Montaigne 2009; Oger 2005; Tribalat et al. 1996). Some of these reports suggest a proclivity for polygamy in particular *banlieues* (Simons 1996).

families where parental authority had broken down. In a press conference, he instructed French parents to "fulfill their responsibilities" and keep children off the streets and away from rioting gangs (*Expatica* 2005). A number of other politicians like Gérard Larcher and Bernard Accoyer made similar comments (Arnold 2005; Belien 2005). Scholars have since pointed to the impact of socio-economic issues in contributing to these tensions (Cesari 2005; Mauger 2006; Moran 2012; Kepel 2012).

## Radicalism

Rather than a 9/11 focus, response to terrorism in France has been more focused on attacks undertaken by Algerian terrorists in 1995, most dramatically in a number of Parisian metro stations. Indeed, there are differing views as to the impact of 9/11 on the perception of Muslims and Islamophobia in France. Some qualify its impact as being more generative of differing policies than necessarily exemplifying pointed discrimination like that experienced by some Muslims in North America (Bowen 2009). Others qualify the fallout more plainly, like Marcel Maussen (2006: 7) who notes how, "In the wake of 9/11, one of the ideas to obstruct Islamic radicalism was to accelerate the incorporation of Islam in France, in order to take away feelings of rejection (especially among younger Muslims)." Recall the creation of the CFCM, as a way to foster greater belonging while creating a formal branch of the organization. The Armed Islamic Group (*Groupe islamique armée*, GIA) sought to bring attention to the Algerian War to specifically cut off French support for the Algerian military (Hargreaves 2007: 110). The GIA's terrorist activities killed eight people and injured more than one hundred others. These incidents instilled fear and concern with the rise of "Islamism," a term which quickly became shorthand for fear of terror and fundamentalist movements. In the French context, these 1995 incidents arguably had a greater immediate impact for French Muslims than 9/11.

The "Mohamed Merah" incident in March 2012 has also been invoked by former President Sarkozy as an example of an Islamist threat in France, who, in his 2012 presidential platform pledged to clamp down on communities which might generate similar terrorism (Hewlett 2012: 409). Merah, a young Frenchman of Algerian origin, killed seven people, three French paratroopers, a rabbi, and three Jewish schoolchildren, and injured five others, four seriously, in Toulouse, France. Merah had a criminal record for petty crimes and claimed ties with Al-Qaeda (Ganley 2012a). France's far-right National Front leader Marine Le Pen claimed that "Islamisation has corrupted the French culture and will change France forever, if no one acts against the influx of Muslim immigrants and the growing demands of Muslims born on French soil" (Associated Press 2012; see also Heneghan 2011). Hewlett (2012) suggests that Sarkozy's attempt to poach votes from the far right on this issue failed, given the relative success of the National Front in the elections and his loss.

For Le Pen, the Toulouse killings reflected what she claims are "whole districts [...] in the grip of Islamists" and undesirable immigration (Trilling 2012). Some evidence suggests that there was a rise in Islamophobic incidents in the wake of the Toulouse events. Laurent Mucchielli, a sociologist from France's National Centre for Scientific Research, noted "the strong showing by the [far-right] National Front, in the recent French presidential elections" (Leduc 2012). The Collective Against Islamophobia also confirmed that the number of anti-Muslim incidents rose after the Merah killings (Leduc 2012).

## Islamic Movements

There has been some scholarship on radical Islamic movements in France (see Amghar 2005, 2008, 2009; Maréchal 2008; Ternisien 2011; Kepel 2004). Samir Amghar's overview chapter of Islamic movements since the 1980s surveys a range of expressions and incidents of religious radicalism. He usefully defines Islamic radicalism as a "composite, heterogeneous movement based on the diverse projects (not always coordinated) of autonomous organisations or individuals acting alone or in small groups" (2009: 27). His six primary active groups in France include the afore mentioned Salafists, who established themselves through ex-militants of the Algerian Islamic Salvation Front in the 1990s (2009: 28); the Albâch, originating in Lebanon, who settled in the country in the 1990s (2009: 31); the Tabligh, the oldest re-Islamization movement in France, founded in India and who established themselves in the late 1960s (2009: 32); Islamic nationalist radicals like the Armed Islamic Group, responsible for a series of bomb attacks in metro stations in Paris in 1995; other Islamo-nationalist jihadists like the GSPC (the Group for Call and Combat or the so-called Al-Qaeda of the Islamic Maghreb) that have organized attacks on France from outside the country and are increasingly oriented within international networks that seek to defend the rights of Muslims (2009: 43); and lastly, secular political radicalism that Amghar links to the a-religious riots in the suburbs of large cities in 2005 (2009: 48). He includes this last category because these radicals do not refer to Islam in their actions, but are often attributed Muslimness by outside observers.

## Securitization and Immigration

As noted, there are differing views on the impact of 9/11 on the perception of Muslims and Islamophobia in France. Some qualify its impact as being more generative of differing policies than necessarily producing specific discriminatory laws and experiences like in North America (Bowen 2009). Marcel Maussen (2006: 7) notes how the period was generative of positive implications, as well: "In the wake of 9/11, one of the ideas to obstruct Islamic radicalism was to accelerate the incorporation of Islam in France, in order to take away feelings of rejection (especially among younger Muslims)." Recall the creation of the CFCM as a way to foster greater belonging and representation.

Even if reported incidents of Islamophobia in France were not greatly impacted by 9/11, three shifts following 9/11 related to securitization laws, immigration policy, and police responses have impacted French Muslims. These numbers should also be contextualized: a greater number of Basques have been convicted of terrorism in France than Muslims (Cesari 2006: 27). In the first place, although its anti-terrorism framework was not impacted, a law was passed on November 15, 2001—the Law on Everyday Security—that explicitly aimed to decrease the threat of terrorism. This November 2001 law addresses domestic security, juvenile delinquency, and terrorism (see Cesari and McLoughlin 2005). More tangibly this legislation has meant that the stop and search of vehicles in the context of terrorism investigations became legal without prior court approval.

The post-9/11 period did lead to more restrictive governmental positions toward immigration. This point was underscored with the 2002 presidential election results obtained by right-wing National Front leader Jean-Marie Le Pen. His upswing in popularity meant that public policy moved more generally to restrict immigration. For instance, a law related to the control of immigration was adopted on November 26, 2003. By 2004, asylum-seeking was rendered more difficult and it became easier for the French government to expel individuals from the country. Also adopted were increased penalties for illegal immigration, more temporary detention centers, and new limits on family reunification.

## Policing and the *Banlieues*

Perhaps because many of those living in suburban areas are of immigrant origin, immigration laws were tightened in response to three weeks of riots in the suburbs of Paris in November 2005. On September 18, 2007, a bill was presented to parliament with President Sarkozy's backing that would authorize DNA testing for immigrants, and require applicants to pass language examinations and prove they can support themselves. The bill coincided with Sarkozy's renewed promise to begin deportation of an estimated 400,000 illegal immigrants. On November 15, 2007, the French Constitutional Court threw out the article in the immigration bill that allowed for the census tracking of ethnic origins. The Court did not challenge the amendment allowing for DNA testing of immigrants, however. The 2005 riots have also been directly linked by Sarkozy to his second anti-immigration law, the "law on immigration and integration," presented to the National Assembly in May 2006. The former President called for "selective immigration" (*immigration choisie*) as opposed to *immigration subie* ("uncontrolled/unwanted immigration").

In addition, a number of scholars have charted increased scrutiny by police of Muslim youth since 2001. Two examples highlight this feeling of scrutiny. The first, from November 2006, is that of seventy Muslim employees at the Charles de Gaulle Roissy airport who were fired because of security concerns (Smith 2006). After 9/11, security and cleaning companies working in airports and public buildings received requests from their employers to conduct background checks on their Muslim employees to ensure that none were members of terrorist networks. Some were asked to fire groups of workers. In a speech delivered at the Sorbonne University on October 21, 2006, Sarkozy explained, "I can't accept that people who have a radical outlook should work in an airport runway area. I prefer the risk of litigation because we have been too strict than having a tragedy on our hands because we have not been strict enough" (Mabut and Lerougetel 2006). *Les mosquées de Roissy: nouvelles révélations sur l'islamisation en France* (2006) by French politician Philippe de Villiers further sensationalized concerns through its claim that there are dozens of illegal mosques at Roissy airport. Subsequently, informal prayer spaces were outlawed at the airport (Spiegel Online 2006).

A second example stems from the 2005 and 2007 suburban riots, where young men living in the disenfranchised suburban regions are often victims of harassment and discrimination. In late October 2005, youth riots in a number of French *banlieues* highlighted this police discrimination and the resulting backlash for more than three weeks created a security crisis for French authorities. Tensions with police, systemic racism, and high unemployment are not newsworthy in the *banlieues* of France's urban industrial cities (see Beaud and Pialoux 2003; Wacquant 2005). Riots broke out in an eastern Parisian *banlieue* after two young boys were accidentally fatally electrocuted; a third young man, aged 21, suffered severe burns. Midway through an afternoon pick-up football match, the three adolescents took refuge in an electricity substation believing they were being chased by police responding to a call about a break-in in a nearby barracks. All three were children of immigrants from North Africa who lived in a suburban *cité* (social housing project) in Clichy-sous-Bois (population approximately 29,000). Despite the relative frequency of police–youth altercations like these,[12] with the initially unacknowledged accidental deaths and with Sarkozy's suggestion that the suburbs' resident "scum" needed to be "hosed down" (Maddox 2005), for some twenty-one days young male *banlieusards* railed against police and their environs in what were the worst civil riots since 1968. The deaths of the young men by electrocution, the relative silence of police, a rarely-imposed curfew, and the aforementioned Islamophobic comments of government officials were among the many factors which contributed to the three-week social unrest in the outskirts of Paris (Selby 2013).

While a number of "hijabophobic" incidents, as well as responses to Islamophobic-fueled concerns at the Roissy airport and to the suburban riots, are notable, there is some indication of a range of public opinion on these matters. The results of a December 2010 IFOP (Dabi and Fourquet 2010) study reveal that 42% of respondents believed that the Muslim population of France was a threat to the identity of the country. A greater percentage, 68%, believed that the Muslim population of France was not well integrated into French society. Fifty-nine percent said they were opposed to the wearing of the headscarf. While these positions do not necessarily translate to Islamophobia, they speak to a common climate of hostility toward Muslims in France.

---

[12] The city of Marseille, which has a large Muslim population (a 2013 *La Croix* article estimates 200,000), did not experience similar riots in 2005 and 2007, some suggest because of its geographic distribution of space, which encourages a certain level of mixing (Laurence 2012; for a more nuanced historicized account of Marseille's Muslim population, see Cesari 2001).

## Conclusion

This overview has highlighted the evolving positions and statuses of Muslims in France. I have emphasized elements that have impacted this religious group in broad strokes. Muslim communities in France have shifted from a once mostly-masculine first-generation group to a heterogeneous population with a variety of practices, backgrounds, and socio-economic levels. A number of factors condition the experiences of individual Muslims in France: the Republican *laïque* context that facilitates and hinders certain kinds of religious expressions and the collection of religiously based demographic information; the institutionalization of government representatives and practices; and a context where fears and notions of radical Islamism and Islamophobia shape the possibilities of Muslims as full members of French society. The foci of academic investigation have also changed since the early twentieth century. Scholarship has moved from a sociology of immigration and social movements that did not focus on the religious backgrounds of those under examination, to a tremendous convergence on the tradition in the 1980s that has examined religious practices, religious dress, as well as the political expressions of Muslims in secular France. In this chapter I have also noted fields of study that have been granted less attention, like political participation, and the religiosity of Muslims of all ages and both genders; men have been studied far less than women. A last notable largely unexplored topic is the interpretation of shariah (Islamic law) by Muslims in France at times of marriage, divorce, for the custody of children, and in finances, among other moments. For instance, how often is a *fiqh* (Islamic jurisprudence) for minorities (*fiqh al-aqalliyyat al-muslima*) dispensed? These chronologies and changing scholarship underscore how experiences of Islam in France are ever-changing.

## Acknowledgment

Thanks to Terry Riche for his bibliographic assistance and to Jocelyne Cesari for her useful suggestions.

## References

Adida, C., Laitin, D., and Valfort, M. 2010. *Les Français musulmans sont-ils discriminés dans leur propre pays? Une étude expérimentale sur le marché du travail* [pdf]. French-American Foundation—United States [online]. Available at: <http://equality.frenchamerican.org/sites/default/files/laitin_discriminationmusulmans_report_fr.pdf> [Accessed December 9, 2012].

Agence France-Presse. 2009. 367 femmes portent la burqa en France. *Le Figaro*, July 29 [online]. Available at: <http://www.lefigaro.fr/flash-actu/2009/07/29/01011-20090729FILWWW00467-367-femmes-portent-la-burqa-en-france.php> [Accessed December 9, 2012].

Agence France-Presse. 2010a. *500 cimetières dégradés en 9 mois.* Le Figaro, November 2 [online]. Available at: <http://www.lefigaro.fr/flash-actu/2010/11/02/97001-20101102FIL-WWW00537-500-cimetieres-degrades-en-9-mois.php> [Accessed December 9, 2012].

Agence France-Presse. 2010b. *Entre 5 et 6 millions de musulmans en* France. Le Point, June 28 [online]. Available at: <http://www.lepoint.fr/politique/entre-5-et-6-millions-de-musulmans-en-france-28-06-2010-471071_20.php> *[Accessed December 9, 2012].*

Agence France-Presse. 2011a. Douai: maillot islamique interdit. *Le Figaro*, July 7 [online]. Available at: <http://www.lepoint.fr/politique/entre-5-et-6-millions-de-musulmans-en-france-28-06-2010-471071_20.php> [Accessed December 9, 2012].

Agence France-Presse. 2011b. France: 41% des musulmans pratiquants. *Le Figaro*, May 13 [online]. Available at: <http://www.lefigaro.fr/flash-actu/2011/05/13/97001-20110513FILWWW00434-france-41-des-musulmans-pratiquants.php> [Accessed December 9, 2012].

Agence France-Presse. 2011c. *Multiculturalism "clearly" a failure:* Sarkozy. *National Post*, February 10 [online]. Available at: <http://www.nationalpost.com/news/Multiculturalism+clearly+failure+Sarkozy/4261825/story.html> *[Accessed December 9, 2012].*

Agence France-Presse. 2011d. Plus de 100 mosquées "en construction." *Le Figaro*, July 2 [online]. Available at: <http://www.lefigaro.fr/flash-actu/2011/08/02/97001-20110802FILWWW00332-plus-de100-mosquees-en-construction.php> [Accessed December 9, 2012].

Alba, R. and Silberman, R. 2002. Decolonization Immigrations and the Social Origins of the Second Generation. *International Migration Review* 36(4): 1169–93.

Allen, C. 2010. *Islamophobia*. Farnham: Ashgate.

Allen, P. 2011. As France issues first fines, burka rebel says: I'll stand for president. *Daily Mail*, September 23 [online]. Available at: <http://www.dailymail.co.uk/news/article-2040494/Burka-ban-defier-Kenza-Drider-run-Nicolas-Sarkozy-President-France.html?ito=feeds-newsxml> [Accessed December 9, 2012].

Amghar, S. 2005. Les salafistes français: une nouvelle aristocratie religieuse? *Maghreb-Machrek* 185 (Spring): 13–31.

Amghar, S. 2008. Le salafisme en France: de l'instauration de l'Etat islamique à la révolution conservatrice. *Critique internationale* 42 (September–October): 95–113.

Amghar, S. 2009. Ideological and Theorical Foundations of Muslim Radicalism in France. In M. Emerson, ed., *Ethno-Religious Conflict in Europe: Typologies of Radicalisation in Europe's Muslim Communities*. Brussels: Ceps, 27–50.

Amghar, S. 2011. *Le salafisme d'aujourd'hui: mouvements sectaires en occident*. Paris: Michalon.

Amiraux, V. 2003a. CFCM: A French Touch? *ISIM Newsletter* 12(1): 24–5.

Amiraux, V. 2003b. Discours Voilés sur les Musulmanes en Europe: Comment les Musulmans sont-ils Devenus des Musulmanes? *Social Compass* 50 (March): 85–96.

Amiraux, A. 2007. The Headscarf Question: What is Really the Issue? In S. Amghar, A. Boubekeur, and M. Emerson, eds., *European Islam: Challenges for Public Policy and Society*. Brussels: Centre for European Policy Studies, 124–43.

Amrani, Y. and Beaud, S. 2004. *Pays de malheur! Un jeune de cité écrit à un sociologue*. Paris: La Découverte.

Arnold, M. 2005. *French Minister Says Polygamy is to Blame for Riots*. Financial Times, November 15.

Assemblée Nationale. 1905. Projet de loi relative à la séparation des eglises et de l'etat [pdf]. Assemblée Nationale. Available at: <http://www.assemblee-nationale.fr/histoire/eglise-etat/1905-projet.pdf> [Accessed December 9, 2012].

Assemblée Nationale. 2010. *Gerin Commission Report [pdf]*. Assemblée Nationale. Available at: <http://www.assemblee-nationale.fr/13/pdf/rap-info/i2262.pdf> [Accessed December 9, 2012].

Associated Press. 2012. French Muslims worry over fallout from Mohamed Merah. *Metro News*, March 22 [online]. Available at: <http://metronews.ca/news/140004/french-muslims-worry-over-fallout-from-mohamed-merah/> [Accessed December 9, 2012].

Bachman, C. and Basier, L. 1984. Le Verlan: Argot d'École ou Langue de Keums? *Mots* 8(1): 169–87.

Barillas, M. 2012. François Hollande: the first Muslim president of France. *Spero News*, May 17 [online]. Available at <http://www.speroforum.com/a/JTMEAPVPLL49/72621-Francois-Hollande-the-first-Muslim-president-of-France> [Accessed December 9, 2012].

Barzegar, K. 2012. "Fed up" French Muslims mobilize to unseat Sarkozy. *Washington Times*, April 19 [online]. Available at: <http://www.washingtontimes.com/news/2012/apr/19/french-muslims-mobilizing-to-unseat-sarkozy/?page=all> *[Accessed December 9, 2012].*

Baubérot, J. 1990. *Vers un Nouveau Pacte Laïque?* Paris: Éditions du Seuil.

Baubérot, J. 1998. La laïcité française et ses mutations. *Social Compass* 45(1): 175–87.

Baubérot, J. 2003. Editorial. *Libération*, December 15: 39.

Beaud, S. and Pialoux, M. 2003. *Violences urbaines, violence sociale: genèse des nouvelles classes dangereuses*. Paris: Fayard.

Begag, A. and Delorme, C., 1994. *Quartiers Sensibles*. Paris: Seuil.

Belghiti, L. 2009. Strasbourg donne le jour à un cimetière musulman. *Sapphirnews*, October 8 [online]. Available at: <http://www.saphirnews.com/Strasbourg-donne-le-jour-a-un-cimetiere-public-musulman_a10608.html> *[Accessed December 9, 2012].*

Belien, P. 2005. Too Many Wives Causes Unrest. *The Brussels Journal*, November 16.

Benn, T. and Jawad, H. 2004. *Muslim Women in the United Kingdom and Beyond: Experiences and Images*. Brill.

Biedermann, F. 2011. Bardot group campaigns against halal animal slaughter. *The National*, January 10 [online]. Available at: <http://www.thenational.ae/news/worldwide/europe/bardot-group-campaigns-against-halal-animal-slaughter> [Accessed December 9, 2012].

Blackler, F. 2010. La polémique sur le halal est-elle dépassée? *Libération*, March 3 [online]. Available at: <http://www.liberation.fr/societe/0101622326-la-polemique-sur-le-halal-est-el> [Accessed December 9, 2012].

Blitz, J. 2010. Poll Shows Support in Europe for Burka Ban, *The Financial Times*, March 1 [online]. Available at: <http://www.ft.com/intl/cms/s/0/e0c0e732-254d-11df-9cdb-00144feab49a.html#axzz1R8ZEUn6q> [Accessed July 4, 2011].

Bloul, R. 1996. Engendering Muslim Identities: Deterritorialization and the Ethnicization Process in France. In B. D. Jones, ed., *Making Muslim Space in North America and Europe*. Berkeley: University of California Press, 234–50.

Borrel, C. and Simon, P. 2005. Les origines des Français. In C. Lefèvre and A. Filhon, eds., *Histoires de famille, histoires familiales*. Paris: INED-PUF, 425–41.

Bowen, J. R. 2004a. Does French Islam Have Borders? Dilemmas of Domestication in a Global Religious Field. *American Anthropologist*, 106(1): 43–55.

Bowen, J. R. 2004b. Muslims and Citizens: France's Headscarf Controversy, *Boston Review: A Political and Literary Forum* [online]. Available at: <http://bostonreview.net/BR29.1/bowen.html> [Accessed December 9, 2012].

Bowen, J. R. 2007. *Why the French Don't Like Headscarves: Islam, the State, and Public Space*. Princeton, NJ and Oxford: Princeton University Press.

Bowen, J. R. 2009. Recognising Islam in France after 9/11. *Journal of Ethnic and Migration Studies* 3(3): 439–52.

Bowen, J. R. 2010. *Can Islam Be French? Pluralism and Pragmatism in a Secularist State*. Princeton, NJ: Princeton University Press.

Boyer, A. 1998. *L'islam en France*. Paris: Presses Universitaires de France.

Bracke, S. and Fadil, N. 2012. Is the Headscarf Oppressive of Emancipatory? Field Notes on the Gendrification of the "Multicultural Debate." *Religion and Gender* 2(1): 36–56.

Bréchon, P. and Mitra S. K. 1992. The National Front in France: The Emergence of an Extreme Right Protest Movement. *Comparative Politics* 25(1): 63–82.

Brochen, P. 2010. Au Quick de Montreuil: "Quoi? J'ai mangé halal?" *Libération*, September 2 [online]. Available at: <http://www.liberation.fr/societe/0101655525-au-quick-de-montreuil-quoi-j-ai-mange-halal> [Accessed December 9, 2012].

Brulard, I. 1997. Laïcité and Islam. In S. Perry, ed., *Aspects of Contemporary France*. London and New York: Routledge, 175–90.

Cabana, A. 2011. Laïcité, le débat qui scinde l'UMP en deux. *Le Point*, April 6 [online]. Available at: <http://www.lepoint.fr/politique/la-politique-par-anna-cabana/06-04-2011-laicite-le-debat-qui-scinde-l-ump-en-deux-06-04-2011-1315808_232.php> [Accessed December 9, 2012].

Caeiro, A. 2003. Debating Fatwas in the Cyberspace: The Construction of Islamic Authority in Four Francophone Muslims Internet Forums. *Sacred Media—Transforming Traditions in the Interplay of Religion and the Media* [online]. Available at: <http://www.sacredmedia.jyu.fi/mainpage.php#caeiro> [Accessed December 9, 2012].

Caeiro, A. 2005a. Religious Authorities or Political Actors? The Muslim Leaders of the French Representative Body of Islam. In J. Cesari and S. McLoughlin, eds., *European Muslims and the Secular State*. Aldershot: Ashgate, 71–84.

Caeiro, A. 2005b. An Imam in France: Tareq Oubrou. *ISIM Review* 15: 48.

Cesari, J. 1998. *Musulmans et républicains: Les jeunes, l'islam et la France*. Paris: Éditions Complexe.

Cesari, J. 2001. Identité religieuse et territoire marseillais. In J. Cesari, A. Moreau, and A. Schleyer-Lindenmann, eds., *Plus marseillais que moi, tu meurs! Migrations, identités et territoires à Marseille*. Paris: L'Harmattan, 123–72.

Cesari, J. 2005. Ethnicity, Islam, and les *banlieues*: Confusing the Issues [online]. Available at: <http://riotsfrance.ssrc.org/Cesari/> [Accessed December 9, 2012].

Cesari, J. 2006. Muslims in Western Europe After 9/11: Why the term Islamophobia is more a predicament than an explanation. *Challenge Liberty and Security* [online]. Available at: <http://www.libertysecurity.org/article1167.html> [Accessed December 9, 2012].

Cesari, J. 2009. Islam in the West: From Immigration to Global Islam. *Harvard Middle Eastern and Islamic Review* 8: 148–75.

Cesari, J. and McLoughlin, S. eds. 2005. *European Muslims and the Secular State*. Burlington: Ashgate.

CEVIPOF. 2011. Les électorats sociologiques: Le vote des musulmans. Centre de recherches politiques, No. 5 (December) [online]. Available at: <http://www.cevipof.com/rtefiles/File/AtlasEl3/NoteDARGENT.pdf> *[Accessed December 9, 2012]*.

Chevalérias, A. 2008. La menace du communautarisme, Le terrorisme depuis le 11 septembre 2001 [online]. Available at: <http://www.recherches-sur-le-terrorisme.com/Analysesterrorisme/communautarisme-france.html> *[Accessed December 9, 2012]*.

Collège Lycée Réussite. 2011. *Premier établissement privé musulman d'enseignement secondaire*. Collège Lycée Réussite [online]. Available at: <http://www.lareussite.net/> [Accessed December 9, 2012].

Costa-Lascoux, J. 1994. Les lois "Pasqua": une nouvelle politique de l'immigration? *Regards sur l'actualité* 199 (March): 19–43.

Couvreur, G. 1998. *Musulmans de France: diversité, mutations et perspectives de l'islam français.* Paris: Éditions de l'Atelier.

Crumley, B. 2011a. French Muslims Confused Over Halal Restrictions. *Time World* [online]. Available at: <http://www.time.com/time/world/article/0,8599,2048589,00.html> [Accessed December 9, 2012].

Crumley, B. 2012. *Fact-Checking: Sarkozy's Campaign for the French Anti-Muslim Vote, Time World [online]. Available at:* <http://world.time.com/2012/04/30/fact-checking-the-french-presidents-xenophobia/#mosque-and-state#ixzz22anuFTEv> *[Accessed December 9, 2012].*

Dabi, F. and Fourquet, J. 2010. Comparative survey France/Germany on Islam [pdf]. Institut Français d'Opinion Publique. Available at: <http://www.ifop.fr/media/poll/1365-2-study_file.pdf> [Accessed December 9, 2012].

Dargent, C. 2003. *Les Musulmans declarés en France: affirmation religieuse, subordination sociale et progressisme politique*, vol. 34. Paris: Cahiers du CEVIPOF.

Dayan-Herzbrun, S. 2000. The Issue of the Islamic Headscarf. In J. Freedman and C. Tarr, eds., *Women, Immigration and Identities in France*. Oxford and New York: Berg, 69–84.

*Débat Halal.* 2011. Saphirnews à la rescousse de ses annonceurs. *Débat Halal* [blog], July 12. Available at: <http://www.debat-halal.fr/blog/2011/01/saphirnews-a-la-rescousse-de-ses-annonceurs/#more-470> [Accessed December 9, 2012].

Dufresne, D. 2007. *Maintien de l'ordre: Enquête.* Paris: Éditions Hachette Littératures.

Euro-Islam. n.d. Islam in France. *Euro-Islam [online]. Available at:* <http://www.euro-islam.info/country-profiles/france/> *[Accessed December 9, 2012].*

Euro-Islam. 2007. President Sarkozy appoints his former spokeswoman Rachida Dati to justice ministry. Available at: <http://www.euro-islam.info/2007/05/18/president-sarkozy-appoints-his-former-spokeswoman-rachida-dati-to-justice-ministry/> [Accessed December 9, 2012].

Euro-Islam. 2009a. First Bricks Laid for Marseille Mosque, France's Largest Mosque. Euro-Islam [online]. Available at: <http://www.euro-islam.info/2010/05/20/first-bricks-laid-for-marseille-mosque-france%E2%80%99s-largest-mosque/> [Accessed December 9, 2012].

Euro-Islam. 2009b. Le Bourget, Europe's largest and most popular Muslim convention, opens outside Paris. Euro-Islam [online]. Available at: <http://www.euro-islam.info/2009/04/15/le-bourget-europe%E2%80%99s-largest-and-most-popular-muslim-convention-opens-outside-paris/> [Accessed December 9, 2012].

Expatica. 2005. Chirac points finger at parents of rioters. *Expatica* [online]. Available at: <http://www.expatica.com/fr/news/local_news/chirac-points-finger-at-parents-of-rioters-25248.html> [Accessed December 9, 2012].

Fausto, G. 1992. *Arabicides*. Paris: La Découverte.

Favell, A. 1998. *Philosophies of Integration: Immigration and the Idea of Citizenship in France and Britain*. New York: St. Martin's Press.

Fernando, M. L. 2010. Reconfiguring Freedom: Muslim Piety and the Limits of Secular Law and Public Discourse in France. *American Ethnologist* 37(1): 19–35.

Fetzer, J. S. and Sopher, J. C. 2005. *Muslims and the State in Britain, France, and Germany.* Cambridge: Cambridge University Press.

Fourest, C. 2004. *Frère Tariq: Discours, stratégie et méthode de Tariq Ramadan*. Paris: Grasset et Fasquelle.

Freedman, F. 2004. *Immigration and Insecurity in France.* Aldershot: Ashgate.

Frégosi, F. 1998. Les problèmes d'organisation de la religion musulmane en France. *Esprit* 239(1): 109–36.

Frégosi, F. 2004. L'Imam, le conférencier et le jurisconsulte: Retour sur trois figures contemporaines du champ religieux islamique en France. *Archives de sciences sociales des religions* 125 (Jan.–Mar.): 131–46.

Frégosi, F. 2011. *L'islam dans la laïcité*. Paris: Pluriel.

Gabizon, C. 2009. Les Français de plus en plus hostile aux mosquées. *Le Figaro* (December 3, 2009) [online]. Available at: <http://www.lefigaro.fr/actualite-france/2009/12/02/01016-20091202ARTFIG00629-les-francais-de-plus-en-plus-hostiles-aux-mosquees-.php> [Accessed December 9, 2012].

Galaud, F. 2011. Laïcité: Copé reproche à Fillon de ne pas «jouer collectif». *Le Figaro*, March 28 [online]. Available at: <http://www.lefigaro.fr/flash-actu2011/03/28/97001-20110328FILWWW00650-cope-adresse-des-critiques-a-fillon.php> [Accessed December 9, 2012].

Ganley, E. 2012a. Le Pen says anti-Islam agenda is vindicated. *Irish Examiner*, March 23 [online]. Available at: <http://www.irishexaminer.com/world/le-pen-says-anti-islam-agenda-is-vindicated-188154.html> [Accessed December 9, 2012].

Ganley, E. 2012b. French Muslims get call to vote for president. *Al Arabiya News*, May 1 [online]. Available at: <http://english.alarabiya.net/articles/2012/05/01/211406.html> [Accessed December 9, 2012].

Gaspard, F. and Khosrokhavar, F. 1995. *Le Foulard et la République*. Paris: La Découverte.

Gauchet, M. 1998. *La Religion dans la Démocratie: Parcours de la Laïcité*. Paris: Éditions Gallimard.

Gauthier, A. 2012. Le salafisme, c'est quoi? *TF1*, March 21 [online]. Available at: http://lci.tf1.fr/france/societe/le-salafisme-c-est-quoi-7082347.html [Accessed March 22, 2013].

Geisser, V. 2010. Islamophobia: A French Specificity in Europe? *Human Architecture: Journal of the Sociology of Self Knowledge* 8(2): 39–46.

Gourévitch, J. 2008. *Le coût réel de l'immigration en France*. Les Monographies de Contribuables Associés [online]. Available at: <http://www.contribuables.org/2008/03/21/le-cout-reel-de-l-immigration-en-france/> [Accessed December 9, 2012].

Guénif-Souilamas, N. 2000. *Des Beurettes*. Paris: Éditions Grasset et Fasquelle.

Hargreaves, A. G. 1998. The Beurgeoisie: médiation or mirage? *Journal of European Studies* 28(1): 89–102.

Hargreaves, A. G. 2007. *Multi-Ethnic France: Immigration, Politics, Culture and Society*. New York and London: Routledge.

Harris Interactive. 2006. *The French take the most supportive stance toward immigration within their country whilst the British take the least supportive stance*. Rochester, NY and London: Harris Interactive [online]. Available at: <http://www.harrisinteractive.com/news/allnewsbydate.asp?NewsID=1107> [Accessed December 9, 2012].

Heiser, J. 2012. French Muslims Overwhelmingly Supported Socialist. *The New American*, May 10 [online]. Available at: <http://www.thenewamerican.com/world-news/europe/item/11347-french-muslims-overwhelming-supported-socialist> [Accessed December 9, 2012].

Heneghan, T. 2007. France fires official for opposing Muslim school. *Reuters*, March 21 [online]. Available at: <http://uk.reuters.com/article/2007/03/21/uk-france-islam-school-idUKL2153373320070321> [Accessed December 9, 2012].

Heneghan, T. 2011. Islam emerges as campaign issue in French local polls. *Reuters*, March 25 [online]. Available at: <http://www.reuters.com/article/2011/03/25/oukwd-uk-france-election-islam-idAFTRE72O5RP20110325> [Accessed December 9, 2012].

Hewlett, N. 2012. Voting in the Shadow of the Crisis: The French Presidential and Parliamentary Elections of 2012. *Modern and Contemporary France* 20(4): 403–20.

Husson, J. 2007. Training imams in Europe: the current status [pdf]. King Baudouin Foundation. Available at: <http://www.kbs-frb.be/uploadedFiles/KBS-FRB/05%29_Pictures,_documents_and_external_sites/09%29_Publications/PUB_1694_TrainingImamsEurope.pdf> [Accessed December 9, 2012].

Innovative Minds. 2004. *Protest French Hijab Ban*. Innovative Minds [online]. Available at: <http://www.inminds.com/french-hijab-ban.html> [Accessed December 9, 2012].

Institut Français d'Opinion Publique. 2007. Minorités Visibles Versus Majorité Invisible: Promotion de la Diversité ou de la Diversion? *Migrations Société* 19 (May–Aug.):5–15.

Institut Français d'Opinion Publique. 2009. *Les Français et la construction des mosquées et des minarets en France* [pdf]. Available at: <http://www.lefigaro.fr/assets/pdf/Sondage-minaret.pdf> [Accessed December 9, 2012].

Institut Français d'Opinion Publique. 2010. *La réaction des français aux déclarations de Marine Le Pen du 10 décembre 2010* [online]. Available at: <http://www.ifop.com/?option=com_publication&type=poll&id=1352> [Accessed December 9, 2012].

Institut Français d'Opinion Publique. 2011a. *Les pratiques religieuses chez les musulmans* [pdf]. Available at: <http://www.ifop.com/media/poll/1499-1-study_file.pdf> [Accessed December 9, 2012].

Institut Français d'Opinion Publique. 2011b. *Enquête sur l'implantation et l'évolution de l'Islam en France* [pdf]. Available at: <http://www.la-croix.com/Religion/S-informer/Actualite/Tous-les-resultats-de-l-etude-Ifop-La-Croix-sur-les-musulmans-francais-_NG_-2011-08-01-694857> [Accessed December 9, 2012].

Institut Montaigne. 2009. *La Polygamie en France: une fatalité?* Report by Sonia Imloul (November) [online]. Available at: <http://www.institutmontaigne.org>. [Accessed December 9, 2012].

Institut national d'études démographiques. 2010. *TeO: Enquête sur la diversité des populations en France* [online]. Available at: <http://www.ined.fr/en/pop_figures/france/immigration_flow/> [Accessed December 9, 2012].

Institut national d'études démographiques. 2011. *TeO: Enquête sur la diversité des populations en France* [online]. Available at: <http://www.ined.fr/fichier/t_telechargement/35196/telechargement_fichier_fr_dt168.13janvier11.pdf> [Accessed December 9, 2012].

Islam Online. 2008. *Islamic Education in Europe*. Islam Online [online]. Available at : <http://www.euro-islam.info/key-issues/education/>.

Jacques, J. 2012. The Muslim Vote Profoundly Changes Europe. *The Trumpet*, May 24 [online]. Available at: <https://www.thetrumpet.com/article/9455.8315.0.0/religion/islam/the-muslim-vote-profoundly-changes-europe> [Accessed December 9, 2012].

Jazouli, A. 1992. *Les années banlieues*. Paris: Seuil.

Joppke, C. 2007. State Neutrality and Islamic Headscarf Laws in France and Germany. *Theory and Society* 36(4): 313–42.

Keaton, T. D. 2006. *Muslim Girls and the Other France: Race, Identity Politics and Social Exclusion*. Bloomington and Indianapolis: Indiana University Press.

Kepel, G. 1987. *Les banlieues de l'Islam: Naissance d'une religion en France*. Paris: Seuil.

Kepel, G. 2004. *The War for Muslim Minds: Islam and the West*. Cambridge, MA: Belknap Press of Harvard University Press.

Kepel, G. 2012. *Banlieue de la République: Société, politique et religion à Clichy-sous-Bois et Montfermeil*. Paris: Gallimard.

Khosrokhavar, F. 1997. *L'islam des jeunes*. Paris: Flammarion.

Killian, C. 2003. The Other Side of the Veil: North African Women in France Respond to the Headscarf Affair. *Gender and Society* 17(4): 567–90.

Killian, C. 2006. *North African Women in France: Gender, Culture, and Identity*. Stanford: Stanford University Press.

King Baudouin Foundation. 2003. What Perspectives for Islam and Muslims in Europe [online]. Available at: <http://www.kbs-frb.be/uploadedFiles/KBSFRB/Files/EN/PUB_1415_Islam_and_Muslims_Europe.pdf>.

Klausen, J. 2005. *The Islamic Challenge: Politics and Religion in Western Europe*. New York: Oxford University Press.

Koven, R. 1992. Muslim Immigrants and French Nationalists. *Society* 29(4): 25–33.

Lacoste-Dujardin, C. 1991. *Des mères contre les femmes. Maternité et patriarcat au Maghreb*. Paris: La Découverte.

Lacoste-Dujardin, C. 1992. *Yasmina et les autres, de Nanterre et d'ailleurs. Filles de parents maghrébins en France*. Paris: La Découverte.

Lacoste-Dujardin, C. 1994. Transmission religieuse et migration: l'Islam identitaire des filles de maghrébins immigrés en France. *Social Compass* 41(1): 163–70.

*La Croix*. 2013. À Marseille, un islam encore fragmenté. *La Croix*, February 2 [online]. Available at: <http://www.la-croix.com/Religion/Actualite/A-Marseille-un-islam-encore-fragmente-_NG_-2013-02-07-908491. [Accessed February 13, 2013].

Lagrange, H. 2013. Pratique religieuse et religiosité parmi les immigrés et les descendants d'immigrés du Maghreb, d'Afrique sub-saharienne et de Turquie en France, *Notes et Documents* 4 (Sept.), 43 pp.

Lainé, F., Okba, M., and Rosbapé, S. 2005. Les difficultés des étrangers sur le marché du travail: effet nationalité, effet quartier? [pdf]. Available at: <http://www.epsilon.insee.fr/jspui/bitstream/1/3927/1/2005.04-17.3.pdf> [Accessed December 9, 2012].

Laurence, J. 2012. A Charmed Life May Not Last. In Islam in the Melting Pot of Marseille. Room for Debate. *The New York Times*. Available at: <http://www.nytimes.com/roomfordebate/2012/03/22/islam-in-the-melting-pot-of-marseille-13/marseilles-charmed-life-may-not-last> [Accessed August 12, 2011]

Laurence, J. and Vaisse, J. 2006. *Integrating Islam: Political and Religious Challenges in Contemporary France*. Washington, DC: Brookings Institution Press.

Le Bars, S. 2012a. 200 projets de mosquées en cours en France. *Le Monde*, July 24 [online]. Available at: <http://www.lemonde.fr/societe/article/2012/07/24/200-projets-de-mosquees-en-cours-en-france_1735970_3224.html> [Accessed December 9, 2012].

Le Bars, S. 2012b. Islam: M. Valls dénonce les « divisions et les égoïsmes » des représentants officiels. *Digne de foi* [blog], July 7. Available at: <http://religion.blog.lemonde.fr/2012/07/07/islam-m-valls-denonce-les-divisions-et-les-egoismes-des-representants-officiels/> [Accessed December 9, 2012].

Leduc, S. 2012. France sees "shocking surge" in anti-Semitic violence. *France 24*, June 7 [online]. Available at: <http://www.france24.com/en/20120606-rise-violence-against-french-jews-revives-anti-semitism-debate-merah-toulouse> [Accessed December 9, 2012].

Lefkowitz, N. 1991. *Talking Backwards, Looking Forwards: The French Language Game Verlan.* Tübingen: Gunter Narr Verlag.

*Le Figaro.* 2009. 367 femmes portent la burqa en France. *Le Figaro*, July 29 [online]. Available at: <http://www.lefigaro.fr/flash-actu/2009/07/29/01011-20090729FILWWW00467-367-femmes-portent-la-burqa-en-france.php> [Accessed December 9, 2012].

*Le Figaro.* 2010. 500 cimetières dégradés en 9 mois. *Le Figaro*, November 2 [online]. Available at: <http://www.lefigaro.fr/flash-actu/2010/11/02/97001-20101102FILWWW00537-500-cimetieres-degrades-en-9-mois.php> [Accessed December 9, 2012].

*Le Figaro.* 2011a. France: 41% des musulmans pratiquants. *Le Figaro*, May 13 [online]. Available at: <http://www.lefigaro.fr/flash-actu/2011/05/13/97001-20110513FILWWW00434-france-41-des-musulmans-pratiquants.php> [Accessed December 9, 2012].

*Le Figaro.* 2011b. Douai: maillot islamique interdit. *Le Figaro*, July 7 [online]. Available at: <http://www.lefigaro.fr/flash-actu/2011/07/07/97001-20110707FILWWW00407-douai-maillot-islamique-interdit.php> [Accessed December 9, 2012].

*Le Figaro.* 2011c. Plus de 100 mosquées "en construction." *Le Figaro*, August 2 [online]. Available at: <http://www.lefigaro.fr/flash-actu/2011/08/02/97001-20110802FILWWW00332-plusde100-mosquees-en-construction.php> [Accessed December 9, 2012].

*Le Monde.* 2008. Une Marocaine trop religieuse pour être française. *Le Monde*, July 12 [online]. Available at: <http://www.lemonde.fr/web/recherche_breve/1,13-0,37-1043780,0.html> [Accessed December 9, 2012].

*Le Monde.* 2009. Une confrérie turque controversée installe son premier collège en France. *Le Monde*, December 20 [online]. Available at: <http://www.lemonde.fr/web/recherche_breve/1,13-0,37-1110337,0.html> [Accessed December 9, 2012].

*Le Monde.* 2010. Le Parlement vote l'interdiction du voile intégral. *Le Monde*, September 14 [online]. Available at: <http://www.lemonde.fr/politique/article/2010/09/14/le-parlement-vote-l-interdiction-du-voile-integral_1411203_823448.html> [Accessed December 9, 2012].

*Le Monde.* 2011a. Mohammed Moussaoui réélu à la tête du CFCM. *Le Monde*, June 19 [online]. Available at: <http://www.lemonde.fr/societe/article/2011/06/19/mohammed-moussaoui-reelu-a-la-tete-du-cfcm_1538042_3224.html> [Accessed December 9, 2012].

*Le Monde.* 2011b. Fadela Amara nommée inspectrice générale des affaires sociales. *Le Monde*, January 5 [online]. Available at: <http://www.lemonde.fr/societe/article/2011/01/05/fadela-amara-nommee-inspectrice-generale-des-affaires-sociales_1461414_3224.html> [Accessed December 9, 2012].

*Le Monde.* 2011c. Mohammed Moussaoui réélu à la tête du CFCM. *Le Monde*, June 19 [online]. Available at: <http://www.lemonde.fr/societe/article/2011/06/19/mohammed-moussaoui-reelu-a-la-tete-du-cfcm_1538042_3224.html> [Accessed December 9, 2012].

*Le Monde.* 2012. Kader Arif, un ex-bébé Jospin, ministre délégué aux anciens combatants. *Le Monde*, May 16 [online]. Available at: <http://www.lemonde.fr/politique/article/2012/05/16/kader-arif-un-ex-bebe-jospin-ministre-delegue-aux-anciens-combattants_1702542_823448.html> [Accessed December 9, 2012].

*Le Nouvel Observateur.* 2008. Aubervilliers: Polémique autour d'un collège musulman. *Le Nouvel Observateur*, December 12 [online]. Available at: <http://tempsreel.nouvelobs.com/societe/20081212.OBS5109/aubervilliers-polemique-autour-d-un-college-musulman.html> [Accessed December 9, 2012].

*Le Nouvel Observateur.* 2012. Yamina Benguigui, une réalisatrice engagée pour la diversité. *Le Nouvel Observateur*, May 16 [online]. Available at: <http://

tempsreel.nouvelobs.com/election-presidentielle-2012/20120516.OBS5749/yamina-benguigui-une-realisatrice-engagee-pour-la-diversite.html> [Accessed December 9, 2012].

Le Parisien. 2009. En France, la place manque. *Le Parisien*, May 30 [online]. Available at: http://www.leparisien.fr/abo-vivremieux/en-france-la-place-manque-30-05-2009-531354.php [Accessed December 9, 2012].

Leveau, R. and Wihtol de Wenden, C. 2000. Les beurs, nouveaux citoyens. In B. Badie and P. Perrineau, eds., *Le citoyen: mélanges offerts à Alain Lancelot*. Paris: Presses de Sciences Po, 267–82.

Leveau, R. and Wihthol de Wenden, C. 2001. *La Beurgeoisie: Les trois âges de la vie associative issue de l'immigration*. Paris: CNRS Editions.

*Libération*. 2011. Le recteur de la Grande Mosquée demande l'annulation du débat sur l'islam. *Libération*, March 11 [online]. Available at: <http://www.liberation.fr/societe/2011/03/11/le-recteur-de-la-grande-mosquee-demande-l-annulation-du-debat-sur-l-islam_720944> [Accessed March 13, 2011].

Lycée-collège Averroès. n.d. Etablissement Privé Musulman sous contrat d'enseignement. Website [online]. Available at: <http://www.lycee-averroes.com/> [Accessed December 9, 2012].

Lyon, D. and Spini, D. 2004. Unveiling the Headscarf Debate. *Feminist Legal Studies* 12(3): 333–45.

Mabut, P. and Lerougetel A. 2006. France: airport workers fired in anti-Muslim campaign. World Socialist Website [online]. Available at: <http://www.wsws.org/en/articles/2006/11/bagg-n11.html> [Accessed December 9, 2012].

McGoldrick, D. 2006. *Human Rights and Religion: The Islamic Headscarf Debate in Europe*. Oxford: Hart Publishing.

Maddox, B. 2005. Sarkozy touches nerve over "unFrench" future. *Times Online*, November 4.

Mamdani, M. 2004. Culture Talk; or, How Not to Talk about Islam and Politics. In *Good Muslim, Bad Muslim: America, the Cold War, and the Roots of Terror*. New York: Doubleday, 17–62.

Maxwell, R. 2010. Political Participation in France among Non-European Origin Migrants: Segregation or Integration? *Journal of Ethnic and Migration Studies* 36(3): 425–43.

Maxwell, R. 2012. *Ethnic Minority Migrants in Britain and France: Integration Trade-offs*. Cambridge: Cambridge University Press.

Maréchal, B. 2008. Universal Aspirations—The Muslim Brotherhood in Europe. *ISIM Review* 22: 36–7.

Mauger, G. 2006. *L'émeute de novembre 2005: Une révolte protopolitique*. Paris: Éditions du Croquant.

Maussen, M. 2006. Representing and regulating Islam in France and in the Netherlands. Muslims in Europe and in the United States Conference. Harvard University [online]. Available at: <http://www.people.fas.harvard.edu/~ces/conferences/muslims/Maussen.pdf>.

Mazawi, A. E. 2010. "Also the School is a Temple": Republicanism, Imagined Transnational Spaces, and the Schooling of Muslim Youth in France. In L. Herrera and A. Bayat, eds., *Being Young and Muslim: New Cultural Politics in the Global South and North*. Oxford: Oxford University Press, 177–88.

Merle, P. 1997. *Argot, Verlan et Tchatches*. Toulouse: Milan.

Ministère de l'éducation nationale de l'enseignement supérieur et de la recherché. 2005. *L'application de la loi du 15 mars 2004 sur le port des signes religieux ostensibles dans les établissements d'enseignement publics.* Rapporteur Hanifa Chérifi [pdf]. Available at: <http://media.education.gouv.fr/file/98/4/5984.pdf> [Accessed August 15, 2012].

Ministère de l'intérieur et de l'aménagement du Territoire. 2005. Machelon Report [pdf]. Available at: <http://www.ladocumentationfrancaise.fr/var/storage/rapports-publics/064000727/0000.pdf> [Accessed December 9, 2012].

Mohammed, M. and Mucchielli, L. 2006. La police dans les "quartier sensibles": un profond malaise. In V. Le Goaziou and L. Mucchielli, eds., *Quand les banlieues brûlent... Retour sur les émeutes de novembre 2005*. Paris: La Découverte, 104–25.

Moran, M. 2012. *The Republic and the Riots: Exploring Urban Violence in French Suburbs*. Oxford: Peter Lang.

Mullally, S. 2010. Gender Equality, Citizenship Status, and the Politics of Belonging. In M. A. Fineman, ed., *Transcending the Boundaries of Law: Generations of Feminism and Legal Theory*. London: Routledge-Cavendish, 47–62.

Nikolas, K. 2011. Veiled Muslim woman to run for French Presidency. *Digital Journal*, September 22 [online]. Available at: <http://www.digitaljournal.com/article/311818#ixzz22oTVgRQC> [Accessed December 9, 2012].

Nixey, C. 2009. A school "condemned to death." *The Guardian*, May 26 [online]. Available at: <http://www.guardian.co.uk/education/2009/may/26/reussite-france-muslim-school> [Accessed December 9, 2012].

Ogden, P. E. 1989. International Migration in the Nineteenth and Twentieth Centuries. In P. E. Ogden and P. E. White, eds., *Migrants in Modern France: Population Mobility in the Later Nineteenth and Twentieth Centuries*. London: Unwin Hyman, 34–59.

Oger, G. 2005. France's polygamy problem. *Deutsche Welle*, July 31. Available at: <http://www.dw-world.de>.

Open Society Foundations. 2011. *Unveiling the Truth: Why 32 Muslim Women Wear the Full-Face Veil in France* [pdf]. New York: Open Society Foundations. Available at: <http://www.opensocietyfoundations.org/sites/default/files/a-unveiling-the-truth-20100510_0.pdf> [Accessed December 9, 2012].

Parvez, Z. F. 2011. Debating the Burqa in France: The Antipolitics of Islamic Revival. *Qualitative Sociology* 34(2): 287–312.

Perrin-Haynes, J. 2008. *"Situation des immigrés et des non-immigrés sur le marché du travail" enquêtes Emploi du 1er au 4e trimestre 2007* [online]. Available at: <http://www.insee.fr/fr/themes/document.asp?ref_id=ip1212> [Accessed December 9, 2012].

Pew Forum. 2011. *The Future of the Global Muslim Population. Region: Europe*. Available at: <http://www.pewforum.org/2011/01/27/future-of-the-global-muslim-population-regional-europe/#1> *[Accessed December 9, 2012].*

Pouchard, A. 2011. Laïcité: trois heures de débat pour clore deux mois de polémique. *Le Monde*, April 5 [online]. Available at: <http://www.lemonde.fr/politique/article/2011/04/05/laicite-trois-heures-de-debat-pour-clore-deux-mois-de-polemique_1503022_823448.html> [Accessed December 9, 2012].

Prada-Bordenave, E. 2008. Conclusions de la commissaire du gouvernement Emmanuelle Prada-Bordenave sous Conseil d'État, 27 juin, Madame Machbour, no. 286798. Available at: <http://www.droitdesreligions.net/conclusions/conclusions_286798.pdf> [Accessed June 10, 2012].

Radio Free Europe. 2011. First Women Convicted in France for Wearing Islamic Face Veil. *Radio Free Europe*, September 22 [online]. Available at: <http://www.rferl.org/content/

veiled_woman_to_run_for_french_presidency/24336391.html> [Accessed December 9, 2012].
Reuters. 2010a. 39% des Français approuveraient les propos de Marine Le Pen. *L'express*, December 15 [online]. Available at: <http://www.lexpress.fr/actualites/2/39-des-francais-approuveraient-les-propos-de-marine-le-pen_945402.html> [Accessed December 9, 2012].
Reuters. 2010b. Le Parlement vote l'interdiction du voile intégral. *Le Monde*, September 14 [online]. Available at: <http://www.lemonde.fr/politique/article/2010/09/14/le-parlement-vote-l-interdiction-du-voile-integral_1411203_823448.html> [Accessed December 9, 2012].
Rey, H. 1996. *La Peur des banlieues*. Paris: Presses des Sciences Po.
RFI. 2010. Facebook anti-Muslim apéros cancelled, protests. *RFI English*, June 18 [online]. Available at: <http://www.english.rfi.fr/france/20100618-facebook-anti-muslim-aperos-cancelled-protests> [Accessed December 9, 2012].
RFI. 2011. Muslims offered disused barracks to stop prayers in the streets. *RFI English*, August 8 [online]. Available at: <http://www.english.rfi.fr/france/20110808-paris-muslims-offered-disused-barracks-stop-prayers-streets> [Accessed December 9, 2012].
Richard, J. L. 2007. Youth of Foreign Origin Entering the Labour Market in France: An Approach of Discrimination against Children of African Immigrants. *Revista Economica* 31(1): 63–80.
Runnymede Trust Commission on British Muslims and Islamophobia. 1997. *Islamophobia: A Challenge for Us All*. Available at: <http://www.runnymedetrust.org/publications/17/32.html>.
Santelli, E. 2007. Les jeunes de banlieue d'origine maghrébine: entre galère et emploi stable, quel devenir? *Revue Européenne des Migrations Internationales* 23(2): 57–77.
Schnapper, D. 1994. *La communauté des citoyens: sur l'idée moderne de nation*. Paris: Gallimard.
Scott, J. W. 2007. *The Politics of the Veil*. Princeton, NJ and Oxford: Princeton University Press.
Selby, J. A. 2011a. French Secularism as a Guarantor of Women's Rights? Islam and Gender Politics in a Parisian banlieue. *Culture and Religion* 12(4): 441–62.
Selby, J. A. 2011b. Islam in France Reconfigured: Republican Islam in the 2010 Gerin Report. *Journal of Muslim Minority Affairs* 31(3): 383–98.
Selby, J. A. 2012. *Questioning French Secularism: Gender Politics and Islam in a Parisian Suburb*. New York: Palgrave Macmillan.
Selby, J. A. 2013. Polygamy in the Parisian Banlieues: Debate and Discourse on the 2005 French Suburban Riots. In G. Calder and L. G. Beaman, eds., *Polygamy's Rights and Wrongs: Perspectives on Harm, Family and Law*. Vancouver: University of British Columbia Press, 89–103.
Shryock, A. 2010. Introduction: Islam as an Object of Fear and Affection. In *Islamophobia/Islamophilia: Beyond the Politics of Enemy and Friend*. Bloomington, IN: Indiana University Press, 1–28.
Silverman, M. 1992. *Deconstructing the Nation: Immigration, Racism and Citizenship in Modern France*. London and New York: Routledge.
Silverstein, P. 2004. Headscarves and the French Tricolor, *Middle East Report Online* [online]. Available at: <http://www.merip.org> [Accessed December 9, 2012].
Simon, P. 2008. The Choice of Ignorance: The Debate on Ethnic and Racial Statistics in France. *French Politics, Culture, & Society* 26(1): 7–31.
Simons, M. 1996. African women in France battling polygamy. *The New York Times*, January 26 [online]. Available at: <http://www.nytimes.com>.
Smith, A. D. 2006. Paris airport strips 70 Muslim staff of security clearance. *The Independent*, November 2 [online]. Available at: <http://www.independent.co.uk/news/world/europe/

paris-airport-strips-70-muslim-staff-of-security-clearance-422576.html> [Accessed December 9, 2012].

Souilamas, N. G. 2000. *Des «beurettes» aux descendantes d'immigrants nord-africains*. Paris: Éditions Grasset & Fasquelle.

Spiegel Online. 2006. Paris Airport Bars Muslim Workers. *Spiegel Online*, November 2 [online]. Available at: <http://www.spiegel.de/international/anti-terror-investigation-paris-airport-bars-muslim-workers-a-446120.html> [Accessed December 9, 2012].

Spiegel Online. 2010. Inventive Imam Caters to Muslims on the Go. *Spiegel Online*, September 17 [online]. Available at: <http://www.spiegel.de/international/zeitgeist/0,1518,718018,00.html> [Accessed December 9, 2012].

The Stasi Commission Report 2003. *Le Monde*, December 12. Available at: <http://medias.lemonde.fr/medias/pdf_obj/rapport_stasi_111203.pdf>.

Stock-Morton, P. 1988. *Moral Education for a Secular Society: The Development of "Morale Laïque" in 19th Century France*. Albany: State University of New York Press.

Stora B. 1992. *Ils Venaient d'Algérie: L'immigration algérienne en France (1912–1992)*. Paris: Fayard.

Ternisien, X. 2011. *Les frères musulmans*. Paris: Fayard.

Tetreault, C. 2000. "Tom-boy talk," Girls in the "Cité," and the Limits to Gender as Performance. In *Texas Linguistics Forum*, Proceedings from the Eighth Annual Symposium about Language and Society. Austin, Texas, 7–9 April.

Tetreault, C. 2001. Ambiguous Authority: Adolescent Girls of Algerian Descent Performing French Cité Styles. *Europaea: Journal of the Europeanists / Journal des Européanistes* 1(2): 117–30.

Thomas, S. 2010. Le collège-lycée musulman Réussite d'Aubervilliers survit au jour le jour. *Le Parisien*, May 31 [online]. Available at: <http://islamenfrance.20minutes-blogs.fr/archive/2010/06/17/le-college-lycee-musulman-reussite-d-aubervilliers-survit-au.html> [Accessed December 9, 2012].

Tribalat, M. 1995. *Faire France: Une Enquête sur les Immigrés et Leur Enfants*. Paris: La Découverte.

Tribalat, M. 1996. *De l'Immigration à l'Assimilation: Enquête sur les Populations d'Origine Étrangère en France*. Paris: La Découverte.

Trilling, D. 2012. Don't frighten the children. *New Statesman* [online]. Available at: <http://www.newstatesman.com/politics/2012/03/don%E2%80%99t-frighten-children> [Accessed December 9, 2012].

Venel, N. 1999. *Musulmanes françaises: Des pratiquantes voilées à l'université*. Paris: L'Harmattan.

Wacquant, L. 2005. *Parias urbains: Ghetto, banlieues, État*, trans. from English by S. Chauvin. Paris: La Découverte.

Weibel, N. B. 2000. *Par-delà le voile: Femmes d'Islam en Europe*. Paris: Éditions Complexe.

Weil, P. 2009. Why the French Laïcité is Liberal. *Cardozo Law Review* 30(6): 2699–714.

Wieviorka, M. 1993. *La Démocratie à l'épreuve: Nationalisme, populisme, ethnicité*. Paris: La Découverte.

Wihtol de Wenden, C. 2011. La creuset de la « beurgeoisie ». *Sciences Humaines*. Available at: <http://www.scienceshumaines.com/le-creuset-de-la-beurgeoisie_fr_12771.html>.

Winter, B. 2006. Secularism Aboard the Titanic: Feminists and the Debate over the Hijab in France. *Feminist Studies* 32(2): 279–98.

Zehraoui, A. 1994. *L'immigration, de l'homme seul à la famille*. Paris: L'Harmattan.

CHAPTER 2

# THE UNITED KINGDOM

SOPHIE GILLIAT-RAY

## Introduction

THE range and quality of quantitative and qualitative data gathered about Muslim communities in Britain since the 1960s has varied, as have methodological and disciplinary approaches. Researchers working in what might now be called 'British Muslim Studies' may be historians, lawyers, sociologists, anthropologists, geographers, educationalists, psychologists, criminologists, cultural theorists, political scientists, or specialists in religious studies, gender studies, inter-faith relations, or racial and ethnic studies. A field of research that was already diverse has become more so in recent years, with the growing contribution of those who specialize in counter-terrorism studies, international relations, and Islamic banking and finance. A notable development has been the growing involvement of British Muslims themselves in this interdisciplinary academic community, and the flourishing of independent Islamic colleges and research organizations.

Even from a very limited survey of the literature produced within 'British Muslim Studies' (and the claim to the evolution of such a field will be explored later in this chapter) a bias towards qualitative approaches and methods is evident. Although Muslims as a distinctive socio-religious category have been included in important quantitative research, not least the bi-centennial national Census (which in 2001 asked a question on 'religion' for the first time since 1851), there is a preponderance towards qualitative research. Consequently, our understanding of Muslim communities in Britain is strongly informed by research involving relatively small sample sizes focused on particular topics, such as schools, conversion, youth, identity, Islamophobia, and gender, as well as the settlement of Muslims in particular cities, such as Manchester, Cardiff, Liverpool, Oxford, Birmingham, and London.[1] In any putative 'mapping' of the literature on Muslims in Britain, some areas would be rich in detail; others would be very

---

[1] References to this literature will be found throughout the chapter.

sketchy. Some cities, perhaps inevitably, have become 'over-researched' (Johansen and Spielhaus 2012; Sanghera and Thapar-Bjorkert 2008). Recognizing the existing gaps in knowledge and research is therefore as important to document, as is the rich array of literature that now exists (Gilliat-Ray 2005a).

This chapter charts the evolving academic and research landscape that now characterizes the study of Islam and Muslims in Britain. Through a range of analytic categories, such as immigration and settlement, multiculturalism and social policy, and Muslim community development and integration, it is possible to identify a clear shift within the research field that mirrors the changing self-understanding of many British Muslims themselves. It is a shift that takes account of the increasing emphasis that many Muslims place on their distinctive religious identity, as Muslims. Many consequences flow from this shift, of course. Muslims who have a loose association with religious organizations may be indirectly excluded from research, simply through lack of affiliation to religious networks or gatekeepers, and this will inevitably shape the outcomes of any study undertaken (Sanghera and Thapar-Bjorkert 2008). Researchers have disproportionate access to particular communities, organizations, or individuals on account of their own personal characteristics and networks (Bolognani 2007; Gilliat-Ray 2005a), while for many reasons, including political ones, some topics of research are regarded as more worthy of funding than others (Gilliat-Ray 2013; Johansen and Spielhaus 2012). Appreciation of the consequences of the political, economic, and social dynamics of the research process is an important prelude to the discussion that follows. This is because understanding of Muslim communities in Britain has been subject to changing views as to 'what counts' as researchable and worthy of investigation.

# Muslim Immigration and Settlement in Britain

## From the Eighth Century to 1945

It is often assumed that the presence of Muslims in Britain and the influence of Islamic culture and history on British society is a recent phenomenon, confined mainly to the post-Second World War era (Gilliat-Ray 2010c). The period after 1945 is certainly distinctive in terms of the scale of Muslim migration to Britain, but the history of Muslim settlement, and wider British engagement with Muslim majority countries, goes back much further. This has been the subject of energetic research activity in the last decade, alongside greater British Muslim engagement in the historical roots of Muslim communities in the UK (Gilliat-Ray 2010c). The following paragraphs map some of the changing contours of the historical writing and research about Islam in Britain. The discussion begins with a critical evaluation of historical records and sources, and then traces the evolution of more settled Muslim communities in Britain, from the late nineteenth century to the present day. This evaluation of sources is of course relevant not only for historical research; it clearly has resonance for knowledge that is drawn from newer forms of data, such as blogs, Twitter feeds, or social networking sites.

It is important at the outset to consider where information about Islam and Muslims in Britain has come from over the course of history, and the limitations and biases that arise as a consequence. Any understanding of Muslims in Britain, or contact between Muslim majority countries and the British Isles is inevitably shaped by the available evidence. So whether we are examining Christian ecclesiastical texts from the eighth and ninth centuries (Scarfe Beckett 2003), travel diaries (Bak 2006; Davies 2011; Murad 2003), sixteenth-century captivity/piracy narratives (Colley 2000, 2001, 2002; Matar 1993, 1997, 2001, 2005; Milton 2004), parliamentary papers, literary fiction, or stage plays, there are inherent limitations. Misunderstandings of Islam or Muslims in one genre have often been reproduced in another. So, for example, in the Anglo-Saxon world, information about Islam was understood within a framework of Christian theological ideas and assumptions that predated Islam (Scarfe Beckett 2003). Perceptions contained within travel diaries in the fifteenth and sixteenth centuries directly influenced later impressions of Islam among playwrights. In the medieval period, alongside prodigious theological and literary writing about Islam that was often negative (and rarely supported by actual personal encounter with Muslims) there was also secular engagement with Muslim states via trade and commerce. Scholars today therefore have access to numerous literary records about Islam produced by medieval ecclesiastics, but they do not have other kinds of data, such as trade records or visual representations, except in the form of material culture such as ceramics or coins (Petersen 2008).

From the mid-nineteenth century onwards, there are more diverse resources available for understanding the place of Islam in British society, and evolving perceptions of Muslims in Britain and abroad. Travel narratives, parliamentary papers, newspapers, novels, poetry, and scholarly studies are supplemented by detailed trading documents, missionary reports (Salter 1873, 1895), oral histories, and photographs. These sources also have limitations and biases, but the scope for comparative analysis opens up possibilities for a greater range of interpretations. Some of these sources, especially literary works, have recently been subject to important critical evaluation (Khattak 2008). What becomes apparent from the mid-nineteenth century is that new sources (mainly newspapers, and newsletters produced by Muslims themselves) began to document the formation of embryonic Muslim communities in Britain itself, rather than discussion of Islam among Muslims based in Muslim majority countries (Beckerlegge 1997). The technical transformations taking place in the merchant shipping industry, principally the change from wind-powered sails to coal-fired steam engines, meant that large British seaports with proximate access to coalfields were important centres for colonial shipping (Evans 1985; Sherwood 1991). Consequently, in cities such as Cardiff, South Shields, and Liverpool, boarding houses were established for seafarers from the Yemen, Somaliland, and the Indian subcontinent (Ansari 2004). These transient male seafaring communities eventually evolved into established, settled British Muslim communities.

Not surprisingly, historians have largely contributed to our understanding of Muslim settlement in Britain prior to 1945 (Ansari 2004; Beckerlegge 1997; Evans 1985; Halliday 1992a, 1992b; Lawless 1994, 1995, 1997; Matar 1998, 1999, 2005; Robinson-Dunne 2003; Seddon 2004), although some British cities with sizeable Muslim populations around the time of the Second World War were of interest to sociologists at the time. For example, the growing population of Yemeni and Somali seafarers in Cardiff was subject to qualitative and quantitative research by Kenneth Little in the 1940s (Little 1942a, 1942b). As well as documenting basic sociological features of the communities, such as housing, education of children, social life, and occupation, Little also recorded developing religious infrastructures, and his work provides a prelude to the work of sociologists and anthropologists who recorded the socio-economic and religious-cultural dynamics of Muslims migrating to Britain after 1945.

As the dates of the references in these early paragraphs indicate, during the decade 2000–10, a number of academic studies were produced by historians about the settlement of Muslims in Britain (and British engagement with the Muslim world) prior to 1945. This development is of intrinsic interest, of course, but what is perhaps of more significance for the present discussion is not so much what these new studies reveal, but the use to which they are now put by British Muslims today. A number of contemporary British Muslim community organizations and websites have shown increasing interest in the history of Islam and Muslims in Britain. Their sites often refer, for example, to the discovery of a coin minted by the eighth-century King Offa of Mercia (757–96 CE), that carried the Islamic declaration of faith (the *shahadah*) on one side, and the Latin formula 'Offa Rex' ('King Offa') on the other.[2] For example, the website www.salaam.co.uk begins its pages about the 'Historical Roots of British Islam' with the Offa dinar; the coin is situated at the beginning of a 'timeline' that charts the history of Muslim settlement/contact in Britain, from the eighth century to the present day. Although there has been endless speculation about the meaning of the coin—was Offa an early convert to Islam?—most historians attribute his decision to mint such a coin as more centrally bound up with his commercial acumen and wish for political self-aggrandizement in the Anglo-Saxon period than any personal affiliation with Islam (Wormald 1982). For the purposes of this present discussion, the significance of the coin lies in the claims that British Muslims make about it (for some, Offa probably was the first British Muslim convert), and its positioning at the beginning of an historical timeline. Such 'timelines' seem concerned with documenting the historicity, heritage, and thus the legitimacy of Muslim settlement in Britain (Gilliat-Ray 2010b). They not only assert a sense of British Muslim history and 'belonging', but also serve as powerful counter-narratives about the supposed 'segregation' and separateness of Muslims, sometimes asserted by the media, by politicians, and by policy-makers (Mirza et al. 2007).

---

[2] Pictures of the coin can be viewed on the website of the British Museum: <http://www.britishmuseum.org/explore/highlights/highlight_objects/cm/g/gold_imitation_dinar_of_offa.aspx> [Accessed 2 November 2012].

Alongside the production of 'timelines', a number of projects emerged during the late 1990s and early 2000s to record the historical presence of Muslims in Britain prior to 1945, via buildings. These include, for example, the Abdullah Quilliam Society founded in 1998, to revive interest in the life and work of Abdullah Quilliam (1856–1932), a Liverpool solicitor and convert to Islam, and the mosque that he established in the city in 1887 (Geaves 2009). Meanwhile, 'Islam in British Stone' (http://www.islaminbritishstone.co.uk/, accessed 2 November 2012), is a web resource devoted to an exploration of 'Britain's Greatest Muslim Heritage Sites', which includes the Shah Jahan Mosque in Woking, Surrey, built in 1889 (Ansari 2002; Salamat 2008), and the early East London Mosque (Ansari 2011). Recent research has also explored the myths that have evolved around a mosque supposed to have been established in Cardiff in 1860 (Gilliat-Ray 2010b). 'Islam in British Stone' notes on its website that significant buildings can provide a way for 'a community to connect to its past and help establish a sense of place within society'. It is the second half of this sentence that is especially poignant; it is indicative of the powerful shift that has taken place in British Muslim self-understanding in recent decades. British Muslim assertions of 'belonging' in the present arguably have far greater legitimacy when they are supported by material evidence indicating the longevity of contact between Muslims and the British Isles that stretches back over centuries, not just decades.

## From 1945 to the Present Day

Muslims who had contributed to the Second World War effort as a consequence of Britain's colonial ties were demobilized in Britain. Some returned to their countries of origin (mainly in the Indian subcontinent), but others became domiciled in Britain. A number of them were drawn to cities with existing Muslim settlement, such as Cardiff, Liverpool, and South Shields, adding to a sense of growth and flourishing in these communities. However, many were also attracted to those cities at the heart of post-war reconstruction, and growth in manufacturing industries. Consequently, cities such as Birmingham and Manchester, and northern towns and cities in Yorkshire and Lancashire, such as Bradford and Leeds, were primary destinations both for demobilized servicemen, and also for new arrivals from the Indian subcontinent. As a result of Britain's colonial ties and links, the Muslim population grew as a consequence of the migration to Britain of Pakistanis, in particular, especially from the Punjab (Gilliat-Ray 2010c). Here the work of anthropologist Pnina Werbner must be mentioned, on account of the meticulous way that she described and theorized the migration of Pakistani Muslims in Manchester (Werbner 1990), their settlement and community formation, and the transnational religious ties that have sustained Sufi practice both in Manchester and other major British cities, such as Birmingham (Werbner 1996a, 1996b, 2002a, 2002b, 2004, 2006).

Compared to the pre-1945 period, there is more familiarity with the post-Second World War phase of Muslim immigration into Britain, not only because it is relatively recent, but also because it has been studied more systematically. Sociologists and anthropologists have charted the 'push' and 'pull' factors that drew Muslims to Britain, such as prospects for economic improvement, and documented the formation of new associations and communities (Adams 1987; Anwar 1976, 1979; Dahya 1965, 1973, 1974; Jeffery 1972; Kalra 2000; Saifullah-Khan 1975, 1976; Shaw 1988, 1994; Werbner 1990). Race and ethnicity provide the predominant analytic points of reference in much of this literature. Researchers at the time were principally concerned with the settlement not of Muslims, but of Pakistanis or Bengalis, who happened to be Muslim. While these studies usually made reference to the practice of Islam, or to the formation of mosques, this was generally part of a wider discussion about community formation and evolving infrastructures.

Once again, however, there has been recent British Muslim interest in this phase of settlement. Concerted efforts are underway to investigate what it meant to be a Muslim in Britain in the 1950s and 1960s. As a generation of post-Second World War migrants enter their twilight years, researchers from the Islamic Foundation Policy Research Centre in Leicester are pro-actively collecting oral histories from these elders about life in Britain in the second half of the twentieth century:

> This project aims to collect narratives from first generation migrants to Britain of Muslim heritage, looking at their experiences, contributions and observations of Muslim life in Britain over the last 40 years. The archives will be web-based and aimed at educational institutions, particularly helpful for young Muslims growing up today, but also a wider audience. It is hoped that this will contribute towards emphasising the Muslim presence in the narrative of Britishness, and show young Muslims that they have a deep heritage in recent British history and therefore a significant stake in this society. (http://policyresearch.org.uk/research, accessed 22 January 2013)

Like their seafaring counterparts in the nineteenth century, many of the early post-Second World War migrants to Britain were single men, who relied upon kinship networks to find housing, employment, and social support as part of a process of chain migration. They mostly intended to remain in Britain temporarily, having earned sufficient money to improve material and economic prospects 'back home'. However, legislative changes intended to curb new immigration (e.g. the 1962 Commonwealth Immigrants Act) led to a dramatic increase in the number of women and children coming to join their menfolk in the UK. In order to 'beat the ban' of the new legislation, large numbers of women arrived in Britain; temporary male residence gave way to more permanent family settlement, and led to what a British Muslim sociologist dubbed 'the myth of return' (Anwar 1979). As children began to be born and educated in Britain, any prospect of returning 'home' became unrealistic and merely a 'myth'. The arrival of women and children, and the more intensive development of community infrastructures as a consequence, such as mosques, educational facilities, and halal/ethnic supplies is reflected in the literature; later anthropological works often pay significant attention to the role of women in these communities (Shaw 1988; Werbner 1990), and the social and economic capital that began to be invested in more long-term community development.

The Muslim population in Britain since the post-Second World War period has grown and diversified. Where the first substantial wave of South Asian Muslim settlement in Britain after 1945 was almost entirely driven by economic motives, the later migration of Muslims from other parts of the world, such as Turkey, Iran, East Africa, and the Middle East in the 1980s and 1990s, rests upon a greater range of factors. Some have come to Britain as refugees, as international traders, or as highly skilled professionals. But as with their South Asian counterparts, wider global political and economic forces have often underpinned their decision to come to Britain (e.g. the Iranian Revolution in 1979). Since the 1990s, asylum-seekers from Bosnia, Somalia, and Kurdistan have also come to Britain. These newer Muslim migrants have tended to be somewhat 'invisible' in the literature on Islam in Britain, which is why an annotated bibliography devoted exclusively to the literature on newer Muslim communities has become a valuable research resource (Hussain 2005). Additionally, in 2008 a government department (Communities and Local Government) commissioned the 'Change Institute' to undertake a survey of thirteen ethnic minority communities in England which are predominantly Muslim, thereby increasing our understanding of the migration and settlement of Algerians, Afghans, Egyptians, Nigerians, and other ethnic groups that are principally Muslim.[3]

## Muslims in Britain: Quantifying Demographic Change

Establishing with some degree of accuracy how many Muslims there are in Britain has been a matter of concern for decades, both within and outside Muslim communities. From the mid-1970s, articles began to appear in British Muslim publications debating the number of Muslims in Britain, then estimated at about 500,000 (Huq 1975). With the gradual realization of the 'myth of return', planning for the future became a priority, and this could not be done without some sense of scale and demographics. Furthermore, Muslims realized that their claims for recognition and support as a distinctive religious minority group (e.g. as part of their efforts to establish voluntary aided Muslim schools) would be more successful if their overall numeric strength was measured. For several decades, this meant extrapolating from Census data on ethnicity/race. For example, in 1991 it was safe to assume that the vast majority of the 476,000 Pakistanis in Britain were Muslim; likewise the 162,835 Bangladeshis. The outcome of this rather haphazard process of guesswork was widely varying estimates of the number of Muslims in Britain. For several decades the range was anything between 550,000 and 3 million (Anwar 1993b; Aspinall 2000), the majority being South Asians. But mutual self-interest on the part of

---

[3] <http://www.communities.gov.uk/documents/communities/pdf/1203896.pdf> [Accessed 2 November 2012].

British Muslims and national government has been a significant driver for gaining better information and statistical evidence in recent years. In 2001, a question on 'religion' was asked in the national Census for the first time since 1851 (Aspinall 2000; Peach 2006b; Sherif 2011; Southworth 2005; Weller 2004). The question was used again in the 2011 Census, with main results becoming publicly available in late 2012. Although detailed analysis is still to be done, the Census gave a figure of 2.7 million Muslims in Britain (up from 1.6 million in 2001). Muslims now constitute almost 5% of the UK population (up from 3% in 2001). These large figures mask important regional differences, of course. In parts of some towns and cities with long histories of Muslim settlement, Muslims will constitute anything up to 50% of the population, whereas the 2001 Census failed to record any Muslims living in some parts of the UK, such as the Scilly Isles, just off the Cornish coastline.

The increase in the Muslim population in Britain between 2001 and 2011 is largely attributed to the higher birth rate in Muslim communities (Beckford et al. 2006), and, to some extent, conversion to Islam (Brice 2010; Moosavi 2012). Census data, as well as other quantitative sources (e.g. the Labour Force Survey) reveal the disproportionately 'youthful' character of Muslim communities. About half of all British Muslims are under the age of 25, meaning that government policy aimed at children and families has a disproportionate impact on Muslim communities. Over time, the gender balance in Muslim communities has become more even between men and women; a greater proportion is now 'British-born', with obvious consequences for language use. For many British-born Muslims, English is their first language. Muslims of South Asian origin dominate the British Muslim population, constituting about three-quarters of all Muslims, the remainder being Arab, African, South East Asian, and European (including an estimated 100,000 converts to Islam; Brice 2010).

The data about Muslims in Britain in the 2001 Census were subject to intensive quantitative investigation (Hussain 2008; Peach 2006a, 2006b). For example, Serena Hussain's monograph *Muslims on the Map* provided a detailed picture of the housing, employment, health, age, ethnicity, and geographical distribution of Muslims in Britain. It is to be hoped that the 2011 Census data in relation to British Muslims will be subject to the same level of scrutiny, in order to measure longitudinal and demographic change. Will the levels of Muslim socio-economic deprivation, educational underachievement, and rates of economic inactivity clearly discernible in the 2001 Census findings be in evidence once again, when 2011 data are analysed? Regardless of the answer to this question, since the 2001 Census data were analysed, qualitative research has explored some of the socio-economic dynamics of Muslim communities which help to illuminate Census findings.

For example, 2001 Census data showed that Muslims tended to live in inner-city, formerly run-down areas with an inherited high level of housing deprivation (Anwar and Bakhsh 2003). The key issues are overcrowding and poor housing quality. It is also clear that there are too few affordable properties that can accommodate Muslim families which are, on average, larger than the national average (Hussain 2008). But residential patterns are strongly determined by historic employment and housing opportunities.

In the post-Second World War period for example, many Pakistani and Bangladeshi migrants lived in cheap private housing located close to textile mills. Their concentration in particular streets and neighbourhoods has been reinforced over time by the desire to live, or to remain living, close to extended family members or associated community facilities (such as mosques).

The perceptions arising from the growing concentration of Muslims in particular socio-economically deprived areas, especially following the urban disturbances in Bradford, Oldham, and Burnley in 2001, have led to unfounded charges of Muslim self-imposed isolationism and 'self-segregation'. In the reports following these events, it was claimed that white and minority ethnic communities were living 'parallel lives' and that the disturbances reflected divisions in patterns of settlement, education, and cultural practices (Cantle 2002). However, some of the assumptions behind this isolationist discourse have recently been challenged (see for example Phillips 2006; Simpson 2004; Simpson and Peach 2009), on the grounds that they fail to take sufficient account of 'the power of structural constraints (economic and institutional racism) and popular racism to shape minority ethnic housing and neighbourhood choices' (Phillips 2006: 29). In other words, it is likely that choices and decisions made by the majority white community exert a greater impact on Muslim residential patterning than the self-determining but 'bounded choices' and decisions of Muslims themselves.

What is rarely mentioned in political and media commentary about supposedly 'self-segregating' Muslim communities is the surprising effect this has on political participation, especially electoral registration and voter turnout. Researchers at the Centre for Census and Survey Research at the University of Manchester have provided clear evidence that 'Muslim registration, like turnout [at General Elections] increased as proportion of the local population that were Muslim increased... we believe the most plausible explanations relate to the process of community mobilization generated through social connectedness and community networks, formal and informal, secular and religious' (Fieldhouse and Cutts 2008: 346). There are therefore both positive and negative outcomes of, and reasons for, the residential clustering of Muslims in some areas of the UK, but among the more significant negative reasons are fear of racism and harassment in areas that are perceived to be 'white'. Among the positive reasons for living in close-knit communities is the availability of social, cultural, and religious support that is simply not provided by indigenous religious and social networks (Simpson 2004). The outcomes of this support in terms of civic participation, especially voting, are generally not well known (see the section on Political Participation).

An important conclusion to be drawn from the 2001 Census data is that one form of social deprivation often compounds another. For example, compared to other faith groups in Britain, Muslims report the highest rates of ill-health. Given the evidence of housing deprivation and overcrowding, poor employment prospects, and the poverty associated with both, poor health outcomes are not surprising (Hussain 2008). In many ways, this can be traced back to migration history; many South Asians arriving in Britain came with little economic capital and limited capacity in English. They were largely confined to employment in areas that would go on to suffer long-term industrial decline.

The types of work available to them then (and to some extent now) not only determined income, but also settlement and residence patterns, educational opportunities, and access to services (Anwar 1993b). The consequences of post-Second World War housing and employment decisions continue to affect Muslims in Britain today, with nearly one-third of Muslims now living in some of the most deprived neighbourhoods in Britain, especially in London (Beckford et al. 2006). Establishing how, and to what extent this situation has changed provides an important future research agenda for geographers and sociologists of Muslim communities in Britain.

Set alongside these issues of segregation and deprivation, there is evidence of entrepreneurialism, creativity, wealth-creation, and very successful social and political achievement among British Muslims. In the current climate, this can easily be overlooked. For example, London is now a major centre for the international 'halal' market (Fischer 2008a, 2008b, 2008c; Lever and Miele 2012) as well as Islamic banking and finance. There is a growth in financial products that appeal not only to Muslims, but also to non-Muslims because of the ethical and trading principles involved (Housby 2011). In his speech to the Islamic Finance and Trade conference in October 2008 the Justice Secretary at the time, Jack Straw MP, claimed that British Muslims contributed over £31 billion to the UK economy.[4] In light of the growth in the British Muslim population since, this figure is likely to have increased yet further.

# Researching British Muslims: Interdisciplinary Perspectives

Since the arrival of large numbers of South Asian Muslims in Britain after 1945, Muslims have increasingly laid claim to a distinctive 'religious' identity (Jacobson 1998). This changing self-understanding has been mirrored in the academic world. If there is a distinctive change of emphasis in the academic research about Muslims in Britain since 1945, it is most evident in the shift from a predominant concern with the ethnic and racial identity of 'immigrants', to a more concentrated focus on the religious dynamics of settled Muslim communities increasingly comprising British-born Muslims. This can be mapped onto the evolving academic centres and research activities of the last forty years, and their associated outputs.

For example, the Centre for Research in Ethnic Relations (CRER) founded by John Rex in 1970 was a leading centre for academic social scientific research on the settlement of ethnic minorities in Britain. For a substantial period (1984–98) CRER received research council funding,[5] and was at the forefront of work on racial discrimination and race relations,

---

[4] <http://www.globalvision2000.com/forums/printthread.php?tid=691> [Accessed 23 January 2013].
[5] CRER was funded by the Economic and Social Research Council (ESRC).

refugees and asylum-seekers, nationalism, cultural identity, and so on. Some of the most important work on Muslims in Britain in the 1980s and 1990s was undertaken by researchers associated with CRER (Anwar 1984, 1993a, 2001; Joly 1995; Rex 1994) at the University of Warwick. While some of their work focused on Muslims as a distinctive religious minority group, a good deal of the work in CRER was more concerned with research about ethnic groups, e.g. Pakistanis, who happened to be Muslim. Amongst the researchers in CRER with a particular interest in British Pakistani Muslims was Muhammad Anwar. Anwar did some important quantitative analysis of Census data (before questions about religion were incorporated) and produced policy papers on topics ranging from education and burial to social policy more broadly, in keeping with the focus on ethnic mobilization and multicultural identity that was a hallmark of Rex's work (Rex 1991, 1994).

It was quite clear from Anwar's research that in the 1970s, Pakistani Muslims living in Britain tended to remain in relative isolation from wider society. Their world-view was shaped by the assumption that they were in Britain to work, to save money, and eventually to return 'home'. This mind-set largely mitigated pro-active resistance to prejudice and discrimination, and inhibited any sense of identity as 'British Muslims'. Religion was an important 'binding force' in Pakistani communities, especially among those living in the northern town of Rochdale where Anwar conducted much of his early work. Islamic injunctions around dress, diet, marriage, relations between genders, and the sense of mutual 'brotherly' obligations were evident, as was a strong sense of moral responsibility towards kin 'back home'. Much of the communal networking revolved around the mosques and Islamic centres in the town, some of which were already beginning to provide religious education for children. Considerable emphasis was placed on teaching children Urdu, in preparation for the assumed return to the Indian subcontinent. As one informant put it: 'without this they will not have patriotic feelings and will be misfits in Pakistani society' (Anwar 1979: 160). Other sociologists with an interest in British Muslims also began to take greater account of Islamic religious life and practice in the 1980s and 1990s as part of larger investigations of ethnic minorities. For example, Tariq Modood led the fourth major study of ethnic minorities in Britain for the Policy Studies Institute (PSI) in the 1990s (Modood et al. 1997). This resulted in a comprehensive social scientific picture of the situation of ethnic minority groups that are predominantly Muslim, especially Bangladeshis and Pakistanis. Where previous PSI studies had tended to focus exclusively on social policy concerns, such as housing and employment, the Fourth Survey had a broader concern with questions of cultural and religious identity as well. For example, the finding that 74% of Muslims reported their religion as being 'very important' to them (Modood et al. 1997: 118) provided important quantitative evidence that supported other qualitative research.[6]

Where CRER was predominantly associated with sociologists, the Community Religions Project (CRP) established at the University of Leeds in 1976 was one of the

---

[6] For example, Jessica Jacobson's qualitative study with young Muslims in Walthamstow, London in the 1990s (Jacobson 1998).

first centres of excellence for the production of research reflecting the interdisciplinary field of Religious Studies. The project engaged in empirical mapping of religion in Leeds, and some of the most important monographs about Muslims in Britain in the 1980s and 1990s were produced by doctoral researchers involved with the project. Much of the work of the CRP revolved around the changes taking place in ethnic minority faith communities as a result of their location in Britain, and specifically, Leeds, and the new inter-religious relations that formed as a result of their new proximity (Prideaux 2009). The CRP work was significant because of the emphasis placed upon 'lived religion' in the day-to-day life of Muslim communities, such as the dynamic of mosques and the work of imams (Barton 1986; Lewis 1994), and the internal religious diversity among South Asian Muslim communities (Geaves 1996). Inevitably, these researchers brought greater 'religious literacy' to the study of Muslim communities in Britain, having been trained in the Study of Religions (rather than Sociology). The religious world-views of Muslims were a central point of focus, enabling the intersections of ethnicity, migration history, locality, and 'school of religious thought' to become apparent. This was especially evident in Barton's detailed study of Bengali Muslims in Bradford, most of whom had originated from the Sylhet region. His work described the establishment of one of the earliest mosques in the city, its evolving role over time, its transnational connections, and the particular place of the imam as the religious figurehead. He observed how the mosque provided 'both a means of and a stimulus to the performance of basic Islamic duties' and that prior to its establishment, religious observance had been 'variable' (Barton 1986: 78). As in many other British cities, the business of establishing mosques (usually by adapting existing buildings) often brought Muslims into direct contact with the local state (especially via planning authorities) for the first time, and required considerable internal organization and pooling of collective resources. It was often the case that distinctions of ethnicity, 'school of religious thought', or tribal loyalties were temporarily shelved. However, as mosque communities grew in size, ethnic and sectarian rivalries and tensions originating from the Indian subcontinent became more evident, leading to the creation of new mosques organized around more distinctive identities.

Barton's work provided a rich ethnographic account of the place of the mosque for the observance of the Five Pillars of Islam, and the celebration of religious festivals. However, there were aspects of religious life that Bengali Muslims in Bradford could not reproduce in Britain. For example, the performance of devotions associated with the shrines of Sufi masters (*pirs*) could only be undertaken via return visits 'home', and Sylhet was the preferred location for other major life-cycle rites, such as marriages, funerals/burials, and celebrations of birth: 'ceremonies relating to the birth and growth of children may be postponed until a return visit or celebrated vicariously by the family in Sylhet' (Barton 1986: 103). Barton's work remains particularly valuable for contemporary scholars because of the degree to which it provides a point of comparison with current trends. For example, the growth of British Muslim funeral services and burial grounds in the last decade is clearly indicative of an important spatial and psychological shift.[7]

---

[7] For example, the 'Gardens of Peace' is one of the largest Muslim cemeteries in Europe, with over 10,000 plots in Ilford, Essex.

Barton's work was largely concerned with the strategies employed by Bengali Muslims to establish religious infrastructures and leadership in Britain. However, as a consequence of her gender, the social anthropologist Pnina Werbner was able to document in intricate detail how Pakistani Muslims established households, neighbourhoods, and communities in Britain in the 1970s and 1980s via her study of Muslims settling in Manchester (Werbner 1990). Her ability to freely access family life and domestic spaces enabled her to show how family homes tended to be simultaneously both private spaces, and also the sites of extensive family-orientated social life. The broad contours of sociability that she described then have changed relatively little, on account of the centrality of the family in Islamic teaching and Muslim cultures. Homes are still important sites for mutual exchange of news and gossip, joking and political debate, the cooperative care of children and the elderly, and the sharing of refreshments (Werbner 1990). This is made all the more possible when families are clustered together in neighbouring houses, streets, or neighbourhoods. It is within the unsegregated, private space of homes that the power (and mutual empowerment) of women is often most evident, since here they share information and act with autonomy and confidence in relation to most family matters. The relationships of trust that are built up through the exchange of information, gifts, hospitality, and mutual support are indicative of the active centrality of women in family life. Werbner showed, however, that the establishment of close-knit social networks was not undertaken solely for utilitarian purposes, but rather to create 'a moral community and [to] transform the space, the house, the neighbourhood, and the city in which they live, into a moral space' informed by Islamic values (Werbner 1990: 150).

Around the same time that Werbner was undertaking her anthropological work in Manchester, the Centre for Research on Islam and Christian–Muslim Relations (CSIC) founded at the University of Birmingham in 1977 was leading efforts to develop the field of Islamic Studies in Britain. CSIC placed particular emphasis on an understanding of the place of Islam and Muslims in European societies (Johnstone 1977), and in particular, relations between Muslims and Christians. Under the leadership of Jørgen Nielsen, CSIC was also at the forefront of empirical research about Muslims in Britain (Nielsen 1991), documenting challenges facing Muslim communities and their interaction with the state. This included, for example, educational challenges (practical, theoretical, and theological) faced by Muslims as they sought to reconcile Islamic world-views and norms with the prevalent assumptions of mainstream educators (Nielsen 1981, 1989). CSIC was similarly supporting the production of graduate dissertations mapping Muslim settlement in Britain, especially in Birmingham (Ally 1979; Amer 1997; North 1996).

Of particular significance was the production of the *British Muslims Monthly Survey* (BMMS), a digest of national and local newspaper reports about Muslims, often themed around issues of significance at the time, such as the building of mosques, provision of halal food in schools, burial facilities, education, and so on. BMMS was produced between 1993 and 2001, and provided researchers and policy-makers with essential information about Muslim community development, especially during the years before widespread use of the internet. Some BMMS archives are still available to view via the World Wide Web, and provide a unique insight into the evolving infrastructure of Muslim communities around the UK.[8] The coverage of local developments in the BMMS was significant; regional negotiations about issues, such as educational provision, often provided a driver for later policy-making at national level (Joly 2012).

When Nielsen left Birmingham University in 2005/6, the CSIC seemed to lose momentum, eventually morphing into a new Centre for Islamic and Middle Eastern Studies in the Department of Theology. However, an important legacy of CSIC continues to flourish. CSIC pioneered the establishment of the Muslims in Britain Research Network (MBRN) in the late 1980s. This informal network of scholars that included researchers from CRER, CSIC, and the CRP became an important locus for the sharing of information resources and research updates. The MBRN remained active at Birmingham until the late 1990s, but then ceased to hold regular meetings. However, at a workshop held for Islamic Studies researchers in Leeds post-9/11, Jørgen Nielsen, Seán McLoughlin, and Sophie Gilliat-Ray agreed that it was important to revive the MBRN. The MBRN was thus relaunched at Cardiff University in 2003 with a keynote address by Pnina Werbner. In 2006, the MBRN won Home Office funding to become a formally constituted professional association, rather than an informal network, and under the current Chair, Seán McLoughlin, the MBRN remains a flourishing academic enterprise. Much of the growth in membership in the last decade has been among postgraduate researchers, many of whom are British Muslims. Where they are conducting research as 'insiders' of Islamic religious movements to which they have unique access, they are inevitably challenged by some particularly interesting methodological questions around issues of reflexivity, positionality, and ethics.

The relaunch of the MBRN in 2003 provided a catalyst for another academic development, namely the establishment of the Centre for the Study of Islam in the UK at Cardiff University in 2005. The Centre was founded explicitly on the basis of collaboration and partnership with local Muslim organizations, including the Muslim Council of Wales. Like some of its forerunners, the Islam-UK Centre is distinctive for its interdisciplinary research activity, and in particular its support of graduate and doctoral students via a well-established scholarship programme. However, its collaborative engagement with local Muslim communities and associations gives it a particular orientation to research which might be characterized as grassroots, and most research is wherever possible conducted in partnership with Muslim organizations. Thus far, major projects have been conducted on the work of Muslim chaplains in Britain (Gilliat-Ray 2008, 2010a, 2011; Gilliat-Ray et al. 2013), religious nurture in Muslim families (Scourfield et al. 2012, 2013), British Muslim environmental action (Gilliat-Ray and Bryant 2011), the history and settlement of Muslims in south Wales (Gilliat-Ray 2010b; Gilliat-Ray and Mellor 2010), British Muslim musicians,[9] and an ethnography of an Islamic social welfare organization.[10]

---

[8] <http://artsweb.bham.ac.uk/bmms/howtouse.asp>.
[9] Sounds Islamic? British Muslims, the Umma and an Islamic Sound Aesthetic, Carl Morris, 2009–12.
[10] A Sociological Study of Islamic Social Work in Contemporary Britain, Roz Warden, 2009–13.

These studies are indicative of some important trends, especially in relation to the increasing professionalization of welfare and pastoral services in Muslim communities, and the innovative and often highly individualistic use of Islamic scholarly traditions and practices. For example, the research about religious nurture in Muslim families established that teaching children of primary school age how to read the Qur'an, in Arabic, is still regarded as an important parental duty among Muslims in Britain (with less emphasis now on learning of community languages, such as Urdu). However, where it was once taken for granted that children would attend the local mosque for this religious instruction, some families are using tutors based abroad who deliver their one-to-one instruction via the internet. Parents are 'shopping around' for teachers and facilities that accommodate the pressures of busy family lives. They remain committed to traditional practices, but exercise individualistic and pragmatic choices about exactly how they should be fulfilled. Furthermore, families are keen that children should know not only how to recite the Qur'an but also appreciate its meaning and application for contemporary twenty-first century Britain.

These changing parental views offer an insight into how some Muslims are choosing to shape the identity of their children in a way that is consonant with their faith, and the society to which they belong. We can observe a shift, from what Castells would term 'resistance identity'—shaped by perceptions of external hostility and rejection of dominant secular-liberal values—to 'project identity', that seeks to redefine the social position of Muslims, not through withdrawal to the 'trenches', but through pro-active engagement within civil society (Castells 1997). Much the same might be said in relation to the evolving role of Muslim chaplains in Britain, of whom there are now around 450. The findings of a major study of Muslim chaplains at Cardiff University (2008–11) found that they are involved in the important process of contextualizing Islamic traditions in the UK. As they go about their daily work, they encounter situations which demand decisions as to how, and to what extent, Islamic practices can be accommodated within the confines of secular, multifaith, public institutions. Decision-making often requires an ability to think and act contextually, and in light of both institutional policies (e.g. around equality and diversity) and the principles of shariah (Islamic legal traditions). We found evidence of considerable interpretive effort (*ijtihad*) as chaplains strive to interpret the principles of shariah into the practice of chaplaincy.

The profile of Islamic Studies in Britain since the mid-to-late 2000s has grown substantially following a decision by the Higher Education Funding Council for England (HEFCE) to nominate the field as a subject of 'strategic importance' in June 2007. Following the publication of the Siddiqui Report in 2007 (Siddiqui 2007), which investigated the teaching of Islam in English universities and pastoral support for Muslim students, it became clear that the interdisciplinary field of Islamic Studies was diffuse and badly networked across the disciplines. The benefit that might be derived from greater investment in terms of curriculum development, professional networking opportunities, digitization of teaching resources, and graduate support was obvious. Under the auspices of the Higher Education Academy, an Islamic Studies Network Advisory Board was formed to support these initiatives, with representation from MBRN, former staff of the CSIC, the British Society for Middle Eastern Studies (BRISMES) as well as leading academics from key universities between 2009 and 2012.[11] A number of independent British Muslim colleges were also represented, such as Markfield Institute of Higher Education in Leicester (MIHE), largely because of the significance of Dr Ataullah Siddiqui's report. One of the outcomes of the Islamic Studies Network was a decision to form the British Association for Islamic Studies (BRAIS), which was launched in Edinburgh in April 2014.

Alongside these efforts in the field of Islamic Studies, there have been important parallel developments in Religious Studies in recent years (especially from 2005 onwards). For example, a number of major government funded initiatives have provided the impetus for new academic research about Muslims in Britain, such as the Diasporas, Migration and Identities Programme (University of Leeds, 2005–10) and the £12 million Religion and Society Programme (2008–12). Within both programmes, a number of projects were concerned with British Muslims, meaning that researchers (and stakeholders) could often collaborate and work cooperatively, rather than in isolation.

It is clear that since the launch of CRER in 1970, there has been a distinctive trajectory in the way that research with, and about, Muslims in Britain has taken place. The field has become both more specialized, but also increasingly interdisciplinary. There is now greater 'stakeholder' involvement, such that Muslim researchers and Islamic colleges are more central to the development of the field. Some of the most significant research that took place via the Islamic Studies Network, as well as central government funded research in the late 2000s, has explored the links that can be made between university-based teaching and learning in Islamic Studies, and Islamic Studies delivered in Islamic colleges and independent seminaries (*dar ul-uloom*).[12] Part of the rationale for this development derives from the fact that ever since Philip Lewis's doctoral research in Bradford in the 1990s, there have been concerns about capacity of Islamic scholars (*'ulama*) and imams to engage effectively with British-born youth. At the time of Lewis's study, nearly all religious leaders serving in British mosques were recruited from overseas, with obvious consequences for their capacity to speak English and to relate to the social context of their congregation (especially youth). These concerns have not diminished with the growth of Islamic seminaries (*dar ul-uloom*) in Britain, most of which reflect the Deobandi 'school of thought' (see the section on Muslim Communities in Britain).[13] Geaves's research with a group of *'ulama* in 2008 found that only 8% were born and educated in the UK, meaning

---

[11] See the Islamic Studies Network homepage: <http://www.heacademy.ac.uk/islamicstudiesnetwork/home>.

[12] Examples include: Mukadam and Scott-Baumann 2010, and work by Ron Geaves ('An exploration of the viability of partnership between dar al-ulum and higher education institutions in North West England focusing upon pedagogy and relevance').

[13] This current of Islamic thought emerged in India (Deoband) in the nineteenth century in response to European colonialism. The scholars associated with this movement placed an emphasis on hadith studies, and the preservation and protection of Islamic law and lifestyles. It is often contrasted with the 'Barelvi' school of thought, which might be regarded as more 'Sufi' in orientation, and where great emphasis is placed on devotion towards the Prophet Muhammad.

that many congregations continue to recruit their religious leaders from overseas (Geaves 2008), despite the growth of religious training facilities in the UK.

In light of this, and an awareness of the fact that imams could be 'part of the solution, not the problem' in relation to radicalization, the British government's Department for Communities and Local Government commissioned a major study, the 'Muslim Faith Leaders Review' in 2008, led by a British Muslim scholar and a university academic. Their brief was to explore, among other things, the 'possibilities of collaborative initiatives between the providers of Muslim faith leadership training and mainstream further education and higher education institutions' (Mukadam and Scott-Baumann 2010). The study found that Muslim faith leadership is now exercised not only by imams based in mosques, but by a wide range of men and women in their capacity as youth workers, chaplains, teachers, and so on, and that greater effort should be invested in supporting the educational and training needs of this diverse group. It was also established that there would be 'substantial advantages if programmes of Muslim faith leadership training were to be validated in accordance with the levels in the national qualifications framework (NQF)' (Mukadam and Scott-Baumann 2010: 13). At least one of these 'advantages' would be some recognition for the years of scholarly effort that some young British Muslims invest in developing their Islamic knowledge. Partly as a consequence of the Review, Muslim organizations and individual Muslim researchers now have far greater involvement in research and in debate about teaching and learning in Islamic Studies.

The sustained output of new publications, conferences, and events, alongside professional associations increasing in membership, means that there are strong grounds for asserting the emergence of a more coherent field of 'British Muslim Studies' that is able to encompass a wide range of disciplines, and that is becoming more methodologically reflexive (Abbas 2010; Bolognani 2007; Gilliat-Ray 2010a, 2011; Khan et al. 2013; Quraishi 2008; Sanghera and Thapar-Bjorkert 2008; Zubair et al. 2012). Researchers who are influenced by 'the subjective turn' in anthropology and qualitative social science research have begun to pay greater reflexive attention to their own position in the fieldwork process, and the way this might shape the outcomes of their work (Coffey 1999; Ellingson 2006; Ellis and Bochner 2000; McLean and Leibing 2007a, 2007b). But while practical, professional, and organizational developments have moved relatively quickly, there is perhaps a longer-term theoretical academic project to be undertaken which brings improved integration and new intellectual rigour to the field.

# British Muslims and Social Policy: Multiculturalism, Social Cohesion, and 'Prevent'

Just as in the academic world, social policy relating to Muslims in Britain has undergone paradigmatic change since the post-Second World War period. These changes reflect the negotiation of new discourses emanating from both within and outside Muslim communities, especially at local level, shaped by changing self-understanding and evolving socio-political realities. Over a period of approximately fifty years, changing categories have been used to 'frame' British Muslims. Terms such as 'colour' and 'race' were followed by 'ethnicity', while today there is a more distinctive emphasis on 'religion' in public life, largely driven by the growing agency and mobilization of British Muslims in response to national and international events (Joly 2012). From being cast as 'black' in the 1960s and early 1970s, the majority of Muslims began to distinguish themselves as more distinctively 'Asian' in the later 1970s and 1980s, with the Rushdie affair providing an important catalyst for the emergence of a more confident public religious identity as 'Muslims' in the 1990s. These developments are mirrored in changing social policies. Joly has noted that 'after a brief period of assimilationism, a class-based race relations paradigm was formulated, followed by the establishment of a multicultural policy... that has since metamorphosed into a Muslim paradigm' (Joly 2012: 5).

An important driver for the changing self-identity of Muslims in Britain in the 1990s was the publication of Salman Rushdie's novel *The Satanic Verses* in 1988, widely held by Muslims as defamatory of the Prophet Muhammad, and calculatedly blasphemous. The publication of the novel served to unite Muslims from a wide range of ethnic, linguistic, intra-religious, and racial backgrounds around a common religious identity, for the first time. Their vulnerable position in Britain, especially in relation to their religious rights and equality vis-à-vis other faiths was placed squarely into the public domain; calls for greater equality in law (especially in terms of blasphemy laws) were clearly articulated as part of the anti-racist discourse of the time (Modood 1989, 1990a, 1990b; Weller 2009). The Rushdie affair provided Muslims with an opportunity for active participation in British society through the public defence of Islam. As Pnina Werbner noted, 'it liberated Pakistani settler-citizens from the self-imposed burden of being a silent, well-behaved minority, whatever the provocation, and opened up the realm of activist, anti-racist and emancipatory politics' (Werbner 2002a: 258). Coinciding with the growing realization of the 'myth of return', the crisis led to an awareness that existing forms of community leadership centred on mosques and their management committees were inadequate for the professional representation of Muslim interests at a national level (McLoughlin 2005). Consequently, the UK Action Committee for Islamic Affairs (UKACIA) was formed in 1988 to coordinate political protest and lobbying; it was the forerunner to the Muslim Council of Britain (MCB) which was established in 1997.

The extent to which the MCB is regarded as 'representative' of British Muslim interests (either by Muslims in Britain, or by government politicians) has varied over the first fifteen years of its existence, with contrasting views largely shaped by unfolding national and international events. But the activities of the MCB provide a valuable lens through which to view British Muslim engagement in social policy and efforts to negotiate with the state at a national level (Adamson 2011; Pedziwiatr 2007; Radcliffe 2004). Thus, one of the earliest MCB initiatives was directed towards the inclusion of a question on 'religion' in the 2001 Census (Sherif 2011). This was followed by calls for stronger legislation on religious discrimination and incitement to religious hatred, and state funding for Muslim schools. The MCB has not been the only player here, of course. Since the 7/7 bombings, the government has tried to give support to other allegedly 'representative' bodies, such as the British Muslim Forum (established in 2005) and the so-called Sufi Muslim Council (established in 2006). Neither has managed to achieve the sustained profile or prominence of the MCB, despite sometimes vehement criticism of the latter (O'Toole et al. 2013).

As part of the emerging 'Muslim paradigm' (Joly 2012), Joly notes the myriad ways in which, since the Rushdie affair, Muslims have successfully negotiated accommodation of religious practices in a range of public spheres and arenas of local and national social policy. These have included education (Hewer 2001; Meer 2007; Parker-Jenkins 2002; Shah 2009; Tinker 2009), publicly funded chaplaincy (Ahmad and Sardar 2012; Beckford and Gilliat 1998; Beckford et al. 2005; Gilliat-Ray et al. 2013), burial and marriage arrangements (Ansari 2007), and banking and finance (Housby 2011). However, the urban riots that erupted in a number of northern towns and cities in 2001, followed by the London bombings in 2005, led to reduced emphasis on multiculturalism (which emphasized anti-discrimination, equal opportunities, and recognition of difference) and more focus upon social and community cohesion as the guiding principle of social policy. A government commission was launched in 2006 to address questions of supposed minority group 'separateness', 'self-segregation', and 'isolation' and this was soon followed by substantial investment in projects to support activities such as inter-faith relations, better integration of new immigrants (e.g. English language support), and staffing of new posts that could underpin these initiatives.

Not surprisingly, the assumptions behind 'community cohesion' have not been without criticism, especially where this policy has intersected with efforts in counter-terrorism (Husband 2012; Husband and Alam 2011; Ratcliffe 2012). More positively, new modes of Muslim debate and participation in public life have come about as one of the by-products of moves toward greater 'community cohesion'. Some of these have been initiated and driven by Muslims, others led by government departments. Examples of the former include institutions such as the Policy Research Centre in Leicester (Ahmed 2009; Hussain 2012), the City Circle (Lewis 2007),[14] the Muslim Institute,[15] the Radical Middle Way, and Muslim involvement in the 'Stop the War' coalition (Phillips 2008), while the latter include the National Muslim Women's Advisory Group (2008) and an equivalent body which sought to engage Muslim youth with government. Younger, British-born Muslim women and youth have been mobilized through these initiatives, and it is clear that they have placed more emphasis on their religious identity and pro-active engagement in contemporary issues in Britain, distancing themselves from the religious institutions created by their elders which were steeped in ethnic networks and traditions originating from countries of origin (Joly 2012).

---

[14] <http://www.citycircle.com> (a professional Muslim network that engages in practical projects and hosts events/debates about a wide range of community issues).

[15] <http://www.themusliminstitute.org.uk> (another professional network, more academic/intellectual in terms of aims and objectives, established in 2009).

This mobilization has been double-edged, however, insofar as it has intersected with narratives of radicalization and countering of violent extremism. The Preventing Violent Extremism (PVE) agenda recasts Muslims as members of a 'suspect community' (Awan 2012), or as 'potential violent extremists' (Khan 2009). These narratives play into the hands of well-funded right-wing think tanks, the reports of which can shape public opinion via the media and, to some extent, social policy (Mills et al. 2011). Consequently, understanding of Muslims in Britain is now informed not only by academic research and better quality investigative journalism, but also by hastily produced, under-researched, unaccountable think-tank reports that typically fail to make reference to academic research.[16] Not surprisingly, therefore, being an empirical researcher of Muslim communities in Britain today has become a more complex and sensitive undertaking, because of the suspicion that Muslim communities justifiably feel towards 'researchers' whose credentials and motives may not always be transparent.

Since 2006, an entire field has emerged which examines British Muslims, policing, and counter-terrorism (Choudhury and Fenwick 2011; Kundnani 2009, 2012; Lambert 2008, 2011; O'Toole et al. 2012; Saggar 2009; Spalek 2011, 2012; Spalek and McDonald 2009; Vidino 2010). If we can crudely summarize the predominant perspectives, it is evident that two major currents of thought currently hold sway. Those in favour of community-based approaches to counter-terrorism suggest that radical extremism is best tackled through negotiation with, and empowerment of, non-violent Muslim activists (e.g. Lambert 2011). Their religious credibility among those more inclined towards violence provides an important 'firewall' (Vidino 2010) that will, it is asserted, ultimately limit actual terrorist action. The opposing perspective instead regards non-violent extremism as simply a 'conveyor belt' (Vidino 2010) towards more radical violence. This view has been propounded by the counter-terrorism think tank, the Quilliam Foundation, which argues that non-violent Islamist groups 'advocate separatist, confrontational ideas that, followed to their logical conclusion, lead to violence' (Quilliam Foundation, *Pulling Together to Defeat Terror*, April 2008). As yet, there is little empirical evidence to support either one of these viewpoints. There is, in contrast, more substantial evidence to support claims that British Muslims feel that their faith has been stigmatized by PVE policy and policing strategies (Spalek 2011), that distrust between communities has increased (often as a consequence of unaccountable funding decisions; Birt 2010), and that PVE policy has been a driver of embitterment and feelings of isolation within British Muslim communities that were not so apparent before these 'measures' were enacted (Bonino 2012; Mythen 2012).

In light of this, it is not surprising to find that some British Muslims feel themselves, both individually and corporately, to be victims of 'Islamophobia', this being a facet of a larger problem of discrimination that may be directed towards Muslims as members of ethnic or racial groups. It is paradoxical that the rise of 'Islamophobia' has happened in

---

[16] Examples of this genre of literature can be found on the websites of CIVITAS [<http://www.civitas.org.uk/>] and Policy Exchange [<http://www.policyexchange.org.uk/>].

parallel with the increasing recognition of Muslims in many other spheres of public life (Vertovec 2002). 'Islamophobia' is a word that first entered the discourse about Muslims in Britain in the early 1990s but went on to receive more formal 'recognition' with the publication of the seminal Runnymede Trust report *Islamophobia: A Challenge for us All* in 1997. Following the Rushdie affair, the second Gulf War, the 9/11 atrocities, the Danish 'Cartoon' controversy (Meer and Mouritsen 2009), and the 7/7 bombings, there is well-documented evidence of increasing Islamophobic attitudes and behaviours, not least through a comprehensive survey of 'opinion polls' about Muslims in Britain carried out by Clive Field (Field 2007).

> A stereotypical picture of British Muslims in the eyes of the majority population has emerged, Muslims being seen as slow to integrate into mainstream society, feeling only a qualified sense of patriotism, and prone to espouse anti-Western values that lead many to condone so-called Islamic terrorism... polls among the Muslim population reveal a community that, despite some softening of attitudes since 7/7, remains ill at ease with the majority British culture and apprehensive about the future... mutual suspicion and fear are fuelling a worsening Islamophobia. (Field 2007: 469)

Islamophobia has become a topic of intensive academic research in the last decade (Abbas 2012; Allen 2010a, 2010b, 2011; Hussain and Bagguley 2012; Meer 2012; Meer and Noorani 2008; Pratt 2011; Taras 2012; Werbner 2012), with more recent publications focusing upon the intersection of Islamophobia with counter-terrorism. The academic institutionalization of this field in terms of the rise of far-right extremism (which is often directed against Muslims) has recently occurred at the University of Teesside which, in January 2013, established a Centre for Fascist, Anti-Fascist and Post-Fascist Studies. British Muslims themselves have been similarly pro-active, establishing organizations and mechanisms to monitor Islamophobic attacks against institutions, individuals, and in the media. Examples include FAIR (Forum Against Islamophobia and Racism) between 2001 and 2008, and calls in most issues of the British Muslim newspaper *The Muslim News* to report Islamophobic attacks.

The coincidence of rising Islamophobia, the emergence of a more confident and articulate Muslim religious identity (especially post-Rushdie), and growing calls for the accommodation of Islamic practice in the public domain (especially in schools) has, unsurprisingly, had major consequences in relation to religious discrimination and calls for the recognition of Islamic law. For many years, Muslims as a distinctive religious minority group were without legal protection on the grounds of their religion. So where Jews and Sikhs, for example, could find recourse in the law as members of distinctive racial/ethnic groups, Muslims could not make similar claims where they had suffered from religious discrimination (Poulter 1986a, 1986b). It was especially in the area of employment that Muslims suffered on account of dress in the workplace (e.g. hijab), the need to pray at particular times, or taking holiday at short notice to celebrate Eid, or simply gaining a job in the first place (Bunglawala 2004; Khaliq 2002; Malik 2004). Following the introduction of incremental law to protect Muslims against religious discrimination in particular settings such as the workplace (via the Employment Equality (Religion or

Belief) Regulations of 2003), much stronger legislation was introduced via the Equality Act of 2010. The new Act harmonizes what was a fragmented range of discrimination legislation, and now includes protection from discrimination on the grounds of 'religion or belief' (or lack thereof). The new Equality and Human Rights Commission provides detailed guidance about the remit of the new legislation, as does the Home Office.[17]

Other legal issues that have been investigated have included the intersection of Muslim personal law in relation to the civil courts, especially in relation to marriage and divorce (Bano 1999, 2007; Douglas et al. 2012; Pilgram 2012; Warraich and Balchin 2006; Yilmaz 2000) and the question of how, and to what extent, Islamic law (shariah) should be recognized more broadly (Williams 2008b; Yilmaz 2002). A lecture given by the Archbishop of Canterbury, Dr Rowan Williams, in February 2008 led to much public discussion about the relationship between religious law—primarily though not exclusively Islamic—and civil law in England and Wales (Williams 2008a). In that lecture, Rowan Williams sought to bring to a higher level of public debate than found in the tabloid press the question of 'what it is like to live under more than one (legal) jurisdiction' and how (and how far) the civil law of the land should recognize or accommodate a legal pluralism based on religious adherence. Part—perhaps much—of the public outcry which greeted the Archbishop's lecture in 2008 reflected a lack of knowledge of how religious courts already operate in Britain. Media-hyped fears over the operation of shariah courts were matched with prejudiced comments about the privileging of Jewish courts which have operated in Britain for over a hundred years (and no one mentioned that the Roman Catholic Church has handed down decrees of nullity of marriage throughout its history).

This provided a context for a project to explore the role and practice of religious courts in England and Wales, especially in relation to marriage and divorce, which included extensive research with the shariah council of the Birmingham Central Mosque. It was clear from this research that religious courts firmly recognize and support the ultimate authority of civil law processes when it comes to marriage and divorce and none seeks greater 'recognition' by the state. We also found evidence of 'forum shopping', especially within the Jewish and Muslim communities, as there is no 'hierarchy' or system of appeal for shariah Councils or the Beth Din. Litigants can choose which tribunal they go to according to the way in which (they think) the law will be applied to them or by what they perceive will be the extent of recognition of the tribunal's decision across their community.

## Political Participation

High concentrations of Muslims in particular towns and cities in Britain have direct implications for local politics, political mobilization, and voting patterns. In the 1970s, when Muslim communities were becoming more established as a result of the

---

[17] <http://www.equalityhumanrights.com/advice-and-guidance/your-rights/religion-and-belief/> or <http://www.homeoffice.gov.uk/publications/equalities/equality-act-publications/equality-act-guidance/vcs-religion-belief?view=Binary>.

reunification of families, their political concerns were particularly related to immediate needs, especially in terms of housing, social welfare, immigration, and education. Organizations were established to lobby and campaign on these issues, and Muslims began to influence local political decision-making by serving as local councillors. Purdam's research outlined the growing trajectory of this involvement, the demographic profile of Muslim councillors (Purdam 2000) and their sometimes controversial relationship to the Labour Party (Purdam 2001).

In May 1996, there were 160 Muslim local councillors in Britain, and their distribution among the main political parties was indicative of historical Muslim community support for different parties with 153 Labour, six Liberal, and one Conservative (Purdam 2001). Their presence reflected areas of Muslim concentration, and so there were twelve Muslim councillors on Birmingham City Council, and eleven in Bradford. Purdam predicted future growth in the number of British Muslim councillors, and indeed, by the mid-2000s there were 230 Muslim local government councillors in Britain (Anwar 2008).

Yet, Muslims remain under-represented in national politics. In 2013, there were eight Muslim MPs (out of a total of 650), meaning they constitute just 1.2% of all MPs. To reflect the fact that nearly 5% of the UK population is Muslim, there should be more like 32 Muslim MPs in Britain today (O'Toole et al. 2013). But one of the success stories of British Muslim political participation we might cite includes the life-peer Baroness Saeeda Warsi, born in Britain in 1971 to parents of Pakistani origin in Yorkshire. Until recently she was Vice-Chair of the Conservative Party and Minister without Portfolio in David Cameron's Cabinet. She was the first Muslim woman to serve as a government minister, and is now the Minister of State for Faith and Communities. This kind of growing political inclusion is reflected in other more symbolic ways; it is routine for British Muslim newspapers to carry greetings from senior politicians at Eid, reflecting the broader 'institutionalization' of Islam in British society.

Examining Muslim involvement in local and national politics first of all, we find that there are now British Muslims of both genders serving in local authority councils, and in both Houses of Parliament.[18] The representation of Muslims in mainstream local and national politics has been of interest to academics for several decades, not least because political incorporation is a significant measure of wider recognition and involvement (Anwar 1979: 136). Furthermore, 'growing numbers of Muslims have come to regard formal political mechanisms as an effective way of getting their problems addressed, if not solved' (Ansari 2004: 234). The evidence to support this assertion can be found in research which has documented the growing involvement of British Muslims in local politics (Anwar 1979; Purdam 2000, 2001). Additionally, new work documents and evaluates Muslim participation in new post 9/11 political parties and movements, such as the Stop the War Coalition and the 'Respect' party (Peace 2012; Phillips 2008).

---

[18] 'Following the election of Britain's first Muslim MP in 1997—Mohammad Sarwar—the number of Muslim MPs in the House of Commons increased to eight following the 2010 General Election, which also marked the election of Britain's first three female Muslim MPs and the first two Conservative Muslim MPs' (O'Toole et al. 2012).

There are various ways and means by which British Muslims have engaged in political action in the last four decades, each of which reflects different understandings of how they should strategically construct their identities and subsequently mobilize in order to achieve particular outcomes (Adamson 2011). A typology for various forms of participation has been set out by Dilwar Hussain from the Islamic Foundation in Leicester (Hussain 2004: 183). He has characterized Muslim political participation as involving: working outside the system; working for an alternative system; joining existing parties; setting up a Muslim party; lobbying; and local action. More recently, important new research has mapped the range of ways in which Muslims have been engaged in contemporary governance in British society, whether this is through participation in the 'faith sector', as part of 'Prevent' projects, or as part of equality, diversity, and social cohesion initiatives (O'Toole et al. 2012, 2013). This research demonstrates that while the presence of Muslims in government may be characterized by rather 'slow progress' (O'Toole et al. 2013: 65) there has been a significant increase in Muslim involvement in other governance structures.

> The current political visibility of Muslims in the UK has been an outcome of *Muslim activism*—in lobbying for state recognition of Muslim distinctiveness and seeking inclusion within governance—as well as significant *institutional innovation* in the ways in which government has recognised and engaged with Muslims since the late 1990s. (O'Toole et al. 2013: 6)

The authors note that, over time, there has been an important recognition of the diversity of Muslim civil society, and the need to work with 'democratic constellations' (O'Toole et al. 2013: 12) of Muslim organizations and interests, depending upon the issues and projects involved. The report provides an invaluable survey of the changing forms of Muslim 'representation' over time, and the ways in which Muslims have been engaged in faith, cohesion, security, or equality initiatives, under both New Labour and the current Coalition government, at both local and national level.

# Muslim Communities in Britain: Diversity, Development, and Integration

The research carried out by Stephen Barton, Muhammad Anwar, Pnina Werbner, and others in the 1970s and 1980s documented the establishment of mosques, facilities for the education of Muslim children, and other institutions that have enabled the flourishing of Islam in Britain. However, it was only with the publication of Geaves's doctoral research in the 1990s that researchers in Britain began to fully appreciate the internal religious diversity within Muslim communities. As an outcome of Geaves's work researchers gained an insight into the range of Islamic religious reform movements present in Britain, each with their particular orientations to belief and practice of Islam. Many of these reform movements had been established in the Middle East or in South Asia during the colonial period. But their subsequent growth and popularity in postcolonial times meant that their action-guiding ideologies and practices were transmitted to Britain as part of the migration of South Asian (and later Middle Eastern) Muslims to the UK.

The main differences between the various 'schools' of Islamic thought in Britain, sometimes fundamental, sometimes a matter of nuance, cannot be readily summarized within the scope of a discussion such as this (with lineaments outlined in Gilliat-Ray 2010c). Furthermore, there is strong evidence that many British Muslims may not even self-consciously identify with any one of them in particular (Scourfield et al. 2013). When non-Muslims enquire about the internal differences in Muslim communities, any diversity in practice or interpretation is often downplayed in favour of an emphasis upon a common allegiance to Islam, in 'a community which would rather regard itself as unified' (King 1997: 55). But it is clear that some movements reactively and defiantly orientate themselves against everything in society that they consider to be 'anti-Islamic'. They moreover call for a new religious-political order to bring about change, often inspired by, or modelled upon, historic methods of Islamic governance, real, imagined, or idealized (Afshar 1998: 55). Other schools of thought might be characterized as more isolationist, seeking to protect and preserve religious identity from the corrupting influences of society using piety, knowledge, and contemplation. Another trend in thought and action seeks to fully engage with the wider society, working through existing political structures but using distinctively Islamic perspectives to try to bring about deliberate social change and the modelling of society upon Islamic values. While there are distinctive perspectives on religious orientation among British Muslims, there are often significant differences of interpretation or practice within these trends. The boundaries of membership are often overlapping and fluid, and as a consequence they are frequently the sites for disputes and vigorous competition for members, resources, or influence (e.g. with government politicians). Most traditions have South Asian roots, and have been characterized as 'the reformist Deobandis, the quietist and revivalist Tablighi Jamaat, the conservative and populist Barelwis, the Islamist Jamaat-i Islami and the modernists' (Lewis 1994: 36).

Not all Muslims accept the 'labels' that have been ascribed to their particular school of thought (Gilliat-Ray 2010c), and since Geaves's research in the 1990s, the meaning of these labels and identifications has arguably changed. To give an example, a number of British Muslim institutions were founded in the 1960s and 1970s by individuals inspired by the South Asian reformer Maulana Maududi and the Jamaat-i Islami movement, such as the UK Islamic Mission and the Islamic Foundation (Geaves 1995; Gilliat-Ray 2010c). However, over time, these institutions have undergone significant development and generational change because of the new recruitment of younger British-born staff from a wide range of ethnic backgrounds, and the appointment of directors with strong links to Britain. In his research at the Islamic

Foundation in Leicester in 2002, Seán McLoughlin found that there is now an evolving generation there who are developing

> innovative, cosmopolitan and self-critical reformulations of their tradition... it is now necessary to speak of a 'third generation' of (diasporic) intellectual-activists who are... reflexive concerning their Islamic lineage (McLoughlin 2005: 64)

In effect, this has meant asking some difficult questions about priorities. For example, 'Is it appropriate to continue to publish the works of Maulana Maududi for a twenty-first-century British audience?' There appears to be no clear consensus about the answer to this and other questions, and the Islamic Foundation appears to maintain a sense of coherence derived precisely from its appreciation of internal diversity.[19]

Relatively little original and field-based research has been undertaken about the varieties of Islamic thought and practice in Britain since Geaves's work, and what little has been done has often focused on the rise of Salafi groups (Hamid 2007, 2008a, 2008b), and movements associated with the international Hizb-ut-Tahrir (HT) (Hanif 2012; Wiktorowicz 2005; Yilmaz 2010). This work has been important for documenting the appeal of these movements to young British-born Muslims, while also noting the fact they are often movements of 'transition'. For example, Hamid notes that HT

> offers little that is constructive beyond vague general prescriptions about the superiority of Islamic systems, and does not have much to say about the pressing social problems and issues affecting Muslim communities at the grassroots hence limiting its mass appeal. Internationally, it represents an intellectual halfway house of sorts between moderate Islamism and violent jihadism. In Britain, it continues to fill a void in the Islamic landscape with a consistent, professionally marketed message. Young people who complete their education and settle down into adult life, and those who can think for themselves, usually leave. HT's long-term appeal will most likely be determined not by the radicalism of its ideas but by the absence of alternatives. (Hamid 2007: 157–8)

This assessment accords with Winter's general observation of the phenomenon of 'Salafi burnout' (Winter 2004: 286), by which he means that the enthusiasm of initial engagement with Islamic movements in one's early twenties loses appeal with greater life-experience, and a realization that it is often impossible to bridge the gap between aspiration and reality.

In the immediate post-Second World War period when Muslims in Britain still thought of themselves as temporary sojourners rather than settlers or citizens (Haddad 2002; Lewis 1994), relatively little investment was made in the development of institutions to support religious practice and community life, and there was certainly little

---

[19] The author is currently a member of the Islamic Foundation's 'Advisory Board', and these impressions are derived from conversations with staff within and outside formal meetings.

account taken of the distinctions between different 'schools of thought', at the time. However, with the realization of the 'myth of return', more energy was directed towards the establishment of mosques, madrassas, and other agencies such as charities, import–export businesses, Islamic bookshops, media, travel agencies (e.g. to facilitate *umrah* and *hajj*), and so on, and this enabled the different currents of religious thought to become more apparent. Anwar, Barton, Werbner, and others noted in their work, from the 1970s onwards, that the process of establishing mosques and associated educational facilities for children took place in earnest. Consequently, there are approximately 1,500 mosques in Britain today, varying in terms of their adherence to a particular school of law or thought (it is estimated that about half of all British mosques are Deobandi), size, architecture, function, and history, with the UK Charity Commission producing one of the first quantitative studies of UK mosques in Britain to date (Coleman 2009; Gilliat-Ray 2010c). Not all mosques are registered as places of worship with local authorities, thus making completely accurate figures difficult to obtain. But it is clear that over time, more of these mosques have been 'purpose-built', not only reflecting the gradual 'Islamisation of space' (Eade 1993) in the urban landscape, but also the increasing range of functions that mosques are seeking to offer to their congregations. For example, large 'central' mosques in major British cities might encompass facilities for funeral services, leisure, and youth activities. But the 'Islamisation of space' has gone well beyond the urban landscape. Public institutions increasingly provide dedicated space for Muslim prayers such as prisons, airports, shopping centres, hospitals, motorway service stations, and leisure attractions (Gilliat-Ray 2005b, 2005c, 2010c).

Much of the academic research about mosques in Britain thus far has concentrated on mosque construction and 'controversies', with a lot of this work being produced by social geographers interested in architectural and planning issues (Birt and Gilliat-Ray 2009; Brown 2008; Eade 2011; Gale 2004; Gale and Naylor 2003; Jones 2010; Nasser 2005, 2006; Nilsson DeHanas and Pieri 2011; Peach and Gale 2003). There is a notable absence of more anthropological work (certainly since Barton's work in the 1980s: Barton 1986), which is why a doctoral project involving an ethnographic study of a single mosque will be of particular value.[20] This is because the internal power dynamics of mosque communities are still poorly understood. Answers to even relatively simple questions about access, keys, use of the office (by whom, when, and why), the use of the prayer hall, and so on, will provide illuminating insights about the flows of power, influence, and authority, and the way these are shaped by economic, social, and political capital within and beyond the building.

Mosques have often been sites for the more formal Islamic education of Muslim children, mainly directed towards teaching them how to read the Qur'an in Arabic. As noted already, between 2008 and 2010, a major study was undertaken at Cardiff University to examine the religious nurture of Muslim children, and the intersection of home-based and community-based sources of religious education (Scourfield et al. 2013). This work

---

[20] 'Understanding the Role of Mosques in Britain: An Ethnographic Study', is being conducted by Abdul-Azim Ahmed at Cardiff University (2012–15).

builds on a longer trajectory of research undertaken by both Muslim and non-Muslim educationalists (Gent 2006, 2011a, 2011b; Mogra 2004, 2005). A distinctive theme in this body of literature is a realization of the 'transferrable skills' to be derived from traditional methods of Islamic education. For example, instead of regarding 'rote-learning' as outdated or irrelevant, it has become apparent that the skill of being able to memorize and publicly recite classical religious texts can be used by Muslim children to help them revise for school exams, or participate in interactive classroom activities. However, this body of research about after-school madrassas is relatively small, in comparison to the extensive work that has been undertaken over the years on Muslim schools in Britain. By now, researchers have mapped the campaigns and the educational and philosophical arguments for and against the state-funding of Muslim schools (Dwyer 1993; Dwyer and Meyer 1995; Halstead 1986; Hewer 2001; Meer 2007, 2009; Tinker 2006, 2009; Tinker and Smart 2011), as well as the efforts that British Muslims have made to support their children in state education, mainly in relation to the curriculum, and practical matters such as provision of halal food or school uniforms (Nielsen 1989; Shah 2009). To some extent, these are campaigns of the past. Particular effort is now being invested in raising the standards of Muslim supplementary schooling (Hafez 2003; Mogra 2004, 2005) and, through a new generation of Muslim educationalists, exploring the scope for cooperation between state-provided and Muslim education.[21]

Alongside the provision of religious education for children, some of the larger mosques in the UK offer the services of a shariah council. The work of these councils/courts has received very little sustained academic attention thus far, but the research that does exist has tended to focus on the provision of Islamic/religious divorce (Bano 1999, 2007, 2012; Douglas et al. 2012; Shah-Kazemi 2001; Shah 2010), and in particular the experiences of Muslim women in their engagement with these religious authorities. An exception to this is the work of Dutch scholar Gerard Wiegers, who examined the legal opinions of the late Syed Ad-Darsh via his 'Ask the Imam' column in the British Muslim newspaper *Q News* (Wiegers 2011). Some shariah councils operate independently of mosques, but may be attached to another kind of Islamic organization (e.g. an Islamic college). The remit of their work is wide, covering financial and business matters (e.g. inheritance laws), worship and religious life (e.g. performance of *hajj*), community relations, as well as marital guidance and mediation. Most shariah councils are constituted by a panel of Islamic scholars (often reflecting a range of 'schools of Islamic law') that meets periodically, but many also offer advice and issue *fatwa* via the internet and television, such as www.darulifta.com—the Institute of Islamic Jurisprudence in Leicester, and the *Q&A* show on the Islam Channel.

British Muslims ask scholars a range of questions pertaining to their religious life and observance of the so-called 'Five Pillars' of Islam. It is surprising that so far relatively little social scientific work has been done to map these fundamental practices in Britain.

---

[21] For more information on Muslim schools and education in Britain see the website of the Association of Muslim Schools, <http://www.ams-uk.org> [Accessed 6 February 2013].

Although the flourishing of British Muslim charities is now well established (Gilliat-Ray 2010c), the actual meaning and practice of charitable giving (*zakat*) remains largely unexplored, as does the practice of formal and informal prayer (a notable exception being a small-scale study of a women's Islamic study circle/*halaqa* (Bhimji 2009)). Apart from a journal article exploring the negotiation and meaning of fasting during Ramadan among Muslim school children in Liverpool, this central religious practice has not been considered in depth, thus far. However, in recent years, valuable new research has begun to examine the practice of pilgrimage, led by Seán McLoughlin (McLoughlin 2009), as part of a larger collaboration with the British Museum's exhibition, 'Hajj: Journey to the Heart of Islam', in 2012. The findings of this project will make a significant contribution to a social scientific appreciation of Muslim religious practice in Britain, and will hopefully serve as a catalyst for more research about the practice of the 'Five Pillars' in Britain.

Since the 1970s, a range of British Muslim organizations have become active producers of knowledge and research about Muslims in Britain. These include well-established media, such as *The Muslim News*, but more especially, Islamic colleges that have academic affiliations with higher education institutions, usually via the degree validation process overseen by the Quality Assurance Agency for Higher Education (QAA). Some of these colleges are involved in the training of Muslim religious specialists via an *'alim* course (or equivalent), while others are more actively orientated towards academic research and publication. Research undertaken by Gilliat-Ray in the late 2000s mapped the array of such institutions in the UK (Gilliat-Ray 2006). Alongside these institutions, single-issue Muslim organizations occasionally produce reports and policy documents that contribute to a broader understanding of Muslim community life. An example of this genre might be the outputs of the Islamic Human Rights Commission (www.ihrc.org.uk) which has produced briefings covering Muslims in Britain, and further afield. In recent decades, Muslims in Britain have made considerable progress in supporting their evolving informational infrastructures, so that it is now a simple matter to locate Muslim schools and colleges, businesses, mosques, charities, and other welfare services via the 'Yellow Pages' publication *The Muslim Directory*, published bi-annually. This is of course an invaluable resource for researchers as well, providing an overview of Muslim community facilities and resources around the UK.

## Conclusion

The foregoing survey demonstrates that the study of Islam and Muslim communities in Britain has become a vibrant and flourishing field of academic research. From the early mapping of South Asian Muslim migration by sociologists and anthropologists, academics from other disciplines have gone on to explore the religious life and evolving infrastructures of more settled Muslim communities. There are now increasing numbers of Muslim researchers engaged in this field, documenting some of the changing dynamics within their communities.

Despite the growth of academic outputs, there are still significant areas that remain under-researched however. We are still to see, for example, any substantial investigation of British Shi'a Muslims, or work that updates Geaves's seminal study on the different sectarian/schools of religious thought in Muslim communities. How have these evolved in the last twenty years through the new involvement of British-born Muslim youth, for example? In the last two decades, British Muslims have become active producers and consumers of their own arts and entertainments, inspired by their faith. These have potential to shed illuminating insights on questions of 'identity' in a society where Muslims have contributed their own cosmopolitan, transnational, and multicultural influences (see especially sections on art, sport, comedy, etc. in Gilliat-Ray 2010c). Scholars with a long involvement in the field of 'British Muslim Studies' are perhaps justified in feeling some concern with the way that Muslims in Britain have become particularly 'researchable' through the lens of 'extremism' and counter-terrorism. Further moves in this direction would distract from the arguably more important task of understanding and appreciating the 'ordinary' lives of the majority of Muslims in Britain.

# REFERENCES

Abbas, T. 2010. 'Muslim-on-Muslim Social Research: Knowledge, Power and Religio-Cultural Identities', *Social Epistemology* 24(2): 123–36.

Abbas, T. 2012. 'The Symbiotic Relationship between Islamophobia and Radicalisation', *Critical Studies on Terrorism* 5(3): 345–58.

Adams, C. 1987. *Across Seven Seas and Thirteen Rivers: Life Stories of the Pioneer Sylheti Settlers in Britain*. London: Eastside Books.

Adamson, F. 2011. 'Engaging or Contesting the Liberal State? "Muslim" as a Politicised Identity Category in Europe', *Journal of Ethnic and Migration Studies* 37(6): 899–915.

Afshar, H. 1998. 'Strategies of Resistance among the Muslim Minority in West Yorkshire: Impact on Women', in N. Charles and H. Hintjens (eds.), *Gender, Ethnicity and Political Ideology*. London: Routledge, 107–26.

Ahmad, W. and Sardar, Z. (eds.) 2012. *Muslims in Britain: Making Social and Political Space*. London: Routledge.

Ahmed, S. 2009. *Seen and Not Heard: Voices of Young British Muslims*. Leicester: Policy Research Centre.

Allen, C. 2010a. 'Fear and Loathing: The Political Discourse in Relation to Muslims and Islam in the British Contemporary Setting', *Politics and Religion* 4(2): 221–36.

Allen, C. 2010b. *Islamophobia*. Aldershot: Ashgate.

Allen, C. 2011. 'Opposing Islamification or Promoting Islamophobia? Understanding the English Defence League', *Patterns of Prejudice* 45(4): 279–94.

Ally, M. 1979. 'The Growth and Organisation of the Muslim Community in Britain'. Birmingham: Selly Oak Colleges, CSIC.

Amer, F. 1997. 'Islamic Supplementary Education in Britain: A Critique'. Ph.D., Birmingham: University of Birmingham.

Ansari, H. 2002. 'The Woking Mosque: A Case Study of Muslim Engagement with British Society since 1889', *Immigrants and Minorities* 21(3): 1–24.

Ansari, H. 2004. *The 'Infidel' Within: Muslims in Britain, 1800 to the Present*. London: Hurst.

Ansari, H. 2007. '"Burying the Dead": Making Muslim Space in Britain', *Historical Research* 80(210): 545–66.

Ansari, H. (ed.) 2011. *The Making of the East London Mosque, 1910–1951*. Cambridge: Cambridge University Press (for the Royal Historical Society).

Anwar, M. 1976. *Between Two Cultures: A Study of Relationships between Generations in the Asian Community in Britain*. London: Commission for Racial Equality.

Anwar, M. 1979. *The Myth of Return*. London: Heinemann.

Anwar, M. 1984. 'Employment Patterns of Muslims in Western Europe', *Journal of the Institute of Muslim Minority Affairs* 5(1): 99–122.

Anwar, M. 1993a. 'Muslims in Britain: Demographic and Social Characteristics', *Journal of the Institute of Muslim Minority Affairs* 14(1–2): 124–34.

Anwar, M. 1993b. 'Muslims in Britain: 1991 Census and other Statistical Sources'. Birmingham: CSIC.

Anwar, M. 2001. 'The Participation of Ethnic Minorities in British politics', *Journal of Ethnic and Migration Studies* 27(3): 533–49.

Anwar, M. 2008. 'Muslims in Western States: The British Experience and the Way Forward', *Journal of Muslim Minority Affairs* 28(1): 125–37.

Anwar, M. and Q. Bakhsh. 2003. 'British Muslims and State Policies'. Coventry: CRER, University of Warwick.

Aspinall, P. 2000. 'Should a Question on "Religion" be Asked in the 2001 British Census? A Public Policy Case in Favour', *Social Policy and Administration* 34(5): 584–600.

Awan, I. 2012. '"I Am a Muslim Not an Extremist": How the Prevent Strategy Has Constructed a "Suspect" Community', *Politics & Policy* 40(6): 1158–85.

Bak, G. 2006. *Barbary Pirate: The Life and Crimes of John Ward*. Stroud: Sutton Publishing.

Bano, S. 1999. 'Muslim and South Asian Women: Customary Law and Citizenship in Britain', in P. Werbner and N. Yuval-Davis (eds.), *Women, Citizenship and Difference*. London: Zed Books, 162–77.

Bano, S. 2007. 'Muslim Family Justice and Human Rights: The Experience of British Muslim Women', *Journal of Comparative Law* 2(2): 38–66.

Bano, S. 2012. *Muslim Women and Shari'ah Councils: Transcending the Boundaries of Community and Law*. Basingstoke: Palgrave Macmillan.

Barton, S. 1986. *The Bengali Muslims of Bradford: A Study of their Observance of Islam with Special Reference to the Function of the Mosque and the Work of the Imam*. Leeds: Community Religions Project, University of Leeds.

Beckerlegge, G. 1997. 'Followers of "Mohammed, Kalee and Dada Nanuk": The Presence of Islam and South Asian Religions in Victorian Britain', in J. Wolffe (ed.), *Religion in Victorian Britain*. Manchester: Manchester University Press, 221–70.

Beckford, J., R. Gale, D. Owen, C. Peach, and P. Weller. 2006. *Review of the Evidence Base on Faith Communities*. London: Office of the Deputy Prime Minister.

Beckford, J. and S. Gilliat. 1998. *Religion in Prison: Equal Rites in a Multi-Faith Society*. Cambridge: Cambridge University Press.

Beckford, J., D. Joly, and F. Khosrokhavar. 2005. *Muslims in Prison: Challenge and Change in Britain and France*. Basingstoke: Palgrave Macmillan.

Bhimji, F. 2009. 'Identities and Agency in Religious Spheres: A Study of British Muslim Women's Experience', *Gender, Place and Culture* 16(4): 365–80.

Birt, J. and S. Gilliat-Ray. 2009. 'Mosque Conflicts in Europe: The Case of Great Britain', in S. Allievi (ed.), *Mosque Controversies in Europe*. Rome: Ethnobarometer, 135–52.

Birt, Y. 2010. 'Promoting Virulent Envy? Reconsidering the UK's Terrorist Prevention Strategy', *RUSI Journal* 154(4): 52–8.

Bolognani, M. 2007. 'Islam, Ethnography and Politics: Methodological Issues in Researching amongst West Yorkshire Pakistanis in 2005', *International Journal of Social Research Methodology* 10(4): 279–93.

Bonino, S. 2012. 'Policing Strategies against Islamic Terrorism in the UK after 9/11: The Socio-Political Realities for British Muslims', *Journal of Muslim Minority Affairs* 32(1): 5–31.

Brice, K. 2010. *A Minority within a Minority: A Report on Converts to Islam in the United Kingdom*. London: Faith Matters.

Brown, K. 2008. 'The Promise and Peril of Women's Participation in UK Mosques: The Impact of Securitisation Agendas on Identity, Gender and Community', *British Journal of Politics and International Relations* 10(3): 472–91.

Bunglawala, Z. 2004. *Aspirations and Reality: British Muslims and the Labour Market*. Budapest: Open Society Institute.

Cantle, T. 2002. *Community Cohesion: A Report of the Independent Review Team*. London: Home Office.

Castells, M. 1997. *The Power of Identity*. Oxford: Blackwell.

Choudhury, T. and H. Fenwick. 2011. *The Impact of Counter-Terrorism Measures on Muslim Communities*. Manchester: Equality and Human Rights Commission Research Report 72.

Coffey, A. 1999. *The Ethnographic Self: Fieldwork and the Representation of Identity*. London: Sage.

Coleman, L. 2009. *Survey of Mosques in England and Wales*. London: Charity Commission.

Colley, L. 2000. 'Going Native, Telling Tales: Captivity, Collaborations and Empire', *Past and Present* 168: 170–93.

Colley, L. 2001. 'Britain and Islam 1600–1800', *Mare Liberun* 20.

Colley, L. 2002. *Captives*. New York: Pantheon Books.

Dahya, B. 1965. 'Yemenis in Britain', *Race* 6(3): 177–90.

Dahya, B. 1973. 'Pakistanis in Britain: Transients or Settlers?', *Race* 14(3): 241–77.

Dahya, B. 1974. 'The Nature of Pakistani Ethnicity in Industrial Cities in Britain', in A. Cohen (ed.), *Urban Ethnicity*. London: Tavistock, 77–118.

Davies, G. 2011. *The Dragon and the Crescent: Nine Centuries of Welsh Contact with Islam*. Bridgend: Seren.

Douglas, G., N. Doe, S. Gilliat-Ray, R. Sandberg, and A. Khan. 2012. 'The Role of Religious Tribunals in Regulating Marriage and Divorce', *Child and Family Law Quarterly* 24(2): 139–57.

Dwyer, C. 1993. 'Constructions of Muslim Identity and the Contesting of Power: The Debate over Muslim Schools in the United Kingdom', in P. Jackson and J. Penrose (eds.), *Constructions of Race, Place and Nation*. London: UCL Press, 143–59.

Dwyer, C. and A. Meyer. 1995. 'The Institutionalisation of Islam in the Netherlands and in the UK: The Case of Islamic Schools', *New Community* 21(1): 37–54.

Eade, J. 1993. 'The Political Articulation of Community and the Islamisation of Space in London', in R. Barot (ed.), *Religion and Ethnicity*. Kampen, the Netherlands: Kok Pharos, 29–42.

Eade, J. 2011. 'Sacralising Space in a Western Secular City: Accommodating Muslims and Catholic Migrants in London', *Journal of Town and City Management* 1(4): 355–63.

Ellingson, L. 2006. 'Embodied Knowledge: Writing Researchers' Bodies into Qualitative Health Research', *Qualitative Health Research* 16(2): 298–310.

Ellis, C. and A. Bochner. 2000. 'Autoethnography, Personal Narrative, Reflexivity', in N. Denzin and Y. Lincoln (eds.), *Handbook of Qualitative Research*. Thousand Oaks, CA: Sage, 733–68.

Evans, N. 1985. 'Regulating the Reserve Army: Arabs, Blacks and the Local State in Cardiff, 1919–1945', *Immigrants and Minorities* 4(2): 68–115.

Field, C. 2007. 'Islamophobia in Contemporary Britain: The Evidence of the Opinion Polls 1988–2006', *Islam and Christian–Muslim Relations* 18(4): 447–77.

Fieldhouse, E. and D. Cutts. 2008. 'Mobilisation or Marginalisation? Neighbourhood Effects on Muslim Electoral Registration in Britain in 2001', *Political Studies* 56(3): 333–54.

Fischer, J. 2008a. 'Feeding Secularism: The Halal Market in London'. <http://www.ku.dk/Satsning/religion/sekularism_and_beyond/pdf/Fischer_Paper.pdf> [Accessed 9 December 2008].

Fischer, J. 2008b. *Proper Islamic Consumption: Shopping among Malays in Modern Malaysia*. Honolulu: University of Hawai'i Press.

Fischer, J. 2008c. 'Religion, Science and Markets', *European Molecular Biology Organisation* 9(9): 828–31.

Gale, R. 2004. 'The Multicultural City and the Politics of Religious Architecture: Urban Planning, Mosques and Meaning-making in Birmingham, UK', *Built Environment* 30(1): 18–32.

Gale, R. and S. Naylor. 2003. 'Religion, Planning and the City: The Spatial Politics of Ethnic Minority Expression in British Cities and Towns', *Ethnicities* 2(3): 387–409.

Geaves, R. 1995. 'The Reproduction of Jamaat-i-Islami in Britain', *Islam and Christian–Muslim Relations* 6(2): 187–210.

Geaves, R. 1996. Sectarian Influences within Islam in Britain with Reference to the Concepts of 'Ummah' and 'Community'. Leeds: Community Religions Project.

Geaves, R. 2008. 'Drawing on the Past to Transform the Present: Contemporary Challenges for Training and Preparing British Imams', *Journal of Muslim Minority Affairs* 28(1): 99–112.

Geaves, R. 2009. *Islam in Victorian Britain: The Life and Times of Abdullah Quilliam*. Leicester: Kube Publishing.

Gent, B. 2006. 'The Educational Experience of British Muslims: Some Life-Story Images', *Muslim Education Quarterly* 23(3–4): 33–42.

Gent, B. 2011a. 'But "You Can't Retire as a Hafiz": Fieldwork within a British Hifz Class', *Muslim Education Quarterly* 24(1–2): 55–63.

Gent, B. 2011b. 'The World of the British Hifz Class Student: Observations, Findings and Implications for Education and Further Research', *British Journal of Religious Education* 33(1): 3–15.

Gilliat-Ray, S. 2005a. 'Closed Worlds: (Not) Accessing Deobandi Dar Ul-Uloom in Britain', *Fieldwork in Religion* 1(1): 7–33.

Gilliat-Ray, S. 2005b. 'From "Chapel" to "Prayer Room": The Production, Use, and Politics of Sacred Space in Public Institutions', *Culture and Religion* 6(2): 287–308.

Gilliat-Ray, S. 2005c. '"Sacralising" Sacred Space: A Case Study of "Prayer Space" at the Millennium Dome', *Journal of Contemporary Religion* 20(3): 357–72.

Gilliat-Ray, S. 2006. 'Educating the 'Ulema: Centres of Islamic Religious Training in Britain', *Islam and Christian–Muslim Relations* 17(1): 55–76.

Gilliat-Ray, S. 2008. 'From "Visiting Minister" to "Muslim Chaplain": The Growth of Muslim Chaplaincy in Britain, 1970–2007', in E. Barker (ed.), *The Centrality of Religion in Social Life: Essays in Honour of James A. Beckford*. Aldershot: Ashgate, 145–60.

Gilliat-Ray, S. 2010a. 'Body-Works and Fieldwork: Research with British Muslim Chaplains', *Culture and Religion* 11(4): 413–32.

Gilliat-Ray, S. 2010b. 'The First Registered Mosque in the UK, Cardiff, 1860: The Evolution of a Myth', *Contemporary Islam* 4(2): 179–93.
Gilliat-Ray, S. 2010c. *Muslims in Britain: An Introduction*. Cambridge: Cambridge University Press.
Gilliat-Ray, S. 2011. '"Being There": The Experience of Shadowing a British Muslim Hospital Chaplain', *Qualitative Research* 11(5): 469–86.
Gilliat-Ray, S. 2013. 'The Ethics and Politics of Fieldwork', in L. Woodhead (ed.), *How to Research Religion: Putting Methods into Practice*. Oxford: Oxford University Press.
Gilliat-Ray, S., M. M. Ali, and S. Pattison. 2013. *Understanding Muslim Chaplaincy*. Aldershot: Ashgate.
Gilliat-Ray, S. and M. Bryant. 2011. 'Are British Muslims "Green"? A Survey of British Muslim Environmental Activism', *Journal for the Study of Religion, Nature and Culture* 5(3): 284–306.
Gilliat-Ray, S. and J. Mellor. 2010. 'Bilad al-Welsh (Land of the Welsh): Muslims in Cardiff, South Wales: Past, Present and Future', *The Muslim World* 100(4): 452–75.
Haddad, Y. (ed.) 2002. *Muslims in the West: From Sojourners to Citizens*. Oxford: Oxford University Press.
Hafez, S. 2003. 'Safe Children, Sound Learning: Guidance for Madressahs'. Huddersfield: Kirklees Metropolitan Council.
Halliday, F. 1992a. *Arabs in Exile: Yemeni Migrants in Urban Britain*. London: I. B. Tauris.
Halliday, F. 1992b. 'The Millet of Manchester: Arab Merchants and the Cotton Trade', *British Journal of Middle Eastern Studies* 19(2): 159–76.
Halstead, M. 1986. 'To What Extent is the Call for Separate Muslim Voluntary Aided Schools in the UK Justifiable?', *Muslim Educational Quarterly* 3(2): 5–26.
Hamid, S. 2007. 'Islamic Political Radicalism in Britain: The Case of Hizb-ut-Tahrir', in T. Abbas (ed.), *Islamic Political Radicalism: A European Perspective*. Edinburgh: Edinburgh University Press, 145–59.
Hamid, S. 2008a. 'The Attraction of "Authentic" Islam: Salafism and British Muslim Youth', in R. Meijer (ed.), *Salafism as a Transnational Movement*. London: Hurst, 384–403.
Hamid, S. 2008b. 'The Development of British Salafism', *ISIM Review* 21 (Spring): 10–11.
Hanif, N. 2012. 'Hizb ut Tahrir: Islam's Ideological Vanguard', *British Journal of Middle Eastern Studies* 39(2): 201–25.
Hewer, C. 2001. 'Schools for Muslims', *Oxford Review of Education* 27(4): 515–27.
Housby, E. 2011. *Islamic Financial Services in the United Kingdom*. Edinburgh: Edinburgh University Press.
Huq, M. 1975. 'How Many Muslims in Britain?', *The Muslim* (August–September): 142.
Husband, C. 2012. 'British Multiculturalism, Social Cohesion and Public Security'. <http://www.isp.org.pl/uploads/filemanager/Ch.Husband.pdf> [Accessed 22 January 2013].
Husband, C. and Y. Alam. 2011. *Social Cohesion and Counter Terrorism: A Policy Contradiction?* Bristol: Policy Press.
Hussain, D. 2004. 'Councillors and Caliphs: Muslim Political Participation in Britain', in M. S. Seddon, D. Hussain, and N. Malik (eds.), *British Muslims Between Assimilation and Segregation: Historical, Legal and Social Realities*. Leicester: The Islamic Foundation, 173–200.
Hussain, D. 2012. 'Social Policy, Cultural Integration and Faith: A Muslim Reflection', *Social Policy and Society* 11(4): 625–35.
Hussain, S. 2005. 'An Annotated Bibliography of Recent literature on "Invisible" Muslim Communities and New Muslim Migrant Communities in Britain'. <http://www.

compas.ox.ac.uk/publications/papers/Muslim%20Communities%20Annotate%20 Bibliography%20090306.pdf> [Accessed 17 April 2008].

Hussain, S. 2008. *Muslims on the Map: A National Survey of Social Trends in Britain*. London: I. B. Tauris.

Hussain, Y. and P. Bagguley. 2012. 'Securitized Citizens: Islamophobia, Racism and the 7/7 London Bombings', *Sociological Review* 60(4): 715–34.

Jacobson, J. 1998. *Islam in Transition: Religion and Identity among British Pakistani Youth*. London: LSE/Routledge.

Jeffery, P. 1972. 'Pakistani Families in Bristol', *New Community* 1: 364–9.

Johansen, B. and R. Spielhaus. 2012. 'Counting Deviance: Revisiting a Decade of Production of Surveys among Muslims in Western Europe', *Journal of Muslims in Europe* 1(1): 81–112.

Johnstone, P. 1977. 'Birmingham: Centre for the Study of Islam and Christian–Muslim Relations, Selly Oak Colleges', *Bulletin (British Society for Middle Eastern Studies)* 4(1): 49–50.

Joly, D. 1995. *Britannia's Crescent: Making a Place for Muslims in British Society*. Aldershot: Avebury.

Joly, D. 2012. 'Race, Ethnicity and Religion: Social Actors and Policies'. <http://hal.archives-ouvertes.fr/docs/00/75/49/59/PDF/FMSH-WP-2012-24_Joly.pdf> [Accessed 22 January 2013].

Jones, R. D. 2010. 'Islam and the Rural Landscape: Discourses of Absence in West Wales', *Social and Cultural Geography* 11(8): 751–68.

Kalra, V. 2000. *From Textile Mills to Taxi Ranks: Experiences of Migration, Labour and Social Change*. Aldershot: Ashgate.

Khaliq, U. 2002. 'The Accommodation and Regulation of Islam and Muslim Practices in English Law', *Ecclesiastical Law Journal* 6(31): 332–51.

Khan, A., J. Scourfield, S. Gilliat-Ray, and S. Otri. 2013. 'Reflections on Qualitative Research with Muslim Families', *Fieldwork in Religion* 7(1): 48–69.

Khan, K. 2009. 'Preventing Violent Extremism (PVE) and PREVENT: A Response from the Muslim Community'. London: An-Nisa Society.

Khattak, S. K. K. 2008. *Islam and the Victorians: Nineteenth Century Perceptions of Muslim Practices and Beliefs*. London: I. B. Tauris.

King, J. 1997. 'Tablighi Jamaat and the Deobandi Mosques in Britain', in S. Vertovec and C. Peach (eds.), *Islam in Europe: The Politics of Religion and Community*. Basingstoke: Macmillan, 129–46.

Kundnani, A. 2009. *Spooked! How Not to Prevent Violent Extremism*. London: Institute of Race Relations.

Kundnani, A. 2012. 'Radicalisation: The Journey of a Concept', *Race & Class* 54(2): 3–25.

Lambert, R. 2008. 'Empowering Salafis and Islamists Against Al-Qaeda: A London Counterterrorism Case Study', *Political Science and Politics* 41(1): 31–5.

Lambert, R. 2011. *Countering Al-Qaeda in London: Police and Muslims in Partnership*. London: Hurst.

Lawless, R. 1994. 'Religion and Politics among Arab Seafarers in Britain in the Early Twentieth Century', *Islam and Christian–Muslim Relations* 5(1): 35–56.

Lawless, R. 1995. *From Ta'izz to Tyneside: An Arab Community in the North East of England in the Early 20th Century*. Exeter: University of Exeter Press.

Lawless, R. 1997. 'Muslim Migration to the North East of England during the Early Twentieth Century', *Local Historian* 27(4): 225–44.

Lever, J. and M. Miele. 2012. 'The Growth of the Halal Meat Markets in Europe: An Exploration of the Supply Side Theory of Religion', *Journal of Rural Studies* 28(4): 528–37.

Lewis, P. 1994. *Islamic Britain: Religion, Politics and Identity among British Muslims*. London: I. B. Tauris.
Lewis, P. 2007. *Young, British, and Muslim*. London: Continuum.
Little, K. 1942a. 'Loudoun Square: A Community Survey I', *Sociological Review* 34 (July): 12–33.
Little, K. 1942b. 'Loudoun Square: A Community Survey II', *Sociological Review* 34 (July): 119–46.
McLean, A. and A. Leibing. 2007a. '"Learn to Value your Shadow!" An Introduction to the Margins of Fieldwork', in A. McLean and A. Leibing (eds.), *The Shadow Side of Fieldwork: Exploring the Blurred Borders between Ethnography and Life*. Oxford: Blackwell, 1–28.
McLean, A. and A. Leibing (eds.) 2007b. *The Shadow Side of Fieldwork: Exploring the Blurred Borders between Ethnography and Life*. Oxford: Blackwell.
McLoughlin, S. 2005. 'The State, New Muslim Leaderships and Islam as a Resource for Public Engagement in Britain', in J. Cesari and S. McLoughlin (eds.), *European Muslims and the Secular State*. Aldershot: Ashgate, 55–70.
McLoughlin, S. 2009. 'Holy Places, Contested Spaces: British Pakistani Accounts of Pilgrimage to Makkah and Madinah', in R. Gale and P. Hopkins (eds.), *Muslims in Britain: Race, Place and Identities*. Edinburgh: Edinburgh University Press, 132–49.
Malik, M. 2004. 'British Muslims—Discrimination, Equality and Community Cohesion'. Budapest: Open Society Institute—EU Monitoring and Advocacy Programme.
Matar, N. 1993. 'The Renegade in English Seventeenth-Century Imagination', *Studies in English Literature* 33(3): 489–506.
Matar, N. 1997. 'Muslims in Seventeenth-Century England', *Journal of Islamic Studies* 8(1): 63–82.
Matar, N. 1998. *Islam in Britain: 1558–1685*. Cambridge: Cambridge University Press.
Matar, N. 1999. *Turks, Moors and Englishmen in the Age of Discovery*. New York: Columbia University Press.
Matar, N. 2001. 'English Accounts of Captivity in North Africa and the Middle East: 1577–1625', *Renaissance Quarterly* 54(2): 553–72.
Matar, N. 2005. *Britain and Barbary, 1589–1689*. Gainesville: University Press of Florida.
Meer, N. 2007. 'Muslim Schools in Britain: Challenging Mobilisations or Logical Developments?', *Asia Pacific Journal of Education* 27(1): 55–71.
Meer, N. 2009. 'Identity Articulations, Mobilization, and Autonomy in the Movement for Muslim Schools in Britain', *Race, Ethnicity and Education* 12(3): 379–99.
Meer, N. 2012. 'Racialization and Religion: Race, Culture and Difference in the Study of Antisemitism and Islamophobia', *Ethnic and Racial Studies*: 1–14. iFirst Article [10.1080/01419870.2013.734392].
Meer, N. and P. Mouritsen. 2009. 'Political Cultures Compared: the Muhammad Cartoons in the Danish and British Press', *Ethnicities* 9(3): 334–60.
Meer, N. and T. Noorani. 2008. 'A Sociological Comparison of Anti-Semitism and Anti-Muslim Sentiment in Britain', *Sociological Review* 56(2): 195–219.
Mills, T., T. Griffin, and D. Miller. 2011. *The Cold War on British Muslims*. London: Spinwatch.
Milton, G. 2004. *White Gold: The Extraordinary Story of Thomas Pellow and North Africa's One Million European Slaves*. London: Hodder & Stoughton.
Mirza, M., A. Senthilkumaran, and J. Zein. 2007. *Living Apart Together: British Muslims and the Paradox of Multiculturalism*. London: Policy Exchange.
Modood, T. 1989. 'Religious Anger and Minority Rights', *Political Quarterly* 60(3): 280–4.
Modood, T. 1990a. 'British Asian Muslims and the Rushdie Affair', *Political Quarterly* 61(2): 143–60.
Modood, T. 1990b. 'Muslims, Race and Equality in Britain: Post-Rushdie Reflections', *Third Text* 11 (Summer): 127–34.

Modood, T., R. Berthoud, J. Lakey, J. Nazroo, P. Smith, S. Virdee, and S. Beishon (eds.) 1997. *Ethnic Minorities in Britain: Diversity and Disadvantage*. London: Policy Studies Institute.

Mogra, I. 2004. 'Makatib Education in Britian: A Review of Trends and Some Suggestions for Policy', *Muslim Education Quarterly* 21(4): 19–27.

Mogra, I. 2005. 'Moving Forward with Makatib: The Role of Reformative Sanctions', *Muslim Education Quarterly* 22(3&4): 52–64.

Moosavi, L. 2012. 'British Muslim Converts Performing "Authentic Muslimness"', *Performing Islam* 1(1): 103–28.

Mukadam, M. and A. Scott-Baumann. 2010. *The Training and Development of Muslim Faith Leaders: Current Practice and Future Possibilities*. London: Communities and Local Government.

Murad, A. H. 2003. 'Ward the Pirate', *Seasons* (Spring/Summer): 61–4.

Mythen, G. 2012. 'Identities in the Third Space? Solidity, Elasticity and Resilience amongst Young British Pakistani Muslims', *British Journal of Sociology* 63(3): 393–411.

Nasser, N. 2005. 'Expressions of Muslim Identity in Architecture and Urbanism in Birmingham, UK', *Islam and Christian–Muslim Relations* 16(1): 61–78.

Nasser, N. 2006. 'Metropolitan Borderlands: The Formation of BrAsian Landscapes', in N. Ali, V. Kalra, and S. Sayyid (eds.), *A Postcolonial People: South Asians in Britain*. London: Hurst & Company, 374–91.

Nielsen, J. 1981. 'Muslim Education at Home and Abroad', *British Journal of Religious Education* 3(3): 94–9.

Nielsen, J. 1989. 'Muslims in English Schools', *Journal of the Institute of Muslim Minority Affairs* 10(1): 223–45.

Nielsen, J. 1991. 'A Muslim Agenda for Britain: Some Reflections', *New Community* 17(3): 467–75.

Nilsson DeHanas, D. and Z. Pieri. 2011. 'Olympic Proportions: The Expanding Scalar Politics of the London "Olympics Mega-Mosque" Controversy', *Sociology* 45(5): 798–814.

North, C. 1996. 'Muslims in Birmingham: Religious Activity in Mosques and Para-Mosques'. Birmingham: Birmingham University.

O'Toole, T., D. N. DeHanas, and T. Modood. 2012. 'Balancing Tolerance, Security and Muslim Engagement in the United Kingdom: The Impact of the "Prevent" Agenda', *Critical Studies on Terrorism*: 1–17. iFirst article [10.1080/17539153.2012.725570].

O'Toole, T., D. N. DeHanas, T. Modood, N. Meer, and S. Jones. 2013. 'Taking Part: Muslim Participation in Contemporary Governance'. Bristol: Centre for the Study of Ethnicity and Citizenship, University of Bristol.

Parker-Jenkins, M. 2002. 'Equal Access to State Funding: The Case of Muslim Schools in Britain', *Race, Ethnicity and Education* 5(3): 273–89.

Peace, T. 2012. 'All I'm Asking, is for a Little Respect: Assessing the Performance of Britain's Most Successful Radical Left Party', *Parliamentary Affairs* [10.1093/pa/gsr064].

Peach, C. 2006a. 'Islam, Ethnicity and South Asian Religion in the London 2001 Census', *Transactions of the Institute of British Geographers* 31: 353–70.

Peach, C. 2006b. 'Muslims in the 2001 Census of England and Wales: Gender and Economic Disadvantage', *Ethnic and Racial Studies* 29(4): 629–55.

Peach, C. and R. Gale. 2003. 'Muslims, Hindus, and Sikhs in the New Religious Landscape of England', *Geographical Review* 93(4): 469–90.

Pedziwiatr, K. 2007. 'Creating New Discursive Arenas and Influencing the Policies of the State: The Case of the Muslim Council of Britain', *Social Compass* 54(2): 267–80.

Petersen, A. 2008. 'The Archaeology of Islam in Britain: Recognition and Potential', *Antiquities* 82(318): 1080–92.
Phillips, D. 2006. 'Parallel Lives? Challenging Discourses of British Muslim Self-Segregation', *Environment and Planning D: Society and Space* 24: 25–40.
Phillips, R. 2008. 'Standing Together: The Muslim Association of Britain and the Anti-War Movement', *Race & Class* 50(2): 101–13.
Pilgram, L. 2012. 'British-Muslim Family Law and Citizenship', *Citizenship Studies* 16(5–6): 769–82.
Poulter, S. 1986a. *English Law and Ethnic Minority Customs*. London: Butterworth.
Poulter, S. 1986b. 'Ethnic Minority Customs, English Law and Human Rights', *International and Comparative Law Quarterly* 36: 589–615.
Pratt, D. 2011. 'Islamophobia: Ignorance, Imagination, Identity and Interaction', *Islam and Christian–Muslim Relations* 22(4): 379–89.
Prideaux, M. 2009. 'The Significance of Identity in Muslim–Christian Encounter', *Islam and Christian–Muslim Relations* 20(2): 153–70.
Purdam, K. 2000. 'The Political Identities of Muslim Local Councillors in Britain', *Local Government Studies* 26(1): 47–64.
Purdam, K. 2001. 'Democracy in Practice: Muslims and the Labour Party at the Local Level', *Politics* 21(3): 147–57.
Quraishi, M. 2008. 'Researching Muslim Prisoners', *International Journal of Social Research Methodology* 11(5): 453–67.
Radcliffe, L. 2004. 'A Muslim Lobby at Whitehall? Examining the Role of the Muslim Minority in British Foreign Policy Making', *Islam and Christian–Muslim Relations* 15(3): 365–86.
Ratcliffe, P. 2012. '"Community Cohesion": Reflections on a Flawed Paradigm', *Critical Social Policy* 32(2): 262–81.
Rex, J. 1991. *Ethnic Identity and Ethnic Mobilisation in Britain*. Coventry: ESRC/CRER.
Rex, J. 1994. 'The Political Sociology of Multiculturalism and the Place of Muslims in Western European Societies', *Social Compass* 41(1): 79–92.
Robinson-Dunne, D. 2003. 'Lascar Sailors and English Converts: The Imperial Port and Islam in Late 19th-Century England', paper presented at Seascapes, Littoral Cultures and Trans-Oceanic Exchanges, Washington DC, 12–15 February. <http://www.historycooperative.org/proceedings/seascapes/dunn.html> [Accessed 31 January 2006].
Runnymede Trust Commission on British Muslims and Islamophobia. 1997. *Islamophobia: A Challenge for Us All*. Available at: <http://www.runnymedetrust.org/publications/17/32.html>.
Saggar, S. 2009. 'Boomerangs and Slingshots: Radical Islamism and Counter-Terrorism Strategy', *Journal of Ethnic and Migration Studies* 35(3): 381–402.
Saifullah-Khan, V. 1975. 'Pakistani Villagers in a British City'. Ph.D., University of Bradford.
Saifullah-Khan, V. 1976. 'Pakistanis in Britain: Perceptions of a Population', *New Community* 5(3): 222–9.
Salamat, P. 2008. *A Miracle at Woking*. Chichester: Phillimore & Co.
Salter, J. 1873. *The Asiatic in England: Sketches of Sixteen Years' Work among the Orientals*. London: Seeley, Jackson & Halliday.
Salter, J. 1895. *The East in the West*. London: Partridge.
Sanghera, G. and S. Thapar-Bjorkert. 2008. 'Methodological Dilemmas: Gatekeepers and Positionality in Bradford', *Ethnic and Racial Studies* 31(3): 543–62.
Scarfe Beckett, K. 2003. *Anglo-Saxon Perceptions of the Islamic World*. Cambridge: Cambridge University Press.

Scourfield, J., S. Gilliat-Ray, A. Khan, and S. Otri. 2013. *Muslim Childhood*. Oxford: Oxford University Press.

Scourfield, J., C. Taylor, G. Moore, and S. Gilliat-Ray. 2012. 'The Intergenerational Transmission of Islam in England and Wales: Evidence from the Citizenship Survey', *Sociology* 46(1): 91–108.

Seddon, M. S. 2004. 'Muslim Communities in Britain: A Historiography', in M. S. Seddon, N. Malik, and D. Hussain (eds.), *British Muslims Between Assimilation and Segregation: Historical, Legal and Social Realities*. Leicester: Islamic Foundation, 1–42.

Shah, P. 2010. 'Between God and the Sultana? Legal Pluralism in the British Muslim Diaspora', in J. Nielsen and L. Christoffersen (eds.), *Shari'a as Discourse: Legal Traditions and the Encounter with Europe*. Aldershot: Ashgate, 117–39.

Shah, S. 2009. 'Muslim Learners in English Schools: A Challenge for School Leaders', *Oxford Review of Education* 35(4): 523–40.

Shah-Kazemi, S. N. 2001. *Untying the Knot: Muslim Women, Divorce and the Shariah: A Study of the Muslim Law Shariah Council, UK*. London: Nuffield Foundation.

Shaw, A. 1988. *A Pakistani Community in Britain*. Oxford: Blackwell.

Shaw, A. 1994. 'The Pakistani Community in Oxford', in R. Ballard (ed.), *Desh Pardesh*. London: Hurst and Co., 35–57.

Sherif, J. 2011. 'A Census Chronicle: Reflections on the Campaign for a Religion Question in the 2001 Census for England and Wales', *Journal of Beliefs and Values* 32(1): 1–18.

Sherwood, M. 1991. 'Race, Nationality and Employment among Lascar Seamen, 1660–1945', *New Community* 17(2): 229–44.

Siddiqui, A. 2007. 'Islam at Universities in England: Meeting the Needs and Investing in the Future'. London: Department for Innovation, Universities and Skills.

Simpson, L. 2004. 'Statistics and Racial Segregation: Measures, Evidence and Policy', *Urban Studies* 41(3): 661–81.

Simpson, L. and C. Peach. 2009. 'Measurement and Analysis of Segregation, Integration and Diversity: Editorial Introduction', *Journal of Ethnic and Migration Studies* 35(9): 1377–80.

Southworth, J. 2005. '"Religion" in the 2001 Census for England and Wales', *Population, Space and Place* 11: 75–88.

Spalek, B. 2011. '"New Terrorism" and Crime Prevention Initiatives Involving Muslim Young People in the UK: Research and Policy Contexts', *Religion, State & Society* 39(2/3): 191–208.

Spalek, B. (ed.) 2012. *Counter-Terrorism: Community-Based Approaches to Preventing Terror Crime*. Basingstoke: Palgrave Macmillan.

Spalek, B. and L. Z. McDonald. 2009. 'Terror Crime Prevention: Constructing Muslim Practices and Beliefs as "Anti-Social" and "Extreme" through Contest 2', *Social Policy and Society* 9(1): 123–32.

Taras, R. 2012. '"Islamophobia never stands still": Race, Religion, and Culture', *Ethnic and Racial Studies*: 1–17. iFirst article [10.1080/01419870.2013.734388].

Tinker, C. 2006. 'Islamophobia, Social Cohesion and Autonomy: Challenging the Arguments against State Funded Muslim Schools in Britain', *Muslim Education Quarterly* 23(1&2): 4–19.

Tinker, C. 2009. 'Rights, Social Cohesion and Identity: Arguments for and against State-Funded Muslim Schools in Britain', *Race, Ethnicity and Education* 12(4): 539–53.

Tinker, C. and A. Smart. 2011. 'Constructions of Collective Muslim Identity by Advocates of Muslim Schools in Britain', *Ethnic and Racial Studies* 35(4): 643–63.

Vertovec, S. 2002. 'Islamophobia and Muslim Recognition in Britain', in Y. Y. Haddad (ed.), *Muslims in the West: From Sojourners to Citizens*. Oxford: Oxford University Press, 19–35.

Vidino, L. 2010. 'The Role of Non-Violent Islamists in the UK', *CTC Sentinel* 3(11–12): 9–11.
Warraich, S. and C. Balchin. 2006. *Recognising the Un-Recognised: Inter-Country Cases and Muslim Marriages and Divorces in Britain*. London: Women Living under Muslim Laws (WLUML).
Weller, P. 2004. 'Identity, Politics and the Future(s) of Religion in the UK: The Case of the Religion Questions in the 2001 Decennial Census', *Journal of Contemporary Religion* 19(1): 3–22.
Weller, P. 2009. *A Mirror for Our Times: The Rushdie Affair and the Future of Multiculturalism*. London: Continuum.
Werbner, P. 1990. *The Migration Process*. Oxford: Berg.
Werbner, P. 1996a. 'Fun Spaces: On Identity and Social Empowerment among British Pakistanis', *Theory, Culture and Society* 13(4): 53–79.
Werbner, P. 1996b. 'Stamping the Earth with the Name of Allah: Zikr and the Sacralizing of Space among British Muslims', *Cultural Anthropology* 11(3): 309–38.
Werbner, P. 2002a. *Imagined Diasporas among Manchester Muslims*. Oxford: James Currey Publishers.
Werbner, P. 2002b. *Pilgrims of Love: The Anthropology of a Global Sufi Cult*. London: Hurst.
Werbner, P. 2004. 'Theorising Complex Diasporas: Purity and Hybridity in the South Asian Public Sphere in Britain', *Journal of Ethnic and Migration Studies* 30(5): 895–911.
Werbner, P. 2006. 'Seekers on the Path: Different Ways of being a Sufi in Britain', in J. Malik and J. Hinnnells (eds.), *Sufism in the West*. London: Routledge, 127–41.
Werbner, P. 2012. 'Folk Devils and Racist Imaginaries in a Global Prism: Islamophobia and Anti-Semitism in the Twenty-First Century', *Ethnic and Racial Studies*: 1–18. iFirst article [10.1080/01419870.2013.734384].
Wiegers, G. 2011. 'Dr Sayyid Mutawalli Ad-Darsh's Fatwas for Muslims in Great Britain: The Voice of Official Islam?', in G. Maclean (ed.), *Britain and the Muslim World*. Cambridge: Cambridge Scholars Press, 178–92.
Wiktorowicz, Q. 2005. *Racial Islam Rising: Muslim Extremism in the West*. Oxford: Rowman & Littlefield.
Williams, R. 2008a. 'Civil and Religious Law in England: A Religious Perspective', *Ecclesiastical Law Journal* 10(3): 262–82.
Williams, R. 2008b, 'Civil and Religious Law in England: A Religious Perspective'. <http://www.archbishopofcanterbury.org/1575> [Accessed 17 April 2008].
Winter, T. J. 2004. 'The Poverty of Fanaticism', in J. Lumbard (ed.), *Islam, Fundamentalism, and the Betrayal of Tradition: Essays by Western Muslim Scholars*. Bloomington, IN: World Wisdom, 283–94.
Wormald, P. 1982. 'The Age of Offa and Alcuin', in J. Campbell (ed.), *The Anglo-Saxons*. London: Phaidon, 101–28.
Yilmaz, I. 2000. 'Muslim Law in Britain: Reflections in the Socio-Legal Sphere and Differential Legal Treatment', *Journal of Muslim Minority Affairs* 20(2): 353–60.
Yilmaz, I. 2002. 'The Challenge of Post-Modern Legality and Muslim Legal Pluralism in Britain', *Journal of Ethnic and Migration Studies* 28(2): 343–54.
Yilmaz, I. 2010. 'The Varied Performance of Hizb ut-Tahrir: Success in Britain and Uzbekistan and Stalemate in Egypt and Turkey', *Journal of Muslim Minority Affairs* 30(4): 501–17.
Zubair, M., W. Martin, and C. Victor. 2012. 'Embodying Gender, Age, Ethnicity and Power in "the Field": Reflections on Dress and the Presentation of the Self in Research with Older Pakistani Muslims', *Sociological Research Online* 17(3): 21.

CHAPTER 3

# GERMANY

RIEM SPIELHAUS

## Introduction

SINCE the mid-1990s academics have produced numerous publications on Islam and Muslims in Germany from a rich variety of perspectives and disciplines. Hence, this subject became a fast-growing research field and it coincides with a growing awareness of the Muslim presence in Germany and Europe in society.

The national level is not always the most relevant in the German context. First, Muslims are unequally distributed in the country, with most Muslims living in major cities and industrial regions and almost none in the eastern part of Germany. Hence, surveys as well as public debates often concentrate on specific regions, cities, or even neighbourhoods. Second, due to the federal principle, German states (*Länder*) are decisive in shaping the relationship between religions and state by determining arrangements on the level of federal states (Rohe 2012), while conversely, concrete accommodation of Islam happens on the communal level.

The recent awareness of the presence of Muslims has led to negotiations of national identity, with some localized debates about mosque buildings arousing nationwide attention. The federal government intervened by establishing the German Islam Conference, a platform for long-term communication between the state and Muslim representatives. In such interactions between local and national levels the nation-state becomes relevant for the study of Muslims in Germany and Islam related politics.

After 9/11, the federal government addressed Islam politics as a topic of national importance though the lens of security, and later under the paradigm of integration. Since then governmental politics towards Islam appears to be heavily intertwined with integration policies and is, to a lesser degree, addressed in the field of religion politics. This political construction of the Muslim is reflected in the scholarship in two ways: directly through funding and indirectly through influencing the questions that are raised and given prominence in public debates. Contemporary political narratives are thus affecting dominant epistemological premises of current research that try to map Muslim populations and Islamic organizations in Germany. The growing scholarly literature on Muslims and Islam has resulted in a thematic diversification that includes: (a) historical perspectives on Islam; (b) descriptions of 'Muslims' as a socio-demographic category; (c) legal aspects of religious life; (d) Islamic organizations, and issues of representative bodies of Islam; (e) governmental politics towards Islam; (f) debates on and attitudes towards the visible presence of Islam and Muslims; (g) Islamic pedagogy for religious instruction in public schools; (h) inner-Muslim debates on major Islamic concepts; and finally (i) reflections on the production of knowledge on Muslims and Islamic organizations. After shortly characterizing the main trends and evolution of academic works on Muslims and Islam Germany, this chapter presents significant studies from each of these thematic fields.

## A Shift in Research from Migrants and 'Guest Workers' to Muslims

With the closure of the Eastern Bloc, a labour shortage led to the guest worker treaties of the Federal German Republic with Greece, Spain, Italy, Morocco, Yugoslavia, and Turkey. Subsequently men and women from these Mediterranean countries accepted the invitation from West Germany in order to work and then return home. An end to immigrant recruitment (*Anwerbestopp*) in 1973, however, inspired many immigrants to stay and from the 1980s onwards possibilities for family reunions stimulated even more migration (Bade 1994, 1996; Herbert 2001). Later immigration of Palestinian refugees from Lebanon in the late 1980s and Bosnian refugees in the early 1990s contributed to the diversity of Muslims in Germany. The growing number of converts and their descendants should also be mentioned, because even though they are considered statistically insignificant compared to Muslim immigrants and therefore often neglected, they play significant roles in several Islamic organizations.

For three decades or so, the same populations in Germany that are studied as 'Muslims' today have been researched in the fields of migration sociology, criminology, and pedagogies as 'guest workers' or refugees. Religion did not play an important role in how they were discussed in public debates (Wilpert 1991; Yurdakul 2009) or in research. Studies concentrated for instance on migrants' performance in education, return migration, and particularly, on working conditions and labour conflicts. Around the year 2000 though, research on migrant individuals as Muslims began to flourish in several disciplines from migration studies to Islamic studies. At this time, the first academic publications on religiosity—especially among young Muslim women and second-generation youth—and surveys on Islamic organizations appeared.

Since that time, we can observe a striking interconnectedness between public debates concerning the perceptions of migrants as driven by their (different) religion and an increasing interest in Muslims in academic research. The growing awareness of the presence of Muslims in Germany in political and media debates triggered the emergence of a new research field (cf. Foroutan 2012). Islamic Studies, after concentrating on the Middle East for a long time, now also turned to Europe and included Muslims at home. Migration sociology or criminology studied populations that were already on their agenda from new perspectives. The new focus on religious aspects of selected immigrants' lives does not simply mean the attention towards another dimension of an existing group of people; it rather triggered the construction of a new group (see also Spielhaus 2011a).

In the 1980s people from around the Mediterranean, both Muslim and non-Muslim, were perceived in politics and academia as connected through their 'Mediterranean culture'. Towards the end of the 1990s, 'Muslim culture' emerged as a separate explanatory category (cf. Sunier 2012). During this process non-Muslim immigrants were left out and new groups of people were regarded as important for research and explaining relevant developments in German society, i.e. Bosnian and Palestinian refugees. Sociological disparities between Muslims of different national origins and religious denominations (Haug et al. 2009) and also the fact that Muslims are failing to meet the request by political actors to provide common organizational structures show that Muslims do not represent an existing collective that only needed to be discovered and described. On the contrary, researchers are contributing to the making of a new collective and to creating and legitimizing or at least approving, Muslim speakers' positions (Spielhaus 2011a, 2011b). This shift in perception led to an increase in research and a thematic diversification of academic literature on Islam and Muslims in Germany.

## Thematic Fields in Research on Islam and Muslims in Germany

While the growing interest in the historical presence of Muslims in Germany is fairly recent, current research often aims at mapping contemporary 'Muslims' as a sociodemographic category, especially with regard to quantitative survey questions on integration, educational levels, and attitudes to democracy, violence, and radicalization. The first studies on Muslim life in Germany in the 1990s, however, were based on qualitative fieldwork and aimed either to give an overview on Islamic organizational structures and milieux or to present in-depth descriptions of different aspects of religiosity and the daily lives of individuals. They were followed by studies on legal aspects concerning Islam and Muslim life and later by analyses of governmental politics towards Islam. Another recent genre investigates debates on the visible presence of Islam and attitudes towards Muslims both in large population surveys on the perception of Islam and in qualitative analyses of conflicts (e.g. about mosque buildings). Finally, it can be expected that the chairs for Islamic Theology at state-funded universities as well as religious instruction in public schools will lead to innovative research in Islamic pedagogies and theological interpretations of major Islamic concepts.

This academic literature is further characterized by different scales of research with a strong focus on the national frame, specific large German cities, and certain neighbourhoods. Several descriptions of mosque landscapes and quantitative studies of

Muslim inhabitants in different cities and regions have been carried out, in federal states like North Rhine-Westphalia (Haug et al. 2010; Chbib 2008) and Baden Württemberg (Schmid et al. 2008) and in the cities Duisburg (Ceylan 2006), Hamburg (Mihçiyazgan 1990; Hieronymus 2010; Spielhaus 2011a; Koch and Reinig 2013), Bad Kreuznach (Thielmann 2003), and Berlin (Jonker and Kappahn 1999; Spielhaus and Färber 2006, Mühe 2010).

Apart from large quantitative surveys of Muslim immigrants and their descendants, numerous qualitative studies focus on specific Muslim groups, movements, communities, and milieux, especially Islamic organizations, mosque associations, and religious 'denominations' or on different segments of Muslim population like gendered age groups—specific girls and young women, female students of pedagogy, boys and young men—but also on women wearing headscarves, converts, men, or imams.

# A Historical Perspective on Islam and Muslims in Germany

The presence of Muslims in Germany is currently discussed in the academic literature as a result of post-Second World War immigration. Most research on Muslims focuses on the time after the 1960s, yet few studies on Muslim communities in the inter-war period document both the flourishing Islamic life during the Weimar Republic and the disruptions caused by Hitler's rise to power. In the inter-war period the first mosque, which is still in operation today, was built in Berlin-Wilmersdorf (1924–7).[1] The Third Reich brought to an abrupt and violent end the growing cultural and religious diversity in Germany, although not all Islamic associations were dissolved.

Some active German members withdrew from community life (Bauknecht 2010; Heimbach 2001). Several foreign members left Germany, even if only Muslims with communist views appear to have been forced to leave the country. The Ahmadiyya and their German-Muslim Society faced pressure because they continued to 'tolerate' Jewish converts among their ranks. Nonetheless, in 1939, the Islamic Community of Berlin united with the Islam-Institute, simultaneously offering a platform for collaboration with the Nazi regime. But it was not until 1942 that the regime decided that Muslims were allowed to play a role in their war (Höpp 1994a, 1994b; Jonker 2014 forthcoming).

---

[1] The Ahmadiyya movement started its da'wa activities in Europe in the 1920s, where the Ahmadiyya Anjuman Ishaat-e Islam, also known as the Lahori branch, which does not support the claim of their founder Ghulam Ahmad to be a prophet, built the first still existing mosque in Germany. Berlin-Wilmersdorf is the headquarters of the German AAII branch until today. In the inter-war period the mosque was open to and frequented by Muslims of a variety of ethno-national and religious backgrounds (Preckel 2008: 310–12). For a description of the two Ahmadiyya movements in Germany see Lathan 2010.

After the end of the Second World War, Muslims, mostly prisoners of war, refugees, and displaced persons including Bosniaks, Albanians, and Muslim minorities from the Soviet Union, founded the first Islamic associations in German refugee camps (Höpp 2004; Bauknecht 2010: 80). The presence of two Muslim communities from the 1950s onwards led to the construction of three other purpose-built mosques.[2] While the history of Muslims in Germany has been the subject of very few studies based on original sources so far, this field is currently attracting growing attention (Cwiklinski 2008; Baer 2013; Jonker 2014 forthcoming).

## Early Studies on the Religiosity of Muslims

In the late 1990s and early 2000s, empirical studies, which were primarily qualitative, focused on the modernization of Islam through individualization. Within the disciplines of Islamic Studies, religion studies, cultural anthropology, or cultural studies, investigations on the individual religiosity among women (Karakaşoğlu-Aydın 2000; Klinkhammer 2000; Nökel 2002; Jouili 2008) and men (Frese 2002; Tietze 2001) of Turkish origin, as well as converts (Wohlrab-Sahr 1999; Özyürek 2008), offer a differentiated picture of primarily Turkish Muslim life in Germany. In these early studies, individual Muslims are depicted as reflective, rational, but nevertheless pious individuals who seek their place in modern German society. They are portrayed as actively seeking religious knowledge either without any attachment to Islamic organizations or networks or by getting actively involved in local mosque associations and youth groups. Researchers emphasize the importance religious knowledge plays in individuals becoming pious and maintaining a pious life. Jeanette Jouili and Schirin Amir-Moazami stress that 'women's augmentation of their roles as educated and religiously instructed believers provides them with a new role in the Islamic community, and thereby with a particular type of agency' and interpret acquisition and distribution of religious knowledge as steps towards the empowerment of Muslim women (Jouili and Amir-Moazami 2006: 637). Both acquisition and distribution of Islamic knowledge are, moreover, described as tools used by young Muslims in negotiating their individual freedom at school and with parents, as well as in promoting understanding for Islam and Muslims in society (Karakaşoğlu-Aydın 2000; Klinkhammer 2000).

## 'Muslims' as a Socio-Demographic Category

In the aftermath of 9/11, the murder of the Dutch filmmaker Theo van Gogh in 2004, and the Madrid and the London bombings in 2005, administrations, politicians, scholars,

---

[2] The Ahmadiyya Muslim Jama'at opened the Fazle-Omar-Moschee in 1957 in Hamburg and the Masğid Nūr'in Frankfurt/M. in 1958. The Imam-Ali-Pasha-mosque in Hamburg's prestigious quarter at the Außenalster was opened by a predominantly shi'i community of merchants and students from Pakistan, Afghanistan, and Iran in 1968.

media, and non-governmental organizations (NGOs) in Germany displayed interest in obtaining and providing factual knowledge about Muslim populations: How do they live, what do they think, how religious and how well integrated are they, and how many are there?

This growing awareness of Muslims' presence in Germany led to the realization that little official statistical data and very little knowledge on Muslims in Germany existed. Since official statistics and population surveys did not classify Muslims, researchers felt compelled to resort to indirect methods to gather information about Muslim populations by referring to the nationality or national background of immigrants and their descendants (Spielhaus 2011b). To map the Muslim population in the country, seven large surveys commissioned by the Federal Interior Ministry and its sub-department the Federal Office for Migration and Refugees have been carried out by scholars from disciplines such as migration sociology, political studies, psychology, and criminology (Haug et al. 2009, 2010; Brettfeld and Wetzels 2007; Frindte et al. 2011; Halm and Sauer 2012; Schmidt and Stichs 2012; Becher and El-Menouar 2013).

Thus, the current knowledge on Muslims in Germany is mainly shaped by the results of large surveys that have been commissioned by governmental institutions to create data on Muslims. In Rogers Brubaker's words 'Muslim' was not only used as a category of social, political, and religious practice but increasingly as a category of analysis (Brubaker 2013). Thus the term was integrated into the existing systems of knowledge and classification as a tool of modern state administration. Muslims became a socio-demographic category.

## Muslim Populations: Numbers and Characteristics

The number of Muslims in Germany remains subject to calculations and estimations, which have been established on the basis of immigration statistics and a recent large-scale survey among immigrants from countries with substantial Muslim population (Deutscher Bundestag 2000, 2007; Haug et al. 2009), because German official authorities do not raise or document the religious affiliation of residents—except for members of the Catholic and Protestant churches.

In 1999, during the debates about a more inclusive regulation in citizenship law, the oppositional parliamentary fraction of the Christian Democrats, in opposing the turn from citizenship rights based on *ius sanguinis* to *ius soli* and even more vehemently objecting to any option for double citizenship, asked the red–green government to provide an official account of the numbers of Muslims living in Germany. The answer to the parliamentary inquiry published in 2000 presented the first official estimate on the number of Muslims in Germany (2.5–2.7 million) and was based on migration statistics (Deutscher Bundestag 2000).

Reliable data on the precise number of Muslims living in the country are of concern to various socio-political actors, including Muslim representatives. The 2011 Census included a voluntary question on religious conviction, the Federal Statistical

Office quantifies self-identified Muslims as 1.9% but refused to publish a total number for Muslims in Germany based on what it assessed as unreliable data due to the high non-response rate (17.4%) to this question (Statistisches Bundesamt 2013).[3]

The number of Muslims in Germany will probably continue to be an issue of debate, especially given the claims of various Islamic organizations to speak for all Muslims in the country, for all immigrants from Turkey or from other Muslim majority countries. These claims are meant to emphasize an organization's importance and point out the pre-eminence of their agenda (Spielhaus 2011b). In turn, the relevance of organizational claims is questioned by Muslims, non-Muslim immigrants, and by government representatives. As a result of these contentions, a representative survey was commissioned by the first German Islam Conference (DIK), a forum for long-term dialogue set up by the German Federal Interior Ministry in 2006. To a larger extent than in other European countries, NGOs, private foundations, and government institutions invested in direct surveys on Muslim life in Germany.[4]

Published in 2007 by the Federal Ministry of Interior Affairs, *Muslims in Germany*, the first large quantitative survey among Muslims in Germany, focused on integration and radicalization (Brettfeld and Wetzels 2007). Another survey, the *Religion Monitor 2008*, which was commissioned and published by the Bertelsmann Foundation, included large-scale surveys in twenty-one countries on five continents. Using a religious studies approach it addressed questions of religious affiliation, belief, and religious or spiritual dimensions of life. A complementary survey of the *Religion Monitor* targeting the Muslim minority population in Germany surveyed 2,007 respondents of Turkish, Arab, Iranian, and Bosnian descent. Different from the other surveys mentioned here, the research design and questionnaire of this study were not designed specifically for Muslims but for a variety of faith groups. This has implications for its content and questions that deal not with integration but with religious practice and belief as well as their consequences for daily life (Bertelsmann Stiftung 2008).

As part of the negotiations about the recognition of Islamic organizations as representative bodies for Muslims in Germany, the German Islam Conference commissioned a third survey *Muslim Life in Germany* (MLG, Haug et al. 2009) designed to quantify self-identifying Muslims with a *Migrationshintergrund* (migration background) living in Germany. The intention was to generate a population estimate based on a representative nationwide sample that does not depend solely on data from immigration statistics, but takes into account the self-perception and identification of individuals. Besides

---

[3] Because of the high non-response rate the Federal Statistical Office expressed the view that Muslims and affiliates of other religious minorities refused to answer this question at a higher rate than among the average population and therefore did not publish the net results. The office also did not indicate the share of respondents who self-classified as Sunni, Shi'i, or Alevi (Statistisches Bundesamt 2013).

[4] The number of surveys with samples of Muslims in Germany created in the 2000s is larger than the four biggest surveys selected for this chapter. For an extensive list of surveys among Muslims in Germany see Johansen and Spielhaus (2014); for a discussion of the challenges in quantifying Muslims see Spielhaus (2011).

Table 3.1 Persons in Germany from Muslim majority countries according to religion and region of origin (%)

| | South-east Europe | Turkey | Central Asia/CIS | Iran | South/South-Eeast Asia | Middle East | North Africa | Other parts of Africa | Total |
|---|---|---|---|---|---|---|---|---|---|
| Muslim | 37.2 | 81.4 | 1.2 | 48.7 | 57.2 | 59.3 | 74.6 | 22.1 | 52.0 |
| Christian | 34.1 | 2.7 | 55.7 | 10.3 | 8.8 | 17.4 | 3.4 | 59.2 | 22.1 |
| Jew | 0.1 | – | 3.0 | 0.7 | – | 1.1 | – | 0.0 | 0.8 |
| Others | 0.6 | 1.2 | 2.0 | 1.9 | 13.9 | 2.8 | 0.0 | 1.4 | 1.9 |
| None | 27.9 | 14.7 | 38.0 | 38.4 | 20.0 | 19.5 | 22.0 | 17.1 | 23.3 |
| Total in % | 100 | 100 | 100 | 100 | 100 | 100 | 100 | 100 | 100 |
| Total (n) | 2.226 | 2.401 | 2.864 | 753 | 2.551 | 3.064 | 1.786 | 1.347 | 16.992 |

*Note:* The dataset of the MLG study was collected in 2008 while the report was published in 2009.
*Source:* MLG (2008). Dataset of all household members, weighted; unweighted cases: 16.992 (Haug et al. 2009: 90, own layout).

quantifying Muslims among the immigrants from countries with relevant Muslim populations, it seeks to measure the integration of Muslim immigrants and their descendants. Grounded in migration sociology, the study 'aims to find out whether there are differences in the integration of the residents' Muslim population that might depend on affiliation with a particular denomination of Islam or on the respective ethnic and national origin of this group' (Haug et al. 2009: 28).

On the basis of a sample that contains 6,000 respondents with a background in one of forty-nine countries with relevant Muslim populations, along with data on almost 17,000 household members, the MLG survey suggests an estimated number of 3.8–4.3 million Muslims in Germany.[5] Approximately 45% of them are German nationals while the other 55% are foreign nationals (Haug et al. 2009: 75).

A little more than half of the 5,232 respondents (52%) stated that they are Muslims. That means that nearly half of the sample that comprised immigrants and descendants of immigrants from countries with relevant Muslim populations do not consider themselves as Muslims. A quarter of the interviewees with a background in a predominantly Muslim country stated they are Christians (26%) (Haug et al. 2009: 104–5; see Table 3.1). This demonstrates that indirect calculations and estimates based on migration or linguistic background cannot be used to make reliable statements about Muslims.

---

[5] A shortcoming of this estimation is that the sample included only interviewees with *Migrationshintergrund* using a name-based procedure method that could not be used to locate Muslims of German origin. The methodology reflects the understanding of Muslims as immigrants that is reflected in the aim of the survey: 'determining the number of Muslims with a migrant background' (Haug et al. 2009: 54; for further discussion of the quantification of Muslims see Spielhaus 2011).

According to the *Mikrozensus* that is conducted by the Federal Statistical Office and since 2005 provides number of persons with a *Migrationshintergrund*, approximately 15.8 million people in Germany have either a personal migration experience or a parent or grandparent who immigrated to Germany (Statistisches Bundesamt 2011). The maximum extrapolation of 4.3 million Muslims therefore indicates that not even a third of the German residents with *Migrationshintergrund* self-identify as Muslims.

As has been pointed out before, taking the (former) nationality of immigrants as a proxy for religious affiliation, and depending on migration statistics as the basis for an estimate of the Muslim population has many drawbacks. In their call for direct instead of indirect measurement methods for religious affiliation Jocelyne Cesari and Jytte Klausen stress that calculations on the basis of nationality would not include all bi-national and naturalized Muslims (Cesari 2004: 9–18; Klausen 2005: 6, 214–15; cf. Brown 2000 and Sander 1997).

Furthermore, as the MLG survey confirms, emigration does not necessarily reflect the religious composition of the countries of origin (Haug et al. 2009: 81). Specific parts of the population seem to be more likely to grab opportunities to emigrate, as other surveys like the *Religion Monitor 2008* indicate (Heine and Spielhaus 2008; see also Brown 2000). This explains why, despite originating from Muslim majority countries, a substantial proportion of the respondents in this survey are not Muslims according to their self-assessment (Haug et al. 2009: 12). Members of religious minorities—those who practise minority religion or a different denomination, practice, or understanding of Islam than the dominant—seem to have been more likely to take the chance to leave when foreign workers were recruited. This applies even more in cases of politically motivated emigration, as the example of respondents from Iran shows. Almost 40% of the respondents with an Iranian background in the survey claim to have no religious affiliations (Haug et al. 2009: 12, 87, 302–20). Similar disproportions can be found regarding denominational minorities.[6] Hence, the findings of the MLG survey confirm 'the necessity of determining the religious composition of important immigrant groups in order to empirically determine the number of Muslims' living in a specific territory (Haug et al. 2009: 82).

The majority of the Muslims who immigrated to Germany are of (former) Bosnian, Turkish, Albanian, Lebanese, Iraqi, Iranian, Afghan, Somalian, and Yugoslav nationality and include Kurdish, Palestinian, Kosovar-Albanian, and other ethnic minorities (see Table 3.2). According to the MLG survey, a clear majority of all Muslims with a *Migrationshintergrund* living in Germany—this includes descendants of immigrants—originate from Turkey (2.5 million, 63%), while nearly 14% have a *Migrationshintergrund* in south-east Europe (Haug et al. 2009: 84). The percentage of Muslims with a *Migrationshintergrund* in South/South-East Asia, the Middle East, or North Africa ranges between 5 and 8% of all Muslims in the country. Muslims from

---

[6] *Religion Monitor 2008* documented that a remarkably high proportion (29%) of the interviewees with an Iranian background classified themselves as Sunnis.

Table 3.2 Religious affiliation of individuals with a *Migrationshintergrund* (migrant background) in Germany according to their country of origin (%)

|  | Muslim | Other religious affiliation | No religious affiliation | Total |
|---|---|---|---|---|
| Afghanistan | 69.4 | 10.2 | 20.4 | 100.0 |
| Egypt | 62.4 | 18.4 | 19.2 | 100.0 |
| Albania | 32.6 | 13.2 | 54.2 | 100.0 |
| Bangladesh | 67.6 | 2.9 | 29.4 | 100.0 |
| Bulgaria | 1.6 | 46.0 | 52.4 | 100.0 |
| Former Yugoslavia | 39.6 | 35.6 | 24.8 | 100.0 |
| India | 7.3 | 66.7 | 26.0 | 100.0 |
| Indonesia/Malaysia | 25.0 | 50.0 | 25.0 | 100.0 |
| Iraq | 58.7 | 24.4 | 16.8 | 100.0 |
| Iran | 48.7 | 12.9 | 38.4 | 100.0 |
| Israel | 21.7 | 39.1 | 39.1 | 100.0 |
| Yemen/Jordan | 80.0 | 4.7 | 15.3 | 100.0 |
| Kazakhstan | 0.5 | 69.3 | 30.2 | 100.0 |
| Lebanon | 74.0 | 7.6 | 18.4 | 100.0 |
| Morocco | 77.8 | 1.8 | 20.3 | 100.0 |
| Pakistan | 86.6 | 1.5 | 11.9 | 100.0 |
| Rest of North Africa | 69.4 | 5.9 | 24.7 | 100.0 |
| Rest of central Asia/CIS | 5.2 | 57.0 | 37.8 | 100.0 |
| Rest of Africa | 22.1 | 60.7 | 17.1 | 100.0 |
| Russian Federation | 1.3 | 57.9 | 40.8 | 100.0 |
| Syria | 40.7 | 37.6 | 21.7 | 100.0 |

*Source*: MLG (2008), dataset covering all household members, weighted (Haug et al. 2009: 82–3, own layout).

'other parts of Africa' and Iranian Muslims each form around 2% of the Muslims with *Migrationshintergrund* in Germany, while the share of Muslims originating from Central Asia/CIS is less than 1% (Haug et al. 2009: 91–2).

The MLG survey gives a sense of the gender distribution among Muslim immigrants. Of the 16,984 total cases, 53% of the sample was male and 47% female, while among the two largest groups of origin, from south-east Europe and Turkey, males and females were comparably even (around 51% male and 49% female). In the case of immigrants from Africa and the Middle East, men are the clear majority. This is most pronounced among immigrants from 'other parts of Africa', as here the share of men (66.4%) is twice as high as that of women (33.6%). This is less true but still significant among Muslims from North Africa (60.0% are male) and the Middle East (55.6% are male) (Haug et al. 2009: 96).

The religious affiliations of female and male respondents from different regions of origin (i.e. whether they are Muslim, affiliated with another religion, or are unaffiliated) differ considerably. For instance, men from south-east Europe, Turkey, and Iran are more likely than women to state that they have no religious affiliation, while men from 'other parts of Africa' are more likely to state they are Muslim. Additionally a larger share of women from North Africa state that they are 'members of other religious communities' (see Haug et al. 2009: 96). This means that it remains unclear whether this uneven distribution of males and females in certain Muslim communities results from different migration patterns or has other causes.

With a distinctly higher proportion of Muslims under the age of 25, the Muslim population in Germany is considerably younger than the general population. However, the age structure of Muslims in Germany from different countries of origin varies. Muslims from South/South-East Asia and the Middle East especially show large shares of persons under the age of 25. Among Muslims from Turkey we can find the largest segment of people beyond the age of 65 (Haug et al. 2009: 99–101).

As indicated by the distribution of the respondents to the MLG survey, Muslim immigrants live throughout western Germany and Berlin with some focal points. The greatest number of Muslim immigrants live in the densely inhabited and industrial area of the federal state of North Rhine-Westphalia (33%), the *Ruhrgebiet*, which includes Cologne, home to the headquarters of four major Islamic umbrella organizations. This state is followed by Baden-Württemberg (16.6%), Bavaria (13.2%), and Hessen (10.3%). Considering the size of their territory, the comparatively high share of the city-states Berlin (6.9%) and Hamburg (3.5%) is also remarkable. Less than 2% of Muslim migrants are living in the eastern part of Germany, on the territory of the former GDR (Haug et al. 2009: 101–2).

Over 70% of the Muslim interviewees and no fewer than 90% of members of other religions with a *Migrationshintergrund* were born abroad. The remaining portion of almost 30% of Muslims and 10% of members of other religions with a *Migrationshintergrund*, were born in Germany as children of immigrants (Haug et al. 2009: 110–11).

The average duration of residence among immigrants is highest among those from Turkey, Morocco, and Tunisia, the countries with which West Germany had signed guest worker programmes (Haug et al. 2009: 113). The proportion of Muslims of Turkish origin born abroad is lower than that of any other origin (Haug et al. 2009: 294). Turkish Muslims are most likely to have attended school in Germany, while at the same time their standard of education is the lowest. Approximately half of them either have no school-leaving qualification at all or only a low-level school-leaving qualification. Nevertheless, Turkish Muslims who were born in Germany show a higher educational standard in comparison to the first generation, yet the relatively low standard of education remains closely connected to the history of immigration (i.e. the recruitment of

Table 3.3 Muslims in Germany according to denomination (%)[a]

|  | % |
| --- | --- |
| Sunni | 74.1 |
| Shiite | 7.1 |
| Alevi | 12.7 |
| Ahmadi | 1.7 |
| Sufis/Mystics[b] | 0.1 |
| Ibadis | 0.3 |
| Other[c] | 4.0 |
| Total (N) | 6.669 |

*Notes:*
[a] The findings are based on the question 'Do you belong to a religious community and, if so, are you... (1) Muslim (Sunni, Shia, Ahmadi, Sufi, Ibadi), (2) Alevi, (3) Christian (Protestant, Catholic, Orthodox), (4) Jewish, (5) Member of a different religious community (Hindu, Buddhist, Druse, Yezidi), (6) No, I do not belong to a religious community, (9) Not specified' (Haug et al. 2009: 379); 'Are You... (1) Sunnite (e.g. Hanafi, Shafi'i, Maliki, Hanbali), (2) Shiite (e.g. 12th Shiite/Imami, 7th Shiite/Ismaili, 5th Shiite/Zaidi, Alawi/Nussairi), (3) Alevi, (4) Ahmadi, (5) Sufi/Mystic, (6) Ibadi, (7) Other, (9) Not specified' (Haug et al. 2009: 380).
[b] According to the questionnaire respondents could only mark one of the given options, hence the number of Sufis/Mystics remains rather problematic, since the respondents who considered the Sunni, Shi'i, etc. denominations could additionally want to describe themselves as Sufis or Mystics.
[c] The MLG survey report informs its readers of the percentage of respondents who answered 'other' for denomination, but it does not reveal the number of respondents who neglected to identify a denomination. As the *Religion Monitor* showed, this information is, however, relevant.
*Source:* MLG 2008, dataset covering all household members, weighted.Unweighted number of cases: 6,669 (Haug et al. 2009: 92, own layout).

unskilled workers) (Haug et al. 2009: 295). Around 40% of Muslims of Turkish origin are German citizens (Haug et al. 2009: 294).

According to the MLG survey, Alevis account for 19% of the household members of respondents with a background in Turkey. Ahmadi, Sufis/Mystics, and Ibadis, taken together, amount to fewer than 3% of the total respondents, while Ahmadis make up 28% of the interviewees from South and South-East Asia who self-identify as Muslims (Haug et al. 2009: 93; see Table 3.3).

The number of respondents who prefer *not* to classify themselves as one of the given choices of 'Islamic denominations' is very instructive, especially in the breakdown of denominations according to regions of origin. Among the Muslims with a background in south-east Europe 25.5%, and in 'other parts of Africa' 17.6%, state that they belong to another 'denomination'. Among those from North Africa this accounts for 9.8% while all Muslims with a background in Iran state that they are either Shi'i (95.5%), Sunni (3%), or Alevi (1.5%). Also among respondents from Turkey a comparatively small share (3.4%)

identify as belonging to another 'denomination', while 74.6% state they are Sunni, and 18.9% identify as Alevis (Haug et al. 2009: 94).[7]

This finding confirms an observation previously made in the study of the *Religion Monitor* among Muslims in 2008. Among the 2,007 Muslims in Germany interviewed in the *Religion Monitor*, 9% classified themselves as Shiites, 65% as Sunnis, and 8% as Alevis. A remarkable percentage (19%) of all interview partners did not classify themselves with any of the denominations listed, but answered 'other denomination' (11%) or 'don't know/no answer' (8%) (Heine and Spielhaus 2008: 24–5). Similar to the results of the MLG survey, Bosnian respondents ranked high among those who did not identify with any of the given choices. More than a third (36%) of the Bosnian respondents and 13% of those of Iranian origin did not agree to self-classify, although—or perhaps because—the concept of a duality between Shi'i and Sunni Islam dominates the academic and political discourse on Islam. The answers of Muslims reveal both a different degree of awareness as well as regional relevance of denominational affiliation. The high number of those who say they belong to other denominations than the choices given in the questionnaires, points to other religious affiliations or further connections on a religious level; that might be mystic movements, Islamic schools of jurisprudence, or transnational networks and religious groups that have acquired global significance over the past decades. As for Germany, it can therefore be ascertained that the polarization between Sunnis and Shiites is either less important, or identities based on the affiliation with Islamic denominations are more complex than commonly suggested in Islamic Studies literature[8] (Heine and Spielhaus 2008: 24–5).

## Religiosity and Membership in Religious Organizations

Most elaborated is the measure for religiosity that is used in the *Religion Monitor*, which includes the self-assessment for religiosity, and categorizes respondents on the basis of answers to six core dimensions of religiosity (intellect, faith, communal practice, private practice, experiences, and consequences). According to this measure, 41% of Muslims in Germany are categorized as highly religious and 49% as religious (Bertelsmann Stiftung 2008). Surveys that compare Muslim immigrants with non-Muslim populations without a *Migrationshintergrund* conclude that Muslims have a higher level of identification

---

[7] The low identification with 'Sufi/Mystics', however, seems questionable, since in praxis the detailed options are not exclusive as one could well identify as Sufi and Sunni or Shi'i at the same time but the survey demanded a decision for one option.

[8] The 2011 Census allowed Muslims only to claim affiliation to Islam if they decided between the three 'denominations' Sunni, Shi'i, or Alevi Islam. It remains uncertain how Muslims who do not care about or oppose subdivisions of Islam answered this question. The Federal Statistical Office valued the answers to this question as not reliable since the non-response rate to the voluntary question on religious conviction was very high (17.4%) (Statistisches Bundesamt 2013).

with religion and a higher level of daily religious practices (Brettfeld and Wetzels 2007; Bertelsmann Stiftung 2008: 6).

Inspired by the debate about the legitimacy of Islamic organizations to represent Muslims in Germany, surveys have been interested in establishing the relevance of religion and the rate of Muslims who are members in an Islamic organization. Comparing Muslims and non-Muslims with a *Migrationshintergrund* in countries with relevant Muslim populations,[9] the MLG survey, however, observes a higher membership rate among non-Muslims (27%) (Haug et al. 2009: 159f.). The share of Muslims who are registered members of a religious organization is lower among people from the Middle East (5%) and other parts of Africa (14%) than those from Turkey (24%) or South/South-East Asia (28%), and is correspondingly lower among Alevis (1%) and Shiites (10%) than among Sunnis (22%). Among the members of other Islamic denominations, such as the Ibadis or Ahmadis, as many as 29% are members of an organization (Haug et al. 2009: 160). The MLG examination of active involvement among Muslims according to denomination suggests that religious minorities within Islam show particularly higher levels of organization.

## Access to the Labour Market

In 2010 the Federal Anti-Discrimination Agency published two studies, one on discrimination of Muslims in the job market based on existing statistical data (Peucker 2010), and one on the legal framework concerning unequal treatment on the basis of religion. Both highlight that not only the lack of data causes difficulties in differentiating between discrimination based on ethnic identity and discrimination motivated by an (assumed) affiliation to Islam, but also the intersection of the two characteristics. Moreover, the reasons for discrimination are not always made explicit. According to Mario Peucker, Muslims are potentially exposed to three different but intersecting forms of discrimination: based on an (assumed) ethnic or national background, religious practices and needs, and ethno-religious discrimination that can aggravate unequal treatment (Peucker 2010: 14); others mention even more (Barskanmaz 2009). Dorothee Frings highlights the structural and legal circumstances that many Muslims were exposed to as immigrants and their lasting effects on the German job market. While labour migrants were mostly employed as unskilled or low-skilled workers until the 1980s, a considerable part of the next generation moved into highly-qualified and academic jobs. In contrast, refugees were excluded from the job market by a ban on employment for asylum-seekers that was introduced in the 1990s to discourage migration to Germany. This caused a structural segmentation of the labour market in which many people of Muslim faith

---

[9] The MLG survey compares non-Muslims and Muslims from specific regions as well as different Muslim religious denominations in order to evaluate not only inter-religious and intra-religious difference concerning membership and active engagement in religious organizations and ritual practice, but also structural and cultural integration.

are still confined to the less-qualified and lower-paid jobs. Parallel to public debates on Islam, long-term residence and naturalization have led to a stronger and more visible presence of Muslims in higher education and employment that triggers frictions and legal conflicts especially concerning the headscarf for Muslim women (Frings 2010: 7).

In 1998, a Muslim woman applied for a job in a public school in the southern German state of Baden-Württemberg and was rejected because she was wearing a headscarf. Her complaint led to a landmark decision of the Federal Constitutional Court (*Bundesverfassungsgericht*) on 30 September 2003. It decided that on the basis of current law it was not legitimate to refuse the woman's request for placement as a teacher on the basis of visible religious affiliation. While pondering the freedom of faith of the teachers and of the pupils affected, the parent's right of education and the state's duty of ideological and religious neutrality, the court pointed out that the regional parliaments of the German federal states (*Länder*) could create the statutory basis to ban the wearing of headscarves for teachers in public schools by laying down the permissible degree of religious references in schools.[10] It indicated two ways of legislation for German states: either a general ban of religious symbols for teachers and state officers or a general permission while stressing that all religions had to be treated equally.

Following this verdict, laws to ban headscarves for teachers in public schools have been introduced in eight out of sixteen German states (Baden-Württemberg, Bavaria, Berlin, Bremen, Hesse, Lower Saxony, North Rhine-Westphalia, and Saarland[11]). According to the legal scholar Matthias Rohe some of the regulations are neutral in their wording but clearly aimed at the Muslim headscarf only (Rohe 2012: 247–8).[12]

The introduction of bans for headscarves in the educational field and public service appears to have had immense effects on the broader labour market (John 2009). The few existing surveys among employers have shown that the headscarf is largely unwanted or considered to be incompatible with professional life (Frings 2010: 7). This attitude is often justified with the anticipated negative reaction of a third party, especially customers (Peucker 2010: 54).

---

[10] Judgment of the Second Senate of the Federal Constitutional Court from 24 September 2003 (2 BvR 1436/02), available at <http://www.bundesverfassungsgericht.de/entscheidungen/rs20030924_2bvr143602.html> [Accessed 8 September 2013, translation by the author]. For a discussion of the case and its socio-political context see: Mahlmann (2003); Fournier and Yurdakul (2006); Berghahn and Rostock (2009).

[11] While Baden-Württemberg apart from teachers includes also nursery staff in the ban, the states of Hesse and Berlin include all state officers and Berlin explicitly banned all kinds of religious symbols for employees in public service (Rohe 2011).

[12] Students are generally allowed to wear headscarves even though several schools have been reported to prevent students from attending classes with headscarf or deny the acceptance of girls who wear a headscarf (Senatsverwaltung für Integration, Arbeit und Soziales 2007; Spielhaus 2012). Debates on the '*burqa*-ban' in France, Belgium, and other European countries had rather small repercussions on the German public debate, but led to an expert hearing in the Committee on Human Rights of the German Bundestag in October 2010. All political parties agreed that a total ban of the face veil would be unconstitutional and regarded the existing laws relating to security measures and work in public institutions sufficient (Rohe 2011: 249).

Several cases concerning employment law in the private sector have been brought to German courts. In most cases decisions turned out in favour of employees who wanted to wear a headscarf during work. These verdicts weighed freedom of faith against the interest of the employers and were supported by the Anti-discrimination Law that was implemented in 2006 on the basis of EU Directives (Rottmann and Ferree 2008). Even though the legal situation seems clear, Muslim women's organizations and anti-discrimination agencies report limited access for women wearing a headscarf to job training and the labour market (Frings 2010).

Still, very few cases are reported or even brought to court. Muslim women show low levels of rights-awareness and knowledge about as well as trust in mechanisms for making complaints (Open Society Institute 2009). They furthermore have developed strategies to avoid discrimination and harassment by not applying for positions when they suspect visibly Muslim women are not welcome, not walking alone in the street and not seeking help or service (Spielhaus 2012: 249–50). These strategies of coping with discrimination underline two aspects: firstly, discrimination renders Muslim women immobile; secondly, the impact of unequal treatment or harassment cannot sufficiently be captured in data on the frequency and nature of discrimination. Researchers also need to consider strategies taken by potential victims to avoid discrimination or harassment in order to assess their relevance in people's everyday lives (Spielhaus 2012: 250).

The MLG survey data sustain these assumptions. By raising both self-assessed religious affiliation and data on education and employment of immigrants from countries with relevant Muslim populations and their descendants, the MLG data can serve for comparisons between immigrants of different faith as well as between immigrants and non-immigrants. In a successive analysis of the survey data concerning the employment of respondents, Stichs and Kreienbrink have concluded that differences appear between migrants and German-born informants, as well as between men and women with different levels of education. Except for Muslim women, faith has apparently no effect on employment status. The unemployment rate among male Muslims (15.1%) is drastically lower than among female Muslims (42.1%) but is similar to male non-Muslims (15.9%). Female non-Muslims (33.1%) are still twice as likely to be unemployed than male non-Muslims from Muslim majority countries, but their unemployment rate is still significantly lower than among female Muslims (Stichs and Kreienbrink 2012: 2).

Independent of the religion, labour force participation is notably higher among German-born residents than among immigrants. This coincides with higher language competencies, German professional education, and access to social networks. Within the second generation gender differences decrease, and this shift is more significant among Muslims than among non-Muslims. Compared to those born and educated in Germany, female Muslims of the first generation show lower rates of labour force participation. Considering the career structure of those gainfully employed, women with *Migrationshintergrund* regardless of their religion, perform poorly when compared to men. They are significantly under-represented in highly qualified or skilled occupations, and compose a higher percentage of part-time employees (*Teilzeitbeschäftige* and *geringfügig Beschäftigte*) (Stichs and Kreienbrink 2012: 3).

Peucker resorts to comparing statistical data of the *Mikrozensus* and the *Socio-Economic Panel*, two large-scale long-term surveys of the German population with conclusive shares of immigrants in the sample, and evaluates labour market access and ethnicity to assess patterns of exclusion (Peucker 2010). With a multivariate regression analysis he tests labour market data for indicators of discrimination. Unlike in the case of Polish or Italian immigrants, the under-representation of Turks in the German labour market cannot be statistically explained with differences in other significant demographic variables like education or socio-economic background. Peucker interprets this as a sign of structural mechanisms of exclusion (Peucker 2010: 25). According to a correspondence test that was carried out in the job market for student internships in economics and management science,[13] applicants with a German sounding name have roughly a 14% greater chance of being called back by a potential employer. In the 1990s, testing results concerning exclusion of ethnic groups in low-skilled segments of the labour market differed from one sector to the other, with the commercial sector rating highest (Goldberg et al. 1996). Both forms of testing conclude that in smaller enterprises with fewer than fifty employees, net discrimination factored into hiring practices (Kaas and Manger 2012). The more information was provided on the applicant's personality, like in reference letters, the less discrimination was significant (Kaas and Manger 2012: 19). As Peucker points out, neither statistics nor tests can reveal religious discrimination on the job or in other spheres of life like education, schooling, housing, or in the service sector. Hence, in these fields researchers have to resort to other empirical methods.

## Experiences of Discrimination

Even though unequal treatment of Muslims in Germany has been acknowledged by anti-discrimination agencies on the federal and regional level, and several surveys have included questions on experiences of discrimination, there remains a considerable lack of official data on the quantity, nature, and severity of discrimination against Muslims. There still appears to be a large gap between the assessment of discrimination by Islamic organizations and the awareness of the problem in the larger public and state government (Spielhaus 2012: 243).

While some of the above-mentioned surveys included questions on experiences of discrimination and on religious practices such as clothing, they do not publish information on a potential connection between the two, and for the most part do not break down experiences of discrimination by gender. Therefore they do not provide useful data to quantify what is often claimed: that women wearing a headscarf suffer from greater exclusion and an increased number of assaults to a larger degree than their male counterparts and when compared to women who do not show any visible traits of their Muslim faith.

---

[13] In this testing more than 1,000 applications have been sent answering to 528 job advertisements (Kaas and Manger 2010).

Several surveys indicate that Muslims in Germany experience high levels of discrimination. In a survey by the Open Society Institute, Muslims in Berlin were asked to compare the past and current levels of religious prejudice. A large majority (86%) of the Muslim respondents said that, 'current levels of religious prejudice are greater than five years ago', while 59% of the non-Muslim control group (including immigrants and non-immigrants) answered that prejudice levels are 'about the same amount' (Mühe 2010: 210). Muslims also reported experiencing ethnic and religious discrimination to a much larger degree than non-Muslims: 74% of the Muslim respondents said that they felt discriminated against within the last year on the basis of their religion, while this was only identified by 25% of the non-Muslims (Mühe 2010: 202). The subjective experience of discrimination is furthermore included in surveys that aim at assessing the potential for radicalization among Muslims. In this context such experiences are interpreted as indicators for radicalization (see Chapter 7).

Meanwhile, the intersectionality of different grounds for unequal treatment of people of Muslim faith continues to be largely under-studied and it remains open in what way and to what extent the multiple elements that play a role in the marginalization like (alleged) foreign nationality, ethnic origin, migration, and social status may amplify disadvantages Muslims are facing in the educational system and the job market (Barskanmaz 2009).

## Surveys with a Specific Focus

Besides the surveys that aim at providing data on Muslim immigrants as such, a few quantitative studies target specific Muslim populations or professions, like women with headscarves (Jessen and Wilamowitz-Moellendorff 2006) and imams (Schmidt and Stichs 2012), or collect data on mosque associations in specific geographical frames ranging from cities like Berlin (Spielhaus and Färber 2006) to regions (Chbib 2008) or the whole state (Halm and Sauer 2012). Such surveys follow and contribute to specific debates in the public discourse on Islam and Muslims in the country, like the headscarf controversy (Berghahn and Rostock 2009) or the growing interest in mosques as spaces and religious functionaries as tutors of integration (Tezcan 2008).

While limiting their access to the job market and other negative effects, the debate on headscarves raised the visibility of Muslim women (Spielhaus 2009). Throughout the conflict about visible Islamic symbols, the need for data on women who wear the headscarf, on their motives, their access to education, etc. has been repeatedly identified. In 2006 the Konrad Adenauer Foundation, a think tank of the Christian Democratic Party, presented a survey of 315 Turkish women who wear a headscarf. In their conclusion the authors of the study stress that the widely published view that the headscarf would stand for the oppression of women could not be sustained. The respondents favoured equitable models of partnership and did not want to stand back behind their male partners. In these attitudes, the answers of the women surveyed corresponded highly with attitudes among the general German society, and yet religion plays an important role in the lives of the respondents (Jessen and Wilamowitz-Moellendorff 2006: 41f.).

As the motivation to wear a headscarf respondents mainly referred to religion, while they considered the influence of male members of the family being of minor importance. In evaluating why many women in the sample showed no interest in obtaining German citizenship the authors conclude that this results from their feelings of being rejected by or discriminated by German society (Jessen and Wilamowitz-Moellendorff 2006: 42). Altogether, 43% of the respondents felt strongly or fairly connected to Germany, 71% with Turkey (Jessen and Wilamowitz-Moellendorff 2006: 18), while 80% of the respondents were convinced that Turks in Germany were treated as second-class citizens (Jessen and Wilamowitz-Moellendorff 2006: 19). The majority (63%) of women with the lowest educational level had only Turkish friends. However, among women with medium or high educational levels this is only the case for 27 or 29%. Stronger than citizenship, educational levels are a greater determining factor in the composition of circles of friends and acquaintances (Jessen and Wilamowitz-Moellendorff 2006: 21).

Among the female respondents of the *Muslim Life in Germany* survey from 2009, 28% identified wearing a headscarf, while the large majority of 72% of female Muslims in the sample did not wear a headscarf in the public sphere. The percentage of women wearing a headscarf increases with age, as one in two Muslim women aged 65 or above wears one (Haug et al. 2009: 186–7). The analysis shows a pronounced positive link between devoutness and the wearing of the headscarf. However, strong religiosity does not automatically lead to the wearing of the headscarf, as half of highly religious Muslim women do not wear a headscarf (Haug et al. 2009: 14, 192).

Among the female respondents from predominantly Muslim countries of origin, women who wear the headscarf are less likely to assess their knowledge of German as good or very good or to be gainfully employed. Their emotional ties to Germany tend to be weaker and they are less likely to be naturalized (Haug et al. 2009: 14, 192f.).The causalities concerning these empirical findings remain a matter of speculation.

Finally, the MLG survey also queried the reasons women give for wearing a headscarf. The vast majority answered that they considered it a religious duty (92.3%). The second most common statement (43.3%) was 'the headscarf gives me a sense of security'; 36% of the respondents agreed with the statement that they wanted 'to be recognizable as Muslim women'; 15% reported they wore the headscarf as a 'protection against harassment by men'. To wear the headscarf 'on fashion grounds' (7.3%) or as the result of the partner's or the family's request or social expectations ranked lowest (6.7%, 5.8%, and 5.8% respectively) (Haug et al. 2009: 14, 196f.).

The German Islam Conference commissioned a second study with two parts: a survey among mosques and cem evi's[14] and a survey among male religious functionaries. The

---

[14] *Cem evi* is the Turkish name for the Alevi community's prayer rooms. Alevis do not hold Friday prayers but usually meet on Thursdays for *cem* rituals that include music and dancing. According to leading scholars, the Alevi community shares the origin and basic belief system but not the religious praxis with the Shi'i denomination. Alevism developed in the region of Anatolia in the thirteenth century. Alevis in Germany disagree about whether they are Muslims, despite not being Muslims still part of Islam, or whether Alevism is not a religion at all but rather a cultural tradition based on an ethical code and cultural practices including the *cem* ceremonies (Sökefeld 2008a, 2008b). Yet the Alevi

samples for this study comprised 1,141 Islamic associations and more than 800 imams and Alevi Dedes. As a result of the survey data, the authors claimed that 2,342 communities with facilities for Friday prayers existed in Germany. Nearly half of them (49%) were telephone interviewed during the survey.

Most mosque associations, especially those run by Turkish-speaking communities (34%), were founded in the 1980s closely followed by the 30% established in the 1990s. Most of these associations are members in one of the four major Islamic umbrella organizations (DITIB, IGMG, VIKZ, and ZMD).[15] About 13% of the participating mosques were founded after 2000. The majority of these 145 mosque associations did not join any of the umbrella organizations and cater to a diversity of non-Turkish communities. The majority of mosques are located in the inner city (54%), with 27% in residential areas and 14% in industrial zones. The biggest share of mosques (37%) host around 20–100 attendants during Friday prayers, 24% host 200–500 male Muslims, and 6% 500–1,000 worshippers. Ninety-five per cent of the mosques have spaces for women and roughly 55% state that women do not attend Friday prayers. Almost three out of ten Islamic prayer rooms in the sample (29%) are owned by their community. Beyond religious services, mosque associations are engaged in manifold activities: seven out of ten associations organize sporting activities for youth, 65% participate in inter-religious dialogue of some kind, and 57% supervise student homework. Nearly every third mosque offers German lessons for youth (31%) and every fourth (23%) for adults (Halm and Sauer 2012).

The survey among religious functionaries showed that most imams and Dedes were educated outside Germany and hold educational degrees far above the average of the total Muslim population. They also rate their knowledge of the German language to be significantly lower than the total Muslim population. A large share of the 835 imams and Dedes in the sample (40%) are working on a voluntary unpaid basis, while 60% are employed either by the local mosque association (67%), by the umbrella organization (19%), or by the Turkish state (14%). According to the survey analysis, the majority of respondents are open for dialogue and most imams and Dedes in the sample are highly interested in further education, especially pastoral care and social counselling (Schmidt and Stichs 2012).[16]

The seventh and so far last survey on Muslims comissioned by the Ministry for Interior Affairs—indirectly by the German Islam Conference—focuses on attitudes towards gender roles among Christian and Muslim 'Germans and immigrants' (Becher and El-Menouar 2013).[17] A minority of respondents—11% among Christians and 17%

---

association insists on being included in dialogue initiatives between the state and Islamic organizations and also shows strong interest in being included in academic surveys like the MLG.

[15] For more information about the organizational structure of Islam in Germany see the next section on 'Islamic Organizational Structures and Milieux'.

[16] Qualitative research was the basis for Melanie Kamp's characterization of imams and their situation in Germany (Kamp 2008).

[17] The survey was carried out among 3,000 respondents including Christians from Germany, Poland, Romania and Italy and Muslims from Iran, Turkey, south-east Europe, South Asia, North Africa, and the Middle East.

among Muslims—show attitutes that were assessed as misogynist by the authors of the survey. Independent of their religion, the offspring of immigrants tend to distance themselves from the 'classical', i.e. the male breadwinner, role model. Norms of chastity remain untouched by this trend towards 'liberalization' among many of the Muslim respondents while they lose their relevance for children and grandchildren of Christian immigrants (Becher and El-Menouar 2013: 5-6). Muslims are living more often (66%) in a constellation in which the man works full-time and the woman part-time or not at all than Christians (38%) (Becher and El-Menouar 2013: 158). Yet more than half of the Muslim respondents state they would prefer to live a different constellation (Becher and El-Menouar 2013: 170). Unfortunately the survey did not ask why respondents live unwanted gender roles but the authors suggest that reasons lie beyond the partner relationship (Becher and El-Menouar 2013: 170).

# Islamic Organizational Structures and Milieux

Between the 1970s and 1990s, Muslim communities in Germany were predominantly divided along ethnic and linguistic lines, rather than religious denominations. In the late 1990s and 2000s, Muslim communities on the local, regional, and national level more or less successfully worked to establish overarching organizations that could represent Muslims to or in administration and society.

Islamic religious life and political representation in Germany is organized according to the German civil law (Rohe 2008). Most of the mosques and Islamic prayer rooms in the country are run by local associations. Many of those form umbrella organizations to pool their strengths, support each other in offering religious and social services for their members and other visitors, and to represent needs and claims of Muslims and Islamic communities to local, regional, and national authorities.

Most prayer rooms are located in former flats, factory buildings, shops, or storage facilities. A research on mosques and prayer rooms estimates 2,400 rooms in Germany are used for Friday prayers and other Islamic rituals or community activities (Halm and Sauer 2012). Around 180 mosques have been built for this purpose since the 1920s with most coming in the second half of the 1990s.

The early academic publications on Muslims in Germany were compiled by researchers from Islamic and Turkish Studies, cultural anthropology, and sociology and focused either on the general organizational structure of Islam or on particular Muslim milieux or organizations. Greatest attention was given to Turks, the biggest national group of Muslims. Many studies concentrate on mapping Islamic organizations according to their political stances and transnational networks, in some cases in a rather simplistic way that does not take into account developments within the organizations over time or distinctions between different local settings (Steinbach and Feindt-Riggers 1997; Seufert

1999; Lemmen 2000, 2002; Sen and Aydin 2002; Halm 2010; Reetz 2010). A few exceptions present internal perspectives or long-term developments like the ethnographic accounts by Gerdien Jonker on the Sülemanci movement (2002), by Werner Schiffauer on the Kaplan movement (2000) and the Islamic Community Milli Görüş (2010), and the network analysis of the Gülen movement by Bekim Agai (2004).

## Phases of Institutionalization

In 2003, cultural anthropologist Werner Schiffauer presented the first historical review of the Turkish Islamic organizations in the country. He described three main phases of institutionalization: Phase 1 (1970–85): establishment of Islam in Germany (Turkish organizations or movements founded mosque associations); Phase 2 (1985 until mid-1990s): consolidation and founding of umbrella organizations that control and support communities, a phase characterized by an orientation to politics concerning Islam in Turkey; Phase 3 (since the 1990s): turn towards problems of Muslims in Germany and formation of positions in debates with the German public (Schiffauer 2003). This list could be continued by a fourth phase (since the early 2000s) that encompasses different initiatives to unify the leading Islamic umbrella organizations on the regional (*Länder*) and the national level. This process (*Einigungsprozess*) has been successful in providing a unified body of most Islamic associations in some states like in Lower Saxony, Hessen, Bremen, and Hamburg. On the national level this process has led to the foundation of the Koordinationsrat der Muslime in Deutschland (KRM, Coordination Council of Muslims in Germany) by the four major Islamic umbrella organizations (DITIB, VIKZ, Islamrat, and Zentralrat der Muslime, ZMD) (Azzaoui 2011). However, so far the KRM has not been successful in establishing itself as the (legitimate) representative of Muslims and which would ensure recognition by state authorities (Rohe 2012).

These nationwide umbrella organizations consist of local mosque associations or other umbrella organizations like the Islamic Community Milli Görüş and the Islamic Community Germany, and include student as well as women's associations. While the local associations of DITIB, IGMG, and VIKZ are clearly dominated by members of Turkish background, Islamrat and ZMD have members from several Muslim ethnic and religious minorities in Germany such as Shi'i communities and the association of Bosniaks (the Islamic Community of Bosniaks in Germany, IGBD, founded in 1978), an associated member in both ZMD and Islamrat. The Islamic Federation of German Shi'i Communities (IGS) that was founded in 2009, however, did not join any of the existing umbrella organizations. Other more marginal religious minorities like Alevis and Ahmadis established their own associations: the Alevitische Community Germany (AABF, in 1986) and the Ahmadiyya Muslim Jamaat (AMJ, in 1955[18]) and appear not

---

[18] According to Thomas Lemmen the organization was founded in 1955 in Berlin and has carried the name Ahmadiyya Muslim Jamaat since 1988 (Lemmen 2000: 72).

very interested in joining any of the umbrella organizations but even more than that by questioning their Muslimness they have been made to feel unwelcome by these organizations.

## Struggling for Recognition

Largely unsuccessful applications by Islamic organizations for recognition as religious communities date back to the late 1970s, 1980s, and early 1990s, when several associations of Turkish Muslims, e.g. Verein Islamischer Kulturzentren (VIKZ) and the Islamrat, applied for recognition as a religious body (*Körperschaft des öffentlichen Rechts*) according to the German law (Albrecht 1995: 1). Citing the requirement to guarantee permanency (*Gewähr der Dauer*),[19] authorities stopped short of formally rejecting the petitions, while implying that applicants would stand little chance. The aforementioned two Islamic organizations therefore adjourned their petitions and have not reapplied. In 2006, the German Islam Conference, a long-term consultation process, was initiated in part to explore this matter and find solutions so that a full recognition of Islam could be achieved. Concomitantly, the German Interior Ministry and its representatives continued to highlight the deficiencies of Islamic organizations, including the inability to provide members lists and their lack of authority to speak for the majority of Muslims in Germany (Azzaoui 2011). Meanwhile, in 2013, the Ahmadiyya Muslim Jamaat (AMJ) became the first Islamic association to be granted the status of a religious body (*Körperschaft des öffentlichen Rechts*) by the German federal state of Hesse.[20] The Ahmadiyya community gave little reason for a rejection: they have existed for more than a hundred years, have a meticulous list of members, and have given rise to no record of suspicious activities among security agencies. While the decades-old applications for recognition by other Islamic organizations in other federal states have not yet been accepted or rejected, the AMJ's admission could potentially pave the way for more successful claims for recognition in other German states (Herzog und Jonker 2013).

With her analysis of the Central Council of Muslims, Islam Council, DITIB, and Islamic Community Milli Görüş, Kerstin Rosenow-Williams examines three nationwide Islamic umbrella organizations from an organizational-sociological perspective. She takes a closer look at organizational decoupling and protest behaviour vis-à-vis current governmental initiatives for a 'dialogue with Islam' and concludes that the state-led, top-down negotiation process is not always accompanied by bottom-up organizational support, since internal and external expectations differ.

Even though the political expectations raised by the German state play an important role in the behavioural patterns of Islamic organizations, Rosenow-Williams observes

---

[19] In legal interpretations the requirement of the guarantee of durability is often understood as a minimum of thirty years' existence, a stable structural constitution, and size that promises stability (Rohe 2012).

[20] The status of a religious body is granted by federal states.

that the organizations both have to meet the expectations of their members and consider the requirements for organizational legitimacy and efficiency. Hence, Islamic organizations can be characterized by similar interests, like the continuing institutionalization of Islam, while at the same time, key political and religious differences among them and differences regarding organizational history, resources, size, and (in)dependence remain. This leads to different possibilities to attain resources in the form of status and financial assistance. Furthermore, organizations have to consider different members' interests (Rosenow-Williams 2012).

All three organizations stress the need to cooperate with the state, while the IGMG is more reserved than the other two. Both ZMD and IGMG voice criticism of the German government, although the latter is much more direct in its criticism and even confrontational in publicly criticizing and legally challenging methods of law enforcement agencies (cf. Schiffauer 2010). While DITIB and ZMD meet the frequent demands to follow the German constitution (*Grundgesetz*) with politeness, IGMG openly rejects and protests security agency accusations that it sanctions anti-constitutional behaviour. Of the three, DITIB is the least involved in making public demands, according to Rosenow-Williams. Milli Görüş can be characterized as mostly protesting, while DITIB and ZMD chose the decoupling strategy to reconcile contradictory expectations; in this way they established a hybrid identity by combining a Muslim identity with German societal norms (Rosenow-Williams 2012: 464f.).

## Transnational Influences

The first attempts to map Islamic organizations in Germany emphasized their history and transnational relations (Lemmen 2002; Feindt-Riggers and Steinbach 1997; cf. Bodenstein and Kreienbrink 2010). Beyond the question of a risk of violence, international relations and networks are relevant for the different ways Islam is lived in Germany. While the influences of global Muslim actors and networks have been identified, Jörn Thielmann argues that they are rarely fully considered in research (Thielmann 2003, 2010). One of the few studies that approaches transnational networks as such, was Dietrich Reetz's. His team portrays selected Islamic networks active throughout Western Europe, including the three South Asian networks of the Tablighi Jama'at, the Da'awat-e Islami, and the Ahmadiyya Muslim Jama'at which had previously been neglected in academic literature on Islam in Germany (cf. Reetz 2010).

A significant implication of Schiffauer's analysis for policy-makers is that Milli Görüş started as a religious-political diaspora movement of Turks in Europe but today unites several competing trends. This makes it difficult to come to one definite conclusion on how to treat the organization (Schiffauer 2010) that is so far regarded as 'a threat to the German constitution' (Henkel 2008: 115) and handled with great caution if not total neglect (Laurence 2007; Schiffauer 2008). While post-Islamists, who advocate for democracy, integration, and pluralism and against terrorism and anti-Semitism, currently hold leading positions the power constellations might well shift. The reactions to the current leadership's engagement will, as Schiffauer argues, affect its future position in the movement as well as its transnational ties and engagement. Despite systematic rejections by German authorities, the movement is currently oriented towards German and European politics (Schiffauer 2010). The organization's headquarters in Cologne is the centre for a European network that includes groups in Austria, France, and the Netherlands. The engagement of Islamic actors on the EU-level seems to be rather underdeveloped, especially if compared to Christian representatives in Brussels (Jentges 2010).

## Muslim Public Spaces

Muslim public spaces like mosque associations, internet networks (Thielmann 2003), youth groups (Bendixsen 2013), women's associations and their journals (Gamper 2011), and media outlets like the *Islamische Zeitung*[21] (Kuppinger 2010; Bentzin et al. 2007) have provided another focal point of research. As Kuppinger summarizes, communication platforms are crucial in the search for consensus among Muslims and thereby play into processes of 'constructing a more coherent community of German Muslims who share certain understandings and opinions' (Kuppinger 2010: 76). Religious identity formation and processes of differentiation are often accompanied by an engagement with the changing role of religion in an urban European setting, the restructuring of religious authority, and the formation of gender identity through religion (Bendixsen 2013).

Utilizing an urban studies framework, cultural anthropologists present findings on mosques and prayer rooms in specific city contexts, and in so doing identify the appropriation of and struggle for space and recognition. Such an approach examines the junction between Muslims' participation in society and their urban visibility (Spielhaus and Färber 2006; Schiffauer 2010; Kuppinger 2011, 2014). As primary constituents for later Islamic organizations, the establishment and diversification of mosques is tightly connected with the institutionalization of Islam. The first prayer rooms of Turkish guest workers were located in flats (Schiffauer 2010: 45) or as Petra Kuppinger coins them 'leftover or marginal locations'. Islamic communities 'often recycle otherwise unwanted spaces, in particular, defunct industrial sites. First tucked away in small backyards locations, many mosques eventually upgraded to smaller or larger industrial facilities'. The localization of mosques, whether visible or hidden in backyards, 'is the result of powerful urban images, [and] economic necessities', rather than deliberate urban planning (Kuppinger 2008: 49).

---

[21] The *Islamische Zeitung* is a newspaper produced by German Muslims for German Muslims that informs about political, cultural, and theological topics. It was founded by a group of German Muslims in 1995 and is published twice a month. Beyond providing information, Kuppinger states, 'the paper aims to create a platform of debate for a growing group of, in particular, younger pious educated Muslims who examine current politics by way of an Islamic and also an anti-globalization perspective' (Kuppinger 2010: 59).

Visibility in urban spaces is thus not a natural consequence of presence, but an expression of power relations that is produced by negotiating legitimate transformations of presence into representation (Färber et al. 2012: 63). Alexa Färber and her colleagues therefore approach Muslim entrepreneurs as urban practitioners who are both a product of and producers of urbanity. On this basis they developed a typology of prayer rooms and mosques that cuts across the religious, national, and linguistic divides and an assessment of mosque associations according to the security risk they potentially pose. Instead their typology follows the mosques' spatial localization within city structures (such as infrastructures, real estate market, and social facilities), the intensity in negotiating these structures, and their daily community life and symbolic references. Färber et al. distinguish between mosque associations that cater to Muslims in a specific neighbourhood, a larger district, or in the whole city and beyond. City mosques are unique since they are run and frequented by religious and/or linguistic, ethnic, or other minorities within the Muslim population. District mosques differ in that they are part of larger umbrella associations with a professionalized routine, while neighbourhood mosques are deeply rooted within the urban residential structures. The target audience is not only indicative of the visitors of prayer rooms, but affects their services as well as their visibility and contacts within the city (Färber et al. 2012).

## Legal Issues Concerning Islam and Muslim Life

Since the mid-1990s legal studies, especially public law (*öffentliches Recht*)[22] and less commonly private law (*Privatrecht*), have engaged with Islam in Germany (Rohe 2012). Both fields focus on interpreting German constitutional law and its principles and explore the ways in which it can accommodate religious pluralization in order to ensure religious freedom. According to the jurist Stefan Muckel, Germany is facing a tension between two major paradigms. On the one hand Germany is shaped by a Christian predisposition that is imprinted onto the legislation; on the other hand, according to its self-conception as a secular state, the Federal Republic cannot discriminate against other religions like Islam to the benefit of Christianity. The German constitution provides that state and church are separate, even though this separation does not prevent cooperation between religious communities and the state. However, the state cannot identify with one religion or religious community (Muckel and Tillmanns 2008).

Authors in this thematic field discuss legal concepts such as religious freedom and religio-ideological neutrality of the state, and assess the legal situation concerning

---

[22] The subfield within public law that engages most with the presence of Islam, was for a long time referred to as 'state-church law' (*Staatskirchenrecht*) but facing growing religious pluralism is increasingly called 'constitutional law of religion' (*Religionsverfassungsrecht*) (Muckel 2008; Oebbecke 2008).

different issues related to Islam and Muslim life in the country. Several topics reappear regularly in these reflections: the Muslim headscarf of teachers in public schools, co-educative sport and swimming classes, the call for prayer, halal slaughtering, Islamic religious instruction according to article 7 of the *Grundgesetz*, Islamic burials (Gartner 2006), and last but not least, a series of questions regarding the establishment of chairs and faculties for Islamic theology (like how to involve Islamic associations or where to set limitations for the content of the subject; Janke 2005, Salama 2010). Most of the texts in the field of legal studies suggest possible accommodations of Islam according to the constitutional structure. In several cases political actors embraced these suggestions, which led to the introduction of religious instruction in schools, to modifications in the burial regulations, and to the establishment of chairs and faculties for Islamic theology. In contrast to those in other countries, Muslims in Germany have not requested the introduction of Islamic arbitration courts. This could be one of the reasons for the absence of a debate on shariah courts in German legal studies.

## Governmental Politics towards Islam

Closely aligned with the work of their legal studies colleagues, political scientists have been analysing and comparing existing laws, and their underlying concepts and legal norms, concerning the accommodation of Islam in Germany and other Western European countries, like France and Great Britain. Matthias Koenig provides a comparison of state–church relations in which he explains the German notion of religion as a component of the public sphere that results in religious organizations being invested with public or state functions. Koenig argues that the state's public policy regarding religion is mainly concerned with regulating the public functions of corporative religious communities, through the *Staatskirchenrecht* (state–church law) that emerged in the Weimar Republic and was further developed in the Federal Republic of Germany. It sets up the rules for the selective cooperation between the state and the churches, as well as the criteria for religious communities to achieve the status of 'corporations of public law' (*Körperschaften des öffentlichen Rechts*) (Koenig 2005: 224–5). In the political dimension Koenig identifies 'a strong influence of the two Christian churches in the public arena, notably in the field of public policies vis-à-vis religious minorities' (Koenig 2005: 225). Since the 1970s Islamic umbrella organizations have been interested in acquiring the status of a corporation of public law mostly in connection with the aim to establish Islamic religious instruction in public schools that—until recently—met resistance by the administration.

> In the state-corporatist polity, which is characteristic of the German case, incorporation has been controlled by the organizational centre of the state. […] The major obstacles to the development of more pluralistic modes of incorporation were particularistic or ethnic codes of national symbols in Germany, which reinforced the public perception of Islam as an essentially foreign religion. (Koenig 2005: 228)

Beyond the field of legal recognition, politics towards Islam comprise top-down initiatives in which the government explicitly or implicitly addresses Muslims and their organizations.

## Intertwinement of Religion and Integration Politics

In 2006, after a long period without specific state policy towards immigrants' religions, and characterized by regular denials to Islamic organizations requesting formal consultations, Dr Wolfgang Schäuble, the Federal Minister for Interior Affairs initiated not only a long-term communication process but a shift in policy towards Islam by convening the German Islam Conference (DIK). It appears that two insights were necessary for this development: first, to accept that Muslim immigrants and their descendants would stay in the country for good, and second, that a considerable percentage of these immigrants were Muslims, who claimed their legitimate right to religious practice and recognition as a religious community.

Researchers have shown great interest in analysing Islam politics on the national level—especially with regard to the DIK—(Brunn 2013; Rohe 2012; Tezcan 2008, 2011, 2012; Amir-Moazami 2009, 2011a, 2011b; Peter 2010) and, even though to a much lesser extent, on the states (*Länder*) and communal levels (Halm 2008; Meyer and Schubert 2011; Eschweiler 2012). Some of the descriptive studies in this field leave intact the dominant political framing of Muslims as immigrants and mosque associations as migrant organizations that will then be *naturally* addressed by integration measures and by religion policies. A number of scholars, however, describe the paradigmatic state politics towards Islam under the Christian-Democratic leadership, as becoming narrowly intertwined with or understood as a part of integration politics (Peter 2010; Tezcan 2012; Brunn 2013: 245–7). In fact, communication with representatives of Islam is not included in religion politics, in contrast to that of its Christian and Jewish counterparts (Spielhaus 2013).

Current politics towards Islam in Germany can therefore be understood as a continuation of the former immigration policy (*Ausländerpolitik*) framed in a new terminology. This new interior Islam policy, hence, follows the paradigm of integration that constructs and addresses immigrants as Muslims (Peter 2010: 119) and Muslims as immigrants (Spielhaus 2012). Contrary to Christian—and other—immigrants, Muslims are perpetually constructed as potentially disintegrated and not fully belonging. Whether religious or not and whether migrants or descendants of immigrants or not, Muslims are approached as potentially in need of integration. As Peter argues, the state combines the recognition of Islam as part of Germany, with the 'project of normalizing Muslim immigrants' (Peter 2010: 119).

> Tolerance asserts the fundamental difference of Muslims and, combined with the variously defined injunction to normalize, results in the natural placement of Muslims at the margins of the national community. (Peter 2010: 119)

This strategy is innovative insofar as it claims to recognize Islam as a part of Germany, and hence displays an inclusive approach. Levent Tezcan, a German sociologist, characterizes the counter-effects of the current governmental concept of integration as both culturalizing and separating the objects of this policy while always keeping the group of those in need of integration in existence (Tezcan 2011: 375). Islam became a very relevant sub-theme of the discourse on integration and migration that has become a fundamental political question of the federal German government under Chancellor Merkel (Brunn 2013).

Several researchers found Foucault's theory of governmentality useful in discussing specific formations of dialogue with Islam or Muslims, like the Islam Conference. Schirin Amir-Moazami describes the initiative of the Federal Interior Ministry as a 'governmental technique which aims at reshaping Muslims according to secular/liberal norms'. She argues that despite the best of intentions to be inclusive, this state-initiated dialogue contains structural deficiencies, which lead to exclusionary mechanisms like one-sided agenda-setting and invitation policy (see also Peter 2010) and the 'process of publishing and recording of the "jointly" achieved results, which are more or less exclusively controlled and screened by representatives of the state, and are largely self-justifying in nature' (Amir-Moazami 2011a: 2). With her analysis of the discussion on Islam and women Amir-Moazami critiques the pedagogical approach of the DIK as a tool of the modern state. It presents as the core problem that Muslims can adapt to existing gender norms *only* with great difficulties and therefore must be disciplined or educated. Here, domestic violence, sham marriages, and the need of immigrants to be subjected to pedagogical measures that would—if necessary by force—acquaint them with liberal values are, rather typically, presented and dealt with as connected. Therefore only, or at least especially, Muslims are portrayed as deficient and needing to be confronted with these subjects, while 'the impression is created that non-Muslims have already absorbed all basic values', including gender equality, in a uniform manner (Amir-Moazami 2011a: 13). Gender equality is just one of several values that Muslims have to commit themselves to before being really welcomed in Germany, as Frank Peter elaborated. The gap separating 'Muslims in Germany' from 'German Muslims' is identified by politicians such as former Interior Minister Schäuble as 'a number of norms which Muslims today do not fulfil sufficiently'. A welcome to the nation can therefore be only conditional 'upon their self-willed normalization' (Peter 2010: 130).

## Surveilling Radicalization

The internal security agency for the protection of constitutional order, *Verfassungsschutz*,[23] publishes a yearly assessment of extremism and a selective

---

[23] The office for the protection of the constitution consists of a federal agency and sixteen regional agencies, one in each German region. Each of them monitors groups and individuals who potentially carry out or promote anti-constitutional activities. The main results of this observation are published

description of the objects of its surveillance. According to this report the agency in 2013 investigated thirty organizations with 43,190 followers (Verfassungsschutz 2014: 205) including the Islamic Community Milli Görüş with 30,000 members, the Muslim Brotherhood Germany, and the Muslim Youth Germany. Continuously the Federal Interior Ministry issues warnings and reports on the risk of Islamic terrorism and threats of terrorist attacks on German soil. The participation of the German army in the 'war against terror' in Afghanistan continues to be the major ground for the risk assessment. Most of the radicalization under scrutiny is 'home-grown', with young Muslims who were raised or born in Germany and recent converts to Islam who joined Jihadist movements and travelled into Syria or the border region of Pakistan and Afghanistan to attend training camps. The returnees, especially, are considered potential terrorists (Verfassungsschutz 2014: 196f.).

Besides risk assessments from its intelligence, the Federal Interior Ministry occasionally commissions academic studies with the aim of measuring the possible security risk posed by specific parts of populations. One of these surveys was carried out by researchers with a background in criminology (Brettfeld and Wetzels 2007) and aimed at evaluating radicalization along with integration barriers, especially in order to map political attitudes and milieux of radicalization among Muslims in Germany.[24] The survey investigated attitudes of Muslims in four categories: integration, religious orientation, democracy and the rule of law, and politically/religiously motivated violence. Depending on their answers respondents were placed in one of several clusters in each of these categories. A small minority of 8–12% of respondents shows ambivalence to democracy (*Demokratiedistanz*), with half aligning with what Brettfeld and Wetzels call a 'fundamental religious orientation' that exhibits 'sweeping devaluation of the West'[25] (2007: 493). As a result the authors estimate the potential for an Islamic radicalization among the respondents at about 10–12%. Individual experiences of social exclusion from the German 'host society' (*Aufnahmegesellschaft*) or particular religious orientations, Brettfeld and Wetzels explain, cannot be assumed to be the only or most effective determinants (Brettfeld and Wetzels 2007: 494). Some Muslim respondents with

---

in annual reports. The annual reports enumerate Islamists in terms of whether they are law-abiding, here called 'legalistic Islamists' or violence-prone. In the case of legalistic Islamic organizations the law-abiding nature is not questioned, as Jonathan Laurence explains. They are accused of practising 'social or political self-segregation and/or promoting intolerant attitudes' even if using legal means to create Islamist milieux that finally could serve as fertile grounds for radicalization. The anti-constitutional component of Islamist's agendas, according to the Verfassungsschutz, is their understanding of God as the highest authority instead of the people (Laurence 2007: 14) and of holy texts as instructions for political and social order (Verfassungsschutz 2011: 202f.).

[24] The sample of the survey comprises 1,725 Muslims living in four German cities (Hamburg, Berlin, Cologne, and Augsburg): 970 were interviewed in a standardized telephone survey, 500 written surveys were filled out by 14- to 18-year-old Muslims (additionally 1,553 native non-Muslims and 630 non-Muslims with migrational background) at school, 195 university students mailed their written surveys, and 60 narrative interviews with adult Muslim men who were active in Islamic organizations were carried out.

[25] Translation by R.S.

higher levels of education also show a higher potential for radicalization. The authors explain this in terms of an identification with victims as a result of what some of the respondents perceive to be the collective national and international marginalization of Muslims. Those respondents who had poorer access to education and experienced discrimination and exclusion are categorized as open to radicalization. A third group withdrew into a 'traditional ethnic milieu', insists on external rituals, and distances itself from the receiving society. Correlating these three pockets of respondents with their answers on 'religio-politically' motivated violence leads the authors to estimate that 6% of Muslim respondents would show acceptance for 'religio-political' violence (Brettfeld and Wetzels 2007: 494). However, equating fundamental orientations or strong religiosity with a potential radicalization would be mistaken (Brettfeld and Wetzels 2007: 498).

In an extensive critique Sarah Dornhof evaluates the underlying concepts of the survey. The importance of this research, she argues, lies in its being the first representative survey to collect and analyse detailed quantitative data about the religious and political attitudes of Muslims living in Germany (Dornhof 2009: 76). Dornhof criticizes the study's categories, the vagueness of its variables and their lack of specificity and nuance, especially those evaluating extremist views. Dornhof concludes her assessment by arguing that the survey 'should be understood in the context of the state's need to provide academic support for the targeting of a religious minority' (Dornhof 2009: 82).

While the first study by the Ministry of Interior Affairs was targeting the general Muslim population, another survey focusing on lifeworlds of young Muslims was presented to the public in spring 2012.[26] It was carried out by a large research team that included scholars trained in psychology, sociology, and communication studies. The main question of this survey was: Which criteria can be empirically grounded to evaluate young Muslims on the basis of their attitudes and actions as integrated, radicalized, or extreme Islamist? The survey used the following attitudes as indicators and predictors for potential radicalization: prejudices against 'the West', prejudices against Jews, religious fundamentalism, negative emotions against how 'the West' is dealing with 'the Islamic World', distance from democracy, and acceptance of ideologically founded violence (Frindte et al. 2011: 431, 613). Based on 923 telephone interviews, the study finds a high level of support for integration among 78% of German and 55% of non-German Muslims, with 22% of Muslim respondents emphasizing the wish to stick to their 'background culture'. Muslims, both German and non-German, express prejudices against 'the West', a higher distance from democracy, and higher acceptance of violence as a tool of defence against the threat that is posed by 'the West' than German non-Muslims in the sample (Frindte et al. 2011: 431). Among Muslim respondents aged between 14 and

---

[26] The presentation of this survey has been accompanied by a controversial media debate in which the authors used the media to distance themselves from the way in which the Interior Ministry and the tabloid *BILD* had presented their results. The study used a complex set of methods including a multi-generation case study, telephone survey, an analysis of internet forums, and a media analysis. The quantitative part of the study was carried out in two waves among 923 respondents aged 14–32 including 206 German non-Muslims, 200 German Muslims, and 517 non-German Muslims in 2010 and 2011 (Frindte et al. 2011).

32, a subgroup of 15% among German Muslims and 24% among non-German Muslims can be characterized as 'strictly religious with strong hostility against the West, tendencies to accept violence and without ambitions for integration'. The survey by Frindte and his team concludes that the level of religiosity appears *not* to be connected to perceptions of a conflict between 'the West' and the 'Islamic World' or attitudes towards terrorism (Frindte et al. 2011: 604).

Both surveys commissioned by the Interior Ministry establish a link between failed integration, discrimination, and radicalization.

> When the Muslim community perceives itself as being discriminated and stigmatized by the receiving society, this is on the one hand jeopardizing a positive Muslim identity and sets hurdles for the identification with the receiving culture. This contains the danger of cultural uprooting and loss of identity that thus can increase the probability for radicalization. (Frindte et al. 2011: 646, translation by R.S.)

Both the 2007 and the 2011 surveys find high rates of anti-Muslim attitudes among the non-Muslim respondents and corresponding experiences of exclusion among those Muslims sampled. The surveys also document that exclusion even affected respondents who did not experience direct discrimination. In fact, vicarious experiences of discrimination and collective marginalization of Muslims score higher than personal experiences (Brettfeld and Wetzels 2007: 495f.; Frindte et al. 2011: 180–3). According to the authors of the surveys, exclusion and being denied cultural identity and belonging to both the country of residence and the country of origin, is a more telling indicator for potential radicalization than religiosity by itself (Frindte et al. 2011: 646). Consequently, the two surveys conceptualize integration as a necessary tool of national security. Thus according to this analysis, discrimination must be fought *primarily* to prevent the potential radicalization of migrant populations.

## Political Participation and Activism

Research on political participation of Muslims in Germany focuses mostly on immigrants' national collectives—especially the Turkish one—and perceives inter-religious and inter-cultural dialogue as a form of engagement in civil society (Klinkhammer et al. 2011; Schmid et al. 2008). Gritt Klinkhammer and her colleagues found 270 dialogue initiatives in Germany that include Muslims.[27] While a number of the sixty-four initiatives selected for their sample date back to 1975, most were founded in or after 2001. Klinkhammer et al. observe residual effects from conflicts like the first Gulf War, 9/11, or the German headscarf affair, but also long-range activities in dialogue like the Religions

---

[27] Out of these initiatives 232 were organized with the main or only aim to provide space for dialogue and were therefore included in the survey (Klinkhammer et al. 2011: 6).

for Peace movement.[28] In their analysis it becomes apparent that inter-religious dialogue is increasingly incorporated into and supported by integration measures. Dialogues that began from private initiatives grew into a socio-political task of large public relevance (Klinkhammer et al. 2011: 39–48). Here, religion is first and foremost discussed in terms of its potential benefits for or negative impacts on society, and not in regard to its stabilizing or meaningful functions for individuals. Even though an engagement in inter-religious initiatives might initially be religiously motivated, this kind of dialogue developed into a new segment of participation in civil society (Klinkhammer et al. 2011: 374).

Another field of study is the engagement in official separate forums and bodies that were installed for foreigners and/or Muslims in order to enable parts of population that were excluded from participation in the democratic system as foreign residents like *Ausländerbeiräte* (foreigner's councils), *Migrationsbeiräte* (migration councils), *Islam Foren* (Islam forums), or *Nationaler Integrationsgipfel* (National Integration Summit) and *Deutsche Islamkonferenz* (German Islam Conference). A number of analyses concentrate on different political approaches to accommodation of Islam in Germany like the German Islam Conference (e.g. Amir-Moazami 2009, 2011a, 2011b; Peter 2010; Tezcan 2008, 2011) or inter-religious and inter-cultural dialogue initiatives (Klinkhammer et al. 2011).

Recently, research projects have focused on describing not only the engagement of Islamic organizations but also Muslim individuals' involvement in secular political parties and parliamentary processes. Interestingly individuals who were formerly referred to as immigrant representatives, are now increasingly studied and in some cases also portray themselves as Muslims or of Muslim background (cf. Spielhaus 2010). Information on politically involved individuals of Muslim faith can be found in research on immigrants' political participation (Schönwälder et al. 2011) along with explicit studies on Muslims' participation as political party members in local and national politics. While immigrants' participation in elections is widely studied, the relationship between voting and religious beliefs has not been given much attention.

This means the shift in perception of Turkish and other immigrants has so far not reached this field of study. One reason for this could be that political activists who happen to be Muslims do not present themselves primarily as such. Even political initiatives by Muslim activists tend to downplay any connection to religion, as Maike Didero showed in her writing on the Confederation for Peace and Fairness (BFF). The BFF voters' association ran for parliament in the local elections of the former West German capital Bonn, North Rhine-Westphalia, in 2009. It was the first local voters' association

---

[28] The international organization with the full name World Conference of Religions for Peace (WCRP) was founded in 1970 as a large international coalition of representatives from the world's religions dedicated to promoting peace. Its International Secretariat headquarters is in New York City and it has Regional Conferences in Europe and Asia, and more than seventy-five affiliates at the national level. The first German local unit was founded in 1988; today thirteen local units are united in an umbrella organization.

founded exclusively by Muslims that was registered for the municipal elections in the city. Still, the Confederation insisted on *not* being a Muslim or even an Islamic party but was challenged on this framing. According to Didero, most media articles on the BFF were less concerned with integration, the topic BFF candidates were stressing throughout their election campaign, but highlighted it as a Muslims' party, despite the BFF's intentional lack of reference to religious issues (Didero 2013: 48). Insisting on being just Muslims interested in politics did not work. The harshest opposition came from 'Pro-Bonn', another voter association and spin-off from the anti-mosque movement 'Pro-Köln' (Shooman and Spielhaus 2010). The anti-Muslim tenor of Pro-Bonn's campaign forced the BFF to take a stand on religious issues.

'Foreigners being equated with Muslims and both being perceived as social out-groups, any political organisation which knowingly positions itself with relation to both of these categories needs to be aware of the severe headwinds it will face', as Didero concludes (Didero 2013: 50). The BFF resorted to talking about peace, unity, and social cohesion and was yet accused of contributing to separation and social disintegration. In the 2009 elections the Confederation won two seats in Bonn's city council and the first woman wearing a headscarf entered a German parliament for the BFF. However, the Confederation could not repeat this success on the country level in the 2010 state elections in North Rhine-Westphalia where a merger of the BFF with two other voter associations fell well below the 5% threshold (Didero 2013: 34, 51).

# ISLAMIC THEOLOGY AND PEDAGOGIES

## Islamic Schools and Islamic Instruction in Public Schools

After family reunifications in the 1970s brought children of guest workers to Germany, Islamic organizations demanded to be allowed to offer religious instruction in public schools comparable to that offered by Christian churches and the Jewish community. The only Islamic school in Germany was founded in 1989 and has been—like other confessional private schools—co-funded by the state since 1995. The primary school in the district of Berlin-Kreuzberg mostly serves the local Turkish Muslim community (Niehaus 2010: 193). Berlin was also the first federal state that introduced Islamic instruction in public schools in the late 1990s. Hamburg is running an inter-confessional model of 'religion for all' (*Religion für alle*) under the oversight of the Protestant church. Through cooperation between the state and the respective religious community, several other states are currently carrying out pilot projects to introduce religious instruction as a regular subject in public schools. Therefore attaining legal recognition as a religious community is a major goal of the larger Muslim organizations. This multi-pronged issue touches on the institutionalization of Islam, the relations and communication between the state and its administration and religious organizations, and the education of teachers and the development of the curriculum for religious instruction. Various initiatives to establish Islamic instruction in schools have been supported by academics from pedagogy, as well as legal and Islamic studies (Özdil 1999; Mohr 2006; Kiefer 2005; Dietrich 2006; Reichmuth et al. 2006; Uslucan 2011).

## Islam in Higher Education

In 2010, after examining and evaluating Theology and Religion Studies at universities for three years, the German Council of Science and Humanities, the most important government advisory body that oversees education, published its recommendations (Wissenschaftsrat 2010). A main recommendation was to establish several centres for Islamic theology in different German regions with significant Muslim population, i.e. in Bavaria, Baden-Württemberg, Hessen, Lower Saxony, and North Rhine-Westphalia.

As part of their integration policy, the Federal Ministry of Education and Science (BMBF) established academic programmes in Islamic theology at German universities. The ministry estimates that 2,200 teachers will be needed in order to ensure a comprehensive introduction of Islamic religious education in Germany (Fuess 2007, 2011). Other sources state that up to 4,500 teachers will be needed in the future (Rohe 2012). According to the ministry it will be impossible to provide suitable training for these instructors without an appropriate academic environment which includes the challenging field of Islamic theology (Fuess 2007, 2011). This led to the 2011 decision to fund four centres of Islamic theology in Tübingen, Frankfurt/Gießen, Münster/Osnabrück, and Erlangen-Nürnberg. All four centres aim to train Islamic theological researchers, social workers, educators, and specialized religious scholars, who could become the future staff of mosques and most importantly school teachers. The University of Osnabrück has established a special course for on-the-job training of imams and other mosque employees.

The creation of Islamic Studies Centres in Germany has been met with some scepticism within neighbouring academic fields and also within German Muslim communities. Despite this, Albrecht Fuess, a German researcher of Islamic Studies, marks the support for Islamic theology as a remarkable decision by the German government and foresees long-lasting irreversible impact in the context of European Islamic thought (Fuess 2011).

## Theological Studies

As a result of these developments, normative texts in the field of Islamic theology are currently becoming established as a new genre in German research on Islam. Because the Federal German Ministry of Education and Research decided to support chairs, academic programmes, and research centres in Islamic Studies, Islamic theology is moving from self-publishing to established academic publishing houses and university libraries. Within five years the German government established four centres of learning and knowledge production. Research activities and academic exchanges led to various publications (Ucar 2010; Borchard and Ceylan 2011), the founding of the academic peer-reviewed journal *Zeitschrift für Islamische Studien* (Journal for Islamic Studies), and the *Jahrbuch für islamische Theologie und Religionspädagogik* (Yearbook for Islamic Theology and Religious Education).

One of the challenges in the establishment of new chairs in Islamic theology, philosophy, and pedagogies was that no scholars had been educated in these fields in Germany. Among the sixteen professors who were recruited for these positions, some studied Islamic sciences at Islamic faculties in Egypt or Ankara, while others pursued sociology or oriental studies at German or British faculties. In a few cases, candidates had studied both. Since 2007 Ömer Özsoy, specialist on Qur'an studies and historical-critical reading of the Qur'an, has held the chair in Islamic Theology in Frankfurt. He studied Systematic Theology, Islamic Philosophy, and Islamic Pedagogy at the Divinity Faculty of Ankara University and joined the Department of Oriental Studies at University of Heidelberg for postdoctoral research. Mouhanad Khorchide, the son of Palestinian refugees, came from Saudi Arabia to Austria at the age of 18 and studied sociology. While living in Vienna he earned a degree in Islamic theology at the Islamic Studies College at University of Al Imam Al Ouzai in Lebanon. He fills the chair in Islamic Pedagogy at the University of Münster. His publication, *Islam is Compassion*, in which he stresses every Muslim's duty is to serve human kind instead of focusing on the hereafter, stirred a tense debate among Muslims in Germany (Khorchide 2012). Reza Hajatpour, chair for Systematic Islamic Theology at the University of Erlangen-Nuremberg, studied at the Theological University of Ghom in Iran and then pursued Islamic Studies at Heidelberg. With his philosophical and ethical analysis of the perfect human being in Islamic thinking, which looks at perception, enhancement, and perfectionism of the self in the context of cloning and gene optimization, Hajatpour makes current debates among Persian and Arab scholars accessible to the German audience (Hajatpour 2013). Katajun Amirpur, a German-born former student of Islamic Studies at University of Bonn and of Shi'i Theology in Teheran, became chair in Islamic Theology at the Academy for World Religions of the University of Hamburg in 2011. Based on ideas of contemporary thinkers of Islam (such as Abdolkarim Soroush, Nasr Hamid Abu Zayd, and Amina Wadud) Amirpur puts forward the concept of *jihad* for democracy, freedom, and gender equality in contrast to the prevalent notion of *jihad* against non-believers (Amirpur 2013). It is to be expected that publications and discussions of this kind will increase and that Islamic Studies from an internal perspective will be established within German academia.

# Debates on the Visible Presence of Islam and Attitudes towards Muslims

Reactions to the fairly recent public presence of Islam have inspired qualitative analyses of conflicts and debates as well as large population surveys on the perception of Islam and attitudes towards Muslims. In an early assessment of major debates about Islam the German sociologist Claus Leggewie concludes that Islam is contested when it becomes visible and claims spaces in the public sphere (Leggewie 2001). This has been exemplified through conflicts on clothing and dress codes like the debate on teachers' headscarves (Mahlmann 2003; Amir-Moazami 2007; Berghahn and Rostock 2009). Disputes on the discrimination of pupils, employees, or potential tenants (Peucker 2012), visible mosque buildings and corresponding conflicts, and the representation of Islamic communities within the political sphere further demonstrate these continuing tensions.

While in many cases mosque building projects have found the support of local actors, others have caused severe conflicts, which have in a few cases reached nationwide attention. A project to build new headquarters for the Islamic umbrella organization DITIB in the 'cathedral city' of Cologne in Germany has given rise to street protests and public meetings and aroused public interest beyond the local region in 2008 (Schmitt 2013). At the same time, a project by the Ahmadiyya Muslim Jamaat to construct the first mosque in East Berlin triggered another heated debate that played out in the national press (Lathan 2010: 103).

Conflicts provoked by mosque building projects have been described and analysed by cultural geographers (Büchner 2000; Schmitt 2003, 2012, 2013) and sociologists (Hüttermann 2006, 2011). Some researchers offer a practical guide for resolutions in mosque conflicts (Leggewie et al. 2002), or provide an introduction to the mosque as an institution (Beinhauer-Köhler and Leggewie 2008), while others concentrate on aesthetic and architectural aspects of specific building projects (Kraft 2002).

These mosque building conflicts (Schmitt 2003; Hüttermann 2006, 2011) have revealed that in many towns no relations existed between mosque associations and the local administration before the beginning of such a controversy; instead they are often established during a conflict. Thus these struggles can contribute to an institutional recognition of Islamic associations. Conflicts about public presence and urban visibility of Islam therefore often establish formal relationships between Muslim representatives and local government, even if the building project ultimately fails (Tezcan 2001; Kraft 2002; Häußermann 2006).

## Surveys on Anti-Islamic Attitudes among the German Population

Detailed studies describe an international network of parties and movements that combines anti-Muslim and polemical anti-EU positions. This network is used to exchange images, texts, and themes along with strategies for public debates (Shooman and Spielhaus 2010).[29] Open forums of the web pages *Grüne Pest* (Green Plague) or *Politically*

---

[29] Images of Islam in the public sphere were also studied in representations of Islam in German public service television programmes by examining non-fictional formats such as magazines, talk shows,

*Incorrect* discuss local, national, and international events and developments like mosque buildings, media reports, and violent incidents (e.g. the murder of a Muslim woman in a German courtroom in 2009 (Shooman and Attia 2010) or the massacre by Breivik in Norway in July 2011). Even though the positions and images exchanged on the internet are more extreme, some stereotypes and themes like 'Muslims parasitically feeding off the welfare system', 'the insidious Islamization of Europe', 'the demographic danger of the child bearing Muslims', or the notion of 'backward Islam' make their way into German mainstream media (Widmann 2009; Shooman 2011).[30]

Core media and academic debates on attitudes towards Islam are concerned with the question of whether discussing anti-Muslim sentiments and stereotypes delegitimizes *any* critique of Islam (cf. Schneiders 2010). Frank Peter calls this the 'ever recurring question about how to distinguish between "legitimate criticism of Islam" and what transcends it' (Peter 2012: 346).

## Measuring Anti-Muslim Sentiments and Critique of Islam

Scholars from sociology, psychology, and pedagogies that engage in studies on sentiments, discrimination, and stereotypes are divided over which terms and concepts should be used to describe and analyse these phenomena. Those most frequently used include *Islamophobia* or *Enmity of Islam* (*Islamfeindlichkeit*, Leibold et al. 2011; Zick et al. 2011; Schneiders 2010), *Islamoprejudice* (Imhoff and Recker 2012), *Critique of Islam* (Attia 2010), and *Anti-Muslim Racism* (Attia 2009; Shooman 2011, 2012). A point of contention is whether the issue should be framed as targeting Muslims or targeting Islam. Some authors argue that Islam as a religion should be open for criticism (Imhoff and Recker 2012), while others point out that even this critique can be used to discredit and exclude Muslims; thus the two phenomena cannot easily be separated (Shooman 2012).

The social psychologists Imhoff and Recker distinguish between Islamoprejudice, a negative and closed view of Islam, and secular critique of Islam, which they define as 'unprejudiced but highly critical views' of the religion. Based on this differentiation they designed and tested scales to measure both attitudes in quantitative surveys. From

documentaries, and reportages. The results show that Islam mainly occurs in connection with violence and conflict-driven issues, thus adding to a negative image of Islam and Muslims in Germany (Hafez and Richter 2009).

[30] One such debate was started by an interview of the former Finance Senator of Berlin, Thilo Sarrazin, published in September 2009 in *Lettre International*, a German cultural quarterly. There and in his bestselling book *Germany Does Away with Itself* that appeared in 2010, the member of the executive board of the German Federal Bank (Bundesbank) and of the Social Democratic Party, argues that as a result of lax immigration policies the nation's racial stock is degenerating. Especially Germany's Muslim population, he maintains, is reluctant to integrate, tends to rely more on social services than to be productive, and has lower intelligence than the average. Sarrazin calculates that their population growth may well overwhelm the 'German population' within a couple of generations (Friedrich 2011; Shooman 2011a). For a substantial critique of Sarrazin's use of statistical data concerning immigrants and specific ethnic groups see Foroutan et al. (2010).

their data Imhoff and Recker suggest that Islamoprejudice is highly related to prejudice against Muslims in general but also to ethnic groups like Turks specifically (Imhoff and Recker 2012: 822). Their study aims at providing validated scales for further research. Several large-scale studies, including a long-term study, have been carried out in order to measure anti-Muslim attitudes.

The 2012 survey 'Die Mitte im Umbruch' ('The middle ground on the move') used Imhoff and Recker's tools to measure what they call *Islamfeindschaft* and *Islamkritik* in the German population. Right-wing movements and parties like the National Democratic Party of Germany (NPD) have transferred their enmity from foreignness to Islam and increasingly try to legitimize their racist resentments by making cultural and religious arguments instead of their previous claims of biological backwardness (Häusler 2008). As the authors of this study that regularly measures right-wing extremist attitudes conclude, combinations of both xenophobic and Islamophobic sentiments are used for mobilization, because they are shared by large parts of the population. According to the survey more than half of the 2,415 respondents (57.5%) agree that Islam is 'backward', 56.3% think that Islam is an 'archaic religion'. All in all between 50 and 59% of respondents agree with anti-Islamic statements, while approval ratings of Islam critique are above 60%. Islamophobic sentiments are higher among respondents who face social deprivation than those who are critical of Islam (Decker et al. 2012).

A survey on religious plurality in Europe that compares attitudes towards people of different faiths in the five Western European countries Denmark, France, Germany, the Netherlands, and Portugal concludes that anti-Muslim sentiments in Germany are significantly higher than in the other nation-states. Moreover Muslims are viewed more negatively than Jews, Buddhists, and Hindus. A majority of respondents in Germany has a positive attitude towards followers of the first three religions. Still, compared to Denmark, France, and the Netherlands the differences between those in the German population that take up a negative stance to other faith groups are considerable, amounting to 15–20 percentage points. The stance on Muslims in all countries is more negative than on Buddhists, Hindus, or Jews. In Germany, however, the general opinion is noticeably more critical: 62% of respondents in East Germany and 58% in West Germany state that they have a negative attitude towards Muslims compared to less than 37% in the other West European countries (Pollack et al. 2012).

# Reflections on the Production of Knowledge on Muslims and Islam

Scholars have repeatedly evaluated the status of research on Muslims in Germany. For a long time the main feature of research has been a Turkish bias. Jörn Thielmann recapitulates that 'a complex and very diverse field of religious actors has emerged, covering all kinds of religious orientation and more and more overcoming national, ethnic or linguistic barriers' (Thielmann 2010: 169). Yet, the perception by academics, politicians, and the media does not fully reflect this diversity, he continues. As the largest ethnic group of Muslims in the country, Turks are still considered the most relevant. Thielmann establishes that while studies developed considerably different research issues over the last years, they are still neglecting big parts of Muslim populations in Germany, including religious ideas and concepts.

Since most Muslims of Turkish origin are Sunnis, there is also a concentration on Sunni Muslims and a scarcity in literature on Shi'is, despite their long-term presence in Germany. Another research desideratum concerns the strong intellectual presence of Arab Muslim leaders and German converts, who are in some cases active in supra-national mosque networks, contributing to their relevance far beyond their sheer number. Hence there is a need for more attention to the dynamics of smaller sub-segments of Muslims in the country (Thielmann 2008, 2010), including Arab, Persian, and South-East Asian as well as African Muslims.

Even though anti-Muslim tendencies, attitudes, and sentiments have received considerable attention in recent research, little work has been done on whether and how these excluding and discriminating narratives are taken up by Muslim and non-Muslim actors on the local level, and what their direct or indirect effects are on everyday Muslim life. Nor has it been investigated which positive historical narratives are presented to counter exclusive images of European history as Christian or at least void of Muslim influences.

While in 2003 the sociologist Levent Tezcan observed a lack of quantitative data on Muslims (Tezcan 2003), others call for more qualitative research on non-organized Muslims, often called the silent majority in political debates. For instance Thielmann argues that while less than 20% of the total Muslim population are members of Islamic organizations, the 'unorganized silent majority', which becomes visible in the recent quantitative surveys, has been ignored by qualitative studies. However, in the light of the existing academic literature—both qualitative and more recently quantitative— and the political focus on the 'silent majority' in the struggle over the recognition of Islamic organizations,[31] it seems necessary to enquire whether this observation is correct. Thielmann mentions two notable exceptions—both *not* with a focus on Muslims in Germany—specifically look into 'silent', 'non-organized', or 'ordinary' Muslims (Amiraux 2006; Otterbeck 2007). Yet, especially the early qualitative works that investigated individual religiosity (Karakaşoğlu-Aydın 2000; Klinkhammer 2000; Nökel 2002; Öztürk 2007) generated their samples beyond the spheres of 'organized Islam'. Even

---

[31] The terms 'silent masses' or 'silent majority' are frequently referred to in the political debates about the recognition of Islam in Germany which basically comes down to the request for recognition by particular representatives of Islam in the form of Islamic associations and umbrella organizations. Existing organizations are regularly disqualified from representing the Muslims in the country because of the low membership rate when considering the whole Muslim population. Accordingly the Federal Interior Ministry invited several 'unaffiliated Muslims' to represent those who are not organized at the table of the German Islam Conference (cf. Spielhaus 2011: 710–11; Peter 2010; Tezcan 2012).

though the authors did not present their works in the terms of the later unfolding political negotiations about visibility and representation, most of their respondents were not part of an organized group. Thielmann's critique is taken even further by the Danish scholar Garbi Schmidt. She argues that because of their accessibility, visible and active Muslims have been the focus of qualitative research (cf. Schmidt 2011). This touches upon a crucial methodological question about how to define research frames and where to search for and find Muslim individuals and communities. No matter how much data we manage to collect, this issue continues to be relevant. It points us to a most relevant aspect of research—how the subject of research is imagined and how much of this imagination is constructed within a particular constellation of research and public discourse.

Schmidt cautions us that a focus on the visible, vocal, and devout practitioners risks reinforcing 'political and public understandings of Muslims as particularly (and dangerously) religious' (Schmidt 2011: 1217). However, searching for the 'invisible', 'ordinary' Muslim, even if its intention is to counter stereotypes, also carries the risk of constructing persons of Muslim faith or background as always Muslim, just as Muslim immigrants became immigrant Muslims (Tezcan 2011).

In this regard the collection of (statistical or quantitative) data on Muslims in Germany seems ambivalent: it facilitates Muslim applications for legal status and can also serve to document discrimination. Meanwhile, because it highlights their faith, such academic knowledge production further solidifies the shift in politics and public debates to an understanding of individuals and communities with a background in Muslim majority countries as Muslims. Those marked and categorized as Muslims are viewed in the context of religion regardless of the concrete subject of inquiry. As Brubaker points out, whether consciously or not, this supports the notion that, in the case of Muslims, religion influences all spheres of life (Brubaker 2012: 6).

## Conclusion

In this review of the academic literature of the last decade, we identified a series of major themes in the research on Muslims and Islam in Germany. Besides the established interest in individual religiosity and organizational structures of Islam, a number of studies are engaged in measuring and evaluating integration of immigrant Muslims, and looking at success, denial, hindrances, and obstacles for integration, recently including anti-Muslim attitudes among the population. Furthermore, researchers critically investigate the integration paradigm as well as the configurations of social hierarchies and power structures that produce certain subject positions among both immigrants and Muslims. Another issue is the involvement of academia in public debates on the presence of Muslims in Germany and the formation of 'Muslims' as a socio-demographic category. The demand for data from this particular part of the population has led to a growing number of surveys and opinion polls targeting Muslims. This quantification is part of a broader process in which 'Muslims' have been turned into a highly politicized category. Hence, the polls and surveys hold valuable information, not only about what Muslims think and do, but also about the current social imaginaries of who these Muslims supposedly are.

The dominant research trends and largest surveys on Islam and Muslims in Germany show how the integration paradigm that shapes current state policy towards Islam influences research in the field. Debates on foreigners have been replaced with debates on Islam (Halm 2008; Foroutan 2012; Brunn 2013), and the (often unreflective) merging of immigrant studies with studies on Islam has had a deep impact on knowledge production. Quantifications of people who are now marked and classified as Muslim are hence effectively embedded in political agendas, discourses of governance, and national identity politics.

Apart from filling the research gaps mentioned in this chapter's last paragraph, it appears all the more important to scrutinize theoretical and methodical approaches to Muslim minorities concerning the concepts of Islam and the categories used to designate Muslim individuals and populations. 'Muslim' and 'immigrant' are terms connected to entirely different concepts, one standing for a specific religious affiliation, the other for the crossing of a national border. In current public discourse as well as in research, too often one is taken as the indicator for the other without recognizing differences between the two. However, both terms serve a certain function in *othering* the subjects of debate and research. This chapter therefore advocates that researchers notice overlaps and incongruities between the categories 'Muslim' and 'immigrant' in their descriptions and analysis, and that they operationalize them methodically. In the light of increased funding for surveys of Muslims and the direct commissioning of studies that try to map Muslim populations and evaluate the risk of disintegration and radicalization, it appears challenging for researchers to refrain from perpetuating the integration paradigm and instead reflect on the effects of the dominant conceptualization of Muslims as immigrants.

## References

Agai, B. (2004). *Zwischen Netzwerk und Diskurs. Das Bildungsnetzwerk um Fethullah Gülen (geb. 1938): die flexible Umsetzung modernen islamischen Gedankenguts* [Between Network and Discourse—The Educational Network of Fethullah Gülen (born 1938): A Flexible Implementation of Modern Islamic Thought]. Schenefeld: EB-Verlag.

Albrecht, A. (1995). 'Die Verleihung der Körperschaftsrechte an islamische Vereinigungen', *Kirche und Recht*, 2(1): 25–30.

Amiraux, V. (2006). 'Speaking as a Muslim: Avoiding Religion in French Public Space', in V. Amiraux and G. Jonker (eds.), *Politics of Visibility*. Bielefeld: Transcript, 21–52.

Amir-Moazami, S. (2007). *Politisierte Religion. Der Kopftuchstreit in Deutschland und Frankreich* [Politicized Religion: The Headscarf Controversy in Germany and France]. Bielefeld: Transcript.

Amir-Moazami, S. (2009). 'Die Produktion des Tolerierbaren: Toleranz und seine Grenzen im Kontext der Regulierung von Islam und Geschlecht in Deutschland' [Producing the

Tolerable: Tolerance and its Limits in the Context of Regulaion for Islam and Gender in Germany], in U. Goel, G. Dietze, C. Brunner, and E. Wenzel (eds.), *Kritik des Okzidentalismus. Transdisziplinäre Beiträge zu (Neo-)Orientalismus und Geschlecht* [Critique of Occidentalism: Transdisciplinary Contriutions on (Neo-)Orientalism and Gender]. Bielefeld: Transcript, 151–67.

Amir-Moazami, S. (2011a). 'Dialogue as a Governmental Technique: Managing Gendered Islam in Germany', *Feminist Review*, 98(1): 9–27.

Amir-Moazami, S. (2011b). 'Pitfalls of Consensus-Orientated Dialogue: The German Islam Conference (Deutsche Islam Konferenz)', *Approaching Religion*, 1(1): 2–15.

Amirpur, K. (2013). *Islam neu denken. Der Dschihad für Demokratie, Freiheit und Frauenrechte* [Rethinking Islam: Jihad for Democracy, Freedom and Women's Rights]. München: C. H. Beck Verlag.

Attia, I. (2009). *Die westliche Kultur und ihr Anderes. Zur Dekonstruktion von Orientalismus und antimuslimischem Rassismus* [Western Culture and Her Other: On Deconstructing Orientalism and Anti-Muslim Racism]. Bielefeld: Transcript.

Attia, I. (2010). 'Islamkritik zwischen Orientalismus, Postkolonialismus und Postnationalismus' [Islam Critique between Orientalism, Postcolonialism and Postnationalism], in B. Ucar (ed.), *Die Rolle der Religion im Integrationsprozess. Die deutsche Islamdebatte* [The Role of Religion in the Integration Process: The German Islam Debate]. Frankfurt am Main: Peter Lang, 113–26.

Azzaoui, M. (2011). 'Muslimische Gemeinschaften in Deutschland zwischen Religionspolitik und Religionsverfassungsrecht—Schieflagen und Perspektiven' [Muslim Communities in Germany between Religion Politics and Constitutional Law of Religion—Imbalances and Perspectives], in H. Meyer and K. Schubert (eds.), *Politik und Islam* [Politics and Islam]. Wiesbaden: VS Verlag, 247–76.

Bade, K. J. (1994). *Homo Migrans—Wanderungen aus und nach Deutschland. Erfahrungen und Fragen* [Homo Migrans—Migrations from and to Germany: Experiences and Questions]. Essen: Klartext Verlag.

Bade, K. J. (1996). 'From Emigration Country without Emigration Law to Immigration Country without Immigration Law: German Paradoxes in the Nineteenth und Twentieth Centuries', in G. Fischer (ed.), *Debating Enzensberger: Great Migration and Civil War*. Tübingen: Stauffenburg Verlag, 155–68.

Baer, M. (2013). 'Turk and Jew in Berlin: The First Turkish Migration to Berlin and the Shoah', *Comparative Studies in Society and History*, 55(2): 330–55.

Barskanmaz, C. (2009) 'Das Kopftuch als das Andere. Eine notwendige postkoloniale Kritik des deutschen Rechtsdiskurses' [The Headscarf as the Other: A Necessary Post-Colonial Critique of the German Legal Discourse], in S. Berghahn and P. Rostock (eds), *Der Stoff aus dem Konflikte sind. Debatten um das Kopftuch in Deutschland, Österreich und der Schweiz* [The Material Conflicts Are Made Of: Debates on the Headscarf in Germany, Austria and Switzerland]. Bielefeld: Transcript, 361–92.

Bauknecht, B. R. (2010). 'Zur Geschichte der Muslime in Deutschland vor der Arbeitsmigration' [On the History of Muslims in Germany before Labour Migration], in B. Ucar (ed.), *Die Rolle der Religion im Integrationsprozess. Die deutsche Islamdebatte* [The Role of Religion in the Integration Process: The German Islam Debate]. Frankfurt am Main: Peter Lang, 61–82.

Becher, I. and Y. El-Menouar (2013). *Geschlechterrollen bei Deutschen und Zugewanderern christlicher und muslimischer Religionszugehörigkeit* [Gender Roles among Germans and Immigrants of Christian and Muslim Religious Affiliation]. Nürnberg: Bundesamt für Migration und Flüchtlinge.

Beinhauer-Köhler, B. and C. Leggewie (2008). *Moscheen in Deutschland: religiöse Heimat und gesellschaftliche Herausforderung* [Mosques in Germany: Religious Home and Challenge for Society]. München: Beck.

Bendixsen, S. (2013). *The Religious Identity of Young Muslim Women in Berlin: An Ethnographic Study*. Leiden: Brill.

Bentzin, A., J. E. Dağyeli, A. Durdu, K. Kosnick, and R. Spielhaus (2007). *Islam auf Sendung. Islamische Fernsehsendungen im Offenen Kanal Berlin* [Islam on Air: Islamic TV Broadcastings on the Open Channel Berlin]. Berlin: Dagyeli Verlag.

Berghahn, S. and P. Rostock (eds.) (2009). *Der Stoff, aus dem Konflikte sind. Debatten um das Kopftuch in Deutschland, Österreich und der Schweiz* [The Material Conflicts Are Made Of: Debates on the Headscarf in Germany, Austria and Switzerland]. Bielefeld: Transcript.

Bertelsmann Stiftung (ed.) (2008). *Religion Monitor 2008: Muslim Religiosity in Germany*. Gütersloh: Gütersloher Verlagshaus.

Bodenstein, M. and A. Kreienbrink (eds.) (2010). *Muslim Organisations and the State: European Perspectives*. Nürnberg: Bundesamt für Migration und Flüchtlinge.

Borchard, M. and R. Ceylan (2011). *Imame und Frauen in Moscheen im Integrationsprozess: Gemeindepädagogische Perspektiven* [Imams and Women in Mosques in the Integration Process: Perspectives of Community Pedagogy]. Osnabrück: V&R Unipress.

Brettfeld, K. and P. Wetzels (2007). *Muslime in Deutschland—Integration, Integrationsbarrieren, Religion sowie Einstellungen zu Demokratie, Rechtstaat und politisch-religiös motivierter Gewalt* [Muslims in Germany—Integration Barriers to Integration, Religion and Attitudes towards Democracy, Rule of Law and Politically-Religious Motivated Violence]. Hamburg: Bundesministerium des Innern.

Brown, M. (2000). 'Quantifying the Muslim Population', *International Journal of Social Research Methodology* 3(2): 87–101.

Brubaker, R. (2013). 'Categories of Analysis and Categories of Practice: A Note on the Study of Muslims in European Countries of Immigration', *Ethnic and Racial Studies* 36(1): 37–41.

Brunn, C. (2013). *Religion im Fokus der Integrationspolitik. Ein Vergleich zwischen Deutschland, Frankreich und dem Vereinigten Königreich* [Religion in the Focus of Integration Politics: A Comparison between Germany, France and the United Kingdom]. Wiesbaden: Springer VS.

Bundesamt für Verfassungsschutz (2014). *Verfassungsschutzbericht 2013* [Report of the Federal Office for Protection of the Constitution 2010]. Berlin: Bundesministerium des Innern.

Büchner, H.-J. (2000). 'Die marokkanische Moschee in Dietzenbach im kommunalpolitischen Streit. Ein Beitrag zur geographischen Konfliktforschung' [The Maroccan Mosque in Dietzenbach in a Dispute: A Contribution to Geographic Conflict Studies], in A. Escher (ed.), *Ausländer in Deutschland. Probleme einer transkulturellen Gesellschaft aus geographischer Sicht* [Foreigners in Germany. Problems of a transcultural Society from a geographical Perspective]. Mainz: Herausgegeben von Anton Escher, 53–67.

Cesari, J. (2004). *When Islam and Democracy Meet: Muslims in Europe and in the United States*. New York: Palgrave Macmillan.

Ceylan, R. (2006). *Ethnische Kolonien. Entstehung, Funktion und Wandel am Beispiel türkischer Moscheen und Cafés* [Ethnic Colonies: Emergence, Function and Change Exemplified by Turkish Mosques and Cafés]. Wiesbaden: Verlag für Sozialwissenschaften.

Chbib, R. (2008). 'Heimisch werden in Deutschland: Die religiöse Landschaft der Muslime im Wandel' [Settling in Germany: The Changing Religious Landscape of Muslims], in M. Hero,

V. Krech, and H. Zander (eds.), *Religiöse Vielfalt in Nordrhein-Westfalen* [Religious Plurality in North Rhine-Westphalia]. Paderborn: Schöningh, 125–39.

Cwiklinski, S. (2008). 'Between National and Religious Solidarities: The Tatars in Germany and Poland in the Inter-War Period', in N. Clayer and E. Germain (eds.), *Islam in Inter-War Europe*. London: Hurst, 64–88.

Decker, O., J. Kiess, E. Brähler et al. (2012). *Die Mitte im Umbruch. Rechtsextreme Einstellungen in Deutschland 2012* [Middle Ground on the Move: Right-Wing Attitudes in Germany 2012]. Bonn: Ralf Melzer Verlag.

Deutscher Bundestag (2000). *Islam in Deutschland. Antwort der Bundesregierung auf eine Große Anfrage* [Islam in Germany: Answer of the Federal Government to a Parliamentary Inquiry]. Berlin: Drucksache 14/4530.

Deutscher Bundestag (2007). *Stand der rechtlichen Gleichstellung des Islam in Deutschland. Antwort der Bundesregierung auf eine Große Anfrage* [Status of Legal Equalization of Islam in Germany: Answer of the Federal Government to a Parliamentary Inquiry]. Berlin: Drucksache 16/5033.

Didero, M. (2013). 'Muslim Political Participation in Germany: A Structurationist Approach', in J. S. Nielsen (ed.), *Muslim Political Participation in Europe*. Edinburgh: Edinburgh University Press, 34–60.

Dietrich, M. (2006). *Islamischer Religionsunterricht* [Islamic Religious Instruction]. Frankfurt am Main: Peter Lang.

Dornhof, S. (2009). 'Germany: Constructing a Sociology of Islamist Radicalisation', *Race & Class*, 50(4): 75–82.

Eschweiler, J. (2012). *Towards Voice in the Public Sphere? Deliberation with Muslim Civil Society in Berlin*. Roskilde Universitet.

Färber, A., R. Spielhaus, and B. Binder (2012). 'Von der Präsenz zur Artikulation: islamisches Gemeindeleben in Hamburg und Berlin aus der Perspektive der Stadtforschung' [From Presence to Articulation: Islamic Community Life in Hamburg and Berlin from an Urban Studies Perspective], in J. Pohlan, H. Glasauer, C. Hannemann, and A. Pott (eds.), *Jahrbuch StadtRegion 2011/2012. Schwerpunkt: Stadt und Religion*. Opladen: Barbara Budrich, 61–78.

Foroutan, N. (2012). *Muslimbilder in Deutschland. Wahrnehmungen und Ausgrenzungen in der Integrationsdebatte* [Images of Muslims in Germany: Perceptions and Exclusions of the Integration Debate]. Berlin: Friedrich-Ebert-Stiftung.

Foroutan, N., I. Schäfer, C. Canan, and B. Schwarze (2010). *Sarrazins Thesen. Ein Empirischer Gegenentwurf zu Thilo Sarrazins Thesen zu Muslimen in Deutschland* [An Empirical Counterdraft to Thilo Sarrazin's Theses on Muslims in Germany]. Berlin: Humboldt-Universität zu Berlin.

Fournier, P. and G. Yurdakul (2006). 'Unveiling Distribution: Muslim Women with Headscarves in France and Germany', in M. Bodemann and G. Yurdakul (eds.), *Migration, Citizenship, Ethnos*. New York: Palgrave Macmillan, 167–84.

Frese, H.-L. (2002). *"Den Islam ausleben": Konzepte authentischer Lebensführung junger türkischer Muslime in der Diaspora*. Bielefeld: Transcript.

Friedrich, S. (ed.) (2011). *Rassismus in der Leistungsgesellschaft. Analysen und kritische Perspektiven zu den rassistischen Normalisierungsprozessen der 'Sarrazindebatte'* [Racism in the Performance Society: Analyses and Critical Perspectives on the Racist Processes of Normalization within the 'Sarrazin Debate']. Münster: Edition Assemblage.

Frindte, W., K. Boehnke, H. Kreikenbom, and W. Wagner (2011). *Lebenswelten junger Muslime in Deutschland. Ein sozial- und medienwissenschaftliches System zur Analyse, Bewertung und Prävention islamistischer Radikalisierungsprozesse junger Menschen in Deutschland* [Lifeworlds of Young Muslims in Germany: A Tool for the Analysis, Evaluation and Prevention of Islamist Radicalisation of Young People in Germany]. Berlin: Bundesministerium des Innern.

Frings, D. (2010). *Diskriminierung aufgrund der islamischen Religionszugehörigkeit im Kontext Arbeitsleben—Erkenntnisse, Fragen und Handlungsempfehlungen Diskriminierungen von Musliminnen und Muslimen im Arbeitsleben und das AGG*. Berlin: Antidiskriminierungss telle des Bundes (ADS).

Fuess, A. (2007). 'Islamic Religious Education in Western Europe: Models of Integration and the German Approach', *Journal of Muslim Minority Affairs*, 27(2): 215–39.

Fuess, A. (2011). 'Introducing Islamic Theology at German Universities: Aims and Procedures'. Manuscript of a lecture held at University of Copenhagen, Copenhagen.

Gamper, M. (2011). *Islamischer Feminismus in Deutschland? Religiosität, Identität und Gender in muslimischen Frauenvereinen* [Islamic Feminism in Germany? Religiosity, Identity and Gender in Muslim Women's Associations]. Bielefeld: Transcript.

Gartner, B. (2006). *Der Islam im religionsneutralen Staat* [Islam in the Neutral State]. Frankfurt am Main: Peter Lang.

Goldberg, A., D. Mourinho, and U. Kulke (1996). 'Labour Market Discrimination against Foreign Workers in Germany', *International Migration Papers 7*. Geneva: International Labour Office.

Hafez, K. and C. Richter (2009). 'The Image of Islam in German Public Service Television Programmes', *Journal of Arab and Muslim Media Research* 2(3): 169–81.

Hajatpour, R. (2013). *Vom Gottesentwurf zum Selbstentwurf: Die Idee der Perfektibilität in der islamischen Existenzphilosophie* [From God's Design to Self-Design: The Idea of Perfectibility in Islamic Existentialism]. Freiburg: Verlag Karl Alber.

Halm, D. (2008). *Der Islam als Diskursfeld. Bilder des Islams in Deutschland* [Islam as a Discursive Field: Images of Islam in Germany]. Wiesbaden: VS Verlag.

Halm, D. (2010). 'Muslimische Organisationen in Deutschland—Entwicklung zu einem europäischen Islam?' [Muslim Organizations in Germany: A Development towards a European Islam?], in L. Pries and Z. Sezgin (eds.), *Jenseits von 'Identität und Integration'. Grenzen überspannende Migrantenorganisationen* [Beyond 'Identity and Integration': Migrant Organizations across Boarders]. Wiesbaden: VS Verlag, 295–319.

Halm, D. and M. Sauer (2012). 'Islamisches Gemeindeleben in Deutschland' [Islamic Community Life in Germany], in D. Halm, M. Sauer, J. Schmidt, and A. Stichs (eds.), *Islamisches Gemeindeleben in Deutschland*. Nürnberg: Bundesamt für Migration und Flüchtlinge, 21–154.

Haug, S., S. Müssig, and A. Stichs (2009). *Muslim Life in Germany: A Study Conducted on Behalf of the German Conference on Islam*. Research Report 6. Nürnberg: Federal Office for Migration and Refugees.

Haug, S. et al. (2010). *Muslimisches Leben in Nordrhein-Westfalen* [Muslim Life in North Rhine-Westphalia]. Düsseldorf: Ministerium für Arbeit, Integration und Soziales des Landes Nordrhein-Westfalen.

Häusler, A. (ed.) (2008) *Rechtspopulismus als 'Bürgerbewegung'. Kampagnen gegen Islam und Moscheebau und kommunale Gegenstrategien* [Rightwing Populism as

'Citizens' Movement': Campaigns against Islam and Mosque Building and Communal Counter-Strategies]. Wiesbaden: VS Verlag.

Häußermann, H. (2006). 'Umkämpfte Symbole. Moscheen in der christlichen Stadt. Ein Einwurf' [Contested Symbols: Mosques in the Christian City—An Intervention], in R. Spielhaus and A. Färber (eds.), *Islamisches Gemeindeleben in Berlin* [Islamic Community Life in Berlin]. Berlin: Beauftragter des Berliner Senats für Migration und Integration, 85–7.

Heimbach, M. (2001). *Die Entwicklung der islamischen Gemeinschaft in Deutschland seit 1961* [The Development of Islamic Communities in Germany since 1961]. Berlin: Klaus-Schwarz Publishers.

Heine, P. and R. Spielhaus (2008). 'Sunnis and Shiites in Germany: A Brief Analysis of the Results of the Study by the Bertelsmann Stiftung', in Bertelsmann Stiftung (ed.), *Religion Monitor 2008: Muslim Religiosity in Germany*. Gütersloh: Gütersloher Verlagshaus, 24–31.

Henkel, H. (2008). 'Turkish Islam in Germany: A Problematic Tradition or the Fifth Project of Constitutional Patriotism?', *Journal of Muslim Minority Affairs*, 28(1): 113–23.

Herbert, U. (2001). *Geschichte der Ausländerpolitik in Deutschland. Saisonarbeiter, Zwangsarbeiter, Gastarbeiter, Flüchtlinge* [History of Immigration Policy in Germany: Seasonal Workers, Forced Laborers, Guest-Workers, Refugees]. München: C. H. Beck.

Herzog, M. and G. Jonker (2013). *Körperschaftsstatus für muslimische Ahmadiyya Muslim Jamaat* [Status of a Corporate Body for the Muslim Ahmadiyya Muslim Jamaat]. www.EZIREfau.de. Available at: <http://www.ezire.fau.de/ahmadiyya_k%C3%B6rperschaftsstatus.pdf> [Accessed 24 August 2013].

Hieronymus, A. (2010). *Muslims in Hamburg*. Budapest: Open Society Institute.

Höpp, G. (1994a). 'Der Koran als "Geheime Reichssache". Bruchstücke deutscher Islampolitik zwischen 1938 und 1945' [The Qur'an as a Secret Reich Business: Fragments of German Foreign Policy between 1938 and 1945], in H. Preißler and H. Seiwert (eds.), *Gnosisforschung und Religionsgeschichte*. Marburg: Diagonal-Verlag, 435–46.

Höpp, G. (1994b). 'Muslime unterm Hakenkreuz. Zur Entstehungsgeschichte des Islamischen Zentralinstituts zu Berlin e.V.' [Muslims under the Swastika: Genesis of the Islamic Central Institute Berlin], *Moslemische Revue*, 14(1): 16–27.

Höpp, G. (2004). 'Arab Inmates in German Concentration Camps until the End of World War II', in W. Schwanitz (ed.), *Germany and the Middle East, 1871–1945*. Madrid: Iberoamericana.

Hüttermann, J. (2006). *Das Minarett: zur politischen Kultur des Konflikts um islamische Symbole* [The Minarett: On the Political Culture of Conflict over Islamic Symbols]. Weinheim and München: Juventus.

Hüttermann, J. (2011). 'Moscheekonflikte in der Einwanderungsgesellschaft' [Mosque Conflicts in the Immigration Society], in W. Schiffauer and M. Krüger-Potratz (eds.), *Migrationsreport 2010. Fakten, Analysen, Perspektiven* [Migration Report 2010: Facts, Analyses, Perspectives]. Frankfurt am Main: Campus Verlag, 39–81.

Imhoff, R. and J. Recker (2012). 'Differentiating Islamophobia: Introducing a New Scale to Measure Islamoprejudice and Secular Islam Critique', *Political Psychology*, 33(6): 811–24.

Janke, K. (2005). *Institutionalisierter Islam an staatlichen Hochschulen. Verfassungsfragen islamischer Lehrstühle und Fakultäten* [Institutionalized Islam at State Universities: Constitutional Questions of Islamic Chairs and Faculties]. Frankfurt am Main: Peter Lang.

Jentges, E. (2010). *Die soziale Magie politischer Repräsentation. Charisma und Anerkennung in der Zivilgesellschaft* [Social Magic of political Representation: Charisma and Recognition in Civil Society]. Bielefeld: Transcript.

Jessen, F. and U. von Wilamowitz-Moellendorff (2006). *Das Kopftuch—Entschleierung Eines Symbols?* [The Headscarf: Unveiling a Symbol?]. St. Augustin: Konrad Adenauer Stiftung.

Johansen, B. S. and R. Spielhaus (2014). *Mapping a Decade's Surveys and Opinion Polls among Muslims in Europe*. Copenhagen: University of Copenhagen.

John, B. (2009). 'Rückblick auf die Initiative "Aufruf wider eine Lex Kopftuch"' [Retrospect on the Campaign 'Against a Lex Headscarf'], in S. Berghahn and P. Rostock (eds.), *Der Stoff aus dem Konflikte sind. Debatten um das Kopftuch in Deutschland, Österreich und der Schweiz* [The Material Conflicts Are Made Of: Debates on the Headscarf in Germany, Austria and Switzerland]. Bielefeld: Transcript, 465–72.

Jonker, G. (2002). *Eine Wellenlänge zu Gott. Der 'Verband der Islamischen Kulturzentren' in Europa* [One Wavelength with God: The 'Association of Islamic Cultural Centers' in Europe]. Bielefeld: Transcript.

Jonker, G. (forthcoming 2014). 'In Search of Religious Modernity: Converts to Islam in Inter-War Berlin', in B. Agai, U. Ryad, and M. Sajid (eds.), *Islam in Interwar Europe and Transcultural History*. Leiden: Brill, 2014 (forthcoming).

Jonker, G. and A. Kapphan (eds.) (1999). *Moscheen und islamisches Leben in Berlin* [Mosques and Islamic Life in Berlin]. Berlin: Beauftragte des Berliner Senats für Ausländerfragen.

Jouili, J. (2008). 'Re-fashioning the Self through Religious Knowledge: How Muslim Women become Pious in the German Diaspora', in A. Al-Hamarneh and J. Thielmann (eds.), *Islam and Muslims in Germany*. Leiden: Brill, 465–88.

Jouili, J. and S. Amir-Moazami (2006). 'Knowledge, Empowerment and Religious Authority among Pious Muslim Women in France and Germany', *TheMuslim World*, 97(4): 615–40.

Kaas, L. and C. Manger (2012). 'Ethnic Discrimination in Germany's Labour Market: A Field Experiment', *German Economic Review*, 13(1): 1–20.

Kamp, M. (2008). 'Prayer Leader, Counselor, Teacher, Social Worker, and Public Relations Officer: On the Roles and Functions of Imams in Germany', in A. Al-Hamarneh and J. Thielmann (eds.), *Islam and Muslims in Germany*. Leiden: Brill, 133–60.

Karakaşoğlu-Aydın, Y. (2000). *Muslimische Religiosität und Erziehungsvorstellungen* [Muslim Religiosity and Pedagogical Concepts]. Frankfurt am Main: IKO-Verlag.

Khorchide, M. (2012). *Islam ist Barmherzigkeit. Grundzüge einer modernen Religion* [Islam is Compassion: Basics for a Modern Religion]. Freiburg im Breisgau: Herder.

Kiefer, M. (2005). *Islamkunde in deutscher Sprache in Nordrhein-Westfalen. Kontext, Geschichte, Verlauf und Akzeptanz eines Schulversuchs*. Münster: LIT-Verlag.

Klausen, J. (2005). *The Islamic Challenge: Politics and Religion in Western Europe*. Oxford and New York: Oxford University Press.

Klinkhammer, G. (2000). *Moderne Formen islamischer Lebensführung. Eine qualitativ-empirische Untersuchung zur Religiosität sunnitisch geprägter Türkinnen in Deutschland* [Modern Forms of Islamic Conduct: A Qualitative-Empirical Study on the Religiosity of Sunny Turks in Germany]. Marburg: Diagonal Verlag.

Klinkhammer, G., H.-L. Frese, A. Satilmis, and T. Seibert (2011). *Interreligiöse und interkulturelle Dialoge mit MuslimInnen in Deutschland. Eine quantitative und qualitative Studie* [Interreligious and Intercultural Dialogues with Muslims in Germany: A Quantitative and Qualitative Survey]. Bremen: Universität Bremen.

Koch, M. and J. Reinig (2013). *Moscheen und Gebetsräume in Hamburg. Untersuchung der räumlichen Situation*. Hamburg: Schura, DITIB and VIKZ.

Koenig, M. (2005). 'Incorporating Muslim Migrants in Western Nation States: A Comparison of the United Kingdom, France, and Germany', *Identity*, 6(2): 219–34.

Kraft, S. (2002). *Islamische Sakralarchitektur in Deutschland. Eine Untersuchung ausgewählter Moscheeneubauten* [Islamic Sacred Architecture in Germany: A Survey on Selected Mosque Buildings]. Münster: LIT-Verlag.

Kuppinger, P. (2008). 'Mosques in Stuttgart Struggling for Space', *ISIM Review*, 21: 48–9.

Kuppinger, P. (2010). 'Between Islam and Anti-Globalization: Cultural, Political and Religious Debates in the German Muslim Newspaper *Islamische Zeitung*', *Contemporary Islam*, 5(1): 59–79.

Kuppinger, P. (2011). 'Vibrant Mosques: Space, Planning and Informality in Germany', *Built Environment*, 37(1): 78–91.

Kuppinger, P. (2014). 'Mosques and Minarets: Conflict, Participation, and Visibility in German Cities', *Anthropological Quarterly*, 87(3).

Lathan, A. (2010). 'Reform, Glauben und Entwicklung: die Herausforderungen für die Ahmadiyya-Gemeinde' [Reform, Belief and Development: Challenges for the Ahmadiyya Community], in D. Reetz (ed.), *Islam in Europa: Religiöses Leben heute. Ein Portrait ausgewählter islamischer Gruppen und Institutionen* [Islam in Europe: Religious Life Today—A Portait of Selected Islamic Groups and Institutions]. Münster: Waxmann, 79–107.

Laurence, J. (2007). *Islam and Identity in Germany*. Brussels: International Crisis Group.

Leggewie, C. (2001). *Römisches Minarett und deutscher Islam: Wie weit geht der religiöse Pluralismus?* Bad Homburg: Herbert Quandt-Stiftung.

Leggewie, C., A. Joost, and S. Rech (2002). *Der Weg zur Moschee. Eine Handreichung für die Praxis* [The Road to the Mosque: Recommendations for the Practice]. Bad Homburg: Herbert Quandt Stiftung.

Leibold, J., S. Thörner, S. Gosen, and P. Schmidt (2011). 'Mehr oder weniger erwünscht? Entwicklung und Akzeptanz von Vorurteilen gegenüber Muslimen und Juden' [More or Less Unwanted? Development and Acceptance of Hostility against Muslims and Jews], in W. Heitmeyer (ed.), *Deutsche Zustände—Folge 10* [German Conditions, 10th edition]. Frankfurt am Main: Suhrkamp, 177–98.

Lemmen, T. (2000). *Islamische Organisationen in Deutschland* [Islamic Organizations in Germany]. Bonn: Friedrich-Ebert-Stiftung.

Lemmen, T. (2002). *Islamische Vereine und Verbände in Deutschland* [Islamic Associations and Federations in Germany]. Bonn: Friedrich-Ebert-Stiftung.

Mahlmann, M. (2003). 'Religious Tolerance, Pluralistic Society and the Neutrality of the State: The Federal Constitutional Court's Decision in the Headscarf Case', *German Law Journal*, 4(11): 1099–116.

Meyer, H. and K. Schubert (eds.) (2011). *Politik und Islam* [Politics and Islam]. Wiesbaden: VS Verlag.

Mihçiyazgan, U. (1990). *Moscheen türkischer Muslime in Hamburg. Dokumentation zur Herausbildung religiöser Institutionen türkischer Migranten* [Mosques of Turkish Muslims in Hamburg: Documentation of the Development of Religious Institutions of Turkish Migrants]. Hamburg: Behörde für Arbeit, Gesundheit und Soziales der Freien und Hansestadt Hamburg.

Mohr, I.-C. (2006). *Islamischer Religionsunterricht in Europa—Lehrtexte als Instrumente muslimischer Selbstverortung im Vergleich* [Islamic Instruction in Europe: Comparing Curricula as Instruments of Muslim Self-positioning]. Bielefeld: Transcript.

Muckel, S. (ed.) (2008). *Der Islam im öffentlichen Recht des säkularen Verfassungsstaates* [Islam and Public Law of the Secular Constitutional State]. Berlin: Duncker & Humblot.

Muckel, S. and R. Tillmanns (2008). 'Die religionsverfassungsrechtlichen Rahmenbedingungen für den Islam' [The Constitutional Framework for Islam], in S. Muckel (ed.), *Der Islam im öffentlichen Recht des säkularen Verfassungsstaates* [Islam and Public Law of the Secular Constitutional State]. Berlin: Duncker & Humblot, 234–72.

Mühe, N. (2010). *Muslims in Berlin*. New York/ London/Budapest: Open Society Institute.

Niehaus, I. (2010). 'Islamische Schulen in Europa' [Islamic Schools in Europe], in D. Reetz (ed.), *Islam in Europa: Religiöses Leben heute. Ein Portrait ausgewählter islamischer Gruppen und Institutionen* [Islam in Europe: Religiouse Life Today. A Portrait of Selected Islamic Groups and Institutions]. Münster: Waxmann, 191–211.

Nökel, S. (2002). *Die Töchter der Gastarbeiter und der Islam. Zur Soziologie alltagsweltlicher Anerkennungspolitiken. Eine Fallstudie* [The Guest Workers' Daughters and Islam: On the Sociology of Daily Politics of Recognition—A Case Study]. Bielefeld: Transcript.

Oebbecke, J. (2008). 'Der Islam und die Reform des Religionsverfassungsrechts' [Islam and the Reform of Constitutional Law of Religion], *Zeitschrift für Politik*, 55: 49–63.

Open Society Institute (2009). *Muslims in Muslims in Europe: A Report on 11 EU Cities*. Budapest: Open Society Institute.

Otterbeck, J. (2007). 'Growing up with Islam in Sweden: Discussing Islam with Young Adult Muslims', *Forum Bosnæ*, 39(7): 151–65.

Özdil, A.-Ö. (1999). *Aktuelle Debatten zum Islamunterricht in Deutschland: Religionsunterricht* [Contemporary Debates on Islamic Instruction in Germany]. Hamburg: EB-Verlag.

Öztürk, H. (2007) *Wege zur Integration. Lebenswelten muslimischer Jugendlicher in Deutschland* [Ways to Integration: Life Worlds of Muslim Youth in Germany]. Bielefeld: Transcript.

Özyürek, E. (2008) 'Convert Alert: German Muslims and Turkish Christians as Threats to Security in the New Europe', *Comparative Studies in Society and History*, 51(1): 91–116.

Peter, F. (2010). 'Welcoming Muslims into the Nation: Tolerance Politics and Integration Germany', in J. Cesari (ed.), *Muslims in Europe and the United States since 9/11*. London and New York: Routledge, 119–44.

Peter, F. (2012). 'Nation, Narration and Islam: Memory and Governmentality in Germany', *Current Sociology*, 60(3): 338–52.

Peucker, M. (2010). *Diskriminierung aufgrund der islamischen Religionszugehörigkeit im Kontext Arbeitsleben—Erkenntnisse, Fragen und Handlungsempfehlungen. Erkenntnisse der sozialwissenschaftlichen Forschung und Handlungsempfehlungen* [Discrimination on the Basis of Islamic Religion in the Worklife Context: Results, Questions and Recommendations]. Berlin: Antidiskriminierungsstelle des Bundes (ADS).

Peucker, M. (2012). 'Differenz in der Migrationsgesellschaft—ethnische Diskriminierung' [Difference in the Migration Society: Ethnic Discrimination], in M. Matzner (ed.), *Handbuch Migration und Bildung* [Handbook of Migration and Education]. Weinheim: Beltz, 75–88.

Pollack, D., O. Müller, G. Rosta, N. Friedrichs, and A. Yendell (2012). *Grenzen der Toleranz: Wahrnehmung und Akzeptanz religiöser Vielfalt in Europa* [Borders of Tolerance: Perceptions and Aceptance of Religious Diversity in Europe]. Wiesbaden: VS-Verlag für Sozialwissenschaften.

Preckel, C. (2008). 'Philosophers, Freedom Fighters, Pantomimes: South Asian Muslims in Germany', in A. Al-Hamarneh and J. Thielmann (eds.), *Islam and Muslims in Germany*. Leiden: Brill, 299–328.

Reetz, D. (ed.) (2010). *Islam in Europa: Religiöses Leben heute. Ein Portrait ausgewählter islamischer Gruppen und Institutionen* [Islam in Europe: Religious Life Today. A Portrait of Selected Islamic Groups and Institutions]. Münster: Waxmann.

Reichmuth, S., M. Bodenstein, M. Kiefer, and B. Väth (eds.) (2006). *Staatlicher Islamunterricht in Deutschland—Die Modelle in NRW und Niedersachsen im Vergleich* [Islamic Instruction by the State in Germany: Comparing Models in NRW and Lower Saxony]. Münster: Lit Verlag.

Rohe, M. (2008). 'Islamic Norms in Germany and Europe', in A. Al-Hamarneh and J. Thielmann (eds.), *Islam and Muslims in Germany*. Leiden: Brill, 49–81.
Rohe, M. (2011). *Brauche ich Yearbook*, Vol. 3. Wirklich.
Rohe, M. (2012). 'Germany', in J. S. Nielsen, S. Akgönül, A. Alibasic, and E. Racius (eds.), *Yearbook of Muslims in Europe*, vol. 4. Leiden: Brill, 245–68.
Rosenow-Wiliams, K. (2012). *Organizing Muslims and Integrating Islam in Germany: New Developments in the 21st Century*. Leiden: Brill.
Rottmann, S. B. and M. M. Ferree (2008). 'Citizenship and Intersectionality: German Feminist Debates about Headscarf and Antidiscrimination Laws', *Social Politics*, 15(4): 481–513.
Salama, I. (2010). *Muslimische Gemeinschaften in Deutschland—Recht und Rechtswissenschaft im Integrationsprozess* [Muslim Communities in Germany: Law and Jurisprudence in the Integration Process]. Frankfurt am Main: Peter Lang.
Sander, Å. (1997). 'To What Extent is the Swedish Muslim Religious?', in S. Vertovec and C. Peach (eds.), *Islam in Europe: The Politics of Religion and Community*. Basingstoke: Macmillan, 269–89.
Schiffauer, W. (2000). *Die Gottesmänner. Türkische Islamisten in Deutschland. Eine Studie zur Herstellung religiöser Evidenz* [God's Men: Turkish Islamists in Germany—A Study in the Making of Religious Evidence]. Frankfurt am Main: Suhrkamp Verlag.
Schiffauer, W. (2003). 'Muslimische Organisationen und ihr Anspruch auf Repräsentativität: Dogmatisch bedingte Konkurrenz und Streit um Institutionalisierung' [Muslim Organisations and their Claim for Representativity: Domatical Rivalry and the Contention for Institutionalisation], in A. Escudier (ed.), *Der Islam in Europa. Der Umgang mit dem Islam in Frankreich und Deutschland*. Göttingen: Wallstein Verlag, 143–58.
Schiffauer, W. (2008). 'Suspect Subjects: Muslim Migrants and the Security Agencies in Germany', in J. M. Eckert (ed.), *The Social Life of Anti-Terrorism Laws: The War on Terror and the Classification of the 'Dangerous Other'*. Bielefeld: Transcript, 55–78.
Schiffauer, W. (2010). *Nach dem Islamismus. Eine Ethnographie der Islamischen Gemeinschaft Milli Görüş* [After Islamism: An Ethnography of the Islamic Community Milli Görüş]. Berlin: Suhrkamp Verlag.
Schmid, H., A. A. Akca, and K. Barwig (2008). *Gesellschaft gemeinsam gestalten: islamische Vereinigungen als Partner in Baden-Württemberg* [Shaping Society Together: Islamic Associations as Partners in Baden-Württemberg]. Baden-Baden: Nomos Verlagsgesellschaft.
Schmidt, G. (2011). 'Understanding and Approaching Muslim Visibilities: Lessons Learned from a Fieldwork-based Study of Muslims in Copenhagen', *Ethnic and Racial Studies*, 34(7): 1216–29.
Schmidt, J. and A. Stichs (2012). 'Islamische Religionsbedienstete in Deutschland' [Islamic Clerics in Germany], in D. Halm, M. Sauer, J. Schmidt, and A. Stichs (eds.), *Islamisches Gemeindeleben in Deutschland* [Islamic Community Life in Germany]. Nürnberg: Bundesamt für Migration und Flüchtlinge, 157–509.
Schmitt, T. (2003). *Moscheen in Deutschland. Konflikte um ihre Errichtung und Nutzung* [Mosques in Germany: Conflicts over their Construction and Use]. Flensburg: Deutsche Akademie für Landeskunde.
Schmitt, T. (2012). 'Mosque Debates as Space-Related, Intercultural, and Religious Conflicts', in B. Becker-Cantarino (ed.), *Chloé—Beihefte zum Daphnis*, 46: 207–17.
Schmitt, T. (2013). 'Moschee-Konflikte und deutsche Gesellschaft' [Mosque-Conflicts and German Society], in D. Halm and H. Meyer (eds.), *Islam und die deutsche Gesellschaft* [Islam and the German Society]. Wiesbaden: VS Verlag für Sozialwissenschaften, 145–66.

Schneiders, T.-G. (ed.) (2010). *Islamfeindlichkeit—Wenn die Grenzen der Kritik verschwimmen* [Islamophobia: When the Boundaries of Criticism Blur]. Wiesbaden: VS-Verlag für Sozialwissenschaften.

Schönwälder, K., C. Sinanoglu, and D. Volkert (2011). *Vielfalt sucht Rat: Ratsmitglieder mit Migrationshintergrund in deutschen Großstädten* [Diversity Searching for Advice: Councillors with Migration Background in Major German Cities]. Berlin: Heinrich-Böll-Stiftung.

Sen, F. and H. Aydin (2002). *Islam in Deutschland* [Islam in Germany]. München: Beck Verlag.

Senatsverwaltung für Integration, Arbeit und Soziales (ed.) (2007). *Mit Kopftuch außen vor?* [Headscarves Excluded?]. Berlin: Landesstelle Für Gleichbehandlung—Gegen Diskriminierung Berlin.

Seufert, G. (1999). 'Die Türkisch-Islamische Union der türkischen Religionsbehörde (DİTİB). Zwischen Integration und Isolation' [The Turkish-Islamic Union for Religious Affairs (DİTİB): Between Integration and Isolation], in G. Seufert and J. Waardenburg (eds.), *Turkish Islam and Europe/Türkischer Islam und Europa*. Stuttgart: Franz Steiner Verlag, 261–93.

Shooman, Y. (2011). 'Keine Frage des Glaubens. Zur Rassifizierung von "Kultur" und "Religion" im antimuslimischen Rassismus' [Not a Question of Belief: On Racification of 'Culture' and 'Religion' in Anti-Muslim Racism], in S. Friedrich (ed.), *Rassismus in der Leistungsgesellschaft. Analysen und kritische Perspektiven zu den rassistischen Normalisierungsprozessen der 'Sarrazindebatte'* [Racism in the Performance Society: Analyses and Critical Perspectives on the Racist Processes of Normalization within the 'Sarrazin Debate']. Münster: Edition Assemblage, 59–76.

Shooman, Y. (2012). 'Vom äußeren Feind zum Anderen im Inneren—Antimuslimischer Rassismus im Kontext europäischer Migrationsgesellschaften' [From the Exterior Enemy to the Interior *Other*: Anti-Muslim Racism in the Context of European Migration Societies], in K. N. Ha (ed.), *Asiatische Deutsche: Vietnamesische Diaspora and Beyond* [Asian Germans: Vietnamese Diaspora and Beyond]. Berlin: Assoziation A, 305–20.

Shooman, Y. and I. Attia (2010). '"Aus blankem Hass auf Muslime", Zur Rezeption des Mordes an Marwa el-Sherbini in deutschen Printmedien und im deutschsprachigen Internet', *Jahrbuch für Islamophobieforschung. Deutschland—Österreich—Schweiz* 1, 23–46.

Shooman, Y. and R. Spielhaus (2010). 'The Concept of the Muslim Enemy in the Public Discourse', in J. Cesari (ed.), *Muslims in Europe and the United States after 9/11*. London: Routledge, 198–228.

Sökefeld, M. (2008a). 'Difficult Identifications: The Debate on Alevism and Islam in Germany', in J. Thielmann and A. Al-Hamarneh (eds.), *Islam and Muslims in Germany*. Leiden: Brill, 267–95.

Sökefeld, M. (ed.) (2008b). *Aleviten in Deutschland. Identitätsprozesse einer Religionsgemeinschaft in der Diaspora* [Alevites in Germany: Identities of a Religious Community in the Diaspora]. Bielefeld: Transcript.

Spielhaus, R. (2009). 'Interessen vertreten mit vereinter Stimme: Der "Kopftuchstreit" als Impuls für die Institutionalisierung des Islams in Deutschland' [Speaking with One Voice: the 'Headscarf Debate' as an Impulse for the Institutionalization of Islam in Germany], in S. Berghahn and P. Rostock (eds.), *Der Stoff, aus dem Konflikte sind. Debatten um das Kopftuch in Deutschland, Österreich und der Schweiz* [The Material Conflicts Are Made Of: Debates on the Headscarf in Germany, Austria and Switzerland]. Bielefeld: Transcript, 413–36.

Spielhaus, R. (2010). 'Media Making Muslims: The Construction of a Muslim Community in Germany through Media Debate', *Contemporary Islam*, 4(1): 11–27.

Spielhaus, R. (2011a). *Wer ist hier Muslim? Die Entwicklung eines islamischen Bewusstseins in Deutschland zwischen Selbstidentifikation und Fremdzuschreibung* [Who is a Muslim Anyway? The Development of an Islamic Consciousness between Self-Identification and Ascription]. Würzburg: Ergon Verlag.

Spielhaus, R. (2011b). 'Measuring the Muslim: About Statistical Obsessions, Categorizations and the Quantification of Religion', in J. S. Nielsen, S. Akgönül, A. Alibašić, B. Maréchal, and C. Moe (eds.), *Yearbook of Muslims in Europe*, vol. 3. Leiden: Brill, 695–715.

Spielhaus, R. (2012). 'Counter-Measures to Religious Discrimination: The Example of a Local Initiative in Berlin', in F. Ast and B. Duarte (eds.), *Discriminations religieuses en Europe: Droit et pratiques*. Paris: L'Harmattan, 237–54.

Spielhaus, R. (2013). 'Vom Migranten zum Muslim und wieder zurück—Die Vermengung von Integrations- und Islamthemen in Medien, Politik und Forschung' [From Migrant to Muslim and Back Again: The Merging of Integration and Islam Issues in Media, Politics and Research], in H. Meyer and D. Halm (eds.), *Islam und deutsche Gesellschaft* [Islam and German Society]. Wiesbaden: VS-Verlag für Sozialwissenschaften, 169–94.

Spielhaus, R. and A. Färber (2006). *Islamisches Gemeindeleben in Berlin* [Islamic Community Life in Berlin]. Berlin: Beauftragter des Berliner Senats für Migration und Integration.

Statistisches Bundesamt (2011). *Bevölkerung und Erwerbstätigkeit. Bevölkerung mit Migrationshintergrund, Ergebnisse des Mikrozensus 2010* [Population and Employment: Population with Migration Background, Results of the Microcensus 2010]. Wiesbaden: Statistisches Bundesamt.

Statistisches Bundesamt (2013). *Zensus 2011. Ausgewählte Ergebnisse. Tabellenband zur Pressekonferenz am 31. Mai 2013 in Berlin* [2011 Census: Selected Results. Tables for the Press Conference on 13 May 2013 in Berlin]. Wiesbaden: Statistisches Bundesamt.

Steinbach, U. and N. Feindt-Riggers (1997). *Islamische Organisationen in Deutschland: eine aktuelle Bestandsaufnahme und Analyse* [Islamic Organizations in Germany: A Current Inventory and Analysis]. Hamburg: Deutsches Orient-Institut.

Stichs, A. and A. Kreienbrink (2012). 'Die Situation von Muslimen am Arbeitsmarkt. Empirische Grundlagen auf Basis der Daten der Studie "Muslimisches Leben in Deutschland" (MLD)' [The Situation of Muslims at the Job Market: Empirical Facts on the Basis of Data from the Survey 'Muslim Life in Germany' (MLG)]. Manuscript of a paper given at the DIK-Fachtagung 2012, Muslime und Arbeitsmarkt—Vielfalt fördern, Potenziale besser nutzen. <http://www.deutsche-islam-konferenz.de> [Accessed 11 October 2012].

Sunier, T. (2012). Domesticating Islam: Exploring Academic Knowledge Production on Islam and Muslims in European Societies. *Ethnic and Racial Studies* [published online].

Tezcan, L. (2001). 'Kollektive Identitätsbildungsprozesse von Muslimen in öffentlichen Konflikten' [Processes of Collective Identity Formation of Muslims in Public Conflicts], *Journal für Konflikt- und Gewaltforschung*, 3(1): 96–108.

Tezcan, L. (2003). 'Das Islamische in den Studien zu Muslimen in Deutschland' [The Islamic in Studies on Muslims in Germany], *Zeitschrift für Soziologie*, 32(3): 237–61.

Tezcan, L. (2008). 'Govermentality, Pastoral Care and Integration', in A. Al-Hamarneh and J. Thielmann (eds.), *Islam and Muslims in Germany*. Leiden: Brill, 119–32.

Tezcan, L. (2011). 'Der säkulare Muslim: Zur Generierung einer Kategorie im Kontext der Deutschen Islam Konferenz' [The Secular Muslim: On the Genesis of a Category in the Context of the German Islam Conference], in W. Schiffauer and M. Krüger-Potratz (eds.),

*Migrationsreport 2010. Fakten, Analysen, Perspektiven* [Migration Report 2010: Facts, Analyses, Perspectives]. Frankfurt am Main and New York: Campus Verlag, 83–108.

Tezcan, L. (2012). *Das muslimische Subjekt: Verfangen im Dialog der Deutschen Islam Konferenz* [The Muslim Subject: Entangled in the Dialogue of the German Islam Conference]. Konstanz: Konstanz University Press.

Thielmann, J. (2003). 'The Shaping of Islamic Fields in Europe: A Case Study in South-West Germany', in S. Nökel and L. Tezcan (eds.), *Islam and the New Europe: Continuities, Changes, Confrontations. Yearbook of the Sociology of Islam 6*. Bielefeld: Transcript, 152–77.

Thielmann, J. (2008). 'Islam and Muslims in Germany: An Introductory Exploration', in A. Al-Hamarneh and J. Thielmann (eds.), *Islam and Muslims in Germany*. Leiden: Brill, 1–29.

Thielmann, J. (2010). 'The Turkish Bias and Some Blind Spots: Research on Muslims in Germany', in A. Kreienbrink and M. Bodenstein (eds.), *Muslim Organisations and the State: European Perspectives*. Nürnberg: Bundesamt für Migration und Flüchtlinge, 169–95.

Tietze, N. (2001). *Islamische Identitäten. Formen muslimischer Religiosität junger Männer in Deutschland und Frankreich* [Islamic Identities: Forms of Muslim Religiosity among Young Men in Germany and France]. Hamburg: Hamburger Edition.

Ucar, B. (ed.) (2010). *Die Rolle der Religion im Integrationsprozess. Die deutsche Islamdebatte* [The Role of Religion in the Integration Process: The German Islam Debate]. Frankfurt am Main: Peter Lang.

Uslucan, H.-H. (2011). 'Islamischer Religionsunterricht: Ein Impuls zur Integration und religiösen Mündigkeit von Muslimen?' [Islamic Istruction: An Impulse for Integration and Religious Maturity for Muslims?], in P. Graf and B. Ucar (eds.), *Religiöse Bildung im Dialog zwischen Christen und Muslimen* [Religious Education in Dialogue between Christians and Muslims]. Stuttgart: Kohlhammer, 240–57.

Widmann, P. (2009). 'Der Feind kommt aus dem Morgenland. Rechtspopulistische "Islamkritiker" um den Publizisten Hans-Peter Raddatz suchen die Opfergemeinschaft mit den Juden' [The Enemy Comes from the Orient: Right-Wing Populist 'Islam Critiques' around the Publicist Hans-Peter Raddatz Searching for Victimhood with Jews], in W. Benz (ed.), *Jahrbuch für Antisemitismusforschung* [Yearbook for Research on Antisemitism], vol. 17. Berlin: Metropol, 45–68.

Wilpert, C. (1991). 'Migration and Ethnicity in a Non-Immigrant Country: Foreigners in a United Germany', *New Community*, 18(1): 49–62.

Wissenschaftsrat (2010). *Recommendations on the Advancement of Theologies and Sciences concerned with Religions at German Universities*. Köln.

Wohlrab-Sahr, M. (1999). *Konversion zum Islam in Deutschland und den USA* [Conversion to Islam in Germany and the US]. Frankfurt am Main and New York: Campus Verlag.

Yurdakul, G. (2009). *From Guest Workers into Muslims: The Transformation of Turkish Immigrant Associations in Germany*. Newcastle: Cambridge Scholars Press.

Zick, A., B. Küpper, and A. Hövermann (2011). *Die Abwertung der Anderen. Forum Berlin: Eine europäische Zustandsbeschreibung zu Intoleranz, Vorurteilen und Diskriminierung* [Devaluation of the Others: A European Investigation in Intolerance, Prejudice and Discrimination]. Berlin: Friedrich-Ebert-Stiftung.

# CHAPTER 4

# THE NETHERLANDS

MAURITS S. BERGER

## INTRODUCTION

THE study of Islam in the Netherlands goes as far back as the sixteenth century, and in the late nineteenth century the country became especially renowned for its scholarship on Islam in the Dutch colony of Indonesia. The study of Islam and Muslims *in* the Netherlands, however, is of recent date because there has been a significant Muslim presence in the Netherlands only since the 1970s.

A quick overview of both academic and semi-academic literature of the period 1970–90 shows the wide array of aspects of Muslims' lives and problems in the Netherlands that have been addressed, discussed, and studied (see for overviews: Bonjour 2010; van Ooije et al. 1990). These studies include legal matters (divorce, status of imams), religious rituals (circumcision, burial, marriage), religious institutionalization (mosques and youth organizations), the social life of youth (including criminal behaviour) and women, education (instruction in Islam, Islamic schools), the theological differentiations among ethnic as well as religious communities, and social and economic aspects of integration. A corresponding range of disciplines was applied to study these matters: law, sociology (including sociology of religion), theology, and anthropology.

One might say that from the 1970s onwards the studies of Muslims and Islam in the Netherlands covered nearly all aspects of Muslim life. In the 1990s, the field of research merely expanded in volume, but not necessarily in topics. This changed with the turn of the millennium, when the prevailing themes of study, namely multiculturalism and integration, were supplanted by the topics of radicalization, security, and Islam in the public domain.

# From Immigrants to Muslims

## 'Not an Immigration Country'

The first reference to Muslims residing in the Netherlands—that is the Netherlands proper, excluding its colonies Indonesia and Surinam—dates from the late nineteenth century. The census of 1889 mentions forty-nine 'Mohammedans' who had migrated from the Dutch Indies, and until the Second World War their number rose but would never exceed several hundred (Forum 2012). After that, the origins of Muslim migrants stemmed from three sources: the labour force from Turkey and Morocco, postcolonial migrants from Indonesia and Surinam, and refugees and asylum-seekers from Muslim majority countries like Iran, Irak, Afghanistan, Somalia, and Bosnia.

The migration movements, in brief, were as follows.[1] In the 1950s, after the independence of Indonesia, an estimated 300,000 Indonesians and 150,000 Moluccans migrated to the Netherlands, of whom only a small number was Muslim. They established the first (wooden) mosque in the Netherlands in 1951, a brick mosque following suit in 1955. In the 1960s, Dutch factories recruited each year several tens of thousands of labourers ('guest workers') from Turkey and Morocco (Forum 2012). Starting in the late 1970s, their number grew rapidly due to family reunification: the labourers' families joined them and with their settlement in the Netherlands their intention to return to their homelands gradually dissipated (Bonjour 2010). In 1975, the colony of Surinam became independent and 300,000 Surinamese opted to migrate to the Netherlands, an estimated 10% of them being Muslim (Forum 2010a). Finally, by the end of the 1980s, the Netherlands started to receive a growing number of refugees and asylum-seekers from countries such as Afghanistan, Bosnia, Egypt, Iran, Iraq, Pakistan, Somalia, and Sudan.

In 2010, the Netherlands counted 907,000 Muslims, that is, 6% of the total population.[2] This number is expected to rise to an estimated 7.6% in 2050 based on immigration and birth rates (Beer 2007). The majority of Muslims live in urban regions of the western Netherlands, in particular in the large cities of Amsterdam, Rotterdam, and The Hague where in some neighbourhoods they constitute a majority of the population.[3] The Muslims are largely made up of Moroccans (36%) and Turks (37%), with Surinamese, Afghans, and Iraqis numbering 3–4% each. An estimated 13,000 native Dutchmen are converts (1% of all Muslims—Forum 2010a). In 2007, the Netherlands

---

[1] For background studies on immigration to the Netherlands, including that of Muslims, see Amersfoort 1974; Justitiële Verkenningen 1979; Lucassen and Penninx 1995; Muus and Penninx 1991; Obdeijn and Schrover 2008.

[2] Statistics on Muslims in the Netherlands are predominantly produced by two semi-governmental institutions, the Social Cultural Planning office (SCP) and the Central Office for Statistics (CBS). Both institutions also publish elaborate annual reports as well as thematic studies on all issues related to immigrants.

[3] In 2011, non-Western allochthones (that includes Muslims) made up 28% of the Amsterdam population and 37% of Rotterdam's (CBS, 25 May 2011).

had an estimated 475 mosques, most of which are existing buildings converted for that purpose (Oudenhoven 2008). Almost all mosques were established and are being used by specific ethnic communities so that there are few mosques with mixed ethnic congregations, and their sermons are mostly in Arabic or the native language of the respective community.[4]

The Dutch government acknowledged on several occasions that the Netherlands was *effectively* an immigration country,[5] but until the day of this writing has not been willing to develop an overall immigration policy (ACVZ 2008). The literature has been critical about this lack of a coherent immigration policy (e.g. Entzinger 1986). Insofar as such policies existed, they were fragmented into different policies for different target groups (Koolen 2010; Rijkschroeff et al. 2003). For instance, the government felt obliged as part of a Dutch postcolonial responsibility to resettle Indonesians in make-shift camps, but left the Surinamese to their own devices. With regard to the Turkish and Moroccan guest workers, the government was at first involved in practical arrangements regarding recruitment and residence permits, as well as the bringing in of imams.[6] Later, in the late 1970s, when family reunification was well under way, the government developed a policy emphasizing the preservation of language and culture of these communities, but with the aim to facilitate their return. During the 1970s, the government formally identified the following target communities: guest labourers, Surinamese, Antilleans, Moluccans, gypsies, and caravan dwellers), each group embedded in different structures and policies and targeting separate groups of migrants (Koolen 2010).

In the early 1980s it became clear that many of these immigrants were in the Netherlands to stay, and that a comprehensive approach might be needed. This became known as 'integration' and will be discussed in the next section. While the Netherlands witnessed a steady increase of immigration from the 1970s onwards, immigration trends changed in the first decade of the millennium. First, between 2001 and 2005, there was more emigration than immigration, which may be attributed to the new strict anti-immigration policies put in place by the 2002 government.[7] In 2010, on the other hand, the Netherlands received 150,000 immigrants, which was the highest number of annual immigrants ever.[8] However, only 24% of these immigrants were of non-Western origin: the remainder were European citizens (40%) and Dutch people returning from abroad (30%, including a substantial number of non-Western allochthones (see the section on

---

[4] An exception is the 'Polder mosque', established in 2008 by young Muslims of mixed ethnic background with the express purpose to speak in Dutch and focus on the issues typical to Dutch Muslims. It closed in 2010 due to a lack of financial means.

[5] This was stated, for instance, in the cabinet's formal responses to the policy recommendations of the Scientific Council for Government Policy (WRR) in 1979 and 1990.

[6] Since there were no imams in the Netherlands, the Dutch government entered into agreements with Turkey and Morocco allowing for imams to be brought in by the Turkish and Moroccan communities in the Netherlands (Koolen 2009).

[7] CBS, 9 February 2011 press release.

[8] CBS, 9 February 2011 press release. According to the CBS, this number of immigrants is the highest since the first record of immigrants dating from 1865.

Nationality, Ethnicity, and Religion)) with Dutch nationality who had emigrated to their homelands but decided to return to the Netherlands.[9]

## Nationality, Ethnicity, and Religion

Almost all Muslims in the Netherlands hold Dutch nationality, although many also maintain the nationality of their country of origin (often, as in the case of Turkey and Morocco, because this nationality cannot be abandoned by its nationals). Interestingly, the term 'Dutchman' is rarely used in governmental, public, and political vocabularies to distinguish between persons with Dutch nationality and foreigners. This is rooted in a particular Dutch logic in categorizing its nationals and foreigners. Until 1996, the general denominator for migrants was their nationality: one spoke of Moroccans and Turks. When these nationalities distinguished themselves on ethnic grounds, these would be used as well: (Turkish) Kurds, (Moroccan) Berber, (Surinamese) Javanese, Creole, or Hindoustani. However, nationality as an indicator of 'foreignness' lost its meaning due to the high number of naturalizations:[10] between 1975 and 1990, naturalization rose from several thousand to an average of 20,000, then peaked to more than 90,000 in 1996.[11] The government therefore introduced terminology that distinguished between 'autochthone' and 'allochthone' Dutchmen. This needs some elaboration since these terms are relevant when speaking of Muslims in the Netherlands.

'Autochthones' are defined as persons whose parents are both born in the Netherlands, and 'allochthones' as persons of whom at least one parent is born outside the Netherlands.[12] (According to these definitions, by the way, the coming (third) generation of Muslims in the Netherlands will be mostly autochthones. However, it appears that the term allochthone has become equated with being coloured.)

Within the official autochthone/allochthone classification, a further distinction is made between 'Western' and non-Western' allochthones, whereby Western allochthones include Europeans and North Americans, but also Japanese and Indonesian nationals.[13] In 2010, of the total of over 3 million allochthones (19–20% of the total population), more than half was non-Western, and half of this group of non-Western allochthones

---

[9] CBS, 9 February 2011 press release.
[10] Observation made by the government itself: <http://www.nationaalkompas.nl/bevolking/etniciteit/wat-is-etniciteit>.
[11] CBS, 'Naturalisatie populair in jaren negentig', CBS webmagazine, 16 October 2000.
[12] Definitions available on the website of the Central Office for Statistics (CBS): <http://www.cbs.nl/nl-nl/menu/methoden>, under 'begrippen'.
[13] According to the CBS, allochthones from Japan and Indonesia are classified as 'Western allochthone' based 'on their social-economical and social-cultural position [...] This pertains in particular to [predominantly Dutch colonial—MB] persons who have been born in the former [colony of the] Dutch Indies, and employees and their families of Japanese enterprises [in the Netherlands—MB]' (CBS, <http://www.cbs.nl/nl-nl/menu/methoden>, 'begrippen').

was Muslim (CBS 2010b; Forum 2012). The largest national-ethnic communities of Muslims are Turks, Moroccans, and Surinamese.[14]

With the turn of the millennium, the categories of 'Turks' and 'Moroccans' were in public and political discourse gradually replaced with the term 'Muslims' as a singular ethnic-religious category. This terminology, however, disregards the strong national, ethnic, linguistic, and religious diversity among Dutch Muslims. Indeed, in academic literature there is a preference for the term allochthones or to use ethnic and national categories, rather than the term 'Muslims'.

Although the Central Bureau of Statistics (CBS) provides counts of the number of Muslims in the Netherlands, it is the first to acknowledge the difficulty of establishing exact figures since there is no Dutch census based on religion, nor is there any other kind of central registration of Muslims (as opposed to church registers, for instance) (van Herten 2009; Schmeets 2010). Counting 'Muslims' is therefore based on estimates, and this has led to different calculations. In the first decade of the twenty-first century the number of Muslims in the Netherlands was estimated by the CBS to be more than 950,000, based on the calculation of nationalities from Muslim majority countries (Moroccans, Turks, Arabs, and Iranians were therefore all automatically classified as 'Muslim'). In 2007, however, the CBS came up with new calculations that lowered the number of Muslims to 825,000, a decrease of more than 10%. This new calculation was based on methodologies showing that, for instance, many Iraqis and most Syrians were not Muslim but Christian, and that some Muslims, in particular Iranians, did not identify themselves as Muslim (van Herten 2009; Schmeets 2010).

# Multiculturalism

The Netherlands has been known as a country that had embraced multiculturalism. Whereas the equally vague and often undefined notion of integration became the term for government policy, multiculturalism was a model that until 2000 provided the foundation of this policy. The main characteristic of multiculturalism is that residents of foreign origin may retain their own culture and that cultural differences need to be considered and, where possible, addressed and facilitated by the government.[15] For instance, the government enabled the translation of all public health, education, administrative,

---

[14] The Muslim Surinamese originated from Java (Indonesia) and India. In the latter case they would also call themselves 'Hindu' in the ethnic meaning of the word.

[15] The literature on multiculturalism is extensive: e.g. Entzinger 2002; Cliteur and Van den Eeckhout 2001; Duijvendak and Veldboer 2001; Duijvendak and Scholten 2011; Gowricharn 2006; Guadeloupe and de Rooij 2007; van Leeuwen and Tinnevelt 2005; Lucassen and Ruijter 2002; Manenschijn 2003; Mooren et al. 2001; Penninx et al. 1998; Shadid 2009c; Slijper 1999. Several researchers have discussed multiculturalism with specific reference to Islam and Muslim minorities (Phalet et al. 2000; Shadid and Koningsveld 1997; Vermeulen 1997).

and other brochures in several languages, and provided financial support for media, festivals, and organizations for the benefit of minority organizations and communities.

Perhaps the most prominent example of governmental multiculturalist policy was the introduction by the Ministry of Education of the primary school programme 'Education in One's Own Language and Culture' (*Onderwijs in eigen Taal en Cultuur*). For specified hours in the week, specially designed language and culture classes were taught to pupils of foreign (primarily Turkish and Moroccan) origin. In the literature extensive attention is paid to the question of what exactly the 'language' and the 'culture' of the respective ethnic communities are, elaborating the linguistic and ethnic diversities within each community (Driessen et al. 1989; Giesbers and Kroon 1986; Kabdan 1987; Kroon 1987; de Moor 1985; Pels 1991). An issue of debate, for instance, was that most Moroccans in the Netherlands are Berber but nevertheless preferred their children to be taught Arabic even though that was not their mother tongue. The government was criticized by scholars for being unclear in this respect, and also for being unclear as to whether this education programme was a goal in itself, or whether it served ulterior policy purposes such as remigration (Lucassen and Köbben 1992). Even before the programme was introduced, the Scientific Council for Government Policy (WRR) in its 1979 report *Ethnic Minorities* warned that a lower socio-economic status may come to coincide with ethnicity and that the policy of maintaining one's culture may be counterproductive as it would reinforce isolation of ethnic groups.

The rationale of the multiculturalism model was twofold. As a matter of policy, it was initially aimed at expressly maintaining the connection with the country of origin in order to facilitate an easy return (Vermeulen 1997). Multiculturalism was also supportive of minority rights, as it was considered a basic human right to maintain one's culture, and as a consequence it was the government's duty to provide the infrastructure to do so (Penninx et al. 1998; Shadid and Koningsveld 1997; Werkgroep-Waardenburg 1983).

The government took the latter approach in its ambitious 1983 Minority Report (*Minderhedennota*). The government specifically mentions a number of minority groups for which it 'feels a special responsibility because of admission [to the Netherlands] or because of a bond with the Netherlands due to a colonial past'. With the 1983 Report, however, a slight change of policy occurred. The government acknowledged the permanent stay of many of these migrants and advocated a specific minority policy that was still aimed at preserving the identity of these groups, although not for the purpose of an easy return to the homeland, but for the purpose of successful participation in Dutch society. As a result, as the Minority Report stated, Dutch society 'will acquire a lasting multicultural character' (see also Coello 2013; Fermin 1997, 2009a; Rijkschroef et al. 2003).

After a phase of benevolent neglect of immigrants in the 1960s and 1970s, followed by the recognition of their presence on a permanent basis in the 1980s, the 1990s were a period in which the socio-economic problems related to the large number of migrants were identified. This observation was first made by the WRR in its 1989 report *Allochthones Policy* (*Allochthonen beleid*). The main source of concern voiced by this study was the so-called 'immigration surplus', i.e. the presence of more immigrants than were needed by the labour market. The government responded in 1994 with an elaborate policy paper entitled *Integration Policy for Ethnic Minorities* (*De Contourennota integratiebeleid etnische minderheden*) in which it recognized the growing dissatisfaction with the increasing numbers of migrants (by now also referred to as 'allochthones' or 'ethnic minorities', but not yet Muslims) and introduced a nationwide programme called 'multicultural society' to be implemented by an alliance of the Ministries of Interior, Education, and Welfare. This programme maintained the earlier policy of emphasizing cultural identity as a source of empowerment for migrants, but this time focused on the need for acceptance of these migrants and of cultural diversity as such by Dutch public, i.e. the autochthones.

While multiculturalism was embraced on an official level, criticism in public and political discourse swelled, culminating in a public debate triggered by a newspaper article entitled 'The Multicultural Drama'.[16] It argued that multiculturalism as a model had failed, because cultural differences in the Netherlands were a source of problems that needed to be eliminated rather than a praiseworthy fact that was to be embraced. Attention in public and political discourse shifted accordingly from immigrants and allochthones to Muslims, who were now identified as being responsible for their 'failure' to integrate. It was the accusatory tone of the debate rather than the facts that dominated this discourse, as can be illustrated with the parliamentary inquiry of 2004 on integration (Commissie Blok 2004). After extensive research and interviews with key officials from government and civil society, the commission concluded that, apart from some minor issues, the integration of allochthones was in general successful. These findings were received with public and political disdain and rejection, however: the social and political climate had changed and was not receptive anymore to positive facts and comments. From that point on, public and political discourse accused multiculturalism of ignoring or even denying the alleged negative impact of allochthones and in particular Muslims on Dutch society.

While the term 'multiculturalism' gained a pejorative meaning, several scholars in the social sciences upheld this term as a frame of reference when discussing Dutch society (Fermin 2009a; Gowricharn 2006; Leeuwen and Tinnvelt 2005; Ruijter and Extra 2002; Shadid 2007, 2008, 2009c; Trappenburg and Pellikaan 2003). For them, multiculturalism was a societal fact—i.e. a plurality of cultural diverse communities within Dutch society—rather than an aim or policy. And even the many scholars who preferred concepts like integration as opposed to multiculturalism, retained culture and ethnicity as concepts needed to describe and analyse the pluriformity of Dutch society and its inhabitants.

# INTEGRATION

Integration was a policy term introduced by the government in the 1980s when it became apparent that migrants were in the country to stay, and as such focused at first

---

[16] Paul Scheffer, 'Het multiculturele drama', NRC Handelsblad, 29 January 2000.

primarily on the socio-economic status of the migrants but gradually shifted to their social-cultural status (Fermin 2007; Rijkschroef 2003). While multiculturalism refers mostly to a state of being of a society and how that society should adjust to that state, integration has a more pragmatic orientation as it refers predominantly to specific demands made by immigrants (or from the allochthones, or the Muslims).

While multiculturalism made a silent exit from public discourse with the turn of the millennium, integration remained centre stage, generating a lot of public debate as well as academic studies as to whether the non-Western allochthones—and in particular the Muslims—had successfully integrated into Dutch society, or how such integration should be accomplished (e.g. van der Burg 2009; Dagevos 2001; Dourleijn et al. 2011; Engbersen and Gabriëls 1995; Entzinger 2009; Esveldt and Traudes 2001; Masselman 1993; Prins 2004). These studies pointed at the lack of a clear definition of integration as the main problem in determining its success or failure. A general and useful distinction, however, is between socio-economic and social-cultural indicators of integration, and this distinction will be used to further discuss the research produced on integration.

## Socio-Economic Indicators of Integration

Until the 1990s, both academics and policy-makers defined integration predominantly in terms of empowerment and participation, in particular as enabling people to take advantage of the opportunities available in Dutch society—hence the emphasis on the socio-economical empowerment of allochthones (Beroud 1989). Research and literature accordingly focused primarily on socio-economic indicators, such as education, employment, and the role of discrimination therein (CBS 2010a, 2010b; Commissie Blok 2004; Dagevos 2001; Gijsberts and Dagevos 2009, 2010, 2011; Jenissen and Oudhof 2007; Justitiële Verkenningen 1997, 2013; SCP 2009, 2011; Veenman 1999; WRR 1989, 2001). We will discuss these indicators separately but, before doing so, a few general remarks are in order.

First, the literature mostly takes an ethnic rather than a religious perspective. In other words, one will find very little on socio-economic issues related to 'Muslims', but more on Moroccans and Turks (or Antilleans and Surinamese, for that matter). Religion, therefore, is neither used to identify persons or communities, nor to explain their behaviour in socio-economic terms. Second, with regard to Turks, Moroccans, and Surinamese—who make up the majority of Muslims in the Netherlands—the aforementioned reports and researches draw the overall conclusion that the second generation is doing much better than the first generation in socio-economic terms (except when it comes to crime rates, as we will see in the subsection on Crime), but they still lag behind in comparison to their autochthone peers. This observation will be elaborated further.

However, socio-economic success is clearly not a guarantee for integration, as disenchantment with Dutch society and radicalization occurs predominantly among Muslim youth who are doing fairly well socio-economically (the killer of Theo van

Gogh is a case in point[17]). These are issues typically related to social-*cultural* indicators of integration, which will be discussed under the heading Social-Cultural Indicators of Integration.

*Language and Education*

One of the factors used to measure successful or failed integration was language. It became less and less acceptable for allochthones in shops and the workplace not to speak (proper) Dutch. This pertained in particular to the first generation of allochthones who had no need of language proficiency since they had come to do unskilled labour, mostly in factories, with no intention to stay. For them there was no need or incentive to learn Dutch—indeed, as we saw before, the government provided multicultural language education, in addition to translators and translated brochures when these people required social or healthcare services. The receding acceptance of the Dutch autochthones with the lack of language proficiency was increasingly voiced in political and public debates. This change in attitude was also reflected in court cases: in 1983, the Court of Cassation ruled that an employer had the responsibility to make sure that his or her guest worker employee had understood the written Dutch contract,[18] while ten years later it became standard jurisprudence that it was the responsibility of guest workers who had lived in the Netherlands for considerable time to understand the Dutch instructions of their employer as well as the content of their contract.

Within the context of language proficiency, two interrelated issues have dominated the research agenda of social sciences and education studies: education and segregation. An education gap exists between the first- and second-generation Muslims in the Netherlands: whereas the first generation had often received little education, the second generation is increasingly entering higher education (Dagevos et al. 2003; Gijsberts and Dagevos 2009; CBS 2010a; SCP 2011).[19]

This relative success is not without problems or effort, however, because these students in most instances had to struggle their way through so-called 'segregated' or, more commonly named, 'black' or 'coloured' schools, that is, schools with a large non-Western allochthone student population. In 2010, 8% of all high schools in the Netherlands had a student population of which more than half was non-Western allochthone. In the four largest cities, however, with a much larger allochthone population, this situation

---

[17] Theo van Gogh, a film director and outspoken critic of many issues including Islam, was stabbed to death in 2004 by a young Muslim radical who was born and raised in the Netherlands.

[18] Hoge Raad; 14 January 1983, NJ 1983, 457.

[19] The Social Cultural Planning office (SCP 2011) distinguishes between four levels of education (that, for the sake of clarity, we will call here 'low', 'middle', 'high', 'academic'), and provides the following statstics for the period 1991–2011: in these twenty years, Turkish allochthones increased their academic education from 2 to 10% and lowered their 'low' education from 72 to 38%; Moroccan allochthones increased their academic education from 1 to 13% and lowered their 'low' education from 85 to 42%; Surinames allochthones increased their academic education from 8 to 22% and lowered their 'low' education from 42 to 15%. In this same period, autochthones increased their academic education from 17 to 25% and lowered their 'low' education from 18 to 8%.

applied to almost 50% of all high schools (CBS 2010b). The 'segregated' or 'black' schools pose considerable problems for regular instruction (Dijkstra et al. 2002; Timmerman et al. 2006). The issue is not so much Islam (although Muslims constitute the majority of these 'black' pupils), but the cultural and socio-economic background of the pupils, often combined with insufficient language skills.

This issue generated a substantial amount of literature, mainly from the side of educational studies but also from social sciences. Some of the literature was policy-oriented, discussing the (dis)advantages of forced pupil selection in order to maintain a 'black–white' balance that would preserve the quality of education of all pupils (Ledoux and Felix 2009; Metselaar 2005; Vermeulen 2001). Although some studies promoted forced selection, it has never been put into practice, partly because it was considered not feasible (based, among others, on the results of similar efforts made in the United States), and partly because schools are meant to represent their neighbourhood rather than society at large (this, in turn, referred the question to the municipality and its willingness to adopt a neighbourhood population planning policy, as will be discussed). Some of the literature was more focused on the educational problems themselves, discussing ways and means to enhance the educational level of these schools (Dijkstra et al. 2002; Metselaar 2005; Ledoux and Felix 2009; Valk and Nimwegen 2003). In these studies the issue was once more raised whether the allochthone pupils should be submitted to exclusively Dutch education (including Dutch history and national holidays), or whether religious and cultural factors should be addressed as well. Most literature tended towards the latter, although the question was then debated (but left undecided) as to whether allochthone culture and history was to be an end in itself, or a means to facilitate the Dutch education programme.

## *Labour Market*

As noted, the second generation of Muslims has overall received more higher education than the first generation. However, statistics show a structural higher unemployment rate among non-Western allochthones, including Muslims, than among their autochthone peers. The figures fluctuate with economic changes, of course, but as a general trend the unemployment among non-Western allochthones is two to three times higher than autochthones (CBS 2010a, 2010b; SCP 2009, 2011). For instance, unemployment among autochthones in 2001 was 2.4%, but was 8% among non-Western allochthones, and in 2009 reached 3.9% among autochthones, but was 10.9% among non-Western allochthones (CBS 2010a, 2010b; SCP 2009, 2011). These figures are much higher for youth (both autochthone and allochthone), who are in particular vulnerable to economic recession (CBS 2010a, 2010b; SCP 2009, 2011).

The reasons for the higher unemployment among non-Western allochthones are a source of continuous research by social scientists, in particular with regard to the higher educated allochthones (Dagevos and Roodenburg 1998; Forum 2007, 2010b; Odé and Dagevos 1999). Studies indicated that these allochthones had less chance to get an internship, and remained longer unemployed after graduation than their autochthone peers (Andriessen et al. 2007; Klaver et al. 2005). Among the explanations mentioned for the high unemployment figures are cultural differences in the workplace, a comparative lack of education, but also social and cultural factors such as different attitudes with regard to authority, hierarchy, and social interaction (Dagevos 1998, 2006; Dagevos et al. 2003; Gils 2002; Klaver et al. 2005; Meerman 1999; Veenman 1995, 1997).

In the particular case of Muslims, discrimination is often mentioned as a serious impediment to entering the labour market (Andriessen et al. 2007; Andriessen 2010; Dagevos et al. 2003; Harchaoui and Huinders 2003; Nievers and Andriessen 2010; Zegers de Beijl 2000). It is not entirely clear to what extent such discrimination is based on ethnicity rather than religion. Indeed, discrimination on the basis of ethnicity seems to be more prevalent, as was indicated by a survey conducted in 2010 showing a preference among employers for Turkish and Surinamese employees rather than Moroccan and Antillean (Andriessen 2010). Nevertheless, all mentioned studies point at negative media coverage of Muslims and Islam as one of the factors contributing to discrimination of Turks and Moroccans (see for further discussion the Islamophobia section). The mentioned studies point out that discrimination in particular takes place during the process of recruitment and hiring (such as the rejection of applicants beforehand because of their names, or because they do not fit the profile of the average Dutch applicant who participates in certain sports and has been a member of a student organization). A 2007 study conducted extensive tests in various forms of job applications, demonstrating that 'non-Western allochthones' were significantly less likely to be invited for job interviews (Andriessen et al. 2007).

Some studies have paid particular attention to the need for diversity among employees, and the consequential methods of recruitment that need to be applied to obtain that goal (Kruisbergen and Veld 2002; Olde Monnikhof and Buis 2001; Verheggen and Spangenberg 2001). Little attention, so far, has been paid to allochthone or Muslim entrepreneurs (an exception is Jansen 2003), possibly because there are few: in 2009, only 5.5% of all private entrepreneurs in the Netherlands were of non-Western origin (SCP 2009).

Allochthone women participate less in the labour market than autochthone women do (CBS 2010a, 2010b; SCP 2009, 2011). Interestingly, Moroccan and Surinamese women do better in the labour market than the men of the same ethnic group—as opposed to Turkish women, who are more often unemployed than Turkish men (CBS 2010b; SCP 2009). An explanation offered by qualitative research is that Surinamese and especially Moroccan men are not reputed among employers as dedicated workers in less-skilled jobs (Klaver et al. 2005). On the other hand, non-Western allochthone women appear to be suffering from specific health issues such as headaches, depression, and anxiety disorders that often lead to long-term sick leave or other impediments to accessing the labour market (Keizer and Keuzenkamp 2011).

## Crime

The occurrence of domestic violence, honour killings, and female circumcision among Muslims (often among certain ethnic groups, as will be demonstrated in this subsection), and the fact that Moroccan youth dominate crime statistics in the

Netherlands has caused some politicians, in particular of the PVV party[20] (which is outspoken in its anti-Islam position) to make a causal link between Islam and criminal or violent behaviour. This link is generally dismissed by the literature, as will be discussed in the following.

Generally speaking, Dutch criminological and legal-anthropological literature focuses primarily on crimes such as theft, assault, and public violence, while social sciences concentrate on crimes such as domestic violence, honour killings, and female circumcision. While all these acts may be considered crimes, we will discuss them in accordance with these two branches of literature.

With regard to the crimes of theft, assault, and public violence, statistics show that non-Western allochthones are relatively more involved in criminal behaviour than autochthones. The number of non-Western allochthone inmates in Dutch prisons is disproportionately large (approximately 40–50%) compared to its percentage of the general population (approximately 10%). Among these, Moroccans and Surinamese constitute the highest percentage, followed by Turks and Antilleans (CBS 2010b). In addition, allochthones, and in particular Moroccans and Antilleans, are more often arrested for criminal behaviour than autochthones (CBS 2010b; SCP 2009). Most of these persons are unemployed and from a low-income background. On the other hand, non-Western allochthones are more often victims of crime and, correspondingly, also feel less secure than autochthones (Korf and Bovenkerk 2007).

There is extensive Dutch criminological and legal-anthropological literature on the relation between ethnicity and crime. In such studies, a distinction is made between circumstances and ethnic inclinations. With regard to the relatively higher crime rates among non-Western allochthones, the overall conclusion of the literature is that these allochthones are more exposed to factors that contribute to criminal behaviour, like demographic and socio-economic background, but also family structures and circumstances (such as absent fathers, or parents lacking authority). Generally speaking, researchers conclude that these factors are universal and not necessarily culturally determined (Blom et al. 2005; Bovenkerk 2003, 2009; Junger et al. 2001). In other words, being a Moroccan or Turk, let alone being a Muslim, does not make a person prone to criminal behaviour, but their social, economic, and specific circumstances do. On the other hand, researchers have pointed out that, once non-Western allochthones are involved in crime, their preference for certain weapons, and ways of settling conflicts or organizing themselves (gang culture, criminal organizations) can be culture-specific (Blom et al. 2005; Bovenkerk et al. 2003; Dijk and Oppenhuis 2002; Foblets et al. 2004; van Gemert 1998; de Jong 2007; Junger et al. 2001; Willemsen 2007). But this observation, again, is not specific for Muslims; it equally pertains to

---

[20] The Party For Freedom (Partij Voor Vrijheid) was established in 2005 by parliamentarian Geert Wilders who had split off from the liberal party VVD. The party calls its ideology 'new realism' and is very critical of migrants and Islam. In the 2010 elections, it jumped from 9 to 24 seats. See for further details the section on Islamophobia.

national-ethnic communities like the Turks, Morrocans, Chinese, 'Yugoslavians',[21] or Antilleans.

In the discussions on crime and culture, the question has been raised whether cultural factors should play a role in the mitigation of punishments (as has been argued by lawyers in the case of honour crimes committed by Turks, for instance). The answer in the literature has been negative, but cultural factors are taken into consideration by the police in developing tailor-made methods to prevent crime, and by the Justice Department in adopting special programmes for adolescent criminals (Bovenkerk 2009; Forum 2011; Komen 2005; Korf and Bovenkerk 2005; Terlouw 1991). In the case of Moroccan youth, for instance, important aspects of these programmes are the presence of authoritative male figures, strict discipline, and vocational training that leads to a quick and successful entry into the labour market.

With regard to crimes that take place in the private sphere, such as domestic and marital violence, honour crimes, and female circumcision, research is limited in particular because researchers indicate the problem of gaining access to the persons involved in order to acquire data and statistics. The issue of domestic and marital violence was repeatedly raised between 2003 and 2006 by the well-known parliamentarian Ayaan Hirsi Ali, and was taken up by several studies (van Dijk and Oppenhuis 2002; Forum 2011; Willemsen 2007). The earliest study from 2002 estimated that the frequency of *domestic* violence among allochthones is similar to that among autochthones. The later studies (2007, 2011), however, particularly pointed at *honour*-related violence as being very high among non-Western allochthones. This type of violence is mostly directed towards young women who allegedly dishonour their families with their behaviour. In the Turkish community in particular this violence has occasionally manifested itself by means of so-called honour-killings of the persons who are accused of having dishonoured the family (the victims being mostly female family members who were intimately involved with a person who was not approved of by the family—Dagdas and Yandouzi 2006; van Eck 2001; Ermers 2007; Simsek 2002).

In 2006, the Dutch police established the National Centre of Expertise Honour Violence[22] that combines anthropological and criminological research in order to develop methods of registration, recognition, and analysis of honour crimes for police use. One of the findings of this ongoing research is that honour violence appears predominantly among people who are members of close-knit communities that adhere to traditional ways, who are dependent on these communities, and who have a low socio-economic status in society; so far, such violence has been registered in Turkish, Morrocan, Iraqi, and Afghan communities in the Netherlands (Janssen 2008; Janssen and Sanberg 2010a, 2010b).

Another form of crime in the private sphere is female genital mutilation which is reportedly practised primarily by migrants from Somalia and less so—or at least in less

---

[21] People from former Yugoslavia who formed criminal gangs that are known for violent crime.
[22] *Landelijk Expertise Centrum Eer Gerelateerd Geweld (LEC EGG)*, in The Hague.

mutilating forms—among Egyptians, Eritrean, Gambians, and Sudanese (E. Bartels 2004; Bartels and Haaier 1995; Kooijman 2008; Kool et al. 2005; Kwaak et al. 2003). The practice gave rise to several court cases (analysed by Rutten 2010) and became the subject of heated public debate after a 1992 report of the Ministry of Health suggested allowing a symbolic 'non-mutilating' form of infibulation rather than prohibiting it altogether. Since 1993, the law forbids the practice in all its forms and since 2006 it is also forbidden to have the operation take place abroad. No follow-up has been given, however, to Ayaan Hirshi Ali's suggestion for an obligatory annual medical check-up of all Muslim girls as a measure to prevent or diagnose instances of female genital mutilation.

In all mentioned instances—domestic violence, genital mutilation, honour crimes— the research studies indicate that the motivation is cultural rather than Islamic, although the perpetrators (and victims, for that matter) very often conflate the two. As one study remarked, the practice 'may be justified by Islam, but that does not make it an Islamic practice' (Kwaak et al. 2003: 16). For that reason several organizations such as Forum[23] and SPIOR[24] have developed programmes to raise awareness among Muslims about the difference between cultural and religious demands regarding marriage and divorce (e.g. SPIOR 2007; Forum 2011).

## *Burdening the Social Welfare System?*

One of the criticisms of the multiculturalism model was that immigrants had been pampered by the social welfare system and, consequently, their claim on the social welfare system had caused it to be overburdened. The relatively high demand on the social security system by non-Western allochthones was confirmed by a 2009 report issued by the Social Cultural Planning office (SCP), albeit with the specification that this applied predominantly to the first generation, in particular the refugees, on the one hand, and first-generation Turkish and Moroccan labourers declared unfit for work, on the other hand (SCP 2009).

This criticism of an overburdened social system has received little academic attention, partly for practical reasons (data files of various governmental and municipal institutions only became available for large-scale research in the 1990s when they were linked up) and partly because of technical reasons (how does one calculate the costs of migrants?). But the main reason for the lack of such research is moral and political: it is considered highly unethical to put price tags on people or groups of people (van de Beek 2010). Thus, a 1999 study calculating that since 1974, Moroccan and Turkish migrants had cost the state an average 30 billion euros[25] per year (Lakeman 1999) was much criticized, not only because of allegedly faulty calculation parameters, but also because the study was conducted in the first place.

---

[23] Forum Instituut voor Multiculturele Vraagstukken (Institute for Multicultural Matters).
[24] Stichting Platform Islamitische Organsiaties Rijnmond (platform of Islamic organizations in the Rotterdam area).
[25] The report mentions 70 billion guilder, the Dutch currency of the time.

This sensitivity explains the storm of indignation in 2009 when the PVV party demanded to know the financial burden of the 'non-Western allochthones' on the state budget. When the Minister of Interior, who was addressed by the PVV to undertake such a study, declared such calculations unethical and refused to carry them out, the PVV commissioned a study by an independent research organization. The report, published in 2010, concluded, on the one hand, that non-Western allochthones rely more on social welfare and pay less tax than autochthones but, on the other hand, that this is particular to the first-generation allochthones due to their lack of integration and unskilled background (Geest and van der Dietvorst 2010). One of the criticisms of this report was that it only relied on costs incurred by the public sector, and included costs for education (which, according to the critics, could also have been considered investment costs).

## Living Environment

An issue of concern among policy-makers and politicians is the segregation between autochthones and allochthones as manifested in residential distribution. Extensive literature has been published on this topic, mainly from semi-governmental and planning institutions (Dugteren 1993; Feijten and van Ham 2009; Gijsberts and Dagevos 2005; Kullberg and Kulu-Glasgow 2009; Kullberg et al. 2009; Roelandt and Veenman 1989; VROM 2004, 2007), the main findings of which will be discussed in this subsection.

While the Dutch government distributed housing to refugees as well as to migrants from the former colony of Indonesia (thereby making sure they were spread out evenly through the Netherlands), Surinamese and labour migrants had to find their own way. This latter category tended to concentrate in the largest cities in the mid-western region, Rotterdam, Amsterdam, and The Hague, where one-third of the population is now of non-Western origin.[26] In certain quarters, non-Western communities even constitute majorities, sometimes over 90% (CBS 2011 press release). The number of such districts is increasing, mainly because newly arriving migrants tend to settle there. These areas are the poorest neighbourhoods, consisting mainly of cheap 'social' (i.e. destined for low-income families) rental housing. Private ownership of houses among allochthones only occurred in the 1990s and has been increasing ever since but not at the same pace as among the autochthones: in 2009, 60% of Dutch autochthones owned their own house, while this is the case for only 14% of the Moroccans and 26% of the Turks (Dugteren 1993; SCP 2009; Roelandt and Veenman 1989).

As a result of the increasing concentration of non-Western communities in certain areas, autochthone residents began moving out to other places (Dagevos 2009; Feijten and van Ham 2009). This development, referred to as the 'white flight', seems to have decreased over time, however, partly because of the active policy of many municipalities to increase the quality of the living conditions of these neighbourhoods. Examples of such activities are the restoration of entire neighbourhoods, and the mixing of private and rental housing in a single residential area in order to mingle populations of different backgrounds (Dagevos 2009; SCP 2009, 2011).

[26] CBS, 25 May 2011.

In addition, numerous initiatives were undertaken by municipalities to upgrade the social living conditions, such as the promotion of contacts between allochthone and autochthone residents by means of joint festivities, discussions, or courses, and to adopt programmes to deal with young criminals and school dropouts (these initiatives were suggested as well as studied by Bolt and van Kempen 2008; Frissen and Harchaoui 2011; Kullberg and Kulu-Glasgow 2009; Kullberg et al. 2009; SCP 2005; Sohilait and Marinelli 2009). Some of these initiatives included so-called 'multicultural architecture' that tries to accommodate the specific cultural needs of the residents (Labyrinth Onderzoek and Advies 2010). In 2007, the Ministry of Interior provided state funds for these initiatives in the case of forty so-called 'problematic neighbourhoods' targeted for a comprehensive improvement of social, economic, and cultural conditions.

## Social-Cultural Indicators of Integration

As noted already, in matters of integration a distinction can be made between socio-economic and social-cultural factors. Policy-makers and academics had difficulties in identifying and quantifying the social-cultural factors, however, resulting in the development of concepts like social cohesion, citizenship, and the untranslatable term *inburgering* (meaning the process of becoming an integrated citizen). These concepts combined notions of commitment to Dutch society, shared values, and national allegiance.

### *Municipalities and Social Cohesion*

Municipalities, especially the larger ones, played an important role in matters of social-cultural integration. They traditionally hold considerable autonomous powers and budgets to determine their own policies, which is why they are also known as 'lower governments' as opposed to the central government. For example, after 9/11 and especially after the murder of Theo van Gogh in 2004, the municipalities rather than the Ministry of Interior took the lead in addressing the issues at hand. In doing so, most municipalities with large non-Western allochthone communities developed extensive social, economic, and cultural policies that were tailor-made to the cultural composition and needs of their particular municipality. The overriding purpose was to maintain or create some sort of social cohesion within the municipality. The diversity and plurality of the municipal populations became the centre of attention, but the way these issues were addressed differed per municipality. This may be illustrated with the titles of the municipal policy papers that were published during this period. The city of Amsterdam, for instance, emphatically omitted any reference to differences but focused on what unites its citizens (its 2004 policy plan was entitled 'We, Amsterdammers'), while the city of Rotterdam clearly felt the need to address the differences head-on (its 2004 policy plan was entitled 'Participate or Stay Behind'). Other large cities considered the diversity of their population as a source of strength rather than division, as is demonstrated by the titles of their policy plans: 'The Strength of Differences' (Utrecht, 2004) and 'Participating in Diversity' (Breda 2005). The various policies of social cohesion will be elaborated here.

In developing policies particularly related to Islam and issues like integration, citizenship, social cohesion, and related topics, municipalities often approached academics as advisers and instructors at workshops or commissioned them to draft policy-oriented reports. Much literature generated by these academics was therefore written in a user-friendly manner, such as booklets containing backgrounds to debating sessions,[27] or manuals for civil servants (e.g. Berger 2008; van der Heijden 2009). On the other hand, some researchers also published academic analyses of the topical and complex matters at hand, such as the meanings and characteristics of social cohesion (e.g. Bochove et al. 2009; Hart et al. 2008; Klop 2010; Lucassen and de Ruijter 2002) and the particular role of Islam in this (e.g. Maussen 2006). The two largest cities, Amsterdam and Rotterdam, were particularly active in this respect, attracting many academics as advisers, the most famous being Tariq Ramadan who was appointed by the municipality of Rotterdam as senior adviser on integration between 2007 and 2009 (we will discuss the effects of these policies further).

## *Identity*

The policy-oriented focus on social cohesion rekindled the interest of both policy-makers and researchers in culture and intercultural communication, which had previously dominated the research on multiculturalism. But this time there was a particular interest in the notion of identity, and more specifically on the question of how people can unify and bond regardless of their different identities, be it in the workplace, on the street, at school, in neighbourhoods, or as Dutch people in general.

Identity became a popular subject of research for social scientists and historians, first with regard to Muslims, but increasingly also with regard to the Dutch autochthones. We will discuss the issue of Muslims' identity in the next section, but will briefly address the issue of Dutch identity here. The interest in this topic can perhaps be interpreted as a reaction to the general demand for Muslims to integrate in Dutch society. Because if allochthones, and in particular Muslims, must adapt to Dutch culture and become part of the Netherlands, as the new policies and public debates demanded, what is it that they have to adapt to? The question in the public debate shifted, if only temporarily, from 'who are they?' to 'who are we?' Consequently, much academic effort focused on Dutch culture, history, and identity. In addition to the many—and very popular—monographs, biographies, and 'ego-documents'[28] on various aspects of Dutch history

---

[27] A year of debates and workshops organized by the municipality of Rotterdam between 2003 and 2004 in which several academics participated culminated in a publication titled *Sociale Integratie... en de islam in Rotterdam* (*Social Integration... and the Islam in Rotterdam*) that consisted of five volumes (1. *Islam in Rotterdam*, 2. *Zo denken ze er over*, 3. *Zo zijn de spelregels*, 4. *Zo informeerden wij elkaar*, 5. *Rotterdam Mozaiek*), published by the municipality of Rotterdam (Projectbureau Sociale Integratie) in 2004.

[28] Very popular were chronicles written by authors about their own families in which family narratives and archives were interwoven with the historical context (the most prominent and successful example being Geert Mak's *De Eeuw van mijn Vader*—'My Father's Century').

and historical personae, the political arena also took an interest in Dutch identity. In 2004, a culture and history test ('inburgeringstest') was made obligatory for all residents of foreign origin, and family members or spouses living abroad had to pass this test at the nearest Dutch embassy in order to be allowed admittance to the Netherlands (e.g. Gowricharn and Nolen 2004).[29] In 2006, a 'canon' of milestones in Dutch history was developed by historians and subsequently officially introduced into the Dutch education system in 2009 (a Museum of National History, endorsed by parliament, ultimately failed to be established due to political and financial controversies). In 2007, the WRR issued reports on Dutch identity in which it concluded that identity based on ethnicity and religion is mostly strong and immutable, and that it would be unwise to demand from allochthones an unequivocal choice for a single, Dutch identity: according to the WRR, the Dutch should therefore realize that their identity in most cases is a plural identity (WRR 2007a, 2007b).

The identification of the Dutch autochthones with their own national and cultural identity, however imaginary, proved to be a sensitive issue, in particular when discussed in relation to the Dutch allochthone. An illustrative example is the speech delivered by Princess Maxima—herself an allochthone of Argentinian origin and wife of the then Dutch crown prince—at the presentation in 2007 of the mentioned reports by the WRR on Dutch identity. Her remark that 'a singular' Dutch identity does not exist since it was composed—in her opinion—of so many facets and identities, caused public indignation.

Identity issues were also reflected in the political debates on double nationality, discussed in parliament during the 1990s as a practical problem for young Dutch men of Turkish origin who were called for military service in Turkey. The issue resurfaced in 2004 with several politicians criticizing double nationality as a hindrance to successful integration.[30] Although almost 7% of the Dutch population held double or multiple nationalities in 2011,[31] the discussion mostly focused on the case of non-Western allochthones. In 2011, 60% of the Dutch population was against double nationality, which was perceived as a symbol of double loyalty and, consequently, as a deliberate choice not to be part of Dutch society.[32] These discussions disregarded the legal problem that double nationality often is not a matter of choice by the holders of those nationalities, but is an imposition by the countries of their birth. The legal complexities of double nationality (Hart 2005) were thus connected with the debates on integration and identity. Several legal scholars reflected on this issue (Dagevos 2008; Groot and Vink 2008), as did the WRR in its 2007 report 'Identifying with the Netherlands', in which it criticized the use of nationality in political and policy terms (WRR 2007a).

---

[29] It appears that quite a few native Dutch people who took the test for fun, failed it.
[30] See parliamentarian documents under search term 'dubbele nationaliteit' at <https://zoek.officielebekendmakingen.nl>.
[31] CBS, 2 May 2011, press release.
[32] CBS, 2 May 2011, press release.

## Shared Values

Parallel to the public debate on Dutch identity, a discussion developed on Dutch (or Western) values. The government took the initiative of publishing several papers elaborating the values that were considered central to Dutch society (BZK 2004; Commissie Uitdragen Kernwaarden van de Rechtstaat 2008). These reports defined core Dutch values as 'freedom, solidarity, and equality'. Between 2004 and 2010, these values became the standard rebuttal by the government of politicians (mainly of the PVV and orthodox-Christian parties) who denounced certain practices by Dutch Muslims as contrary to what they considered the 'Jewish-Christian values' of Dutch society. Examples of such criticized behaviour was the refusal to shake hands with the opposite sex, the insistence on wearing Islamic attire at work, and the claim that one or more national holidays should be Islamic festive days.

The proclaiming of these political and legal values (which were in fact a rephrasing of fundamental rights) never made an impact on public or political discourse, however. This discourse remained dominated by those advocating the upholding of Dutch cultural values. The difference between political-legal values, on the one hand, and cultural values, on the other, reflected the two basic positions that were taken on the issue of integration. Those propagating political and legal values advocate personal freedom and allow for religious and cultural freedoms, and consequently restrict the demand for integration to the socio-economic domain. Those propagating cultural values, on the other hand, demand subjugation to a single Dutch culture and therewith expand the need for integration to the social-cultural domain. The supporters of this position are willing to restrict personal freedoms in order to safeguard social cohesion and the integrity of the nation (Fermin 2007; Rijkschroef 2003). It is clear that with the turn of the millennium, the latter gained the upper hand.

# Religion, Secularism, and Public Space

## Dutch Muslims and their Islam

As mentioned before, Islamic studies have been carried out for many years and became a well-established discipline in the Netherlands. Starting in the 1980s, scholars gradually turned their attention to the religious beliefs and practices of Muslim migrants in the Netherlands (Broex 1982; Custers 1985; Koningsveld and Shadid 1997; Moslim Informatiecentrum 1980; Shadid and van Koningsveld 1992). The focus of interest at first was predominantly Islam in general (Jansen 1987; Koningsveld 1982), and the ways it was being practised by the Muslims in the Netherlands (e.g. Waardenburg 1983; Landman 1992). Some literature provided guidance on how this new religion needed to be instructed in schools (Wagtendonk 1987; Esch and Roovers 1987). In the 1990s, a tradition of anthropological and ethnographic research developed concerning the

Muslims' experiences of their religion and religious identity (Andree et al. 1990; Brons 1990; Sunier 1996, 1997; Dessing 2001). We will elaborate their findings here.

When at the turn of the millennium public and political debate regarding integration focused on Muslims, academic research rose to the challenge in order to answer basic questions such as: Who are the Muslims?, What do they want?, and What is the role of Islam in their life? This research into the praxis of Islam was soon to dominate the study of Islam in the Netherlands, resulting in studies on a diversity of issues, such as religion and culture (Buitelaar 2006; Buijs 2009; Phalet and van der Wall 2004), Muslim youth (Bartels 2000; van der Heijden 2009; Pels et al. 2006a; Korf et al. 2007, 2008; Nabben et al. 2006; Pels and Lahri 2008; Phalet et al. 2000), mosque architecture (Roose 2009), female circumcision (Aalst 2002; Bartels 2004), choice of marriage partners (Hooghiemstra 2003; de Koning and Bartels 2005), the headscarf (Moors 2009a; Motivaction 2011), homosexuality (Nahas 2005), psychological problems (Hoffer 2009), burial (Kadrouch-Outmany 2014), use of multi-media (Konijn et al. 2010), and upbringing (Pels and Gruijter 2005). In a later stage many studies appeared on radicalization and orthodox trends among young Muslims (see the subsection Radicalism under the heading Security and Terrorism).

## *Muslims' Identities*

The aforementioned studies show a clear divide between the first and second generation of Muslims in the Netherlands in their relation to Islam (in the case of the Indonesians, one must add the third generation since they arrived earlier). The first generation identifies mainly with ethnicity and nationality and to them Islam has mostly cultural value. The second generation, on the other hand, identifies less with ethnicity or nationality, but much more with Islam, both as a religion and as an identity marker. Indeed, the second generation generally is more pious, to the point of being strict in their observation of the rules of Islam and their search for an authentic or 'pure' Islam (de Koning 2008), that is, an Islam based on its theological sources and devoid of cultural practices (Bartels 2000; Buijs et al. 2006; Buitelaar 2006; Buijs 2009; Korf et al. 2007, 2008; de Koning 2008; Pels and Lahri 2008). However, research shows that the multiple identities of Dutch Muslims—Dutch nationality, ethnicity, religion—are being used interchangeably, depending on the circumstances: the Dutch nationality is often used in conflicts with parents, the ethnic and religious identities to differentiate between the in-group and out-group, and the religious identity also in case of real or perceived loyalty conflicts with the autochthone society (Phalet and van der Wall 2004).

If we combine these observations with the fact that the second generation is socio-economically much better integrated into Dutch society than the first generation, then this divide is a veritable generation gap (Harchaoui 2006). This may also explain the fact that the second generation visits the mosque less than the first generation (Phalet and van der Wall 2004) because the latter dominate and regulate these mosques which, by consequence, do not provide the source of religious and societal answers that the second generation is craving for. (At the time of writing, however, it appears that mosque attendance by Muslim youth is increasing, but this has not yet been researched.)

In 2004, the elaborate study *Muslims in the Netherlands* (Phalet and van der Wall 2004) was published, which was commissioned at the request of parliament in the immediate aftermath of the events of 9/11. This 2004 study studied the religious identity of Dutch Muslims, its connection with ethnic identity and acculturation, and the influence of Islam on the private and public domain. One of the main problems that the researchers faced, however, was that Muslims were reluctant to cooperate, so that the researchers extrapolated the findings of quantitative surveys from 1998 and 2002 on the basis of observations and theories made in similar migrant–religion contexts outside the Netherlands. (The suspicion of the Dutch Muslims towards the intentions of the researchers is in itself telling, because it demonstrates their sense of insecurity vis-à-vis Dutch interest in them.) It is interesting to briefly discuss this study, because it identified trends that did not concur with later developments. One of the main findings, for instance, was that the importance attached to Islam by Dutch Muslims, and in particular the second generation, was decreasing. This observation was based on the lessening participation of young Dutch Muslims in religious rituals and organizations and a decrease in mosque attendance. The study predicted that this trend would continue, mainly because of the increasing level of education and individualization of the second generation. However, as the abovementioned studies of later date indicated, the second generation attached more importance to religion than the first generation, but did so mostly as an individual experience, often outside the traditional religious structures of mosques and rituals. In this respect, the expression of religiosity by Muslim youth was not much different to that of their Dutch Christian or Jewish peers (Gruijter et al. 2011; Pels 2003).

Within the context of this newly developed Muslim identity with its strong emphasis on 'pure' Islam it is yet unclear to what extent Dutch Muslims adhere to, or want to adhere to, the legal precepts of Islam (shariah). Little research has been conducted in this field with the exception of religious rituals like prayer, birth, and burial (Dessing 2001; Landman 1992), and the needs and demands among Muslims in this respect therefore remain to be researched (e.g. Berger 2007). Two government-commissioned researches, one on Islamic marriages (2009) and one on shariah courts (2010), were meant to provide this kind of information, but unfortunately were allotted too little time to conduct comprehensive research in this respect. Nevertheless, the report on Islamic marriages indicated that such marriages were highly valued among younger Muslims. With regard to the so-called shariah courts, the second report concluded that apart from authoritative persons like imams whose counsel is being sought by Muslims in matters of marital and other disputes, there were no judiciary institutions in the Netherlands that administered justice in accordance to Islamic law. We will discuss shariah in more detail in the subsection on Islamic Law.

## Religious Authorities

The search for 'pure Islam' posed a number of problems for second-generation Muslims, as to what its sources are, how it applies in a contemporary Dutch context, and who are the authoritative voices to explain Islam. In finding the authoritative texts and people to answer these questions, Dutch Muslims encounter the problem of a lack of political as well as religious authorities. This is typical for the Dutch conext—as opposed to that in Germany, France, or the United Kingdom—since Dutch Muslims are from a working-class background of guest labourers who expressed little use for, and had little capacity to produce such authorities. With the exception of a few knowledgeable imams, there are hardly any Islamic scholars or institutions in the Netherlands with sufficient knowledge of Arabic and Islamic theology to serve as sources of authority among the Muslim community (Boenders 2007). Dutch society and government often overrate the authority and influence of imams; although imams are mostly respected within their community, their counsel is limited to religious affairs and hardly applies to societal or other practical matters (Boenders 2007). Apart from Boenders no comprehensive studies have yet been conducted on the impact of imams or religious scholars, whether active inside or outside the Netherlands, on Dutch Muslims.

Muslim scholars in the Netherlands with sufficient knowledge are mostly foreigners who have come to the Netherlands as imams. Almost all imams in the Netherlands are from abroad, and most are recruited on a temporary basis: imams from Morocco are approached by individual mosques in the Netherlands, while imams from Turkey are sent by the Turkish Ministry of Religious Affairs (*Diyanet*) under the coordination of the Turkish embassy in the Netherlands (BZK 1997–8; Rath et al. 1996; Sunier et al. 2011). Only the Surinamese imams tend to stay longer or even permanently, due to the former colonial relations between the Netherlands and Surinam (BZK 1997–8; Rath et al. 1996).

This lack of any centralized form of religious authority in combination with the thirst of the second generation for knowledge of 'pure Islam' has been a source of social-scientific research. Researchers have pointed at the rise of a phenomenon called Muslim 'Protestantism' or 'cut-and-paste Islam' whereby young Muslims search for answers, mostly on the internet, while lacking a basic knowledge of the theological framework of Islam that would otherwise guide them through the host of information that they encounter (de Koning 2008; Sunier 2010b; Vellenga et al. 2009).

No wonder, then, that the internet plays an important role among young Muslims, especially those of the second generation. Several Dutch sites, such as Maroc.nl, Nieuwemoskee.nl ('new mosque'), and Wijblijvenhier.nl ('We remain here'), are frequently visited by Muslims, and they provide information as well as discussion platforms on religious and social matters related to Islam. Very little research so far exists on the cyber activity of Dutch Muslims on foreign sites (de Koning 2008), except when pertaining to radicalism (AIVD 2012; Becker 2009), so that the question of the role of the internet in the religiousness and religious identity of Dutch Muslims remains unanswered.

In 2002, attention focused on several so-called 'radical imams' whose sermons in Arabic were secretly recorded by journalists and broadcasted (subtitled) on national television. These imams will be discussed further the section Security and Terrorism but the point of interest here is that these imams and their mosques attracted relatively large crowds of young Muslims who apparently gave them the status of authority figures. Another matter of concern to security agencies was that these mosques in particular had attracted and trained young, second-generation Muslims as preachers who were fluent in Dutch but also very well versed in Islam and Arabic (AIVD 2004a). This combination apparently made them very popular among the second generation of Muslims, although this has not been researched yet. However, it can be observed that the preference of young Muslims to develop individual piety and find their own answers, detached from the mosque or clergy, is a phenomenon that has also been observed within the Dutch religious landscape (Becker and de Hart 2006; Borg et al. 2008; Schmeets and Van der Bie 2009; WRR 2006b). Whether this is coincidental or a causal phenomenon has not yet been researched.

## Religious, Political, and Other Organizations

The Muslim community counts numerous civic organizations that are fragmented on the basis of ethnic, local (municipal), religious, and leaders' personality differences. For instance, one will find Moroccan, Surinamese, and Turkish organizations, secular as well as religious, in each municipality, some of which are united in larger regional umbrella organizations (Heelsum et al. 2004; Landman 1992; Shadid and Koningsveld 1997; Sunier 1996). Recent and overall data are lacking, however, although it has been observed that changes are taking place among the second generation: ethnic differences are gradually being replaced by a single 'Muslim' identity, and the higher level of integration and education of these youngsters makes them more skilful in formulating their needs, finding funds, and engaging with society and politics (Bartels 2007; Maussen 2006; Rath et al. 2008; Sunier 2009b, 2010c). The aforementioned survey into Muslims in the Netherlands observed that religious organizations play a more important role in the Turkish and Moroccan communities than cultural and political organizations (Phalet and van der Wall 2004).

The government has always thought it important to maintain institutionalized forms of communication with these organizations. In 1997, the government created a national platform for consultation with ethnic organizations in the so-called National Minorities Conference (Landelijk Overleg Minderheden). Since organizations could only take part under the umbrella of a single ethnicity, they were forced to form so-called 'alliances' with organizations with the same ethnic background. Currently eight 'alliances' take part in this conference: Chinese, Turkish, Caribbean, Moluccan, Moroccan, Surinamese, South European, and refugees.

In a similar manner, the government in 2001 invited the Muslim community (as well as the Hindu and Buddhist communities) to form a single and representative body on a religious basis that could act as a communication channel with the government. Such consultation platforms for religious communities already existed for the Catholics, Protestants, and Jews, and the intention was to create similar bodies for the 'new' religions. The divisions among the Muslim organizations were such that it took three years of intensive internal negotiations to finally establish in 2004 not one but two Islamic umbrella organizations to participate in this platform.[33] However, these bodies appear

---

[33] CMO (Contactorgaan Moslims en Overheid) and CGI (Contact Groep Islam).

to have relatively little clout in terms of lobbying on a political level or in responding to incidents or media. The reasons for this weakness have not been researched, but it may be caused by a conjunction of different factors, such as a lack of experience and funds, as well as lack of representation since their constituency is mosques rather than Muslim organizations at large (and, as we have seen, the second generation of Muslims is less mosque-oriented than the first generation).

As opposed to the many and fragmented civic organizations of Muslims along religious and ethnic divides, there is little interest among Muslims to organize politically. The few Muslim political parties that have participated in municipality elections in several of the larger cities did so with very little success. The Dutch branch of the Arab European League[34] stated in 2003 its intention to participate in the municipal council elections of 2006, but ultimately withdrew before the elections due to a lack of support, and has not been politically active since. The Dutch Muslim Party (*Nederlandse Moslim Partij*), established in 2007 by a Dutch convert who had already been active in local politics, did participate in the 2010 municipal council elections in seven municipalities, but failed to win any seats. In the same 2010 municipality elections, however, one local Islamic party won a seat in The Hague and in the elections of 2014 local Islamic parties won two seats in The Hague and two seats in Rotterdam.[35] On a national level, where a low threshold and proportional representation make it relatively easy for small parties to gain access to parliament, no initiatives have been taken by a political party with an Islamic programme. The reason for this apparent lack of interest in political participation on an Islamic ticket has to date not been researched.

On the other hand, Muslims are more active in municipal and national politics by means of demonstrations, petitions, contacting media, meetings, or other activities. In this respect, the non-Western allochthones (that includes the Muslims) score almost as high as the autochthones, that is 25–30% (CBS 2010b). These figures are not much different from those reported by a 2002 survey, although young Moroccans then stood out with 50% showing willingness to take political action (Phalet and van der Wall 2004). An interesting aspect of this 2002 survey was the enquiry into the motives for which one was willing to undertake political action: if it is the defence of human rights, 51% of autochthones are motivated, 28% of the Turks, and 38% of the Moroccans; if it is the defence of Islam, 59% of the Moroccans will take action, Turks 29%, and autochthones nil (Phalet and van der Wall 2004).

In casting votes in elections, on the other hand, non-Western autochthones are less active than autochthones: in parliamentarian elections of 2010, 77% of the autochthones voted and 69% of the non-Western allochthones (CBS 2010b). In all elections, an average of half of all the non-Western allochthones vote for the Social Democratic Party (CBS 2010b; Brasse and Huinder 2011; Koenen 2011). With regard to active political

---

[34] This organization was founded in Belgium in 2000 under the charismatic leadership of Abu Jahjah.
[35] The Islamic party in The Hague is the Islam Democraten (Islam Democrats), established in 2006 with a distinct local (The Hague) programme and constituency. The Islamic Party *Al Nida* in Rotterdam was newly established in 2014.

participation, all large political parties—socialists, social democrats, liberals, Greens, Christian-democrats—have several Muslim candidates in parliament as well as in numerous municipality councils.[36]

## *Islamic Education*

Religious education in the Netherlands can be provided by private institutions like mosques or by religious schools. Little research has been conducted into religious education in mosques, but three case studies indicate that their educational methods are relatively child friendly and related to the Dutch context (Doğan et al. 2006; Pels et al. 2006b, 2006c). The religious schools—primary as well as secondary—are established by private organizations, and are free to determine their own religious upbringing and education, but are required by law to adhere to the national standards of education. In the Dutch educational system all religious schools receive state funding equal to public schools. Since 1988, Islamic primary and secondary schools have been established (e.g. Beemsterboer 2009; Shadid 2006), resulting in over forty Islamic primary schools and two Islamic high schools in 2011. At the time of writing, several PhD studies are being conducted about the origins and identity of these Islamic schools.

From the moment of their establishment, these Islamic schools received a lot of public and political criticism and attention on a number of grounds, including the alleged lack of quality of their education, but mostly that the 'Islamic education' would impede the integration of the pupils or even indoctrinate them against Dutch society. This debate was rekindled after 9/11, with the Dutch national security agency in 2002 reporting that the teaching programmes of these schools were not contributing to, and were sometimes even against, the integration of their pupils in Dutch society (BVD 2002). These allegations were rebutted on several occasions by the School Inspection of the Ministry of Education that judged these schools quite positive in their focus on 'social cohesion' (Inspectie Onderwijs 2002, 2003, 2009). However, the Inspection concluded in several reports that many of these schools indeed had problems related to the overall quality of their education and the poor management by their school boards (Inspectie Onderwijs 2008).

In addition to the religious schools that reside under the formal scrutiny of the Ministry of Education, several private institutions have emerged where Islam is being taught. One of the more successful and popular initiatives is Dar al-Ilm that provides evening courses on subjects of Islamic theology in several large cities. There is as yet no research into these forms of education. So far, we can only observe that these institutions are very

---

[36] There is little use in naming these candidates because as politicians they come and go, but two social-democrats have become seasoned politicians and executives: Ahmed Aboutaleb served as alderman in Amsterdam, as under-secretary of social affairs in the 2007 government, and became mayor of Rotterdam in 2008; Nebahat Albayrak was under-secretary of justice in the 2007 government and belongs to the top of the social-democrat party. Both are children of migrant workers who had moved to the Netherlands, and both were born abroad, respectively in Morocco and Turkey, and their double nationality has led to protests from the aforementioned PVV party against their appointment as under-secretaries.

popular among the young Muslims given the large attendance at their courses. An interesting observation in this respect is that interest among Muslims is lacking in the Islamic theology courses taught at Leiden and Amsterdam universities.[37] This discrepancy may be explained by the fact that, as we have seen, second-generation Muslims are entering higher education and choosing subjects with job potential—like law, medicine, engineering, and business administration—and they prefer to fulfil their need for knowledge on Islam in the private educational sphere rather than through full-time university degrees.

The aforementioned lack of religious authorities combined with a lack of comprehensive Islamic theological training within the Netherlands has given rise to a political call in the late 1990s for 'home-grown imams'. In 1998 the government deemed it important that funds would be made available for imam training within the Netherlands and that imams from abroad should take exams on Dutch society (the so-called 'inburgeringscursus'), but no follow-up was given to this initiative (BZK 1997–8). Then, after 2001, the debate was rekindled when several imams were accused of preaching radical views, but a commission appointed to investigate the possibilities of imam training within the Netherlands came to the conclusion that there was little interest among the Muslim community for such training (OC&W 2003). Parliament then decided that funds should be made available for Dutch colleges and universities to establish such training parallel to that of priests and ministers. As mentioned, the theology faculties of the universities of Amsterdam and Leiden, as well as the vocational college of Amsterdam have set up such training courses in 2006 (Ghaly 2008), but the response so far has been disappointing. Consequently, the 'imam-training' course in Leiden was discontinued in 2011, and at the vocational college in Amsterdam in 2013. Parallel to these initiatives, which received accreditation within their respective universities, two self-named 'Islamic universities' have been established in Rotterdam but have yet received only partial accreditation for their programmes.[38]

## Headscarf Issues and the Burqa

The public domain's confrontation with Islam has centred predominantly on the issue of the headscarf. The headscarf has generated not only much public and political discussion, but also legal cases.

While research among Muslim women about their wish or refusal to wear the headscarf has been scarce and mostly of a qualitative nature (Buitelaar 2009) more has been published on Dutch autochthone perceptions (e.g. Moors 2009a). The only quantitative study so far among Muslim women themselves was conducted in 2011 (Motivaction

---

[37] In addition to the general Islamic Studies programmes at several universities, Islamic theology is taught only at Leiden University and the Free University of Amsterdam. The Leiden University programme was discontinued by 2012 and is party subsumed by the Islamic Studies programme.

[38] The Islamic University of Rotterdam was established in 1997, and the Islamic University of Europe in 2001. In 2006, the Masters programme 'Islamic Spiritual Care' of the Islamic University of Rotterdam was accredited by the Ministry of Education. In 2014, the 'Al Huraa' institute in The Hague that called itself a university was accused of forging academic diplomas.

2011).³⁹ According to this research, six out of ten Dutch Muslim women of Turkish and Moroccan origin (the survey does not distinguish between the two ethnic groups) between the ages of 15 and 35 wear a headscarf; nine out of ten do so out of their own free will, one out of ten experiences pressure from parents or peer groups. Two-thirds of the women wearing a headscarf do so because it is a religious obligation, 40% consider it (also) a part of their cultural tradition. But the primary identity of the overall majority of these women (83%) is that of 'Muslima' (Motivaction 2011).

The headscarf has been a source of discrimination, abusive words in the streets or refusal to be allowed in cafés or restaurants. Discrimination is also experienced on the labour market: sometimes applicants were rejected because they wore a veil, and sometimes employees were fired because they started to wear one (see, for example, the annual *Rascism Monitor* by Donselaar and Rodrigues 2002, 2004, 2005, 2007, 2008, 2009, 2010). In the latter situation some women raised their case with the court or, more often, with the Commission for Equal Treatment (CGB 2003–11).⁴⁰ Interestingly, the issue of the headscarf was legally mostly framed as a question of equal treatment rather than freedom of religion. The yardstick used by the Commission is that prohibition of headscarves in general is not allowed unless it is functional (for instance, in a chemical lab), or when uniforms are prescribed for a public function (e.g. police or judiciary). In case of religious (as opposed to public) schools, however, the context was different. Here it was argued by the Commission that teachers as well as pupils wearing the headscarf could be refused (or fired) at schools that had a distinct and expressly articulated Christian (or otherwise non-Muslim) identity as long as this was clearly stipulated in the school's articles (CGB 2003–11). Court cases argued in a similar fashion, but in addition were willing to allow schools—confessional as well as public—to prohibit certain 'Islamic' behaviour like headscarves or the refusal to shake hands if such conduct or fashion was contrary to an explicit school policy aimed at promoting social interaction.⁴¹ The requirement for pupils and female teachers at most Islamic schools to wear headscarves even if they were not Muslim, received some media attention but did not become an issue, possibly because it was done so with consent.

While the wearing of the headscarf is practised by an estimated 60% of Dutch Muslim women, as we have seen, according to another study an estimated 500 women in the Netherlands also wear the full-face veil, known as niqab, but in popular parlance as *burqa* (Berger 2010d; Moors 2009b). The study by Moors was conducted as a qualitative research, but estimated that 100 women wear the niqab 'full time', and 'no more than 400' wear the niqab 'part time', i.e. on certain occasions (Moors 2009b). The majority

---

³⁹ It was the first survey of this kind and this scale in the Netherlands, involving 338 women of Turkish and Moroccan origin in the age group of 15 to 35 years with different educational backgrounds, and 1,019 Dutch autochthone women in the age group of 15 to 70 years (see for details <http://www.motivaction.nl/content/samenvatting-nationaal-hoofddoek-onderzoek>).

⁴⁰ This commission was established in 1994 to uphold the Equal Treatment Act. Although its rulings are formally 'advises' without any legal force, they are often adhered to by the parties.

⁴¹ See e.g. the ruling of the Centrale Raad van Beroep, 7 May 2009 (LJN: BI2440).

(60%) of the interviewed women are Dutch authochthone converts, often from mixed parentage, while the remainder is exclusively Moroccan. Most of these women are younger than 30, and the remainder is not older than 40. Their marital and educational status is quite mixed: the women come from all educational backgrounds ranging from university to hardly any education at all, and are married, divorced, as well as single. All interviewed women wear the niqab of their own free will, sometimes even against the will of their husbands, and mainly for purely religious reasons, although some women have indicated that others—not they themselves—may wear the niqab as an act of provocation or 'adolescent fancy' (Moors 2009b).

In 2012, a bill known as the *burqa* ban was submitted by the Minister of Interior banning full face veils as well as full casket helmets and balaclavas from Dutch public places (including streets) with a penalty of a 390 euro fine for wearing them. Several months later, when the cabinet had fallen, the bill was retracted. A *burqa* ban has been submitted twice in the Netherlands before, in 2007 and 2008, but both came to naught, not least because a state-appointed committee (Vermeulen 2006) as well as the State Council[42] strongly advised against it. One of the main problems raised against banning full face veils was that the proposed bills were not consistent in their arguments on why such veils ought to be banned in the first place since the exact harm done by them could not be legally defined, and that many of the objections raised against them did not warrant a legal ban (see analysis of discussions by van Sasse van Ysselt 2010).

# Relations between State and Islam

## Separation of State and Church

In the Dutch context, the separation of state and church imposes more restrictions on the state than on religious organizations, because the latter are allowed much leverage to get involved in all kinds of state matters, including politics: churches have campaigned vigorously against abortion and euthanasia laws, and have at times practised the ancient rule of immunity by giving shelter to asylum-seekers who were to be returned to their homelands. The state, on the other hand, needs to observe strict neutrality towards religion and is not to interfere with the dogmas or internal affairs of religious organizations. These two restrictions are based on the Dutch constitution that requires the state to treat everyone equally (Article 1) and to guarantee freedom of religion (Article 6). Basically, this means that the state has no opinion on religion and, consequently, may not favour or condemn any religion, nor interfere with the doctrines or internal organization of religious institutions[43] (e.g. Berger 2010b).

---

[42] Raad van State, zaaknummer W03.07.0219/II, 21 September 2007.
[43] The Law on Equal Treatment, for instance, does not apply to religious institutions, for that would require the Catholic Church to allow women to become priests and the orthodox Christian political party SGP to allow women as parliamentarians, to name but a few examples.

State neutrality vis-à-vis religion is not as simple as it sounds, however, especially now that the Dutch government under international law is duty-bound to protect freedom of religion, and has also developed policies that increasingly involve issues of religion. Examples of what the Dutch government understands as its obligations under international law are the adaptations made in laws of burial and animal slaughter in order to accommodate specific religious practices,[44] and allowing for full freedom of religion for persons in state institutions like prisons or army barracks (this will be elaborated in the next section).

With regard to the government policies involving religion, two main trends will be mentioned here and elaborated in the following paragraph with regard to Muslims. First, the government in its Minority Paper of 1983 (BZK 1983) indicated the role of religion as a possible factor of empowerment and integration of allochthones. This applied at the time to Muslims in particular, but by the first decade of the twenty-first century there was also a large number of allochthone Christians who had organized themselves in so-called 'migrant-churches'. Second: parallel to these policy developments was the government policy of transferring certain state obligations that pertained to the welfare state back to the private domain. The Societal Support Act (Wet Maatschappelijke Ondersteuning) of 2007 was the main example of this policy, allowing non-governmental organizations to obtain state support in order to undertake activities that would otherwise be the obligation of the state. Since religious organizations were traditionally involved in such activities, they were the ones that applied for state support.

These two policies represent a trend of government involvement into matters that pertain, directly or indirectly, to the religious domain. This raised the question of to what extent such government activitiy constitutes a violation of the separation of church and state. The government took the position that state involvement or cooperation with religious organizations is allowed when it involves *societal* activities, but not when it involves *religious* activities: the latter would compromise the state's neutrality vis-à-vis religion, while the former would not.[45] However, this distinction did not always prove workable in practice. For instance, the municipality of Rotterdam argued that it could reproach imams if their sermons were considered inappropriate, other municipalities have refused to subsidize mosques for literacy classes because they had separate male and female classes, and several individual municipal aldermen announced at public meetings and on talkshows that they intended to actively promote a liberal Islam.

Several handbooks and policy papers were published to assist municipal civil servants in addressing these complex issues in the context of the separation of religion and state (Amsterdam 2008; Berger 2010b; Kiem 2005; VNG 2009). This literature tried to

---

[44] In 2011, the Animal Rights Party proposed a bill banning ritual animal slaughter as practised by Muslims and Jews. At the time of writing, this bill is still under discussion.

[45] This position was (re)confirmed in the 2004 report issued by the Ministry of Interior 'Fundamental right in a pluriform society' (Grondrechten in een pluriforme samenleving), that refers to earlier cabinet resolutions (Kamerstukken II 1989/90, 20 868, nr. 2, p. 3) and the ruling of the State Council (RvS 18 December 1986, AB 1987, 2601986).

clarify the distinction between 'religious' and 'societal' activities from a variety of cases and angles (integration, social cohesion, education, public order). One of the contentious issues, however, was the question of whether government neutrality vis-à-vis religion should be explained as an obligation of the government to first establish social and economical equality among the religious organizations before one could actually exert neutrality. According to this position, equal treatment of Muslims and Catholics, for instance, will only be possible once Muslims are in a position similar to the Catholics in terms of financial means, mosques, and social-political infrastructure. The obligation of the government to correct this inequality has been called 'compensating neutrality' (van der Burg 2009), a notion which has not found broad support in government circles except in a policy paper of the municipality of Amsterdam on the issue of separation of church and state (Amsterdam 2008).

## Islam and Government Policy

From the 1980s onwards, religion in general and Islam in particular became the subject of government attention, for a variety of reasons. Already in 1983 the government stated in its Minority Paper that religion has a function for the development and strengthening of the self-esteem of ethnic minorities and as such can contribute to their empowerment and integration (BZK 1983). This position was repeated in consecutive policy papers of the Minister of Interior until 1999, sometimes with specific reference to Islam (discussed by Koolen 2010; Phalet et al. 2000; Shadid and van Koningsveld 1997).

The position on religion by the Minority Paper of 1983 was reiterated by two research committees appointed by the government (Werkgroep-Waardenburg 1983; Commissie Hirsch Ballin 1988) as well as the WRR (1989), all arguing strongly in favour of a religion-oriented integration policy. In particular, they suggested that the government should finance the building of mosques, since such religious centres would stimulate empowerment and integration of Muslims. But after initial subsidies the financing of mosques was stopped in the early 1990s because of political opposition from the liberal VVD[46] arguing that financial support by the state of only one group of recipients (that is, Muslims) and not other religious communities was a violation of the constitutional rule of non-discrimination.

However, the role of religion in matters of integration and empowerment re-entered the political debate halfway during the first decade of the twenty-first century. By this time, the notions of 'active citizenship' and 'social cohesion' had become important elements in integration policies, and in 2006 both became mandatory topics to be taught at high school. The WRR distinguished four 'styles' of citizenship—dependent, active, anticipating, and detached (WRR 2005)—although other categorizations of styles are also used (e.g. Hurenkamp and Tonkens 2011; Tonkens 2009; Tonkens and Kroese 2008).[47] The advantage of these notions was that they circumvented the exclusive focus

---

[46] 'Liberal' in the Dutch political context is often equated with 'right-wing' which, in turn, generally denotes the need for freedom of and self-regulation by the individual and the market.
[47] Such as over-challenged—active—follower—not-challenged; or: obedient—responsible—pragmatic—outsider.

on allochthones, Muslims or immigrants, and emphasized the individual responsibility of each citizen to participate in society. Nevertheless, several religious organizations and political parties argued that religion does not oppose such participation but, to the contrary, contributes to good and active citizenship. One of these voices in the context of Islam was the government-funded foundation 'Islam and Citizenship' that was established in 1999 with government funding.

The two major cities, Amsterdam and Rotterdam, both with the largest allochthone communities,[48] have put a lot of effort and funds into developing policies regarding social cohesion with particular attention to the role of religion therein, although they did so in very different ways. In Amsterdam, the policy paper *Wij Amsterdammers* made no mention of religion or any other quality that distinguishes people, on the one hand, but in its implementation strongly favoured ethnic and religious diversity as means to reach the municipal cohesion, on the other hand. The mayor Job Cohen was a driving force behind this policy and he became a forceful, albeit controversial advocate of religion as a source of social cohesion (Cohen 2009), on the other hand, in its policy paper *Meedoen of Achterblijven* ('Join in or Stay Behind') specifically identified Islam as one of the issues of municipal controversy and organized in 2003–4 a municipal-wide discussion titled 'Islam and Integration' with the intention to get all the information, concerns, and needs out in the open.[49] As already mentioned, the municipality of Rotterdam in 2007 hired the Muslim intellectual Tareq Ramadan as the city's 'bridge builder' and paid for his appointment as visiting professor in 'citizenship and identity'.

However, the enthusiasm for this policy approach quickly wore off. In the case of Amsterdam, the city council became entangled in the financing of a mosque-building project by a Dutch-Turkish Muslim organization suspected of fundamentalism and embezzlement; and in Rotterdam where Ramadan's role was repeatedly questioned,[50] he was finally fired in 2009 on the grounds of his side-job as a host in a London-based news channel of the Iranian government in which Ramadan allegedly failed to criticize the Iranian government crack-down of the 'Green' demonstrations in 2009 (see analysis by Zessen 2010). In 2008, the foundation 'Islam and Citizenship' was dissolved due to discontinuation of government funding.

At the time when policy initiatives linking social cohesion with religion ended, research came out that actually corroborated the initial argument that religion does play a social cohesive role, and contributes to political, social, and economic participation (Castillo Guerra et al. 2008; Blauw 2010; Schmeets and de Bie 2009). These researches, although predominantly focused on Christian communities, demonstrated that participation in elections was higher among citizens affiliated to religious communties than the national average, and that they were actively involved in social welfare and local

---

[48] See the section on Not an Immigration Country.
[49] For the published findings of these debates see note 16.
[50] The recurring suspicion raised by the municipal political party Leefbaar, as well as by the Dutch gay magazine *Gay Krant* and several national politicians (like Bolkestein) and commentators, was the alleged duplicity of Ramadan in posing as a liberal Muslim to the autochthone public while expressing conservative views to the Muslim public.

initiatives aimed at social cohesion. Another study demonstrated that in the case of the Danish Cartoons (2006) and the Dutch film *Fitna* (2008), when Muslim anger and indignation was heavily criticized by many autochtones, religious organizations made a considerable effort to counter manifestations of social polarization based on religion (Vellenga and Wiegers 2011).

## *Representative Muslim Organizations*

In order to guarantee the freedom of religion of prison inmates and soldiers, the government has taken it upon itself to provide chaplains in prisons and the military. However, since the state cannot appoint these clerics, it has entered into close cooperation with Jewish, Catholic, and Protestant institutions to designate such clerics who are then employed by the state. With the increasing number of Muslim inmates and military personel,[51] the government in 1988 expressed the need for imams. However, as we have already seen, there was no organization at the time representing the entire Muslim community in the Netherlands.

The need for a representative Muslim body also became urgent after several incidents (teachers at kindergarten wanting to wear the *burka*, an imam comparing homosexuals with pigs, several incidents of women with headscarves refused at the workplace or at school) had caused heated public debates, and especially after 9/11. The Dutch government was not only in constitutional need of clerics for its prisons and army barracks; it now also had a pressing societal and political need to be able to communicate with the Muslim community as a whole. The ethnic fragmentation and theological diversity among Dutch Muslims was such, however, that they could not reach consensus on a representative body. Finally, as we have seen already, two bodies were formed in 2004 and 2005, respectively, with much help from the Dutch government, and recognized by the government as official interlocutors of the state for the Dutch Muslim population and as official suppliers of imams to government facilities like prisons and army barracks (Berger 2010b). After 2008, only one body remained: the CMO ('contact body Muslims–government'). The composition of this body was based not on elections, but on the cooperation of mosque organizations, similar to the existing representative bodies of the Catholics, Protestants, and Jews.[52]

It could be argued that the government in its active involvement with the establishment of this Muslim body, and its demands regarding the composition of its board

---

[51] The Ministry of Defence does not register the religion of its personnel, so the number of Muslims is unknown. However, for several years the Ministry has employed two Muslim 'spiritual caretakers'.

[52] The CMO at the time of writing is composed of nine umbrella organizations of cooperating mosques, some of which are based on ethnicity (Turkish, Moroccan, and Surinamese), some on religious denomination (Sunni and Shi'a), one is regional (the Islamic organization of the province of Limburg), and another professional (Union of Dutch Imams). In addition the Dutch government, as the main financial sponsor of the CMO, has required the thirteen members of the executive board of the CMO to also include a representative number of women and youth.

(which must include women and youth), has overstepped boundaries that separate church and state, but this issue has not been raised or researched.[53]

## Islamic Law

In the 1980 and 1990s a fair amount of legal literature was produced on the application of Islamic family law (in particular Moroccan law) by Dutch courts as a matter of private international law (Bakelen 1983; Groot 1983; Hensen 1989; Jordens-Cotran 2000, 2007; Rutten 1983–2011). A particular issue was the invocation of public order in typical cases of Islamic law, such as repudiation (*talaq*) (Rutten and Foblets 2006; Velden 2003), inheritance (Rutten 1997, 2008a), and polygamous marriages (Boele-Woeki et al. 2009; Groot and Rutten 1996): while Moroccan (Islamic[54]) family law as such could be deemed applicable by Dutch courts, these specific rules are considered contrary to Dutch public policy and therefore not enforceable by Dutch courts. The double nationality of many Moroccan Dutch nationals allowed for a continuation of Dutch courts applying Moroccan family law, until the private international law concept of 'strong societal ties' determined that when a Moroccan had developed strong ties with Dutch society, application of Dutch family law rather than Moroccan law was justified.

Parallel to Islamic rules of foreign laws applied by Dutch courts, discussion arose on the existence of an indigenous form of shariah in the Netherlands. The literature on this aspect of Islamic law is limited, but assesses that only a limited number of shariah rules are being practised by Dutch Muslims, and that this practice mostly fits within the Dutch legal framework (Berger 2005, 2007, 2010c; Rutten 2005). Most of these Islamic rules pertain to the devotional rules of shariah (prayer, fasting, burial, etc). In addition, many Muslims (figures are not known) enter into an Islamic marriage, sometimes with a corresponding civil marriage, but sometimes not, whereby the latter is not necessarily deliberate or otherwise politically motivated (Leun and Avalon 2009).

The indigenous form of shariah and Islamic marriage in particular gained public attention in 2004, when the Canadian case of 'shariah courts' in Ontario made headlines in the Dutch news. Questions were asked in parliament about possible application of shariah in the Netherlands. The issue emerged again with the 2006 court case against the Hofstad Group, the alleged Dutch Islamic terrorist organization (discussed in the next section), where it became clear that concluding an 'Islamic marriage' was an important facet of the sectarian life of the group members. Consequently, parliamentarians voiced concerns about Muslims concluding Islamic rather than civil marriages and to what extent this might be a sign of extremist tendencies. The latter allegation was denied by the aforementioned study (Leun and Avalon 2009).

Little is yet known about the social dimensions regarding marriage (for celebrational rituals, see Dessing 2001), but some of the more negative aspects have received

---

[53] An evaluation report by M. S. Berger, commissioned by the then-Ministry of Justice and Integration in 2005, does address these issues, but has not been published.

[54] This is the Mudawannah, which applies only to Muslim Moroccans; Jewish Moroccans have their own family statute.

considerable academic and political attention, like marriage to partners from the countries of origin (so-called 'import marriages') and forced marriage. The import marriages were perceived as an unwelcome continuation of immigration and, by consequence, a perpetuation of integration problems (Hooghiemstra 2003). According to statistics, almost 90% of second-generation Moroccans and Turks marry partners from the same ethnic community (Hooghiemstra 2003; Huis 2007; de Koning and Bartels 2005).[55] Before 2004, almost 60% of these marriages were with partners from the countries of origin, and 30% from their own community in the Netherlands; by 2011 these figures had reversed, however, and now 30% choose marriage partners from the countries of origin, and 60% from their own community in the Netherlands (Hooghiemstra 2003; Huis 2007). Since this reversal took place around 2004, it is tempting to explain these changes by the government restrictions implemented in that year,[56] but that disregards the fact that the trend had already set in several years before (Hooghiemstra 2003; Huis 2007). So far, no explanations have been offered for this change, but research into the preference among second-generation Turks and Moroccans for marriage partners shows a complex combination of psychological and economic factors, as well as an interaction of traditional backgrounds and 'modernization processes' (Sijses 2003). Examples of the traditional backgrounds are family pressure and giving in to parental and cultural expectations (Sijses 2003). Also, Dutch Moroccan and Turkish men often prefer brides from their country of origin because they allegedly have a guaranteed unblemished reputation (as opposed, in their view, to the girls of their own ethnic community in the Netherlands); many Dutch Moroccan and Turkish women, on the other hand, prefer grooms from their country of origin because they are considered more modern and liberated than the men of their own ethnic community in the Netherlands (Hooghiemstra 2003; Sijsen 2003).

Closely connected to traditional backgrounds motivating the choice for a marriage partner is the issue of forced marriage. Research has yielded little quantitative results regarding the extent and motivations of this phenomenon since it takes place behind the closed doors of family units and is invariably connected to family honour (Cornelissens et al. 2009; de Koning and Bartels 2005). The problem of identifying such marriages is that the degree of force may vary considerably, ranging from the use of force and violence, to coercion and blackmail, to social pressure (Cornelissens et al. 2009; de Koning and Bartels 2005). For that reason, women's organizations and police authorities have not developed efficient indicators to report such marriages. Moreover, forced marriages are hardly reported by the victims. A research conducted among young students confirms this hesitance to report forced marriage, and indicates that the few students who

---

[55] This report was much more elaborate than a similar report of 1994 into trends of partner choice in the context of family reunification (Schoorl et al. 1994) that had as its primary conclusion that digitalization of registration was to be awaited in order to provide a fuller account of actual figures and numbers in this respect.

[56] These restrictions were, inter alia, the raising of the marriage age to 24 years, conditions to the income of the Dutch partner, and a test to the immigrating partner to be taken successfully before migrating to the Netherlands.

have come forward with information mostly refer to the possibility that they might have to accept a marriage against their wishes, rather than that the forced marriage had actually taken place (Kuppens et al. 2008).

Islamic finance is another legal matter of importance to Muslims in the Netherlands. The topic has received some academic interest (Berger 2011a; Sinke 2009; Visser 2009), although these studies were more directed to Dutch bankers and lawyers who are increasingly interested in this category of Islamic law. A private endeavour called *bi-la riba* ('without interest') devised financial-legal instruments to make Islam-conform mortgages possible, but the initiative failed in 2008 when the Tax Authority indicated its unwillingness to adopt the laws to accommodate such legal-financial construction.

Whereas these Islamic rules are being practised by Muslims in the Netherlands—again, there are no figures available—there are no institutionalized religious-legal bodies like 'shariah tribunals' to solve disputes (Bakker 2010; Berger 2010a). In the case of divorce in particular this has proved problematic for women who remain 'locked' in their marriage when their husbands refuse to divorce them; in some instances, when the couple was already divorced according to civil law, civil judges deemed the husband's refusal to divorce their wives in accordance with Islamic law an abuse of rights, and ordered that they would pronounce the religious divorce by means of *talaq* (Berger 2011b; Rutten 2008b).

## Security and Terrorism

In the first decade of the twenty-first century, the Netherlands witnessed two terrorist murder attacks, one against the right-wing politician Pim Fortuyn in 2002, committed by an animal rights activist, and the other against film director Theo van Gogh in 2004, committed by a Muslim militant. The two victims of these attacks were known for their criticism of Muslims and Islam and although only the second attack was committed by a Muslim, both attacks fuelled fierce debates about Muslims' alleged lack of integration and their consequential proneness to radicalization.

In the case of the murder of Theo van Gogh, it appeared that the killer, Mohamed Bouyeri, belonged to the Hofstad group, a group of young Muslims with allegedly terrorist intentions. Its members were subsequently arrested and six were sentenced for 'attempted terrorist crimes', although the Court of Cassation in 2012 overturned two verdicts because the 'membership of a terrorist organization' had been insufficiently proven. Other attacks by Muslim militants have not taken place (or might have been thwarted successfully, but that is classified information).

Parallel to these debates, legislature and the judicial establishment tried to come to terms with the exact meaning of 'terrorism'. The Dutch legislature had copied the definition of 'terrorism' adopted by the European Union 2002,[57] and this definition was

---

[57] According to Article 1(1) of the Framework Decision of 13 June 2002 on combating terrorism (2002/475/JHA), terrorist intent of crimes committed is shown in the aim of either 'seriously

first used against the Hofstad group. More anti-terrorist legislation followed suit. The Minister of Justice in 2003 tabled a law that criminalized 'recruitment for jihad', but retracted this law soon afterwards, possibly because it was hard to define 'jihad' for legislative purposes.[58] Also, police and intelligence agencies were given more freedom to monitor suspects and to act pre-emptively, surveillance cameras were positioned at public places, and data systems of criminal as well as non-criminal records were linked up.

The few voices of criticism during these first years of counter-terrorism were drowned in the general mood that 'something had to be done'. The literature on violations of civil rights and breaches of privacy was very limited, and mainly produced by lawyers and scholars of human rights (e.g. Baehr 2008; Böhler 2004). The debate on the interrelation between anti-terrorism measures and the safeguarding of human rights arose later, around 2005, following the international debates on this issue, but was mostly a debate between policy-makers and lawyers, and never made it to a general public discourse.[59]

## Radicalism

Aside from all the legal measures enabling law enforcement agencies to act promptly in cases of terrorism, the emphasis in security and police circles quickly switched from apprehension of the terrorist to prevention of terrorist acts. This generated a lot of research, as we will see shortly, because in order to prevent acts by Muslim extremists, 'profiling' of suspects is needed: who are these people and what makes them prone to becoming extremists or even terrorists? The process of preparatory actions and behaviour leading up to terrorist acts was identified as 'radicalization'. Numerous reports and studies were produced on radicalism and radicalization, whereby Islam and Muslims were put centre stage—although the Dutch security apparatus emphatically indicated that it was equally concerned with two other categories of terrorists: 'right-wing extremism' and 'animal rights activism'.[60]

The Dutch intelligence agency AIVD, which had already in 1998 produced an extensive analysis on political Islam in the Netherlands (AIVD 1998), after 9/11 quickly dominated the discourse on radicalism by publishing several studies of considerable quality, thereby setting the definitions of several terms, like radicalism, da'wa, jihad, and the like (AIVD 2004a, 2006, 2007, 2010a, 2010b).

According to the AIVD, radicalism is not confined to the process leading to violent action, but also poses a danger as 'a creeping segregation between different (ethnic or

intimidating a population, or unduly compelling a Government or international organization to perform or abstain from performing any act, or seriously destabilising or destroying the fundamental political, constitutional, economic or social structures of a country or an international organization'.

[58] The amendment to the Dutch Criminal Code to include 'recruitment for jihad' was proposed by the Minister of Justice in his letter to the parliament, 'Terrorism and the protection of society', of 24 June 2003.

[59] For example, in 2005, the Dutch section of the International Commission of Jurists convened the conference 'Combating Terrorism with Human Rights'.

[60] The man who murdered the politician Pim Fortuyn in 2002 had a track-record of animal rights activism.

religious) communities and the emergence of parallel societies that undermine social cohesion and therewith, in the long term, democratic rule of law' (AIVD 2006: 66). This is a broader definition than those used by other Western European security services that mostly confine radicalism to the use of violence.

In addition to these first AIVD reports, academic research produced in-depth studies on radicalism of young Muslims (Bos et al. 2009; Buijs et al. 2006; Fermin 2009b; Hachraoui 2006; Pligt and Koomen 2009; Poot and Sonnenschein 2010; Tillie 2006; Veldhuis and Bakker 2009), and some studies paid particular attention to the issue of salafism among Dutch Muslims (Koning 2008; Roex et al. 2010; Slootman 2009). In addition, investigative journalism also produced several books that gave a good insight into these young Muslim radicals at a time when such information was lacking (Groen and Kranenberg 2006, 2008; Kleijwegt 2005).

In a relatively short time, a comprehensive picture emerged of the young Muslims who had adopted radical notions of Islam. A combination of social factors was identified as contributing to this development: experiences of discrimination, a sense of alienation, identity crisis, international politics, and criticism of Islam. These factors coincided with a general tendency among the second generation to turn to Islam as their new identity. However, while all these factors explained the resentment and anger among young Muslims and their identification with Islam, researchers could not explain why one Muslim would become a radical while the other turned to politics or merely to orthodoxy (Buijs et al. 2006). Indeed, most young Muslims who fitted the profile of anger and Islamic orthodoxy did not turn to radicalism, and researchers have pointed out that Islamic orthodoxy is not a necessary prelude to radicalism, so that a clear distinction therefore needed to be made between Islamic orthodoxy, on the one hand, and Islamic radicalism, on the other (e.g. Roex et al. 2010).

The intelligence service AIVD as well as the newly established Netherlands Coordinator for Combating Terrorism (NCTb[61] found that the best prevention strategy against radicalization was integration: a Muslim who was successfully integrated, both social-culturally and socio-economically, was deemed less prone to radical ideas. Indeed, the newly developed policy of 'de-radicalization and de-polarization' (see, for example, BZK 2007) was nothing less than a renewed effort of integration. However, while the net effect might be the same, there was a distinct difference in the motivation: integration as promoted by the Ministry of Interior and municipalities served a mixed social, cultural, and economic cause, while the integration promoted by the AIVD served the cause of national security.

## Parallel Societies

The definition of radicalism by AIVD centred on so-called 'parallel societies' (AIVD 2004b, 2006, 2007), that is, communities who isolate themselves from society at large. In a similar fashion, the Dutch Prime Minister had already indicated several years earlier,

---

[61] In 2012 renamed National Coordinator for Security and Counterterrorism (NCTV).

in 2003, that Islamic organizations and schools could impede integration as they might become 'prisons for those staying behind'.[62] Concern for Muslim 'parallel societies' as a breeding ground for radicalism was one of the main reasons for parliament to have the Ministry of Justice commission the aforementioned studies on Islamic marriage (van der Leun and Avalon 2009) and shariah courts (Bakker et al. 2010). However, apart from these studies, the existence and particularities of Muslim parallel societies have to date not been researched.

These concerns deserve closer attention because they illustrate the changes that have taken place in Dutch thinking on religious minority communities. Only thirty years earlier, the government had introduced the programme of 'Education in One's Own Language and Culture' (discussed in the section on Multiculturalism) whereby at given moments of the day children would be called from their classes for special instruction in their native language and culture. And until the 1970s, Dutch society was structured by means of so-called 'pillars' that in fact constituted parallel societies. The latter deserves some elaboration, because it was a structure deeply embedded in the Dutch social and political fabric during the twentieth century. In this system, each confessional and ideological community—Catholics, Protestants, socialists, liberals—had organized themselves as a separate community from grassroots level up to the political arena (hence the pillar image) with its own schools, shops, sports clubs, unions, media, and political parties, and only its leaders would meet to communicate on matters of common or national concern. The Dutch Christian reformist community had introduced this concept in the early twentieth century as a means of empowerment. They had established their own newspaper, political party, and even university—all as part of the newly coined concept of 'sovereignty in one's own circle' meaning that state power should not extend to all facets of life. These concepts and ideas gradually disappeared in the 1970s, only to be resuscitated by some sociologists and politicians who suggested it as a model for the empowerment and integration of the Muslim community (see analyses by Hoogenboom and Scholten 2008; Penninx and Entzinger 1998; Rath et al. 1996; Sunier 2010b). But as we have seen, by the turn of the millennium the dominant public and political opinion deemed any form of structural internal organization and community formation by Muslims to be not only contrary to integration but also suspect of possible radicalization.

## *'Securitization'*

Developments as described already, such as integration policies becoming a means to prevent radicalization, and suspicion of organizational initiatives by the Muslim community that in other times would have been applauded as a means of empowerment, have led Dutch terrorist experts to use the term 'securitization' of Dutch society, meaning the tendency to see everything that is related to Islam and Muslims in terms of security (de Graaf 2010, 2011). While securitization has been defined as related to a specific

---

[62] 'Premier: zuil moslims blokkeert integratie', interview with daily *Trouw* on 3 November 2003.

debate of policy-making vis-à-vis a particular group or situation (Cesari 2009), in the Dutch case it is discussed in the specific context of state security: the concern by the state security services for Islamic 'orthodoxy' has evolved from a 'general threat' in the 1990s until 2004 into a 'public security problem' since the murder of Theo van Gogh by a Muslim extremist in 2004 (Cesari 2009). In its development of security strategies, the government has turned from the protector of national security to the protector of national identity (Cesari 2009).

Such securitization can also be detected in the academic research on Muslims and Islam. One of the effects of 9/11 and the killing of Theo van Gogh (2004) was the call from all segments of society for more information on Muslims and Islam, in particular in relation to radicalization and integration. Numerous parties, ranging from ministries and parliament to municipalities, the mayor's office, health care institutions, and the police and justice department, allocated funds for research into these terrains. Indeed, most of the research undertaken in this period was commissioned, and only few research projects were initiated by academics themselves.

While this research was academically sound and independent, academics could not avoid the societal turmoil regarding Islam and Muslims. Similarly, when they applied for research to the national Organization for Scientific Research (Dutch universities do not have their own research funds), the applicant faces the demand of valorization, i.e. the need to indicate the practical relevance of the project. There was no avoiding, then, to somehow link the project proposal to the current political and societal issues of Muslims and Islam. As a result, the academics undertaking either commissioned or independent research enjoyed full academic freedom in the scholarly sense, but not necessarily in the choice or framing of their research topic, which was ultimately security-related.

## Islamophobia

Discrimination in the Netherlands is well documented by several organizations active in this terrain. The 'Racism Monitor' (*Monitor Rascisme*) is the most known and comprehensive annual publication in this respect (Donselaar and Rodrigues 2002, 2004, 2005, 2007, 2008, 2009, 2010). In addition, the Social Cultural Planning office issues extensive studies that include surveys on discrimination of non-Western allochthones in the labour market (*Discriminatiemonitor niet-westerse allochthonen op de arbeidsmarkt*). These reports, as well as others (Kruisbergen and Veld 2002; Lindner et al. 2003), have observed an increase of discrimination against Muslims since 2001. By 2008, the term 'Islamophobia' had become part of the Dutch discrimination jargon (Donselaar and Rodrigues 2008; ECRI 2008).

The attacks of 9/11 marked a turning point in the attitude towards Muslims in the Netherlands. One of the main Dutch polling and research centeres, NIPO, observed that after these events, 95% of the Dutch population had a negative image of Muslims

(45% already had that opinion before 9/11), and 85% indicated that Muslims were not sufficiently integrating into Dutch society.[63] These concerns and feelings of unease were mirrored by the Muslims: in 2003, 58% of the Muslims interviewed felt not welcome in the Netherlands, and 69% indicated that they would always remain an outsider in the Netherlands regardless of their efforts to integrate.[64] This corresponds with about half of the Turkish and Moroccan allochthones reporting experiences with discrimination (Donselaar and Rodrigues 2005). These polls are corroborated by several reports indicating that a substantial number of autochthones hold negative views on the presence of allochthones, and many think that the lifestyle of Muslims is not consistent with a Western lifestyle (Gijsberts and Dagevos 2004, 2005; Gijsberts and Vervoort 2007).

The surveys are sometimes explicitly focused on Islam and Muslims, but mostly on allochthones in general, sometimes specifying non-Western allochthones ethnic minorities. When it comes to the generic terms 'migrants' and 'allochthones' (which appear to be interchangeable in the public perception), two-thirds of the Dutch autochthones in 2005 were of the opinion that there are too many allochthones in the Netherlands (interestingly, this opinion was shared by over half of the Turkish allochthones—SCP 2005), and another survey six years later indicated that 56% of the Dutch population was of the opinion that measures ought to be taken to limit 'the immigration of Muslims'.[65]

Although not specifically researched and therefore not substantiated, it appears that the source of these fears and concerns has shifted gradually from 'Muslims' towards 'Islam'. In 2007, 50% of the Dutch population indicated that Islam and democracy 'do not go well together' as opposed to 42% that believes they do.[66] In a July 2011 poll, 63% of the Dutch were concerned about the 'ever increasing influence of Islam in Western European countries'.[67] In a poll that same year, more than half of the Dutch populations considered Islam a threat to Dutch society.[68]

These anti-Islam sentiments were also reflected in politics, in particular Geert Wilders's Party for Freedom (PVV) and to a lesser extent by the orthodox Christian State Reformed Party (SGP). The latter repeatedly emphasized that Islam should not have the same protection as reformed (Protestant) Christianity (Brouwer 2005). The PVV, on the other hand, continuously labelled Islam as a violent and abject religion, as was reflected in numerous interviews and op-ed articles, the film *Fitna* (2008), and by the book written by the PVV-ideologue Bosman (2011). This position can be summarized with the statement of the PVV 2010 party programme: 'Islam is mostly a political ideology: a totalitarian doctrine aiming at domination, violence and suppression. [...] Of course there are moderate Muslims, but a substantial number of the Muslims

---

[63] NIPO, 11 September 2002.
[64] NIPO, 11 September 2003.
[65] Peil, 25 March 2011.
[66] Poll of 30 July 2011 by Peil, better known by the name of its director Maurice de Hond who is the main provider of quick-poll information (published on the website <https://n9.noties.nl/peil.nl>).
[67] Peil, 25 March 2011.
[68] NIPO, 9 August 2007.

are not.'[69] In the 2010 elections, the PVV won a landslide victory, rising from nine to twenty-four seats, and became the third largest party in Dutch politics.[70] In addition, the PVV became indirectly part of the government by means of the so-called 'permissive partnership', whereby the PVV was not officially part of the cabinet, but became part of the majority coalition in parliament supportive of the cabinet.[71] In May 2012, this coalition collapsed and with the new elections that same year a coalition was formed without participation of the PVV.

## Muslims and Islam as 'the Other'

The other aspect of discrimination that has received scholarly attention is that of perception of Muslims as 'others', that is not-Dutch, non-Western, or not-integrated (Esveldt and Traudes 2001; Pinto 2004; Poorthuis and Salemink 2011; Shadid 2009c). Some of the research has focused on whether the negative image of the other can be attributed to the lack of contact of the autochthone and allochthone communities: studies estimate that Turkish, Moroccan, and Somalian allochthones spend 70%, 60%, and 50% of their free time, respectively, interacting with members of their own community (Gijsberts and Dagevos 2005). The so-called 'ethnic concentration' in certain neighbourhoods was considered the main culprit in this respect (see the subsection on Living Environment under the heading Socio-Economic Indicators of Integration). Some studies brought some nuance, however. First, the relative lack of interaction does not necessarily have a negative impact on the perceptions of each other (autochthones and allochthones judge each other generally in positive terms, although the higher educated are more negative about the 'social climate' that deprives them of opportunities), but it does have a negative impact on social-cultural integration of the allochthones (Gijsberts and Dagevos 2005). In a later report by one of the same authors, the following addition was made: it is not the number of allochthones in a neighbourhood that causes a negative perception of them, but the speed by which a neighbourhood is 'colouring' due to the influx of allochthone newcomers (Dagevos 2009).

Several researches have studied the role of the media as contributing to the negative image of Islam and Muslims (Shadid 2009a, 2009b; Vliegenthart 2007). While media outlets themselves may very well be objective in their reporting, a lot of criticism on Islam and Muslims was expressed in their columns and op-ed pages. Many of these critics were quite famous as public intellectuals, Islam-specialists, or politicians. Several of

---

[69] *De agenda voor hoop en optimisme. Een tijd om te kiezen: PVV 2010–2015* ('The agenda for hope and optimism. A time to choose: PVV 2010–2015)', p. 13.

[70] The three traditional large parties until then had been the liberals (VVD), social-democrats (PvdA), and Christian-Democrats (CDA). The latter was sept away in the 2010 elections.

[71] While most 'leftist' parties refused to form a government with the PVV, the other winning party, the liberals (VVD), formed a coalition with the Christian-Democrats that had lost significantly in the elections, and together with the PVV formed the 'permissive partnership'.

them, such as the politicians Bolkestein[72] and Pim Fortuyn who were the first to raise the issue of Islam as a problematic factor in Dutch society, followed later by Bosman, the ideologue of Wilders's PVV party, and the Islamologist and university professor Hans Jansen (who in 2014 became official PVV candidate for the EU parliament elections), elaborated their views in books that received much attention (Bolkestein 1997; Bosman 2010; Fortuyn 1997; Jansen 2008). These 'popular' books and the op-ed articles and television talkshows became more dominant in the public debate than the numerous academic studies already mentioned.

The sentiment of Muslims being the 'other' was reflected in a study demonstrating that Muslims would never be able to fully integrate, regardless of their efforts, because they would never be able to become 'us'. This study was a repetition of an earlier study conducted in the late 1990s on the social and economic status of integration among allochthones (Entzinger and Dourleijn 2008). While the earlier study had identified significant socio-economic differences between autochthones and allochthones, this study observed that now, more than ten years later, with the rising level of education, 'Turks and Moroccans in all kinds of ways become increasingly similar to the autochthone Dutch.' But, the authors pointed out, regardless of these accomplishments there was still a lack of acceptance of allochthones among the autochthones: 'Autochthones and allochthones therefore appear to turn away from each other, each increasingly emphasizing his own innateness' (Entzinger and Dourleijn 2008: 142, 155).

Irrespective whether the negative view of Muslims and Islam was correct or not, it imposed a burden on the Muslim community, in particular the higher educated ones of the second generation. Not only was the negative image contributive to discrimination on the labour market (see the beginning of this section on Islamophobia), but also to feelings of alienation and being unwanted. Indeed, researchers have pointed at the fact that the importance of Islam for Muslims may only increase with the Muslims' perception of being discriminated against (e.g. Phalet and van der Wall 2004). The combination of these two factors—alienation and Islam—was considered by the Dutch intelligence service to be a cause of radicalization. This was a concern expressed in 2004 by the Minister of Interior (responsible for the intelligence service) with the statement that 'a growing number of Muslims feels pestered by opinion makers and opinion leaders [...] the group of pestered youngsters forms an important breeding ground for radicalization'.[73]

The Minister's remark raised a lot of protest, however, for even if it were true, the curtailing of such opinions was considered a violation of the freedom of opinion. This debate, in turn, fuelled the discussion on the limits to the freedom of opinion, as we will discuss in the section on Insulting Believers or Beliefs?.

---

[72] Frits Bolkestein had been member of several cabinets in the 1980s, but became known for his criticism of multiculturalism and Islam as leader of the VVD party from 1990 until 1998.

[73] Report 'Recruitement for Jihad' by the Minister of Interior to parliament, 10 March 2004.

## Insulting Believers or Beliefs?

After the turn of the millennium, the criticism on immigrants, Islam, and Muslims reached an unprecedented pitch. Whereas a member of parliament named Janmaat[74] was convicted by the court in the 1990s for making such statements as 'Full is full' and 'We will, as soon as we have the possibility and the power, abolish the multicultural society', similar statements—or worse—could be used with impunity after the turn of the millennium.[75] The 'debate had become harsher' as the expression went but, although regretted by many, this became the new style of public and political debate. Discussions were waged in the media on whether this new style constituted a possible abuse of the freedom of opinion, or perhaps even a violation of the freedom of religion, but these considerations ultimately had to succumb to the legal argument of the freedom of opinion. Indeed, the many legal cases on offensive language, discrimination, and incitement of hatred were discussed predominantly in legal literature that provided little analysis of the (un)desirability of the tone of the public debate (Berger 2006; Nieuwenhuis 2011; Stokkom et al. 2006).

The legal arguments did reverberate among Muslims as well. In a poll conducted in 2000, when anti-Islamic polemics in the media was at its height, 56% of second-generation Turks supported the freedom of opinion unconditionally, 43% of the autochthones, and 25% of the Moroccan youth (Phalet and van der Wall 2004). According to the researchers, these statistics indicate that ethnic-national identities in this respect have a stronger influence than religious identity (Phalet and van der Wall 2004). On the other hand, one of these researchers observes with regard to the other important freedom, namely the freedom of religion, that second-generation Muslims emphasize the freedom of religion, 'even if this results in a treatment that protects their being different rather than their equality' (Phalet van der Wall 2004). These two observations show the conflict of freedoms that Muslims experience: they make use of the freedom of religion, on the one hand, to shape their religious identity to their personal liking and needs but, on the other hand, must endure the criticism of their religion that is made under the aegis of the freedom of opinion.

The legal setting of this debate became prominent with the court cases against parliamentarians Hirshi Ali (2004)[76] and Geert Wilders (2011).[77] In both cases, the court had to decide whether public derogatory comments on Islam and—although much less—on Muslims, were tantamount to insult or discrimination or incitement of hatred of a group

---

[74] Hans Janmaat was leader of the Centrum Partij, later renamed Centrum Democraten, a party with a nationalist and anti-migration programme. He was member of parliament during 1982–6 and 1989–98, but was mostly isolated and boycotted by his fellow MPs.

[75] In a televised interview on 23 Februari 2011, Dutch prime minister Rutte when asked about his opinion of the multicultural society, answered: 'We buried this experiment in the eighties.'

[76] Pres. Rb.'s-Gravenhage, 15 March 2005, KG 05/123 (Moslimorganisaties/Hirsi Ali).

[77] Rechtbank Amsterdam, 23 June 2011, LJN BQ9001, and Gerechtshof Amsterdam 21 January 2009, LJN BH0496.

on the basis of their religion (all criminal offences under Dutch penal law). The legal considerations were twofold. One was pertinent to the jurisprudence of the European Court of Human Rights that allows for offensive and even shocking opinions if they are relevant to national debates.[78] Islam, it was ruled in the mentioned cases, was one such national debates, and hence more freedom was allowed to express opinions about it. The second consideration is particular to Dutch criminal law that only protects against discrimination or incitement of hatred of people, not of their religions or ideologies. The Court of Cassation had already ruled in 2010 that a banner with an anti-Islamic text was therefore not punishable under the law, even though Muslims felt insulted, and even if one might assume that insulting Muslims was the motive behind that banner.[79] This shows one of the distinct differences between anti-Semitism and Islamophobia in the Dutch legal context: while the first is directed against people (Jews) and as such is punishable by law, the latter is directed against a religion (Islam) and therefore is not punishable by law (see Berger 2010a).

These legal decisions, combined with the major election victory of Geert Wilders's PVV party in 2010 and his subsequent partnership with the next government, put a lid on the efforts of the previous cabinet to make legal adjustments in order to somehow regulate offensive Islam-criticism.

# Conclusion

## Major Findings

While the Netherlands has a long-standing tradition of academic research into Muslims and Islam in general, the study of Muslims and Islam *in* the Netherlands is of recent date, as it corresponds with the arrival of 'guest workers' from Turkey and Morocco in the 1960s. Before that date, very few Muslims lived within the Netherlands. The rapid increase of these communities was accompanied by an equally growing volume of research. Most of this research was conducted within the discipline of social sciences, and to a limited extent within the disciplines of theology and religious studies. Specific fields of interest, in particular law and education, were covered by the scholars of those fields. Scholarship in this field was—and still is—quite extensive: there is hardly a topic relating to Muslims or Islam that has not been researched (although we will see in this Conclusion that there still remain some blanks).

There is a general preference among all scholars—except, for obvious reasons, those of theology and religious studies—to approach their topics of study from the perspective of culture and ethnicity rather than religion. This perspective remains dominant,

---

[78] ECHR 7 December 1976, Handyside vs. United Kingdom, Series A no. 24, par. 49
[79] Hoge Raad, 10 March 2009, LJN BF0655.

even though the second generation of Muslims is distinctively more pious and observant of religious rules than their parents. To most scholars the ethnic differences are apparently more explanatory of certain behaviour than religious convictions.

In contemporary Dutch scholarship on Muslims and Islam in the Netherlands a progression of themes can be discerned that generally follows the development of the social and political situation of Muslims in the country. First, in the 1960s and 1970s, 'Muslims' (better known as Turks and Moroccans at the time) were seen in the context of temporary labour migration: the guest workers were assumed to remain in the Netherlands for a limited period of time, and the academic focus was predominantly on issues of law, culture, and language. With the growing number of migrants in the 1980s, primarily because of family reunification, the emphasis switched to multiculturalism and, gradually, to integration. Integration at first was studied in socio-economic terms, but later also in social-cultural terms. And with the attacks of 9/11 and the murder of Theo van Gogh in 2004, scholarly focus turned to the religious identity of Muslims and processes of radicalization.

Research on Muslims and Islam in the Netherlands took place in close conjunction with governmental policies in that field. There was significant interaction between the two, not least because the government—both the 'central' government and the large municipalities—commissioned numerous studies and engaged many scholars in order to develop their policies. However, complaints have been voiced in the academic community that scholarship on Islam and Muslims has become too policy-driven and that research funds are often linked to issues of radicalization and security.

## Research to be Continued

As said, most topics of research related to Muslims and Islam in the Netherlands have been covered by academic research. It would be presumptuous, however, to claim that certain topics of research have been studied in full. The presence of Muslims and their Islam in the Dutch context is a rapidly changing situation, and this needs continuous academic monitoring. These developments can be mostly attributed to the fact that in the Netherlands the second generation of Muslims is establishing itself and does so in ways that are often different from those of the first generation. We will mention four fields of research that deserve further academic exploration, bearing in mind that there are of course many more.

The first field of research is the political domain. The lack of political mobilization and lobbying initiatives among Dutch Muslims is striking when compared, for instance, with the Muslims in the United States. We may guess at the why and how—the second generation still being too intimidated by or too reverential vis-à-vis the first generation that lacks the know-how and capabilities to assert themselves politically—but little study has been conducted in this respect.

Second, there is the issue of gender and gender dynamics within the Muslim community. Among the second generation, girls and women are doing better in school and on the labour market than boys and men. This will most probably have its effects on the choice of marriage partners, but also on the Muslim women's role in society compared to that of Muslim men. At the same time, both men and women of the second generation are still finding their way among the demands and expectations of tradition, religion, and Dutch society.

Third, the topic of authority needs elaboration. This field of research has been mostly approached from the security angle (how do young Muslims get recruited by radical preachers, and why are they receptive to a radical Islamic message?), but needs extension in the domain of social and religious studies: what are the authoritative people and sources that Muslims of the second and third generation are receptive to, and why? In this respect, the roles of foreign influences and in particular the internet is most relevant and in need of further research.

Fourth and finally, the studies into the labour market need to be continued, especially because of the emerging class of highly educated Muslims, but research also needs to be expanded into the domain of entrepreneurship for it is to be expected that a new class of allochthone entrepreneurs will emerge. In that case it will be interesting to see to what extent transnational ties will contribute to their success or, as has been indicated by some, to what extent in particular young Turkish entrepreneurs might prefer to take their business to Turkey.

## Research to be Initiated

In addition to research that needs to be continued and widened, we suggest that research needs to be initiated in several additional fields. In doing so we are fully aware that these topics are not entirely novel since they may have already been touched upon by scholars. However, we argue that a larger international, transnational, and Dutch context is needed in order to understand certain developments of Muslims and Islam within the Netherlands. This is in particular the case with the following fields of research.

The first field of research proposed here is that of the arts, like literature, paintings, cabaret, hip-hop music, and architecture—a field that has received limited attention so far but is rapidly evolving. The international and transnational context in this respect is self-evident.

Second, while Islam is often approached as a separate or even foreign religion in the Netherlands, it may very well be argued that with the emergence and self-assertion of the second generation Muslims, their religiosity is becoming merged with the Dutch religious landscape. Islam may essentially remain the same, but the Muslims are distinctively Dutch in their education, their presentation in the public domain, and their outlook on the world. What effect does this have on the religiosity of Dutch Muslims?

Closely connected hereto is the next field of research: the impact of religion on social bonding and isolation. Given the fact that religiosity is resurging in the Netherlands—albeit not in its traditional forms—the impact of religion on social structures will become important in the near future. The expression of this religiously motivated bonding or isolation may be social, political, and even economic. In Dutch scholarship, research is only gradually emerging on this topic. While in the context of Islam these issues have been researched in terms of integration and radicalization, with the next generations of Muslims the question becomes more pertinent whether and how they compare and relate to other religious communities in the Netherlands.

The fourth field of research that deserves more attention is that of the Dutch Muslim religious infrastructure, in particular with regard to education, counselling, and adjudication. As has become clear in this chapter, this infrastructure is almost non-existent in the Netherlands, but with the decidedly religious, educated, and assertive second generation it is foreseeable that such infrastructure will be established. That infrastructure does not necessarily have to emerge as a united, singular system—indeed, one can already discern numerous initiatives in this respect, in particular with regard to religious education—but the apparent need among the Muslims for established religious authorities and institutions may very well push current developments in new directions.

## Bibliography

Aalst, C. van 2002. *Vrouwenbesnijdenis in Nederland*. Amsterdam: VU Wetenschapswinkel.
Advies Commissie Vreemdelingen Zaken (ACVZ) 2008. *Nederland migratieland, ook in 2025 (g)een probleem*. The Hague: SDU.
AIVD. 1998. *De Politieke Islam in Nederland*. The Hague: Ministerie van Binnenlandse Zaken.
AIVD. 2004a. *From Dawa to Jihad*. The Hague: Ministry of Interior.
AIVD. 2004b. *Saoedische invloeden in Nederland—Verbanden tussen salafistische missie*. The Hague: Ministerie van Binnenlandse Zaken.
AIVD. 2006. *De gewelddadige jihad in Nederland. Actuele trends in islamitisch-terroristische dreiging*. The Hague: Ministerie van Binnenlandse Zaken.
AIVD. 2007. *The Radical Dawa in Transition: The Rise of Islamic Neoradicalism in the Netherlands*. The Hague: Ministry of Interior.
AIVD. 2010a. *Resilience and Resistance*. The Hague: Ministry of Interior.
AIVD. 2010b. *Local Jihadist Networks in the Netherlands: An Evolving Threat*. The Hague: Ministry of Interior.
Amersfoort, J. M. M. van. 1974. *Immigratie en minderheidsvorming: een analyse van de Nederlandse situatie 1945–1973*. Alphen aan den Rijn: Samsom.
Amsterdam, G. van. 2008. *Notitie Scheiding Kerk en Staat* (online publication: <http://www.amsterdam.nl>).
Andree, T., A. van Dijk, and K. de Jonge. 1990. *De moskee is om de hoek. Ontmoetingen met islamitische jongeren*, The Hague: Boekencentrum.
Andriessen, I., J. Dagevos, E. Nievers, and I. Boog. 2007. *Discrimnatiemonitor niet-westerse allochtonen op de arbeidsmarkt*. The Hague: SCP.
Andriessen, I., E. Nievers, L. Faulk, and J. Dagevos. 2010. *Liever Mark dan Mohammed? Onderzoek naar arbeidsmarktdiscriminatie van niet-westerse migranten via praktijktests*. The Hague: SCP.
Baehr, P. R. 2008. 'Human Rights and Counterterrorism from a Transatlantic Perspective: The Cases of the United States and the Netherlands'. Conference paper, University of Pittsburg. <http://www.ucis.pitt.edu/euce/events/conferences/PDFs/Baehr.pdf>.

Bakas, A., R. Kip, V. David, and H. van Wolde. 2000. *Polderpalet: Management van diversiteit*. Alphen aan den Rijn: Samsom.
Bakelen, F. A. van. 1983. 'Implementatie van het recht van de islam in het Nederlandse recht en wetgeving', in *Recht van de Islam*. Maastricht: RIMO.
Bakelen, F. A. van. 1984. 'De imam in het Nederlandse arbeidsrecht', in *Recht van de Islam*. Maastricht: RIMO.
Bakker, L., K. van Mourik, A. J. Gehring, M. M. Claessen, and E. Harmsen. 2010. *Sharia in Nederland. Een studie naar islamitische advisering en geschilbeslechting bij moslims in Nederland*. The Hague: WODC.
Bartels, E. 2000. '"Dutch Islam": Young People, Learning and Integration', *Current Sociology* 48(4): 59–73.
Bartels, E. 2004. 'Female Circumcision among immigrant Muslim Communities: Public Debate in The Netherlands', *Journal of Muslim Minority Affairs* 24(2): 393–9.
Bartels, E. 2007. 'Civil Society on the Move in Amsterdam: Mosque Organisations in the Slotervaart District', *Journal of Muslim Minority Affairs* 27(3): 455–71.
Bartels, K. and I. Haaier. 1995. *Vrouwenbesnijdenis en Somalische vrouwen in Nederland*. Utrecht: Stichting Pharos.
Baumann, G. and T. Sunier (eds.) 1995. *Post-Migration Ethnicity: Cohesion, Commitments, Comparisons*. Amsterdam: Het Spinhuis.
Becker, C. 2009. '"Gaining Knowledge": Salafi Activism in German and Dutch Online Forums', *Masaryk University Journal of Law and Technology* 3(1): 79–98.
Becker, J. and J. de Hart. 2006. *Godsdienstige Veranderingen in Nederland*. The Hague: SCP.
Beek, J. H. van de. 2010. *Kennis, Macht en Moraal: de productie van wetenschappelijke kennis over de economische effecten van migratie naar Nederland, 1960–2005*. Amsterdam: UvA.
Beemsterboer, M. 2011. 'Geloven in onderwijs. Het kennisgebied geestelijke stromingen in Nederland', *Tijdschrift voor Religie, Recht en Beleid* 2(3): 18–31.
Berger, M. S. 2005. 'Sharia in Canada: An Example for The Netherlands?' in P. van der Grinten and T. Heukels (eds.), *Crossing Borders: Essays in European and Private International Law, Nationality Law and Islamic Law in Honour of Frans van der Velden*. Deventer: Kluwer,173–84.
Berger, M. S. 2006. 'Religieuze grenzen aan de vrijheid van meningsuiting: De Deense spotprenten voor de Nederlandse rechter', *NJCM-Bulletin* 31(5): 664–75.
Berger, M. S. 2007. 'Sharia in Nederland is heel Nederlands', *Ars Aequi* (June): 506–10.
Berger, M. S. 2008. *Islam binnen de dijken: Gids voor gemeentebeleid inzake islam, sociale cohesie en de-radicalisering*. Utrecht: Forum.
Berger, M. S. 2010a. 'Bescherming van gelovigen, of ook van godsdiensten en godsdienstige gevoelens?' *Tijdschrift voor Religie, Recht en Beleid* 1(1): 68–74.
Berger, M. S. 2010b. *Monografie Naturalisatie and Integratie "Religie"*. The Hague: SDU.
Berger, M. S. 2010c. 'Sharia en religieuze familierechtspraak in Nederland', *Tijdschrift voor Religie, Recht en Beleid* 1(2): 49–62.
Berger, M. S. 2010d. 'Overzicht van burka-wetgeving in Frankrijk, Belgie en Nederland', *Tijdschrift voor Religie, Recht en Beleid* 1(3): 96–106.
Berger, M. S. 2011a. 'Islamitisch bankieren in Nederland'. *Rechtstreeks* 4: 79–85.
Berger, M. S. 2011b. 'Het afdwingen van een islamitische verstoting', *Tijdschrift voor Religie, Recht en Beleid* 2(2): 99–104.
Beroud, H. 1989. 'Het spel meespelen of buitenspel komen te staan. Politieke en maatschappelijke participatie van minderheden in Nederland', in R. Haleber (ed.), *Rushdie-effecten: Afwijzing van moslim-identiteit in Nederland?* Amsterdam: SUA.
Berting, J. 2006. *De versplinterde samenleving*. Delft: Eburon.

Bijsterveld, S. C. van. 2008. *Overheid en Godsdienst. Herijking van een Onderlinge Relatie*. Nijmegen: Wolf Legal Publishers.

Blauw, W. 2010. 'Kansen voor Utrechtse kerken binnen de Wmo', *Tijdschrift voor Religie Recht en Beleid* 1(2): 63–75.

Blom, M., J. Oudhof, R. V. Bijl, and B. F. M. Bakker (eds.) 2005. *Verdacht van criminaliteit. Allochtonen en autochtonen nader bekeken*. The Hague/Voorburg: CBS and WODC.

Bochove, M. van, K. Rusinovic, and G. Engbersen. 2009. 'Lokaal of transnationaal: actief burgerschap bij de allochtone middenklasse', in K. Rusinovic and M. van Bochove (eds.), *Tijdschrift voor Beleid. Politiek en Maatschappij* 36(1): 27–39.

Boele-Woeki, K., I. Curry-Sumner, and W. Schrama. 2009. *De juridische status van polygame huwelijken in rechtsvergelijkend perspectief*. Utrecht: Utrecht Centre for European Research into Family Law.

Boenders, W. 2007. *Imam in Nederland: Rol, gezag en binding in de samenleving*. Amsterdam: Bert Bakker.

Böhler, B. 2004. *Crisis in de Rechtsstaat*. Amsterdam: Arbeiderspers.

Bolkestein, F. 1997. *Moslim in de polder*. Amsterdam: Contact.

Bonjour, S. 2010. *Grens en gezin: beleidsvorming en gezinsmigratie in Nederland 1955–2005*. Amsterdam: Aksant.

Borg, E. A. (ed.) 2008. *Religie in Nederland*. Zoetermeer: Uitgeverij Meinema.

Bos, K. van den, A. Loseman, and B. Doosje. 2009. *Waarom jongeren radicaliseren en sympathie krijgen voor terrorisme: onrechtvaardigheid, onzekerheid en bedreigde groepen*. The Hague: WODC.

Bosman, M. 2011. *De schijn-élite van de valse munters*. Amsterdam: Bert Bakker.

Bovenkerk, F. 2003. 'Over de oorzaken van allochtone misdaad', in F. Bovenkerk, M. Komen, and Y. Yesilgöz (eds.), *Multiculturaliteit in de strafrechtspleging*. The Hague: Boom Juridische uitgevers, 29–58.

Bovenkerk, F. 2009. *Etniciteit, criminaliteit en het strafrecht*. The Hague: Boom Juridische Uitgeverij.

Bovenkerk, F., M. Komen, and Y. Yesilgöz (eds.) 2003. *Multiculturaliteit in de strafrechtspleging*. The Hague: Boom Juridische uitgevers.

Brasse. P. and C. Huinder. 2010. *Opkomst- en stemgedrag van nieuwe Nederlanders: Gemeenteraadsverkiezingen 2010*. Utrecht: Forum.

Broex, S. (ed.) 1982. *Moslims in Nederland. Religieuze en sociale achtergronden*. The Hague: Regionaal Centrum Buitenlanders.

Brons, F. 1990. *Marokkaanse vrouwen en islam. Onderzoek naar geloofsbeleving van enkele Marokkaanse vrouwen in Zwolle*. Utrecht: Rijksuniversiteit Utrecht.

Brouwer, E. J. 2005. *De islam in huis. Een politieke positiebepaling*. The Hague: Staatkundig gereformeerde Partij (SGP).

Brug, W. van der, M. Fennema, S. van Heerden, and S. L. de Lange. 2009. 'Hoe heeft het integratiedebat zich in Nederland ontwikkeld?', *Migrantenstudies* 25(3): 198–220.

Brugman, J. 1990. 'De Alphense hoofddoekjesaffaire', in *Recht van de Islam*. Maastricht: RIMO.

Bruin, J. de 2005. *Multicultureel drama? Populair Nederlands televisiedrama, jeugd en etniciteit*. Amsterdam: Otto Cramwinckel Uitgeverij.

Buijs, F. 1998. *Een moskee in de wijk*. Amsterdam: Het Spinhuis.

Buijs, F. J. 2009. 'Muslims in The Netherlands: Social and Political Developments after 9/11', *Journal of Ethnic and Migration Studies* 35(3): 421–38.

Buijs, F. J., F. Demant, and A. Hamdy. 2006 *Strijders van eigen bodem: Radicale en democratische moslims in Nederland* Amsterdam: Amsterdam University Press.

Buitelaar, M. 2006. *Islam en het dagelijks leven. Religie en cultuur onder Marokkanen.* Amsterdam: Atlas.
Buitelaar, M. 2008. 'Islamisering van identiteit onder Marokkaanse jongeren', in E. A. Borg (ed.), *Religie in Nederland*. Zoetermeer: Uitgeverij Meinema, 239–52.
Buitelaar, M. 2009. *Van huis uit Marokkaans. Levensverhalen van hoogopgeleide migrantendochters.* Amsterdam: Bulaaq.
Burg, W. van der, K. Schuyt, and H. Nieuwenhuis. 2008. *Multiculturaliteit en Recht.* Deventer: Kluwer Juridisch.
Buskens, L. 2011. 'Wat rechters over sharia en moslims willen weten', *Rechtstreeks* 4: 113–19.
Buskens, L. P. H. M. 2004. 'De gemeenschap der moslims. Opvattingen over islamitische saamhorigheid in theorie en praktijk', in B. C. Labuschagne (ed.), *Religie als bron van sociale cohesie in de democratische rechtsstaat? Godsdienst, overheid en civiele religie in een post-geseculariseerde samenleving.* Nijmegen: Ars Aequi, 119–44.
BVD (Binnenlandse Veiligheids Dienst). 2002. *De democratische rechtsorde en islamitisch onderwijs: buitenlandse inmenging en anti-integratieve tendensen.* The Hague: Ministerie van Binnenlandse Zaken.
BZK (Ministry of Interior). 1983. *Minderhedennota.* The Hague: Ministerie van Binnenlandse Zaken.
BZK (Ministry of Interior). 1997–8. *Integratiebeleid betreffende etnische minderheden in relatie tot hun geestelijke bedienaren.* Tweede Kamer, vergaderjaar 1997–1998, 25 919, nos. 1–2.
BZK (Ministry of Interior). 2004. *Nota Grondrechten in een pluriforme samenleving.* The Hague: Ministerie van Binnenlandse Zaken.
BZK (Ministry of Interior). 2007. *Actieplan Polarisatie en Radicalisering 2007–2011.* The Hague: Ministerie van Binnenlandse Zaken.
Castillo Guerra, J., M. Glashouwer, and J. Kregting. 2008. *Tel je zegeningen. Het maatschappelijk rendement van christelijke kerken in Rotterdam en hun bijdrage aan sociale cohesie.* Nijmegen: NIM.
CBS (Centraal Bureau voor Statistiek). 2010a. *Jaarrapport Integratie 2010.* The Hague: CBS.
CBS (Centraal Bureau voor Statistiek). 2010b. *Jaarrapport Allochtonen 2010.* The Hague: CBS.
Cesari, J. 2009. *The Securitization of Islam in Europe.* CEPS CHALLENGE programme, Research Paper No. 15.
CGB (Commissie Gelijke Behandeling) 2003–11. *Gelijke Behandeling: oordelen en commentaar.* Utrecht: Wolf Legal Publishers (annual publication of rulings and commentaries). Utrecht: CGB.
Cliteur, P. B. 2004. *De neutrale staat, het bijzonder onderwijs en de multiculturele samenleving.* Leiden (oratie).
Cliteur, P. B. and V. van den Eeckhout (eds.) 2001. *Multiculturalisme, cultuurrelativisme en sociale cohesie.* The Hague: Boom Juridische uitgevers.
Coello, L. (ed.) 2013. *Het Minderhedenbeleid voorbij. Motieven en gevolgen.* Amsterdam: Amsterdam University Press.
Cohen, J. 2009. *Binden.* Amsterdam: Bert Bakker.
Commissie Bestrijding Vrouwelijke Genitale Verminking. 2005. *Bestrijding vrouwelijke genitale verminking. Beleidsadvies.* Zoetermeer: Commissie Bestrijding Vrouwelijke Genitale Verminking.
Commissie Blok. 2004. *Onderzoek Integratiebeleid.* The Hague: Tweede Kamer, Vergaderjaar 2003–4, TK 28689-9.
Commissie Hirsch Ballin. 1988. *Overheid, godsdienst en levensovertuiging, rapport van de Commissie van Advies inzake de Criteria voor Steunverlening aan Kerkgenootschappen en*

*andere Genootschappen op Geestelijke Grondslag*. The Hague: Ministerie van Binnenlandse Zaken.

Commissie Meijers. 2006. *Notitie van de Permanente Commissie van deskundigen in internationaal vreemdelingen-, vluchtelingen- en strafrecht naar aanleiding van de motie Wilders die een verbod van het openbaar gebruik van een burka voorstaat*. Utrecht.

Commissie Uitdragen Kernwaarden van de Rechtstaat. 2008. *Onverschilligheid is geen optie. De rechtsstaat maken we samen*. The Hague: Ministerie van Binnenlandse Zaken.

Cornelissens, A., J. Kuppens, and H. Ferwerda. 2009. *Huwelijksdwang: een verbintenis voor het leven? Een verkenning van de aard en aanpak van gedwongen huwelijken in Nederland*. The Hague: WODC.

Custers, M. 1985. 'Muslims in The Netherlands: Newcomers in an Established Society', *Journal of the Institute of Muslim Minority Affairs* 6(1): 167–80.

Dagdas, A. and W. el-Yandouzi. 2006. *Eergerelateerd geweld en percepties van de Islam* Amsterdam: Aletta.

Dagevos, J. 1998. *Begrensde mobiliteit: Over allochtone werkenden in Nederland*. Assen: Van Gorcum.

Dagevos, J. 2001. *Perspectief op integratie: over de sociaal-culturele en structurele integratie van etnische minderheden in Nederland*. The Hague: WRR.

Dagevos, J. 2006. *Hoge (jeugd)werkloosheid onder etnische minderheden*. The Hague: SCP.

Dagevos, J. 2008. *Dubbele nationaliteit en integratie*. The Hague: SCP.

Dagevos, J. 2009. *Ruimtelijke concentratie van niet-westerse migranten: Achtergronden, gevolgen en aangrijpingspunten voor het beleid*. The Hague: SCP.

Dagevos, J. and M. Gijsberts. 2010. *Integration in ten trends*. The Hague: SCP.

Dagevos, J., M. Gijsberts, J. Kappelhof, and M. Vervoort. 2007. *Survey integratie minderheden 2006: Verantwoording van de opzet en de uitvoering van een survey onder Turken, Marokkanen, Surinamers, Antillianen en een autochtone vergelijkingsgroep*. The Hague: SCP.

Dagevos, J., M. Gijsberts, and C. van Praag. 2003. *Rapportage minderheden 2003: Onderwijs, arbeid en sociaal-culturele integratie*. The Hague: SCP.

Dagevos, J., A. W. M. Odé, and T. Pels. 1999. *Etnisch-culturele factoren en de maatschappelijke positie van etnische minderheden: Een literatuurstudie*. Rotterdam: EU Rotterdam—ISEO.

Dagevos, J. and A. Roodenburg. 1998. *Ongekend talent: Hoog opgeleide allochtonen en hun kansen op instroom, door- stroom en uitstroom bij de ministeries van VROM, OCandW en VandW*. Rotterdam: ISEO—EU Rotterdam.

Dam, G. ten. 2002. 'Sociale competentie in de multiculturele samenleving. Een beschouwing', *Pedagogiek* 22(1): 70–81.

Dekker, G., J. de Hart, and J. Peters. 1997. *God in Nederland, 1966–1996*. Amsterdam: Anthos.

Dessing, N. 2001. *Rituelen van geboorte. Besnijdenis, huwelijk en overlijden bij moslims in Nederland*. Leuven: Peeters.

Dijk, T. van and E. Oppenhuis. 2002. *Huiselijk geweld onder Surinamers, Antillianen en Arubanen, Marokkanen en Turken in Nederland: Aard, omvang en hulpverlening*. The Hague: WODC.

Dijkstra, A. B., P. Jungbluth, and S. Ruiter. 2002. 'Verzuiling, sociale klasse en etniciteit: segregatie in het Nederlands basisonderwijs', *Sociale Wetenschappen* 44(4): 1–25.

Doğan, G., T. Pels, and H. El Madkouri. 2006. *Pedagogiek in moskee Ayasofya*. Utrecht: Forum.

Donselaar, J. and P. R. Rodrigues. 2002. *Monitor Rascisme and Extreem Rechts: Ernstiger Incidenten*. Amsterdam: Pallas Publications.

Donselaar, J. and P. R. Rodrigues. 2004. *Monitor Rascisme and Extreem Rechts: Extreemrechts groeit*. Amsterdam: Pallas Publications.

Donselaar, J. and P. R. Rodrigues. 2005. *Monitor Rassendiscriminatie: Discriminatie Ervaringen*. Amsterdam: Pallas Publications.

Donselaar, J. and P. R. Rodrigues. 2007. *Monitor Rascisme and Extremisme: Andere Aanpak*. Amsterdam: Pallas Publications.

Donselaar, J. and P. R. Rodrigues. 2008. *Monitor Rascisme and Discriminatie: Islamofobie neemt toe*. Amsterdam: Pallas Publications.

Donselaar, J. and P. R. Rodrigues. 2009. *Monitor Rascisme and Discriminatie: Discriminatie niet gemeld*. Amsterdam: Pallas Publications.

Donselaar, J. and P. R. Rodrigues. 2010. *Monitor Rascisme and Extremisme: Botsing van grondrechten*. Amsterdam: Pallas Publications.

Dourleijn, E. et al. 2011. *Vluchtelingengroepen in Nederland: Over de integratie van Afghaanse, Iraakse, Iraanse en Somalische migranten*. The Hague: SCP.

Douwes, D., M. de Koning, and W. Boender. 2005*Nederlandse moslims: van migrant tot burger*. Amsterdam: Amsterdam University Press.

Driessen, G., K. de Bot, and P. Jungbluth. 1989. *De effectiviteit van het onderwijs in eigen taal en cultuur: prestaties van Marokkaanse, Spaanse en Turkse leerlingen*. Nijmegen: Instituut voor Toegepaste Sociologie.

Dugteren, F. van. 1993. *Woonsituatie minderheden. Achtergronden en ontwikkelingen 1982-1990 en vooruitzichten voor de jaren negentig*. Rijswijk: SCP.

Duyvendak. J. W. and L. Veldboer. 2001. *Meeting point Nederland: Over samenlevingsopbouw. Multiculturaliteit en sociale cohesie*. Amsterdam: Boom.

Duyvendak, W. G. J. and P. W. A. Scholten. 2011. 'The Invention of the Dutch Multicultural Model and its Effects on Integration Discourses in The Netherlands', *Perspectives on Europe* 40(2): 39–45.

Eck, C. van. 2001. *Door bloed gezuiverd—eerwraak onder Turken in Nederland*. Amsterdam: Bert Bakker.

ECRI (European Commission against Racism and Intolerance). 2008. *Third Report on the Netherlands*. Strasbourg: European Commission.

Engbersen, G. and R. Gabriëls (eds.) 1995. *Sferen van integratie: naar een gedifferentieerd allochtonenbeleid*. Amsterdam: Boom.

Entzinger, H. B. 1986. *Het Minderhedenbeleid: Dilemma's voor de overheid in Nederlanden zes andere immigratielanden in Europa*. Meppel/Amsterdam: Boom.

Entzinger, H. B. 2002. *Voorbij de multiculturele samenleving*. Assen: Van Gorcum.

Entzinger, H. B. 2009. 'Integratie, maar uit de gratie. Multi-etnisch samenleven onder Rotterdamse jongeren', *Migrantenstudies* 1: 8–23.

Entzinger, H. B. and E. Dourleijn. 2008. *De lat steeds hoger: de leefwereld van jongeren in een multi-etnische stad*. Assen: Van Gorcum.

Ermers, R. 2007. *Eer en Eerwraak*. Amsterdam: Uitgeverij Bulaaq.

Ersanilli, E. 2009. 'Identificatie van Turkse migrantenjongeren in Nederland, Frankrijk en Duitsland', *Migrantenstudies* 25(1): 42–58.

Esch, W. and M. Roovers. 1987. *Islamitisch godsdienstonderwijs in Nederland, Engeland, Belgie en West-Duitsland*. Nijmegen: Instituut voor Toegepaste Sociologie.

Esveldt, I. and J. Traudes. 2001. *Kijk op en contacten met buitenlanders: immigratie, integratie en interactie*. The Hague: WRR.

EUMAP. 2009. *Muslims in EU Cities: Background Research Reports (Netherlands)*. New York: Open Society Institute.

Feijten, P. and M. van Ham. 2009. 'Neighbourhood Change... Reason To Leave?' *Urban Studies* 46(10): 2103–22.
Fermin, A. 1997. *Nederlandse Politieke Partijen over Minderhedenbeleid 1977–1995* (thesis). Amsterdam: Thesis Publishers.
Fermin, A. 2009a. 'Burgerschap en multiculturaliteit in het Nederlands integratiebeleid', in K. Rusinovic and M. van Bochove (eds.), *Tijdschrift voor Beleid. Politiek en Maatschappij* 36(1): 12–26.
Fermin, A. 2009b. *Islamitische en extreem-rechtse radicalisering in Nederland: Een vergelijkend literatuuronderzoek.* The Hague: WODC.
Foblets, M.-C., B. Djait, and K. Pieters (eds.) 2004. *Mietjes en machos: allochtone jeugddelinquentie.* Leuven/Voorburg: Acco.
Fortuyn, P. 1997. *Tegen de islamisering van onze cultuur: Nederlandse ideniteit als fundament.* Amsterdam: Bruna.
Forum. 2007. *Onverzilverd talent: Hoogopgeleide allochtonen op zoek naar werk.* Utrecht: Forum.
Forum. 2010a. *Fact Book. The Positie van moslims in Nederland.* Utrecht: Forum.
Forum. 2010b. *Onverzilverd Talent II: Marktkansen van hoogopgeleiden die starten vanuit achterstand.* Utrecht: Forum.
Forum. 2011. *Bewust omgaan met samenwerking: Verslag congres tegen huiselijk geweld en eergerelateerd geweld.* Utrecht: Forum.
Frissen, R. and S. Harchaoui. (eds.) 2011. *Integratie en de Metropool.* Amsterdam: Forum and Uitgeverij van Gennep.
Geest, L. van der and A. J. F. Dietvorst. 2010. *Budgettaire effecten van immigratie van niet-westerse allochtonen.* Utrecht: Nyfer.
Gemert, F. van. 1998. *Ieder voor zich. Kansen, cultuur en criminaliteit van Marokkaanse jongens.* Amsterdam: Aksant.
Gemert, F. van and M. S. Fleisher. 2002. *In de greep van de groep: Een onderzoek naar een Marokkaanse problematische jeugdgroep.* The Hague: WODC.
Ghaly, M. M. 2008. 'The Academic Training of Imams: Recent Discussions and Initiatives in the Netherlands', in W. B. Drees and P. S. Van Koningsveld (eds.), *The Study of Religion and the Training of Muslim Clergy in Europe.* Leiden: Leiden University Press, 369–402.
Giesbers, H. and Kroon, S. 1986. 'Intercultureel onderwijs, moedertalen anders dan standaard-Nederlands en taalbeschouwing', *Moer* 2(3): 116–24.
Gijsberts, M. and J. Dagevos. 2005. *Uit elkaars buurt. De invloed van etnische concentratie op integratie en beeldvorming.* The Hague: SCP.
Gijsberts, M. and J. Dagevos. (eds.) 2007. *Interventies voor integratie: The tegengaan van etnische concentratie en het bevorderen van interetnisch contact.* The Hague: SCP.
Gijsberts, M. and J. Dagevos. 2009. *At Home in the Netherlands? Trends in Integration of Non-Western Migrants.* The Hague: SCP.
Gijsberts, M. and J. Dagevos. 2010. *Integration in ten trends.* The Hague: CBS.
Gijsberts, M. and J. Dagevos. 2011. *At home in the Netherlands: Trends in Integration of Non-Western Migrants: Annual Report on Integration 2009.* The Hague: CBS.
Gijsberts, M. and M. Vervoort. 2007. 'Wederzijdse beeldvorming', in J. Dagevos and M. Gijsberts (eds.), *Jaarrapport Integratie 2007.* The Hague: SCP, 282–310.
Gils, B. A. A. van. 2002. *Allochtonen op de arbeidsmarkt*, in CBS, *Allochtonen in Nederland 2002.* Voorburg/Heerlen: Centraal Bureau voor de Statistiek.
Gowricharn. R. (ed.) 2006. *Falende instituties. Negen heikele kwesties in de multiculturele samenleving.* Utrecht: De Graaff.

Gowricharn, R. and R. Nolen. 2004. *Inburgering: mensen, instellingen en lokaal beleid.* Apeldoorn: Garant.
Graaf, B. de. 2010. 'How to Counter Radical Narratives: Dutch Deradicalization Policy in the Case of Moluccan and Islamic Radicals', *Studies in Conflict and Terrorism* 33(5): 408–28.
Graaf, B. de. 2011. 'Religion bites: religieuze orthodoxie op de nationale veiligheidsagenda', *Tijdschrift voor Religie, Recht en Beleid* 2(2): 62–80.
Groen, J. and A. Kranenberg. 2006. *Strijdsters van Allah. Radicale moslima's en het Hofstadnetwerk.* Amsterdam: Meulenhof.
Groen, J. and A. Kranenberg. 2008. *De opstand der gematigden. De groeiende waarheid van Nederlandse moslims.* Amsterdam: Meulenhof.
Groot, G.-R. de. 1983. 'Juridische vragen bij Nederlands-islamitische huwelijken', in *Recht van de islam.* Maastricht: RIMO, 43–58.
Groot, G.-R. de and S. Rutten. 1996. 'Polygamie, Naturalisatie, Bigamie?' in *Recht van de Islam.* Maastricht: RIMO, 19–60.
Groot, G.-R. de and M. Vink. 2008. *Meervoudige nationaliteit in Europees perspectief: een landenvergelijkend overzicht.* The Hague: Adviescommissie voor Vreemdelingenzaken.
Gruijter, M. de, E. Smits van Waesberghe, D. Bulsink, and C. van Middelkoop. 2011. *Jongeren en hun geloof. Geloofsbeleving van religiuze jongeren in de Nederlandse samenleving.* Utrecht: Forum.
Guadeloupe, F. and V. de Rooij (eds.) 2007. *Zo zijn onze manieren: visies op multiculturaliteit in Nederland.* Amsterdam: Rozenberg Publishers.
Haleber, R. (ed.) 1989. *Rushdie-effecten: Afwijzing van moslim-identiteit in Nederland?* Amsterdam: SUA.
Harchaoui, S. (ed.) 2006. *Hedendaags radicalisme: verklaring en aanpak.* Amsterdam: Het Spinhuis.
Harchaoui, S. and C. Huinder. (eds.) 2003. *Stigma: Marokkaan! Over afstoten en insluiten van een ingebeelde bevolkingsgroep.* Utrecht: Forum.
Hart, B. de. 2005. 'Het probleem van dubbele nationaliteit. Politieke en mediadebatten na de moord op Theo van Gogh', *Migrantenstudies* 21(4): 224–38.
Hart, J. de. 2006. *Meer geloof, minder kerk.* The Hague: SCP.
Hart, J. de, P. Schnabel, and R. Bijl (eds.) 2008. *Betrekkelijke betrokkenheid. Studies in sociale cohesie: sociaal en cultureel rapport 2008.* The Hague: SCP.
Heijden, F. van der. (ed.) 2009. *Jongeren en hun Islam: Aanbevelingen voor lokaal beleid.* Utrecht: Forum.
Hensen, A. J. F. M.1989. 'Islamitisch recht in en buiten rechte: de behandeling van Turkse en Marokkaanse boedels'. in *Recht van de Islam.* Maastricht: RIMO.
Hermans, P. 2004. 'Contranarratieven van Marokkaanse ouders: een weerwoord op discriminatie, paternalisme en stigmatisering', *Migrantenstudies* 20(1): 36–53.
Hoffer, C. 2009. *Psychische ziekten en problemen onder allochtone Nederlanders: beleving en hulpzoekgedrag.* Assen: Van Gorcum.
Hoogenboom, M. and P. Scholten. 2008. 'Migranten en de erfenis van de verzuiling in Nederland: een analyse van de invloed van de verzuiling op het Nederlandse migrantenbeleid', *Beleid en Maatschappij* 35(2): 107–24.
Hooghiemstra, E. 2003. *Trouwen over de grens: Achtergronden van partnerkeuze van Turken en Marokkanen in Nederland.* The Hague: SCP.
Hooven, M. ten. (ed.) 2006. *Ongewenste goden. De publieke rol van religie in Nederland.* Amsterdam: Boom/Sun.

Huis, M. van. 2007. 'Partnerkeuze van Allochtonen', in *CBS Bevolkingstrends 4e kwartaal 2007*. The Hague: CBS.

Hurenkamp, M. and E. Tonkens. 2011. *De onbeholpen samenleving. Burgerschap aan het begin van de 21e eeuw*. Amsterdam: Amsterdam University Press.

Immerzeel, G. van and A. C. Berghuis. 1983. *Leden van etnische minderheden in detentie: Een onderzoek naar Turkse, Marokkaanse en Surinaamse gedetineerden*. The Hague: WODC.

Inspectie Onderwijs. 1999. *Islamitisch basisonderwijs in Nederland*. The Hague: Ministerie van OC&W.

Inspectie Onderwijs. 2002. *Islamitische scholen en sociale cohesie*. The Hague: Ministerie van OC&W.

Inspectie Onderwijs. 2003. *Islamitische scholen nader onderzocht*. The Hague: Ministerie van OC&W.

Inspectie Onderwijs. 2008. *Bestuurlijke praktijken in het islamitisch onderwijs*. The Hague: Ministerie van OC&W.

Inspectie Onderwijs. 2009. *Islamitische scholen nader Onderzocht*. The Hague: Ministerie van OC&W.

Jansen, H. and J. J. G. Jansen. 2008. *Islam voor varkens, apen, ezels en andere beesten*. Amsterdam: Uitgeverij Van Praag.

Jansen, J. J. G. 1987. *Inleiding to Islam*. Muiderberg: Coutinho.

Jansen, P. A. A. M. 2003. 'Allochtone ondernemers in Nederland', in *Handboek Minderheden*. Houten and The Hague: Bohn Stafleu Van Loghum and Sdu/Koninklijke Vermande.

Janssen, J. 2008. *Je Eer of Je Leven? Een verkenning van eerzaken voor politieambtenaren en andere professional*. The Hague: Staple and De Koning.

Janssen, J. and R. Sanberg. 2010a. *Mogelijke eerzaken nader bekeken. Een onderzoek naar casuïstiek uit 2006*. The Hague: Ministerie van Binnenlandse Zaken.

Janssen, J. and R. Sanberg. 2010b. *Inzicht in Cijfers. Mogelijke eerzaken in 2007, 2008, 2009*. The Hague: Ministerie van Binnenlandse Zaken.

Jenissen, R. P. W. 2011. 'Arbeidsmigratie en de daarmee gepaard gaande gezinsmigratie naar Nederland: Een kwalitatieve toekomstverkenning', *TPEdigitaal* 5(4): 17–36.

Jennissen, R. P. W. and M. Blom. 2007. *Allochtone en autochtone verdachten van verschillende delicttypen nader bekeken*. The Hague: WODC.

Jennissen, R. P. W. and J. Oudhof. (eds.) 2007. *Ontwikkelingen in de maatschappelijke participatie van allochtonen: Een theoretische verdieping en een thematische verbreding van de Integratiekaart*. The Hague: Boom Juridische Uitgevers.

Jong, J.-D. de. 2007. *Kapot moeilijk: Een etnografisch onderzoek naar opvallend delinquent groepsgedrag van 'Marokkaanse' jongens*. Amsterdam: Amsterdam University Press.

Jordens-Cotran, L. 2000. 'De kwalificatie van de bruidsgave', *Nederlands Internationaal Privaatrecht* 4: 391–6.

Jordens-Cotran, L. 2007. *Nieuw Marokkaans Familierecht en Nederlands IPR*. The Hague: SDU Juridisch.

Junger, M., K. Wittebrood, and R. Timman. 2001. 'Etniciteit en ernstig en gewelddadig crimineel gedrag', in R. Loeber, W. N. Slot, and J. A. Sergeant (eds.), *Ernstige en gewelddadige criminaliteit in Nederland. Omvang, oorzaken en interventies*. Houten: Bohn Stafleu en Loghum, 97–128.

Justitiële Verkenningen. 1979. *De tweede generatie gastarbeiders*. The Hague: WODC.

Justitiële Verkenningen. 1997. *Integratie*. The Hague: WODC.

Justitiële Verkenningen. 2007. *Religie en Grondrechten.* The Hague: WODC and Boom Juridische Uitgeverij.
Justitiële Verkenningen. 2013. *Arbeidsmigratie.* The Hague: WODC.
Kabdan, R. 1987. *Het onderwijs in de Turkse taal en cultuur.* Amsterdam: Universiteit van Amsterdam.
Kadrouch-Outmany, K. 2014. 'Burial Practices and Desires among Muslims in the Netherlands: A Matter of Belonging', *Canadian Journal of Netherlandic Studies* (Special issue: *Islam in the Netherlands: Entering the Twenty-First Century*) 33–4(2.1): 107–28.
Keizer, M. and S. Keuzenkamp. 2011. *Moeilijk werken: Gezondheid en de arbeidsdeelname van migrantenvrouwen.* The Hague: SCP.
KIEM. 2005. *Religie binnen stedelijk beleid.* Kenniscentrum Grote steden / Kennisnet Integratiebeleid en Etnische Minderheden (KIEM) i.s.m. Kenniscentrum Maatschappij en Religie (KCMR).
Klaver, J., J. Mevissen, and A. Odé. 2005. *Etnische Minderheden op de Arbeidsmarkt: Beelden en Feiten, Belemmeringen en Oplossingen* (onderzoek in opdracht van Ministerie van Sociale Zaken een Werkgelegenheid). Amsterdam: Regioplan Beleidsonderzoek.
Kleijwegt, M. 2005. *Onzichtbare ouders—de buurt van Mohammed B.* Amsterdam: Atlas-Contact.
Klop, C. J. 2010. 'Religie of etniciteit als bindmiddel?', *Migrantenstudies* 26(4): 246–54.
Koenen, B. 2011. *Etnische voorkeuren bij prvinciale verkiezingenn. Stemgedrag van allochtonen en autochtonen.* Utrecht: Forum.
Komen, M. (ed.) 2005. *Straatkwaad en jeugdcriminaliteit: Naar een algemene of een etnisch-specifieke aanpak?* Amsterdam: Het Spinhuis.
Konijn, E., D. Oegema, I. Schneider, B. de Vos, M. Krijt, and J. Prins. 2010. *Jong en multimediaal: mediagebruik en meningsvorming onder jongeren, in het bijzonder moslimjongeren.* The Hague: WODC.
Koning, M. de. 2008. *Zoeken naar een. 'Zuivere' islam. Geloofsbeleving en identiteitsvorming van jonge Marokkaans-Nederlandse moslims.* Amsterdam: Uitgeverij Bert Bakker.
Koning, M. de and E. Bartels. 2005. *Over het huwelijk gesproken: partnerkeuze en gedwongen huwelijken onder Marokkaanse Turkse en Hindoestaanse Nederlanders.* The Hague: ACVZ.
Koningsveld, P. S. van. 1982. *De islam.* Utrecht: De Ploeg.
Koningsveld, P. S. van and W. A. R. Shadid. 1997. 'Islam als minderheidsgodsdienst in Nederland', in J. E. Overdijk-Francis (ed.), *Handboek Minderheden.* Houten: Bohn Stafleu Van Loghum, 11–46.
Kooijman, H. 2008. 'Besneden uit liefde. Meisjesbesnijdenis landelijk aangepakt', *JeugdenCo* 2(4): 22–3.
Kool, R. S. B., A. Beijer, C. F. van Drumpt, J. M. Eelman, and G. G. J. Knoops. 2005. *Vrouwelijke genitale verminking in juridisch perspectief. (Rechtsvergelijkend) onderzoek naar de juridische mogelijkheden ter voorkoming en bestrijding van vrouwelijke genitale verminking.* Utrecht: Willem Pompe Instituut, sectie Strafrecht.
Koolen, B. 2010. 'Integratie en religie: Godsdienst en levensovertuiging in het integratiebeleid etnische minderheden', *Tijdschrift voor Religie, Recht en Beleid* 1(1): 5–26.
Korf, D. and F. Bovenkerk. (eds.) 2005. *Van de straat; Politie, multiculturaliteit en criminaliteitspreventie.* Politieacademie onderzoeksreeks. Apeldoorn: Elsevier Overheid.
Korf, D. J. and F. Bovenkerk (eds.) 2007. *Dubbel de klos. Slachtofferschap van criminaliteit onder etnische minderheden.* The Hague: Boom Juridische Uitgeverij.
Korf, D. J., M. Wouters, S. Place, and S. Koet. 2008. *Geloof en geluk: Traditie en vernieuwing bij jonge moslims.* Utrecht: Forum.

Korf, D. J., B. Yesilgoz, T. Nabben, and M. Wouters. 2007. *Van vasten tot feesten. Leefstijl, acceptatie en participatie van jonge moslims*. Utrecht: Forum.

Kroon, S. 1987. 'Leraren Nederlands en intercultureel onderwijs', in G. Extra, R. van Hout, and T. Vallen(eds.), *Etnische minderheden: Taalverwerving, taalonderwijs, taalbeleid*. Dordrecht: Foris.

Kroon, S. and J. Sturm. 1996. 'Davut, Canan en de schildpad: over (taal)onderwijs in een meertalige klas', *Spiegel* 14(1): 27–53.

Kruisbergen, E. W. and T. Veld. 2002. *Een gekleurd beeld: Over beoordeling en selectie van jonge allochtone werknemers*. Assen: Van Gorcum.

Kullberg, J. and I. Kulu-Glasgow. 2009. *Building Inclusion, Housing and Integration of Ethnic Minorities in the Netherlands*. The Hague: Sociaal en Cultureel Planbureau.

Kullberg, J., M. Vervoort, and J. Dagevos. 2009. *Goede buren kun je niet kopen. Over de woonconcentratie en woonpositie van niet-westerse allochtonen in Nederland*. The Hague: Sociaal en Cultureel Planbureau.

Kuppens, J., A. Cornelissens, and H. Ferwerda. 2008. *Leren van eer op scholen. Een onderzoek naar vroegsignalen van eergerelateerd geweld*. Arnhem: Advies- en Onderzoeksgroep Beke.

Kwaak, A. van der, E. Bartels, F. de Vries, and S. Meuwse. 2003. *Strategieën ter voorkoming van besnijdenis bij meisjes. Inventarisatie en aanbevelingen*. Amsterdam: Vrije Universiteit.

Laan, P. H. van der, A. A. M. Essers, and M. Smit. 1983. *Tehuisplaatsing van jongeren uit etnische minderheden: Een onderzoek naar de problematiek rond de plaatsing in tehuis of internaat van Surinaamse, Turkse en Marokkaanse jongeren*. The Hague: WODC.

Labyrinth Onderzoek and Advies. 2010. *Diversiteit in Wonen*. Utrecht: Forum.

Lakeman, P. 1999. *Binnen zonder kloppen: Nederlandse immigratiepolitiek en de economische gevolgen*. Amsterdam: Meulenhoff.

Landman, N. 1992. *Van mat tot minaret: de institutionalisering van de islam in Nederland*. Amsterdam: VU Uitgeverij.

Ledoux, G. and C. Felix. 2009. *Bestrijding van segregatie in het onderwijs in gemeenten. Verkenning van lokaal beleid anno 2008*. Universiteit van Amsterdam, uitgave Forum.

Leeuwen, B. van and R. Tinnevelt. (eds.) 2005. *De multiculturele samenleving in conflict: Interculturele spanningen, multiculturalisme en burgerschap*. Leuven: Acco.

Leun, J. van der and L. Avalon. 2009. *Informele huwelijken in Nederland: een exploratieve studie*. Leiden: Universiteit van Leiden.

Leuw, E. 1997. *Criminaliteit en etnische minderheden; een criminologische analyse*. The Hague: WODC.

Lindner, L., R. Schriemer, and J. Silversmith. 2003. *Kerncijfers discriminatie 2002. Klachten en meldingen over ongelijke behandeling: Een overzicht van discriminatieklachten en -meldingen*. Amsterdam: Landelijke Vereniging Anti Discriminatie Bureaus.

Lucassen, J. and R. Penninx. 1995. *Nieuwkomers, nakomelingen, Nederlanders: immigranten in Nederland 1550–1993*, 2nd edn. Amsterdam: Het Spinhuis.

Lucassen, J. and A. Ruijter. (eds.) 2002. *Nederland multicultureel en pluriform? Een aantal conceptuele studies*. Amsterdam: Aksant.

Lucassen, L. and A. J. F. Köbben. 1992. *Het partiële gelijk: Controverses over Onderwijs in Eigen Taal en Cultuur en de rol daarbij van Wetenschap en Beleid, 1951–1991*. Amsterdam: Swets & Zeitlinger.

Manenschijn, G. 2003. *Levenslang mores leren: de uitdaging van de multiculturele samenleving*. Amsterdam: Uitgeverij Ten Have.

Masselman, R. 1993. *Islam en integratie: Marokkaanse moskeeën en het integratieproces*. Amsterdam: Vrije Universiteit.

Maussen, M. 2006. *Ruimte voor de islam? Stedelijk beleid, voorzieningen, organisaties*. Amsterdam: Het Spinhuis.

Meerman, M. 1999. *Gebroken wit: Over acceptatie van allochtonen in arbeidsorganisaties*. Amsterdam: Thela Thesis.

Metselaar, T. 2005. *Een zwarte of een witte school? Een onderzoek naar de opvattingen van ouders over etniciteit bij de keuze van een basisschool voor hun kind*. Universiteit van Tilburg: Tilburgse Wetenschapswinkel.

Miedema, S., D. de Ruiter, and M. de Koning. 2008. 'De moskee als partner in het onderwijs? Een pedagogische casus interdisciplinair belicht', *Pedagogiek* 28(1): 3–10.

Moor, E. de. (ed.) 1985. *Arabisch en Turks op school: discussies over eigen taal- en cultuuronderwijs*. Muiderberg: Coutinho.

Mooren, P. and K. Ghonem-Woets (eds.) 2001. *De smalle marge van de multiculturele samenleving: De multiculturele leescultuur in onderwijs en bibliotheek, boekproductie en beleid*. The Hague: Biblion Uitgeverij.

Moors, A. 2009a. 'The Dutch and the Face Veil: The Politics of Discomfort', *Social Anthropology* 17(4): 393–408.

Moors, A. 2009b. *Rapport 'Gezichtssluiers: Draagsters en Debatten'*. Amsterdam: Universiteit van Amsterdam.

Moslim Informatiecentrum. 1980. *Gids voor moslims in Nederland*. The Hague: Moslim Informatiecentrum.

Motivaction. 2011. *Nationaal Hoofddoek Onderzoek*. Utrecht: Motivaction.

Muus, P. J. and R. Penninx. 1991. *Immigratie van Turken en Marokkanen in Nederland: een analyse van de ontwikkeling tussen 1970–1990, een vooruitblik op te verwachten immigratie en de consequenties voor beleid*. The Hague: Ministerie van Binnenlandse Zaken.

Nabben, T., B. Yesilgoz, and D. J. Korf. 2006. *Van Allah tot Prada. Identiteit, leefstijl en geloofsbeleving van jonge Marokkanen en Turken*. Utrecht: Forum.

Nahas, O. 2005. *Homo en moslim—hoe gaat dat samen? 1001 vragen over islam en homoseksualiteit*. Utrecht: Forum.

Nieuwenhuis, A. J. 2011. *Over de grens van de vrijheid van meningsuiting (3e druk)*. Nijmegen: Ars Aequi Libri.

Nieuwenhuis, A. J. and C. M. Zoethout. (eds.) 2009. *Rechtsstaat en religie: staatsrechtconferentie 2008, Universiteit van Amsterdam*. Nijmegen: Wolf Legal Publishers.

Nievers, E. and I. Andriessen. (eds.) 2010. *Discriminatiemonitor niet-westerse migranten op de arbeidsmarkt 2010: De tweede editie van de Discriminatiemonitor*. The Hague: SCP.

Obdeijn, H. and M. Schrover. 2008. *Komen en gaan: immigratie en emigratie in Nederland vanaf 1550*. Amsterdam: Bert Bakker.

OC&W (Ministry of Education). 2003. *Imams in Nederland: wie leidt ze op?* Adviescommissie Imamopleidingen, December.

Odé, A. W. M. and J. M. Dagevos. 1999. *Vreemd kapitaal: Hoger opgeleide minderheden op de arbeidsmarkt*. The Hague: Min. van Sociale Zaken en Werkgelegenheid.

Olde Monnikhof, M. and T. Buis. 2001. *De werving en selectie van etnische minderheden: Een onderzoek naar het zoekgedrag van werkzoekende etnische minderheden en het wervings- en selectiegedrag van werkgevers in zes sectoren*. Doetinchem: Elsevier Bedrijfsinformatie.

Oldenhuis, F. T. 2007. *Schurende Relaties tussen Recht en Religie*. Gorinchem: Uitgeverij van Gorcum.

Oudenhoven, J. P. van, et al. 2008. *Nederland deugt*. Groningen: Van Gorcum.
Pels, T. 1991. *Marokkaanse kleuters en hun culturele kapitaal: Opvoeden en leren in het gezin en op school*. Amsterdam/Lisse: Swets & Zeitlinger.
Pels, T. 2003. *Tussen leren en socialiseren. Afzijdigheid van de les en pedagogisch-didactische aanpak in twee multi-etnische brugklassen*. Assen: Van Gorcum.
Pels, T. and M. de Gruijter. 2005. *Vluchtelingengezinnen: opvoeding en integratie*. Assen: Van Gorcum.
Pels, T., M. de Gruijter, G. Dogan, and J. van der Hoek (eds.) 2006a. *Emancipatie van de tweede generatie: Keuzen en kansen in de levensloop van jonge moeders van Marokkaanse en Turkse afkomst*. The Hague: WODC.
Pels, T. and F. Lahri. 2008. *Jongeren en hun Islam: Onderzoeksrapport*. Utrecht: Forum.
Pels, T., F. Lahri, and H. El Madkouri. 2006b. *Pedagogiek in moskee Othman*. Utrecht: Forum.
Pels, T., F. Lahri, and H. El Madkouri. 2006c. *Pedagogiek in moskee Al Wahda*. Utrecht: Forum.
Penninx, R., H. Münstermann, and H. B. Entzinger. 1998. *Etnische minderheden en de multiculturele samenleving*. Groningen: Wolters-Noordhoff
Phalet, K., C. van Lotringen, and H. Entzinger. 2000. *Islam in de multiculturele samenleving: Opvattingen van jongeren in Rotterdam*. Utrecht: Ercomer.
Phalet, K. and J. van der Wall. (eds.) 2004. *Moslim in Nederland. Religie en migratie: sociaalwetenschappelijke databronnen en literatuur* (5 vols.). The Hague: SCP.
Pinto, D. 2004. *Beeldvorming en integratie: Is integratie het antwoord? Beeldvorming van Turken, Marokkanen en Nederlanders over elkaar*. Houten: Bohn Stafleu Van Loghum.
Pligt, J. van der and W. Koomen. 2009. *Achtergronden en determinanten van radicalisering en terrorisme*. The Hague: WODC.
Poorthuis, M. and T. Salemink. 2011. *Van Harem tot Fitna, Nederland 1848-2010*. Nijmegen: Valkhof Pers.
Poot, C. J. de and A. Sonnenschein. 2010. *Jihadi Terrorism in the Netherlands: A Description Based on Closed Criminal Investigations*. The Hague: WODC.
Prins, B. 2002. 'Het lef om taboes te doorbreken: Nieuw realisme in het Nederlandse discours over multiculturalisme', *Migrantenstudies* 18(4): 241–54.
Prins, B. 2004. *Voorbij de onschuld: het debat over integratie in Nederland*, 2nd edn. Amsterdam: van Gennep.
Rath, J., A. Meyer, and T. Sunier. 2008. 'The Establishment of Islamic Institutions in a De-pillarizing Society', *Tijdschrift voor Economische en sociale geografie* 88(4): 389–95.
Rath, J., R. Penninx, K. Groenendijk, and A. Meijer. 1996. *Nederland en zijn Islam: Een ontzuilende samenleving reageert op het ontstaan van een geloofsgemeenschap*. Amsterdam: Het Spinhuis.
Rijkschroeff, R., J. W. Duyvendak, and T. Pels. 2003. *Bronnenonderzoek Integratiebeleid*. Utrecht: Verwey-Jonker Instituut.
RMO (Raad voor Maatschappelijke Ontwikkeling). 1998. *Integratie in perspectief: Advies over integratie van bijzondere groepen en van personen uit etnische groeperingen in het bijzonder*. The Hague: SDU uitgevers.
RMO (Raad voor Maatschappelijke Ontwikkeling). 2004. *Over insluiting en vermijding: twee essays over segregatie en integratie*. The Hague: SDU uitgevers.
RMO (Raad voor Maatschappelijke Ontwikkeling). 2005. *Eenheid, verscheidenheid en binding: Over concentratie en integratie van minderheden in Nederland*. The Hague: SDU uitgevers.
RMO (Raad voor Maatschappelijke Ontwikkeling). 2010. *Naar een open samenleving? Recente ontwikkelingen in sociale stijging en daling in Nederland*. The Hague: SDU uitgevers.

Roelandt, T. and J. Veenman. 1989. *Minderheden in Nederland: positie op de woningmarkt.* Rotterdam: Instituut voor Sociologisch-Economisch Onderzoek.

Roex, I., S. van Stiphout, and J. Tillie. 2010. *Salafisme in Nederland: aard, omvang en dreiging.* Universiteit van Amsterdam: IMES.

Roosblad, J. 2002. *Vakbonden en immigranten in Nederland (1960-1997).* Amsterdam: Aksant.

Roose, E. 2009. *The Architectural Representation of Islam: Muslim-Commissioned Mosque Design in the Netherlands.* Amsterdam: Amsterdam University Press.

Ruijter, A. de and G. Extra. (eds.) 2002. *De multiculturele samenleving als uitdaging.* Amsterdam: Amsterdam University Press.

Rutten, S. W. E. 1983-2011. 'Rechtspraakoverzicht moslim/islam', in *Recht van de Islam.* Maastricht: RIMO.

Rutten, S. W. E. 1997. *Erven naar Marokkaans recht. Aspecten van Nederlands internationaal privaatrecht bij de toepasselijkheid van Marokkaans erfrecht* (thesis). Schoten: Intersentia.

Rutten, S. W. E. 2005. 'Cultuur en familierecht in eigen kring', in *Preadvies voor de Nederlandse Vereniging voor Rechtsvergelijking.* Deventer: Kluwer, 39-94.

Rutten, S. W. E. 2008a. 'Het gelijkheidsbeginsel bij Shari'ah-testamenten', *Migrantenrecht* 5: 156-64.

Rutten, S. W. E. 2008b. 'Het recht van de gescheiden vrouw om verlost te worden uit het huwelijk', *NJCM-bulletin* 33(6): 755-69.

Rutten, S. W. E. 2010. 'Besnijdeniszaken voor de Nederlandse rechter', in *Recht van de Islam.* Maastricht: RIMO, 67-78.

Rutten, S. W. E. 2011. 'Wat de Nederlandse rechter van de sharia weten moet', *Rechtstreeks* 4: 88-110.

Rutten, S. W. E. and M.-C. Foblets. 2006. 'De toelaatbaarheid van de verstoting: recente ontwikkelingen in Nederlands, Frans en Belgisch internationaal privaatrecht', in P. van der Grinten and T. Heukels (eds.), *Crossing Borders: Essays in European and Private International Law, Nationality Law and Islamic Law in Honour of Frans van der Velden.* Deventer: Kluwer, 195-213.

Sasse van Ysselt, P. van. 2010. 'Over het verbod op het dragen van gezichtssluers en andere gezichtsbedekkende kleding', *Tijdschrift voor Religie, Recht en Beleid* 1(3): 5-28.

Schmeets, H. 2010. 'Het belang van religieuze binding in sociale statistieken', *Tijdschrift voor Religie, Recht en Beleid* 1(3): 29-35.

Schmeets, H. and R. van der Bie (eds.) 2009. *Religie aan het Begin van de 21ste eeuw.* The Hague: CBS.

Schoorl, J. J., M. van de Klundert, and R. F. A. van den Bedem. 1994. *Een partner van verre.* The Hague: Gouda Quint.

SCP (Sociaal en Cultureel Planbureau). 2005. *Uit elkaars buurt: De invloed van etnische concentratie op integratie en beeldvorming.* The Hague: Sociaal en Cultureel Planbureau.

SCP (Sociaal en Cultureel Planbureau). 2009. *Jaarrapport Integratie 2009.* The Hague: Sociaal en Cultureel Planbureau.

SCP (Sociaal en Cultureel Planbureau). 2011. *Jaarrapport Integratie 2011.* The Hague: Sociaal en Cultureel Planbureau.

Shadid, W. A. R. 2006. 'Islamic Religious Education in the Netherlands', *European Education* 38(2): 76-88.

Shadid, W. A. R. 2007. *De multiculturele samenleving in ontwikkeling.* The Hague: SDU.

Shadid, W. A. R. 2008. *De multiculturele samenleving in crisis.* Heerhugowaard: Gigaboek.

Shadid, W. A. R. 2009a. *Het multiculturalismedebat en de islam in Nederland*. Tilburg: Universiteit van Tilburg.
Shadid, W. A. R. 2009b. 'Moslims in de media: de mythe van de registrerende journalistiek', in S Vellenga et al. (eds.), *Mist in de Polder. Zicht op ontwikkelingen omtrent islam in Nederland*. Amsterdam: Aksant, 173–93.
Shadid, W. A. R. 2009c. 'Het multiculturalismedebat en de islam in Nederland: Stigmatisering. uitsluiting en retoriek'. Rede uitgesproken ter gelegenheid van het afscheid als bijzonder hoogleraar in de interculturele communicatie aan de Universiteit van Tilburg op 30 oktober 2009. Tilburg: Universiteit van Tilburg Faculteit Geesteswetenschappen Tilburg.
Shadid, W. A. R. and P. S. van Koningsveld. 1992. *Islam in Dutch Society: Current Developments and Future Prospects*. Tilburg: Kok Pharos.
Shadid, W. A. R. and P. S. van Koningsveld. 1995. *De mythe van het islamitische gevaar: Hindernissen bij integratie*, 2nd edn. Kok: Kampen.
Shadid, W. A. R. and P. S. van Koningsveld. 1996. 'Islam in the Netherlands: Constitutional Law and Islamic Organizations', *Journal of the Institute of Muslim Minority Affairs* 1: 111–28.
Shadid, W. A. R. and P. S. van Koningsveld. 1997. *Moslims in Nederland. Minderheden en religie in een multiculturele samenleving*. Houten: Bohn Stafleu Van Loghum.
Shadid, W. A. R. and P. S. van Koningsveld. 2008. *Islam in Nederland en België. Religieuze institutionalisering in twee landen met een gemeenschappelijke voorgeschiedenis*. Leuven: Peeters.
Sijses, B. 2003. *Het importhuwelijk: dilemma's en oplossingen*. Utrecht: Forum.
Sinke, M. van. 2009. 'Islamitisch financieren', in *Recht van de Islam*. Maastricht: RIMO.
Slijper, B. 1999. 'Twee concepties van liberale tolerantie in een multiculturele samenleving', *Migrantenstudies* 15(2): 83–95.
Slootman, M. 2009. *Salafi-jihadi's in Amsterdam*. Utrecht: Forum.
Sniderman, P. and L. Hagendoorn. 2007. *When Ways of Life Collide: Multiculturalism and its Discontents in the Netherlands*. Princeton: Princeton University Press.
Sohilait, R. and V. Marinelli (eds.) 2009. *Atelierboek 2: Wijken op stand*. Utrecht: Forum en Uitgeverij van Gennep.
SPIOR. 2007. *Hand in hand tegen huwelijksdwang*. Rotterdam: SPIOR.
Stokkom, B. van, H. Sackers, and J.-P. Wils. 2006. *Godslastering, discriminerende uitingen wegens godsdienst en haatuitingen. Een inventariserende studie*. The Hague: Ministerie van Justitie.
Storms, O. and E. Bartels. 2008. *'De keuze van de huwelijkspartner'. Een studie naar partnerkeuze onder groepen Amsterdammers*. Amsterdam: VU.
Sunier, J. T. 1996. *Islam in beweging: Turkse jongeren en islamitische organisaties*. Amsterdam: Het Spinhuis.
Sunier, J. T. 2005a. 'Interests, Identities, and the Public Sphere: Representing Islam in the Netherlands since the 1980s', in J. Cesrai and S. McLoughlin (eds.), *European Muslims and the Secular State*. Aldershot: Ashgate, 85–98.
Sunier, J. T. 2005b. 'Constructing Islam: Places of Worship and the Politics of Space in the Netherlands', *Journal of Contemporary European Studies* 13(3): 317–34.
Sunier, J. T. 2009a. 'Islam in the Netherlands: Dutch Islam', in A. Triandafyllidou (ed.), *Muslims in 21st Century Europe: Structural and Cultural Perspectives*. London: Routledge, 121–36.
Sunier, J. T. 2009b. 'Milli Gorus and Suleymancis in the Netherlands', in F. Peter (ed.), *Manual of Islamic Movements*. Madrid: Casa Arabe, 235–46.
Sunier, J. T. 2009c. '"No white sugarbread in our neighborhood": Houses of Worship and the Politics of Space in Amsterdam', in J. Rath (ed.), *Ethnic Amsterdam: Immigrants and Urban Change in the Twentieth Century*. Amsterdam: Amsterdam University Press, 159–76.

Sunier, J. T. 2010a. 'Assimilation by Conviction or by Coercion? Integration Policies in the Netherlands', in A. Silj (ed.), *European Multiculturalism Revisited*. London: Zed Press, 214–35.
Sunier, J. T. 2010b. 'Islam in the Netherlands: A Nation Despite Religious Communities?' in J. T. Sunier and E. Sengers (eds.), *Religious Newcomers and the Nation State: Political Culture and Organized Religion in France and the Netherlands*. Delft: Eburon, 115–31.
Sunier, J. T., N. Landman, H. van der Linden, N. Bilgili, and A. Bilgili. 2011. *Diyanet: The Turkish Directorate for Religious Affairs in a Changing Environment*. Amsterdam: Universiteit Utrecht en Vrije.
Terlouw, G. J. (ed.) 1991. *Criminaliteitspreventie onder allochtonen: Evaluatie van een project voor Marokkaanse jongeren*. The Hague: WODC.
Tillie, J. 2006. *Processen van radicalisering. Waarom sommige Amsterdamse moslims radicaal worden*. Universiteit van Amsterdam: Instituut voor Migratie- en Etnische Studies.
Timmerman, C., P. Hermans, and J. Hoornaert (eds.) 2006. *Allochtone jongeren in het onderwijs: Een multidisciplinair perspectief*, 2nd edn. Apeldoorn: Garant.
Tonkens, E. 2009. *Tussen onderschatten en overvragen. Actief burgerschap en activerende instituties in de wijk*. Amsterdam: SUN Trancity—deSTADSWIJKstudies.
Tonkens, E. and G. Kroese. 2008. *Oefeningen in burgerschap in de multiculturele Samenleving. Case study Omwana (Oudere Migranten Werken aan een Nieuw Amsterdam)*. Amsterdam: Universiteit van Amsterdam / Stichting Actief Burgerschap.
Trappenburg, M. and H. Pellikaan. 2003. *Politiek in de multiculturele samenleving*. Amsterdam: Boom.
Tubergen, F. van and I. Maas. (eds.) 2006. *Allochtonen in Nederland in internationaal perspectief*. Amsterdam: Amsterdam University Press.
Turkenburg, M. 2002a. *Onderwijs in allochtone levende talen: Een verkenning in zeven gemeenten*. The Hague: SCP.
Turkenburg, M. 2002b. *Taal lokaal: gemeentelijk onderwijs in allochtone levende talen (OALT)*. The Hague: SCP.
Valk, H. de and N. van Nimwegen. 2003. 'De allochtone bevolking van Nederland: een uitdaging voor het onderwijsachterstandenbeleid', in W. Meijnen (ed.), *Onderwijsachterstanden in basisscholen*. Apeldoorn: OOMO/Garant.
van der Burg, W. 2009. *Het ideaal van de neutrale staat. Inclusieve, exclusieve en compenserende visies op godsdienst en cultuur* (oratie). Rotterdam: Erasmus Universiteit Rotterdam.
van Herten, M. 2009. 'Het aantal islamieten in Nederland', in CBS (ed.), *Religie aan het begin van de 21ste eeuw*. The Hague: CBS, 35–40.
van Ooije, H., R. Penninx, T. Rath, and T. Sunier. 1990. *Islam in Western Europe, with Special Reference to the Netherlands: A Bibliography of Islam and Islamic Immigrants and Society's Reactions, 1970–1991*, 2nd revised edn. (online publication).
Veenman, J. 1995. *Onbekend maakt onbemind: Over selectie van allochtonen op de arbeidsmarkt*. Assen: Van Gorcum.
Veenman, J. 1997. *Arbeidsmarkt en maatschappelijke ongelijkheid: Over oorzaken en gevolgen*. Assen: Van Gorcum.
Veenman, J. 1999. *Participatie en perspectief: Verleden en toekomst van etnische minderheden in Nederland*. Houten: Bohn Stafleu Van Loghum / Koninklijke Vermande.
Veenman, J. and T. Roelandt. 1994. *Onzeker bestaan: de maatschappelijke positie van Turken, Marokkanen, Surinamers en Antillianen in Nederland*. Amsterdam: Boom/ISEO.
Velden, F. J. A. van der. 2003. *Talaq in de rechtszaal? Verstoting en openbare orde* (oratie). Stichting tot Bevordering der Notariële Wetenschap.

Veldhuis, T. and W. Bakker. 2009. *Muslims in the Netherlands: Pensions and Violent Conflict*. MICROCON Policy Working Paper 6. Brighton: MOICROCON.

Vellenga, S., H. El Madkouri, and B. Sijsjes (eds.) 2009. *Mist in de polder. Zicht op ontwikkelingen omtrent de islam in Nederland*. Amsterdam: Amsterdam University Press.

Vellenga, S. and G. Wiegers. 2011. *Religie, binding en polarisatie: de reacties van de leiding van levensbeschouwelijke organisaties op islamkritische uitingen*. Amsterdam: Amsterdam University / WODC.

Verheggen, P. P. and F. Spangenberg. 2001. *Nieuwe Nederlanders: Etnomarketing voor diversiteitsbeleid*. Alphen aan den Rijn: Samsom.

Vermeulen, B. P. 2001. *Witte en zwarte scholen: Over spreidingsbeleid, onderwijsvrijheid en sociale cohesie*. The Hague: Elsevier.

Vermeulen, B. P. 2006. *Overwegingen bij een boerka verbod: Zienswijze van de deskundigen inzake een verbod op gezichtsbedekkende kleding*. The Hague: Ministerie van Justitie.

Vermeulen, H. (ed.) 1997. *Immigranten beleid voor de multiculturele samenleving:integratie-, taal- en religiebeleid voor immigranten in vijf West-Europese landen*. Amsterdam: Het Spinhuis.

Visser, H. 2009. 'Islamitisch bankieren: financieren met hindernissen', in *Recht van de Islam*. Maastricht: RIMO.

Vliegenthart, R. 2007. 'Immigratie en integratie: Relaties tussen maatschappelijke ontwikkelingen, parlement, media en steun voor anti-immigratiepartijen in Nederland', *Tijdschrift voor Communicatiewetenschap* 35(4): 369–84.

VNG (Vereniging Nederlandse Gemeenten). 2009. *Tweeluik Religie en Publiek Domein. Handvatten voor Gemeenten*. The Hague: Ministerie van Binnenlandse Zaken.

VROM (Ministry of Housing). 2004. *Zwarte vlucht. De (sub)urbane locatiekeuze van klassieke allochtonen in Amsterdam*. The Hague: Ministerie van Volkshuisvesting, Ruimtelijke Ordening en Milieubeheer.

VROM (Ministry of Housing). 2007. *Kiezen voor de stad. Kwalitatief onderzoek naar de vestigingsmotieven van de allochtone middenklasse*. The Hague: Ministerie van Volkshuisvesting, Ruimtelijke Ordening en Milieubeheer.

Waardenburg, J. 1983. 'The Right to Ritual: Mosques in the Netherlands in Analysis and Interpretation of Rites'. Essays to D. J. Hoens, *Nederlands Theologisch Tijdschrift* 37(3): 253–65.

Wagtendonk, K. (ed.) 1987. *Islam in Nederland, Islam op school*. Muiderberg: Coutinho.

Werkgroep-Waardenburg. 1983. *Religieuze voorzieningen voor etnische minderheden*, rapport van de niet-ambtelijke werkgroep o.l.v. Prof. Dr. Waardenburg; ('werkgroep Waardenburg'). The Hague: Ministerie van Binnenlandse Zaken.

Willemsen, F. 2007. *Huiselijk geweld en herkomstland: Een verkennend onderzoek naar de incidentie van huiselijk geweld en allochtone daders en slachtoffers*. The Hague: WODC.

WRR (Wetenschappelijke Raad voor het Regeringsbeleid). 1989. *Allochtonenbeleid*. The Hague: SDU.

WRR (Wetenschappelijke Raad voor het Regeringsbeleid). 2001. *Nederland als immigratiesamenleving*. The Hague: SDU.

WRR (Wetenschappelijke Raad voor het Regeringsbeleid). 2003. *Waarden, normen en de last van het gedrag*. Amsterdam: Amsterdam University Press.

WRR (Wetenschappelijke Raad voor het Regeringsbeleid). 2005. *Geloven in het Publieke Domein. Verkenningen van een Dubbele Transformatie*. Amsterdam: Amsterdam University Press.

WRR (Wetenschappelijke Raad voor het Regeringsbeleid). 2006a. *Dynamiek in islamitisch activisme: Aanknopingspunten voor democratisering en mensenrechten*. Amsterdam: Amsterdam University Press.

WRR (Wetenschappelijke Raad voor het Regeringsbeleid). 2006b. *Geloven in de Publieke Ruimte*. Amsterdam: Amsterdam University Press.

WRR (Wetenschappelijke Raad voor het Regeringsbeleid). 2007a. *Identificatie met Nederland*. Amsterdam: Amsterdam University Press.

WRR (Wetenschappelijke Raad voor het Regeringsbeleid). 2007b. *Nationale Identiteit en meervoudig verleden*. Amsterdam: Amsterdam University Press.

Zegers de Beijl, R. (ed.) 2000. *Documenting Discrimination against Migrant Workers in the Labour Market: A Comparative Study of Four European Countries*. Geneva: ILO.

Zessen, N. van 2010. 'Wat deed Ramadan in Rotterdam?' *Tijdschrift voor Religie, Recht en Beleid* 1(2): 32–48.

Zorlu, A. 2002. *Absorption of Immigrants in European Labour Markets: the Netherlands, United Kingdom and Norway*. Amsterdam: Thela Thesis.

## CHAPTER 5

# BELGIUM

### NADIA FADIL, FARID EL ASRI, AND SARAH BRACKE

## Introduction

WITH its estimated 500,000 followers, Islam has become a significant and visible religious tradition in the linguistically and regionally fractured kingdom of Belgium. This is most visible in the capital, where Muslims comprise approximately 17–25% of the population. Such an Islamic presence has effectively transformed the shape of the city: there is a growing presence and visibility of Muslim shops, Halal restaurants, Islamic libraries, or mosques in certain '*quartiers*', which Felice Dassetto describes as the 'Islamic territories' of Brussels (2011: 352). Moreover, 32% of babies born in Brussels (in contrast to 5.3% in Wallonia or 15.1% in Flanders) were given Muslim forenames such as Muhammad or Fatima (Dassetto 2011: 22). This new socio-geographical reality has stirred a number of controversies, including alarming predictions of a gradual Islamization of the capital.[1] In April 2011, the widely read Francophone daily *Le Soir* devoted one episode of its special series on the capital entitled '*The 7 capital clichés on Brussels*' to the Islamic presence in Brussels.[2] The special issue purportedly sought to downplay existing fears, yet the adverse way in which the subject was framed served, in fact, to confirm such fears. The results of a poll included in the online version of the special issue were revealing: 77% of the respondents agreed with the suggestion that Brussels was turning into a Muslim city.

This public attention to the presence of Islam in Belgium does not stand alone: Islam has become a crucial 'subject of debate' all over Western Europe, where the rise of post-1989 civilizational narratives, punctuated by global events such as 9/11 and campaigns such as the 'war on terror', engendered new frames which tightly connect security threats to Islam as well as problematize the demographic presence (and growth) of Muslims and Islam in Europe. This is the junction in which scholars began to explore the sociological contours

---

[1] See for instance Van Amerongen (2008) or Bawer (2006).
[2] 'Bruxelles, ville Musulmane?' ['Brussels, a Muslim town?'], *Le Soir*, 11 April 2011.

of a newly settled population and the production of knowledge on Islam in Europe has developed—a contextualization which is particularly salient for the Belgian case, where research on Muslims originates in the early 1980s, in contrast to neighbouring countries where an older Orientalist scholarship already existed due to former colonial ties (France or the Netherlands) or interactions with the Ottoman Empire (Germany). Research on Muslims in Belgium can therefore be characterized as fairly recent scholarship, which is strongly connected to recent public debates on Islam in Belgium.[3]

This chapter reviews scholarship published on Muslims in Belgium, and does so with two aims in mind. Firstly, we seek to offer an extensive—albeit non-exhaustive—overview of the literature produced in the last thirty years—which covers a wide range of issues from socio-economic integration, to Islam and secularism. Secondly, we seek to show how a large part of this literature is traversed by a central concern with integration. This is expressed through the two major tropes underlying discussions about Muslims in Belgium: the question of socio-economic integration of Muslims and that of their compliance to the liberal and secular structure of dominant forms of citizenship. While these different ways of addressing the question of integration resonate, to a certain extent, with regional and linguistic fractures within Belgium (Francophone vs. Dutch speaking), it is important to note that they reflect a broader epistemic fracture that characterizes the scholarship on Muslims in Europe that addresses Muslims either as low-skilled migrants or as a religious minority.

We have structured this chapter in the following way. In the first section, we briefly invoke the historical context in which scholarship on Islam in Belgium emerged. The second section discusses the two distinct notions on integration that underpin the literature on Islam in Belgium. After this brief theoretical contextualization, we discuss the existing scholarship on the socio-economic situation of Muslims in Belgium, the political and institutional aspects of the Muslim presence in Belgium, and the tensions between Islam and a secular public sphere. The sixth section deals with the scholarly concern with radical Islam, and is followed by the final section on Islamophobia.

# ISLAM IN BELGIUM: A HISTORICAL CONTEXT

The presence of Islam on Belgian soil is first registered in 1829, i.e. a year before Belgium's national independence (1830). A statistical report by the Turkish consul based

---

[3] The study of Islam was mostly restricted to Oriental and Islamic studies, with some exceptions (Hitchinson 1978; Dobbelaere and Billiet 1974), under the auspices of the Societé Belge d'Etudes Orientales (established in 1921) until about 1989. These studies were focused on historical and archaeological accounts of Muslim societies or a textual analysis of the Arabic language, rather than contemporary sociological realities of Islam. These textual analyses, furthermore, often failed to engage with century-old hermeneutical debates within the Muslim tradition, as well as the 'lived' experiences of Muslims. A notable exception is the work of Armand Abel (1903–73), who produced one of the most important French Qur'an translations (in 1951) and introduced Islamic studies at the Université libre de Bruxelles.

in Antwerp estimated the number of individuals originally from the Muslim world at 6,000 (Panafit 1999). During the Second World War a special regimen of Muslim soldiers from the French colonies in North and sub-Sahara Africa briefly operated in the east-southern part of the country.[4] Yet the visibility of Muslims remains rather limited, something that changes profoundly in the second half of the twentieth century.

In 1964, bilateral labour migration agreements were signed between Belgium on the one hand, and the Maghreb countries (with Tunisia and Algeria in 1967) and Turkey on the other. Tens of thousands of workers from these countries subsequently migrated to Belgium to be employed in low-skilled jobs in the coalmine, steel, and car industries. These migration flows, moreover, were also driven by a 'demographic factor'—an often-neglected dimension in the discussion of these immigration policies. The sociologist Albert Martens shows, in a study published in 1973, that several policy documents at that time reveal a desire for the 'definitive settlement' of immigrants in the host countries as a way to compensate for the anticipated demographic shortage and ageing of the population. Workers were encouraged to bring their spouses and children to Belgium and to view their residence in Belgium as permanent rather than temporary (Martens 1973: 238). The overwhelming majority of the Muslim population in Belgium are thus the descendants of post-1964 workers who migrated to Belgium either through a job contract or through family reunion.[5] This might account for the fact that initially the scholarship was primarily concerned with the socio-economic predicaments of this population rather than its religious or cultural components.

The recruitment of what then was called 'guest workers' from the Maghreb and Turkey came to an abrupt end with the unilateral closing of the Belgian borders for foreign manual labour forces in 1974.[6] In the same year Islam joins the ranks of the officially recognized confessions in Belgium. Both of these amendments of existing policies and regulations indicate a significant shift in migration policy, which is related to a transformation of the imaginary of temporary guest workers who at some point return to their country into an imaginary of a 'foreign' minority settled in Belgium. Another important policy shift occurs a decade later, in 1984, when the Minister of Justice, the liberal Jean Gol, prepared a law on immigration which sought to further limit the access to the Belgian territory, to limit access of migrants to social welfare, and to bring family reunions to a halt. The proposal was denounced as right-wing and racist, and incited

---

[4] The regimen briefly passed through the Belgian village of Gembloux between May and June 1940, which is documented in the museum of Cortil-Noirmont, and left an impact upon the collective memory of Belgian-born Muslims. More recently, various events were organized at the military cemetery in order to commemorate the Muslim soldiers who died at the front. Such moments of commemoration signal not only the celebration of an anti-fascist Islam, but also provide ground for the construction of a collective Belgian Islamic memory.

[5] Anne Morelli suggests that 50,000 Maghrebi women moved to Belgium between 1961 and 1977, which amounts to half of the Maghrebi population which settled in Belgium (Morelli 1992).

[6] The closure of Belgian borders occurred in the wake of the 1973 oil crisis, which reached heights of 100,000 unemployed at the beginning of the 1970s, only to rise to 300,000 unemployed a decade later.

various political demonstrations gathering millions of people, as well as a hunger strike. The Law Gol, approved in 1985, also accelerated the process of acquiring Belgian citizenship, thereby fostering Muslims' interrogations about their presence, their settlement, and the question of roots. Many families who had sought a definitive return home to their countries of origin, ended up settling in Belgium or finding ways to settle in both (or in-between) countries.

A first important dimension we want to highlight in this respect concerns the ways in which local realities of Islam in Belgium are gradually and increasingly connected, in complex and diverse manners, with international predicaments. Questions of attachment with countries of origin, sympathy for certain causes in the Muslim world, identification with a global community of believers or the presence of transnational religious movements in Belgium began to shape the dominant perception of this newly settled population who were previously merely seen as 'workers'. In the early years, Islam in Belgium was primarily mediated by 'foreign' rather than domestic agendas. A case in point is the symbolic donation, in 1969, of the Oriental pavilion of the Cinquantenaire Park in Brussels to the Saudi King Faisal, for the purpose of hosting the Islamic Cultural Centre (ICC), which was founded in 1968 and figured as a non-official interlocutor to the state (Kanmaz and Zemni 2008). The intensive role of home countries such as Morocco and Turkey in the organization of the Muslim population further underlined the predominance of this 'foreign perspective'.[7] Moreover, this period is characterized by a number of rapid changes in the Arab world, with ideas such as 'Islamic revolution' or 'Muslim state' installing themselves in the political imaginary as an alternative to previously prevailing nationalist (pan-) Arab discourses. In 1969 two important institutions, which both articulate an Islamic identity project in tension with Arab nationalist ideological projects, were created: the Organization of the Islamic Conference (OIC) and the World Muslim League (WML). The succession of global events, such as the oil crisis initiated by Saudi Arabia or the establishment of the first Republic in the Middle East by Ayatollah Khomeini, contributes to a shift in the local perception of Muslims.

From the late 1980s onwards, the interplay between local and international events informing the organization of Muslim communities in Belgium is increasingly framed in terms of 'radicalization'. Several commentators and politicians began expressing their fears of a growing sympathy of Muslims for 'fundamentalist' or 'radical' Islam. A first important event in this context was the pro-Libya demonstration in Brussels, in April 1986, in response to the bombing of Tripoli and Benghazi by the Americans, who accused the Qaddafi regime of standing behind an attack on American soldiers in Berlin. This demonstration gathered a large crowd, among them a significant number of Muslims. The sight of hundreds of Muslims marching in the streets of Brussels attracted much media attention, mostly in the Francophone press, and several commentators

---

[7] It suffices here to refer to the strong role of the Turkey-sponsored *Diyanet* in the religious organization (mosques, Islamic instruction, etc.) of the Turkish community (<http://www.diyanet.be>) or the role of the *Widadiya* (Amicales) in the early years of the Moroccan community (for a fuller account see Bousetta 2001).

and politicians, who saw this as a pro-fundamentalist demonstration, warned against the presence of militant groups in the capital.[8] A second important event occurred a few years later, on 29 March 1989, when Abdallah Al-Ahdal, the director of the ICC who was considered a 'moderate' voice in the debate on Islam, and his librarian Salem al-Buhairi, were found dead in the offices of the Centre. The murder occurred a few days after Al-Ahdal publicly took a critical stand on the Iranian fatwa against Salman Rushdie. While the case was never solved, it fuelled existing fears and fantasies of violent militant Muslim groups in Belgium. Last but not least, 1989 is also the year in which the headscarf debate, which first occurred in France, found its way to Belgium. This debate is characterized by a sense of discomfort over the headscarf, which was largely perceived by the opponents as a sign of a return to tradition or a rejection of Western norms and values.[9]

A second dimension we want to highlight is the way in which the history of Islam in Belgium is shaped by a nationalist reform of the Belgian state apparatus. In 1980 the country went through a major state reform in which the different regions and linguistic communities were granted increased legislative powers. Building on previously existing different sensibilities with respect to questions of religion or language, this institutional and legal reform effectively rendered an important part of migration policy, and notably the question of 'integration', into a communitarian matter (whilst maintaining an immigration policy at the federal level). As a result, more regionally based initiatives were set up and different kinds of migration policy developed in the different parts of the country. In Flanders the establishment of a wide network of integration centres emerged throughout the 1980s, which is complemented after 1998 by the recognition of minority organizations (the federations). In Wallonia, regional integration centres are locally and individually organized and address questions of integration mostly through the concept of social cohesion (*cohésion sociale*) rather than ethno-cultural difference (Gsir 2006; Jacobs 2004). As a result, two distinct models of integration emerged in the Belgian landscape.[10] In the Francophone part of the country an elaborate political and media discourse that 'others' migrants, notably through the lens of 'radicalization', developed. This discourse is influenced by the Francophone intellectual debates (in France and the postcolonial Maghreb region) where concerns about radical Islam were prominent since the late 1970s (Kepel 1987). In the meantime, Flanders was spellbound by another important political phenomenon: the electoral break-through (1991) and subsequent electoral successes of the right-wing party Vlaams Blok. What began as a scission of the Flemish nationalist party in the late 1970s quickly grew, throughout the 1980s and early

---

[8] Dassetto and Bastenier (1987) provide a detailed analysis of the way in which the media, and more particularly the RTBF (the Francophone national broadcasting service), had a crucial share in the moral panic around the pro-Libya demonstration.

[9] Noteworthy in this respect is the essay by Foulek Ringelheim 'Les voiles de l'intolerance' ['The Veils of Intolerance'] published in 1989, which defends the thesis that veiling is incompatible with liberal democracy.

[10] For an elaborate account of this question see Adam (2013).

1990s, into one of the main right-wing political parties in Belgium and Western Europe. With electoral successes attaining 33% in its hometown Antwerp (2000) and 24.2% at a regional Flemish level (2004), the political party succeeded in turning the 'migration question' into an urgent political issue.

Thus the rise of Vlaams Blok played a crucial role in the making of Belgian migration policy: notwithstanding earlier initiatives to support migrants,[11] it is only in the early 1990s that a more coherent migration policy became an important political preoccupation. This concern resulted in the establishment of the Royal Commissariat for Migration Policy in 1989 (see also Blommaert and Verscheuren 1992), an institutional body which provided the first state-authorized definition of the question of integration, and can be seen as the first step towards the institutionalization of the integration apparatus which—particularly in Flanders—was further developed through a number of special decrees (in 1998 and 2004).[12] One of the tasks of the Royal Commissariat was to ensure that the project of a representative body of Muslims was realized. In the northern part of the country such a representative body was considered as a way to tackle the 'problem of integration' (see Martens 1993: 42), while the Francophone part of the country (and particularly Brussels) viewed this as a way to address fears of 'radical elements' (Dassetto 1997; Leman and Renaerts 1996). The activities of the Royal Commissariat ran until 1993, when it was discontinued and succeeded by the establishment of the Centre for Equal Opportunities and Opposition to Racism (CEOOR), which has a different function and structure than the Royal Commissariat, but continues to be the main body on the federal level concerned with the condition of ethnic and religious minorities.

# Setting the Epistemological Terrain: Muslims as the Ethnic and Religious Other

Before mapping out more systematically the scholarship on Islam in Belgium, it is important, we believe, to pause on the analytical grids through which Muslims are studied, and indeed construed as an object of study. As the critical tradition of sociology of knowledge has taught us, social scientific accounts of social reality do not merely describe or reflect social phenomena, but also co-constitute this reality (Berger and

---

[11] Previously, labour unions, local organizations (such as churches or charities), and provincial organizations (especially in the province of Limburg) provided a minimal degree of support for immigrants and their families.

[12] After the minority decree of 1998, which granted a representative status to minority organizations coordinated by the umbrella organization Minderhedenforum, the integration policy in Flanders—inspired by the policy paradigm shift in the Netherlands—developed an *inburgering* (civic integration) decree in 2004, which made attendance at integration courses and language classes mandatory for all new arriving non-EU immigrants.

Luckmann 1966). While this holds true for all social scientific efforts, we observe that the topic of 'Islam in Belgium', precisely because of the ways in which Muslims' presence and political claims in Belgian society are often problematized, is particularly subject to the intricacies between the production of knowledge and the production of the social. As mentioned, we discern two distinct analytical perspectives, which situate and construct Islam in Belgium in different ways: one in which Muslims are addressed through the paradigm of ethno-cultural integration, while a second one is mostly concerned with Muslims' religious and civic integration.

## Muslims as 'Allochthons': Cultural Integration through (Socio-Economic) Integration

In the first trope, Muslims are primarily framed as an ethno-cultural minority that occupies an underprivileged position and whose integration is seen to be conditioned by its social and economic position. Yet more than simply addressing and viewing Muslims as an underprivileged working class, this social and economic integration becomes also tied with their capacity to endorse the prevailing cultural values (see also Schinkel 2007). Consequently, Muslims are not primarily understood as a religious minority, but rather as 'migrants' whose full inclusion within society (i.e. cultural assimilation) is seen to be conditioned by their socio-economic background (see also Arnaut and Ceuppens 2009; Ceuppens and Geschiere 2005). A large part of this literature commonly relies on theories of ethnic stratification and social assimilation of minorities (Alba and Nee 1997), yet it also shows a particular concern with the case of Muslims. In a 1993 essay, for instance, the labour sociologist Albert Martens considers the idea of an Islamic pillar as a strategy of integration for Muslim immigrants. While he argues that Italians and Greeks could successfully be integrated through the existing structures (such as the trade unions) he sees Muslims to be confronted with a more important challenge because of a larger degree of hostility they face due to their religious difference and the bad socio-economic conjuncture of the early 1990s (Martens 1993: 45).

While all Belgian studies initially engage with the presence of Muslims through this socio-economic lens (Martens and Moulaert 1985; Bastenier and Dassetto 1981, 1982a, 1982b; Bastenier et al. 1982), this focus gradually shifts in a differentiated way: until the end of the 1990s, the scholarship in Flanders remains largely structured along this concern with cultural and socio-economic integration (see Clycq 2008; Timmerman 1999; Güngör et al. 2011; Agirdag et al. 2011) while from the second half of the 1980s onwards the Francophone literature shifts to a concern with Islam and secularism.

## Muslims as Religious Other: A Challenge for Secularism

The second analytical trope attends to the extent to which Muslim communities adapt to the secular contours of the public sphere. Here religious particularities become the primary ground for identification and definition of this minority, and the ways in which Muslims relate to dominant liberal and secular models of citizenship are scrutinized. Such a perspective shares a great deal with established individualized and contractual understandings of citizenship, as exemplified by the French Republican model, and addresses the question of integration primarily in political and religiously privatized terms. In this vein, the emergence of religious communities is not merely considered as an indication of 'failed integration', but also as a potential *threat* to the homogeneity and unity that a secular model seeks to establish (Scott 2007). Influenced by French academic knowledge production on Muslims and Islamic movements, this analytical perspective is to a large extent devoted to the socio-political organization of Muslim communities (Dassetto and Bastenier 1984; Dassetto 2001), their negotiation with state actors (Leman 1992b; Leman et al. 1992a; Torrekens 2008; Bousetta 2001), and the presence of Islamic networks and their influence within Muslim communities (Dassetto 1996; Maréchal 2008). The seminal *Islam transplanté* by Dassetto and Bastenier (1984), which is the first study that systematically investigates the socio-political realities of Islam and Muslim communities in Belgium, is exemplary in this respect. Besides offering a historical account of the arrival of Muslims in Belgium, it also maps out different tendencies within the community, the mosques, socio-political networks, and their relationship with dominant society. A similar perspective characterizes the important overviews by Dassetto (1997) *Facettes de l'Islam belge* and Maréchal and El Asri (2012) *Islam belge au pluriel*, which provide a comprehensive overview of social scientific work on Muslims in Belgium. Strikingly, both volumes primarily address the religious components and identity of this community, its religious practices (Touag 2012; Fadil 2012a; Lesthaeghe 1997), the political mobilization of this community towards existing institutions (Pedziwiatr 2012; Torrekens 2009; Zibouh 2011, the problem of radicalization (Manço 2012; Grinard 2008), and the legal challenges that accompany the steady integration of this religious reality (Foblets 1994, 2012). Most studies seek to account for the ways in which Muslims integrate or can be accommodated with a liberal secular regime. The challenge of 'integration' is posed at the level of contradictions between some of the 'radical' tendencies within Islam and liberal democracy. Here controversies around the establishment of a representative body for Muslims or Islam in schools (such as the question of the headscarf, halal food, or Darwinism; see El Asri 2009b) figure as case studies and become important structuring themes in this type of study.

# THE SOCIO-ECONOMIC INTEGRATION OF MUSLIMS

Considered through a socio-economic lens, Muslim minorities are primarily seen as an underprivileged ethnic group that faces a number of structural forms of exclusion such as unemployment, poverty, school drop-out, etc. The seminal study of Martens and Moulaert (1985), *Buitenlandse minderheden in Vlaanderen-België*, offers one of the first systematic and comprehensive accounts of the socio-economic insertion of the 'foreign minorities' (at the level of education, unemployment, housing, etc.) and calls for urgent political measures. This lays the ground for a body of literature examining the weak socio-economic insertion of these minorities through a regular monitoring of socio-economic data. While much of the early literature addresses this population as foreign nationals, more recent reports identify them as an ethno-cultural minority. This shift is strongly related to the growing unreliability of nationality statistics, as a result of the high degree of naturalization of Turkish and Moroccan minorities. Subsequently, different methods are adopted to identify the contours of this population ranging from 'name identification' in particular databases (Van Robaeys et al. 2007; Almaci et al. 2007) to random sampling in particular neighbourhoods (Vandezande et al. 2008).

## Weak Socio-Economic Integration

All studies examining the socio-economic status of Turkish and Moroccan minorities confirm the structurally precarious condition of this group. The study by Van Robaeys et al. (2007), which is the first that systematically focuses on the question of poverty among the Turkish and Moroccan population, shows that the level of poverty among this population balances around the 55% mark (56% for the Moroccans and 59% for the Turks)—hence amounting to almost four times the national poverty level (estimated at 15%). With respect to employment, several studies show a greater difficulty of access to the job market for Turkish and Moroccan minorities—with an unemployment degree of 29–38% (Van Robaeys et al. 2007: 30). The TIES (The Integration of the European Second Generation) survey, an international survey on the structural integration of the descendants of Turkish, Moroccan, and Yugoslavian immigrants aged between 18 and 35 years in Belgium, the Netherlands, Germany, and Sweden, shows for the Belgian data (based on a survey among 569 Moroccan and 608 Turkish second-generation youth in Brussels and Antwerp, compared to 574 white respondents) an underrepresentation of this population in higher job categories (3–17% compared to 25–31% for the white population) and an overrepresentation in non- or lower qualified jobs (59–60% compared to 38% for the white population). This led some analysts to conclude that the Belgian job market is characterized by a growing ethnic stratification (Ben Abdeljelil 1997: 145), with ethnic minorities overrepresented at the lower strata of the job market and whites maintaining its upper segments.

One argument to account for these figures pertains to the realm of education, as most studies show a weaker academic career of Moroccan and Turkish minorities compared to their white peers. Only 6–13% of these ethnic minorities make it to either university or another form of higher education (Vandezande et al. 2008; Almaci et al. 2007). The study of Duquet et al. (2006) shows that the difference in the academic careers between Muslim and non-Muslim pupils begins with a higher degree of school drop-out at high school (about 50%), and an unequal representation of Turkish and Moroccan minorities in the more general sections of high school (20% compared to a general average of 50%), with an overrepresentation in the more technical and vocational orientations (Duquet et al. 2006: 24; see also Vandezande et al. 2008 and Almaci et al. 2007). A 2009 analysis of the European 2006 PISA survey (which examines the degree of socio-economic inequality in various European schools through standardized tests),[13] reveals that the inequality between ethnic minorities and white pupils in Belgium is one of the highest in Europe (Jacobs et al. 2009: 29). The authors also emphasize the high degree of school segregation in Belgian cities, which they consider one of the main explanatory factors for the difference in school performance (Jacobs et al. 2009: 61, 84). A second set of arguments that seek to explain the unequal socio-economic position between Muslims and non-Muslims revolves around the *question of discrimination*. Several reports document systematic experiences of unequal treatment or discrimination, which significantly affect the chances on the job market (Vandezande et al. 2008: 68; Martens et al. 2005; Saaf et al. 2009; Kaya and Kentel 2007). A study commissioned by the King Baudouin Foundation and conducted by a Moroccan research team reports that the respondents cited discrimination as one main reason for their precarious job condition (Saaf et al. 2009: 49–50). The researchers, however, tend to downplay this explanation, privileging instead low educational skills and patriarchal dynamics within the community (hampering women from full participation) as a more solid explanation (2009: 138). A study by Martens et al. (2005), which followed the job application procedure of 321 ethnic minority applicants (compared to white applicants) over a period of several months, yielded more conclusive evidence: in 27% of the cases they observed the presence of plausible unequal treatment (2005: 30).

## Islam and Culture as Cause of Failed Integration?

In recent years, several opinion-makers have defended the claim that the religious or cultural background of ethnic minorities should be taken into account when explaining their weak socio-economic conditions—a development branded by some analysts as the 'crisis of multiculturalism' (Lentin and Titley 2011). In Belgium this development was largely mediated by predicaments in the Netherlands where, since the beginning of the 1990s, well-known political and academic figures across the political spectrum further elaborated the discourse of multiculturalism's end (Fadil 2010). A case in point is the sociologist and Labour politician Paul Scheffer and his widely debated 2000 essay entitled 'Het Multiculturele Drama' ('The Multicultural Disaster'). The emergence of this discourse occurs in relation to a paradigm shift within Dutch migration policy, from the previous prevailing 'Ethnic Minorities Policy' to the 'Integration Policy' that went

---

[13] The Programme for International Student Assessment is a research programme launched in 1997 by the OECD and has as its main aim to evaluate the performance of the educational systems on a world-wide basis. See <http://www.oecd.org/pisa/aboutpisa/> [Accessed March 2013].

into effect at the end of the 1980s (Duyvendak and Scholten 2009). In this shift, minority cultures in general, and Islam in particular, were profoundly problematized and framed in terms of how they impede the integration of ethnic or religious minorities in Western Europe. Within academic scholarship, this new paradigm can be traced in studies that examine the relationship between Islam and the question of integration. The controversial study by the criminologist Marion Van San on the relationship between Moroccan ethnicity and youth criminality in Belgium figures as a case in point.[14] Van San observes a significant relationship between ethnic background and type of criminal conduct, and suggests that 'Moroccan culture' can contribute to account for this variation. Another example is the study by the Dutch sociologist Dronkers who observes, on the basis of his analysis of the earlier-mentioned PISA data, that schools with a high concentration of Muslim pupils negatively impact upon the school performances of all children. He accounts for this observation in terms of 'Islamic norms and values—such as male–female relationships or honour and shame—which are counterproductive for modern Western societies' (Dronkers cited in Agirdag et al. 2011: 2).

Such arguments, however, are criticized for their weak conceptualization of 'ethnicity' or 'culture' in the case of Van San (Verscheuren 2001), or because of the absence of any empirical data on Muslim religiosity in the case of Donkers (Agirdag et al. 2011). Other empirical studies, such as that of Agirdag et al. (2011), effectively show that religiosity does not relate in any clear or direct way with school performance. Measuring the degree of religiosity through mosque visits, attending Qur'an school, and self-identification, the authors observe a more complex picture among Muslim children around the age of 10 whereby 'very high' and 'very low' degrees of religiosity correlate positively with school performance, while 'moderate' religious orientations show a slightly negative relationship (a relationship they describe as curvilinear).[15] The study by Fleischmann and Phalet (2012), which analyses data gathered under the TIES survey (albeit restricted to Turkish young adults between 18 and 35 years in Belgium, the Netherlands, Germany, and Sweden), equally observes an absence of any clear correlation between Islamic religiosity and socio-cultural integration, which is measured through employment, education, and intermarriage.[16] Rather, their findings seem to suggest that the degree

---

[14] The study was commissioned by the Belgian Minister of Interior at the time, Marc Verwilghen, and was considered polemical, not necessarily because of its (rather limited) findings but rather due to a discourse unfolding around this report about its 'taboo' character. See Steven De Foer, 'Koudwatervrees over de studie van allochtone criminaliteit. Rapport van criminologe is al 10 maanden klaar', *De Standaard*, 30 October 2001.

[15] Islamic religiosity was measured on the basis of three indicators. Respondents were asked how important their religion was to them (with five possible answers ranging from 'very important' to 'not important at all') and how often they went to the mosque and to Qur'anic school (both questions with five possible answers ranging from 'never' to 'very often'). An average of these three responses was taken as an indicator of religiosity.

[16] This study operationalized the degree of religiosity through self-categorization (considering oneself Muslim or not), religious identification (attaching a great value to Islam), religious practice (measured through the upholding of dietary practices, participation in Ramadan, and praying at home or at mosques), and the support of the political role of Islam (Fleishmann and Phalet 2012).

of societal openness and recognition of Islam is a more important factor in determining how Islamic religiosity impacts upon the socio-economic integration of Muslims.[17] In countries more hostile to public expressions of Islam (such as Germany), the researchers observe a negative relationship between Islam and integration: 'the lack of recognition and accommodation of the Muslim minority implies that Islam is treated as a second-class religion, leaving little room for a positive attachment to and active practice of this religion among integrated Turkish Germans' (Fleischmann and Phalet 2012: 331). These tentative observations effectively clear the path for new research agendas examining how dominant socio-political contexts facilitate or hamper the extent to which minorities can integrate without abandoning their cultural or religious attachments.

## Cultural Integration and Identity

Several studies examine processes of integration and identification with Belgium and their relationship with ethnic identity (Swyngedouw et al. 1999; Timmerman 1999), and show a gradual sense of identification with the Belgian context, accompanied by a higher sense of belonging at the local context. Experiences of racism and discrimination, however, strongly impede these processes of identification. The Open Society Foundation report *Muslim in Antwerp* (2011), based on a study conducted by Noël Clycq which consisted of 200 individual in-depth interviews with 100 Muslims and 100 non-Muslims, shows a strong sense of belonging among Muslims to the neighbourhood where they live and the city of Antwerp, yet a less intensive sense of identification as Belgian. Clycq accounts for the latter in terms of experiences of discrimination (2011: 58–9). He furthermore notes that a strong sense of identification with the local context stands in sharp contrast with a profound distrust towards local authorities. Several respondents reported feeling by-passed by local authorities, which tend to privilege first-generation men as interlocutors (2011: 49), and the measure to ban the headscarf for city personnel in public functions equally affected their degree of trust (2011: 124).

Two significant reports on patterns of integration among Turkish and Moroccan minorities in Belgium are those of Kaya and Kentel (2007) and Saaf et al. (2009), both commissioned by the King Baudouin Foundation. The reports present the results of a survey conducted with 800 Turkish and Moroccan Muslims (400 of each) and thus provide, despite methodological flaws, a unique set of data about several aspects of their social and cultural integration. Regarding the question of identification with the dominant society, the Moroccan report seems structured by a perspective of gradual assimilation. Hence the observations that 62% of the respondents return on a yearly basis to Morocco and that the majority of the respondents identify with Belgium and Morocco

---

[17] The degree of openness here refers to the extent to which Islam, as a minority religion, is provided a degree of institutional or legal space. The authors emphasize that while countries such as Belgium, the Netherlands, or Sweden provide a certain degree of institutional or legal recognition, this is not the case for Germany where the state does not accommodate a minority cult (Fleishmann and Phalet 2012).

(Saaf et al. 2009: 105) are interpreted as an intermediary phase towards full identification with Europe, and Belgium, as a primary and sole identity (2009: 107). In contrast, the report on the Turkish community observes a similar kind and amount of dual identification, but here the researchers consider this dual identity to be characteristic of the Turkish community (Kaya and Kentel 2007: 73). Both studies, however, fail to account in a satisfactory way for the selection of the respondents, which occasionally results—especially in the Moroccan study—in some remarkable findings. The Moroccan study shows for instance that only 21% of the interviewed Belgian Moroccans living in Flanders declare having a good level of written and spoken Dutch (2009: 46), or that Moroccan media are more popular than Belgian media among the respondents (2009: 130). The absence of bivariate or multivariate analysis (in which social background is crossed with language proficiency or media consumption) leaves us in the dark about the possible reasons behind such observations. These findings beg the question about the composition of the sample, in terms of income and education, and in fact seem suggest that a large part of the interviewees consisted of first-generation Moroccans.

## POLITICAL AND INSTITUTIONAL ASPECTS OF THE MUSLIM PRESENCE IN BELGIUM

The growing visibility of Muslims and Islam in the public sphere is an important topic within the available studies on Islam in Belgium, which address controversies around the institutionalization of Islam, the participation of Muslim actors in political life or the public manifestation of Muslim identity, and notably religious 'symbols' at schools or the workplace. There is a growing interest in the religious dimension of this minority, yet this interest is focused on the public facets of Muslim identity and stands in contrast with a relatively limited attention to religious experiences. This focus on the political and institutional aspects of Islam is tightly connected to the public debate on Islam in Belgium, but is also due to the disciplinary background of these scholars (mostly trained in political and social sciences or law rather religious studies), as well as the peculiar structure of the Belgian institutional landscape (with questions of institutional representation at the heart of any political concern in Belgium).

Unlike France, Belgium is not characterized by a model of *laïcité* and the restrictions it imposes on the relations between religion and state, but rather by a neutrality model, in which the principle of pro-active recognition and state support of religious denominations is constitutionally ingrained (article 181 of the Belgian constitution). This means that the state recognizes and financially supports confessional traditions,[18] whilst refraining from intervening in their internal organization. At the time of writing

---

[18] This consists, for the case of Belgium, primarily of the funding of mosques and the payment of salaries of the recognized imams and Muslim chaplains. For a fuller account see Fadil (2012b).

there are seven officially recognized confessions (Catholicism, Judaism, Protestantism, Orthodox Church, Islam, Anglican Church, and Secular denomination), and one is in the process of being recognized (Buddhism). This pluralistic approach was born out of the historical compromise, central to Belgium's establishment, between liberals and Catholics in which the principle of recognition and funding of religious institutions ensured political support from the clerical authorities and in exchange liberals were granted the principle of freedom of faith and separation between church and state (arts. 19–20 of the Belgian constitution). Besides being fractured along linguistic (Flemish, Francophone, and German) and regional lines (Flanders, Wallonia, and Brussels), Belgian civil society is traversed and organized along a number of ideological cleavages—a phenomenon which has come to be known as the principle of pillarization (*verzuiling*).[19] The educational system is, for instance, largely divided between Catholic schools and state schools,[20] and the trade unions, civil organizations, healthcare system, and media are equally organized according to ideological lines that largely correspond with those found in political life (socialist, liberal, and Christian-democratic). This peculiar institutional composition of the Belgian state is crucial to take into account when considering what facilitates, and also what impedes, the mobilization and organization of the Muslim community.

## Institutionalization of Islam: Between Recognition and Regulation

The development and recognition of places of worship is an important dimension of the institutionalization of Islam. The influential 2004 report by Meryem Kanmaz and Mohamed El Battiui, commissioned by the King Baudouin Foundation, estimates the number of mosques in Belgium at 328 (162 in Flanders, seventy-seven in the Brussels region, and eighty-nine in Wallonia). Of these, 162 are Arab speaking, 134 Turkish speaking, and thirty-two belong to other Muslim communities such as Pakistani or Eastern Europeans (Kanmaz and El Battiui 2004: 13–17). Some forty-three of these mosques are currently recognized for funding by the Walloon regional government, twenty-four by the Flemish government, and eight by the Brussels regional government, while nineteen imams are recognized for the attribution of a salary by the federal authorities. These funding procedures, achieved in 2007, are the result of decades of mobilization by Muslim and non-Muslim actors since the constitutional recognition of Islam by the Belgian state in 1974. Before this period, financial measures were restricted to the appointment of Islam teachers in public schools and Muslim chaplains in hospitals and prisons (see also Fadil

---

[19] Pillarization implies the organization of the social body along confessional or sectarian lines in a segmented polity; it represents a politics of accommodation and pacification, in which different faiths and ideologies are organized in a structurally similar way. For a comprehensive study of pillarization see Lijphart (1968).

[20] Catholic schools represent more than 70% in Flanders and up to 50% in Wallonia.

2012b). This delay can be partially explained by the absence of an effective body that was capable of administrating such public funding.[21]

This brings us to a second dimension of institutionalization: the question of official representation. Whilst the idea of a representative body of Muslims was discussed from the early 1970s onwards, it was only in 1999 that the Executive of Muslims of Belgium (EMB) was established, following a general election among the Muslim community in the autumn of 1998. This was the first representative body for Muslims in Western Europe, and attracted a considerable amount of scholarly attention (Panafit 1999; Dassetto 1997; Foblets and Overbeeke 2002; Kanmaz and Zemni 2008). The EMB effectively brought to an end a long period of unsuccessful attempts to settle the question of representation,[22] yet did not signify the end of a representative crisis. Several analysts observed that the EMB never entirely achieved a degree of 'moral legitimacy', as both internal and external actors keep challenging its operation and decision-making process (Dassetto 2011: 78). The continuous debates over the start or end of Ramadan are a case in point: while the competence of this decision is attributed to the Theological Council of the Executive, it is annually challenged by significant segments of the Muslim community who give preference to decisions taken in home countries (such as Turkey) or by other authorities (such as Saudi Arabia).

Whereas some have attributed the absence of a representative body for Muslims to a lack of strong and 'mature' leadership,[23] the existing literature suggests two main factors. Firstly, the institutional requirements of the Belgian law are modelled on the hierarchical structure of the Catholic Church and ill adapted to the heterogeneous composition of the Muslim community (Foblets and Overbeeke 2002; Panafit 1999; Kanmaz and Zemni 2008). A representative body, therefore, implies the establishment of a structure that is capable of integrating various ideological tendencies and ethnic groups within the community in order to achieve full representation. While ethnic diversity within the community has been taken into account (through ethnic quota), the doctrinal heterogeneity remains unaddressed (Maréchal 2003: 165). A second explanation invokes the political sensitivity of the question of Muslim representation, reflected in the strong interventionism of the political authorities (Kanmaz and Zemni 2008; Boender and

---

[21] Boender and Kanmaz rightly note that the absence of a representative structure did not impede the appointment of Islam teachers since 1974. This has largely to do with the fact that, in the same period, the question of (proper) religious teaching in public schools figured as the object of political struggles: 'The urgency of the "education annex teachers" case was not so much the result of the concern about the needs of the Muslim communities, but of specific Belgian political delicacies. It is striking that the argument that is used for the non-treatment of the "imam-case", i.e. the absence of a Head of Cult who has to appoint the imams, does not hold for teachers' (Boender and Kanmaz 2002: 175).

[22] As mentioned, from 1968 onwards the (Saudi-funded) ICC in Brussels figured as the privileged interlocutor by the Belgian state, yet its legitimacy was challenged by several (mostly secular) Muslims. This resulted in various attempts at establishing a representative body, initiated either by Muslim actors (such as the elections for the High Council for Muslims in Belgium organized by the ICC in 1991) or by Belgian authorities (such as the Temporary Council of Elders in 1990) (see Maréchal 2003: 164 and Kanmaz and Zemni 2008).

[23] Dassetto, for instance, argues that the internal competition and various tensions between the leadership stand in the way of the establishment of a new representative body (Dassetto 2011: 78).

Kanmaz 2002; Panafit 1999). Thus, while the idea of a representative body is partially explained by the institutional requirements of the Belgian landscape, societal controversies about the integration of Muslims and their visibility in the public sphere equally play a crucial role. A strong representative body for Muslims is indeed considered by several policy-makers as a good instrument to institute a dialogue with the Muslim community and regulate a number of problems. The historical and legal study by Lionel Panafit, *Quand le droit écrit l'islam* (1999), which retraces the history of the institutionalization of Islam in Belgium from the late 1960s, documents in a detailed manner the importance of the shifting political climate around the 1980s in this respect. The public funding of mosques, as well as the appointment of an official representative body, emerged as a means to foster a Belgian Islam that would be acceptable to all (see also Kanmaz and Zemni 2008: 117–18). Hence the strong interventionist role adopted by the national authorities, which is illustrated by the federal state's attempt in 1985 to establish a representative body,[24] the non-recognition of the 1991 elections organized by the ICC,[25] and the state security screenings after the 1998 elections which resulted in the exclusion of some candidates.

While all analysts question the legality of such interventions (Foblets and Overbeeke 2002; Maréchal 2003), some commentators insist on the desire by state authorities to adopt a pragmatic and pro-active stance in the light of internal disputes, in order to solve a number of issues (such as the legalization of Islam teachers), at the risk of trespassing the neutrality principles (Foblets and Overbeeke 2002: 118–19). Other commentators take the interventionism as an illustration of shifting geopolitical realities and the gradual 'domestication' of Islam, in which a strong representative body is considered as a way to regulate 'malicious' tendencies within Islam (Panafit 1999; Kanmaz and Zemni 2008; Zemni 2011). Significantly, Muslim actors themselves seem to be divided on the necessity of such a governmental intervention. The study by Jonathan Debeer et al. (2011), conducted among sixty Imams and eight Islamic consultants in Flanders, shows that several respondents considered the interventionism undesirable (Debeer et al. 2011: 85). Yet the difficult negotiations about a renewal procedure for the EMB also show that in some cases Muslims were proponents of a limited degree of state intervention.[26]

---

[24] The Conseil Superieur des Musulmans de Belgique, established by a Royal Decree set out by Minister Gol, was declared non-constitutional by the State Council that same year (Rea 1999: 269).

[25] These elections were driven by the ICC's fear of losing its leadership position, as it felt threatened by initiatives taken by the Royal Commission for Migration Policies. On 13 January 1991, the ICC organized elections and 26,000 Muslims (or 18% of adult Muslims) cast their vote. The High Council of Muslims in Belgium (Hoge Raad van Moslims van België) was established. The Belgian Minister of Justice, however, refused to recognize this body, while Turkish and Moroccan authorities called for a boycott of these elections (Kanmaz and Zemni 2008).

[26] A new board of the Executive for Muslims in Belgium was installed in April 2014, after years of difficult negotiations on the right procedure concerning its renewal since 2005. In the new procedure, a delegation model was followed whereby the mosques act as the main recruiting basis for members of the general assemblee and board of the EMB.

The question of state intervention is more complicated than a simple juxtaposition of non-Muslim state actors versus the Muslim community, as is generally suggested in the literature.

## Muslims as Civil and Political Actors

A second thread in the literature on the public role of Islam concerns the participation of Muslims as civic and political actors. In line with studies conducted elsewhere in Europe (Cesari 1994; Modood 1998; Vertovec 1998), scholars of Islam in Belgium observe a growing reference to Islamic identity within processes of political mobilization. A first set of studies in this respect focuses on the emergence of Muslim elites as a new political entity, and their role in articulating political claims towards local or national authorities (Bousetta 2001). Besides figuring as an important segment of the local population in certain cities such as Brussels (where estimates vary between 162,000 and 235,000), the demographic weight of Muslims in concentrated urban areas effectively turns them into an important political force. Hence several studies examine the political involvement of Muslims and their relationship to elected Muslim (and non-Muslim) elites. Fatima Zibouh's research (2011) shows that the number of MPs in the Brussels parliament has grown considerably, starting with 5.3% in 1995, growing to 12% in 1999 and 19.1% in 2004, and reaching 21.3% in 2009 (Zibouh 2011: 5). This can be explained, she argues, by the specific Brussels demographic, political, and institutional landscape, which is composed of a large diversity of minorities, and by the proportional Belgian electoral structure as well as the dense presence of Muslim civil organizations in certain communes of Brussels (such as Schaerbeek, Molenbeek, or Saint-Josse) and their large mobilizing capacities. Other studies focus on the role of Turkish and Moroccan community organizations, in relation to a more general discussion within the political sciences about the degree of social capital minorities can draw out of these networks for their political participation within society (see e.g. Jacobs et al. 2002). In their analysis of the Brussels Minority Survey (conducted in 1999 among 587 individuals of Moroccan origin and 391 of Turkish origin), Jacobs et al. (2004) observe that membership of ethnic organizations and networks does not guarantee political involvement. In the case of Turkish minorities, they note a strong involvement in ethnic networks, yet a relatively low interest and participation in Belgian political life (measured through questions such as one's interest in Belgian political life, the extent to which one follows Belgian media and is aware of Belgian political life). Moroccan minorities, on the other hand, display a lower degree of integration in ethnic networks, yet a higher involvement with Belgian political life. The authors suggest that this difference in degree of involvement with Belgian politics can be explained by Moroccans' better knowledge of French as well as their historical postcolonial ties to France and the Francophone world (2004: 555). The study by Hassan Bousetta displaces the exclusive focus on institutional, 'visible', or dominant political channels (e.g. trade unions, political parties, etc.) to mobilization strategies *within* Muslim communities, thus taking communitarian resources into consideration. His study adopts a comparative perspective on the political mobilization of Moroccans in Antwerp, Liège, Utrecht, and Lille (2000, 2001). While the representation of these minorities in more established political bodies might be limited, Bousetta observes a larger degree of mobilization in what he describes as the 'infra-political domain' (or the community-based networks).[27] He criticizes the prevailing tendency within the political sciences in general, and the studies of political opportunity structures in particular, to limit the domain of the political to the realm of 'official' institutional politics, hence disregarding the complex community-based political strategies of Muslim minorities (2000: 238).

In a similar vein, a number of other ethnographies document how this emerging demographic and political group impacts upon local public policies. In her study on the local realities of Islam in Brussels, Corinne Torrekens (2009) observes a striking ambiguity in the way local authorities relate to this minority. While forced and compelled to accommodate and engage with Muslim claims—not least considering their electoral weight—a manifest or latent hostility towards the growing visibility of Muslims nevertheless impedes a consistent, open, and constructive engagement. Local authorities often invoke procedural and administrative criteria (e.g. urban regulations) as reasons not to meet certain Muslim demands (e.g. the building of new mosques or small minarets). In a paradoxical way, these strict administrative criteria have engendered a younger and more educated generation of Muslim actors who become specialized in administrative and juridical matters and can act as negotiators with local authorities (Torrekens 2008: 173). Similarly, in their desire to keep certain Muslim claims outside the polarized political arena, local authorities often create consultative bodies with (appointed) representatives of the Muslim community. Torrekens sees such bodies as an alternative public sphere, in which Muslim actors (especially mosque representatives) emerge as new representatives vis-à-vis local authorities, and as direct competitors to political representatives of Muslim background (Torrekens 2008: 179).

Other studies focus on the ways in which political mobilization results in the creation of Muslim autonomous spaces, and trace the changing role of Muslim spaces such as mosques, which are no longer simply a place of worship but emerge as an alternative or subaltern public sphere (Fraser 1992) that plays an increasing role in the civic, political, and public integration and participation of Muslims. In her ethnography of mosques in Ghent, Kanmaz (2009) discerns a gradual differentiation between mosques according to the social function they fulfil as well as the type of public they aim for—differences that also converge with generational and ideological distinctions. While communitarian-traditional mosques (which Kanmaz links with the first generation) tend to primarily focus on a religious function and target members of their own ethnic community, younger generations have a more global vision on the mosque's social

---

[27] Bousetta defines infra-political strategies as 'essentially hidden forms of mobilisation aimed at increasing control of and power over community organisation'. He distinguishes these from more visible organizations which he defines as follows: 'visible organisational political mobilisation is aimed at increasing control of and power over public political decision-making bodies' (2000: 236).

function, both towards the Muslim community as well as non-Muslims. Here mosques become 'centres' that should provide for a set of services, both religious and social (Kanmaz 2009: 29–31).

Many studies observe a shift in the ways in which Muslim identity is lived and conceived (Kanmaz 2002; Fadil 2005, 2006; Dassetto 1996): younger Belgian-born Muslims increasingly turn Islam into a civic identity that plays a constitutive role in how they relate to society at large. At times this results in positions that conflict with dominant understandings of neutrality/secularism or women's emancipation, such as in the case of the headscarf (see Brion 2000). The study by Konrad Pedziwiatr (2010) on Muslim elites in Brussels and London examines how Muslims act as bridging figures between different communities and how they adopt a pro-active citizenship discourse as an integral part of their pious commitment. He describes this identity model as '*Muslim civicness*', which is characterized, among other things, by an activism that insists on the right of sameness and the elaboration of solidarity ties beyond the Muslim community. Hence, being a good Muslim implies being a good and engaged citizen. In contrast to this model, Pedziwiatr distinguishes less prevalent tendencies (which he calls 'uncompromising Muslimness') that are more inwardly oriented, with an emphasis on difference and a focus on solidarity solely within the Muslim community. Important in these two different models is a politicized understanding of Islam as not only a personal but also a civic affair (Pedziwiatr 2010: 411).

## Legal and Institutional Aspects of the Muslim Reality

The increasing visibility of Muslim practices in the public sphere is often framed as a 'new' and 'challenging' development, as illustrated by the successive headscarf debates, the controversy around halal meat at school, or the emergence of Islamic political parties (such as Sharia4Belgium or the political party ISLAM in Brussels during the 2012 elections). Much of the scholarship is informed by the question of how existing institutions can engage with and accommodate this increasing religious diversity. Some responses approach this question from a legal perspective. The legal anthropologist Marie-Claire Foblets, who seeks to develop a socio-anthropological perspective on the intersections of various legal regimes, including non-Western ones, on Belgian soil, offers a pioneering juridical account of the negotiations and conflicts that emerge from the distinct legal traditions informing Muslim lives in Europe. In particular the contradictions that might emerge in relation to specific values of autonomy and emancipation between Belgian personal and family law, to which Muslims are subject as European and Belgian citizens, and those informed by Islamic law, to which they are subjected as Moroccan citizens (such as Moroccan personal and family law also known as the *Mudawana*), are important objects of analysis, as in the cases of polygamy or repudiation (Foblets 1994).[28] Foblets is the only Belgian legal scholar to consider the

---

[28] The Mudawana, or Moroccan personal and family law, was established shortly after the independence of Morocco in 1956. Contrary to other legal domains (such as criminal law or private

possibility of integrating elements of shariah in the existing legislative arsenal (Foblets 2012: 299), provided that these do not conflict with reigning principles such as gender equality, democracy, and pluralism. Foblets' work has also laid the grounds for a more general analysis of how the 'challenge of pluralism' is negotiated on a daily basis on legal grounds (Foblets and Dundes Renteln 2009). Noteworthy in this respect is the work of Katayoun Alidadi (2012; Alidadi et al. 2012), whose doctoral research investigates the desirability and feasibility of 'reasonable accommodation'—a legal concept that travelled to Belgium from Canada, and has been proposed as a possible route to dealing with increasing religious diversity at the workplace, in schools, and in other institutional settings (see Foblets and Kulakowski 2010). After reviewing the contested status of this legal concept, Alidadi adopts a strong stand in favour of it, arguing that it could provide an added value to the existing legal arrangements on non-discrimination when it comes to matters of religious pluralism (2012: 695).[29]

Other reports engage with the notion of reasonable accommodation from a sociological perspective. Adam and Rea (2010) conducted 102 (mostly) phone interviews with employers on their policies towards religious diversity at the workplace and found that flexible schedules during Ramadan, praying at the workplace, specific dietary requirements (halal), the possibility to veil, and some issues pertaining to a gender-mixed environment emerged as the main issues employers had to deal with. The study also finds that most employers are hostile to the idea of some clear and uniform regulations on these issues, preferring a pragmatic case-by-case approach. A similar observation runs through the study by Younous Lamghari (2012) on the STIB/MIVB, the main public transportation company of Brussels and one of the largest employers in the capital. The choice of the STIB/MIVB is a particularly interesting one, as more than half of its drivers are of ethnic minority background (56.29%), including a substantial proportion of Muslims (2012: 35). Because of its strong multicultural composition, the company has adopted a diversity policy and also branded itself as a recruiter of ethnic minorities.[30] However, the religious—and more particularly Muslim—orientation of a large part of its personnel seems to be a more challenging matter. In response, the company adopted a clear neutrality policy that does not allow the display of religious signs (i.e. hijab) or the performance of religious practices, such as praying, at work (Lamghari 2012: 77). Despite these strict regulations, a more pragmatic approach seems to prevail on the

---

law), it is largely structured according to shariah and has been the object of various attempts at reform, culminating in the major 2004 reform, which was the outcome of years of mobilization by feminist and non-feminist civil actors.

[29] She observes that law on equal opportunity or discrimination rarely provides satisfying alternatives when it comes to religious matters, whether it is the question of veiling, praying at work, or other religious claims. Alidadi's work is part of the broader RELIGARE research programme, a consortium between seven European universities and one university from Turkey, funded within the 7th Framework Programme of the European Commission, which investigates the question of religion and diversity from a sociological and legal perspective.

[30] It should be noted that this diversity stops at the higher echelons, as only 3–6% of the upper-level personnel is of ethnic minority background (Lamghari 2012: 35).

ground, as many employees do negotiate the possibility of discrete places to fulfil their religious duties (i.e. praying) in between shifts (Lamghari 2012: 51).

The question of veiling (headscarf and face-veiling) figures, finally, as an important case in these various debates on religious pluralism. Fadil (2004, 2011), Longman (2003), and Brion (2004) provide an account of the different arguments put forward in the debates, examining how the question of women's oppression, neutrality, or the need for an 'enlightened' or 'modern' Islam figure in defence of a ban. Another important study is the one conducted under the direction of the human rights legal scholar Eva Brems on the 'Burqa Ban'. While parts of this study focussed on the legal aspects of the ban (Brems and Oulad Chaib 2011; and Vrielink et al. 2011), they also interviewed twenty-seven face-veiled women. A central finding in their research is that of a clear gap between the lived realities of the face veiled women and the arguments given by the proponents of the ban (Brems et al. 2014, forthcoming).

# Living Islam in a Secular Context: Challenging Liberal Assumptions

As mentioned, the religious practice of Muslims, if and when examined, often figures as a dimension of more general studies on the political and social integration of Muslims (see for instance Fleischmann and Phalet 2012). When religious beliefs and practices of Muslims are examined, we discern two important threads in the literature. A first set of studies aligns with a more conventional sociological discussion on secularization and individualization and tries to assess the degree of these processes among Muslims. A second research line examines the relationship between Muslim (religious) practices and Islamic normative traditions.

## Patterns of Secularization and Religious Individualization

One of the first quantitative investigations of the cultural, social, and religious practices of Turkish and Moroccan minorities in Belgium is the survey conducted by Ron Lesthaeghe (2000) between 1994 and 1996 among 2,748 men of Turkish and Moroccan background (see also Manço 2001 for the Turkish community). The study found an overall gradual process of religious decline—measured as decreasing mosque participation, the importance attached to a religious education or the degree of 'strength' drawn from Islam and their religious practice (amongst other veiling)—among the younger generations compared to the first generation (Lesthaeghe and Neels 2000; Lesthaeghe 2000: 35). The authors also note a striking ethnic difference: Turkish minorities are more attached to certain political religious groups (such as Milli Görüş) while Moroccans display a lower degree of affiliation to political religious groups (i.e. Adl Wal Ihsane). This correlates with an 'overall pattern of tighter Turkish community cohesion and its organization around mosques as institutions of community service' (Lesthaeghe 2000: 35). As part of the earlier-mentioned TIES comparative research project, a more recent study by Güngör et al. (2011) examines patterns of religious identification, belief, and practice among second-generation Turkish and Moroccan Belgians in Brussels and Antwerp.[31] The authors examine the impact of religious socialization (measured through parents' mosque visits and childhood attendance at Qur'an schools) on the degree of religiosity,[32] and its relationship to the degree of identification with dominant culture and society (what the authors call acculturation). They found that the degree of religious identification and practice is strongly mediated by the extent to which second-generation Turkish and Moroccan respondents were exposed to a religious education. The researchers also observed that strong degrees of religious identification and practice do not necessarily impede the respondent's capacity to identify with the dominant society, thus not finding any clear evidence for so-called 'reactive pattern religiosity', i.e. a sense of 'cultural conflict between multiple cultural commitments' among the respondents who strongly identify with Islam. They do observe a very weak negative correlation between these two items in the case of Belgian Turks (i.e. strongly practising Belgian Turks would be less inclined to identify with the dominant society), yet one that is too weak to conclude that Islamic identification would hinder the adoption of Belgian cultural values (Güngör et al. 2011: 138). The earlier-mentioned reports commissioned by the King Baudouin Foundation (Kaya and Kentel 2007; Saaf et al. 2009) on the Turkish and Moroccan communities equally scrutinize the question of religious identification and practice. Both studies show a high amount of identification with Islam and a high degree of practice. Among 401 Moroccan respondents 68% indicate they tried to follow religious prescriptions (praying, halal food, Ramadan) and 18% stated they effectively followed them (Saaf et al. 2009). Only 0.2% of the respondents considered themselves non-believers. Interestingly, 44% of the Moroccan respondents reported experiencing an increasing sense of religiosity. Regarding the relationship between religion and politics, most respondents adopted a secular perspective, with a

---

[31] 'Religious identification' was measured through the following statements: 'Being Muslim is an important part of myself', 'The fact that I am Muslim is something I often think about', 'I see myself as a true Muslim', 'When someone says something bad about Muslims, I feel personally hurt'. 'Religious practice' refers to what the researchers call dietary practices (i.e. participation in Ramadan and the restriction to halal food). 'Beliefs' are measured through the following statements: 'There definitely exists only one correct answer to all religious questions', 'All that can be found in the Koran should be taken literally as written' (Güngör et al. 2011: 130).

[32] The degree of religiosity was measured through the following indicators: (1) the degree of identification as Muslim (five items); (2) knowledge and acceptance of religious doctrines (two items); (3) dietary practices (participation in Ramadan and the consumption of Halal food); and (4) worship (daily prayer and mosque visit).

majority (52%) defending the separation between religion and the state, 37% stating that Islam and Christianity stand on an equal footing, and only 11% considering that secular individuals should adapt to religious conservatives (Saaf et al. 2009: 110–11). The study of Turkish minorities showed a smaller degree of practice among the 400 interviewees: 39% reported trying to follow the prescriptions while only 6% considered themselves religious and practising; 5% saw themselves as not-believing (Kaya and Kentel 2007: 76). Significantly, 45% of the respondents reported believing, yet not practising. The researchers consequently conclude that Islam has become more of a symbolic marker of difference rather than a religious orientation (Kaya and Kentel 2007: 75).

Most studies on the religious aspects of the Muslim community rely on qualitative methodologies (Brion 2000; Van der Heyden et al. 2005; Pedziwiartr 2010; Fadil 2005; Timmerman 1999). An important observation throughout these studies is the persistent identification of younger generations with Islam, yet with some marked transformations compared to the 'traditional Islam' of their parents. Central to these changes is a process of individualization, which is not so much expressed as a gradual detachment from religious practice, but rather as an individualized reclaiming of Islamic tradition and legacy. In her study with Muslim women in Antwerp, Els Vanderwaeren observes the cultivation of new forms of *ijtihad* (interpretation) that results in the emergence of an Islamic feminism that continuously balances between the desire for strong piety and for a life as a modern and emancipated woman. Some scholars such as Pedziwiatr (2010) insist on how this religious individualization remains bounded by the Islamic normative tradition. In this context he speaks of 'limited' individualization, observing an unequal degree of individualization in different social areas. While his interlocutors were open to the idea of religious freedom and the fact that Muslims should be able to abandon their religion if they no longer believed, the question of a marital alliance between a Muslim woman and a non-Muslim man (prohibited according to dominant interpretations of the Islamic scripture) seemed a more thorny issue. This leads Pedziwiatr to conclude that 'processes of modernization are advancing in different areas with dissimilar swiftness' and that while Muslim practices are individualizing, this does not necessarily translate into an equal individualization in all areas of life (Pedziwiatr 2010: 183).

Other studies have sought to examine the extent to which Islamic religious norms direct the everyday conduct of Muslims, and Islamic theological scriptures act as an authoritative reference guide. In his doctoral research in religious studies, Stef Van den Branden (2006) examined Muslim views on the process of dying and the interruption of life. Besides reviewing different positions on this matter within contemporary Anglophone Sunni theological writings, Van den Branden also conducted qualitative interviews with Muslim elders (N = 11) of Moroccan background in Antwerp, and observes a striking parallel between the position held by these elders and the reigning Islamic prescriptions. Euthanasia or other forms of deliberate life ending were strongly condemned by all interviewees, who insisted on God's ownership of life. Moreover, while all interviewees argued that one should seek medical assistance when developing an illness or growing old, they also underlined the limits of medical treatment, pointing towards God's ultimate competence over one's health and the length of one's life (Van den Branden 2006: 404). Van den Branden frames the combination of valorizing medical assistance and simultaneously insisting on God's competence over these matters as a 'paradox', for which he accounts in terms of the low literacy degree and educational background of the interviewees and their relative unfamiliarity with medical sciences (Van den Branden 2006: 482–3). The studies of Karijn Bonne and Wim Verbeke (2006, 2008), at the intersection of STS (Science, Technology, and Society) studies, religious studies and anthropology, are also noteworthy. They observe how both first-generation and Belgian-born Muslims attribute a strong significance to halal (licit) slaughtering techniques. Yet the precise understanding of what counts as halal undergoes significant transformations across generations. While the first-generation respondents draw their judgement of the quality of meat from their own senses and experience (assessing the meat's colour or odour) and the trust they give to the Islamic butcher, an increased commodification of those criteria can be observed among younger generations who rely more on quality and halal labels rather than the place of purchase (Bonne and Verbeke 2008: 44). Hence this study shows how a particular religious practice, i.e. the consumption of halal meat, maintains an intergenerational continuity while shifting from a culturally entrenched practice (revolving around senses and trust) to a more objectified and technical understanding (i.e. the 'halal label').

Finally, the work of Nadia Fadil (2008, 2011) can also be mentioned in this rubric. Her doctoral research as well as other studies critically engages with the religious individualization narrative, by adopting a Foucaultian perspective that takes the latter not so much as a growing process of detachment from religious tradition, but rather as a particular mode of subjectification (*assujettissement*), which produces a particular religious subject and relationship to the religious authorities. In other words, rather than investigating if and how Muslims 'detach' themselves from religious tradition, Fadil's work examines to what extent the religious practice of Muslims is informed by an idealized understanding of the religious self, which is primarily understood in liberal terms, i.e. as an autonomous, authentic, and critical subject. From this theoretical angle Fadil traces how a liberal subject position informs the religious discourse of pious and non-pious Muslims, hence offering a unique contribution to the literature on Islam in Europe, by equally including so-called 'secular Muslims'. Fadil also investigates how the liberal subject position is continuously troubled by a non-liberal understanding of the self, one which takes religion or practising not simply as an outcome of one's 'will', but as something tied to an entity external to the self, i.e. God. Fadil (2011, 2008) examines how distinct modes of the self emerge in relation to the question of belief, religious knowledge, religious praxis, and the relationship to political life.

## Examining Renewed Engagements with the Muslim Tradition

The latter point introduces us to a distinct thread in the scholarship on Muslim religiosity, which focuses on the Islamic tradition, as well as the role of Muslim networks and intellectuals, in a post-migratory context (understood as a shifting and dynamic normative structure). Here special attention is given to the effect of *Islamic revivalist movements* on the Muslim community.[33] The work of Leila El Bachiri, who collected preaching materials and discourses of male and female Muslim leaders in Brussels between 2008 and 2011, is exemplary in this respect. On the basis of participant observation and textual analysis she discerns three broad tendencies: (1) Salafi-oriented tendencies with an emphasis on *daʿawa* (proselytizing) and correct behaviour; (2) Muslim Brotherhood-oriented tendencies with an emphasis on active citizenship and participation; and (3) Islamic feminist discourses that articulate forms of gender activism through a complex engagement with the Muslim tradition.[34] With regard to the latter, she observes an increasing tension around the women's question, and suggests that a 'power struggle' might emerge within the Islamic field between male and female activists (2012: 166). Another noteworthy study in this respect is the important work of Brigitte Maréchal (2008) on the Muslim Brotherhood. Adopting a socio-anthropological perspective, Maréchal maps out more than five decades of mobilization by key figures of the Muslim Brotherhood and the establishment of the network in Western Europe (France, the UK, Germany, and Belgium). The study shows how this network successfully managed to set up a number of influential Muslim organizations (Muslim student organizations, teaching institutes and umbrella organizations, or the European Council for Fatwa Research) that played a key role in carrying the Islamic Revivalist movement throughout Europe and shaping new forms of Muslim identity drawing on active participation within society (2008: 62–3). Maréchal also observes a gradual fragmentation of this network across generations, which she relates to the emergence of a young Muslim elite that might have been shaped by the collective memory of the Brotherhood yet keeps its distance towards its organizational structure, as well as the increasing competition with other piety movements (such as the *Wahabiyya* or *Salafiya*).[35] The Brotherhood, she concludes, lives more as a 'heritage' that left profound imprints upon how Muslims constitute their religious

---

[33] Islamic revivalist movements refer to socio-political organizations that emerged throughout the second half of the twentieth century and have incorporated a political language that understands questions of citizenship and participation in society to be intimately tied with a renewed commitment to Islam. These movements came to Western Europe through the refugees, political activists, and intellectuals from the Middle East and North Africa as well as new media (cassettes and satellite).

[34] El Bachiri draws a distinction between Muslim feminists who adopt a general critique of patriarchy and those who do so through a theological and juridical engagement with the texts (El Bachiri 2012).

[35] Maréchal uses the term *Salafiyya* as a generic term to refer to piety movements that insist on a close imitation of the examples of the Prophet and his followers and hold hostile positions towards any form of innovation in the Islamic tradition (*bidʿa*). The *Wahabiyya* are those Salafi groups that closely follow the teachings of Saudi-based scholars that are close to the Saudi regime.

identity, than an active organization with a coherent ideological programme and organizational structure (Maréchal 2008: 80, 305, 314).

Other studies look at how the existing religious dynamics and networks have an impact on everyday practices of Muslims in a secular context. Significant in this respect is a paper by Hanifa Touag on healing practices within Muslim communities. While her doctorate study focuses on in *Salafi* movements in Brussels, Lille, and Paris, in this paper she offers a focus on the shifting role of *raqi* or healers within this community. Touag observes a gradual democratization of what used to be a highly secretive and exclusive practice as well as the changing role of the healer into a counsellor who provides not only therapeutic but also social and psychological support to the (often female) members of the community (Touag 2012: 210). Another significant study is that by Iman Lechkar (2012a, 2012b), which investigates in- and out-group conversions of non-Muslims to Sunni Islam and Sunni (Moroccan) Muslims to Shi'ism. Besides providing unique ethnographic insights into the underexplored phenomenon of Sunni–Shi'a conversion within the Moroccan-Muslim community, Lechkar's work also challenges prevailing models of conversion that tend to frame these processes as moments of 'radical change'. She shows how processes of conversion were experienced by her Shi'a interlocutors as a 'return' to Maghrebi culture rather than as an abrupt change, and more specifically how the effort to position Shi'ism within a Maghrebi-Islamic traditional legacy allowed some of her interlocutors to understand their conversion as reconnecting with a 'lost' cultural heritage (Lechkar 2012b: 113). Conversion, Lechkar argues, implies a continuous process of self-fashioning of one's embodied dispositions, which is marked by moments of strength and weaknesses as well as sentiments of increase and decrease in the belief of one's own power to act. Finally, the work of Farid El Asri (2009a, 2011) explores the aesthetic and artistic expression of Muslims in the musical field and its intersection with the Muslim tradition, through an ethnographic account of three emerging musical genres within the Islamic field: *Anasheed* (spiritual songs), *Al-Andalus* (a Moroccan musical genre that can be traced back to the Spanish Andalus), and Hip Hop. El Asri analyses the ways in which these musical genres are informed by a continuous commitment to Islamic values and ethics as well as the dialectics between the artist's work and the Islamic normative tradition. This allows for an understanding of how the Islamic normative tradition is constituted and re-enacted as a 'living tradition', continuously transformed and challenged by various dynamics and processes that traverse it (see also Amir-Moazami and Salvatore 2003).

# Shifting International Context and the Growing Concern with 'Radical' Islam

The fear of radical Islam in Belgium dates from at least the mid-1980s, when the earlier-mentioned demonstration against US military interventions in Libya took place in

Brussels. The main catalysts for this fear, however, were the World Trade Center attacks in September 2001, after which a concern with international terrorism increased significantly, and several networks were dismantled and individuals arrested. A well-known case is that of Nizar Trabelsi, a former professional football player who was arrested in September 2001 and condemned to ten years in prison for plotting an attack on the American military base in Brussels. The Trabelsi case was, however, one of the few in which someone was accused of directly plotting an attack; other arrests targeted groups or individuals who were accused of international terrorism in a broad sense, according to the 2004 anti-terrorism law. An important example is the trial against Moroccan-Belgians who were accused of supporting the Groupe Islamique Combattant Marocain, a Moroccan militant group considered responsible for the Madrid attacks in March 2004.[36] Despite a lack of conclusive evidence, they were condemned to five to eight years of imprisonment on the grounds of direct or indirect links with some of the Madrid perpetrators and stays in Syria and Afghanistan. Another well-known example is the case of Malika El Aroud, widow of Abdessattar Dahmane, a Belgian-Tunisian who committed a deadly suicide attack against the Afghan opposition leader Ahmad Shah Masood in September 2001. After her return to Belgium, El Aroud, also known as Umm Obeyda, turned into a vocal advocate of *jihad* on the internet. She was arrested in December 2008, together with thirteen other people, on the charges of organizing and funding terrorist groups and was condemned in May 2010 to eight years of imprisonment. This concern with radicalization, moreover, also extends to socio-political groups that are considered extremist, as illustrated in the case of Sharia4Belgium, a group that emerged in 2010. This small political group, which aims to introduce shariah in Belgium, was given a large amount of media coverage because of its viewpoints on homosexuality, women, and the position of infidels. Led by the Antwerp-born Fouad Belkacem, who wears a *djellaba* and long beard, this movement stirred a number of controversies including the disruption of a public talk by the Flemish writer Benno Barnard known for his anti-Islam sentiments, as well as the release of a YouTube film insulting right-wing Vlaams Belang MP Anke Vandermeersch in the wake of the publication of her book about the liberation of Muslim women. The movement was tried for hate speech and in April 2012 the court of Antwerp condemned Belkacem to two years of imprisonment. The annual report of the Centre for Equality Opportunity and Opposition to Racism (CEOOR), a federal body that monitors, registers, and administers legal plaints against racism and discrimination, confirmed the growing public concern around Sharia4Belgium: 609 of the 5,185 complaints recorded in 2011 dealt with Sharia4Belgium (CGKR 2012: 71–4). The CEEOR was consequently one of the prosecuting parties in the trial against Sharia4Belgium.

## The Emergence of an Expertise of Fear

The shifting local and international context has resulted in countless newspaper articles, documentaries, and statements by public commentators on the danger of 'radical

---

[36] Jeroen Van Der Kris, 'België test anti-terreurwet', *NRC Handelsblad*, 16 November 2005.

Islam'—a discursive shift which also feeds into what analysts have called the growing *securitization* of Islam (Cesari 2009). This genre can be divided into two types. The first one consists of journalistic investigations that seek to unravel the predicaments of 'radical Islam' in Belgian or Brussels Muslim networks. Examples are found in the writings of Hind Fraihi (2006) and Arthur Van Amerongen (2008), which embody a particular genre in which the journalists narrate in a highly personalized way their journey among Muslim communities and experiences with radical and fundamentalist Islam. Other journalistic writings focus on the live stories of 'suicide bombers' such as Chris De Stoop's *Vrede zij met u, zuster* (Peace Be Upon You, Sister), published in 2010, which recounts the story of a high-profile Belgian convert to Islam, Muriel Degauge, who committed a suicide attack in Iraq. By weaving local observations and autobiographies together with the fear of a global Muslim terrorist threat, the idea of the proximity of such a threat is made tangible. A second genre in this security discourse consists of the work of security experts and think tanks, which adopt a hybrid position somewhere mid-way between academic expertise and advocacy. An important figure in this regard is Alain Grignard, who has been working for the anti-terrorist unit of the Federal Police since 1980 and is considered one of the chief Belgian experts on Islamic radicalization. His publications (e.g. 2008) elaborate on the changing nature of Islamic terrorism, which in his view has expanded both in reach—strengthening and intensifying international linkages between groups who were previously nationally organized—as well as in depth since the early twenty-first century. He warns of the global intensification of social exclusions, which exacerbates sentiments of marginalization (both among Muslims in Belgium and more internationally) thus facilitating the recruitment of *jihadis* (Grignard 2008: 92). Another noteworthy figure, less cautious and discrete in tone, is Claude Moniquet, director of the European Centre for Strategic Information and Security. This journalist, specialized in terrorism, intervenes on a regular basis with alarming statistics on the terrorist threat in Belgium. Besides its high-profile and vocal public analysts, his centre plays a pivotal role in the screening process of Moroccan preachers travelling to Belgium.[37]

## Radicalization Studies

The explosion of journalistic writings on the 'Islamic threat' stands in stark contrast with the relatively modest academic contributions on this question. When radicalization is addressed in the academic literature, most studies tend to downplay the prevailing fears by taking them as a case of analysis (see Zemni 2008), or by deconstructing the very term radicalization and the assumptions of threat this would pose (Coolsaet 2011). An important early reference in this regard is the work of Dassetto and Albert Bastenier *Medias u Akbar* published in 1987. In this book, the authors offer an analysis of the media controversy about Islam in Belgium in the wake of the earlier-mentioned demonstrations against US military interventions in Libya. Dassetto and Bastenier offer a detailed account of the role of various

---

[37] Guiterrez Ricardo, 'Prédicatrices marocaines en campagne', *Le Soir*, 28 October 2010.

media actors (most notably the Francophone Belgian broadcasting service, RTBF) in manufacturing this event through the prism of fear and setting the stage for the subsequent debate about the threat of Islamist political movements among the Muslim community of Brussels.

The fear of radical Islam has nevertheless resulted in a number of studies (especially in the Francophone part of the country) that scrutinize the grounds of such a potential threat in a more scholarly manner. Significant here is the strong normative impetus of these studies, with notably a reliance on the question of secularism or Israel/Palestine as indicators of 'radicalization'. The relevance of such indicators or their potential link with violence is rarely explained but merely assumed, and one's position towards democracy, secularism, or international conflicts is often understood in a dualistic manner, ignoring the spectrum of positions vis-à-vis these questions within society at large. A report by Koutroubas et al. (2009) is worth mentioning here. In this study, the researchers offer an overview of several associations that might be considered radical because of the conflict they (might) generate. The authors distinguish between political radicalization on a religious basis (including Islamic political parties such as the PCP, PJM, or MDP) and non-Islamic radical groups such as the Arab European League. However, they remain rather vague about the criteria used to characterize these groups as radical, while suggesting that relativizing the virtues of democracy as a mode of governance (in the case of the PJM), or the presence of explicit anti-Israeli rhetoric (in the case of the AEL) are important distinctive features. While pointing at potential sources of conflict, the authors conclude that there is little reason to be concerned about what they call political, religious, or ethnical radicalization in Belgium, and they observe a stark contrast between media sensationalism of these groups and their actual popularity on the ground. As evidenced by the weak electoral successes of these parties, the authors argue that most Muslims disapprove of such discourses as they 'appreciate what they experience as being the benefits of living in Belgium' (Koutroubas et al. 2009: 28). Also important is the report by Maréchal (2008), which offers a detailed survey of different 'fundamentalist' networks in Belgium which she categorizes as: pietistic movements (i.e. Tabligh), socio-political movements (Muslim Brotherhood, Milli Görüş, Suleymanli, Adl Wal Ihsane), Islamic political parties (such as the political party Noor or Parti de la Citoyenneté et de la Prosperité), politically radical movements (what she calls neo-Salafi tendencies), and movements that resort to military action to pursue their goals (like Al-Qaeda). The author defines fundamentalism as a world-view that seeks to revitalize the origins of religion through a close reading of the scriptures, the prioritization of this religious world-view, the extension of religious doctrines to all aspects of life, and the active organization and mobilization around this world-view (Maréchal 2008: 66). Maréchal finds a clear distinction between networks mobilizing around Islamic questions on intellectual, pietistic, and organizational grounds and political militant networks which lie at the heart of military attacks. While she observes ideological connections between members of these different organizations,[38] her overview shows that

---

[38] This is especially the case between those she designates as the 'ideological fraction' of the Muslim brotherhood and the mobilization for the Mujahedeen in Afghanistan (Maréchal 2008: 73).

these connections consist of loose internationally organized networks, mostly composed of refugees and other migrants rather than Belgian-born citizens (2008: 76).

## ISLAMOPHOBIA AND DISCRIMINATION

Few studies exist on Islamophobia, despite the political prevalence of this term since the 2000s. This is due, to a large extent, to the fact that research on racism and discrimination in Belgium has traditionally focused on nationalist discourses, akin to the political successes of the right-wing party Vlaams Blok (Billiet et al. 1990; Blommaert and Martens 1999; Blommaert and Verscheuren 1992). Moreover, Islamophobia is a contested concept, both in and outside of academia, which also accounts for the reluctance in its adoption.[39] There are, nevertheless, a number of studies that seek to measure the existence of anti-Muslim sentiments and the persistence of such sentiments in shifting political contexts.[40] The Institute for the Study of Political Organization (ISPO, KU Leuven) conducted one of the few surveys that directly address the question of Islamophobia, and observed, in 2007, that 49% of Flemish respondents consider 'Islam as a threat to European values' (Billiet and Swyngedouw 2009). Another source that provides insight into the extent of Islamophobia is the annual report of the Centre for Equality Opportunity and Opposition to Racism. The 2012 report shows that Islamophobia figures as one of the primary grounds for concerns and complaints in 2011. Moreover, the report registers an increased prevalence compared with previous years: 164 of the 198 registered complaints about religious prejudices dealt with Islam, and the Centre considered that 58% of these complaints were clear evidences of Islamophobia (2012: 80–2).

Studies with a broad focus on structural exclusions and discrimination of Muslims confirm that most Muslims in Belgium report experiencing systematic patterns of discrimination on a regular basis (see also the earlier discussion of the labour market). The earlier-mentioned Open Society study by Clycq (2011) found that 74% of the interviewed Muslims report being confronted with a large to relatively large amount of prejudice while only 13% report never experiencing any prejudice (2011: 58–9). And while most respondents value the quality of education, 30% did feel that the schools did not respect their religious identity—mostly referring to the prohibition to veil (2011: 75). The King Baudouin Foundation studies on Turkish and Moroccans in Belgium show that one-third experienced racism (Kaya and Kentel 2007: 48), and that only 32% of the interviewed Moroccans view Belgium as a tolerant country (Saaf et al. 2009: 80).

---

[39] See for instance the report by Amnesty International (2012) which privileges the terms 'discrimination against Muslims' and 'stereotypical discourse and views on Islam and Muslims' rather than Islamophobia (2012: 8).

[40] See for instance the study of Vincent Legrand (2014) who examines 'anti-islamization activism' amongst Christian faith-based organizataions at international conferences on an EU level.

Last but not least, some studies draw attention to the profoundly gendered dimensions of processes of racialization at the heart of Islamophobia. In a reflection on how feminist theory relates to the study of Islam, Sarah Bracke (2007) analyses a number of op-eds about women and Islam in the Flemish daily *De Standaard*, relying on Said's seminal understanding of Orientalism and further developing how gender as a category of analysis operates in relation to Islamophobia. Bracke lays out the mechanisms of representation through which 'women's emancipation' is used as a boundary marker of Western civilization and how Muslim women end up being the objects of rescue narratives. Clycq's study (2008, 2012) of the presence of ethnic and gender differentiations in the education of children from Belgian, Italian, and Moroccan parents in Flanders reveals that 'the Muslim question' emerges as a strong boundary marker, notably in the case of inter-ethnic and inter-religious marriage. While Belgian and Italian parents were open to the idea of their sons marrying a Muslim woman, they opposed it in the case of their daughters. Their refusal was justified by stereotypical representations of Muslim men and Islam as women-unfriendly. Besides highlighting the presence of stereotypical representations of women within Islam, these kinds of observations show, Clycq argues, how the maintenance of ethnic boundaries and the racialization of the 'other' are deeply gendered (2012: 165; see also Bracke and Fadil 2012). In a similar vein, Saroglou et al. (2009) address anti-Muslim prejudices through the question of veiling. While conflating anti-veiling sentiments and anti-Muslim sentiments is controversial (as some consider positions hostile to the veil to reflect anti-religious sentiments rather than racial prejudice), this study explores the validity of an 'anti-veil' indicator for Islamophobia. The study consists of two surveys (N = 166 and 147) on the position of Francophone (non-Muslim) Belgians towards the veil and shows that anti-veil sentiments largely depend on one's position towards religion and the presence of anti-immigrant prejudices. Individuals who were either strongly anti-religious or very orthodox (Christian) in their practice held more hostile positions towards the veil. Similarly, anti-immigrant sentiments strongly correlated with anti-veil sentiments. Consequently, the authors see the anti-veil hostility in Western Europe as a case of subtle anti-immigrant prejudice (Saroglou et al. 2009: 427). Moreover, a recent report by Amnesty International on prejudice and discrimination experienced by Muslims in various European countries singles out the Belgian case for the difficulties experienced by veiled Muslim women in finding a job, as well as the exclusions they face at school. The report identifies these incidents as acts of discrimination and infringement of the freedom of religion, in contrast to various rulings by domestic courts (2012: 38). In this vein, Amnesty International condemns the national ban on full-face veiling that was passed in Belgium in 2011 as a violation of the freedom of exercising one's religiosity (2012: 94).

# Conclusion

Academic production on Islam in Belgium emerged relatively late compared to other European countries. Besides a long-standing Orientalist tradition, sociologists, political scientists, and legal scholars have begun studying Muslims in Belgium from the second half of the 1980s onwards. The development of this scholarship is uneven between the Francophone and Flemish region: Francophone interests have from a very early period been stirred by concerns of secularism and neutrality, whereas the Flemish literature was initially marked by a focus on socio-economic and cultural integration (although a focus on religion and secularism emerges in a more recent period). These different studies converge, however, on documenting the high level of discrimination and exclusion on religious and ethnic grounds experienced by Muslims as well as their precarious socio-economic conditions. With respect to the institutional organization of Muslims, most studies detail the often-difficult negotiations between Muslim actors and state representatives, although the case of Brussels provides an exception as Muslims are well represented in various political bodies, which is due to the decentralized political structure of the capital. In terms of religious experiences, most studies point at an increasing degree of individualization vis-à-vis parents yet this does not necessarily result in a higher degree of detachment from the Islamic legacy.

As a general concluding remark, we would like to draw attention to the close intertwinement that initially existed, and continues to exist, between the scholarly production of knowledge about Muslims and public concerns (of the ethnic majority). Most research on Muslims in Belgium is directly or indirectly policy-oriented: ranging from research on integration and political participation of Muslims to work within the field of legal studies. At the heart of these different accounts lies a direct, practical, and political relevancy rather than an attempt at unpacking the frames through which subjects and concerns come into being, or conceptualizing broader processes that affect these subjects. While this has the merit of producing 'relevant' scholarship that might also appeal to a wider audience, its main drawback is a neglect of questions other than integration, security, or secularism and the reproduction of prevailing normative conceptions that traverse these questions. Little, for instance, is known about the type of knowledge Muslims produce, and how these also are carriers of alternative notions of agency, citizenship, or secularism. Most studies, furthermore, tend to focus on visibly active and religious Muslims—hence neglecting the less religious ones (see Fadil 2011). Finally, because of the outspoken focus on civic and political questions, other domains of the everyday lives of Muslims (such as fashion, the halal industry, or culture) remain understudied—although some new research projects have begun to investigate these questions (Zibouh and Costanzo forthcoming; El Asri 2011). Despite its social relevancy, not enough is known about the extent and nature of Islamophobia in Belgium, such as the way it is articulated and spread in society, the everyday exclusions of Muslims on the ground of their religious practices, as well as the ways in which Muslims deal with

Islamophobia and resist it. In sum, because of the history of its emergence (out of a concern about Muslims' integration or in response to fears of radicalization) the literature on Muslims in Belgium remains tightly bound by dominant concerns about the integration of this minority. Strikingly, and not unrelated, the literature is predominantly empirical and descriptive, and rather limited in its theoretical engagement. A path for further research would therefore consist of a more profound theoretical and empirical engagement with the new realities Muslims fashion in their various interactions with Belgian society. Instead of simply advocating the further development of an interdisciplinary field of study on Islam in Belgium, we believe that a process of de-centring from dominant theoretical and normative concerns with integration or secularism is needed in order to render the scholarship about Muslims and Belgian society, intellectually, academically, and politically, more challenging and vibrant.

# Bibliography

Adam, Ilke (2013). *Les entités fédérées belges et l'intégration des immigrés. Politiques publiques comparées*. Brussels: Éditions de l'Université de Bruxelles.

Adam, Ilke and Andrea Rea (2010). *La diversité culturelle sur le lieu de travail. Pratiques d'aménagements raisonnables*. Brussels: Centre pour l'égalité des chances et la lutte contre le racisme.

Agirdag, Orhan, Maarten Hermans, and Mieke Van Houtte (2011). 'Het verband tussen islamitische religie, religiositeit en onderwijsprestaties', *Pedagogische Studieën* 88: 339–53.

Alba, Richard and Victor Nee (1997). 'Rethinking Assimilation Theory for a New Era of Immigration', *International Migration Review* 31(4): 826–74.

Alidadi, Katayoun (2012). 'Reasonable Accommodations for Religion and Belief: Adding Value to the Article 9 ECHR and the European Union's Anti-Discrimination Approach in Employment', *European Law Review* 37: 693–715.

Alidadi, Katayoun, Marie-Claire Foblets, and Jogchum Vrielink (2012). *A Test of Faith? Religious Diversity and Accomodation in the European Workplace*. Aldershot: Ashgate.

Almaci, Meyrem, Marlies Lacante et al. (2007). *Allochtonen in het Hoger Onderwijs. Factoren van studiekeuze en studiesucces bij allochtone eerstejaarsstudenten*. Leuven/Brussels: KU Leuven and VUB.

Amir-Moazami, Schirin and Armando Salvatore (2003). 'Gender, Generation, and the Reform of Tradition: From Muslim Majority Societies to Western Europe', in Stefano Allievi and Jorgen Nielsen (eds.), *Muslim Networks and Transnational Communities in and across Europe*. Leiden: Brill, 52–77.

Amnesty International (2012). *Choice and Prejudice: Discrimination against Muslims in Europe*. London: Amnesty International.

Arnaut, Karel, Sarah Bracke, Bambi Ceuppens, Sarah De Mul, Nadia Fadil, and Meryem Kanmaz (2008). *Leeuw in een Kooi. De Grenzen van de Multiculturele Verbeelding in Vlaanderen*. Antwerp: Meulenhoff-Manteau.

Arnaut, Karel and Bambi Ceuppens (2009). 'De ondiepe gronden en vage grenzen van de raciale verbeelding in Vlaanderen', in Karel Arnaut et al. (eds.), *Leeuw in een Kooi. De Grenzen van het Multiculturele Vlaanderen*. Antwerp: Meulenhoff-Manteau, 28–47.

Bastenier, Albert and Felice Dassetto (1981). 'La deuxième generation d'immigrés en Belgique', *Cahier Hebdomadaire du CRISP* (23 January): 907–8.
Bastenier, Albert and Felice Dassetto (1982a). *Aspects particuliers de la pathologie dans le milieu migratoire*. Louvain-la-Neuve: UCL, Groupe d'étude des migrations.
Bastenier, Albert and Felice Dassetto (1982b). *La consommation des soins ordinaires par les immigrés en Belgique. Enquête complémentaire auprès des policliniques et autres institutions médicales pratiquant le tiers-payant*. Louvain-la-Neuve: UCL, Groupe d'étude des migrations.
Bastenier, Albert, Annick De Rongé, and Felice Dassetto (1982). *Les immigrés et les accidents de travail*. Louvain-la-Neuve: UCL, Groupe d'étude des migrations.
Bawer, Bruce (2006). *While Europe Slept: How Radical Islam is Destroying the West from Within*. New York: Broadway Books.
Ben Abdeljelil, Youssef (1997). 'Arbeid, burgerschap en inburgering: onmin in een verstandshuwelijk', in Marie-Claire Foblets (ed.), *Nieuwe burgers in de samenleving? Burgerschap en inburgering in België en Nederland*. Leuven: Acco, 131–54.
Berger, Peter and Thomas Luckmann (1991 [1966]). *The Social Construction of Reality: A Treatise in the Sociology of Knowledge*. London: Penguin.
Billiet, Jaak, Ann Carton, and Luc Huyse (1990). *Onbekend of onbemind? Een sociologisch onderzoek naar de houding van de Belgen tegenover migranten*. Leuven: Sociologisch Onderzoeksinstituut KU Leuven.
Billiet, Jaak and Marc Swyngedouw (2009). *Etnische minderheden en de Vlaamse kiezers. Een analyse op basis van de postelectorale verkiezingsonderzoeken*. Leuven: Centrum voor Sociologisch Onderzoek, KU Leuven.
Blommaert Jan and Albert Martens (1999). *Van blok tot bouwsteen. Een visie voor een nieuw lokaal migrantenbeleid*. Antwerp: Epo.
Blommaert, Jan and Jef Verschueren (1992). *Het Belgische Migrantendebat. De pragmatiek van de abnormalisering*. Antwerp: International Pragmatics Association.
Boender, Welmoet and Meryem Kanmaz (2002). 'Imams in the Netherlands and Islam Teachers in Flanders', in W. A. R. Shadid and P. S. Van Koningsveld (eds.), *Intercultural Relations and Religious Authorities: Muslims in the European Union*. Leuven: Peeters, 169–80.
Bonne, Karijn and Wim Verbeke (2006). 'Muslim Consumer's Motivations towards Meat Consumption in Belgium: Qualitative Exploratory Insights from Means-End Chain Analyses', *Anthropology of Food* 5 (May). <http://aof.revues.org/index90.html>.
Bonne, Karijn and Wim Verbeke (2008). 'Religious Values Informing Halal Meat Production and the Control and Delivery of Halal Credence Quality', *Agriculture and Human Values* 25: 35–47.
Bousetta, Hassan (2000). 'Institutional Theories of Immigrant Ethnic Mobilization: Relevance and Limitations', *Journal of Ethnic and Migration Studies* 26(2): 229–45.
Bousetta, Hassan (2001). 'Immigration, Post-Immigration Politics and the Political Mobilization of Ethnic Minorities: A Comparative Case-Study of Moroccans in Four European Cities'. Ph.D. Brussels: KUB.
Bracke, Sarah (2007). 'Feminisme en islam: intersecties', in Inge Arteel, Heidy Margrit Müller, Machteld De Metsenaere, and Sarah Bossaert (eds.), *Vrouw(on)vriendelijk? Islam feministisch bekeken*. Brussels: VUB-Press, 13–38.
Bracke, Sarah and Nadia Fadil (2012). 'Is the Headscarf Oppressive or Emancipatory? Field Notes from the "Multicultural Debates"', *Religion and Gender* 2(1): 36–56.
Brems, Eva and Saila Oulad Chaib (2011). 'Gender in de Multiculturele Samenleving: Het Genderdiscours in de Debatten Rond een Hoofddoekverbod op Vlaamse Scholen en een

Niqaabverbod op de Belgische Straten', in E. Brems and L. Stevens (eds.), *Recht en Gender in België*. Brugge: Kluwer, 181-98.

Brion, Fabienne (2000). 'Des jeunes filles à sauver aux jeunes filles à mater: identité sociale et islamophobie', in Ural Manço (ed.), *Voix et voies musulmanes de Belgique*. Brussels: Publications des facultés universitaires de Saint-Louis, 115-49.

Brion, Fabienne (2004). *Féminité, minorité, islamité. Questions autour du Hijâb*. Louvain-la-Neuve: Academia-Bruylant.

Cesari, Jocelyne (1994). *Être musulman en France*. Paris/Aix-en-Provence: Karthala/Iremam.

Cesari, Jocelyne (2009). 'The Securitisation of Islam in Europe'. *Challenge Research Paper*, No. 15 (April). Brussels: CEPS Challenge Programme.

Ceuppens, Bambi and Peter Geschiere (2005). 'Autochthony: Local or Global? New Modes in the Struggle over Citizenship and Belonging in Africa and Europe', *Annual Review of Anthropology* 34: 385-407.

CGKR (2012). *Discriminatie—Diversiteit. Jaarverslag 2011*. Brussels: Centrum voor Gelijkheid van Kansen en Racismebestrijding/Centre pour l'égalité des chances et la lutte contre le Racisme/Center for Equality Opportunity and Opposition to Racism.

Clycq, Noël (2008). ,Habitus in de gezinssocialisatie. Een Bourdieuaanse analyse van de betekenisgevingsprocessen van Belgische, Italiaanse en Marokkaanse moeders en vaders'. Ph.D. Universiteit Antwerpen.

Clycq, Noël (2011). *Muslims in Antwerp*. Open Society Foundation [At Home in Europe Project]. New York and London: Open Society Foundation.

Clycq, Noël (2012). '"My daughter is a free woman, so she can't marry a Muslim": The Gendering of Ethno-Religious Boundaries', *European Journal of Women's Studies* 19: 151-71.

Dassetto, Felice (1996). *La construction de l'Islam européen. Approche socio- anthropologique*. Paris: L'Harmattan.

Dassetto, Felice (1997). *Facettes de l'islam belge*. Louvain-la-Neuve: Bruylant-Academia.

Dassetto, Felice (2001). *Belgique, Europe et nouvelles migrations*. Louvain-la-Neuve: Éditions Academia-Bruylant.

Dassetto, Felice (2011). *L'iris et le croissant. Bruxelles et l'islam au defi de la co-inclusion*. Louvain: UCL Presses Universitaires de Louvain.

Dassetto, Felice and Albert Bastenier (1984). *L'Islam transplanté: vie et organization des minorités musulmanes de Belgique*. Berchem: EPO.

Dassetto, Felice and Albert Bastenier (1987). *Medias u Akbar. Confrontations autour d'une manifestation*. Louvain-la-Neuve: CIACO.

Debeer, Jonathan, Patrick Loobuyck, and Petra Meier (2011). *Imams en Islamconsulenten in Vlaanderen. Hoe zijn ze georganiseerd?* Steunpunt Gelijke Kansen Beleid. Antwerp: Universiteit Antwerpen / Universiteit Hasselt.

Dobbelaere, Karel and Jaak Billiet (1974). *Godsdienst in België: een sociologische verkenning*. Leuven: Sociologisch onderzoeksinstituut.

Duquet, Nils, Ignace Glorieux, Ilse Laurijssen, and Yollis Van Dorsselaer (2006). *Wit krijt kleurt beter. Schoolloopbanen van allochtone jongeren in beeld*. Antwerp: Garant.

Duyvendak, Jan-Willem and Peter Scholten (2009). 'Le "modèle multiculturel" d'intégration néerlandais en question', *Migrations Société* 122: 77-115.

El Asri, Farid (2009a). 'L'expression musicale de musulmans européens. Création de sonorité et normativité religieuse', *Revue Européenne des Migrations Internationales* (REMI) 25(2): 35-50.

El Asri, Farid (2009b). 'Les origines de l'humain et sa problématique actuelle dans l'enseignement. Entre sciences modernes, convictions et (re)lectures du Coran', in Brigitte Maréchal, Felice Dassetto, and Philippe Muraille (eds.), *Adam et l'évolution. Islam et christianisme confrontés aux sciences*. Brussels: Academia Bruylant, 183–98.

El Asri, Farid (2011). 'Islam en musiques: constructions identitaires et champ musical européen'. Ph.D. Louvain-la-Neuve.

El Bachiri, Leila (2012). *Les féministes de l'islam. De l'engagement religieux au féminisme islamique. Etude des discours d'actrices religieuses 'glocales' à Bruxelles*. Brussels: Université des Femmes, Éditions Pensées Féministes.

Fadil, Nadia (2004). 'Het hoofddoekendebat. Meer dan een debat over een stukje stof?' *Ethische Perspective/Ethical Perspectives* 14(4): 373–86.

Fadil, Nadia (2005). 'Individualizing Faith, Individualizing Identity: Islam and Young Muslim Women in Belgium', in Jocelyne Cesari and Seán McLoughlin (eds.), *European Muslims and the Secular State*. Aldershot: Ashgate, 143–54.

Fadil, Nadia (2006). 'We Should Be Walking Qurans: The Making of an Islamic Political Subject', in Valérie Amiraux and Jonker, Gerdien (eds.), *The Politics of Visibility: Young Muslims in European Public Spaces*. Bielefeld: Transcript Verlag, 53–78.

Fadil, Nadia (2008). 'Submitting to God, Submitting to the Self: Secular and Religious Trajectories of Second-Generation Maghrebi in Belgium'. Ph.D. Leuven.

Fadil, Nadia (2010). 'Breaking the Taboo of Multiculturalism: The Belgian Left and Islam', in Vakil Abdoolkarim and Salman Sayyid (eds.), *Thinking Through Islamophobia: Global Perspectives*. New York: Columbia University Press, 235–50.

Fadil, Nadia (2011). 'On Not/Unveiling as an Ethical Practice', *Feminist Review* 98: 83–109.

Fadil, Nadia (2012a). 'Les pratiques religieuses publiques—remise en question ou articulation d'une nouvelle sphère publique', in Brigitte Maréchal and Farid El Asri (eds.), *Islam belge au pluriel*. Louvain: Presses Universitaires de Louvain, 221–58.

Fadil, Nadia (2012b). 'Belgium', in Jørgen Nielsen, Samim Akgönül, Ahmet Alibašić, and Račius Egdūnas (eds.), *Yearbook of Muslims in Europe*. Leiden: Brill, 69–93.

Fleischmann, Fenella and Karen Phalet (2012). 'Integration and Religiosity among the Turkish Second Generation in Europe: A Comparative Analysis across Four Capital Cities', *Ethnic and Racial Studies* 35(2): 320–41.

Foblets, Marie-Claire (1994). *Famille Maghrébines et la Justice en Belgique. Anthropologie Juridique et Immigration*. Paris: Karthala.

Foblets, Marie-Claire (2012). 'L'islam définitivement installé en Belgique, atout pour un droit de la famille repensé', in Brigitte Maréchal and Farid El Asri (eds.), *L'Islam belge au pluriel*. Louvain-la-Neuve: Presses Universitaires de Louvain, 291–317.

Foblets, Marie-Claire and A. Dundes Renteln (2009). *Multicultural Jurisprudence: Comparative Perspectives on the Cultural Defense*. Oxford and Portland, OR: Hart.

Foblets, Marie-Claire and Christiane Kulakowski (2010). *Assises de l'Interculturalité*. Rapport remis a Joëlle Milquet, Vice-Première Ministre et Ministre de l'Emploi et de l'Egalité des Chances. Brussels.

Foblets, Marie-Claire and Adriaan Overbeeke (2002). 'State Intervention in the Institutionalisation of Islam in Belgium', in W. A. R Shadid and P. S. Van Koningsveld (eds.), *Religious Freedom and the Neutrality of the State: The Position of Islam in the European Union*. Leuven: Peeters, 113–28.

Fraihi, Hind (2006). *Undercover in Klein-Marokko. Achter de gesloten deuren van de radicale Islam*. Leuven: Van Halewyck.

Fraser, Nancy (1992). 'Rethinking the Public Sphere: A Contribution to the Critique of Actually Existing Democracy', in Craig Calhoun (ed.), *Habermas and the Public Sphere*. Cambridge, MA and London: MIT Press, 109–42.

Grignard, Alain (2008). 'The Islamist Networks in Belgium', in Rik Coolsaet (ed.), *Jihadi Terrorism and the Radicalisation Challenge in Europe*. Aldershot: Ashgate, 85–93.

Gsir, S. (2006). 'Belgique: intégration et cohésion sociale. Bienne: Exposé dans le cadre la journée nationale de la Commission fédérale des Etrangers (CFE)', unpublished paper. <http://www.ekm.admin.ch/content/dam/data/ekm/aktuell/Veranstaltungen/ArchivVeranstaltungen/ref_gsir.pdf>.

Güngör, Derya, Fenella Fleischmann, and Karen Phalet (2011). 'Religious Identification, Belief, and Practices among Turkish Belgian and Moroccan Belgian Muslims: Intergenerational Continuity and Acculturative Change', *Journal of Cross-Cultural Psychology* 42(8): 1356–74.

Hermans, Philip (1992). 'De inpassing van Marokkaanse migrantenjongeren in België. Een vergelijkend antropologisch onderzoek bij geslaagde en niet geslaagde Marokkaanse jongens'. Ph.D. KU Leuven.

Hitchinson, Frans (1978). *De Islam in België. Sociologische probleemstelling*. Eindverhandeling Sociale Wetenschappen, KU Leuven.

Jacobs, Dirk (2004). 'Alive and Kicking? Multiculturalism in Flanders', *International Journal on Multicultural Societies* 6(2): 189–208.

Jacobs, Dirk, Marco Martiniello, and Andrea Rea (2002). 'Changing Patterns of Political Participation of Immigrants in the Brussels Capital Region: The October 2000 Elections', *Journal of International Migration and Integration* 3(2): 201–21.

Jabobs, Dirk, Karen Phalet, and Marc Swyngedouw (2004). 'Associational Membership and Political Involvement among Ethnic Minority Groups in Brussels', *Journal of Ethnic and Migration Studies* 30(3): 543–59.

Jacobs, Dirk, A. Rea, C. Teney, L. Callier, and S. Lothaire (2009). *De sociale lift blijft steken/ L'ascenseur social reste en panne. Les performances des élèves issus de l'immigration en Communauté française et en Communauté flamande*. Brussels: King Baudouin Foundation.

Kanmaz, Meryem (2002). 'Onze nationaliteit is onze godsdienst. Islam als "identity marker" bij jonge Marokkaanse moslims in Gent', in Marie-Claire Foblets and Eva Cornelis (eds.), *Migratie, zijn wij uw kinderen?* Leuven: Acco, 115–33.

Kanmaz, Meryem (2009). *Islamitische ruimtes in de stad*. Gent: Academia Press.

Kanmaz, Meryem and Mohamed El Battiui (2004). *Moskeeën, imams en islamleerkrachten in België. Stand van zaken en uitdagingen*. Brussels: Koning Boudewijn Stichting.

Kanmaz, Meryem and Sami Zemni (2008). 'Moslims als inzet in religieuze, maatschappelijke en veiligheidsdiscours. De erkenning en institutionalisering van de islamitische eredienst in België', in Christiane Timmerman and Els Vanderwaeren (eds.), *Islambeleving in de Lage landen*. Leuven: Acco/Apeldoorn.

Kaya, Ayhan and Ferhat Kentel (2007). *Belgische Turken. Een brug of een breuk tussen Turkije en de Europese Unie?* Brussels: Koning Boudewijn Stichting.

Kepel, Gilles (1987). *Les banlieues de l'Islam: Naissance d'une religion en France*. Paris: Éditions du Seuil.

Koutroubas, Theodoros, Ward Vloeberghs, and Zeynep Yanasmayan (2009). *Political, Religious and Ethnic Radicalisation among Muslims in Belgium*. MICROCON Policy Working Paper, Brighton.

Lamghari, Younous (2012). *L'islam en entreprise. La diversité culturelle en question*. Louvain-la-Neuve: L'Harmattan Academia.

Lechkar, Iman (2012a). 'Striving and Stumbling in the Name of Allah: Neo-Sunnis and Neo-Shi'ites in a Belgian Context'. Ph.D. Leuven.
Lechkar, Iman (2012b). 'Quelles sont les modalités d'authentification parmi les chiites belgo-marocains?' in Brigitte Maréchal and Farid El Asri (eds.), *L'Islam belge au pluriel*. Louvain-la-Neuve: Presses Universitaires de Louvain, 113–26.
Leman, Johan and Monique Renaerts (1996). 'Dialogues at Different Institutional Levels among Authorities and Muslims in Belgium', in W. A. R. Shadid and P. S. Van Koningsveld (eds.), *Muslims in the Margin: Political Responses to the Presence of Islam in Western Europe*. Kampen: Kok Pharos Publishing House, 164–81.
Leman, Johan, Monique Renaerts, and Dirk van den Bulck (1992a). 'De Rechtspositie van de Islamitische Praxis in België', *Cultuur en Migratie* 2: 43–84.
Leman, Johan, Monique Renaerts, Dirk van den Bulck, and Mohamed Boulif (1992b). 'De integratie van de islam in Belgie anno 1993', *Cultuur en Migratie* 1992-2: 43–84.
Lentin, Alana and Gavan Titley (2011). *The Crises of Multiculturalism: Racism in a Neoliberal Age*. London: Zed Books.
Lesthaeghe, Ron (1997). *Diversiteit in sociale verandering. Turkse en Marokkaanse vrouwen in België*. Brussels: VUB Press.
Lesthaeghe, Ron (2000). 'Transnational Islamic Communities in a Multilingual Secular Society', in Ron Lesthaeghe (ed.), *Communities and Generations: Turkish and Moroccan Populations in Belgium*. Brussels: VUB-Press, 1–55.
Lesthaeghe, Ron and Karen Neels (2000). 'Islamic Communities in Belgium: Religious Orientations and Secularization', in Ron Lesthaeghe (ed.), *Communities and Generations: Turkish and Moroccan Populations in Belgium*. Brussels: VUB-Press, 129–64.
Lijphart, Arend (1968). *The Politics of Accommodation: Pluralism and Democracy in the Netherlands*. Berkeley: University of California Press.
Longman, Chia (2003). 'Over our Heads? Muslim Women as Symbols and Agents in the Headscarf Debate in Flanders, Belgium', *Social Justice, Anthropology, Peace and Human Rights* 4(3–4): 300–32.
Manço, Ural (2001). *Relgiosité islamique et intégration chez les jeunes hommes turcs de belgique en 2001*. Available at <http://www.cie.ugent.be/umanco/umanco7.htm> [Accessed April 2013].
Manço, Ural (2012). 'Identification religieuses de jeunes schaerbeekois issues de l'immigration', in Brigitte Maréchal and Farid El Asri (eds.), *L'Islam belge au pluriel*. Louvain-la-Neuve: Presses Universitaires de Louvain, 67–84.
Maréchal, Brigitte (2003). 'Institutionalisation of Islam and Representative Organisations for Dealing with European States', in Brigitte Maréchal, Stefano Allievi, and Felice Dassetto (eds.), *Muslims in the Enlarged Europe*. Leiden: Brill, 151–82.
Maréchal, Brigitte (2008). *The Muslim Brothers in Europe: Roots and Discourses*. Leiden: Brill.
Maréchal, Brigitte and Farid El Asri (eds.) (2012). *L'Islam belge au pluriel*. Louvain-la-Neuve: Presses Universitaires de Louvain.
Martens, Albert (1973). *25 jaar wegwerparbeiders: het Belgisch immigratiebeleid na 1945*. Leuven: KUL Sociologisch onderzoeksinstituut.
Martens, Albert (1993). 'De integratieproblematiek binnen een multiculturele samenleving: het verzuilingsmodel als hypothese', in Frank Demeyere (ed.), *Over Pluralisme en Democratie. Verzuiling en integratie in een multiculturele samenleving*. Brussels: VUB Press, 39–50.
Martens, Albert and Frank Moulaert (1985). *Buitenlandse Minderheden in Vlaanderen-België*. Antwerp and Amsterdam: Uitgeverij De Nederlandsche Boekhandel.

Martens, Albert, Nouria Ouali, Marjan Van De Maele, Sara Vertommen, Philippe Dryon, and Hans Verhoeven (2005). *Etnische discriminatie op de arbeidsmarkt in het Brussels Hoofdstedelijk Gewest: onderzoek in het kader van het Sociaal Pact voor de Werkgelegenheid van de Brusselaars.* Brussels: BGDA.

Modood, Tariq (1998). 'Anti-Essentialism, Multiculturalism and the "Recognition" of Religious Groups', *Journal of Political Philosophy* 4(98): 378–99.

Morelli, Anne (2008 [1992]). *Histoire des Etrangers et de l'immigration en Belgique de la préhistoire à nos jours.* Mons: Éditions Couleur Livres.

Panafit, Lionel (1999). *Quand le droit écrit l'Islam. L'integration juridique de l'islam en Belgique.* Louvain-la-Neuve: Bruylant Academia.

Pedziwiatr, Konrad (2010). *The New Muslim Elites in European Cities: Religion and Active Social Citizenship Amongst Young Organized Muslims in Brussels and London.* Saarbrücken: Verlag Dr. Müller.

Pedziwiatr, Konrad (2012). 'Citoyenneté et nouvelles elites musulmanes a bruxelles et a londres', in Brigitte Maréchal and Farid El Asri (eds.), *L'Islam belge au pluriel.* Louvain-la-Neuve: Presses Universitaires de Louvain, 129–46.

Rea, Andrea (1999). 'La reconnaissance et la représentation de l'Islam', *L'Année sociale*: 269–75. Available at <http://www.ulb.ac.be/socio/germe/documentsenligne/3Rea99.pdf> [Accessed April 2013].

Saaf, Abdallah, Bouchra Sidi Hida, and Ahmed Aghbal (2009). *Belgische Marokkanen. Een dubbele identiteit in ontwikkeling.* Brussels: Koning Boudewijn Stichting.

Saroglou, Vassilis, Bahija Lamkaddem, Mattieu Van Pachterbeke, and Coralie Buxant (2009). 'Host Society's Dislike of the Ilsamic Veil: The Role of Subtle Prejudice, Values and Religion', *International Journal of Intercultural Relations* 33: 419–28.

Schinkel, Willem (2007). *Denken in een tijd van sociale hypochondrie. Aanzet tot een theorie voorbij de maatschappij.* Kampen: Klement.

Scott, Joan W. (2007). *The Politics of the Veil.* Princeton: Princeton University Press.

Swyngedouw, Marc, Karen Phalet, and Kris Deschouwer (eds.) (1999). *Minderheden in Brussel.* Brussels: VUB Press.

Timmerman, Christiane (1999). *Onderwijs maakt het verschil. Socioculturele praxis en etniciteitsbeleving bij Turkse jonge vrouwen.* Minderheden in de Samenleving, no. 7. Leuven: Acco.

Torrekens, Corinne (2008). 'La visibilité de l'islam au sein de l'espace public bruxellois: transaction, reconnaissance et identité'. Ph.D. Université Libre de Bruxelles/Université Catholique de Louvain.

Torrekens, Corinne (2009). *L'Islam a Bruxelles.* Brussels: Éditions de l'Université de Bruxelles.

Touag, Hanifa (2012). 'Géurir par l'Islam: l'adoption du rite prophétique—roqya—par les salafistes en France et en Belgique', in Brigitte Maréchal and Farid El Asri (eds.), *Islam belge au pluriel.* Louvain-la Neuve: Presses Universitaires de Louvain, 201–17.

Van Amerongen, Arthur (2008). *Brussels/Eurabia.* Amsterdam: Kemper.

Van den Branden, Stef (2006). 'Islamitische ethiek aan het levenseinde. Een theoretisch omkaderde inhoudsanalyse van Engelstalig soennitisch bronnenmateriaal en een kwalitatief empirisch onderzoek naar de houding van praktiserende Marokkaanse oudere mannen in Antwerpen'. Ph.D. Leuven.

Van der Heyden, Katrien, Johan Geets, Els Vanderwaeren, and Christiane Timmerman (2005). *Islambeleving bij Hoogopgeleide Moslimjongeren in Vlaanderen.* Antwerp: Steunpunt Gelijkekansenbeleid—Consortium Universiteit Antwerpen en Universiteit Hasselt.

Van Robaeys, Bea, Jan Vranken, Nathalie Perrin, and Marco Martiniello (2007). *De Kleur van Armoede. Armoede bij personen van buitenlandse herkomst*. Leuven and Antwerp: Acco/ Oases.

Vandezande, Veronique, Fenella Fleischmann, Gülseli Baysu, Marc Swyngedouw, and Karen Phalet (2008). *De Turkse en Marokkaanse tweede generatie op de arbeidsmarkt in Antwerpen en Brussel. Resultaten van het TIES onderzoek*. Leuven: Centrum voor Sociologisch Onderzoek (CeSO).

Verscheuren, Jef (2001). 'Nogmaals: het rapport-Van San'. Available at <http://www.flw.ugent.be/cie/CIE/verschueren1.htm>.

Vertovec, Steven (1998). *Muslim European Youth: Reproducing Ethnicity, Religion, Culture*. Aldershot: Ashgate.

Vrielink, Jogchum, Saïla Ouald Chaib, and Eva Brems (2011). 'Boerkaverbod. Juridische aspecten van lokale en algemene verboden op gezichtsverhulling in België', *Nieuw Juridisch Weekblad* 244: 398–414.

Zemni, Sami (2008). *Het Islamdebat*. Berchem: EPO.

Zemni, Sami (2011). 'The Shaping of Islam and Islamophobia in Belgium', *Race and Class* 53(28): 28–44.

Zibouh, Fatima (2011). 'La représentation politique des musulmans à Bruxelles', *Brussels Studies* 55 (December).

Zibouh, Fatima and Joe Costanzo (forthcoming). 'A Single Philosophy and Policy of Public Culture for a Cosmopolitan and Multicultural City?' *Identities* 13.

# PART II

# THE ARRIVAL OF ISLAM AS POST-1974 MIGRATION

CHAPTER 6

# ITALY

## CHANTAL SAINT-BLANCAT

The presence of Islam in Italy goes back to the Middle Ages with the conquest of Sicily (Amari 2002) from 827 to 1061, the beginning of Norman rule on the island. Muslims cannot be considered as a new presence but as historical actors in the making of the national cultural heritage as pointed out by Allievi and Dassetto (1993) in their aptly named book *The Return of Islam*.

Italy has a strong tradition of Oriental studies best illustrated by Caetani's (1905–26) ten volumes based on Arabic material of the reconstruction of Islamic access to power and the following Caliphate period or Bausani's (1955) insightful translation of the Qur'an. Orientalist tradition first focused on the translation of religious texts, the analysis of mystical thinking, and poetry from Arabic and Persian literature, and then on theological or juridical aspects of Islam in contemporary Muslim countries such as Vercellin's (1996) *Institutions of the Muslim World*. When Muslim migrants flowed into Italy in the 1980s, such disciplines largely contributed to a better understanding of Muslim requests and expectations, providing an anthropological insight along ethnic lines for social scientists dealing with Muslim issues.

Until the end of the 1990s, Italian society was relatively indifferent to the religious dimension of migrants coming from Egypt, Somalia, or Morocco. The so-called 'Muslim exception' (Saint-Blancat and Perocco 2006; Perocco 2008) where Islam coincides with ethnic and national identity was not yet apparent in the public arena.

It is only since the 2000s that the question of Islam has been at the centre of Italian public debate, becoming a scapegoat for unresolved national and regional problems (Schmidt di Friedberg 2001). This began with the 2000 Lodi mosque conflict (Saint-Blancat and Schmidt di Friedberg 2005) and later on, after 9/11, intensified with the publication of a book by political analyst Giovanni Sartori's *Pluralism, Multiculturalism and Foreigners* (2002) and the well-known journalist Oriana Fallaci's bestseller *The Rage and the Pride* (2001). Both works contributed strongly to the social construction of Muslims as public enemies (Allievi 2009b; Sciortino 2002).

'Clandestine' could be the keyword to describe the peculiarities of the Italian case. The current obsession about 'irregular immigrants' and security issues overlaps with the absence of an official recognition of Islam in the growing religious pluralism of the country. The ambiguous attitude of Italian society towards immigration, and particularly Italian Muslims, is embedded in its own contradictions, as we shall see in this chapter.

On the one hand, the Italian government and Italian citizens are convinced that immigrants are necessary to Italy's economy and society; on the other, they often tend to downplay their dynamic contribution to taxes and pensions and as a demographic resource (Sciortino 2012; Fondazione Leone Moressa 2012). In the same manner, Italian society has built one of the most extended inter-faith relationships with Muslims, but remains one of the last countries to deny them their institutional space in the national religious landscape. It is still difficult for Italian Muslims to open a new mosque, but Italy has had no headscarf affair so far and has never faced terrorist attacks or violence as in other European countries. Despite a lack of full legal recognition, numerous empirical researches show that Muslims have found their way into Italian civil society and are slowly but steadily involved as Italians in shaping the cultural and religious national frame.

This paradoxical setting explains why one finds extensive literature on Islamophobia, mosque conflicts, political and media debates around Islam, but not the same amount of research and data on who are Italian Muslims, on their socio-economic status and their religious practices, on how they view their social and religious inclusion in the country, or how Italian public opinion perceives them.

No national survey, such as those found in the Netherlands or France, exists on these crucial issues in Italy, except the long overdue 2012 ISTAT study on 'how migrants are perceived by Italian citizens'. Such surveys could have improved the knowledge and policies of inclusion. By contrast, regional and local institutions, lay and religious voluntary associations, dioceses, trade unions, and above all Catholic networks strongly involved in immigration issues, such as Caritas, have funded and commissioned empirical studies on a range of issues: from Muslim associations, religious organizations, education and gender issues, to social marginalization and deviancy.

These types of work have produced myriad interesting local data on various topics, sometimes going deep into unresolved problems. But studies are heterogeneous in terms of scientific methods of enquiry, and being mostly based on qualitative approaches and focused on regional or micro local context, they do not always provide a representative assessment of the sociological profile of the populations involved or potential national extension of the problematic investigated.

This is partly due to the fact that Italy has become an immigration country only recently, over the last thirty years, and the Italian governments have never developed any specific model of integration like France or advocated a multicultural policy like other European countries such as Great Britain or the Netherlands. Even during the 2011 celebration of 150 years of national unity, Italian society did not take the opportunity to open a debate on the new ethnic and religious pluralism of the country (Naso and Salvarini 2012).

This explains also why the research agenda initially tends to operate a deconstruction of the stereotyped representation of Muslim residents, producing empirical data and analysis to invert the stigmatic vision of Islam in Italy. It is only in the last decade that research on Italian Islam has widened its perspective from the public perception of the Muslim challenge in terms of integration.

Academic research on Italian Muslims is still young. The first discipline involved in this field was canonical law which still provides today the most extensive and refined work on legal aspects of Italian Islam (Ferrari and others). Other disciplines such as political science, human geography, anthropology, and sociology, in particular sociology of migration, are also active in this field of study. But since the 1990s, sociology of religion addressed Muslim issues in general, producing the most relevant amount of studies and becoming a growing field of research interest.

Both academic and non-academic research has contributed to draw a line and a clear distinction between the national rhetoric/political debate which regularly invades newspapers and TV headlines from the end of the 1990s and the silent local ways of dealing with Islam observed among Italian civil society: the progressive building of positive social interactions in everyday life between Italian citizens and Muslim residents, which can be very different and much more inclusive and tolerant than is currently perceived.

This chapter will highlight the manifold aspects of past empirical research and recent literature on Italian Islam. Studies have mainly focused on how Italian Muslims have faced the lack of inclusion policies and Islamophobia, their ethnic heterogeneity and plural religiosity, and the leading role of young Muslims in the battle for citizenship, access, and visibility in the public space. The failure of the institutional recognition of Italian Islam is discussed and linked to Italian ambiguities and contradictions. While radicalism and Islamic movements remain marginal, interactions with the local civil society at all levels and inter-faith dialogue abound.

# From Immigrants to Citizens: Facing Italian Migration Policies

## Who are Italian Muslims? Estimation More Than Exact Figures

As elsewhere in Europe, the challenge in any statistical study of Muslims is how we define them. As Nadia Jeldtof reminds us (2009: 12), we are facing a categorization of 'Muslims' who can be distinguished from other social groups by virtue of their 'Muslimness'. The way Muslims deal with their individual relationship with Islam is often left unaddressed or worse, taken for granted. The only accurate way to get available data is a national demographic census which allows citizens to declare freely their religious belonging.

Italy has no official census based on religious affiliation. So counting Muslims residents means working on estimates, calculated on the basis of the number of migrants coming from societies considered as Muslim majority countries, yet knowing that a percentage of them are Christians or Jews. Such labelling does not do justice to the ethnic and religious diversity of the Muslim diaspora and to individual religious self-identification. The Albanese case is emblematic: most of them declare themselves as Christians or Muslims, but many do not express religious affiliation.

The main characteristic of the 4,570,317 foreigners living legally in the country at the end of 2010 (7.5% of the total population) is their extreme diversity and the Muslim population is no exception.

Table 6.1 gives a first estimation of the heterogeneity of Italian Muslims and the increase/decrease of the different nationalities of provenance in the last twenty years.

The first Muslim immigrant groups consisted of students from the Middle East (Syrian, Egyptian, Jordanian, and some Iranians) and a small percentage of Somalians, Libyans, and Eritreans coming from former Italian colonies. Then arrived the Moroccan population, one of the earliest settlements of migrant workers in the country: men came first and family reunification began in the 1990s. Tunisians, the second longest standing group, came from their nearby country and settled mainly in Sicily, in particular in Mazara del Vallo where the successive generations amount today to 3% of the population. The Senegalese group followed, then more recently migrants from Bangladesh, Pakistan, and Nigeria (Zincone 2001). As underlined already, not all of them are Muslims.

The first works on Muslim groups have been mainly 'community studies' such as the pioneer work of Ottavia Schmidt di Friedberg on the Italian Senegalese community (1994), focused on *murid* socio-religious organizations and work life, Saint-Blancat's first study on Iranians in Italy and Italian Shi'ism and the plural relationship of Persians with religion (1989, 1990), and Ambrosini and Abbattecola's work on Egyptians in Milan (2002).

The bi-annual collection *Stranieri in Italia* (*Foreigners in Italy*) edited by Colombo and Sciortino since 1991, has largely contributed to the knowledge of the various national migrant groups, including those of Muslim origin, with data and empirical studies, and is still today one of the best reviews of anthropological and sociological research in this field. The Caritas annual publication (since 2001) provides a wide range of statistical, economic, and demographic data on Italian migrants, focusing every year on a different national group, giving particular attention to social and legal insertion, women and youth studies, and the new Italian religious pluralism. Since 2004 the ISMU Foundation in Milan (Initiatives and Study on Multi Ethnicities) has published an annual report and database on migrants.

In the early years 'Italian governments have "made a deal" with the main sending and transit countries such as Albania, Tunisia and Morocco. Since 1998, Italy has reserved a large proportion of the entry slots for citizens of these countries in exchange for their collaboration in emigration control and readmission of their deported citizens' (Sciortino 2012: 87). This strategy worked relatively well until the events of the Arab Spring revolution and the arrival on the island of Lampedusa, first of clandestine young Tunisians (2011), then African refugees from Libya (2012) despite the recent improvement of control on clandestine entries from the sea, the weakest Italian border.

Table 6.1 Foreign citizens in Italy from Muslim majority countries

| Year | Morocco | Albania | Tunisia | Senegal | Egypt | Bangladesh | Pakistan | Algeria | Bosnia-Herzegovina | Iran | Nigeria | Turkey | Somalia |
|---|---|---|---|---|---|---|---|---|---|---|---|---|---|
| 1990 | 80,495 | 2,034 | 42,223 | 25,268 | 20,211 | – | – | – | – | – | – | – | – |
| 1992 | 83,292 | 24,886 | 41,547 | 24,194 | 18,473 | 5,542 | 6,983 | 3,458 | – | 6,821 | 5,627 | 3,617 | 9,265 |
| 1993 | 66,526 | 22,474 | 27,356 | 19,235 | 14,647 | 4,129 | 4,359 | 2,435 | 2,063 | 5,840 | 4,067 | 3,107 | 10,881 |
| 1994 | 72,464 | 23,732 | 28,856 | 19,973 | 14,663 | 4,295 | 4,559 | 2,482 | 5,816 | 5,753 | 4,328 | 3,243 | 10,994 |
| 1995 | 73,076 | 25,245 | 27,751 | 19,383 | 14,796 | 4,100 | 4,467 | 2,514 | 7,825 | 5,645 | 4,371 | 3,348 | 9,415 |
| 1996 | 81,247 | 30,183 | 30,666 | 20,816 | 15,530 | 4,877 | 5,147 | 2,807 | 8,250 | 5,802 | 4,828 | 3,502 | 9,047 |
| 1997 | 115,026 | 66,608 | 40,002 | 31,543 | 23,547 | 11,090 | 10,133 | 11,311 | 9,108 | 5,823 | 12,587 | 3,924 | 8,637 |
| 1998 | 122,230 | 72,551 | 41,439 | 32,037 | 23,606 | 12,140 | 10,661 | 11,643 | 8,928 | 5,915 | 12,911 | 4,364 | 7,841 |
| 1999 | 128,297 | 87,595 | 41,137 | 31,420 | 23,811 | 12,044 | 10,802 | 11,011 | 10,042 | 5,910 | 13,001 | 5,479 | 8,653 |
| 2000 | 155,864 | 133,018 | 46,773 | 40,890 | 34,042 | 18,980 | 17,237 | 13,413 | 11,485 | 6,179 | 20,056 | 6,277 | 7,353 |
| 2001 | 162,254 | 146,321 | 45,972 | 39,170 | 32,381 | 20,820 | 18,551 | 13,038 | 12,093 | 5,791 | 19,489 | 6,402 | 6,281 |
| 2002 | 215,430 | 216,582 | 59,528 | 37,204 | 33,701 | 20,607 | 22,257 | 12,587 | 16,669 | 5,793 | 20,963 | 7,183 | 5,305 |
| 2003 | 253,362 | 270,383 | 68,630 | 46,478 | 40,583 | 27,356 | 27,798 | 15,493 | 20,152 | 6,405 | 26,383 | 9,130 | 5,963 |
| 2004 | 294,945 | 316,659 | 78,230 | 53,941 | 52,865 | 35,785 | 35,509 | 18,736 | 22,436 | 6,550 | 31,647 | 11,077 | 6,094 |
| 2005 | 319,537 | 348,813 | 83,564 | 57,101 | 58,879 | 41,631 | 41,797 | 20,202 | 24,142 | 6,566 | 34,310 | 12,359 | 6,249 |
| 2006 | 343,228 | 375,947 | 88,932 | 59,857 | 65,667 | 49,575 | 46,085 | 21,519 | 26,298 | 6,850 | 37,733 | 13,532 | 6,414 |
| 2007 | 365,908 | 401,949 | 93,601 | 62,620 | 69,572 | 55,242 | 49,344 | 22,672 | 27,356 | 6,913 | 40,641 | 14,562 | 6,237 |
| 2008 | 403,592 | 441,396 | 100,112 | 67,510 | 74,599 | 65,529 | 55,371 | 24,387 | 30,124 | 6,983 | 44,544 | 16,225 | 6,663 |
| 2009 | 431,529 | 466,684 | 103,678 | 72,618 | 82,064 | 73,965 | 64,859 | 25,449 | 31,341 | 7,106 | 48,674 | 17,651 | 7,728 |
| 2010 | 452,424 | 482,627 | 106,291 | 80,989 | 90,365 | 82,451 | 75,720 | 25,935 | 31,972 | 7,444 | 53,613 | 19,068 | 8,112 |

*Note*: Estimation of the number of foreign people resident in Italy refers to 01/01 from 1992 to 2001 and on 31/12 from 2002 to 2010. The data considered the legal migrants with residence permit.
*Source*: F. Cerchiaro's elaboration on ISTAT data (<http://www.demo.istat.it>).

Apart from this last episode, since 2007 immigrants from Muslim countries do not form the majority of the new contingents of workers which have been mainly reserved for domestic labour, housekeepers, or care workers, essentially women from Romania, Ukraine, and other eastern countries, the result of a demanding and strained welfare regime (Einaudi 2007; Zincone 2006; Sciortino 2012).

At the time of writing, Italy counts 1,505,000 Muslims depending on the various and sometimes contradictory estimates (ISTAT, Caritas, ISMU). Migrants' religious affiliation remains difficult to evaluate. Caritas, on the basis of Ministry of Home Affairs data, provides every year one of the best available statistics. At 1 January 2011 half of total legal resident migrants were Christians (2,465,000) with a growing prevalence of Orthodox (1,221,955), while over a third (32.9%) belong to plural Islam, Sunni, Shi'ite, and Sufi confraternities. Islam has become Italy's second religion, including 10,000 Italian converts. But in a few years the Orthodox could easily outnumber them.

The majority of Italian Muslims live in the northern part of the country, in rank order Lombardy and Piedmont and then Veneto. But many are resident in the central part of Italy, particularly in Emilia Romagna. A significant percentage of Muslim populations live in cities like Milan, Turin, or Rome but most of them are scattered over all the Italian provinces. Compared to the rest of Europe, the social location of migrants in Italy is quite peculiar because residence is linked to the Italian dispersed industrial setting. Muslim populations often live in very small provincial towns where the composition of neighbourhoods and school classes do not reflect a strong concentration of migrants. This scattered habitat tends to prevent forms of ghettoization and accelerates social interaction with the local population, above all among youths.

Family reunification, progressive settlement, and the presence of school children born in Italy (Colombo and Sciortino 2008) show evidence of the fact that Muslim groups are here to stay. In the 2011/12 academic year Moroccan students numbered 95,912 (12.7% of the foreign student population) just behind Albanese (13.59%) and Romanians (18.66%) (MIUR 2012: 17). So far, compared to other European countries, no public discourse underlines the threat of Muslim demography, except the North League's newspaper *La Padania*.

Since 2008–11 Italy has hosted refugees (58,000 in 2011) from several countries such as Nigeria (6,208), Somalia, Eritrea, Afghanistan, Pakistan, and recently Tunisia (4,558), Mali, and Ghana, but the procedure to become Italian citizens is a trying experience (UNHCR, Caritas Migrantes 2012).

## Socio-Economic Status: Indicators of Integration

Specific statistical national data on Muslim employment rate, housing, labour market mobility, and social status do not exist in Italy. This is due to a lack of interest from official institutions to conduct national statistical surveys with broader social scopes even if the Italian National Institute of Statistics (ISTAT) has done a good job in the recent years in providing data on the immigration phenomenon. This ineffective policy is also linked to the general precarious status of migrants as a result of the contradictory logic of Italian immigration policies. In contrast with the rest of Europe, Italian governments have always acknowledged the demand for foreign labour and still maintain irregular immigration as a convenient and deep structural phenomenon (Finotelli and Sciortino 2008). Three combined factors are at the root of this contradictory policy: the lack of an active recruitment channel for foreign labour, ineffective internal controls, and above all an extended and structural informal economy, part of a national civic culture generally tolerant towards shadow employment (Finotelli and Sciortino 2008: 3).

Immigration was an answer to the country's labour market needs rather than the result of a clear immigration policy. The first immigration law was drawn up only in December 1986 (Foschi Law) and its title, 'Legislation concerning the employment and treatment of *extra communitarian* immigrants and against *clandestine* immigration', strongly reflects the Italian social representation of the phenomenon. Then came the Martelli Law (1990) which introduced the systematic process of 'regularization' (the famous 'sanatorie'), followed by the Turco-Napolitano Law (1998), the first 'non-emergential legislature frame' (Allievi 2010a: 156), and the first attempt to take care of foreigners' rights and to involve them politically. Finally in 2002 the Bossi-Fini Law was passed and dismantled these tentative juridical moves, introducing a political change focused on order, security, and social fear (Ambrosini and Caneva 2010). By linking the residence permit to a regular job the law had the paradoxical result of '*producing* irregularity *via* the legislation' (Allievi 2010a: 157). Since this period, Muslim residents, like other migrants, have to face the repressive dimension of the country's control policy. If a migrant loses his or her job he or she immediately joins the contingent of irregular immigrants, even if the individual migrant has been a regular resident for ten years.

Actually the fight against irregular migration has always involved the use of regularization policies (seven in thirty years). 'Italy has regularized the largest number of foreign immigrants among all the European countries in the last twenty years' (Ambrosini and Caneva 2010: iii). Since 1986, Italian governments have regularized almost 1.4 million foreigners and most of them still have their residence permits (Finotelli and Sciortino 2008: 4). The 'Italian habit of enacting frequent amnesty programs has allowed the transfer of a large number of immigrants from the shadow economy to the formal, low-skilled labour sector, where they were badly needed' (Sciortino 2012: 81). This policy, systematically used from the late 1990s, coincides with a 'generalized expectation, shared by employers and immigrants alike that hiring an irregular immigrant and waiting for the next amnesty was the easiest and cheapest option' (Sciortino 2012: 87).

Today nearly half of the legal migrants (46%, ISTAT 2012) have received a permanent visa. Moroccans are the first group in number (279,904), followed by Tunisians (65,519), Egyptians (56,021), and Bangladeshi (50,896), clear signs of Italian Muslims' stable residence and level of income. Regarding sectors of wage earning employment, Moroccans and Tunisians are working mainly in industry (respectively 44.7% and 41.1%). Egyptians are mainly shop assistants or waiters (31%), Bangladeshi are in both industry (35.5%) and construction (26.9%). Few Italian Muslims are employed in agriculture, with the exception of Tunisians in Sicilian fishery (Ministero del Lavoro e delle Politiche Sociali 2012).

## Access to Citizenship

The other main obstacle faced by migrants is access to citizenship. Italy has one of the most restrictive laws in Europe in terms of inclusion. The original law (1912) was revised only in 1992 and did not take into account the recent transformation of the Italian context as a land of immigration. The law is still based on *ius sanguinis* defining the national membership in strict tribe-ethnic terms, the so called 'familismo legale' (Zincone 2006). Two main procedures allow migrants to obtain citizenship. The first one is through marriage (article 5), which is still the easiest method compared to other European legislations and the most used: 84.3% of the total number of citizenships granted in 2006, and still 63.2% in 2008 (Caritas Migrantes 2008 and 2009). The second one (article 9) is a real obstacle race whereby citizenship is granted through legal and continuous residence but only after a minimum period of ten years for non EU nationals (the so-called 'extracomunitari' which form the majority of the migrant population) and after four years for European citizens. Moreover the application process is very tricky and often takes more than four or five years. At the end the concession given officially by the President of the Italian Republic is totally discretionary (Ambrosini and Caneva 2010: 20). Finally for people born in Italy from foreign parents (i.e. the second generation) they can apply for citizenship between the ages of 18 and 19 but only if they have lived *continually* in the country since birth. This restriction is the most debated issue and object of protest among young migrants as we shall see later on.

Italy has one of the lowest rates of naturalization compared to the rest of Europe. The total number of citizenships granted was only 11,945 in 2004, but grew to 19,266 in 2005, with an amazing peak in 2006 (35,766). Since this period numbers have grown regularly, reaching 40,084 in 2009 (Ministero dell'Interno 2009) and 66,000 in 2010, but still behind the 124,000 registered in Spain in the same year (Caritas 2012: 116). Who are the winners in this endurance contest? Since the beginning the first group has always been either the Moroccan population or the Albanians as in 2009. Muslim groups, such as Moroccans (5,917), Tunisians (1,256), and Egyptians (926) have obtained Italian citizenship mainly through residence (article 9), especially men over the age of 40 who arrived in the 1980s (Ministero dell' Interno 2009). It is worth noting that Filipino women who arrived in the same years have a much lower rate of application, compared to Muslim families who are in the country to stay. The paradox of such a non-inclusive procedure is that the law tends to exclude migrants who have been part of Italian society and accustomed to its values for many years, such as the second generation, by giving priority to newcomers, mainly women who acquire citizenship after only six months through marriage.

## Women's Migration

Muslim women have not been passive actors in the migration process as underlined in one of the first studies on women's role in Italy (Schmidt di Friedberg and Saint-Blancat 1998). This study was the beginning of a rich field of research dedicated to women's expectations and strategies. The literature takes an ethnic/gender rather than religious perspective. As actors of mediation between their community and the Italian local environment, women have been active in building their own networks (often transnational) and demonstrate significant agency in transmitting their culture and helping the second generation to perform in the Italian school system. Less common than Filipino or Central and Eastern European women in the labour market, in particular in domestic employment (14,738 Moroccans versus 103,979 Ukrainians in 2010; Labour Report 2012), despite linguistic difficulties and less autonomy (only in the case of the first generation), Muslim women learned quickly to find space for themselves inside kinship networks and Italian non-governmental organizations (NGOs). In migration, women have begun to rethink gender roles and to question the frames of the traditional and patriarchal authority. On these issues see Decimo's works on Moroccan and Somalian women (2005, 2007, 2008), Salih's extensive studies on Moroccan women in Emilia Romagna, in particular the means and conduct they adopt confronting modernity (2000, 2001a, 2001b, 2003, 2009), and Errichiello (2008) on Northern African women in Campania.

*Entrepreneurship*

Migrant workers, and in particular Moroccans, Egyptians, and Tunisians, have a significant presence in free enterprise. Extensive research funded by the Italian Ministry of Research and coordinated by Chiesi (2011) provides statistical data and qualitative results on migrants' strategy in small and medium enterprises. Muslim entrepreneurs analysed are the Egyptians in construction work (Milan), North Africans in the mechanics industry (Reggio Emilia), and Moroccans in the food business (Turin). The report provides an interesting insight into the individual biographies, networks, and dynamism of this growing sector of activity. Foreign entrepreneurs numbered 213,267 at the end of 2010; 87% have their business in the northern and central part of Italy, with Lombardy constituting 23% of these enterprises. Moroccan entrepreneurs amount to 16.6% of the total. Sectors mainly involved are building, fast food outlets, and mechanics. In contrast, Chinese are dominant in the textile industry. Egyptian owners of pizza restaurants (64%) have become more numerous than 'pizzaioli' from Campania (19%) or from Naples (24%) (Caritas 2010: 55). Egyptians and Moroccans were the first migrants to become entrepreneurs and usually have dual citizenships. Their social capital is also relevant: multilingual knowledge, educational status, strong kinship networks and family solidarity, good social interactions with Italians, and capacity to build a good name and socio-economic credibility are important components of their success.

Other studies have taken an ethnographic approach involving in-depth interviews, such as Riccio on Senegalese '*vu cumprà*' activities in Italian towns, and along tourist beaches in summertime (2007), and the Moroccan bazaar economy in Turin (Semi 2006). The research on kebab shops in Padua and Treviso (Veneto) underlines the pragmatic conduct of Muslim businessmen in dealing with halal and haram products (Saint-Blancat et al. 2008).

# Learning to Deal with Islamophobia

Islamophobia has been the issue most debated and source of most conflicts in the Italian context. Between 2000 and 2002 the term progressively displaced the broader xenophobia discourse. Politicians, media, policy-makers, the Catholic Church, the rich mixture of lay and religious associations, and also researchers became involved in the debate. However, one actor was largely missing, invisible, and silent: the Italian Muslim. Today Muslim associations are better organized and more visible in the public space, their leaders having acquired legitimate status, but above all because the young generation born or socialized in the country would never remain silent as was the case before.

The Italian case is inscribed in the more general frame of xenophobia and widespread negative perceptions of Islam which pervaded European societies since the beginning of the twentieth century. Increasingly perceived as enemies within (see the opinion polls analysis by Ayhan Kaya in this book), and as the quintessence of otherness, 'the overly culturalist understanding of European Muslim communities has remained mostly unchanged and rarely challenged in the last sixty years' (Marranci 2012: 300). This comment could still be applied to the Italian public and political debate, orchestrated by the media coverage, at least until recently.

Islamophobia and discrimination against Muslims have received much scholarly attention. The immigration issue has been treated as a socially relevant problem since the 1990s, but ten years later Moroccans or Egyptians were no longer considered in the same terms as other national migrant groups. Their social inclusion was observed through the lens of their cultural and religious diversity, strangely overlapping with the fear of Islam. That kind of social construction is not casual. In the Italian context, the public visibility of Islam is not due to Muslims' activism but is mainly the product of the socio-political mobilization of which Islam has been made the target (Pace 2007: 94). It reflects Italian society's contradictions: a fragile national identity and collective memory characterized by deep socio-economic imbalances and ideological fractures where the institutional weakness of the state coexists with the strength and vitality of civil society (Pace 1998; Ambrosini and Caneva 2010). The anti-Muslim stigmatization has been finely discussed and studied by numerous authors. Allievi (2010a: 162) reminds that it all started 'when three important events occurred at three different levels. On the political level, the Northern League started the most aggressive and pervasive anti-Muslim campaign ever seen in Italy, and which still continues. At the religious level, Cardinal Biffi, Archbishop of Bologna, gave voice—with a letter addressed to his parishioners but intended for national readership, which has achieved significant popularity—to Catholic anti-Muslim opinion. At the cultural level, politologist Giovanni Sartori, with no specific expertise on the subject, published a pamphlet against multi-ethnic society (Sartori 2002), followed by Oriana Fallaci's books with millions of copies sold.' Sciortino's paper, 'Islamofobia all'italiana' (2002), scrutinizes the gap between empirical evidence and discourse in Sartori's and Fallaci's books, showing how these two public intellectuals have opened the door for the legitimation of the social construction of Muslims as the paradigmatic other. Other researches have pointed at the link between securitization and discrimination policies against Italian Muslims such as Perocco (2008, 2010) who analyses the media impact on the public construction of Islam. Others underlined the state racism and the criminalization of Muslim immigrants (Basso 2010). Few national enquiries give an analysis of Italian public opinion on migrants and Muslims in particular as explained below. The most complete ISTAT survey of 2012 underlines that 59.5% of Italians affirm that immigrants are discriminated against, 91.4% of them maintain that long-term residents should obtain Italian citizenship, but 60% still recognize a reciprocal climate of distrust between Italians and immigrants and 65.2% declare that foreigners living in the country are too numerous. Clear evidence of these contradictions is revealed by the fact that the results of the first national research on discriminative attitudes and experienced discriminations on the basis of gender, sexual orientation, and ethnic belonging, described as novel and sensitive issues, have not yet been published (ISTAT 2011: 20).

## Two Main Players: Media and the Northern League Party

Throughout Europe the myths and rhetoric against Muslim residents have been largely fuelled by right-wing parties. Unlike other populist parties, which have rarely achieved long-term representation in government either at national or local level in Italy, the Lega Nord (Northern League) (2001–11, except for a brief left parenthesis in 2006–8) held several key cabinet positions in Prime Minister Berlusconi's centre-right coalition, including Minister of Justice and Home Affairs Minister (Roberto Maroni, currently Lombardy's regional governor). The Northern League started as a regional protest movement in the late 1980s and later developed into a secessionist party against the government in Rome. Violently xenophobic, its electoral successes can be partly explained by the instrumentalization of fear and hostility towards migrants, in particular Muslim residents. Confined to its original territory (Lombardy and Veneto) it started to spread out into traditionally left-oriented regions such as Emilia-Romagna, campaigning on issues of political security. The League referred constantly to the boundaries between Italians citizens, the legitimate 'owners of the land', and the 'others', who are threatening safety and public order, the recipients of benefits by a local welfare system whose resources are already limited, and last but not least the cultural and religious identity of the country (Ambrosini and Caneva 2010: 26). The League's initiative led to a political climax, the repressive Bossi Fini Law and above all the Security Package, a set of norms introduced in 2008 and 2009 which have introduced 'local policies of exclusion' (Ambrosini and Caneva 2010: 26).

The Italian media have been the other crucial actor in giving visibility to Muslims as the paradigmatic outgroup. Press and TV coverage has largely contributed to coordinate the public and political discourse on Muslim communities' representation. For a fine analysis of press material and TV debates see Triandafyllidou (2006).

# Being Muslim in Italy: The Heterogeneity of Local Policies and Micro Politics of Discrimination

To understand Muslim conditions and strategies it is necessary to size up the discrepancy between, on the one hand, the national discourse and declared policies, and on the other the variety of concrete policies at the local level, a sort of arena of confrontation between different actors and political traditions of the civil society (see Saint-Blancat and Schmidt di Friedberg 2005). In this perspective, the laws on urban safety (law no. 125/2008 and Ministry Decree 5 August 2008), part of the Security Package, which delegated to mayors the opportunity to introduce by-laws and decrees without any form of public debate with other political actors, have changed radically the Italian mapping of concrete policies of discrimination and xenophobia (Ambrosini 2013b; Caritas 2012). It is estimated that between August 2008 and July 2009, 788 by-laws were introduced in 5.5% of all local administrations, in particular in the Lombardy region. Some municipalities, mainly in the wealthiest and most advanced areas of the northern part of the country (Lombardy, Veneto, Friuli, Piedmont but also in a small part of Emilia-Romagna), where migrant workers and Northern League administrators are concentrated, have used these new regulations to implement discriminative sanctions and measures against legal and particularly illegal migrants, with the pretext to take in hand the defence of the local citizens.

Substantive data on these new 'institutionalized forms of intolerance' enforced by local power can be found in Ambrosini et al.'s research (ACCEPT Pluralism 2012a, 2012b); some of these results have also been presented in two journals (Ambrosini 2013a, 2013b). The study includes discourse analysis of political representatives and media, court judgements, and qualitative in-depth interviews with mayors and local social actors in the small and medium size municipalities of Milan and Brescia provinces. Three issues of policies of exclusion are scrutinized: urban security, the selective policy in welfare provisions, and the means to defend Italian identity and culture.

In the process of exclusion all migrants are directly or indirectly targeted but Italian Muslims have received special treatment. The strategies adopted covered new rules and excessive controls on public spaces and housing, permits to open a food shop or business, rules on places of worship, the exclusion of migrants' children from public competition at school, the denial of access to migrant mothers to the bonus for newborn babies, and worse still, the requirement of a minimum income to register in the Registry Office. The logic is clear: first Italians, then the new 'guests', the immigrants. To avoid complications some mayors produced internal guidelines for their administrative staff when dealing with migrants or urban planning, modifying local police regulations or trading rules (Ambrosini 2012a: 17). As a result, Moroccans can no longer sit on the 'bridge' benches of Treviso centre (taken away by the mayor for urban security and decency), and Pakistani youths cannot play cricket anymore in some Lombardy public parks. One of the best ways to preserve Italian traditions and culinary culture has been the 'anti-kebab regulations' introduced in Brescia and Bergamo, in Bussolengo closed to Venice, and in Prato and Lucca in Tuscany. Always citing the pretext of hygiene and public health, some mayors banned the opening of kebab shops in Italian urban centres 'whose activity can be linked to different ethnic groups, in order to preserve the traditions related to foods and the architectural, structural, cultural, historical and decorative traditions' (resolution of the City Council of Lucca no. 12, 22 January 2009). Fear of food contamination is also at the core of this same policy of obstruction against Muslim entrepreneurs in north-east Italy as observed in Padua and Treviso (Saint-Blancat et al. 2008).

Italian civil society reacted firmly to these discriminatory practices. Left-wing parties, social movements, trade unions such as CGIL and CISL, voluntary associations, non-profit associations, the Catholic institutions, Caritas, the Association of Pro-Bono Lawyers, the Association for Juridical Studies on Immigration (ASGI), politicians, and various anonymous citizens, all formed a coalition of protest against 'racist acts' and 'apartheid climax' using the defence of human rights (Ambrosini 2012a: 22). The same social actors were also involved in the mosque conflict analysed more fully in the next section.

Although these regulations were effective only in specific municipalities, they found resonance in the national debate through media and political debates and attracted the attention of the Constitutional Court (judgement no.115/2011 and no. 40/2011 against illegal exclusion of the social welfare provided by the Regional Law of Friuli 2006) (Caritas 2012: 208) and obviously of the National Office Against Racial Discrimination (UNAR). As is frequently the case in the Italian context, the local frame can produce totally contradictory settings. In response to these micro politics of discrimination some regions and municipalities (such as Rome and Florence) have chosen to modify their statutes, introducing autonomously the right to vote for non-EU migrants in district councils and in municipal consultative bodies, against judgements of the State Council.

In recent years the Northern League administrators have promoted grotesque campaigns of control to increase suspicion and hostility towards migrants, and in particular Muslims, among the public by becoming the scrupulous defenders of the presence of the crucifix in schools and other public spaces, or by promoting the display of the nativity scene during the Christmas period. The last initiative, condemned by courts of justice, was the 'White Christmas' initiative to control and identify, house by house, the presence of illegal migrants in small cities. Using Catholicism as the symbol of shared cultural traditions and unity, these new crusaders ('nuovi crociati') (Guolo 2000, 2011) in their battle against mosques often find themselves in opposition with the Church, despite its internal divisions. The mosque issue, in its symbolic dimension, is the best example of all the contradictions and reluctance faced by Italian society in recognizing the country's new ethnic and religious pluralism.

## Mosque Conflict: A Paradigmatic Issue

In Italy the constitution guarantees the right of freedom of religion. 'Everyone is entitled to freely profess religious beliefs in any form, individually or with others, to promote them, and to celebrate rites in public or in private, provided they are not offensive to public morality' (article 19). The construction or the conversion of other spaces for places of worship is mainly regulated by regional laws. Every municipality can plan or concede an urban space to any religious community asking for it.

Estimates of Italian mosques present difficulties quite similar to those encountered when identifying Italian Muslims. Only three mosques are officially recognized, one in Milan, the second in Rome, and the third in Catania (Sicily). Despite the Muslim communities' requests, many places of worship, being mostly simple prayer halls in the most unexpected buildings, are not registered. According to the Home Minister there are 258 Muslim places of worship; the police have identified 735 such places (ISMU 2010). The most accurate and recent data can be found in the comparative research on mosques in Europe (Allievi 2010b) which identifies 764 Muslim places of worship in Italy. In a last survey and mapping of the religion's worship places in the country, which does not take into account the smallest unofficial prayer rooms, the number amounts to 655 (see Map 6.1; Pace 2013).

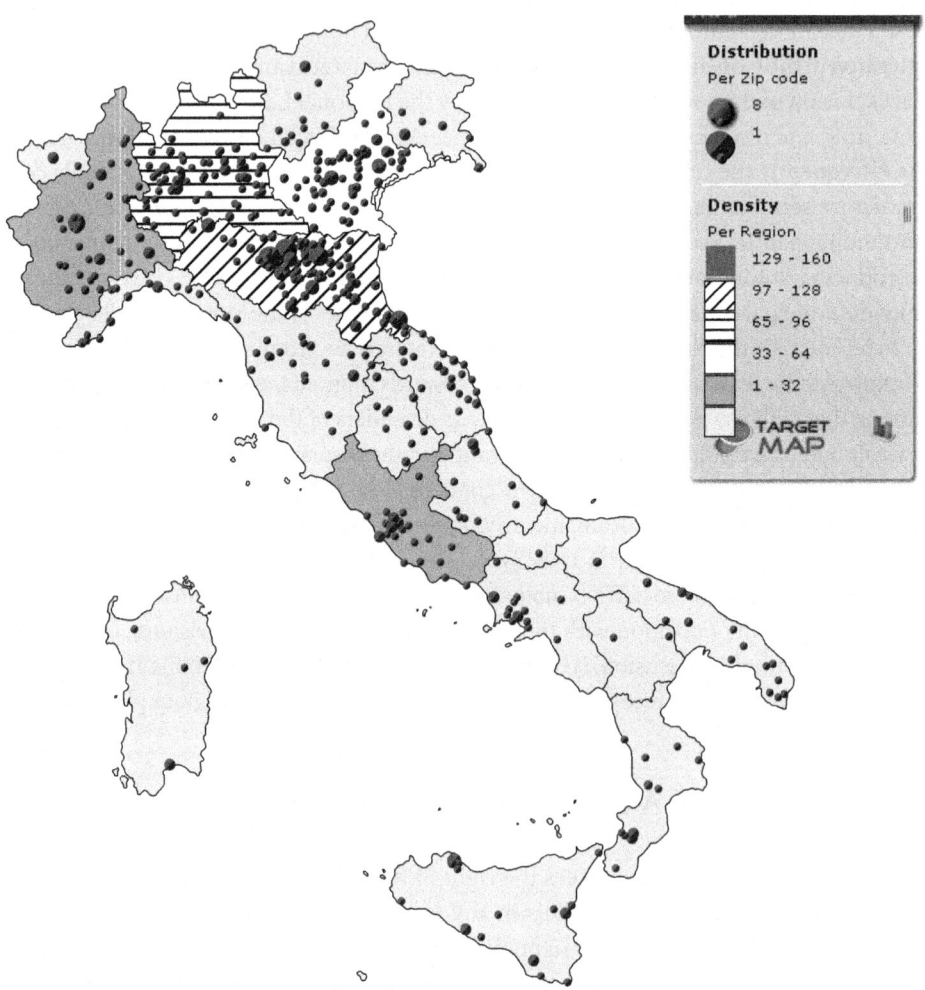

MAP 6.1 Muslim places of worship in Italy by region

Studies on the mosque issue provide not only numbers but a full analysis of the role and function of mosques for Italian Muslims, together with a critical study of the socio-political and cultural reasons behind the mosque conflict and the main players involved, including the media (for the media's role in constructing 'moral panics' see Triandafyllidou 2006). Interrogating what is at stake in this impasse provides valuable information, from both the Muslim and Italian perspectives. Today, just as ten years before, Italian Muslims still encounter a lot of difficulties in opening a new mosque.

Much research focuses on this topic and it is the rare field where longitudinal analysis can be found. Unfortunately in the first paradigmatic case of Lodi, studied by Saint-Blancat and Schmidt di Friedberg (2005) and in the case studies analysed by Allievi (first with Eurobarometer 2009 and NEF 2010), the scenario is roughly the same.

The opening of Sikh temples (Denti et al. 2005) has led to no controversy, in contrast to the opening of mosques in many Italian towns. Why this 'Muslim exception'? As Ottavia Schmidt di Friedberg reminds us (2001: 27), 'for a part of Italian secular public opinion, Islam is a threat to democracy and pluralism (status of women, family law, individual rights), for others it is a threat to the local Catholic identity. It is interesting to note that often both arguments are used together and people do not seem to consider this contradictory or, at least, are not worried by it.'

Mosque conflict initially is always a local affair. It becomes a national controversy when it receives attention from media and political parties. The centre-left municipalities have to face the protest of the Northern League and despite the support of the other religious communities whether Jewish, Protestant, or Catholic, the public debate is on, resulting in petitions, signatures, and finally a call for a local referendum for or against the mosque. In Padua 5,868 signatures were recently gathered in three months (Allievi 2010c; Bombardieri 2011). In some cases, in an action both ritualized and grotesque, members of the League take a pig to the area allocated for the mosque to make the place 'impure'.

In Italy fear of immigration and Islam overlaps, showing that the society is not yet ready for the challenging multiethnic and multireligious setting that could change the social and power balance in urban areas. This concern remains strongly linked to contradictory migration policies, insecurity, and unemployment and this type of anxiety can only grow with the present economic crisis. The mosque provides an excellent pretext and works as a symbolic catalyst for all the undeclared fears held by an Italian society having to deal with socio-economic and cultural changes. In most cases, what is refused is the granting of a piece of communal land to the 'other'. In fact the 'mosque' catalyses the fears of demographic and cultural invasion, and of the physical inscription of Islam—in other words, the fear of a foreign form of sacredness entering Italy's public arena (Saint-Blancat and Schmidt di Friedberg 2005; Branca 2009).

Beyond these controversies the mosque issue paradoxically has been the way forward to a progressive normalization of Islam in the public sphere. It has also been an opportunity for Muslims to gain visibility in the public arena, to negotiate the legitimacy of their presence through conflict and/or negotiation (Saint-Blancat and Perocco 2006; Allievi 2009b). This is attested by the frequent initiatives of some mosque officials, who opt for public clarity by organizing 'open mosque days' which achieve great success among local society, the best way to show to the population at large that a mosque is not a den of terrorists or a centre of occult activities (see on this point the 'hot' case of the Viale Jenner mosque in Milan; Branca 2009), but a versatile structure offering social assistance, religious instruction, and community socialization structured around a place of worship, the same—no more, no less—as in a traditional Catholic parish building (Saint-Blancat and Schmidt di Friedberg 2005).

The issues surrounding the building of mosques reflects the evolution of the social perceptions of the Muslim population by Italian citizens. The first studies were conducted by the research foundation ISMU, and published in their annual 'report on migrants' (see in particular Valtolina 2004, 2005, 2010), which highlighted the usual public security issue. The IPSOS survey (2005) shows that Italians' public attitudes to immigration, similar to those observed in five other European countries, are largely negative: 67% of respondents state that migrants are too numerous. More recent research has been carried out by the Ministry of Home Affairs. The results show that 55.3% of Italians interviewed consider migration from Islamic countries to be the most problematic, because Muslims display more visible social, religious, and cultural differences. In addition, 31.4% of Italians interviewed declared themselves to be against the building of mosques.

ISTAT (2012) has provided the first national survey on 'migrants seen by Italian citizens' with very interesting data on religious cohabitation. Religious tolerance is expressed in positive terms by 59.3% of the population who disagree with the following statement: 'some migrants' religious practices threaten our way of life'. About the opening of a worship place close to home, such as a synagogue, an orthodox church, or a Buddhist temple, 51% declare themselves indifferent to this prospect and 26.9% against it. But in the case of a *mosque* opening, numbers change noticeably: 41.1% of Italians are still opposed to the opening of a mosque next to their home, and only 41.8% are indifferent to it. The main reasons advanced are the following: 28.3% maintain that 'the mosque would create security and public order problems', 26.6% think that 'Muslims are intolerant and would not allow the building of a Catholic church in their own country', and 18.3% declare that 'the mosque would attract more immigrants in the neighbourhood'; 7.8% think that 'their religion and culture are too different from the Italian one' (ISTAT 2012: tables 19, 20, and 21).

In the Italian frame, the state has never addressed the mosque issue at a national level, leaving always the local institutions to deal with the problem on a case-by-case basis. Never taking a clear stand on the mosque conflict is largely due to the ambiguous relationship between church and state, which partly explains why the Italian state (the last one in Europe) has not yet given official recognition to Islam. We deal with this problem in the next section dedicated to Muslims in public space.

# Muslims in the Public Sphere

Italian Muslims' visibility and requests are challenging the state's capacity to cope with the necessary management of the country's growing religious diversity. Public space being the symbolic arena where identity and the process of boundary making are inscribed, the Muslim presence questions the so-called neutrality of the Italian public sphere (Casanova 2000; Ferrari and Pastorelli 2012). Access to public space means also social recognition and acceptance, the possibility to cross institutional and informal thresholds.

## Institutional Relations between State and Religion

In Italy, faiths other than Catholicism are regulated by the 1984 revised Concordat and non-Catholic denominations still encounter many obstacles to obtain institutional recognition and equality of treatment. The only procedure for these minority religions is to sign an official bilateral agreement between the confession's representatives and the Italian State, or 'intesa' (article 8 of the constitution) so clearly analysed by jurists like Silvio Ferrari (2000, 2010b) and Roberta Aluffi (2004) (see also Ferrari and Bottoni Chapter 14 in this book). So far, Italian governments have only signed a few agreements with other religions: Waldensian and Methodist churches (1984), Adventist churches and Assemblies of God (1986), the Jewish representative body (1987), the Jehovah's Witnesses and the Buddhists (2000), the Apostolic Church, the Church of Jesus Christ of Latter-Day Saints, the Orthodox Exarchate for Southern Europe, and the Italian Hindu Union (2007). But most of them (in particular Buddhist and Jehovah's Witnesses) have been waiting for parliamentary approval since the end of the 1990s, the period of their first legal recognition. Most of these agreements are not yet concretely enforced as Paolo Naso (2012) underlines with the mocking title 'Religious Liberty: Slow, Very Slow, without Brilliance'. The series 'Zoom Italia', published by Emi (Editrice Missionaria Italiana) and edited by P. Naso and B. Salvarini, have published two well-informed and critical reports on Italy's religions. The first one, *Il muro di vetro* ('The Glass Wall', 2009) provides statistics, legal documents, bibliography, and critical papers on the complex religious panorama of the country. The second one, *Un cantiere senza progetto* ('A Worksite without Planning or Vision', 2012) criticizes the lack of a clear policy of religious pluralism and trustee supervising, and offers an analysis of the new religious actors in Italian public space. For other statistics and analysis see also the annual Dossier Caritas, and the work of Introvigne and Zoccatelli on 'The Religions of Italians' (2001/2006).

## The Never Ending 'Intesa': Do Muslims Get Special Treatment?

Italian Muslims have tried to sign an agreement since 1992. The first draft was sent by the main Muslim association UCOII (Union of Islamic Organizations and Communities in Italy); three others followed, each one presented by a different association, a fragmented and random way of proceeding which damaged seriously the Italian Muslims' image (Pacini 2000). Muslims have never met success until now in this complex procedure because of a mix of political and institutional variables addressed in this section. Without a joint agreement, Italian Islam is subject to the 1929 Admitted Religions Act.

Without the 'intesa', Muslims are not granted the same rights as the dominant religion, the Catholic Church. These rights essentially concern: chaplaincy in jail and in hospitals, recognition of religious ministers, religious education within public schools (in that case paid by the state), religious holy days, and last but not least the fiscal advantage according to which Italian citizens can devote part of their taxes (the famous 8/1000) to the state or to any recognized confession. To give an idea of the amount of money distributed between the various confessions the parliament has published recent data (2009) quoted by Naso (2012): nearly 40% of tax forms have given to the Catholic Church a total amount of 913 million euros, but only 4.85% have given to the state which apparently does not deserve similar trust. The Waldensian Church, one of the first to get access to 8/1000 received 8.2 million euros. Without an 'intesa' Muslim communities or other minority religions cannot receive any piece of the pie.

In these conditions, the position of Italian Islam is made more difficult on many issues related to religious life: from mosques and cemeteries—even if some separate sectors have been conceded (Schmidt di Friedberg 2002)—to the celebration of *al-'id al-kabir* (holiday marking the end of the month of Ramadan), ritual slaughtering, and halal food at school or in jail (Islamic private schools are also an issue as we shall see later on). Legally speaking, however, Muslims can rent, buy, or build places of worship, receive donations and display their religion in public space. But material benefits and symbolic affirmation are missing.[1]

It would take too long to give a detailed account of the legal and political uphill struggle faced by Muslims from day one. Some authors, such as Pacini (2000), Guolo (2000, 2005), and Silvestri (2012) have done an excellent reconstruction of the political dynamics of this endless battle. It is worth remembering that from the beginning in 2005, Italian Muslim leaders have been appointed and not elected by their communities in an Islamic Council (*Consulta Islamica*), a sort of 'government-sponsored consultative body' (Silvestri 2012: 178; Ferrari 2007). The step is always taken top-down and is firmly in the hands of the Ministry of Interior; first Giuseppe Pisanu (centre-right), then Giuliano Amato (in the left parenthesis of 2006–8), who tried to make the sixteen members of the board agree on a common Charter of Values of Citizenship and of Integration, and the recent Lega leader Maroni who, dismissing the previous *Consulta*, created in 2010 the 'Committee for Italian Islam' (*Comitato per l'Islam italiano*), including among the nineteen members Muslim leaders from the different associations, but excluding the main one (UCOII), and some university experts in Islam and law. Despite the work done, neither Muslims nor Italians seem really convinced by this technical board which should represent Italian Islam but is always looking for the right way to integrate the 'good Muslims' or so-called 'moderates', without consulting those most concerned. We shall discuss this crucial issue for Italian Islam later, from the young Muslims' point of view.

---

[1] For all aspects of legal treatment of Muslim rights in Italian public sphere see Botta et al. (2000) and Aluffi Beck-Peccoz (2004).

More relevant may be the complex mix of interpretations given to this constant practice of exclusion. Sociologists of religion, jurists, and political scientist have tried to elucidate the main reasons behind this failure. Why are Muslims systematically kept at bay? Some studies attribute a leading responsibility to the Northern League strategy which has consistently blocked the legitimation of Italian Islam in the public sphere, taking advantage of the Muslims' internal divisions and playing on a moral panic strategy linked to the Muslim threat to national identity and integrity (for a detailed review on this moral crusade against the 'Islamic Folk Devil' see Testa and Armstrong 2012). But other variables could be considered.

## The Catholic Church: Ambiguities and Contradictions

Other readings privilege a macro level of analysis linked to the central position of the Catholic Church in the Italian frame. The Catholic Church still maintains a powerful monopoly on the national and local religious landscape. This is due to the fact that the majority religion plays 'a central role in granting national cohesion' (Ferrari 2008a). The resonance of the Lautsi Affair[2] among Italian opinion and the symbolic relevance of the Cross in the collective memory of the country show clearly that Catholicism still continues to perform a public role above and beyond ideological divisions and ethnic and cultural tensions, as a master of public ethics and a guardian of shared national values (Pace 1998; Pace and Frisina 2011).

However, the politics of recognition of other religions reveal the ambiguity and the complexity of the Catholic Church's control and interference in the presumed 'natural' public sphere (Pace 2007; Itçaina and Burchianti 2011). According to article 7 of the constitution, Italy has no established national church. Italy is a secular Republic but the Concordat system makes the relationships confused. The position of Islam, like all the other confessions which have not signed an agreement, would be strengthened by the adoption of a statute on religious liberties intended to substitute the 1929 Concordat (Aluffi 2004: 138 note 16). Up to now this legal project has never passed the parliament's approval. The Bill, introducing equality between all religions, would compromise the Catholic Church's dominant position, in particular the religious teaching at schools funded by the state. In a paradoxical convergence, the Northern League and part of the Catholic hierarchy, have firmly opposed the text (Pace and Frisina 2011). The ambiguous relationship between church and state explains the Catholic Church's internal divisions. The Catholic hierarchy is split

---

[2] *Lautsi* v. *Italy* (no. 30814/06). On 3 November 2009, the European Court of Human Rights in response to Mrs Lautsi's application, an Italian national, concluded that 'the display of the crucifix in the State school attended by her two children, is contrary to parents' right to educate their children in line with their convictions and to children's right to freedom of religion, a violation of Article 2 of protocol No. 1 (right to education) taken jointly with Article 9 (freedom of thought, conscience and religion)'. The Catholic Church made only comments but the Italian state, through the Berlusconi government, appealed against the Court's decision and won (18 March 2011) against the first judgement.

between a position of openness towards inter-faith dialogue, its role of mediation between other faiths and Italian society, and its fear of losing its monopoly at the heart of Italian religious space. The church tries today 'to govern the growing ethical, cultural and religious pluralism of the country through the values of Catholicism raised to the rank of civil religion' (Pace 2007: 89). On the one hand the Lega encourages the church to play the part of the state religion and on the other, has to face the firm and constant Catholic opposition to all the discriminations against Muslims promoted by the party. In such a ranked framework and without a legal imprimatur, Italian Muslims are still considered as 'second-class citizens in the religious economy' (Toronto 2008: 68) and do not get access and voice to media and public space.

Other studies maintain that Muslims bear also part of the responsibility for this total deadlock, not being able to find an internal consensus.

## Muslim Lay and Religious Organizations in Public Space: Who Represents Whom?

According to Sara Silvestri (2012: 181) 'the failure of the "intesa" can be put down to several factors: the lack of a hierarchical organization with an institutional leadership in Islam, the modest number of Italian citizens practising Islam and involved in the negotiation process, and the internal competition (between Muslim associations and between them and Muslim states) for the social and political hegemony over Italy's heterogenous Islam'. Every European state has tried, with moderate success, to constrain Muslim populations to build artificial 'alliances' to form a unique recognized representative body, without really taking into account their concrete and legitimated representation. Italy is no exception.

Italian Muslims count several national organizations (mainly religious ones) and many local civic and religious associations, more organized on an ethnic/national basis (see Schmidt di Friedberg 2002). These structures' purposes were—and still are—to give answers to social, cultural, and religious needs, to provide a place to share traditions and identity and to sustain their members' integration. With few financial resources, often mono-ethnic, they built up progressively first interactions with the host society through trade unions, Catholic organizations, or NGOs. The first national data can be found in Saint-Blancat and Schmidt di Friedberg (2002) where Moroccan, Tunisian, Egyptian, Senegalese, Pakistani, Bangladeshi, and Somalian associations are reported as localized geographically mainly in urban areas of the northern and central parts of Italy. Fava and Vicentini's survey (2001), focused on all immigrant associations, reported that 893 foreign organizations have been registered in the country; today studies are more accurate but, as usual, lack national representativity. Empirical local studies show the typology of Italian associations where migrants participate actively and analyse the process of self-organization and thus social empowerment of specific national groups. A good example is the research on Muslim communities in Sicily (Melfa 2006). In the Veneto region, for instance, Mantovan (2006, 2007) compares two 'Muslim' groups,

Senegalese and Bangladeshis, highlighting how the first one is characterized by a high level of associationalism, both secular and religious, a strong work ethic, and a displayed willingness to respect the rules of Italian society as already demonstrated by Schmidt di Friedberg in previous studies. In contrast, Bangladeshis are more community oriented and still strongly linked to the internal divisions of their country of origin. In her book, besides the analysis of variables influencing the emergence of migrants' associations and mobilization, the author provides an update bibliography of the studies on migrant self-organization and associations, included Muslim ones, and European projects involved on this topic (2007: 114–23).

At the end of the 1990s, Muslim immigrants (Moroccans and Senegalese) were already very active in Italian labour trade unions which welcomed and supported them from their arrival; women were also present in many Italian intercultural associations and in school mediation between families and Italian schools. However, Muslim associations already displayed a peculiar typology: 72% of the migrant religious associations in Italy were Muslim. Following family reunification and the growing of the second generation, the necessity of cultural and religious transmission (through mosques and Qur'anic schools) has progressively become the focus of the various Muslim national communities. The structure of the organizations also reflects the social space and types of interaction allocated to Muslims by the Italian society's representations.

The main organizations are the following. The UCOII (Union of Islamic Organizations and Communities in Italy) set up in 1990, with its two affiliated entities ADMI (Association of Muslim Women in Italy) and more recently the GMI (Young Muslim of Italy) born in 2001; 205 mosques present on the national territory are linked to the UCOII network (Rhazzali and Equizi 2013: 65 and see Map 6.2). The COREIS (Islamic Religious Community established in 1997) and the AMI (Association of Italian Muslims established in 1982) are two small but active associations founded by and mainly composed of Italian converts. The Islamic Cultural Centre of Italy, based at Rome's symbolic mosque, is the unique registered legal Islamic body. On 21 March 2012, a new actor subtly and quietly appeared on stage: the Islamic Confederation of Italy (Confederazione Islamica Italia) (CII) which claims to unify 209 mosques and to bring together ten regional federations. The organization is officially sustained by the Rome Great Mosque but also by the Moroccan government. The new president is Moroccan; the members present themselves as followers of the Malekite tradition and as moderate Muslims, in agreement with the Charter of Values spirit, promoted in 2007 by the Italian Home Affairs Minister.[3] This new confederation represents an integrated network between Moroccan local mosque leaders looking for increased cooperation and

---

[3] The Charter was conceived for Italian citizens and migrants as a document to remind them of the principles of the Italian constitution and the Italian choice to work for a pacific treatment of international conflicts (including the issue of Israel–Palestine); the other intent which may appear rather 'paternalistic' (Silvestri 2012: 184) was a first brainstorming on the new multiculturalism. The UCOII judged it discriminatory, because intended mainly for Muslims and did not subscribe to it.

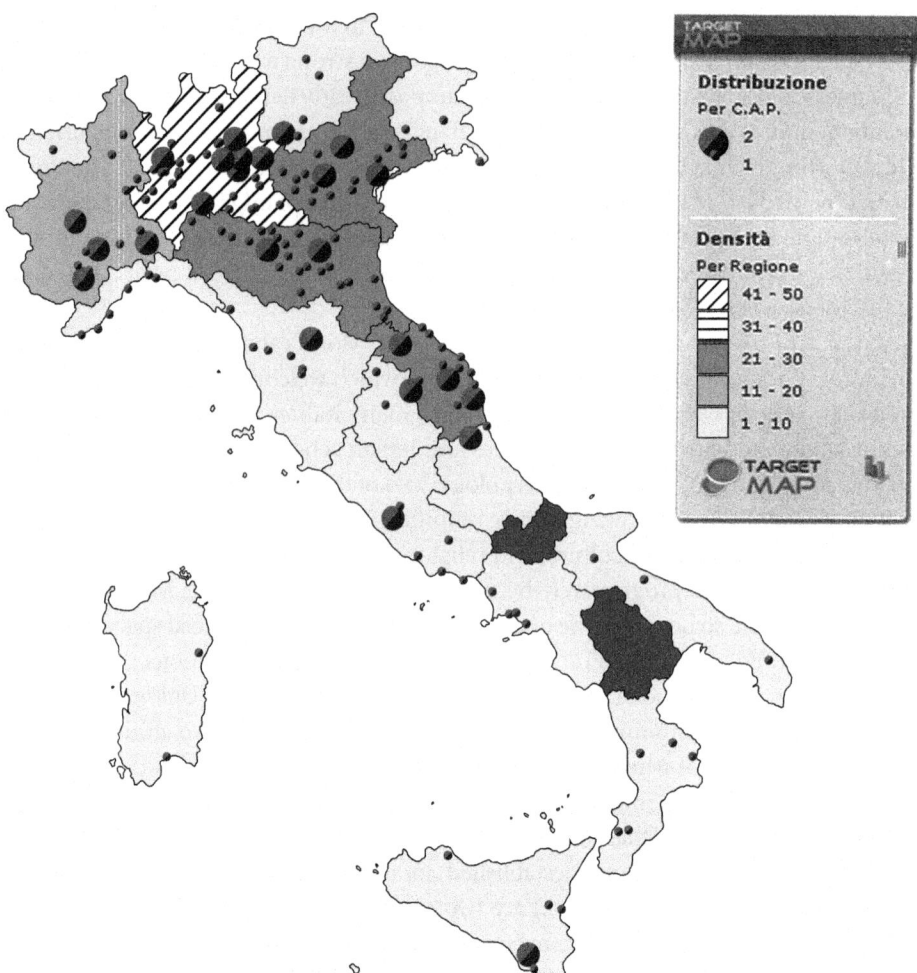

MAP 6.2 Places of worship in Italy affiliated to the Union of Islamic Organizations and Communities in Italy

public visibility (see Map 6.3). At the time of writing, it is too early to say what part this new leadership will play in the plural complexity of Italian Islam.

As observed in other European contexts, the history of Italian Muslim organizations underlines the determinant role of Italian converts in the first phase of mediation between Italian institutions and Muslim populations (Allievi 1998). An accurate description of the main associations and intricate relationships can be found in Guolo (1999a, 2000). Guolo (2005) and Pacini (2008) provide an analysis of the political issues, especially the relationships between Muslim organizations and the national institutions. Comparing the various associations Guolo (2005) and Allievi (2010a) examine the different religious and normative affiliations and membership characteristics. Italian Muslim representatives and imams' sociological profile, style of

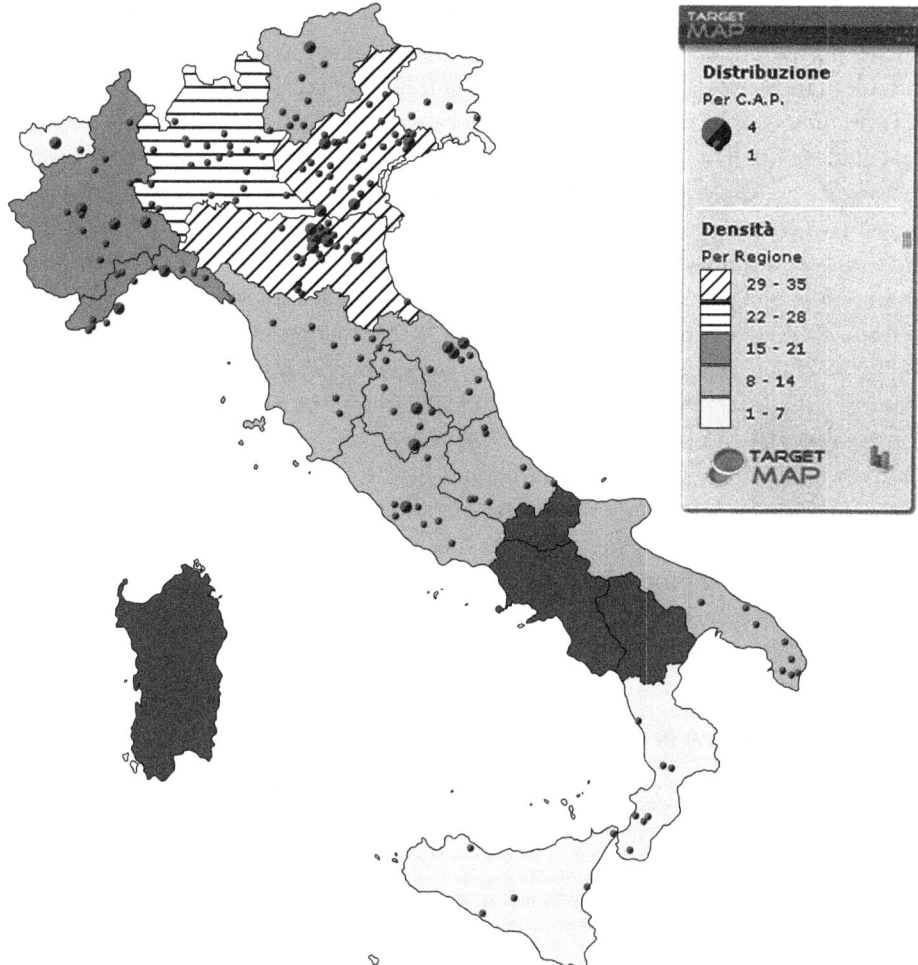

MAP 6.3 Places of worship in Italy affiliated to the Islamic Confederation of Italy

leadership, and strategies of interactions with the Italian local society are instead investigated by Saint-Blancat and Perocco (2006) and Saint-Blancat (2008). UCOII is considered as the main umbrella organization but does not cover the complexity and plurality of Italian Islam, especially at the local level. Despite its national visibility and management of Italian Muslims' tensions and rivalries, the organization has never been able to obtain complete legitimated control of Italian reality. No monographic study has been dedicated so far to this relevant association; the alleged connection or influence of the Muslim Brotherhood on UCOII's practices and organizational typology have not been analysed.

There has been very limited study of the Sufi galaxy, of which very little is known until now. However, among the various mystical brotherhoods, the *Muridiyya* confraternity founded in Senegal by Ahmadu Bamba (1850–1927) and dominant among Senegalese migrants in Italy, has been studied by Schmidt di Friedberg (1994), and by Bruno Riccio (2004), mostly in Lombardy. We shall deal in more detail with the *dahira's*[4] structure and role in the next section dedicated to the pluralism of Italian Islam.

Two unpublished Ph.D. theses provide a rare in-depth analysis of leaders and spiritual guides of Italian Muslims (Perocco 2003 in Venetia and Tuscany; Conti 2011a in Tuscany, Lazio, Umbria, and Emilia Romagna; see also Conti 2011b, 2012). Both studies give a whole picture of Muslim leaders' theological knowledge, flexibility, autonomy, and variety in dealing with the contradictory expectations, on the one hand of their own communities and, on the other, of the Italian institutional bodies and actors of the local civil society. What is particularly interesting is that, taking place in different regions and in two different periods, the data underline two main facts: aside from generational change in the leadership and a better understanding and good practices of interaction with the Italian context, above all in the Moroccan diaspora, few variations can be observed in the global scenario. As underlined before, the lack of recognition has driven Italian Islam not only to clandestine status but also reduced it to a low and silent profile, apart from a few exceptions and moments such as the public protest in 2009 during the Gaza war. The young generation's activism, as we shall see later on, is inscribed in an entirely different vision.

# ITALIAN MUSLIMS AND RELIGION: A PLURAL ISLAM

In some ways Islam in Italy remains a fragmented and unknown territory. One way to get an in-depth understanding of its sociological reality has been to conduct empirical researches among Muslims in a bottom-up approach, letting the actors themselves define their personal link with their faith. In that case, the objective is not to explore the collective and public identity of Italian Muslims but their own relationship to and self-understanding of the place of religion in their everyday life. Studying Muslim belief and religiosity through ethnic/national dimensions, age, status, and gender as in any other religion, could contribute to go beyond the usual representation of a monolithic Islam.

However, despite the richness of anthropological and sociological studies on ethnic communities, including some Muslim groups, the religious dimension is not the central aspect. Most studies address issues such as the migrants' dynamic transnational networks as a resource, the transformations of the relationships between parental structure,

---

[4] In diaspora the *dahira* is both a religious urban association that groups *Mouride* disciples (*taalibes*) on the basis of Marabout's (spiritual guide) mystical allegiance and a religious circle or place where they ritually meet to pray together instead of going to the mosque.

gender, and norms of conduct, the difficult emergence of foreigners' political participation at the local level (see in particular the Senegalese selection of their leaders; Pizzolati 2008), or the interactions between migrants' families and school system.

## Diversity of Origins, Diversity of Practices, and Gender Difference

Few works address Muslim religiosity. One study (Saint-Blancat 1999c) examines the fluctuating relationship between belief, religious practices and rituals, ethics, and normative conduct among Muslims living in the Veneto region. The study also explores the question of exogamy and the main Muslim requests to the Italian state. The sample includes 400 respondents (314 men, 86 women; 241 Moroccans, 25 Tunisians, 19 Algerians, 96 Senegalese; 157 interviewees were single, 233 married, 11 divorced, 3 remarried, and 5 polygamous). Asiatic Muslims had not yet arrived in that period. The questionnaires were prepared through extensive in-depth interviews and distributed in prayer rooms, *dahira* meetings, workplaces, cultural associations, and other existing contacts. The results (Saint-Blancat 1999a, 1999c) show the manifold and complex modalities through which Muslims relate to their faith and provide the first analysis of women's religiosity. Four different profiles emerge: the so-called 'secularized' (23%), mainly married men from Maghreb who privilege the ethical dimension of Islam, are open to exogamy and prefer religious teaching at school to mosque education; those (49%) more 'inclined to religious practice and norms' like prayers, attending mosque, and respect of haram prohibitions, mostly Moroccan men who do not accept exogamy and demand first mosques and halal shops; the youngest ones (7%), sometimes in situations of deviance who have 'put in brackets' any form of practice, and inverted prohibited conducts putting at the top stealing and dealing with drugs; lastly the 'cultural Muslims' (10%), mainly Senegalese men and Moroccan women, attached to norms, ethics, and transmission of faith. For the majority, Islam remains a relevant part of their identity, inspires their conduct and personal coherence, and is a patrimony to preserve and to transmit; that is why mosques are considered as essential in an Italian context, which 84.5% of the sample do not consider at all as an obstacle to their practice and religiosity. Senegalese men and Moroccan women highlight spirituality, the centrality of 'the faith from the heart', and sincerity behind behaviour; but women also underline the necessity to respect normative conduct which they feel responsible for. On that point 67.5% of the respondents answered that it is not a problem to transmit Islam to their children even in a different context, but 85% underline that the family should take care of it, and 37% would prefer Islam teaching in Italian schools more than in a Qur'anic school (23%).

Piedmont's unpublished study (2000), with a very similar questionnaire, confirms these first data; in particular, 82% of the sample of the 300 Muslims interviewed recognize that Islam affects directly their life. Results about the observance of the Five Pillars and the Ramadan fast are slightly higher: 46% attend the mosque close to home, only

12% go to a mosque because of the imam, but 84% declare giving zakat primarily to the mosque, which is quite a large number but can be explained by the more organized structure of Turin's mosques than anywhere else. All researches[5] highlight the pluralism of Italian Islam and the fact that often Muslims do not join the formal Muslim associations and feel free to choose the mosque to attend, giving also (as we will see in the next point) legitimacy to the state school for the teaching of Islam. An interesting analysis of the place and role of women inside the Senegalese *dahira* is provided by Blanchard's study in Pisa (Tuscany), with an original ethnography piece on the annual liturgy in the most popular Italian *murid* centre in Brescia (2008).

In contrast with the mosque conflict studies, no follow-up research has been funded to address the evolution of practices, both on a private level and in collective and organized settings in an Italian religious context which has also evolved in more than ten years. We have no studies on the meanings given by Muslim actors to their subjective belief, the real content of their Islamic knowledge, or how they negotiate their religious identity in everyday life, at school and at work. No in-depth investigation enlightens the way Muslims redefine their normative conduct as 'good Muslims' after twenty years of Italian experience, or how they combine *ijtihad* and spirituality. These are all issues that need to be addressed to understand the changing religious landscape of Italian Islam. Studies about young Muslims, introduced in the next section, have begun to give some answers. Another promising field of enquiry to investigate religious identity is the prison context.

## Religion in Prison

Mohammed Khalid Rhazzali's research on 'Islam in Prison' (2010) is the first Italian empirical study on this issue. Of 36,565 detainees in Italian prisons in 2008, 21,562 are foreigners, mainly men and migrants, and three-quarters of them come from Maghreb. Not all convicts declare their religion, but among those who do, Muslims constitute more than 40% of the total, 9,589 in 2009 (Rhazzali 2010: 46). The sample of the research is quite revealing: from more than 200 convicts approached, fifty agreed to be interviewed: eighteen Moroccans, twelve Tunisians, six Algerians, four Albanese and the rest from Pakistan, Egypt, and other countries. They are men aged from 22 to 35, living in Italy for five to twenty years, but very few are members of the so-called second generation. Most of them have been imprisoned for drug dealing (for the link between migration and criminality see Barbagli 1998, 2002). The study focuses on lived Islam in a segregated institution. Part of the research investigates how Islam can be organized in a prison where nothing is legally organized, including the delicate boundary between halal and haram food in the common fridge among detainees (Rhazzali 2010: 97–8). The analysis of the convicts' narrations reveals the complex puzzle of multiple

---

[5] See also the Center Peirone survey of the Turin diocese (2003–4), the results of which are published in Negri and Scararanari (2005) and Allam and Gritti's enquiry among 1,000 Muslims (2001).

identities (ethnic and above all linguistic) and Islam appears as a broad tradition, which gives confidence and peace and rebuilds self-esteem, and which is easy to understand and to practise. Religion coincides with a process of self-reconstruction and provides meaning to the individual project of life. Prison, as much as migrant condition, becomes the frame where lived Islam is renegotiated through individual experience (Rhazzali 2010: 105). Compared to the British and French studies the Italian case is more a male and clandestine microcosm in contrast with the Muslim population at large. Again this regional study has not been extended to the national level due to lack of financial support from governmental organizations or the National Research Council.

## Religion at School

Religion at school instead has received more scholarly attention and has been sponsored by several public local and academic funding organizations. The presence of foreign children at school is well documented by the Ministry of Education statistics (MIUR 2007, 2011). Foreign students constituted only 0.7% of all students in 1996/97 and reached 7.9% in the academic year 2010/11; among them 42.2% were second-generation students, concentrated in nursery and primary schools. Three groups—Romanians, Albanians, and Moroccans—represent about 45% of all foreign students (Ambrosini 2011). Education is a political issue in Italy as anywhere in Europe. Contrasting with the ambiguities and contradictions observed in migration policies and access to citizenship, the intercultural approach has been a clear and firm choice of education since the arrival of foreign children in classrooms. The right to education is guaranteed to foreign students, regardless of their citizenship, their legal status or that of their parents. The Italian educational system is based strongly on state schools. The few private schools are mostly Catholic, especially nursery schools (never enough to satisfy parental demand), and these are generally recognized by the state.

In their analysis of tolerance in discourses and practices observed in Lombardy schools, Ambrosini and Caneva (2010: 36–41) underline that *interculturalism*, integrated in regular school programmes and teaching, has become the normal approach to prevent racism and intolerance. In their case studies, the authors highlight the discrepancy between the formal but vague concepts at the institutional level and the lack of teachers' training. As usually observed and experienced in Italy most is left to the 'good practices and will from below'. The risk is that every teacher builds his or her own strategy. Still the teachers firmly resist the Northern League proposal (2008) to introduce separate classes for foreign students and find many creative ways to integrate religious festivities and rituals, culture, food, and traditions into everyday school life. Tensions emerge when religious norms (girls in sports activities, swimming classes, mixed recreations outside, organized travel in Italy or abroad) or religious practices, such as fasting during Ramadan, could generate prejudice towards the children or make them feel excluded from their peers' rights. Mediation is often the solution. Inter-faith dialogue, the constant focus of Italian attention, begins at school.

By contrast, Italian society does not seem ready for other faith schools, as suggested by the case of Via Quaranta school, an Egyptian and Arab school in Milan where Muslim parents asked for the use of different language than Italian and a diverse curriculum. 'After a lengthy debate and various conflicting episodes, the school was obliged to close' in October 2005 (Ambrosini and Caneva 2010: 3). Muslim demand in that case appears as a threat to secularism in the Italian educational system; supporting faith schools, above all Muslims ones, is perceived as risking self-segregation and implicit resistance to social and cultural inclusion (Branca and Santerini 2008). Let us remember that Muslim parents have always strongly identified the Italian state school, not only as the ideal place for their children's social mobility but also as the best location for an official transmission of Islam, during the weekly hour of religion (70% of Muslim families in Piedmont are in favour) as shown by Guolo (2009) and Negri and Scaranari Introvigne (2008). See also on this point Alessandro Ferrari's analysis (2008) on the necessity to devise good practices between the education about religion and the education into religion where teachers' training and selection should be revised, as has been already underlined for Catholicism.

## Inter-Faith Dialogue and Mixed Marriages

We only have to search the item 'inter-religious dialogue' on Google or on websites such as www.il dialogo.org or www.confronti.net to measure the amount of initiatives and occasions for inter-faith gatherings in the Italian context. The offer goes from theological conferences, days of spirituality sharing, and church institutional conferences to multicultural and peace events. The main actor who promotes dialogue with Muslims is the Catholic Church, from top to bottom, from the famous symbolic Assisi meeting with all the religious leaders in 1986, repeated in 2011, to the micro exchanges in the smallest parishes of Italian provinces. Catholic structures such as Caritas, Sant'Egidio, Pisa, and many other centres show an unexpected vitality and are joined by Protestant churches and sometimes by the Union of Italian Jewish Communities (UCEI), in particular among members of youth organizations. Islam–Christian dialogue arises from the Second Vatican Council's famous *Nostra aetate* declaration and recently from the impetus given by the late Archbishop of Milan, Carlo Maria Martini, in his episcopal letter of 1990 'Us and Islam'. Since this period bishops, the powerful Episcopal Italian Conference (CEI), priests, and anonymous Catholics have encouraged education to inter-dialogue, reciprocal collaboration for peace, and above all promoted knowledge and divulgation of Muslim spirituality and faith. Towns such as Milan, Turin, Palermo, and Venice have been particularly engaged in this process. A list and historical synthesis of all these initiatives can be found in Courtens (2009, 2012), a review and critical update in Ayuso Guixot (2008) as well as a look to the future in Zatti (2008). Inter-faith dialogue with Islam is organized in annual venues such as the International Christian–Islam conference (organized by the

Focolari) and the ecumenical Day of Islamic and Christian Dialogue, established in 2001, just after 9/11 thanks to Protestant, Catholic, and lay associations' initiative. Participants to this annual appointment have tripled since the recurrent meeting fixed on 27 October, in memory of Assisi. 'Multi faiths under the sky' organized by Italian lay associations meets great public interest as much as 'Equal but different', established in Reggio Emilia to give visibility to cultural and religious pluralism. 'Confronti' has recently organized a conference with the four main Italian Muslim associations, including secular Muslims: indeed a diplomatic and constructive success.

Since the beginning, inter-faith dialogue has been linked to the issue of mixed marriages, whose number has been regularly growing over the last ten years. This is a trend which 30.4% of Italians consider positively, but with less tolerance when their daughters are involved! (ISTAT 2012). Mixed marriages involve mainly Italian men marrying women from Central/Eastern Europe (2,550 with Romanians, only 377 with Moroccan women) but marriages of Italian women with Moroccans numbered 240 in 2010. Catholic hierarchy has officially expressed concern about this type of union without, however, slowing down the process. Good in-depth studies have been recently carried out on the typologies of conflicts and negotiations among mixed couples, in particular Catholic women married to Muslims, regarding everyday life, religious rituals, cultural and food habits, linguistic strategies, and cultural and religious transmission to the children (Cerchiaro 2013; Odasso 2013). For the legal aspects (Italian law and Islamic law) see Zilio-Grandi (2006) and Ghirighelli and Negri (2008) whose work is more focused on religious education and Catholic pastoral practice among mixed couples.

There are no recent or past studies on specific groups such as Tabligh or Salafi in the Italian context. These forms of Islamic thought are not representative of the Italian Islam mainstream. Although present in the country, the Sufi galaxy has not been analysed so far and neither have secular Muslims.

In contrast, there is some literature by jurists and sociologists on Muslim legal aspects and the potential conflict with Italian law (see Zilio-Grandi 2006; A. Ferrari 2008a, 2012 on *burqa* and niqab). But analyses are only linked to the few case studies just mentioned. Debates on these specific issues have not been the focus of deep interest such as in France or in other European contexts. This is partly due to the lack of Muslim demands and requests and to the absence of a strong orthodox informal movement in the Italian public space. Let us remember that Italian Muslims are still fighting for institutional and public recognition, for recognition of mosques, and for equal rights of citizenship.

Looking more closely at how individual Muslims shape, interpret, and express their relationship with religion in everyday life allows us to go beyond the imposed stereotypes which describe them as passive 'followers of Islam' (Marranci 2012). From the same logic it does not make sense to study young Muslims born and socialized in Italy through the usual paradigm developed to study migrants, neglecting their agency, creativity, and consciousness.

# Young Italian Muslims: The New Frontier and a Work in Progress

Being a key issue in all European societies, the second generation of children of immigrants have drawn the attention of many Italian scholars. Research has been focused mainly on self-identifications, belongings, and tactics or strategies used by youths in everyday social interactions with their context of residence (Colombo et al. 2009; Colombo and Semi 2007; Colombo 2010; Barbagli and Schmoll 2011). In the case of Muslim youths this field of research has given more attention to youths' agency, self-organization, visibility in public space, uses of difference, and partly to reinterpretation of gender roles. Issues such as social mobility or religious attitudes have been more neglected.

## Who Are They? What Do They Want?

Again it is difficult to find statistical data on how many young Muslims there are. The first estimate was of approximately 300,000 (Frisina 2005). On the other hand, all studies show the cross-national belongings of the youths interviewed. Most of them were born in Italy or arrived at an early age and thus socialized in the Italian system of education. The best way to attempt an accurate analysis is to study the first association of young Muslims of Italy (GMI) set up in 2001 soon after 9/11, remembering that the members were more involved in religious and civic activities than the average Muslim youths of the same age. Frisina's long-term empirical studies on the organization (2007a, 2007b, 2009, 2010a, 2010b) provide a rich portrait of this dynamic young generation. The GMI association counts about 350 members aged from 16 to 28, mainly of Moroccan origin; some are Egyptian, Syrian, and Palestinian. Girls are more numerous than boys but leaders have always been men who are generally students at Italian universities. The national group is organized in local sections, the most active being in the northern and central part of the country, especially in Milan and in Bologna. The generational gap is quite evident. The initial breakaway from the UCOII adult organization was motivated by youths' strong will for autonomy to get space to build an 'Italian Islam', breaking down the usual dichotomy between the Italian context and Muslim otherness. The desire is also to challenge the negative collective image of Italian Muslims and to demonstrate that the young generation intends to claim a more inclusive destiny. Another distinctive factor compared to the first migrant generation is the youths' strategy to enter Italian public space by gaining direct access to mass media, a key issue in the national framework. In contrast with the communication style of imams or traditional Muslim representatives, young Muslims know how to deal with journalists, TV, and media in general, in a self-assured and even cynical manner. They certainly gain visibility for Islam and present a different profile on television programmes, participating in many interviews and obtaining political attention and interest. Their own website is always well informed and stimulates participation. They act as a pressure group against institutional indifference, having even been received by the President of the Italian Republic.

Obviously this public visibility is mainly in the hands of new Muslim protagonists whose performances are echoed on the national level. For example, Khalid Chaouki, ex leader of GMI, was recently elected as member of the parliament at the last elections (February 2013) with the left-wing Democratic Party. He became famous with his book *Salaam Italia* (2005), a biographical work addressed to Italian and Muslims citizens with a provocative demand for both groups: 'Muslim Brothers or Italian Brothers?' Other celebrities unexpectedly include two young women. Randa Ghazy, born in Lombardy from Egyptian parents, published at the age of 21 her third book *Perhaps I Won't Kill Anyone Today* (2007: 147–8), the story of young Jasmine, an ironic protester, who resists Fallaci's rhetoric and male chauvinism, reminding the reader that any Muslim woman has 'a note on her forehead saying: "work in process, emancipation process running"!' Sumaya Abdel Qader, born in Umbria, published *I Wear the Veil and Adore the Queen* (2008) which tells the story of Sulinda, a young girl of Palestinian/Jordanian origin who fights to find her place as a Muslim in Italian society. Both women work on the lively *Yalla Italia!*, a magazine for the second generation which deals with a great variety of subjects, including the taboo issues often considered as haram, such as gender freedom, or homosexuality. This active minority's courage benefits all anonymous young Muslims with fewer cultural resources and who are dispersed in the many isolated small towns of the Italian province.

## A Demanding Generation: Inter-Faith Dialogue and Activism, Contestation of Religious Authorities, Gender Issues, Generational Conflicts, Italian Identity, and More...

Everything begins at school, facing and fighting all the stereotypes on the veil or Ramadan or radicalism. Young Muslims improve their discursive and linguistic competences, and gain a better understanding of and confidence in the Italian local society. Difference becomes a resource and mixed friendship networks help to engage in horizontal bridging. The migration experience and transnational ethnic networks are transformed into positive assets (Saint-Blancat and Zaltron 2013). All researches underline the importance of young Muslims' participation at the local level to gain credibility and legitimacy in the public sphere. Focus groups organized by Frisina (2009) in several different geographical settings show how young Muslims deal with pragmatism and capacity for conflict management, demonstrating competency in mediation and negotiation around critical issues, exemplifying self-distance and reflexivity, 'global citizens' who tend to put Islam in perspective.

Pioneers in inter-faith dialogue, the GMI meet regularly with the ACLI (Italian Christian Workers' Associations), but also with Waldensians, Jews (UGEI), and

Buddhists, exchanging views about controversial issues and learning to know each other's opinions, and organizing common protest initiatives for peace (Bertani 2004; Frisina 2007b).

Strongly linked to their families and kinship networks which youths evaluate as their main source of social capital and emotional support, young Muslims, especially girls (more engaged in grammar schools and university studies while males are technically or vocationally oriented), underline gender inequalities and the limits of their parents' normative prescriptions and traditions (Saint-Blancat and Zaltron 2013). Tensions, frustrations, and clashes emerge in topics such as spare time, first work experiences, and obviously partner choice, all social interactions out of family control. These discussions often lead to different conceptions and interpretations of religious meanings. The veil rarely appears as a central issue. Girls feel free to wear it or not. Those who prefer to avoid the visibility of difference among Italian friends and in public contexts stand up for the veiled ones when they become the target of peers' derision (Mazzega-Ciamp 2012).

Religiosity, lack of theological knowledge, and religious authorities among young Muslims are issues which should be more widely addressed by researchers. Young Muslims express their need to take their place both emotionally and culturally inside a 'line of faith'. Even those who practise scarcely declare that Islam gives them confidence, or a sense of peace and security. Shared experiences give a meaning to their past and provide them with a set of 'existential instructions' for building their future and reterritorializing Islam. But they do not find enough theological support around them, and looking on Islamic sites on the internet does not always satisfy them. Many youths underline the weakness of their religious leaders' training and their normative approach. Without religious skills, it becomes critical to undertake the necessary reinterpretations. Examples of everyday *ijtihad* have been analysed by Maddanu (2009). What is striking when one reads the biographical narrations collected by Frisina and others is the fact that Italian young Muslims have the same expectations, needs, self-distancing, individual spirituality, and research of coherence as their European Muslim and Christian peers.

They differ instead in their relentless battle for recognition and inclusion in the Italian public arena.

## 'L'Italia sono anch' io' (Italy, That's Me Too): The Battle for Italian Citizenship

Very active in the public sphere, young Muslims have strongly participated in the referendum campaign of 2011 to obtain the 50,000 necessary signatures to propose a new law of citizenship. The GMI association, member of the G2—*Seconde Generazioni*, a national network which gathers adolescent children of immigrants in Italy, and has a 'growing role in representing the voice of "new Italians" in the public sphere' (Colombo et al. 2009: 43)—have contributed to introduce in the public debate new issues such as civic commitment and political participation instead of the recurrent topics on security, deviancy, and control linked to the migrants' presence (Frisina 2010b). Italian civil society actors, such as trade unions, non-profit and voluntary associations, juridical and religious organizations dealing with immigration issues (Caritas, Fondazione Migrantes, Avvocati), and left-wing parties have supported the proposal to reduce the period of residence required and to make naturalization easier for the second generation. It has been a real success: 110,000 signatures have been collected to modify the 1992 law but only a change in political coalitions in power could break the deadlock; this topic was largely left aside in the last electoral campaign. The GMI have also expressed some perplexity over the *Consulta* composition and methods of work.

## Emergence of a 'Muslim' Elite? The Labour Market Will Tell

Going to universities and technical schools, finding a job, these are the next goals of young Muslims. Few studies have been dedicated to young Muslims' entrance into the labour market or their social mobility. The second generation has just begun to look for employment in a time of economic crisis which has hit Italian youths the hardest. Economic insertion will be the real test for equal opportunities. Zanfrini (2006) has provided statistical data on young immigrants in general and Girardi's Ph.D. thesis is one of the first researches on young Moroccans and Romanians but the results are specific to the Veneto region (2012). However, youths show ambition, a strong work ethic, and entrepreneurial spirit, the main characteristics requested by the national labour market. Muslim graduate students' participation in a masters study on 'Islam of Europe' (established in 2012 at the University of Padua) suggests that they find room, besides work hours, to become more informed about their rights, knowledge, and potentialities as Muslims, conscious that Italian Islam will need quickly an elite likely to be included in Italian governance, economic partnership, and involved in religious or juridical consultations. Very few have already got access to research at the university or moved into Italian political party organization (Allam 2006).

## RADICALIZATION

Used to dealing with strong domestic security issues linked to the historical Mafia presence on the territory and more recently to the ten years' period of Red Brigades terrorism in the 1970s, Italy has always kept an attentive and expert eye on potential radicalism in Italian mosques and other informal or clandestine networks. The Italian Intelligence Agency's interest in identifying the mosques affiliated to Tabligh demonstrates it. Yet, even after 9/11 Islam terrorism has not been at the top of the political agenda and the scarce *jihadist* or Salafi groups' activity seems regularly monitored and under control. From time to time some news about arrests of radical cells in Milan, or some imam deported (Porta Palazzo Turin mosque's imam Bouchta in 2005 to Morocco) or expelled (his successor in 2008) make the headlines. The case of Abu Omar, the Egyptian imam of the Milan Islamic Cultural Institute was at the centre of public and media debate in 2003, more because the CIA was involved with Italian intelligence, than the result of a fear of terrorism. Italian radical networks appear more as recruiting and logistical support for international *jihad* (falsification of public documents and fund raising) than a national threat. With the exception of some mosques in Milan such as the one in Via Quaranta or the Islamic Cultural Institute of Viale Jenner and a few centres in Turin, Bologna, and Cremona which have been identified as dens of radical networks, accused of having links with international *jihadists*, Italian Islam has never been directly involved with Salafi movements' extremism. The lax use of deportations by the government has stirred a critical debate in public opinion (Corbucci 2003; Stancanelli 2006).

Italy has ratified the main international conventions against terrorism and collaborates actively with European countries against terrorism but so far no counterterrorism programmes have been organized at a national level. Despite the high level of Islamophobia and the usual supposed link between Islam and terrorism among public opinion, the prejudices have not given way to a concrete policy. At least securitization has not substituted the missing integration policies. Seldom involved with radicalism, the majority of Italian Muslims have other priorities: institutional recognition, youths' social mobility, and the training of their religious leadership.

If the new generations of young Muslims should lose their battle against political and cultural exclusion and see the process of their full integration slowed down, this type of failure could increase the risk of inside radicalism.

# Conclusion

As Grace Davie reminds us, 'a full understanding of the place of new religious movements in any given society... [is] important as much for the religious movements themselves as for what they reveal about the societies of which they are part' (2008: 16). In Italy, the relevance of institutional aspects—the ambiguous relationships between state and religion, the weakness of government inclusion policies—and negative social perceptions of Islam have influenced and indirectly determined Muslims' attitudes and strategies, blurring the internal frontiers and plurality of Islam and obliging Italian Muslims to deal with and react to the external and selective imagery arbitrarily constructed by Italian society (Saint-Blancat 2008b; Allievi 2011).

In the Italian context much has been said and published on *Islam*, less on *Muslims* (Marranci 2012), without bothering too much to produce empirical data concerning their social mobility, religious practices, or social and political exclusion. We had to wait for 2012 to get the first national statistical survey on how Italians view Muslim presence and we cannot count on a diachronic perception. After thirty years of migration part of Italian society still needs more time to recognize that the country has now to live with cultural and religious pluralism, learning to consider Italian Muslims more as a resource than as a social problem.

No national study reports the multifaceted nature of Italian Islam, excepted Allievi's informed diary travel (2003a) among the many different Muslim urban and regional settings scattered across the peninsula; some groups such as Turkish or Pakistani have not been studied at all.

In the future the themes of research should focus more on Italian Muslims' agency, in particular among young Muslims who consider themselves as Italian citizens without receiving equal recognition as such. More ethnographic observation and in-depth interviews should give voice to the actors through the narration of their experience, strategies, internal conflicts, and expectations regarding their socio-economic inclusion in the country as much as their individual redefinition of their relationship with Islam. We still know very little about the new meanings Italian Muslims give to crucial notions such as *ijtihad* or halal/haram, how they value the change underway in gender roles and family structures, what significance they give to secularization involving their community, what they expect in terms of religious authority, and how they intend to support their emerging intelligentsia and artistic leadership.

Moreover, the topics of research on Italian Muslims, in particular statistical surveys, should be commissioned by central government and institutions in interaction with multidisciplinary scholars' experience in the field. How the Italian Muslim diaspora uses transnational links in Europe and networks abroad could be a positive asset for the country in building economic and cultural interactions in the Mediterranean area and in Asia.

At the end what deserves more attention is this young Muslim's comment:

> By knowing me better, my classmates change their views about me and Moroccans in general; they got the idea that Moroccans were drug dealers or thieves but it is because they never had Moroccan friends before! (Moroccan male, technical school, age 17, Treviso, quoted in Saint-Blancat and Zaltron 2013)

Change is a by-product of knowledge after all.

# Bibliography

### Immigration/Ethnicities/Integration

Amari, M. (2002 [1854]). *Storia dei Musulmani di Sicilia*. Firenze: Le Monnier.
Allievi, S. (2003a). *Islam italiano. Viaggio nella seconda religione del paese*. Turin: Einaudi.
Allievi, S. (2003b). 'Sociology of a Newcomer: Muslim Migration to Italy. Religious Visibility, Cultural and Political Reactions', *Immigrants & Minorities* 22(2–3): 141–54.

Allievi, S. (2005). 'How the Immigrant has Become Muslim: Public Debates on Islam in Europe', *Revue européenne des migrations internationales* 21(2): 135–63.

Allievi, S. and Dassetto, F. (1993). *Il ritorno dell'Islam: I musulmani in Italia*. Rome: Edizioni Lavoro.

Ambrosini, M. and Abbatecola, E. (2002). 'Reti di relazione e percorsi di inserimento lavorativo degli stranieri: l'imprenditorialità egiziana a Milano', in A. Colombo and G. Sciortino (eds.), *Stranieri in Italia. Assimilati ed esclusi*. Bologna: Il Mulino, 195–223.

Ambrosini, M. and Abbatecola, E. (2004). *Immigrazione e metropoli. Un confronto europeo*. Milan: Franco Angeli.

Bertani, M. (2012). 'Il capitale sociale nello studio delle migrazioni: riflessioni introduttive', in M. Bertani and P. Di Nicola (eds.), *Migration Studies e capitale sociale*. Sociologia e Politiche sociali, vol. 15/1. Milan: Franco Angeli, 9–29.

Carchedi, F., Ruggerini, M. G., and Scaramella, C. (eds.) (2008). *Quale parità per i migranti? Norme, prassi e modelli di intervento contro le discriminazioni*. Milan: Franco Angeli.

Caritas/Migrantes. (2000–12). *Immigrazione. Dossier statistico*. Rome: Idos.

Caritas/Migrantes. (2010). *Immigrazione. Dossier statistico*. Rome: Idos.

Chiesi, A. M., De Luca, D., and Mutti, A. (2011). *Il profilo nazionale degli imprenditori immigrati*. Rome: Consiglio Nazionale dell'Economia e del Lavoro.

Colombo, A. and Sciortino, G. (2004a). 'Alcuni problemi di lungo periodo delle politiche migratorie italiane', *Le Istituzioni del Federalismo* 5: 763–88.

Colombo, A. and Sciortino, G. (2004b). 'Italian Immigration: The Origins, Nature and Evolution of Italy's Migratory Systems', *Journal of Modern Italian Studies* 9(1): 49–70.

Colombo, A. and Sciortino, G. (eds.) (2008). *Stranieri in Italia. Trent'anni dopo*. Bologna: Il Mulino.

Cvajner, M. and Sciortino, G. (2010). 'A Tale of Networks and Policies: Prolegomena to an Analysis of Irregular Migration Careers and their Developmental Paths', *Population, Space and Place* 16(3): 213–25.

Decimo, F. (2005). *Quando emigrano le donne: Percorsi e reti femminili della mobilità transnazionale*. Bologna: Il Mulino.

Decimo, F. (2007). 'Globalizing Immigrant Networks: Somali Female Workers in Italy', in A. Kusow and S. R. Bjork (eds.), *From Mogadishu to Dixon*. Trenton, NJ: Red Sea Press, 97–117.

Decimo, F. (2008). 'Immigrazione, riproduzione e identità: prospettive di ricerca sulla fecondità degli stranieri in Italia', *POLIS* 2: 307–29.

Einaudi, L. (2007). *Le politiche dell'immigrazione dall'unità a oggi*. Bari: Laterza.

Errichiello, G. (2008). 'Le donne arabo-musulmane immigrate: Background socio-culturale e ricerca nel Casertano', *Studi Emigrazione/Migration Studies* 45(172): 945–66.

Eve, M. (2008). 'Some Sociological Bases of Transnational Practices in Italy', *Revue européenne des migrations internationales* 24(2): 67–90.

Fondazione Leone Moressa. (2012). *Rapporto annuale sull'economia dell'immigrazione-Immigrati una risorsa in tempo di crisi*. Bologna: Il Mulino.

Finotelli, C. and Sciortino, G. (2008). *New Trends in Italian Immigration Policies: 'To change everything in order to keep everything the same'*. ARI (Real Instituto Elcano) 161, 1–5.

FRA (European Union Agency for Fundamental Rights) (2009). *Indagine dell'Unione Europea sulle minoranze e la discriminazione (EU-MIDIS): relazione «dati in breve»: i musulmani*. Vienna: FRA.

Frisina, A. (2005). 'Famiglie musulmane a scuola', in A. Marazzi (ed.), *Voci di famiglie immigrate*. Milan: Franco Angeli, 119–28.

Guarneri, A. (2008). 'Muslim Diversity in Italy: An Unacknowledged Reality', *The International Spectator* 43(3): 117–35.

Jeldtof, N. (2009). 'On Defining Muslims', in J. S. Nielsen, S. Akgonel, and B. Marechal (eds.), *Yearbook of Muslims in Europe*. Leiden: Brill, 9–14.

Kaag, M. (2008). 'Mouride Transnational Livelihoods at the Margins of a European Society: The Case of Residence Prealpino, Brescia, Italy', *Journal of Ethnic and Migration Studies* 34(2): 271–85.

Ministero dell' Interno. (2009). Direzione Centrale per I diritti civili, la cittadinanza e le minorance- Cittadinanza Italiana Statistiche anni 2004–2009. Rome.

Ministero del Lavoro e delle Politiche Sociali (2012). *Secondo Rapporto annuale sul mercato del lavoro degli immigrati—2012*. Rome: Ministero del Lavoro e delle Politiche Sociali.

Pace, E. (2004). *L'Islam in Europa: modelli di integrazione*. Rome: Carocci.

Paci, F. (2004). *L'Islam sotto casa: l'integrazione silenziosa*. Venice: Marsilio.

Paterno, A., Terzera, L., and Strozza, S. (eds.) (2006). *Sospesi tra due rive. Migrazioni e insediamenti di albanesi e marocchini*. Milan: Franco Angeli.

Pojmann, W. (2010). 'Muslim Women's Organizing in France and Italy: Political Culture, Activism, and Performativity in the Public Sphere', *Feminist Formations* 22(3): 229–51.

Regalia, C. and Giuliani, C. (2012). *Esperienze di donne nella migrazione araba e pakistana*. Milan: Franco Angeli.

Riccio, B. (2001). 'From "Ethnic Group" to "Transnational Community"? Senegalese Migrants' Ambivalent Experiences and Multiple Trajectories', *Journal of Ethnic and Migration Studies* 27(4): 583–99.

Riccio, B. (2007). *'Toubab' e 'vu cumprà'. Transnazionalità e rappresentazioni nelle migrazioni senegalesi in Italia*. Padua: Cleup.

Riccio, B. and Russo, M. (2011). 'Everyday Practised Citizenship and the Challenges of Represeentation: Second-Generation Associations', *Journal of Modern Italian Studies* 16(3): 360–72.

Saint-Blancat, C. (1989). 'Nation et religion chez les immigrés iraniens en Italie', *Archives de Sciences Sociales des Religions* 68(1): 27–37.

Saint-Blancat, C. (1990). 'L'immigrazione iraniana in Italia: vera o falsa parentesi?' in G. Cocchi (ed.), *Stranieri in Italia*. Bologna: Misure, Materiali di Ricerca dell'Istituto Cattaneo, 109–25.

Saint-Blancat, C., Rhazzali, K., and Bevilacqua, P. (2008). 'Il cibo come contaminazione: tra diffidenza e attrazione: Interazioni nei kebab padovani e trevigiani', in F. Neresini and V. Rettore (eds.), *Cibo, cultura, identità*. Rome, Carocci, 67–77.

Salih, R. (2000). 'Shifting Boundaries of Self and Other: Moroccan Migrant Women in Italy', *European Journal of Women's Studies* 7(3): 321–35.

Salih, R. (2001a). 'Confronting Modernities: Muslim Women in Italy', *ISIM Newsletter* 7(1): 1–32.

Salih, R. (2001b). 'Moroccan Migrant Women: Transnationalism, Nation-States and Gender', *Journal of Ethnic and Migration Studies* 27(4): 655–71.

Salih, R. (2003). 'Shifting Meanings of Islam and Multiple Representations of Modernity: The Case of Migrant Women of Muslim Origin in Italy', in J. Andall (ed.), *Gender and Ethnicity in Contemporaney Europe*. Oxford: Berg, 119–39.

Salih, R. (2009). 'Muslim Women, Fragmented Secularism and the Construction of Interconnected "Publics" in Italy', *Social Anthropology* 17(4): 409–23.

Scarcia Amoretti, B. (1981). *Il mondo Islamico tra interazione e acculturazione*. Rome: Erder.

Schmidt di Friedberg, O. (1994). *Islam, solidarietà e lavoro. I muridi senegalesi in Italia*. Turin: Fondazione Agnelli.

Schmidt di Friedberg, O. and Saint-Blancat, C. (1998). 'L'immigration au féminin: les femmes marocaines en Italie du Nord. Une recherche en Vénétie', *Studi Emigrazione/Migration Studies* 35(131): 483–98.

Schmoll, C. (2005). 'Pratiques spatiales transnationales et stratégies de mobilité des commerçantes tunisiennes', *Revue européenne des migrations internationales* 21(1): 131–54.

Sciortino, G. (2012). 'Immigration in Italy: Subverting the Logic of Welfare Reform?' in G. Brochmann and E. Jurado (eds.), *Europe's Immigration Challenge*. London and New York: I. B: Tauris, 77–94.

Sciortino, G. and Colombo, A. (eds.) (2003). *Stranieri in Italia. Un'immigrazione normale*. Bologna: Il Mulino.

Sciortino, G. and Colombo, A. (2004). 'The Flow and the Flood: Immigrants in the Italian Newspaper Discourse', *Journal of Modern Italian Studies* 9(1): 94–113.

Semi, G. (2006). 'Il ritorno dell'economia di bazar. Attività commerciali marocchine a Porta Palazzo, Torino', in F. Decimo and G. Sciortino (eds.), *Stranieri in Italia. Reti migranti*. Bologna: Il Mulino, 89–113.

Silvestri, S. (2011). 'Faith Intersections and Muslim Women in the European Microcosm: Notes towards the Study of Non-organized Islam', *Ethnic and Racial Studies* 34(7): 1230–47.

Vercellin, G. (1996). *Istituzioni del mondo musulmano*. Turin: Einaudi.

Westoff, C. F. and Frejka, T. (2007). 'Fertility and Religiousness among European Muslims', *Population and Development Review* 33(4): 785–809.

Zincone G. (ed.) (2001). *Secondo rapporto sull'integrazione degli immigrati in Italia*. Bologna: Il Mulino.

Zincone, G. (2006). *Familismo legale. Come (non) diventare italiani*. Bari: Laterza.

Zincone, G. (2006). 'The Making of Policies: Immigration and Immigrants in Italy', *Journal of Ethnic and Migration Studies* 32(3): 347–75.

## Islamophobia and Discrimination

Allievi, S. (2009a). *Conflicts over Mosques in Europe: Policy Issues and Trends*. London: Alliance Publishing Trust/Network of European Foundations.

Allievi, S. (ed.) (2009b). *I musulmani e la società italiana. Percezioni reciproche, conflitti culturali, trasformazioni sociali*. Milan: Franco Angeli.

Allievi, S. (2010a). 'Multiculturalism in Italy: The Missing Model', in A. Silj (ed.), *European Multiculturalism Revisited*. London: Zed Books, 147–80.

Allievi, S. (2010b). *Mosques in Europe: Why a Solution Has Become a Problem*. London: Alliance Publishing Trust/Network of European Foundations.

Allievi, S. (2010c). *La guerra delle moschee. L'Europa e la sfida del pluralismo religioso*. Venice: Marsilio.

Ambrosini, M. (2013a). 'Immigration in Italy: Between Economic Acceptance and Political Rejection', *Journal of International Migration and Integration* 14(1): 175–94.

Ambrosini, M. (2013b). '"We are Against a Multi-Ethnic Society": Policies of Exclusion at the Urban Level in Italy', *Ethnic and Racial Studies* 36(1): 136–55.

Ambrosini, M. and Caneva, E. (2010). *Tolerance and Cultural Diversity Discourses in Italy*. ACCEPT PLURALISM Research Project. Florence: European University Institute, Robert Schuman Centre for Advanced Studies.

Ambrosini, M. and Caneva, E. (2012a). *Local Policies of Exclusion: The Italian Case*. ACCEPT PLURALISM Research Project. Florence: European University Institute, Robert Schuman Centre for Advanced Studies.

Ambrosini, M. and Caneva, E. (2012b). *Overview Report on Tolerance and Cultural Diversity Concepts and Practices in Italy*. ACCEPT PLURALISM Research Project. Florence: European University Institute, Robert Schuman Centre for Advanced Studies.

Basso, P. (ed.) (2010). *Razzismo di stato. Stati Uniti, Europa, Italia*. Milan: Franco Angeli.

Bombardieri, M. (2011). *Moschee d'Italia: il diritto al luogo di culto: il dibattito sociale e politico*. Bologna: Emi.

Branca, P. (2009). 'Mal di moschea', *Mondi Migranti* 1: 213–24.

Bruno, M. (2008). *L'Islam immaginato. Rappresentazioni e stereotipi nei media italiani*. Milan: Guerini.

Caritas Migrantes. (2012). *Immigrazione. Dossier Statistico 2012, XXII Rapporto*. Rome: Idos.

Cere, R. (2002). '"Islamophobia" and the Media in Italy', *Feminist Media Studies* 2(1): 133–6.

Denti, D., Ferrari, M., and Perocco, F. (eds.) (2005). *I Sikh Storia e immigrazione*. Milan: Franco Angeli.

Fallaci, O. (2001). *La rabbia e l'orgoglio*. Milan: Rizzoli.

Fiorita, N. (2011). 'Uguaglianza e libertà religiosa negli "anni zero"', *Diritto, immigrazione e cittadinanza* 1: 30–49.

Guolo, R. (2000). 'I nuovi crociati: la Lega e l'Islam', *Il Mulino* 5: 890–901.

Guolo, R. (2003). *Xenofobi e xenofili. Gli italiani e l'Islam*. Roma-Bari: Laterza.

ISMU. (ed.) (2010). *Sedicesimo rapporto sulle migrazioni 2010*. Milan: Franco Angeli.

ISTAT (National Institute of Statistics). (2011). *Discriminazioni in base al genere, all'orientamento sessuale e all'appartenenza etnica*. Rome: Istituto Nazionale di Statistica.

ISTAT (National Institute of Statistics). (2012). *I migranti visti dai cittadini*. Rome: Istituto Nazionale di Statistica.

Marzano, A. (2011). 'Reading the Israeli-Palestinian Conflict through an Islamophobic Prism: The Italian Press and the Gaza War', *Journal of Arab & Muslim Media Research* 4(1): 63–78.

Pace, E. (1998). *La nation italienne en crise*. Paris: Bayard Editions.

Pace, E. (2007). 'A Peculiar Pluralism', *Journal of Modern Italian Studies* 12(1): 86–100.

Pace, E. (ed.) (2013). *Le religioni nell'Italia che cambia*. Rome: Carocci editore.

Paci, F. (2006). *Islam e violenza. Parlano i musulmani italiani*. Roma-Bari: Laterza.

Padovan, D. and Alietti, A. (2012). 'The Racialization of Public Discourse', *European Societies* 14(2): 186–202.

Perocco, F. (2008). 'L'enjeu "Islam" en Italie', in A. Capelle-Pogăcean, P. Michel, and E. Pace (eds.), *Religion(s) et Identité(s) en Europe. L'é preuve du pluriel*. Paris: Sciences Po, 141–57.

Perocco, F. (2010). 'Dall'Islamofobia al razzismo anti-musulmano', in P. Basso (ed.), *Razzismo di stato. Stati Uniti, Europa, Italia*. Milan: Franco Angeli, 467–91.

Perocco, F. (2012). *Trasformazioni globali e nuove disuguaglianze. Il caso italiano*. Milan: Franco Angeli.

Saint-Blancat, C. and Schmidt di Friedberg, O. (2005). 'Why are Mosques a Problem? Local Politics and Fear of Islam in Northern Italy', *Journal of Ethnic and Migrations Studies* 31(6): 1083–104.

Sartori, G. (2002). *Pluralismo, multiculturalismo e estranei. Saggio sulla società multietnica*. Milan: Rizzoli nuova edizione aggiornata.

Scalvini, M. (2011). 'Italian Islamophobia: The Church, the Media and the Xenophobic Right', in S. Hutchings, C. Flood, G. Miazhevich, and H. Nickels (eds.), *Islam in its International Context: Comparative Perspectives*. Newcastle-upon-Tyne: Cambridge Scholars Publishing, 151–67.

Schmidt di Friedberg, O. (2001). 'Sentimenti anti-Islamici in Italia e in Europa', *Europa/Europe* 10(5): 26–36.
Sciortino, G. (2002). 'Islamofobia all'italiana', *Polis. Ricerche e studi su società e politica in Italia* 16(1): 103–23.
Triandafyllidou, A. (2006). 'Religious Diversity and Multiculturalism in Southern Europe: The Italian Mosque Debate', in T. Modood, A. Triandafyllidou, and R. Zapata-Barrero (eds.), *Multiculturalissm, Muslims and Citizenship*. London: Routledge, 117–42.
UNAR (Ufficio Nazionale Antidiscriminazioni Razziali) (2010). *Studio per la definizione e l'organizzazione di un sistema di indicatori per la misurazione dei fenomeni di discriminazione razziale sul territorio nazionale e la costituzione di un centro di ricerca permanente.* Rome: UNAR.
UNAR (Ufficio Nazionale Antidiscriminazioni Razziali). (2011). *Relazione al Parlamento sull'effettiva applicazione del principio di parità di trattamento e sull'efficacia dei meccanismi di tutela.* Rome: UNAR.
Valtolina, G. (2004). 'Atteggiamenti e orientamenti degli Italiani nei confronti del fenomeno immigratorio', in ISMU, *Nono rapporto sulle Migrazioni 2003: dieci anni di immigrazione in Italia*. Milan: Franco Angeli.
Valtolina, G. (2005). 'Atteggiamenti e orientamenti della società italiana', in ISMU, *Decimo rapporto sulle Migrazioni 2004*. Milan: Franco Angeli.
Valtolina, G. (2010). 'I cittadini europei e l'immigrazione: gli italiani sono i più "preoccupati"', *Libertà civili* 6: 92–102.

**Muslims in the Public Sphere**

Allam, K. F. (2006). *La solitudine dell'Occidente*. Milan: Rizzoli.
Allievi, S. (1998). *I nuovi musulmani. I convertiti all'Islam*. Rome: Edizioni Lavoro.
Aluffi Beck-Peccoz, R. (2004). 'The Legal Treatment of the Muslim Minority in Italy', in R. Aluffi Beck-Peccoz and G. Zincone (eds.), *The Legal Treatment of Islamic Minorities in Europe*. Leuven: Peeters, 133–58.
Belluati, M. (2007). *L'Islam locale. Domanda di rappresentanza e problemi di rappresentazione*. Milan: Franco Angeli.
Botta, R. (2000). '"Diritto alla moschea" tra "intesa Islamica" e legislazione regionale sull'edilizia di culto', in S. Ferrari (ed.). *Musulmani in Italia: la condizione giuridica delle comunità Islamiche*. Bologna: Il Mulino, 109–30.
Carchedi, F. and Mottura, G. (2010). *Produrre cittadinanza. Ragioni e percorsi dell'associarsi tra immigrati*. Milan: Franco Angeli.
Casanova, J. (2000). *Oltre la secolarizzazione: Le religioni alla riconquista della sfera pubblica*. Bologna: Il Mulino.
Conti, B. (2011a). 'L' émergence de l'Islam dans l'espace public italien: les leaders musulmans entre integration et intégrisme'. Ph.D. Thèse de doctorat en sociologie, EHESS Paris, Università di Bologna.
Conti, B. (2011b). 'Les musulmans en Italie, entre crise identitaire et réponses Islamistes', *Revue Européenne des Migrations Internationales* 27(2): 183–201.
Conti, B. (2012). 'L' émergence de l'Islam dans l'espace public italien', *Archives de sciences sociales des religions* 158: 119–36.
Coppi, A. and Spreafico, A. (2008). 'The Long Path from Recognition to Representation of Muslims in Italy', *The International Spectator* 43(3): 101–15.

Fantelli, P. (2011). *Islam en Italie. Relations entre Etat et culte musulman à la lumière de l'expérience française*. Sarrebruck: Editions Universitaires Européennes.
Ferrari, A. (ed.) (2008a). *Islam in Europa/Islam in Italia. Tra diritto e società*. Bologna: Il Mulino.
Ferrari, S. (ed.) (2000). *Musulmani in Italia: la condizione giuridica delle comunità Islamiche*. Bologna: Il Mulino.
Ferrari, S. (2007). 'La Consulta Islamica', in Fondazione ISMU (eds.), *Dodicesimo rapporto sulle migrazioni 2006*. Milan: Franco Angeli, 249–64.
Ferrari, S. (2009). 'Le moschee in Italia tra ordine pubblico e libertà religiosa', in Fondazione ISMU (eds.), *Quattordicesimo rapporto sulle migrazioni 2008*. Milan: Franco Angeli, 219–36.
Ferrari, S. (2010a). 'La formazione degli imam', in Fondazione ISMU (eds.), *Quindicesimo rapporto sulle migrazioni 2009*. Milan: Franco Angeli, 237–50.
Ferrari, S. (2010b). 'The Creation of Muslim Representative Institutions in the "Secular" European States', *Review of Faith & International Affairs* 8(2): 21–7.
Ferrari, S. and Bradney, A. (eds.) (2000). *Islam and European Legal Systems*. Aldershot: Ashgate/Dartmouth.
Ferrari, S. and Pastorelli, S. (eds.) (2012). *Religion in Public Spaces: A European Perspective*. Farnham: Ashgate
Guolo, R. (1999a). 'Attori sociali e processi di rappresentanza nell'Islam italiano', in C. Saint-Blancat (ed.), *L'Islam in Italia. Una presenza plurale*. Rome: Edizioni Lavoro, 67–90.
Guolo, R. (1999b). 'Le tensioni latenti nell'Islam italiano', in C. Saint-Blancat (ed.), *L'Islam in Italia. Una presenza plurale*. Rome: Edizioni Lavoro, 159–73.
Guolo, R. (2000). 'La rappresentanza dell'Islam italiano e la questione delle intese', in S. Ferrari (ed.), *Musulmani in Italia: la condizione giuridica delle comunità Islamiche*. Bologna: Il Mulino, 67–82.
Guolo, R. (2005). 'Il campo religioso musulmano in Italia', *Rassegna Italiana di Sociologia* 4: 631–58.
Guolo, R. (2009). 'La sharia in Italia. Il diritto parallelo nelle comunità Islamiche', *Diritto, immigrazione e cittadinanza* XI 01/2009: 15–28.
Introvigne, M. and Zoccatelli, P. L. (eds.) (2001/2006). *Enciclopedia delle religioni in Italia*. Turin: Elledici.
Itçaina, X. and Burchianti, F. (2011). 'Between Hospitality and Competition: The Catholic Church and Immigration in Spain', in J. Haynes and A. Henning (eds.), *Religious Actors in the Public Sphere: Means, Objectives, and Effects*. London and New York: Routledge, 57–76.
Mantovan, C. (2006). 'Le diverse anime dell'Islam. Alcuni esempi in Veneto', *Studi Emigrazione* 43(162): 445–64.
Mantovan, C. (2007). *Immigrazione e cittadinanza: auto-organizzazione e partecipazione dei migranti in Italia*. Milan: Franco Angeli.
Melfa, D. (2006). 'Le comunità musulmane di Sicilia tra reti interne alla umma al-islāmiyya e interazione con la società ospite', in F. Decimo and G. Sciortino (eds.), *Reti migranti*, IV volume della serie 'Stranieri in Italia'. Bologna: Il Mulino, 151–80.
Musselli, L. (2000). 'La rilevanza civile delle festività Islamiche', in S. Ferrari (ed.), *Musulmani in Italia: la condizione giuridica delle comunità Islamiche*. Bologna: Il Mulino, 187–200.
Naso, P. (2012). 'Libertà religiosa. Piano, pianissimo, senza brio', in P. Naso and B. Salvarini (eds.), *Un cantiere senza progetto—L'Italia delle religioni Rapporto 2012*. Bologna: EMI.
Naso, P. and Salvarini, B. (eds.) (2009). *Il muro di vetro*. Bologna: EMI.
Naso, P. and Salvarini, B. (eds.) (2012). *Un cantiere senza progetto—L'Italia delle religioni Rapporto 2012*. Bologna: EMI.

Pace, E. (ed.) (2013). *Le religioni nell'Italia che cambia*. Rome: Carocci Editore.
Pace, E. and Frisina, A. (2011). 'Italian Secularism Revisited? Muslim Claims in the Public Sphere and the Long Struggle towards Religious Equality', in T. Kestin (ed.), *The Sociology of Islam: Secularism, Economy and Politics*. New York: Ithaca University Press, 291–315.
Pacini, A. (2000). 'I musulmani in Italia. Dinamiche organizzative e processi di interazione con la società e le istituzioni italiane', in S. Ferrari (ed.), *Musulmani in Italia: la condizione giuridica delle comunità Islamiche*. Bologna: Il Mulino, 21–52.
Pacini, A. (2008). 'I musulmani in Italia: una presenza plurale', in A. Pacini (ed.), *Chiese e Islam in Italia*. Milan: Paoline, 15–41.
Perocco, F. (2003). 'L'Islam nella società locale. Un'indagine sugli "stili di riconoscimento della differenza culturale"' (Toscana e Veneto)'. Ph.D. thesis, Department of Sociology, University of Padua.
Pizzolati, M. (2008). 'Selezione e rappresentazioni della leadership in una comunità immigrata. Il caso dei senegalesi a Ravenna', in A. Colombo and G. Sciortino (eds.), *Stranieri in Italia*. Bologna: Il Mulino, 235–53.
Rhazzali, K. and Equizi, M. (2013). 'I musulmani e i loro luoghi di culto', in E. Pace (ed.), *Le religioni nell'Italia che cambia*. Rome: Carocci Editore, 47–72.
Riccio, B. (2004). 'Transnational Mouridism and the Afro-Muslim Critique of Italy', *Journal of Ethnic and Migration Studies* 30(5): 929–44.
Roccella, A. (2000). 'Macellazione e alimentazione', in S. Ferrari (ed.), *Musulmani in Italia: la condizione giuridica delle comunità Islamiche*. Bologna: Il Mulino, 201–22.
Saint-Blancat, C. (2008a). 'Imam e responsabili musulmani in relazione con la società locale', in A. Pacini (ed.), *Chiese e Islam in Italia*. Milan: Paoline, 57–82.
Saint-Blancat, C. (2008b). 'L'Islam diasporique entre frontières externes et internes', in A. Capelle-Pogăcean, P. Michel, and E. Pace (eds.), *Religion(s) et Identité(s) en Europe. L'épreuve du pluriel*. Paris: Sciences Po, 41–57.
Saint-Blancat, C. and Perocco, F. (2006). 'New Modes of Social Interaction in Italy: Muslim Leaders and Local Society in Tuscany and Venetia', in J. Cesari and S. McLoughlin (eds.), *European Muslims and the Secular State*. Burlington, VT: Asghate, 99–112.
Saint-Blancat, C. and Schmidt di Friedberg, O. (2002). 'Mobilisations laïques et religieuses des musulmans en Italie', *Cahiers d'études sur la méditerranée orientale et le monde turco-iranien* 33: 91–106.
Schmidt di Friedberg, O. (2002). 'Being Muslim in the Italian Public Sphere: Islamic Organisations in Turin and Trieste', in W. A. R. Shadid and P. S. van Koningsveld (eds.), *Intercultural Relations and Religious Authorities: Muslims in the European Union*. Leuven: Peeters, 87–106.
Silvestri, S. (2012). 'Institutionalising British and Italian Islam: Attitudes and Policies', in Y. Hakan and Ç. E. Aykaç (eds.), *Perceptions of Islam in Europe: Culture Identity and the Muslim 'Other'*. London: I. B. Tauris, 159–94.
Spreafico, A. and Coppi, A. (2006). *La rappresentanza dei musulmani in Italia*. Rome: XL.
Testa, A. and Armstrong, G. (2012). '"We are against Islam!": The Lega Nord and the Islamic Folk Devil', *Sage open*. Available at <http://sgo.sagepub.com/content/2/4/2158244012467023>.
Toronto, J. A. (2008). 'Islam *Italiano*: Prospects for Integration of Muslims in Italy's Religious Landscape', *Journal of Muslim Minority Affairs* 28(1): 61–82.
Vicentini, A. and Fava T. (eds.) (2001). *Le associazioni di cittadini stranieri in Italia*. Venice: Fondazione Corazzin.

## Studies on Religion

Allam, M. and Gritti, R. (eds.) (2001). *Islam, Italia: chi sono e cosa pensano I musulmani che vivono tra noi*. Milan: Guerini.
Allievi, S. (2011). 'Muslim Voices, European Ears: Exploring the Gap between the Production of Islamic Knowledge and its Perception', in M. van Bruinessen and S. Allievi (eds.), *Producing Islamic Knowledge*. London and New York: Routledge, 28–46.
Ambrosini, M. and Caneva, E. (2011). *The Embodiment of Tolerance in Discourses and Practices Addressing Cultural Diversity in Italian Schools*. ACCEPT PLURALISM Research Project. Florence: European University Institute, Robert Schuman Centre for Advanced Studies.
Ayuso Guixot, M. A. (2008). 'Il dialogo Islamo-cristiano: bilancio di un'esperienza e prospettive', in A. Pacini (ed.), *Chiese e Islam in Italia*. Milan: Paoline, 109–34.
Barbagli, M. (1998). *Immigrazione e criminalità in Italia*, Bologna: Il Mulino.
Barbagli, M. (2002). *Immigrazione e reati in Italia*. Bologna: Il Mulino.
Bausani, A. (1955). *Il Corano*. Firenze: Sassoni.
Blanchard, M. (2008). 'Donne senegalesi in Italia. Migranti muridi tra iniziativa femminile e controllo delle confraternità', in A. Colombo and G. Sciortino (eds.), *Stranieri in Italia. Trent'anni dopo*. Bologna: Il Mulino, 147–76.
Brambilla, C. and Rizzi, M. (2011). *Migrazioni e religioni. Un 'esperienza locale di dialogo tra cristiani e musulmani*. Milan: Franco Angeli.
Branca, P. and Santerini, M. (eds.) (2008). *Alunni arabofoni a scuola*. Rome: Carocci.
Caetani, L. (1905–26). *Annali dell'Islam*. Milan: Hoepli.
Cerchiaro, F. (2013). 'Fare casa fuori casa. Processi di mixité coniugale nei racconti di vita delle coppie miste in Veneto'. Ph.D., Dottorato di ricerca in Scienze Sociali: interazioni, comunicazione e costruzioni culturali, Ciclo XXV, Università di Padova.
Courtens, G. (2009). 'Annale interreligioso. Eventi 2008', in P. Naso and B. Salvarini (eds.), *Il muro di vetro L'Italia delle Religioni Primo rapporto*. Bologna: EMI, 184–99.
Courtens, G. (2012). 'Annale ecumenico e interreligioso. Dialogo tra fedi in Italia. Quale vitalità?' in P. Naso and B. Salvarini (eds.), *Un cantiere senza progetto L'Italia delle Religioni Rapporto 2012*. Bologna: EMI, 251–69.
Davie, G. (2008). 'Thinking Sociologically about Religion: Contexts, Concepts and Clarifications', in E. Barker (ed.), *The Centrality of Religion in Social Life: Essays in Honour of James A. Beckford*. Aldershot: Ashgate, 15–28.
Ferrara, M. (2011). 'Food, Migration, and Identity: Halal Food and Muslim Immigrants in Italy'. Master's thesis. Retrieved from ProQuest Dissertations and Theses.
Ferrari, A. (2008b). 'La scuola italiana di fronte al paradigma musulmano', in A. Ferrari (ed.), *Islam in Europa/Islam in Italia tra Diritto e Società*. Bologna: Il Mulino, 171–98.
Ghirighelli, B. and Negri, A. (2008). *I matrimoni Cristiano-Islamici in Italia: gli interrogativi, il diritto, la pastorale*. Milan: EDB.
Guolo, R. (2001). 'L'Islam nascosto. Adattamento e trasformazione della religiosità nella confraternita senegalese muride in Italia', *Sociologia urbana e rurale* 64–65: 265–73.
Guolo, R. (2009). 'Islam e scuola pubblica: orientamenti di genitori di religione Islamica in Piemonte', *Ricerche di Pedagogia e Didattica* 4(2): 1–16.
La Torre, G. and Tomassone, L. (eds.) (2009). *Dialoghi in cammino. Protestanti e musulmani in Italia oggi*. Turin: Claudiana.
Marranci, G. (2012). 'Studying Muslims of Europe', in U. Kockel, M. Nic Craith, and J. Frykman (eds.), *A Companion to the Anthropology of Europe*. Malden, MA: Wiley-Blackwell, 295–309.

Menin, L. (2011). 'Bodies, Boundaries and Desires: Multiple Subject-Positions and Micro-Politics of Modernity among Young Muslim Women in Milan', *Journal of Modern Italian Studies* 16(4): 504–15.

MIUR. (2007). 'La via italiana per la scuola interculturale e l'integrazione degli alunni stranieri'. Available at <http://archivio.pubblica.istruzione.it/news/2007/allegati/pubblicazione_intercultura.pdf>[Accessed 9 February 2011].

MIUR. (2010). *'Focus in breve sulla scuola. La presenza degli alunni stranieri nelle scuole statali'*. Available at <http://www.istruzione.it/web/ministero/index_pubblicazioni_10> [Accessed 18 February 2011].

MIUR. (2011). *Gli alunni stranieri nel sistema scolastico italiano, anno scolastico 2010/2011*. Available at <http://www.istruzione.it/web/istruzione/intercultura-pubblicazioni> [Accessed 30 October 2011].

MIUR. (2012). *Gli alunni stranieri nel sistema scolastico italiano, anno scolastico 2011/2012*. Ufficio statistico.

Naso, P. and Salvarani, B. (2002). *La rivincita del dialogo. Cristiani e musulmani in Italia dopo l'11 settembre*. Bologna: EMI.

Negri, A. T. and Scaranari Introvigne, S. (2005). *Musulmani in Piemonte: in moschea, al lavoro, nel contesto sociale*. Milan: Gerini e Associati.

Negri, A. T. and Scaranari Introvigne, S. (eds.) (2008). *I ragazzi musulmani nella scuola statale: il caso del Piemonte*. Turin: L'Harmattan.

Odasso, L. (2013). 'La mixité conjugale: une expérience de migration. Approche comparée des effets de la stigmatisation sur les natifs et leurs partenaires «arabes» en Vénétie et en Alsace'. Ph.D. Dottorato di ricerca in Lingue e civiltà dell'Asia e dell'Africa mediterranea, Ciclo XXIV. Université de Strasbourg et Università Ca' Foscari Venezia.

Pace, E. (2004). *Sociologia dell'Islam*. Rome: Carocci.

Rhazzali, M. K. (2010). *L'Islam in carcere. L'esperienza religiosa dei giovani musulmani nelle prigione italiane*. Milan: Franco Angeli.

Saint-Blancat, C. (1999a). 'Le donne fra transizione e alterità', in C. Saint-Blancat (ed.), *L'Islam in Italia. Una presenza plurale*. Rome: Edizioni Lavoro, 141–57.

Saint-Blancat, C. (1999b). 'Studiare l'Islam', in C. Saint-Blancat (ed.), *L'Islam in Italia. Una presenza plurale*. Rome: Edizioni Lavoro, 25–45.

Saint-Blancat, C. (1999c). 'Tra identità e fede: una religiosità plurale', in C. Saint-Blancat (ed.), *L'Islam in Italia. Una presenza plurale*. Rome: Edizioni Lavoro, 119–40.

Speziale, F. (2005). 'Adapting Mystic Identity to Italian Mainstream Islam: The Case of a Muslim Rom Community in Florence', *Balkanologie* 9(1–2): 195–211.

Zatti, G. (2008). 'La Chiesa italiana e le relazioni cristiano-Islamiche', in A. Pacini (ed.), *Chiese e Islam in Italia*. Milan: Paoline, 135–61.

Zilio-Grandi, I. (ed.) (2006). *Sposare l'altro. Matrimoni misti nell'ordinamento italiano e nel diritto Islamico*. Venice: Marsilio.

## Young Muslims

Abdel Qader, S. (2008). *Porto il velo, adoro i Queen: Nuove italiane crescono*. Milan: Sonzogno.

Barbagli, M. and Schmoll, C. (eds.) (2011). *Stranieri in Italia. La generazione dopo*. Bologna: Il Mulino.

Bertani, M. (2004). 'Muslims in Italy: Social Change and Educational Practices', in B. van Driel (ed.), *Confronting Islamophobia in Educational Practice*. London: Trentham Books House, 95–109.

Chaouki, K. (2005). *Salaam Italia. La voce di un giovane musulmano italiano.* Rome: Alberti Editore.

Colombo, E. (ed.) (2010). *Figli di immigrati in Italia.* Turin: Utet.

Colombo, E., Leonini, L., and Rebughini, P. (2009). 'Different But Not Stranger: Everyday Collective Identifications among Adolescent Children of Immigrants in Italy', *Journal of Ethnic and Migration Studies* 33(1): 37–59.

Colombo, E. and Semi, G. (eds.) (2007). *Multiculturalismo quotidiano. Le pratiche della differenza.* Milan: Franco Angeli.

Frisina, A. (2005). 'Musulmani e italiani tra le altre cose. Tattiche e strategie identitarie di giovani figli di immigrati', in J. Cesari and A. Pacini (eds.), *Giovani musulmani in Europa.* Turin: Fondazione Giovanni Agnelli, 139–60.

Frisina, A. (2007a). *Giovani Musulmani d'Italia.* Rome: Carocci.

Frisina, A. (2007b). 'La diversità religiosa come critica sociale? Un processo di convergenza tra giovani ebrei e musulmani, italiani ed europei', in E. Colombo and G. Semi (eds.), *Multiculturalismo quotidiano. Le pratiche della differenza.* Milan: Franco Angeli, 77–98.

Frisina, A. (2009). 'Luoghi e attori di trasformazione sociale', in S. Allievi (ed.), *I musulmani e la società italiana. Percezioni reciproche, conflitti culturali, trasformazioni sociali.* Milan: Franco Angeli, 94–121.

Frisina, A. (2010a). 'Young Muslims' Everyday Tactics and Strategies: Resisting Islamophobia, Negotiating Italianness, Becoming Citizens', *Journal of Intercultural Studies* 31(5): 557–72.

Frisina, A. (2010b). 'Young Muslims of Italy: Islam in the Everyday Life', in G. Giordan (ed.), *Youth and Religion, Annual Review of the Sociology of Religion*, vol. 1. Leiden and Boston: Brill, 329–51.

Ghazi, R. (2007). *Oggi forse non ammazzo nessuno: Storie minime di una giovane musulmana stranamente non terrorista.* Milan: Fabbri.

Girardi, D. (2012). *Gioventù 'corte'. Giovani adulti di origine straniera.* Milan: Franco Angeli.

Guolo, R. (2007). 'Diventare cittadini. I giovani musulmani in Italia', in G. Cacciavillani and E. Leonardi (eds.), *Una generazione in movimento. Gli adolescenti e i giovani immigrati.* Milan: Franco Angeli, 107–19.

Maddanu, S. (2009). 'L'Islamità dei giovani musulmani e l'«ijtihad» moderno: nuove pratiche per una nuova religiosità europea', *Rassegna Italiana di Sociologia* 4: 655–80.

Mazzega-Ciamp, S. (2012). 'Muoversi tra frontiere simboliche. Differenza e differenze religiose nell'esperienza di giovani musulmani del Trevigiano'. Master's thesis in Sociology. FISPPA University of Padua.

Saint-Blancat, C. and Zaltron, F. (2013). '"Making the most of it": How Young Romanians and Moroccans in North-Eastern Italy Use Resources from their Social Networks', *Ethnicities* 13(6): 759–817.

Zanfrini, L. (2006). 'Il lavoro', in Fondazione ISMU (eds.), *Undicesimo Rapporto sulle migrazioni.* Milan: Franco Angeli.

## Radicalization

Allievi, S. (2006). *Europe's Muslim Communities: Security and Integration post-11 September. The Italian Report.* Rome: Ethnobarometer.

Björkman, C. (2010). *Salafi-Jihadi Terrorism in Italy.* Geneva: World Economic Forum.

Bleich, E. (2009). 'State Responses to "Muslim" Violence: A Comparison of Six West European Countries', *Journal of Ethnic and Migration Studies* 35(3): 361–79.

Corbucci, C. (2003). *Il terrorismo Islamico in Italia. Realtà e finzione*. Rome: Agorà.

Diamanti, I. (ed.) (2011). *La sicurezza in Italia e in Europa. Significati, immagine e realtà. Quarta indagine sulla rappresentazione sociale e mediatica della sicurezza*. Rome: Fondazione Unipolis.

Ferrari, A. (2012). 'La lotta dei simboli e la speranza del diritto (Parte Seconda): la guerra «italiana» al «burqa» e al «niqab»', *Quaderni di diritto e politica ecclesiastica* 1: 39–61.

Stancanelli, B. (2006). *Quindici innocenti terroristi: com' è finita la prima grande inchiesta sull'estremismo Islamico in Italia*. Venice: Marsilio.

Zilio Grandi, I. (ed.) (2006). *Il dialogo delle leggi*. Venice: Marsilio.

CHAPTER 7

# SPAIN

ANA I. PLANET CONTRERAS

## INTRODUCTION[1]

ENTERING the words 'Muslims in Spain' into an internet search engine produces an overwhelming number of results referring to the different dynasties that ruled the country from the eighth to the fifteenth centuries. Particularly noteworthy are the number of pages devoted to the architectural and monumental legacy of this period, much of which is now included on the list of World Heritage Sites. The long history of Spain's relationship with Islam has played a symbolic role in the construction of the Spanish nation, as emphasized by numerous historians, a role that is now—like it or not—at the root of the debate over what Islam has meant in Spain.

A great deal of literature on Islam is currently published in Spain. During the period 2001–10, over 400 published books were catalogued at the National Library under the subject heading 'Islam'. Glancing at the titles, it appears that the vast majority are publications about specific aspects of the country's history between the eighth and the fifteenth centuries. Other works continue the debate over how to include this phase of history in the common course of events. And still others, scarcely a few dozen perhaps, analyse the presence of Muslims in contemporary Spain from a social science perspective. These works analyse Islam in relation to immigration, to the debate on the clash of civilizations, and, as we shall see, to the new reality of religious pluralism in Spain. It is therefore appropriate to begin this chapter with a reflection on Islam in the history of Spain as portrayed in some of these works before going on to examine the reality of

---

[1] This chapter is a result of the research project, *El mundo árabe-islámico en movimiento: migraciones, reformas y elecciones y su impacto en España* [The Arab-Islamic World in Movement: migrations, reforms and elections and their impact on Spain] (CS02011-29438-C05-01), financed by the Ministry of the Economy and Competitiveness' Secretary of State for Research, Development and Innovation for which the author is a senior researcher.

Islam in modern-day Spain, associated with the country's transformation into a country of immigration in the last third of the twentieth century.

This chapter offers an overview of the state of Islam in Spain, taking as its point of departure the relationship between the current presence of Islam in Spain and the transnational migrations of the 1980s and 1990s. This recent presence is combined with the existence of an indigenous Islam, born of conversions that took place towards the end of General Franco's dictatorship and which represented significant defiance of the Catholic Church's morals and the religious monopoly championed by the regime. It also analyses the legal framework regulating Islam in Spain, which is a product of this same social and political context and can be characterized as an attempt to offer a more perfect and comprehensive recognition of religious pluralism, but which emerged at a time when Muslim demographics and social dynamics were far different from those existing today. In addition, the chapter sheds light on an aspect specific to Spain, which recent research takes explicitly into account: regional specificity in the country's different regions. The topics of Islam in schools and Muslim political participation remain marginal, due to the fact that Muslim immigration is only a recent phenomenon. Finally, the chapter will deal with the issue of Islamophobia and discourses on Islam and Muslims in public opinion.

# Social Status and Class: Beyond the Focus on Islam as a Migrant Phenomenon

Determining the exact number of Muslims living in Spain is difficult because, as in many European countries, censuses do not ask about religion. Article 16.2 of the 1978 Spanish constitution categorically states that 'no-one can be obliged to declare their ideology, religion or beliefs'. There is a clear contrast between the dominant perception of Muslims as a monolithic group and the wide diversity of their origin, culture, and language, as well as the ways in which they practice their religion. As noted in *Muslims in Spain: A Reference Guide*, published by Casa Árabe in 2009, 'classifications, although revealing, often fail to reflect a much more complex context, namely that the practice of Islam and the plural reality of communities and citizens identified as Muslims are not monolithic blocks' (Casa Árabe-IEAM 2009: 10).

Interestingly, despite the long centuries of Islamic history in the Iberian Peninsula, Spain's Muslim population is relatively small compared with other European countries. It has already been noted that the key to understanding the slow constitution of a Spanish Islam in twentieth-century Spain is perhaps both ideological and economic. From an ideological perspective, the state Catholicism imposed by Franco may well have delayed the institutionalization of Spanish Islam. Spain did not become a destination for migrants until recently, coinciding with its entry into the EEC and the closure of European borders to migrations from third countries. Spain's transformation into a country of immigration should not be understood in a postcolonial context as in other neighbouring countries.

From the early 1970s onwards, people from Arab countries—countries with which the Franco regime had established cordial political relations from the late 1940s—began to settle in Spain. These early newcomers were the embryo of a religious minority without any specific legal status. Most of them were students at Spanish universities, many of whom put down roots in Spain once they had completed their studies and ended up taking Spanish nationality. This period provided the focus for early studies on Muslims in Spain, for example a Ph.D. thesis (González Barea 2003) looking at Moroccans who came to study at the University of Granada, their integration into the city's society, and their involvement in cultural and religious associations. These early arrivals during the 1970s were followed by immigrants from countries with majority Muslim populations who also obtained Spanish nationality. In addition, Ceuta and Melilla, two Spanish enclaves on the North African coast whose geographical proximity to Morocco has engendered a particular set of population and identity dynamics, form a peculiar cross-border area that requires specific analysis, as shown in Planet Contreras (1998). Both have played an important role in the process of the legal recognition of Islam in Spain. Not only have they mediated with the state, but they have also made great efforts to promote the first associations and places of worship.

In the second half of the 1980s, the economic development that took place in Spain led to a notable growth in the number of North Africans living in the country (López García and Planet Contreras 2002). Other influxes of immigrants from sub-Saharan Africa and Asia, specifically Pakistan, further enriched the landscape.

Despite the lack of available data, attempts have been made to quantify the situation. A case in point is the *Observatorio Andalusí*. Founded in 2003, the observatory is an independent non-profit organization associated with one of the largest federations of Muslim communities, the Union of Islamic Communities in Spain, and defines itself as an 'institution for observing and monitoring the situation of Muslim citizens and Islamophobia in Spain'. In terms of Muslims with Spanish nationality, the observatory distinguishes between 'nationalized Muslims' and their descendants, called 'Hispano-Muslims' and estimated at 413,178 (a figure that includes the residents of Ceuta and Melilla), and citizens from countries belonging to the Organization of Islamic Cooperation (OIC) who have been granted Spanish nationality. However, blanket categorizations about the religious identities of the children, grandchildren, and great-grandchildren of Muslims who have been in Spain since the 1950s may prove problematic and is a subject that requires more in-depth examination and studies of religious practice and reference, which have yet to be carried out (Observatorio Andalusí 2011).

Spanish converts to Islam have formed numerous associations in the Andalusian provinces of Cordoba, Granada, and Seville, as well as in Barcelona and Valencia. These associations played a very important role as mediators with the Spanish authorities in the 1980s and 1990s. These 'new Muslims' are very active on a cultural level in projects linked with historical 'Muslim Spain' and some of their associations have been instrumental in contributing to the current institutionalization of Islam in Spain, as will be explained. The observatory considers these Spanish converts as 'reverts' in that they have 'simply recovered their original natural religion', and together with those born in the former Spanish provinces of what the observatory calls the Caliphate, their numbers reach 18,728 (Observatorio Andalusí 2011). Beyond estimates made by members of the media, no other figures are available.

Conversion to Islam has been the subject of several academic studies (Sánchez Nogales 2004). In these works, the process is explained as the result of the spiritual monopoly and monolithic nature of Catholicism that prevailed during the Franco years and the process of spiritual and political liberation that followed (López Barrios and Hagherty 1983; Valencia 2003). This research reflects on how these conversions took place and how political militancy in *andalucismo* (the search for a specific regional identity like that found in other regions in the country, particularly linked to the reformulation of the relationship between the central state and the regions during the first years of democracy) and conversion to Islam came together in some remarkable cases (Aya 2000). Now relegated to the dusty back rooms of bookstores, these studies have been replaced by new publications casting doubt on the conversion process that incorporate the discourse of 'betraying Spain' in their analysis (Rodríguez Magda 2005).

Some academic experts question this narrative of conversion by these 'new Muslims'. For example, converts claim that the conversions occurred in the last third of the twentieth century, while scholars of religion assert that they took place over a much longer period (Sánchez Nogales 2004). However, the narrative of the new Muslims is an appropriate object of study in itself. Since part of the institutionalization process of Islam in Spain was guided by these men and women, a critical reading of their histories undoubtedly provides information that can help to shed light on the way in which Islam was institutionalized in Spain (Del Olmo 2000). Further analysis of this issue may go some way in explaining the current state of conflict and lack of cooperation between different generations of converts and their very different presence in the public sphere. Information about international contacts and the funding of different projects may also be found in these narratives, but a more analytical and comprehensive study of this topic has not yet been undertaken. Consider, for example, the following fragments from the testimony published in the Muslim magazine, *Verde islam*:

> The first generation of converts was the driving force. These men and women were simply full of hope, they were excited. They were members of the counterculture—extreme left, yoga, psychedelic drugs—and they knew nothing whatsoever about Islam, but their generous hearts intuitively felt that Islam was a more effective liberation formula than others they had tried [...]. The second generation of Spanish Muslims was level headed. They did not yet speak Arabic and they didn't know much about Islam, but at least they were sane. The argument they most frequently used was that if something seemed strange, it was not Islamic, because Islam was the rule not the exception. They played a key role in making Islam possible in Spain by ensuring that 'Islamisation' was not identified with 'Arabisation' [...]. Then along came a third generation of Muslims who tried to strip those who had preceded

them of their authority but who lacked the spontaneous brilliance of the first group and the common sense of the second. These were the 'men of Arabic'; they were completely bilingual and had generally studied for a few years in Islamic countries. They tried to limit experiments to 'adapt Islam to Spanish reality' and for a while they succeeded. They were imams, and tried to lead communities and bored those who sought to approach Islam. But for the same reasons they had managed to adapt themselves to countries like Saudi Arabia and Kuwait when they went there to study with grants and scholarships, the Spanish did not rally round them: they had no Islamic blood in their veins. Their translations were useful because, despite being plagued with a Christianising vocabulary, they provided us with the first materials translated by Spaniards. A new generation followed, the fourth, those who were not only completely bilingual but who also sought to infuse our Islam with the strength and vitality that had always characterised it and which was lacking in the Islam preached by the previous generation. They provided the basis for the blind intuitions of the men of good sense, and I call them 'the men of wisdom' [...]. There followed a fifth generation of Spanish Muslims who made up for the drawbacks of their predecessors: their excessive cerebrality [...]. Then along came 'the men of light', men who came to Islam in a pure and clean state without ever knowing how much effort their predecessors had put into every detail of the normality they now enjoyed, personifying the light that gives us all strength, in a way that only Allah can know. (Aya 2000: 50)

Spanish Muslims aside, the presence of Islam in Spain is basically a 'migrant Islam', which affects both the practice of Islam in Spain and its management by the government. It affects issues such as religious authority, community leadership, and the presence of actors in public debates, as shall be shown. As already noted, the number of individuals involved is difficult to specify, though an estimate of around 1 million seems reasonable, taking into account the statistics on migrants from different OIC countries. Moroccans are the most numerous (746,760 according to the December 2010 census), followed by Senegalese (61,383), Pakistanis (56,402), and Algerians (56,129) (figures available at <http://www.ine.es> [National Statistics Institute, in Spanish] and referred to by the Observatorio Andalusí 2011) (see Table 7.1).

Despite the lack of data on non-foreign Muslims living in Spain, we do have some information about Muslims of foreign origin, as part of the annual statistics on foreigners. In 2010 the population of these workers numbered 467,662. Most are concentrated in the service sector, followed by construction and industry. Figures are low for the agricultural sector, in which cases of exploited workers and unregulated employment still exist. The Ministry of Labour and Social Affairs' Permanent Immigration Observatory monitors the relationship between the labour market and immigration (Table 7.2).

Current economic trends have also had an impact on employment figures, which are falling at this time. The last survey of the active population, carried out in April 2010, shows that unemployment among foreigners is increasing, standing at around 30%. These figures confirm the job loss trend but it is still difficult to ascertain the origin of the workers who are losing their jobs due to a lack of disaggregated data.

Table 7.1 Immigration to Spain from Muslim countries

| Country of origin | Foreigners | Spaniards |
|---|---|---|
| Morocco | 644,688 | 103,249 |
| Algeria | 51,145 | 5,740 |
| Pakistan | 46,649 | 1,746 |
| Senegal | 46,077 | 1,527 |
| Mali | 19,439 | 98 |
| Gambia | 19,233 | 969 |
| Mauritania | 9,805 | 433 |
| Bangladesh | 7,833 | 149 |
| Egypt | 2,656 | 892 |
| Iran | 2,413 | 1,547 |
| Syria | 2,357 | 2,448 |
| Turkey | 2,062 | 432 |
| Tunisia | 1,718 | 459 |
| Libya | 1,386 | 1,458 |
| Jordan | 1,103 | 1,193 |
| Iraq | 956 | 504 |
| Total | 859,520 | 122,844 |

Source: Instituto Nacional de Estadística (census 2010) (<http://www.ine.es>).

Table 7.2 Employees in Spain of Muslim origin

|  | Agriculture | Construction | Industry | Services |
|---|---|---|---|---|
| 2007 | | | | |
| Algerians | 182 | 3,640 | 2,495 | 6,888 |
| Moroccans | 3,251 | 66,894 | 22,413 | 77,720 |
| Senegalese | 244 | 4,523 | 3,147 | 6,526 |
| Pakistanis | 91 | 4,601 | 1,683 | 9,106 |
| 2010 | | | | |
| Algerians | 132 | 1,227 | 1,578 | 5,130 |
| Moroccans | 2,120 | 27,695 | 16,840 | 72,140 |
| Senegalese | 172 | 1,473 | 2,297 | 5,243 |
| Pakistanis | 22 | 2182 | 1,110 | 8,810 |

Source: Anuario estadístico de inmigración (2007 and 2010), Secretaría de Estado de Inmigración y Emigración, Ministry of Employment and Immigration. Compiled by the author.

Very little research has been conducted analysing the specific situation of Muslims in the workplace and the impact of the laws governing religious freedom at work. A study carried out by Jiménez-Aybar and Barrios (2006) concludes that the effectiveness of the legal framework on the practice of Islam in Spain will continue to be limited because neither workers nor small businesses have much information. At the time of writing, 52% of Muslim workers polled by Jiménez-Aybar and Barrios mentioned the complete lack of any facilities provided by their employers for Friday prayers.

## Religion in the Public Arena: The Dynamics of the Presence of Islam in the Context of Religious Pluralism

On 14 July 1989, the Advisory Commission on Religious Freedom, a consultative body within the Ministry of Justice, bequeathed '*notorio arraigo*' on Islam, establishing it as a 'deeply-rooted' and widespread religion in Spain. The Muslim Association of Spain had submitted an application a few months earlier on the grounds that Islam is 'one of the spiritual beliefs that has shaped the historic personality of Spain' and that 'the Islamic religion has been present in Spain since the eighth century, broadly disseminated in the initial centuries and subsequently surviving on a bigger or smaller scale depending on the historical period and circumstances, having remained in Spain uninterruptedly since then' (Jiménez-Aybar 2004: 68). Recognition of Islam as a deeply-rooted religion paved the way for negotiations on agreements concerning Islamic worship in Spain, geared at normalizing the presence of Islam against a backdrop of long centuries of intolerance and ignorance.

Legal recognition brought with it more general changes in the Spanish society's relationship with religion, a development that has been closely examined over the last few decades. Analysing this relationship is a complex matter, due to the combination of secularization and new forms of religiosity. As noted by the sociologist of religion Pérez Agote (2006), three different and interrelated social dynamics must be taken into account when considering religion and society in present-day Spain: firstly, what might be termed the secularization of religious awareness, beginning in the 1960s, but which some date as far back as the beginning of the twentieth century; secondly, the secularization of society, defined by Pérez Agote as a long and still incomplete process that has been part of modern state building since the seventeenth century; and thirdly, the breakup or definitive fracture of a previously homogeneous religious community, caused mainly by immigration. The twenty-first century has brought a new wave of secularization, with the number of both those who define themselves as practising Catholics and those who consider themselves cut off from religion (atheists, agnostics, and people indifferent to religion) continuing to fall.

Current data on religious beliefs and practices in Spain show the impact of the processes just described. From 98% of the population identifying itself as Catholic in 1965, the figure fell to 79.7% in 2002 (CIS data). The Centre for Sociological Research (CIS) has been investigating Spaniards' relationships with religion since 1996, asking two basic questions as to how they identify themselves from a religious standpoint and the extent to which they practise their religion. According to the results of the last survey, conducted in April 2011, 72.6% of Spaniards declared themselves Catholic, 13.4% non-believers, 9.3% atheists, and 2.7% believers of other religions (CIS No. 2885, April 2011). Because the number of non-Catholics remains small, no specific surveys have been carried out on other religions, apart from a series of surveys of Muslims of migrant origin, the results of which are discussed in this section.

Since the enactment of the 1978 constitution, the legal framework governing individual and collective religious freedom in Spain has become complex. Legal recognition of religious pluralism means that the public authorities are required to recognize all religious denominations and to cooperate with them. In this framework, cooperation between public institutions and Muslims is regulated within the general framework of the 1980 Organic Law on Religious Freedom and the cooperation agreements with the various minority religions. These laws regulate the exercise of religious freedom and facilitate the institutionalization process along much the same lines as the provisions governing relations with the Catholic Church. Not only do they specify the general framework for exercising religious freedom, they also stipulate the conditions and recognition of these freedoms: places of worship and religious staff, religious assistance in public centres, the civil effects of religious marriage, and the right to receive religious education in public and grant-assisted private schools (Suárez Pertierra 2006; Contreras Mazarío 2006).

The recognition of Islam within the Spanish framework of religious pluralism created the need for a unified Muslim institution to negotiate with the state, following the model of dialogue and negotiation shaped by the interactions between the state and the Catholic Church. As a result, Muslim organizations and leaders formed groups in order to achieve greater bargaining power with the government in a process that has, as yet, received insufficient analysis (Jiménez-Aybar 2004; Planet Contreras and Moreras 2008). The creation of associations for religious purposes according to the 1980 Organic Law on Religious Freedom is a phenomenon that grew during the 1990s and continues actively today; there are 1,005 groups of this nature recorded in 2011.

This type of institutionalization process has a deep effect on the fragmented nature of Muslim associations in Spain, which is a reflection of the heterogeneous composition of the Muslim populations at the end of the 1980s described already. Two months after Islam was officially recognized as 'having deep roots in Spain' and work began on drafting the text of the agreement, the Spanish Federation of Islamic Religious Entities (FEERI) was created. This federation, mainly made up of associations of Spanish converts, began talks with the Spanish administration aimed at finalizing the agreement. But instead of joining together to create a single negotiator, one of the founding entities of the FEERI, the Association of Muslims in Spain (AME), created eight Muslim organizations in different areas of Spain within just a few weeks and, a few months later, these eight organizations formed the Union of Islamic Communities in Spain (UCIDE). Finally, the FEERI and the UCIDE united to form a single entity, the Islamic Commission of Spain (CIE). This commission signed the Cooperation Agreement with the authorities on 28 April 1992 and became the only recognized institution that can negotiate with the state.

The dual aim of this recently created Islamic commission was set out in its founding statutes and remains in force today, despite increasing criticism from other federations about its monopoly. In July 2011, a new federation, the Islamic Council of Spain, was founded with the explicit goal of changing the dynamics of representation. However, the Islamic Commission of Spain remains up to now the sole interlocutor between Muslims and the Spanish state for the purposes of negotiating, signing, and monitoring the Cooperation Agreement. From a religious or doctrinal perspective, it is committed to facilitating the practice of Islam in Spain as per the precepts of the Qur'an and the Sunnah. This organization accommodates all the various Islamic currents and groups. Very few groups are not included in the commission for ideological reasons, including, most notably, the Granada Murabituns (members of the Islamic Community of Spain and the Granada Mosque Foundation) and the Ahmadiyya community (part of the Jamaat Ahmadiyya association in Spain in Pedro Abad, Cordoba).

Until recently, the structure of the CIE was based on a founding institution represented by the two initial governing bodies, the standing committee and the general secretariat. These acted on behalf of two federations that were initially unequal in size, both in terms of the number of members and geographical representation. The number of associations in the UCIDE has steadily grown and it has an important presence throughout the country. Over the last few years, the number of Muslim communities included in the Ministry of Justice's Registry of Religious Organizations has increased exponentially. The number has grown from 262 registered in 2005, to 559 in 2008 and 643 in 2009 (see Map 7.1). Of these, 356 belonged to the UCIDE and fifty-five to the FEERI, while 218 communities do not belong to either of the federations. Although the UCIDE clearly attracts more groups than the FEERI, both have failed to attract a growing number of new entities and associations to their ranks, as the number of associations that have decided to stay independent or support groups different to the two historic federations has increased (Arigita Maza 2006). The latest data available in June 2011 show a total of 1,005 associations. Of them, 517 are in the UCIDE, eighty-four in the FEERI, and 392 do not belong to either group. In addition to the two large federations, there are forty-four smaller ones, mostly regional in nature, which indicates new organizational trends for groups outside of the umbrella federations.

As of 2004, the dynamics of the CIE paved the way for the emergence of new federative entities, twenty-three in total. Some were the outcome of UCIDE initiatives as the dominant CIE federation, whereas others sprang from new requirements for negotiating with local administrations, and others to meet the demands of numerous associations that did not agree with the CIE's organizational principles and wished to promote a new framework for negotiating with the administration. A new Islamic Council of Spain was created in April 2011 to incorporate 850 associations of the 913 that exist at this time and is registered at the same postal address as the UCIDE.

This new institution was initiated by the leaders of some of the new federations—especially in Madrid, Valencia, and Murcia—who have been unable to find a way to

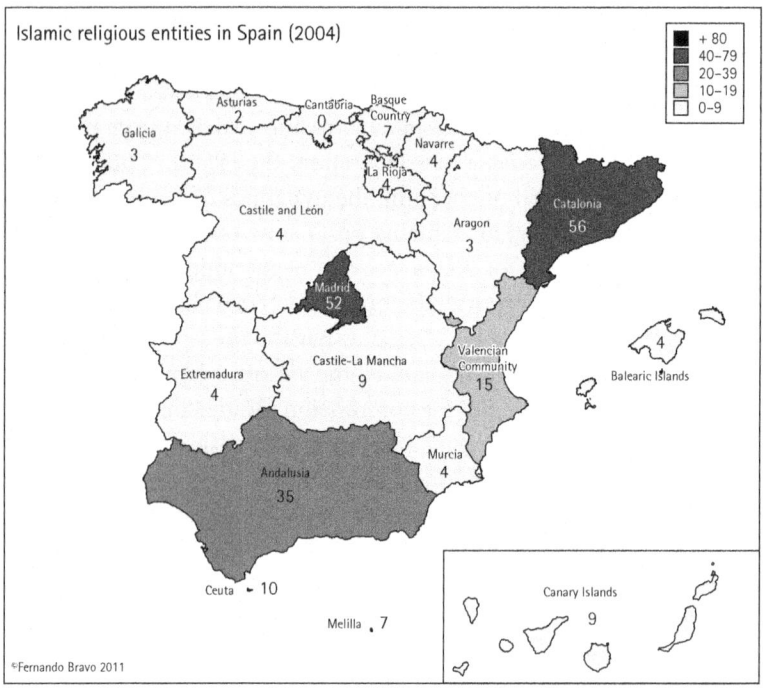
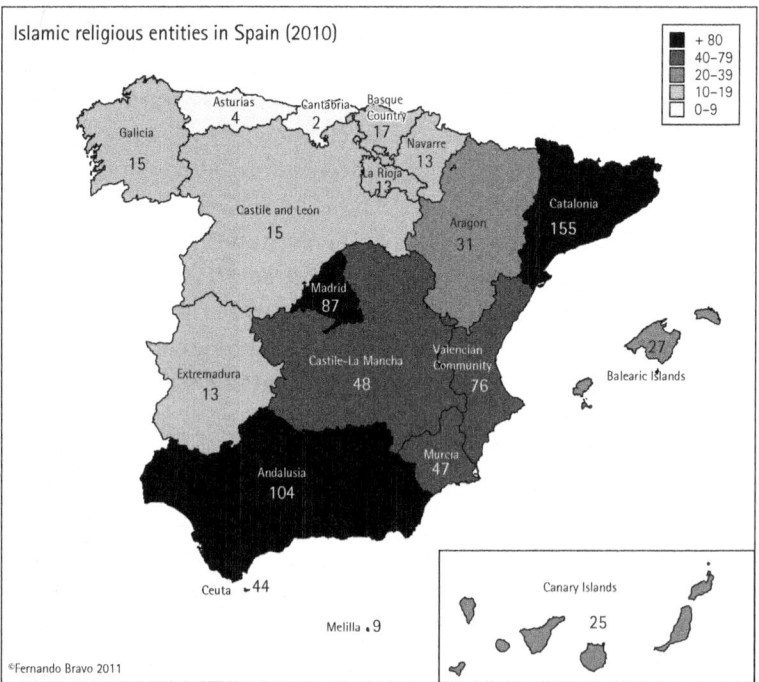

MAP 7.1 Islamic communities in Spain registered with the Ministry of Justice

participate in the CIE. However, these federations, being keenly aware of the importance of the CIE as a legal liaison with the authorities, have opted for rapprochement with its leaders and accepting the inclusion of the UCIDE on the new council.

The current legal framework has engendered what might be called a 'parochial' institutionalization and organization of Islam. As with the Catholic Church, the key elements of the institutionalization process were, on the one hand, the professional figure of the imam or religious leader, and on the other, the organization of places of worship. In other words, these places of worship need to be attached to an association and be under the responsibility of an imam, as is the case with Catholic parishes.

Mosques and other premises used by the Islamic Commission are likewise exempt from paying taxes, as are all religions that have an agreement with the state. The agreement also sets out the social security and military service requirements for 'Islamic religious leaders and imams [sic]'.

This double formulation reflects the suggestions put forth by some associations—especially the earliest members of the FEERI—that considered that a group may not be led by an imam. Finally, with regard to the rights of Muslims in Spain, it stipulates rights to Islamic religious education in infant, primary, and secondary schools, the right to be taught by teachers selected by the Islamic Commission (article 10); the right of Muslim military personnel, prison inmates, and hospital patients to receive Islamic religious assistance (article 8); the adaptation of food in military, penitential, and hospital establishments to meet Islamic religious precepts and the application of the halal denomination to certain products (article 14); and labour rights. The agreement also establishes the validity of marriages conducted according to Muslim rites, provided the parties concerned meet the requirements set out in the Civil Code and register the marriage in the corresponding Civil Registry (article 7) (Jiménez-Aybar 2004). The possibility of including shariah principles in civil law in relation to marriage and divorce was not assessed during the negotiations that led to the agreement; instead it was decided that marriages held in authorized mosques should simply be registered, as Catholic marriages are.

From a legal point of view, one of the questions that jurists have focused on is that of Islamic family law and its relationship to the Spanish legal system (Motilla and Lorenzo 2002). Spain has no experience with religious arbitration, perhaps because the civil law system is rights-based and is not open to the effects of inter-legality (Colom 2012).

A study carried out by Colom in 2012 on this question, however, found that the courts have been forced by private international law to interpret and make pronouncements on the civil validity of some aspects of Islamic law. Colom discusses some sentences regarding the registration of religious marriages conducted abroad, the recognition of the civil effects of polygamy, the recognition of Islamic divorce initiated by a man (*talaq*) as an irrevocable way to dissolve a marriage, and the custody of minors or *kafalah* (Colom 2012).

When private international law is applied—even though Spanish legislation does not allow for polygamy and bigamy is a crime—the effects of a marriage of this type can be recognized when it is allowed by the national law of both spouses (Labaca 2005).

These effects apply to family reunification, inheritance rights, alimony after divorce, and widow's pensions (Carrascosa González 2003). In fact, several sentences have recognized the right to widow's pensions when the deceased has more than one spouse (Colom 2011). Regarding *kafalah*, some cases have recognized the correspondence of effects with Spanish law (Andalusia High Court of Justice sentence dated 14 September 2004, 1014/2003), although not admitting that parentage and kinship were established (Colom 2011).

## Religion in Diverse Public Spheres: Islam in the Autonomous Regions

Spain's economic growth in the late 1980s and 1990s turned the country into an *El Dorado* for immigrants from North Africa, especially Morocco. The uneven economic development in the different regions of Spain favoured the settlement of Moroccans in Catalonia, the Basque Country, and Madrid, and later in Valencia, Andalusia, and Aragon (López García and Planet Contreras 2002). In the regions of early settlement—principally Catalonia—debates on Islam and the resulting religious pluralism have been a reality for over a decade, with policy developing accordingly. In addition, the debate over difficulties in integrating Muslim immigrants has formed part of the last three local election campaigns (Guedioura 2012), with specific campaigns against the construction of mosques around the time of elections (Astor 2009). As will be explained, the settlement rhythm and the complexity of institutionalization in other regions differ greatly from that seen in Catalonia. Spain's other regions share a common institutionalization dynamic, although accompanied by specific characteristics related to the history of the particular region, resulting in resources being made available to associations in their search for greater cultural and social insertion.

The emergence of religious pluralism in Spain has been concomitant with increased academic interest in minority religious groups in Spanish society. A research project on religious pluralism in Spain has been underway since 2006, conducted by interdisciplinary research teams from several universities in the different autonomous regions. These teams include scholars from social anthropology, politics, sociology, and social work. This project 'aims to draw attention to religious minorities in Spain, drawing the map of religious pluralism and showing how religious factors can promote or hinder the construction of a plural society open to dialogue and harmonious coexistence and committed to equality'.[2] The project is financed by the Foundation for Pluralism and Coexistence (created in December 2004 by the Council of Ministers). This foundation

---

[2] See <http://www.pluralismoyconvivencia.es/publicaciones/>.

aims to cooperate with deeply-rooted religions in Spain and supports the development of educational and cultural projects, in addition to projects fostering the integration of communities belonging to the three minority religions with which the state has signed cooperation agreements—Muslims, Protestants, and Jews.

The map of religious pluralism is being drawn in the different regions in the country. The research conducted by this foundation shows that minority religious communities are being set up in a variety of ways, albeit on the basis of a common legal framework. These studies contain a great deal of empirical data, figures, local studies, and up-to-date directories of centres of worship and associations. Muslim communities are closely scrutinized in all the studies published to date, whether on the basis of their size, as in Andalusia and Catalonia, specific institutionalization processes, as is the case in Valencia, or ongoing social debates, as in Catalonia.

The study of Islam in the different autonomous regions is unearthing a picture in which an initial phase of settlement is followed by a long search for recognition and visibility by these groups. As the research shows, the migrant status of many of the individuals concerned slows this process, and is associated primarily with the opening of places of worship, for which requests have grown significantly over the last ten years. The history and sociology of all the places of worship are well documented in this research, as is the community work and relationships with other religious groups and with society at large.

As can be seen from these studies, so-called *Islam inmigrado* (the Islam of immigrant communities) is not the only—but perhaps the latest—manifestation of religious pluralism in Spain. Understanding the connection between Spain's new religious pluralism and immigration is key to understanding the institutionalism processes of Islam. The numerical importance of immigrant Muslims is quite large, giving a new dynamic to Islam in the country and contributing to its visibility (Planet Contreras 2009). It must be noted that this is not an issue that solely affects Muslim communities. Evangelical churches of different denominations and Jewish communities have also increased in number and diversified in recent decades with the arrival of immigrants to the country.

A number of initial methodological difficulties arose in the research on Catalonia which have also appeared in research conducted elsewhere. As already mentioned, legal restrictions make it difficult to count and numerically evaluate the importance of these groups. Monitoring an institutionalization process underway at the level of both religious and cultural associations is also a task fraught with difficulty and one that clearly mirrors the different relationships Muslims have with their religion. The final classification of the areas and projects identified targeted mosques and prayer facilities, Sufi centres and religious federations (Estruch et al. 2006: 199).

The research shows how Islamic projects in Catalonia have been promoted with different aims and by different types of actors. Mosques and prayer facilities—Catalonia lacks a single large mosque—spring from initiatives championed by individuals or small groups. Legal immigrants with stable jobs and steady incomes and who have brought their families over want to ensure that their children do not lose the core values rooted in their parents' identities during the socialization process in the country of settlement.

Mosques are opened and managed in Catalonia by immigrants from Morocco, Pakistan, and to a lesser extent sub-Saharan Africa (Gambia, Senegal, Mali, and Mauritania). In towns with a sufficient number of Muslims, the tendency is for people from the same country or region to pray together. For that reason, many towns have more than one mosque—one opened for and by Moroccans and another for and by sub-Saharan Africans. Exceptions are a mosque in Barcelona attended mostly by Pakistanis but led by a Moroccan imam with Spanish nationality, and another where university students congregate, but whose exact location is not specified in the study (Estruch et al. 2006: 200-4). Spanish converts do not figure prominently in any of these initiatives, whereas their presence is very significant in Sufi centres.

Imams across Spain have been the subject of very few specific analyses, but the situation of imams of Catalonia was studied by Moreras (2007) who discovered that half the mosques in Catalonia are managed by a full-time imam. As he pointed out, these religious leaders have different backgrounds and divide their time between their community duties and other work. Furthermore, many lack full religious training. After conducting in-depth interviews with imams, community leaders, and members, as well as local administration officials, Moreras was able to paint a detailed picture of the profiles, trajectories, and functions of imams in Catalan mosques, the conflicts and complementarities that emerge with visiting imams and other transnational Islamic authorities, and the new tasks these imams must shoulder in the Catalan context. According to the Islamic and Cultural Council of Catalonia, fewer than 50% of active imams assigned to a house of worship can produce a certificate to demonstrate that they have studied religion. Moreras classified the imams working in Catalonia into three types: doctorate-imams (with academic studies), immigrant-imams (who began working as imams in their new place of residence without having done so before), and itinerant-imams (who appear on specific holidays). However, further study of imams and their work in other regions in Spain is necessary to obtain a full picture.

In Catalonia, few Islamic centres offer regular activities beyond prayer. Those that do offer a fairly standard set of activities: religious literacy for adults, Spanish and Catalan classes, legal advice and assistance for immigrants, discussions about Catalan society, and debates on the difficulties of integration. Some centres are beginning to offer meetings and activities specifically for women. The large number of mosques in Catalonia—over 140 at the end of 2010 (updated Ministry of Justice official data available at <http://www.observatorioreligion.es>)—and the need for people to liaise with the regional authorities has paved the way for federative projects. The goal of these projects is not to establish common theological positions or to network but rather to guarantee optimum communication with regional and local authorities (Estruch et al. 2006).

Lastly, there are three Sufi centres in Catalonia, all founded relatively recently (1988, 1999, and 2000), catering mainly to non-immigrant Catalan congregations and providing devotional practices consisting of recitation and meditation, which also take place in social centres and private homes. Some activities are open to the general public. The three centres belong to different *tariqas*: Darqawa, Mevlevi, and Naqshbandi (Estruch et al 2006).³ The Darqawi centre is the oldest and is frequented by several dozen Spanish converts who organize recitation activities and Islamic training. The centre belonging to the Mevlevi brotherhood offers courses in calligraphy, recitation, and Islam and attracts almost only Spanish followers, as does the Naqshbandi centre. None of these centres have more than fifty people involved in their activities. No specific research has yet been carried out on Sufism in present-day Spain, with the exception of the article by López Barrios and Hagherty on Muslim converts in Andalusia (López Barrios and Hagherty 1983).

In Catalonia growing tension is being sparked by the construction of places of worship, a dynamic that has also been the subject of specific analysis (Astor 2009; Planet Contreras and Moreras 2008). Astor examines neighbourhood opposition movements to building mosques in Catalonia and Madrid. Of the fifty-one municipalities in which *SOS Racisme* detected cases of opposition to mosques between 1985 and 2009, thirty were located in Catalonia. Empirical work conducted in 2009 reveals some of the factors that account for these dynamics. What particularly catches Astor's attention is the opposition to mosque construction in municipalities in Catalonia and the neighbourhood dynamics of these districts, compared with the metropolitan areas of Madrid with similar numbers of Moroccans and where opposition to mosques is conspicuously absent. A wave of 'No to the mosque' protests in Catalonia has taken place in small towns that received large numbers of Spanish migrants from other regions in the 1950s and which, decades later, have become the targets of new migratory movements. The proliferation of these movements and their absence in other areas of Spain can be ascribed to the lack of resources in Catalonia, the feeling that former domestic migrants have of not belonging, their fear that the new migration will upset the balance of neighbourhoods, and their desire to press politicians into prioritizing their needs and improving neighbourhood infrastructures. 'No to the mosque' is often articulated through the feeling that other services and facilities are needed more urgently (Astor 2009).

Research conducted in Andalusia was beset by the same difficulties as the research in Catalonia, compounded by the fact that there are more mosques to start with (150 in total). In addition, 20% of the religious associations that exist in the region have no place of worship or meeting places now (Tarrés and Salgado 2010a: 296).

---

³ The Darqawa tariqa is a branch of the Shadhili Sufi order founded by Abul Hasan Ali ash-Shadhili (1196–1258). His teachings were compiled by the third sheikh Ahmad Ibn Ata Allah al-Iskandari (d. 1309). The order is characterized by individualism and asceticism. Along with other Sufis like the Tijani, followers share an extreme veneration of the blessings of their sheiks, who they regularly visit during their lives and make ritual visits to their former homes or tombs after their deaths. The Mevlevi tariqa is a Sufi order based on the doctrines of Jalal al-Din Rumi (1207–73). During the Ottoman Empire, the Mevlevi disseminated their *tariqa* across the land, thanks to the support of the sultans, where it took root with intellectuals and the commercial classes of Cairo, Damascus, Nicosia, and Sarajevo. They are characterized by their *dhikr* ritual involving whirling dervishes who use dance as part of their mystical pursuit. The striking nature of their ceremonies has brought them fame in the West. The Naqshbandi *tariqa* is another Sufi order founded by Baha al-Din al-Naksibendi (d. 1389). This *tariqa* very quickly spread from Bukhara among the Turks of Central Asia, Anatolia, and even India. The Naqshbandi prefer a silent mental *dhikr* that prohibits the music that is characteristic of other Sufi orders. They adhere to a basically spiritual rule of order whose precepts include 'solitude in a crowd', with work being the way to purification and involvement in social life the path to God (Gómez García 2010).

Muslim communities in Andalusia have a long history that can be divided into two phases. In the first phase, from 1960 to 1995, the Muslims who lived in Andalusia formed part of two defined groups. On the one hand, there were the students mainly from Jordan, Iraq, and Syria during the 1980s—and late 1980s and 1990s from Morocco—who came to study at the University of Granada, while on the other hand, there were projects led by Spanish Muslims with very different perspectives on Islam, such as Yama'a Islamica de Al-Andalus/Liga Morisca, the Islamic Community of Spain, Morabitum, and Junta Islámica. Junta Islámica, for example, is an organization created in 1993 rooted in present-day Spain while the Islamic Community of Spain focuses on recovering the symbolic aspects of Islam in Spanish culture. Their visibility strategies also differ, ranging from the highly symbolic opening of a strategically located mosque in the Albaicin neighbourhood of Granada, to specific communication actions like the creation of a platform, Junta Islámica's Webislam, to disseminate plural Islam and the launch of a short-lived Islamic university (Tarrés and Salgado 2010a: 304–11). Also classified under the Islam of Spanish converts are the Sufi brotherhoods of whom there are many in the Alpujarra Mountains of Granada and whose members also include Muslims from other European countries. Tarrés and Salgado looked at the establishment of these *turuq*, whose followers are located in Granada's Albaicin district and whose projects are mostly cultural, such as the Kulturhaus with its radio channel and the Naqshbandiya, which has been located in the town of Órgiva since 1990 and from there has spread to other towns in the region. This study by Tarrés remains unique.

A prominent feature of Islam in Andalusia is the presence of well-organized Muslim communities prior to the 1990s, linked with specific waves of immigration, as in the case of the Pakistanis who came to work in the lead mines of Jaen in the 1970s. A numeric minority compared to the Moroccans, the Pakistani community has been largely overlooked by researchers, except for some purely descriptive work carried out in relation to the community in Barcelona, showing the settlement process in a downtown location and the changes this has meant for the neighbourhood (Moreras 2004; Solé and Rodríguez 2004). Other relevant factors include geographic positioning, as in the case of the al-Huda mosque in Algeciras created in 1978 (a beacon for Moroccans in transit from their homeland to the European cities north of the Pyrenees), and the development of a structure of magnificent proportions and meticulous architectural design for Muslim worship on Malaga's Costa del Sol, now the area used by Saudi royals for vacations (Tarrés and Salgado 2010a).

Islam in Andalusia has been particularly affected by the waves of immigration experienced by the country since 1992, when the region's economic development began to attract Moroccan neighbours from across the Strait of Gibraltar. In this region, the religion is characterized by its ideological pluralism. Some works have highlighted the presence of specific transnational groups, like Jamaat al-Tabligh.[4] Tarrés, in her study of

---

[4] A twentieth-century proselytizing movement based on the Sunni mandate of *tabligh*, i.e. the imperative to spread faith through the propagation of the Revelation, founded by Mohamed Ilyas (1885–1944) in India. The purpose is to re-Islamize by spiritual instead of political means, using the

Tabligh in Spain, notes that Spain's proximity to Morocco has made Spain, along with Portugal, an ideal place for this group to carry out its activities, attracting Moroccans in Spain, not only in the Iberian Peninsula, but also in the North African enclaves of Ceuta and Melilla. Comprised of mostly males, there are very few Spaniards in the movement. Quantifying the number of groups is a difficult task. Jamaat al-Tabligh can be found in some mosques in Ceuta, Catalonia, Valencia, and Andalusia, but there are no mosques specifically maintained by the group. The criminal activities that some members of Jamaat have carried out in mosques in Catalonia have resulted in their actions being monitored by the state security forces (Tarrés and Jordán 2007).

In Andalusia, the large number of associations has also paved the way for federal initiatives. As in Catalonia, there is a movement to reproduce the institutional representation system in order to liaise with the local government. The Islamic Council of Granada, for example, is a local initiative that arose for the specific purpose of requesting a Muslim cemetery in the city. In this case, the goal was to recover the *Patio Musulmán*, or Muslim cemetery, of the Alhambra, an area used as a cemetery during the Spanish Civil War (1936–9). In 2002, after protracted negotiations, an agreement was signed between the city hall, the Islamic Council of Granada, and the company responsible for burials (Tarrés and Salgado 2010b: 481).

In Andalusia, the presence of women in Muslim associations is more prominent, with female members holding positions on the steering committees of groups and associations of converts, as well as running women's associations which work in collaboration with other mosques. In 2003, two associations of women converts to Islam, the Barcelona-based Insha Allah and An-Nisa, first headquartered in Granada and then in Madrid, filed a lawsuit against one of the country's best-known imams, Mohamed Kamal Mustafa, the so-called Imam of Fuengirola, a seaside resort in Malaga. This imam was sentenced to prison after a court found him guilty of inciting violence against women, following the publication of a book about women in the Koran called *Women in Islam*, published by a small publishing house in Barcelona in 2000 (Tarrés and Salgado 2010a: 343).

In February 2000, television networks from all over the world covered the events in El Ejido, in the Andalusian province of Almeria, where a race riot—a '*Moro* hunt'—took place after a young Spanish woman was killed by a mentally ill Moroccan. Acts of vandalism took place with scenes of lynching, the looting of stores run by Moroccans, and the firebombing of substandard immigrant homes being broadcast around the world. In this agricultural region, which has been intensively developed for market gardening and where workers labour in very difficult conditions, relationships between foreigners and locals became increasingly fraught. Their segregation paved the way for

---

Prophet as the reference point both in external aspects, such as attire, and internal ones. The force and simplicity of its principles have caused the doctrine to spread around the world among more socially or economically disadvantaged Muslims. The Tablighis have been criticized by Salafis, who accuse them of proselytizing, and by anti-Wahhabis, who accuse them of colluding with the Salafis, but also by defenders of socially-committed Islam, who accuse the Tablighis of being pietistic (Gómez Barcía 2009).

racist-type discourses with no religious content whatsoever, reviving distrust of the *moros* (Martínez Veiga 2001).

The development of Islam in the Canary Islands can be traced to two specific periods and two different islands. The first was in the late 1960s in Santa Cruz de Tenerife, linked with the development of a duty-free bazaar and street vending trade in the interior of the islands, and the second from the 1990s onwards in Las Palmas in connection with the construction boom and the massive arrival of immigrants. Islands like Fuerteventura and Lanzarote have a residual population of Muslims. Quantification is an arduous task owing to the difficulty of obtaining data for a highly mobile population of undocumented workers and the presence of a transitory population awaiting relocation in the case of illegal immigrants. Contreras Ortega has shown that the scattered nature of this community led to the emergence of many small local meeting centres with little power to bring people together and low levels of activity (Contreras Ortega 2008: 122–5). The study provides information on the history of the legally established communities, closely linking the presence of Moroccans in the Canary Islands to the geography of emigration from Morocco, both northern Morocco and by sea from the city of Tarfaya at its southernmost tip. In the last ten years, some cultural and educational projects directed by women have also been undertaken in the islands.

Furthermore, there is the specific case of Muslims from Senegal grouped around a socio-cultural association, Bamba Ascasac, which fosters national-religious transnationality through the religious and social activities of the Mouride brotherhood,[5] which has been studied at length by Evers Rosander (2006). The association was founded in 2005 and currently has three offices and over 600 members. The fieldwork of Eva Evers, carried out in 1996, 1998, 2000, and 2001 with Senegalese women, shows how financial contributions of women to the brotherhood earn them respect in the community in relation to men. These groups, men and women, do not attend mosques regularly and undertake religious activities such as giving talks and recitation meetings (Evers Rosander 2006).

Islam in the Basque Country, Spain's other major industrial region along with Catalonia, has been analysed by Ruiz Vieytez and his team from the Institute for Human Rights at the University of Deusto. Religious pluralism in the Basque Country, except for the presence of some Protestant churches associated with industrial expansion during the nineteenth century, is a recent phenomenon almost exclusively linked with immigration, and has developed since the 1980s alongside the institutionalization of cultural associations. The first of these was a Moroccan cultural association created in 1982. However, it was not until 1996 that the Islamic communities of the Basque Country

---

[5] Sufi *tariqa* based on the Qadiri *tariqa* founded by Ahmmadu Bamba Mbake in Senegal around 1896. This *tariqa* clashed with French colonialism because of its emphasis on manual labour and the acquisition of land. They make annual visits (*ziyara*) to holy sites. At this time, a fourth of the country's population belongs to this *tariqa*, which has undergone a process of re-Islamization brought about by urbanization and the intensity of emigration to France and North America. Their *marabouts* have travelled the world, supporting the faithful and raising money for the brotherhood (Gómez García 2009).

began to seek religious recognition and access to public funds by enrolling in the Ministry of Justice's Registry of Religious Organizations. A new approach appeared in Bilbao in 2003, with the birth of Islamic Socio-Cultural Centre of the Basque Country, aimed at enhancing the organization of the Muslim communities in the Basque Country and building relationships with Basque society, including the participation of converts and the use of Basque—one of the region's two official languages—as the language of communication. As in other regions, federal processes have been underway since 2007, leading to the introduction of Islamic religious teaching in one school, under the initiative of the Ministry of Education. Likewise, there is a movement to encourage the participation of women in these associations. The presence of brotherhoods—notably the Mourides—has also been reported in the Basque Country (De la Fuente Pereda 2011: 170–5).

In the region of Madrid, Islam essentially stems from the arrival of students and workers from majority Muslim countries, but it can also be ascribed to other social development patterns related to Madrid's status as the capital of Spain. Research into religious pluralism has been conducted by a multidisciplinary group from the Autonomous University of Madrid led by the historian and expert in Islam Bernabé López García. As in other studies, the research done in Madrid includes a parallel study of the different minority religions present in the region, focusing on their settlement, activities, education, and initiatives for dialogue and social cooperation.

In the case of Islam, Madrid is home to the two biggest mosques in the country, the Abu Bakr mosque and Madrid's Islamic Cultural Centre. The former is one of the largest Islamic complexes in the world belonging to the Islamic League. Opened in 1992, the cultural centre offers a broad programme of activities and houses a school and a funeral parlour, and is considered to be the visible manifestation of the 'Islam of the embassies'. The Abu Bakr mosque in Madrid—commonly known as *Mezquita de Estrecho* after the neighbourhood it is in—is the headquarters of one of the two large Islamic federations and forms part of a large cultural complex mostly financed by individual donations (López García et al. 2007).

Muslim communities in the region of Madrid have settled primarily in suburban areas on the outskirts of the city, as well as in downtown neighbourhoods. In Madrid, given the existence of the two large mosques just mentioned, smaller mosques have not proliferated. The most common establishment are small oratories, located close to the downtown neighbourhoods where migrant-run retail activities can be found, such as the well-known district of Lavapiés (López García et al. 2007).

In his recent study featuring young second-generation Moroccans living in Madrid's central neighbourhoods, Justin Gest examined the dynamics of integration in the host societies of young Muslims of migrant origin. Based on fieldwork, this study compares the behaviour of these youths with that of young Bangladeshis in London's East End. The Lavapiés neighbourhood of Madrid, where the young Moroccans live and hang out, features a specific open-air socialization scenario in which the street is a space shared by the inhabitants of a neighbourhood that has had very little associative fabric, both before and since the arrival of immigration. Gest ascribes these immigrants' lack of engagement in politics and their 'non-belonging' to a set of specific circumstances, namely the long legal process to obtain nationality (the basic requirement is a continuous ten-year residence period in Spain), their declared lack of time for participating in civic activities, and low levels of social trust in each other 'because of the atomised scramble for survival, but also with regard to Moroccan associations which are commonly perceived to be corrupt and self-serving' (Gest 2010: 172). There are many signs that the presence of these youths in Spain is decided on an almost day-to-day basis and their inability to decide whether to settle down here for good or return to Morocco is constantly preying on their minds. The political disorientation of these youths and, arguably, of society overall vis-à-vis their presence is not much of an incentive in terms of getting them to commit themselves one way or another (Planet Contreras 2009). As González Enríquez has pointed out, 'The majority of the immigrants in Spain are still in very precarious situations as they have been in the country for too short a period of time and this hinders any kind of civic participation. Probably belonging to a Church (Islamic, Catholic, Orthodox, Adventist) is the only "civic" activity common among immigrants' (González Enríquez 2005).

Islam in the region of Valencia was studied by a group of sociologists from the Centre for Social Integration and Migrant Training and the University of Comillas. The surveys consist of an in-depth examination of each of the communities currently residing in the region, drawing on indirect sources but also on detailed interviews with people involved in these communities, paying particular attention to what they were able to recount from memory about the communities' presence in the region. The number of Muslims who settled in the Valencia region began to grow from the 1980s onwards, not only as a result of immigration but also due to its geographical proximity to Algeria and the arrival of Algerian traders and students who settled in the region in the 1990s. The difference between the heads of the mosque and the heads of some of the services led to a clash and the creation of new groups beginning in 2004. Two different federations (the Higher Islamic Council of the Autonomous Region of Valencia and the Muslim Federation of the Autonomous Region of Valencia) came into being in a bid to enhance liaisons with municipal and regional authorities (Buades and Vidal 2007: 136–40).

Islam in Aragon has been strongly marked by the area's economic development and its transformation into a region of migration. The study of religious pluralism in this region is led by a team of professors from the Sociology Department of the University of Zaragoza. As in other regions, the pioneers of Islam were university students in Zaragoza, who maintained links with like-minded groups in Granada, Madrid, and Valencia. The initiatives that have been developed in Aragon are similar to those in these other regions and the diversification of activities in these associations is due to immigration, family reunification, and conflicts related to maintaining leadership in the community against the local authorities (Gómez Bahillo and Franco de Espés 2009: 268–70).

Other research studies have focused on Aragon's Muslim past to explain the continued presence of Islam in the region (Vicente 2004). A programme to teach Islam in public schools is currently being developed in Aragon in line with the Cooperation Agreement currently in force. Because religious education in Aragon comes under the jurisdiction of the national Ministry of Education—rather than the regional government—over 500 pupils receive Islamic religious education in public schools following the model designed by the ministry. These classes are requested by Muslim families and financed by public resources, although the Islamic Commission must recommend the names of the instructors (Gómez Bahillo and Franco de Espés 2009: 284–5).

The presence of Islam in Castile-La Mancha, as in other regions, is a result of economic development and, above all, its proximity to Madrid and cheaper housing prices. At the University of Castile-La Mancha, an interdisciplinary team—GRESAM—has given special emphasis to this geographical and political factor (proximity to the capital) which, when coupled with the presence of certain industries in specific areas, has increased prosperity in the region and engendered associative dynamics that are very similar to those in other regions, closely examined in the research conducted. The extensive fieldwork led to a mapping of religious pluralism in industrial zones where the presence of places of worship does not raise problems with residents.

Difficulties with finding imams willing to live in these communities permanently is also documented along with accounts of visits by imams from Qatar or those sent by the Hassan II Foundation for Moroccans Abroad, under the auspices of the Moroccan embassy.

Proximity to Madrid facilitates interaction with other communities outside the region, not only for those in positions of authority but also for youth groups. As in other regions, the ineffectiveness of the Islamic Commission of Spain and the need for effective communication with the municipal authorities has engendered new joint federal initiatives in the region (Bravo López et al. 2009).

As can be seen from the works presented here, the study of Islam in Spain has grown over the last fifteen years. Together, the studies show how immigration from countries with an Islamic majority has enhanced the visibility of the religion. The existence of a legal framework recognizing Islam, applicable nationwide, has been used with varying degrees of success by Muslim communities in their relationships with the Spanish authorities during their settlement process. This presence, closely linked with immigration and not with historical elements, is not always conducive to the creation of a positive social image.

# Islam in School and the Hijab Question

One of the most complex issues to emerge from the presence of Islam in Spain has been the teaching of the Islamic religion in schools, which has its legal basis in the definition of the Spanish state as non-denominational in the constitution of 1978 and the subsequent signing in 1992 of the Cooperation Agreement between the state and the Islamic Commission of Spain. Having Islam taught in the public schools is one of the most fundamental aspects in the struggle of Spanish Muslims for the recognition of their rights. Article 10 of the 1992 Agreement guarantees Muslim students and their parents that state schools, if requested, will impart classes in Islamic religion at primary and secondary levels, a right that may be extended to grant-assisted schools[6] as long as this does not affect their ideology. Two decades since the agreement was signed, there are still significant difficulties in the selection of teaching staff, their remuneration, and the evaluation of the teaching.

More broadly, this right to Islamic religious education has been affected by the overall debate over the presence of religion in schools. The complexity of the Spanish teaching model and the decentralization of education, as well as political resistance, have made it very challenging to institute the teaching of Islam. In effect, only children enrolled in schools in Ceuta and Melilla, as well as in some cities in Andalusia, Aragon, the Canary Islands, and the Basque Country, currently receive Islamic religious teaching in public schools. The Observatorio Andalusí annually issues an assessment of the situation and presents data on the development of Islamic religion classes in schools. Once again, the figures provided should be interpreted with caution as they reflect the total number of Muslim students in schools and not the number of families interested in receiving classes (Observatorio Andalusí 2011). For the academic year 2009/2010, the Ministry of Education hired forty-seven teachers (fourteen in Ceuta, eleven in Melilla, and sixteen in Andalusia).

The legal framework for religious education in schools made it possible for the Spanish Ministry of Education to publish a legal text on the contents of Islamic teaching in 1996 as well as an agreement on the appointment and economic conditions of the teaching staff. Twenty years later, a first textbook *Descubrir el islam* (Discovering Islam) was published by a recognized national publishing house, Akal Editions, with the collaboration of the Islamic Commission of Spain and financed by the Foundation for Pluralism and Coexistence, to give teachers of Islam materials in Spanish, in accordance with the national curriculum. The curriculum released in 1996 reflected two different approaches that emerged during discussions over the contents between the Islamic Commission of Spain and the Ministry of Education. The first sought to emphasize the philosophical and historical aspects of Islam and promoted a focus on Islam from a purely religious perspective, including teaching rituals and practices. The second considered the theological and ritualistic aspects of the religion. These objectives, contents, and orientations can be adapted to existing teaching frameworks, including or excluding the teaching of Arabic as the sacred text's language of Revelation. The primary level includes four thematic areas (Knowing the One, Eternal, and Incomparable Allah; The Revelation; The Qur'an, Sacred Book of God; The Prophet: Life, Works, and Example to Follow); the lower secondary level has two areas (Knowledge of Islam and its Principles; Islamic Ethics and Morals); and the higher secondary level contains two additional areas (Knowledge of Islam and its Principles; Society, Religion, and Economics) (Planet Contreras 2000).

---

[6] The Spanish educational system includes public schools maintained by funds from the central administration (the state and regional governments) and private schools, many of which are run by religious groups, whose funds come directly from the administration.

However, the recognition of Islam as part of the curriculum in schools has been somewhat slowed by social tensions and debates related to the presence of Muslim girls wearing the hijab in school. In 2002, the first conflict came to light after a Muslim student was expelled for wearing the hijab in a village school in the mountains of Madrid (Ramírez and Mijares 2008). The girl was first accepted and then turned away from two schools in the town, one public and the other a private religious school. Several group leaders, school authorities from the Comunidad de Madrid, and school directors participated in the debate. Although the girl was able to attend school in the end, she did not continue her studies the following year.

The conflict, as simplified by the press, contained some elements that have appeared in other conflicts on the same issue: schooling a young girl, recently arrived in Spain and with almost no knowledge of Spanish, tension between public and private schools, and mediation by a local Muslim association.

However, a detailed examination of this case reveals other fundamental problems relating to the complexity of the current school system in Spain. The need to find school places for foreign children, even when they arrive in the middle of the school year and have no knowledge of Spanish, as well as tensions between state schools and government funded private schools, have generated significant tensions. The conflict over the hijab must therefore be viewed against this backdrop. Along with resistance from schools, there is the unresolved debate over the hijab as a religious symbol—which as such would be protected by law—or as a cultural element, which would make its use subject to debate and predictably rejected by wide sectors of society (Ramírez 2011).

Conflict over the hijab has also emerged in other social domains such as photos for official documents. Several months of debate on the issue ended with the enactment of Royal Decree 1586/2009, which established that Muslim women can cover their heads and leave their face uncovered for official identity document photographs. The decree was accompanied by a ministerial edict stating that individuals should have 'the head completely bare and without dark glasses or any other garment that could prevent or make the identification of the person difficult'. However, the edict made an exception for the use of the hijab, provided the face could be easily identified.

The issue of Islamic dress does not end here. Towards the end of 2010, municipal by-laws were approved in twelve municipalities in Catalonia banning the wearing of the niqab in official buildings. As has been noted by some commentators, this trend is related less to the presence of women wearing the niqab and more to ultranationalist political groups in the complex structure of the political playing field in Catalonia and the opposition to immigration (Elizondo 2010; Guedioura 2011).

# Religiosity and Political Participation

Interest in Islam and the Muslims living in Spain has triggered a growing number of opinion surveys on the subject. In some, Spain is just one country among others (the

Pew Global Attitudes Project and the work conducted by the Council for the Moroccan Community Abroad). Others focus specifically on Muslim immigrants in Spain.

In May 2005, an initial poll was conducted by the Pew Global Attitudes Project with a view to gauging appraisals of Islamic extremism: 'Islamic Extremism: Common Concern for Muslim and Western Publics', with some of the answers subsequently used for comparative purposes in the 2006 survey. The interviews in the later survey took place in April, after the cartoon crisis in Denmark, and sought to evaluate the impact of the London terrorist attacks, the cartoon controversy, and the wars in Iraq and Afghanistan in terms of how Westerners and Muslims view one another. The questions seek general opinions of Muslims, Jews, and Christians (e.g. 'Do you have a very favourable, favourable, or unfavourable opinion of Muslims, Jews, and Christians?'), appraisals of democracy as a Western product and how the West goes about things (the 'Western approach'), current relations between Muslims and Western countries, why Muslim nations are not more prosperous, extremism, etc.

In June 2006, another report was published from the Pew Global Attitudes Project entitled *The Great Divide: How Westerners and Muslims View Each Other* which sparked media headlines stating that anti-Muslim and anti-Jewish sentiment is 'on the rise in Spain'. The survey set out to determine the extent to which images of Muslims and Westerners clash in various countries around the world, to which end 979 individuals were polled in Spain, including 402 Muslims, with a 4% margin of error for the general public and 5% for Muslims. As the research pointed out, Muslims in Spain are the least concerned about European anti-Muslim sentiment (31% say most or many Europeans have hostile attitudes compared with 64% who see only some or very few as hostile). On the other hand, nearly twice as many in the overall population (60%) see most or many Europeans as hostile to Muslims (Pew Global Attitudes Project 2006).

Both studies detected a rift, a sort of permanent failure to see eye-to-eye, with the resident Muslim community emerging as a closed community but with a positive image of the people surrounding it, who in turn come across as having a relatively negative view of the Muslim community, as the following conclusions taken from the study show:

Thirty-one per cent of the Muslims interviewed in Spain believe that Europeans are hostile to Islam and 25% report having had a bad personal experience. While 82% of Muslims in Spain say they have a favourable opinion of Christianity, only 29% of the Spanish population say they have a favourable opinion of Muslims.

Regarding the compatibility between religion and modernity, 58% of Spaniards believe that there is a natural conflict between being a devout Muslim and living in a modern society, while 71% of Muslims in Spain do not agree with this idea. There is some agreement, however, when the questions concern Christianity: 72% of Spaniards and 74% of Muslims in Spain believe that there is no conflict between being a devout Christian and living in a modern society.

Thirty per cent of the Muslims interviewed stated that they were very concerned about the future of Muslims in the country while 39% were quite concerned. Fifty-three per cent said that they supported adopting national customs while 27% preferred to be distinct from society. On the other hand, 67% of the Spaniards interviewed believed that

Muslims prefer to be distinct from society and 21% that they wish to adopt national customs. Eighty-three per cent of the Spaniards said that they associate Islam with fanaticism, 70% with intolerance, and 60% with violence.

Regarding extremism, 35% of the Spanish public is concerned about the rise in Islamic extremism in the country. A smaller percentage of the Muslim population shares this concern (21%). Five years later, Pew repeated the same study, finding very similar results (Pew Global Attitudes Project 2011).

In addition to conducting annual opinion polls on religion, referred to earlier, the Centre for Sociological Research (CIS) has also done specific research into the status of minority religions, such as Survey #2759. This was conducted as part of the CIS's collaboration with the General Directorate for Religious Affairs at the Ministry of Justice. The survey was designed and analysed by a group of sociologists under the direction of Pérez Agote and aimed at completing studies on secularization in Spain by undertaking a comparative study on the religious practices and sense of belonging among the indigenous and foreign populations in relation to secularization. The results were not analysed by religious confession, but of those polled, 50% of the interviewees were Spanish and 47.7% Moroccans and Muslims, half of whom said they had lived in Spain for more than ten years. In the interview, they were asked about topics being debated at the time the study was conducted: belief (91.6% have no doubt about their belief), religious practices and affiliation (77% are willing to give everything, including their lives, for their religion and the same percentage practise their religion at least one day a week), social dynamics in religious spaces (68% attend places of worship to practice, but 26.8% also think it is important that they meet with compatriots and family members there), interest in religion in schools (80% of the interviewees want their children to receive religious education in school), relationships between people of the same sex, the evaluation of state–religion relations, and the presence of religion in the public sphere (Pérez Agote and Santiago 2009).

In 2004, a survey entitled 'Survey of Muslims in Europe' was conducted by a research team from the Complutense University of Madrid. It was a comparative study of religious practices among Bangladeshi migrants in London, Turkish migrants in Berlin, and Moroccan migrants in Madrid. The main conclusion of the research was the existence of a sense of unity and collective identity based on national common origins but a great difference in religious beliefs and practices among different groups. Commercial and family links with countries of origin were very important in the host society (Pérez-Díaz et al. 2004). As for Moroccan residents in Madrid, 81% of the participants considered it very important 'for others to know who I really am, it is important that they know I am Muslim'; 36% said they had 'very strong' beliefs, while 20% declared that they had weak beliefs, and only 3% said they did not have any. As for daily prayers, 57% of the interviewees in Madrid declared that they pray on a daily basis. However, communal prayer is only practised by 27% of the respondents either on Fridays (14%) or for major holidays (10%).

In spring 2009, the Council for the Moroccan Community Abroad (CCME) commissioned a survey in the countries with the largest concentrations of Moroccan immigrants. This survey, which tackles the subject of religion as part of a broader social reality, is quite fascinating in that it provides a sharper image of the Moroccans living in Spain. This is significant since, though not the only Muslims of foreign origin in the country, Spanish society's conception of 'Muslims' usually corresponds with 'Moroccans'.

In this CCME survey, the Moroccans in Spain are mainly men, 40% of whom are unskilled workers at risk of not being able to find a job: 60% said they had been without work for a period of time. They come from rural areas and own land in their own country, more than in the case of Moroccans in other European countries. They do not socialize much with their host community in daily life: 75% mainly mix with other Moroccans. They have clearer ideas about returning home than Moroccans in other countries, 70% in Spain as opposed to an average 52% elsewhere. Moroccans in Spain feel more rejected by their host society than Moroccans in Germany and France but less so than those in Italy or Holland. Compared with work or housing, religion is not perceived as a particularly complex issue or an area of discrimination, with only 17% saying they found it more difficult to practise their religion, as opposed to 80% who spoke of the difficulty of finding a job and 67% of the difficulty of finding a place to live. Only 17% of those polled in Spain said it was harder to practise their religion as opposed to an average of 34% in the other countries.

Moroccans in Spain go to the mosque more frequently than Moroccans in the other countries surveyed—55% as opposed to 23% in France. Second-generation Moroccans visit mosques less than their parents than in any other country, except the Netherlands. The Moroccans in Spain do not appear to be unhappy with the quality of religious practice or places of worship: 73% consider that the Islam preached in these places is suited to the country in which they live. Appraisals of the physical characteristics and number of these places of worship are not unanimous: 58% consider them sufficient as opposed to 39% who do not. Italy and Spain are the countries where places of worship are singled out as insufficient, as well as France, but to a lesser extent. In Spain, 413 people were interviewed for the survey (CCME 2009).

Metroscopia, a social research and survey institute in Madrid, has been conducting annual polls on Muslims in Spain since September 2006 under the heading 'Barometer of opinion of the Muslim community of immigrant origin in Spain'. The most recent results were published in March 2010. Commissioned by three ministries linked with immigration and religious pluralism (Interior, Labour and Social Affairs, and Justice), the survey takes as its starting point that 'broadening our knowledge of socio-cultural and religious groups can contribute to a better understanding of these groups and mutual rapprochement' (Metroscopia 2010). The percentage of Muslims polled for the purpose of this survey broke down as follows: Moroccans 57%, Senegalese 13%, Pakistanis 11%, and Algerians 5%.

On average, the answers to the four surveys show a relatively recently established Muslim immigrant community: 50% have been living in Spain for two to ten years. Mostly workers (76%), they consider that they have adapted to the Spanish way of life and customs, an opinion held by as much as 95% of those who have been in the country over ten years. In Spain, freedom, the level of state healthcare, standard of living, and respect for beliefs are appraised in particularly positive terms (78%). In terms of personal religiosity, the survey speaks of people who consider themselves religious (7.6 on a scale of one to ten), with 41% defining themselves as seriously practising Muslims.

The study states that the way in which the Muslim immigrant community defines itself religiously more or less matches the way the Spanish population defined itself thirty years ago: in 1976, 48% of the Spanish population defined itself as seriously practising Catholics versus 22% in 2008. Thirteen per cent of the immigrants polled said they had faced obstacles in the practice of their religion; most often mentioning the lack of a mosque as being the biggest hurdle (8%). The 'social desirability' bias, which refers to a tendency to present a more favourable picture of the situation insofar as respondents often tend to exaggerate their conformity with what they perceive as socially accepted norms, is noted by Metroscopia and corrected.

The need to understand Muslim immigrants who live in Spain comes across in the Metroscopia surveys. It refers to the level of religious self-definition and religious practice among these immigrants in Spain and how this differs from that of the host population (see Table 7.3). The research tries to address the main concerns raised by the

Table 7.3 Religious definition in Spain

'In religious terms, do you describe yourself as...' (%)

| | Muslims immigrants | | | Spanish population | | | |
| --- | --- | --- | --- | --- | --- | --- | --- |
| | October 2008 (n = 2000) | July 2007 (n = 2000) | September 2006 (n = 1500) | 2008 | 2007 | 1988 | 1976 |
| Very regular practising Muslim | 49 | 49 | 41 | – | – | – | – |
| Practising Catholic | – | – | – | 22 | 20 | 31 | 48 |
| Occasional practising Muslim | 36 | 34 | 39 | – | – | – | – |
| Occasional practising Catholic | – | – | – | 31 | 28 | 27 | 29 |
| Non-practising Muslim | 13 | 16 | 18 | – | – | – | – |
| Non-practising Catholic | – | – | – | 20 | 31 | 29 | 17 |
| Non-Muslim | – | – | – | – | – | – | – |
| Unbeliever | – | – | – | 22 | 18 | 9 | 2 |
| Other definition | – | – | – | 5 | 3 | 1 | 0 |
| NA | 2 | 1 | 2 | – | – | 3 | 4 |

Source: Metroscopia, *Valores, actitudes y opiniones de los inmigrantes de religión musulmana. Cuarta oleada del Barómetro de opinión de la comunidad musulmana de origen inmigrante en España* (<http://www.mir.es/PNAC/actividades_integracion/comunidad_musulmana/Informe_2009.pdf>).

presence of foreign Muslims from the Muslim immigrants' point of view: mosques and their use, religious authority and religious loyalty/citizen loyalty, the degree of commitment to democratic values as formulated in twenty-first century Spain, and the thorny issue of the status of women in Islam.

Muslim immigrants who go to the mosque obviously do so because it is the best place to pray (87%) but also because they can find people 'from their country or who share their customs' (73%), or because they find peace of mind (84%) and can seek the advice of imams regarding the problems they encounter in their daily lives (61%). These imams are considered to be friendly (67%)—not aloof—and well integrated in Spanish society (62%). However, appraisals of whether these imams help people in adjusting to Spanish customs are not unanimous (51%).

To conclude with the scenario that emerges from the Metroscopia surveys, as stated in the accompanying notes, Muslim immigrants living in Spain unanimously believe that the Islamic faith is compatible with democracy, Spanish identity, and the secularity of the state: 94% state that violence should never be used to defend or disseminate religious beliefs; 89% that it is possible to simultaneously be a good Muslim and a good Spaniard; 87% feel that Islam is perfectly compatible with democracy and human rights; and 83% favour a state that is absolutely neutral regarding religion, without supporting or defending one religion over another.

Moreover they reject all acts of violence related to the propagation of their faith. The degree to which they identify with Spain is striking (6.9 out of ten) and with the area where they live (7.2 out of ten), but also with their country of origin (8.7 out of ten). On this occasion, the question was formulated in the following terms: 'To what extent do you identify with your country of origin? And with Spain?'

Regarding voting trends among Muslims residing in the country, it should be noted that their status as foreigners prevents them from voting and standing for election. Recent changes to the Moroccan constitution in June 2011, however, will make it possible, once the necessary legal adjustments have been made, for Moroccan residents in Spain to vote in local elections. Up to now, only the political participation of Muslims in the North African cities of Ceuta and Melilla has been studied in detail. An analysis of elections from 1986 to 1997 was carried out by Planet Contreras, working with censuses and election results at the level of the electoral colleges. In these constituencies, the appearance of political parties specifically catering to the Muslim vote (for example, the Coalition for Melilla, born out of the local elections of 1995 and with results of around 20% in the different elections) has triggered a reconfiguration of voting structures, with the emergence of other local parties and generally a disintegration of the left that has favoured conservative local governments (Planet Contreras 1998).

In the case of the Moroccan immigrants who are in the process of settling in Spain, as with immigrants from other countries, the relationship with the country of origin is very important when it comes to religious life. Since Spain is a secular state, one that is neutral in terms of religion and 'ignorant' in terms of key issues such as religious authority, countries of origin (or others, as we have seen in the fieldwork carried out) have a specific sphere of influence, such as on the preference for imams from those countries, both for everyday activities and during the month of Ramadan, and on the organization of the pilgrimage to Mecca from their country of origin and not from Spain.

When observing social dynamics among Moroccan immigrants in Spain, it appears that the political tensions and dynamics of the society of origin are present and reproduced in the migratory context. Spain is seen, for example, as a breeding ground for the development of a national project for an Islamic transnational movement such as the Moroccan movement al-Adl wa-l-Ihsan (Justice and Spirituality). In interviews on this topic, the author found that along with a commitment to the movement in Morocco, arguments were given regarding Islam's need to adapt in Spain. The interviewees were young people active in the social sphere, but not representatives of Islam in Spain on an institutional level at the time. Once established in Spain, they officially cease to belong to the movement and call themselves 'members of al-Adl wa-l-Ihsan in Spain'. In any case, although the basic political commitment to the movement is Moroccan, the movement's main objective is to adapt itself to the Spanish social and legal framework so that they can operate here (Arigita 2010).

As Tarrés notes in the case of Andalusia and as has been noted in other research, such as that focusing on Castile-La Mancha, the active presence of Moroccan groups such as al-Adl wa-l-Ihsan and the representatives of Jamaat al-Tabligh facilitates links with the specific national religious reality of the country of origin and new currents of religious practice, without harming the development of local strategies to promote their presence and participation (Tarrés and Salgado 2010a; Bravo López et al. 2009).

# Islamophobia and Public Opinion: Historical and Contemporary Aspects

For a long time, the history of al-Andalus has been presented as the history of the destruction of Spain. Medieval chronicles speak of a succession of holy wars between the Christians of Spain and the Moors to recover a lost Spain. This and other stories of the time effectively expel the Arabs and Islam from Spanish history and historiography, writing them off as the 'invaders' who were responsible for all the ills that had befallen the nation. As demonstrated by recent public opinion surveys in Spain, these arguments may be timeworn but remain extremely topical.

The eighteenth century and the Enlightenment marked a turnaround, a period in which Spain ushered in new discoveries and new discourses. Tentative initiatives were launched to reinstate the country's past history and its geographic and political relationships with Islam. Throughout the nineteenth century, Spanish historians were divided between those who wanted to give this long-standing Muslim presence its rightful place in Spanish history and those who did not. Some authors wanted to rewrite Spanish history with other protagonists in an attempt to do away with the historic injustice of always narrating [history] from the perspective of the conqueror (López García 1990). They were assisted in this task by Arabists and translators who, through their translations and studies of Arab sources, contributed to constructing an alternative history that never managed to hold sway over the dominant view projected by historians that summarized eight centuries of Muslim history in the Iberian Peninsula as a combat (López García 1990).

But it is not Spain alone that is guilty of omitting or failing to recognize the role played by the Islamic world in transmitting classical knowledge and skills to the West. Ignorance of what took place in these centuries in the Peninsula—and by extension in the Mediterranean—fuels the idea of a fracture between continents and civilizations, with the result that history must be studied in leaps and bounds. Once again, it is the Spanish Arabists who have tried to shed some light on this matter. In 1999, a new edition appeared of *Lo que Europa debe al Islam de España*, a reference work by the Arabist Juan Vernet, who makes an inventory of what culture owes to 'Spanish Arabs'. Vernet presents these centuries of history as centuries of *convivencia*—a Spanish term used to describe the period in Spanish history from about 711 to 1492 when Jews, Muslims, and Catholics in Spain lived together in relative peace—marked by permanent rivalry over control of territories, but also a period in which common ground was established in the cultural domain and, to a large extent, in the social, economic, and political spheres (Vernet 1999).

Nineteenth-century history in Spain and the difficulties of Spain's colonial adventure did little to change the prevailing negative image (Martín Corrales 2002). The Spanish–Moroccan war of 1959–60 was to accentuate the presence of Muslims as enemies, leading even such a highly respected historian as José María Jover to declare that the historic antagonism between the Spaniard and the *Moro* is 'the most intensely socialized notion of the Spaniard's historical awareness' (Jover 1986). *Moro* is the term commonly used to refer to the Muslims who live in Spain and although deemed pejorative, the *Dictionary of the Spanish Royal Academy of Language* allows any of the following definitions: '1. Native of Northern Africa bordering Spain. [...] 3. By extension, he who professes the Islamic faith. 4. Term used for the Muslims who lived in Spain from the eighth to the fifteenth century [...]'.

Deep-rooted negative sentiments towards all Muslims in close geographic proximity really became established in the twentieth century. The distrust with which the average Spaniard views what comes from the other side of the Mediterranean—from the Orient closest to home—is a recurrent element in conflicts associated with immigration and with the demands and claims of Muslim groups and their attempts to make themselves visible, as well as in bilateral relations between Spain and Morocco (Moreras 2002; Hernando de Larramendi and Planet Contreras 2003). The intensity of these discourses differs from one region to another, depending on the degree of the physical proximity and presence of the Muslim immigrants.

The question as to what extent this historic image still holds true and whether it can affect the presence of Islam in Spain today was raised in a research study conducted in 2008 by a team from the Institute for Advanced Social Studies at Spain's national research council, the Spanish National Research Council (CSIC). The research study, entitled *Discourses of Non-Muslim Spaniards on Immigrants, Islam and Muslims*, was conducted using qualitative methods with discussion groups representing the country's social and geographic diversity. Five major discursive spheres were identified in Spanish society: an intrinsically primitive and generally negative perception of Islam associated with fanaticism; the ethnic-religious *Moro* bias; incomprehension of the religiosity ascribed to Muslims (even among those who say they have no personal contacts with any Muslims); doubts concerning their capacity for integration; and the subordination of Muslim women (Desrues 2009: 8).

This research clearly shows that rejection of the *Moro* is expressed in different ways in the discourses of the non-Muslim population, who resort to a combination of mostly stereotypical and essentialist arguments, continually swinging from immigration to religion and back again. Essentially, the arguments are as follows. Firstly, the *Moros* keep to themselves, do not like outsiders, and they do not integrate easily, integration being understood by the target audience as the process of being accepted and adopting Spanish customs. Secondly, their attitude towards Spaniards denotes a lack of respect in that they continue to speak their mother tongue and they are anti-social—an attitude basically linked with financial difficulties—living as they do in severely overcrowded and cramped housing both in the country and in cities where there are many seasonal workers. Thirdly, perceptions of delinquency are also noted in association with these individuals, including the odd reference to their presence as a specific threat, citing the Madrid terrorist attacks of March 2004 in this context. Then there are arguments concerning their bad reputation, their *machismo* or chauvinism, their low educational and cultural levels and lack of professional skills. The most interesting argument, because of its link with Islam, is the 'invasion' argument consisting of a rather vague evaluation of their presence in the Peninsula, concentrated in Andalusia, one respondent even going so far as to assert that 'when they wake up, they will climb up onto the Meseta', the vast highland plateau in the centre of Spain. This invasion tends to take shape more as a scramble for space—as was the case in the past with al-Andalus, say respondents in some discussion groups—and the experience is now being repeated with Moroccan immigration. The content with regard to Islam in the construction of the *Moro* is somewhat vague, but it is important to highlight the specific use of the past, the 'myth of al-Andalus', in line with the debates of historians referred to at the outset (Desrues 2009: 124–6).

In the September 2007 survey conducted by the CIS on *Attitudes Towards Discrimination Based on Racial and Ethnic Origin*, respondents were asked whether they thought there were ethnic, religious, or cultural groups 'that don't mix with the rest of society' and what groups sprang to mind. In the results, those that can be identified as 'Muslims' are identified thus in at least four different ways: 15.7% of those polled singled out 'Moroccans, North Africans, and Algerians' as those who do not integrate; 18.2% said 'Muslims and Mohammedans'; 11.1% said 'Arabs'; and 7.9% 'Moros'. If all these identities are pooled under the label 'Muslims', it would appear that at least 52.9% of those polled were thinking about Muslims when they said there were ethnic, religious, and cultural groups that did not mix with society, a far cry from the 18.3% that said Romanians and the 17.2% that singled out gypsies.

In an attempt to separate rejection and distrust of Muslims from Islamophobic discourse, a new argument emerges on analysing the data compiled in the Elcano Royal Institute's barometer survey to gauge Spaniards' opinions and attitudes towards Islam: religious Islamophobia does not exist in Spain, but rather a growing secularism affecting all religions, with only 37% of those polled in February 2005 professing to have a negative opinion of Islam. But what does exist is a rejection of certain Islamic practices: 61% of Spaniards are against Muslim girls wearing headscarves to school. This same analysis examined another episode that has been relevant in terms of shaping the image of Islam and Muslims, this time on the basis of the debate about freedom of expression, religious freedom, and Islam sparked by the so-called cartoon crisis. The 2006 Elcano barometer shows that 90% of those polled considered Muslims to be authoritarian—10% more than two years earlier—while 68% felt they were violent, also 10% more than two years earlier. In the intervening period, the international situation contributed to reinforcing negative stereotypes of Muslims, although some data in the analysis of this crisis introduce a nuance of 'solidarity between believers': the Spaniards who identified themselves as more religious criticized the publication of the cartoons more strongly than the Spaniards who are less religious. In addition, 38% of those polled considered that the violent reaction to the publication of the cartoons was not entirely spontaneous, but manipulated by governments. The barometer does not note any irreconcilable conflict between religions or a clash of civilizations, and suggests that there are substantial differences in the broad group of Muslim countries. Spaniards are still profoundly ignorant 'even of the Muslim countries closest to Spain'. And while including Muslims as fully-fledged citizens in Spanish society does not appear to pose any particular problem, the egalitarian culture that has taken root in Spain is mirrored in criticisms of certain aspects of Islam, such as gender inequality (Noya 2007).

## Post-9/11 Situation and Radicalization

Although the 9/11 terrorist attacks against the World Trade Center shook Spanish public opinion and augmented interest in issues related to Islamic-inspired international terrorism, they aroused relatively little interest among Spanish academics. However, the attacks of 11 March in Madrid and the subsequent suicide of members of a supposed *jihadist* cell in a municipality close to the capital did generate important reactions in Spanish society, whose analysis has not yet been calmly carried out.

Muslim communities in Spain felt directly affected from the beginning by what happened. In Madrid, where the attacks took place, after the first moments of fear of reprisal, different initiatives from civil society appeared, highlighting the reaction of associations of young Muslims in the city. During the months that followed the attacks, some existing associations were revived and others created (Téllez 2008). The CSIC developed a project titled *Mourning Archive. Creating an ethnographic archive of the terrorist attacks of 11 March in Madrid*, gathering objects left at the sites of the attacks. This material, currently on loan to the Spanish Railway Foundation, could be the subject of analysis in the future (Sánchez Carretero 2011).

Early research was carried out on the socio-demographic profile of the 188 individuals imprisoned in Spanish penitentiaries between 2001 and 2005 who were suspected of being involved with *jihadist* terrorism. This first study showed that they were young men, born between 1966 and 1975, mainly migrants of North African origin, legally residing in Madrid, Barcelona, and on the Mediterranean coast, with low levels of education and few work qualifications (Reinares 2006). The study of the expert material compiled for judicial reasons, as well as the numerous police reports which had been produced by Spanish state security forces since the late 1980s, has been used to analyse behavioural similarities and differences, the use of social media, and the functioning (causes, funding, organization) of *jihadist* networks based in or linked to Spain (Jordán 2005). The presence of those involved in different *jihadist* terrorist acts in Spanish prisons has been taken as starting point for reflections on radicalization processes among this prison population, inspired by studies carried out in other countries and based on information provided by the prison authorities (Gutiérrez et al. 2008) or on extensive fieldwork carried out using questionnaires.

As has been shown, the study of the contemporary presence of Islam in Spain up to this point has focused on writing the history of the process of community formation against the backdrop of Spain's transformation into a destination for immigration. Much effort has been made to reveal the processes by which communities have constituted themselves, built mosques, and increased the visibility of this old religion now increasingly present on the country's streets. However, few studies analyse the different factors that have influenced these developments. In my opinion, the way in which negotiating the legal framework has affected institutionalization processes has not been fully analysed. The influence and dynamics of identity construction given the proximity of Morocco, a phenomenon partially studied in Arigita Maza (2010) and Planet Contreras (2011), also needs to be analysed in greater detail. Finally, more attention should be paid to the way in which this Islam has evolved in recent years in ideological terms; little is known about ideological references. Likewise, little research has been done into the identities of young Muslims, with the exception of the work by Téllez (2008).

In recent years, Spain's Muslims have found new avenues of communication and information in technology, harnessing a variety of communication tools to provide greater visibility. The creation of cyberspace has affected communities already present in the Islamic public sphere, but has also opened doors to many communities and individuals that previously had insufficient avenues or resources to express their perspectives on Islam. A look at these new means of communication demonstrates the existence of a dynamic cyberspace peopled by new actors, largely cut off from institutionalized Islam, who use the internet to show how they understand Islam and demonstrate their rejection of the dynamics of associations or the absence of women in that sphere, among other things (Guerrero Enterría 2011).

## Conclusion

As this chapter has shown, academic interest in the analysis of Islam in Spain in the contemporary period is closely linked to the presence of a new Islam, of immigrant origin, occurring at the same time as the processes of religious change experienced by Spanish society over the last thirty years. The legal framework of liberties that facilitates the institutionalization of Islam has taken different forms in different regions of the country, taking into account the needs, possibilities for dialogue, and the political dynamics provided by Spain's regional system of government. These regional dynamics have been the focus of research more than studies on a national scale.

Despite the existence of some partial studies of this historical process, a complete reconstruction of the history of the institutionalization of Islam in Spain remains to be undertaken. The fight against global terrorism sparked by the 11 September attacks has resulted in a shift in academic analysis away from transnational elements affecting Spanish Islam. Beyond questions of fanaticism and terrorism, a more detailed study remains to be done of the ideological reference points for the accommodation of Islam and its practice within Spanish society.

## Bibliography

### Social Status and Class

AAVV (2009). *Muslims in Spain: A Reference Guide*. Madrid: Casa Árabe-IEAM.

Aya, A. (2000). 'El islam del próximo milenio', *Verde Islam* 13: 50 <http://www.webislam.com/biblioteca/59344-verde_islam_13.html>.

Colectivo Ioé (2008). *Inmigrantes, nuevos ciudadanos. ¿Hacia una España plural e intercultural?* Estudios de la Fundación de las Cajas de Ahorros-Confederación Española de Cajas de Ahorro, Madrid.

Del Olmo Pintado, M. (2000). 'Los conversos españoles al Islam: De mayoría a minoría por la llamada de Dios'. *Anales del Museo Nacional de Antropología* 7: 13–40.

Del Olmo Pintado, M. (2004). 'Un efecto inesperado de la globalización: los conversos españoles al islam', in C. Ortiz (ed.), *La ciudad es para ti*. Barcelona: Anthropos, 119–34.

González Barea, E. (2003). 'El proceso migratorio de los/as estudiantes marroquíes a la Universidad de Granada: ¿Hacia una comunidad trasnacional?' Ph.D. dissertation. Granada: Universidad de Granada <http://ldei.ugr.es/cddi/uploads/tesis/GonzalezBarea2003.pdf>.

Jiménez-Aybar, I. and Barrios Baudor, G. L. (2006). 'La conciliación entre la vida laboral y la práctica de la religión musulmana en España. Un estudio sobre la aplicación del Acuerdo de cooperación con la Comisión Islámica de España y otras cuestiones relacionadas', *Revista de Trabajo y Seguridad Social* 274: 3–42.

López Barrios, F. and Hagherty, M. J. (1983). *Murieron para vivir. El resurgimiento del Islam y el Sufismo en España*. Barcelona: Argos Vergara.

Observatorio Andalusí (2011). *Estudio demográfico de la población musulmana*. Madrid: Unión de Comunidades Islámicas de España.

Planet Contreras, A. I. (2009). 'Pluralismo religioso e inmigración: ¿una propuesta de construcción ciudadana', in A. Viana Garcés (ed.), *Repensar la pluralidad. Red iberoamericana de justicia constitucional. Atlas plural*. Valencia: Tirant Lo Blanch, 63–90.

Rodríguez Magda, R. M. (2005). *La España convertida al Islam*. Barcelona: Altera.

Sánchez Nogales, J. L. (2004). *El islam entre nosotros. Cristianismo e islam en España*. Madrid: Biblioteca de autores cristianos.

Valencia, R. (2003). 'Los nuevos musulmanes', in M. A. Roque Alonso (coord.), *El islam plural*. Barcelona: Icaria-Antracyt, 361–8.

## Religion in the Public Arena

Arigita Maza, E. (2006). 'Representing Islam in Spain: Muslim Identities and the Contestation of Leadership', in F. Peter and E. Arigita (eds.), *The Muslim World*, Special Issue: *Authorizing Islam in Europe* 96(4): 563–84.

Carrascosa González, J. (2003). 'Nuevos modelos de familia y derecho internacional privado en el siglo XXI', *Anales de Derecho. Universidad de Murcia* 21: 109–43.

Colom González, F. (2012). 'Entre el credo y la ley. Procesos de "interlegalidad" en el pluralismo jurídico de base religiosa', *Revista de Estudios Políticos (nueva época)* 157: 83–103.

Contreras Mazarío, J. M. (2006). 'La libertad de conciencia y convicción en el sistema constitucional español', *Revista CIDOB d'Afers Internacionals* 77: 41–63.

Jiménez-Aybar, I. (2004). *El Islam en España. Aspectos institucionales de su estatuto jurídico*. Pamplona: Navarra Gráfica.

Labaca Zavala, M. (2005). 'El matrimonio polígamo islámico y su trascendencia en el ordenamiento jurídico español', *Noticias jurídicas* <http://noticias.juridicas.com/articulos/45-Derecho%20Civil/200501-6557171110453510.html>.

Pérez-Agote Poveda, A. (2006). 'El proceso de secularización en la sociedad española', *Revista CIDOB d'Afers Internacionals* 77: 65–82.

Pérez-Agote Poveda, A. and Santiago, J. (2009). *La nueva pluralidad religiosa*. Madrid: Ministerio de Justicia.

Planet Contreras, A. I. and Moreras, J. (2008). *Islam e inmigración*. Madrid: Centro de Estudios Políticos y Constitucionales, Colección Foro 17.

Suárez Pertierra, G. (2006). 'La ley orgánica de libertad religiosa, 25 años después', in *La nueva realidad religiosa española: 25 años de la ley orgánica de libertad religiosa*. Madrid: Ministerio de Justicia, 45–58.

## Religion in the Public Sphere

Astor, A. (2009). '"¡Mezquita No!": The Origins of Mosque Opposition in Spain'. GRITIM-UPF Working Paper Series, 3.

Bravo López, F. et al. (2009). 'Comunidades islámicas', in M. Hernando de Larramendi Martínez and P. García Ortiz (dir.), *Religion.es. Minorías religiosas en Castilla-La Mancha*. Barcelona: Icaria, 245–78.

Briones Gómez, R. (ed.) (2010). *¿Y tú (de) quién eres? Minorías religiosas en Andalucía*. Barcelona: Icaria.

Buades Fuster, J. and Vidal Fernández, F. (2007). *Minorías de lo mayor. Minorías religiosas en la Comunidad Valenciana*. Barcelona: Icaria.

Contreras Ortega, V. (2008). 'La diversidad de las comunidades musulmanas en Canarias', in F. Díez de Velasco (ed.), *Religiones entre continentes. Minorías religiosas en Canarias*. Barcelona: Icaria, 115–78.
De la Fuente Pereda, P. (2011). 'El Islam', in E. Ruiz Vieytez (ed.), *Pluralidades Latentes. Minorías religiosas en el País Vasco*. Barcelona: Icaria, 164–83.
Díez de Velasco, F. (ed.) (2008). *Religiones entre Continentes. Minorías religiosas en Canarias*. Barcelona: Icaria.
Estruch, J. et al. (2006). *Las otras religiones: minorías religiosas en Cataluña*. Barcelona: Icaria.
Evers Rosander, E. (2006). 'Sacralizing Hotels in Spain: Murid Marabuts in Motion', *Awraq. Estudios sobre el mundo árabe e islámico contemporáneo* 23: 131–52.
Gest, J. (2010). *Apart: Alienated and Engaged Muslims in the West*. London: Hurst & Company.
Gómez Bahillo, C. (ed.) (2009). *Construyendo redes: minorías religiosas en Aragón*. Barcelona: Icaria.
Gómez Bahillo, C. and Franco de Espés, C. (2009). 'El Islam', in C. Gómez Bahillo (ed.), *Construyendo redes: minorías religiosas en Aragón*. Barcelona: Icaria, 247–287.
González Enríquez, C. (2005). 'Active Civic Participation of Immigrants in Spain'. Country Report prepared for the European research project POLITIS, Oldenburg. <http://www.uv.es/CEFD/12/Spain.pdf>.
Guedioura, H. (2012). 'La forte croissance de Plataforma per Catalunya: À l'aube d'un nouveau national-populisme en Espagne?', *Hérodote. L´extreme droite en Europe* 144: 163–81.
Hernando de Larramendi Martínez, M. and García Ortiz, P. (dir.) (2009). *Religion.es. Minorías religiosas en Castilla-La Mancha*. Barcelona: Icaria.
Lacomba Vázquez, J. (2001). *El islam inmigrado. Transformaciones y adaptaciones de las prácticas culturales y religiosas*. Madrid: Ministerio de Educación, Cultura y Deporte.
López Barrios, F. and Hagherty, M. J. (1983). *Murieron para vivir. El resurgimiento del Islam y el Sufismo en España*. Barcelona: Argos Vergara.
López García, B. et al. (2007). *Arraigados. Minorías religiosas en la Comunidad de Madrid*. Barcelona: Icaria.
López García, B. and Planet Contreras, A. I. (2002). 'Islam in Spain', in S. Hunter (ed.), *Islam, Europe's Second Religion : The New Social, Cultural and Political Landscape*. Westport, CT: Praeger, 157–74.
Martínez Veiga, U. (2001). *El Ejido, discriminación, exclusión social y racismo*. Madrid: Los Libros de la Catarata.
Moreras, J. (1999). *Musulmanes en Barcelona: espacios y dinámicas comunitarias*. Barcelona: CIDOB.
Moreras, J. (2004). '¿Ravalistán? Islam y configuración comunitaria ente los pakistaníes de la ciudad de Barcelona', *Revista CIDOB de Relaciones Internacionales* 68: 119–32.
Ruiz Vieytez, E. (ed.) (2011). *Pluralidades Latentes. Minorías religiosas en el País Vasco*. Barcelona: Icaria.
Solé, M. and Rodríguez, J. (2004). 'Pakistaníes en España. Un estudio basado en el colectivo de la ciudad de Barcelona', *Revista CIDOB de Relaciones Internacionales* 68: 98–118.
Tarrés, S. and Jordán, J. (2007). 'Movimientos musulmanes y prevención del yihadismo en España: La Yama'a at-Tabligh Al-Da'wa'. *Athena Paper*, vol. 2, no. 1.
Tarrés, S. and Salgado, O. (2010a). 'Musulmanes en Andalucía', in R. Briones Gómez (ed.), *¿Y tú (de) quién eres? Minorías religiosas en Andalucía*. Barcelona: Icaria, 289–347.
Tarrés, S. and Salgado, O. (2010b). 'Espacios de culto y cementerios de las confesiones minoritarias en Andalucía', in R. Briones Gómez (ed.), *¿Y tú (de) quién eres? Minorías religiosas en Andalucía*. Barcelona: Icaria, 466–81.

Vicente, A. (2004). *Musulmanes en el Aragón del siglo XXI*. Zaragoza: Instituto de Estudios Islámicos y de Oriente Próximo.

## Islam in School and the Hijab Question

Elizondo, I. (2010). 'España y Cataluña, el desvelo de un debate no resuelvo', in W. Tamzali (ed.), *El burka como excusa. Terrorismo intelectual y moral contra la libertad de las mujeres*. Barcelona: Saga Editorial, 97–134.

Moreras, J. (2007). *Els imams de Catallunya rols, expectatives i propostes de formació*. Barcelona: Biblioteca Universal Empúries.

Planet Contreras, A. I. (2000). 'L'enseignement de l'Islam dans le système educatif espagnol', in F. Sanagustin (ed.), *Le fait religieux, est-il enseignable?* Toulouse: AFDA-Association Française des Arabisants, 229–39.

Ramírez, A. (2011). *La trampa del velo. El debate sobre el uso del pañuelo musulmán*. Madrid: Libros de La Catarata.

Tarrés, S. and Salgado, O. (2010a). 'Musulmanes en Andalucía', in R. Briones Gómez (ed.), *¿Y tú (de) quién eres? Minorías religiosas en Andalucía*. Barcelona: Icaria, 289–347.

## Religiosity and Political Participation

Arigita Maza, E. (2010). 'Al-Adl wa-l-Ihsan en España: ¿Un proyecto nacional para un movimiento islámico transnacional?' *Revista de Dialectología y Tradiciones Populares* 65(1): 113–36.

Bravo López, F. et al. (2009). 'Comunidades islámicas', in M. Hernando de Larramendi Martínez and P. García Ortiz (dir.), *Religion.es. Minorías religiosas en Castilla-La Mancha*. Barcelona: Icaria, 245–78.

Conseil de la Communauté Marocain à l'étrangère (2009). *Enquête auprès de la population marocaine résidant en Europe (France, Espagne, Italie, Belgique, Pays-Bas et Allemagne* <http://www.ccme.org.ma/fr/Evénements-du-CCME/événements-du-CCME/Résultats-de-l'étude-CCME---BVA.html>

*Estudio de opinión entre La comunidad musulmana de origen inmigrante en España realizado por Metroscopia para el Gobierno de España, Ministerio del Interior y Ministerio de Trabajo y Asuntos Sociales*, Madrid, 2006, 2007, and 2008 <http://www.oberaxe.es/files/datos/49afb64d486f3/2008%20INFORMELACOMUNIDADMUSULMANA.pdf>.

Metroscopia (2010). *Valores, actitudes y opiniones de los inmigrantes de religión musulmana. Cuarta oleada del Barómetro de opinión de la comunidad musulmana de origen inmigrante en España* <http://www.mir.es/PNAC/actividades_integracion/comunidad_musulmana/Informe_2009.pdf>.

Pew Global Attitudes Project (2006). *The Great Divide: How Westerners and Muslims View Each Other* <http://pewglobal.org/reports/display.php?ReportID=253>.

Pew Global Attitudes Project (2011). *Common Concerns About Islamic Extremism: Muslim–Western Tensions Persist* <http://pewglobal.org/2011/07/21/muslim-western-tensions-persist/5/>.

Planet Contreras, A. I. (1998). *Melilla y Ceuta, espacios-frontera hispano-marroquíes*. Melilla: Universidad Nacional de Educación a Distancia-Ciudad Autónoma de Melilla-Ciudad Autónoma de Ceuta.

Tarrés, S. and Salgado, O. (2010a). 'Musulmanes en Andalucía', in R. Briones Gómez (ed.), *¿Y tú (de) quién eres? Minorías religiosas en Andalucía*. Barcelona: Icaria, 289–347.

## Islamophobia and Public Opinion

Bravo López, F. (2005). 'Culturalismo e inmigración musulmana en Europa', in A. Planet and F. Ramos (eds.), *Relaciones hispano-marroquíes. Una vecindad en construcción*. Guadarrama: Ediciones del Oriente y del Mediterráneo, 305–51.

Desrues, T. (2009). *Percepciones y actitudes hacia el Islam y los musulmanes en España. Los discursos de los españoles no musulmanes sobre los inmigrantes, el islam y los musulmanes*. Córdoba: Instituto de Estudios Sociales Avanzados.

Guerrero Enterría, A. (2011), *e-Islam. The Spanish Public Virtual Sphere*. Electronic document <http://www.cyberorient.net/article.do?articleId=6206>.

Hernando de Larramendi Martínez, M. and Planet Contreras, A. I. (2003). 'Maroc-Espagne: la crise de l'îlot du Persil', in R. Leveau (dir.), *Afrique du Nord Moyen-Orient. Espace et conflits*. Paris: Les Etudes de la Documentation Française, 133–40.

Jover, J. M. (1986). 'La percepción española de los conflictos europeos: notas históricas para su entendimiento', *Revista de Occidente* 57: 13–42.

López García, B. (1990). 'Arabismo y orientalismo en España: radiografía y diagnóstico de un gremio escaso y apartadizo', *Awraq* 11: 35–69.

Martín Corrales, E. (2002). *La imagen del magrebí en España*. Barcelona: Bellaterra.

Moreras, J. (2002). 'Muslims in Spain: Between the Historical Heritage and the Minority Construction', *The Muslim World* 92(1–2): 129–42.

Noya,J.(2007).'LosespañolesyelIslam',AnálisisdelRealInstitutoElcano,no.105/2007<http://www.realinstitutoelcano.org/wps/portal/rielcano/contenido?WCM_GLOBAL_CONTEXT=/Elcano_es/Zonas_es/Imagen+de+Espana/ARI+105-2007>.

Vernet, J. (1999). *La cultura hispanoárabe en Oriente y Occidente*. Barcelona: El Acantilado (original 1979).

## Post-9/11 Situation and Radicalization

Arigita Maza, E. (2010). 'Al-Adl wa-l-Ihsan en España: ¿Un proyecto nacional para un movimiento islámico transnacional?' *Revista de Dialectología y Tradiciones Populares* 65(1): 113–36.

Centro Investigaciones Sociológicas (2007). Estudio no. 2731: 'Actitudes ante la discriminación por origen racial o étnico'. Observatorio Español del Racismo y la Xenofobia de la Dirección General de Integración de los Inmigrantes <http://www.cis.es>.

Gutiérrez, J. M., Jordán, J., and Trujillo, H. (2008). 'Prevention of Jihadist Radicalization in Spanish Prisons: Current Situation, Challenges and Dysfunctions of the Penitentiary System', *Athena Intelligence Journal* 3-1 <http://www.athenaintelligence.org>.

International Centre for the Study of Radicalization and Political Violence (ICSR) in partnership with the National Consortium for the Study of Terrorism and Responses to Terrorism (START) (2010). *Prisons and Terrorism: Radicalisation and De-radicalisation in 15 Countries*. London: King's College <http://www.icsr.info>.

Jordán, J. (2005). 'El terrorismo islamista en España', in A. Blanco, R. Del Águila, and J. M. Sabucedo (eds.), *Madrid 11-M. Un análisis del mal y sus consecuencias*. Madrid: Trotta, 79–112.

Jordán, J. (2009). 'El terrorismo yihadista en España: evolución después del 11-M'. Working Paper 7/2009. Madrid: Real Instituto Elcano.

Ortuño, J. M. (2006) in J. Cesari (coord.). *Securitization and Religious Divides in Europe: Muslims in Western Europe After 9/11: Why the Term Islamophobia is More a Predicament than an*

*Explanation*. Submission to the Changing Landscape of Citizenship and Security 6th PCRD of European Commission.

Pérez-Díaz, V., Álvarez-Miranda, B., and Chuliá, E. (2004). *La inmigración musulmana en Europa. Turcos en Alemania, argelinos en Francia y marroquíes en España*. Estudios Fundación La Caixa nº 15 <http://www.estudios.lacaixa.es>.

Planet Contreras, A. (2011). 'El Estado marroquí ante sus emigrantes y la ciudadanía marroquí en la diáspora'. Análisis del Real Instituto Elcano, no. 59/2011 <http://www.realinstitutoelcano.org/wps/portal/rielcano/Imprimir?WCM_GLOBAL_CONTEXT=/elcano/Elcano_es/Zonas_es/ARI59-2011>.

Reinares, F. (2006). 'Towards a Social Characterisation of Jihadist Terrorism in Spain: Implications for Domestic Security and Action Abroad'. Análisis del Real Instituto Elcano, no. 34/2006 <http://www.realinstitutoelcano.org/analisis/929/929_Reinares.pdf>.

Sánchez Carretero, C. (2011). *El archivo del duelo*. Madrid: CSIC.

Téllez, V. (2008). 'La juventud musulmana de Madrid responde: lugar y participación social de las asociaciones socioculturales formadas o revitalizadas después de los atentados del 11-M', *Revista de Estudios Internacionales Mediterráneos* 6: 133–43.

Trujillo, H., Jordán, J., Gutiérrez, J. A., and González-Cabrera, J. (2009). 'Radicalization in Prisons? Field Research in 25 Spanish Prisons', *Terrorism and Political Violence* 21(4): 558–79.

CHAPTER 8

# GREECE

VENETIA EVERGETI, PANOS HATZIPROKOPIOU, AND NICOLAS PREVELAKIS

## INTRODUCTION

CONTEMPORARY encounters with the Muslim 'Other' in the Greek context carry a loaded historical burden related to the place of the Orthodox Christian religion as a determining component of Greek national identity.[1] The roots of the relationship between nation and religion lie in Greece's Ottoman legacy and the fact that modern Greek national identity emerged initially out of the Ottoman *millet* system, i.e. the organization of non-Muslim communities along religious lines, of which the largest was the Orthodox and Grecophone *Rum millet*. Greek nationalism emerged in opposition to Ottoman Islam as the religion of the ruler, with Orthodoxy forming an essential element of 'Greekness' (Hatziprokopiou forthcoming).

One of the specificities of Greece in regard to Islam is that its Muslim population today comprises two broad groups: an indigenous Muslim minority, often referred to as the 'old' Islam, a heritage of the Ottoman period as is the case in many neighbouring Balkan countries, and Greece's 'new' Islam, which resulted from recent migrations to the country and bears similarities to Muslim communities in Western Europe. Due to the differences between these two groups, a separate section will be dedicated to each of them.

## THE 'OLD' ISLAM: THE MUSLIM MINORITY OF THRACE

The historical presence of Islam in Greece has been studied mainly by historians and political scientists who have explored the emergence of the Greek nation-state and the

---

[1] e.g. Triandafyllidou (1998); Herzfeld (2001); Trubeta (2003); Mavrogordatos (2003); Fokas (2009); Roudometof (2010); Christopoulos (2012); Tsitselikis (2012).

importance of the Greek Orthodox Church in the development of Greek national identity (Polis 1992; Triandafyllidou 1998; Koliopoulos and Veremis 2002; Psomiades 1968; Mavrogordatos 2003). In addition to these, academic studies that focus on the indigenous Muslim minority in Thrace have been written by sociologists, anthropologists, legal scientists, and educationalists. Early work on the Muslim minority in Thrace was mainly political and socio-historical in nature; it was often motivated by a nationalist agenda and reflected the state of Greek–Turkish relations (Alexandris 1991; Andreades 1956; Soltaridis 1990). Such work would often deal with the historical establishment of the minority through the Treaty of Lausanne, describe Turkish nationalism in the area of Thrace, and attempt to give a positive image of the living standards of the minority. Political developments in Greece and the turbulent relations between Greece and Turkey have always had a noticeable impact on Greek minority policies and the research produced within this context. A major shift, both in terms of policies and in academic research, came in the early 1990s, when the political and academic promotion of multiculturalism in Europe resulted in an increased European pressure to respect minority rights in Greece (Mantouvalou 2009; Anagnostou 2001). Sociological and anthropological studies on the Muslims of Thrace reflected this shift: moving away from stereotypical discourses, they started to cover a plethora of issues including the ethnic composition and political participation of the minority, legal and religious issues, and aspects of the educational system.

This section will first review the historical studies that deal with the presence and status of Islam following the establishment of the modern Greek state, then move to the research that deals specifically with the indigenous Muslims of Thrace.

## Historical Context: Islam and the Greek Nation-State

There is a long list of recent historical and political studies on the construction of the modern Greek nation-state and the role of Ottoman Islam in defining Greek national identity. During the Greek war of independence, religion was a major line of demarcation between the warring sides, as Muslims typically identified with the Ottoman Turks, and Orthodox Christians readily identified with the Greek cause (Mavrogordatos 2003: 128). Upon independence, some of the few Muslims who had remained in the freed Greek territory converted to Christianity in order keep their properties (e.g. Koliopoulos and Veremis 2002: 250). Most of them, however, had no other option than to leave their ancestral lands.

The gradual expansion of Greece in the course of the century that followed would constantly add new Muslim populations, whose status was determined by the international treaties defining borders and peace terms. With the annexation of Thessaly in 1881, 35,000–40,000 Muslims became subjects of the Greek kingdom, bringing the share of its Muslim population to about 8.2% (Tsitselikis 2004b; Immig 2009a). The Treaty of Istanbul 'defined in detail the obligations of Greece towards the Muslim community' (Ziaka 2009: 155), and included provisions for the building of a central mosque in Athens (Triandafyllidou and Gropas 2009: 963). With the annexation of the 'New Lands' at the end of the Balkan Wars in 1912–13, over half a million Muslims became citizens of the expanded Greek state (Tsitselikis 2004b). In Macedonia alone, some 475,000 'Turks' formed nearly 40% of the population in 1912, while approximately 84,000 Muslims were recorded in Western Thrace by the 1920 Greek census (Milios 2000: 224, 226). The 1913 Treaty of Athens obliged Greece 'to provide freedom of worship to its Muslims… and freedom of contact between these populations and the supreme Muslim clergy of Istanbul' (Katsikas 2009: 181) and included provisions for the establishment of mosques in Athens and in four areas in northern Greece (Triandafyllidou and Gropas 2009: 963). The 1920 Treaty of Sèvres, which established Greek administration over Western Thrace and the province of Izmir in the Anatolian Coast, following the First World War, obliged the Greek state to provide legal equality to all its citizens 'regardless of their language or religion', to respect minority rights 'such as the familial laws and customs of Greek Muslims', and to fund 'the establishment of mosques and Muslim benevolent organisations' (Katsikas 2009: 181–2).

These provisions, however, were abandoned in the aftermath of Greece's defeat in the 1919–22 Greco-Turkish War. The 1923 Treaty of Lausanne not only delimited borders anew, but also decisively reshuffled the ethno-religious landscape in both Greece and Turkey through an accompanying convention that determined a compulsory population exchange between the two countries. This exchange was done on the basis of religion, understood as a criterion of ethnicity: as a result, an estimated total of 350,000– 500,000 Muslims were defined as Turks and forced to leave Greece for Turkey; up to 1.5 million Orthodox Christian citizens of Turkey were defined as Greeks and had to follow the reverse path (Baldwin-Edwards and Apostolatou 2008; Katsikas 2009; Greenfeld and Prevelakis 2010: 2527).

This exchange of populations made an exception for the Muslim minority of Thrace, which was considered permanently established in Greece, and which will be addressed in detail in the next sub-section. The Treaty of Lausanne conditioned the status and rights of this population. The terms of Lausanne were, however, not applied in the case of two other Muslim groups. The first comprised 25,000 Albanophone Muslims (Chams) living mostly in coastal Epirus (north-western Greece) (Baldwin-Edwards and Apostolatou 2008: 24). The Greek state had begun deporting Chams to Turkey, causing Albania's reaction and a subsequent 1924 League of Nations ruling that exempted them from the exchange. Local tensions, reinforced by the settlement of Asia Minor refugees in the area and open state repression in the 1920s and 1930s, led many Chams to collaborate with occupation forces in the Second World War (Katsikas 2009), leading to conflict with nationalist guerrilla forces (EDES) in 1944 and mass expulsions by the post-war Greek government. The second group comprised 12,000 Muslims, who were added as a result of the cession of the Dodecanese islands to Greece by Italy in 1947 (Tsitselikis 2010). From this group, 7,000 'Turks' live today in the islands of Kos and Rhodes; they have a 'semi-minority' status, which excludes young men from compulsory military service, and allows the construction of mosques and the administration of *vakif* properties (Tsitselikis 2007).

Today, Muslims of Greek citizenship number roughly 110,000: 80,000 in Thrace, 15,000 in Athens, 5,000 in Thessaloniki, and 7,000 in Rhodes and Kos (Tsitselikis

2004b: 406; Tsitselikis 2007). However, figures vary and are even more complicated by the lack of official data. For example, Hüseyinoglu (2010) estimates their number at 145,000, whereas others speak of approximately 120,000 people (Evergeti 2006; Mantouvalou 2009).

## The Muslim Minority of Thrace

Many scholars have written on the Muslim minority in Greece in comparison with similar minorities in other Balkan states and have studied it within the context of wider historical and socio-political developments in the area.[2] For example, Immig (2009b) has explored the situation of Muslim populations in Greece between 1881 and 1886—the very beginning of the establishment of the Greek nation-state. Katsikas (2009) has given a detailed historical exploration of Islam in the Balkans and the multiethnic and linguistic character of the Muslim populations which were established in the area during and after the Ottoman times (see also Mentzel 2000).

Other studies which have looked at the Muslim minority within the wider historical context of collections provide very general outlines of the Muslim communities of Thrace, although they do offer an important insight into the Greek national culture and the way in which religious, ethnic, and linguistic minorities are treated in Greece. In particular, Renee Hirschon (2003) edited a volume which deals with the exchange of minorities between Greece and Turkey and its political and socio-historical effects on both countries. Hirschon argues that although the Lausanne Treaty had often been used as a reference in international politics and had thus set a precedent for subsequent population displacements, its serious effects on the two countries had not yet been fully explored. To fill this gap, the chapters by Hirschon (2003) and Oran (2003) deal with the various problems that the Muslim communities faced, both in the aftermath of the exchange and afterwards. According to Hirschon, the consequences of the population exchange for Greece were much greater than for Turkey. According to the author, the population exchange 'constituted a major humanitarian emergency... which resulted in an on-going process of long-term economic, political, cultural and social adjustment and assimilation... For the tiny Greek state, a nation totalling 4.5 million, the influx represented a massive increase by one-quarter of its population in just two years' (2003: 14). The aforementioned volume also describes how the Muslim communities in Western Thrace became a small minority in the area: their official status was determined in religious (Muslim) rather than linguistic or ethnic terms. Their rights were regulated by an international treaty and, as a result, their situation was influenced by tensions between Greece and Turkey. According to Oran, those exempted from the population exchange were never accepted by their host countries as part of the nation and 'have always been

---

[2] For an elaborated discussion on minorities in the Balkans see Poulton (1994). Poulton provides an extensive coverage of the history of the area and its respective states and minorities.

forced to live a separate life, sometimes subjected to harassment' (2003: 101). They were always viewed as the enemy, or the 'other within'.

More recent historical research on the minority has unravelled very important aspects of the area and its peoples, whilst exploring various socio-political developments that affected the minority at important historical times. For example, a recent study (Featherstone et al. 2011) explores the minority's role and position during the 1940s, one of the most turbulent decades in Greek history due to the Second World War and the Greek civil war that followed. It explains why Muslims remained loyal to Greece during these difficult times of war, based on an impressive analysis of archives and official documents. By placing the minority within its local context, rather than within the context of Greco-Turkish relations and wider geopolitical developments, the authors found that a number of important factors worked together and resulted in the minority's passivity during the Second World War and the Bulgarian occupation. Turkey's 'active neutrality' towards the minority's plight during the war, the decision, by many, to flee to Turkey, and, more importantly, the absence of a common ethnic identity and shared interests within the minority, were some of the main reasons which explain why the Muslims in Thrace remained royal to Greece and largely passive during the war.

## Ethnic Composition and Demographic Description of the Minority

The ethnic composition of the minority is one of the most extensively covered issues in Greek, but also Turkish and Bulgarian (Neuburger 2000) studies. It is also the most controversial topic within academic and political circles in Greece, both at a local and national level. Influenced by the Ottoman *millet* system of governance, the Treaty of Lausanne recognized the minority as a religious (Muslim) group. However, the minority consists of three different ethno-linguistic groups: Turks, Pomaks, and Roma. The formation of their diverse identities has not been without tensions and conflicts, especially for the Turks, part of whom (especially the educated elite) identifies with the secularism of Kemalist Turkish politics. The question of whether the Muslim minority of Thrace should be viewed as a homogeneous religious community or as a set of diverse ethno-linguistic groups, has been debated for many decades in Greece (see Evergeti 2006, 2011; Molokotos-Liederman 2007; Borou 2009; Meinardus 2002).

Thrace has often been described as a politically and nationally sensitive area by both academics and politicians (Borou 2009; Yiakoumaki 2006). The presence of a Muslim minority close to the Turkish borders has been seen as problematic and the two countries have strived to present it under two antithetical homogenizing titles: as 'a unified Muslim minority' according to the Greek official discourse and as 'one Turkish minority' according to the Turkish discourse (Demetriou 2004; Evergeti 2006).

Political factors as well as issues related to language, ethnicity, and religious practice are all intertwined, making this a very complex situation (Dragonas 2013). The ethnic Turks are the dominant group within the minority not only because of their number

(56,000) but also because of the socio-historical and political developments in the area. The Pomaks (38,000) and the Roma (18,000) thus face the problem of being a minority within a minority. For the Pomaks, this problem became apparent during the Greek civil war, when they were regarded as 'the fifth column of Bulgaria and of Communism' (Brunnbauer 2001: 48). This image of them was probably wrong, as many Pomaks were persecuted by Bulgaria and supported the Greek annexation of Thrace (Michail 2003; Featherstone et al. 2011).

In general, the Pomak population is concentrated in the mountainous regions of Rodopi and Xanthi, while the Turks live in the plains, and the Romas mainly in villages around the urban centres (Ziaka 2009: 147). Most members of the Muslim minority are farmers, employed in agriculture (mainly tobacco) or raising livestock. Despite the fertile soil, the region remains one of the least developed in the EU (Antoniou 2003: 164). This underdevelopment has led to an 'internal migration' towards the major cities of Athens and Thessaloniki, where the Muslims (mainly from the Pomak and Roma groups) find work as labourers, technicians, and street vendors (Evergeti and Hatziprokopiou forthcoming a and b). Only recently have some Muslims begun working in the public sector, and their number remains quite small (Tsitselikis 2004a: 86).

Recent ethnographic studies in Thrace have shown that there exists an inner hierarchy among the Muslim populations of the area. Those who claim to have a Turkish origin often look down on the other two groups and try to impose a unifying Turkish ethnic origin on the entire minority (Evergeti 2006). The Pomaks come second. They are often seen as the most religious of the three groups and have a very traditional lifestyle. Ethnographic work has confirmed that religion is one of the most important elements in their self-definition and that, in the remote Pomak villages, their dress remains religious, with headscarves for young girls and women and the small white cap for boys and men (Trubeta 2001; Evergeti 2006; Michail 2003). The Roma come third in the 'hierarchy' and are in many instances socially excluded from the other two groups (Mavromatis 2005).

The origin of the Pomaks is obscure and has been interpreted differently by Bulgarian, Greek, and Turkish historians,[3] reflecting the fact that each country has tried to claim the 'origin' of this Slavophone group. Anthropological research has shown that Pomak-ness is generally attributed to the Muslim populations of the Rodopi mountains (Tsibiridou 1994; Demetriou 2004; Fragopoulos 2007). However, as Demetriou has argued '... it is the move out of the mountain and into the valley villages that caused Pomaks to become differentiated' (2004: 104). In other words, their difference gained a historical and ethnic substance and became more apparent once they started moving away from their remote villages in the mountains of Rodopi and mixing with the Turkish part of the minority in the urban areas of Thrace. Some members of the minority's Turkish political elite have even accused the Greek state of trying to weaken the Turkish presence in the area of Thrace by dividing the minority into these three ethnic groupings and by 'celebrating' the Pomak distinct culture and language. Pomak origin and language is often seen by

---

[3] On the different views on the Pomaks' origin see Seyppel (1989: 41–9) and Hidiroglou (1991).

leading members of the Turkish community as a sign of inferiority. Anthropological studies have shown that many Pomaks will subsequently try to diminish or deny their Pomak identity when interacting with Turkish members of the minority (Demetriou 2004; Michail 2003). Their public denial is the result of years of ridicule which they have experienced, coming mainly from local Turkish urbanites (Trubeta 2001; Demetriou 2004).

Ethnographic research indicates that Pomak identity is largely locally-specific and gains rigidity in social interactions with other members of the minority, thus resulting in boundary formations and constant negotiation of what comprises Pomak-ness (Michail 2003; Evergeti 2006). This negotiation is in fact quite complex. For example, in their social encounters with urban Turks, many Pomaks define themselves as Turks instead of Pomaks (Demetriou 2004); on the other hand, anthropological studies of the Pomak mountainous villages (Michail 2003; Tsibiridou 1994; Fragopoulos 2007) and recent studies on Pomaks who have migrated to Athens (Evergeti and Hatziprokopiou forthcoming a and b) show that when among themselves, Pomaks display their Pomak-ness openly. Although the whole of the minority is unified under the umbrella of Sunni Islam, studies focusing on religious trends in Thrace have shown that many Pomaks follow the Bektashi mystical order.[4] The secularist, Kemalist leanings of the Turkish state have not always sat well with Muslims (especially Pomaks) in Thrace, who tend to be conservative and traditional (Michail 2003: 141). According to Karakasidou (1995) 'the clash between Islamist religious leaders and Kemalist reformers in Thrace focused on competing notions of transnational religion and secular nationhood'. This created internal tensions within the three groups of the minority, with the more 'progressive' Turkish group pushing for religious and language reforms following the national Turkish model.

Antoniou (2003) confirms that the three ethnic categories are not clearly defined. He points out that 'most Pomaks and Gypsies usually view themselves as Turks and state that they belong to the Turkish ethnic group because, for these Pomaks and Gypsies, Turkish identity offers a higher social status' (Antoniou 2003: 155). He allows that this tendency may be partially driven by the minority education system, which prioritizes Turkish over Pomak. Michail makes a similar point about the Pomaks, suggesting that 'their Muslim religion, their Slavic language, their socio-economic marginalization over a long period of time, and the fact that they have ethnically been claimed by three different countries, have created a rather movable situation and a flexible ethnicity, which adapts to a variety of inter-group interactions and corresponding changes in their environment' (Michail 2003: 144).

The Muslim Roma, also referred to as Gypsies or Athiganoi in academic and public discourse, are primarily a nomad group, moving from town to town depending on seasonal agricultural work in the fields. This being said, there are also permanent Roma settlements around the town of Komotini. Their inhabitants speak the Greek and Turkish languages together with their own dialect of Romany. They are

---

[4] For an exploration of Bekashism in Western Thrace see Zenginis (1988).

considered to be the least religious of the three groups of the minority and have been subjected to racial prejudice both from within the minority and from the wider Greek society. It was very rare for early research on Thracian Muslims to include a detailed study of the Roma group. This is because, in contrast to the Pomaks, there was very little national interest in superimposing an ethnic origin on the community of the Muslim Roma. Although there are no systematic surveys on discrimination, current research has revealed that due to prejudices and stereotypes, the Roma are one of the most marginalized and socially excluded groups in Greece (Mavromatis 2005; Trubeta 2001, 2008; Zenginis 1994). This exclusion has created a culture of low educational achievement and of lifelong unemployment. In his study of Kalkantza, a small settlement of Roma people outside the town of Komotini, Mavromatis (2005) examined how the educational system reinforces the multiple layers of exclusion experienced by children and young people from the community.

The Roma ethnic identity is very fluid. In an attempt to escape the negative stereotypes and social exclusion that it attracts, Roma display multiple or plural identities, often claiming an ethnic Turkish identity and/or a dominant Greek one (Mavromatis forthcoming; Ioannidou 2009), depending on the social context. In comparison to the other two groups, their relationship with their religion is not strong. Recent research of Thracian Muslims in Athens has shown that, whereas Pomaks have strong community networks which are reinforced through their religious organization, Muslim Roma in Athens have little knowledge of their religion and very rarely practise it (Evergeti and Hatziprokopiou forthcoming a and b). Their marginalization and resulting stigmatized identities are reinforced within the Athenian urban space (Avramopoulou and Karakatsanis 2002).

## Legal Status and Greek Minority Policy

As mentioned in the sub-section on Ethnic Composition and Demographic Description of the Minority, the basic document defining the legal status of the Muslim minority is the Treaty of Lausanne. Together with the Greek constitution, the European Convention of Human Rights, and special legislation passed in accordance with the Treaty's premises, it still forms the basis of minority protection today. There has been a plethora of studies on the minority from a legal perspective. Tsitselikis (2004b, 2006) and Christopoulos (2000) have provided extended analyses of the legal status of Islam in Greece especially as regards the historical minority. Baltsiotis and Tsitselikis (2001) have also put together a collection of all the laws and relevant legal documents on minority schools which have passed in the Greek parliament since the signing of the Treaty of Lausanne.

Islam is legally recognized as an official religion in Greece but provisions for Muslims only exist in the area of Thrace. The Greek law stipulates that Islam is taught in minority schools (Baltsiotis and Tsitselikis 2001), and recognizes the existence of Muftis and mosques in the three provinces of Thrace, but these requirements are always specified and safeguarded by law only in relation to the Muslim minority of the area.

As Greek citizens, Muslims in Thrace enjoy full civil rights, including the freedom to establish political parties, vote, and run for office (Antoniou 2003: 163). Muslims are well represented at the local and municipal level. Aarbakke's (2000) work on the political organization and representation of the minority provides a detailed historical analysis of the political trends over the years and the inter-ethnic differences and polarizations within the minority. For instance, he shows in a systematic way how the minority's political organization has been characterized by internal religious and ethnic oppositions between the conservative Muslims and the modernists who adopted Kemalist reforms (Aarbakke forthcoming).

Prohibition against discrimination and freedom of religion are provided for in articles 5 and 13 of the Greek constitution. Freedom of the press is guaranteed, a variety of minority newspapers and magazines are published (Aarbakke forthcoming), and Muslim Greeks of Thrace have the right to use their own language in the courts' oral proceedings. However, although such freedoms and provisions are officially recognized, Thracian Muslims and especially members of the Turkish community have often been treated as the 'others within' (Triandafyllidou and Paraskevopoulou 2002). For example, although they have the legal freedom to establish their own associations and unions, they are not allowed to officially call these 'Turkish'. This has created serious tensions both within the different groups of the minority and between them and the Greek state. It has also resulted in intensified efforts by the minority's elite to unify the whole minority under an ethnic Turkish identity.

Interestingly, during the Cold War, Greek authorities had pursued an aggressive policy of 'Turkification', hoping to encourage Muslim Greeks to identify with Turkey, a NATO ally, rather than communist Bulgaria. However, with rising tensions between Greece and Turkey over Cyprus, Greece changed its tactic and refrained from defining the Muslims as 'Turks'. According to various studies (Antoniou 2003; Karakasidou 1995; Evergeti 2006; Aarbakke 2000), fears emerged that Western Thrace could become 'a second Cyprus'. Indicative of such fears is the fact that Muslims of Greek citizenship were often denied re-entry to Greece if they left the country for a temporary period. Article 19 of the Greek Nationality Law stated that 'a person of non-Greek origin who leaves Greece with the intention of not returning, may be declared as having lost Greek nationality' (Christidis 1996: 159). A significant change in Greek minority policies occurred in the early 1990s when Greece received international pressure to respect minority rights (Mantouvalou 2009; Anagnostou 2001). According to Yakoumaki, 'the year 1991 marked a turning point, when Greece introduced "*isonomi'a*" (equality before the law) and "*isopoliti'a*" (equal civil rights) for all Greek citizens of Thrace, on the initiative of Prime Minister Konstantinos Mitsotakis' (2006: 148). Greece's integration into the EU coincided with the emergence of a plethora of important studies on ethnic and national identity, migrants and minorities, nationalism and cultural diversity in Greece (Triandafyllidou and Paraskevopoulou 2002; Christopoulos 2000; Fragoudaki and Dragonas 1997, to name but a few). These studies raised awareness of the complex socio-political and cultural issues surrounding migrant and minority identities and situated the case of the indigenous Muslims in Greece within the wider context of European reforms.

The Muslim minority in Thrace has a unique judicial system, with origins in the Ottoman *millet* system. Formally established by Law 2345 of 1920, this system establishes one-judge courts, presided by the local Mufti, which resolve disputes in matters of inheritance or family according to the Islamic law (Tsitselikis 2004b: 417). Some legal scholars (Mekos 1991, 1995) have raised concerns that the Islamic jurisdiction and legal decisions of the Muftis are often unconstitutional because they contradict the Greek legal system, and are particularly detrimental to women. This is allegedly the case in matters pertaining to child custody, divorce, and inheritance. However, the Muftis' decisions are not legally binding unless validated by the Greek judicial authorities. Ioannidou (forthcoming) points out that in all the three prefectures of Thrace, the Mufti's decree must be validated by the local First Instance Courts. Many scholars point out that following a family and inheritance legal system based on Islamic law rather than the laws passed in the Greek parliament intensifies gender inequalities and reinforces the social exclusion of the minority. In particular, there are concerns that women are forced to submit to Islamic law, which often privileges males: for instance, under Islamic law, men can obtain a divorce much more easily than women (Mekos 1995; Tsitselikis 2004a: 104). However, some ethnographic research has shown that formal Islamic rules are typically adapted to local customs. Ioannidou's (forthcoming) ethnographic work on divorce rates and cases in the area has shown that the rate of *talaq* divorces (initiated by men) has been much lower than *khul* ones (initiated by women). This fact is due to a local socio-cultural specificity: under a *talaq* divorce, the man has to compensate his wife, whereas under a *khul* divorce, he does not (Ioannidou forthcoming).

## The Organization of Mosques and the Role of the Muftis

There are currently approximately 300 mosques in Thrace. We do not have any systematic studies on their current state, but there are numerous references to the role of local Imams and mosques in anthropological studies of minority villages (Michail 2003; Evergeti 2006). Some scholars have explored the topic from a legal perspective (Tsitselikis 2004; Mekos 1995). In this tradition, Kurban and Tsitselikis's (2010) study of the minority *waqfs* in Greece and Turkey provides a detailed historical analysis of the legislation about Muslim properties in Thrace, where imams are employed by the government but selected and paid (out of *waqf* income) by the local Muftis.

One of the biggest controversies regarding the religious organization of the minority concerns the election versus appointment of the Muftis. Officially, Muftis are civil servants, just like priests of the Orthodox Church. Since 1985, Muftis have been appointed by the state, through a Presidential Decree of the Greek government, after nomination by the Greek Ministry of Education and Religion. There are currently three state-appointed Muftis, one for each prefecture of Thrace. However, many Muslims in the area believe that they should be allowed to elect their Muftis as is done in Bulgaria and the Former Yugoslav Republic of Macedonia, though not in most Muslim-majority countries, including Turkey (Tsitselikis 2004b: 417). Turkey, however, does not recognize the state-appointed Muftis in Western Thrace (Tsitselikis 2004a: 93). This tension came to head in 1990, when people from the minority organized their own unofficial elections in Komotini and Xanthi. As a result two 'independent' Muftis were elected locally, in addition to the three state-appointed. The elected Muftis were eventually convicted on charges of engaging 'pretension of religious authority'. They appealed to the European Court of Human Rights in Strasbourg, which found that the Greek Court's appeal to a 'pressing social need' was 'not justified in the circumstances', and that Greece was therefore in violation of article 9 para 2 of the European Convention on Human Rights, which stipulates that 'freedom to manifest one's religion or beliefs shall be subject only to such limitations as are prescribed by law and are necessary in a democratic society in the interests of public safety, for the protection of public order, health or morals, or for the protection of the rights and freedoms of others' (Tsitselikis 2004b: 419). At the time of writing the situation has not changed and there are still two independent and three official state-appointed Muftis in Thrace.

The controversy over the elected (also called '*pseudo muftis*') versus the state-appointed Muftis has also revealed the political tensions and religious differences within the minority. For example, the state-appointed Mufti of Xanthi is from a Pomak village and has studied in Saudi Arabia and Iraq, whereas the elected one (up until 2006) was an ethnic Turk who had studied in Turkey. Borou (2009) points out that the elected Muftis were supported mainly by the Turkish section of the minority and were elected with non-representative procedures and by a show of hands in some mosques in Thrace.

# Education

Articles 40 and 41 of the Treaty of Lausanne have given the Muslim minority of Western Thrace the right to establish and manage educational institutions in any language of instruction (Ziaka 2009: 166). In practice, Turkish and Greek are the main languages of minority instruction, while Pomak and Roma are underemphasized. The use of the Turkish language has no doubt been aided by Turkey's involvement with minority education (starting with a bilateral Greek–Turkish Agreement in 1968), through the supply of books, funds for school construction, and education of teachers (Ziaka 2009: 166). This fact has spurred concerns within the Greek state about a possible 'Turkification' of the Muslim Greek minority. Öktem (2010) alleges that, 'especially in the 1980s, the Greek state has tended to endorse education in Pomak to counter-act the weight of Turkish'. This view has been supported by other researchers who have explored and analysed the state's interest in reviving and promoting the Pomak language (Mantouvalou 2009).

Minority education includes elementary and high schools. There are no legislative measures for nursery schools/kindergartens; as a result, most Muslims attend public Greek-language kindergartens. Despite an abundance of minority primary schools, only two minority high schools remain, leading many students to either attend Greek schools or emigrate to Turkey in order to complete their secondary education. Muslim instructors teach in Turkish, while Christian teachers teach in Greek. Muslim teachers are trained at a two-year programme at the Greek state's Special Academy of Thessaloniki, while their Christian colleagues graduate from a four-year programme at the University Departments of Primary Education—an often-noted disparity (Tsitselikis 2004b: 424, 425)

Since the 1990s, Muslims of Greek citizenship have had increasing access to tertiary education, thanks to an affirmative action policy enacted by the Greek Ministry of Education, which reserves 0.5% of admission slots at universities and institutes of higher technical education for the minority (Ziaka 2009: 149). However, it is still very difficult for minority students to enter higher education in Greece (Tsitselikis 2004a: 99), mostly due to 'socio-economic and language issues'; official statistics show that, from 1996 to 2002, less half of the 400 seats reserved for Thrace's Muslims were actually filled by students from the Minority (Tsitselikis 2012: 503).

One of the biggest reforms in the minority education came in 1997 with the Programme for the Education of Muslim Children (known in Greek as PEM) (Dragonas and Fragoudaki 2006, 2008). This programme was initially introduced in order to improve Greek language skills among pupils in Muslim minority schools, and therefore facilitate their integration within the wider Greek society (Mantouvalou 2009). Since its beginnings, it has employed more than 100 experts from a variety of disciplines who have organized and implemented training seminars for minority teachers, rewritten Greek textbooks for minority high schools, and sought to take seriously into account the needs of the children of the minority whilst attending to their diverse linguistic and cultural identities.

## Greece's New Islam: Recent Muslim Immigrants

In addition to the indigenous Muslims of Greek citizenship, Greece has been, during the last decades, the recipient of a significant number of Muslim economic immigrants and refugees. Considering the novelty of immigration in that country, academic studies on Greece's 'new' Islam and Muslim migrants have been limited to date. The main perspectives come from sociological studies, and to a lesser extent from anthropology, political science, and human geography, though one often encounters interdisciplinary approaches. One could classify the state of the art in relevant research under the following four categories:

The first category deals with *the general relationship between religion and immigrants in Greece*. This remains a marginal topic, with just one known study so far (Hatzopoulos and Kambouri 2010) and a few others where aspects of religion feature as minor issues (e.g. Hatziprokopiou 2006: ch. 8; Petronoti and Papagaroufali 2006; Noussia and Lyons 2009).

The second category entails research on *immigrants from Muslim countries* with no particular focus on religion. One finds information on the background of these migrant populations in terms of migratory history, work, legal status, social incorporation, language, and identity. One encounters overviews of official data on immigrants from Asian (Tonchev 2007) or Muslim countries (Baldwin-Edwards 2008), as well as studies on specific groups, such as Egyptians (Iosifides and King 1998; Gogonas 2010), Pakistanis (Broersma and Lazarescu 2009; Leghari 2009; Salvanou 2009; Kambouri 2009; Liakos and Salvanou 2010), Bangladeshis (Broersma and Lazarescu 2009; Fouskas 2012), and various refugee communities including Iraqis (Wanche 2004), Turkish and Iraqi Kurds (Papadopoulou 2003), Palestinians (Mavroudi 2007), and Afghanis (Bathaïe 2009).

The third category encompasses *issues related to Islam and Muslim migrants*. One finds publications that deal primarily with legal matters (e.g. in respect to religious rights) and general overviews of the place of Islam in the Greek public sphere and public discourse (Tsitselikis 2004a, 2004b, 2009, 2010, 2012; Triandafyllidou 2010; Anagnostou and Gropas 2010). Some studies in this category specifically address the construction of a central mosque in Athens, with varying foci and methods ranging from ethnography (Antoniou 2010) to discourse analysis (Triandafyllidou and Gropas 2009; Anagnostou and Gropas 2010; Skoulariki 2010). Another focus of these studies has been the representations of Islam and Muslim immigrants in public discourses. An example of these is the portrayal of Pakistani migrants in press reports and images: interestingly, while the Pakistani migrant press in Greece emphasizes narratives of success in the community, the Greek press typically shows photos of Pakistanis as victims (Kambouri 2009). Another example is the coverage of the Danish Cartoons controversy, often presented in the Greek media as an opposition between a Christian (Western) Europe and a Muslim East, with Greece belonging in the former (Triandafyllidou 2009).

The fourth category looks specifically at Muslim migrants, based on primary fieldwork research and reflecting on various *dimensions of religiosity and Islamic practice*. The pioneering 2007 study entitled 'In search for spaces of coexistence' mapped informal mosques and religious discrimination of Muslim migrants in Athens by the Centre for Support of Repatriate Migrants and Ethnic Greeks (KSPM 2007; Papantoniou 2009); it was followed by Evergeti's and Hatziprokopiou's 2010–11 project 'Islam in Greece: religious identity and practice among indigenous Muslims and Muslim immigrants' (Hatziprokopiou and Evergeti 2014; Hatziprokopiou 2014; Evergeti and Hatziprokopiou forthcoming a and b). Recent research has focused on Muslim religious organizations (Antoniou 2003, 2005; Kassimeris and Samouris 2012), South Asians' transnational religious networks (Leghari 2009), everyday rituals and transnationalism among Pakistanis in Athens (Salvanou 2009; Liakos and Salvanou 2010), as well as comparative religious and ethnic identities of Egyptians, Palestinians, and Pakistanis (Papanastasiou forthcoming).

This typology underlines the structure of this section, though not strictly. The section begins by situating the case of Muslim immigrants within the recent history of immigration to Greece, then gives an account of the state of the research regarding perceptions about Islam and Muslims in Greek society, the debates around the establishment of a central mosque in Athens, religious organizations and practice, and the identities of the Muslim populations.

## Migration to Greece: Historical Overview and Composition

Immigration to Greece is a fairly recent phenomenon. For most of its post-war history, Greece had been a country of emigration. Although labour immigrants started arriving in the early 1970s, it remained largely a transit country until the late 1980s, when new migratory flows from Eastern Europe and the former Soviet Union following the collapse of the regimes in 1989–91 transformed it *de facto* into a new major destination (Hatziprokopiou 2006). Greece's economy, characterized by a large informal sector, high seasonality of key industries such as agriculture, construction, and tourism, as well as various socio-economic developments since the 1970s (including rising prosperity and the widening of the middle classes, women's growing labour market participation, and the increased educational attainments of the youth) have left labour shortages and gaps in specific regions or sectors of the economy and created new needs for cheap and flexible labour (Cavounidis 2006).

The development of Greek immigration policy since the early 1990s gave way to an exclusionary, fragmented, and selective legal framework, distinguishing between various 'categories' of migrants partly on the basis of national identity considerations (Triandafyllidou and Veikou 2002). Differential treatment was reserved for ethnic Greek migrants, while the majority remained in an ambiguous status of irregularity for nearly a decade. It was not until 1998 that a first regularization programme was applied, followed by two more amnesties in 2000 and 2005 accompanying two subsequent Immigration Bills, which included general provisions on immigrants' integration. Almost no further steps have been taken since. A law providing access to citizenship for long-term regular migrants and the second generation has been ineffective since it was passed in 2010, while the voting of a new framework for asylum in 2011 has not yet been put into practice. This, together with Greece's obligations arising from the Second Dublin Regulation,[5] is keeping many newcomers in a limbo of irregularity and hardship, at a time of deepening crisis and rising xenophobia.

A first, and major, flow of immigrants came from neighbouring Albania, while a second one included ethnic Greek migrants originating mostly from former Soviet republics. These two waves dominated the picture throughout the 1990s and still weight much today. Since 2005, international geopolitical currents and shifts in the entry

---

[5] The Second Dublin Regulation establishes the criteria for determining the member state which is responsible for examining asylum applications by non-EU nationals. These criteria have to do with the location of the applicant's family, the country that has issued the applicant's visa, and/or the country through which the applicant has entered the European Union. This means that Greece cannot send asylum-seekers who fall under its jurisdiction to other European countries; and that asylum-seekers who are caught attempting to move from Greece to another European country are sent back to Greece.

channels into the EU have directed growing waves of immigrants from more distant lands of Asia and Africa into Greece, either as a final destination, or as a transit country towards some wealthier European state. It is very probable that the recent economic crisis in Greece has led many settled immigrants to return to their home countries or re-migrate, though no academic evidence is available to document the existence of such trends.

In terms of numbers, the 2001 census recorded 761,191 foreign nationals living in Greece, corresponding to roughly 7% of the country's population.[6] Around half of them were between 20 and 39 years old; more than half declared that they had migrated for economic reasons; 57.5% had come from Albania, nearly 20% from other Balkan, East European, and former Soviet countries, and some 13% from the EEA, North America, and Oceania. Anagnostou and Gropas (2010: 92) report on data on the 'religious denominations' of immigrants. They argue that Muslims form nearly 30% of the total, but it remains unclear how the authors came to this number, since no official statistics on religious beliefs are recorded in Greece. In fact, nationality-based statistics provide the only proxy for any estimation.[7] The 2001 census registered nearly 52,400 immigrants from predominantly Muslim countries,[8] about 7% of the total migrant population. Around 23,620 of those were from Mediterranean countries, another 9,450 from elsewhere in the Middle East, and nearly 16,000 from South Asia. The five most numerous nationalities—namely Pakistanis, Bangladeshis, Egyptians, Syrians, and Iraqis—formed a share of 4.7% of the total number of immigrants. Data from other sources towards the end of the decade are indicative of their growing proportions: these five groups account for 7.3% of the migrants holding a residence permit in August 2007; 7.7% of the foreign labour force in the third quarter of 2009; and 8.2% of the foreign workers registered with IKA, Greece's largest social security fund, in June 2011.[9]

By 2008, estimates brought the total number of legal immigrants to about 1–1.1 million people, including 700,000 third country nationals and EU citizens, at least 150,000 naturalized 'repatriates' from the former Soviet Union, and nearly 200,000 ethnic Greek Albanians subject to a special legal status (Gropas and Triandafyllidou 2009). The turnaround of the mid-2000s weights substantially in the emerging picture: Figure 8.1 presents official data on 'undocumented aliens' apprehended by Greek police and border authorities in the past decade.[10] Evidently, numbers double in the second half of the

---

[6] Detailed data on immigrants from the recent census of May 2011 have not yet been made publicly available.

[7] Nationality statistics should be considered safe enough in migration research in Greece with respect to the novelty of immigration and the limited access of immigrants and their children to naturalization.

[8] These include countries with more then 50% Muslim population (according to the CIA World Factbook: <http://www.cia.gov/library/publications/the-world-factbook>, accessed 15 June 2012).

[9] Residence permit data are from Maroukis (2008: 5–6, tables 1 and 1a); data on foreign workers come from Labour Force Survey statistics (multiple years) kindly provided by the Greek Statistical Authority; insurance data are from the IKA website (<http://www.ika.gr>, accessed 25 June 2012).

[10] Data on apprehensions (i.e. arrests) should be treated with caution; they may be indicative of migratory trends, but not of actual numbers, since they depend on the extent and efficacy of policing

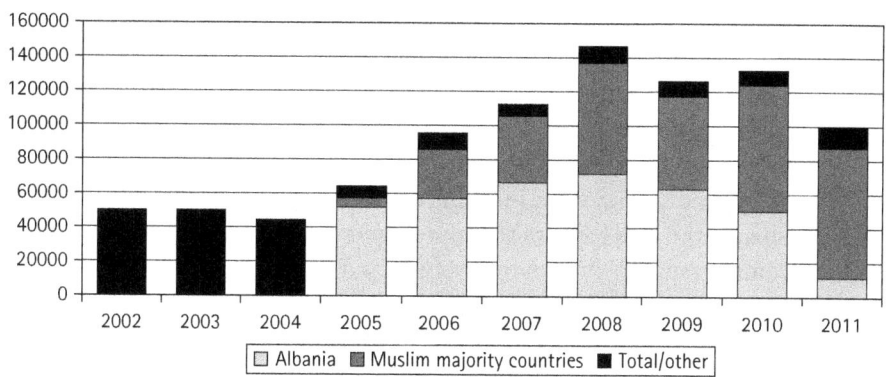

FIGURE 8.1 Apprehensions of undocumented aliens in Greece, 2002–11

Source: 2006–11: Greek police website (<http://www.hellenicpolice.gr>, accessed 3 July 2012); 2002–5: Maroukis (2008: 66, table 15); authors' elaboration.

decade; based on these data, the estimated figure for undocumented migrants in Greece at the end of 2011 approaches 400,000 people (Maroukis 2012).

Recent immigration comprises a large number of migrants from Muslim countries. Data on apprehensions of illegal immigrants by the police show a gradual decline of the shares (and absolute numbers since 2008) of Albanian immigrants and a respective proportional and numerical growth of immigrants from Muslim countries, from 28.7% in 2006 to 76.6% in 2011. During those years, the aggregate share of nationals of predominantly Muslim countries among the total number of apprehensions approaches 47%, among whom one finds 16.4% Afghanis, 7.3% Iraqis, 6.4% Pakistanis, 4.6% Palestinians, and 4.1% Somalis. In 2009, migrant community organizations estimated the total number of immigrants at roughly 70,000 Pakistanis, 25,000 Bangladeshis, 20,000 Afghanis, 15,000 Syrians, 12,000 Jordanians and Palestinians, and 40,000 from other Arabic countries, mostly Egypt, Lebanon, and Iraq (Tsitselikis 2010: 235).[11] By 2010, the total immigrant Muslim population was estimated at 200,000–300,000 (Tsitselikis 2010; Skoulariki 2010). It is reasonable to suspect that this number has increased since then.

## Key Features of the Immigrant Muslim Population

As mentioned, the vast majority of Greece's immigrants originate from Albania, a country in which 70% of the population is nominally Muslim. One would rightly wonder why this group is not counted in the account of official data given in the previous subsection. The reason is that most scholars writing on Greece's 'new' Islam (e.g. Trubeta 2003; Tsitselikis 2010; Triandafyllidou 2010; Anagnostou and Gropas 2010) agree that

and count apprehensions rather than people. Thus an undocumented immigrant may have been apprehended at least twice, e.g. on the border upon entry and in Athens.

[11] Reporting on a press article in the newspaper *To Vima*, 31 May 2009.

Albanians exhibit limited religiosity and that even those who are of Muslim background are largely non-practising. In addition, a significant proportion of Albanian migrants have ethnic Greek roots and a Christian Orthodox background. These are subject to a privileged status and are generally more easily accepted by Greek society. For this reason, non ethnic-Greek migrants would often develop peculiar adaptation strategies consisting in changing their names from Muslim to Christian Orthodox ones, and converting to Christianity through baptism (Hatziprokopiou 2006: ch. 8.2.3). Recent fieldwork on Muslim immigrants in Athens by Evergeti and Hatziprokopiou (2010–11) found a very small number of Albanians attending prayers in the city's informal prayer sites. Moreover, Albanians are not generally perceived as Muslims by the host society, but rather as members of a different nation (Antoniou 2003: 156). With the exception of one study indicating mistrust towards their Muslim faith (Kafetzis et al. 1998), the racialization of Albanian immigrants in Greece during the 1990s has not involved any emphasis on religion (Hatziprokopiou 2006: ch. 9.1.1).

Besides Albanians, immigrants from former Central Asian Soviet republics have also been excluded: these may be Muslim majority countries, but most of their nationals who migrated to Greece[12] are of Greek ethnic origin (Diamanti-Karanou 2003). Other groups have been included, for which, however, the exact number of Muslims is unclear. For instance, the proportion of Muslims among Nigerians in Greece remains unknown, as well as that of Christians among Arabic speakers from Egypt, Syria, Lebanon, or elsewhere. Turkish nationals may comprise Turks and Kurds, but also Muslims from Thrace who were deprived of their Greek citizenship in earlier decades, and ethnic Greeks who migrated to Greece after 1955 'and were refused Greek citizenship' (Baldwin-Edwards 2008: 30).[13]

Returning to the five most numerous nationalities, Table 8.1 illustrates some of their key features in terms of migration and work as recorded in the 2001 census. Evidently, despite common patterns, there were some variations in the number of years they had spent in Greece, their stated reasons of migration, and their relation to the labour market. To some extent these reflect key demographic characteristics as well as different migratory patterns and routes. In their majority, these groups consist overwhelmingly of young males of working age, but there are significant variations in this respect as well: among Pakistanis and Bangladeshis, women and children were less then 5%; among Iraqis, the largest refugee community, the share of women was 30% and that of children

---

[12] Nearly 3,240 were recorded in the 2001 census, 70% from Kazakhstan and 25% from Uzbekistan.

[13] Article 19 of the Greek Citizenship Code, based on a 1927 presidential decree, 'provided the means to sever the links between the Greek state and those who did not assimilate', namely 'non-ethnic Greeks' (*allogeneis*), i.e. those without (ethnic) Greek ancestry, but also those lacking 'Greek consciousness' (Anagnostou 2005: 338). In the aftermath of the Greek civil war, this legislation was primarily applied to communists. Following the 1955 riots against the Greek Orthodox minority of Istanbul, it has been extensively applied to Thracian Muslims: between 1955 and 1998, about 50,000 of the latter were deprived of their Greek nationality (Anagnostou 2005: 339). The 1955 riots in Istanbul also led many local Greeks to migrate to Greece; however, many of them were denied citizenship by the Greece state, in an effort to maintain the Greek minority within Turkey.

Table 8.1 Key features of the five most numerous nationalities of Muslim migrants in Greece, 2001

|  | ALL MIGRANTS | EGYPT | SYRIA | IRAQ | PAKISTAN | BANGLADESH |
|---|---|---|---|---|---|---|
| YEARS IN GREECE | | | | | | |
| Up to a year | 12.2 | 11.3 | 13.0 | 42.3 | 10.7 | 9.5 |
| 1–5 years | 46.8 | 38.6 | 48.7 | 47.4 | 61.6 | 76.2 |
| More than 5 years | 41.0 | 50.2 | 38.2 | 10.3 | 27.7 | 14.3 |
| REASON FOR MIGRATION | | | | | | |
| Employment | 50.1 | 63.9 | 61.0 | 40.5 | 90.9 | 91.0 |
| Family reunion | 12.3 | 7.7 | 8.2 | 6.1 | 1.8 | 1.1 |
| Education | 2.6 | 1.7 | 5.2 | 0.8 | 0.3 | 0.4 |
| Asylum | 1.3 | 0.2 | 0.9 | 28.5 | 3.5 | 3.0 |
| Refugee | 0.3 | 0 | 0.3 | 5.9 | 0 | 0.1 |
| Other reason | 27.1 | 23.1 | 19.7 | 8.4 | 1.5 | 1.1 |
| Multiple reasons | 6.3 | 3.4 | 4.7 | 9.8 | 2.0 | 3.3 |
| RELATION TO LABOUR MARKET | | | | | | |
| Employed | 51.4 | 64.8 | 66.3 | 38.4 | 83.0 | 84.5 |
| Seeking employment | 5.3 | 4.1 | 3.7 | 15.8 | 8.6 | 9.3 |
| Pupil/student | 11.2 | 4.1 | 6.4 | 7.8 | 1.4 | 1.1 |
| Pensioner | 4.0 | 3.6 | 0.9 | 1.0 | 0.5 | 0.2 |
| Housework | 14.2 | 10.9 | 10.4 | 15.2 | 1.3 | 0.9 |
| Other | 3.3 | 3.5 | 2.3 | 10.4 | 4.0 | 3.3 |
| <10 years old | 10.6 | 9 | 10 | 11.4 | 1.2 | 0.7 |

Source: 2001 census, author's elaboration (available at <http://www.statistics.gr>, accessed 30 June 2012).

18%; among fairly long-established groups, such as Egyptians or Syrians, women were around 20–5% and children about 11–12%.

In terms of employment and living conditions, studies of specific immigrant groups have shown that the majority performs hard manual tasks in specific economic sectors, often through informal arrangements and thus without social security and with very modest rewards. According to data from the Labour Force Survey of the second quarter of 2011, the principal sectors of employment are construction (for Pakistanis, Iraqis, and especially Syrians), manufacturing (for South Asians), trade (for Egyptians, Iraqis, and South Asians), catering (for Egyptians, Syrians, and Bangladeshis), and to a lesser extent agriculture (for Pakistanis) and transport/storage (for Egyptians). Certain groups, especially Iraqis and Bangladeshis, show a high propensity to be self-employed

(17.5% and 25.8% respectively). Since 2009, the unemployment rate among immigrants has exceeded that of Greeks.[14] South Asians seem to have been particularly affected. It is impossible to estimate the extent of informal employment, but one could assume that newcomers, transit migrants, and asylum-seekers are particularly vulnerable, and that, because of their precarious situation, they also work for low wages. Looking at those among these groups who were insured with IKA (the main social security organization in Greece) in June 2011, South Asians, Iraqis, and Afghanis were amongst the lowest paid.

The vast majority of Muslim immigrants in Greece are concentrated in Greater Athens and Piraeus: this is true of more than 90% of the Bangladeshis and Iraqis recorded in the 2001 census, of more than two-thirds of the Egyptians and Syrians, and of roughly 68% of the Pakistanis. Most live in neighbourhoods with low rents, either traditional working-class districts or areas that have been gradually abandoned by indigenous Greek residents who moved to the suburbs. Although housing segregation of immigrants is generally low, mostly due to the overwhelming presence and spatial dispersal of Albanians, smaller national groups such as the ones from Muslim countries have formed specific and rather visible concentrations, especially in central Athens and its western surroundings (Arapoglou et al. 2009). In particular, the historic commercial core of downtown Athens (around Omonoia square) concentrates spaces of mass temporary settlement of newcomers, a diversity of ethnic businesses including many established by Muslim immigrants, offices of migrant community organizations, and multiple sites of worship (Arapoglou et al. 2009; Noussia and Lyons 2009).

Legal status has been the major issue of concern for the majority of immigrants in Greece, including Muslims (Evergeti and Hatziprokopiou forthcoming b). Muslim immigrants are subject to the general laws that apply to all immigrants: theoretically, this means both general human rights and the legal framework for third country nationals ('aliens') under Greek law. Their legal statuses range from citizenship for the rather few migrants who have been settled in Greece for several decades, to long-term stay permits for the majority. Many of those who arrived between the late 1990s and mid-2000s are subject to a short-term stay permit which is renewable every one or two years; however, maintaining this status has become a problem in the context of the recent economic crisis since renewal depends on proven formal employment, which has become scarcer. Some Muslim immigrants have been granted refugee status or asylum; those whose applications are still pending have the right to stay under the temporary status of 'asylum-seekers'. The vast majority of newcomers in the last few years, however, remain undocumented.

Last, a related phenomenon concerns the internal migration of Thracian Muslims towards urban centres, mostly Athens and Thessaloniki. Although this migration has been mostly motivated by economic reasons, it was encouraged by state policy in the

---

[14] According to Labour Force Surveys, unemployment rates in Greece for Greek and foreign nationals respectively jumped from 9.2% and 9.9% in the third quarter of 2009, to 24% and 32.8% in the third quarter of 2012.

1980s (by supplying interest-free loans and public sector employment), with the objective of weakening politician participation in Western Thrace and facilitating the integration of the minority into Greek society (Antoniou 2003, 2005). Though Greek citizens, these internal migrants face similar problems to those of foreign immigrants, not only in terms of precarious and badly-paid employment, but chiefly in respect to religious rights and facilities, access to which is lost once outside the region of Thrace (Antoniou 2005; Evergeti and Hatziprokopiou forthcoming a and b).

## Contentious Issues in Perceptions of Islam and Muslim Immigrants

So far religion has not been a major issue in respect to the public discourse on immigrants in Greece (Hatziprokopiou 2014). As elsewhere in Europe, however, Islam stands quite exceptional, since 'public debates on the question of religion and migration in Greece have primarily focused on the impact of Muslim migration in Greek society' (Hatzopoulos and Kambouri 2010: 3). For a good part since the late 1990s, such debates have been monopolized by reactions over the construction of a central mosque in Athens. Much of the 'mosque debates' reflect the role of the church in Greek decision-making, the influence of religion in the Greek public sphere, and the historical association of Islam with Turkey (Triandafyllidou and Gropas 2009; Skoulariki 2010). We have earlier commented on the historical weight of Orthodoxy in Greek national identity, while the ways in which the non-separation between church and state affects the status of Islam and the construction of mosques are addressed in the next two sub-sections. References to Turkey have been a recurring argument against the building of a central mosque: they focus on Turkey's alleged intervention in Greek domestic affairs by favouring the building of a central mosque, which they contrast to its inadequate respect of Orthodox churches and institutions within its territory (Triandafyllidou and Gropas 2009). These arguments are typically raised by moderate conservative, ultra-nationalist, and extreme right political parties, as well as church circles, while the centre and left of the political spectrum are generally less reluctant or even supportive to the building of the mosque (Triandafyllidou and Gropas 2009; Skoulariki 2010), as we are going to see later on.

A particularly contentious issue is the aforementioned Law (3838) of 2010 facilitating access to citizenship for the second generation and long-term immigrants. Reactions from sections of the church and conservative politicians focused partly on the challenge of Muslims becoming Greek citizens (e.g. Hatzopoulos and Kambouri 2010). Despite such reactions from some members of the clergy, the Church of Greece did not adopt a single official stance: the moderate archbishop avoided intervening in what he saw as an essentially civic matter; opinions given by individual bishops varied from positive views acknowledging the 'multicultural character of contemporary Greek society' and 'the need for respecting alterity', to a 'growing preoccupation with Islam as a potential destabilising force' (Hatzopoulos and Kambouri 2010: 5).

In general, mistrust vis-à-vis Muslims seems to be primarily connected to perceptions of national identity, and the peculiar 'entanglement of Muslim difference with Turkish ethnicity' in the Greek context (Triandafyllidou and Gropas 2009: 212). The complex daily negotiations between mixed Greek–Turkish couples in Athens, studied by Petronoti and Papagaroufali (2006: 568, 574), reveal 'how the interplay between gender and kinship overshadows resistance to religious diversity', since 'inbreeding with "infidels" tends to be seen as a "monstrous" act endangering the norms pertaining to the integrity of the nation-state'.[15] The aforementioned study, an ethnography focusing on two married couples permanently settled in Greece, shows the ways in which these couples make sense of their relationship and negotiate it in contexts of family, friendship, and work, rationalizing their choice by either appealing to their 'modern' approach in respect to religion, namely that they are non-religious or non-practising, or to the cultural proximity between Greece and Turkey, which transcends their religious differences. In less intimate situations, Papantoniou (2009: 355) records the complaints of Muslim interviewees 'about their indiscriminate equation to the Turks, which often activates consciously or subconsciously nationalistic reflexes from the part of the Greeks'.

Suspicion towards Muslims in daily encounters entails stereotypical assumptions that Muslim immigrants are religious, devout, and practising rather than fears of Islam-related terrorism that may be the case elsewhere in Europe (KSPM 2007). Such stereotypes relate to the place of women in Islam, or dietary habits in relation to pork meat and alcohol, which may become contentious issues in everyday interactions between Muslim immigrants and Greeks (KSPM 2007; Papantoniou 2009; Evergeti and Hatziprokopiou forthcoming a and b). For instance, Gogonas (2010) reports that Coptic Egyptian families appear to be closer to the host population, whereas Egyptian Muslims face prejudice associated with their religious habits, such as fasting during Ramadan.

Until recently, most of the discrimination experienced by Muslims appeared to relate to their very position and status as immigrants. Anagnostou and Gropas (2010: 92) remind us that Greeks have been among the Europeans holding the most negative views on immigration in Eurobarometer surveys[16] and there has been rising xenophobia and racism in the context of the recent economic crisis. This being said, negative views may also be linked to perceived aspects of Islam and Muslim societies, reflecting a great deal of ignorance, more than broad Islamophobic sentiments. A 2009 opinion poll to a sample of 622 people across the country recorded some 77% of respondents having minimal knowledge of Islam (Public Issue 2010). The same poll registered large shares of negative reactions to the concepts of 'jihad', 'burka', and the 'Islamic veil', but relatively limited

---

[15] Inter-religious marriages, sometimes involving the conversion of one of the partners, appear to be a very limited though growing phenomenon. No research has been done on this to date, though a doctoral study is currently taking place in Middlesex University (UK) by Ms D. Papadopoulou.

[16] e.g. see Eurobarometer 71, national report Greece (European Commission 2009). Eight out of ten Greek citizens disagree with the notion that 'people from other ethnic groups enrich the cultural life of their country' and think that their presence is instead 'a cause of insecurity' and that it 'increases unemployment in Greece', while 70% do not believe that 'immigrants contribute more in taxes than they benefit from health and welfare services' (European Commission 2009: 31).

shares reacting negatively to 'Qur'an', 'Mosques', 'Muslims', 'Prophet Muhammad', or 'Islam' (between 19% and 23% of responses, and a similar range of shares declaring positive views towards the same concepts). About half agreed that 'Islam leads to violence more easily than other religions' (as opposed to nearly 40% disagreeing with that statement), but close to 70% did not think that Islam poses a real threat for Greece.

This being said, recent research indicates that a shift may be underway, as emerging discourses do not simply reflect dominant constructions of national identity, but also echo Orientalist perceptions of Islam and Muslims as backward, incompatible with 'Western' democracy and secularism, and oppressive towards women, thus reproducing prejudices which associate Islam with fanaticism and portray Muslim immigrants as a potential threat (Hatziprokopiou 2014). Recent developments include the entrance in the Greek parliament of 'Chrisi Avgi' (Golden Dawn) in the elections of May 2012. Golden Dawn is an ultranationalist party with expressed sympathies to Nazism, an openly racist and Islamophobic agenda, and involvement in physical attacks. Press reports are indicative of a rise in violent racist attacks since 2011, with eighty Pakistani victims just in September that year, including beatings and stabbings, the majority of incidents taking place in downgraded parts of central Athens (such as the neighbourhoods of Aghios Panteleimon and Attica Square) or working-class districts of Greater Athens.[17] According to a 2012 report by Human Rights Watch, 'far-right extremists rampaged through immigrant neighborhoods in May [2011], leaving at least 25 people hospitalized with stab wounds or severe beatings' (HRW 2012). The latest such incident that gained public attention was the sad case of the 26-year-old Pakistani S. Luqman, who was stabbed to death on his way to work at about 4 a.m. in the morning on 17 January 2013; electoral pamphlets of the Golden Dawn were found in the house of one of the murderers.[18]

There have also been reports on xenophobic and Islamophobic prejudice among police officials, as well as incidents of human rights violations (HRW 2012). Antonopoulos et al. (2008: 363) quote from an interview with a police detective stating: 'In a few years they may say that they are 5,000,000 Muslims and they want mosques. Imagine if that happens'. On 20 May 2009, a policeman tore up pages of a migrant's Qur'an during a routine documents inspection (Hatzopoulos and Kambouri 2010: 5), causing an angry reaction by many Muslim migrants, whose demonstration two days later in the centre of Athens could be termed the first migrant 'riot' in Greece (Hatziprokopiou 2014).

Last, issues of Islamic extremism that are a concern elsewhere in Europe are nearly absent in Greece. The only case that gained wide public attention concerned allegations of abductions and interrogations of eight innocent Pakistani men in the summer of 2005 by Greek intelligence services on behalf of the British ones, following the London terrorist attacks (Kambouri 2009). This case made the front pages in many Greek newspapers, which raised concerns about the methods used by the Greek secret services. In

---

[17] *Eleftherotypia* newspaper of 26 September 2011: <http://www.enet.gr/?i=issue.el.home&date=26/09/2011&id=312844>.
[18] <http://www.kathimerini.com.cy/index.php?pageaction=kat&modid=1&artid=119743&show=Y>.

2010, a court found that there was lack of evidence and the secret services were subsequently freed of charges. Religious leaders appear to be concerned with radicalization, which they see as a potential problem that they try to resist by excluding radical elements and promoting 'the true Islam of peace and justice' (Kassimeris and Samouris 2012: 187; also Evergeti and Hatziprokopiou forthcoming b). Lately, Greece has not escaped angry Muslim demonstrations against the insulting online video about the Prophet Muhammad that shook many countries across the globe in September 2012.

## Religious Rights

Officially, religious tolerance is safeguarded by the Greek constitution and a number of international treaties. As explained by Tsitselikis (2004b, 2009, 2010, 2012), the framework for religious freedom in Greece is determined by articles 5 (paragraph 2) and 13 of the Greek constitution, articles 9 and 14 of the European Convention on Human Rights, articles 18 and 27 of the International Covenant on Civil and Political Rights, articles 14 and 30 of the Convention on the Rights of the Child, etc. However, despite the formal recognition of Islam as the second most important religion in the country and of Muslim immigrants as entitled to their religious rights, several issues remain.

The Greek Orthodox Church is by constitution (article 3) the prevailing religion in Greece and enjoys a privileged position vis-à-vis other religious denominations; it also maintains the authority to control their activities (Tsitselikis 2004a, 2009, 2010; Anagnostou and Gropas 2010). On these grounds, the church has the status of 'a special branch' of the state and of its civil service (Mavrogordatos 2003: 121). As a legal entity, it is incorporated under public law: religious affairs are managed by the Ministry of Education and clerics are paid by the state. Within this context, Islam (as well as Judaism) enjoys the status of a 'known' religion and is officially recognized as a public law entity (Anagnostou and Gropas 2010; Tsitselikis 2012). However, while the Orthodox Church reserves the right to issue building permits for its own churches and chapels, the construction of any religious building associated with a different ('known') religion required its permission until 2006, and still needs its consultation. Moreover, Orthodoxy is taught in state schools, though pupils not adhering to it may be exempted; Islamic education is formally available only in the designated minority schools in Thrace.

Skoulariki mentions that in practice, despite its 'long experience in dealing with Islamic institutions' in respect to the minority of Thrace, the Greek state has not yet managed 'to provide equal religious rights' to Muslim immigrants (Skoulariki 2010: 302). This affects migrant Muslims in a number of ways, from complications in family law issues, to the lack of formal mosques and cemeteries outside Thrace (and the islands of Rhodes and Kos). For instance, a Muslim couple needs to travel to Thrace in order to have an Islamic ceremony recognized by the state; to avoid this, many couples choose to perform a civil marriage instead (according to 2010–11 research by Evergeti and Hatziprokopiou). Legal disputes are usually resolved by members of the community or in the home country, not by the Greek courts (Tsitselikis 2004a: 90). Tsitselikis (2010: 242) mentions that Greek courts 'can apply Islamic Family Law through the rules of International Private Law', though no such cases have been so far reported.

## Mosques and Cemeteries

In recent years, the Athens mosque 'controversy' and relevant debates have been one of the most important issues concerning Muslim migrants in Greece and have spurred a vast academic interest.[19] In short, while mosques are common in Western Thrace (and the islands of Rhodes and Kos), no mosque or Islamic prayer venue functions officially elsewhere in the country. Discussions about establishing a central mosque in the Greek capital started more than a century ago and have included a series of never-applied provisions and abandoned plans. The first such provisions came as early as the 1880s, followed by a second wave in 1913–14, and a third in the 1930s—all remaining on paper (Triandafyllidou and Gropas 2009). The framework established by the Treaty of Lausanne in the 1920s has certainly made things difficult by blocking the construction of mosques outside Thrace (Tsitselikis 2004b, 2012). The legal provision determining the establishment of non-Orthodox venues of worship dates back to 1938–9 and requires a permit issued by the Ministry of Education and Religious Affairs, after hearing the (non-binding) opinion of the Church of Greece (Triandafyllidou and Gropas 2009: 962–3; Anagnostou and Gropas 2010: 95). The question of establishing a central mosque in the capital emerged anew in the 1970s, mostly raised by diplomatic representatives of Arab countries (Skoulariki 2010; Anagnostou and Gropas 2010); in the 1980s, it was also promoted by a deputy of the minority in Thrace, as well as by a group of Sudanese students (Triandafyllidou and Gropas 2009; Skoulariki 2010). The government responded by offering a plot in Marousi, a northern Athens suburb, then in the south-eastern area of Alimos, but these plans were rejected by the (conservative) opposition (Skoulariki 2010: 305).

The construction of the mosque came close to materializing with a relevant Law (2833) which was passed in parliament in the year 2000, with the aim to have the venue functioning during the 2004 Olympic Games. Even though the church resisted the foundation of an Islamic cultural centre associated with the mosque, it had a relatively positive view about building the mosque itself. However, some church officials and the local bishop raised concerns about the location that was ultimately chosen, namely the district of Paiania, near Athens airport. They argued that foreign visitors arriving in Greece might get the false impression that Greece is a Muslim country (Triandafyllidou and Gropas 2009; Anagnostou and Gropas 2010; Skoulariki 2010). As a result, the Law did not lead to any concrete action, and the public debate went on. A short-lived

---

[19] Antoniou (2003); Tsitselikis (2004a); KSPM (2007); Papantoniou (2009); Triandafyllidou and Gropas (2009); Salvanou (2009); Antoniou (2010); Skoulariki (2010); Anagnostou and Gropas (2010); Tsitselikis (2012); Hatziprokopiou and Evergeti (2014).

proposal to have the mosque established in an eighteenth-century Ottoman mosque in the Monastiraki area of downtown Athens, literally in the shadow of the Acropolis, also drew negative reactions: the public discourse focused on the symbolism of that particular location, but there have also been objections from Muslim communities who rejected the plan because of the small size and unsuitability of the venue (Skoulariki 2010: 309–10).

Eventually, the church proposed to have the mosque built in Elaionas, a sparsely populated industrial area at the western fringe of the Municipality of Athens, subject to a massive regeneration project. This proposal was taken forward with Law 3512 of 2006 despite opposition; it determines specific procedures for building the mosque, provides for its funding by the Greek state, and describes its future operation under state management and with state-appointed imams. This Law was passed with a parliamentary majority, with different parties basing their support on different grounds; only the ultranationalist party LAOS voted against it. The plan was viewed positively by church authorities, as well as by the police and security services. A ministerial decision to begin construction was approved in parliament in late 2011, but procedures were blocked anew in January 2012, after an appeal to the Council of State by the (conservative) bishop of Piraeus, who objected to the plan on financial and legal-constitutional grounds. The bishop raised questions of public order and fears that the construction of the mosque might 'trigger a series of events' which would 'dismantle the cohesion of the Greek nation as a Christian Orthodox people'.[20] Meanwhile, however, Greece's worsening economic difficulties seem to be the main reason why the construction of the mosque, estimated at nearly one million euros, has been officially postponed, as the government announced in late September 2012.[21] About a year later, the government announced that funds of 946,000 euros had been allocated, yet there was reluctance from construction companies to undertake the project.[22] A newly formed partnership placed a successful bid in November 2013, and the mosque was scheduled to be ready by the summer of 2014.[23]

In the absence of either a central mosque or of officially recognized sites of worship, the daily religious needs of the Muslim immigrants are covered by numerous prayer sites operating mainly in Athens and its suburbs, but also in other locations of Greece with a sizeable or religiously active local Muslim community. Informal mosques have been the subject of some studies (Antoniou 2003; KSPM 2007; Papantoniou 2009; Salvanou

---

[20] *Kathimerini* English edition (3 January 2012) 'Bishop appeals against mosque project in central Athens', <http://www.ekathimerini.com/4dcgi/_w_articles_wsite1_1_03/01/2012_420959> (accessed 12 October 2012).

[21] *To Vima* newspaper, 26 September 2012, <http://www.tovima.gr/society/article/?aid=476474&wordsinarticle=τέμενος> (accessed 12 October 2012).

[22] *To Vima* newspaper, 24 October 2013, <http://www.tovima.gr/society/article/?aid=536491> (accessed 16 April 2014).

[23] *Ta Nea* newspaper, 14 November 2013, <http://www.tanea.gr/news/greece/article/5053834/brethhke-anadoxos-gia-to-temenos-ston-botaniko> (accessed 16 April 2014); *Kathimerini* newspaper, 27 January 2014, <http://www.kathimerini.gr/750756/article/epikairothta/ellada/amesa-h-ypografh-ths-symvashs-gia-to-temenos-sto-votaniko> (accessed 16 April 2014).

2009; Leghari 2009; Hatziprokopiou and Evergeti 2014), which point out that most of them operate in flats, basements, storerooms, garages, or abandoned small industrial sites, lacking 'all the architectural characteristics of a mosque, especially the minaret used for the ezan' (Skoulariki 2010: 311). They are, more correctly, prayer halls or sites of worship, as denoted by the terms *masjid* or *mescit*.

While informal mosques do not operate illegally as such, they do not have a proper permit as religious venues, and are therefore often referred to as 'semi-legal' (Hatzopoulos and Kambouri 2010: 6). Given the very complex legal framework regulating non-Orthodox sites of worship (the need to submit a request for a permit, which has to be approved by the church, and then wait for a ministerial decision), these sites are typically registered in the name of an association and officially presented as its premises or activity venue. Salvanou (2009) and Skoulariki (2010: 313) have studied one of these 'unofficial' mosques, run and frequented by Pakistanis, in the Athens district of Nea Ionia. The mosque had to pay a fine of 87,000 euros because it operated as a prayer hall while it was rented as a library. Unpublished 2010–11 fieldwork by Evergeti and Hatziprokopiou revealed similar stories elsewhere in Athens, such as the case of a Pakistani mosque on which planning authorities imposed a fine after discovering that it included water taps for washing before prayer.

A pioneering 2007 study by the Centre for Returning Migrants and Ethnic Greeks, linked to the Church of Greece, mapped twenty-six places of worship (*masjids*) in central Athens alone (KSPM 2007; Papantoniou 2009), while estimations of their total number range from about sixty (Skoulariki 2010: 312) to over a hundred (Gogonas 2010: 8). Increased migration and the informal status of these venues make their number tough to determine. The studies by the aforementioned NGO in 2007 and by Evergeti and Hatziprokopiou in 2010–11 reveal a huge diversity of different *masjids*, depending on the venue and location, the sources of funding, as well as the history and composition of the local communities.

Moreover, the few studies available so far show a shift from multiethnic prayer publics to a more segregated situation, not unrelated to growing immigration and the resulting ethnic and linguistic diversity among the migrant Muslim population. Such segregation is expressed by lines of nationality, e.g. between Pakistanis, Bangladeshis, and migrants from Arabic countries (KPSM 2007; Papantoniou 2009; Kassimeris and Samouris 2012; Hatziprokopiou and Evergeti 2014). In a recent paper, Kassimeris and Samouris (2012: 178) reported that of a total of some one hundred informal mosques, about half were established by South Asians (thirty to thirty-two by Pakistanis and twenty to twenty-two by Bangladeshis). Segregation may also relate to location: one encounters, for instance, a more 'multiethnic' public during the Friday prayers in central Athens, and single-group prayer attendees in specific districts (Salvanou 2009; Evergeti and Hatziprokopiou forthcoming b). And it may further reflect differences in religious denomination (Leghari 2009; Hatziprokopiou and Evergeti 2014). For example, Evergeti and Hatziprokopiou (2014) located two Sunni Pakistani mosques operating in the same location, at a distance of about 500 metres of each other in the district of Egaleo, attracting followers of different Islamic traditions (orthodox Hanafi and Sufi). There are also two Shi'a mosques maintained by Pakistani migrants and situated very close to Sunni Pakistani mosques. In addition, there seems to be a shift in the ways imams are selected: while typically this role would be undertaken by a member of the community commonly accepted as more knowledgeable in theological matters, in the last few years imams have been invited from the immigrants' countries of origin and supported by the communities, despite their varying knowledge of Greek language and limited contact with the wider society (KSPM 2007; Papantoniou 2009: 353; Evergeti and Hatziprokopiou 2014).

Fieldwork evidence shows that informal mosques perform multiple functions, rather than attending to spiritual needs only (Hatziprokopiou and Evergeti 2014), similar to what is the case in many other European countries and, in varying ways, in Muslim countries as well. In some cases they may host educational programmes for children; more often, they support and help the most disadvantaged among the faithful. In that sense, but also symbolically, they become central points of reference for locally based communities in specific districts (KPSM 2007; Papantoniou 2009; Leghari 2009; Noussia and Lyons 2010; Salvanou 2009; Liakos and Salvanou 2010, Hatziprokopiou and Evergeti 2014).

Legal scholarship shows that the issue of burial remains problematic as there are no cemeteries outside Thrace and the Dodecanese islands. Muslims wishing to observe traditional funerary practices have to arrange burials in these regions, which is often prohibitively expensive (Tsitselikis 2004b, 2010). The alternative is either not to have ceremonial burial, or to engage in the far more expensive and bureaucratic process of transporting the body to the country of origin. Research by Evergeti and Hatziprokopiou over 2010–11 has shown that the latter does take place, but it is hard to estimate how widespread it is. Overall, transporting the body to Thrace is the most frequent practice, especially by immigrants who are quite settled and have families in Greece. This is one of the few issues bringing together the institutions of the minority in Thrace and Muslim immigrants. Moreover, with the rise in border crossings over the last few years, the Muftis in Thrace, especially the one of Didymoteicho, which borders Turkey, are often assigned the task of burying the refugees who died in their attempt to cross the border, and who often remain unnamed.[24] Since the mid-2000s, the Church of Greece has donated a piece of land (about 30 hectares) in Schisto, a western Athens suburb, for the creation of an Islamic cemetery (Skoulariki 2010), but the procedures for its establishment have been moving slowly.

## Religious Organizations

There is, expectedly, not a single body addressing Greece's migrant Muslims, but there have been several studies that document the organization of various communities along religious lines or around religious issues. Antoniou (2003: 167) reports that

---

[24] Screened on a Net TV documentary entitled 'Evros, the other bank', presented by M. Tsokli (10 June 2011).

'diplomatic representatives of Muslim countries in Greece, as well as an international Islamic non-governmental organization, have... shown interest in the welfare of these emerging Muslim communities'. In respect to the former, he refers to lobbying for the establishment of a central mosque; in respect to the latter, he mentions the *Lahore Ahmadiyya* movement which, according to the author, was 'interested in translating several books on Islam into the Greek and Albanian languages, as well as turning the Albanian immigrants in Greece into devote Muslims' (Antoniou 2003: 167). In 1997, an organization named Panhellenic Federation of Supporting Muslims in Greece, 'Filotita', was set up in Athens in 1997 by Thracian Muslims and managed to enlist members from various migrant groups, claiming to represent the entire Muslim population (Imam and Tsakiridi 2003), but remains rather inactive in recent years.

The largest and perhaps most influential organization at present is the Muslim Association of Greece (MAG), founded in Athens in 2003 and headed by Egyptian businessman Naim El-Ghandour, who has been living in Greece for about forty years, has Greek citizenship, and is married to a Greek convert to Islam. The MAG comprises long-settled migrants and Greek converts, as well as recent immigrants and refugees, mostly (though not exclusively) originating from Arabic countries; it represents several informal prayer sites (Evergeti and Hatziprokopiou forthcoming b). Since June 2007, the Greek–Arabic Cultural Centre, a member of the Federation of Islamic Organizations in Europe, operates in the Moschato neighbourhood of Athens. It is run by Egyptians and functions as a community centre that hosts meetings, social events, as well as prayers (Triandafyllidou and Gropas 2009). Moreover, three virtual organizations, i.e. websites on Islam in the Greek language, were active as of early 2012, offering general information on Islam addressed primarily to the Greek public, second-generation migrants, and Greek converts to Islam.[25] As far as academic research is concerned, little is known on the religious and theological influence of these groups.

Immigrants from South Asian countries have established their own associations and religious organizations in the last ten years or so. Unpublished research by Evergeti and Hatziprokopiou (2010–11) located seven Pakistani religious organizations of diverse religious denominations and Islamic traditions, including two Shi'a associations, which run their own sites of worship. The majority of Pakistani migrants tend to identify either with different tendencies of the Barelvi movement and their transnational Sufi networks (such as Minhaj-ul-Quran, or the Sultan Bahu Trust), or with missionary networks originating from the Deobandi movement such as Tablighi Jamaat[26] (Leghari 2009).

---

[25] The URLs for these websites are <http://www.islam.gr>, <http://islamforgreeks.org>, <http://www.greeksrething.com>.

[26] The origins of both Barelvis and Deobandis lie in the mid-nineteenth-century Islamic reformist movements in British India (Leghari 2009). According to Leghari (2009: 10) Barelvis are influenced by 'folk' Islam of the South Asian Sufi tradition (including 'veneration of saints, idolization of the prophet... and popular and festive display of syncretic religious rituals'), while Deobandis are 'followers of Hanafi Islam' and with 'a puritanical bent in their interpretation of Islam' (opposing most rituals observed in various Sufi traditions). The latter are mostly represented in Greece by Tablighi Jamaat, an international missionary network formed in the 1920s in the Indian subcontinent. The former are represented by

Kassimeris and Samouris (2012) draw a more complex picture, distinguishing between organizations such as Tablighi Jamaat, Dawat-e-Islami, and the Sufi neo-brotherhoods, which, despite their doctrinal differences, have a 'bottom-up' approach to *dawah* (proselytization), and focus on grassroots awareness; and organizations which relate to the Islamic Forum of Europe and the Minhaj ul-Quran, operate with a 'top-down' approach, and are more political in terms of structure and goals. In both types of organizations, the authors acknowledge the distinction mentioned by Leghari (2009) between neo-Sufi groups and missionary networks generally opposed to Sufism. Informal mosques are to a lesser or greater extent run by one such organization: for instance, about one-third of Pakistani mosques are controlled by Minhaj ul-Quran, while nearly 80% of Bangladeshi *masjids* are related to the Tablighi Jammat (Kassimeris and Samouris 2012: 178). Similar differentiations exist in respect to the practice of *dawah*, the 'main tool used by Islamic associations in Greece in their effort to help the Muslim immigrants cope with the requirements of their new life'; divisions between organizations and their approaches to *dawah*, however, may result in blurred lines of halal (permitted) and haram among lay people, i.e. confusion over what is permissible and what is prohibited in living as migrants in a non-Muslim country (Kassimeris and Samouris 2012: 182–3).

Some of the nationality-based (non-religious) immigrant community organizations have ties with these religious organizations. In this sense, religious differences alongside political ones, in respect to both home-country politics as well as to political alliances in Greece, explain representational splits within immigrant groups, as we have observed among Pakistani migrant organizations, whose ways of mobilization include seeking alliances with radical left groups or with the government (Evergeti and Hatziprokopiou forthcoming b). In fact, there are various nationality-based associations and community organizations established by migrants and refugees from a wide range of Muslim countries,[27] often more than one per nationality, even by numerically small and recently established immigrant groups. Their primary functions entail mostly social and cultural activities, including legal support and information, lobbying and advocacy, assistance with employment issues, care and education for children, and organization of cultural events and festivals. In many cases, however, religion enters the frame of their activities either as an issue of advocacy or struggle, or as a matter of responding to the mundane and daily religious needs of the community, or even as a domain of culture and memory in the occasion of religious feasts (Evergeti and Hatziprokopiou forthcoming a and b). The leaders of such organizations, as well as those of many religious associations, typically belong to the tiny elites of the groups that they represent: they have been in Greece for a longer period, possess a long-term legal status, and are educated and financially comfortable (Kassimeris and Samouris 2012: 180; Evergeti and Hatziprokopiou forthcoming b).

---

a number of groups, each adhering to a specific Sufi saint, the main one being Minhaj-ul-Quran, an international NGO founded in Lahore in 1981.

[27] Including Algerians, Tunisians, Moroccans, Libyans, Egyptians, Syrians, Lebanese, Jordanians, Palestinians, Iraqis, Kurdish, Iranians, Afghanis, Pakistanis, Bangladeshis, Sudanese, Somalis, etc.

In short, one observes a fragmentation of Muslims on the basis of nationality, different Islamic traditions, different localities in Athens and beyond, different politics reflecting diverging allegiances in their countries of origin, as well as different political tactics and alliances in Greece. This fragmentation has so far left little space for the organizations to come together in a single formal body of collective representation (Antoniou 2003). The single issue around which the different organizations mobilized together is that of the Athens central mosque. Should the mosque be eventually built, divisions both between and within different communities, organizations, and Islamic traditions are not expected to fade out but may rather come to the fore.

## Special Celebrations and Everyday Religious Practice

In general, the immigrants' attachment to transnational religious networks allows for the maintenance of ties with places of origin and provides a source of identity and a space for organizing informal prayer sites in Athens (Leghari 2009). Religious associations appear to play an important role in the migrants' acculturation in the host society (Kassimeris and Samouris 2012) and religious feasts become points of reference for the communities (Hatziprokopiou and Evergeti 2014). Evergeti and Hatziprokopiou's fieldwork during 2010–11 showed that prayers during the Ramadan period are attended by more people than during the rest of the year, while major and minor festivals are specially celebrated in most informal prayer sites. In the absence of a central mosque, Muslims hold Eid-ul Fitr and Eid-al-Adha, which concentrate large numbers of believers in large venues such as stadiums, after obtaining a relevant permit from local municipal and police authorities (Skoulariki 2010: 312). The MAG, as well as the Pakistani community Unity and other organizations, have organized various such celebrations over the last few years, which inevitably attracted large public attention.

Over the last few years, Shi'a Pakistanis have been celebrating the day of Ashura[28] in the streets outside their mosque premises, in an area of warehouses and storerooms near the port of Piraeus (Terzopoulou 2008). A similar strategy of public prayer in the open space was followed recently by the MAG in respect to major festivals, attracting even more attention and media coverage (Hatziprokopiou and Evergeti 2014). On the occasion of the Prophet's birthday on 26 February 2010, for example, a public prayer was held in Constitution Square, at the heart of Athens; the prayer took place the Sunday that followed 26 February, to allow more people to attend. The Eid-ul-Fitr (Feast of Ending the Ramadan Fast) prayer that took place on 9 October 2010 at the square across from Athens Town Hall, with imams invited from Egypt, generated headlines such as 'Kotzia

---

[28] The day of Ashura is a Muslim religious observance occurring every year on the tenth day of Muharram (the first month of the Islamic calendar). Ashura was instituted as a day of fasting by Prophet Muhammad, but for Shi'a Muslims, Ashura is also a day of mourning for Hussein, the Prophet's grandson, who was murdered on that day in 680 AD, in a battle against the ruling Caliph.

Square turned to Mecca' and multiple reactions from conservative circles.[29] The Eid-al-Adha (Feast of the Sacrifice) on 16 November 2012 was also celebrated publicly in open space, provoking similar reactions. Muslim community leaders justified their choice to pray in public by referring to the lack of a formal place of worship, but as Hatziprokopiou and Evergeti (2014) and Hatziprokopiou (2014) argue, the performance of Islamic identity in landmark locations may be read as a protest statement, an active claim of rights and recognition.

A very limited number of studies have so far focused on the importance of religion in the immigrants' daily lives (KSPM 2007; Papantoniou 2009; Evergeti and Hatziprokopiou forthcoming a and b; Papanastasiou forthcoming). These studies show that the immigrants' primary concerns have to do with legal status, employment, and housing, i.e. issues that relate to their migrant condition, and that any references to Islam are generally made in terms of custom and identity. Information coming from research on specific immigrant groups in the following paragraph points to the diversity and complexity of daily negotiations of Islamic identity and practice, and to the multiplicity of ways in which these groups associate with and practise Islam.

Comparing Egyptian pupils of different religious background, Gogonas (2010) found that the importance attributed to Islam by Muslim parents, especially the practice of after-school Qur'anic education, helps their children to maintain Arabic as their mother tongue, which is not the case for their peers in Christian (Coptic) families, whose parents associate with the dominant religion, and who tend to experience language shifts. Papanastasiou (forthcoming) analyses the role of class in Egyptians' feelings about Islam: while educated Egyptians perceive their religious identity as a continuation of what they experienced before migration, less educated immigrants shift from a rather cultural-customary association with Islam to stronger religious feelings, especially once they become conscious of discrimination. Pakistanis, on the other hand, appear to be affected by the re-Islamization movement in their country, although their rather traditionalist approach to religion seems to be also related to their experience of living in a non-Muslim country and to their marginalization and discrimination in Greek society (Salvanou 2009; Papanastasiou forthcoming). In general, the immigrants' attachment to transnational religious networks not only shapes their diasporic religious identities, but also allows the maintenance of ties with places of origin (Leghari 2009) and provides a source of identity and a familiar space in an otherwise alien and often hostile environment (Salvanou 2009). Wanche's (2004) research on Iraqis in Greece exposes the religious diversity within the community; it compares Christian and Muslim Iraqis and shows that the latter have a sense of not being well received by the host population because of their religion. Papanastasiou's (forthcoming) account of Palestinians found them quite secular and not particularly inclined to associate with Islam as a group, confirming earlier studies analysing the Palestinians' transnational modes of constructing

---

[29] *Ethnos* newspaper, 10 September 2010. The same newspaper quoted the reaction of the bishop of Piraeus stating: 'With feelings of affliction we have watched... the irresponsible concession by the Municipal authority of Athens of Kotzia square to persons of Muslim religious confession.'

their national identity in the diaspora (Mavroudi 2007), where religion appears to play a very marginal role.

The nature and degree of religious faith, practice, and custom varies from one individual to another, depending on multiple factors. Location is one of them, since the non-existence of a prayer hall locally may result in individuals praying alone or in small groups in the afternoon only, or not praying at all. Work is another factor, since many employers may not allow for prayer breaks at all. In general, earlier studies (KSPM 2007; Papantoniou 2009) revealed a rediscovery of religion, in the context of migration and life in a Western and Christian country. Papanastasiou (forthcoming) interprets this retreat to Islam as a kind of 'reactive ethnicity': immigrants become conscious and self-aware of their religious identity partly as a result of experiences of discrimination.

# Concluding Remarks and Directions for Future Research

While there is a decent amount of information about the Muslim minority in Thrace, academic research on Muslim immigrants and Greece's 'new Islam' is severely lagging behind and is mostly done by independent scholars with relatively limited means. Based on the state of research presented in the second section, and taking the cue from the relevant literature in other European contexts, we could sketch some possible directions for future research in the Greek context along three basic axes.

The first concerns the expansion of knowledge of Greece's 'new' Islam and Muslim immigrants, though follow-up studies on issues already analysed (e.g. the public discourse, the central mosque, informal prayer sites, religious practices) and on specific groups that have attracted academic interest (Egyptians, Pakistanis, Bangladeshis), but also through additional research on other groups (Syrians, Bangladeshis, Afghanis, Somalis, etc.) or issues (e.g. gender, dietary habits, etc.). The second relates to a deeper understanding of the complex organizational dimensions of the various communities, their transnational ties and their theological underpinnings. While some work on that has been done in respect to South Asian groups (Leghari 2009; Kassimeris and Samouris 2012), very little is known about the Arab communities. The third axis entails a broader need in respect to migration research in the Greek context, focusing on the daily interactions and intimate encounters amongst different groups of Muslims, and between them and indigenous Greeks, whether religious or secular, in shared spaces. Certain dimensions of this have been studied in relation to specific Athens districts (Noussia and Lyons 2009; Salvanou 2009; Liakos and Salvanou 2010) or to Greek–Turkish couples (Petronoti and Papagaroufali 2006), while a doctoral project looking at identity negotiations and conversion in mixed couples (Muslim–Christian) is being currently undertaken at Middlesex University (UK) by Dora Papadopoulou.

Last, there is also a need for integrated, combined, and comparative accounts of indigenous Thracian Muslims and Muslim immigrants, in the tradition initiated by Trubeta (2003) and Antoniou (2003) and brought forward by Triandafyllidou (2010) and Evergeti and Hatziprokopiou (forthcoming a and b). As Muslim immigrants enter the country, gradually outnumber the minority, and feature prominently in the public sphere (Hatziprokopiou 2014), there is a need to focus more thoroughly on the contacts and communication (or lack thereof) between these two groups.

## Bibliography

Aarbakke, V. (2000). 'The Muslim Minority of Western Thrace'. Ph.D. thesis, Norway: Bergen University.
Aarbakke, V. (forthcoming). 'The Political Writings of the Minority Press', in V. Evergeti (ed.), *Indigenous Muslims in Greece: Case Studies of Europe's Autochthonous Muslims*. London: Springer.
Agtzidis, V. (2001). 'Μία άλλη εκδοχή για την επανάσταση του 1821: πώς αντιμετώπισαν οι Μουσουλμάνοι την νίκη των Ελλήνων και τα γεγονότα που ακολούθησαν' (An alternative version of the 1821 revolution: how did the Muslims received Greek victory and the events that followed). *Kathimerini* newspaper, 25 March 2001 [in Greek].
Alexandris, A. (1991). 'Το μειονοτικό ζήτημα: 1954–1987' (The Minority Question), in A. Alexandris, Th. Veremis, P. Kazakos, V. Koufoudakis, Ch. Rozakis, and G. Tsitsopoulos (eds.), *Οι Ελληνοτουρκικές Σχέσεις: 1923–1987* (Greek–Turkish Relations: 1923–1987). Athens: Gnosi, 493–552.
Anagnostou, D. (2001). 'Breaking the Cycle of Nationalism: The EU, Regional Policy and the Minority of Western Thrace, Greece', *South European Society and Politics* 6(1): 99–124.
Anagnostou, D. (2005). 'Deepening Democracy or Defending the Nation? The Europeanisation of Minority Rights and Greek Citizenship', *West European Politics* 28(2): 335–57.
Anagnostou, D. and Gropas, R. (2010). 'Domesticating Islam and Muslim Immigrants: Political and Church Responses to Constructing a Central Mosque in Athens', in V. Roudometof and V. N. Makrides (eds.), *Orthodox Christianity in 21st Century Greece: The Role of Religion in Culture, Ethnicity and Politics*. Farnham: Ashgate, 89–109.
Andreades, K. G. (1956). *The Moslem Minority in Western Thrace*. Thessaloniki: Institute for Balkan Studies.
Antoniou, D. (2003). 'Muslim Immigrants in Greece: Religious Organisation and Local Responses', *Immigrants and Minorities* 22(2–3): 155–74.
Antoniou, D. (2005). 'Western Thracian Muslims in Athens: From Economic Migration to Religious Organization', *Balkanologie* 9(1–2): 79–101.
Antoniou, D. (2010). 'The Mosque That Was Not There: Ethnographic Elaborations on Orthodox Conceptions of Sacrifice', in V. Roudometof and V. N. Makrides (eds.), *Orthodox Christianity in 21st Century Greece: The Role of Religion in Culture, Ethnicity and Politics*. Farnham: Ashgate, 155–74.
Antonopoulos, G. A., Tierney, J., and Webster, C. (2008). 'Police Perception of Migration and Migrants in Greece', *European Journal of Crime, Criminal Law and Criminal Justice* 16: 353–78.

Arapoglou, V., Kavoulakos, K. I., Kandylis, G., and Maloutas, Th. (2009). 'Athens' New Social Geography: Migration, Diversity and Conflict', *Syghrona Themata* 107 (October–December): 57–67 [in Greek].
Avramopoulou, E. and Karakatsanis, L. (2002). 'Διαδρομές της Ταυτότητας: Από τη δυτική Θράκη στο Γκάζι. Αναστοχασμοί και συγκρούσεις στη διαμόρφωση συλλογικών ταυτοτήτων. Η περίπτωση των τουρκόφωνων μουσουλμάνων στο Γκάζι' (Identity Trajectories: From Western Thrace to Gazi. Reflections and Conflicts in the Construction of Identities. The Case of Turkish-Speaking Muslims in Gazi). *Theseis* 79 [in Greek].
Baldwin-Edwards, M. (2008). 'Immigrants in Greece: Characteristics and Issues of Regional Distribution'. *Mediterranean Migration Observatory Working Paper Series*, W.P. no. 10. Athens: Panteion University.
Baldwin-Edwards, M. and Apostolatou, K. (2008). 'Ethnicity and Migration: A Greek Story', in M. Baldwin-Edwards (ed.), *Ethnicity and Migration: A Greek Story*, Special issue of *Migrance* 30: 5–17.
Baltsiotis, L. and Tsitselikis, K. (2001). 'Η μειονοτική εκπαίδευση της Θράκης: Συλλογή νομοθεσίας—Σχόλια' (The Minority Education of Thrace: legislation Collection—Comments). Athens: Sakkoula Publications [in Greek].
Bathaïe, A. (2009). 'La Grèce, une étape cruciale dans le parcours migratoire des Afghans depuis la frontière iranienne jusqu'en Europe', *Méditerranée* 113: 71–7.
Borou, C. (2009). 'The Muslim Minority of Western Thrace in Greece: An Internal Positive or an Internal Negative "Other"?', *Journal of Muslim Minority Affairs* 29(1): 5–26.
Broersma, F. and Lazarescu, D. (2009). 'Pakistani and Bangladeshi Migration to Greece: "Chasing the Dream"'. IDEA Project, Research Brief, June. <http://www.eliamep.gr/migration/idea/publications-idea/diktia-ke-diadromes-epta-metanasteftikon-omadon-stin-ellada> [Accessed 13 June 2012].
Brunnbauer, U. (2001). 'The Perception of Muslims in Bulgaria and Greece: Between the "Self" and the "Other"', *Journal of Muslim Minority Affairs* 21(1): 39–61.
Cavounidis, J. (2006). 'Labor Market Impact of Migration: Employment Structures and the Case of Greece', *International Migration Review* 40(3): 635–60.
Cella, E. (1996). 'Albanian Muslims, Human Rights and Relations with the Islamic World', in G. Nonneman, T. Niblock, and B. Szajkowski (eds.), *Muslim Communities in the New Europe*. Reading: Ithaca Press, 139–52.
Christidis, G. (1996). 'The Muslim Minority in Greece', in G. Nonneman, T. Niblock, and B. Szajkowski (eds.), *Muslim Communities in the New Europe*. Reading: Ithaca Press, 153–66.
Christopoulos, D. (ed.) (2000). *Νομικά ζητήματα θρησκευτικής ετερότητας στην Ελλάδα* (Legal Issues of Religious Difference in Greece). Athens: Kritiki [in Greek].
Christopoulos, D. (2012). *Who is a Greek citizen? The Citizenship Framework from the Formation of the Greek State to the Beginnings of the 21st Century*. Athens: Bibliorama [in Greek].
Clogg, R. (ed.) (2002). *Minorities in Greece: Aspects of a Plural Society*. London: Hurst & Co.
Demetriou, O. (2004). 'Prioritizing Ethnicities: The Uncertainty of Pomak-ness in the Urban Greek Rhodope', *Ethnic and Racial Studies* 27(1): 95–119.
Diamanti-Karanou, P. (2003). 'Migration of Ethnic Greeks from the Former Soviet Union to Greece, 1990–2000: Policy Decisions and Implications', *Southeast European and Black Sea Studies* 3(1): 25–45.
Divani, L. (1995). *Ελλάδα και Μειονότητες* (Greece and Minorities). Athens: Nefeli [in Greek].
Dragonas, T. (2013). 'Ταυτότητες και η διαχείρισή τους στην πολυπολιτισμική Θράκη' (Identities and their Management in Multicultural Thrace), in V. Evergeti and P. Hatziprokopiou

(eds.), *Το Ισλάμ στην Ελλάδα: Θρησκευτική ταυτότητα και πρακτική μεταξύ γηγενών και μεταναστών Μουσουλμάνων* (Islam in Greece: Religious Identity and Practice among Indigenous and Migrant Muslims). Athens: Okto Publishers [in Greek] (in preparation).

Dragonas, T. and Fragoudaki, A. (2006). 'Educating the Muslim Minority of Western Thrace', *Islam and Christian Relations* 17(1): 21–41.

Dragonas, T. and Fragoudaki, A. (eds.) (2008). *Πρόσθεση όχι αφαίρεση/Πολλαπλασιασμός όχι διαίρεση* (Addition, Not Subtraction/Multiplication, Not Division). Athens: Metehmio [in Greek].

European Commission (2009). 'National Report: Greece', *Eurobarometer: Public Opinion in the European Union* 71 (Spring). See <http://ec.europa.eu/public_opinion/archives/eb/eb71/eb71_el_el_nat.pdf>, for the report in Greek, and <http://ec.europa.eu/public_opinion/archives/eb/eb71/eb71_el_en_exec.pdf>, for an executive summary in English [Accessed 7 October 2012].

Evergeti, V. (2006). 'Boundary Formation and Identity Expression in Everyday Interactions: Muslim Minorities in Greece', in J. Stakul, C. Moutsou, and H. Kopnina (eds.), *Crossing European Boundaries: Beyond Conventional Geographical Boundaries*. Oxford: Berghahn Books, 176–96.

Evergeti, V. (2011). 'Discrimination and Reaction: The Practical Constitution of Social Exclusion', *Symbolic Interaction* 34(3): 377–97.

Evergeti, V. and Hatziprokopiou, P. (forthcoming a). '"New" and "Old" Islam in Greece: Forming and Performing Religious Identities and Practices', in V. Evergeti and P. Hatziprokopiou (eds.), *Islam, Ethnicity and Belonging in the Balkans*, Special Issue of *Contemporary Islam: Dynamics of Muslim Life* (in preparation).

Evergeti, V. and Hatziprokopiou, P. (eds.) (forthcoming b). *Το Ισλάμ στην Ελλάδα: Θρησκευτική ταυτότητα και πρακτική μεταξύ γηγενών και μεταναστών Μουσουλμάνων* (Islam in Greece: Religious Identity and Practice among Indigenous and Migrant Muslims). Athens: Okto Publishers [in Greek] (in preparation).

Featherstone, K., Papadimitriou, D., Mamarelis, A., and Niarchos, G. (2011). *The Last Ottomans: The Muslim Minority of Greece, 1940–1949*. Basingstoke: Palgrave Macmillan.

Fokas, E. (2009). 'Religion in the Greek Public Sphere: Nuancing the Account', *Journal of Modern Greek Studies* 27(2): 349–74.

Fouskas, Th. (2012). 'Low Status Work and Decollectivization: The Case of Bangladeshis in Athens', *Journal of Immigrant and Refugee Studies* 10: 54–73.

Fragopoulos, I. (2007). 'Τζαμί, πλατεία, καφενείο: κοινωνική μετάβαση και χωρική οργάνωση σε μία ορεινή μειονοτική κοινότητα της Θράκης' (Mosque, Square, Coffee-Shop: Social Mobility and Spatial Organization in a Mountainous Minority Community of Thrace), *Ethnologia* 13: 5–48 [in Greek].

Fragoudaki, A. and Dragonas, T. (eds.) (1997). *Τι είν'η πατρίδα μας: Εθνοκεντρισμός στην εκπαίδευση* (What's Our Country: Ethnocentrism in Education). Athens: Alexandria Press [in Greek].

Gogonas, N. (2010). 'Religion as a Core Value in Language Maintenance: Arabic Speakers in Greece', *International Migration* 50(2): 113–29.

Greenfeld, L. and Prevelakis, N. (2010). 'The Formation of Ethnic and National Identities', in R. A. Denemark (ed.), *The International Studies Encyclopedia*. Oxford: Blackwell Publishing, 2516–31.

Gropas, R. and Triandafyllidou, A. (2009). 'Immigrants and Political Life in Greece: Between Political Patronage and the Search for Inclusion'. *EMILIE Project Policy Brief*. <http://emilie.

eliamep.gr/wp-content/uploads/2009/11/emilie_political_rights_policy_brief_greece_en.pdf> [Accessed 7 July2012].

Hatziprokopiou, P. (2006). *Globalisation and Contemporary Immigration to Southern European Cities: Processes of Social Incorporation of Balkan Immigrants in Thessaloniki.* Amsterdam: Amsterdam University Press.

Hatziprokopiou, P. (2014). 'Muslim immigrants in contemporary Greece', in T. Martikainen, J. Mapril and A. Khan (eds.), *Muslims at the Margins of Europe: Finland, Greece, Ireland and Portugal*, Leiden: Brill. (under review)

Hatziprokopiou, P. (forthcoming). 'Migrants, Islam and Greek National Identity', in V. Evergeti (ed.), *Indigenous Muslims in Greece: Case Studies of Europe's Autochthonous Muslims.* London: Springer (in preparation).

Hatziprokopiou, P. and Evergeti, V. (2014). 'Negotiating Religious Diversity and Muslim Identity in Greek Urban Spaces', *Social and Cultural Geography*, published online on 28 March 2014 (DOI: 10.1080/14649365.2014.894114).

Hatzopoulos, P. and Kambouri, N. (2010). 'National Case Study: Thematic Study on Religion'. Ge.M.IC. research project (Gender, Migration and Intercultural Communication in South-East Europe), WP 6—Greece, Panteion University of Political and Social Sciences.

Herzfeld, M. (2001). 'Towards an Ethnographic Phenomenology of the Greek Spirit', *Mediterranean Historical Review* 16(1): 13-26.

Hidiroglou, P. (1991). *The Greek Pomaks and their Relation with Turkey*. Athens: Proskinio.

Hirschon, R. (2003). 'The Consequences of the Lausanne Conventions: An Overview', in R. Hirschon (ed.), *Crossing the Aegean: An Appraisal of the 1923 Compulsory Population Exchange between Greece and Turkey*. Oxford: Berghahn Books, 13-20.

Hirschon, R. (ed.) (2003). *Crossing the Aegean: An Appraisal of the 1923 Compulsory Population Exchange between Greece and Turkey*. Oxford: Berghahn Books.

HRW (Human Rights Watch) (2012). Hate on the Streets: Xenophobic Violence in Greece. <http://www.hrw.org/sites/default/files/reports/greece0712ForUpload_0.pdf> [Accessed 12 July 2012].

Hüseyinoglu, A. (2010). 'Islam in Western Thrace after 1923: The Role of Internal and External Actors'. Working paper presented at the conference After the Wahhabi Mirage: Islam, politics and international networks in the Balkans, European Studies Centre, University of Oxford.

Imam, M. and Tsakiridi, O. (2003). *Muslims and Social Exclusion*. Athens: Livanis.

Immig, N. (2009a). '"Forced Migrations" in Greece and Turkey: The Twisting Way of Historiography', paper presented at the 4th PhD Symposium on Contemporary History of Greece and Cyprus, Hellenic Observatory, LSE, 25-26 June.

Immig, N. (2009b). 'The "New" Muslim Minorities in Greece: Between Emigration and Political Participation, 1881-1886', *Journal of Muslim Minority Affairs* 29(4): 511-22.

Ioannidou, N. (2009). 'Αναδυόμενες ταυτότητες στις παρυφές της "μουσουλμανικής μειονότητας" στη Θράκη: η σημασία της 'εμπειρίας' στο πλαίσιο της εθνογραφικής έρευνας' (Emerging Identities in the Borders of the 'Muslim Minority' in Thrace: The Importance of 'Experience' in the Context of Ethnographic Research), in F. Tsimpiridou (ed.), *Μειονοτικές και Μεταναστευτικές εμπειρίες: βιώνοντας την 'κουλτούρα του κράτους'* (Minority and Migratory Experiences: Living the 'State Culture'). Athens: Kritiki, 55-92 [in Greek].

Ioannidou, N. (forthcoming). 'Identities at Stake: Divorces and Marriages in the "Mahalas" Muslim Settlement in Komotini (Thrace—Greece)', in V. Evergeti (ed.), *Indigenous Muslims in Greece: Case Studies of Europe's Autochthonous Muslims.* London: Springer.

Iosifides, Th. and King, R. (1998). 'Socio-Spatial Dynamics and Exclusion of Three Immigrant Groups in the Athens Conurbation', *South European Society and Politics* 3(3): 205–29.

Kafetzis, P., Michalopoulou, E., Manologlou, E., and Tsartas, P. (1998). 'Εμπειρικές διαστάσεις της ξενοφοβίας' (Empirical Dimensions of Xenophobia). In E. Michalopoulou, P., Tsartas, M. Giannisopoulou, P. Kafetzis, and E. Manologlou (eds.), *Μακεδονία και Βαλκάνια, Ξενοφοβία και ανάπτυξη* (Macedonia and the Balkans: Xenophobia and Development). Athens: EKKE & Alexandria, 171–222 [in Greek].

Kambouri, H. (2009). 'Images of Pakistani Migrants in the Greek and the Pakistani Migrant Press'. Report on the project Culture, Identity and Movement: a study in the social anthropology of the everyday life and popular representations of migrants from Pakistan in Nea Ionia. Athens: Latsis Foundation <http://www.latsis-foundation.org/files/Programmes2008-2009/Dermentzopoulos%20FINAL%20REPORT.pdf> [Accessed 29 April 2012], pp. 87–131.

Kapllani, G. (2002). 'Θρησκεία και αλβανική εθνική ταυτότητα: Μύθοι και πραγματικότητες' (Religion and Albanian National Identity: Myths and Realities), *Synhrona Themata* 81: 50–8 [in Greek].

Karakasidou, A. (1993). 'Politicizing Culture: Negating Ethnic Identity in Greek Macedonia', *Journal of Modern Greek Studies* 11(1): 229–35.

Karakasidou, A. (1995). 'Vestiges of the Ottoman Past: Muslims Under Siege in Contemporary Greek Thrace', *Cultural Survival* 19(2), Special issue on Nationalism in Eastern Europe <http://culturalsurvival.org>.

Kassimeris, G. and Samouris, A. (2012). 'Examining Islamic Associations of Pakistani and Bangladeshi Immigrants in Greece', *Religion, State and Society* 40(2): 174–91.

Katsikas, S. (2009a). 'European Modernity and Islamic Reformism among Muslims of the Balkans in the Late-Ottoman and Post-Ottoman Period (1830s–1945)', *Journal of Muslim Minority Affairs* 29(4): 435–42.

Katsikas, S. (2009b). 'Millets in Nation-States: The Case of Greek and Bulgarian Muslims, 1912–1923', *Nationalities Papers* 37(2): 177–201.

King, R. (2000). 'Southern Europe in the Changing Global Map of Migration', in R. King, G. Lazaridis, and Ch. Tsardanidis (eds.), *Eldorado or Fortress? Migration in Southern Europe*. Basingstoke: Macmillan, 1–26.

Koliopoulos, I. and Veremis, Th. (2002). *Greece: The Modern Sequel. From 1831 to the Present*. London: Hurst & Company.

KSPM (2007). 'In Search of Spaces of Coexistence', project report by the Centre for Support of Repatriate Migrants and Ethnic Greeks <http://www.kspm.gr/> [Accessed 17 May 2012] [in Greek].

Kurban, D. and Tsitselikis, K. (2010). *Μια ιστορία αμοιβαιότητας: Τα μειονετικά βακούφια ατην Ελλάδα και την Τουρκία* (A Story of Reciprocity: Minority Vakifs in Greece and Turkey). Istanbul: TESEV Publications [in Greek].

Leghari, I. U. (2009). 'Pakistani Immigrants in Greece: From Changing Pattern of Migration to Diaspora Politics and Transnationalism'. Paper presented at the 4th LSE Ph.D. Symposium on Contemporary Greece, LSE-Hellenic Observatory. 25–26 June 2009. Available at <http://www.lse.ac.uk/collections/hellenicObservatory/pdf/4th_%20Symposium/PAPERS_PPS/ETHNICITY_IMMIGRATION/LEGHARI.pdf> [Accessed 8 October 2010].

Liakos, A. and Salvanou, E. (2010). 'Citizenship, Memory and Governmentality: A Tale of Two Migrant Communities', in A. K. Isaacs (ed.), *Citizenships and Identities: Inclusion, Exclusion, Participation*. Pisa: Plus-Pisa University Press, 155–72.

Macartney, C. A. (1934). *National States and National Minorities*. Oxford: Oxford University Press.
Mantanika, R. and Kouki, H. (2011). 'The Spatiality of a Social Struggle in Greece at the Time of the IMF', *City: Analysis of Urban Trends, Culture, Theory, Policy, Action* 15(3-4): 482-90.
Mantouvalou, K. (2009). 'Equal Recognition, Consolidation or Familiarization? The Language Rights Debate in the Context of the Minority of Western Thrace in Greece', *Ethnicities* 9(4): 477-506.
Maroukis. Th. (2008). 'Country Report: Greece'. Report prepared for the project *CLANDESTINO Undocumented Migration: counting the uncountable—data and trends across Europe*, EU 6th Framework Programme. <http://irregular-migration.net/typo3_upload/groups/31/4. Background_Information/4.4.Country_Reports/Greece_CountryReport_Clandestino_Nov09_2.pdf> [Accessed 16 April 2014].
Maroukis, Th. (2012). 'Update Report Greece: The Number of Irregular Migrants in Greece at the end of 2010 and 2011'. Database on Irregular Migration, Update Report <http://irregular-migration.net/index.php?id=229>.
Mavrogordatos, G. (2003). 'Orthodoxy and Nationalism in the Greek Case', *West European Politics* 26(1): 117-36.
Mavromatis, G. (2005). *Τα Παιδιά της Καλκάντζας. Εκπαίδευση, φτώχεια και κοινωνικός αποκλεισμός σε μια κοινότητα μουσουλμάνων της Θράκης* (Children of Kalkantza: Education, Poverty and Social Exclusion in a Muslim Community of Thrace). Athens: Metaihmio Publications [in Greek].
Mavromatis, G. (forthcoming). 'Stigmatised Identity and Social Exclusion in the Muslim Community of Kalkantza', in V. Evergeti (ed.), *Indigenous Muslims in Greece: Case Studies of Europe's Autochthonous Muslims*. London: Springer.
Mavroudi, E. (2007). 'Learning to be Palestinian in Athens: Constructing National Identities in Diaspora', *Global Networks* 7(4): 392-411.
Meinardus, R. (2002). 'Muslims: Turks, Pomaks and Gypsies', in R. Clogg (ed.), *Minorities in Greece: Aspects of a Plural Society*. London: Hurst & Co, 81-93.
Mekos, Z. (1991). *Οι αρμοδιότητες του Μουφτή και η Ελληνική νομοθεσία* (The Responsibilities of the Mufti and the Greek Legislation). Athens: Sakkoulas [in Greek].
Mekos, Z. (1995). *Θράκη, συνιστώσες του μειονοτικού προβλήματος* (Thrace, Aspects of the Minority Problem). Komotini: Hrodotos [in Greek].
Mentzel, P. (2000). 'Introduction: Identity, Confessionalism and Nationalism', *Nationalities Papers* 28(1): 7-11.
Michail, D. (2003). 'From "Locality" to "European Identity": Shifting Identities among the Pomak Minority in Greece', *Ethnologia Balkanica* 7: 140-57.
Milios, J. (2000). *The Greek Social Formation: From Expansionism to Capitalist Development*. Athens: Kritiki [in Greek].
Molokotos-Liederman, L. (2007). 'Looking at Religion and Greek Identity from the Outside: The Identity Cards Conflict through the Eyes of Greek Minorities', *Religion, State and Society* 35(2): 139-61.
Neuburger, M. (2000). 'Pomak Borderlands: Muslims on the Edge of Nations', *Nationalities Papers* 28(1): 181-98.
Noussia, A. and Lyons, M. (2009). 'Inhabiting Spaces of Liminality: Migrants in Omonia, Athens', *Journal of Ethnic and Migration Studies* 35(4): 601-24.
Öktem, K. (2010). 'New Islamic Actors after the Wahhabi Intermezzo: Turkey's Return to the Muslim Balkans'. European Studies Centre, University of Oxford. Available at <http://balkanmuslims.com/pdf/Oktem-Balkan-Muslims.pdf>.

Oran, B. (2003). 'The Story of Those Who Stayed: Lessons from Articles 1 and 2 of the Convention', in R. Hirschon (ed.), *Crossing the Aegean: An Appraisal of the 1923 Compulsory Population Exchange between Greece and Turkey*. Oxford: Berghahn Books, 97–116.

Papadopoulou, A. (2003). '"Give us asylum and help us leave the country!" Kurdish Asylum Seekers in Greece and the Politics of Reception', *Immigrants and Minorities* 22(2–3): 346–61.

Papanastasiou, A. (forthcoming). 'Conceptualising the Ummah: The Case of Muslim Immigrants in Greece', in V. Evergeti and P. Hatziprokopiou (eds.), *Islam, Ethnicity and belonging in the Balkans*, Special Issue of *Identities: Global Studies in Culture and Power* (in preparation).

Papanikolaou, A. (forthcoming). '"A claim to fail": The Case of the Turkish Minority Associations in Western Thrace (Greece)', in V. Evergeti (ed.), *Indigenous Muslims in Greece: Case Studies of Europe's Autochthonous Muslims*. London: Springer.

Papantoniou, A. (2009). 'Μουσουλμάνοι μετανάστες στην Αθήνα' (Muslim Migrants in Athens), *Ekklisia*, 86th year, vol. 5: 348–60 [in Greek].

Petronoti, M. and Papagaroufali, E. (2006). 'Marrying a "Foe": Joint Scripts and Rewritten Histories of Greek-Turkish Couples', *Identities: Global Studies in Culture and Power* 13: 557–84.

Polis, A. (1992). 'Greek National Identity: Religious Minorities, Rights, and European Norms', *Journal of Modern Greek Studies* 10: 171–95.

Poulton, H. (1994). *Balkans: Minorities and States in Conflict*. London: Minority Rights Publication.

Psomiades, H. J. (1968). *The Eastern Question: The Last Phase*. Thessaloniki: Institute for Balkan Studies.

Public Issue (2010). 'Οι Έλληνες και το Ισλάμ: Τι γνωρίζει και τι πιστεύει η κοινή γνώμη' (Greeks and Islam; What Public Opinion Knows and Believes). Public Issue Opinion Surveys, November <http://www.publicissue.gr/1395> [Accessed 2 February 2013].

Roudometof, V. (2010). 'The Evolution of Greek Orthodoxy in the Context of World Historical Globalisation', in V. Roudometof and V. N. Makrides (eds.), *Orthodox Christianity in 21st Century Greece: The Role of Religion in Culture, Ethnicity and Politics*. Farnham: Ashgate, 23–38.

Salvanou, E. (2009). 'Pakistani Migrants at N. Ionia: A Community at the Procedure of Forming: Narratives and Representations through Space and Time'. Report on the project *Culture, Identity and Movement: a study in the social anthropology of the everyday life and popular representations of migrants from Pakistan in Nea Ionia*. Athens: Latsis Foundation. <http://www.latsis-foundation.org/files/Programmes2008-2009/Dermentzopoulos%20FINAL%20REPORT.pdf> [Accessed 29 April 2012), pp. 12–87.

Seypel, T. (1989). 'Pomaks in Northeastern Greece: An Engangered Balkan Population', *Journal Institute of Muslim Minority Affairs* 10(1): 41–9.

Skoulariki, A. (2010). 'Old and New Mosques in Greece: A New Debate Haunted by History', in S. Allievi in collaboration with Ethnobarometer (eds.), *Mosques in Europe: Why a Solution Has Become a Problem*. Network of European Foundations Initiative on Religion and Democracy in Europe. London: Alliance Publishing Trust, 300–17.

Soltaridis, S. (1990). Η Δ. Θράκη και οι Μουσουλμάνοι: Τι ακριβώς συμβαίνει (Western Thrace and the Muslims: What Exactly is Happening?). Athens: Nea Synora—Livanis [in Greek].

Stathis, P. (2010). 'Μουσουλμάνοι και ιδιότητα του πολίτη στην ελληνική επανάσταση' (Muslims and Citizenship in the Greek Revolution), *Avgi* newspaper, 28 March 2010. <http://

www.avgi.gr/ArticleActionshow.action?articleID=531975> [Accessed 2 February 2011] [in Greek].

Terzopoulou, M. (2008). 'Ιερά δάκρυα, ιερός πόλεμος. Ποιητική και πολιτική της σιιτικής λατρείας των Πακιστανών μεταναστών στην Ελλάδα' (Holly Tears, Holly War: Poetics and Politics of Shi'a Worship of Pakistani Migrants in Greece', in *Ετερότητες και μουσική στα Βαλκάνια* (Otherness and Music in the Balkans), special issue of *Tetradia*, no. 4: 91-9. Arta: TEI Epiros & KEMO [in Greek].

Thornberry, P. (1991). *International Law and the Rights of Minorities*. Oxford: Clarendon Press.

Tonchev, P. (2007). 'Asian Migrants in Greece: Origins, Status and Prospects'. Report prepared at the Asian Studies Unit, Institute of International Economic Relations, Athens, January <http://www.idec.gr/iier/new/asian_migrants_gr.pdf> [Accessed 8 June 2012].

Triandafyllidou, A. (1998). 'National Identity and the Other', *Ethnic and Racial Studies* 21(4): 593-612.

Triandafyllidou, A. (2009). 'The Mohammed Cartoons Crisis in the British and Greek Press: A European Matter?', *Journalism Studies* 10(1): 36-53.

Triandafyllidou, A. (2010). 'Greece: The Challenges of Native and Immigrant Muslim Populations', in A. Triandafyllidou (ed.), *Muslims in 21st Century Europe: Structural and Cultural Perspectives*. Abingdon: Routledge, 199-217.

Triandafyllidou, A. and Gropas, R. (2009). 'Constructing Difference: The Mosque Debates in Greece', *Journal of Ethnic and Migration Studies* 35(6): 957-75.

Triandafyllidou, A. and Paraskevopoulou, A. (2002). 'When is the Greek Nation? The Role of Enemies and Minorities', *Geopolitics* 7(2): 75-98.

Triandafyllidou, A. and Veikou, M. (2002). 'The Hierarchy of Greekness: Ethnic and National Considerations in Greek Immigration Policy', *Ethnicities* 2(2): 189-208.

Trubeta, S. (2003). '"Minorization" and "Ethnicization" in Greek Society: Comparative Perspectives on Moslem Migrants and the Moslem Minority', in S. Trubeta and Ch. Voss (eds.), *Minorities in Greece: Historical Issues and New Perspectives*, special edition of *History and Culture of South Eastern Europe: An Annual Journal/Jahrbücher für Geschichte und Kultur Südosteuropas* 5 (2003/2004): 95-112.

Trubeta, S. (2001). *Κατασκευάζοντας ταυτότητες για τους Μουσουλμάνους της Θράκης: Το παράδειγμα των Πομάκων και των Τσιγγάνων* (Constructing Identities for the Muslims of Thrace: The Example of Pomaks and Gypsies). Athens: Kritiki.

Trubeta, S. (2008). *Οι Ρομά στο Σύγχρονο Ελληνικό Κράτος: Συμβιώσεις, αναιρέσεις, απουσίες* (The Roma in the Contemporary Greek State: Symbiosis, Withdrawals, Absences). Athens: Kritiki.

Tsibiridou, F. (1994). 'Χώρος: δομές και αναπαραστάσεις -ανθρωπολογική πρόταση ανάγνωσης του χώρου στα Πομακοχώρια του νομού Ροδόπης' (Space: Structures and Representations: An Anthropological Proposal for Understanding Space in the Pomak Villages of Rodopi), *Ethnologia* 3: 5-31.

Tsitselikis, K. (2004a). 'Muslims in Greece', in R. Potz and W. Wieshaider (eds.), *Islam and the European Union*. Leuven: Peeters, 79-107.

Tsitselikis, K. (2004b). 'The Legal Status of Islam in Greece', *Die Welt des Islams* 44(3): 402-31.

Tsitselikis, K. (2006). 'Μουσουλμανικές κοινότητες στην Ελλάδα πριν και μετά το 1923: Δικαιϊκές συνέχειες και ιδεολογικές ασυνέπειες' (Muslim Communities in Greece before and after 1923: Legal Continuations and Ideological Discrepancies), in K. Tsitselikis (ed.), *Η Ελληνοτουρκική Ανταλλαγή Πληθυσμών: Πτυχές μιας εθνικής σύγκρουσης* (The Greek-Turkish Exchange of Populations: Aspects of a National Conflict). Athens: Kritiki, 368-87.

Tsitselikis, K. (2007). 'The Pending Modernization of Islam in Greece: From Millet to Minority Status', *Südosteuropa* 55(4): 354–72.
Tsitselikis, K. (2009). 'Greece', in J. S. Nielsen, S. Akgönül, A. Alibašić, B. Maréchal, and Ch. Moe (eds.), *Yearbook of Muslims in Europe*, vol. 1. Leiden: Brill, 151–61.
Tsitselikis, K. (2010). 'Greece', in J. S. Nielsen, S. Akgönül, A. Alibašić, B. Maréchal, and Ch. Moe (eds.), *Yearbook of Muslims in Europe*, vol. 2. Leiden: Brill, 233–44.
Tsitselikis, K. (2012). *Old and New Islam in Greece: From Historical Minorities to Immigrant Newcomers*. Leiden: Brill.
Vickers, M. (2006). *The Albanians: A Modern History*. New York: I. B.Tauris.
Wanche, S. I. (2004). 'An Assessment of the Iraqi Community in Greece'. Report commissioned by the UNHCR Representation in Greece and supported by the Evaluation and Policy Analysis Unit <http://www.aina.org/reports/aoticig.pdf> [Accessed 13 June 2012].
Yiakoumaki, V. (2006). 'Ethnic Turks and "Muslims" and the Performance of Multiculturalism: The Case of the Dromeno of Thrace', *South European Society and Politics* 11(1): 145–61.
Zenginis, E. (1988). *Ο Μπεκτατισμός στη Δυτική Θράκη -Συμβολή στην ιστορία της διάδοσης του μουσουλμανισμού στον ελλαδικό χώρο* (Baktashism in Western Thrace: Contribution to the History of the Distribution of Islamism in the Greek Space). Thessaloniki: IMXA.
Zenginis, E. (1994). *Οι Μουσουλμάνοι Αθίγγανοι της Θράκης* (The Muslim Athigganoi of Thrace). Thessaloniki: IMXA.
Ziaka, A. (2009). 'Muslims and Muslim Education in Greece', in E. Aslan (ed.), *Islamische Erziehung in Europa/Islamic Education in Europe*. Vienna: Böhlau, 141–78.

# CHAPTER 9

# SCANDINAVIAN COUNTRIES

## GARBI SCHMIDT AND JONAS OTTERBECK

THE Scandinavian countries (in this case defined as Denmark, Norway, and Sweden) share similar experiences of their respective Muslim populations—which within all three national contexts must be categorized as a recent phenomenon. Most Muslims living in the three countries arrived as immigrants (as labour migrants, refugees, or through family reunification), but a growing number (yet still small) of the majority population are converts to Islam (see e.g. Jensen and Østergaard 2007; Roald 2004). Some Muslims also formally leave Islam, a process that has not been researched but written about in different news media. Pathways to residency in Scandinavia look different before and after the global oil crisis and recession in the early 1970s. From a modest start in the early 1960s up until the early 1970s, migrants with a Muslim family background came as labour migrants from southern Europe to Sweden and Denmark, most of them from Yugoslavia or Turkey. Labour migrants from Pakistan also came to Denmark. The first labour migrants with a Muslim background came to Norway in the late 1960s (Vogt 2000). The Muslim labour migrants were predominantly males in their 20s. All Scandinavian countries eventually introduced restrictions on labour migration, reducing it drastically in numbers in the first half of 1970s. During the 1970s, as a result of family reunification, a higher degree of family members, especially women and children came to Scandinavia—primarily ending up in the major cities. The proportion of refugees among Muslim migrants started to increase in the 1980s, bringing both individuals and families to Scandinavia. Another way to enter Scandinavia was on the basis of asylum (see also Bevelander 2009: 57; Schmidt and Jacobsen 2000, 2004; Brochmann and Hagelund 2010; NOU 2011: 67ff.).

The demographic changes in the three countries have also had a noticeable impact on research and knowledge production across these contexts. Scandinavia has a long history of Oriental/Islamic Studies research, but before the late 1980s such disciplines predominantly focused on Islam and Muslim as national outsiders. Including a perspective on Muslims as groups living in Scandinavia is undoubtedly connected to the intensified political focus on the impact of immigration and cultural diversity from the mid-1980s onward. As is often the case, research agendas develop according to societal perceptions of particular aspects of human coexistence as particularly problematic, challenging, or (negatively) transformative (Jacobsen 2006: 365ff.; Schmidt 2008b).

Although a Muslim presence in Scandinavia is a recent phenomenon, historical records show that Muslims lived in Scandinavia long before the second half of the twentieth century. One example comes from the Danish national censuses. In 1880 eight individuals were recorded as 'Muhammadans' (B. A. Jacobsen 2009). In Denmark, national censuses were carried out until 1970, but after 1880 the category of Muhammadan or Muslim for that matter was not used. There are two possible explanations for the lacking registration of Muslims in Denmark between 1880 and 1921, when the state stopped registering people according to their religion. One may be that there were no Muslims living in Denmark in the thirty-year period; another that Muslims were simply registered under the category 'other religions' (B. A. Jacobsen 2009). However, the police records of citizens in Copenhagen from 1890–1923 include the names of immigrants from countries with Muslim majorities that indicate a Muslim heritage. For example, we find sixteen immigrants from Morocco, all registered as living in Copenhagen between 1913 and 1923 (and all artists), bearing names such as Ben Ali Mohamad and Hajd Hamed (<http://www.politietsregisterblade.dk>). A similar situation applies to Sweden where police registers from the early twentieth century include persons from Muslim majority countries who had been expelled from Sweden (Lundborg 1919[1]). However, it was never a sizeable population. The last time the Swedish state performed a religious census was in 1930. Only some two to eleven persons registered as Muslims; the number is uncertain due to the classification 'Muhammadans and other Asian communities' in the original rapport (Statistics Sweden 1937). According to our research, Norwegian scholars have not yet looked into the possibility of finding Muslims through historical archives. Laws were also slightly different as 'non-Lutherans were excluded entry' into Norway and 'baptism and confirmation were compulsory for all inhabitants until 1912' (C. M. Jacobsen 2011: 19). We know, however, that Norway signed a trade treaty with the Tunisian Sultan al-Mustansir in the thirteenth century, making it likely that sailors went ashore in the major harbour towns of Norway, and at times stayed on for a while, during that period (Lower 2007: 216). But those visits, including Ottoman envoys visiting Sweden in the eighteenth century, did not lead to any permanent settlements and will not be discussed further here.

Specific statistical demographic data on the number of Muslims, their social standard, housing, and labour market performance, do not exist in the Scandinavian countries, even though the countries are world renowned for their extensive population data, available from governmental institutions like SCB (Statistics Sweden), DST (Statistics

---

[1] Herman Lundborg was a committed racial biologist who became the head of the State Institute for Racial Biology that was inaugurated in 1922. In this book that preceded the institute, he collected images from what he claimed were different racial types. He included images of foreigners expelled from Sweden after having lived in the country for some time. They include, among others, a Tunisian and an Egyptian. Nothing is yet written about these, thus far nameless, persons.

Denmark), and SSB (Statistics Norway).[2] The main reason is that the religious affiliation of residents in these countries has not been registered since the early or mid-twentieth century. However, since many Scandinavians are paying members of a 'congregation' of their respective faiths, some statistics covering the majority of the citizens are available. For example, in Sweden in 2011, more than 7.3 million people, 77% (of a total population of 9.5 million) were registered members or active in a religious community (Swedish Church 2013; SST 2013). Current numbers show that in Norway (2011), 83% of 4.4 million are members of the Norwegian state church (C. M. Jacobsen 2011: 18). Unfortunately, many migrant denominations do not register their members. Further, many migrants do not have a tradition of joining a religious association through membership. Instead, much of the statistical data on Muslims in Scandinavia is derived on the basis of the (former) citizenship of the individual and the citizenship of his or her parents. Such figures are rough estimations since it is difficult to know how many of, for example, the Turkish citizens who have immigrated to Sweden actually are Muslims. The majority of the Turkish population are Muslims (estimated to 99%) but a large proportion of Turkish migrants to Sweden have a Christian family background (some 30–40% according to Sander 1993: 10).

The Muslim population of Scandinavia is generally heterodox. No specific ethnicity or national belonging dominates, but some immigrant groups are more represented in some countries than others. For example, Muslims of Pakistani origin are more likely to settle in Denmark and Norway, while Sweden has received a larger proportion of Iraqi refugees. (For detailed information on the estimation of the number of Muslims, see the section on Immigration and Assimilation in Statistics.)

In the wider public and media, Muslims are frequently portrayed as a cultural, ethnic group, not as a heterogeneous population segment, where different understandings of Islam are represented and practised. Looking at Islam in Scandinavia one does well to notice that the first purpose-built mosques in Denmark and Sweden belonged to Ahmadiyya Muslims (Copenhagen, 1967, Gothenburg, 1976) who, while being few in numbers, have had a Scandinavian *dawa*-mission since the 1950s (Otterbeck 2000a; Vogt 2000). In Norway, Ahmadiyyas converted a villa into a mosque in the late 1970s, one of the earliest mosques in the country. A Pakistani Deobandi group inaugurated a mosque in Oslo already in 1974. Different kinds of Shi'a Muslims (though most are Twelver Shi'a) are also active in Scandinavia, besides from Sunni Muslims of all schools, Sufis of several different orders, and also traditions which can be called Alids, i.e. especially Kurdish/Turkish/Iranian/Iraqi groups with a very high esteem for Ali. There are also different pietistic, reformist, or resurgence groups or trends such as Tablighi Jamaat, the Fethullah Gülen movement, Salafis, Muslim Brotherhood supporters, Shabaab supporters, Deobandis, etc. Furthermore, Islam is preached and practised through a great variety of languages and regional differences. Finally, defining who is a 'Muslim' on the basis of family background and history sometimes clashes with individual self-identification: religious belonging is by no means hereditary. Identification can

---

[2] Visit their webpages at <http://www.scb.se>, <http://www.ssb.no>, <http://www.dst.dk>.

also be situational, meaning that 'Muslim' is a relevant label in certain spheres or times, but irrelevant in others (Otterbeck 2010a).

Below, we will highlight the situation for the Muslim populations of Scandinavia by discussing aspects of immigration, socio-economic issues, active citizenship and representation, and discrimination and violence.

# Immigration and Assimilation in Statistics

## Denmark

Statistical evidence of immigration from countries with Muslim majorities is scarce in the period 1950–74 when migration to Denmark from such countries gained pace. We do have some indications of the amount of migration from the period from existing sources, as illustrated by Table 9.1.

In 1973, the Danish government formally stopped free migration to the country. Before then immigrants could, if they found a job, apply for work and a residence permit at the local police station (Simonsen 1990: 15). In 1974 the rules were eased somewhat, making it possible for people who already had family living in Denmark, or who were marrying someone living in the country (family reunification), or who sought asylum (refugees) to settle in Denmark.

Immigrant statistics underline the increase in migration to Denmark from countries with Muslim majorities. Table 9.2 highlights this increase, including also the category of descendants (Danish: *efterkommere*). Particularly groups of refugees increased from 1990 onwards, including people from Iran, Iraq, Somalia, and Lebanon.

Table 9.1 Foreign citizens in Denmark 1965–75

| Year | Turkey | Pakistan | Former Yugoslavia | Morocco |
|---|---|---|---|---|
| 1965* | 85 | 616** | 218 | – |
| 1970* | 1,852 | 1,512** | 2,495 | – |
| 1975* | 8,129 | 4,982 | 6,892 | 1,292 |

*All based on Pedersen and Selmer (1991: 33). Tables based on data from Statistics Denmark.
** Until 1971 Statistics Denmark did not include Pakistan as a single country, but included immigrants from that country as people from Asia. Numbers marked with ** therefore include all immigrants from Asia in the period.

Table 9.2 Foreign citizens and descendants in Denmark 1980–2005

| Year | Turkey | Pakistan | Former Yugoslavia | Morocco | Iran | Iraq | Somalia | Lebanon |
|---|---|---|---|---|---|---|---|---|
| 1980 | 14,086 | 7,845 | 7,452 | 2,104 | 241 | 160 | 133 | 222 |
| 1985 | 18,995 | 9,485 | 8,166 | 2,977 | 984 | 266 | 168 | 280 |
| 1990 | 29,442 | 12,014 | 10,518 | 4,295 | 8,591 | 2,427 | 531 | 7,945 |
| 1995 | 39,222 | 14,692 | 13,006 | 5,955 | 11,157 | 6,415 | 5,280 | 15,110 |
| 2000 | 48,773 | 17,509 | 17,176 | 7,813 | 12,980 | 14,902 | 14,856 | 19,011 |
| 2005 | 54,859 | 19,301 | 17,528 | 8,974 | 14,289 | 26,351 | 16,952 | 22,232 |

Source: Based on Mikkelsen (2008: 37).

Although we have statistics on immigration to Denmark and people with immigrant background, we do not have any exact statistics on the number of Muslims living in the country. A qualified estimate was made by sociologist of religion Brian Jacobsen, in 2007 (B. A. Jacobsen 2007, 2009). According to Jacobsen's calculations, based on immigration statistics and estimates of converts to Islam, around 190,000 people or 3.5% of the total Danish population were Muslim.

## Sweden

The first Muslim group to arrive in Sweden was the Russian-Baltic Tatars who came as refugees during the 1940s. Most Tatars went to Finland where the Tatars had had an organization for decades, but a few families made their way to Stockholm. These Muslims formed the first Islamic 'parish'[3] in 1949 (Otterbeck 1998). Eventually their initiative merged with other Turkic groups arriving as labour migrants. The Tatar group came at a time when Swedish emigration was lower than immigration for the first time in decades due to the decrease of the large emigration of Swedes, primarily to the USA (Lundh and Olsson 1994). Today, a result of a continuous immigration is that 19.5% of the population (of 9.5 million) were not born in Sweden, or have parents who were both born outside the country (Statistics Sweden 2013).

At the end of 2010, 633,292 persons residing in Sweden had a foreign citizenship, approximately 7% of the total population (Statistics Sweden 2010). Among the top seven foreign citizenships, all were neighbouring countries apart from Iraqi citizens (56,581, number two on the list) and Somali citizens (30,807, number six). It is possible to obtain Swedish citizenship if fulfilling certain criteria that vary a little depending on

---

[3] The Tatars themselves used the Swedish Christian word 'församling' which translates into English as 'parish'.

circumstances. But the general rule is, firstly, to obtain a permanent residence permit and then live five years consecutively in Sweden. Since 1980, roughly between 20,000 and 50,000 individuals are granted Swedish citizenship every year. In 2010, Iraqi was the single most common citizenship background when changing citizenship to Swedish (Statistics Sweden 2010).

Åke Sander has estimated the number of Muslims in Sweden in numerous publications over the last decades. In his latest book on Muslims in Sweden, he and his co-author gave an overview of the demographic development as presented here in Figure 9.1 (Larsson and Sanders 2007).

It is reasonable, judging from migration, that the Muslim population in Sweden might have numbered some 450,000 in 2011. From Figure 9.1 we can deduce that approximately 75% of the Muslim population have either migrated to Sweden or were born in the country after 1992, i.e. during the last twenty years. Further, a third of the Muslims living in Sweden is expected to be of school age or younger, many of them born in Sweden (Anwar et al. 2004: 224). Since the Swedish state supports religious organizations economically, we also have available figures of the number of Muslims registered as members in the religious (Muslim) associations that the state supports. The governmental department, set up in 1971, called SST (the Commission for State Grants to Religious Communities) is in charge of giving support. According to SST's statistics for 2011, the department supports some 110,000 members of Muslim associations divided into approximately 120 different associations, organized through six national umbrella organizations (SST 2013). Some local associations have refrained from joining the umbrella organizations and are not supported through SST. The most well-known of these, the Islamic Centre, is in charge of the only purpose-built mosque in Malmö.

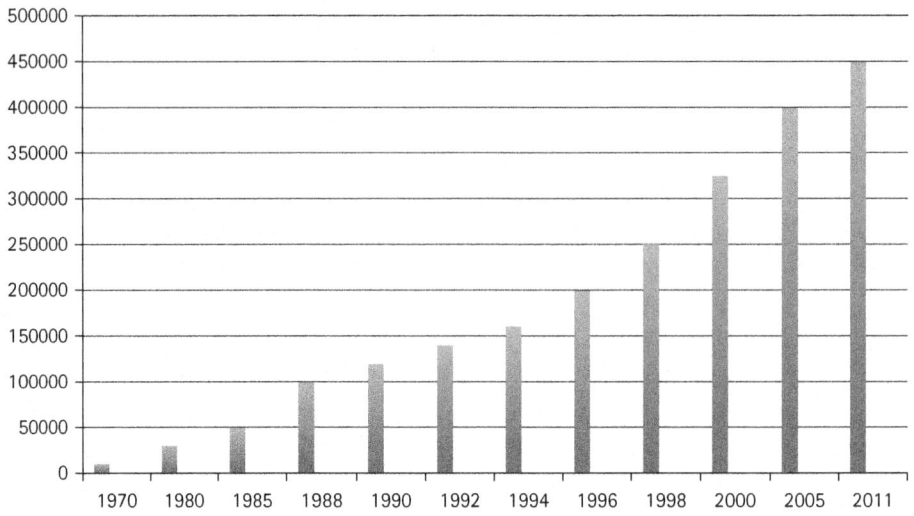

FIGURE 9.1 Number of Muslims in Sweden: estimation

*Source*: Based on Larsson and Sander (2007: 74) with 2011 addition.

Table 9.3 Immigration of some size to Sweden from Muslim majority countries (absolute numbers)

|  | 2000 | 2001 | 2002 | 2003 | 2004 | 2005 | 2006 | 2007 | 2008 | 2009 |
|---|---|---|---|---|---|---|---|---|---|---|
| Afghani. | 524 | 484 | 498 | 515 | 443 | 299 | 1,241 | 465 | 603 | 869 |
| Bosnia-H. | 776 | 936 | 1,134 | 1,349 | 884 | 668 | 1,066 | 603 | 630 | 592 |
| Iran | 1,143 | 1,456 | 1,515 | 1,131 | 1,311 | 1,207 | 2,124 | 1,720 | 2,116 | 2,813 |
| Iraq | 4,938 | 4,802 | 5,175 | 3,447 | 2,054 | 2,549 | 9,732 | 13,045 | 9,203 | 6,346 |
| Jordan | 842 | 752 | 845 | 826 | 493 | 265 | 736 | 798 | 760 | 555 |
| Lebanon | 480 | 493 | 459 | 516 | 601 | 641 | 1,964 | 705 | 610 | 749 |
| Pakistan | 334 | 394 | 468 | 478 | 589 | 760 | 1,042 | 1,331 | 1,574 | 1,849 |
| Somalia | 331 | 416 | 630 | 1,075 | 728 | 949 | 2,355 | 2,537 | 2,522 | 4,965 |
| Syria | 890 | 1,006 | 1,294 | 1,403 | 1,093 | 865 | 1,685 | 1,984 | 3,048 | 3,062 |
| Turkey | 1,032 | 1,192 | 1,290 | 1,420 | 1,421 | 1,209 | 1,809 | 1,653 | 1,752 | 2,164 |

Source: Based on Statistics Sweden (2009).

Instead of gaining partial support from the Swedish state, the organization has relied on donations (not least from the Islamic Call society of Libya) and temporary revenues from different projects.

The majority of the Muslims in Sweden were born in Sweden, Bosnia, Turkey, Albania, Lebanon, Iraq, Iran, Afghanistan, and Somalia. While their ethnicity does not necessarily mirror their citizenship, they are likely to be, for example, Kurdish, Palestinian, or Kosovo-Albanian. Figures for immigration between 2000 and 2009 from predominantly Muslim countries are presented in Table 9.3.

As is clear from the above, immigration to Sweden is a continuous process. The exceptions are the results of political crises in the different countries. It might be added that return migration is substantially smaller, seldom more than 100 persons and often much less. The exceptions are Iran (130 to 330 return migrants a year) and Iraq from 2003 onwards (120 to 470 returnees a year).

# Norway

Immigration to Norway from countries with a Muslim majority resembles what we see in both Denmark and Sweden. Many of the same immigrant groups are represented in significant numbers. One exception is that whereas Turks are a larger demographic group than Pakistanis in both Sweden and Denmark, the reverse tendency can be seen in Norway (see Table 9.4).

To the statistics in Table 9.4 should be added that Somali migrants numbered 23,600 in 2008 (Leirvik 2014). Another significant demographic trend of the Norwegian case

Table 9.4 Total number of immigrants to Norway (selected countries)

| | 1970 | 1980 | 1990 | 2000 | 2010 |
|---|---|---|---|---|---|
| Pakistan | 163 | 6,828 | 15,488 | 22,831 | 31,061 |
| Iraq | 20 | 38 | 759 | 7,664 | 26,374 |
| Iran | 43 | 135 | 5,381 | 10,354 | 16,321 |
| Turkey | 236 | 2,384 | 6,155 | 10,481 | 15,998 |
| Bosnia-Herzegovina | 0 | 0 | 3 | 12,614 | 15,918 |
| Afghanistan | 0 | 3 | 266 | 804 | 10,475 |
| Morocco | 401 | 1,286 | 3,064 | 5,409 | 8,058 |

*Source*: NOU (2011, no. 7: 177).

is that the presence of some immigrant groups has increased significantly from 1990 onwards. Whereas only three individuals from Bosnia-Herzegovina lived in Norway in 1990, the number had increased to 12,614 in 2000. Another group where we see a similar increase from 2000 onwards is the Afghan group. Whereas only 804 Afghan immigrants lived in Norway in 2000, the number was 10,475 in 2010. The rapid demographic increase of Afghanis, Bosnia-Herzegovinians, and Iraqis underlines a growing prevalence of refugees in Norway, primarily from countries where Norway is partaking actively in military operations.

The number of Muslims living in Norway is estimated in 2009 to be 160,000, making Muslims 3% of the total population (of 4.8 million). Out of these, 92,700 were registered members of a Muslim association (Leirvik 2014). As in the other Scandinavian countries, these figures are estimations and for example in C. M. Jacobsen (2011), similar but not identical figures are given. However, the Muslim population in Norway has gradually increased over the last three decades, as reflected in recent research. For 1980, Leirvik (2006) gave a figure of 10,000 Muslims, for 2000, Vogt (2000, 2002) estimated that 67–70,000 Muslims lived in Norway, for 2005, C. M. Jacobsen (2009) stated 120,000, and for 2007, Jacobsen and Leirvik gave the estimate of 150,000 Muslims in Norway (Jacobsen and Leirvik 2009). In an admittedly rough estimation, Vogt (2000) stated that probably 20% of the Muslim population in Norway was Shi'a and 80% Sunni Muslims.

## Assimilation

The concept of assimilation is highly contested and debated in the Scandinavian contexts. Most frequently politicians, the media, and also researchers use the concept of integration, although the implications of the concept are far from clear (Emerek 2003). Researchers, on one hand, use the concept as a way to determine a two-way process, where the access to resources and participation in societal arenas are equally distributed among the majority and minority (e.g. Kjeldstadli 2008: 106). Among politicians, on the other hand, the concept is frequently used synonymously with assimilation: as a demand on immigrants to adapt to norms and values understood as, for example, inherently Danish (Hervik 2002; Schmidt 2008b). In some politicians' rhetoric 'national' norms and values are considered so crucial for active citizenship and inclusion that anything but an unconditional submission to these norms is considered a challenge to social cohesion and the very fabric of the welfare state (Otterbeck 2010b; Schmidt 2011b).

Debates over immigrants' integration in Scandinavian societies shows a blurring of (1) what the term 'integration' actually implies, (2) what parameters immigrants should follow when integrating, focusing on either involvement in the labour market or the educational system, or adopting certain social and cultural norms of 'Danishness', 'Swedishness', or 'Norwegianness', and (3) understandings of the easily or problematically integrated immigrant. Especially the third category shows a complicated overlap between immigration and religious identity. As noted in several research publications, Muslimness is often portrayed as contrary to Scandinavian national cultures and thus, Muslims are, at least within parts of the political spectrum, understood as not only difficult, but impossible to integrate (Schmidt 2007; Cato and Otterbeck 2011; C. M. Jacobsen 2011: 160ff.; Cato 2012).

As elsewhere in Europe, the political debate over the integration of Muslim immigrants is based on a hegemonic understanding of what a Muslim *is*. The debate is analysed in a vast amount of academic publications (for Denmark, see: Schmidt 2007, 2011a; Holtug 2012; Hedetoft 2006a, 2006b; Hedetoft et al. 2006; Hervik 2002; Jensen 2011; for Sweden, see: Otterbeck and Bevelander 2006; Larsson and Sander 2007; Malm 2009; Gardell 2010; Cato 2012; for Norway, see: C. M Jacobsen 2011; Markussen and Natvig 2005). Two trends are discernible: one trend homogenizes Muslims, claiming Muslimness to be the core identity of any individual with a Muslim religious background; another trend claims Muslim identity to be diverse, even implying completely contradictory things for different individuals. While the first trend always essentializes Muslim identity (often in a dissatisfying way to most individuals with a Muslim background), the other runs the risk of oversimplifying and ignoring complex issues about religious and cultural belonging and the migration experience.

One central political player in the articulation of Muslim immigrants as a 'problem' is the Danish People's Party (DPP, Danish: Dansk Folkeparti). The DPP was established in 1995 as an offspring of the now dissolved Progress Party, among other things sharing its predecessor's anti-immigrant and anti-Muslim rhetoric. Until the late 1990s the party had little political influence, and was described by then-prime minister Poul Nyrup Rasmussen in 1999 as 'never acceptable' (Danish: *aldrig stuerene*). A couple of years later the scenario changed, when a new government took office, from then onwards supported by the DPP (see also Østergaard-Nielsen 2003; Rydberg 2004). During the 2001 national elections the DPP received 12% of all votes, increasing to 13.3% in 2005. The anti-Muslim, anti-immigrant ideas of the DPP have been an important precondition for the political success of the party. MPs from the Danish People's Party have among others claimed that Islam could not be seen as a civilization; that Islam was a plague over Europe; and that owning a Danish citizenship should not least depend on people's religious belonging. Being a Muslim, according to this rhetoric, is incompatible with being Danish (Schmidt 2007: 103, 2009: 46). Further, members of the DPP have claimed that since Danish culture in all respects is determined by Christianity, the granting of citizen rights to a Muslim can only be looked upon with scepticism (see Schmidt 2007: 108). Concrete effects of the anti-immigrant/anti-Muslim politics of the DPP include the tightening of the Danish family reunification regulations (see Schmidt et al. 2009) (a way for many non-Western immigrants to settle in Denmark), and increasing legislative demands put on people who apply for Danish citizenship.

The rhetoric and success of the DPP has influenced populist parties in Sweden (for example the Swedish Democrats (SD), see Hellström 2010) and has its equivalent in Norway (the Progress Party, see Aslaksen 2006). In Sweden, the SD, inspired by DPP but also by other European right-wing populist parties, has presented a simplistic anti-Islamic rhetoric during the last two national elections in 2006 and 2010, claiming Islam to be the greatest threat to Sweden since the Second World War, or that Muslims are inherently violent and prone to criminality because of Islam. The party made it to parliament in 2010 (5.7 %). Using all means of communication available to them (especially through individuals sympathetic to the SD or part of the party active on the internet[4]) the party makes sure their message of Islam (and Muslims) as incompatible with Swedish society is read and heard (Cato and Otterbeck 2011; Kiiskinen and Saveljeff 2010; Hellström 2010). Even so, there are differences between how Islam is presented and debated in Denmark, Norway, and Sweden, stemming among other things from differences in public discussions at large. Public political debates in both Denmark and Norway are generally of a harsher and more drastic nature than public debates in Sweden, which are more low-key (Arvidsson 2007; Alsmark 2007). In Denmark, members of parliament (representing the DPP) have, for example, portrayed Islam as a plague and argued that the Islamic headscarf is equivalent to the Nazi Swastika. In Sweden, such emotional and hyperbolic argument in parliament would not be tolerated and a person claiming such things would be likely to be excluded from their party. But with the introduction of the SD in parliament in 2010, this kind of discourse has partly slipped into political discussions.

The study of Islamophia as a phenomenon and a concept in the Danish context is almost non-existent. The concept is under-analysed and with little or no reference to empirical, context-specific data.

An important, yet frequently underestimated aspect of the integration debate in Scandinavia is the voice of municipalities with large immigrant populations, in particular larger/metropolitan cities such as Copenhagen (Schmidt forthcoming) and Malmö (Hvenegård-Lassen 2007). While national political debates over immigration (coming from outside the EU and North America) frequently focus on the phenomenon as

---

[4] See for example <http://kentekeroth.se/ or http://imittsverige.blogspot.com/>.

problematic or even as a threat to social cohesion, the two mentioned municipalities (and others) represent alternative understandings, focusing on inclusion of immigrant citizens, and seeing ethnic and religious diversity as a resource. The municipality of Copenhagen, for example, is known for its celebration of Muslim holidays (as well as the holidays of other religious minorities in the city) (Schmidt 2014). Another important aspect are the many collaborations between Muslim and non-Muslim actors in civil society. For example, in Sweden, the Christian Council of Sweden (formed in 1994) frequently invites Muslim leaders to participate in projects and in making statements. Bosnia-Herzegovina's Muslim Youth Association has on occasion collaborated with the temperance movement for at least the last ten years. The largest Christian scout organization (KFUM) helped Muslims to organize Muslim scout groups and eventually was instrumental in setting up a Muslim national scout organization in 2008 (Sweden's Muslim Scouts) (Otterbeck 2010b: 114ff.).

Some common indicators of assimilation include housing, success on the labour market (which will be dealt with below), and also voting patterns. Foreign nationals have the right to vote in Swedish municipal elections; however, the participation of immigrants in these elections is very low and has decreased over time. In 1976, 60% of foreign voters participated; in the 2002 election the number was only 35% (Larsson and Sander 2007: 235). Geographical areas with the lowest participation rates are the so-called 'housing projects'. Immigrants living there are either fairly new in Sweden, have not been successful on the labour market, and live fairly isolated from Swedish society at large. Since 'Muslim' is not a category in official statistics it is difficult to differentiate those with a Muslim family background from these general figures, but since all current research demonstrates that most Muslims settle in major city areas and especially in the housing projects, a large proportion of Scandinavian Muslims are included in the trends we have sketched here. In any case, these socially segregated areas of Scandinavian cities—where social isolation, low political participation in official politics, and low socio-economic assets tend to be conflated with being an immigrant—trouble politicians and the institutions of the respective welfare states. Therefore, much effort is put into trying to alter conditions and combat negative patterns. These efforts have been carefully studied by, for example, Bunar (2001), Bevelander et al. (2003), Andersson et al. (2003), and Børresen (2006). While these governmental or municipality initiated efforts often have a positive effect for individuals, the general trends of non-participation, segregation, and unemployment have not been broken so far.

## SOCIAL STATUS AND CLASS

Describing the social status and class of Muslims in Scandinavia is far from simple. Several researchers underline how the hegemonic understanding of Muslims, present in both politics and research, creates categories that people cannot necessarily—yet are forced to—identify with (Jeldtoft and Nielsen 2011; Otterbeck 2010a). The problem with counting Muslims is that such counting (especially when we assume that immigrants coming from certain countries and regions can be counted as Muslims) contributes to an 'ethnification of Islam'. However, there is no one-to-one relationship between ethnicity/nationality on the one hand and religion on the other (Jeldtoft 2009: 12). Although family affiliation with Islam can be taken as an argument for counting such family members as Muslims, such a strategy does not take the individual understanding of religious belonging (or not belonging) into account. Further, Christians from the Middle East, for example Turkey and Iraq, might end up being counted as Muslims if and when we use the method of seeing immigrants from particular countries or regions of the world as Muslims *per se* (Sander 1993). A sensitive approach to the identifier 'Muslim' is also underlined by existing statistics. For example, in 2008, immigrants and descendants from Turkey, Pakistan, ex-Yugoslavia, Iran, Iraq, and Somalia, all living in Denmark, were asked about their self-defined religiosity (based on telephone interviews with more than a thousand respondents, and carried out by the consultancy company Catinet). In the survey, 37% considered themselves very little/little religious, 33% considered themselves moderately religious, and 24% considered themselves very religious (Mikkelsen 2008: 139). Compared to other religious minority groups, the religious practice of Muslims (immigrants) is, according to other surveys carried out in Denmark, far from the most intense. Another survey from Denmark, conducted in 2005 (published in Gundelach and Nørregård-Nielsen 2007),[5] shows that whereas more than 60% of Roman Catholic immigrants and descendants participated in religious ceremonies/services once a month, less than 40% of Muslims did so. More Roman Catholic immigrants and descendants than Muslim immigrants and descendants described themselves as religious (Gundelach and Nørregård-Nielsen 2007: 119–20). However, both studies show that there is a growing tendency among Muslim immigrants/descendants to understand themselves as being very religious (Ministry of Refugee, Immigration and Integration Affairs 2007: 208; Mikkelsen 2008: 140).

Only a few statistical studies on religious praxis exist, and none with a more sophisticated methodology using multivariate analysis. A Danish study of youth in upper secondary school (Andersen et al. 2003; Jensen 2002) concludes that while only a few of the Muslim informants are members of a religious organization (two out of fifty-eight while 79% of all youth were members, most often of the Danish Church) Muslims tend to rate very high when asked about their beliefs. While 52% of all youth believed in God, 100% of the Muslims claimed a belief in God. Muslims made up 3% of all who answered. The same large differences were repeated when asked about heaven, hell, the devil, and angels. Some 90% of the Muslims claimed to believe in these phenomena, while only 15–25% of all respondents shared this view. In this light it is interesting to note that only half of the Muslims said

---

[5] The survey was conducted among majority Danes and immigrants from the following countries: Turkey, Pakistan, West-Balkan, Iran, Iraq, Vietnam, as well as descendants from Turkey, and descendants from Pakistan. All respondents had lived in Denmark for at least three-and-a-half years. All respondents were under 50 years of age. A total of 4,478 people participated in the survey (Gundelach and Nørregård-Nielsen 2007: 15ff.).

they pray often; the rest pray occasionally, irregularly, or not at all. A third claimed to visit a mosque at least once a month. Prayers are likely to be performed at home. Another study of youth carried out in Sweden (Otterbeck 2010a: 17) had less precise questions but far more respondents (558 Muslims). However, it paints a similar picture.

Granted that Muslims are far from a homogeneous group, even in countries as small as the Scandinavian, a critical survey of social aspects of 'the group' is linked with challenging methodological and also ethical questions. It is far more reasonable, in line with Roy (2004), to talk about a Muslim population (only signalling that a number of diverse people happen to nominally share religious belonging) than of Muslims as a group (implying social interaction and shared interests) in the respective countries, thereby avoiding homogenization and ethnification (Otterbeck 2010a). One growing trend in Scandinavian research of Muslims, undoubtedly reacting against a national, hegemonic, ethnified understanding of Muslimness—and the abundance of research literature across Europe and the United States describing organized Muslims—points to the necessity of (1) focusing on non-organized Muslims (Jeldtoft 2008, 2009; Jeldtoft and Nielsen 2011; Otterbeck 2010a), and (2) critically scrutinizing and questioning the category of 'Muslim', far too often used in a homogenizing way and at times used instead of more relevant categories signalling ethnicity, national background, human capital, etc. (Larsson and Sander 2007; Otterbeck and Bevelander 2006).

## Denmark

In Denmark, one larger survey of Muslims was carried out in 2008 (Hussain 2011). The survey was carried out in the Copenhagen neighbourhood Nørrebro, known for its diverse ethnic and religious population (Schmidt 2011b, 2011c). The survey, funded by the Open Society Institute, was a part of a larger study examining the level and nature of Muslim integration in Europe.[6] The overall project defined Muslim as a diverse population: '... although there are a common belief systems and possibly experiences as Muslims, this report relies on its Muslim respondents' identification of themselves as Muslims. Furthermore, this term includes Muslims who view themselves in a cultural rather than a religious context' (Hussain 2011: 18). Responding to the question 'Do you actively practise your religion?' thirty-seven respondents within the Muslim group responded 'no'. The number was forty-six within the group of non-Muslims (Hussain 2011: 29).

Comparing the Nørrebro study with existing reports on the social profile of immigrants in Denmark underlines a complicated picture. Variables affecting the employment rate of immigrants in Denmark include aspects of gender, age, length of residency, and whether the person comes from a Western or non-Western country.[7] Statistics

---

[6] <http://www.soros.org/initiatives/home/about>.
[7] Defined as countries outside the EU and Nordic countries, as well as USA, Canada, Australia, New Zealand, Andorra, Liechtenstein, Monaco, San Marino, Switzerland, and the Vatican State.

Table 9.5 Employment rates among immigrants and the Danish majority population 2009

| Age/Gender | Immigrants, Western | | Immigrants, non-Western | | Descendants, Western | | Descendants, non-Western | | Danes | |
|---|---|---|---|---|---|---|---|---|---|---|
| | M | W | M | W | M | W | M | W | M | W |
| 16–24 | 42 | 37 | 58 | 49 | 57 | 62 | 59 | 63 | 68 | 70 |
| 30–39 | 75 | 70 | 68 | 53 | 81 | 77 | 80 | 68 | 89 | 85 |
| 60–64 | 49 | 39 | 35 | 16 | N/A | N/A | N/A | N/A | 53 | 35 |

Source: Statistics Denmark (2010: 86).

Denmark has since 2007 published a yearly report describing various areas of immigrant life in Denmark (Statistics Denmark 2008, 2009, 2010, 2011) including employment rates, levels of education, and crime rates among immigrants and descendants. Based on the report from 2010, we can gain an understanding of the complexity of labour market attachment among immigrants, according to the variables of age, gender, whether the person is born in Denmark or not, and whether he/she descends from a Western or non-Western country (Table 9.5). As Table 9.5 shows, non-Western immigrants are to a lesser degree employed than Western immigrants, Danes and descendants. Immigrant women, aged 60–64, constitute the group with the lowest employment rate.

Both among young men and women of non-Western background, there is a growing tendency to complete both high school and vocational training (see e.g. Schmidt et al. 2009: 138ff.). Yet, a 2011 study of discrimination in the vocational training system underlines that the step from education to employment is far from easy for young people with ethnic minority backgrounds. In her Ph.D. dissertation, sociologist Line Vikkelsø Sloth (2011) asked teachers in the vocational training system which assists students to obtain trainee jobs whether the ethnic background of the students had an effect on companies' willingness to offer such jobs or not. Forty per cent of the teachers replied that the ethnic background of the student was often or sometimes an aspect that the companies saw as important. Almost half of the companies explained their concern as based on the (expected) limited language proficiency of ethnic minority students. More than 40% of the teachers explained that their impression was that the companies thought that the Islamic headscarf (or other religious garments) did not fit into the workplace (Sloth 2011: 78). Although only 19% of the companies, according to the teachers, often or sometimes placed any importance on the religious background of the student (Sloth 2011: 67), dressing according to religious traditions played a noticeable role for the companies accepting or rejecting a student. While Sloth's study undoubtedly grants a view of discrimination of ethnic minorities in Danish workplaces, the study suffers from a lack of data, particularly interviews or survey data from both students and companies.

## Sweden

In Sweden, there are no major statistical studies of the socio-economic conditions of Muslims. The Open Society planned a study of the Muslim population in an area of Stockholm, similar to the Copenhagen study, but has, as of now, not succeeded in conducting it. Instead, different pieces of research performed by mainly labour market researchers have to be patched together to gain some insight. When looking at employment rate, ever since 1985 Swedish-born men and women have had a similar level (women slightly less), while the rate for foreign-born men and women has been between 10% and 25% lower (again, women slightly less). In 2005, the employment rate for native-born men and women aged 16–64 was 73% and for foreign-born 53%, a gap of 20%. However, European-born migrants had a higher employment rate than non-Europeans (Bevelander and Pendakur 2009). Since most Muslims are of non-European origin the research stresses the harsh reality of a higher unemployment rate. According to another study, Bosnians do significantly better on the labour market than Iraqis (Bevelander and Lundh 2007). Somalis are among the least successful on the labour market with an employment rate of only 20% as of 2009 (Hussein et al. 2011). Thus, unemployment is unlikely to be a question of Muslimness, but rather reflects different variables such as migration history, and social and human capital as valued in the new country. Still, being categorized as religiously different might create barriers in daily life and may lead to lower chances in the housing and labour markets (Agerström and Rooth 2008; Carlsson and Rooth 2007). Several cases of discrimination at work, school, or when applying for a job directed towards Muslims (particularly women with headscarves) have been dealt with by the Swedish Discrimination Ombudsman (DO 2011). According to Larsson and Sander (2007) who have tried to create an overall picture of the situation, Muslims are exposed to discrimination on both the labour market and the housing market leading to fewer opportunity and segregated cities. Especially the housing projects of the 1960s and 1970s, built on the outskirts of mid-size and larger cities, have a completely new demography compared to when they were built. The rapid transformation during the later part of the twentieth century has led to a segregation of several of the larger cities only comparable with how the poor districts of Swedish larger cities were once created through urbanization during the first half of the twentieth century. This general sketch should of course be contrasted with individual stories of success, even though these are statistically less common.

## Norway

As in both Denmark and Sweden, we do not have any Norwegian studies focusing explicitly on the socio-economic conditions of Muslims. Also in this national context, a picture can be pieced together on the basis of available data and studies describing the labour marked attachment and status of non-Western immigrants. In 2011, a large national report on welfare and migration in Norway appeared (NOU 2011). The report showed that labour market attachment among immigrants from countries such as Iran, Turkey, Morocco, Afghanistan, Iraq, and Somalia was significantly lower than among members of the majority population, but also among groups of Western immigrants. Whereas 76.4% of the majority population was working, the total was 59.9% among immigrants from Iran, 54.1% among immigrants from Turkey, and as low as 31.9% among immigrants from Somalia. The proportion of employed women among immigrant (but also non-immigrant, majority) women was lower than among men: whereas 61.3% of men with Turkish background were working, the number was 53.3% among the women. Among Pakistan immigrants, 64.5% of the men were working, and 31.7% of the women. Within the majority population the number was 78% among men and 74.7% among women (NOU 2011: 185). As is the case in Denmark and Sweden, studies of the possible discrimination of immigrants in the Norwegian labour market (a tendency that can explain the lower employment rate within these groups) are scarce. One survey-based study from 2008 showed that 18% of a population representing ten non-Western immigrant groups in Norway felt that their immigrant background had hindered them in obtaining a job they had applied for, and for which they were qualified (NOU 2011: 209; Blom and Henriksen 2008). According to the NOU report, non-Western immigrants in Norway are more frequently over-qualified for the jobs they obtain than what is seen among other groups of immigrants (NOU 2011: 209).

## Religion in Public Space

The role that Muslims play in public spaces in Scandinavia is threefold: (1) in and through Muslim institutions, including religious associations and mosques, (2) as tokens of difference within political debates and discourses, (3) through everyday life engagement with the majority population.

As noted in the previous section, the term 'Muslim, is' when we deal with public spaces, neither easily nor coherently defined. Some Muslims vigorously participate in the life of mosques or institutions or associations that in one way or another signal a focus on a shared religious background (e.g. schools, ethnic minority associations), while others do not participate at all in such institutions or associations, or do so occasionally (see also Jeldtoft 2012). In Scandinavia, studies of Muslim organizations and their members are almost exclusively based on qualitative methods, making any representative assessment of the ethnic, age, and class-based composition *across* the spectrum of these organizations difficult. Still, the existing qualitative studies show how persons with a Muslim family background, as all other citizens, can choose different pathways to engage with broader society or with their local area, e.g. through political associations (Togeby 2003), civic society institutions (Otterbeck 2010b), or simply meeting people who do not share their faith in their workplace, but how relevant their identity as Muslims is in such meetings undoubtedly differs. Actually, Scandinavian studies—as is the case in many other European contexts—still show a lack of focus on the arenas where Muslims play roles, *but not necessarily* as Muslims, e.g. as heterogeneous implementations of their being Muslims. However, a steadily growing number of researchers show caution towards essentializing or 'ethnifying' a Muslim identity, not least in a political climate where hegemonic understandings of such an identity play a central, yet skewed, role in national debates over the impact of immigration (Schmidt 2011a; C. M. Jacobsen 2011; Jeldtoft 2012; Cato 2012), multiculturalism (Holtug 2012), and religious and ethnic diversity for national identity and the welfare state (Otterbeck 2010b; Cato and Otterbeck 2011).

# Denmark

Several studies describe organized Muslim life in Denmark and engagement with public (majority) institutions. Studies include Simonsen (1990), Kühle (2006), and Helqvist (2010). In 2007, Garbi Schmidt (Schmidt 2007) described Sunni Muslim youth organizations in the Copenhagen context, including analysis of the roles that these organizations and prominent spokespersons within these organizations played within the public debate. The analysis showed how many of the youth organizations focused extensively on establishing positive contacts with the surrounding society, e.g. through inviting neighbours or high school classes to the local mosques, or giving talks about Islam at schools or other private institutions. Portraying a positive image of Islam and the role Muslims played in Danish society was described by organization members as crucial. Some individuals within the organizations chose to become active in majority political parties: a move that most of these parties were open to, until media attention on such Muslim candidates, often focusing on an argued incompatibility between Islam and secular democratic values, forced them to withdraw their candidacy (primary cases took place in the late 1990s and the early 2000s). Schmidt's book also described how one Muslim youth organization (the Hizb ut-Tahrir) chose not to engage with the surrounding society, and even advocated that such interaction was—according to their interpretation—prohibited by Islam. The role and agency of the Hizb ut-Tahrir in Denmark is a recurring element in scholarly works in Denmark, not least due to the large amount of media and political attention that the organization receives (see e.g. Grøndahl et al. 2003; Sinclair 2010). Hizb ut-Tahrir has not managed to establish itself in Norway or Sweden.

A few studies describe mosques and other types of organized Muslim life in Denmark. In 2006 sociologist of religion Lene Kühle published a study of mosques and Muslim places of worship[8] across the country (Kühle 2006). Kühle reported that 115 mosques existed in Denmark, eleven of which were Shi'i. The mosques were located all over Denmark, notable in the larger cities. Three mosques were purpose-built—one being Denmark's oldest mosque: the Ahmadiyya Nusrat Djahan Mosque in the Copenhagen

---

[8] Muslim places of worship included institutions/associations facilitating a place where Muslim prayer could take place.

suburb of Hvidovre (see also B. A. Jacobsen 2009: 97, 103). Other researchers have described independent Muslim schools. Notable is Annette H. Ihle's study (2007) of so-called 'Free Schools' (Danish: *Friskoler*). Ihle's study underlines the variation in both the quality of the teaching and leadership of the schools (also Shakoor 2008; Schmidt 2008a). Some schools, however, do extremely well in terms of preparing their students for high school. A study carried out by the Ministry of Education in 2006 showed that whereas 26% of the students in national public schools continued into high school, the average for Muslim private schools was 41% (B. A. Jacobsen 2009: 104).

As noted by Kühle, eleven mosques in Denmark are Shi'i. Still, Shi'i Muslim life and engagement with Danish society are so far fairly ignored in Danish (and Scandinavian) research. A few exceptions include Marianne Holm Pedersen's Ph.D. thesis on Shi'i Iraqi refugee women in Copenhagen, and to some extent Garbi Schmidt's studies of Muslim engagement with the Copenhagen neighbourhood of Nørrebro (Pedersen 2009; Schmidt 2011c). Shi'a Muslims are not a new strain of the Muslim community in Denmark (the first Shi'ite mosque was established around 1970, see Kühle 2006), but until the mid-2010s Shi'ites have been fairly silent in Denmark. The tendency of silence has changed with a growing, publicly engaging profile of some Shi'ite youth organizations (most notably the Young Muslim Group—*Unge muslimer gruppen*). Further, as described by Pedersen and Schmidt, Shi'a Muslims have become publicly visible through their annual 'Ashura parade through the Copenhagen neighbourhood Nørrebro. During the parade around 3,000 Shi'a Muslims walk through the streets, shouting paroles and waving banners. The parade ends at the Shi'i Imam Ali mosque at the north end of the neighbourhood. The growing attention of researchers on the Shi'i community is adding a much-needed dimension to Danish research of the country's Muslim communities, and is an aspect that will hopefully be expanded in further research. One lesson to be learned from the recent development in research of Shi'ites in Denmark is that research interest often increases in the wake of public visibility and (as is the case with Muslim private schools, mosques, and youth organizations and activism) where public interest and debate is intense.

Just as research intensifies in fields where there is particular public and political attention, Danish researchers of Islam and Muslims are frequently turning their attention towards the content of these very debates and discourses. Studies include descriptions of the role that Muslims and Islam play as '(dangerous) strangers' in the media (Hervik 2002). Within the political debate, some see Islam and Muslims as absolutely 'integrationable', while others see them as a threat to Danish values, the welfare state, and the very essence of a Danish national identity (Schmidt 2007). One highly interesting study by Brian Arly Jacobsen (2008) compares parliamentary debates over Islam during the years 1967–2005 with parliamentary debates of Jewish immigrants to Denmark in 1903–25. Jacobsen concludes that both groups, as immigrants, have been seen as aliens, yet their role and compatibility with Danish society was presented differently. Jews were, in the early twentieth century, seen as biologically and racially different, but were still (perhaps as a consequence of the existence of a well-established Jewish community and bourgeoisie) understood as 'integrationable'. In contrast, Muslims were and are by the early twenty-first century (at least by some segments of the Danish political establishment), seen as carriers of a culture that cannot be compatible with Danishness (and thus non-integrationable). Further, there is growing attention within Scandinavian research on the politicized role that research in Islamic minorities presently plays, including how research may take over the vocabulary of political discourses, and how researchers of Islam are increasingly seen as political agents (e.g. C. M. Jacobsen 2006; B. A. Jacobsen 2008; Schmidt 2008b). Included in this debate is how researchers tend to address questions that are relevant from a political point of view (Muslim communities as problems, difficult to integrate, etc.), for example as a means to obtain research funding. Further, the role that researchers of Islam play as experts in public—emotionally heated—debates is often complicated. Looking, for example, at postings and debates on right-wing, anti-Islamic websites in the Scandinavian countries, such as the Danish uriasposten.net, shows that researchers are frequently seen as blindly defensive of Islam, 'halal-hippies', and out of touch with a social reality that, arguably, exposes explicit signs of the danger of Islam and the Muslim wish to conquer Western countries.

# Sweden

In Sweden, organized Muslims started with lobbyism, added cooperation, and have now started to develop an active citizenship and political participation (Cato and Otterbeck 2011). In the 1970s Muslim associations started small-scale lobbying to achieve separate treatment by certain key societal institutions like schools and healthcare. Issues such as alternative diet were at the top of the agenda. Muslims started to organize nationally in 1974 to meet the requirements of the already mentioned state institution, SST, in charge of governmental economic support to religious organizations. The umbrella organization, the Union of Islamic Congregations in Sweden (FIFS), was founded in 1974. However, it was not until FIFS and another umbrella organization (SMF—Sweden's Muslim Association, founded in 1982) formed a lobbying branch called SMR (Muslim Council of Sweden) in 1990 that a new phase of activism was instituted. In an open letter sent out in 1994, SMR approached various political parties offering to cooperate with anyone on integration issues. Only the Social Democrats accepted and the party delegated the responsibility of cooperation to its Christian subgroup, the Christian Social Democrats, better known as the Brotherhood Movement, to organize the cooperation which is still ongoing. For example, the collaboration has resulted in joint reports and statements, seminars on Islam and democracy, and leadership training courses, not least for Muslim women (Cato and Otterbeck 2011). Early in 2011, the Brotherhood movement changed its official name to 'Social Democrats for Faith and Solidarity', marking that it is now multi-religious. This is mainly a result of the extensive cooperation with and inclusion of Muslims in the movement.

Due to the structure of having umbrella organizations, Swedish governmental institutions have cooperated with these when in need of opinions or representatives from Muslim organizations. This cooperation has created a platform for some Muslims to negotiate their interests from. Even though no common Muslim political opinion exists, the umbrella organizations' representatives have skilfully used the government's need for 'a (or even *the*) Muslim voice' to promote their own views in certain instances. Some of the representatives of the Muslim groups have thus gained experience of Swedish politics over decades. In the last national election (autumn 2010) a couple of high-profile Muslim leaders decided individually to run for office. One made it to parliament as a representative of the Moderates. There are other persons of Muslim background in the parliament who have not profiled themselves specifically as Muslims in the election campaign (Cato and Otterbeck 2011).

Since 1992 all governments of Sweden have liberalized the country's economic rules and legal structures responding to the global neo-liberal economic trend. This has created some new opportunities in the civil society sector. Muslim entrepreneurs have mainly taken an interest in starting independent schools (sixteen Muslim schools in 2009 according to Berglund 2009: 18). Other tendencies are an interest in creating a Muslim parallel to diaconal work in, for example, healthcare, in prisons, and in military service (Otterbeck 2004: 250) and Islamic business including slaughter houses and travel agencies specializing (among other things) in pilgrimage travels.

Muslim associations are getting more and more experience in dealing with municipal and state administrations, and quite a few associations take an active part in the surrounding society. A survey investigating the activities of 105 Muslim congregations in Sweden (Borell and Gerdner 2011) shows that it is fairly common for these congregations to organize what in a Christian context is called diaconal work, on a voluntary basis. For example, almost half of them were engaged in organizing hospital visits to support Muslims who had fallen sick. Further, Muslim associations often arrange activities for children and youths like summer camps, sports, etc.

The increased visibility of Muslims in society brings about reactions. Mosque projects, Muslim schools, Muslim politicians, and Muslim dress codes all signal changes in the public sphere and have caused heated debates in media, politics, but also in the private sphere. Four major arguments have emerged in the discussions (among non-Muslims): (1) *Sweden is being Islamized*. This is proposed by populist parties, locally, regionally, and nationally. Views are mainly spread by internet, local radio, and small print media. The subtext is that the established politicians are selling out Sweden to Islamism; distrust of the established is classical populist politics, in this instance using Islam and Muslims as a scare to break into politics (Otterbeck and Bevelander 2006; Malm 2009; Gardell 2010). (2) *Islam is part of a multicultural, new Sweden*. This viewpoint is taken by many of the established parties, much of the established 'old' media like dailies and major TV channels. Avoiding contradictions or problematic issues like Islamism is typical of this position according to Carlbom (2006). (3) *Islam is not an issue, but Islamism and Islamic terrorism is truly a threat*. This view is taken by some politicians both from the left and the right. Some researchers have taken this stance and tend to argue for it forcefully. This has triggered some investigations of Islamic radicalism in Sweden and a discourse on securitization (Carlbom 2006; Ranstorp and Dos Santos 2009). Since 2006, the discussion about Islamism has taken a new turn and gained prominence in Swedish political debate (Cato 2012). (4) *Religion is a private issue and as such not a problem.* This is the general opinion of most Swedes judging from opinion polls. If religion is de-privatized and brought out into the streets or to work through clothing or publicly visible rituals, tolerance is reduced. This is clearly visible in several different quantitative attitude studies. When respondents are asked if Muslims (as a category) should have the right to vote, or any similar issues, answers are tolerant. For example, only 10% of a group of 10,599 youth disagreed with the statement: 'Most Muslims are probably decent people'. But if questions asked include religious rights in the public sphere (like always having the right to wear the veil), views are significantly less tolerant. For example 23% of the same youth questioned disagreed with the statement: 'Muslims in Sweden should have the right to build mosques' (Otterbeck and Bevelander 2006: 43). Qualitative studies demonstrate a similar tendency (Otterbeck 2010a; Sixtensson 2009).

Looking at the discourse on Islam and Muslims in Swedish popular culture, media, school textbooks, or the like, it is easy to find examples of how Islam is 'othered' (Berg 1998; *Muslimer och islam i svenska nyhetsmedier* 2002; Otterbeck 2005; Kamali 2006). Apart from certain specific national events that have caused strong reactions, like the honour killing in 2002 of 26-year-old, Kurdish Fadime Sahindal by her father because of her life choices (Wikan 2004) and the attempt to cause turmoil in Stockholm in 2010 by suicide bomber Taimour Abdulwahab, Swedish othering of Muslims is strongly influenced by international discourses and events.

# Norway

In Norway, we also find strong public scepticism towards Muslims. In 2006, a national survey, the so-called 'Integration barometer' showed that eight out of ten respondents were against authorities facilitating Muslim religious practices in Norway (Jacobsen and Leirvik 2009: 266). As mentioned by Jacobsen and Leirvik, the 2008 European Commission against Racism and Intolerance (ECRI) urged Norway to take action against Islamophobia. ECRI based its judgement on increasing examples of media linkage between Islam and terrorism/violence, discrimination against Muslims in the labour market, and resistance among the public and local authorities to building mosques (ECRI 2009: 29).

Kari Vogt (2000) published a study on Islam in Norway including information on mosques and organizations stressing the heterogeneity of such institutions. A homepage operated by scholar Leirvik states that as of 2009 some 130 different Muslim organizations exist in Norway (Leirvik 2009). Most of them are Sunni but according to Vogt (2000) some 20% are Shi'a. The main umbrella organization for Norwegian Muslims is the Islamic Council of Norway set up in 1993. The council is acknowledged as a spokesperson for Muslims by both the Norwegian church and the political authorities. It has, since 2007, received financial support from the Norwegian government (Jacobsen and Leirvik 2010).

# Qualitative Perspectives on Muslim Individuals and Groups

Although research of Muslim communities in the Scandinavian countries is a fairly young academic niche, the amount of particularly qualitative research on various aspects of these communities is both significant and varied. The qualitative focus is, if anything, a key characteristic of how research of Muslim immigrant communities is carried out in the Scandinavian countries. The background for this particular approach is most likely that whereas quantitative researchers (e.g. economists and quantitative sociologists) have been preoccupied with researching aspects central to the core factors of the welfare state (income, labour market attachment, educational level), qualitative researchers representing disciplines such as anthropology, ethnology, qualitative sociology, and humanistic approaches to religion have focused on religion as an aspect of culture. It might be added as a footnote that few major research grants have been given for post-doctoral studies in this field. Instead major contributions have been Ph.D. theses. In Scandinavia, Ph.D. theses are often published as books and are easy to find at libraries or on sale. Examples of qualitative research include: for Denmark: Bektovic (2004); Galal and Liengaard (2003); Jensen and Østergaard (2007); Schmidt (2002, 2004, 2005, 2007, 2011a, 2011c); Pedersen (2009); Jeldtoft (2012). For Sweden: Karlsson Minganti (2007); Larsson (2003); Larsson and Sander (2007); Otterbeck (2010a); Ouis and Roald (2003); Roald (2004); Sultan Sjöqvist (2006); Svanberg and Westerlund (1999). For Norway: C. M. Jacobsen (2006, 2011); Østberg (2005). Theoretically, these studies are mainly based in different anthropological and sociological approaches, especially taking gender, power practices, postcolonial critique, ritual practices, and identification issues into account. The studies give examples of individual strategies to live Muslim lives in Scandinavia trying to cope with how to practise and believe in Islam without throwing convictions overboard.

Some studies focus on the issue of interpreting Islam, e.g. when religious interpretation is carried out by religious authorities or persons seeking religious authority (including researching what constitutes religious authority as such). For Denmark: see e.g. Liengaard (2007). For Sweden: Otterbeck (2000a). For Norway: C. M. Jacobsen (2011). In these studies the dynamics of interpretation and context is of importance.

Other studies concentrate on a wider focus on Islamic organizations and their interaction with wider majority society (e.g. Islamic schools, mosques). For Denmark: e.g. Simonsen (1989, 1990); Pedersen and Selmer (1991); Kühle (2006); Schmidt (2007). For Sweden: Berglund (2009); Gustafsson (2004); Karlsson and Svanberg (1995); Otterbeck (2000b); SOU (2009). For Norway: Vogt (2000); Anderson (2009). These studies tend to present historical processes in detail. Some try to interpret these by contextualizing both organizations and majority societies, for example, through postcolonial power theories or Bourdieusian or Foucauldian (or the like thereof) paradigms of the political power of societies.

Some recent studies have addressed the issue of shariah law as a part of a legal plurality (Hjärpe 2005; Roald 2009; Sayed 2009). This is a growing field of research interest since migration, the presence of foreign citizens, and international treaties sometimes cause complicated situations for the jurists of Scandinavia. For example, issues of inheritance and divorce often no longer simply fall within the jurisdiction of one nation-state but might affect families in several different countries. What is the role of religiously motivated family law codes in the countries of origin? Research interests in this field are still in their infancy, and the field needs to be developed further, not least to answer the demands of multicultural Scandinavian nation-states. (See Chapter 15 by Mathias Rohe on 'Sharia in Europe'.)

Other researchers have described the phenomenon of Islamophobia and how Islam is represented through different media. For Denmark: Hussain et al. (1997); Hervik (2002); Andreassen (2007). For Sweden: Bevelander and Otterbeck (2010); Larsson (2003, 2010); Otterbeck and Bevelander (2006); Malm (2009); Gardell (2010). For Norway: Markussen and Natvig (2005). See also Horsti (2008) for a broader perspective on Scandinavian research in the media's coverage of immigrant issues. Most studies tend to support Edward Said's well-known ideas of widespread, dominant stereotypical representations of Muslims or Islam. These studies very often lean towards discourse studies or postcolonial anthropology.

While the concept of Islamophobia is a frequently used element of mainly Swedish research, the concept is less frequently used by researchers in, for example, Denmark. We can explain the difference according to the variation in public debate climate in the two countries: an aspect that also has an impact on research. While both the public and researchers in Sweden show sensitivity to discrimination as a social phenomenon (i.e. Islamophobia), researchers in Denmark are situated in a political/public discourse where discrimination is frequently questioned, and where a too blunt (even research-based) pointing to the existence of this phenomenon is seen as a sign of political (non-objective) correctness.

Even though the concept of Islamophobia is not directly mentioned, research studies of, for example, parties and organizations representing what we determine as Islamophobic world-views are numerous (e.g. Schmidt 2007; Hervik 1999, 2002). Importantly, researchers pointed to the existence of radical right-wing networks and organizations long before the tragic events of Oslo and Utøya on 22 July 2011 (e.g. Karpantshof 2003). What the effects of the 2011 events will be on Islamic and migration studies in Scandinavia in the long run is still to be seen. However, publications appearing after the event show that it will come to play a role in future research (e.g. Andersson 2012; Ingregard 2012; Eide 2012).

# INTERNATIONAL CONSTRAINTS

## Denmark

After the terror attacks of 9/11, Denmark has become an active international player in the war against terrorism. Denmark has sent troops to both Afghanistan and Iraq, and most recently to Libya and Mali. Simultaneously with such international engagement, Denmark's reputation as a country with a very restrictive immigration policy and a country where anti-Muslim sentiment is a constant element of public and political debates has grown. In spite of its size, Denmark is neither an innocent nor invisible player on the international political scene. The attention did, undoubtedly, reach its zenith during the so-called Cartoon controversy in 2005. The crisis escalated when the newspaper *Jyllands-Posten* decided to publish twelve cartoon drawings relating to either Muslims or the Prophet Muhammad in particular. *Jyllands-Postens*' cultural editor, Flemming Rose, argued the publishing to be an act of defence for freedom of expression, and a reaction towards the censoring effects of Islamist fanaticism. The effect of the cartoons, however, was a crisis of international proportions that affected Denmark for several months (and where the long-term effects during the writing of this book are still felt). Danish flags were burned publicly in countries from the Middle East to Asia, and Danish embassies in Syria, Libya, and Iran were attacked by angry protesters (Klausen 2009).

Given the nature of the crisis, the cartoons play a role in several studies after 2005 (e.g. Lindekilde et al. 2009; Lindekilde and Larsson 2009; Lægaard 2009). Also—and both affected by and detached from the Cartoon controversy—Denmark's involvement in various battlefields of the world has caused a growing attention on radicalization and terror attacks. A number of terror attacks that would arguably have been carried out in the name of Islam have been prevented since 2005. Not surprisingly, an increasing number of studies of radicalization among (young) Muslims in the Danish context have been published in the same period (see e.g. Kühle and Lindekilde 2010; Hemmingsen 2011; Lindekilde 2010; Goli and Rezaei 2010; Hemmingsen 2012). A shared ambition of these studies is to understand radicalization as a phenomenon, how it is constituted, and even—as is the case for Goli and Rezaei's study—to present quantitative parameters according to which radicalization can be measured. The studies as such underline the problem with defining and framing radicalization as a practice and linking the phenomenon to causality (as illustrated by reviews of some of the mentioned studies: see Crone 2010; Schmidt 2010).

## Sweden

In Sweden, the interrelated debates on Islamophobia and radicalization have polarized opinions and made fruitful, analytical discussion difficult. Recently, two major books on Islamophobia have been written (Malm 2009; Gardell 2010). Both authors are strongly associated with the political left in Sweden. Instead of being treated as studies by academics (which both authors are), the books were received as heavily biased. Both books are essayistic in style and at times bantering, but are grounded in research. What is obvious from these and from studies by Borell (2012), Otterbeck and Bevelander (2006), and Bevelander and Otterbeck (2010, 2012) is that Islamophobia is not a constant, but rather changing phenomenon. Up until 2006, the most reasonable way of describing Islamophobia in Sweden was that it meant the discrimination of Muslims on the housing and labour market, that Muslims were exposed to verbal slurs, and at times to violence or had their property damaged. From 2007 and onwards, Bat Ye'or's ideas about Eurabia (from 2005) have gained a tremendous influence, mostly through other authors who have processed and expanded the original idea (Malm 2009). The Eurabia thesis includes, apart from a conspiracy theory of an Arab-Muslim takeover of Europe, a harsh critique of Islam which is portrayed as a violent, anti-democratic, sexist, political ideology equivalent to fascism and Nazism, rather than as a religion comparable to other religions. This addition to the repertoire of Islamophobia is of great importance to populist parties and radical right-wing parties who, while they would risk being charged with hate speech if attacking Muslims *per se*, virulently attack Islam at any given moment to get at Muslims specifically or everyone who is foreign in general. This strategy can be called a political economy of hate (Otterbeck and Bevelander 2006). But it is not only the populists and the radicals that pave the way for this dubious discourse. The Eurabia discourse has also a place in the liberal press and some of its proponents are published as interesting debaters by, for example, the magazine *Neo* (Malm 2009).

At the same time, it must be stated that the Islamophobia research has thus far not been very sophisticated. Rather it operates too much with anecdotes and general criticism instead of larger text collections or questionnaires. Most quantitative studies are bivariate analyses and generate at best some useful indications. The only multivariate analysis of larger quantitative data using logistic regression analysis is on youth (9,498 persons) between 14 and 18 years old (Otterbeck and Bevelander 2006; Bevelander and Otterbeck 2010). In this study, contrary to assumptions made in much other research, the general level of tolerance is quite high among youth. Those who do have a negative attitude tend to share some attitudes and social conditions. They generally have few or no (friendly) contacts with Muslims. They tend to be more restless and aggressive than other youth. Further, they tend to have more stereotypical understandings of gender and a negative perception of society in general and school in particular. Contrary to most bivariate analyses, intolerance cannot be attributed to sex in a simple way. If the aforementioned profile is filled, regardless of sex, the youth tends to have negative views. However, more men than women fill the profile. Other factors that stand out are on a more structural level. The economic position of parents affect the views held (the worse the situation, the likelier are harsh views). Living in mid-size cities with a degenerating industry sector but a population increase due to migration also makes harsh opinions likelier (Bevelander and Otterbeck 2010).

The discourse on radicalization and securitization has also grown in Sweden as some terrorist experts and the national security police SÄPO have issued warnings and reports on Islamic terrorism. Much of the discourse is similar to other European countries. In a much cited report from 2010, SÄPO claimed that there are fewer than 200 Muslim radicals that they keep under surveillance. The report is interesting since it is not alarmist but carefully prepared. Further, none of these 200 people are considered to be interested in Sweden as a target for terrorism. Rather, their prime interests are conflict areas in different Muslim majority environments. The report was commissioned by the government which gave SÄPO the task of mapping radical Islamist environments. However, SÄPO reinterpreted the task claiming that their prime function is to find out real threats to national security, not to chart radical environments. This took the edge off the political discussion on radicalism for a couple of days. However, the report was issued only weeks before the first suicide bomber blew himself up in Stockholm on 11 December 2010. As can be imagined, the discussion on radicalization quickly gained momentum.

The Cartoon crisis mentioned in relation to Denmark also affected Sweden to some extent. Many sympathized with the Danes and felt that the collective punishment of Danish industries was unfair or specifically called for the need to protect freedom of speech. Some of the cartoons were published in marginal media in Sweden. Others felt that this was the result of a harsh attitude (if not downright racist) towards Muslims that had been building up over time in Denmark. At the height of the crisis, some Swedish companies were boycotted.

As a result of the Cartoon crisis, post-modern conceptual artist Lars Vilks produced a series of pictures for an exhibition portraying Muhammad as a roundabout dog. A roundabout dog was at the time a part of spontaneous, very popular, folk art in Sweden. Someone simply built a funny looking or cute dog (or other animal), often out of wood, painted it, and put it in the centre of a roundabout. Vilks combined this popular trope with another one understood as forbidden to use: Muhammad. According to Vilks, his original thought was to provoke a Swedish gallery owner who had asked Vilks to do a series of art on the theme 'dogs'. Vilks's drawings and sketches were, however, noticed by others and he has since then received several threats from Muslims worldwide and also been attacked a couple of times. This, of course, feeds the discussion on radicalization and makes the claimed threats from Islamists realistic.

## Norway

Norway was also affected by the Cartoon crisis. A paper in Norway called *Magazinet* published all twelve cartoons from *Jyllands-Posten* in an alleged defence of freedom of expression drawing attention to Norway among Muslim activists and Arab governments (Weldeghebriel 2008). Norway was not of prime interest though, but the Cartoon crisis was domestically important for the othering of Muslims. But it was also an impulse for dialogue and collaborations (Weldeghebriel 2008). This pattern—of collaboration and conflict often walking hand in hand—is discussed further by Otterbeck (2010b). Norwegian internet pages have, as in both Denmark and Sweden, been flooded with anti-Muslim and anti-Islamic rhetoric. In the summer of 2011, after the terrorist attack on Oslo centre and the massacre at Utøya on 22 July, the perpetrator's (Anders Breivik) 1,500-page manifesto posted a few hours before the attack quoted not only American anti-Islamic sources but also Norwegian. For example, the anti-Islamic blogger Fjordman's (pseudonym of Peder Jensen) webpage became well known for being quoted extensively. The manifesto can be said to contain a radical version of Eurabia conspiracy theories.

Further, all Scandinavian countries also have moderate, secular, or former Muslims criticizing radical or conservative Muslims especially for encouraging segregation, sexism, homophobia, and violence. This kind of critique is often broadcasted in mass media, such as television and newspapers.

# The Scandinavian Case(s)

Denmark, Norway, and Sweden share similar languages and post-war developments (including becoming immigration countries). All three countries are economically successful welfare states with fairly small populations. Not surprisingly, Muslim populations in the three countries share quite similar experiences too. Being fairly new population segments that have yet to establish themselves firmly on the labour and housing markets, Muslims in Scandinavia are still socially marginal. Such social marginality is furthered by low political participation in elections, social segregation, discrimination, and the often psychologically troublesome process of relating to a personal history of refugeeship (Magnusson 2011). Still, Muslim associations (locally and nationally) and Muslim individuals strive to make a mark through collaborations, public debate, entrepreneurship, and of course community work.

Muslim organizations and associations have been established since the 1970s and created substantial changes: from the lone initiative taker to fully professionally run organizations; from no mosques to several purpose-built ones and hundreds of prayer halls; from acting completely outside of mainstream society to dialogue and collaborations. At the same time, Muslims have—by becoming socially visible—become the favourite target of populist groups and ultra-nationalists, making conflict and discrimination on the grounds of religion a prevalent phenomenon across Scandinavia. In this complex situation the discourses on radicalization, Islamophobia, and securitization are conflated. The rise of populist, anti-Muslim, and anti-immigrant parties in all three countries post-9/11 underlines the existence of such conflation, although the 'mainstreaming' of the ideas and the power of such parties—so far—differ across Scandinavia.

## What We Don't Know

The research on Islam and Muslims in the Scandinavian countries is extensive. Still, areas exist where more research needs to be done. A list of suggestions for further research is as follows.

*Variation in religious interpretation and discourse*: Although a few studies exist presenting how Scandinavian Muslims interpret Islam, much remains to be done. Most mosques have libraries—what kind of books do they contain? Larger mosques tend to sell books, audio and video cassettes, and CDs—what kind of Islam do these represent? All mosques have *khutbas* (Friday sermons)—what is preached in different mosques over a year? The internet has been studied by some but the amount and variety of Islamic web pages in Sweden alone merits at least a monograph.

A further aspect in need of research is devout Muslims' engagement in creative arts. For example, in all Scandinavian countries we find Muslim musicians creating engaged religious music in such music genres as hip-hop, reggae, and soul.

*Transnational ties*: While organizational structures and organization history have been studied, few studies take into account the fact that immigrants also are emigrants and try to understand religious transnational ties and exchange. For example, what were the opinions on the profiled Bosnian Grand Mufti (1993–2012) Mustafa Cerić among Scandinavian Bosnians? And what are their opinions about the new Grand Mufti Hussein Kavazovic? Some have tried to understand the influence of global or transnational Islamic groups, but thus far, researchers have not written the Scandinavian history of, for example, the Ahmadiyya movement, the Süleymanlis, the Gülen movement, the Salafi trend, the Habashi movement, the Muslim Brotherhood, the Tablighi Jamaat, or various Sufi networks.

Another aspect of emigration and translocal lives are treasured letters 'home' and from 'home', photographs, and memories of elders that could be used to create individual-centred histories of Muslim migration and resettlement in Scandinavia. These could help write the history of the first Muslims to arrive. Only a few such studies have been preformed.

*Non-organized Muslims*: The already mentioned focus on organized Muslims is self-evident and necessary. Still, the majority of Muslims are not organized or deeply devout. These merit some attention not least since such studies might counter the stereotype of the always religiously serious Muslim who cannot, and will not, accept any other understanding of Islam than as a religion covering all aspects of life.

*Sexuality and gender issues*: Several of the quantitative studies of Muslims in Scandinavia skilfully apply gender theories to understand their empirical material. However, few studies engage in in-depth questions about sexuality as such. The issues revolving around sexual preferences, lifestyle choices, and religiosity are still to be explored. Further, masculinity and Islam is far less developed as a study field that gender-sensitive studies of Muslim women.

*Political participation and activism*: One remarkable gap in the existing research on Muslim participation in Scandinavian societies is that of political participation. While we find an abundance of studies describing Muslim organizations and Muslim activism, we lack studies of Muslims' engagement in secular political parties and parliamentary processes. Thus, whereas several studies document the role that Islam and Muslims play as (mainly) objects of difference in national political debates, we lack studies of the roles that Muslims as political party members play in local and national politics. What, for example, are the barriers for Muslims' participation in secular political parties, and for their becoming parliamentary candidates? How many people of immigrant/Muslim background are at all involved in secular politics, and within which political parties? A few attempts have been made, as mentioned already, but we need further studies of this area to understand, thoroughly, the societal integration of Muslims in Scandinavian countries.

## References

Agerström, J. and Rooth, D.-O. (2008). 'Implicit Prejudice and Ethnic Minorities: Arab-Muslims in Sweden'. Working Paper IZA DP No. 3873. <http://www.iza.org> [Accessed 16 June 2009].

Alsmark, G. (2007). 'Integrationspolitik på svenska', in G. Alsmark, T. Kallehave, and B. Moldenhawer (eds.), *Migration och tillhörighet: Inklusions- och exklusionsprocesser i Skandinavien.* Göteborg: Makadam, 53–98.

Andersen, P. B., Fredriksen, S., Jensen, T., and Olsen, N. L. (2003). '3.g´ere og hf´eres religiøse profil og holdning til religionsfaget', *Religion. Tidskrift for Religionslærerforeningen for Gymnasiet og HF* 1 (February): 37–55.

Anderson, M. (2009). 'Religion in Inner City Oslo', *Street Signs* (Spring): 5–7.

Andersson, B., Liedholm, M., Otterbeck, J., Salameh, E.-K., Sörensson, J., Trulsson, J., and Ullberg, S. (2003). *Fyra stadsdelar—fyra vägar mot integration.* Malmö: Malmö stad.

Andersson, M. (2012). 'The Debate about Multicultural Norway before and after 22 July 2011', *Identities: Global Studies in Culture and Power* 19(4): 418–27.

Andersson, P. and Wadensjö, E. (2004). 'Self-Employment Immigrants in Denmark and Sweden: A Way to Economic Self-Reliance?' IZA Discussion Paper No. 1130 <http://www.iza.org> [Accessed 16 June 2009].

Andreassen, R. (2007). *Der er et yndigt land. Medier, minoriteter og danskhed.* Copenhagen: Tiderne Skifter.

Anwar, M., Blaschke, J., and Sander, A. (2004). *State Policies towards Muslim Minorities: Sweden, Great Britain and Germany.* Berlin: Edition Parabolis.

Arvidsson, H. (2007). 'Skandinavisk modernisering: Särdrag och likheter', in G. Alsmark, T. Kallehave, and B. Moldenhawer (eds.), *Migration och tillhörighet: Inklusions- och exklusionsprocesser i Skandinavien.* Göteborg: Makadam, 23–52.

Aslaksen, T. M. (2006). 'Plass til islam i Norge? En studie av Fremskrittspartiets holdning til muslimer og islamsk praksis i Norge'. Master's thesis in History of Religions, IKOS/UiO.

Bektovic, S. (2004). *Kulturmøder og religion: Identitetsdannelse blandt kristne og muslimske unge.* Copenhagen: Museum Tusculanum.

Berg, M. (1998). *Hudud: Ett resonemang om populärorientalismens bruksvärde och världsbild.* Stockholm: Carlsson.

Berglund, J. (2009). *Teaching Islam: Islamic Religious Education at Three Muslim Schools in Sweden.* Uppsala: Uppsala University.

Bevelander, P. (2009). 'In the Picture: Resettled Refugees in Sweden', in P. Bevelander, M. Hagström, and S. Rönnqvist (eds.), *Resettled and Included? The Employment Integration of Resettled Refugees in Sweden.* Malmö: Malmö University, 49–80.

Bevelander, P., Broomé, P., Carlson, B., and Lindberg, G. (2003). *Variationer på framtidsmelodi.* Malmö: Malmö stad.

Bevelander, P. and Lundh, C. (2007). 'Employment Integration of Refugees: The Influence of Local Factors on Refugee Job Opportunities in Sweden'. IZA-Discussion Paper No. 2551.

Bevelander, P. and Otterbeck, J. (2010). 'Young People's Attitudes towards Muslims in Sweden', *Ethnic and Racial Studies* 33(3): 404–25.

Bevelander, P. and Otterbeck, J. (2012). 'Islamophobia in Sweden: Politics, Representations, Attitudes and Experiences', in M. Helbling (ed.), *Islamophobia in the West: Measuring and Explaining Individual Attitudes*. London: Routledge, 70–82.

Bevelander, P. and Pendakur, R. (2009). 'The Employment Attachment of Resettled Refugees, Refugees and Family Reunion Migrants in Sweden', in P. Bevelander, M. Hagström, and S. Rönnqvist (eds.), *Resettled and Included? The Employment Integration of Resettled Refugees in Sweden*. Malmö: Malmö University, 227–46.

Blom, S. and Henriksen, K. (eds.) (2008). *Levekår blant innvandrere i Norge 2005/2006*. Oslo: Statistisk sentralbyrå.

Borell, K. (2012). *Islamofobiska fördomar och hatbrott: En kunskapsöversikt*. SST:s skriftserie nr. 1. Stockholm: Nämnden för statligt stöd till trossamfund.

Borell, K. and Gerdner, A. (2011). 'Hidden Voluntary Social Work: A Nationally Representative Survey of Muslim Congregations in Sweden', *British Journal of Social Work* 41: 968–79.

Børresen, S. (2006). *Etniske minoriteters bosætning: Hvad viser forskningen?* Copenhagen: Danish Building Research Institute.

Brochmann, G. and Hagelund, A. (2010). *Velferdens grenser: Innvandringspolitikk og velferdsstat i Skandinavia 1945–2010*. Oslo: Universitetsforlaget.

Bunar, N. (2001). *Skolan mitt i förorten: Fyra studier om skola, segregation, integration och multikulturalism*. Stockholm/Stehag: Symposion.

Carlbom, A. (2006). 'Mångkulturalism och den politiska mobiliseringen av islam', in U. Hedetoft, B. Petersson, and L. Sturfelt (eds.), *Bortom stereotyperna? Invandrare och integration i Danmark och Sverige*. Göteborg: Makadam, 26–65.

Carlsson, M. and Rooth, D.-O. (2007). 'Evidence of Ethnic Discrimination in the Swedish Labour Market Using Experimental Data', *Labour Economics* 14(4): 716–29.

Cato, J. (2012). *När islam blev svenskt: Föreställningar om islam och muslimer i svensk offentlig politik 1975–2010*. Lund Studies in History of Religions 33. Lund: Lund University.

Cato, J. and Otterbeck, J. (2011). 'Aktivt medborgarskap bland muslimer', in P. Bevelander, C. Fernández, and A. Hellström (eds.), *Vägar till medborgarskap*. Lund: Arkiv.

Crone, M. (2010). 'Book review: Lene Kühle and Lasse Lindekilde, *Radicalization among Young Muslims in Aarhus*', *Tidsskrift for Islamforskning* 2: 120–30.

DO (2011). <http://www.do.se> [Accessed 8 July 2011].

Eide, E. (2012). 'The Terror in Norway and the Multiculturalist Scapegoat', *Journal of Contemporary European Studies* 20(3): 273–84.

Emerek, R. (2003). *Integration eller inklusion? Den danske debat om integration*. AMID Working Paper Series No. 31. Aalborg: AMID/Aalborg University.

ECRI (2009). *ECRI Report on Norway* (4th monitoring cycle). <http://www.coe.int/t/dghl/monitoring/ecri/Country-by-country/Norway/NOR-CbC-IV-2009-004-ENG.pdf> [Accessed 30 June 2011].

Galal, L. P. and Liengaard, I. (2003). *At være Muslim i Danmark*. Copenhagen: Forlaget Anis.

Gardell, M. (2010). *Islamofobi*. Stockholm: Leopard.

Goli, M. and Rezaei, S. (2010). *House of War: Islamic Radicalisation in Denmark*. Research Report. Aarhus: Aarhus University Press.

Grøndahl, M., Rasmussen, R. R., and Sinclair, K. (2003). *Hizb ut-Tahrir i Danmark: farlig fundamentalisme eller uskyldigt ungdomsoprør?* Aarhus: Aarhus University Press.

Gundelach, P. and Nørregård-Nielsen, E. (2007). 'Etniske gruppers værdier—Baggrundsrapport'. Copenhagen: Ministry of Refugee, Immigration and Integration Affairs.

Gustafsson, K. (2004). *Muslimsk skola, svenska villkor. Konflikt, identitet & förhandling*. Umeå: Boréa.

Hedetoft, U. (2006a). 'More than Kin and Less than Kind: The Danish Politics of Ethnic Consensus and the Pluricultural Challenge', in J. Campbell, J. Hall, and O. K. Pedersen (eds.), *National Identity and the Varieties of Capitalism: The Danish Experience*. Montreal: McGill-Queens University Press, 398–430.

Hedetoft, U. (2006b). 'Denmark: Integrating Immigrants into a Homogeneous Welfare State'. Migration Information Source. <http://www.migrationinformation.org/Profiles/display.cfm?id=485> [Accessed 8 June 2011].

Hedetoft, U., Petersson, P., and Sturfelt, L. (eds.) (2006). *Bortom Stereotyperna? Invandrare och integration i Danmark och Sverige*. Gothenburg: Makadam.

Hellström, A. (2010). *Vi är de goda: Den offentliga debatten om Sverigedemokraterna och deras politik*. Hägersten: Tankekraft förlag.

Helqvist, I. (2010). 'Muslimske interesseorganisationers samarbejde med Integrationsministeriet', *Tidskrift for Islamforskning* 2: 104–16.

Hemmingsen, A.-S. (2011). 'The Attractions of Jihadism: An Identity Approach to Three Danish Terrorism Cases and the Gallery of Characters around Them'. Ph.D. thesis. Copenhagen: University of Copenhagen.

Hemmingsen, A.-S. (2012). *Anti-demokratiske og voldsfremmende miljøer i Danmark, som bekender sig til islamistisk ideologi. Hvad ved vi?* DIIS report 2012:06: København: Danish Institute of International Studies.

Hervik, P. (ed.) (1999). *Den generende forskellighed: Danske svar på den stigende multikulturalisme*. København: Hans Reitzels forlag.

Hervik, P. (2002) *Mediernes muslimer: En undersøgelse af mediernes dækning af religioner i Danmark*. Copenhagen: Council for Ethnic Equality.

Hjärpe, J. (2005). *Sharia: Gudomlig lag i en värld i förändring*. Stockholm: Nordstedts.

Holtug, N. (2012). 'Danish Multiculturalism, Where Art Thou?', in R. Taras (ed.), *Challenging Multiculturalism: European Models of Diversity*. Edinburgh: Edinburgh University Press, 190–215.

Horsti, K. (2008). 'Overview of Nordic Media Research on Immigration and Ethnic Relations: From Text Analysis to the Study of Production, Use and Reception', *Nordicom Review* 29(2): 275–93.

Hussain, M. (2011) *Muslims in Copenhagen*. London: Open Society Foundations.

Hussain, M., Yılmaz, F., and O'Connor, T. (1997). *Medierne, minoriteterne og majoriteten: en undersøgelse af nyhedsmedier og den folkelige diskurs i Danmark*. Copenhagen: Council for Ethnic Equality.

Hussein, A., Abdirahman, M., Sandberg, P., Brinkemo, P. and Carlsson, B. (2011). 'Somalier flyr svenska affärshinder', *Sydsvenskan*, 17 June.

Hvenegård-Lassen, K. (2007). 'Viljen til valg: Kommunalt integrationsarbejde i Sverige og Danmark', in G. Alsmark, T. Kallehave, and B. Moldenhawer (eds.), *Migration och tillhörighet: Inklusions- och exklusionsprocesser i Skandinavien*. Göteborg: Makadam, 160–93.

Ihle, A. H. (2007). *Magt, medborgerskab og muslimske friskoler i Danmark: traditioner, idealer og politikker*. Copenhagen: University of Copenhagen.

Ingregard, S. (ed.) (2012). *Motgift: Akademisk respons på den nye høyreekstremismen*. Oslo: Flamme Forlag.

Jacobsen, B. A (2007). 'Muslimer i Danmark: en kritisk vurdering af antalsopgørelser', in M. Warburg and B. A. Jacobsen (eds.), *Tørre tal om troen: religionsdemografi i det 21. århundrede*. Højbjerg: Forlaget Univers, 45–66.

Jacobsen, B. A. (2008). 'Religion som fremmedhed i dansk politik: En sammenligning af italesættelser af jøder i Rigsdagstidende 1903–45 og muslimer i Folketingstidende 1967–2005'. Ph.D. thesis. Copenhagen: University of Copenhagen.

Jacobsen, B. A. (2009). 'Denmark', in J. S. Nielsen et al. (eds.), *Yearbook of Muslims in Europe*. Vol. 1. Leiden: Brill, 97–109.

Jacobsen, C. M. (2006). 'Staying on the Straight Path: Religious Identities and Practices among Young Muslims in Norway'. Ph.D. thesis. Bergen: University of Bergen.

Jacobsen, C. M. (2008). 'Theory and Politics in Research on Muslim Immigrants in Norway', *Tidsskrift for islamforskning* 2. <http://islamforskning.dk/Tidsskrift_2_2008/Theory_and_Politics_in_Research_on_Muslim_immigrants_in_Norway.pdf> [Accessed 11 July 2011].

Jacobsen, C. M. (2009). 'Norway', in G. Larsson (ed.), *Islam in the Nordic and Baltic Countries*. London: Routledge, 18–39.

Jacobsen, C. M. (2011). *Islamic Traditions and Muslim Youth in Norway*. Leiden: Brill.

Jacobsen, C. M. and Leirvik, O. (2009). 'Norway', in J. S. Nielsen et al. (eds.), *Yearbook of Muslims in Europe*. Vol. 1. Leiden: Brill, 257–66.

Jacobsen, C. M. and Leirvik, O. (2010). 'Norway', in J. S. Nielsen et al. (eds.), *Yearbook of Muslims in Europe*. Vol. 2. Leiden: Brill, 387–400.

Jeldtoft, N. (2008). 'Andre muslimske identiteter: et studie af ikke-organiserede muslimske minoriteter i Danmark', *Tidsskrift for islamforskning* 1: 59–83.

Jeldtoft, N. (2009). 'On Defining Muslims', in J. S. Nielsen et al. (eds.) *Yearbook of Muslims in Europe*. Vol. 1. Leiden: Brill, 9–14.

Jeldtoft, N. (2012). 'Everyday Lived Islam: Religious Reconfigurations and Secular Sensibilities among Muslim Minorities in the West'. Ph.D. thesis. Copenhagen: University of Copenhagen, Faculty of Theology.

Jeldtoft, N. and Nielsen, J. (2011). *Muslim Minorities: Methods and Contexts*. London: Routledge.

Jensen, T. (2002). 'The Religiousness of Muslim Pupils in Danish Upper-Secondary Schools', in W. A. R. Shadid and P. S. van Koningsveld (eds.), *Intercultural Relations and Religious Authorities: Muslims in the European Union*. Leuven: Peeters, 123–37.

Jensen, T. G. (2011). 'Context, Focus and New Perspectives in the Study of Muslim Religiosity', in N. Jeldtoft and J. S. Nielsen (eds.), *Methods and Contexts in the Study of Muslim Minorities*. London: Routledge, 43–58.

Jensen, T. G. and Østergaard, K. (2007). *Nye Muslimer i Danmark: Møder og Omvendelser*. Højbjerg: Univers.

Kamali, M. (2006). 'Skolböcker och kognitiv andrafiering', in L. Sawyer and M. Kamali (eds.), *Utbildningens dilemma—Demokratiska ideal och andrafierande praxis*. SOU 2006:40. Stockholm: Fritzes, 47–101.

Karlsson, P. and Svanberg, I. (1995). *Moskéer i Sverige: En religionsetnologisk studie av intolerans och administrativ vanmakt*. Tro & tanke no. 95:7. Uppsala: Svenska kyrkans forskningsråd.

Karlsson Minganti, P. (2007). *Muslima: Islamisk väckelse och unga muslimska kvinnors förhandlingar om genus i det samtida Sverige*. Stockholm: Carlsson.

Karpantshof, René (2003) 'Højreradikalismen i Danmark—en politisk model på historisk-sociologisk grund', *Dansk Sociologi* 14(3): 25–41.

Kiiskinen, J. and Saveljeff, S. (2010). *Att dansa i otakt med väljarna: Socialdemokraternas och Moderaternas strategiska bemötande av Sverigedemokraterna*. Malmö: Malmö University.

Kjeldstadli, K. (2008). *Sammensatte samfunn: Innvandring og inkludering*. Oslo: Pax Forlag.

Klausen, J. (2009). *The Cartoons that Shook the World*. New Haven: Yale University Press.

Kühle, L. (2006). *Moskeer i Danmark—islam og muslimske bedesteder*. Højbjerg: Univers.

Kühle, L. and Lindekilde, L. (2010). *Radicalization among Young Muslims in Aarhus.* Aarhus: University of Aarhus.

Lægaard, S. (2009). 'Normative Interpretations of Diversity: The Muhammad Cartoons Controversy and the Importance of Context', *Ethnicities* 9(3): 314–33.

Larsson, G. (2003). *Muslimer i Sverige ett år efter 11 september 2001. Diskriminering, mediebilder och alternativa informationskanaler.* Uppsala: Swedish Science Press.

Larsson, G. (2010). 'From Aesthetic Conflict to Anti-Mosque Demonstrations: The Institutionalisation of Islam and Muslims in Sweden', in S. Alievi (ed.), *Mosques in Europe. Why a Solution Has Become a Problem.* London: Alliance Publishing Trust, 355–72.

Larsson, G. and Sander, A. (2007). *Islam and Muslims in Sweden: Integration or Fragmentation? A Contextual Study.* Berlin: Lit.

Leirvik, O. (2006). *Islam og kristendom: Konflikt eller dialog?* Oslo: Pax.

Leirvik, O. (2009). <http://folk.uio.no/leirvik/tekster/IslamiNorge.html#statistikk> [Accessed 8 July 2011].

Leirvik, O. (2014). 'Muslims in Norway: Value Discourses and Interreligious Dialogue', *Tidskrift for islamforskning* 8(1): 137–61.

Liengaard, I. (2007). '"Normalt er islam jo en fælles ting…" Religiøse autorieter og etableringen af et islamisk felt i Danmark'. Ph.D. thesis. Aarhus: Aarhus University.

Lindekilde, L. (2010). 'Forebyggelse af radikalisering, miskendelse og muslimsk minoritetsidentitet', *Tidsskrift for islamforskning* 3(2): 7–29.

Lindekilde, L. and Larsson, G. (2009). 'Muslim Claims-Making in Context: Comparing the Danish and the Swedish Muhammad Cartoons Controversies', *Ethnicities* 9(3): 361–82.

Lindekilde, L., Mouritzen, P., and Zappata-Barero, R. (2009). 'The Muhammad Cartoon Controversy in Comparative Perspective', *Ethnicities* 9(3): 291–313.

Lower, M. (2007). 'Conversion and St Louis's Last Crusade', *Journal of Ecclesiastical History* 58(2): 211–31.

Lundborg, H. (1919). *Svenska folktyper.* Stockholm: H. W. Tullbergs förlag.

Lundh, C. and Ohlsson, R. (1994). *Från arbetskraftsimport till flyktinginvandring.* Stockholm: SNS.

Magnusson, N. (2011). *Refugeeship: A Project of Justification. Claiming Asylum in England and Sweden.* Stockholm: Department of Education, Stockholm University.

Malm, A. (2009). *Hatet mot muslimer.* Stockholm: Atlas.

Markussen, H. I. and Natvig, R. J. (eds.) (2005). *Islamer i Norge.* Uppsala: Swedish Science Press.

Mikkelsen, F. (2008). *Indvandring og Integration.* Copenhagen: Akademisk Forlag.

Ministry of Refugee, Immigration and Integration Affairs (2007). 'Værdier og normer—blandt udlændinge og danskere. Tænketanken om udfordringer for integrationsindsatsen i Danmark'. Copenhagen: Ministry of Refugee, Immigration and Integration Affairs.

*Muslimer och islam i svenska nyhetsmedier—Om rapporteringen av terrorattackerna i USA den 11 september 2001* (2002). Integrationsverkets skriftserie III. Norrköping: Integrationsverket.

NOU (Norges offentlige utredninger) (2011). *Velferd og migrasjon—Den norske modellens framtid.* Oslo: Departementne servicesenter, informajonsforvaltning.

Østergaard-Nielsen, E. (2003). 'Counting the Cost: Denmark's Changing Migration Policies', *International Journal of Urban and Regional Research* 27(2): 448–54.

Otterbeck, J. (1998). 'The Baltic Tatars: The First Muslim Group in Modern Sweden', in K. Junefelt, M. Peterson, and L.-L. Wallenius (eds.), *Cultural Encounters in East Central Europe.* Stockholm: FRN, 145–53.

Otterbeck, J. (2000a). *Islam på svenska. Tidskriften Salaam och islams globalisering.* Stockholm: Almqvist & Wiksell International.

Otterbeck, J. (2000b). *Islam, muslimer och den svenska skolan.* Lund: Studentlitteratur.

Otterbeck, J. (2004). 'The Legal Status of Islamic Minorities in Sweden', in R. Aluffi B.-P. and G. Zincone (eds.), *The Legal Treatment of Islamic Minorities in Europe.* Leuven: Peeters, 233–54.

Otterbeck, J. (2005). 'What is Reasonable to Demand? Islam in Swedish Textbooks', *Journal of Ethnic and Migration Studies* 31(4): 795–812.

Otterbeck, J. (2010a). *Samtidsislam.* Stockholm: Carlsson.

Otterbeck, J. (2010b). 'Sweden: Cooperation and Conflict', in A. Triandafyllidou (ed.), *Muslims in 21st Century Europe: Structural and Cultural Perspectives.* European Sociological Association Studies in European Societies vol. 12. London: Routledge, 103–20.

Otterbeck, J. and Bevelander, P. (2006). *Islamofobi—En studie av begreppet, ungdomars attityder och unga muslimers utsatthet.* Stockholm: Forum för levande historia.

Ouis, P. and Roald, A. S. (2003). *Muslim i Sverige.* Stockholm: Wahlström & Widstrand.

Pedersen, L. and Selmer, B. (1991). *Muslimsk indvandrerungdom.* Aarhus: Aarhus University Press.

Pedersen, M. H. (2009). 'Practices of Belonging: Ritual Performances and the Making of Place and Relatedness among Iraqi Women in Copenhagen'. Ph.D. thesis. Copenhagen: Department of Anthropology, University of Copenhagen.

Ranstorp, M. and Dos Santos, J. (2009). *Hot mot demokrati och värdegrund: En lägesbild från Malmö.* Report from Centrum för assymetriska hot och terrorismstudier.

Roald, A. S. (2004). *New Muslims in the European Context: The Experience of Scandinavian Converts.* Leiden: Brill.

Roald, A. S. (2009). *Muslimer i nya samhällen: Om indivuduella och kollektiva rättigheter.* Göteborg: Daidalos.

Roy, O. (2004). *Globalized Islam: The Search for a New Ummah.* New York: Columbia University Press.

Rydberg, J. (2004). 'Explaining the Emergence of Radical Right-Wing Populist Parties: The Case of Denmark', *West European Politics* 27(3): 474–502.

Sander, A. (1993). *I vilken utsträckning är den svenske muslimen religiös?* Göteborg. Göteborgs universitet.

SÄPO (2010). *Våldsbejakande islamisk extremism i Sverige.* Report.

Sayed, M. (2009). *Islam och arvsrätt i det mångkulturella Sverige: en internationellt privaträttslig och jämförande studie.* Stockholm: Iustus.

Schmidt, G. (2002). 'Dialectics of Authenticity: Examples of Ethnification of Islam among Young Muslims in the United States and Denmark', *The Muslim World* 1–2: 1–17.

Schmidt, G. (2004). 'Islamic Identity Formation among Young Muslims in Denmark, Sweden, and the United States', *Journal of Muslim Minority Affairs* 24(1): 31–45.

Schmidt, G. (2005). 'The Transnational Umma: Myth or Reality? Examples from the Western Diasporas', *The Muslim World* 95(4): 575–86.

Schmidt, G. (2007). *Muslim i Danmark, muslim i Verden.* Stockholm: Swedish Science Press.

Schmidt, G. (2008a). 'Islam på Nørrebrosk', *Tidsskrift for islamforskning* 1. <http://islamforskning.dk/Tidskrit_1_2008/Islam_paa_Noerrebrosk.pdf> [Accessed 11 July 2011].

Schmidt, G. (2008b). 'From Granting the Right (?!) Answers to Posing Odd Questions: Perspectives on Studying and Presenting Muslim Minorities in a Politicized, Western Context', *Tidsskrift for islamforskning* 2: 11–26.

Schmidt, G. (2009). 'Denmark', in G. Larsson (ed.), *Islam in the Nordic and Baltic Countries*. London: Routledge, 40-55.
Schmidt, G. (2010). 'Book review: Marco Goli and Shahamak Rezaei: *House of War: Islamic Radicalisation in Denmark*', *Tidsskrift for Islamforskning* 2: 125-7.
Schmidt, G. (2011a). 'Law and Identity: Transnational Arranged Marriages and the Limits of Danishness', *Journal of Ethnic and Migration Studies* 37(2): 257-75.
Schmidt, G. (2011b). 'Understanding and Approaching Muslim Visibilities: Lessons Learned from Fieldwork-Based Study of Muslims in Copenhagen', *Ethnic and Racial Studies* 34(7): 1216-29.
Schmidt, G. (2011c). 'Lived, Negotiated Spaces: Muslims in Nørrebro, Copenhagen', in J. Egholm Feldt and K. Sinclair (eds.), *Lived Space: Reconsidering Transnationalism among Muslim Minorities*. Frankfurt am Main: Peter Lang, 65-82.
Schmidt, G. (2011d). 'Nørrebro as a Multicultural Neighborhood: Space, Politics and Genealogy'. Inaugural lecture, University of Roskilde, 8 March.
Schmidt, G. (2014). '"Let's Get Together": Perspectives on Multiculturalism and Local Implications in Denmark', in P. Kivisto and Ô. Wahlbeck (eds.), *Debating Multiculturalism in the Nordic Welfare States*. Basingstoke: Palgrave Macmillan, 197-218.
Schmidt, G. and Jakobsen, V. (2000). *20 år i Danmark: En undersøgelse af nydanskeres situation og erfaringer*. Report 00:11. Copenhagen: Danish National Centre for Social Research.
Schmidt, G. and Jakobsen, V. (2004). *Pardannelsesmønstre blandt etniske minoriteter*. Report 04:09. Copenhagen: Danish National Centre for Social Research.
Schmidt, G., Liversage, A., Jakobsen, V., Jensen, T. G., and Graversen, B. (2009). *Ændrede familiesammenføringsregler. Hvad har de nye regler betydet for pardannelsesmønstret blandt etniske minoriteter?* Report 09:28. Copenhagen: Danish National Centre for Social Research.
Shakoor, T. (2008). 'Formål for muslimske friskoler i Danmark—udviklinger i formålserklæringer og vedtægter i danske friskoler for muslimske børn', *Tidsskrift for Islamforskning* 3: 29-43.
Simonsen, J. B. (1989). *Religiøs organisering blandt muslimer i Danmark: om moskeer, koranskoler og privatskoler for muslimer i Danmark*. Dokumentation om indvandrere no. 3. Copenhagen: Mellemfolkeligt Samvirke.
Simonsen, J. B. (1990). *Islam i Danmark, muslimske institutioner i Danmark 1970-1989*. Aarhus: Aarhus University Press.
Sinclair, K. (2010). 'The Caliphate as Homeland: Hizb ut-Tahrir in Denmark and Britain'. Ph.D. thesis. Odense: University of Southern Denmark.
Sixtensson, J. (2009). *Hemma och främmande i staden: Kvinnor med slöja berättar*. Mapius 4. Malmö: Malmö University.
Sloth, L. V. (2011). 'Diskrimination på arbejdsmarkedet—og hvad så?' Ph.D. thesis. Copenhagen: University of Copenhagen.
SOU (2009). *Staten och imamerna—Religion, integration, autonomi*. SOU 2009:52. Stockholm: Fritzes.
SST (2013). 'Statistik över antalet betjänade'. <http://www.sst.a.se/statistik.4.7501238311cc6f1 2fa580005236.html> [Accessed 18 February 2013].
Statistics Denmark (2008). *Indvandrere i Danmark 2007*. Copenhagen: Statistics Denmark.
Statistics Denmark (2009). *Indvandrere i Danmark 2008*. Copenhagen: Statistics Denmark.
Statistics Denmark (2010). *Indvandrere i Danmark 2009*. Copenhagen: Statistics Denmark.
Statistics Denmark (2011). *Indvandrere i Danmark 2010*. Copenhagen: Statistics Denmark.

Statistics Sweden (1937). *Folkräkningen den 31 december 1930. V. Trosbekännelse, främmande stam, främmande språk*. Stockholm: P. A. Norstedt & Söner.

Statistics Sweden (2009). <http://www.scb.se/statistik/_publikationer/BE0101_2009A01_BR_10_BE0110TAB.pdf> [Accessed 8 July 2011].

Statistics Sweden (2010). *Medborgarskap*. <http://www.scb.se/Statistik/BE/BE0101/2010A01L/Medborgarskap.pdf> [Accessed 8 July 2011].

Statistics Sweden (2013). <http://www.scb.se/Pages/ProductTables.aspx?id=25795> [Accessed 18 February 2013].

Sultan Sjöqvist, M. (2006). *'Vi blev muslimer': Svenska kvinnor berättar: En religionssociologisk studie av konversionsberättelser*. Uppsala: Acta Universitatis Upsaliensis.

Svanberg, I. and Westerlund, D. (eds.) (1999). *Blågul islam? Muslimer i Sverige*. Nora: Nya Doxa.

Swedish Church (2013). 'Medlemsstatistik'. <http://www.svenskakyrkan.se/default.aspx?id=645562> [Accessed 18 February 2013].

Togeby, L. (2003). *Fra fremmedarbejdere til etniske minoriteter*. Magtudredningen. Aarhus: Aarhus University Press.

Vogt, K. (2000). *Islam på norsk: Moskeer og islamiske organisajoner i Norge*. Trondheim: Cappelens.

Vogt, K. (2002). 'Integration through Islam? Muslims in Norway', in Y. Haddad (ed.), *Muslims in the West*. Oxford: Oxford University Press, 88–100.

Weldeghebriel, F. K. (2008). 'En rammeanalyse av karikatursaken i Norge'. Master's thesis in History of Religion. Oslo University.

Wikan, U. (2004). *En fråga om heder*. Stockholm: Ordfront.

# PART III

# THE OLD EUROPEAN LAND OF ISLAM

CHAPTER 10

# BOSNIA AND HERZEGOVINA

## AHMET ALIBAŠIĆ

The symbolic value and power of the Bosnian indigenous European Muslim community by far outweigh its statistical importance. Although statistically insignificant in the ocean of 1.5 billion Muslims at the end of the twentieth century this small community became globally famous for the way in which it struggled to defend its homeland and uphold its Islamic identity. That trial came at the end of 200 years of intensive changes that witnessed former Muslim Ottoman subjects of Bosnia and Herzegovina become a modern European nation of Bosniaks. During that period Bosnian Muslims, among other things, opposed and then implemented Ottoman modernizing reforms. After 1878 they initially resisted and fled but eventually accepted Austro-Hungarian occupation and rule, particularly after the Balkan wars of 1912. However, in 1918 that multinational empire dissolved. Between two world wars Bosnian Muslims found themselves in the kingdom of Yugoslavia where they were vastly marginalized.

Immediately after the Second World War, communist Yugoslavia was very unfriendly towards all religious communities. The situation of Bosnian Muslims was particularly difficult because of the denial of their separate national identity and the absence of any national institutions. By late 1960s the process of recognition of a "Muslim" nation was initiated and anti-religious policy significantly relaxed.[1] Eventually, however, it was the tragic dissolution of Yugoslavia (1991–2) that brought the community to the brink of extinction. Since the end of the war (1995), the community has recovered to some extent but has struggled to come to terms with new demographic realities whereby it now lives as a minority in around 70% of its homeland. That is the result of the utter failure to implement Annex VII of the Dayton Peace Accords pertaining to the return of refugees and displaced persons.[2]

---

[1] On religion in Yugoslavia see Esad Ćimić, *Drama a/teizacije* (Sarajevo: Šahinpašić, 2007).

[2] The Dayton Peace Accords were negotiated in Dayton (Ohio, USA) and signed in December 1995 in Paris. This agreement is credited with ending the Bosnian war but blamed for creating a dysfunctional state with two "entities" (Federation of B&H and Republic of Srpska) and a district of Brčko with asymmetric solutions and elements of systemic discrimination of minorities. On the Dayton Accords see Richard Holbrooke, *To End a War* (New York: Random House, 1998). On the inter-religious relations

Today this community is at another important junction in its history and facing a new challenge—EU integration. A part of that challenge is its image in the post-9/11 world. To some this community is a source of hope and inspiration, to others it is a source of concern and threat. In the aftermath of genocide, the community itself is uncertain about its future and its place in the hearts and minds of its neighbors. Why that is so we will try to show in the rest of this chapter.

The main themes of studies on Islam and Muslims in Bosnia Herzegovina since the mid-twentieth century have been: (1) the conversion of a large portion of the local population to Islam during the Ottoman era, (2) the encounter of Bosnian Muslims with modernity and their evolution from a religious community into a modern nation, (3) the specific Bosnian tradition of understanding and living of Islam, (4) Bosnian Islamic institutions, (5) the religious revival particularly since the fall of communism, (6) ethnic cleansing and genocide in the 1990s, and (7) Islamophobia.

## Conversion to Islam in Ottoman Bosnia

Islam has been continuously present in Bosnia and Herzegovina since the early fifteenth century. Ottomans started invading the country from the south-east in the late fourteenth century, took what is today Sarajevo in 1453 but managed to take the then Bosnian capital Jajce only in 1463 before losing it soon after. The Ottoman conquest was not completed until the late sixteenth century when lands surrounding the western Bosnian town of Bihać were finally taken. During the fifteenth and especially sixteenth centuries the majority of Bosnians accepted Islam. However, due to a combination of wars, plagues, and migrations, by the time Austrians occupied the country in 1878 Muslims were the majority no more.[3]

While almost everything in Bosnian history evades consensus among the three major communities (Bosniak, Serb, and Croat), the Islamization process is one of the most hotly contested topics in the Balkan historiographies.[4] The disagreements start with the terminology to define this process (Islamization vs. Conversion) and continue over the

---

in Bosnia before the war see the excellent Tone Bringa, *Being Muslim the Bosnian Way: Identity and Community in a Central Bosnian Village* (Princeton: Princeton University Press, 1995). As to what war did to that life, see the movies: *We Are All Neighbours* (1993) and *Returning Home: Revival of a Bosnian Village* (2002), which Tone Bringa helped produce.

[3] Justin McCarthy, "Ottoman Bosnia, 1800 to 1878," in Mark Pinson (ed.), *The Muslims of Bosnia-Herzegovina: Their Historic Development from the Middle Ages to the Dissolution of Yugoslavia* (Cambridge, MA: Harvard University Press, 1996), 81; *Popis žiteljstva u BiH od 22 aprila 1895 sa podacima o teritorijalnom razdjeljenju, javnim zavodima i rudnim vrelima* (Sarajevo: Zemaljska vlada BiH, 1896).

[4] For an annotated bibliography of 202 works on Islamization in Bosnia see: Gilles Grivaud and Alexandre Popovic (eds.), *Les conversions à l'islam en Asie Mineure et dans les Balkans aux époques seldjoukide et ottomane: Bibliographie raisonnée (1800–2000)* (Athènes: École française d'Athènes, 2011), 509–697. It is telling that the bibliography contains more items on Islamization in Bosnia than on any

pre-Islamic religious identity of the Bosnian population, the reasons for the conversion, and the freely chosen or forced nature of it. Some Bosniak historians defend "an hour of faith" thesis; the thesis of mass conversion of mainly Bogumil population soon after Ottoman conquest when allegedly tens of thousands of Bogumil families oppressed by Christian rulers had joyfully accepted Islam.[5] Many non-Muslim historians deny the existence of such a community or process at the time of Ottoman conquest.[6] The most ideological Serbian nationalist historiography presents Bosnian Muslims as the progeny of greedy landlords, thieves, slaves, poor, mentally ill, lazy, outcasts, prisoners, or at best defeated and confused Serbs who chose to follow the religion of their enemies. One such account concludes that Islamization was "an act of human confusion and collective feeble-mindedness (*maloumlja*)."[7]

According to more serious scholarship,[8] the Islamization process seems to have been a gradual one of mainly voluntary conversion of the local population assisted by church persecution of Christian heretics in some areas and weak church presence in others, the weakness of Christian belief of Bosnians of the time, favorable socio-economic conditions, the intellectual appeal of a simple and clear message of a victorious religion, and limited Muslim immigration. The definitive truth about the relative percentage of Catholics, Orthodox, and heretics among the pre-Ottoman Bosnian population might be impossible to establish as Ottoman censuses—the main sources of information on the population of early Ottoman Bosnia—made a distinction only between Muslims and non-Muslims without going into any further subdivisions.[9]

Unfortunately, in the Balkans, these discussions on a long ago completed process are not only a matter of historiography but have had immediate consequences for living people. Of them Michael Sells writes:

> In the nineteenth century, the three myths—conversion to Islam based only upon cowardice and greed, stable ethnoreligious groups down through the centuries, and complete depravity of Ottoman rule—became the foundation for a new religious ideology, Christoslavism, the belief that Slavs are Christian by nature and that any conversion from Christianity is a betrayal of the Slavic race.

---

other country. For instance, only eighty-six items deal with Islamization in Bulgaria, eighty-four among the Albanians, and forty-three in Macedonia.

[5] Salih Jalimam, *Historija bosanskih bogomila* (Tuzla: Hamidović, 1999), 246. See also: Midhat Spahić, "Proces prihvatanja islama u Bosni i Hercegovini," *Glasnik Rijaseta Islamske zajednice u BiH* 64(3–4) (2002): 327–38; Adem Handžić, *Studije o Bosni* (Istanbul: IRCICA, 1994).

[6] Srećko M. Džaja, *Konfesionalnost i nacionalnost Bosne i Hercegovine: Predemancipacijsko razdoblje 1463.–1804.* (Mostar: ZIRAL, 1999); Dubravko Lovrenović, *Povijest est magistra vitae: o vladavini prostora nad vremenom* (Sarajevo: Rabic, 2008).

[7] Quoted from Mustafa Imamović, *Historija Bošnjaka* (Sarajevo: Bošnjačka zajednica kulture Preporod, 1998), 148.

[8] Noel Malcolm, *Povijest Bosne* (Zagreb-Sarajevo: Erasmus Gilda, 1995), 71–92; John V. A. Fine, "The Medieval and Ottoman Roots of Modern Bosnian Society," in Mark Pinson (ed.), *The Bosnian Muslims*, 11–21; Imamović, *Historija Bošnjaka*, 138–180; Nedim Filipović, *Islamizacija u Bosni i Hercegovini* (Tešanj: Centar za kulturu i obrazovanje, 2005).

[9] Ahmed Zildžić, "Fenomen zvani Srečko M. Džaja," *Znakovi vremena* 9(32) (Summer 2006): 136–56.

He goes on to say:

> Christoslavism... was critical to the genocidal ideology being developed in 1989. Christoslavism places Slavic Muslims and any Christian who would tolerate them in the position of the Judas figure of Kosovo, Vuk Branković. It sets the Slavic Muslims outside the boundaries of nation, race, and people. As portrayed in *The Mountain Wreath* it demonstrates what can be done to those defined as nonpeople and what is, under certain circumstances, a religious duty and a sacred, cleansing act. ...In their acts of genocide from 1992 through 1995, Radovan Karadžić and his followers integrated the Kosovo tradition, as it was handed down through Vuk Karadžić and transformed by Njegoš and Andrić, into the daily rituals of ethnoreligious purification.[10]

The historiographic disputes regarding Islamization have found their way into history textbooks currently used in Bosnian schools which present divergent truths about Islamization as one of the most important historical and cultural processes in the country. Serb and Croatian nationalist historians occasionally still deny its voluntary nature and associate Islam explicitly with the conquering army. In the Bosnian language textbooks, the scale of conversion is explained by the absence of a strong unified church organization in Bosnia, mounting pressure from neighboring church centers on the Bosnian church, and persecution of the same church by the two last Bosnian kings. At the end of the process, the old BH religious triangle—Bosnian, Catholic, and Orthodox Churches—was replaced by a new religious mosaic in which Islam took the place of the Bosnian church. The overall picture of the Islamization painted in Bosnian language schoolbooks is somewhat idealized, and quite unnecessarily so.[11]

## The Encounter of Bosnian Muslims with Modernity

During the Ottoman era, Bosnian Muslims were somewhat privileged over non-Muslim subjects in that their tax load was lighter and they had an opportunity to advance

---

[10] Michael Sells, *The Bridge Betrayed: Religion and Genocide in Bosnia* (Berkeley: University of California Press, 1998), 36, 51. See also: Miodrag Popović, *Vidovdan i časni krst* (Beograd: Slavoljublje, 1976); Branimir Anzulović, *The Heavenly Serbia: From Myth to Genocide* (New York: New York University Press, 1999); Safet Bandžović, "Bošnjaci u postjugoslavenskoj srpskoj historiografiji," *Prilozi Instituta za istoriju*, no. 29, Sarajevo 2000; Azher Mihrović, ur., *Nacionalno mitomansko prokletstvo* (Sarajevo: Kaligraf, 2002).

[11] Ahmet Alibašić, "Images of the Ottomans in History Textbooks in Bosnia and Herzegovina," in Christian Moe (ed.), *Images of Religious Other: Discourse and Distance in the Western Balkans* (Novi Sad: CEIR, 2008), 39–71 and *Islam Arastirmalari Dergisi* (*Turkish Journal of Islamic Studies*) 17 (2007): 103–37. It is probably beyond the scope of this survey but Yugoslav textbooks also treated Ottomans as arch-enemy. See: Wolfgang Hoepken, "War, Memory, and Education in a Fragmented Society: The Case of Yugoslavia," *East European Politics and Societies* 13(1) (1999): 197–8.

socially. However, most of them to a large extent shared the destiny of hard-working and taxpaying Ottoman subjects (*ra'aya*). In addition they had to fight within the ranks of the Ottoman armies.[12] Towards the end of the Ottoman times, out of conservatism and self-interest they opposed modernizing reforms, revolted under the leadership of Husein-kapetan Gradaščević (1831–2),[13] and were mercilessly suppressed by Omer Pasha Latas (1850–1). However, they simultaneously participated in attempts to salvage the Ottoman Empire and therefore partook in the Ottoman losses, dying on the many battlefields or migrating with the withdrawing Ottoman soldiers and administrators.

Things changed dramatically for them in 1878 when the Ottomans under international pressure and internal uprisings handed over Bosnia to the Austro-Hungarian Empire. That was the beginning of a process during which at one point Bosnian Muslims were completely separated from the *Ummah* and turned into a dispossessed minority. After initial confusion and wavering between migrating and staying, the majority decided to stay and started to work within the existing political system.[14] This has intensified the Bosnian Muslims' encounter with modernity and Europe which had already started in the late Ottoman times. Over the next 130 years Bosniaks developed a distinct Islamic tradition—more on which below—and evolved from a religious community (*millet*) into a European nation accepting most of the European values and institutions as their own.

The evolution of Bosnian Muslims into a modern nation of Bosniaks and the denial of their separate identity and belonging to Europe by sections of Serb and Croat nationalists is one of the key narratives of the contemporary history of this community.[15] After the departure of the Ottomans the nationalist elites of neighboring nations continued to identify Bosnian Muslims with the hated Ottoman occupation which meant that Serb and Croat nationalisms have since been not only anti-Ottoman but anti-Muslim as well. According to sociologist Šaćir Filandra this fact is of fundamental importance since it has resulted in a systematic effort especially by Serbian nationalists to deny Bosnian Muslim identity and occasionally negate their right to live in the Balkans.[16] From time to time such attitudes have erupted into genocides and ethnic cleansings.[17] Two most

---

[12] Ferid Muhić, "The Ottoman Legacy as a Common Layer of the Balkan Muslim Identities," in Halit Eren (ed.), *The Ottoman Legacy and the Balkan Communities Today* (Istanbul: BALMED, 2011), 29–36.

[13] Ahmed Aličić, *Pokret za autonomiju Bosne od 1831. do 1832. godine* (Sarajevo: Orijentalni institut, 1996).

[14] Fikret Karčić, *Bosniaks and the Challenge of Modernity: Late Ottoman and Hapsburg Times* (Sarajevo: El-Kalem, 1999b). Enes Karić, *Contributions to Twentieth Century Islamic Thought in Bosnia and Herzegovina*, vol. 1 (Sarajevo: El-Kalem, 2011).

[15] Marko Atilla Hoare, *The History of Bosnia: From the Middle Ages to the Present Day* (London: Saqi, 2007).

[16] Šaćir Filandra, *Bošnjaci nakon socijalizma: O bošnjačkom identitetu u postjugoslavenskom dobu* (Sarajevo, Zagreb: BZK Preporod i Synopsis, 2012), 306–8. For the image of Ottomans in the Bosnian textbooks see: Alibašić, "Images of the Ottomans in History Textbooks in Bosnia and Herzegovina." See also: Safet Bandžović, *Bošnjaci i deosmanizacija Balkana* (Sarajevo, Author, 2012).

[17] Norman Cigar, *Genocide in Bosnia: The Policy of "Ethnic Cleansing"* (College Station, TX: Texas A&M University Press, 1995); Fikret Karčić, *Muslimani Balkana: Istočno pitanje u XX vijeku* (Tuzla: Behram-begova medresa, 2001).

difficult periods in the twentieth century were from the early 1940s to the mid-1960s and in the 1990s. In the bloodbath of the Second World War Muslims of Yugoslavia were second only to the Yugoslav Jews in terms of percentage demographic loss. Many of them were killed by the Serb extremist movement of Chetniks (*četnici*).[18] About 8.1% of them died in the war. It is important to mention that they also perpetrated war crimes against the Serb population mostly as members of the Croat extremist movement of Ustasha (*ustaše*), which some Bosnian Muslims joined.[19] These crimes were systematically used by Serbian war propaganda in the 1980s and 1990s to mobilize Serbs for war against Bosniaks.[20] This calamity was followed by another disaster in the form of communist rule, which in its first two decades was particularly harsh on all religious communities. While religious freedom was formally guaranteed and religious communities legally registered, most of their property was nationalized, almost all of their schools closed down, religious practices forcibly changed, and the clergy were often harassed.[21]

For over a century Bosnian Muslims themselves have wavered between rejecting self-identify in national terms and opportunism, i.e. siding with Croats or Serbs. Eventually in the late 1960s the communist authorities allowed the formation of a "Muslim" nation in Yugoslavia which most Bosnian Muslims embraced as their national identity. In 1993 the meeting of their leaders appropriated the old historical name "Bosniaks."[22] By the 1990s Bosnian Muslims had reached a point whereby even the religious amongst them preferred residence in Western Europe to any of the Muslim countries offering them shelter, including Turkey and Malaysia. For the first time Balkan Muslim war refugees were migrating westward. This raises the question of the religious tradition which has supported such a development.

## Islamic Tradition of Bosniaks

Accepting Islam from the hands of the Ottoman scholars and Sufis meant adoption of the traditional Islamic legal and theological thought and practice prevalent in the

---

[18] Vladimir Dedijer and Antun Miletić, *Genocid nad Muslimanima 1941–1945, Zbornik dokumenata i sjećanja* (Sarajevo: Svjetlost, 1990), pp. xxiv–xxxi; Bernard Bruneteau, *Stoljeće genocida: Nasilje, masakri i genocidne metode od Armenije do Ruande* (Zagreb: Politička kultura, 2005) or *Le Siècle des génocides: Violences, massacres et processus génocidaires de l'Arménie au Rwanda* (Paris: Armand Colin, 2004).

[19] Enver Redžić, *Muslimansko autonomaštvo i 13. SS divizija* (Sarajevo: Svjetlost, 1987). On Muslim declarations against Nazi oppression see Safet Bandžović, *Bošnjaci i antifašizam: ratni realizam i odjek rezolucija građanske hrabrosti (1941.)* (Sarajevo: Author, 2010).

[20] For instance the novel *Nož* (*Knife*) written by (former) Serbian minister of foreign affairs (2004–7) and (former) extremist Vuk Drašković in 1982.

[21] Denis Bećirović, *Islamska zajednica u Bosni i Hercegovini za vrijeme avnojevske Jugoslavije (1945–1953)* (Zagreb: Bošnjačka nacionalna zajednica za grad Zagreb i Zagrebačku županiju i Islamska zajednica u Hrvatskoj—Medžlis IZ Zagreb, 2012).

[22] On the evolution of the Bosniak nation from a religious community into a modern nation see Filandra, *Bošnjaci nakon socijalizma*, 131–51; Muhamed Hadžijahić, *Od tradicije do identiteta* (Sarajevo: Svjetlost, 1974); Atif Purivatra, Mustafa Imamović, and Rusmir Mahmutćehajić,

Ottoman state. The years since the fall of communism have brought significant changes to Islam and Muslims in Bosnia, as will be discussed later in the chapter. One thing of interest is the reintegration of Bosnian Muslims into the wider Muslim world community. In that process all sorts of ideas from the Muslim world—and elsewhere—came to Bosnia and disturbed the homogeneity of Islamic practice in the country especially in the field of rituals.[23] Many local Muslims as well as foreign observers perceived this as a threat to "Bosnian Islam" without defining it. Nor was everybody happy with this ethno-geographic qualification of what is usually perceived as a universal religion. While not negating the usefulness of this term as a sociological tool some have preferred to use a phrase from the constitution of the Islamic Community (*Islamska zajednica*, see below) "Islamic tradition of Bosniaks." So far the most significant attempt at its definition was that of a lay member of the Islamic Community's Executive Body (*Rijaset*) and historian of law Professor Fikret Karčić (b. 1955) whose thoughts on the topic have been well received and went almost unchallenged.[24]

According to Karčić six elements constitute the Islamic tradition of Bosniaks. First, it is Sunni Islam of Maturidi[25] variation in Islamic doctrine, Hanafi school of Islamic Law and relevant Sufi orders.[26] Second is belonging to the Ottoman Islamic cultural zone characterized by—among other things—strong central authority and institutionalization of *'ulama* into a tightly knit hierarchy. Third is the presence of "Islamized" pre-Islamic Bosnian culture such as performing prayers in the open on certain days of the solar calendar. These elements are present even today and have been constantly evolving. The case of the annual June gatherings and prayers in the open field at Ajvatovica (near Prusac in Central Bosnia) is an interesting case in this regard.[27] Fourth is the tradition of Islamic reformism since the mid-nineteenth century. It was an attempt to revive *ijtihad* (interpretation of Islamic sources) and reform the socio-political conditions of Muslims. In the second half of the twentieth century this reformism became

---

*Muslimani i bošnjaštvo* (Sarajevo: Ključanin, 1991); Šaćir Filandra, *Bošnjačka politika u XX stoljeću* (Sarajevo: Sejtarija, 1998).

[23] Ahmet Alibašić, "Traditional and Reformist Islam in Bosnia-Herzegovina." <http://www.academia.edu/2564570/Traditional_and_Reformist_Islam_in_Bosnia>.

[24] Fikret Karčić, "Šta je to 'islamska tradicija Bošnjaka'," *Preporod*, no. 23/841, Dec. 1, 2006 (English translation available at: <http://cns.ba/cns-izdanja/what-is-islamic-tradition-of-bosniaks-fikret-karcic/>) and *Rezolucija Islamske zajednice u Bosni i Hercegovini o tumačenju islama i drugi tekstovi* (Sarajevo: El-Kalem, 2006), 51–9.

[25] The Maturidi school of Islamic theology is a school established by Abu Mansur al-Maturidi (853–944), usually adhered to by the followers of Hanafi school of Islamic law.

[26] One of the major schools of Islamic jurisprudence established by Abu Hanifa (d. 767). Many Bosnian Muslims including many intellectuals believe that Hanafi *madh'hab* is significantly more liberal than the other schools of Islamic law and that most problems in Islamic practice today are the result of departure from Hanafi *madh'hab*, which is an oversimplification of the situation and hardly a defensible position. It might, however, be legitimately claimed that this school is the most rational(ist) Sunni law school.

[27] Nusret Abdibegović and Zoran Filipović (eds.), *Ajvatovica: 500 godina dovišta* (Sarajevo: Naklada Zoro, 2010).

"the official intellectual tradition in interpreting Islam in BiH.". This tradition is not homogeneous. It includes religious modernist as well as more conservative trends. The fifth defining element of Bosniak Islamic tradition is the institutionalization of Islamic religious authority in the form of an "Islamic Community," described below.[28] And sixth is the practice of living Islam in a secular state. The dynamic relationship—and sometimes tension—between these elements still exists. Karčić also observed that two of these elements—Islamic institutions and Islamic thought—could be the main elements for further development.

In this respect, the responses of Bosnian Muslim intellectuals to the challenges of modernity and European culture are potentially interesting to the outside world.[29] However, these responses have still to be systematically studied and presented in major European languages. At the moment this legacy can be defined by the following traits. First, these responses to modernity were formed under absence of freedom and in isolation from the *Ummah*, which sometimes was a blessing in disguise since it forced creativity upon local Muslim thinkers. Second, it is evolving as Bosnian Muslim thought is "digesting" new input from the wider Muslim world into which it has been reintegrated.[30] One can only hope that Bosnian Islamic thought will regain its creativity and authenticity. Third, Bosnian Muslim scholars still need to rethink, justify, and legitimize many Bosnian Islamic practices if they do not want to be seen and written off by their fellow Muslims as weak and lax Muslims.

## Main Characteristics of "Bosnian Islam"

Since 1878 Bosnian Muslims have lived in secular states. Austria (1878–1918) and royal Yugoslavia (1918–41) implemented shariah in personal matters of Muslims but from 1945 until 1990 Bosnian Muslims lived in an often aggressively atheistic state. Its attitude towards religion fluctuated from harsh treatment of the late 1940s and 1950s when most of Islamic endowment (*waqf*) property was nationalized, shariah courts and most Islamic schools (madrasas) closed, many *'ulama* were imprisoned and many mosques destroyed, Sufi orders banned, and every aspect of the work of Islamic Community (IC) was closely watched, to the 1970s when the anti-religious policy was relaxed and Islamic

---

[28] Asked about the precise meaning of institutionalization of Islam former Rais al-Ulama Mustafa Cerić once said: "I am not sure I know what it means but I understand it as a way of disciplining Muslims in religious matters. Muslims respect norms in society but do all sorts of things in their mosques and do not respect any norms inside them."

[29] Xavier Bougarel, 'The Role of Balkan Muslims in Building a European Islam," European Policy Centre Issue Paper no. 43, November 22, 2005.

[30] A working bibliography of Islamic literature in Bosnian prepared by Azra Hadžić, Amela Lepir, and Ahmet Alibašić lists some 2,500 titles published since 1990. See also: Ahmet Alibašić, "Pravci i elementi razvoja islamske tradicije Bošnjaka u bosanskom kontekstu," *Zbornik radova naučnog skupa 'Islamska tradicija Bošnjaka: izvori, razvoj i institucije, perspektive'*, 14–16. Nov. 2007 (Sarajevo: Rijaset IZ u BiH, 2008), 491–509.

life in was Yugoslavia reinvigorated. Since 1990, Muslims have been part of the effort to establish a liberal democracy.

In January 2004, Bosnia and Herzegovina completely overhauled its legal framework for state–church relations. The basic principles of the new Law on Freedom of Religion and the Legal Position of Churches and Religious Communities in today's Bosnia are: (1) religious communities are separate from the state; (2) religious communities are equal in rights and obligations; (3) religious communities are independent in defining their own internal organization; (4) religious communities have the status of legal persons; (5) religious communities and their organizations are not tax-exempt; (6) the state may provide material assistance for healthcare activities, educational, charitable, and social services offered by religious communities, on the condition that those services are provided without any discrimination; and (7) the state may also pay the pensions, disability, and health insurance for religious personnel.

This law was drafted in an unusually wide process of consultation between Bosnian religious communities and public authorities, as well as international experts and organizations.[31] The result is a law that takes into account the highest international standards of religious freedom. The Law can safely be said to uphold the principle of separation with cooperation between state and religious communities. The state has signed the agreements with the Vatican and the Serbian Orthodox Church. Similar agreement is currently been negotiated with the IC. Religious education is an optional course in Bosnian public schools.[32] Chaplains are present in the armed forces and are paid by the state. There is no state law on holidays yet but there is a consensus on how to celebrate religious holidays on state level. However, the law on holidays of one of the two Bosnian entities, that of the Republic of Srpska adopted in November 2005, clearly prefers Orthodox Christianity by proclaiming Orthodox patron saint days as official holidays of the Republic of Srpska, its police and army units. Bosniak members of parliament strongly protested the adoption of the law.

Since the abolition of shariah courts in 1946 Bosnian Muslims have to abide by the religious and moral norms of the shariah. As for "legal" shariah norms, i.e. those norms where the state's intervention is needed for their implementation or for the execution of sanctions in the case of their violation, those norms have also been transformed into moral norms with individual conscience being the only authority supervising their implementation.[33] The IC itself has repeatedly stated its commitment to the separation

---

[31] Emir Kovačević, "The Legal Position of Churches and Religious Communities in Bosnia and Herzegovina," in Silvo Devetak et al. (eds.), *Religion and Democracy in Moldova* (Maribor-Chisinau: ISCOMET and ASER, 2005), 286.

[32] Ahmet Alibašić, "A Problem that Does Not Have to Be: Religious Education in Public Schools in Bosnia and Herzegovina," in Ahmet Alibašić et al. (eds.), *Religija i školovanje u otvorenom društvu: Preispitivanje modela religijskog obrazovanja u Bosni i Hercegovini* (Sarajevo: Fond otvoreno društvo Bosna i Hercegovina, 2009), 107–10.

[33] More on this in Fikret Karčić, "Secular State and Religion(s): Remarks on the Bosnian Experience in Regulating Religion and State Relations in View of the New Law on Freedom of Religion," in Stefan Schreiner (ed.), *Religion and Secular State* (Zurich and Sarajevo: European Abrahamic Forum and Interreligious Institute in B&H, 2008), 15–24.

of state and religious communities.[34] In practice, for instance, so called "shariah marriages" are not recognized by the state and are in principle conducted only after a civil marriage.

Given their recent experience, Bosnian Muslims have been reasonably peaceful, non-violent, civic, respectful of the laws and norms of the country, open, and tolerant. There has been no massive revenge against Serbian or Croatian targets, or serious attacks on Western targets, or extra-judicial quest for justice despite the disappointment in Europe and the very strong sense of victimization and betrayal. It has been suggested that Ottoman normative culture might be one of the factors contributing to this stance.[35] In this regard Xavier Bougarel has also suggested that Bosnian Muslims have adapted to the condition of non-sovereignty and power-sharing in a multi-religious environment.[36]

Bosnian Islam is essentially democratic, meaning participatory, inclusive, and pluralistic. A telling indicator of the situation in the community in this regard is public discussion of statements and actions of the top leadership unheard of in other religious communities. The inclusive and participatory nature of the IC begets pluralism.[37] A plethora of Islamic trends have always been present inside the IC: the Traditionalists who trust inherited ways, i.e. old religious authorities, more than the reasoning of new generations; Reformists who seek to simultaneously remain faithful to the Islamic sources and requirements of their times and therefore aim at reforming both Islamic teachings (through *ijtihad*, i.e. independent reasoning) and society; religious Modernists who advocate acceptance of modernity in its European edition by providing religious justification for it; Salafis who would rather revive the Islam of the first three Muslim generations than follow later religious authorities; Sufis who give priority to spirituality over juristic formalities; and a small group of extremists who tolerate no other opinion and even occasionally justify use of violence to settle theological disputes.[38] All are in there. Many of the IC officials with university diplomas are graduates of non-Bosnian universities such as those in Morocco, Tunisia, Algeria, Libya, Egypt, Saudi Arabia, Jordan, Syria, UAE, Kuwait, Iraq, Iran, Turkey, Malaysia, Pakistan, Spain, USA, Serbia, Croatia, and others. In a sense, the IC is a melting pot. It is premature to

---

[34] Rijaset IZ u BiH, "Platforma IZ u BiH za dijalog," available at the official website of the IC (<http://www.rijaset.ba>).

[35] Personal conversation with Dr. Fikret Karčić. This is not to deny the war crimes committed by Muslims, both local and foreign, in uniforms of the Bosnian army. However, evidence suggests that local Islamic authorities actually reined in the destructive impulses. An analysis of the texts published in *Glasnik*, the official journal of the IC during last twenty years, did not discover any significant case of intolerance or chauvinism. See Omer Kovačević, "Muslimani i drugi: analiza tekstova objavljenih u *Glasniku Islamske zajednice*" (Muslims and Others: Analysis of the *Herald of Islamic Community* articles), graduation paper no. 401, Faculty of Islamic Studies in Sarajevo, June 2006.

[36] Xavier Bougarel, "The Role of Balkan Muslims in Building a European Islam," p. 7.

[37] Ahmet Alibašić, "Izdavačka djelatnost Islamske zajednice u BiH 1993.–2011. God.," in Aziz Kadribegović et al. (eds.), *Islamska zajednica u Bosni i Hercegovini: Dvije decenije reisu-l-uleme Dr. Mustafe ef. Cerića* (Sarajevo: Centar za napredne studije, 2012), 177–84.

[38] For more see Tariq Ramadan, *Western Muslims and the Future of Islam* (Oxford: Oxford University Press, 2004), 24–30.

say for how long it will manage to keep together Salafis, Sufis, and modernists. In the near future one or the other group might have more say in running the Community. However, any sort of massive exclusion based on ideological differences seems to be out of question.

Bosnian Islam might be pluralistic when it comes to various Islamic orientations but it is thoroughly nationalized and Bosnian Muslims are very pragmatic when it comes to balancing patriotism and allegiance to their religious principles. Religious and national identities in their case are reinforcing each other and it is often difficult to say where Islam stops and national culture begins. Sometimes it seems that Islam is at the service of Bosniak nationhood as much as the other way around. More secular Bosniaks are protesting against this situation and would like to see Bosniak national identity clearly separated from Islam as religion. According to Šaćir Filandra this Islamic component has since 1990 been downplayed and its central place has been overtaken by belonging to Bosnia as Bosniak homeland. The very change of national name of Bosnian Muslims in 1993 from "Muslims" into "Bosniaks" is indicative of this secularizing trend.[39]

According to Christian Moe:

> Bosnian Muslims position themselves as European Muslims whose tradition embodies multicultural values. Seeing their future security and prosperity in European integration, they are concerned over Europe's image of Islam. Some have voiced ambitions for contributing to a "Euro-Islam." Important assets in this regard are their experience with orderly institutionalization and representation of Islam, indigenous Islamic higher education, and a relaxed Islamic lifestyle adapted to European secular societies. However, Bosnian Islam is not easily packaged for export to heterogeneous Muslim contexts in Western Europe.[40]

Having said all this, one should also note that the Islamic tradition of Bosniaks is not static and the struggle over the nature of Islam in Bosnia is ongoing. Currently the challenge seems to be most pronounced at two levels: theological interpretation of Islam and the administration of Islamic affairs. At the interpretation level, the influx of Islamic literature, missionaries, and Bosnian graduates of Islamic studies from the Arab world during the 1990s has for a moment created a significant challenge. However, by the 2000s it is obvious that thanks to the strong presence of the IC as the guardian of the Bosnian Islamic tradition, this challenge was successfully rebutted.[41] In that regard, the very clear position of the IC on the use of violence in the name of religion, the identification of violent Muslim groups with an early Muslim militant sect of *kharijites*, the internal differentiation within the Salafis between the majority of more mainstream oriented

---

[39] Filandra, *Bošnjaci nakon socijalizma*. See also: Husnija Kamberović (ed.), *Rasprave o nacionalnom identitetu Bošnjaka* (Sarajevo: Istorijski institut, 2009).

[40] Christian Moe, "A Sultan in Brussels? European Hopes and Fears of Bosnian Muslims," *Südosteuropa* 55(4): 374–94.

[41] Juan Carlos Antunez, *Foreign Influences in Islam in Bosnia and Herzegovina since 1995* (Sarajevo: Centar za napredne studije, 2010). See also section on foreign influence below.

groups and a very small minority of militants, as well as a few violent acts carried out by local extremists on a police station in Bugojno in 2010 and on the American embassy in Sarajevo in 2011, have delegitimized the extremist Islamic discourse in the eyes of vast majority of Bosnian Muslims.[42]

The other challenge also coming from some Salafis was directed at the way Islamic affairs are organized and managed in Bosnia, questioning the "exclusive right" or "monopoly" of the IC to operate mosques, train imams, provide basic religious education in mosques, collect *zakah* (almsgiving), or organize the hajj (pilgrimage to Mecca). It is principally a clash of two Islamic administrative cultures: one that is more commonly present in the Arab world with individualistic tendencies verging on anarchism and a centralized one that is based on the Ottoman tradition of structured religious hierarchy (but is not strictly speaking only Turkish). And although there has been a lot of talk by local politicians, religious leaders, and security experts in the late 1990s and early 2000s about the magnitude of this challenge or "Wahhabi threat," many observers have now concluded that critical years were the late 1990s when "Wahhabis" had money, people, and organizations on the ground.[43] In the 2000s the status and independently minded conduct of the IC has also been heavily criticized by radical secularists who would like to push religious communities back onto the margin and religion into the private space. However, despite all these pressures only minor readjustments seem to be feasible in the future precisely because of the stability of the IC to which we turn next.

## Bosnian Islamic Institutions

The way Islamic affairs are administered in Bosnia is, in fact, a combined legacy of Ottoman, Austrian, and Yugoslav periods. The establishment of the IC was supported and even initiated by the Austrian authorities as part of their strategy to separate Bosnian Muslims from Istanbul but would not be possible without the Ottoman *'ilmiyya* hierarchy tradition.[44] In 1882 the Austrian emperor appointed the first Bosnian Grand Mufti (*Rais al-'Ulama*), the supreme religious leader. During the following three decades Bosnian Muslims struggled for autonomy in their educational affairs and administration of religious endowments (*awqaf*) which they eventually won in 1909, i.e.

---

[42] Enes Karić et al., *Islamic Scene in Bosnia and Herzegovina* (Sarajevo: Udruženje ilmijje IZ u BiH, 2011).

[43] Kerem Öktem, *New Islamic Actors after the Wahhabi Intermezzo: Turkey's Return to the Muslim Balkans* (St Antony's College, University of Oxford, 2010) <http://www.balkanmuslims.com/pdf/Oktem-Balkan-Muslims.pdf>; Ahmet Alibašić, "Traditional and Reformist Islam in Bosnia and Herzegovina."

[44] The 1997 Statute of the IC simply states that the autonomy of the IC is based on the religious and legal institutions of Bosnian Muslims from the time of Ottoman administration in Bosnia.

a year after Bosnia was formally annexed by Austro-Hungary.[45] Today the IC in Bosnia and Herzegovina is probably the best-organized Islamic administration in Europe. It is independent from the state or any international Islamic organization, self-financed, headed by an elected leader and an elected assembly. Its structures combine representative and hierarchical principles of leadership; it controls all the mosques in the country, trains and appoints all the imams, has exclusive right to administer *waqf* property, and organizes hajj.

According to its statute,[46] the IC in Bosnia and Herzegovina is "the sole and united" community of Muslims in Bosnia and Herzegovina, of Bosniaks outside their homeland, and of other Muslims who accept it as their own. The IC is an inseparable part of the world Muslim community (*Ummah*). The organization of the IC and its activities are derived from the Holy Qur'an and the Sunnah, Islamic traditions of Bosniaks, and the requirements of the time. The IC is independent in regulating its activities (e.g. rituals, Islamic education, management of Islamic endowments, publishing, and charity) and the management of its property.

Furthermore, the aim of the IC is that all of its members should live in conformity with Islamic norms. The IC protects the authenticity of the Islamic norms and assures their interpretation and application. In the interpretation and performance of the Islamic religious rituals the Hanafi *madh'hab* is to be applied. The IC dedicates itself to the preservation of the values of marriage and family life and takes care of the Islamic education and upbringing of its members. The IC is supposed to take care of the religious rights of Muslims and provide necessary conditions for its members so that they may perform their Islamic religious obligations. The IC should also organize and support activities that improve social and financial living conditions of Muslims.

According to the same document, the IC establishes and maintains contact and cooperation with Islamic communities, institutions, and organizations worldwide and cooperates with other religious communities and organizations promoting peace, justice, and good will among all people. The IC is financed by membership fees, *zakah*, *sadaqat al-fitr*, *waqfs*, proceeds from *qurban* (sacrificial animal), revenue of its profit-generating agencies, funds, gifts, and testaments. The statute was slightly amended in April 2012 and again in April 2014.

The organizational structure of the IC consists of *jama'ahs* (community of at least a hundred households), *majlises* (usually a group of not less than seven *jama'ahs*),

---

[45] For a comprehensive account of the institutionalization of Islam in Bosnia during this period see Enes Durmišević, *Uspostava i pravni položaj Rijaseta Islamske zajednice u Bosni i Hercegovini 1882–1899* (Sarajevo: Magistrat, 2002); Omer Nakičević (ed.), *Istorijski razvoj institucije Rijaseta* (Sarajevo: Rijaset IZ u BiH, 1996); Adnan Jahić, *Islamska zajednica u Bosni i Hercegovini za vrijeme monarhističke Jjugoslavije 1918–1941*. (Zagreb: Bošnjačka nacionalna zajednica za grad Zagreb i Zagrebačku županiju i Islamska zajednica u Hrvatskoj—Medžlis IZ Zagreb, 2010).

[46] Muhamed Salkić, *Ustavi Islamske zajednice* (Sarajevo: El-Kalem, 2001).

*muftiluks* (*mufti* districts, eight of them in Bosnia, one in the BH armed forces and one in each of Slovenia, Croatia, Serbia, and Germany),[47] the *Riyasat* (Bosnian: *rijaset*), main executive body headed by Rais al-Ulama (the Grand Mufti),[48] the Assembly of the IC (*Sabor*), and the Constitutional Court.[49]

In 2010 there were 2,202 mosques and *masjids* (mosques without minarets, hereafter mosques) in Bosnia and Herzegovina and 1,395 active *jamaʿats*.[50] Out of 1,701 mosques and *masjids* before the war, 832 were completely destroyed during the aggression on Bosnia in 1992–5 while another 348 were damaged. All the mosques in the territory under the control of the Army of Republic of Srpska, with exception of two small ones, were destroyed. Overall 45% of the IC's total pre-war mass of buildings and monuments (including schools, tekkes, turbes, and religious endowment property—*awqaf*) was damaged or destroyed.[51] Many are still to be reconstructed. The IC employs 1,150 imams on a full-time basis, 338 on a part-time basis, and a few hundred administrators and teachers in its madrasas and faculties.

Major educational institutions of the IC are: the Faculty of Islamic Studies in Sarajevo (est. 1887/1977), Gazi Husrevbey Library (est. 1537), Faculties of Islamic Pedagogy in Zenica and Bihać, Gazi Husrevbey madrasa in Sarajevo (est. 1537), five other madrasas in Bosnia (Tuzla, Travnik, Mostar, Visoko, and Cazin), and the First Bosniak Gymnasium in Sarajevo (est. 1995). In general, the Islamic education system run by the IC combines religious and secular, modern and traditional Islamic education.[52]

Other institutions of the IC are: The Waqf Directorate (est. 1894),[53] Gazi Husrevbey Waqf (est. 1531), El-Kalem Publishing Center (1974), Center for Islamic Architecture (est. 1993), Agency for Halal Quality certification (est. 2005), the Association of the "Ulama"

---

[47] The relations between these "branches" and Sarajevo are not always well spelled out and there are many lacunas and inconsistencies. Karčić, Fikret et al., *Organizacija islamskih zajednica u regionu* (Organizing Islamic Communities in the Region) (Sarajevo: Udruženje ilmijje IZ u BiH, 2008).

[48] See Fikret Karčić, "The Office of Raʾis al-'Ulamaʾ Among the Bosniaks (Bosnian Muslims)," *Intellectual Discourse* 5(2) (1997b): 109–20. The current Grand Mufti is Husein Kavazović, elected to the office in 2012.

[49] Fikret Karčić, "Administration of Islamic Affairs in Bosnia and Herzegovina," *Islamic Studies* 38(4) (1999a): 541–2, 544.

[50] "Izvještaj o radu Rijaseta IZ u BiH za 1430.–1431. H.g./2010. Godinu" (Riyasat of the IC Report 2010), *Glasnik Rijaseta IZ u BIH* 73(5–6) (2011): 596.

[51] Muharem Omerdić, *Prilozi izučavanju genocida nad Bošnjacima, 1992–1995* (Sarajevo: El-Kalem, 1999).

[52] See Ahmet Alibašić and Asim Zubčević, "Islamic Education in Bosnia and Herzegovina," in Ednan Aslan (ed.), *Islamic Education in Europe* (Vienna: Böhlau, 2009), 43–57; Stepan Machacek, "'European Islam' and Islamic Education in Bosnia and Herzegovina," *Sudost Europa.* 55(4) (2007): 395–428; Stepan Machacek, "Islamic Education in the Post-Communist Balkans in the Period from 1990 to 2005," *Archiv orientální* 74(1) (2006): 65–93.

[53] The number of *waqfs* has continuously been reduced since the beginning of twentieth century until the 1990s. In 1909, when the Austro-Hungarian Empire granted autonomy to the IC *waqf* was the biggest private owner in the country with 1,050 individual *waqfs*. In the 1930s that number rose to 1,647. However, in 1945 and 1958 almost every important *waqf* was expropriated and nationalized. Karčić, "Administration," 541–2, 544.

of the IC (1910), Council for Fatwa (est. 2005), Radio of the Islamic Community "BIR" (est. 2008), and the Center for Dialogue—*Wasatiyya* (est. 2012). Sufi orders (*tariqahs*) established in accordance with shariah and *Tariqah* rules are also part of the IC, provided they ask for such a status.

The IC has published its official journal *Glasnik* (Herald) almost continuously since 1933. *Takvim*, the annual prayer timetable and a collection of essays has probably been the most widely circulated publication in the country since 1950. The fortnightly newspaper *Preporod* (<http://www.preporod.com>) has been published since 1970. The journal *Novi Muallim*, under various titles and interruptions, has been published since 1910.

The Bosnian model of Islamic religious affairs administration seems to be performing better than alternative solutions: Russian independent muftis, South-East Asian Islamic movements, European Islamic societies and NGOs, Arab *Wizarat al-Awqaf*, and state-appointed *shuyukh* (*'ulama al-sultah*). It is an asset that needs to be further developed and theoretically legitimized in order to ensure its sustainability against the challenge of other concepts and models. This model is considered important because its structures, institutional setup, and procedures influence the brand of Islam that is affirmed. First, a single Islamic structure means more powerful organization and a better negotiating position *vis-à-vis* state and other actors. Second, self-financing makes such an organization more resistant to unwelcome outside or state influences, whatever they might be. These two together mean more autonomous and consequently more credible Islamic authority that is able to prevent radicalization. This does not exclude some sort of relationship between local IC and transnational Islamic authority once and if it is established. Bosnian Muslims had very positive experience in this regard from 1909 until the end of caliphate in 1924 when a three-stage arrangement was in place for electing Bosnian Grand Mufti. At the outset of the process the local Muslim scholars would recommend a shortlist of three names to the head of state (e.g. the Austrian Emperor in Vienna), who would pick out one name and send it to Istanbul so that the Caliph issued to him a letter of appointment (*manshur*). Third, universal, inclusive membership makes the organization lean towards mainstream, moderation, and the middle path.

The Bosnian model has its limitations too with the main one being the unclear boundaries of the exclusive powers of the IC and the nature of its relations with Islamic NGOs. While the IC's authority over the training of imams and management of mosques has been almost universally accepted, its monopoly on organization of *qurban* (sacrificial animal) or *zakah* (almsgiving) collection has been challenged. There have also been issues regarding the limits of the IC's authority over Islamic informal education, fatwa giving, and Islamic literature publishing. Other shortcomings of its current setup include lack of institutional capacity to respond adequately to the newly acquired social roles, limited human and financial resources, old administrative culture, and lack of strategic planning. For instance, despite the fact that Bosnian state is no longer a welfare state the IC has not significantly increased its charitable activities. It is true that financial resources are significantly smaller than usually thought but more attention paid to charitable projects would certainly bring in more funds. This issue has been acknowledged in recent debates about the mission of the community.[54]

## THE RELIGIOUS REVIVAL

The religious revival in Bosnia since the 1970s and particularly since the fall of communism has attracted some scholarly and a lot more of political attention both in the region and outside it. The debate has included issues such as levels of private and public religiosity, desecularization, reintegration of Bosnian Muslims into the Muslim world community, foreign influences, and radicalization to which we turn next.

The contemporary Islamic revival in Bosnia started in the 1970s due to several factors: the liberalization of the then Yugoslav regime, recognition of Bosnian Muslims as a "nationality," an improved economic situation, the graduation of a new generation of young Muslim intellectuals from Yugoslav and Middle Eastern universities, and global trends in the Muslim world which culminated in the Iranian Revolution in 1979. The main manifestations of revival until 1992 were: (a) (re)construction of mosques financed by local money except in a few cases (such as Zagreb mosque), (b) (re)opening of new education institutions (Faculty of Islamic Studies and female section of Gazi Husrev Bey Madarasah in Sarajevo), (c) publishing of Islamic texts and periodicals (e.g. the fortnightly *Preporod*), (d) intensified personal religiosity and use of Islamic social symbols (mosque attendance, hijab for women, and beard for men), (e) establishment of Muslim political organizations (Democratic Action Party—SDA), and (f) emergence of Muslim solidarity institutions. The research of Fikret Karčić, Enes Karić, and Cornelia Sorabji on these issues stands out.[55] The dominant feature of the Islamic revival in Bosnia during this period was that its only institutional framework was the IC. Alternative organizations were practically unheard of since the forced closing down by the communists of the Young Muslims Society in the 1940s. This would dramatically change after April 1992 with the arrival of Muslim aid agencies and *mujahids*.

The greater visibility of Islam in post-communist Bosnia and Herzegovina has been the subject of many media reports but scholarly work on this topic has been limited.[56]

---

[54] See the election program of the grand mufti of Bosnia Husein Kavazović at <http://www.rijaset.ba/images/stories/Programi-kandidata-za-izbor-reisu-l-uleme/PROGRAM_RADA-Husein_ef_Kavazovic.pdf>.

[55] Fikret Karčić, "Islamic Revival in the Balkans 1970–1992," *Islamic Studies* 36(2–3) (1997a): 565–81; Karić, *Contributions to Twentieth Century Islamic Thought in Bosnia and Herzegovina*; Cornelia Katherine Sorabji, "Muslim Identity and Islamic Faith in Sarajevo," Ph.D. Thesis, University of Cambridge (1988); Cornelia Sorabji, "Islamic Revival and Marriage in Bosnia," *Institute of Muslim Minority Affairs Journal* 9(2) (1988): 331–7.

[56] See, for instance: Xavier Bougarel and Nathalie Clayer, *Le Nouvel Islam balkanique: Les musulmans, acteurs du post-communisme 1990–2000* (Paris: Maisonneuve et Larose, 2001); Harun Karčić, "Islamic Revival in Post-Socialist Bosnia and Herzegovina: International Actors and Activities," *Journal of Muslim Minority Affairs* 30(4) (2010b): 519–34; Harun Karčić, "Globalization and its Impact on Islam in Bosnia:

The security perspective has dominated the writing on this phenomenon. The overall importance of foreign factors in this revival and the potential security threat coming from more radical elements has been commonly overstated by journalists and observers. For instance, Bulgarian security expert Velko Attanassoff concluded that Islamic revivalism is mainly an imported phenomenon maintained through financial and ideological support from the Middle East. Although he could not prove causal relationship between Islamic revivalism and global Salafi *jihad* he went on to argue that the current Islamic revival poses a security threat to the region due to its potential of developing into viable Islamic movements on the ground.[57] Others such as Vienna-based military expert Alfred C. Legert have been a little more optimistic concluding that there is no risk that significant numbers of Muslims in the Balkans might support Islamic extremists since such a development would contradict their religious traditions, their political views, and their lifestyles, which are emphatically Western. Nevertheless, the activities of some Islamic organizations in Bosnia and Kosovo may present a security threat.[58]

Although the Islamic revival in former Yugoslavia started initially in the 1970s it was the transition and the war that had a drastic impact on the re-awakening of Bosnian Muslim masses. The arrival of Islamic aid agencies and *mujahideen* (fighters) during the war opened a channel for the transfer of Islamic ideas and resources from Arab and other Muslim countries.[59] New legislation adopted in the country during the post-war period secured greater religious freedom and paved the way for greater manifestation and practice of religion.[60]

## Manifestations of Islamic Revival

The Islamic revival after 1990 manifested itself in education, (re)construction of mosques, publications, media, work of *Tariqas* (Sufi orders), and Islamic faith-based organizations. The traditional way of teaching Islam to children has been through *mektebs* which never really stopped and has been on the increase since 1990. *Mektebs* are

---

Foreign Influences and Their Effects," *Politics, Religion & Ideology* 11(2) (2010a): 151–66. This section has benefited a lot from Harun Karčić, "Islamic Revival in Bosnia and Herzegovina 1990-2010," *Context* 1(1) (2014), forthcoming.

[57] Velko Attanassoff, "Islamic Revival in the Balkans," MA Thesis (Naval Postgraduate School, Monterey, California, 2006). See also his "Bosnia and Herzegovina: Islamic Revival, International Advocacy Networks and Islamic Terrorism," *Strategic Insights* 4(5) (May 2005) <http://www.hsdl.org/?View&did=453894>. Also Esad Hećimović, "Radical Movements: A Challenge for Moderate Balkan-Islam?" in Walter Feichtinger and Predrag Jureković (eds.), *Religiöser Extremismus vs. Internationale Friedensbemühungen: Lessons Learned und präventive Strategien im Nahen Osten und am Westbalkan* (Vienna: Landesverteidigungsakademie (LVAK), 2008).

[58] Alfred C. Legert, *Preventing and Combatting Terrorism in Bosnia and Hercegovina* (Vienna: National Defence Academy, 2002), 32.

[59] Dženana Karup, "Kuran je naš ustav," *Dani* 72, March 30, 1998.

[60] Law on the Freedom of Religion and the Legal Position of Churches and Religious Communities in Bosnia and Herzegovina (2004).

voluntary weekend classes organized by the IC and usually held in mosques by the local imam or its assistant. According to the 2009 statistics of the IC, classes were held at 1,825 *mektebs* which was an increase of 31 *mektebs* over 2008.[61] Islamic religious education was initially introduced in a number of public schools in Sarajevo in 1991 and has since been part of public school curricula as an elective course with around 95% of elementary school pupils attending it.[62]

The collapse of communism also led to the reopening of several traditional Islamic *madrasas* (boarding schools) which were closed down during the period of communism as well as the opening of new ones. Before the 1946 communist takeover there were more than 40 *madrasas* in Bosnia and Herzegovina. All of them, except for one—the Gazi Husrev Beg *madrasa*—were shut down. Five of them were reopened in the 1900s. Previously, *madrasas* were educating imams only; today, however, their aim is to teach young Bosnian Muslims both secular and traditional Islamic courses and hence prepare them not only for imam profession but for further university study in general.[63]

In order to cater for the greater need of Islamic-education teachers, in addition to the Faculty of Islamic Studies in Sarajevo, two Islamic pedagogical faculties were established by the IC during and immediately after the war, in Zenica (1993, <http://www.ipf.unze.ba>) and Bihać (1996, <httyp://www.ipf.unbi.ba>). The curricula and teaching staff of all these institutions are provided by the IC. They combine traditional Islamic sciences of Islamic doctrine, Qur'anic exegesis, Prophetic tradition, and Islamic law and ethics (*'aqidah, tafsir, hadith*, and *fiqh*) with training in humanities and social studies, especially in pedagogy, psychology, sociology, and philosophy. Since the 1990s Bosnian Muslim students have continued to pursue university education abroad mainly in Saudi Arabia, Syria, Egypt, Jordan, Iran, and Turkey.[64] The post-war period also witnessed the establishment of non-religious colleges and schools often run by foreign parties in Bosnia and Herzegovina, most notably by Iran and Turkey (the Persian–Bosniak College near Sarajevo <http://www.pbk.edu.ba>, the Turkish–Bosnian colleges and schools in Sarajevo, Tuzla, and Bihać, <http://www.bosnasema.com>).[65] No study has been done on the post-graduation lives of the students from these institutions.

Mosques symbolize the presence of Islam in a given territory and therefore their destruction is closely related to the annihilation of Muslims in this given territory. The reconstruction of mosques started immediately after the war and was, due to the lack of local funding, significantly aided by foreign Muslim donors from Turkey, Saudi Arabia,

---

[61] *Glasnik Rijaseta Islamske zajednice u BiH* 72(5–6) (2010): 521.

[62] Alibašić and Zubčević, "Islamic Education in Bosnia and Herzegovina," pp. 43–57; Ahmet Alibašić, "Islamic Higher Education in the Balkans: A Survey," in Yorgen Nielsen (ed.), *Yearbook of Muslims in Europe* (Leiden: Brill, 2010), 619–34; Alibašić, "A Problem that Does Not Have to Be," 107–10.

[63] For more on Islamic education in Bosnia see special issue of *Novi Muallim* 3(8) (2002.).

[64] Machacek, "'European Islam' and 'Islamic Education in Bosnia-Herzegovina,'" 419, footnote no. 61.

[65] Anne Ross Solberg, "The Gulen Schools: A Perfect Compromise or Compromising Perfectly?," available at <http://kotor-network.info/papers/2005/Gulen.Solberg.pdf> [accessed February 15, 2013].

Kuwait, Malaysia, Jordan, Indonesia, Iran, Qatar, Emirates, Egypt, and several other countries. According to the 2010 IC statistics, 319 mosques were under (re)construction. By 2010 an estimated 95% of all the mosques had been reconstructed.[66] This figure is somewhat misleading as it refers to the physical reconstruction of mosques while their congregations (*jamaats*) have not returned in large numbers. Several hundred *jamaats* have been permanently destroyed in the Republic of Srpska during the war.

The vast majority of Bosnian Muslims rely completely on the Bosnian language for information and knowledge on Islam. Therefore publishing was always an important aspect of Islamic life in Bosnia. Again, the first decades of communist rule witnessed little activity in this regard. The situation improved somewhat in the 1970s and 1980s but stalled again in the first years of war 1992–5. Since then about 900 titles have been published inside the IC and about same number of titles by independent publishers. Among the IC publications religious textbooks have the highest print run. In the period 1994–2011 the IC's publishing center El-Kalem printed 1,300,000 copies of *mekteb* and religious education textbooks, and religious instruction manuals. Almanac *Takvim* was printed in 857,000 copies. Unlike private publishers the ICBH has resisted the temptation of populist literature on eschatological themes, conspiracy theories, and occultism. The same cannot be said of so called "scientific" interpretations of the holy texts. About one-third of titles published by the IC (295/906) are translations, mainly from Arabic (c.200), English (58), and Turkish (13). This ratio between local and foreign authors is most probably the inverse in privately published books.

The main characteristic of these publications is plurality of orientations. Practically all the Islamic trends mentioned above are represented with Salafi authors being rarely published by the IC. Abu Hamid al-Ghazali (d. 1111) is by far the most translated classic with twenty books in forty-seven editions published in Bosnian, including two full and one abridged translation of *Ihya'*. Of those, 90% have been published since 1994 and they represent three-quarters of all Al-Ghazali translations into Balkan languages; 14% of all translation of theological works from Arabic into Bosnian since 1990.[67] Then comes Ibn Qayyim al-Jawziyya (d. 1350, who is favored by both Sufis and Salafis). The following classics are also translated: Imam Abu Hanifa (d. 767), Imam Malik ibn Anas (d. 795), Imam Al-Bukhari (d. 870), Imam Muslim (d. 875), Imam Abu Dawud (d. 889), Imam Al-Tirmidhi (d. 892), Imam Al-Nasa'i (d. 915), Al-Tahawi (d. 935), Abu Bakr al-Bayhaqi (1066), Abu Abdullah al-Qurtubi (d. 1273), Ibn Kathir (d. 1373), Al-Nawawi (d. 1278), Ibn Khaldun (d. 1406), Jalal al-Din Al-Suyuti (d. 1505), and Muhammad Al-Shawkani (d. 1834). The Egyptian popular preacher Amr Khalid (b. 1967) and Saudi scholar 'A'id al-Qarni (b. 1960) are reportedly the best-sellers with thirty and ten titles to their names in

---

[66] "Izvještaj o radu Rijaseta IZ u BiH za 1430.-1431. H.g./2010. godinu" (Riyasat of the IC Report 2010), *Glasnik Rijaseta IZ u BIH*, 73(5–6) (2011): 596 and *Glasnik Rijaseta Islamske zajednice u BiH* 72(5–6) (2010): 521.

[67] Emina Ćeman i Azra Hadžić, "Pogled na prijevode djela imama Ebu Hamida Muhammeda el-Gazalija objavljenih na području Balkana do 2011. Godine, sa posebnim osvrtom na prijevode na bosanski jezik," Dec. 2011, manuscript.

Bosnian respectively. While popular among many scholars, shaykh Yusuf Al-Qaradawi's books are not always best-sellers perhaps because of the repetitive nature of some of his writings. Although most authors are Sunnis, Shi'a scholars too are on the list of both the IC and Iranian supported independent publishers such as the Mulla Sadra Foundation, Ibn Sina Institute, and Cultural Center of the Iranian Embassy (an Iranian scholar living in Bosnia Akbar Eydi, Muhammad H. Tabatabai (1904–81), former Iranian president M. Khatami (b. 1943), Ayatollah Morteza Mutahhari (1920–79), and others). Among Western scholars, German Annemarie Schimmel (1922–2003), John L. Esposito (b. 1940) of Georgetown University, British author Karen Armstrong (b. 1944), and French Islamologist Henry Corbin (1903–78) are favorites. Of local authors the best selling are: Sarajevo Imam of Kosovo origin Sulejman Bugari (b. 1966), professor of Prophetic tradition Šefik Kurdić (b. 1958), Zenica professor of Qur'anic exegesis Safvet Halilović (b. 1968), Zenica Imam Husein Čajlaković (b. 1963), and Sarajevo native preacher Sanin Musa (b. 1972). Absent are radical (post-)modernists French professor Mohamed Arkoun (1928–2010), Egyptian scholar exiled in the Netherlands Nasr Hamid Abu Zayd (1943–2010), German scholar of Syrian origin Bassam Tibi (b. 1944), and Abdullahi A. An-Na'im of Emory University (b. 1946 in Sudan) while UCLA law professor of Kuwaiti origin Khaled Abou El Fadl (b. 1963) is fragmentarily translated. This variety is reflective of the pluralism inside the Bosnian Muslim community that has developed since 1990.[68]

The situation is significantly different with the literature subsidized by donors, which is mostly supply, not demand driven. This is a (post-)war phenomenon whereby both Islamic and other interest groups, Salafi, Sufi, Shi'a, and others, have spent a significant part of their energy and resources on the translation and distribution of their literature into the Bosnian language. However, such efforts to convert Bosnian Muslims away from the traditional Bosnian practice of Islam have largely failed due to the presence of the firmly established IC.

Another visible sign of Islamic revival has been an increased public presence of hijab (head covering) for women and beards for men, shariah marriages, religious songs concerts, and the emergence of Islamic faith-based organizations. The increase in the number of headscarved women compared to the communist period is obvious; however percentage-wise this number is still tiny while niqab (face covering) is donned by only a fraction of those. (The niqab was worn by Bosnian Muslim women until they were banned by the communist government in the early 1950s.) The MA thesis of Djermana Šeta on hijab in the Bosnian job market in 2009, which is a rare serious study in the field—found that hijab-wearing Bosnian Muslim women are not different from other Bosnian women in terms of education and competencies. However, discrimination in the job market is evident. It is mainly explained by stereotypes of the employers but far too often Muslim women are ready to accept discrimination as normal.[69]

---

[68] Alibašić, "Izdavačka djelatnost Islamske zajednice u BiH 1993.–2011. god."
[69] Đermana Šeta, *Zašto marama? Bosanskohercegovačke muslimanke o životu i radu pod maramom* (Sarajevo: CNS and CIPS, 2011).

So called "shariah marriages," a marriage ceremony administered by an imam, have also become more common. Their numbers over the last decade have been gradually increasing from 4,639 in 2004 to 5,355 recorded shariah marriages in 2009.[70] Another form of public manifestation of Islam has been the organization of large concerts featuring recitations of the Qur'an and Islamic spiritual music, known locally as *ilahije* and *kaside*. The concert marking 600 years of Islam in Bosnia on 28 July 2007 at the biggest football stadium in the country was one such manifestation.

The post-communist Islamic revival in Bosnia and Herzegovina has also been marked by the (re)emergence of *tariqas*, Muslim women organizations, and youth associations. Historically, Sufi orders or *tariqas*[71] played an important role in the Islamization of Bosnia and in the Ottoman military, but also in several reform and protest movements.[72] The orders that have endured in Bosnia have typically been more "sober," Sunni, and orthodox than their Albanian counterparts. Today, Sufi orders are mainly found in central Bosnia (Travnik, Fojnica, Kiseljak, Visoko, Zenica, Sarajevo) and the Neretva valley (Mostar, Blagaj). There are now some 107 places of *dhikr* (up from 40 in 1981[73] and 50 in 2005) of which 29 are Sufi lodges (*tekkes*). Publications include the annual *Šebi Arus* and the new monthly *Kelamu'l Šifa'*.

The IC banned the activities of *tariqas* in Bosnia in 1952. Their property was taken over either by the IC or the state. They continued as a clandestine movement, meeting in private homes. The situation improved under the IC presidency of Ahmed Smajlović (1975–85).[74] In May 1977, the IC leadership met with the *tariqa* leaders, and decided to establish an official Tariqa Center, coordinated by Fejzulah Hadžibajrić (1913–90), then one of the most widely respected Sufis in Bosnia.[75] In part, this move probably aimed to keep Bosnian dervishes away from joining the Kosovo-based dervish organization ZIDRA. However, the IC officially recognized and included the *tariqas* only in 1989.[76] They have never been tightly integrated, though the present constitution of the IC mentions *tariqas* among its institutions (article 71).

Bosnian Sufis today gather in 107 places belonging mainly to the Naqshibandiyyah and Qadiriyyah orders. There are also some Rifa'is, and lately some Shadhiliyyah. Mawlawis and Khalwatis were historically important orders.[77] On the one hand, we find

[70] *Glasnik Rijaseta IZ u BiH* 72(5–6) (May–June 2010): 521.
[71] Ar. *Tariqa*, "way," pl. *Turuq*; Bos. *Tarikat*, pl. *Tarikati*. In Bosnian, Sufis are generally known as dervishes (*derviši*).
[72] Džemal Ćehajić, "Društveno-politički, religiozni, književni i drugi aspekti derviških redova u jugoslavenskim zemljama," *Prilozi za orijentalnu filologiju* 34 (1984): 93–113, at 105, 108.
[73] F. Hadžibajrić, "Naših četrdeset medžlisi zikira danas na početku XV stoljeća po Hidžri," *Takvim* 1981: 145–55.
[74] F. Hadžibajrić, "Djelatnost tarikatskog centra u Sarajevu," *Šebi arus* 12 (1990): 17–32.
[75] Hadžibajrić studied oriental languages, and worked for the IC as librarian, school secretary, teacher, imam, and Friday preacher (*khatib*). He was initiated into the Qadiriyya in 1939, and was recognized as shaykh in Istanbul in 1965. He also collected *khilafa-nama* certificates from five other orders. He authored textbooks, and held regular lectures on Rumi's *Mathnawi* from 1966.
[76] Beglerović, "Fejzulah efendija Hadžibajrić."
[77] Salih Smajlović, "Rad u skladu sa hanefijskim mezhebom u okvirima Islamske zajednice," <http://www.preporod.com/index.php/vjera/islamske-teme/1354-rad-u-skladu-sa-hanefijskim>

traditional Bosnian Sufi groups who are grouped around the IC-affiliated Tariqa Center (75% of all Sufi groups). Many Sufis, including well-known commanders, fought in the recent war, and some politicians have publicly attended *dhikr* sessions, but for the most part, the *tariqas* project a quietist or apolitical stance. Since the revival of Sufism is a relatively new phenomenon there are no studies on the social or educational profile of Sufis in Bosnia. On the other hand, there are more independently minded Sufi groups, led by shaykhs whose credentials are questioned and who refuse to integrate into the Tariqa Center. Currently the most popular preacher in Bosnia, Sulejman Bugari, comes from the ranks of Sufis. He is a Medina graduate of Kosovan origin, whose sessions and books have attracted huge audience and readership. His message is one of love and optimism conveyed in a very accessible language.

The IC runs no special program for women. A number of independent Muslim women's organizations have sprung up to fill this gap. Two of the most significant are "Nahla" and "Kewser." The Education and Research Center "Nahla" (Honey Bee) in Sarajevo was established in 2001 as a center where Muslim women could gain motivation, knowledge, skills, and self-confidence for this world and the hereafter (<http://www.nahla.ba>). Its activities fall into four categories: research,[78] general education, religious education, and sports and recreation. The center has helped to establish similar centers in a few other towns in Bosnia. The center was established and is successfully run by a small, dedicated group of local women. Unlike other Islamic women's groups, it does not rely on an outside male ideological patron. Although major projects, like the building of the new center, are sponsored by foreign donors, a significant part of the operating costs are covered by service charges and membership fees. The center's open-mindedness, local human resources, financial sustainability, and ideological independence augur well for its future.

The women's education organization "Kewser" was established in 1994 in Zenica, but is now based in Sarajevo. It resembles "Nahla" in several ways: its moving force is a strong female personality, and it runs much the same kind of activities, focusing on the education of women and children in the spirit of Islamic religion and culture. A distinctive feature of Kewser is its Shi'i affiliation and devotion to the Prophet's family (*ahl al-bayt*). This is evident in the organization's main annual event, "the Musk of the Prophet" (*Mošus Pejgamberov*), which celebrates the birthday of the Prophet's daughter

---

-mezhebom-u-okvirima-islamske-zajednice.html> [accessed March 10, 2013]. For historical overview see Džemal Ćehajić, *Dervički redovi u jugoslovenskim zemljama sa posebnim osvrtom na Bosnu i Hercegovinu* (Sarajevo: Orijentalni institut, 1986). See also Dž. Ćehajić, "Aspekti derviških redova"; Muharem Omerdić, "Derviši i tekije u Sarajevu," in Dževad Juzbašić (ed.), *Prilozi historiji Sarajeva* (Sarajevo: Institut za istoriju and Orijentalni institut, 1997), 129–40. The Naqshibandiyyah order was founded by Muhammad Baha al-din al-Naqshabandi (d. 1388), Qadiriyyah by Abd al-Qadir al-Kilani (d. 1166), Rifa'iyya by Ahmad al-Rifa'i (d. 1181), Shadhiliyyah by Abu al-Hasan Ali al-Shadhili (d. 1258), Mawlawiyya by Jalal al-Din al-Rumi (d. 1273), and Khalwatiyya by 'Umar al-Khalwati (d. 1397).

[78] See for instance an annotated bibliography on Bosnian women 1990–2010: Fahira Fejzić et al., *Prilozi za istraživanje sociokulturnog položaja žene u BiH: Izabrana bibliografija (1900–2010)* (Sarajevo: Nahla, 2011).

Fatima. The organization also publishes the magazine *Zehra* and runs Zehra TV and Radio Zehra.[79]

Among the youth organizations, the now defunct Active Islamic Youth (AIY, active 1995–2006) gained much popularity among youth as well as criticism by the more mainstream segments of the post-war Bosnian society. It was registered as an NGO in Zenica in October 1995. In a 1998 interview with the then president of the organization Adnan Pezo, it appears that the core members, just out of high school, were profoundly impressed by their foreign *mujahideen* fellow-fighters.[80] The IC has given the AIY the cold shoulder and distanced itself from it. The AIY's golden era were the years 1997–9. From the start, the association met with resistance from both secular and traditional Bosniaks, and some Serb and Croat publications portrayed the AIY as a major terrorist organization.[81] In the summer of 2001, the AIY's spiritual mentor and charismatic leader Imad al-Misri (b. 1964 in Egypt) was extradited to Egypt at the request of Egyptian government, where he was sentenced to a ten-year prison term from which he was released in May 2009. In the anti-terrorist campaign that followed 9/11 the AIY was often questioned and its premises searched, but it was never formally charged for anything. In 2006 under enormous security and social pressure it formally deregistered itself. However, the magazine *Saff* that was associated with the organization continued as an independent magazine.[82]

The relationship between the IC and other Islamic actors has not always been a smooth one. There have been several reasons for occasional friction between them. First, the IC has proclaimed itself in its constitution to be the sole community of Muslims in Bosnia on the basis of which the IC advocates the idea that the state should not register any organization with the attribute "Islamic" in its name. Second, belonging to the universal community of the Ummah is put side by side with the belonging to the particular country and ethnic group. Third, the Hanafi *madh'hab* (school of jurisprudence) is said to be binding in interpretation and application of Islamic norms. Fourth, reference in this context is made to "the Islamic tradition of Bosniaks." Each of these provisions has to some extent been controversial outside the IC. The provision about the Hanafi *madh'hab* (school of law) is problematic with some Salafis while others claim that they would be happy with the application of any authentic Sunni *madh'hab* in Bosnia. Much more controversial with the reformists is the provision about the Islamic tradition of Bosnian Muslims since that tradition—like any other popular religious practice—occasionally contradicts the scholarly explication of Islam, in this case that of the Hanafi *madh'hab*.

In terms of orientation, although traditional Sunni Islam dominates the scene, the post-communist spectrum of Islamic ideas (and practices) is wide and includes

---

[79] <http://www.zehra.ba/zehra/index.php> [accessed February 15, 2013].
[80] Dž. Karup, "Kur'an je naš ustav," *Dani* 72, March 30, 1998.
[81] E. G. D. Trifunović, *Islamic Fundamentalists' Global Network* (Banja Luka: Bureau for Relation with ICTY of the Republic of Srpska, 2002), 75–7.
[82] <http://www.saff.ba>.

reformists, religious modernists, Salafis, Sufis, and a very small group of extremists. So a kind of Islamic pluralism is developing in Bosnia. However, despite all this diversity there has not been any serious organization calling for the state implementation of shariah in the public domain or for the establishment of an Islamic state. Anyway, when analyzed in the context of other processes in the country (e.g. the transition from communism to democracy, war to peace, liberalization, reconstruction, and European Union integration) and when compared to the revival of other religions, the revival of Islam certainly does not seem to be an exceptional or the most important process going on in the country.[83]

Geographically speaking, whatever Islamic revival is there it is taking place only on the third of the Bosnian territory that was under the control of Bosnian government forces during the war and where Muslims are still either a majority or significantly present. Bosnia is a wounded, torn, and in many respects divided country. Every community is a minority in some part of the country which often translates into an unequal status and discrimination—legal assurances notwithstanding. Therefore, it is not always useful to treat Bosnia and Herzegovina as one unit of analysis.

In terms of agency, Islam has experienced a sort of revival mainly under the auspices of the IC in Bosnia and Herzegovina. Four major agents of Islamic revival have been (1) the imams of the IC, who are perhaps most responsible for spreading the message of Islam to the masses; (2) the IC institutions, i.e. its *madrasas*, faculties, and media; (3) Bosnian students of Islamic studies abroad who played a major role in transmitting Islamic ideas and literature from Muslim countries and translating them into the Bosnian language; (4) foreign factors such as Islamic (humanitarian) agencies, Islamic preachers, and foreign fighters. When the *mujahids* first arrived in 1992 they brought some hope and encouragement to Bosnian Muslims at a time when they felt alone in their fight against aggressors.[84] However, as time passed they slowly became "foreign Arabs" instead of being "fellow Muslims." Their presence became a problem in the relation with the West and especially the USA which several times asked President Alija Izetbegović (1925–2003) to send them back home.[85] That was one of the provisions of the Dayton Agreement. In a 2002 interview, in the wake of post-9/11 assault on anything that has to do with *jihad*, ex-president Izetbegović opined "on the whole, they did more harm than good."[86] However, his former minister of foreign affairs and later member of the Bosnian presidency Haris Silajdžić (b. 1945) expressed reservation towards such a judgment.[87] Anyhow, while other Muslim actors—sometimes branded as alternative—such

---

[83] Harun Karčić, "Islamic Revival in Bosnia and Herzegovina 1990–2010," <http://www.cns.ba/docs/islamic_revival_in_Bosnia_and_Herzegovina_1992-1995.pdf>.

[84] Esad Hećimović, *Garibi: Mudžahedini u BiH 1992–1999* (Zenica: Fondacija Sina, 2006).

[85] On the evolution of Bosnian Muslim attitudes towards Arabs in 1990s see the excellent article by Darryl Li, "A Universal Enemy? 'Foreign Fighters' and Legal Regimes of Exclusion and Exemption Under the 'Global War On Terror,'" *Columbia Human Rights Law Review* 41(2) (2010): 355–427, esp. 382–92.

[86] Senad Pećanin, Intervju sa Alijom Izetbegovićem, "Caco je i heroj i zločinac," *BH Dani*, March 1, 2002, 11.

[87] Interview with Dr Haris Silajdžić, *Saff*, no. 140, March 15, 2005, 28–31.

as Islamic faith-based, missionary, and charitable organizations contributed to the revival the primacy of the IC in that process is unquestionable.[88]

## The Growth of Mainstream Scholarship

While security concerns have focused attention in recent years on "new forms of Islam" in Bosnia, developments within the "mainstream" Islamic scholarship have been far more significant. The mainstream has come a long way. Immediately after the Second World War, the IC was incapacitated by the killing or imprisonment of its most able cadres, mostly at the hands of communists.[89] Until the 1970s, the intellectual output of the IC was meager.[90] Things started changing slowly with the liberalization of Yugoslavia, the return of the first graduates from Egypt (often of Arabic, not Islamic studies), and the graduation of a group of religious Muslims from secular universities.[91] Still, until the late 1980s, Islam was "spoon-fed" and publications on Islam were rare. The real breakthrough in mainstream scholarship happened in the late 1980s and early 1990s. However, since then no single scholar has been able to dominate the Islamic intellectual scene the way Husein Đozo (1912–82)[92] did in the 1970s. This graduate of Al-Azhar and intellectual follower of Muhammad Abduh (1849–1905) during 1960s and 1970s became the foremost Islamic authority in Yugoslavia, issuing fatwas, writing exegesis of the Qur'an, commenting on current issues, and teaching at the newly opened Islamic Theological Faculty in Sarajevo all from the viewpoint of Muslim religious modernism.[93]

The main concern of new generation of scholars who came on the scene in the late 1980s has been to establish a baseline of religious knowledge in Bosnian by making available important works in translation, as well as writing surveys and compendia of whole fields of study. For instance, Enes Karić (b. 1958) has translated and edited a large

---

[88] Antunez, *Foreign Influences in Islam in Bosnia and Herzegovina*.

[89] For instance, Mustafa Busuladžić (1914–45), Mehmed Handžić (1906–44), Kasim Dobrača (1910–79), Husein Đozo (1912–82), and others. See for instance: Đevad Šošić, "Islamska pedagoška misao i praksa Derviš-ef. Spahića," MA Thesis defended at the Faculty of Islamic Studies in Sarajevo, 2011.

[90] Ahmet Alibašić, "Izdavačka djelatnost Islamske zajednice u BiH 1993.–2011. godina."

[91] These important developments have not been properly studied. Some information can be found in Jusuf Ramić, *Bošnjaci na univerzitetu El-Azher* (Sarajevo: Muftijstvo sarajevsko, 2002); Fikret Karčić, "Islamic Revival in the Balkans." The Yugoslav authorities preferred the Arab world as a destination for Islamic studies rather than Turkey probably for all or some of the following reasons: Turkey was a successor state of the Ottoman "occupier" and member of NATO. On the other hand, Egypt, Libya, and Iraq were all members of Non-Alignment Movement with socialist leanings whose markets were open for Yugoslav companies and products.

[92] Husein Đozo (1912–82) is the most influential Islamic scholar in socialist Yugoslavia. In 1939 he graduated from Al-Azhar where he studied with respected Islamic scholars of the time such as Rashid Rida (1865–1935), Mustafa Maraghi (1881–1945), and Mahmud Shaltut (1893–1963). From 1960 until his death in 1982 he worked tirelessly in promoting reformist Islamic thought and building Islamic institutions. See his selected writings in Husein Đozo, *Izabrana djela*, 5 vols. (Sarajevo: El-Kalem, 2006).

[93] Omer Nakičević (ed.), *Život i djelo Husein ef. Đoze* (Sarajevo: Fakultet islamskih nauka, 1998).

body of important studies on the Qur'an, arguing for a modern hermeneutic approach and the multivocality of the sacred text.[94] Rešid Hafizović (b. 1956) has written surveys of Shi'i and Sufi thought.[95] There have also been some collaborative scholarly efforts to edit, publish, and study the heritage of important twentieth-century *'ulama* such as Džemaludin Čaušević (1870–1938), Mehmed Handžić (1906–44), and Husein Đozo.[96] Historical surveys of Bosnian twentieth-century reformism and opposition to it have been made by Enes Karić and Fikret Karčić.[97] Thanks partly to these efforts and partly to the general opening up of the country, Islamic studies in Bosnia now draw on a vastly greater range of materials than was available when these scholars started their careers.

The mainstream continues to be defined by Bosnian tradition combined with modernist leanings. Islamic legal historian Fikret Karčić (b. 1955) has perhaps been the most consistent in his exposition of Islamic ideas, and has articulated important basic positions of the IC. He is of the opinion that the future of Islam in Bosnia is in incremental change and reform that should be rooted in local Islamic tradition while benefiting from the experience of global Islamic reformism.[98] Karić, too, has been consistent in his opposition to "reductionist" interpretations of the multivocal Qur'an, whether Islamist or Salafi. Karić and other members of this generation, however, take a more critical view of Islamic modernism's faith in reason and progress than did their teacher Đozo. They find part of their inspiration in the intellectual mysticism of the "perennial wisdom" school, with its misgivings about the project of modernity.[99]

For long the IC and the mainstream Islamic scholars have failed to offer official fatwa, answers to the believers' questions on points of Islamic law, despite the fact that it is a self-imposed duty of the IC. Some within the IC would even claim that the IC has a monopoly on this function. Until 2005 fatwa giving was not institutionalized, and there was always some uncertainty as to the authority behind answers provided by individual scholars from within the IC institutions at their own initiative. Concern about the lack of clear authority has surfaced from time to time; e.g. in 1987, there was inconclusive talk

---

[94] Enes Karić, *Tumačenje Kur'ana i ideologije XX stoljeća* (Sarajevo: Bemust, 2002); Enes Karić, *Semantika Kur'ana* (Sarajevo: Bemust, 1999); Enes Karić, *Kur'an u savremenom dobu* (Sarajevo: Bosanski Kulturni Centar/El-Kalem, 1998).

[95] Rešid Hafizović, *Temeljni tokovi Sufizma* (Sarajevo: Bemust, 1999); R. Hafizović, *Znakovi šiijske duhovnosti* (Sarajevo: Bosanska knjiga, 1997).

[96] Enes Karić and Enes Duraković (eds.), *Izabrana djela Mehmeda Handžića* (Sarajevo: Ogledalo, 2000); Enes Karić and Mujo Demirović (eds.), *Reis Džemaluddin Čaušević: prosvjetitelj i reformator* (Sarajevo: Ljiljan, 2002).

[97] Karić, *Contributions to Twentieth Century Islamic Thought in Bosnia and Herzegovina*; Fikret Karčić, *The Bosniaks and the Challenges of Modernity: Late Ottoman and Habsburg Times* (Sarajevo: El-Kalem, 1999).

[98] Karčić, "Islamic Revival," 565–81.

[99] Christian Moe identifies "perennialists" as "a small, international line of scholar-believers concerned with *sophia perennis* or perennial wisdom they claim can be found in the authentic core of all religious traditions." Rene Guenon (1886–1951), Frithjof Schuon (1907–98), Martin Lings (1909–2005), and Seyyed Hossein Nasr (b. 1933) are some of the best-known perennialists. C. Moe, "A 'Bosnian Paradigm' for Religious Tolerance?," paper given at the EASR conference in Bergen, May 9, 2003.

of establishing a fatwa committee.¹⁰⁰ During the war, the then *reisu-l-ulema* (head of the *'Ulama*) Cerić ordered a compilation of existing fatwas, and in 1999–2000 he briefly tried to give his own answers in *Glasnik*.¹⁰¹ In the meantime, others had established themselves as reasonably credible sources of fatwa. Most important was the now defunct *Novi Horizonti's* "Fatwas and advice" (1998–2007) column of Šukrija Ramić (b. 1960), then dean of the Islamic Pedagogical Academy in Zenica, and the column in the *Saff* magazine, of collective and anonymous authorship.¹⁰² Finally in 2005 the IC established a Fatwa Council, with Enes Ljevaković (b. 1959), professor of Islamic law at the Faculty of Islamic Studies in Sarajevo, as its secretary and the *de facto* fatwa giver. According to Ljevaković the number of questions is rising at an annual rate of 50% and has gone from 180 questions in 2005 to 1,000 in 2008. Questions are asked by institutions and individuals (including non-Muslims asking about burial of people from multi-religious families or health problems) and concern religious duties (*'ibadat*), family issues, property rights, food and attire, death-related questions, doctrine, community life, health issues, and business ethics—generally in that order. They come in from old and young, men and women, by mail and email, phone or through personal contact.¹⁰³

## Where Do the Mainstream and the Alternative Differ?

While there is a continuity between Islam espoused by the "mainstream" represented by the IC and the "alternative" Islamic actors such as faith-based organizations, and a diversity of positions within each side, there are also substantial differences, which are well brought out by three issues: gender relations, inter-religious relations, and attitudes to popular and mystical Islam. We will take the practice in IC institutions and statements in the IC publications *Preporod* (published since 1970) and *Glasnik* (published since 1933) as a statement of the mainstream. They will be contrasted with writings in *Saff*, which quite faithfully reflect the Salafi position on the above issue, and with *Novi horizonti*, which used to represent an intermediate reformist position.¹⁰⁴ We cite indicative examples, but attempt no exhaustive systematic comparison.

---

¹⁰⁰ Sabor meeting March 28, 1987, *Preporod* 399, 1 and 4; E. Alić, "O pisanoj riječi Islamske zajednice," *Preporod* 400, 5.
¹⁰¹ *Glasnik* 61 (1999): 5–6 until 62 (2000): 9–10.
¹⁰² Both mainstream and fringe also increasingly face competition from the globalization of Islamic authority in cyberspace, a point we cannot pursue here. See e.g. Fikret Karčić, "Main Trends in the Interpretation of the Shari'a in Bosnia and Herzegovina 2000–2005," lecture held at Copenhagen University, Sept. 15, 2010, <http://islam.ku.dk/lectures/Karcic150910final.pdf/>.
¹⁰³ Enes Ljevaković, "Fikhski diskurs kakav imamo (kroz prizmu pitanja i odgovora)," in Mehmedalija Hadžić (ed.), *Islamski diskurs u Bosni i Hercegovini* (Sarajevo: Institut za proučavanje tradicije Bošnjaka, 2011), 23–40.
¹⁰⁴ The fortnightly *Saff* was published by the Salafi Active Islamic Youth until it deregistered itself in 2006. Today it is published independently by a group of like-minded Salafis. The Reformist monthly *Novi horizonti* (<http://www.novihorizonti.ba/hm/>) was published by reformist non-governmental

## Gender Relations

Both the mainstream and the alternative groups tend to emphasize, to differing degrees, that men and women are different by nature, that men are meant to be breadwinners, and that women's primary roles are as wives and mothers. The mainstream, though, holds a range of views on women's employment, including the view that women can hold any job and position that does not involve immorality. The low representation of women in the institutions or organs of the IC may have more to do with the general patriarchal nature of Bosnian society than with perceived Islamic norms.[105] In practice, the IC seems to have long since come to terms with women's employment outside the home. For Salafis, on the other hand, the principal rule is that a woman should stay at home unless there is a good reason for her to go out (*Saff* 118: 6; 126: 8). Mixing of the sexes is to be forbidden as a source of tragedy and catastrophe (16: 12–13; 106: 7; 129: 7–8). The IC practice differs: The Gazi Husrev Bey's *madrasa* prides itself on the graduation of the first mixed class of pupils in 2012, and at the Faculty of Islamic Studies, students sit together in the classroom, sing together in the Faculty's chorus, and mingle on all other occasions.

The Salafis consider the covering of a woman's face (niqab) to be a religious duty (*Saff* 99: 13–15). The IC's position is that it is a woman's Islamic duty to cover her hair and body except for the face, hands, and feet. In its own practice, however, the IC has not stood on a dress code. A few years ago, there was an attempt to impose "Islamic norms of clothing" in the IC's offices, but the order was subverted in various ways by female employees, and IC authorities soon stopped insisting on it. In the *madrasa*s, though, female pupils have for some time been required to wear headscarves. At the Faculty of Islamic Studies most female students wear ordinary hijab, but some do not; there has been inconclusive debate on whether niqab should be banned, as it is in the Sarajevo *madrasa*. The young generation tends to place greater emphasis on hijab than those who grew up under socialism.

Sometimes *Saff* agrees with the prevalent IC position on women issues, e.g. that informal "shariah marriage" is not sufficient in Bosnia (*Saff* 101: 12–13). Opinions seem to converge also on the wife's right to dispose of her own salary (*Saff* 120: 6); and on domestic violence (*Saff* 106; 107; 142: 7). *Saff* also argues, on shariah grounds, the "feminist" position that women should not change their surname upon marriage (*Saff* 109: 7).

## Inter-Religious Relations

Since its establishment, and especially during the last ten years, the IC has had inter-religious dialogue as a strategic orientation, and has been very active in this

---

organization "Salam" in Zenica. Its publication was discontinued for financial reasons in late 2012 after 160 issues. This disappearance of organizations and publications outside the IC testifies to the preeminence of the IC.

[105] Four of the eighty-three members of the current IC Assembly are women. There are no women on the main board of the Association of Islamic Scholars. Women hold teaching posts at the Faculty of Islamic Studies in Sarajevo and in some of the Islamic schools (*madrasas*). Two seats of fifteen in the new Fatwa Council are statutorily reserved for women.

field.[106] The *Saff* circle, however, holds that it is forbidden to greet non-Muslims on their holidays, as that would imply condoning unbelief (111: 7, 115: 12–15). The IC and *Saff* agree, however, that Muslims are not to celebrate New Year. On Pope John Paul II's death in 2005, the IC sent its condolences to the Catholic community, while *Saff* said that condolences for a non-Muslim are allowed if he did not infringe on the rights of Muslims (143: 8)—leaving open whether that applied to the Pope. *Saff* also holds that attending a non-Muslim funeral is in principle forbidden (101: 7).

The IC and *Saff* seem to agree on the permissibility of distribution of *qurban* meat to non-Muslims, the general purity of meat slaughtered by Christians and Jews, the permissibility of visiting a non-Muslim either to offer him Islam or to maintain good neighborly relations.[107] *Saff* also says it is acceptable to receive donations from non-Muslims for the building of mosques if that money has been legitimately earned, but stresses that the non-Muslims nonetheless will not have any reward in the hereafter (106: 6). *Saff* also often reminds its readers that it is strictly forbidden to imitate or follow the manners of non-Muslims (63: 4; 111: 13). The official *Preporod* fatwa column has frequently based its answers on the same principle.

Students at the Faculty of Islamic Studies are customarily encouraged to read the sacred texts of other religions, and many mainstream Muslims would see this as part of a well-rounded education. According to *Saff* (113: 7), on the other hand, the Bible should be read only for the purpose of guiding Christians to the truth. The Salafis are generally more likely to dwell on how Jews and Christians have distorted their scriptures (*tahrif*), and also more likely to invite non-Muslims to accept Islam. Mainstream imams tend to think it impolite to do so.

## *Intra-Religious Relations: Popular and Mystical Islam*

Nothing has been as contentious in relations between the IC and Salafis in Bosnia as the issue of popular religious practice. Though the IC's regional officials caution against excesses, they not only condone, but also sponsor, organize, and control several annual mass religious events derived from popular and/or Sufi tradition. Among these are the afore-mentioned gatherings and prayers at Ajvatovica and the May celebration of Prophet's birthday (*mevlud*) at the *tekke* at the source of Buna river near Mostar. Both traditions have pre-Islamic roots.

Salafis, on the other hand, consider the fight against un-Islamic Muslim practices—as a form of associationism (*shirk*)—their priority. *Saff* regularly deals with these issues. Thus it writes that "Bosniak practice is not consistent with *Shari'ah*" (70: 8–9). Ajvatovica, the central Bosnian Muslim gathering in the open near Prusac (Central Bosnia) under the auspices of the IC is condemned as an "Islamized Bogumil sanctuary/shrine" (*Saff* 8: 23–4; 122: 26–8). Furthermore, according to *Saff*, *Laylat Raghaib*, the 15th night of the 8th month of the Islamic calendar is man-made (*Saff* 127: 4) and

---

[106] See *Platforma Islamske Zajednice u BiH za dijalog* (the Platform of the IC for dialogue).
[107] *Saff*: 13: 10–12 and 24–5; 99: 6; 111: 13; 113: 6; 126: 7–8; 101: 7; cf. Omerdić in *Preporod* 749 (on *qurban*), 757 (food of non-Muslims); cf. Ramić in *NH* 2 and 23 (neighborly and family relations).

not divinely blessed. Very popular religious songs accompanied by music are said to be forbidden (*Saff* 100: 6, see also 91: 38–40). Recitation of parts of the Qur'an and other Islamic prayers for the dead is said to be "prohibited deformation of the religion" (*Saff* 116: 42–5). It is particularly wrong when done for money (cf. *Saff* 135: 8). Mausoleums (*turbe*) are forbidden (*Saff* 21: 6–8; 119: 6–7). So is the recitation of the Qur'an over the grave and the erection of tombstones (*Saff* 122: 9; 142: 8). Commemorations on the 40th day after death is also un-Islamic practice (*Saff* 133: 6).

Some IC authorities share some of these views, e.g. on commemorating the 40th day after death, or on paid Qur'an recitation—a long-debated issue, and one in which fringe criticism may have influenced mainstream views.[108] But these views are not widely advocated in the IC. The IC considers existing mausoleums (*turbe*) part of its cultural heritage and property. As for new tombs, *Preporod*'s fatwa column (766) approves of simple gravestones without decorations and ostentation.

Another contentious issue is the *mevlud*, which refers both to the annual celebration of the Prophet's birthday (Ar. *mawlid*), the poetry recited on that occasion, and similar gatherings held anytime to mark important family events.[109] An annual *mevlud* that has become a mass event is held under IC auspices at the Sufi shrine in Blagaj near Mostar. In the mainstream, as reflected in *Preporod*, the Prophet's birthday is celebrated as an occasion to reflect on all aspects of his life and mission. Even a former IC leader sometimes described as a Salafi argues in these terms for celebrating *mevlud*.[110]

There are other intra-religious issues that are the subject of difference between the IC and Salafis, the most important of them being Salafis' antagonistic attitude toward Shi'a and Sufism. Prayers should be performed in Sufi lodges (*tekije*) only where there is no mosque (*Saff* 134: 7). Salafis and the IC, however, concur in condemning black magic, fortune-telling (*Saff* 23: 5–7; 98: 13–15), and the use of amulets (*Saff* 56: 13; 22: 6, 40). Surprisingly, *Saff* writes that the use of a rosary (*tespih*) is not a prohibited innovation (100: 7); neither, the IC agrees, does it bring any added value to worship (*Preporod* 770).

## Contested Religious Authority in a Crowded Market

There is no doubt that ideology plays a role in the tensions between the mainstream and fringe organizations. However, the importance of a more social factor is increasingly obvious: the crowded Islamic job market in Bosnia. This is a new development. Until 1992 the Bosnian IC was short of human resources. A majority of the IC employees were graduates of the only Islamic high school in the country, many lacked even a high school diploma, and very few had higher education. Despite changes from the late 1970s, the

---

[108] Cf. Fadil Fazlić, "Nagrađivanje za učenje Kur'an," *Takvim za 2006*. (Sarajevo: Rijaset IZ, 2005), 75–86.

[109] Bringa, *Being Muslim the Bosnian Way*, 169–71, 189–93, 221–2; Džafer Obradović (ed.), *Mevlud u životu i kulturi Bošnjaka* (Sarajevo: BKZ Preporod, 2000).

[110] Salih Čolaković, "Da li mevlud ima uporište u Kur'anu?," in Obradović (ed.), *Mevlud*, 23–31.

shortage of qualified personnel was still apparent in 1990. Between 1977 and 1992 the Faculty of Islamic Studies produced only 92 graduates, and there was a limited number of overseas students.

All this changed in 1992–5: seven new *madrasas* opened, and the number of students abroad increased sharply.[111] In addition, two teacher-training academies in Zenica and Bihać, plus a department for Islamic education teachers in Mostar,[112] have produced several hundred graduates, to meet the initial demand created by the introduction of religious education in public schools. The Faculty of Islamic Studies has produced far more graduates in recent years (almost 800) in its three departments: imam training, Islamic theology, and religious pedagogy. For a combination of ideological and job-related reasons, the IC decided to employ as imams only those who have attended a Bosnian *madrasa* prior to their enrolment in a university level Islamic Studies program. Then, in 2004, it was decided that *madrasas* in future will not confer certificates of *"imam, khatib,* and *muallim"* (prayer leader, Friday preacher, and teacher) on their graduates. To become an imam, one now has to first complete a Bosnian *madrasa*, and then go for higher Islamic education. As educational requirements have tightened, older IC employees have had to enroll as part-time students to keep their jobs.

In a tightening market, the traditional *ulama* face a double challenge to their jobs and influence in the IC: from better-qualified overseas students, some of whom will have picked up Salafi ideas, and from educated laymen with the organization and communication skills the IC needs. If the traditional *ulama* were first challenged in the 1970s by mainstream Muslim intellectuals who combine a secular and religious education, they are also challenged by the new, foreign-educated fringe. First, the new fringe rejects as *bid'a* (innovation) or even *shirk* (associationism) various customs that traditional imams have condoned, perpetuated, and practiced for additional income. Second, the new fringe has a number of highly educated people. Not only are their formal credentials better, they also tend to specialize in core Islamic sciences such as Prophetic tradition and to be fluent in Arabic, skills more rarely mastered in the Bosnian mainstream. It is of course debatable whether it is these skills, or a broader humanist learning of the kind that informs the Faculty of Islamic Studies, that best enable one to interpret Islam for the needs of contemporary Bosnia. That being the case, the foreign-educated fringe is a challenge not only to the job security of mainstream teachers and imams, but also to the religious authority of long-time IC employees, including the regional Muftis. This matters less as long as the latter's functions remain chiefly administrative, but becomes more of an issue when, as recently, they are *ex officio* made responsible for the IC's fatwa-giving.[113]

---

[111] Nobody has statistics on the number of graduates in the Muslim world since 1992. The Faculty of Islamic Studies has since 2002 recognized around 160 certificates from the Muslim world. This is not a precise indicator since many who have graduated abroad have not asked for recognition (*nostrifikacija*).

[112] The Mostar department for Islamic Education teachers stopped admitting freshmen in 2003.

[113] On the challenges to the religious authority of the IC see Enes Ljevaković, "Vjerski autoritet Islamske zajednice u Bosni i Hercegovini," in *Islamska zajednica u Bosni i Hercegovini: Dvije decenije reisu-l-uleme Dr. Mustafe Cerića* (Sarajevo: Centar za napredne studije, 2012), 40–51.

## Actual Religious Practice and Religiosity

Since 1946 and the closure of shariah courts, which had until then jurisdiction over Muslim personal status affairs, the practice of Islam in Bosnia has been reduced in scope to rituals (*'ibadat*), education, and to some extent to *waqf* administration since most *awqaf* were confiscated or nationalized in the 1940s and 1950s. All aspects of shariah requiring any state intervention have been either suspended or downgraded from legal to ethical norms. This transition in understanding of shariah from legal to ethical code is probably the most significant development in understanding Islam in the second half of the twentieth century.[114]

Perhaps the least researched and documented aspect of the studies on Islam in Bosnia is religiosity trends over the last several decades. Practically all claims about a huge surge in religiosity among Bosnian Muslims since the 1990s are impressionistic. Our understanding of current religiosity and its consequences among Bosnian Muslims is somewhat better thanks to a recent Pew Research Center survey report.[115] That survey found that Bosnian Muslims if judged by how much they pray, read the Qur'an, fast, or go to mosques or Mecca are far less religious than Arabs, Turks, or South Asian Muslims but are among the most religious in the region they share a common communist past with—Southern and Eastern Europe, and Central Asia. Almost all (96%) profess belief in one God and Prophet Muhammad (p. 38 of the report), 83% belief in the afterlife (p. 62), while 81% give alms (*zakat al-fitr* and *zakat*, p. 52) which is the highest percentage in South-East Europe and Central Asia. The reason for this is perhaps the focus of the IC on this aspect since its financial survival depends to a large extent on the collection of alms. In addition, 75% say they fast during Ramadan (p. 54) which is among the highest rates in this group of countries. Overall, religion matters very much to 36% of them (p. 40), compared to 15% in Albania, 44% in Kosovo and Russia, and 67% in Turkey. However, only 14% say they pray five times a day while another 4% pray several times a day (p. 43). Only 30% pray once a week in the mosque (p. 46) compared to 44% in Turkey. However, the number of those who never attend a mosque (10%) is much lower than in other countries of the group (p. 47).

Belonging to Sufi *tariqas* remains a marginal phenomenon (2%, p. 31). Only 1% were not Muslims at birth (p. 33); 38% self-identify as Sunnis while 54% say they are "just Muslims" (p. 35). They are also amongst the least superstitious (21% believe in witchcraft, 13% wear a talisman, and 16% use religious healers—pp. 71, 75, and 80). However, and probably because of the presence of a strong religious organization, 75% believe that there is only one interpretation of Islam (p. 85). Visiting shrines is acceptable to 68% while reading poetry in praise of God is acceptable to 61% (pp. 96, 98).

---

[114] Fikret Karčić, "Secular State and Religion(s)."
[115] Pew Research Center's Forum on Religion and Public Life, *The World's Muslims: Unity and Diversity* (Washington: Pew Research Center, 2012).

However, many aspects of traditional Bosnian Muslim religiosity such as celebrations of the birthday of the Prophet (*mevlud*), prayers for the dead (*tevhid*), prayers in open fields (*dove* and *dovišta*), new mosque opening ceremonies, listening to recitation of the Qur'an during Ramadan in the mosques (*mukabela*), Qur'an recitation competitions, and concerts of religious songs (*ilahije i kaside*) remain outside the scope of this and similar surveys.[116]

Besides this survey, during the last few years a number of scholarly studies have focused on the relevance of religiosity to evaluate social distance between members of different ethnic groups. Aid Smajić of the Faculty of Islamic Studies attempted to examine correlations between different aspects of religiosity and inter-ethnic tolerance. His findings have confirmed that the individual differences in religiosity cannot account for ethnic (in)tolerance of religious individuals.[117] Another study concluded that Bosnia fits both global and regional pattern of revitalization of religion especially in the public sphere. That does not mean that individual religiosity is resurging at the same pace. Bosnian Muslims are not particularly observant. Although most of them consider religion as very important to them they would rather not have politicians meddle in politics and media.[118]

It is very difficult to speak of Islamic politics proper in Bosnia in any meaningful sense if by Islamic politics we mean politics that takes Islam as its primary frame of reference. When Islamic symbols and motives are used in everyday political discourse in Bosnia it is done in order to achieve national Bosniak (Muslim) political objectives, not Islamic ones. So it is more appropriate to call it Muslim rather than Islamic politics.

The role of Islam in voting patterns and other forms of political participation is not sufficiently explored. Election results often suggest that the support of the IC is no guarantee of political success.[119]

## The Role of Foreign Islamic Actors[120]

Bosnia was largely unknown to the Muslim world prior to 1992. However, once the tragedy of Bosnia became top news in Muslim media, aid was mobilized both by official and by private donors. We are never likely to know for certain how much was disbursed, for two reasons. First, part of it was spent in violation of the UN-imposed arms

---

[116] Cornelia Sorabji, "Mixed Motives: Islam, Nationalism and Mevlud in an Unstable Yugoslavia," in Camillia Fawzi El-Solh and Judy Mabro (eds.), *Muslim Women's Choices: Religious Belief and Social Reality* (Oxford: Berg Publishers, 1995), 108–27; Bringa, *Being Muslim the Bosnian Way*.

[117] Aid Smajić, "Psihosocijalni aspekti religioznosti kao determinante međunacionalne tolerancije," Ph. D. Dissertation, Faculty of Arts in Sarajevo (2010).

[118] Dino Abazović, *Bosanskohercegovački muslimani između sekularizacije i desekularizacije* (Zagreb-Sarajevo: Synopsis, 2012), 7, 167–72.

[119] Filandra, *Bošnjaci nakon socijalizma*, 128.

[120] For a good analysis of foreign influences in Islam see Juan Carlos Antunez, *Foreign Influences in Islam in Bosnia and Herzegovina*.

embargo. Second, another part was unofficial aid that came from private donors and NGOs to individual persons. The fragmentary available data suggest that some of the biggest donors came from Saudi Arabia, Iran, Malaysia, Turkey, Pakistan, United Arab Emirates, and Kuwait.

## Saudi Arabia

Saudi Arabia was one of the fastest countries to react to the Bosnian crisis. In early June 1992 the Saudi government created the High Saudi Committee for Assistance to Bosnia and Herzegovina (HSC) which first operated from Zagreb and then inside Bosnia as well. The HSC may have been the largest single Muslim donor to Bosnia.[121] According to its own estimates, it delivered some 450 million USD out of 560 million USD which is estimated Saudi assistance to Bosnia until 2001. Aid was spent on refugees, orphans, the needy, students, reconstruction of hospitals, infrastructure, schools and faculties, houses, mosques, medical equipment and drugs, and cultural, educational, and religious activities, which included sending targeted groups of people on pilgrimage.[122]

The educational and cultural activities of the HSC included restoration of damaged mosques and building of new ones, including a few big mosques (e.g. the King Fahd mosque in Sarajevo). They also supported schools, teachers, and students, as well as distribution of books, in Arabic and Bosnian. Particularly important was the HSC's project of translation and mass distribution of some thirty books in Bosnian. These were mostly by Salafi authors, though non-Salafis including several Bosnians were also included. As with all services of the King Fahd Center in Sarajevo, HSC publications have been distributed free of charge, including about 500,000 copies of the Qur'an, Ibn Kathir's *Tafsir*, and 6,000 copies of *Sahih al-Bukhari*.[123]

Clearly, Salafis have benefited from Saudi sponsorship of publication. However, this is not the full picture. First, there were non-Saudi agencies such as the Kuwaiti Salafi

---

[121] Other important donors from Saudi Arabia and the Gulf included the Jeddah-based Islamic Development Bank (IDB) of the OIC, the Saudi Development Fund, and the wealthy al-Ghazzaz family, as well as a raft of others: the strongly Salafi Al-Haramayn Foundation, the less ideological Ighatha and Al-Muwaffaq, the Saudi-sponsored World Association of Muslim Youth (WAMY/NADWA), Taibah (Saudi Arabia), Human Appeal and the Red Crescent of UAE, Qatari Charitable Organization, Kuwaiti Committee, Mercy International, etc. Some have been closed (Al-Haramayn, Al-Muwaffaq), others have left (Qatar), while some continue taking care of orphans (Human Appeal, Red Crescent, Kuwaiti Committee) or students (NADWA). Contrary to some expectations, the Muslim World League (Rabita) has not played a significant role in Bosnia since 1992.

[122] HSC Final Report, *Al-Hay'ah al-'Ulya li Jam' al-Tabarru'at li Muslimi al-Busna wa al-Harsak: Juhud wa Injazat*, 2nd edn. (Riyadh, 2001), 97–8.

[123] Evidence suggests that Bosnians translate and publish books for other than ideological or intellectual reasons. They may do so for money, or because they fail to grasp the implications, as when a book by a prominent Ahmadi author was translated by a local Mufti and recommended to Bosnian readers by a top IC official who had written a number of articles against the Ahmadiyya. Some Salafi organizations find mainstream scholars to translate uncontroversial books. Sometimes local scholars recommended books only with reservations that were not respected or printed by the publishers. See Šukri Ramić, "Fetve i savjeti," *Novi horizonti* 17, with reference to A. El-Džezairi, *Put pravog muslimana* (AIO, 2001).

Society for the Revival of Islamic Heritage (*Jam'iyyat Ihya' al-Turath al-Islami*) that also supported the distribution of Salafi literature. Second, Salafi ideas were not the only ones that enjoyed the support of foreign agencies. Books of various other authors are distributed for free (e.g. Nazim Haqqani, Bediuzzaman Sa'id al-Nursi,[124] Fethullah Gulen,[125] Ayatollah Khomeini).[126] Third, not all Salafi books were distributed for free. Some were translated and published on a commercial basis and well received. Fourth, many non-Muslim organizations too distributed religious literature from the New Testament to Bill Graham's book in Bosnian.[127] On more than one occasion Bosnian children received New Year's gifts with books on Christianity in the bag distributed by Western agencies. Fifth, a good part of the literature sponsored by Saudis or other Salafi groups, like Hadith collections, is not specifically Salafi but part of the common Islamic heritage. And sixth, this boom in Salafi literature was partly offset by the huge rise in other Islamic literature referred to earlier.

The HSC at times supported Salafi organizations. However, after 9/11 things changed. The pressure led to the closure of a number of those organizations while the King Fahd Cultural Center invested in establishing closer relations with the IC. In turn, the IC leader spoke out against the incrimination of Muslim solidarity, and visited several Islamic aid projects, including an orphan village and school whose accounts had been frozen.

After the opening of the King Fahd Cultural Center in September 2000, the HSC has been phasing itself out, and seeking to finalize incomplete projects. The HSC main office in Riyadh submitted its final report in January 2001. The Committee was formally closed in Bosnia in 2010.

## *Iran*

Iran has been one of the biggest donors to Bosnia. During the war, Iran—with tacit approval of the USA[128]—provided arms, and took wounded people for medical treatment. Iranian aid has also built some mosques, and assisted refugee return. Of particular interest here is that Iran has been the most active state when it comes to cultural and academic exchange. The Iranian presence has been distinguished by its systematic nature and coordination with relevant local counterparts including the Islamic

---

[124] Bediuzzaman Sa'id al-Nursi (1878–1960) is a Turkish Muslim thinker who authored *Risale-i Nur* and founded neo-Sufi Nurcu movement.

[125] Fethullah Gulen (b. 1941) is a popular Turkish religious author and leader living in the USA heading a movement with associations in most part of the world. The movement runs hundreds of educational institutions around the globe. Gulen's message focuses on peace and dialogue.

[126] Nazim Haqqani (b. 1922) is a controversial Turkish Cypriot Sufi sheikh.

[127] According to Christian missionary websites there has not been lack of effort by Christian missionaries to work in Bosnia since 1995 but their efforts have not been very successful. <http://www.cumorah.com/index.php?Target=missiology_articles&story_id=192#_ftnref15 and http://www.pray.om.org/bosnia-herzegovina/>.

[128] Douglas Jehl, "U.S. Looks Away as Iran Arms Bosnia," *The New York Times*, April 15, 1995, <http://www.nytimes.com/1995/04/15/world/us-looks-away-as-iran-arms-bosnia.html>.

Community, academic circles, and municipalities. Due to these efforts, and despite the occasional disputes, it is a widespread perception in some circles of Bosnia that—besides Americans—Iranians are the best friends of Bosnia. We will briefly discuss three Iranian and Bosnian-Iranian cultural entities.

The Cultural Center of the Iranian Embassy (<http://sr.sarajevo.icro.ir/>) presents Iranian culture to Bosnians and arranges visits of Bosnian academics, journalists, and other professionals to Iran, and vice versa. Since 2001 the Center has published the journal *Beharistan*, which focuses on Persian literature and Bosnian-Iranian cultural ties. The Ibn Sina Institute (<http://www.ibn-sina.net/>) has been very active in academic exchange between Iran and Bosnia, in encouraging local research on Islamic or Muslim topics, and in translation of Iranian literature. In addition, since 1997 it has been publishing the journal *Znakovi vremena* (*Signs of the Times*) which deals with philosophy, culture, and sociology.

The Mulla Sadra Foundation (<http://www.mullasadra.ba/>) is an NGO devoted to the promotion of "progressive Islamic teaching, the Qur'an, and enlightened thought of reputed Islamic scholars," which seems to mean Shi'a scholars. The focus of this NGO is lectures and translation of Iranian authors on topics such as Islamic doctrine and ethics, logic, Qur'anic epistemology, gnosis, and Islamic law.

Iranians have also sent many Bosnian students to Iran. It is not clear how many of them (or of those working with Iranians in ventures such as the above) have "converted" to Shi'ism. Some have done so, openly; others were clearly disaffected by their stay in Iran; and there might be dozens who practice *taqiyya* (hide their Shi'i beliefs). Certainly, a number of mainstream Bosnian Muslim intellectuals have found much to study and admire in Iranian tradition. So far several dozen Shi'i books have been printed in Bosnia. No study has been done as to the impact of Iranian activism in Bosnia.

## Turkey

Due to a variety of reasons which mainly had to do with its internal politics Turkey has been very slow to return to Bosnia after the dissolution of Yugoslavia. However, the ascendance of AKP to power and especially the appointment of Dr. Ahmet Davutoglu to the post of Minister of Foreign Affairs in May 2009 have brought significant change. The official Turkish presence has risen significantly both diplomatically and in the form of developmental assistance through the Turkish Development Agency (TIKA) and loans supporting sustainable return of refugees and displaced persons. Equally significant has been its business and civic society presence. While charities like Milli Görüş[129] have supported Bosnian Muslims during and after the war, over the last ten years new actors have emerged—various Sufi brotherhoods, NGOs, and networks, some of them with links to Turkey. Their presence is particularly visible in the education sector. While the Gulen movement successfully runs fifteen schools, Burch University (<http://bosnasema.ba/en/o-nama/10140>), and a publishing house, another group of Said Nursi followers

---

[129] A major Turkish Diaspora organization inspired by former Turkish Islamist political leader Necmettin Erbakan (1926–2011).

publish his books in Bosnian (<http://www.rejhan.net/>). An informal Turko-Bosnian group allegedly close to AKP runs one of the best private universities teaching in English (<http://www.ius.edu.ba/>). The Yunus Emre Center runs Turkish language courses (<http://yunusemreenstitusu.org/bosnia>), the Center for Balkan Civilization—BALMED—supports students and research (<http://balmed.ba>), to name just a few. All this has led some observers to conclude that presence of "Wahhabis" in 1990s was nothing but intermezzo.[130]

## Ethnic Cleansing, Genocide, and Islamophobia

As has been indicated, the twentieth century proved to be extremely difficult for Bosnian Muslims as they continued to struggle for the preservation of their identity and, at times, their very survival, first in the Royal Yugoslavia (1918–41), then in the Independent State of Croatia (1941–5),[131] the communist Yugoslavia (1945–91), and eventually in independent Bosnia and Herzegovina (since 1991), each time facing a different set of challenges and threats. The dissolution of Yugoslavia proved to be particularly bloody.

By the early 1980s the Yugoslav communist regime was already going through its final crisis and the first problems in Kosovo started in 1981. Since 1985 the Serbian nationalists led by the Serbian Academy of Sciences and Arts, Slobodan Milošević and allied media, church officials,[132] and military men galvanized Serbs for the idea of a Serb-dominated Yugoslavia or else Greater Serbia and a war to achieve that goal.[133] Plans to establish homogeneous ethnic nation-states (with less than 5% of "others") in a multiethnic environment of the Balkans inevitably led to a bloodbath. Very soon Croatian and Bosniak/Muslim towns and villages including their places of worship were burning, tens of thousands of women and men were put into concentration camps with thousands of them being raped, some burned alive.[134] Millions were moved from their homes. For a while the Croatian leadership too was induced by Serb leaders to accept the division of Bosnia as a "solution" which led to the Croat–Bosniak conflict from late 1992 until early 1994.

---

[130] Öktem, *New Islamic Actors after the Wahhabi Intermezzo*.
[131] On the disorientation and tragic mistakes of Bosnian Muslim leadership in the Second World War see Redžić, *Muslimansko autonomaštvo i 13. SS divizija*.
[132] Milorad Tomanić, *Srpska crkva u ratu i ratovi u njoj* (Beograd: Medijska knjizara Krug, 2001).
[133] International Commission on the Balkans, *Unfinished Peace: Report of the International Commission on the Balkans* (Washington, DC: Carnegie Endowment for International Peace, 1996); Samantha Power, *"A Problem from Hell": America and the Age of Genocide* (New York: Basic Books, 2002).
[134] The ICTY was the first international tribunal based in Europe to pass convictions for rape as a crime against humanity: <http://www.icty.org/sid/10312>. For life burning of 120 women, children, and old men see the ICTY final ruling sentencing Milan Lukić to life in prison: <http://www.icty.org/sid/11162>.

Towards the end of the war in July 1995 the army and police of the Republic of Srpska assisted by state military troops from Serbia and Montenegro committed genocide in the Srebrenica region killing over 8,200 Muslim men and women. The consequences of the war were devastating for the whole country and the Muslim community in particular. By March 2008, the most careful count of total causalities of war, not yet complete, stood at 97,207.[135] Estimates done for the International Criminal Tribunal for the Former Yugoslavia (ICTY) put the number of war casualties at 104,732 dead persons.[136]

While these figures came as a surprise to many observers and the affected people as too small, Marko Attila Hoare is right in observing that "The most striking fact to emerge from the study is that 83.33% of civilian deaths in the Bosnian war were Muslims (Bosniaks)…In Podrinje (Eastern Bosnia), 94.83% of civilian casualties were Muslims…"[137] Once predominantly or significantly Muslim towns in eastern, northern, and southern Bosnia (Bijeljina, Zvornik, Vlasenica, Bratunac, Srebrenica, Rogatica, Višegrad, Foča, Prijedor, etc.) have been "ethnically cleansed" of Muslims.[138]

A large section of the Serb population in the region questions or denies such an interpretation of events. Serb war leaders indicted by the ICTY are often celebrated as national heroes.[139] Chances are great that decades will pass before the majority of Serbs acknowledge what really happened in the Balkans in the 1990s and the role Serbian authorities, institutions, and large sections of the community played in it. Probably the best-known example of denial at the highest level is the Republic of Srpska government's report on the Srebrenica massacre which infamously concluded in 2002: "…the remaining figure in the missing list would be the number of Muslims soldiers who were executed by Bosnian Serb forces for personal revenge or for simple ignorance of the international law. It would probably stand less than 100."[140] Discussing the role of the commander of the RS Army, General Ratko Mladić, the report said (errors in the original text, AA):

> The existence of Mladzic in Potočari can be considered to discourage Serbs to take their wild revenge, taking into consideration the vengeful mind of relatives of Serbian victims that were massacred in 1992 and 1993. Several old Serbs whom the author met in January of 1998 said that they personally was too harsh and strict in discipline to overlook any unlawful behaviors of his soldiers. Although these were

---

[135] Jan Zwierzchowski and Ewa Tabeau, "The 1992–95 War in Bosnia and Herzegovina: Census-Based Multiple System Estimation of Casualties' Undercount," <http://www.idc.org.ba/index.php?Option=com_content&view=section&id=35&Itemid=126&lang=bs> [accessed Dec. 26, 2012].

[136] <http://www.diw.de/documents/dokumentenarchiv/17/diw_01.c.350596.de/tabeau_%20conflict_gecc.pdf>.

[137] Marko Atilla Hoare, "What do the Figures for the Bosnian War Dead Tell Us?," <http://www.bosnia.org.uk/news/news_body.cfm?Newsid=2336> [accessed Aug. 16, 2012].

[138] Edina Bećirović, *Na Drini genocid* (Sarajevo: Buybook, 2009); Smail Čekić, *Agresija na Republiku Bosnu i Hercegovinu: planiranje, priprema, izvođenje* (Sarajevo: Institut za istraživanje zločina i Kult B, 2004).

[139] Norman Cigar, *Genocide in Bosnia*.

[140] <http://www.slobodan-milosevic.org/documents/srebrenica.pdf>, p. 34.

the statements of Serbs, it must be remembered that the existence of Mladzic does not necessarily mean the systematic killings and could be the deterrance to revengeful killings. Of course, however, Mladzic, who failed to stop killings perfectly, would be responsible as a superior, and those Serbs who directly committed the crimes should be punished accordingly.[141]

In such circumstances, the rulings of the ICTY,[142] the International Court of Justice,[143] and other courts in the region seem to provide the most accurate account of the wars of the 1990s. Those rulings confirm beyond reasonable doubt the narrative given above. This is not to deny that on a number of occasions the Army of the Republic of Bosnia and Herzegovina or its allies committed war crimes.

However, ICTY justice is often of little help to the survivors or children of victims. While experts estimate that some 10,000 persons need to be investigated for war crimes the figures for those brought to justice so far are much lower. All indicators suggest that impunity rather than justice will be the rule this time as well. Furthermore, most of those who were sentenced to various prison terms have since been released (e.g. Biljana Plavšić) while Srebrenica and other ethnically cleansed territories are left under permanent control of the perpetrators of war crimes; where the children of victims of genocide have to sing the songs to "mother Serbia." The fear is that many will conclude that war crimes pay off while others will opt for extrajudicial pathways to justice.

Truth be told, the Dayton Accords (Annex VII) envisaged the return of refugees and displaced persons. However, the refugee return has been largely unsuccessful. Reliable statistics are lacking but there are many indications that in only a few towns has the return been successful (Brčko, several central Bosnian towns). The environment was particularly hostile for returnees in the early post-war years. The pre-1990s pluralistic Bosnia that had been multi-confessional before the Ottomans and remained so throughout the Ottoman, Austrian, and Yugoslav periods was largely destroyed by the Army of the Republic of Srpska. While the Croat Defense Council and Bosnian army also committed war crimes they were nowhere as systematic as those committed by the Army of the RS. For instance, of hundreds of mosques in the territories under the control of the Serb army only two survived the war. Even those enjoying the status of cultural heritage and deep in the territories without hostilities were destroyed and their remains completely removed.[144]

For all the aforementioned reasons, according to Šaćir Filandra of the University of Sarajevo the fear of physical extinction has become the defining socio-psychological frame of reference for Bosniaks, as well as the source of many political mistakes committed by their leaders. The genocide in Srebrenica demonstrated what Serbian neo-fascists want to do to Bosniaks and that fact is the real basis for that fear. The fear has become a constitutive element of the Bosniak national identity. The experience of genocide warns

---

[141] <http://www.slobodan-milosevic.org/documents/srebrenica.pdf>, p. 31.
[142] <http://www.icty.org/>.
[143] <http://www.icj-cij.org/docket/files/91/13685.pdf>.
[144] Omerdić, *Prilozi izučavanju genocida nad Bošnjacima*.

that annihilation of an ethnic group is indeed possible in Europe at the beginning of the twenty-first century.[145] The full impact of the 1992–5 war will be easier to assess after the publication of results of the 2013 census, the first census conducted since 1991.

In the post-war period, several incidents have become symbolic of intolerance towards Muslims in the Republic of Srpska. Among dozens of returnees who have been killed or have died in suspicious conditions the killing of 16-year-old Meliha Durić in Vlasenica while she was watching TV in her home is the most infamous. Like most other killings this one has not been resolved to this day.[146] The last European stoned to death for his religious beliefs was a Bosnian Muslim, Murat Badić.[147] He was stoned at a ceremony marking the beginning of the reconstruction of destroyed Ferhadija mosque in Banja Luka on 7 May 2001. Several young men were sent to jail for a few months but were later pardoned by the Republic of Srpska president Dragan Čavić. In addition to this, after the war the Serbian Orthodox Church built a church in Divič near Zvornik on the foundations of a destroyed mosque. In Konjević Polje an Orthodox church was constructed in the private courtyard of a Muslim family (Fata Orlović).[148] Unfortunately these are not the only examples of rampant discrimination.[149]

The media has been criticized by academics[150] and the IC[151] for its biased coverage of Islam. The war on terror in the post-9/11 world was misused by some to renew their attacks on Islam and Muslims in a way that was not possible before. The thing that was new this time was libel: now the culprit is Islamic terrorism while previously it was pan-Islamism or Fundamentalism.

# Conclusion

Research on Islamic history and heritage in Bosnia and Bosniak national identity development accounted for most of the scholarship on Bosnian Muslims prior to the

---

[145] Filandra, *Bošnjaci nakon socijalizma*, 316–17; Sells, *The Bridge Betrayed*.

[146] UNHCR, "Bosnia murder of a 16-year-old Bosniak returnee," <http://www.unhcr.org/3b4f08754.html>; BBC, "Muslim shot dead near Srebrenica," <http://news.bbc.co.uk/2/hi/europe/1435597.stm>.

[147] Ivan Lovrenović, "Poslije kraja," *BH Dani* 208, June 1, 2011, <http://www.bhdani.com/arhiva/208/kraj.shtml>.

[148] On this case see US Department of State, "International Religious Freedom Report for 2011," at <http://www.state.gov/documents/organization/193003.pdf> and a documentary "The House Fata Didn't Build," <http://www.aljazeera.com/programmes/aljazeeracorrespondent/2012/10/201210311243956401.html>.

[149] For regular updates check Jorgen S. Nielsen, *Yearbook of Muslims in Europe* (Leiden: Brill, 2009 onwards).

[150] Davor Marko, *Zar na Zapadu postoji neki drugi Bog? Stereotipi i predrasude u medijima prema islamu* (Sarajevo: Media Plan Institut, 2009); Fatmir Alispahić, *Reisofobija* (Tuzla: Offset, 2010).

[151] Rijaset Islamske zajednice u BiH, "The First Report on Islamophobia, Discrimination and Intolerance on the Territory of the Islamic Community in B-H 2004–2011" (Sarajevo, April 2011), <http://www.rijaset.ba/images/stories/Za-download/The%20First%20Report%20on%20Islamophobia%20-%202004-2010.pdf>.

1990s. Since then genocide and security studies have been more prominent. There is comparatively little sociological and political research although lately a few younger Bosnian scholars have started working on it. Recently there has been more scholarly interest in contemporary Islamic thought, education, and administration in Bosnia as the most relevant aspects of Bosnian Islamic tradition to the outside world. However, the research in this area is in its early stage and much more needs to be done. Despite all the focus on Bosnian Muslims after 9/11 there is little serious scholarly work on Islamic revival in the post-socialist Bosnia especially in comparative perspective. The role of the Bosnian Diaspora in the interaction between Europe, European Muslims, and Bosnian Muslims is hardly addressed in scholarly research. Similarly the role of the internet in the exchange between the Muslim world and Bosnia and in the work of Islamic actors in Bosnia is largely uncharted territory except for a few security oriented papers. Another theme escaping researchers' attention is the place of Islam in popular culture. It is expected that the autumn 2013 census will make socio-economic analysis of all sorts much easier including the impact of new demographic realities in "ethnically cleansed" territories on local Islamic life.

## Bibliography

Abazović, D. (2012). *Bosanskohercegovački muslimani između sekularizacije i desekularizacije*. Zagreb-Sarajevo: Synopsis.
Abdibegović, N. and Filipović, Z. (eds.) (2010). *Ajvatovica: 500 godina dovišta*. Sarajevo: Naklada Zoro.
Alibašić, A. (2008a). "Images of the Ottomans in History Textbooks in Bosnia and Herzegovina," in C. Moe (ed.), *Images of Religious Other: Discourse and Distance in the Western Balkans*. Novi Sad: CEIR, 39–71.
Alibašić, A. (2008b). "Pravci i elementi razvoja islamske tradicije Bošnjaka u bosanskom kontekstu," in *Zbornik radova naučnog skupa 'Islamska tradicija Bošnjaka: izvori, razvoj i institucije, perspektive', 14–16. Nov. 2007*. Sarajevo: Rijaset IZ u BiH, 491–509.
Alibašić, A. (2009). "A Problem that Does Not Have to Be: Religious Education in Public Schools in Bosnia and Herzegovina," in A. Alibašić et al. (eds.), *Religija i školovanje u otvorenom društvu: Preispitivanje modela religijskog obrazovanja u Bosni i Hercegovini*. Sarajevo: Fond otvoreno društvo Bosna i Hercegovina, 11–34, 107–10.
Alibašić, A. (2010). "Islamic Higher Education in the Balkans: A Survey," in Y. Nielsen (ed.), *Yearbook of Muslims in Europe*. Leiden: Brill, 619–34.
Alibašić, A. (2012). "Izdavačka djelatnost Islamske zajednice u BiH 1993.–2011. God." in Aziz Kadribegović et al. (eds.), *Islamska zajednica u Bosni i Hercegovini: Dvije decenije reisu-l-uleme Dr. Mustafe ef. Cerića*. Sarajevo: Centar za napredne studije, 177–84.
Alibašić, A. and Zubčević, A. (2009). "Islamic Education in Bosnia and Herzegovina," in E. Aslan (ed.), *Islamic Education in Europe*. Vienna: Böhlau, 43–57.
Aličić, A. (1996). *Pokret za autonomiju Bosne od 1831. do 1832. godine*. Sarajevo: Orijentalni institut.
Alispahić, F. (2010). *Reisofobija*. Tuzla: Offset.

Antunez, J. C. (2010). *Foreign Influences in Islam in Bosnia and Herzegovina since 1995*. Sarajevo: Centar za napredne studije.

Anzulović, B. (1999). *The Heavenly Serbia: From Myth to Genocide*. New York: New York University Press.

Attanassoff, V. (2005). "Bosnia and Herzegovina: Islamic Revival, International Advocacy Networks and Islamic Terrorism," *Strategic Insights* 4(5): 1–10.

Attanassoff, V. (2006). "Islamic Revival in the Balkans." MA Thesis. California: Naval Postgraduate School, Monterey.

Bandžović, S. (2000). "Bošnjaci u postjugoslavenskoj srpskoj historiografiji," *Prilozi Instituta za istoriju* 29.

Bandžović, S. (2010). *Bošnjaci i antifašizam: ratni realizam i odjek rezolucija građanske hrabrosti (1941.)*. Sarajevo: Author.

Bandžović, S. (2012). *Bošnjaci i deosmanizacija Balkana*. Sarajevo: Author.

BBC (2001). "Muslim shot dead near Srebrenica." <http://news.bbc.co.uk/2/hi/europe/1435597.stm>.

Bećirović, D. (2012). *Islamska zajednica u Bosni i Hercegovini za vrijeme avnojevske Jugoslavije (1945-1953)*. Zagreb: Bošnjačka nacionalna zajednica za grad Zagreb i Zagrebačku županiju i Islamska zajednica u Hrvatskoj—Medžlis IZ Zagreb.

Bećirović, E. (2009). *Na Drini genocid*. Sarajevo: Buybook.

Beglerović, S. (2005). "Fejzulah efendija Hadžibajrić—njegov život i borba za povratak tekija u okrilje Islamske zajednice." MA Thesis, Sarajevo: Faculty of Islamic Studies in Sarajevo.

Bougarel, X. (2005). "The Role of Balkan Muslims in Building a European Islam," *European Policy Centre Issue Paper* 43: 1–31.

Bougarel, X. and Clayer, N. (2001). *Le Nouvel Islam balkanique: Les musulmans, acteurs du post-communisme 1990-2000*. Paris: Maisonneuve et Larose.

Bringa, T. (1995). *Being Muslim the Bosnian Way: Identity and Community in a Central Bosnian Village*. Princeton: Princeton University Press.

Bruneteau, B. (2004). *Le Siècle des génocides: Violences, massacres et processus génocidaires de l'Arménie au Rwanda*. Paris: Armand Colin.

Ćehajić, Dž. (1984). "Društveno-politički, religiozni, književni i drugi aspekti derviških redova u jugoslavenskim zemljama," *Prilozi za orijentalnu filologiju* 34: 93–113.

Ćehajić, Dž. (1986). *Dervički redovi u jugoslovenskim zemljama sa posebnim osvrtom na Bosnu i Hercegovinu*. Sarajevo: Orijentalni institut.

Čekić, S. (2004). *Agresija na Republiku Bosnu i Hercegovinu: planiranje, priprema, izvođenje*. Sarajevo: Institut za istraživanje zločina i Kult B.

Cigar, N. (1995). *Genocide in Bosnia: The Policy of "Ethnic Cleansing."* College Station, TX: Texas A&M University Press.

Ćimić, E. (2007). *Drama a/teizacije*. Sarajevo: Šahinpašić.

Čolaković, S. (2000). "Da li mevlud ima uporište u Kur'anu?," in Dž. Obradović (ed.), *Mevlud u životu i kulturi Bošnjaka*. Sarajevo: BKZ Preporod, 23–31.

Dedijer, V. and Miletić, A. (1990). *Genocid nad Muslimanima 1941-1945, Zbornik dokumenata i sjećanja*. Sarajevo: Svjetlost.

Đozo, H. (2006). *Izabrana djela*, 5 vols. Sarajevo: El-Kalem.

Durmišević, E. (2002). *Uspostava i pravni položaj Rijaseta Islamske zajednice u Bosni i Hercegovini 1882-1899*. Sarajevo: Magistrat.

Džaja, S. M. (1999). *Konfesionalnost i nacionalnost Bosne i Hercegovine: Predemancipacijsko razdoblje 1463-1804*. Mostar: ZIRAL.

Fazlić, F. (2005). "Nagrađivanje za učenje Kur'an," *Takvim za 2006*: 75–86.
Fejzić, F. et al. (2011). *Prilozi za istraživanje sociokulturnog položaja žene u BiH: Izabrana bibliografija (1900–2010)*. Sarajevo: Nahla.
Filandra, Š. (1998). *Bošnjačka politika u XX stoljeću*. Sarajevo: Sejtarija.
Filandra, Š. (2012). *Bošnjaci nakon socijalizma: O bošnjačkom identitetu u postjugoslavenskom dobu*. Sarajevo and Zagreb: BZK Preporod and Synopsis.
Filipović, N. (2005). *Islamizacija u Bosni i Hercegovini*. Tešanj: Centar za kulturu i obrazovanje.
Fine, J. V. A. (1996). "The Medieval and Ottoman Roots of Modern Bosnian Society," in M. Pinson (ed.), *The Muslims of Bosnia-Herzegovina: Their Historic Development from the Middle Ages to the Dissolution of Yugoslavia*. Cambridge, MA: Harvard University Press, 1–21.
Grivaud, G. and Popovic, A. (eds.) (2011). *Les conversions à l'islam en Asie Mineure et dans les Balkans aux époques seldjoukide et ottomane: Bibliographie raisonnée (1800–2000)*. Athens: École française d'Athènes.
Hadžibajrić, F. (1981). "Naših četrdeset medžlisi zikira danas na početku XV stoljeća po Hidžri," *Takvim 1981*: 145–55.
Hadžibajrić, F. (1990). "Djelatnost tarikatskog centra u Sarajevu," *Šebi arus* 12: 17–32.
Hadžijahić, M. (1974). *Od tradicije do identiteta*. Sarajevo: Svjetlost.
Hafizović, R. (1997). *Znakovi šiijske duhovnosti*. Sarajevo: Bosanska knjiga.
Hafizović, R. (1999). *Temeljni tokovi Sufizma*. Sarajevo: Bemust
Handžić, A. (1994). *Studije o Bosni*. Istanbul: IRCICA.
Hećimović, E. (2006). *Garibi: Mudžahedini u BiH 1992–1999*. Zenica: Fondacija Sina.
Hećimović, E. (2008). "Radical Movements: A Challenge for Moderate Balkan-Islam?," in W. Feichtinger and P. Jureković (eds.), *Religiöser Extremismus vs. Internationale Friedensbemühungen: Lessons Learned und präventive Strategien im Nahen Osten und am Westbalkan*. Vienna: Landesverteidigungsakademie (LVAK).
High Saudi Committee (2001). *Al-Hay'ah al-'Ulya li Jam' al-Tabarru'at li Muslimi al-Busna wa al-Harsak: Juhud wa Injazat*, 2nd edn. Riyadh: High Saudi Committee.
Hoare, M. A. (2007). *The History of Bosnia: From the Middle Ages to the Present Day*. London: Saqi.
Hoare, M. A. "What do the Figures for the Bosnian War Dead Tell Us?" <http://www.bosnia.org.uk/news/news_body.cfm?Newsid=2336> [accessed Aug. 16, 2012.
Hoepken, W. (1999). "War, Memory, and Education in a Fragmented Society: The Case of Yugoslavia," *East European Politics and Societies* 13(1): 190–227.
Holbrooke, R. (1998). *To End a War*. New York: Random House.
Imamović, M. (1998). *Historija Bošnjaka*. Sarajevo: Bošnjačka zajednica kulture Preporod.
International Commission on the Balkans (1996). *Unfinished Peace: Report of the International Commission on the Balkans*. Washington, DC: Carnegie Endowment for International Peace.
Jahić, A. (2010). *Islamska zajednica u Bosni i Hercegovini za vrijeme monarhističke jugoslavije 1918.–1941.* Zagreb: Bošnjačka nacionalna zajednica za grad Zagreb i Zagrebačku županiju i Islamska zajednica u Hrvatskoj—Medžlis IZ Zagreb.
Jalimam, S. (1999). *Historija bosanskih bogomila*. Tuzla: Hamidović.
Jehl, D. (1995). "U.S. Looks Away as Iran Arms Bosnia." *The New York Times*, April 15, 1995. <http://www.nytimes.com/1995/04/15/world/us-looks-away-as-iran-arms-bosnia.html>.
Kamberović, H. (ed.) (2009). *Rasprave o nacionalnom identitetu Bošnjaka*. Sarajevo: Istorijski institut.
Karčić, F. (1997a). "Islamic Revival in the Balkans 1970–1992," *Islamic Studies* 36(2–3): 565–81.

Karčić, F. (1997b). "The Office of Ra'is al-'Ulama' Among the Bosniaks (Bosnian Muslims)," *Intellectual Discourse* 5(2): 109–20.
Karčić, F. (1999a). "Administration of Islamic Affairs in Bosnia and Herzegovina," *Islamic Studies* 38(4): 535–61.
Karčić, F. (1999b). *The Bosniaks and the Challenges of Modernity: Late Ottoman and Habsburg Times*. Sarajevo: El-Kalem.
Karčić, F. (2001). *Muslimani Balkana: Istočno pitanje u XX vijeku*. Tuzla: Behram-begova medresa.
Karčić, F. (2006). "Šta je to 'islamska tradicija Bošnjaka," *Preporod* 23/841.
Karčić, F. (2008). "Secular State and Religion(s): Remarks on the Bosnian Experience in Regulating Religion and State Relations in View of the New Law on Freedom of Religion," in S. Schreiner (ed.), *Religion and Secular State*. Zurich and Sarajevo: European Abrahamic Forum and Interreligious Institute in B&H, 15–24.
Karčić, F. (2010). "Main Trends in the Interpretation of the Shari'a in Bosnia and Herzegovina 2000–2005," lecture held at Copenhagen University, Sept. 15, 2010. <http://islam.ku.dk/lectures/Karcic150910final.pdf/>.
Karčić, F. et al. (2008). *Organizacija islamskih zajednica u regionu*. Sarajevo: Udruženje ilmijje IZ u BiH.
Karčić, H. (2010a). "Globalization and its Impact on Islam in Bosnia: Foreign Influences and their Effects," *Politics, Religion & Ideology* 11(2): 151–66.
Karčić, H. (2010b). "Islamic Revival in Post-Socialist Bosnia and Herzegovina: International Actors and Activities," *Journal of Muslim Minority Affairs* 30(4): 519–34.
Karčić, H. (2011). "Islamic Revival in Bosnia and Herzegovina 1990–2010." <http://www.cns.ba/docs/islamic_revival_in_Bosnia_and_Herzegovina_1992-1995.pdf>.
Karić, E. (1998). *Kur'an u savremenom dobu*. Sarajevo: Bosanski Kulturni Centar/El-Kalem.
Karić, E. (1999). *Semantika Kur'ana*. Sarajevo: Bemust.
Karić, E. (2002). *Tumačenje Kur'ana i ideologije XX stoljeća*. Sarajevo: Bemust
Karić, K. (2011). *Contributions to Twentieth Century Islamic Thought in Bosnia and Herzegovina*. Sarajevo: El-Kalem.
Karić, E. and Demirović, M. (eds.) (2002). *Reis Džemaluddin Čaušević: prosvjetitelj i reformator*. Sarajevo: Ljiljan.
Karić, E. and Duraković, E. (eds.) (2000). *Izabrana djela Mehmeda Handžića*. Sarajevo: Ogledalo.
Karić, E. et al. (2011). *Islamic Scene in Bosnia and Herzegovina*. Sarajevo: Udruženje ilmijje IZ u BiH.
Karup, Dž. (1998). "Kur'an je naš ustav," *Dani* no. 72, March 30, 1998. <http://www.bhdani.com/arhiva/72/tekst172.htm>.
Kovačević, E. (2005). "The Legal Position of Churches and Religious Communities in Bosnia and Herzegovina," in S. Devetak et al. (eds.), *Religion and Democracy in Moldova*. Maribor-Chisinau: ISCOMET and ASER, 275–91.
Kovačević, O. (2006). "Muslimani i drugi: analiza tekstova objavljenih u *Glasniku Islamske zajednice*." Graduation paper no. 401, Sarajevo: Faculty of Islamic Studies.
Legert, A. C. (2002). *Preventing and Combatting Terrorism in Bosnia and Hercegovina*. Vienna: National Defence Academy.
Li, D. (2010). "A Universal Enemy? 'Foreign Fighters' and Legal Regimes of Exclusion and Exemption Under the 'Global War On Terror'," *Columbia Human Rights Law Review* 41(2): 355–427.

Ljevaković, E. (2011). "Fikhski diskurs kakav imamo (kroz prizmu pitanja i odgovora)," in M. Hadžić (ed.), *Islamski diskurs u Bosni i Hercegovini*. Sarajevo: Institut za proučavanje tradicije Bošnjaka, 23–40.

Ljevaković, E. (2012). "Vjerski autoritet Islamske zajednice u Bosni i Hercegovini," in A. Kadribegović et al. (eds.), *Islamska zajednica u Bosni i Hercegovini: Dvije decenije reisu-l-uleme Dr. Mustafe Cerića*. Sarajevo: Centar za napredne studije, 40–51.

Lovrenović, D. (2008). *Povijest est magistra vitae: o vladavini prostora nad vremenom*. Sarajevo: Rabic.

Lovrenović, I. (2001). "Poslije kraja," *BH Dani*, Jan. 1, 208. <http://www.bhdani.com/arhiva/208/kraj.shtml>.

McCarthy, J. (1996). "Ottoman Bosnia, 1800 to 1878," in M. Pinson (ed.), *The Muslims of Bosnia-Herzegovina: Their Historic Development from the Middle Ages to the Dissolution of Yugoslavia*. Cambridge, MA: Harvard University Press, 54–83.

Machacek, S. (2006). "Islamic Education in the Post-Communist Balkans in the Period from 1990 to 2005," *Archiv orientální* 74(1): 65–93.

Machacek, S. (2007). "'European Islam' and Islamic Education in Bosnia and Herzegovina," *Sudost Europa* 55(4): 395–428.

Malcolm, N. (1995). *Povijest Bosne*. Zagreb-Sarajevo: Erasmus Gilda.

Marko, D. (2009). *Zar na Zapadu postoji neki drugi Bog? Stereotipi i predrasude u medijima prema islamu*. Sarajevo: Media Plan Institut.

Mihrović, A. (ed.) (2002). *Nacionalno mitomansko prokletstvo*. Sarajevo: Kaligraf.

Moe, C. (2003). "A 'Bosnian Paradigm' for Religious Tolerance?" Paper presented at the 3rd EASR conference in Bergen.

Moe, C. (2007). "A Sultan in Brussels? European Hopes and Fears of Bosnian Muslims," *Südosteuropa* 55(4): 374–94.

Muhić, F. (2011). "The Ottoman Legacy as a Common Layer of the Balkan Muslim Identities," in H. Eren (ed.), *The Ottoman Legacy and the Balkan Communities Today*. Istanbul: BALMED, 29–36.

Nakičević, O. (1996). *Istorijski razvoj institucije Rijaseta*. Sarajevo: Rijaset IZ u BiH.

Nakičević, O. (ed.) (1998). *Život i djelo Husein ef. Đoze*. Sarajevo: Fakultet islamskih nauka.

Nielsen, J. S. (2009). *Yearbook of Muslims in Europe*. Leiden: Brill.

Obradović, Dž. (ed.) (2000). *Mevlud u životu i kulturi Bošnjaka*. Sarajevo: BKZ Preporod.

Öktem, K. (2010). *New Islamic Actors after the Wahhabi Intermezzo: Turkey's Return to the Muslim Balkans*. Oxford: European Studies Centre, University of Oxford.

Omerdić, M. (1997). "Derviši i tekije u Sarajevu," in Dž. Juzbašić (ed.), *Prilozi historiji Sarajeva*. Sarajevo: Institutu za istoriju/Orijentalni institut, 129–40.

Omerdić, M. (1999). *Prilozi izučavanju genocida nad Bošnjacima, 1992–1995*. Sarajevo: El-Kalem.

Pećanin, S. (2002). "Caco je i heroj i zločinac: Intervju sa Alijom Izetbegovićem." *BH Dani*, March 1, 246.

Pew Research Center's Forum on Religion and Public Life (2012). *The World's Muslims: Unity and Diversity*. Washington, DC: Pew Research Center.

Popović, M. (1976). *Vidovdan i časni krst*. Beograd: Slavoljublje.

Power, S. (2002). *"A Problem from Hell": America and the Age of Genocide*. New York: Basic Books.

Purivatra, A., Imamović, M., and Mahmutćehajić, R. (1991). *Muslimani i bošnjaštvo*. Sarajevo: Ključanin.

Ramadan, T. (2004). *Western Muslims and the Future of Islam*. Oxford: Oxford University Press.

Ramić, J. (2002). *Bošnjaci na univerzitetu El-Azher*. Sarajevo: Muftijstvo sarajevsko.
Redžić, E. (1987). *Muslimansko autonomaštvo i 13. SS divizija*. Sarajevo: Svjetlost.
Rijaset Islamske zajednice u BiH (2005). "Platforma IZ u BiH za dijalog." <http://www.rijaset.ba>.
Rijaset Islamske zajednice u BiH (2006). *Rezolucija Islamske zajednice u Bosni i Hercegovini o tumačenju islama i drugi tekstovi*. Sarajevo: El-Kalem.
Rijaset Islamske zajednice u BiH (2011). "Izvještaj o radu Rijaseta IZ u BiH za 1430.–1431. H.g./2010. godinu," *Glasnik Rijaseta IZ u BIH* 73(5–6): 574–652.
Salkić, M. (2001). *Ustavi Islamske zajednice*. Sarajevo: El-Kalem.
Sells, M. (1998). *The Bridge Betrayed: Religion and Genocide in Bosnia*. Berkeley: University of California Press.
Šeta, Đ. (2011). *Zašto marama? Bosanskohercegovačke muslimanke o životu i radu pod maramom*. Sarajevo: CNS and CIPS.
Smajić, A. (2010). "Psihosocijalni aspekti religioznosti kao determinante međunacionalne tolerancije." Ph.D. Dissertation, Faculty of Arts in Sarajevo.
Solberg, A. R. (2005). "The Gulen Schools: A Perfect Compromise or Compromising Perfectly?" <http://kotor-network.info/papers/2005/Gulen.Solberg.pdf> [accessed February 15, 2013].
Sorabji, C. (1988). "Islamic Revival and Marriage in Bosnia," *Institute of Muslim Minority Affairs Journal* 9(2): 331–7.
Sorabji, C. (1988). "Muslim Identity and Islamic Faith in Sarajevo." Ph.D. Thesis, Cambridge: University of Cambridge.
Sorabji, C. (1995). "Mixed Motives: Islam, Nationalism and Mevlud in an Unstable Yugoslavia," in C. F. El-Solh and J. Mabro (eds.), *Muslim Women's Choices: Religious Belief and Social Reality*. Oxford: Berg Publishers, 108–27.
Šošić, Dž. (2011). "Islamska pedagoška misao i praksa Derviš-ef. Spahića." MA Thesis defended at the Faculty of Islamic Studies in Sarajevo.
Spahić, M. (2002). "Proces prihvatanja islama u Bosni i Hercegovini," *Glasnik Rijaseta Islamske zajednice u BiH* 64(3–4): 327–38.
Tomanić, M. (2001). *Srpska crkva u ratu i ratovi u njoj*. Beograd: Medijska knjizara Krug.
Trifunović, E. G. D. (2002). *Islamic Fundamentalists' Global Network*. Banja Luka: Bureau for Relation with ICTY of the Republic of Srpska.
UNHCR (2001). "Bosnia murder of a 16-year-old Bosniak returnee." <http://www.unhcr.org/3b4f08754.html>.
Zemaljska vlada BiH (1896). *Popis žiteljstva u BiH od 22 aprila 1895 sa podacima o teritorijalnom razdjeljenju, javnim zavodima i rudnim vrelima*. Sarajevo: Zemaljska vlada BiH.
Zildžić, A. (2006). "Fenomen zvani Srečko M. Džaja," *Znakovi vremena* 9(32): 136–56.
Zwierzchowski, J. and Tabeau, E. (2010). "The 1992–95 War in Bosnia and Herzegovina: Census-Based Multiple System Estimation of Casualties' Undercount." <http://www.idc.org.ba/index.php?Option=com_content&view=section&id=35&Itemid=126&lang=bs> [accessed Dec. 26, 2012].

CHAPTER 11

# ALBANIANS' ISLAM(S)

ISA BLUMI AND GËZIM KRASNIQI

## INTRODUCTION

ALBANIANS[1] in the Balkans represent a rather unique socio-political case. Today, Albanians live as majorities in the independent and sovereign state of Albania and in the newly independent and contested state of Kosovo. Nominally, both these countries have an Albanian Muslim majority, thus being a rare instance in Europe. As much as these countries warrant study in the context of a larger survey on European Islam, Albanian Muslims do not inhabit these countries alone. They also make up numerically significant minorities in neighboring countries once part of Yugoslavia—Serbia, Macedonia, and Montenegro (Ellis 2003; Krasniqi 2011; Babuna 2000). Moreover, as a result of ongoing political and economic tensions in these territories, many Albanian Muslims have migrated elsewhere, now making large diasporas in Western Europe, Greece, Turkey, and North America.[2]

One of the main problems that inhibits a true understanding of the complexities of Albanians' Islam is related to the predominance of "methodological nationalism" (Wimmer and Schiller 2002) that has characterized how different fields of inquiry and mainstream social science are applied to the study of Islam in the Balkans. Of the three variants of methodological nationalism identified by Wimmer and Schiler—ignorance, naturalization, and territorial limitation—the idea that a nationally bounded society is considered a "natural" entity of study (naturalization) unnecessarily reduces the analytical focus to the boundaries of the nation-state (territorial limitation) (Wimmer and Schiller 2002: 302–8). In this respect, it appears clear that such methods have been predominant in the study of Islam in the Balkans.

---

[1] The authors would like to thank the editor and Gent Cakaj for constructive comments on earlier versions of this chapter.

[2] These Albanian Muslims living abroad form a diaspora that, in some estimates, constitutes half of Europe's Albanians (Blumi 2011a).

On the other hand, scholarship in local languages is conditioned by two main factors. First, since the very creation of new "nation-states" starting from the mid-nineteenth century, national historiographies have been dominated by an ethno-nationalist agenda. Due to the fact that most of these new states were created as a result of violence against other communities within the predominantly Muslim Ottoman Empire, sectarianism has constantly been the means by which Balkan nations were perceived. In this context, all the countries in the post-Ottoman Balkans continuously and systematically demonized and misrepresented Islam and Muslims living as minorities in these new states. As a result, political identities fit within national discourses that indiscriminately constructed the nation-state as an opposition to the Ottoman Empire. In this context, scholarship on Islam in the Balkans and its role in the development of the various communities in that part of Europe has thus been neglected.

The "ethno-nationalist" paradigm has been the predominant method of reading and telling the past in the Balkan states. As a result, politically manufactured and anachronistic terms and concepts, linked today to ethno-national affiliations and selecting, became prevalent in historical studies instead of the local terminology individuals used to self-identify in various contexts. More specifically, the spatial, cultural, and economic units used in ethno-national frames by "national" historiographies of the twentieth century prove to be restrictively self-referential and internalist, and they selectively ignore the intersecting forces that make the Ottoman Balkans so unambiguously valuable to studying the larger issues related to "modernity" in greater Europe (Blumi 2011b: 7). This has been the case with the official historiography in the states inhabited by Albanians after the fall of the Ottoman Empire—Albania, Yugoslavia, and Greece. Modern concepts of nation and "nation-state"—perceived as culturally and politically homogenous—were frequently projected into the past at the detriment of the terminology individuals used to self-identify in an ever changing socio-political Balkan context.

Another impediment to studying Islam in the Balkans is linked to the communist experience in the second half of the twentieth century. Due to the underlying tensions and antagonisms between communist states and religion, scholarship on Islam was limited and often partisan. While in socialist Yugoslavia, the liberalization of the system in the late 1960s resulted in an increase in studies on Islam and Muslim communities, communist Albania banned religion altogether. In such settings a major rupture in the development of religion and scholarship took place. Thus, states' hostile approach towards religion in general and Islam in particular played a great part in the way local historians read and analyzed the past and present.

Nonetheless, after the fall of communism in Eastern Europe and the "opening-up" of the region to Europe and the world, new scholarship did emerge in different disciplines (Clayer 1990, 2006, 2010; Popović 1990; Norris 1993; Duijzings 2000). Many of these new sociological and anthropological studies on Islam and Muslims in the Balkans shed light on various, previously neglected or outright ignored religious and social aspects that animate the life of Albanian Muslims in the region. Although these studies are limited in number and often superficial, they remain important for they represent a counterbalance to the ideologically motivated local scholars and journalists dealing with the issue of religion. However, in the aftermath of the Yugoslav wars and the 9/11 events, ideologically motivated scholars preaching ethnic separation, the "war on terror," or the clash of civilizations have initiated a new wave of challenges to the corrective scholarship emerging from outside the region. Therefore, the present social, political, and cultural cleavages and tensions in the region are seldom put in a wider context of the "clash of civilizations" (where Islam is indiscriminately portrayed as foreign and primitive) and Islam's "incompatibility" with democracy and modern European and Western values. This has contributed to the increasing level of Islamophobia in the region.

Thus, when put in the context of this larger survey on European Islam, it is crucial to appreciate that Albanian Muslims constitute a diffuse and complex set of stories that, it is argued in this chapter, make any understanding of the larger issues under study in this project dependent on differentiating distinctive Muslim (and ethno-national) communities using various tools. By offering an interdisciplinary approach that brings nuance to otherwise normative historical analysis and social scientific codification, this chapter will help scholars and policy-makers to differentiate between Albanian Muslims and situate their political, socio-economic, and spiritual diversity in the larger context of state and regional life over the last century of European and Balkan life.

In general, the relationship Albanians—who profess faith as both Christians (Catholic or Orthodox) and Muslims of various sects—had with most post-Ottoman states was directly influenced by their larger legal status as ethnic, as well as religious, minorities in each country. In Greece and Yugoslavia, for instance, Muslim Albanians were labeled as "minorities," whose added affiliation with an "alien," "Turkish" faith like Islam resulted in decades of persecution that was not necessarily the case for Bosniaks (who eventually became integrated into larger Yugoslav society) or even Pomaks in Bulgaria (Ghodsee 2009). For Albanians, being both religious and ethnic minorities often meant being labeled as "threats" to the national security of Greece and Yugoslavia throughout the Cold War (and later in the break-away countries of Serbia, Montenegro, and Macedonia).

This is in contrast to Muslim Albanians living inside the country of Albania, an independent state, in theory if not in practice, since 1912. Albanians who were "Muslims," when grouped into a single religious category, were often assumed to make up a "majority" of the country's population. This did not translate, however, into protection from religious persecution. Depending on the era and regime in power, only certain subgroups of Albanian Muslims were persecuted on the grounds of their religious (sectarian) affiliation. In other words, although Albania was in one way a "Muslim" country, the diverse practices that emerged during 500 years of Ottoman rule meant that only a selected group of Muslims, at any given time, enjoyed protection from the more general trend of persecution in the larger Balkans. More importantly to recent events, even this distinction changed inside Albania with the insertion of Stalinist "reforms" in 1967 when Albania was declared the world's first "atheist state" (Doja 2000). From that point onward, all openly practicing Muslims, as well as Christians, faced often brutal state persecution (Pllumi 2008).

With this in mind, the chapter aims to cover two crucial aspects of Albanian Islam in the Balkan/European context. The first one is the diversity of interactions with various twentieth-century states experienced by Albanian Muslims in the Balkans. The second is Albanians' relationship with Islam. As will become clear throughout, the kinds of Islam practiced by Albanians have changed dramatically over the decades, often in direct response to state persecution in Albania, Greece, or Yugoslavia (post-Yugoslavia). As explained in the following, hostility towards Albanian Muslims often compelled them to modify how they practiced their faith, be it embracing regional traditions more strongly, or being drawn to a new kind of Islamic practice coming from Turkey or Saudi Arabia since the region has "opened up" to the world with the fall of communist regimes in the early 1990s. Finally, as there were very different experiences for Albanian Muslims living in Albania and Yugoslavia, these two aspects of Albanian Islam mentioned already will be explained in distinctive subsections in what follows.

# Charting a History of Difference in Balkan States

This part of the chapter is divided into five different sections analyzing: (i) the uniqueness of the Islam among Albanians in Europe; (ii) religious diversity; (iii) the experience of Albanian Muslims in inter-war and socialist Yugoslavia; as well as different trajectories and developments among (iv) Albanian Muslims in Kosovo and (v) Macedonia.

Albanian Muslims have faced many forms of persecution due to both their ethnic and religious identities. The scale of this persecution, however, is difficult to gauge. To a large extent, religious identity and/or Albanian ethnicity was not recorded in official state documentations since Ottoman times. This policy to strategically disguise demographic imbalances often protected the state from outside calls for greater protection of such large (but denied) groups. The logic was that the larger the Albanian population in these territories—often reluctantly incorporated into post-Ottoman, self-identified "Christian" states—the more grounds these Albanians had to claims for cultural and ultimately political rights. Indeed, after periods of forcible conversions of Muslims into Christians, states in the Balkans also pursued forced migration, thus contributing to yet another set of factors that distorted realistic demographic statistics. In many ways, the very fact that the states persecuting Muslims in the Balkans refused to provide documented records of these violent policies challenges the very nature of our research. The result is that an entirely different set of analytical tools are available to the social scientist.

## What Makes Albanian Muslims Unique in Europe?

As members of the Orthodox, Catholic, and Evangelical Christian, as well as Sunni, various Sufi, and Shi'a Muslim spiritual traditions, Albanians are often considered unique among the ethno-national groups of the Balkans (Roux 1992; Clayer 1990;

Doja 2000; Poulton 1998; Lakshman-Lepain 2002). Many scholars recognize that this religious diversity has not been a barrier to Albanians who sought to form a common sense of belonging to a single ethno-national group, requisite in the twentieth century (Babuna 2004; Bougarel 2007; Blumi 1998). In stark contrast to how religiously different Albanians forged a common ethno-national identity, southern Slavs—Serbs, Croats, Bosniaks, Macedonians, Bulgarians—as well as Greeks and Romanians became permanently distinctive on these same sectarian grounds (Banac 2006; Poulton 1997; Mazower 2002). In the post-Ottoman Balkans, the rise of the nation-state led to the calculation that previously "mixed" communities were a liability in countries where the political elite deemed ethnic (thus religious) uniformity crucial for national survival (Poulton 1998).

This fate imposed by the victors of the First World War proved especially traumatic for Albanian Muslims. It was the Albanian Muslims who became the primary targets of those ascendant (self-declared "Orthodox Christian") states—Montenegro, Serbia, Bulgaria, and Greece—which captured most of the former Ottoman Balkan territories (Mazower 2002: 113–44). Much of the post-First World War period thus became a tragic story of forced "population exchanges" whereby "foreigners" were "repatriated" to their "ethnic homelands."[3]

Balkan history is often presented today by many local and foreign scholars in terms of such monolithic "ethnic" terms, which implicitly suggest communities retain the presumptions of distinct, quasi-primordial cultural identities that have supposedly persisted fundamentally unchanged over centuries (Popović 1986; Deliso 2007). Embedded in this logic is the assertion that religious affiliation specifically determines the contours of an ethnic community (Banac 2006; Iveković 2002). But as demonstrated next, Albanian Muslim faith is far more diverse and varied than can be captured by a reductionist analysis of just who was being persecuted in, for instance, twentieth-century Yugoslavia or Albania.

## Albanian Muslim Diversity in Sect and Practice: Inside the Republic of Albania

Most conventional studies of the region recognized that the current Albanian state is Muslim, a view based on calculations drawn from the 1940s, according to which 70% of people were declared/considered to be Muslim, 20% Christian Orthodox, and 10% Christian Catholic. However, a 2011 census revealed a slightly different picture.

---

[3] The most studied case of this process is that of Christian "Greeks" indigenous to the towns and villages of western Anatolia being "exchanged" for "Turks" (Muslims) living in the Balkans (Mazower 2002; McCarthy 1995). Less appreciated, this history of negotiated "repatriation" of Muslims (claimed to be Turks) similarly led to the violent persecution of Albanians (and other indigenous Muslims) throughout Greece and Yugoslavia from the late 1920s onwards (Roux 1992; Schwandner-Sievers 2004; Stefanović 2005). Such widespread persecution resulted in the creation of an Albanian diaspora in Turkey alone estimated to be more than 1.4 million today (Blumi 2011a: 162).

According to the census data, 56.7% of the residents declared themselves as Muslims, 10% Catholics, 6.7% Orthodox, 2% Bektashi, while 13.7% did not declare their religious affiliation.[4] While the percentage of Catholics remained almost intact, this census indicates a decrease in the percentage of Muslims and Orthodox Christians. However, the large percentage of people who did not declared their religious affiliation leaves space for various interpretations as to the real religious composition of the country.

Nonetheless, largely missing from recent scholarship on Islam in the Balkans is the appreciation for quite different spiritual traditions that have shaped the way Muslims have lived in the region (Clayer 1990; Bougarel 2005). In territorial Albania throughout the twentieth century, for example, there have been three significant subcategories of practicing Muslims that require attention. Perhaps the most important group was a persecuted Muslim sect, the *Bektashiyya* (Bektashi), which settled in the thirteenth century in what is today larger cultural Albania (Blumi 2003b; Clayer 1992; Doja 2006; Duijzings 2000; Malcolm 1999; Norris 1993; Popović and Veinstein 1995; Rexhepagiqi 2003). The Bektashi, unlike other Sufi orders inhabiting the Balkans, though officially considered Sunni by way of their affiliation with legal traditions, were regarded as Shi'a by fellow Muslims because of their "esoteric" practices with a special reference to 'Ali, the cousin, and son-in-law, of the Prophet Muhammad, and his two sons Hasan and Hussayn.[5] In reality, due to the lack of a clearly defined theology, Bektashism could provide enough room to accommodate local influence and tradition, thus becoming, as Lakshman-Lepain argues, "the purest expression of Albanian religiosity" (2002: 38). Since the early nineteenth century, as a result of the entrenchment of the persecuted elite of the order in the south-western Balkans, the Bektashi became a crucial element in the social, cultural, economic, and political life of Muslims living in what is today southern Albania and northern Greece (Doja 2006: 90–105; Clayer 1992: 273–89).

After the formal collapse of the Ottoman Empire and the creation of a small, vulnerable Albanian Republic, only loosely controlled by competing factions, the state in the inter-war period took several steps towards the "nationalization" of religion, leading to the cutting of ties with Islamic institutions in Istanbul. Religious life was organized on four main principles: (a) laity of the state; (b) religious freedom; (c) equality among religions; and (d) recognition of three "national churches" (Islam, Christian Orthodoxy, and Catholicism) (Odile 1990; Lakshman-Lepain 2002; Lederer 1994; Clayer 2008). The internal doctrinal disputes between Bektashi and Sunni Albanians were seen as a source of weakness and state leaders desperately attempted to keep sectarianism out of inter-war Albanian politics. By the end of the Second World War, which saw the rise of the

---

[4] This census was boycotted by some of Albania's ethnic minorities (Greeks above all). For the complete results of the census see Instat, *Population and Housing Census*, 2011. Available at <http://www.instat.gov.al/media/177354/main_results__population_and_housing_census_2011.pdf>.

[5] Sunni Islam has four basic legal schools (*madhhab*). The Hanafi *madhhab*, founded by Abu Hanifa in the eighth century was the official *madhhab* of the Ottoman Empire, and was the only one represented in the Balkans until the 1990s. Present-day Salafists most actively involved in the Balkans are often considered to be close to the stricter Hanbali *madhhab*, founded by Ahmad ibn Hanbal at the beginning of the ninth century.

Enver Hoxha regime, elite membership to the Bektashi and Orthodox communities was strategically foregrounded by party affiliation (Blumi 1997).

In the aftermath of the fall of communism in 1991, Albanian society went through a process of multiple social, political, and identity transformations. In part, this took the form of an exodus of people beginning in July 1990, when hundreds of thousands of Albanians crashed the Italian and Greek borders in search of work and better living conditions in Europe (G. Krasniqi 2010; Mai 2008; Chiodi 2005). The two most dramatic examples are the more than 400,000 Albanians who have migrated to Italy and the 500,000 who have relocated to Greece (Antoniou 2007: 155). This has had an immense impact on the way these people identified themselves and interacted with the others in their countries of admission. Among those in Greece, for example, many have chosen to change their Muslim names into "Greek Christian" ones in order to avoid discrimination (de Rapper 2008; Puto 2006; Ceka 2006). Population shifts in concert with these fluid conditions of religious identification thus make it virtually impossible for the various Sufi orders that traditionally were based in the southern regions of the country to survive. As reported by the Grand Mufti of Albania, Hafiz Sabri Koçi (himself of the Tijani Sufi order) in an interview in January 2000, most of the Sufi orders (*tekkes*) in Albania have more or less disappeared due to a lack of funds and followers. Moreover, he noted, the more mainstream Sunni Muslim and Bektashi communities, while having a broader base of faithful to rely on, are not fairing much better in respect to retaining their followers, with Albanians "returning" to their so-called "Christian European roots" (Clayer 2006; Doja 2003; Lakshman-Lepain 2002).

One important source of this slow demise of local Islam in Albania is the legacy of the communist regime that ruled from 1944 to 1991. In this period, the brutal persecution of religious leaders forced followers underground, leaving the dissemination of "tradition" in the hands of largely isolated, uneducated individuals. As a result, knowledge in the practice of Islam was all but lost as thousands of religious leaders were either murdered or arrested by the regime and the faithful compelled to worship in secret (Dizdari and Kasollja 1992). To those who were able to observe the first few months of Albania's "liberation" from communist-imposed isolation, the consequences of such long persecution were glaringly evident when the first religious services took place. Both in the northern city of Shkodër on November 16, 1990, and then in Tirana on November 23, places of worship were reinstated but the ceremonies proved far from conventional (Blumi 2003b). It was clear that knowledge of even the most basic Islamic practices was virtually unknown to the youth.

In the same year, the Muslim Community of Albania (*Komuniteti Musliman i Shqipërisë*)—MCA—resumed its activities, claiming in its literature to be the main Muslim main organization in Albania.[6] Not long after, however, the Bektashi community reestablished the World Headquarters of the Bektashi Order in Tirana.[7] While the MCA formally includes all the Muslim sects of Albania—article 14:61 of its statute states

---

[6] <http://www.kmsh.al/index.php>.
[7] <http://www.komunitetibektashi.org>.

that "All the sects are integral parts of the Islamic Community of Albania"—the Bektashi Community, having cut its ties with Turkey in 1929, reminded the world that its statute (adopted at the fourth congress of May 1945) declares the movement's independence from the Sunni community. The reiteration of this independence has since 1990 caused tensions as rival groups of leaders conflicted over competing claims of legitimacy (Lederer 1994). In the end, the Bektashi Community in Albania has successfully kept its status as the "fourth religion" or "fourth church" in Albania, the other three being Sunni Islam, Orthodox, and Catholic (Lederer 1994; Lakshman-Lepain 2002).

While internal debates, often resurfacing after decades of suppression during the communist period, raged within Albania, the void created during the communist era also offered many foreign Muslim organizations an opportunity to spread their particular brand of Islam into largely "ignorant" Muslim Albanian communities. Representatives from Iran, Saudi Arabia, and Turkey rushed to a materially, and, to many, spiritually impoverished Albania (Blumi 2003a; Solberg 2007; Trix 1995; Deliso 2007; Bougarel 2003).

The results from this "invasion" of Muslim (and Christian) charities were immediate. According to a study conducted in the two universities of Tirana in 1994, three-quarters of the students asked stated they believed in God while only one-quarter of the professors who were instructing them claimed to be believers (Blumi 2003b; Tomo 1996). This "rebirth" of faith may have reflected a rebirth in religious institutions and a surge of attendance in religious-based schools that followed the 1990 opening of the country to foreign donors.

As a consequence of the perception that Albanians are in need of religious reintegration, the region has been a point of intense rivalry between competing "Islamic traditions." The best example of this competition may again be found in Albania with the emergence of a Turkish network of both religious and secular schools, part of the Gülen movement, which has nearly monopolized the education of Albanian Muslims from the early 1990s (Agai 2002: 44–6). Fethullah Gülen (1938–) and his vast economic, pedagogical, and spiritual empire has been very successful in exporting his "Turkish" type of Islam (Solberg 2007; Öktem 2011).[8] In Albania, Gülen's "secular" private schools, known by the name of Mehmet Akif, have emerged throughout the country since 1991, practically serving as an effective counterweight to more conservative Arab organizations coming to Albania at the time. From the very beginning, generous scholarship programs, a world-class English language instruction, and promises of a paid university education in Turkey have attracted thousands to these schools, which at their height numbered eight throughout the country. These schools do not put a heavy emphasis on Islamic education, and as many students confirm, Gülen's message is decidedly more "liberal" than his more orthodox rivals funded by charities based in the Arab world.

This apparent "tolerant" religious education is part of the well-established Gülen role in thwarting radical Islamic influences around the world (Yavuz and Esposito 2003).

---

[8] For more on Gülen, his mission, and activities see his official website <http://www.fgulen.com/>.

Indeed, throughout Gülen's writings and pronouncements, "Arab" literalism (better known as Wahhabism[9] or Salafism) is not the Islam for the modern era and is openly condemned in his schools. This counterweight to Wahhabi values is clearly playing an important role in how Islam is reintegrated into the lives of Muslims in Albania, as throughout Central Asia and parts of Europe (Yavuz 2012). Specific to Albania, unlike in other parts of the world, Saudi-funded schools have not gained a dominant position in the education of Muslims, a factor largely attributed to the success of these Gülen-inspired schools. As a result of this failure, Arab charities have redirected their money and attention to Kosovo, especially after 1999, leaving Albania to Fetullah Gülen and the "Christians" who include large numbers of Protestant evangelical and Orthodox programs (Blumi 2005).

A crucial agent in this indigenous campaign to thwart "foreign" and "intolerant" interpretations of Islam was the Grand Mufti of Albania, Hafiz Sabri Koçi (1921–2004). Koçi was one of a handful of Albanian Muslim intellectuals who survived the communist era. Born on May 14, 1921, he passed his formative years in the northern Albanian city of Shkodër, once the epicenter of Albanian Islamic and Catholic culture. Too poor to continue his theological studies, he worked as the imam of the village mosque in Drisht and then as Mufti of Kavaja in central Albania. On July 4, 1966, he was arrested and given a prison sentence of 23 years for "threatening" the order of society. His legacy as a prominent theologian was not forgotten, however, and in 1990 his former colleagues and followers sought him out and asked him to return to perform his spiritual duties. From 1990 until his death in 2004 Hafiz Sabri Koçi, as the head of the Muslim Community of Albania, worked to link Albania to the Islamic world. Through his tireless lobbying, he successfully secured financial assistance for the building of religious institutions and the training of religious personnel. Raised in local religious institutions and a strong believer in religious tolerance, it is believed he will have been the last of the Albanian-trained Muftis in Albanian history to practice what many outsiders have called "unorthodox" local forms of Islam.

Albanian Muslims have also contributed to ongoing theological debates among many European Muslim communities. Perhaps the preeminent figure is Nasir al-Din al-Albani (1914–99) whose scholarship and public speeches have been decisive in positioning Albanians in the imaginations of Muslims around the world. Shaykh al-Albani was born in the Northern Albanian city of Shkodër and educated by his father, Al-Hajj Nooh Said Al-Burhani, the premiere Hanifi scholar of Albania at the time. Under persecution of the inter-war ruler of Albania, the family migrated to Syria where Shaykh al-Albani established himself as one of the Islamic world's most important scholars of *fiqh* and *hadith*. Upon moving to Amman, Jordan in the 1970s, al-Albani cultivated his following into a veritable empire of scholarship which was disseminated by affiliated schools in several countries. Until his death, al-Albani attracted students from throughout the

---

[9] So-called after its spiritual leader, Muhammad b. 'Abd al Wahhab (1703–92), who aimed to invigorate Islam by sweeping away corruptive and sinful practices. See Blumi (2005).

Islamic world, including many Albanians from the Balkans. His hundreds of hours of recorded sermons, teachings, and conversations are for sale in every Muslim city of the world today and his dozens of publications are the focus of intense debate among theologians. While his death has probably marked the end of his particular importance in modern Albanian Islam, it does not mean his legacy is in any way erased. Shaykh al-Albani represented a link between the Middle East and the Balkans that has produced a generation of Albanian theologians who may eventually influence the future of Islam in the Balkans. Although today al-Albani is not widely known among Albanian practitioners of Islam in the Balkans, some of his former students are actively engaged in spreading his ideas and teachings.

Similarly, Shuayyib Muharrem Arnauti, (1928–) offers an important theological link between the Arabic-speaking world and current Salafist groups operating inside Albanian communities. Shuayyib, being from a family of Albanian decent learned the foundations of Islam from his father in his birthplace, Damascus. Like Shaykh al-Albani, Shuayyib specialized in *hadith* and sought to bring this form of scholarship to a larger reading public in what were the earliest forms of modern populist Islamic literature (Blumi 2005). In 1955 he started to work as a lecturer of Arabic language and Islamic morality and then became a curator of a prominent library in Damascus. In 1982, like Shaykh al-Albani, he left for Amman and joined the *Risale* foundation as the chief of the cultural section, a position he still holds today. His extensive publications of over 160 volumes containing commentary on *hadith*, *fiqh*, and *tafsir*, have solidified Shuayyib's reputation as one of his generation's greatest theologians. Partly due to their cultural and ethnic affiliation, many students and theologians from the Balkans have come to study under his guidance.

## Albanian Muslim Diversity in Sect and Practice: Yugoslavia as a Whole

In contrast to these politically crucial Muslim community leaders from present-day Albania, other Muslim constituencies—Sufis—have played a largely misunderstood role in Albanian spiritual life because of a lack of such prominent, internationally recognized personalities (Clayer 1990; Blumi 2003b). As discussed further in the Kosovo section, Sufism was long seen by the Slavic Muslim elite based in Yugoslavia's designated Islamic center—Sarajevo—as a theological and political threat. As such, Albanian Muslim traditions were condemned by the state-funded, Sarajevo-based religious authorities (Blumi 2003a; Doja 2000; de Rapper 2008; Morrison 2008; Trix 1995).

A crucial phase of direct hostility from Yugoslavia's religious establishment was when Albanians responded to these attacks from Yugoslavia's state-backed Muslim Orthodoxy with the creation in the 1970s of underground Muslim networks, including an association of Sufi (Dervish) orders (*Bashkësia e Rradhëve Dervishe Islame Alijje*, henceforth BRDIA), which was headed by Shaykh (*Sheh*) Xhemali Shehu of the Rufai *tekke* (lodge) based in Prizren (Blumi 2003b). The BRDIA, vilified by the Sunni Islamic leaders based in Sarajevo, quickly became a cultural force in Kosovo's public life as locals flocked to these Albanian institutions. By 1984, 126 Sufi lodges throughout Kosovo joined the BRDIA, representing 50,000 dervishes, which in 1998 reached a membership of 100,000 (Djurić 1998: 107; Rexhepagiqi 2003).

These numbers give us a sense of the vastness of this phenomenon and the richness of pre-1998–9 Kosovar Islamic life. Crucially, in face of this organizational resistance to formal state efforts to control Albanian religious practice, authorities in Sarajevo, representing the state and Slav Muslims in general, declared as "un-Islamic" the orders that operated in Kosovo until the mid-1990s—the Rufai, Kaderi, Halveti, Sadi, Bektashi, Nakshibendi, Sinani, Mevlevi, and Shazili.[10] This hostility left open the door for full-scale persecution as efforts to suppress Albanian nationalist ambitions fused with direct campaigns at physically eliminating Albanian spiritual autonomy from state influence (Blumi 2003b).

The influence enjoyed by Sufi organizations in rural Kosovo became not only a direct threat to the Muslim hierarchy based in Sarajevo, but by the 1970s, the "un-Islamic" Sufis also threatened the Kosovo-based wing of the Yugoslav Islamic Community. Indeed, throughout the 1970s and 1980s, members of the latter openly accused local Sufi *shaykhs* of "stealing" the faithful away from Sunni orthodox (Albanian-managed) mosques. They eagerly campaigned against these *tekkes* by accusing rural Albanians of "mysticism and primitivism." In many ways, the largely urban Albanian Muslim "establishment" shared first with Yugoslav and later with Serbian state authorities an open hostility towards the Sufi orders' organizing role in rural Kosovar society (Halimi 2000). This role posed a long-term threat to Belgrade's attempts to assert more control over rural Kosovo during the tumultuous 1990s, thereby providing the pretext for a persistent, institutional animosity still evident today in Kosovo (Poulton 1998).

The modern history of Albanians in Yugoslavia, therefore, represents a complicated intersection of state discrimination against certain kinds of Muslims and the specific use of administrative power to reconstitute the distribution of "ethno-national" communities in modern Balkan territories (Clayer 2001; Roux 1992; Norris 1993; Stefanović 2005). While acknowledged in the scholarship generally, the specific traumas experienced by very different Muslim Albanian communities throughout the twentieth century have often been ignored by scholars who focus on "Slavic" Yugoslavia. State policies addressing religious affairs prevented the unification of Yugoslavia's Muslims under one religious authority. Until 1929, all Muslims of Bosnia-Herzegovina and other ex-Habsburg territories were placed under the supreme authority of the office of the *Reis ul-ulema* in Sarajevo, while the supreme Mufti in Belgrade headed the Muslims of Serbia and Montenegro, which had occupied Kosovo since 1912 (Radić 2003: 199). Only in 1930 was a new law on the Islamic Religious Community passed, uniting Muslims in one Independent Islamic Religious Community (*Samostalna Islamska Verska Zajednica*)

---

[10] *Buletin HU* (1978), vol. 2, p. 6. See also Rexhepagiqi (2003).

based in Belgrade. In 1936, as part of the state's concession to Bosnian Muslim leaders, the office of the *Reis ul-ulema* returned to Sarajevo.

State-sponsored attempts to "Slavicize" or deny Albanians influence in the Islamic institutions in Kosovo and Macedonia actually intensified after the creation of socialist Yugoslavia in 1945. The status of the Islamic Community and the *Reis ul-ulema*, which was not functional during the war, was restored in 1947 under the control of Bosnian Muslims willing to collaborate with the new socialist elite in Belgrade. Between 1957 and 1958, the Islamic hierarchy was reorganized, leading to a new form of centralization of religious affairs in Yugoslavia.

Following the fall of communism and the subsequent dissolution of the socialist Yugoslavia in 1992, Albanians in Yugoslavia were divided between two new independent states, Macedonia and the Federal Republic of Yugoslavia, comprising Montenegro and Serbia, which included Kosovo. For Albanians in Kosovo and Macedonia, this new reality also meant communities had to change the way they organized their lives around their religion. Likewise, the dissolution of Yugoslavia meant the end of the dependence on the *Riyaset* (office of the *Reis ul-ulema*) and control from Sarajevo. This newly found independence in terms of religious organization soon led to the emergence of competing factions that distinguished the role of Islam in politics in Kosovo (still occupied by Serbia) from the Republic of Macedonia (G. Krasniqi 2011: 194).

## Albanian Muslims in Kosovo

As in Albania proper, the diversity of religious/spiritual practices in Kosovo complicates otherwise simplistic explanations of Muslim life in this landlocked territory. According to the last census conducted with any accuracy prior to NATO intervention in 1999, Albanians made up 90% of the population in Kosovo, of which 92% were Muslim and 8% Catholic (Roux 1992; Doja 2000; King and Mason 2006).[11] There are smaller communities, such as the Turks, Bosniaks, Roma, Ashkali, Egyptians, and Gorans that form part of the Muslim majority in Kosovo. Much as in Albania proper, Kosovo was once a vibrant spiritual area where a great variety of Sufi orders intermingled with more conventional groups of Muslims linked to communities loyal to one of the four Sunni legal traditions. Indeed, before the wars of 1998–9, many of Kosovo's rural communities practiced forms of Sufism that actively resisted the Sunni orthodoxy imposed from Belgrade through its centralized Islamic authority (*Zajednica*) first established in Sarajevo. This history of resistance resulted in a particularly heavy dosage of violence that exploded

---

[11] A new census was carried out in Kosovo in 2011, but was boycotted by most of the members of the Serb community. According to data from this census, Albanians constitute 92.9 % of the overall population of 1.7 million. As regards religion, Muslims constitute 95.6% of the overall population in Kosovo. See the final results of the 2011 census in Kosovo, available at <http://esk.rks-gov.net/rekos2011/?cid=2,1>.

with the war of 1998–9 in Kosovo, where Serbian forces seemed to target Sufi places of worship and their visitors especially harshly.

This situation has dramatically changed since June of 1999 with the end of the Milošević regime in Kosovo. In the post-war recovery, Arab charity groups not interested in helping rebuild these "unorthodox" practices diverted all their money to establishing mosques and schools that would promote a universalistic rather than a local form of Islam. Much as in Albania, therefore, the future of Kosovo's Sufi heritage is at serious risk because so few people attend their centers any more. In its place has been an aggressive Salafism promoted by wealthy outside donors (Blumi 2005).

The distraction of Kosovo's rural spiritual tradition, far more tolerant of cultural diversity and inter-sectarian cohabitation than the Islam propagated by Saudi-based humanitarian agencies dominating Kosovo's spiritual life today, creates a clear fissure in Kosovar society. In the devastation brought on rural Kosovo by war and post-war economic changes, little has been done by the international community (IC) to address these spiritual voids. Such neglect by those charged by UN resolution 1244 to administer Kosovo has resulted in long-term problems for the region. Instead of disinterested UN agencies providing the necessary support to Kosovo's destitute people, the provision of much-needed aid has been "outsourced" to wealthy Gulf-based charities who have supplied the material needs of Kosovar Albanian's poor. Although no accurate figures are available, it is estimated that Middle Eastern charities have invested some $800 million in Kosovo (Poggioli 2010). On the other hand, the UN administration in Kosovo even praised the work of such organizations in providing relief assistance to people (*Saudi Press Agency* 2004).

Ironically, Rexhep Boja (1946–), the rebellious Mufti of the Islamic Community of Kosovo (*Bashkësia Islame e Kosovës*)—ICK—until being removed in 2003 by a more pliant Naim Tërnava, could have filled the spiritual void.[12] Born in the period immediately following the reassertion of Serbian domination over Kosovo, Rexhep Boja lived very much in conditions of spiritual deprivation and political oppression. Perhaps due to his experience as a student studying in semi-illegality, he left for Medina where he finished his doctorate in 1985 with a dissertation on Islam in Yugoslavia. After receiving his doctorate, he returned to Kosovo to begin teaching Islamic jurisprudence (*fiqh*) at the "Alauddin" school in Prishtina, of which he would become dean in 1992 and later helped administer as appointed Grand Mufti of Kosovo from 1990 to 2003.

His importance for Albanian Islam has been his active struggle to secure autonomy from Serbian control during the 1990s, publishing widely in journals that reached large Muslim audiences and balancing the needs of Arab money with local desires to remain culturally autonomous. He has been very active in promoting religious tolerance and the preservation of locally built mosques. Also he has been decidedly non-antagonistic

---

[12] Boja has remained on the sidelines of Kosovo's spiritual life ever since. Since 2008 he is Kosovo's ambassador to Saudi Arabia. See <http://www.bislame.net>.

and has cooperated with the IC, meeting European officials and visiting clergy from the Vatican.

The problem was that, under the leadership of Boja, representing the last remnants of a once strong, rural-based spiritual infrastructure, the ICK itself had little material resources to rebuild a religious and educational infrastructure. Since the election in 2003 of Tërnava as Mufti, however, the theological/doctrinal battle with Saudi-backed Salafists has practically ended and the ICK seems to be especially well equipped to undermine what is left of Kosovo's Sufi traditions.[13] Instructively, the efficiency with which this flurry of "locally run" programs has gone about filling a void in rural Kosovo (not directly linked to the political machines created since 1999) hints at a sophisticated and global agenda something akin to a multinational cooperation seeking a dominant "market share."

The current tensions within Kosovo's Muslim communities are the direct result of the IC charged with managing post-war Kosovo, permitting Saudi organizations to operate in Kosovo without much supervision. As a result, individuals directly linked to these well-funded (and thus materially generous—with direct cash payments, no-interest loans, and scholarships to study in Saudi Arabia) organizations have been emboldened (or encouraged) to display an open hostility towards Kosovo's religious traditions. In many ways, the current clashes taking place between "bearded Salafists" who publicly flaunt their growing numbers during daily (public) prayers and with the large number of women fully veiled (a practice never seen in Kosovo in the twentieth century) and the traditional "moderate" Albanian Muslims reflect the tensions instigated by the Yugoslav state against Sufis in the 1945–91 period. As during the twentieth century, the struggle today is for control over the formal institutions of the Kosovar Albanian *ulama*, the actual way Islam is practiced as ritual, and how Muslims are allowed to dress.

## Albanian Muslims in Macedonia

Islam in Macedonia, in contrast to Albania and Kosovo, has been politicized since the beginning of the 1990s. Overt nationalist policies have sought to stir up fears among the Christian and non-Albanian population about the "Albanization" of Macedonia through Islam (Gaber 1997). Albanian political leaders representing the main parties as well as the head of the Islamic Community, Sulejman Rexhepi, have constantly denied these accusations (Rexhepi 2002).[14] Despite the realities in local Albanian politics where Rexhepi (and Islam) plays a modest role, the Skopje government has persistently

---

[13] Naim Tërnava, born in 1961 in Fushë Kosovë, finished the "Alauddin" *madrasa* in Prishtina and continued his studies at the "Al-Azhar" University in Cairo. In 2005 he finished his Master studies at the American Open University in Cairo. From 1995 to 2003 Tërnava served as the dean of the "Alauddin" school in Prishtina before being elected as the Grand Mufti of Kosovo, a position he still holds.

[14] Sulejaman Rexhepi was born in 1947 in Skopje. He studied in Prishtina (Kosovo), Sarajevo (Bosnia and Herzegovina), and then in Kuwait. He was one the co-founders of the "Isa Beu" *madrasa* in Skopje, as well as of the Faculty of Islamic Studies in Skopje.

framed the issue to the outside world, in particular since September 11 (9/11), as one in which Macedonia is facing a wave of political Islamic fundamentalism. This suggests that, as was evidenced in Milošević's Yugoslavia, post-war Kosovo, and recently even in Albania, the politicization of Islam does not have to originate from Muslims, but can be—and often is—stirred up by non-Muslim politicians seeking to exploit current perceptions about Islam in the larger world.

Macedonia has a particularly long history of this kind of politics. The post-1991 period was experienced as a time of insecurity both in terms of the Albanian national and religious identity, as both Albanian ethnicity as well as Islam were deemed incompatible with the Macedonian elite's vision for a national Orthodox Macedonian state (G. Krasniqi 2011: 201). The 1991 Macedonian constitution established a privileged position for the ethnic and religious majority (Macedonia was defined as a national state of the Macedonian nation and the constitution makes explicit reference only to the Orthodox Church).

In Macedonia, according to the last population census of 2002 (contested by both the Albanian and Macedonian sides) there were 674,015 Muslims out of a total population of 2,022,547. From those, 509,083 were stated to be ethnic Albanians or roughly 25% of the total population.[15] As in the other two cases where large numbers of Albanian Muslims still reside in the Balkans, relying on disputed census data alone makes it difficult to appreciate the actual significant intra-group distinctions that have often made the experience of being "Muslim" in the Albanian context both tenuous and violent. In the case of Macedonia, ethnic numbers and percentages have been a contentious issue since the country's independence in 1991. Formal requirements for citizenship often change at the discretion of Macedonian Slav authorities aiming to assure the Albanian share of the entire population never reaches levels that could lead to new protections/rights for a segment of society no longer considered "a minority" deserving "tolerance" rather than power (Brown 2006).

For their part, the leaders of the Albanian community in Macedonia have since independence sought to influence future mediations between local interested parties by asserting Albanians actually constitute more than 40% of the population (ICG 1999). Tensions last rose again in 2011, when Macedonia's census was officially stopped after the Balkan country's census law was repealed by its government. This came as a result of increasing tensions between the two major political parties (representing the two main ethnic communities) in the government. In a situation of delicate ethnic balance within this fragile Balkan state, numbers and percentages have direct bearing on the political weight of the different ethnic communities.

It is instructive to note that these tensions over Albanian demographics in Macedonia have mirrored much the same concerns of nationalist Serbian officials in Kosovo throughout the Yugoslav era. In the 1970s and 1980s, the Macedonian authorities launched a number of initiatives to prevent the Muslim community of Macedonia

---

[15] <http://www.stat.gov.mk>.

from becoming what they called "Albanianized" rather than remaining loyal to their "faith" or even the universal Yugoslav identity (Roux 1992). In 1970, for instance, the Association of the Macedonian Muslims was formed with the blessing of authorities in order to effectively split the Muslim community along ethno-national lines (Poulton 1997: 94). By 1981, these efforts to drive a wedge between non-Albanian Muslims and Albanian Muslims took the form of a new bureaucracy which state officials helped establish in Macedonia's third city, Gostivar. In creating this so-called "scientific circle" of different Muslim groups, authorities claimed there was a dire need to study more carefully Muslims in Macedonia as parts of disparate groups. At the same time, once-suppressed religious institutions, such as the "Isa Beu" *madrasa*, was reopened in Skopje in order to expand direct state authority over Muslim affairs in general. In addition, authorities launched a state-funded Muslim newspaper—*El Hilal*—in three languages: Macedonian, Albanian, and Turkish, to expand and complement the ongoing theme of halting Albanian cultural "hegemony" over the faithful (Popović 1990: 25–6).

Of course, as elsewhere in the Balkans, Muslims in Macedonia are not homogeneous in religious terms. The majority of them are Sunni Muslims, belonging to the Hanafiyya school of jurisprudence,[16] but a sizeable minority, of which there are no official numbers, also belong to one of the six Sufi orders still in operation in Macedonia. There are also some Bektashi who further perplex the spiritual environment for Macedonia's Muslims.

Today, the Islamic Religious Community of the Republic of Macedonia (IRC) is the main organization of the Sunnis and is currently led by Haxhi (Hajji) Sulejman Effendi Rexhepi.[17] Thanks to state support, the IRC claims to be the legitimate authority over all Muslims in Macedonia. It has a dervish (*tekke*) section, despite efforts by most Sufi orders to remain independent, constituting an ongoing source of tension. For their part, the Sufi Orders are organized by the Islamic Dervish Religious Community, which was created in 1993 but is not recognized by the state. In practice, the Bektashi Community does not belong to any of those religious organizations, but has an independent status and thus is often the victim of hostility from Sunni imams and followers.

It must be stressed that the officially registered Islamic Religious Community is ruled by a 1994 statute. Unlike in Albania or Kosovo, the Executive Council of the IRC in Macedonia consists of twenty-three members (persons) and works in six main sectors: religious education, science and culture, information and publications, administrative, financial sector, and the sector dealing with the property of pious foundations (*awqaf/ waqf*). It is comprised of all the Muftis, the director of the Islamic High School, the rector of the Islamic Theological Faculty (established in 1997), the director of the humanitarian organization "El Hilal," all the directors of the six sectors mentioned above, the president of the Association of the Imams, and five lay people, who are selected personally by Haxhi (Hajji) Sulejman Effendi Rexhepi, the current *Reis ul-ulema*. Four additional members are the Muftis from the diaspora in Switzerland, Germany, the Scandinavian countries, and the United States.

---

[16] The Hanafiyyah school is one of the four orthodox Sunni schools of law.
[17] <http://www.bim.org.mk/>.

Although the Islamic Religious Community claims to unify all the Muslims in Macedonia, regardless of their ethnic origin or branch of Islam, there are credible claims by non-Albanian Muslims as well as Macedonian politicians that this institution unifies mainly Albanians and much less so people from other ethnic groups due to its political connection to the Albanian Democratic Party (*Partia Demokratike Shqiptare*—PDSH). In fact, a Muslim Albanian has led the Islamic Religious Community since 1994, when the latter became independent from the Islamic Community of Yugoslavia.

However, the ascendant role of Albanians in the organization of religious life of Macedonia's Muslims was challenged in the 1990s with the creation of a separate Muslim Religious Community (MRC), led by former Sarajevo *Reis ul-ulema*, Jakub Selimoski, who was Slav Macedonian.[18] The MRC viewed itself as the rival organization to the Islamic Religious Community (IRC), since the former not only unified the Torbeshi (Slav Macedonian Muslims), Turks, Bosnians, and Roma, but also some Albanians. Despite the financial and political support he received from the state, however, Selimoski eventually gave up on his parallel organization and decided to merge with the Islamic Religious Community in 1994, where he later acted as senior coordinator for religious education.

As a result of the democratization of Macedonia and an increased level of communication and interaction with the outside world, the Islamic Religious Community has recently become an arena of struggle between different interest groups, be it in the form of religious sects or political parties (G. Krasniqi 2011: 202–3). A power struggle seems to have begun within the Islamic Religious Community between the moderate mainstream and the radical (usually referred to as the "Wahhabi") wing. Leaders of the Islamic Religious Community in Macedonia do not deny the presence of the Wahhabis in the country; indeed, according to the more moderate Muslims demonstrating the same kind of concern as their Kosovar neighbors, the Wahhabi sect now "controls" several mosques in Skopje. Several incidents, including physical confrontations, have taken place in different mosques over the last few years, reflecting the contentious process of laying claim to both physical properties in the form of mosques and schools, but also the worshipers who frequent them. Despite the fact that the presence of Wahhabis in Macedonia is undeniable, these claims and counter-accusations might also have political connotations. Major political parties representing Albanians in Macedonia, especially the Democratic Union for Integration (*Bashkimi Demokratik për Integrim*—BDI) and the PDSH have often clashed over the control of religious institutions (Iseni 2007). There is another arena, however, where the tensions within Albanian Muslim communities are playing out, and that is the focus of the next section, one that will try to offer some explanations for some key segments of Albanian Muslim society gravitating towards "foreign" influences linked to Salafism.

---

[18] Jakub Selimoski (1946–2013) was born in Kicevo (Macedonia). He studied in Skopje, Sarajevo, as well as at the Al-Azhar University in Cairo. In March 1991 he was elected head of the united Yugoslav Islamic Community. In the same year, he became the head of the short-lived Islamic Council for Eastern Europe.

# Social Dynamics among Muslim Albanians

Deep and multiple social and political transformations that occurred in the Balkans in the aftermath of the fall of communism have created new social dynamics among Balkan Muslims, including Albanians. Despite the fact that there is an ever increasing number of studies on the transition from communism to democracy and free market economies, as well as on migration, the effects of these multiple transformations on religion and the lives of the Muslims in the region remain uncharted. As will be shown, in the absence of more comprehensive and systematic studies and surveys measuring and depicting social dynamics among Muslim Albanians, the predominant superficial journalistic-type works in the region draw far too much attention to the asserted alarming "radicalization" and "the threat coming from the Middle East." By adopting an essentialist and generalizing approach to presenting Islam, such studies/reports, which dominate local and international media, have contributed to the creation of a simplified and mostly negative tableau of Islam and Muslims in the region. Thus, the root causes of the problem of the nascent radicalization in the region are often ignored.

Thus, in this part of the chapter we discuss some of the social dynamics that delineate the lives of Albanian Muslims in the Balkans today. The first section looks at different forms of religiosity present among Albanians in the Balkans. The second section looks at the presence of different and often opposing religious trends/interpretations. The last section looks at the issue of gender/ethnic/class differences among Albanian Muslims.

## (Re)religionization of the Balkans

The Balkans is known for its plurality of religious traditions, languages, and ethnicities. Decades of wars, conflicts, and migration and attempts by the post-Ottoman (Christian) states to erase the Ottoman legacy and mainstream religions have transformed the landscape of the Balkans and pushed various religious denominations to the verge of extinction. In addition, decades of secularizing policies pursued by socialist Yugoslavia and more so by communist Albania have resulted in a highly secularized population.

Nonetheless, since the early 1990s, the pendulum began to swing in the opposite direction. Faced with serious political crisis, conflict, and almost permanent social and economic insecurity, many individuals in the Balkans' transition societies turned to religion. As a result, the role of religion appears to be growing among Albanians in the Balkans (Figure 11.1). In the case of Albania, the share of people stating that religion played an important part in their lives has risen from 32.5% in 2006 to 48.4% in 2011. In the case of Albanians in Kosovo and Macedonia, the share of people stating that religion plays an important role in their lives is even higher. In the case of the former it varies from 67.9% in 2006, to 89.5% in 2009, and 82.7% in 2011. In the case of Macedonia, in

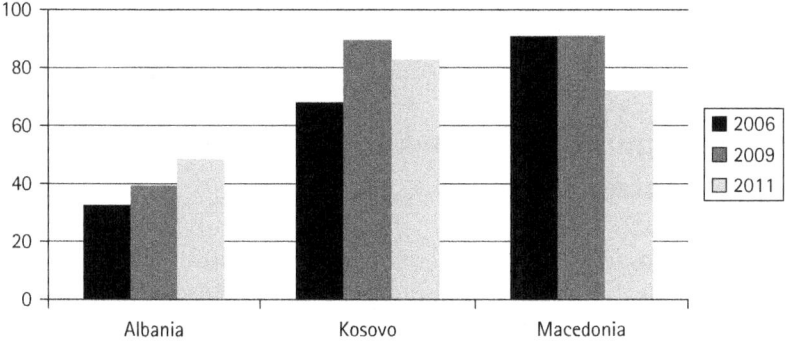

FIGURE 11.1 Importance of religion among Albanians in the Balkans

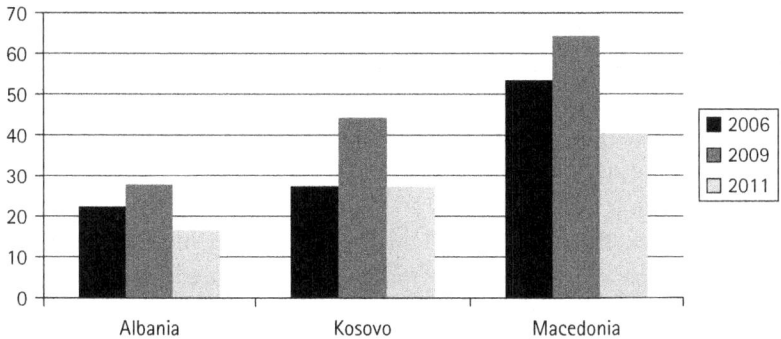

FIGURE 11.2 Attended religious service among Albanians in the Balkans

2006 and 2009 some 91% of Albanians stated that religion was important in their lives, whereas in 2011 the percentage fell to 72.1.

Nonetheless, when it comes to attendance of religious services, percentages are smaller in all the three countries and show tendencies of further decline (Figure 11.2). Again, the share of people who attend religious services in Albania is smaller than the one in Kosovo and Macedonia. In 2011, the share of people in Albania who declared that they attend religious service fell to 16.6% from 27.7% in 2009. Likewise, in the case of Kosovo the percentage fell from 44.2 in 2009 to 27.2 in 2011. Although the share of people among Albanians in Macedonia who attend religious services is the highest among the three, nevertheless it fell from 64.3% in 2009 to 40.4% in 2011.

However, the increased role of religion in public space and the occasional politicization of religion do not always translate into positive public attitudes towards Muslims. Indeed, new opportunities that were created after the fall of communism for many "faith-based" international organizations and agencies to get involved in the process of transforming societies and identities, as well as the new post-9/11 global context, have had direct impact on the way Islam and Muslims are perceived. The general increase of the inter-confessional prejudice in the region in the aftermath of the fall of communism

(Koinova n.d.: 22) was followed by an increase of prejudice towards Islam, especially the new (radical) tradition that is gradually making headway in the region.

## Different Religious Trends and the Root Causes of Albanians' Failure to Confront Salafists

Some Albanians—usually in poor, rural communities—choose to appeal to "Wahhabis" for representation because they see no other viable option.[19] With the dying Sufi orders incapable of attracting younger followers and the large amounts of money available to Salafist groups to spend on any number of projects in the utterly impoverished rural areas of Kosovo, the future of Islam in Kosovo seems one in which the socio-economic gap between rich and poor, rural and urban found in any Third World country will determine the relative success of radical Islamic groups in south-eastern Europe. As argued by scholars studying the post-conflict performance of the United Nation's Mission in Kosovo (UNMIK), policies adopted by the international community have contributed to the marginalization of many of Kosovo's rural poor, a result of political opportunism among cultural or economic elites closely linked to the United States and European Union (EU) (King and Mason 2006; Morrison 2008; V. Krasniqi 2007).

The main local beneficiaries of this UNMIK order, now members of parliament or in government after Kosovo's declaration of independence, have adopted much of the same hostility towards the rural poor in Kosovo as their UNMIK predecessors. Indeed, many have exploited the current sentiment towards the outbreak of "radical Islam" throughout the world to justify partnerships with European and American interests who openly assist in the persecution of opponents who happened to be labeled "Muslim" as well. Ironically, this strategic use of "Islamophobia," similar to that practiced by far-right parties elsewhere in Europe, is creating large sections of Kosovar society who have no means to survive other than accepting relief from the very radical organizations deemed "a threat" among Kosovo's political and cultural elite (Ceka 2006; Puto 2006).

As a result of the radically changed post-9/11 international context, the loyalties of many people being educated in well-funded religious schools and mosques no longer remain in a Kosovo or Albanian context, but are universal in nature (Blumi 2003b). Indeed, similar dynamics are quietly emerging throughout Europe's younger generation of Muslims, now detached from traditional, more tolerant, forms of practice. Such possible resentment had already manifested itself by 2003, articulated by various personalities, such as imam Shefqet Krasniqi.[20] One of his early students initiated perhaps the

---

[19] The majority of Albanian Muslims in Kosovo and Macedonia live in rural areas. For statistics on population in Kosovo and Macedonia see <http://esk.rks-gov.net/rekos2011> and <http://www.stat.gov.mk/Default_en.aspx> respectively.

[20] Shefqet Krasniqi, imam of the Central Mosque in Prishtina and close associate of Mufti Tërnava, is perhaps the most outspoken public religious figure (<http://www.krenaria.com/>). He received a Ph.D. from the Islamic University in Medina in Saudi Arabia. He rose to prominence in Kosovo when he engaged in public debates over the veiling issue and the need to declare Kosovo an Islamic state.

first open debate about what had largely been going on unnoticed in Kosovo among its most directly affected Muslims being trained by Salafists. In 2003, Armend Podvorica, a student at the Faculty of Islamic Studies in Prishtina, in 2003 instigated a public campaign through a series of public letters against the then Grand Mufti of Kosovo, Rexhep Boja, who had been complaining loudly about the growing power of Saudi agencies. Podvorica's public attacks on Boja, in theory his spiritual guide, revealed the underlying tensions that Wahhabi ascendancy in some parts of Kosovo created for the region, at that time still under UNMIK administration. Within the next few years, such open attacks were commonplace; indeed, Boja, who was trying to warn the world of the growing threat of "Salafist extremism" in Kosovo, was formally expelled from his position in 2003 by Tërnava.

Revealingly, in Podvorica's words, Kosovars never learned the "true" Islam. Instead, they inherited the "bastardized" form from Turkey [sic] which "has nothing to do with religion." Podvorica goes on to challenge Rexhep Boja's stated concerns with extremism by qualifying the acts of "these Muslims" (interestingly, implying Boja is not one) who are running schools and "are well respected in Arabia." That "they follow the authentic path" was a crude attempt to assuage any concerns readers of the daily *Koha Ditore* that published Podvorica's letter may have had about the legitimacy of Wahhabi doctrine. As Podvorica's pious Arab Muslims were rhetorically distinguished from what he is clearly identifying as Boja's "bastardized" Islamic tradition, Podvorica exhibits a tell-tale sign of doctrinal rigidity that fails to accommodate the interpretations of other Muslims, let alone talk to them.[21]

Podvorica's letter perfectly highlights the underlying indoctrination and exposure to new and radical interpretations of Islam that were occurring in Kosovo's most impoverished neighborhoods and villages by 2003. Podvorica crudely demarcated a border which separated the faithful and the true followers from those who are not. This method of differentiation quickly became the expected format in which to discuss Islam in Kosovo. Indeed, a number of incidents have occurred in which Wahhabi-trained Albanians have disrupted community meetings by verbally attacking those who did not subscribe to their doctrine. This led to a tacit "mosque war"— i.e. competition between traditional practitioners and imams and Salafi ones over the control of the mosques. For instance, in 2008, Xhabir Hamiti, a professor of Islamic studies in Prishtina and a prominent critic of the Wahhabis, was beaten up by masked men. Similarly, in January 2009, a group of nine Albanians, apparently belonging to a group of followers of the more radical imams, severely beat Imam Osman Musliu while he was entering a mosque in a central Kosovo village.[22] Imam Musliu's crime was that he criticized the head of the Islamic Community of Kosovo, Naim Tërnava, for

---

[21] Armend Podvorica, "Besimi i denjë nuk është ekstremizëm," *Koha Ditore* (January 7, 2003), 11.
[22] United States Department of State, *2009 Report on International Religious Freedom—Kosovo*, October 26, 2009, available at <http://www.unhcr.org/refworld/docid/4ae8612d91.html> [accessed April 10, 2012].

not standing up against Wahhabism and warned the latter would soon take control of more mosques.

Some of the more prominent imams that stand out for their radical interpretation of Islam include Fadil Sogojeva, Dr. Shefqet Krasniqi, and Mazllam Mazllami (Haraqija and Duriqi 2012). Sogojeva has studied at the Al-Imam Muhammad ibn Saud University in Riyadh, Saudi Arabia, and now works as imam of the Ebu Bekr Es-Sidik in Prishtina. As previously mentioned, Dr. Krasniqi studied in Medina and later became a professor at the Islamic Studies Faculty and imam of the Grand Mosque in Prishtina. Imam Mazllami, on the other hand, works in the region of Prizren in southern Kosovo. All these religious figures maintain a regular public presence and make extensive use of social media to convey their message and communicate with their followers and the public in general. In addition to frequent public meetings with their followers, these figures occasionally travel to Western Europe in order to pursue their campaigns among the large Albanian diaspora.

At the other end of the spectrum is a group of self-anointed "traditionalists"[23] such as Xhabir Hamiti, Mullah Osmani, Idriz Bilalli, Lulëzim Esati, Avni Sinani, etc. who openly question the motivations of faith-based charity groups in general and "foreign" religious practices imported to Kosovo in particular (Maxhuni 2012). These antagonist groups, as well as "secularists," have shaped the contours of political debate in Kosovo.[24] The result has been several years of quiet community building, with an occasional outburst of rhetoric that animates anti-"Salafist" sentiments.

While there is a growing sense of organization among such groups, the promotion of what are perceived as "foreign" Islamic practices by a number of vocal, self-declared "secularists" and "traditionalists"—the forced segregation of women from social activities, dress codes, "Islamic" cultural values—is still viewed with mistrust among the vast majority of Albanians in Kosovo and Albania. These kinds of debates have also taken place in other regions of the former Yugoslavia, but with a decidedly different set of motivations behind the polemic, as evident in neighboring Macedonia and Serbia, where ethnic tensions between Albanians and Macedonians and Serbs and Bosniaks respectively have taken an Islamophobic character since the early 1990s. Due to the existing almost clear-cut religious and ethnic differences in these societies, ethnic and social unrest and tensions have led to increasing Islamophobia.

---

[23] They see new and foreign influences as being detrimental to the old and tolerant tradition of Islam once dominant in the region. Some of these regional religious leaders were engaged in forming a separate organization—the Union of Workers of the Islamic Community of Kosovo (*Shoqata Sindikale e Punëtorëve të Bashkësisë Islame të Republikës së Kosovës*) in September 2011. They criticized Naim Tërnava for his links with radical organizations and toleration of foreign influences. See M. Mulaj, "Themelohet Shoqata Sindikale e Punëtorëve të Bashkësisë Islame," *Kosovapress*, September 6, 2011, available at <http://kosovapress.com/?cid=1,26,134609> [accessed September 10, 2012].

[24] A growing number of politicians, MPs, and women's rights activists openly criticize the "foreign" Islamic practices applied in Kosovo.

## Religion and Gender/Ethnic/Class Differences

One thing that surfaces after reviewing the underlying tensions within and between distinct Muslim communities is that local social dynamics in many ways mirror the Muslim experience in Europe. This is especially true for Muslim women (V. Krasniqi 2007). Women have traditionally played a prominent role in urban Albanian history while having long been subordinate to men socially and economically in rural areas. Much has changed in all three Albanian societies in the twentieth century as extensive migration pressures, war, and state policies to integrate women into the workforce altered the "traditional" role of Albanian women living in towns. Urban women are generally well integrated into the secular educational system, seek employment, and live lives much like their Western European counterparts. In contrast, women and children in rural areas in particular are vulnerable to rural poverty, trauma, and a lack of a stable household as mothers struggle to make ends meet, often without a husband. As noted earlier, the plight of rural Kosovo after the war has been something Western international aid agencies have, in particular, neglected to address. In their absence, Islamic relief groups supported by the Saudi government have taken over the responsibility for the education of rural children (albeit entirely religious in content) and for their nourishment and are seen as trustworthy providers among the population. This is especially crucial for rural widows who seem to have little political support from the major parties.

In all three areas where Albanian Muslims predominate, women are in theory legally protected from discrimination by the state but culturally they are often marginal in their male-dominated communities. This is particularly true of rural areas, a situation which today is being reinforced by a growing bifurcation between rural and urban women as the segregationist ideologies of Saudi-based funding agencies in rural Kosovo pursue conservative agendas that limit women's access to the outside world. This explains the growing number of women who wear hijab or, on some rare occasions, niqab. In addition, followers of some of the indigenous Salafi groups demanded education reform in Kosovo's secular schools. These groups have expressed opposition, for example, to the teaching of human biology in public meetings throughout the country as inappropriate for young girls and young boys who are still seated together in the classroom. In this respect, calls for the segregation of the classroom by sex and the required teaching of religious texts tie into concerns about "immoral" influences. So far, there has been little public support for these initiatives. Many of these debates take place increasingly in blogs and other social media such as Facebook, replacing what were, until the early 2000s, the normal methods of community building: the printed journal/newspaper/magazine. Social media such as internet forums and Facebook have become an invaluable tool in the hands of religious organizations and local imams in their attempt to raise awareness of what they consider are proper religious practices (Haraqija and Duriqi 2012).

Education, therefore, is an area of great concern for Albanians eager to exclude Arab Salafi influences. Indigenous Muslim pedagogical traditions still exist but are based mostly in the region's larger towns. In Kosovo, the ICK has organized the "Alauddin" *madrasa* since the 1960s in Kosovo's capital city, Prishtina. However, there is little incentive for local children to attend this school as there are many more attractive options, such as studying in a Gulf country. Alauddin, therefore, draws most of its students from the rural migrant families who have little or no money to support their children's education. This leads to a constant money shortage as traditional donors like Saudi Arabia and other Gulf Arab states are clearly directing their resources towards their own schools based in rural areas, far away from the influence and the inspection of Kosovo authorities.

In Macedonia, the previously mentioned "Isa Beu" *madrasa* network is at present the only secondary school providing Islamic religious instruction. It operates under the organizational structure of the Islamic Community set up in Macedonia and it has successfully kept Arab Islamic influences at arm's length. Instead, the school offers a more indigenous approach to the study of Islam, with far more openness to allowing outside influences to shape the way Muslims understand religion and engage in religious practice. The reason for girls' studying at home is a continued belief that girls should be separated from boys, an indication that Albanians in Macedonia live up to their reputation as being the most conservative of the three Albanian societies in the region.

Ten *madrasas* were opened in the main cities of Albania within three years of the fall of the communist regime. As of 2000, 1,504 students attended these schools, out of which 148 are girls.[25] The reason for the small number of girls may attest to the fact that families in Albania prefer their girls to attend the under-funded state schools, or if they are lucky enough, to send their children to the Turkish Mehmet Akif schools on scholarship. Female students are particularly keen on attending these schools as they usually facilitate subsequent entrance into secular Turkish universities and do not impose the rigid gender segregation demanded by the more orthodox *madrasas*.

# Religion in Public Space

Throughout the modern history of Albania and the former Yugoslavia where the majority of Albanian Muslims lived, Islam as a doctrine of political activism has never played a major role. This is in spite of clear trends towards mobilizing religion in the Balkans in the service of realizing political ends (Babuna 2004). As a result of this, but also reflecting states' attempts to underplay the role of religion, especially under communism, scholars have neglected to study the presence of Islam in public spaces and society at large. With the exception of some studies on the position and rights of the Albanian minority in inter-war Yugoslavia (see the historic section), the relationship between Islam, Albanians, and the state, both in Albania and Yugoslavia, has been mostly neglected or touched upon only briefly in those studies focusing in inter-ethnic relations in Yugoslavia. As a result of the "resurgence" of Islam in the aftermath of the fall of communism and the creation of new states in the territory of Yugoslavia, the region is

---

[25] Information tabulated from materials available at the Islamic Community Union located in Tirana.

experiencing an ever increasing presence of Islam in public spaces. Hence the increase in scholarly attention on the role of religion in general and Islam in particular in public space and society (Gaber 1996; Doja 2000; Babuna 2000; Gjuraj 2000; Alibašić 2010; G. Krasniqi 2011; Öktem 2011).

What many scholars argue is that throughout the struggle against anti-Albanian nationalism in Kosovo and Macedonia, Albanians never reverted to using their sectarian identity to challenge totalitarian rule. Scholars have long made this assertion because of the assumption that Albanians of Orthodox, Catholic, and Muslim faith were collectively being victimized and that their ethnic loyalties superseded their religious (Duijzings 2000: 153–61; Young 1999: 5–14). This assumption did not change substantially even after the fall of communism in Europe and the consequent reemergence of religion as an important personal signifier and identity marker. This is in contrast to other predominantly Christian states such as Greece, Croatia, and Serbia where religion and nationalist sentiment were utilized by different national elites to shape and reshape national and state identities in order to suit their interests.

## Legal and Institutional Status of Islam

As regards formal legal status, Albania, Kosovo, and Macedonia constitutionally are defined as secular states whose laws are neutral in matters of religious beliefs. Likewise, these states' constitutions guarantee freedom of belief, conscience, and religion, including the right to accept and manifest religion, the right to express personal beliefs, and the right to accept or refuse membership in a religious community or group. These provisions guarantee an equal position for Muslims in these states and societies, at least in principle. However, the treatment of Islam and Muslims within these polities is contingent on state policies as well as inter-ethnic, intra-ethnic, and religious power dynamics.

In the case of Albania, according to the constitution, there is no official religion in the country and the state is neutral in questions of belief and conscience; it also guarantees the freedom of their expression in public life. According to the law, the state recognizes the equality of religious communities and relations between the state and religious communities are regulated on the basis of agreements entered into between their representatives and the Council of Ministers and ratified by the Assembly. The Albanian government signed such agreements with the main religious communities: the Roman Catholic Church (in 2002), the Muslim Community of Albania (2008), the Orthodox Church of Albania (2008), the Bektashi community (2008), and more recently (2010) with the Evangelical Brotherhood of Albania (VUSH), a Protestant umbrella organization (Bureau of Democracy, Human Rights and Labor 2011a: 2).

Although the government does not require registration or licensing of religious groups—religious movements may acquire the official status of a juridical person by registering with the Tirana District Court under the Law on Nonprofit Organizations—the State Committee on Cults, under the jurisdiction of the Ministry of Tourism, Culture,

Youth, and Sports, is charged with regulating relations between the government and religious communities. Religious communities are juridical persons. They have independence in the administration of their properties according to their principles, rules, and canons.

When it comes to the issue of education, public schools are secular and the law prohibits ideological and religious indoctrination. Religion is not taught in public schools. However, religious communities may establish their schools or educational institutions, which should be licensed by the Ministry of Education of Albania. According to official figures, religious communities, including the MCA and the Bektashi Community, organizations, and foundations had 135 affiliated associations and foundations managing 102 educational institutions (Bureau of Democracy, Human Rights and Labor 2011a: 3). Apart from the numerous Islamic schools and training centers for imams administered by the Albanian Muslim Community (MCA), a new Theological Islamic University was established in Tirana in 2011.

The constitution of the Republic of Kosovo guarantees freedom of belief, conscience, and religion, including the right to accept and manifest religion, the right to express personal beliefs, and the right to accept or refuse membership in a religious community or group. The state also ensures and protects religious autonomy and religious monuments within its territory. Religious denominations are free to independently regulate their internal organization, religious activities, and religious ceremonies, as well as to establish religious schools and charity institutions in accordance with this constitution and the law.

Nonetheless, Kosovo still does not have a legal mechanism to register religious groups thus creating a number of practical challenges for religious groups in Kosovo in owning and registering property and vehicles, opening bank accounts, and paying taxes on employees' salaries (Bureau of Democracy, Human Rights and Labor 2011b: 2). This fact, together with the specific status of the Orthodox Church of Serbia in Kosovo (which does not recognize the state of Kosovo), have created a particular situation where religious groups act unhindered and unregulated by the law.

The field of religious education remains unregulated by the law as well. Nonetheless, various religious communities organize their religious schools. Apart from the regular Friday sermons organized in mosques around Kosovo, ICK managed the religious high school "Alauddin" *madrasa* (established in 1949) based in Prishtina but with branches in other major cities as well. Its curriculum is a mixture of religious and non-religious subjects. Up to 2009 some 1,100 students had graduated from that school (Hamiti 2009: 235). ICK also runs the Faculty of Islamic Studies in Prishtina. This faculty attracts students from Kosovo but also Albanian students from Albania, Macedonia, Serbia, Montenegro, etc. Some 118 students, of whom 20% are female, have graduated from this faculty since its establishment in 1992 (Hamiti 2009: 237).

Despite the fact that the legal status of religious communities is not yet regulated properly, graduates' diplomas were accepted and recognized by the Ministry of the Education of Kosovo, but the faculty is currently experiencing some problems with accreditation (Alibašić 2010: 626). In terms of the curriculum, with the exception of Arabic language and a couple of Islamic philosophy courses, only courses in the traditional Islamic disciplines of Qur'an recitation, *tafsir, hadith, 'aqida*, Islamic jurisprudence, etc., are offered at this faculty in Prishtina, thus making it the least open to non-religious courses of all the Islamic faculties in the Balkans (Alibašić 2010: 625).

In Macedonia, likewise, the state is secular and guarantees freedom of religion and religious organization. Although there is no official religion in Macedonia, the Macedonian constitution (amended in 2001) specifically lists five religious groups: the Macedonian Orthodox Church, the Islamic Religious Community of Macedonia, the Roman Catholic Church, the Jewish Community, and the Evangelical Methodist Church.

The law requires religious groups to register in order to acquire status as legal entities. The law provides detailed information about the materials for new registrants and a timeline in which the court must issue its rulings and also requires that the registered leaders of religious groups be Macedonian citizens (Bureau of Democracy, Human Rights and Labor 2011c: 3). Although the law is quite detailed, the Bektashi Community of Macedonia (Tetovo), an Islamic Sufi order that is involved in a long-running property dispute with the IRC, and which continues to occupy the Bektashi compound in Tetovo thus limiting Bektashis' ability to worship, has been unable to register (Bureau of Democracy, Human Rights and Labor 2011c: 3).

Private religious primary schools are not allowed under the law, but there are no restrictions on private religious schools at the secondary level and above, or on religious education that takes place in religious spaces. IRC manages the religious high school "Isa Beu" based in Skopje but with branches in other towns in Macedonia, as well as the Faculty of Islamic Studies, established in 1997. According to data from IRC's official website, from 1984 to 2011 some 1,850 pupils graduated from the "Isa Beu" *madrasa* and in the academic year 2011/2012 the school enrolled some 750 full-time and 300 part-time pupils.[26] In comparison, 130 students have graduated from the Faculty of Islamic Studies so far and at present there are 230 students enrolled. Following a decision by Ministry of Education and Science of Macedonia, from 2010, Isa Beu *madrasa* would become a publicly funded school operating under the ministry's supervision, a move that entailed changes in the curriculum, including the introduction of a large number of non-religious courses (Alibašić 2010: 626).

In all three countries there is a serious problem related to the restitution of religious properties expropriated by the former socialist and communist government in Yugoslavia and Albania. While ownership of religious objects has been restored to the appropriate religious communities, most other properties, such as land and *waqf*-s, have not. Moreover, central government and local authorities are often selective when it comes to granting permission to religious communities to erect objects of worship.

Finally, regarding shariah, the religious law of Islam, none of the countries provide for partial or full implementation of it. Albania, Kosovo, and Macedonia are organized

---

[26] <http://www.bim.org.mk/bimbroshur.pdf>.

on the principles of civil law and their constitutions do not allow existence of any sort of religious-based courts. Indeed, no such requests have been put forward by local Muslims or official religious organizations in these countries.

## The Role of Religion in Society

In the case of Albania, religion in general and Islam in particular did not occupy a prominent position in the public sphere and political life. Even prior to all religion being banned in 1967, a thoroughly secular set of institutions was developed since the 1920s. Although culturally marginalized as a result of the hostile attitude of the communist regime towards religion, Albania's religious plurality and a sense of inter-sectarian tolerance and unity were mostly preserved. While today this inter-sectarian sense of unity exists, the most important reason for a lack of outright sectarianism (such as in the form of religious parties) in Albanian political life is the fact that such parties are legally banned. However, in the early 1990s, exponents close to President Sali Bershia and the Democratic Party, such as Abdi Baleta[27] and Bashkim Gazidede,[28] were proponents of the idea that Albania should take its place in the great family of Islamic nations and states (Misha 2008: 146–7). Albania's membership at the Organization of the Islamic Conference (OIC) is an expression of such a vision.

Nonetheless, since the fall of communism in Albania, religion has never become a contentious issue in everyday politics and public life. Regardless of the state's secularism and non-interference in the organization of religious life in Albania, deep transformations in the constitution of the population caused by almost half a century of orthodox communist rule and successive waves of emigration have hampered a faster recovery of religious communities and life, including the organization of Muslims. In the case of the Muslim Community of Albania (MCA), restitution of land and property seized by the state during communism remains one of the main challenges. A case in point is the prolongation of the decision to provide the MCA with land to build a mosque in the centre of Tirana. Despite continual promises by both political camps in the local and central institutions of governance, the issue is yet to be resolved.

In the case of Kosovo, even during the period under direct Serbian rule and oppression, religion did not play a major role in public space. As a declared socialist state, religion was relegated to a personal issue with state laws and educational policies aggressively avoiding reference to religion. In fact, throughout the 1990s, religious identity and institutions were never utilized by political leaders to achieve political and national cohesion. Although the ethnic and linguistic commonalities that bound Albanians together, as well as the threat coming from the Serb state, helped to supersede religious

---

[27] Abdi Baleta is a former diplomat and publicist from Albania.
[28] Bashkim Gazidede directed the National Intelligence Service (SHIK) during the rule of Sali Berisha (1992–7).

differences between Catholic and Muslim Albanians, no Kosovar Albanian political party or association of any importance rallied around Islamic symbols, let alone a language of Islamic fundamentalism in opposition to the Serbian regime. Nonetheless, religious motives—in this case Muslim ones—did play a role in defining and constructing the self-image of many Albanians in opposition to the Serbian (Orthodox) "Other" (G. Krasniqi 2011: 196).

However, in the aftermath of the 1999 war, ICK made various attempts to increase its role in social and political life. One of the ways to increase the presence of Islam in post-1999 public space and social life was through the revitalization and extension of its network of mosques and other religious organizations. The last war in Kosovo left approximately 200 (of the more than 600) mosques damaged or destroyed along with other Sufi lodges and Islamic schools (*madrasas*), archives, and libraries (Herscher 2006: 41). Since 1999, the Islamic Community of Kosovo, through various funding channels, has been reconstructing 113 war-damaged mosques and building 175 new ones.[29] An investigation by *Balkan Insight* reveals that almost all have been erected illegally. Most of these mosques, especially the ones in rural areas, have been built without any permission from local authorities.

Undoubtedly, this increased the presence of Islamic symbols in the public space in Kosovo. But debates about mosques did not take centre stage until 2011 when various Muslim organizations, with tacit support from the Islamic Community, stepped up street protests demanding a location for a new city-center mosque. For many years now, various organizations of Muslims have been asking for a location and permission to build a new mosque in the center of Prishtina, opposite the newly erected Albanian Catholic Cathedral named after Mother Teresa.[30] While denying accusations that the protest was against the cathedral, the organizers of the protest, a newly created movement called *Bashkohu* (Unite),[31] complained that Catholics, though a small minority in Kosovo, are more privileged than the majority Muslims when it comes to obtaining permits for places of worship.[32] Finally, in late 2012, ICK and the Municipality of Prishtina reached an agreement to build the new mosque in the location proposed by the latter.

This is not the only example of mobilization of Kosovo's Muslims against what they consider discrimination from the state. Similar protests, attracting considerable

---

[29] Besiana Xharra, "Kosovo Turns Blind Eye to Illegal Mosques," *Balkan Insight* (January 12, 2013). <http://www.balkaninsight.com/en/article/kosovo-turns-blind-eye-to-illegal-mosques> [accessed January 15, 2013].

[30] The idea to build a cathedral emerged more from political than religious needs as it is interpreted as an example of the pro-Western orientation of the (Muslim) majority and inter-religious tolerance of Albanians.

[31] *Bashkohu* was created in 2010 and it advocates a more prominent role of Islam in Kosovar state and society. So far it has staged protests to demand the building of a grand mosque in Prishtina, introduce religious education in schools and allow women to wear headscarf in school. In early 2013 it announced the creation of an Islamic party. See <http://www.bashkohumene.org>.

[32] Petrit Çollaku, "Kosovo Muslims Step Up Mosque Protests," *BalakanInsight* (June 30, 2011). <http://www.balkaninsight.com/en/article/muslim-community-demand-for-new-mosque-in-pristina-centre> [accedded December 15, 2011].

media attention both locally and internationally, were organized in 2010 against an Administrative Instruction (No. 6/2010) adopted by the Ministry of Education which introduced a ban on headscarves in public elementary and secondary schools. The issue of the headscarf (hijab), which, together with requests to introduce religious education in public schools, caused considerable debate in Kosovo; thanks to the presence (for the first time) of the only political party that is often identified as an Islamic leaning party—the Party of Justice (*Partia e Drejtësisë*—PD).[33] Supported by 27 MPs from both the ruling coalition and opposition parties, the Party of Justice initiated changes in the "Law on Pre-University Education" in Kosovo that would allow the use of the headscarf and the introduction of religious education in public schools. Amid heated debates in the parliament and press,[34] the Assembly of Kosovo voted in August 2011 not to permit the Islamic headscarf (hijab) or any religious instruction in public schools.[35] The parliamentary and public debate on these issues was framed as a choice between "the past" and "the future." Likewise, both camps invoked human rights and non-discrimination laws in support of their position (Schwartz 2011).

These debates, as well as the attitude of the Albanian politicians in Kosovo, are symptoms of growing tensions between a rather conjectural tendency of "self-negation" (to convince Europeans that Albanians are not really Muslims) and the increasing role of Islam in Kosovar society and politics (G. Krasniqi 2011: 199). Kosovo's political leaders have often gone too far in suppressing and undermining the Islamic layer of Albanian identity. Surveys show that 8% of people point to Islam as the religion discriminated against (Centre for Humanist Studies "Gani Bobi" 2011).

In Macedonia, like in other Orthodox-majority states in the region, religion came to play a decisive role in the definition of modern national identity. Likewise, in the aftermath of the fall of communism, religion experienced a revival and the Macedonian Orthodox Church occupied a more prominent role in the public sphere (Babuna 2000; G. Krasniqi 2011). Especially under the right-wing government in Skopje, the Orthodox Church of Macedonia received very privileged treatment, reminiscent of the alliances between "the altar and the throne." In a situation of an almost clear-cut religious, ethnic, and linguistic distinction and delicate balance between the Slav Macedonians and ethnic Albanians, this increased presence of Orthodox religious symbols in public life in Macedonia mobilized the Muslim Community, which demanded equal treatment. After the 2001 conflict, under the Ohrid Framework Agreement and the subsequent constitutional changes[36] that improved the position of Albanians within Macedonia, the Islamic Religious Community received explicit constitutional recognition by being mentioned

---

[33] See its official site: <http://www.drejtesia.org/>.

[34] Nebih Maxhuni, "Ligji i debateve," *Gazeta Express* (August 29, 2011), 8–9.

[35] See the transcript from the plenary session of the Kosovo Assembly on August 29, 2011, available at <http://www.assembly-kosova.org/?cid=1,177,3643>.

[36] This agreement was signed in 2001 after months of sporadic fighting between Albanian rebels and the Macedonian army and police, which claimed hundreds of lives. It paved the way for major political reforms that improved the rights of the Albanian minority in Macedonia.

alongside the Orthodox Church in article 19 of the new constitution as one of the country's religious communities.

In situations where religious communities act as organized structures of respective ethnic groups, the erection of various religious objects and symbols has become a way of ethno-religious demarcation in Macedonia. A case in point is the ongoing debate on the urban revitalization project "Skopje 2014," which foresees the erection of a series of historical monuments in the city center, together with a new church. Initiated by the right-wing party VMRO, the aim of this project is to erect as many monuments as possible to prove the Macedonian and Orthodox character of the capital city. This project, as well as the previous project to erect a 66-meter cross, known as the "Millennium Cross," on the top of Skopje's surrounding mountains, overlooking the city, has outraged Albanians who see it as an attempt by Orthodox Macedonians to symbolically appropriate the landscape and territory. This process of "religionization" of landscape through the erection of symbols sustains the argument that the main struggle in Macedonia is between Christianity and Islam (Robelli 2011: 152). Thus, Albanian NGOs (such as "Zgjohu" [Wake Up], "Illiricum Libertas," etc.) and the Islamic Religious Community have reacted by demanding permission to rebuild an old mosque in the city center, which had been destroyed decades before by the Kingdom of Yugoslavia (before the Second World War).

Indeed, religious symbols and objects in Macedonia serve as "proxies" in the political and national battle between Macedonians and Albanians for the control of territory and state institutions. In a situation where the contested nation-building of the Macedonian majority is deeply intertwined with the reemergence of Orthodoxy as an important pillar of identity in Macedonia, various requests coming from Macedonia's Albanians, deemed to be national in their essence, often assume religious connotations.

Despite animosities and competition, the Orthodox Church and the Religious Islamic Community in Macedonia were successful in pushing for the introduction of religious education in elementary schools. The 2008 decision of the Macedonian government to introduce religious education as an elective subject provided both these organizations with opportunities to provide instructors for classes on Islam and Christianity. Some opposition parties and civil society groups challenged the decision and took the decision to the constitutional court of Macedonia, which repealed article 26 of the Law on Primary Education that allowed religious education for different religious groups.[37]

The increased presence of Islam in public space in Macedonia is mostly due to a specific political and constitutional system of power-sharing that enables Albanian Muslims to demand the same treatment as the majority Orthodox population. Thus, paradoxically, the enhanced role of the Orthodox Church in Macedonia and its attempts, mostly supported by the state, to increase social role of Christian Orthodox religion in the Macedonian society has provided a leeway for the Islamic Religious Community to do the same.

---

[37] See decision 202/2008 of the Constitutional Court of the Republic of Macedonia, dated April 15, 2009.

As regards religious promotion and propaganda, apart from the official journals published by the official religious institutions, in recent years there has been a mushrooming of religious publishers. Publishers such as "Logos-A" (Skopje), "Furkan ISM" (Skopje), "Lib-Art" (Prishtina), "Progresi Botime" (Tirana), etc., have been very productive in translating foreign religious scholars into Albanian and publishing other religious books and journals. Profiting from the almost completely unregulated and uncontrolled publication sphere in the region, as well as from foreign donations, these new publishers have created a very effective circulation network, thus increasing the presence of religious-themed publications in local bookshops and book fairs.

Likewise, proponents of an "Islamic revival" among Albanians have managed to establish a TV channel dedicated to Islam and religious education. Coordinated by the Kosovar "Center for Islamic Studies,"[38] Peace TV, an enterprise directed from India, Saudi Arabia, and Dubai by a hardline Islamist preacher, Zakir Naik, has established a 12-hour daily program in Kosovo. It also includes interviews in the Albanian language with Kosovo Muslim figures under the influence of Wahhabism. As argued by Al-Alawi, the entry into Kosovo of Naik's Peace TV, known for its hardline interpretations of Islam and insults directed at spiritual Sufis, Shi'a Muslims, non-fundamentalist Sunnis, Jews, Christians, and Hindus, represents an additional tool in a novel campaign by South Asian Islamists backed by Saudi money to establish a foothold among Europe's indigenous Balkan Muslims.[39]

In short, Islam, together with other religions in the region, has resurged in public space in the Balkans in the aftermath of the fall of communism. As a result, religious objects, mostly funded with money from foreign religious organizations and networks, have mushroomed in recent years, transforming an urban and rural landscape which once was dominated by its old Ottoman stone mosques. On the other hand, new opportunities offered by internet, social media and digital TV platforms have been utilized by radical Islamist interlopers and their financiers, mainly from Saudi Arabia and other Gulf states, in order to "awaken" Balkan Muslims and "connect" them to a larger world community of Muslims.

# INTERNATIONAL CONSTRAINTS AND ISLAMOPHOBIA

Since 9/11, there has been a tendency by local commentators to see social, political, and cultural and religious cleavages and tensions in the region through the ideological lens

---

[38] This centre appears to exist only online and via television. For more see <http://www.qsi-ks.com/webi/index.php>.

[39] Irfan Al-Alawi, "Extremists Establish Foothold in the Balkans," *Gatestone Institute* (September 24, 2012). <http://www.gatestoneinstitute.org/3360/kosovo-peace-tv> [accessed January 15, 2013].

of the "clash of civilizations" (where Islam is indiscriminately portrayed as foreign and primitive). This often results in assertions that Islam's "incompatibility" with democracy and modern European and Western values can in part account for the tensions in these post-socialist societies. Linked to this is the renewed interest in the role of Islam in the formation of the modern Albanian national and political identity and its position vis-à-vis Europe. Study has also begun to focus on the increasing public hostility towards Islamic institutions amounting to populist forms of Islamophobia. Whereas the relationship between Islam and the Albanian nation and state(s) attracts wide academic interest, the issue of Islamophobia remains largely neglected by scholars from different disciplines. In contrast, the issue of Islamophobia has constantly remained high on the agenda of the local media.

The increased presence of many "faith-based" international organizations which engaged in the process of transforming societies and identities after the fall of communism and the post-9/11 context has reactivated the debate on the issue of Albanian identity and belonging. There is a tendency among some Albanian intellectual and political circles to view the past (under the Ottoman Empire) and the present religious composition of the population as incompatible with the EU and "Western civilization" in general. This is best exhibited in the public hostility towards Islamic institutions in Albania today. It is, for example, quite acceptable today among non-Muslims and southern Albanians in particular to claim that its 500-year relationship with Islam is a by-product of "foreign" invasion (i.e. Ottoman) and should be abandoned (de Rapper 2008; Kadare 2006; Lubonja 2004; Poulton 1997; Brisku 2006; Welton and Brisku 2007; Sulstarova 2007). This sentiment is articulated by Albanian academics with links to the old communist regime and the famous author Ismail Kadare in particular (Jazexhi 2007; Brisku 2006; Kostovicova and Prestreshi 2003; Öktem 2011; G. Krasniqi 2011; Qosja 2006; Doja 2003). Indeed, since 1997, the ruling "Socialist Party" has been particularly eager to stress Albania's non-Islamic identity (Gjuraj 2000).

Albanian elites and populations in Albania, Kosovo, and Macedonia are among the most pro-European and pro-American residents of the region.[40] This vision seems to be supported by central religious organizations as well. Islamic actors in Albania such as MCA publicly endorse democracy and European integration in their statements, seeing it as the best "shield" against past repression as well as a survival strategy in the dominant anti-Islamic atmosphere that has characterized post-communist transition (Elbasani and Saatçioglu 2011). Likewise, a recent survey conducted in Kosovo suggests that some 91.5% of the people in Kosovo support Kosovo's pro-Western orientation and

---

[40] According to the data assembled by Gallup Balkan Monitor, Albanians in Kosovo, Macedonia, and Albania show the highest support for the US leadership. In 2012, the support for the US among Albanians in Kosovo was 92.2%, in Albania 80.2%, and among those in Macedonia 55.5%. Likewise, Albanians in the Balkans show the highest level of support for the EU membership of their respective countries. Data from 2011 reveal that support for EU integration among Albanians in Kosovo is 95.4%, in Macedonia 72.3%, and in Albania 87.1%. Source: Gallup Balkan Monitor. Survey data available at: <http://www.balkan-monitor.eu/index.php/dashboard>.

exclude other cultural and ideological alternatives; only 1.8% think that religion and Islam are the only values to be followed (Center for Humanist Studies "Gani Bobi" 2011).

Nonetheless, the predominance of secular-minded political elites among Albanians combined with the ever-increasing "anti-Islamic" discourse in Europe, have had a noticeable impact on the way Muslims are perceived by local people, both Albanians and the others, in the region. Thus, the increase in the number of mosques built with international Islamic organizational money is seen by Albanian politicians and people as detrimental to the vision of a modern Albanian identity that is above all "European" and "Western." Consequently, any acts of implicit or explicit expression of Islamic leaning, especially that influenced by external radical networks or movements from the Gulf region, is perceived by Albanian media, intellectuals, and many other people as a direct attack on this pro-European and pro-Western political vision promoted by elites. Even isolated cases, such as that of a radicalized 21-year-old of Kosovo-Albanian origin living in Germany, Arid Ukaj, who in March 2011 opened fire on a busload of American troops at Frankfurt airport, killing two and severely wounding another pair, suffice to renew debates on potential links between Albanian Muslims, radical Islam, and terrorism.[41] The survey conducted by the Center for Humanist Studies "Gani Bobi" (2011) reveals that 40% of people in Kosovo are of the opinion that radical Islam is gaining strength in Kosovo, while 24.3% see it as a threat to Kosovar society and its pro-Western orientation.

In Macedonia, with the global effect of the 9/11 bombings, religion would eventually become the key criterion of distinction among Macedonia's population. In other words, for many nationalistic Macedonian politicians, the religious belonging of Albanians (Muslim) provided legitimate grounds for discrimination. In line with this logic, various Macedonian politicians sought to capitalize on the "war on terror" and thereby strengthen their position vis-à-vis Albanians by trying to give a religious connotation to the Albanian demands for more rights and equality within the state. The state and security apparatus has appropriated "anti-terrorism" discourse in order to portray the mostly Muslim Albanians as suspicious. Evocative of Samuel Huntington's concept of the "clash of civilizations," nationalist Macedonian circles tend to draw a line of essential difference between the "right side" and the "wrong side," with the Albanians occupying the latter (G. Krasniqi 2011: 202; Robelli 2011: 152).

In the modern history of Albanians, religion was an important element of their identity but mostly it was kept separate from national identity. In many respects, their nationhood superseded their religious identities. This is why they hardly ever felt part of a broader Muslim transnational community of believers (*umma*). The traditional form of Islam practiced by Albanians provided enough room for religious tolerance and coexistence. The majority of religious leaders as well as people still seem to favor the

---

[41] The Kosovar institutions and printed media described the attack as "shameful", which will damage the image of Albanians. See "The Frankfurt shootings: the Kosovo connection," *The Economist* (March 3, 2011). <http://www.economist.com/blogs/newsbook/2011/03/frankfurt_shootings> [accessed December 20, 2011].

traditional form of practicing Islam.⁴² However, different state experiences, as well as different socio-political contexts, have left their scars in the three major Albanian milieux in the Balkans. In addition, attempts by various radical transnational networks to "re-Islamize" Albanians expose these societies to new and mostly radical forms of Islam, thus risking instilling radical ideas among the new generations of Muslim Albanians.

Decades of foreign influence and tireless underground work have allowed religious extremists to establish a foothold in the Balkans while growing with the cooperation of international radical networks. These groups have produced an army of young people with a proven readiness to join the international cause of "Islam." As earlier in Libya and Iraq, once the conflict in Syria erupted, local radical leaders mobilized hundreds of Albanians to join the anti-Assad oppositions, in particular the Jabhat al-Nusra and the Islamic State of Iraq and al-Sham (ISIS)—the two militant groups that are sometimes linked to Al-Qaeda (Zelin 2013). The growing number of Albanian "jihadists" contributing to this campaign against the Assad regime has led to a number of *shahids* (martyrs) discussed by radical groups in Kosovo in their online media. Such exposure to the deaths of Kosovar Albanians in Syria has raised public concerns and prompted the reaction from Albanian and Kosovar institutions, which undertook in early 2014 legal changes aimed at criminalizing future participation in foreign religious and sectarian wars.

## Conclusion

One century after the fall of the Ottoman Empire in the western Balkans, the latter's Muslims have undergone a process of multiple social and political transformations. The spillover from one regime to another, followed by state-enforced measures to "domesticate" Islam, has left an indelible trace in the traditional and heterodox Islam practiced among Albanians. Likewise, developments in regional and international politics, especially after the fall of communism, have resulted in the emergence of three interconnected, yet distinct Muslim milieux among Albanians in Albania, Kosovo, and Macedonia. Despite the fact that all these countries are defined as secular states the relationship between the state and religious institutions has not always been one of neutrality. This has been conditioned by the type of regime, the share of Muslims in the overall population, as well as the international context and constraints.

In the case of Albania, religion was banned for many decades and even after the introduction of political pluralism, state institutions and politicians often showed signs of hostility towards Islam and Muslims. In the case of Kosovo and Macedonia, Muslims in these two countries have been for a long time governed by a Slav-dominated central religious organization in Yugoslavia. Since the early 1990s, the newly found

---

⁴² A survey conducted in Kosovo shows that 61% of people favor the traditional way of practicing Islam (Centre for Humanist Studies "Gani Bobi").

independence in terms of religious organization also quickly led to the emergence of differential trajectories of Islam and politics in Kosovo and Macedonia. In the former, in the period of ethnic tensions and war, religion was superseded by ethnicity in the process of ethno-national mobilization and homogenization. After 1999, however, new dynamics have evolved in the relationship between religion and politics. Dreaming of a "European" identity for Kosovo, Kosovar elites have often been hostile towards an increased role of Islam in social and political life. This is exemplified by backlashes over the location for new mosques in Prishtina, or the use of headscarves and the introduction of religious education in public schools. In Macedonia, on the other hand, Muslims are in a minority position and for two decades now have sought to build an alliance with the Albanian parties in the battle for equal treatment in society.

In this respect, mastery over the cultural landscape commanding the loyalties of Albanian Muslims constituted a primary administrative goal of the state. Indeed, throughout the modern history of Albania and the former Yugoslavia where the majority of Albanian Muslims lived, Islam as a doctrine of political activism has never played a major role. This is in spite of clear trends towards mobilizing religion in the Balkans towards realizing political ends (Babuna 2004). Throughout the struggle against anti-Albanian nationalism in Kosovo and Macedonia, for instance, Albanians never reverted to using their sectarian identity to challenge totalitarian rule. Scholars have long made this assertion because of the assumption that Albanians of Orthodox, Catholic, and Muslim faith were collectively being victimized and that their ethnic loyalties superseded their religious identities (Duijzings 2000: 153–61; Young 1999: 5–14).

Political Islam as it has emerged in other parts of the world, therefore, is still in its infancy and struggles for a foothold on otherwise hostile political terrain (Halimi 2000; G. Krasniqi 2011). That said, there are indications that small groups are actively trying to create an Islamic political party in Kosovo, Macedonia, and Albania. In Kosovo, for instance, one can follow in the Islamic Community of Kosovo's journal *Takvimi*, the occasional debate over the merits of an Islamic party in dealing with the political and social issues plaguing Kosovo today (Blumi 2005). In any case, it is the overall political and social context that shapes the development and transformation of identity, and in this context, religious identities as well. In the case of the Albanians, the growing foreign influence after the dissolution of Yugoslavia has left many traces in the region and has introduced followers of traditional forms of localized Islam to a new and radically different form of Islam known as Salafism or Wahhabism. These largely foreign practices of a faith that has long existed in the Balkans have led to important tensions in a part of Europe that is increasingly marginalized as economic crisis exasperates long-held prejudices towards Europe's indigenous Muslims.

Although an increasing number of works have been published on Albanians in recent years, the issue of religion as well as everyday practices among Albanians in the Balkans still is under-researched. In fact, most of the works take a historical approach, focusing on the institutional aspect of religious organization through history. On the other hand, the fall of communism, the dissolution of Yugoslavia, and the post-9/11 contexts have triggered a new and immense process of overall cultural and socio-political transformations. Therefore, more study is needed to gauge the changing landscape of religion in the Balkans and Albanian's relationship to Islam in a broader internationalized context. In order for scholars to grasp the new dynamics in the region, it is necessary to focus on sociological and anthropological studies that use various qualitative data, as well as ethnography. In this vein, we would be able to gain a better understanding about the values and principles that inform Albanian Muslims' lives today and shape their understanding of religion, attitudes, behaviors, and religious practices. Only in this way will we be able to elucidate the endangered rich fabric of Albanian religious tradition(s).

# References

Agai, Bekim (2002). "Fethullah Gulen and his Movement's Islamic Ethic of Education," *Critique: Critical Middle Eastern Studies* 11(1): 27–47.
Alibašić, Ahmet (2010). "Islamic Higher Education in the Balkans: A Survey," in Yorgen Nielsen (ed.), *Yearbook of Muslims in Europe*, vol. II. Leiden: Brill, 619–34.
Antoniou, Dimitri A. (2003). "Muslim Immigrants in Greece: Religious Organization and Local Responses," *Immigrants & Minorities* 22(2–3): 155–74.
Babuna, Aydin (2000). "The Albanians of Kosovo and Macedonia: Ethnic Identity Superseding Religion," *Nationalities Papers* 28(1): 67–92.
Babuna, Aydin (2004). "The Bosnian Muslims and Albanians: Islam and Nationalism," *Nationalities Papers* 32(2): 287–321.
Banac, Ivo (2006). "The Politics of National Homogeneity," in B. K. Blitz (ed.), *War and Change in the Balkans*. Cambridge: Cambridge University Press, 30–43.
Blumi, Isa (1997). "The Politics of Culture and Power: The Roots of Hoxha's Postwar State," *East European Quarterly*, 31(3): 409–28.
Blumi, Isa (1998). "The Commodification of Otherness and the Ethnic Unit in the Balkans: How to Think About Albanians," *East European Politics and Societies* 12: 527–69.
Blumi, Isa (2003a). "The Islamist Challenge in Kosova," *Current History* 101(2): 124–8.
Blumi, Isa (2003b). "Negotiating Globalization: The Challenges of International Intervention Through the Eyes of Albanian Muslims, 1850–2003." *UCLA Center for European and Eurasian Studies*, Occasional Lecture Series, Paper 2. <http://repositories.edlib.org/international/cees/ols/2> [Accessed December 2011].
Blumi, Isa (2005). *Political Islam among the Albanians: Are the Taliban Coming to the Balkans?* Prishtina: Kosovar Institute for Policy Research and Development.
Blumi, Isa (2011a). "Neither Eastern nor Welcome: The Confused Lives of Berlin's Balkan Migrants, 1950–2000," in Marc Silberman (ed.), *The German Wall: Fallout in Europe*. Basingstoke: Palgrave Macmillan, 145–64.
Blumi, Isa (2011b). *Reinstating the Ottomans: Alternative Balkan Modernities, 1800–1912*. New York: Palgrave Macmillan.
Bougarel, Xavier (2003). "Islam and Politics in the Post-Communist Balkans (1990–2000)," in Dimitris Keridis and Charles Perry (eds.), *New Approaches to Balkan Studies*. Dulles: Brassey's, 345–60.
Bougarel, Xavier (2005). "The Role of Balkan Muslims in Building a European Islam." EPC Issue Paper no. 43: 1–25.

Bougarel, Xavier (2007). "Introduction: Balkan Muslims and Islam in Europe," *Southeast Europe Journal of Politics and Society* 4: 339–53.

Brisku, Adrian (2006). "Occidentalising the Past and Orientalising the Present: Ismail Kadare's and President Moisiu's 'European' Albanian Identity," *Albanian Journal of Politics* 2(2): 82–103.

Brown, Wendy (2006). *Regulating Aversion: Tolerance in the Age of Identity and Empire*. Princeton: Princeton University Press.

Bureau of Democracy, Human Rights and Labor (2011a). *International Religious Freedom Report for 2011: Albania*. <http://www.state.gov/documents/organization/192989.pdf> [Accessed January 15, 2013].

Bureau of Democracy, Human Rights and Labor (2011b). *International Religious Freedom Report for 2011: Kosovo*. <http://www.state.gov/documents/organization/193037.pdf> [Accessed January 15, 2013].

Bureau of Democracy, Human Rights and Labor (2011c). *International Religious Freedom Report for 2011: Macedonia*. <http://www.state.gov/documents/organization/193047.pdf> [Accessed January 15, 2013].

Ceka, Egin (2006). "Die Debatte zwischen Ismail Kadare und Rexhep Qosja um die nationale Identität der Albaner," *Südosteurope. Zeitschrift für Gegenwartsforschung* 54: 451–60.

Center for Humanist Studies "Gani Bobi" (2011). *Interesi publik dhe religioni*. Prishtina: Forum 2015.

Chiodi, Luisa (ed.) (2005). *The Borders of the Polity: Migration and Security across the EU and the Balkans*. Ravenna: Longo Editore.

Clayer, Nathalie (1990). *L'Albanie, pays des derviches: Les ordres mystiques musulmans en Albanie a l'epoque post-ottomane, 1912–1967* (Balkanologische Veroffentlichungen, 17). Berlin–Wiesbaden: Osteuropa-Institut der Freien Universität Berlin.

Clayer, Nathalie (1992). "Bektachisme et nationalisme albanais," *Revue des Etudes Islamiques* 60(1): 271–300.

Clayer, Nathalie (2001). "L'islam facteur des recompositions internes en Macédoine et au Kosovo," in Xavier Bougarel and Nathalie Clayer (eds.), *Le nouvel islam balkanique. Les musulmans, acteurs du post-communisme (1990–2000)*. Paris: Maisonneuve et Larose, 177–240.

Clayer, Nathalie (2006). "Saints and Sufis in Post-Communist Albania," in Masatoshi Kisaichi (ed.), *Popular Movements and Democratization in the Islamic World*. London and New York, Routledge, 33–42.

Clayer, Nathalie (2008). "Behind the Veil: The Reform of Islam in Inter-War Albania and the Search for a 'Modern' and 'European' Islam," in Nathalie Clayer and Eric Germain (eds.), *Islam in Inter-War Europe*. London: Hurst & Company, 128–55.

Clayer, Nathalie (2010). "Adapting Islam to Europe: The Albanian Example," in Christian Voss and Jordanka Telbizova-Sack (eds.), *Islam und Muslime in (Sudost)Europa im Kontext von Transformation und EU-Erweiterung*. Munchen: Sagner.

Daniel, Odile (1990). "The Historical Role of the Muslim Community in Albania," *Central Asian Survey* 9(3): 1–28.

Deliso, Christopher (2007). *The Coming Balkan Caliphate: The Threat of Islam to Europe and the West*. Westport, CT: Praeger Security International.

Dizdari, Nasuf and Kasollja, Faik (1992). "Persekutimi i klerit musliman në Shqipëri," *Drita Islame* 21: 1–2.

Djurić, Sladjana (1998). *Osveta i Kazna. Sociološko istrazivanje krvne osvete na Kosovu i Metohiji*. Nish: Prosvetas.

Doja, Albert (2000). "The Politics of Religion in the Reconstruction of Identities: The Albanian Situation," *Critique of Anthropology* 20(4): 421–38.

Doja, Albert (2003). "Confraternal Religion: From Liberation Theology to Political Reversal," *History and Anthropology* 14(4): 349–81.

Doja, Albert (2006). "A Political History of Bektashism in Albania," *Totalitarian Movements and Political Religions* 7(1): 83–107.

Duijzings, Ger (2000). *Religion and the Politics of Identity in Kosovo*. New York: Columbia University Press.

Elbasani, Arolda and Saatçioglu, Beken (2011). "Islamic Actors' Support for Democracy and European Integration: A Case for Power-Seeking?" *Discussion Paper SP IV 2011-801*. Berlin: Wissenschaftszentrum Berlin für Sozialforschung.

Ellis, Burcu Akan (2003). *Shadow Genealogies: Memory and Identity among Urban Muslims in Macedonia*. New York: Columbia University Press.

Elsie, Robert (1995). *History of Albanian Literature*, vol 1. Boulder: Social Science Monographs.

Gaber, Natasha (1996). "Muslims, State and Society in the Republic of Macedonia: The View from Within," in Gerd Nonneman, Tim Niblock, and Bogdan Szajkowski (eds.), *Muslim Communities in the New Europe*. New York: Ithaca Press.

Gaber, Natasha (1997). "The Muslim Population in FYROM (Macedonia): Public Perceptions," in Hugh Poulton and Suha Taji-Farouki (eds.), *Muslim Identity and the Balkan State*. London: Hurst & Company, 103–14.

Ghodsee, Kirsten (2009). *Muslim Lives in Eastern Europe: Gender, Ethnicity, and the Transformation of Islam in Postsocialist Bulgaria*. Princeton: Princeton University Press.

Gjuraj, Tonin (2000). "A Stable Ecumenical Model? How Religion Might Become a Political Issue in Albania," *East European Quarterly* 1: 21–40.

Halimi, Kadri (2000). "Dervishët dhe tempujte e tyre në përgjithësi dhe në Kosovë," in *Trajtime dhe studime etnologjike*. Pristina: Instituti Albanologjik i Prishtinës.

Hamiti, Xhabir (2009). "Islamic Education in Kosovo," in Ednan Aslan (ed.), *Islamic Education in Europe*. Vienna: Böhlau Verlag, 233–8.

Haraqija, Artan M. and Duriqi, Visar (2012). "Radikalizimi i Islamit, rrezik apo fobi?" *Preportr*. <http://preportr.com/sq/Sociale-Kulture/Radikalizimi-i-Islamit-rrezik-apo-fobi-186> [Accessed September 15, 2012].

Herscher, Andrew (2006). "Is it True that Albanians are Responsible for an Orchestrated Campaign to Destroy Kosova's Cultural Heritage in Modern Times?" in A. D. Lellio (ed.), *The Case for Kosova: Passage to Independence*. London and New York: Anthem Press, 37–42.

International Crisis Group (ICG) (1999). "Macedonia: Towards Destabilization?" May 17, 1999.

Iseni, Bashkim (2007). "Entre nationalisme laïc et instrumentalisation Bashkim des institutions religieuses islamiques," in Olivier Haener, Bashkim Iseni, and Xavier Bougarel (eds.), *Islam et politique dans les Balkans occidentaux* (Politorbis No. 43). Bern: Swiss Federal Department of Foreign Affairs, 13–38.

Iveković, Ivan (2002). "Nationalism and the Political Use and Abuse of Religion: The Politicization of Orthodoxy, Catholicism and Islam in Yugoslav Successor States," *Social Compass* 49(4): 523–36.

Jazexhi, Olsi (2007). "The Political Exploitation of Islamophobia in Post-Communist Albania." <http://www.reocities.com/olsi.rm/islamofobia.htm> [Accessed December 27, 2011].

Kadare, Ismail (2006). *Identiteti Evropian i Shqiptarëve*. Tirana: Onufri.

King, Iain and Mason, Whit (2006). *Peace at Any Price: How the World Failed Kosovo*. Ithaca, NY: Cornell University Press.

Koinova, Maria (n.d). *Minorities in Southeast Europe: Muslims of Macedonia.* Center for Documentation and Information on Minorities in Europe—Southeast Europe (CEDIME-SE).

Kostovicova, Denisa and Prestreshi, Albert (2003). "Education, Gender and Religion: Identity Transformations among Kosovo Albanians in London," *Journal of Ethnic and Migration Studies* 29(6): 1079–96.

Krasniqi, Gëzim (2010). "Citizenship in an Emigrant Nation-State: The Case of Albania." *CITSEE Working Paper 2010/13.* Edinburgh: CITSEE/University of Edinburgh.

Krasniqi, Gëzim (2011). "The 'Forbidden Fruit': Islam and Politics of Identity in Kosovo and Macedonia," *Southeast European and Black Sea Studies* 11(2): 191–207.

Krasniqi, Vjollca (2007). "Imagery, Gender and Power: The Politics of Representation in Post-War Kosova," *Feminist Review* 86: 1–23.

Lakshman-Lepain, Rajwantee (2002). "Albanian Islam: Development and Disruptions," in Karl Kasser and Frank Kressing (eds.), *Albania: A Country in Transition—Aspects of Changing Identities in a South-East European Country.* Baden Baden: Nomos Verlag, 34–65.

Lederer, Gyorgy (1994). "Islam in Albania," *Central Asian Survey* 13(3): 331–59.

Lubonja, Fatos (2004). "Albania after Isolation: The Transformation of Public Perceptions of the West," in Andrew Hammond (ed.), *The Balkans and the West: Constructing the European Other, 1945–2003.* Aldershot: Ashgate, 127–35.

McCarthy, Justin (1995). *Death and Exile: The Ethnic Cleansing of Ottoman Muslims, 1821–1922.* Princeton, NJ: Darwin Press.

Mai, Nicola (2008). "Albanian Migrations: Demographic and Other Transformations," in J. Batt (ed.), *Is There an Albanian Question?* (Chaillot Paper no. 107). Paris: Institute for Security Studies, 61–72.

Malcolm, Noel (1999). *Kosovo: A Short History.* New York: Harper Perennial.

Maxhuni, Nebih (2012). "Viktimë e vahabistëve," *Gazeta Express.* <http://www.gazetaexpress.com/index.php?cid=1,15,80933> [Accessed September 17, 2012].

Mazower, Mark (2002). *The Balkans: A Short History.* New York: Modern Library.

Misha, Pirro (2008). *Arratisje nga burgjet e historisë. Ç'do të thotë sot të jesh shqiptar.* Tirana: Botimet Toena.

Morrison, Keneth (2008). *Wahhabism in the Balkans.* Defence Academy of the United Kingdom, Balkans Series 08/06.

Norris, H. T. (1993). *Islam in the Balkans: Religion and Society between Europe and the Arab World.* London: Hurst & Company.

Öktem, Kerem (2011). "Between Emigration, de-Islamization and the Nation-State: Muslim Communities in the Balkans Today," *Southeast European and Black Sea Studies* 11(2): 155–71.

Pllumi, Zef (2008). *Live to Tell: 1944–1951, A True Story of Religious Persecution in Communist Albania.* New York: iUniverse.

Poggioli, Sylvia (2010). "Radical Islam Uses Balkan Poor To Wield Influence." National Public Radio. <http://www.npr.org/templates/story/story.php?storyId=130801242> [Accessed September 5, 2012].

Popović, Alexandre (1986). *L'Islam balkanique. Les musulmans du sud-est européen dans la période post-ottomane* (Balkanologische Veröffentlichungen, 11). Berlin-Wiesbaden: Otto Harrassowitz Verlag.

Popović, Alexandar (1990). *Posrednici i metafore. Jugoslovenski muslimani (1945–1989).* Belgrade: Akvarius.

Popović, Alexandre and Veinstein, Gilles (eds.) (1995). *Bektachiyya: études sur l'ordre mystique des Bektachis et les groupes relevant de Hadji Bektach*. Istanbul: Isis.

Poulton, Hugh (1993). *The Balkans: States and Minorities in Conflict*. London: Minority Rights Group Publications.

Poulton, Hugh (1997). "Changing Notions of National Identity among Muslims in Thrace and Macedonia: Turks, Pomaks and Roma," in Hugh Poulton and Suha Taji-Farouki (eds.), *Muslim Identity and the Balkan State*. London: Hurst & Company, 82–102.

Poulton, Hugh (1998). *Minorities in Southeast Europe: Inclusion and Exclusion*. London: Minority Rights Group International Report.

Puto, Artan (2006). "Fryma romantike dhe nacionaliste në debatin për 'identitetin shqiptar,'" *Përpjekja* 23: 13–33.

Qosja, Rexhep (2006). *Ideologjia e Shpërbërjes*. Tirana: Botimet Toena.

Radic, Radmila (2003). "Religion in a Multicultural State: The Case of Yugoslavia," in Dejan Djokic (ed.), *Yugoslavism: Histories of a Failed Idea 1918–1922*. London: Hurst & Company, 196–207.

Rapper, Gilles de (2008). "Religion in Post-Communist Albania: Muslims, Christians and the Idea of 'Culture' in Devoll, Southern Albania," *Anthropological Notebooks* 14(2): 31–45.

Rexhepagiqi, Jashar (2003). *Dervishët dhe teqetë në Kosovë, në Sanxhak e në rajonet e tjera përreth*. New and updated edition. Peja: Dukagjini.

Rexhepi, Haxhi Sulejman (2002). *Reis ul-ulema* of the Islamic Religious Community of the Republic of Macedonia, interview on May 12, 2002 in Skopje.

Robelli, Enver (2011). *Arbën Xhaferi rrëfen: Në Tetotvë në kërkim të kuptimit*. Prishtina: Koha.

Roux, Michel (1992). *Les Albanais en Yougoslavie. Minorite nationale, territoire et developpement*. Paris: Editions de la Maison des Sciences de l'Homme.

Saudi Press Agency (2004). "Kosovo's U.N. Administration praises Saudi Relief Committee," *Saudi Press Agency*. <http://www.saudinf.com/display_news.php?id=1958> [Accessed September 5, 2012].

Schwandner-Sievers, Stephanie (2004). "Albanians, Albanianism and the Strategic Subversion of Stereotypes," in Andrew Hammond (ed.), *The Balkans and the West: Constructing the European Other, 1945–2003*. Aldershot: Ashgate, 110–26.

Schwartz, Stephen (2011). "Kosovo Bans Islamic Headscarf and Religious Instruction in Public Schools," *Weekly Standard*. <http://www.weeklystandard.com/blogs/kosovo-bans-islamic-headscarf-and-religious-instruction-public-schools_592759.html?page=1> [Accessed December 18, 2011].

Selimoski, Hadzhi Jakub (2002). Head of the Muslim Religious Community in Macedonia, interview on May 11, 2002 in Skopje.

Solberg, Anne (2007). "The Role of Turkish Islamic Networks in the Western Balkans," *Südosteuropa* 55(4): 429–62.

Stefanović, Djordje (2005). "Seeing the Albanians through Serbian Eyes: The Inventors of the Tradition of Intolerance and their Critics, 1804–1939," *European History Quarterly* 35: 465–92.

Sulstarova, Enis (2007). *Arratisje Nga Lindja: Orientalizmi Shqiptar nga Naimi te Kadareja*, 2nd edn. Tirana: Botimet Dudaj.

Tomo, Adem (1996). "Attitudes towards Religion and the Religious Motivations of Students and Intellectuals." Appearing in the first volume of *Social-Pedagogical Reflections*, published by a group of authors in Tetova Macedonia, 15–22.

Trix, Frances (1995). "The Resurfacing of Islam in Albania," *East European Quarterly* 28(4): 533–49.
Welton, George and Brisku, Adrian (2007). "Contradictory Inclinations? The Role of 'Europe' in Albanian Nationalist Discourse," in Balihar Sanghera, Sarah Amsler, and Tanya Yarkova (eds.), *Theorising Social Change in Post-Soviet Countries: Critical Approaches*. Oxford and New York: Peter Lang, 87–110.
Wimmer, Andreas and Schiller, Nina Glick (2002). "Methodological Nationalism and Beyond: Nation-State Building, Migration and the Social Sciences," *Global Networks* 2(4): 301–34.
Yavuz, M. Hakan (2012). *Toward an Islamic Enlightenment: The Gülen Movement*. New York: Oxford University Press.
Yavuz, M. Hakan and Esposito, John L. (eds.) (2003). *Turkish Islam and the Secular State: The Global Impact of Fethullah Gulen Nur Movement*. New York: Syracuse University Press.
Young, Antonia (1999). "Religion and Society in Present-Day Albania," *Journal of Contemporary Religion* 14(1): 5–16.
Zelin, Aaron Y. (2013). "Up to 11,000 foreign fighters in Syria: steep rise among Western Europeans," ICSR Insight. <http://icsr.info/2013/12/icsr-insight-11000-foreign-fighters-syria-steep-rise-among-western-europeans/> [Accessed April 10, 2013].

# CHAPTER 12

# RUSSIA

## STÉPHANE A. DUDOIGNON

WITHIN Europe, Russia stands out for her exceptionally long and deep engagement with Islam and with the world of Islam. The modern Russian state itself was erected through the conquest of Muslim polities, from the Kazan Khanate in 1552 to the Tekke Turkmens in 1881. Conversely, many an upheaval has been brought about in the country's modern history by disasters inflicted by Muslim powers and strengths—oftentimes backed by Western superpowers—from the Ottoman Empire in the Crimean War of 1853–6 to the Afghan *mujahid* resistance of 1979–89 (to say nothing of the conflicts hazardously managed against Chechnya in 1994–6 and 1999–2009 by the Yeltsin and Putin administrations). Another historical legacy consists of Tsarist and Soviet Russia's state interventionism in the religious field, characterized in the USSR by the denunciation of all religious faiths. Religion at the same time was mobilized by the Tsarist and Soviet states for the sake of their external relations—as for Islam, from the efforts by Catherine II's administrations to make Russia look more Muslim-friendly at the eve of the empire's expansion southwards, to early Soviet diplomacy's vain endeavours to appeal to nascent Saudi monarchy in the 1920s, or much more recently to Russia's adhesion in 2005, as an Observer, to the Organisation of the Islamic Conference.[1]

Despite this length and depth of Russia's commitment to Islam, her Muslim believers rarely make the headlines of international media. When they do so, it is through denunciations by the country's officialdom of some excess or drift of their Muslim citizenry towards 'extremism' or 'fanaticism'. Such was again the case on 8 August 2012 in Kazan, the capital of the Republic of Tatarstan 500 km east of Moscow. During an inquiry on the murder of the Republic's Vice-Mufti Wali-Allah Ya'qupov (b. 1963) and an assassination attempt against Mufti Ildus Fayzov (also b. 1963) on 19 July of the same year, the police discovered the troglodyte sect of Fayz al-Rahman Satarov (b. 1927) who, according to police officers, had been waiting for the Apocalypse in an underground bunker

---

[1] Renamed in 2011 Organisation of Islamic Cooperation (<http://www.oic-oci.org/page_detail.asp?p_id=179>, accessed 25 September 2012).

since 1996, surrounded by seventy followers.² A chemist by training and the holder of a Ph.D. in history, Ya'qupov was posthumously saluted by Russia's press as a staunch opponent of Islamic 'radicalism' and of sectarian shifts embodied by Satarov and his like. His assassination was imputed to his work in the service of 'moderate' Islam impregnated with Russia's age-old tradition of cohabitation between different faiths, and the accommodation of religious practice with modern European economic and social rationality.³

In present-day Russia, the terms of reference of the public discourse such as 'confessional tolerance' and 'acceptance of progress' are, in fact, intended to point out all sorts of 'deviancies'. They have been forged with the participation of parts of the country's research networks in the context of the late 1990s campaigns against Muslim 'terrorism', 'extremism', and 'separatism'. As such, they bear the trace of the recent development by Russia with China of the Shanghai Cooperation Organisation (SCO), an assembly of authoritarian regimes for which anti-establishment Islam is a common *bête noire*.⁴ The adoption by the Shanghai Five, since 2003, of repressive policies against a range of transnational Islamic movements (cf. Ambrosio 2008; Aris 2009) entailed Russia's further criminalization of every kind of 'imported' religious practice and thought—opposing *Russia's* Islam (if not *Russian* Islam) to Islam *in Russia*, and perceiving cross-border religious trends as a danger to established orders and national cultures. Besides this, the SCO's specious extradition rules have put Russia in regular breach of her engagements with the Council of Europe, to which the country adhered on 29 February 1996—two months ahead of the creation of the Shanghai Five on 26 April of the same year.

In the present tentative synthesis, we shall deal with the contribution of the scholarship on Islam in Russia to a limited set of key issues tackled by the other chapters of the present volume: (1) the renewal of the history of Islam in Russia in the Tsarist, Soviet, and current periods, and the deep change brought about in representations by the mass labour immigration of the 1990s–2000s from the Caucasus and Central Asia; (2) the issue of the integration of vernacular and migrant Muslims from diverse socioeconomic and sociocultural viewpoints—with insights on the issues and challenges of carrying out a demographic census of confessions; (3) the sociology of religious practices through the quantitative survey of the Soviet and current periods as well as through recently developed qualitative approaches to individual practice; (4) the impacts exerted by social and political sciences on religious policies; (5) studies dealing with the place of religion in Russia's public sphere and with the question of secularism, in a country where the 'private' legal status endowed to religion allows the state to intervene massively, as in the Soviet times, in religion's public aspects; (6) the question of Islam in politics, through the development of studies on political parties and protest movements; (7) the current impact on the field of prevailing security and terrorism approaches, with an insight into

---

² e.g. <http://www.guardian.co.uk/world/2012/aug/09/islamist-fayzarahmanist-sect-underground-kazan>.

³ e.g. <http://www.interfax-religion.com/?act=news&div=9534> (posted 19 July 2012).

⁴ See Chung 2006, with considerations on SCO as an instrument of preservation of the political status quo within the member states.

the development of Islamophobia since the mid-1990s and the embryonic Islamophile reactions to this challenge through original forms of association between academic, religious, and civic actors.

# Reappraising Some Legacies of History

## Antagonism or Accommodation? History's Break with Dialectics

A distinct feature of Russia's Islam is the ancient character and extreme diversity of the country's Muslim populations, combined with a tradition of heavy state intervention into religious affairs. The cradle of modern Russian states, Muscovy had experienced long submission to a Muslim empire, the Turko-Mongol 'Golden Horde' in the fourteenth and fifteenth centuries.[5] The modern memory of this era deeply politicizes Russia's relationship to Islam and contributes to structure this relationship in terms of a complex power struggle. This memory also identifies Muslim culture as a vector of unity in Eurasia. This identification explains the special interest shown since the end of the Soviet period by Russia's ruling circles in Islamic religion and culture as a possible foil to lost political cohesion. It also explains the interest of Russia's 'new right' in conversion to Islam as a possible tool for the invoking and revival of past continental empires. Studies on modern-day Russia's relationship to the Orient also emphasize the recurring identification by many Russian authors of the 'East' with Tsarist and Soviet Russia's Muslim south. In so doing, they highlight too the strong pragmatism of Russia's modern Oriental scholarship and the overt priority it gives to aspects of political dominance (e.g. de Meaux 2010: 135ff.). The continuity of Russia's expansion east- and southwards from the fifteenth to the twentieth century explains, conversely, the radical newness of challenges like the Chechen independence of 1991–2000 and the increase of mass labour immigration from Central Asia and from the Southern Caucasus since the mid-2000s—introducing a sharply felt cleavage between 'our' and 'their' Islam.

The issue of Russia as a secular multi-ethnic and multi-confessional state underlies the domestic and international historical literature devoted to Russia's Islam. The historical works of the 1990s–2000s are distinguished by their diversity. The dialectical approach inherited from the Cold War period, with its concomitant dichotomies of 'high' and 'low', 'learned' and 'popular', 'reformist' and 'traditionalist', 'official' and 'parallel' Islam, has been systematically revisited. This critical reappraisal gave way to historical works encompassing a diverse typology of interactions between the different protagonists of the religious field, and between them and the Russian state.

---

[5] On Muscovy's vision of Islam, see the recent evolution of modern historiography from Ostrowski 1998: 144–63; to Schimmelpenninck van der Oye 2010: 24–30.

Indeed this does not mean that the old framework has been completely erased from history writing. In ethnic republics like Tatarstan or Bashkortostan, in the Middle Volga and the Western Urals, historical research was goaded on in the 1990s by the impacts of the wars of Chechnya. The ensuing exemplification by regional historians of antagonisms between, on the one hand, Muslim populations and, on the other hand, the Russian state, the Orthodox Church, and the Slavic settlers, gave way to essentialist and ahistorical readings of Islam as a vector of resistance and of preservation of the ethnic self. Against such a backdrop, the dominance of ethnocentric perspectives and the regionalization of historical discourse do not always favour innovation, in spite of impressive amounts of documentary discoveries by local researchers.[6]

As a result, some of the subtlest historical approaches to the interactions between the state and the Muslim populations of the Russian Empire and the USSR, among Tatars especially, developed outside the ethnic republics, far from Kazan in particular. Within Russia, the School of Omsk for example has since the 1960s promoted pioneering historical research on Muslim adjustments to the setting of the Tsarist society into different estates (*sosloviia*, sing. *soslovie*) and on Muslim adaptations to the evolution of the imperial tax system.[7] Now key in both Western and Russian historical scholarship, the notion of 'cooperation and mutual accommodation' between the Russian authorities and the Muslim natives (Frank 2009: 380; Bobrovnikov 2012: 158) has facilitated a renewal of imperial history.[8] In parallel, historians of Russia's Islam have also developed a sensitivity to the many side effects of the restrictions put on public Islamic practice during several periods of the Tsarist and Soviet eras, for instance to the role of women in the transmission of Islamic learning as a result of the closure of *madrasa*s (e.g. Kefeli 2001). As we shall see, female participation in Islamic religious life in the USSR has also attracted the interest of sociologists. Surveys implemented in the 2000s explain this increased participation of women by the demographic gender disproportion of the post-Second World War period and by the proliferation of alcoholism among men in villages, transforming *abïzta*s (female Muslim religious scholars)[9] able to read the Qur'an as proficiently as men into authorities invited to oversee religious rituals and sociability (e.g. Sabirova 2011: 337).

---

[6] As a prominent émigré historian of Central Asia, Yuri Bregel (b. 1925) had warned already seventeen years ago in a landmark essay (1996) that passed unnoticed, apparently, among Russia's researchers.

[7] See for instance the synthetic presentation by Tomilov 2000; on imperial Russia's political differentiation between Orthodox and non-Orthodox religious personnel through estate differentiation, see recently Werth 2010.

[8] It suggests for instance that in the nineteenth century the struggle for the shariah enhanced the authority of Oriental scholars, who were estimated by the Muslim believers themselves more authentic on Islam's fixed codes than Muslim intermediaries who, 'after all, had trouble agreeing with one another' (Crews 2006: 189–91).

[9] The feminine form of Tatar word (*abïz*), derived from Arabic *hafiz*, 'Qur'an memorizer'.

## Islamic Reform: The Temptation of Historicism

Nineteenth- and early twentieth-century movements of Islamic reform in the Russian Empire have also lately been criticized by international scholarship as yet another offspring of Soviet dialectics adopted by Western scholars of the Cold War period. In the late 1920s, it had been established by Soviet historians that Islam was 'feudal' in character (Kemper 2009). In the Stalinist period (from the early 1930s to the early 1950s), the notion of the 'friendship of peoples' consecrated the leading position of Russians as purveyors of progress. In the years following Stalin's death (1953) and again in the mid-1970s, young academics from the Soviet south promoted a selective rehabilitation of pre-revolutionary and early Soviet reformist ('Jadid') intellectuals. Implemented within a revaluation of the national cultural 'heritages' of the peoples of the USSR,[10] this rehabilitation opposed 'reformist' and 'traditionalist' Muslim thinkers in a dichotomy that is widely vigorous today, especially in the Volga region and Dagestan.

This rehabilitation was led initially by specialists without a background in Oriental studies, who based their works on secondary materials in Russian. For a long period, it remained focused on the study of 'public thought' (Rus. *obshchestvennaia mysl'*) and societal issues such as schooling and the press in the Muslim-peopled regions of the Russian Empire. In so doing, it produced a reading of Islamic sources that neglected their properly Islamic background, introducing the nineteenth- and twentieth-century Muslim religious reformers in the Volga-Ural, the Caucasus, and Central Asia as secular advocates of social progress through adaptation to the norms of Russian society and 'civilization' (cf. Bustanov and Kemper 2012a: 36). It is only in the mid-1990s that the study of late Tsarist Russia's Islamic literature within the conceptual framework of Islamic studies really began. The new experts of 'Islamic discourse' are historians who work simultaneously with Arabic, Persian, Turkic, and Russian documents and texts, and develop methods that aim to understand concepts and practices of Islam and Islamic communities on the believers' terms rather than through the projection towards the past of present-day dialectical categories (DeWeese 2002). Throwing out the baby with the bathwater, the same experts, focusing usually on manuscript sources valued for their authenticity, are often less interested than their predecessors in the multiple changes brought about in the late nineteenth and early twentieth centuries by the development of Muslim philanthropy, the appearance of new media, the diffusion of new intellectual trends, and the resulting multiplication of cleavages and tensions within local and regional communities and networks of Muslim believers.

From another viewpoint, the sociology of present-day Russian Islam also suggests (e.g. Omel'chenko and Sabirova 2003a: 170) that the late Soviet and early post-Soviet rehabilitations of Islamic thinking through the revaluation of modern reform and early twentieth-century 'Jadidism' expressed the way Islam was viewed within Soviet Muslim educated urban milieux of the 1960s to 1980s—namely as a largely secularized 'culture' equivalent to modern Russian civilization. In the period of time from Khrushchev to

---

[10] Designed among Turkic-speaking peoples by the Arabic loanword *mirath* = 'heritage'.

perestroika, religion in the USSR had lost its status as a social imperative. And the tradition of handing down the Muslim legacy within distinct linguistic communities helped maintain religiosity on an ethnic and cultural level. Such a phenomenon explains this understanding of Islam as something 'inherited' and as part of a sense of belonging. Unfortunately, since the 1990s the late Soviet identification of nineteenth- and early twentieth-century Islamic reform with the respective cultural heritages of distinct peoples of Russia and the former USSR also reinforced the criticism of this legacy by those who advocate varied forms of transnational Islam—especially young Salafis who turn away from all religious and philosophical teachings associated with Soviet things, notably from 'Jadidism' in its Soviet reinterpretations.

## Rediscovering the Impact of Soviet Mass Resettlements

The overall criticism of the dialectical approaches of Soviet Oriental studies and of the ahistorical stereotypes of Islam that are still dominant in the ethnic republics was recently extended to the so-called 'stagnation' period (1964–87) of the history of the USSR. This criticism does not deny the tremendous impact of the closure of Islamic teaching institutions in the 1920s, and of periods of massive repressions in the early 1930s (and again, though with lesser impact, in the early 1960s) on the decline of Muslim religious practice in the USSR.[11] Historians of the late Soviet period now cast light, however, on the extreme variations in time and space of Soviet state coercion against Islam. Most recently, some have demonstrated how the mass resettlements of the 1930s to 1970s in Dagestan (and the Central Asian republics of Tajikistan and Kazakhstan) contributed under Brezhnev (1964–82) to the propagation of Islamic religious teachings in newly settled territories (cf. Dudoignon and Noack 2013). In the very last years, historical studies confirmed that in the 1970s–80s the concentration of Islamic practice in Russia's countries benefited from protection networks within the kolkhoz system, notably in isolated Muslim communities surrounded by ethnically and religiously different populations.[12]

As far as Soviet mass resettlements are concerned, combinations of archival research, private source discoveries, and oral history suggest that it is in districts where anti-collectivization protests were the most active in the 1930s that Soviet anti-religious campaigns took the most aggressive forms. As a result, the Soviet and early post-Soviet Islamic revivals of the 1960s to 1990s took place in villages either forgotten by the economic planners of Stalin's time, or well integrated in the kolkhoz economy, or still set up in new territories after the mass resettlements of the post-Second World War decades.[13] At the forefront of the current Islamic boom, many of these new religious centres remain

---

[11] This decline has been well underlined, notably, by the documentary rediscoveries of archival historians such as Ro'i (2000) and Arapov (2009).

[12] As in Muslim Tatar villages of the predominantly Orthodox Finno-Ugric and Slavic-peopled Ural region: e.g. Minnullin 2013.

[13] On Dagestan see the sociological study by Omel'chenko and Sabirova 2003b: 197, 203–4: these authors briefly evoke the village of Gubden whose inhabitants, nowadays, are proud that their mosque

deprived, for very good reasons, of a distinct memory of resistance against Bolshevik rule. A consequence of this legacy of Soviet history is the situation of new holy places in locations previously unknown to Muslim pilgrims.[14]

In some occurrences, global historical reappraisals permit us to understand how Soviet mass resettlements and present-day labour migration endow Muslim congregations and religious networks with varying ethnic contents. In Dagestan, recent research suggests how, as a result of the massive resettlements of the late 1950s to early 1970s, highlander Avar-speaking Sufi leaders became the transmitters of Islamic practice among Kumyk autochthonous dwellers in the Republic's northern flatlands. It also shows how the Kumyks ultimately refuted the 'Avar' model of Islam, impregnated by Sufi teaching. Inter-ethnic tension in immigration zones between autochthonous Kumyk and immigrant Avar-speaking populations was related to allocations of resources with advantage to the migrants. When in the 1990s inter-ethnic issues deteriorated into open conflicts, it is among Kumyks that Salafi ideas spread the most rapidly, as an ideological counterbalance to the Sufi teachings propagated by well-to-do Soviet migrants (Shikhaliev 2013). Interestingly, some of the most convincing approaches to the transformation of the sociology of post-Soviet Islam are proposed not by social scientists but by scholars in Oriental studies. In so doing, the latter also shed light on a period, from Khrushchev to Gorbachev, that was until recently decried by international critique as eventless and dull.

## Immigration and Integration

### The Demographic Aspect: Is Russia Still More 'Muslim' than the USSR?

In the early 1990s, on his way back to Russia, writer and dissident Alexander Solzhenitsyn (1918–2008) advocated the country's separation from its former southern colonies. For decades, the hermit of Vermont had inveighed against Islam as a reactionary religion.[15] This turned out to be a pure waste of effort, since after the self-dissolution of the Soviet system in 1991, Russia has found herself with a percentage of 'ethnic Muslim' nationals even larger than the USSR's—to say nothing of the massive influx in the 1990s–2000s of labour migrants from the former Soviet south. These evolutions once incited President Putin to suggest that Russia possesses more than 20 million Muslim citizens (cf. Moroz 2005: 119–20).

---

was never closed down, even during the darkest years of Stalin's times. The building remained the focal point of the congregation's life, especially on the festivals of the Islamic calendar.

[14] For Dagestan by Bobrovnikov 2013; about Tajikistan for instance, see Dudoignon 2013.
[15] e.g. Joseph Pearce, 'An Interview with Alexander Solzhenitsyn', *St Austin Review* 2(2) (February 2003, reprinted at <http://www.catholiceducation.org/articles/arts/al0172.html>).

A demographic heritage of the Tsarist and Soviet periods is the concentration of a large majority of 'ethnic Muslims' (viz. opposed to non-Muslim Russians, Russian converts, and Muslim migrants from outside Russia) within the territories of their former Soviet national republics. Significant discrepancies can still be observed in terms of ethnic Muslim population density between Russia's territories: from 0.2% in the centre of the country to 50% in Bashkortostan and Tatarstan and 80% in Dagestan. Indeed for present-day Russia, religion is a question of each citizen's personal choice (cf. Radvanyi 2005)—as it already was in Soviet times,[16] enabling then and now state restrictions on public expressions of religiosity. Concentration on ethnic data still allows observers to highlight a permanent increase of the proportion of 'Muslims' within Russia's population. Even after modern censuses have proved instrumental in the production of ethnic and racial identities in the former Soviet domain, their innumerable comments today continue to fuel equivalence between national and confessional affiliation.[17] The 1990s surveys used to insist on the equivalence between ethnic and religious identities, in connection with the ethnic 'revivals' so typical of the late Soviet and early post-Soviet periods (e.g. Musina 2001). More recently, the sociology of Russia's Islam shifted to the study of the mobilization of Islamic symbols within a much wider range of social discourses (cf. Omel'chenko and Sabirova 2003a and Chapter 3 in this volume).

Census data suggest that if in Russia 'ethnic Muslims' made up 6% of the population in 1937, they were more than 8% in 1989, and 10.8% in 2010, with more than 14.8 million people representing some sixty different national groups[18]—the balance between different groups being questioned by recent immigration from the former southern periphery of the USSR.[19] Besides natural growth and migration, and indeed the recent developments in the self-identification strategies of entire groups, another cause for such variations is found by demographers and sociologists in the manipulations of statistics.[20] Demographic studies in fact cast light on overall discrepancies between ethnic affiliations and religious sentiments—definitely underlying the vanity of extrapolations which gather confessional

---

[16] Cf. Prozorov 1994: 232; Malashenko 2001: 64.

[17] Even in the situations, as in Ukraine, where on the occasion of censuses the citizens take a defensive stance towards a state they neither trust nor respect (cf. Uehling 2004).

[18] The numerically largest national/confessional group of the Russian Federation after the Russians are the Volga Tatars (5.3 million in 2012, making up 3.9% of the Federation's population), followed by the Bashkirs in the Ural region (1.6 million—1.15% of the population), after whom come the numerically most important populations of the Northern Caucasus: the Chechens (1.4 million—1.05%); the Avars (912,000—0.66%); the Darghis (590,000—0.43%); the Kabards (517,000—0.38%); the Kumyks (503,000—0.37%); the Lezghis (474,000—0.35%); the Ingush (445,000—0.32%); the Karachais (218,000—0.16%); the Laks (179,000—0.13%); the Tabasarans (146,000—0.11%); the Balkars (113,000—0.08%); the Turks (105,000—0.08); and the Noghais (104,000—0.08%). It should be noted that at the time of the 2010 census, 5.629 million people (3.94% of the population) did not declare a specific national affiliation (Rus. *natsional'nost'*). See <http://www.perepis-2010.ru/results_of_the_census/tab5.xls> (accessed 25 September 2012).

[19] Sociologist R. Lunkin puts forwards the figure of 14 million Muslims in Russia, but as many as 20 million if including legal and illegal migrants from the former Soviet south (<http://Kommersant.ru/doc/1997068>), a figure curiously as overestimated as Vladimir Putin's.

[20] As in the 1990s in Dagestan by regional authorities who overestimated the population of their regions or districts for obtaining more subsidies or appointments (e.g. Radvanyi 2005: 164-5).

information out of ethnic data. Surveys like the 'Atlas of Russia's Religions and National Groups' (ARENA) prepared by the 'Sreda' Research Centre[21] also highlight profound analogies between Islam and Russia's other 'traditional' religions, beginning with the contrast between the confessional zeal of 'born again' migrant mosque-goers with the ritual apathy among the majority of vernacular believers.

## The New Challenges of Post-Soviet Immigration

At the same time, as suggested by many observers, the available demographic figures on Russia's Muslim population need to be qualified by those on Southern Caucasian and Central Asian migrants, whose seasonal or permanent presence in the Russian Federation remains imperfectly reflected in statistics. Two changes revealed by the studies of the late 1990s are the decrease in the numbers of Russians among immigrants from the former Soviet south, replaced by nationals of the emigration countries (except for Kazakhstan), and these migrants' more durable installation in Russia. The 2010 census of Russia's population provides overtly underestimated figures for Southern Caucasian and Central Asian migrants settled in the country.[22]

These southern migrants are a focus of public attention due to their potential mobilization by transnational Salafi movements and by protest confessional parties (e.g. Bulatov 2007). Such is the case of Tajik citizens, more than one million of whom were estimated in the mid-2000s to be working outside Tajikistan.[23] Substantial studies have underlined the presence in the early 2000s of groups of seasonal 'workers' coming to Russia to earn money for *jihad*.[24] Other studies more generally underline the migrants' distrust of the political institutions of their countries of origin.[25] Religious practice among Central Asian and Caucasus migrants recently raised interest from the viewpoint

---

[21] See the project's presentation at <http://sreda.org/arena/about-project>. Highlighting the fact that only 40% of Russia's population adhere to Orthodox Christianity (in contrast to a proportion of 80% of ethnic Russians), the atlas questions the equation of national or ethnic and confessional affiliations, which is traditional in the former USSR and in Western studies on religion in the Soviet Union (see <http://rus.ruvr.ru/2012_09_04/V-Rossii-sostavlen-Atlas-religii>; <http://kommersant.ru/doc/1997068>).

[22] Namely: 603,000 Azerbaijanis (0.44% of Russia's population); 290,000 Uzbeks (0.21%); 200,000 Tajiks (0.15%); 103,000 Kyrgyz (0.08%); and 36,000 Turkmens (0.03%)—let alone a substantial amount of 648,000 Kazakhs (0.47% of Russia's population). Among other available figures, those of the aforementioned Centre for Migration Studies in Moscow mention a shift from 1 million labour migrants in 2006 to 2 million only two years later. The over-dominance of CIS countries in Russia's labour migrants' contingents (79% in 2009, 90% for women migrants) must be further qualified by the major part devoted to three Central Asian countries—Kyrgyzstan (10% in 2009, according to official statistics), Tajikistan (21.8%), Uzbekistan (35.3%)—with one-third of Russia's labour migrant population in 2009, and more than half in 2010 (Tiuriukanova 2011: 4; Mkrchian 2011: 9).

[23] Viz. some 18% of the country's adult population identified as 15 years of age or older, and more than 95% of them in Russia (cf. Olimova and Bosc 2003; Olimova and Olimov 2007).

[24] On the presence in Russia in the early 2000s of former fighters of the so-called 'Islamic Movement of Uzbekistan' and militants on the Hizb al-Tahrir al-Islamiyya, see Babadjanov and Islamov 2013.

[25] On Tajikistan see Olimova and Olimov 2007.

of the organization of bazaar workers' dormitories into congregations, and of the diffusion of religious information on this basis and through electronic media (e.g. Roche 2012)[26]—highlighting the internet audience of anti-establishment Muslim preachers like theologian and Sufi master Ishan Nur al-Din Jan Turajanzada (b. 1953) among Moscow's Tajik migrant workers.

Russian researchers on this topic, especially authors linked to the country's Muslim establishment, demonstrate concern at the recent surpassing, in number and in religious influence, of Russia's historical or 'ethnic' Muslim nations by Central Asian migrants. Even in the Middle Volga region, in past times one of Russia's cradles of Islamic erudition and thought, studies on Islamic religious teaching institutions denounce a reduction in the number of Tatar and Bashkir imams, replaced by Tajik and Uzbek clerics, and the replacement of the Tatar language by Russian as the main idiom for preaching Islam (e.g. Mukhametshin 2007)[27]... although the decisive factor for adopting Russian in the majority of Tatarstan's and Dagestan's *madrasa*s is these diverse institutions' mutual competition for attracting students from all over the former USSR. Albeit quite imprecise on the notion of 'religiosity', available statistics also suggest a high level of religious practice among migrants from the Southern Caucasus and Central Asia.[28]

Research materials on the Muslim migrants' situation in present-day Russia also insist on their alleged isolation from the country's autochthonous Muslims—despite attempts to show the migrants' participation in the life of local congregations (e.g. Larina and Naumova 2007). Some statistics also underline phenomena such as weak levels of intermarriage between migrants and Muslim autochthones, and the high sense of exposure to racism developed in Russia's big cities by Chechens, Azerbaijanis, and Tajiks. Rare case studies confirm that in Russian towns, a hostile climate encourages migrants coming from one region to establish more intimate relations with each other than at home, religion being frequently at the centre of 'immigrant alliances' established during prayers in local mosques (cf. Babadjanov and Islamov 2013). Conversely, when migrants do participate in the operation of mosques of regional Muslim spiritual boards, this participation is oftentimes denounced as the expression of an alien force opposed to 'national', mainly Tatar, confessional establishments.[29] The temporary, sometimes seasonal character of migration for many migrant workers (e.g. Ruget 2008) and the role played by enlarged kinship networks in the organization of migrant groups (e.g. Olimova and Bosc 2003) are also invoked for explaining the relative mutual

---

[26] I am particularly grateful to Dr Sophie Roche for having shared with me her promising study of religious practices and affiliations among Moscow's Tajik labour migrants.

[27] And my critical review of this book in *Central Eurasian Reader* 1 (2008): 370–1.

[28] More than 92% of believers in each migrant national group of the Volga region at the eve of the post-2008 burst, contrasting with much lower figures on autochthonous Muslim populations (e.g. V. V. Semenov 2007).

[29] Silant'ev 2002: 5; Yemelianova 2003, and my critical review in *Central Eurasian Reader* 1 (2008): 371–2.

isolation sometimes observed between migrant and autochthonous practitioners of Islam.

## Other Quantitative Approaches of Religious Affiliations and Practices

Research on confessional identities and ritual practice among Russia's Central Asian and Caucasian labour migrants remains poorly developed. Experts seem primarily concerned with avoiding the contagion of Russia by Islamist ideologies allegedly born in the Caucasus and Central Asia.[30] Rare opinion surveys highlight the propagation of 'fundamentalist' ideas and leanings among Russia's Muslims, in the North Caucasus especially (e.g. Abdulagatov 2007). The prevalence of such opinions explains the orientation of substantial part of research about Russia's migrants towards political mobilization among seasonal workers (e.g. Olimova and Olimov 2007) and mutual interactions between vernacular and migrant mosque-goers (e.g. Silan'tev 2002).

Quantifying confessional affiliations remains a sharply discussed issue in the sociology of religions.[31] As we have seen, the 'Atlas' conducted by Sreda underlines the variations in time and space of religious identities within confessional groups. The same atlas also casts light on the decreasing audience of traditional or 'ethnic' religions.[32] It reveals that, while non-Orthodox Christians multiply parishes in Siberia and the Russian Far East, in parallel Muslims increasingly disclaim affiliation to an accredited *madhhab* (traditional theological and legal school of Islam).[33] For Islam as well as for Christianity, it is in the 'born again' populations linked with non-centralized worldwide networks—Salafi Muslim or Protestant Christian—that, according to Sreda's observers, religious practice reaches its highest level. Such an activism, however, does not prevent those mosque-goers who appeal to unity of a wider umma to show extreme mistrust towards Muslim migrants from the Caucasus and Central Asia. From this viewpoint, the yet nascent sociology of Russia's Islam underlines the emergence of multiple cleavages within the country's umma, and an extreme diversity of confessional practices and identities.

In a country where the notion of 'ethnic Muslims' remains central, substantial room is given by sociological surveys to ethnic *cum* confessional affiliations as

---

[30] The Palestinian-born transnational pro-Caliphate party Hizb al-Tahrir al-Islamiyya ['Party of the Islamic Liberation'] was introduced in 2008 as an organization whose 'ideology was engendered by the conditions of present-day Uzbekistan' by Ruslan Nurmametov, of the Spiritual Board of the Muslims of the Chelyabinsk Region, east of the Ural Mountains (cf. Shikhov 2008).

[31] On Russia's case see for instance Musina 1997.

[32] According to a federal inquiry implemented at federal level in 2002 by the All-Russia Centre for the Study of Public Opinion (VTSIOM), at that date 58% of Russia's citizens were declaring themselves Orthodox, 31% atheist, 5% Muslim, 1% non-Orthodox Christian, and 2% of other religions—only 6% of the whole admitting regular attendance of a worship place (cf. Radvanyi 2005: 161).

[33] Even if the respective figures given by the atlas for Muslim believers—viz. 2.4 million Sunnis; 300,000 Shiites; and 6.7 million Muslims refuting affiliation to either group—rely too exclusively on ethnic statistics (cf. <http://www.facebook.com/media/set/?set=a.10151008601181857.414677.139349786856&type=1>).

vectors of integration or self-isolation, with a special interest in migrants, youth, and women. From the viewpoint of socioeconomic integration, however, the evolution of the labour market, at the centre of interests in the 1990s, now seems of lesser importance. Pioneering studies implemented in the bi-national (Tatar/Russian) Republic of Tatarstan on unequal access for Muslim Tatar and Orthodox Russian workers to management and welfare in the regions' new industrial cities (e.g. Garipov 1997), for example, have not been continued and their authors rarely showered with praise.[34] Equality of treatment between Russians and other ethnic groups, a key issue of the Volga Tatar intelligentsia's discourse under Yeltsin, faded with the dissolution of this intelligentsia's major organization, the 'Tatar Civic Centre', in the early 2000s. Yet extremely vivid in the Volga-Ural region, studies on Christian–Muslim relations have been shifting towards identity construction, mutual tolerance,[35] and more lately 'integration' within the one and indivisible Russian nation.

If surveys on the implication of Russia's most diverse Muslim-background populations in crime remain conspicuous by their absence in sociological literature, a rising number of sociological studies of Russia's youth and on the impacts of public discourses on the younger generation's self-construction strategies (on personal story-telling among Muslim-background migrants, especially) provide us with an outline of developments. These approaches show, first, that it is not only young Muslim radicals, but post-Soviet young people as a whole who are dealt with in Russia's common discourse 'with a ring of panic' (Sabirova 2011: 30). The dominant rhetoric of the 1990s on drug problems, criminalization, and moral laxity seems to have given way to sententious discourses on alcoholism, a retreat to subculture, and political apathy. Recent studies suggest that the adoption of radical identities does not always imply the existence of an ideological constituent. In Russia's largest suburbs, Tatar migrant young women in headscarves sometimes enjoy turning themselves into 'part of an overall atmosphere of risk' and provocation (Sabirova 2011: 34).

# Sociologists' Islam: Integrator and/or Isolator?

## Qualitative Parameters: Gender, Generation, and Location

Since the late 1990s initiatives have highlighted the way socio-demographic factors like gender, generation, and location have been stratifying ethnic communities. Two figureheads of the 'Region' Centre in Ulyanovsk, Elena Omel'chenko (b. 1957) and Guzel

---

[34] Despite the potential interest of comparative studies of the situations in the mid-1990s and early 2010s: electronic correspondence with sociologist Iagfar Garipov, 10 October 2012.

[35] e.g. Musina 2001, 2009, 2012; Garipov and Nurulina 2011; Sabirova 2011; and infra chapter 6.D.

Sabirova (b. 1971), demonstrate the central role of the nuclear family in the transmission of religious knowledge and identity. They highlight a strong differentiation between families where traditions were maintained and those associated with rapid urbanization and exposed to stronger generational cleavage (Omel'chenko and Sabirova 2003a: 169–70).

A recent inquiry on the students of Tatarstan's *madrasa*s suggests that confessional socialization could take place in the post-Soviet decades (Garipov and Nurulina 2011: 125–6). However, present-day young adults already belong to the second generation of Muslim believers since the Soviet period. Many were educated by 'born again Muslim' parents. The same survey also casts light on the significance of family education dispensed in national language[36]—confirming the prevalence, among *madrasa* students, of recent migrants from rural Tatar-speaking areas. The families' diverse relationship to Islamization is reflected in their varying perception of a daughter's reversion/Islamization—this experience being lived either as continuation of ancestral traditions or, on the contrary, as a rejection of 'ethnic' Islam (e.g. Sabirova 2011: 338). Comparing and contrasting the narratives of respondents from varied ethnic republics, such studies tend to show varying relationships between Islam and ethnicity in different regions.[37] Breaking with the cult of objectivity still representative of the 1990s, they cast light on the essentially interactive processes at work in the fluid constructions of the self and the other in present-day Russia.

In the field of religious authority and transmission of learning, historical studies have also revealed the deepest impacts of the Soviet and current periods. In the North Caucasus, historians and political sociologists show religious dynasties struggling against the emergence of new protagonists. Among these newcomers, observers come across other genealogy owners. Such is the case in Circassia for example, in the Northwest Caucasus, a region where since the 1990s descendants of Adyghes settled in Kosovo during the Ottoman period have Islamized the initially secular Circassian national movement (cf. Bram 2008; Nefliasheva 2009). Prominent 'returnees' increased the regional authorities' panic in the face of this new 'tribal' and 'pan-Islamic' danger. The role played by Dagestani émigré populations who had left early Soviet Russia and settled in Turkey, Cyprus, and present-day Jordan and Saudi Arabia in the 1920s–1930s was also highlighted in the early phases of the open conflicts in Chechnya—many observers underlining at the same time the poor mutual understanding between the *jihadist* fighters of émigré background and the local Muslim populations.[38]

---

[36] Most informants belonged to exclusively Tatar-speaking families (44%) or bilingual Tatar-and-Russian-speaking families (39%).

[37] Notably in two different entities often taken as comparative tools: Tatarstan—a bi-ethnic republic where Islam is inseparable from Tatar ethnic identity by opposition to Orthodox Russians—and Dagestan—an ethno-linguistic mosaic where Islam has potentially supra-ethnic identification, while customs and traditions undermine any single vision of religion (Sabirova 2011: 181).

[38] Overviewed by Filiu 2006: 190–1; see also Souleimanov and Ditrych 2008; Williams 2008.

## Some Issues of Language and Discourse

Immediately related to the religious field, language policies have remained a key issue in the contemporary history and social sciences of Russia. Recently research has shown how the promotion of national languages by some ethnic republics in the 1990s divided their populations, most notably in bi-ethnic and bilingual Tatarstan. Promoted as one of Tatarstan's two state languages on a more equal footing with Russian, Tatar became a compulsory subject in the Republic's schools. Several studies cast a harsh light on internal factors of weakness (lack of motivation, insufficient public investment, etc.: e.g. Cashaback 2008). Russian speakers, including many Tatars, felt discriminated against. Even Tatar speakers of the older generation or those returning from other parts of the former USSR, Central Asia in particular, have had difficulties reading modern written Tatar, characterized by abundant use of Arabic words, not always consistently and in total absence of standardization (cf. Wertheim 2005).

Combined with these weaknesses, the expansion of digital communication and the influx of migrant populations from the former Soviet South reinforced the Russian language's position as the idiom of Islamic preaching at the all-Russia level, alongside the flourishing of confessional media in national languages within ethnic republics. A nascent interest in these media has recently developed, dealing especially with those in Tatar language (e.g. Usmanova et al. 2010: 52–7). Despite the aforementioned decisive contribution by international historians to the reconstruction of Russia's modern and contemporary Islamic discourses, very little systematic research has been devoted to the internet and its decisive role in the evolution of present-day Islamic discourses and the restructuring of believers' networks.[39] As to fictional literature with Muslim religious themes, in Russian or national languages, it seems to be as yet ignored by the academy.

Public interest in rituals and their role in the transmission of learning, morals, and identity decreased after the global decline of religious practice observed in the 2000s. The as yet extremely rare inter-regional comparative studies (e.g. Omel'chenko and Sabirova 2003b) highlight the diversity of observance of Islamic or Islamized rituals and festivals in Russia's territories and social groups. Many apparent contradictions are underlined: while food prohibitions are seldom rigorously enforced, for instance, the Ramadan fast became a key vector of social prestige. In connection with the growing significance of a selective individual approach to religious affiliation and practice, increasing tension too is highlighted between traditional vernacular models and the desire to standardize ritual practice. The adoption of new dress codes 'in the Turkish manner', in the Middle Volga's new industrial city of Naberezhnye Chelny for example, is locally perceived as an innovation, against the backdrop of a revaluation of national cultural heritages. In parallel the rapid stratification of post-Soviet society makes the

---

[39] Despite recent attempts at discourse analysis—e.g. Kemper 2012b on the Kavkaz Center, the main propaganda tool of the Caucasus Emirate which, in 2007 under the leadership of Chechen militant Dokku Umarov succeeded the defunct independent Republic of Ichkeria-Chechnya, displaying a wide spectrum of style–contents relations.

observance of traditions such as the payment of the *kalïm* (dowry) in Dagestan much more awkward. Attentive to ethical and ritual change induced by rapid social differentiation, Russia's sociology paves the way for diachronic studies in fields where anthropologists are curiously conspicuous by their complete absence.

## Gender Issues: Going to Market

The highly charged discursive context of gender and Islam is sometimes put forward for explaining 'the failure of Russian sociological literature to fully explore the intersection of gender and Islam' (Omel'chenko and Sabirova 2003c: 242). In their comparative inquiry on Tatarstan and Dagestan, Omel'chenko and Sabirova, however, unveil discrepancies between stereotypes and self-narratives. They show the different impacts of these two republics' respective ethnic and social situations on discursive practices.[40] Analyses of recent adherence to new images of the perfect Muslim women imported from Middle Eastern countries question the concept of 'retraditionalization' so typical of the sociology of post-Soviet Islam. The now salient external image of the *shakhidka* (female suicide bomber, from Arabic *shahid*, 'martyr') also raises parents' prejudices against headscarves, in European Russia especially (cf. Sabirova 2011).

Comparative surveys also reflect the weight of regional backgrounds in respective portraits of the 'genuine' Muslim family. Tatarstan's respondents almost universally consider that marriage ought to be 'mono-ethnic'—mixed unions coming up against children's religious initiation and funeral rites, both important community markers in a bi-ethnic *and* bi-confessional republic. In multiethnic and multilingual Dagestan, it is the issue of language that appears at the forefront of discussions on mixed marriage, and the mutual compatibility of diverse customary traditions (*'adat*). On issues like polygyny and clothing, the small number of sociological works underline the same inter-regional variations: in Tatarstan where polygyny is poorly attested, its criticism is articulated prominently by young, non-religious, and unmarried women; in Dagestan where bigamy is practised among small groups of well-to-do businessmen, public demonstration by *nouveaux riches* of male superiority can be perceived by other men as personal insult.

An item of primary symbolic significance in Russia, especially in bi-confessional regions like Tatarstan and the country's biggest suburbs, women's clothing appears in comparative approaches through the impacts of varying ethnic contexts. In Tatarstan, surveys suggest that the adoption of a specifically Muslim dress code is problematic for middle-aged people since it is associated with the memory of Soviet-style folklore

---

[40] Because of the tremendous change of the past two decades on the labour market, the household has become a refuge value and the enlarged family a key vector of protection and influence, but through unseen gendered distributions of roles: see Sokirianskaia (2005) on Chechnya; Garipov and Nurulina (2011) on Tatarstan; to be compared with analogous data in V. E. Semenov (2007) on the Russian Federation as a whole.

events. In Dagestan, stricter attitudes are observed towards Muslim dress in religious villages (cf. Omel'chenko and Sabirova 2003c: 258–61). Rarely taken into account by public discourses, the motivations of women wearing the scarf recently became an object of systematic surveys showing the importance of 'tying the scarf forward' among migrant Tatar women in Russia's big cities (Sabirova 2011: 334)—for expressing a higher degree of faith and against the sexual objectification of women. Among Tatar women in the 2000s, tying the scarf around one's head in an untraditional way (that is, folded into two halves and tied under the chin) also appears as a symbol of female modernity if compared with the larger white scarf borne by elder women (also tied under the chin, but left unfolded with two tips hanging in the back).

# Social Sciences and the Fluidity of the Religious Field

## Studying Islam and Muslims

Ethnography and Oriental studies, both endowed with strong Orthodox missionary backgrounds, are the two disciplines that since the Tsarist period have dominated the study of non-Christian religious practice in Russia. Both give credit to Soviet and post-Soviet Muslims for their alleged superficial knowledge of their own religion. As for Islamic religious education, it is perceived as a forgotten scholarly legacy, fully replaced by 'popular' forms of Islam since the mass suppression of religious personnel by Stalin's purges.[41] Moreover, Russia's young mosque-goers are commonly reproached by a number of the country's academic experts for their borrowings of elements of ritual from Islamic legal schools (Ar. *madhhabs*) alien to the Muslim traditions developed in the Russian Empire and the USSR. Many observers, both domestic and international, denounce especially the irruption in Russia of the rigid Hanbali *madhhab* from the Arab Near East. The Hanbaliyya is opposed by these authors to the more adaptable Hanafi tradition that continues to prevail in Russia and Siberia and to the Shafii theology and law that predominates in the North Eastern Caucasus.

These varied assertions also suggest that for being a proper Muslim, one must show a sound knowledge of those Islamic dogmas and laws cultivated during sometimes more than a millennium on the soil of the present-day Russian Federation, and act strictly within their framework. Historian Vladimir Bobrovnikov mischievously observes that Russia's imams are now supposed to demonstrate accomplishments in the translation of the Qur'an from Arabic whilst nobody would have expected a party committee secretary of the Soviet period to know by heart Marx's *Capital* in the German original (Bobrovnikov

---

[41] On the North-Western Caucasus (Circassia), see Babich 2008: 24; critically reviewed by M. Kemper in *Central Eurasian Reader* 2 (2010): 547.

2007). Besides, few experts on Islam in the former Soviet realm have yet studied the believers' expectations of their religious leaders as they have been expressed for decades in a rich hagiography and obituary literature (e.g. Dudoignon 2011a).

Indeed, 'popular' forms of Islam are still felt to be uninteresting by many specialists. A great pity since, as shown by history and by sociology, it is precisely in non-verbal and ritual practice that a great deal of the 'learned' tradition of Islam, in personal ethics in particular, has been preserved through the alleged hiatus of the Soviet period. In the rare cases of durable observation, Russian ethnography has shown an eagerness to revisit the dialectics of 'learned' vs. 'popular' Islam.[42] This opposition was recently questioned through the study of a wider typology of figureheads of the religious field, for example through the Noghai *yïllï mollas*: specialists of Islamic theology who are also reputed to command to the spirits and heal people with their help (Iarlykapov 2008). In this figure and in many others, Muslim Russia's ethnographers now observe the perfect interlink of 'orthodox' and 'popular' elements of Islam, impossible in many instances to detach from one another, far from the dialectic oppositions so characteristic of Soviet scholarship on religions.

## Rediscovering the Diversity of Russia's Islam

Since 1991, academic efforts have been made to recover the pre-Soviet tradition of Russia's Muslim peoples and to highlight its pluralism and extreme regional and social differentiation (cf. Dannreuther 2010a).[43] It is true that the past two decades have seen the emergence of a plurality of protagonists in expertise and publication on Russia's Islam.[44] Financed by domestic capital, new private Islamic foundations often rely on central or regional muftiates while trying to make academics their partners in their edition and propagation work. In parallel, secular experts have been brought to participate in judicial expertise. Often reproaching prosecuted Muslim activists and organizations for their religious 'incompetence',[45] a number of these secular experts have paradoxically opened the way for the treatment of Russia's civil and criminal procedures in Islamic theological terms.

---

[42] See the plea by Sergei Abashin for a renewed ethnography of Russia's Islam in *Central Eurasian Reader* 2 (2010): 348–53.

[43] These efforts are notably reflected by the vogue for collective volumes and conferences about inter-confessional relations in Russia. On the paradigmatic value of the Middle Volga region as an 'ideal model for a Eurasian synthesis reflecting the coexistence of the three most important ethno-linguistic (Slavic, Turkic, and Finno-Ugric) and confessional (Russian Orthodox, Sunni Muslim, and Polytheist) communities of Russia', see Grachev et al. 2005: 9.

[44] Let's notably mention private Muslim foundations like 'Marjani' in Moscow, endowed since 2011 with a 'Cabinet of Islamic Studies' (<http://mardjani.ru/ru/601.html>), 'Medina' in Nizhny Novgorod, a major editor of regional encyclopaedias on Islam in Russia (see for instance the set of book reviews in *Central Eurasian Reader* 2 (2008): 54–6, 359–65), the 'Abubakarov' Foundation in Makhachkala, an active publisher of Islamic literature and the organizer of a yearly concourse of Arabic calligraphy, and the 'Ahmad-Hajji Qadïrov' Foundation in Grozny, subsidized by the pro-Russian Chechen administration.

[45] Shikhov 2008.

Sometimes closely involved in the writing of Arabic textbooks for public educational institutions,[46] the academic world is present too within several state consultative institutions created in the mid-2000s, such as the Committee for Freedom of Conscience of the National Assembly of the Russian Federation and the Council of Experts for State Expertise on Religion, both established in 2006. Breaking with the prudent secular legislative practice of the early 1990s, the appearance of these councils manifested the adoption by Russia's executive of an interventionist stance in confessional matters. This turn must be resituated in the wake of the 1997 law On Freedom of Conscience and Religious Organizations[47] which, well before Putin's advent, already insisted on the 'peculiar role' of Orthodox Christianity in Russia's history and established a catalogue of the country's 'traditional religions'—Orthodoxy, Islam, Buddhism, and Judaism, in the respective traditional forms of these religions cultivated for centuries within Russia. It is only in these admitted 'traditional' forms that these global religious systems are entitled to receive financial support from Russia's central, regional, and local administrations. It is only these forms that enjoy teaching in the Federation's primary, secondary, and higher public education institutions. Such typological prerequisites still reinforce the state's permanent need for historical and theological expertise, and explain the predominance of Arabic and Oriental scholars in the public discourse on Islam.

This distinction between 'traditional' and 'non-traditional' Islam remains a critical issue for many scholars and experts. While the former is approximately identified with the vernacular state-controlled practice of the Islamic faith by Russia's 'ethnic' Muslims, the latter, defined primarily since the late 1990s in terms of Salafi movements, is viewed by many Russian commentators (and by many of their Western counterparts) as a threat to Russia's integrity. Soviet-inherited dualism reduces Islam's pluralism into a political opposition between state-approved and state-opposed practice. Another Soviet legacy consists, as we have seen, of equating ethnicity with nationality—strengthening the dichotomy of 'moderate Russian Islam' vs. 'extremist foreign Islam'. Since the 1920s Islam has often been seen by the Soviet ruling circles as a non-democratic other, ontologically related to the culture and tradition of 'Oriental despotism' (cf. Kemper 2009; Dannreuther 2010a). These colonial and Soviet representations have been reinvigorated by the poisonous climate of the post-Chechen wars period.

## The Interplay of Ethnic and Confessional Identities

The growing traditionalism shown by Russia's Muslim confessional establishments does not prevent central power institutions—Russia's diplomacy and national security, especially—to show benevolence if not keen interest in some of the country's most radical anti-establishment Islamist trends. If Muslim 'extremism' is perceived as alien and

---

[46] As for the elementary and secondary schools of Dagestan (Bobrovnikov et al. 2010: 149–50).

[47] *O svobode sovesti i religioznykh organizatsiiakh*, federal law 125-F3 of 26 September 1997 (cf. Kovalskaya 2013).

hostile to Russia, 'fundamentalist Islam, though antagonistic to Russian secular values, can potentially be consonant with Russian strategic interests' (Dannreuther 2010a: 15)—as it has been and remains in the Near and Middle East for a range of Western powers. Already in the early 1990s, this rhetorical distinction between extremism and fundamentalism permitted convergences between the upper military and intelligence staff, part of the Muslim religious establishment, and the Islamic Revival Party of the USSR created in Astrakhan in June 1990 with the participation of Dagestani and Tajik militants. Heydar Jemal (b. 1947) in particular, an IRP founding father of Azerbaijani origin, raised interest by his biography, which associated political Islam, neo-Nazism, and occultism.[48] These convergences were then spreading out in Russian periodical publications such as *Elementy*, *al'-Kods*, and *Den'* prolonged by present-day *Zavtra* and its link *Den' TV*—the most steadfast media bridges between Russia's 'new right' (Rus. *novye pravye*) and a handful of active Islamist circles.[49] Since Russia's anti-Western strategic turn of 2003, the consecration of these ideological experiments helped the gradual conceptualization of Russia as a Eurasian polity.

With the beginning of Vladimir Putin's first presidential term on 1 January 2000, the Soviet-inherited dualism of a 'foreign extremist Islam' vs. 'loyal Russian Islam' could be resurrected, as a research paradigm for political science scholars and as a decision-making yardstick for the political and judicial powers. Within Russia, the authorities had already begun in the late 1990s to ban most foreign Muslim charities and organizations suspected of propagating transnational radical trends. Presenting the resolution of the Chechen issue as a struggle against 'foreign extremism' and for the restoration of Russia's 'traditional' Islam committed to peaceful coexistence with other confessions, the Putin administration has co-opted since 2000 Ahmad Qadïrov (1951–2004), a former Mufti of Chechnya and a religious head of the Chechen independence, and after him his son Ramzan (b. 1976), as the leaders of Chechnya's pro-Russian government. For critical observers, the Kremlin's oscillating alliance system confirmed that the North Caucasus 'Wahhabism' widely disparaged by Russia's mass media was a mere 'catch-all term' (Knysh 2004), a 'parasite word' (Bobrovnikov 2007) finally banned as such from serious academic literature and part of the media (Sabirova 2011: 331).[50]

Everywhere in Russia the public ban on vaguely defined 'Wahhabism' incriminates a wide range of Islamist groups, from Nurcu missionary cells to embryonic networks

---

[48] Cf. Sedgwick 2004: 222–4, 257–60; Moroz 2005: 128–9.

[49] Highlighting the anti-Western sentiment of geopolitical thinkers looking back to undivided Eurasia, these newspapers and their websites laud to the skies Iranian Shi'ite fundamentalism, while insisting on Russia's fair struggle against Western-backed transnational networks of Sunni *jihad* fighters, from Afghanistan to Chechnya, and singing praise of those Chechen *jihadists* who since 2000 are in power in Grozny. See for instance the explicit address 'To the Saviours of Chechnya' signed R. Madueva and published in *Zavtra* on 15 February 2000 (still available on 25 September 2012 at <http://zavtra.ru/content/view/2000-02-1572/>).

[50] On the exploitation of the 'Wahhabi' accusation in the disputes between Russia's rival Muslim boards during the 1990s and early 2000s, see the astute remarks by Khabutdinov 2005: 151ff.

of the Hizb al-Tahrir al-Islamiyya.[51] Initially derogatory, the 'Wahhabi' epithet is sometimes adopted as a positive identity marker. Such is the case among the Chechen youth for whom Russian counterpropaganda (especially the equation nationalism = separatism = terrorism = international terrorism) transformed a decade of war in Chechnya from 1999 to 2009 into a blood feud with hopelessly blurred lines (e.g. Sokirianskaia 2008). Ironically, surveys carried out in the decisive years 1999–2000 in ethnic republics clearly indicated weak support for separatism even among members of the titular nations (e.g. Hagendoorn et al. 2008).

The polarization of the public discourse on Islam in Russia does not help to explain the typological diversity of modern Salafism. This set of reformist currents of Islam includes a quietist form which has remained non-violent and mostly apolitical (e.g. Rougier 2008: 15–19).[52] This means that in many instances Salafism shows much less politicized than the ex-*jihadist* networks now supported by the Kremlin in Chechnya. In its quietist forms it proves less interested in politics than the traditional regional and local Muslim establishments. Partly inherited from the Tsarist and Soviet times, Russia's muftiates have been for two decades in mutual competition for the control of mosques and tithes. The action of these competing central, regional, and local Muslim religious boards explains the expansion of violence *within* Russia's Islam since the return of the mosques' assets in 1993. The obligation of a legal accreditation for local Muslim congregations raised endless debates on their affiliation with one or another of the quickly multiplying and competing muftiates—either all-Russian as in the case of the Soviet-inherited Muftiate of Ufa; ethnic or national as in the case of Dagestan or Tatarstan; or regional outside of an ethnic republic as with the Muslim board of Nizhny Novgorod, in the Middle Volga region. Issues such as the return of mosques' assets and the collection of Muslim tithes also deepened the competing Muftis' collusion with the local, regional, and central political power. They explain, too, the energy Russia's Muftis, old and new, expended during these decisive decades for the disqualification or elimination of potential rivals and dissidents.

## Secular Reform: Rise and Fall

Another feature of the late Soviet and current periods is the emergence of religious Muslim intelligentsias, with two distinct approaches towards Islam and multiple intermediary gradations: reformism (secular or fundamentalist, both often apolitical) and traditionalism (often politicized and staunchly opposed to both reformisms). Contrary to many experts' assertions, reformism has been exerting an influence on Russia's general Muslim population since the rehabilitation of a wide range of vernacular nineteenth- and early

---

[51] e.g. Silant'ev 2007: this article denouncing a 'union' of Russia's Salafis with the Hizb al-Tahrir al-Islamiyya is based exclusively and uncritically on local press releases and on police and public prosecutor's sources.

[52] See also the interesting but exceptional case study of apolitical Salafism in Western Siberia by Cherepanov 2009.

twentieth-century 'Jadid' Muslim thinkers in the most varied Muslim-peopled regions of the USSR, during the 1970s–1980s (cf. Dudoignon 2011b). The most discussed example of Russia's secular Islamic reform is the 'Euro-Islam' project developed since the mid-1990s by philosopher Raphael Hakimov (b. 1947). A theoretician of Russia's federalism and the main political adviser to Mintimer Shaimiev, the President of Tatarstan from 1991 to 2010, Hakimov long directed the Institute of History of the newly created Academy of Sciences of Tatarstan in Kazan. He systematically promoted the study of vernacular Islamic reform as a possible great ancestor to Euro-Islam. Institutionally, Euro-Islam in fact presents a striking continuity with the Soviet practice of co-opting religion as an ideological support for the secular political order (cf. Dannreuther 2010a). It also illustrates the development of numbers of intellectual bridges between national movements and regional political establishments. It is not by chance if historical research developed in Kazan since the 1990s deals with themes such as: Islam as a national Tatar culture that unites the religious and the secular; insistence on knowledge acquisition as a Muslim duty; equality between men and women; and above all inter-confessional toleration.

In parallel the Islamic concept of *ijtihad*, a catchword for the free questioning of tradition, has been in Tatarstan not only transmuted to the secular sphere, but also attached by the academic discourse to a particular national identity (cf. Bustanov and Kemper 2012a: 49–52). In this perspective, nineteenth- and early twentieth-century Islamic reform is reinterpreted as a tentative elaboration of a model of adaptation to European industrial society. Dagestan itself, the centre of a Muslim reformist trend during the last decades of the Tsarist period, has only recently begun to reappraise this side of its religious legacy.[53] However, in the 2000s the initially enthusiastic rediscovery of Islamic reform has given room in these regions to more careful approaches, after nineteenth-century thinkers like 'Abd al-Nasir Abu'l-Nasr Qursawi and Shihab al-Din Marjani, identified by historians of Russia's Muslim public thought with Islamic reform, were recently adopted as reference authors by neo-fundamentalist trends.[54]

Today as in the late Tsarist period, secular reformists are criticized by their traditionalist opponents for their alleged heterodoxy and for their rejection of the traditional schools of Islamic theology and law (Ar. *madhhab*s). Initially supported by Tatarstan's government and fashionable in the Volga-Ural region and the North-East Caucasus till the early 2000s, Euro-Islam faced the consequences for religious and national cultures of the Putin administration's growing opposition to everything Western. The initial accusations launched against Euro-Islam for its overt collusion with Tatarstan's political apparatus have been replaced since 2003 by denunciations of its cultivation of Western ideas. Such accusations are now relayed simultaneously by traditional religious boards and by Salafi

---

[53] Notably through the gradual reprint of early twentieth-century periodicals: see notably Navruzov 2007, esp. 27–44.

[54] See for instance the tribune by historian Aidar Khabutdinov, 'Vakhkhabizm v Tatarstane: segodniashniaia situatsiia v istoricheskoi retrospective' [Wahhabism in Tatarstan: The Present Situation in Historical Retrospect], *Vestnik Evrazii* 2000/2 (also available at <http://islamrf.ru/news/history/culture/24673>).

fundamentalist reformers, mutually opposed but rounded up by a common hostility to everything European. The case illustrates well the influence of a certain academic discourse on Islam and modernity, and this discourse's partial failure—linked with Russia's changing policies as much as with the rapidly changing and contradictory expectations of the country's Muslim audience.

# Islam in the Public Space and Secularism

## Echoing the Fragmentation of the Religious Field

The succession of state-Islam legal arrangements adopted since the end of the Soviet period have not yet become the subject of systematic studies, save assessments of the infringements inflicted to the principle of secularity proclaimed in the constitution of 1993 (cf. Rousselet 2008, 2009; Fagan 2012). These assessments underline the strong regional and local variations observable throughout the country—a consequence of the strong clientele relationship established during the past two decades between clerics of all 'traditional' confessional systems and Russia's political class. Bigger interest has been shown by historians in the practices of the Muscovite, Tsarist, and Soviet administrations towards 'foreign faiths', and these practices' impacts on the religious field.[55] Islam's withdrawal to the private sphere from the 1930s onwards was no novelty for Russia's Muslims: since the seventeenth century, the transformation of Orthodoxy into the state religion had led to the self-seclusion of local Muslim communities. The autonomy that these congregations enjoyed in Tsarist and Soviet Russia was different, though. The recognition of the legitimacy of religious conviction by the state in Tsarist Russia meant that the Muslims had institutions at their disposal. Their inner autonomy was largely preserved through their mono-ethnic settlements in parts of the towns and in the countryside. In Soviet Russia, communist ideology and forced industrialization led to internal migration, intensive inter-ethnic contacts, and the spread of Soviet culture (Dudoignon and Noack 2013).

As shown in the early 2010s by pioneering historical studies, a constitutive factor of Soviet policy came into play: the individual forms in which the leaders ruled the country in the 1960s–1980s. In ethnic enclaves especially, some religious institutions and practices could be preserved throughout the whole Soviet period under permanent threat of sanctions. In her study on the Tatar Muslim-peopled village of Srednjaia Eliuzan', in the Orthodox Slavic-peopled Penza region of the Ural Mountains, sociologist Liliya Sagitova demonstrated the resilience of the institution of the family and the stimulation by collectivized agriculture of the reproduction of social and cultural conservatism

---

[55] e.g. on Muscovy and the early Russian Empire see Nogmanov 2005; on the late Tsarist period Werth 2002; on the Soviet period Ro'i 2000: 9–55 and Arapov and Kosach 2010; on the Soviet and current periods Arapov 2007—denouncing the current administration's illiteracy (*bezgramotnost'*) in ethnic and confessional matters, and its Islamophobia.

(cf. Sagitova 2013). This heritage of autonomy provides us with a historical explanation for the current subdivision of Russia's Muslim establishment into a multitude of varied trends. Since the multiplication of muftiates in the early 1990s, these trends have been in fierce competition for the definition of religious standards, in many instances with participation of research institutes and universities.

Appointed by the Soviet state in 1980, Mufti Taj al-Din emerged as a supporter of unified Russia against the national sovereignties of the 1990s. The Tatar academic intelligentsia shook his authority through the promotion of an alternative Muslim Spiritual Board of Tatarstan (DUMRT in Russian acronyms: cf. Usmanova et al. 2010: 50–2). Moreover, a Council of 'Ulama was set up in Kazan in 1995 with participation of researchers, intellectuals, and national leaders. They encouraged the conception of a national Muslim education, specifically in the Tatar language, while Tatarstan's government was financing the rapid growth of mosques. Kazan's autonomous government received the support of local authorities and entrepreneurship, especially in Tatarstan's oil-producing districts, so for eighteen mosques officially operating in Tatarstan before perestroika, about 1,000 could be counted in the late 1990s and some 1,300 in the mid-2000s (Mukhametshin 2005: 122). In parallel to DUMRT's extension, the 'Iman' Foundation was initially favouring the publication and diffusion of the historiography of Islamic reform and of the Euro-Islamic trend, opposing the traditionalist line defended in Ufa.

## The Mutations of Religious Authority

In the early 1990s a number of foreign charities were supporting quickly multiplying Islamic foundations, schools, and places of worship. These developments were rapidly perceived by numerous experts, oftentimes linked to Muslim boards, as covers for 'separatism' (e.g. Mukhametshin 2010: 41). The result was a succession of bans on foreign financing of Russia's congregations. A consequence was the reduction of the number of *madrasas*, accompanied by the standardization of their teaching programmes under tight scrutiny of the Muslim spiritual boards (e.g. Usmanova et al. 2010: 56). In parallel, sociologists observed a quick diversification of the channels of transmission of Islamic religious learning. The enlarged family and kinship networks reinforced by mass labour migrations play a pivotal role in this phenomenon (cf. Omel'chenko and Sabirova 2003b: 196–7). Alongside extended kinship relations, the media also play a central role in the propagation of religious discourses. For many, television remains the only source of authoritative discourse on religion.

Since the mid-1990s, Moscow's attempts to recentralize Russia's political apparatus brought about a redistribution of roles in former autonomous republics. These quick transformations lie at the core of an abundant political and political science literature. In Kazan conflicts finally arose between the aforementioned Spiritual Board of the Muslims of Tatarstan (DUMRT) and the republic's government. Prefiguring Putin's early-2000s discourse on the 'multi-ethnic people of Russia', the Tatarstani President Shaimiev shrewdly propagated the idea of a 'multi-ethnic people of Tatarstan'. While DUMRT finally sided with the government, the 'Ittifaq' Tatar nationalist party and its leader Fawziya Bayramova abandoned their previous support for secular Islamic reform and rejected Western democratic ideals. Central Russia's Islam being based on the Hanafi *madhhab*, after 1998 all the other Islamic movements in Tatarstan henceforth became 'unofficial'. Under the appellation of 'Wahhabism', DUMRT as well as a whole range of national and regional Muslim boards began actively to target a variety of denominations. The main ones throughout Russia were and remain: the Tablighi Jama'at,[56] the Nurcu movement,[57] and the Hizb al-Tahrir al-Islamiyya.[58] Since 2011 the 'Arab Springs' have only aggravated these movements' situation in the Russian Federation, because of their association by local pundits with US and EU support to Near Eastern Saudi- and Qatar-backed Sunni revolutionary movements.

In Chechnya, political and religious sociology contributed to the identification of new solidarity structures. The inner migrations of the Soviet period concentrated manpower in the foothills of the Caucasus, where traditional religious and sub-ethnic divisions were replaced by wider social groups and networks, by enlarged *wird*s (branches of a Sufi *tariqa*) in particular (cf. Sokirianskaia 2005; Khizrieva 2009). Growing numbers of Muslim practitioners started to perform massive pilgrimages to holy places, and formerly confidential rituals such as Sufi *dhikr*s (ceremonies of recall of the name of God) came to assume a public character. Unlike Dagestan, however, Chechnya's *wird*s did not produce charismatic personalities able to overcome organizational fragmentation. This absence of authoritative traditional Sufi leaders ultimately permitted the rise of the militias (*jama'at*s) set up during the wars against Russia in 1994–6 and 1999–2009. In Dagestan, the independent 'Islamic communities' (also called *jama'at*s) established in the 1990s were suppressed militarily in 1999 under cover of Russia's second post-Soviet war against Chechnya, with the support of local Sufi authorities. More than opposition between Salafis and Sufis, the violent competition between Sufi masters themselves raised scholarly interest in the confessional motives of public violence as well as in discourses by prominent Sufi leaders. Among the latter must be mentioned Shaykh Sa'id Afandi of Chirkey (1937–2012), an Avar Naqshbandi-Mahmudi master who used to denounce any Dagestani anti-establishment Muslim leader as a 'Wahhabi' (cf. Kemper 2012a, 2012b). The assassination of this influential figure in August 2012 struck the popular imagination throughout Russia even more than Vice-Mufti Ya'qupov's murder in Kazan had two months earlier.

---

[56] A missionary movement created in India in 1926 for struggling against Hindu religious propaganda, the TJ has been labelled 'extremist' by Russia's Supreme Court since 2006.

[57] Created in post-Second World War Turkey for the modernization of Islam—for the Islamization of modernity, correct its detractors—continued by the Fethullah Gülen international school network, the Nurcu movement endeavours since the early 1990s to re-Islamize the Turkic-speaking and other peoples of the former USSR. It was forbidden by the Supreme Court of Russia on 10 April 2008.

[58] A Sunni Muslim political party created in Palestine in the 1950s for restoring the Caliphate through non-violent means, the Hizb al-Tahrir became in the mid-2000s SCO's *bête noire*; on the history of the Tahrir's deployment in the former USSR, see Karagiannis 2010: 58–72.

## Towards Global Appraisals: Studying the Impacts of Privatization

The appearance in Dagestan of independent, self-segregated 'Islamic communities' (Ar. *jama'at islami*) during the 1990s in the flatlands of Buinaksk, Khasav Yurt, and Kizil Yurt is explained by historians and political scientists by the exclusion, as in Chechnya, of the resettled populations of the Soviet period from the profits of privatization. Aki Chechens in particular, whose upper valleys had been peopled by Lak dwellers after their deportation to Central Asia in 1944, had resettled in 1958 in the nearby lowland cities of Khasav Yurt and Kizil Yurt. Investing their market gardening know-how in private cultivation in the margins of the kolkhoz system (cf. Gammer 2005b; Kisriev 2007: 82–95), they had gradually freed themselves simultaneously from collective agriculture and from the religious authority of the Dagestani Muslim Spiritual Board. Political science largely reflects the same struggle, elsewhere in the North Caucasus, by mosques against national Muslim spiritual boards. Such is the case of the congregations of young Balkar mosque-goers of the southern rural district of the Elbrus in Kabardo-Balkaria (Iarlykapov 2009: 213–14). Even in this region, long reputed for its allegedly superficial Islamicization, one could observe in the 2000s a rapid spread of the idea of *jihad* and of the Salafi practice of *takfir wa hijra*,[59] the ideological basis of the 'Islamic communities' of the 1990s.

Lasting public violence in Dagestan raised the interest of a diverse group of scholars in the rekindled rivalry within the Shafii Sunni community for the control of Dagestan's Muslim Spiritual Board between Avar migrants and Kumyk lowlanders (on them, see above; cf. Silant'ev 2002: 7–8; Gammer 2005b). Avars, especially the disciples of the late Sufi master Shaykh Sa'id Afandi of Chirkey, held the key positions in the Board, leading to the multiplication of alternative ethnic muftiates.[60] As in Chechnya one can feel here the impact of the mass resettlements of the post-Second World War decades on the institutional life of Islam. The internecine conflicts for the profitable control of each republic's muftiate also reflect the effects of the quick privatizations operated in the early 1990s and the concentration of resources in the hands of limited numbers of oligarchs of faith.

Studies on collective memory show how this substratum was made more sensitive in the 1980s–1990s by the recollection, borne by the baby-boom generation, of the deportations of the 1940s–1950s. These studies highlight the fostering of the 'memories

---

[59] 'Anathema and self-exile', on the model of Prophet Muhammad leaving Mecca for Yathrib, the future Medina, in 622—the Hegira (*hijra*) marking the beginning of the Islamic era.

[60] A 'national' Kumyk spiritual board in Dagestan's capital Makhachkala was followed by a Lak board, a Darghi qadiship, a Nogay directorate, ..., all soon neutralized by powerful Mufti Sayyid Muhammad Hajji Abu-Bakr (Abubakarov, assassinated himself already in August 1998). Sayyid Muhammad Hajji was then the envied controller of a number of Islamic educational institutions within the Republic, but also of more than one thousand Dagestani students in religion outside Russia (cf. Bobrovnikov et al. 2010: 141–2; see also the interesting praise of Sa'id Afandi on <http://www.islamdag.ru/lichnosti/7269>).

of grievance' by independent Chechnya's President Jokhar Dudayev (1991–6) and the attraction to militancy of the young generation through feelings of revenge (cf. Sokirianskaia 2008; Campana 2009). It is the rift between Dagestani and Chechen identities that ultimately turned the spotlight to Dagestani resistance to Chechen pretence to political and religious leadership in the 1990s–2000s, and to the ultimate failure of *jihad* mass mobilization. Chechen attempts to export 'decolonization' and to create a 'single Islamic nation' on the basis of the Caucasus finally alienated the Dagestani public (Gammer 2005a). As shown by historians and political scientists, Islam ultimately fails to be a unifying force in the region, notably because of the contrasting and changing attitudes of different segments of the Sufi world towards Russia's political establishment and the issue of 'infidel' rule.[61]

# Islam in the Political Landscape

## Political Parties and the Expression of Discontent

Studies on political parties in Russia rarely address the Islamist organizations that have emerged since 1990. In the early 2000s an inquiry partly dedicated to the Volga region kept completely silent on the Tatar and other nationalist organizations of the 1990s, including the then influential Kazan-based 'Tatar Civic Centre' (Hutcheson 2003: 45–54). Insisting on the political parties' 'fairly small role', this study highlights the ethnic republics' frequent support of the federal 'party of power' in the 2000s and the fact that non-establishment parties, although numerous and active, achieve little. Albeit working together on the model of the oppositional fronts of the late 1980s, Tatarstan's Democrats, communists, and nationalists, for instance, were frequently criticized in the 2000s by international observers for being unable to relay the claims of the region's Muslim populations (cf. Daucé 2005).

In the 1990s, the same authors noticed that no independent Muslim political party had brought off any electoral breakthrough. Created in 1990 but already eclipsed in Russia four years later, the Islamic Revival Party had been succeeded in the mid-1990s by the Nur ('Light') Party, which managed to obtain 5% of the votes in Tatarstan and 15% in Chechnya in Russia's general elections of 1995. The Refah ('Prosperity') Party created in 1998 was distinguished by a strategy of association with power in the framework of the control of political life set up by the Putin administration. The adoption in 2001 of a new law 'On political parties' banning organizations founded on a professional, ethnic, national, or religious basis closed this period of history (Daucé 2005: 174)—although the

---

[61] Breaking with the dialectical approach of the Cold War period, which identified Sufism *per se* as a vector of political resistance in the North Caucasus, recent historians of modern Sufism notably demonstrated that, in the nineteenth century, the Naqshbandiyya/Khalidiyya and the Qadiriyya/Kunta-Hajji had successively, and alternatively, opposed and accepted Russian conquest and dominance (Kemper 2002; Reynolds 2005).

continuation of organizations like Fawziya Bayramova's Ittifaq in Naberezhnye Chelny[62] and Dokku 'Umarov's more radical self-proclaimed virtual state 'Caucasus Emirate' in the cyberspace since 2007 suggest the ultimate failure of the repressive strategy adopted by the Kremlin on the pretext of 9/11.

This relative weakness of confessional parties and their ultimate though incomplete ban after 2001 have turned scholars' interests to other forms of political claims and discontent among Russia's Muslims. Although they have been credited with limited influence by political science and political sociology, the mushrooming Muslim boards and muftiates of the 1990s retain significant lobbying strengths, especially at the regional and local scales where they sometimes manage to play their role as representative bodies (cf. Rousselet 2008). Functioning, like political parties themselves, as part and parcel of federal, regional, or district political power, Muslim religious boards and muftiates cannot appear as oppositional forces, which brought about growing calls among academics for alternative lobbying strengths.[63] For many observers, the presidential elections of December 2003 in Bashkortostan, for example, confirmed the political utilization of confessional identities in the Volga region and the wide participation of influential religious organizations, thus further blurring the boundary between the public and political spheres.[64]

Curiously, no academic study has yet been devoted to a rich typology of Muslim protest organizations. This is even more surprising in that some have cross-border dimensions that should have earned them the attention of experts. These organizations mainly target migrant populations, and they are based outside the Russian Federation, but within the CIS and the SCO. Such is the case of the Islamic Revival Party of Tajikistan, which since the end of Tajikistan's civil war in 1997 is officially, though asymmetrically, associated with political power in Dushanbe and, as a result, enjoys official recognition within the CIS despite the 2001 ban on religious political parties in Russia. Well aware of the potential weight of the vote reserves in Russia's Tajik emigration, the IRPT is active in the mobilization of students, young workers, and more largely Central Asian migrants in Russia's biggest cities. Another category of transnational networks, the traditional Central Asian Sufi paths, which are presently active among Russia's Central Asian migrants through deeply redefined master–disciple connections, remain totally absent from the academic landscape.

## Islamic Education: A Major Political Issue

Spurred by a number of historical works on *madrasa* teaching in the late Tsarist period, research on Islamic religious education was made more actual by the spectacular boom

---

[62] See the critical appraisals by Mukhametshin 2002, 2007.
[63] See the interview with young Muslim political scientist and columnist Rinat Mukhametov, 'Ekstremizm vs. islamofobii' [Extremism vs. Islamophobia], *Medina al'-Islam* 55 (8–14 February 2008): 4.
[64] Notably through the rivalry of the Muslim Spiritual Board of the Muslims of Bashkortostan, autonomous since 1992, with the Soviet-inherited, Ufa-based Central Spiritual Board of the Muslims of Russia led by Mufti Taj al-Din (e.g. Azamatov 2005, esp. 141).

of the 1990s. Such measures as Yeltsin's decree of 23 April 1993 'On the Transmission to Religious Organizations of Worship Buildings and Other Assets' or debates in ethnic republics on the restoration of *waqf* mortmain deeds[65] have put financial aspects at the centre of academic attention and stirred historical research on Islamic philanthropy. Still, the recent mushrooming of Islamic teaching institutions is observed throughout Russia with 'a panic horror' (Navruzov 2010: 150), bringing about more restrictive sets of measures.

The rare non-apologetic studies on Islamic education in Russia highlight the tight interconnections between Islamic 'universities' created since the 1990s, regional Muslim boards, and, in the case of Dagestan at least, the main leaders of traditional Sufi paths. These studies also shed light on the links between the boards and particular ethno-linguistic groups. Conversely, they insist on the appeal of Dagestan and Chechnya's Russian-language *madrasa*s on the all-Russian scale.[66] These studies also underline the conservative nature (and low quality) of the teaching offered in these institutions, besides the modesty of their infrastructure (of libraries in particular, not compensated for by the internet and social networks). Despite the direct access granted to *madrasa* and Islamic university graduates to secular universities (e.g. Navruzov 2010: 155), access to the work market for ever-growing contingents of students in religion has become an overall concern for the experts in religious studies.[67]

Islamic theology was adapted to Russia's state norms of higher education—from the standardization of theology as a university discipline to the more recent interest of law faculties in Islamic jurisprudence and banking. Although initiated by Orthodox Christians, who still hold most departments of studies on religion, this adaptation has been extended to higher Islamic educational institutions (such as the Islamic University of Russia in Kazan, the Islamic University of Dagestan in Makhachkala; research centres like the academic Institutes of Oriental Studies in St Petersburg, Moscow, and Kazan; and regional and local *madrasa*s often supported by powerful private foundations). Institutional diversity, the presence of Islamic theology in public higher education, and the Russian state's intervention in the regulation of Islamic religious studies appear as key features of the current period when compared with the developments of the late Tsarist era—still a period of reference for many protagonists (cf. Navruzov 2010; Bobrovnikov et al. 2010).

---

[65] See the chronicle by the Rector of the Husayn-Fayzkhan Islamic Institute of Nizhny Novgorod, Dämir Muhetdinov, 'Vosstanoviat li vakfy?', <http://islamrf.ru/news/expert/analytics/7324> (posted 6 February 2009). The decree was followed on 24 September 1993 by the Sate Duma's vote of the law on the gratuitous transmission to religious organizations in permanent use of the lands attached to buildings of worship significance.

[66] Notably on Tatar *madrasa* graduates from Tatarstan's main industrial towns of Naberezhnye Chelny, Almetyevsk and Elabuga (Navruzov 2010; Usmanova et al. 2010: 55–6).

[67] A recent inquiry on Tatarstan's Islamic religious teaching institutions and on the self-financing of Muslim religious personnel, published by the Iman Foundation related to this Republic's Muslim Board, deplored that only a minority of their students pursue a religious career (cf. Garipov and Nurulina 2011: 126).

## 2012: A Turning Point?

Another key feature of present times, underlined by a set of studies published in the early 2010s, is the strong contestation of established religious teaching by the younger generation of Muslim believers. A consequence specific to the former Soviet realm is the resulting favour enjoyed by graduates of the Oriental faculties of secular public universities, of Kazan and Makhachkala in particular, who nowadays have better chances to find employment in the expanding field of religious education and expertise than former *madrasa* and Islamic university students.[68] Illustrating the connections between academic scholars of Oriental studies and the religious field in the former USSR, this evolution also confirms the growing role of mosques as the unique professional prospect for excessive numbers of *madrasa* and Islamic university graduates.

Since 1997 and the Kremlin's overt promotion of a pro-Orthodox policy, the issues of the separation of state and church and of Islam's place in the public sphere have occupied the headlines and underpinned research activity. Since Russia's adoption in 2003 of restrictive measures against transnational religious trends of Islam, rapidly reflected at the scale of the SCO, state censorship has also been heavily discussed. In March 2012, the banning of sixty-five Islamic publications by the Lenin District Court in the Southern Urals city of Orenburg, at the initiative of the FSB (Federal Security Service, the KGB's successor organization in the Russian Federation)—considered the largest single banning of religious literature in a single Russian court decision so far—provoked widespread outrage from human rights defenders and Islamic religious scholars.[69] By censuring translations of classical, pre-modern Islamic theology and jurisprudence (of authors like al-Ghazali, al-Nawawi, and Ibn al-Kathir), such measures were seen as a direct attack against Muslim culture in general, in its most traditional aspects and contents.

## Tradition vs. Radicalization?

The opposition by the Patriarchate of the Russian Orthodox Church to the publication of statistics on confessional membership deprives us of reliable figures about 'Russian' Islam. Helped by the boom of Islamic literature in the 1980s–1990s, and by the acquaintance of Russian speakers with Russian translations of the Qur'an, a first generation of converts had come to light.[70] However, it rapidly faced the emergence of a new one, more

---

[68] Navruzov 2010; on Central Asia Dudoignon 2011b; on the Southern Caucasus Göyüshov et al. 2011.

[69] Some considered the event 'a crucial turning point' for Russia's Muslims and engaged in a fierce appeal battle: see F. Corley, 'Absurd Bans', <http://www.forum18.org/Archive.php?article_id=1726> (posted 30 July 2012).

[70] A generation personified by figures such as Qur'an translator Iman-Valeriia Pokhorova, a vibrant supporter of Russia's policy in Chechnya: see <http://www.rtkorr.com/news/2011/09/22/265259.new> (interview posted on 22 September 2011, on the occasion of the transfer with great pomp of 'the Prophet Muhammad's Cup' to the city of Grozny).

politicized and more active in the country's emerging Muslim blogosphere. This second generation was decisively influenced by the Islamist media of the early post-Soviet period such as the brothers Shamil and Kamil Sultanovs' newspaper *al-Kods*[71] or the tribunes of aforementioned Heydar Jemal, now the head of a ghostly 'Islamic Committee of Russia',[72] in the newspapers *Den'* and *Zavtra*, or by Jemal's TV broadcasts 'Minaret' and 'Now' (*Nyne*).

The anti-liberal ideas advocated by this second generation of Russian converts provide an ideological bridge with Russia's new right.[73] The National Organization of Russian Muslims (NORM) created in 2004 has been led by Vadim Sidorov, alias Harun al-Rusi, a Russian nationalist searching to rejuvenate Northern Eurasia, first through Salafi Islam, then Sufism.[74] While NORM's ideologists had been initially oriented towards neo-paganism and the neo-Nazi Solidarist Movement (cf. Sedgwick 2004: 222–4; Moroz 2005: 123–6), Sidorov claimed adherence to a European anti-modernist neo-Sufi network, the Murabitun World Movement.[75] Endeavouring to regroup an organization for Sunni and Shi'ite Russians, NORM faces difficulties to maintain unity as well as to form links with the organizations of Russia's Muslims. Russian Shi'ites themselves are divided between French Islamic scholar Henry Corbin's apolitical readers, Qom-educated enlighteners, and staunch advocates of Khomeini's political heritage. Besides its utopian nature, the ambition of Jemal's continuators to unite anti-Western forces through conversion to Islam seems jeopardized by NORM itself and its rooting in the most radical movements of Russian nationalism: 'Less than ever conversion offers a way out of marginality', was the warning of political scientist E. Moroz in 2005 (pp. 131–2).

The choice by a number of Russian converts to radical Islam also brought public attention to the Russian-Muslim leadership of present-day terrorist movements of the North Caucasus region. In late August 2012 the killing of the prominent Dagestani Sufi master

---

[71] Shamil (b. 1952) is sometimes introduced as an active intermediary between Islamist thinkers, Russia's 'new right', and figureheads of the Security Council of the Russian Federation like former presidential adviser and prominent oligarch Iurii Skokov: cf. <http://persona.rin.ru/view/f/0/11474/sultanov-shamil-zagitovich>.

[72] A denouncer of Western influence in Russia's former Central Asian and Caucasian periphery, the ICR had one of its authors condemned in 2009 for apology of terrorism, after the publication on its site of an article praising the acts of female Chechen suicide bombers (<http://www.gazeta.ru/social/2012/09/13/4768049.shtml>, posted 13 September 2012).

[73] See the retrospective testimonies by Russian Shi'ite convert and proselyte Anastasiia Ezhova (b. 1983), a doctoral student in religion and religious studies at Moscow State University, the editor of the Russian Muslim journal *Musul'manka* ['The Muslim Woman'] and a regular collaborator of *Zavtra*—in the journal *Chetki* ['Rosary'] published since 2007 in Moscow by the 'Marjani' Foundation (Ezhova 2008, 2009, 2011; and *Central Eurasian Reader* 2 [2008]: 353–4).

[74] See his recent chronicle 'Tatarskii islamskii proekt: sovety so storony' [The Tatar Islamic Project: Advice from Aside], <http://v-sidorov.livejournal.com/#post-v_sidorov-252200> (posted 3 September 2012).

[75] The movement has been headed since its creation in the early 1980s by Scottish Darqawi Sufi master and Maliki Sunni theologian Ian Dallas (alias 'Abd al-Qadir al-Sufi, b. 1930): see the introduction on the movement's site <http://sunnizm.blogspot.fr/> (accessed 25 September 2012)—which does not mention any Russian disciples.

Shaykh Sa'id Afandi of Chirkey by a Russian female suicide bomber once again raised the issue of the conversion of ethnic Russians to Islam (e.g. Vatchagaev 2012). The phenomenon is interpreted by many as the response of Russian youth to the compromises of the Orthodox Church with the Putin administration. Rare analyses of the anti-establishment converts' motivations insist on Islam's appeal as an egalitarian community more independent from the government, with a fraternal connection with the wider Muslim world. Such is the case for Sa'id the Buryat (Aleksandr Tikhomirov, 1982–2010), an inspirer of the 'Caucasus Emirate' who is said to have been popular among the rebels, or Amir 'Abd al-Malik (born Aleksei Pashintsev in 1990 in Belgorod, a leader of the 'Riyad al-Salihin' suicide bomber battalion in Dagestan).[76] Though limited in demographic terms, the movement has brought some analysts to question the absence of alternative to *Jihadism* among the Russian youths disgusted by present-day politics in Russia, to criticize again the appalling weakness of established political parties, and to raise the issue of a fundamental reform of Russia's purely formal democracy.[77]

# Security and Terrorism

## Kremlin-Approved Extremism?

Despite the modesty of the means at his disposal, Heydar Jemal, a founding father of the Islamic Revival Party of the USSR in 1990, endeavours now to mobilize the former Central Asian branches of this organization. After two decades of autonomous operation, these branches are invited to denounce the Western presence in the former southern backyard of the USSR.[78] Russian Islam sees itself as a potential bridge between Russia, the 'Muslim' republics of the ex-USSR, and regional powers like Turkey and Iran (countries with good mutual relations until the Syrian civil war). Heydar Jemal's tortuous biography and Vadim Sidorov's unpredictable reasoning suggest the existence of numerous connections between Russia's most divergent Islamic and non-Islamic currents and trends, from neo-Nazism to neo-Sufism, against the backdrop of spiritual and

---

[76] Tikhomirov has recently been endowed with a rather detailed page on Wikipedia's Russian edition (<http://ru.wikipedia.org/wiki/>) and his Russian-language exhortations in favour of *jihad* are still available on an internationally famous site of video sharing: <http://www.youtube.com/watch?v=0Dte7TgHcUI&feature=related>; on Pashintsev's claim for the assassination of Dagestani Sufi master Sa'id Afandi of Chirkey on 28 August 2012 and for elements of biography on him, see the North Caucasian *jihadist* sites <http://vDagestan.com/?p=7187> (posted 26 September 2012) and <http://www.kavkaz.org.uk/russ/content/2012/09/27/93330.shtml> (posted 27 September 2012).

[77] e.g. Nikolai Petrov, 'Nadutye grubo' [Deeply Cheated], <http://www.carnegie.ru/experts/?fa=499> (posted 18 October 2012).

[78] For instance, by Jemal as one of the numerous guest stars of the Ninth Congress of the Islamic Revival Party of Tajikistan on 23–4 September 2011 (e.g. <http://www.islamnews.ru/news-87421.html>, posted 24 September 2011).

philosophical quests not supervised by traditional confessional institutions like muftiates, *madrasa*s, and Sufi paths.

Despite the recent rise of criticism against the Russian Orthodox Church, notably in the year 2012 in connection with the developments of the 'Pussy Riot' trial,[79] several commonplace perceptions must still be qualified. This is the case of allegations over this body's real audience in Russian society, and on the recent evolution of its relations with Russian Islam. Indeed in 1994, at the beginning of the war won by the small Republic of Chechnya against the Kremlin, the TV-broadcasted images of priests blessing the MIG aircraft that were bombing Grozny had a deep impact on the minds of millions of Russia's Muslim television viewers. Since then, the widespread negative rhetoric against Islam and Muslims, in Russia's state-controlled media, does not help to put right mutual prejudices between Christians and Muslims. At the same time, during the past twenty years, marked notably by the squabbles between multiplying Muslim spiritual boards for the control of mosques, the inner-confessional cleavages in multiethnic Russia have often proved more productive of public violence than inter-confessional tensions (as suggested by the murders of Wali-Allah Ya'qupov and of Sa'id Afandi of Chirkey in the summer of 2012).

Yet the most significant forms of Russia's right-wing extremist violence are identified as ad hoc hate crimes, local ethnically motivated conflicts, the activities of organized gangs, the existence of paramilitary units and terrorist tendencies (e.g. Larys and Mares 2011). Islamophobia and the racist violence developed by extremist groups— among which the powerful associations of Putin's supporters—remain focused against the migrant populations from the former Soviet south (including Russian citizens from Chechnya, Ingushetia, or Dagestan). Available surveys fully reveal the strengthening of the migrants' sentiment of extreme precariousness and isolation. Added to Russia's extradition policy of Central Asian Muslim practitioners and activists,[80] the overall situation leads the migrants' religious field into diverse forms of underground. The Orthodox Church's attitude oscillates now between benevolence towards the traditional Islamic establishment and fierce hostility against possible threats of migrant and foreign Muslim proselytizing.[81] Political science studies have also cast light on the Orthodox establishment's hostility to the constitution of a politicized lobby searching to convert

---

[79] Launched against the feminist punk rock collective of this name after their anti-Putin performance of 21 February 2012 in the Saviour-Christ Orthodox Cathedral of Moscow, the procedure against three of them resulted on 17 August in a sentence to two years of imprisonment for 'hooliganism motivated by religious hatred'. Their trial and conviction attracted considerable criticism, in Russia as well as in the West; see the panoramic chronicle by Forum 18's correspondent for Russia Geraldine Fagan, 'Pussy Riots, Blasphemy and Freedom of Religious Belief', <http://www.forum18.org/Archive.php?article_id=1754> (posted 15 October 2012).

[80] Curbed in September 2012 by a first postponement of trial by the country's General Prosecutor's Office (circular correspondence by Elena Ryabinina of the Institute of Human Rights [*Institut prav cheloveka*] of Moscow about the Mamir Nematov affair, dated 14 September 2012).

[81] Comparative inter-regional studies show that, while more centralized, the Orthodox establishment shows the same hostility towards the development of Islamic practice in neighbourhoods and in districts peopled by Caucasian and Central Asian labour migrants (Verkhovskii 2007).

Russians to Islam, and the Patriarchate's quest for support by Muslim boards against the rapid expansion, in the 2000s, of a range of new creeds, confirmed by the 2012 'Atlas of Religions and Nationalities in Russia'. If confessional solidarity finds a means of expression, it is essentially between the respective establishments of different 'traditional' religions through their common loathing against transnational missionary organizations.

## Barriers against Islam's Politicization

Together with Soviet ethnographers, Russia's Islamic religious establishments long regarded ethnic tradition as the best possible barrier against Islam's politicization.[82] Here lies the explanation of the largely benevolent attitude of Russia's civil and religious officialdom to Muslim customary practice. This official benevolence towards familiar and reassuring vernacular traditions of Islam grew further in the 1990s after the irruption of new, unknown, transnational Muslim networks, media, and discourses, and in the 2000s after the massive influx towards Russia's largest cities of new Muslim populations bearing unknown religious trends. Contrary to expectation, the eventful 1990s, through the shaking of tradition and social codes, have permitted a rapid Islamicization of national movements, in Chechnya especially, through the radicalization of warlords after the secessionist Republic's first conflict against Russia in 1994–6 (Filiu 2006: 161–76). Respect for the elders, a cornerstone of traditional Chechen society, had been shaken during the conflict, and the ageing local Sufi leaders gave up part of their charisma to 30-year-old 'Arab' *mujahideen*.

The same generational cleavage can be observed throughout the whole former Soviet realm. Everywhere parents unprepared to shoulder the responsibility for educating children brutally confronted with the mutation of the labour market must face an abrupt loss of prestige in their offspring's critical eyes (cf. Sabirova 2011: 331). This new cleavage was rapidly reflected in the religious field by new conflicting lines. Such is the case even in the most 'peripheral' zones of Russia's Islam. In Mordovia, for example, a monographic study in local history showed how the sunflower seed-trading Soviet Muslim Tatar bourgeoisie of the market town of Belozerye was confronted by the schism of the local congregation through construction of a new mosque in the mid-1990s, the 'second mosque' gathering the middle-aged and young population, among them people endowed with *madrasa* education (cf. Minnullin 2013).

In cases such as the peripheral, minority and poorly sovietized Belozerye, nonconformist youth established connections with remote avant-gardist groups—here with the anti-establishment Muslim congregation (*jama'at*) led by Ayyub 'Umarov (Omarov, a former aid of Chechen President Jokhar Dudayev) in Astrakhan.[83] 'Umarov sent to

---

[82] For instance in the case of the *adïghage*, the customary code of the Adyghes in the North-Western Caucasus (cf. Lyagusheva 2005; Nefliasheva 2009).

[83] On the trans-regional political activism of the Astrakhan community, and the connections denounced by Russian and Kazakhstani police between the congregation, the Tablighi Jama'at, and

Mordovia as his emissary a Russian convert and proselyte called Oleg Marushkin, alias Abu-Dhar. Under the latter's authority, the new congregation mutated into a strongly united solidarity group attracted by international *jihadist* networks. However, a majority of the congregation's members finally chose to leave and to cooperate with local authorities while the group's leaders were opting for exile. These developments in Belozerye provide us with an illustration of the strong generational gap that influences part of the Muslim youth's expectations. The case also highlights the interconnections between small groups, rural and urban, on the all-Russian scale through mobile telephony and electronic media. However, and contrary to the common assessments by Russia's experts on religions, it also shows the still limited capacity of *jihadists*, either Russian converts like 'Abu-Dhar' in Mordovia, autochthonous Muslims like 'Umarov in Astrakhan, or international fighters like the more famous Khattab in Chechnya, to find common language with vernacular believers.

## Securitization

The generalized rhetoric of 'Islamic extremism', sanctioned and qualified at the same time by Barack Obama's June 2009 Cairo discourse, has blurred the boundaries between diverse currents and trends. Few specialists have ventured to suggest a positive definition of what 'extremism' means in the case of Islamic militancy. Recent studies on European radical organizations highlight the central place of hierarchy, violence, and transgression as key features of extremist behaviour. They underline a recurring thematic scheme from rejection of the present to the designation of scapegoats, ending with calls to a saviour for the establishment of a new order (discussed by Bourseiller 2012: 31–44). Such criteria amply suggest that a number of those Muslim groups and movements prosecuted in present-day Russia do not belong to this category. Conversely, as we have seen, certain Islamist groups holding openly extremist views enjoy benevolence from officialdom in Vladimir Putin's Russia—of course, as long as they do not embark on advocacy of *jihad within* the country's territory.

Sparking off a world panic with durable repercussions, the 9/11 attacks legitimated the aggressive stance adopted by the early Putin administration towards transnational Sunni Islam. Like classical Sovietology, current 'religiology' or *religiovedenie*, a new discipline of its own, yet poorly codified, ultimately conveys a vision of Islam as a vector of conflict with European values and identity. Academic intelligentsias have been playing an ever-growing role in the denunciation of 'nonconformist' religious practices, 'to the extent that Soviet official studies on Islam have become, for today's young Muslims,

---

international smuggling networks (of black caviar, in the present case), see for instance the alarmed chronicle by Oleg Gorelov, 'Astrakhanstvo' ['Astrakhanism'], <http://www.vahhabizm.ru/stat/astrhan.html> (posted in 2008; last accessed 25 September 2012)—as indicated by its name, this site specializes on the criticism of Salafism in Russia and shows also particular interest in the repression of the Tablighi Jama'at, Hizb al-Tahrir, and Nurcu 'pan-Turkist' [sic] movement.

more influential in matters of history and creed than the village mullahs of yesteryear' (Kisriev 2007: 42). Indeed Islamic radicalization represented a serious threat to Russia at the turn of the twenty-first century, and the Putin administration is often given credit for successes in stemming this danger while improving Russia's image in the wider world of Islam (Dannreuther 2010b). One wonders, however, whether past Islamist violence has not been replaced by delayed-action devices.

Establishment Islam and its academic supporters have embarked on the simultaneous denunciation of radicalism, transnational proselytism, and pro-European Muslim liberal trends—a stance analogous, in fact, to that of the Orthodox Church. More globally, the policy of repression against a range of non-accredited religious entrepreneurs has fatally confined many phenomena to new forms of underground where, as underlined by sociologist Roman Lunkin, they completely escape the scrutiny of social sciences. In the North Caucasus in particular, all observers agree that the overt corruption of regional governments and the absence of popular support paved the way for more violent upheavals. In Chechnya in particular, entrusted by Moscow to a fundamentalist Sunni satrap, writers demonstrate how endless years of war and depopulation have dismantled the structure of social codes (e.g. Littell 2009: 108–9). Moreover, if the Qadïrov administration installed in Grozny since 2000 is credited by some with stabilization of the former secessionist Republic, social violence has migrated towards new, more marginal territories, Astrakhan for instance, with Islamic insurgency spreading again to Dagestan and opening new fields in neighbouring Ingushetia, while peaceful Tatarstan seems not to be spared anymore by the settling of scores between antagonistic visions of Islam.

## Islamophobia and Tentative Islamophile Echoes to It

Since autumn 2012, the present author's correspondence with colleagues in Russia has consisted of observations about the constant rise of ethno-confessional hatreds and tensions in the country. Since the mid-1990s these tensions have notably taken the shape of Islamophobia, contrasting with the low level of radicalization observed among religiously active Muslims in the country's largest cities and suburbs, the place of many acts of violence against southern migrants.[84] After inquiries in the early 2000s into the damage done by Chechen terrorist violence to public opinion on Islam,[85] and the peak

---

[84] Already noticed by Alekseev et al. (2004); these authors' inquiry among Moscow's practising Muslims had suggested in the early 2000s a low identification, among their informants, of the notion of *jihad* with armed struggle for the Islamic faith, and highlighted weak religious practice among the apologists of an abstract 'shariah'.

[85] An inquiry by the prestigious All-Russia Centre for the Study of Public Opinion (VTSIOM in Russian acronyms) revealed in the autumn 2004, in the wake of the tragic event in the Beslan elementary school and of a wave of terror acts throughout Russia, a peak of 79% of respondents convinced that the expansion of Islam is a threat for Russia (quoted by Moroz 2005: 118).

of inter-community tensions in 2005,[86] Islamophobia as such has become a taboo in present-day Russia. When anti-Muslim violence is denounced in the mass media, it is now in its Western manifestations.[87] Studies by domestic scholars on Islamophobia have not been flourishing despite the emergence of new research on 'mutual tolerance' at the federal level (e.g. Musina 2009, 2012; Garipov and Nurulina 2011). The rare studies on Russia's mass media (e.g. Kuznetsova-Morenko and Salakhatdinova 2006)[88] observe that on the all-Russian TV channels Islam appears mainly in reports on international conflicts and in the form of critical assessments of actions by Muslims. Rare exceptions are offered by the media in the national languages of the ethnic republics like Tatarstan, Bashkortostan, and Dagestan, which concentrate on regional issues and distinguish themselves by a general lack of negative assessments of Islam and the Muslims.

In correlation with the multiplication of voices on Islam, a nascent Islamophile current and apologetic discourse emerged within Russian academic circles, spurred by the aftermaths of the wars in Chechnya. Lack of public support, of ambition, and of media coverage, however confines such generous undertakings to tiny circles of initiates. The recent appearance of prestigious academic tribunes such as the journal *Pax islamica* do not entirely compensate for this lack of echo.[89] Such is the case also of the high-quality but poorly distributed encyclopaedias such as the fascicules edited by the Institute of Oriental Studies in Saint Petersburg on Islam in the former Russian Empire (Prozorov 2006), or the volumes dedicated by the Muftiate of Nizhny Novgorod and the Medina Foundation in the same city about Islam in Russia's regions (e.g. Mukhetdinov 2007)— in this case, through cooperation of regional academics with Muslim religious personnel, under the leadership of an influential regional Mufti.[90] Many other publications, notably those by the 'Logos' publishing house in Moscow, also give considerable space to the Muftis, regional or central, and to their role in the preservation of Islam in the twentieth century against Soviet repression, and in the twenty-first against the threat of radicalism (e.g. Asadullin 2007; Iunusova 2007).

---

[86] e.g. M. Belen'kaia, 'Lechit'sia ot ksenofobii pridetsia dolgo' [It Will Take a Long Time to be Cured of Xenophobia], *Rianovosti* (20 January 2006) <http://ria.ru/analytics/20060117/43044047.html>.

[87] See for instance O. A. Kolobov, 'Sindrom islamofobii v sovremennoi politike SShA: spetsifika proiavleniia i vozmozhnye posledstviia' [The Syndrome of Islamophobia in the USA's Current Policy: The Features of Its Emergence and Its Possible Consequences], <http://islamrf.ru/news/politics/analytics/114/> (posted 16 May 2007); Ivan Mutkoglo, 'Islamofobiia: zhizn' s musul'manami no bez islama' [Islamophobia: Life with Muslims but without Islam] <http://www.islam.ru/content/obshestvo/islamofobiya-mir-s-musulmanami-no-bez-islama> (posted 4 July 2012).

[88] See also the critical comments on this study by historian from Kazan Ilnur Minnullin in *Central Eurasian Reader* 1 (2008): 351–2.

[89] Cf. <http://paxislamica.ru> and my review of volume 1 in *Central Eurasian Reader* 2 (2010): 50–1.

[90] An exceptionally prolific writer, Damir Ways-ughli Muhi al-Din (Mukhetdinov, b. 1977), a religious teacher since 1996, has since 2009 been the Chair of the Council of *'Ulama* of the Nizhny Novgorod Region. He became in the mid-2000s the director of several Islamic foundations and, as such, one of Russia's main private financers of research in both Islamic and Turkic studies. The numerous Russian-language electronic information portals he also manages on Islam in Russia and in the CIS (islamrf.ru; islamsng.com; dumrf.ru) welcome regular columns by specialists of the Tatar Muslim cultural heritage.

The succession of repression campaigns that since 2003 have fallen on Russia's transnational Islamic movements incited legal chambers and human rights defence associations to coordinate their actions, and to appeal to the researchers' expertise. The 'Memorial' association, the 'Civic Action' (*Grazhdanskoe sodeistvie*) Committee and the Institute of Human Rights, as well as organizations specializing in the defence of freedom of conscience like 'Forum 18' in Oslo and the SOVA Centre in Moscow, both regular producers of information on present-day confessional repression in Russia, have been combining their efforts, and not without result, despite a modest global impact. In parallel, a number of actors are now involved in the defence of migrants' interests, highlighting for instance the consequences of registration problems for children's schooling (e.g. Florianskaia 2011: 59–60). Despite the deep pessimism often expressed by liberal experts in Moscow, Kazan, or Ulyanovsk about the weak impact of their discourse on Russia's religious policy, the judgment invalidations obtained by the Institute of Human Rights suggest, on the contrary, the necessity of a dissociation of ideas between autonomous cross-border Muslim religious trends and a potential 'threat' of religious 'extremism'.

# Conclusions

## Major Findings

In Russia Islam was perceived in the Tsarist and Soviet periods as a mere survival, bound for disappearance as a result of modernization. Social and political science approaches to the world of Islam were for long reserved to foreign countries, with significant investments in the Maghreb and the Near East after decolonization. It is only recently that Islam in Russia has become the object of a rediscovery by Oriental scholars redeployed from Yemen, Egypt, or Algeria to their homeland. The dissolution of the USSR and the triggering of the war with Chechnya were rapidly followed by still another shock with the influx of labour migrants from the former Soviet south. These changes entailed a rapid differentiation of disciplinary approaches to Russia's Islam. Oriental studies could preserve their leadership but one also observes a gradual investment of social sciences and law (in the framework of reflection on 'Islamic banking' or of the defence of Muslim migrants' rights). A paradox of post-Soviet research, however, remains the dominance of literalist approaches centred on the Qur'an, even among researchers of the Institute of Ethnography and Anthropology of the Academy of Sciences of Russia, who seem educated in the principal aim of providing replies to Muslim radical preachers.

Another heritage of the Tsarist and Soviet periods is no doubt the concept of 'ethnic Muslims' and the subsequent association by many studies of confessional and ethnic identities. For most scholars of Russia's Islam, ethnic differences continue to be more explanatory of certain behaviours than religious convictions. Two decades of endemic public violence in the North Caucasus—in Dagestan, Chechnya, and more recently Circassia—have further conditioned these discourses. A consequence of these conflicts has been since 1996 (i.e. five years before 9/11) the overvaluation of security approaches. In the early 2010s, public research funding often remained related to issues of Islamization of nationalist movements. At the same time, one can observe a perceptible evolution and enrichment of the thematic orientation of research on Russia's Islam during the past twenty years.

The elimination of foreign Muslim charities since the late 1990s has been partly balanced during the following decade by the growing role of domestic Muslim foundations financed notably by the hydrocarbon extraction industry of the Volga-Ural region. Moreover, the new significance given by Russia's government to 'federal' campuses provided several major regional academic centres like Kazan, Ufa, Nizhny Novgorod, or Ulyanovsk in the Volga-Ural region, Makhachkala in the Northern Caucasus, with an increase in research funding. Besides this, the ever wider practice of international cooperation and exchanges further strengthened scholars' autonomy and capacity for inter-regional comparative study. The participation of international researchers also contributed towards the diversification of disciplinary approaches and to the enlargement of perspectives. At the same time, the decisive character of interpersonal links between sponsors and scholars, in the context of increasing private financing of research, sometimes restricts the range of opinions and over-represents establishment discourses—those of regional muftiates especially, which support growing numbers of research initiatives.

## Some Fields to be Developed

Backed by these Muslim boards, efforts have been produced by the private foundations for the valuation of the modern and contemporary Islamic art and literature of Russia. Such efforts pave the way for a possible Islamophile current. Epistemological reflection, however, only begins about Islam as an object of study in the Tsarist and Soviet periods, and about the role of academic experts in the recent developments of the Islamic religious field. The issue of the transformation of authority also remains to be developed, even if inter-regional comparative approaches have already been promoted for the historical sociology of the religious personnel of Islam since de-Stalinization, or on the role of family in the transmission of religious learning during the past twenty years. Mutations also remain to be observed as far as the recent decades are concerned from the viewpoint of authoritative people and sources that Russia's Caucasian and Central Asian migrants show themselves receptive to.

In early post-Soviet Russia, the key political issue of the privatization and redistribution of once collectivized church assets and possible restoration of mortmain deeds (*waqf*s) has turned the spotlight on the petty squabbling between competing muftiates and religious boards at federal, regional, and even local levels. In parallel, the issue of secularity in educational reforms was attracting international interest in the Islamic religious learning provided by *madrasa*s and teaching cells. In the North Caucasus in particular, the role of traditional Sufi paths and their transformations in the wake of Soviet modernization have recently become the object of systematic study. At the same time, the present redeployment of varied historical branches of traditional Sufism throughout Russia and its inter-relations with more or less formal anti-Sufi currents such as the Salafiyya and the Tabligh remain beyond the vision of present-day research. As far as the Salafiyya, the Tabligh, and other transnational missionary networks and social movements like the Nurcu conglomeration or the Hizb al-Tahrir party are concerned, the repressive policy adopted since 2003 does not favour independent social science approaches.

At the core of sociological analyses developed in the 1990s, studies into the labour market in Russia's multiethnic areas need to be continued. The development of the 'Ittifaq' nationalist party in a city like Naberezhnye Chelny in Tatarstan suggests that in certain regions of Russia the ethnic *cum* confessional resentment observed since the 1970s has not been mollified. 'Ethno-sociology' developed in Tatarstan, instead, is now rather invited to focus on mutual toleration and the integration of the Russian nation. In parallel, comparative inter-regional studies remain to be undertaken on the transformation of migrant economic *cum* religious entrepreneurs into community leaders as in the case of these Tajik migrants recently settled in Russia's Far East and affiliated, through internet connections, to Tajikistan-based leaders of varied Sufi paths. Besides economic, social, cultural, and religious aspects, these evolutions—and the development of anti-migrant Islamophobic discourses and attitudes among the host populations, of either Orthodox or Muslim background—also assume a geopolitical aspect through the impact that they exert on the countries of origin of Russia's Muslim migrants.

## Some Yet Unexplored Tracks

Russia's intimate relation with Islam is an ancient phenomenon. However, the massive presence of young, predominantly male Muslim economic migrants in Russia is a much more recent one, in contrast with Western European countries. This phenomenon, its geopolitical significance for those Central Asian countries dependent on remittances, and the necessities of human rights defence increase the need for further monitoring. Strategy differences between varied generations of migrants in Russia, and continuous public allegations on the specific religiosity developed by newcomers, also appeal for further assessments. The political mobilization of Muslim migrant youths in Russia also remains terra incognita. The recent evolution of the basis of the Islamic Revival Party of Tajikistan and the current efforts by the Qadïrov administration in Grozny to neutralize Russia's Chechen diaspora, suggest the importance of the matter. Conversely, the lack of social bonding and the isolation of many Muslim migrants will have to be assessed from the viewpoint of their social, cultural, and political impacts (Russia offering, in this matter, an exceptional diversity of local situations).

As far as the social sciences are concerned, one can only be surprised by the paucity of observation practice, still a fundamental dimension of any anthropology worthy of the name. In the total absence of a truly anthropological approach, social science scholarship has remained classically dependent on the collection of discourses and of story-telling, notably in the field of ethno-sociology. A discipline deeply influenced by the taxonomies of the Tsarist and Soviet periods, ethno-sociology concentrates on expressions of identities, dialectic constructions of the self, and the emission of alternative ethical norms intended to facilitate coexistence between populations tightly defined in ethnic and confessional terms, and ultimately requested to conform to these terms. So the heritage of Soviet ethnography continues to prosper in the shade of Oriental studies. Never at any time is the issue of the interaction between the inquirer and the inquired raised, which could inform an epistemological departure and help researchers to put social and political demand at a distance. Conversely, the interest shown by a few sociologists in the dynamic processes at work in the construction of the self among Russia's recent Muslim-background migrant populations paves the way for a better account of the complex motivations of the most diverse actors of the religious field, far from essentialist approaches. This interest provides us too with an example of a genuinely significant contribution of research to the ongoing public debate about the place of Islam and Muslims in the Russian society.

# Acknowledgements

The author would like to express his warm thanks for their kind assistance and helpful answers, during the preparation of this chapter, to Igor Alekseev (Moscow), Vladimir Bobrovnikov (Moscow), Yagfar Garipov (Naberezhnye Chelny), Michael Kemper (Amsterdam), Kristina Kovalskaya (St Petersburg and Paris), Rozalinda Musina (Kazan), Muzaffar Olimov and Saodat Olimova (Dushanbe), Sophie Roche (Berlin), Guzel Sabirova (St Petersburg), Liliya Sagitova (Kazan), and Shamil Shikhaliev (Makhachkala and Bochum). Special gratitude goes to Alexander Morrison (University of Liverpool and All Souls, Oxford) for his generous help to make this chapter look more English. Indeed, all the errors and approximations that could be found in the text remain the author's property.

# Bibliography

Abdulagatov, Z. (2007). 'Fundamentalistskie Sostavliaiushchie Soznaniia Dagestanskogo Veruiushchego (po Materialam Sotsiologicheskikh Oprosov' [The Fundamentalist Component of the Dagestani Believer's Consciousness (through the Data of a Sociological Inquiry)], *Vestnik Evrazii* 3: 90–106.

Alekseev, I. L., Khalturina, D. A., and Korotaev, A. B. (2004). 'O Sootnoshenii Islamskogo Fundamentalizma, Politicheskogo Radikalizma i Religioznoi Neterpimosti (po Materialam Sotsioantropologicheskogo Obsledovaniia Musul'man Moskvy)' [On the Correspondence between Islamic Fundamentalism, Political Radicalism and Religious Intolerance (through the Data of a Socio-Anthropological Study of the Muslims of Moscow)], in T. V. Evgen'eva (ed.), *'Chuzhie' zdes' ne Khodiat: Radikal'naia Ksenofibiia i Politicheskii Ekstremizm v Sotsiokul'turnom Prostranstve Sovremennoi Rossii*. Moscow, 175–98.

Ambrosio, T. (2008). 'Catching the "Shanghai Spirit": How the Shanghai Cooperation Organization Promotes Authoritarian Norms in Central Asia', *Europe-Asia Studies* 60(8): 1321–44.

Arapov, D. (2007). 'Etnicheskoe i Konfessional'noe v Rossiskom "Musul'manstve": Islamskaia Politika Gosudarstva v xx–xxi vekakh' [The Ethnic and the Confessional in Russia's 'Muslimhood': The State Islamic Policy in the Twentieth and Twenty-First Centuries], *Vestnik Evrazii* 3: 58–67.

Arapov, D. (2009). 'Musulmanskii triptikh: Islam i Sovetskaia Vlast' (1917, 1949, 1982)' [A Muslim Triptych: Islam ad the Soviet Power (1917, 1949, 1982)], *Pax Islamica* 1(2): 248–66.

Arapov, D Iu. and Kosach, G. G. (2010). *Islam i Sovetskoe Gosudarstvo (1917–1936)* [Islam and the Soviet State (1917–1936)]. Moscow: Mardzhani.

Aris, S. (2009). 'The Shanghai Cooperation Organisation: "Tackling the Three Evils" (A Regional Response to Non-Traditional Security Challenges or Anti-Western Block?)', *Europe-Asia Studies* 61(3): 457–82.

Asadullin, F. (2007). *Islam v Moskve* [Islam in Moscow]. Moscow: Logos.

Azamatov, D. (2005). 'Le Facteur Religieux aux Elections Présidentielles Bachkires de 2003', in M. Laruelle and S. Peyrouse (eds.), *Islam et Politique en Ex-URSS*. Paris: L'Harmattan, 135–44.

Babadjanov, B. and Islamov, S. (2013). 'The Enlighteners of Koni-Zar: Islamic Reform in a Cotton Kolkhoz', in S. Dudoignon and C. Noack (eds.), *Allah's Kolkhozes: Migration, De-Stalinisation, Privatisation, and the Emergence of New Muslim Congregations in the USSR and After (1950s–2000s)*. Berlin: Klaus Schwarz Verlag (Islamkundliche Untersuchungen), 265–306.

Babich, I. (2008). 'Islam and the Legal System in the North-Western Caucasus', in M. Gammer (ed.), *Ethno-Nationalism, Islam and the State in the Caucasus*. Abingdon: Routledge, 19–27.

Bobrovnikov, V. (2007). 'Sovieticum vs. Islamicum: Nekotorye Itogi i Perspektivy Izucheniia Islama v Rossii' [*Sovieticum* vs. *Islamicum*: Some Conclusions and Perspectives of the Study of Islam in Russia], *Vestnik Evrazii* 3(37): 8–21.

Bobrovnikov, V. (2012). 'Rossiiskii Postsovetskii Islam v Vostokovedenii i Etnografii: Podkhody i Problemy' [Russia's Post-Soviet Islam in Oriental Studies and Ethnography: Approaches and Issues], in *Islam v mul'tikul'turnom mire: 1-yi Kazanskii Mezdunarodnyi Nauchnyi Forum*. Kazan: KPFU, 156–68.

Bobrovnikov, V. (2013). 'Withering Heights: Micro-History of the Relocation and Re-Islamisation of a Kolkhoz Village in Daghestan', in S. Dudoignon and C. Noack (eds.), *Allah's Kolkhozes: Migration, De-Stalinisation, Privatisation, and the Emergence of New Muslim Congregations in the USSR and After (1950s–2000s)*. Berlin: Klaus Schwarz Verlag (Islamkundliche Untersuchungen), 367–97.

Bobrovnikov, V., Navruzov, A., and Shikhaliev, S. (2010). 'Islamic Education in Soviet and Post-Soviet Daghestan', in M. Kemper, R. Motika, and S. Reichmuth (eds.), *Islamic Education in the Soviet Union and its Successor States*. Abingdon: Routledge, 107–67.

Bourseiller, C. (2012). *L'Extrémisme: Une Grande Peur Contemporaine*. Paris: CNRS Editions.

Bram, C. (2008). '"Re-Islamisation" and Ethno-Nationalism: The Circassians (Adyghe) of the Northwestern Caucasus and Their Diaspora', in M. Gammer (ed.), *Ethno-Nationalism, Islam and the State in the Caucasus: Post-Soviet Disorder*. Abingdon: Routledge, 28–49.

Bregel, Y. (1996). *Notes on the Study of Central Asia*. Bloomington: Indiana University (Papers on Inner Asia: 28).

Bulatov, A. (2007). 'Rossiiskoe Gosudarstvo i "Vnutrennie Migranty-Musul'mane": Osnovnye Tendentsii Vzaimodeistviia i Strategii Adaptatsii' [The Russian State and the 'Inner Muslim Migrants': The Main Interaction Tendencies and the Adaptation Strategies], *Vestnik Evrazii* 3: 68–77.

Bustanov, A. K. and Kemper, M. (2012a). 'From Mirasism to Euro-Islam: The Translation of Islamic Legal Debates into Tatar Secular Cultural Heritage', in A. K. Bustanov and M. Kemper (eds.), *Islamic Authority and the Russian Language: Studies on Texts from European Russia, the Caucasus and Western Siberia*. Amsterdam: Pegasus, 29–54.

Bustanov, A. K. and Kemper, M. (eds.) (2012b). *Islamic Authority and the Russian Language: Studies on Texts from European Russia, the Caucasus and Western Siberia*. Amsterdam: Pegasus.

Campana, A. (2009). 'Collective Memory and Violence: The Use of Myths in the Chechen Separatist Ideology, 1991–1994', *Journal of Muslim Minority Affairs* 29(1): 43–56.

Cashaback, D. (2008). 'Assessing Asymmetrical Design in the Russian Federation: A Case Study of Language Policy in Tatarstan', *Europe-Asia Studies* 60(2): 249–75.

Cherepanov, M. (2009). 'Otrazhenie Sotsial'nogo Instituta Svobody Sovesti v Soznanii Musul'manskikh Aktivistov Tiumenskoi Oblasti' [The Reflection of the Social Institution of Freedom of Conscience among the Muslim Activists of the Tyumen Region], in I. L. Alekseev et al. (eds.), *Mir islama: Istoriia, obshchestvo, kul'tura*, Moscow: Izdatel'skii dom Mardzhani, 200–5.

Chung, C.-P. (2006). 'China and the Institutionalization of the Shanghai Cooperation Organization', *Problems of Post-Communism* 53(5): 3–14.

Crews, R. D. (2006). *For Prophet and Tsar: Islam and Empire in Russia and in Central Asia*. Cambridge, MA and London: Harvard University Press.

Dannreuther, R. (2010a). 'Russian Discourses and Approaches to Islam and Islamism', in R. Dannreuther and L. March (eds.), *Russia and Islam: State, Society and Radicalism*, New York and London: Routledge, 9–25.

Dannreuther, R. (2010b). 'Islamic Radicalization in Russia: An Assessment', *International Affairs* 86(1): 109–26.

Dannreuther, R. and March, L. (eds.) (2010). *Russia and Islam: State, Society and Radicalism*. New York and London: Routledge.

Daucé, F. (2005). 'Les Revendications Musulmanes en Russie: Entre Mobilisation et Défection Politique', in M. Laruelle and S. Peyrouse (eds.), *Islam et Politique en Ex-URSS*. Paris: L'Harmattan, 171–88.

Demintseva, E. B. (ed.) (2009). *Islam v Evrope i v Rossii* [Islam in Europe and in Russia]. Moscow: Izdatel'skii Dom Mardzhani.

DeWeese, D. (2002). 'Islam and the Legacy of Sovietology: A Review Essay on Yaacov Ro'i's *Islam in the Soviet Union*', *Journal of Islamic Studies* 13(3): 298–330.

Dudoignon, S. A. (2011a). 'From Revival to Mutation: The Religious Personnel of Islam in Tajikistan, from De-Stalinisation to Independence (1955–91)', *Central Asian Survey* 30(1): 53–80.

Dudoignon, S. A. (2011b). 'Un orientalisme "Progressiste" et Ses Effets Collatéraux: Les Suds de l'URSS après Staline', in F. Pouillon and J.-C. Vatin (eds.), *Après l'Orientalisme: L'Orient Créé par l'Orient*. Paris: Karthala—IISMM, 61–78.

Dudoignon, S. A. (2013). '"They Were All from the Country": The Revival and Politicisation of Islam in the Lower Wakhsh River Valley of the Tajik SSR (1947–1997)', in S. Dudoignon and C. Noack (eds.), *Allah's Kolkhozes: Migration, De-Stalinisation, Privatisation, and the*

*Emergence of New Muslim Congregations in the USSR and After (1950s–2000s)*. Berlin: Klaus Schwarz Verlag (Islamkundliche Untersuchungen), 47–122.

Dudoignon, S. A., Mukhametshin, R., and Iskhakov, D. (eds.) (1997). *Islam v Tatarskom Mire: Istoriia i Sovremennost'* [Islam in the Tatar World: Past and Present]. Kazan: Panorama.

Dudoignon, S. A. and Noack, C. (eds.) (2013). *Allah's Kolkhozes: Migration, De-Stalinisation, Privatisation, and the Emergence of New Muslim Congregations in the USSR and After (1950s–2000s)*. Berlin: Klaus Schwarz Verlag (Islamkundliche Untersuchungen).

Ezhova, A. (2008). '"Starye" i "Novye" Litsa na Avanstsene Rossiiskogo Islama: Tendentsii, Personalii, Perspektivy' ['Old' and 'New' Faces on the Proscenium of Russia's Islam: Tendencies, Personalities, Perspectives], *Chetki* 2: 159–67.

Ezhova, A. (2009). 'Dvizhenie "Murabitun": Verouchenie i Sotsial'naia Doktrina' [The 'Murabitun' Movement: Its Theological and Social Doctrine], *Chetki* 4: 118–31.

Ezhova, A. (2011). 'Russkii Islam: Sredy, Motivy, Tendentsii i Perskektivy' [Russian Islam: Its Means, Motives, Tendencies and Perspectives], *Chetki* 11–12: 211–25.

Fagan, G. (2012). *Believing in Russia: Religious Policy after Communism*. London and New York: Routledge.

Filiu, J.-P. (2006). *Les Frontières du Jihad*. Paris: Fayard.

Florinskaia, Iu. S. (2011). 'Obrazovanie Detei Migrantov' [Educating the Migrants' Children], in E. V. Tiuriukanova (ed.), *Zhenshchiny Migranty iz Stran SNG* [Women Migrants from the CIS Countries in Russia]. Moscow: Tsentr migratsionnykh issledovanii—Fond Tadzhikistan, 49–60.

Frank, Allen J. (1998). *Islamic Historiography and 'Bulghar' Identity among the Tatars and Bashkirs of Russia*. Leiden, Boston, and Köln: Brill.

Frank, Allen J. (2009). 'Russia and the Peoples of the Volga-Ural Region: 1600–1850', in N. di Cosmo, A. J. Frank, and P. B. Golden (eds.), *The Cambridge History of Inner Asia: The Chinggisid Age*. Cambridge: Cambridge University Press, 380–91.

Gammer, M. (2005a). 'Between Mecca and Moscow: Islam, Politics and Political Islam in Chechnya and Daghestan', *Middle Eastern Studies* 41(6): 833–48.

Gammer, M. (2005b). 'The Road Not Taken: Daghestan and Chechen Independence', *Central Asian Survey* 24(2): 87–108.

Gammer, M. (ed.) (2008). *Ethno-Nationalism, Islam and the State in the Caucasus: Post-Soviet Disorder*. Abingdon: Routledge (Central Asian Studies Series).

Garipov, Ia. Z. (1997). 'Molodye Goroda: Formirovanie Naseleniia, Mezhnatsional'nye i Mezhkonfessional'nye Otnosheniia' [New Towns: The Formation of Their Population, the Interethnic and Inter-Confessional Relations], in S. A. Dudoignon, R. Mukhametshin, and D. Iskhakov (eds.), *Islam v Tatarskom Mire: Istoriia i Sovremennost'* [Islam in the Tatar World: Past and Present]. Kazan: Panorama, 266–77.

Garipov, Ia. Z. and Nurulina, R. V. (2011). 'Musul'manskaia Molodezh' Tatarstana: Konfessional'naia Sotsializatsiia i Tsennostnye Orientatsii' [The Muslim Youth of Tatarstan: Confessional Socialisation and Values Orientations], *Sotsiologicheskie issledovaniia* 8: 123–31.

Göyüshov, A., Caffee, N., and Denis, R. (2011). 'The Transformation of Azerbaijani Orientalists into Islamic Thinkers after 1991', in M. Kemper and S. Conermann (eds.), *The Heritages of Soviet Oriental Studies*. London and New York: Routledge (Routledge Contemporary Russia and Eastern Europe Studies), 306–19.

Grachev, S. V., Martynenko, A. V., and Shilov, N. V. (2005). *Pravoslavnoe Khristianstvo i Islam v Mordovii: Problemy Mezhkul'turnogo Dialoga* [Orthodox Christianity and Islam in

Mordovia: Issues of Inter-Confessional Dialogue]. Moscow: Institut Etnologii i Antropologii RAN (Issledovaniia po Prikladnoi i Neotlozhnoi Etnologii: 177).

Hagendoorn, L., Poppe, E., and Minescu, A. (2008). 'Support for Separatism in Ethnic Republics of the Russian Federation', *Europe-Asia Studies* 60(3): 353–73.

Hutcheson, D. (2003). *Political Parties in the Russian Federation*. London and New York: Routledge–Curzon.

Iarlykapov, A. (2008). *Islam u Stepnykh Nogaitsev* [Islam among the Steppe Noghais]. Moscow: Institut Etnologii i Antropologii.

Iarlykapov, A. (2009). 'Islamskoe Vozrozhdenie v Kabardino-Balkarii: Problemy i Techeniia' [The Rebirth of Islam in Kabardo-Balkaria: Issues and Tendencies], in E. B. Demintseva (ed.), *Islam v Evrope i v Rossii* [Islam in Europe and in Russia]. Moscow: Izdatel'skii Dom Mardzhani, 200–14.

Iunusova, A. B. (2007). *Islam v Bashkortostane* [Islam in Bashkortostan]. Moscow: Logos.

Karagiannis, E. (2010). *Political Islam in Central Asia: The Challenge of Hizb ut-Tahrir*. London and New York: Routledge.

Kefeli, A. (2001). 'The Role of Tatar and Kriashen Women in the Transmission of Islamic Knowledge (1800–1870)', in M. Khodarkovsky and R. P. Geraci (eds.), *Of Religion and Empire: Missions, Conversion and Tolerance in Tsarist Russia*. New York: Cornell University Press, 250–73.

Kemper, M. (2002). 'Khalidiyya Networks in Daghestan and the Question of Jihad', *Die Welt des Islams* 42(1): 41–71.

Kemper, M. (2009). 'The Soviet Discourse on the Origin and Class Character of Islam, 1923–1933', *Die Welt des Islams* 49(1): 1–48.

Kemper, M. (2012a). 'The Discourse of Said-Afandi, Daghestan's Foremost Sufi Master', in A. K. Bustanov and M. Kemper (eds.), *Islamic Authority and the Russian Language: Studies on Texts from European Russia, the Caucasus and Western Siberia*. Amsterdam: Pegasus, 167–218.

Kemper, M. (2012b). 'Jihadism: The Discourse of the Caucasian Emirate', in A. K. Bustanov and M. Kemper (eds.), *Islamic Authority and the Russian Language: Studies on Texts from European Russia, the Caucasus and Western Siberia*. Amsterdam: Pegasus, 265–94.

Kemper, M. and Conermann, S. (eds.) (2011). *The Heritages of Soviet Oriental Studies*. London and New York: Routledge (Routledge Contemporary Russia and Eastern Europe Studies).

Kemper, M., Motika, R., and Reichmuth, S. (eds.) (2010). *Islamic Education in the Soviet Union and the Successor States*. London and New York: Routledge.

Khabutdinov, A. (2005). 'Les Diverses Instrumentalisations Politiques de l'Islam au Tatarstan', in M. Laruelle and S. Peyrouse (eds.), *Islam et Politique en Ex-URSS*. Paris: L'Harmattan, 145–56.

Khizrieva, G. (2009). 'Sotsial'naia Organizatsiia Musul'manskikh Obshchin Virdovykh Bratstv Tarikata Kadiriia v Svete Issledovanii Nekropolei Ingushetii' [The Social Structure of the Muslim Communities of *Wird* Brotherhoods of the Qadiriyya *Tariqat* in the Light of Studies on the Necropolises of Ingushetia], in E. B. Demintseva (ed.), *Islam v Evrope i v Rossii* [Islam in Europe and in Russia]. Moscow: Izdatel'skii Dom Mardzhani, 134–45.

Kisriev, E. (2007). *Islam v Dagestane* [Islam in Daghestan]. Moscow: Logos.

Knysh, A. (2004). 'A Clear and Present Danger: "Wahhabism" as a Rhetorical Foil', *Die Welt des Islams* 44(1): 3–26.

Kovalskaya, K. (2013). 'Sainte Connaissance? Les Discours d'Experts du Fait Religieux et Leur Impact sur les Identités et les Pratiques Confessionnelles en Fédération de Russie depuis 1991'. Master 2 dissertation. Paris: Ecole des Hautes Etudes en Sciences Sociales.

Kuznetsova-Morenko, I. B. and Salakhatdinova, L. N. (2006). 'Islam i Musulm'ane v Obshcherossiiskikh i Tatarstanskikh Televizionnykh Programmakh' [Islam and the Muslims in All-Russia's and Tatarstan's TV Programmes]. *Sotsiologicheskie Issledovaniia* 2: 120–8.

Larina, E. and Naumova, O. (2007). '"Islam Imamov" i Traditsionalizm u Kazakhov Rossii' [The Imams' Islam and Traditionalism among Russia's Kazakhs]. *Vestnik Evrazii* 3: 115–36.

Laruelle, M. and Peyrouse, S. (eds.) (2003). *Islam et Politique en Ex-URSS (Russie d'Europe et Asie Centrale)*. Paris: L'Harmattan.

Larys, M. and Mares, M. (2011). 'Right-Wing Extremist Violence in the Russian Federation', *Europe–Asia Studies* 63(1): 129–54.

Littell, J. (2009). *Tchétchénie, an III*. Paris: Gallimard.

Lyagusheva, S. (2005). 'Islam and the Traditional Moral Code of the Adyghes', *Iran and the Caucasus* 9(1): 29–36.

Malashenko, A. V. (2001). *Islamskie Orientiry Severnogo Kavkaza* [The Islamic Landmarks of the North Caucasus]. Moscow: Carnegie Centre.

Malashenko, A. V. (ed.) (2007). *Islam v Rossii: Vzgliad iz Regionov* [Islam in Russia: The Vision from the Regions]. Moscow: Aspekt Press.

Meaux, L. de (2010). *La Russie et la Tentation de l'Orient*. Paris: Fayard.

Minnullin, I. (2013). 'Sunflowers and Moon Crescents: Soviet and Post-Soviet Islamic Revival in a Tatar Village of Mordovia', in S. Dudoignon and C. Noack (eds.), *Allah's Kolkhozes: Migration, De-Stalinisation, Privatisation, and the Emergence of New Muslim Congregations in the USSR and After (1950s–2000s)*. Berlin: Klaus Schwarz Verlag (Islamkundliche Untersuchungen), 421–53.

Mkrchian, N. V. (2011). 'Profil' Trudovykh Migrantov iz Stran SNG' [The Profile of Labour Migrants from CIS Countries], in E. V. Tiuriukanova (ed.), *Zhenshchiny Migranty iz Stran SNG* [Women Migrants from the CIS Countries in Russia]. Moscow: Tsentr migratsionnykh issledovanii—Fond Tadzhikistan, 7–18.

Moroz, E. (2005). '*L'Islam Habite Notre Avenir!* Le Prosélytisme Musulman en Russie: Conversions, Institutionnalisation et Stratégies Politiques', in M. Laruelle and S. Peyrouse (eds.), *Islam et Politique en Ex-URSS*. Paris: L'Harmattan, 117–34.

Mukhametshin, R. (2002). 'Islam i Obshchestvenno-Politicheskie Organizatsii v Tatarstane' [Islam and the Public and Political Organisations in Tatarstan], in R. M. Mukhametshin (ed.), *Islam i Musul'manskaia Kul'tura v Srednem Povolzh'e: Istoriia i Sovremennost'*. Kazan: Master Lain, 333–40.

Mukhametshin, R. (2005). *Islam v Obshchestvennoi i Politicheskoi Zhizni Tatar i Tatarstana v xx veke* [Islam in the Tatars' and Tatarstan's Public and Political Life in the Twentieth Century]. Kazan: Tatarskoe Knizhnoe Izdatel'stvo.

Mukhametshin, R. (2007). *Islam v Tatarstane* [Islam in Tatarstan]. Moscow: Logos.

Mukhametshin, R. (2010). 'Islamic Discourse in the Volga-Urals Region', in G. Yemelianova (ed.), *Radical Islam in the Former Soviet Union*. London and New York: Routledge, 31–61.

Mukhetdinov, D. (ed.) (2007). *Islam na Nizhegorodchine: Entsiklopedicheskii Slovar'* [Islam in the Nizhny Novgorod Region: Encyclopaedic Dictionary]. Nizhny Novgorod: Izdatel'skii Dom Medina ('Islam v Rossiiskoi Federatsii', 1).

Musina, R. (1997). 'Islam i Musul'mane v Sovremennom Tatarstane' [Islam and the Muslims in Present-Day Tatarstan], in S. A. Dudoignon, R. Mukhametshin, and D. Iskhakov (eds.), *Islam v Tatarskom Mire: Istoriia i Sovremennost'* [Islam in the Tatar World: Past and Present]. Kazan: Panorama, 211–18.

Musina, R. (2001). 'Musul'manskaia Identichnost' kak Forma "Religioznogo Natsionalizma" Tatar v Kontekste Etnosotsial'nykh Protsessov i Etnopoliticheskoi Situatsii v Tatarstane'

[Muslim Identity as a Form of 'Religious Nationalism' for the Tatars in the Context of Ethno-Social Processes and of the Ethno-Political Situation in Tatarstan], in M. Iordan, R. Kuzeev, and S. Chervonnaia (eds.), *Islam v Evrazii: Sovremennye Etnicheskie i Esteticheskie Kontseptsii Sunnitskogo Islama, Ikh Transformatsiia v Massovom Soznanii i Vyrazhenie v Iskusstve Musul'manskikh Narodov Rossii*. Moscow: Progress-Traditsiia, 291–303.

Musina, R. (2009). 'Islam i Problemy Identichnosti Tatar v Postsovetskii Period' [Islam and the Tatars' Identity Problems in the Post-Soviet Period], in *Konfessional'nyi Factor v Razvitii Tatar: Kontseptual'nye Issledovaniia*. Kazan: Institut Istorii AN RT, 86–100.

Musina, R. (2012). 'Religiia v Strukture Identichnosti Tatar-Musul'man (po Materialam Etnosotsiologicheskikh Issledovanii v Tatarstane)' [Religion in the Identity Structure of Muslim Tatars (through the Data of Ethno-Sociological Surveys in Tatarstan)], in *Traditsii i Novatsii v Politicheskoi Kul'ture Postsovetskogo Perioda: Sfera Etnokonfessional'nogo Vzaimodeistviia*. Kazan: Institut istorii AN RT, 146–9.

Navruzov, A. R. (2007). *Gazeta 'Dzharidat Dagistan' (1913–1918) kak Istoriko-Kul'turnyi Zhurnal* [The Newspaper *Jaridat Daghistan* as a Historical and Cultural Journal]. Makhachkala: 'Epokha'.

Navruzov, A. R. (2010). 'Ziaiushchie Vysoty: Problemy Islamskoi Vysshei Shkoly v Postsovetskom Dagestane' [Yawning Heights: Problems of Islamic Higher Education in Post-Soviet Daghestan], in V. Bobrovnikov and A. Navruzov (eds.), *Dagestan i Musul'manskii Vostok* [Daghestan and the Muslim East]. Moscow: Izdatel'skii dom Mardzhani, 150–64.

Nefliasheva, N. (2009). 'Islam v Adygee: Ot Traditsii k Modernizatsii [Islam in Adyghea: from Tradition to Modernisation], in E. B. Demintseva (ed.), *Islam v Evrope i v Rossii* [Islam in Europe and in Russia]. Moscow: Izdatel'skii Dom Mardzhani, 146–66.

Nogmanov, A. (2005). *Samoderzhavie i tatary: ocherki istorii zakonodatel'skoi politiki vtoroi poloviny xvi–xviii vekov* [Autocracy and the Tatars: Sketches on the History of the Legal Policy from the Second Half of the Sixteenth to the Eighteenth Century]. Kazan: Tatarskoe knizhnoe izdatel'stvo.

Olimova, S. and Bosc, I. (2003). *Labour Migrations from Tajikistan*. Dushanbe: Mission of the International Organisation for Migration.

Olimova, S. and Olimov, M. (2007). *A Survey of Political Engagement and Enfranchisement of Labour Migrants from Tajikistan*. Washington, DC: International Foundation for Electoral Systems.

Omel'chenko, E. and Sabirova, G. (2003a). 'Islam and the Search for Identity', in H. Pilkington and G. Yemelianova (eds.), *Islam in Post-Soviet Russia: Public and Private Faces*. London and New York: Routledge, 167–82.

Omel'chenko, E. and Sabirova, G. (2003b). 'Practicing Islam: Rituals, Ceremonies and the Transmission of Ethno-Islamic Values', in H. Pilkington and G. Yemelianova (eds.), *Islam in Post-Soviet Russia: Public and Private Faces*. London and New York: Routledge, 183–209.

Omel'chenko, E. and Sabirova, G. (2003c). 'Gender Discourse within Russian Islam', in H. Pilkington and G. Yemelianova (eds.), *Islam in Post-Soviet Russia: Public and Private Faces*. London and New York: Routledge, 242–63.

Omel'chenko, E., Pilkington, H., and Sabirova, G. (2003). 'Islam in Multi-Ethnic Society: Identity and Politics', in H. Pilkington and G. Yemelianova (eds.), *Islam in Post-Soviet Russia: Public and Private Faces*. London and New York: Routledge, 210–41.

Ostrowski, D. (1998). *Muscovy and the Mongols: Cross-Cultural Influences on the Steppe Frontier*. Cambridge: Cambridge University Press.

Pilkington, H. and Yemelianova, G. (eds.) (2003). *Islam in Post-Soviet Russia: Public and Private Faces*. London and New York: Routledge.

Prozorov, S. M. (1994). 'Islam Ediny, Islam Regional'nyi' [Islam One, Islam Regional], in S. Kh. Kimilev and I. M. Smilanskaia (eds.), *Islam i Problemy Mezhtsivilizatsionnykh Vzaimodeistvii*. Moscow: Akademiia Kul'tur i Obshchechelovecheskikh Tsennostei.

Prozorov, S. M. (ed.) (2006). *Islam na Territorii Byvshei Rossiiskoi Imperii, Entsiklopedicheskii Slovar'* [Islam on the Territory of the Former Russian Empire: An Encyclopaedic Dictionary]. Moscow: Izdatel'skaia Firma 'Vostochnaia Literatura' RAN.

Radvanyi, J. (2005). 'Quelques Réponses à une Question non Posée: L'Islam et le Recensement de la Population de Russie en 2002', in M. Laruelle and S. Peyrouse (eds.), *Islam et Politique en Ex-URSS*. Paris: L'Harmattan, 59–71.

Reynolds, M. (2005). 'Myths and Mysticism: A Longitudinal Perspective on Islam and Conflict in the North Caucasus', *Middle Eastern Studies* 41(1): 41–54.

Roche, S. (2012). 'One Day at the "Paradise" Market'. Manuscript text.

Ro'i, Y. (2000). *Islam in the Soviet Union: From World War II to Perestroika*. London: Hurst & Company.

Rougier, B. (2008). 'Introduction', in B. Rougier (ed.), *Qu'est-ce que le Salafisme?* Paris: PUF.

Rousselet, K. (2008). 'Printsip Svetskosti v Rossii: Stolknovenie Norm i Tsennostei' [The Principle of Secularism in Russia: Confronting Norms and Values], in K. Rousselet et al. (eds.), *Religiia i Svetskoe Gosudarstvo : Printsip Laisite v Mire i v Evrazii*. Moscow: Franko-Rossiiskii Tsentr Gumanitarnykh i Obshchestvennykh Nauk v Moskve, 167–86.

Rousselet, K. (2009). 'Les Figures de la Laïcité Postsoviétique en Russie', *Critique internationale* 44: 51–64.

Ruget, V. and Usmanalieva, B. (2008). 'Citizenship, Migration and Loyalty towards the State: A Case Study of the Kyrgyzstani Migrants Working in Russia and Kazakhstan', *Central Asian Survey* 27(2): 129–41.

Sabirova, G. (2011). 'Young Muslim-Tatar Girls of the Big City: Narrative Identities and Discourses on Islam in Postsoviet Russia', *Religion, State and Society* 39(2–3): 327–45.

Sagitova, L. (2013). 'Traditionalism, Modernism and Globalisation among the Volga Muslims: The Case of Sredniaia Eliuzan', in S. Dudoignon and C. Noack (eds.), *Allah's Kolkhozes: Migration, De-Stalinisation, Privatisation, and the Emergence of New Muslim Congregations in the USSR and After (1950s–2000s)*. Berlin: Klaus Schwarz Verlag (Islamkundliche Untersuchungen), 454–93.

Schimmelpenninck van der Oye, D. (2010). *Rusian Orientalism: Asia in the Russian Mind from Peter the Great to the Emigration*. New Haven and London: Yale University Press.

Sedgwick, M. (2004). *Against the Modern World: Traditionalism and the Secret Intellectual History of the Twentieth Century*. Oxford and New York: Oxford University Press.

Semenov, V. E. (2007). 'Tsennostnye Orientatsii Sovremennoi Molodezhi' [The Values Orientation of Present-Day Youth], *Sotsiologicheskie Issledovaniia* 4: 37–44.

Semenov, V. V. (2007). 'Etnicheskie Musul'mane i Mezhnatsional'nye Otnosheniia v Povol'zhe' [Ethnic Muslims and Interethnic Relations in the Volga Region], in A. V. Malashenko (ed.), *Islam v Rossii: Vzgliad iz Regionov* [Islam in Russia: The Vision from the Regions]. Moscow: Aspekt Press, 85–102.

Shikhaliev, Sh. Sh. (2013). 'Downwards Mobility and Spiritual Life: The Development of Sufism in the Contexts of Migrations in Daghestan, 1940s–2000s', in S. Dudoignon and C. Noack (eds.), *Allah's Kolkhozes: Migration, De-Stalinisation, Privatisation, and the Emergence of*

*New Muslim Congregations in the USSR and After (1950s–2000s)*. Berlin: Klaus Schwarz Verlag (Islamkundliche Untersuchungen), 398–420.

Shikhov, K. (2008). 'Khizb ut-Takhrir: Drug ili vrag? Mnenia ekspertov i sviashchennosluzhitelei' [Hizb al-Tahrir: Friend or Foe? The Opinions of Experts and Divines]', *islamrf.ru* (25 April) <http://islamrf.ru/news/vsluh//2634> [Accessed 25 September 2012].

Silant'ev, R. (2002). *Etnicheskii Aspekt Raskola Islamskogo Soobshchestva Rossii* [The Ethnic Aspect of the Schism of Russia's Islamic Community]. Moscow: Institut etnologii i antropologii RAN (Issledovaniia po Prikladnoi i Neotlozhnoi Etnologii: 149).

Silant'ev, R. (2007). 'Islamistskaia Oppozitsiia protiv Muftiiatov' [The Islamist Opposition to the Muftiates], *Vestnik Evrazii* 3: 43–57.

Sokirianskaia, E. (2005). 'Families and Clans in Ingushetia and Chechnya: A Fieldwork Report', *Central Asian Survey* 24(4): 453–67.

Sokirianskaia, E. (2008). 'Ideology and Conflict: Chechen Political Nationalism prior to, and during, Ten Years of War', in M. Gammer (ed.), *Ethno-Nationalism, Islam and the State in the Caucasus: Post-Soviet Disorder*. Abingdon: Routledge, 102–38.

Souleimanov, E. and Ditrych, O. (2008). 'The Internationalisation of the Russian–Chechen Conflict: Myths and Reality', *Europe-Asia Studies* 60(7): 1199–222.

Tiuriukanova, E. V. (ed.) (2011). *Zhenshchiny Migrant iz Stran SNG v Rossii* [Women Migrants from the CIS Countries in Russia]. Moscow: Tsentr migratsionnykh issledovanii—Fond Tadzhikistan.

Tomilov, N. A. (2000). 'Ethnic Processes within the Turkic Population of the West Siberian Plain (Sixteenth–Twentieth Centuries)', in S. A. Dudoignon (ed.), *En Islam sibérien*. Paris: Editions de l'EHESS (*Cahiers du monde russe* 41[2–3]: 221–32).

Uehling, G. (2004). 'The First Independent Ukrainian Census in Crimea: Myths, Miscoding and Missed Opportunities', *Ethnic and Racial Studies* 27(1): 149–70.

Usmanova, D., Minnullin, I., and Mukhametshin, R. (2010). 'Islamic Education in Soviet and Post-Soviet Tatarstan', in M. Kemper, R. Motika, and S. Reichmuth (eds.), *Islamic Education in the Soviet Union and its Successor States*. Abingdon: Routledge, 21–66.

Vatchagaev, M. (2012). 'Caucasus Emirate's Ethnic Russian Suicide Bombers', *North Caucasus Analysis* 13(20) (18 October).

Verkhovskii, A. M. (2007). 'Publichnye Otnosheniia Pravoslavnykh i Musul'manskikh Organizatsii na Federal'nom Urovne' [The Public Relations of Orthodox and Islamic Organisations at Federal Level], in A. V. Malashenko (ed.), *Islam v Rossii: Vzgliad iz Regionov* [Islam in Russia: The Vision from the Regions]. Moscow: Aspekt Press, 123–53.

Werth, P. (2002). *At the Margins of Orthodoxy: Mission, Governance, and Confessional Policy in Russia's Volga-Kama Region, 1827–1905*. Ithaca: Cornell University Press.

Werth, P. W. (2010). '*Soslovie* and the "Foreign Clergies" of Imperial Russia: Estate Rights or Service Rights?' *Cahiers du monde russe* 51(2–3): 419–40.

Wertheim, S. (2005). 'Islam and the Construction of Tatar Sociolinguistic Identity', in J. Johnson, M. Stepaniants, and B. Forest (eds.), *Religion and Identity in Modern Russia: The Revival of Orthodoxy and Islam*. Burlington, VT: Ashgate, 105–22.

Williams, B. G. (2008). 'Allah's Foot Soldiers: An Assessment of the Role of Foreign Fighters of Al-Qa'ida in the Chechen Insurgency', in M. Gammer (ed.), *Ethno-Nationalism, Islam and the State in the Caucasus: Post-Soviet Disorder*. Abingdon: Routledge, 156–78.

Yemelianova, G. (2003). 'Russia's *Umma* and Its Muftis', *Religion, State and Society* 31(2): 139–50.

CHAPTER 13

# BULGARIA

ANTONINA ZHELYAZKOVA

## Introduction

Two factors of a methodological nature influence any scholarly analysis of the current state of knowledge on Islam and Muslim minorities in Bulgaria.

Firstly, during the period of communist rule (1944–89) and especially up until the end of the 1970s, research of Islam and the Muslim population in Bulgaria was hindered by various restrictions, including limited access to works of foreign authors. Such scholarly literature and archive documents were confined to classified archives accessible to a small number of experts working for the communist government. The official state ideology branded religion as 'opium for the people', and considered faith in God and observation of religious rites as harmful and improper. An 'ordinary' social scientist could conduct independent research on issues such as Islamic movements and schools among Bulgarian Muslims, their social and economic status, or Islam in public space only if they had accepted the state propaganda and the official Socialist policy line.

Even today, the Faculty of Theology at the Sofia University 'Kliment Ohridski' teaches only Christianity (and predominantly its Eastern Orthodox tradition). No experts in Islam are trained, regardless of the fact that Muslims have comprised between 8% and 12% of the Bulgarian population through the years.

Secondly, after the fall of the Berlin Wall (1989), social scientists and scholars in humanities focused on the formerly 'prohibited' topics related to minorities and attempted to remove the ideological connotations from the scientific research on Islam and minorities in Bulgaria. Numerous independent think tanks, research NGOs, and foundations producing sociological or political analyses were established in the very beginning of the democratization process.[1] These organizations were independent of

---

[1] Center for the Study of Democracy, Center for Liberal Strategies, International Center for Minority Studies and Intercultural Relations, Center for Interreligious Dialogue and Conflict Prevention, Vitosha Research, and others.

state funding, and provided opportunities for scholars who were not influenced by the 'atheist propaganda'.

The first initiatives included researches, round tables, and publications. For example, the Center for the Study of Democracy (CSD)[2] organized with the financial support of the German Friedrich Ebert Foundation the round table *Aspects of the Ethnic-Cultural Situation in Bulgaria* (1992). The International Center for Minority Studies and Intercultural Relations (IMIR) started interdisciplinary research, organized an international conference, and published a collection of works on the subject of *Relations of Compatibility and Incompatibility between Christians and Muslims in Bulgaria* (Zhelyazkova, Nielsen, and Kepel 1995). Scholars from the traditional scientific institutions such as universities and the Bulgarian Academy of Sciences (BAS) began to take interest in the initiatives organized by CSD, IMIR, and other NGOs. One of the downsides of economic transition was shortage of state funds for all walks of life, including scientific research. Thus, scholars with independent thinking and good expertise were attracted by the funding provided by American and European donor organizations and the opportunity to conduct research and publish free of ideological mentoring or censorship.

As a result, historical and social studies became decentralized. There was no proper planning or coordination among the newly sprung institutes on either the domains of research or the choice of subjects. The scientific approach also changed. Empirical researches became popular and anthropology, which was non-existent or was practised under the disguise of ethnography or folklore studies during the communist period, was introduced. Another long-neglected field, which appeared after 1989, was the study of Islam and Muslims in Bulgaria. Their place in Bulgarian society, some specific features of Muslim religion, and the relations between Christians and Muslims became new priorities.

The emergence of Muslim minorities in Bulgaria and the Ottoman cultural heritage had a major historical impact on the Bulgarian society. Understandably, these factors triggered much interest among scholars as early as the end of the nineteenth century and continuing to date. In the past, most of the researches were in the fields of history and ethnography. It is only over the past twenty years that social and cultural anthropologists, sociologists, and political analysts have also had their say. Contemporary Bulgarian analyses and scholarly literature are characterized by the following trends:

- Debates on and rethinking of the Ottoman period of Bulgarian history, when the indigenous Muslim minorities were formed through the processes of colonization and Islamization.
- Comprehensive works by ethnographers, anthropologists, and folklore experts, analysing the traditions and customs of the Muslim communities in Bulgaria.
- Increasing numbers (since mid-1990s) of sociological and politological analyses of the status of Muslims in public space, of the stereotypes and prejudices they encounter, and of their political representation.

---

[2] Founded in late 1989, the Center for the Study of Democracy is one of the first independent, non-governmental public policy institutes in Bulgaria.

- The study of Islam as a philosophy, theology, and religious practice continues to be marginalized and underdeveloped. It has been undertaken mainly by theologians and spiritual leaders, while secular studies are few.

Immigration is a new phenomenon for the Bulgarian society and research of Muslim immigrants and refugees (the so-called 'new minorities') is in its early stages. Sociologists, economists, experts in statistics, and researchers interested in interdisciplinary approaches and collection of empirical data are most often drawn to studies of the customs, culture, religion, and presence in public space of such groups. There is a visible disproportion in the quantity of researches on the two Muslim groups: immigrants and indigenous populations. The weak interest in the immigrant communities is due to their insignificant number and the fact that Bulgaria is mainly a transit state for migration flows.

Islamophobia is a new phenomenon in Bulgaria that appeared after 9/11. There are of course historical prejudices vis-à-vis local Muslim communities, perceived as unwanted heritage of the Ottoman Empire and as a population related and loyal to its 'fatherland'—the neighbouring Turkey. These stereotypes have also strengthened the newly appeared Islamophobic perceptions.

A very visible manifestation of these developments is the ongoing debate on the radicalization of Muslims in Bulgaria. Since 1989, the Muslim minorities have acquired self-confidence and a sense of freedom to profess their religion and traditions. Sometimes the public, especially the nationalist fragments of society, perceive this assertiveness as radicalization. It could be argued that the debate has been transplanted to Bulgaria under the influence of events in other Balkan countries and worldwide.

Very few scientists in Bulgaria understand and study Islam as a theological system and a philosophy. Usually such data are collected by social and cultural anthropologists, ethnographers, and sometimes sociologists. None of them, for that matter, is an expert in Islam—they are familiar only with the local cults and traditions and the stereotypes prevailing among the religious communities (Jeliazkova and Georgieva 1994; Kyurkchieva 2004; Troeva 2011). Such anthropological and ethnological field research has the advantage of allowing systematic monitoring and registration of cultural changes, of modernization, of conditions and changes in the Muslim community with all its regional and ethnic specific features. Even if not theoretically familiar with the theology of Islam, anthropologists know in detail the Muslim practices and other religious issues of the community.

# History

The position and role of Islam and Muslims in the Bulgarian society cannot be fully comprehended without presenting the historical background. In 1396, the Bulgarian Kingdom was conquered by the Ottoman Empire. Bulgaria remained part of the European provinces of the Empire until 1878.

One of the most important dimensions of the Bulgarian national identity and of the national consolidation is the absolute repudiation of Ottoman rule. Despite living for almost five centuries under the Ottoman/Muslim law (Arnaudov 1872–81), and isolated from the rest of the Christian world, Bulgarians managed to preserve their traditions and culture—that of a Christian nation. Becoming a part of an Islamic Empire also meant that new Muslim communities have emerged alongside the majority Christian population. Some appeared through colonization by the Ottoman military and civil settlers, while others were created gradually through conversion.

The Ottoman conquest brought numerous profound changes into the life of Bulgarians. shariah norms and courts were introduced. The Bulgarian Christians became *dhimmis*, a second-rate population, which was obliged to pay special additional taxes levied on non-Muslims. Many Christian children were recruited to be trained, Islamized, and enrolled in the Ottoman army (Zhelyazkova 1998a; Castellan 1999; Sadulov 2000). However, Islam that has penetrated the Bulgarian lands after the Ottoman conquest has also experienced changes, adapting to local beliefs and customs.

Under Ottoman rule, Bulgarians became part of the *millet* system—a relatively tolerant form of government. The system guaranteed them the right to profess and practise their religion, a limited self-governance in the fields of education, culture, religion, and often also in management of local administrative affairs. On the other hand, the non-Muslim population had specific fiscal, labour, and military duties to the state. Ernest Gellner considers the *millet* system a specific feature of the Ottoman Empire. According to Gellner, the *millet* performed best in those parts of the Empire where there was a strong government and was weaker in the periphery (Gellner 1996; for more about the Ottoman Empire see Sugar 1977; Hosch 1995; Mantran 1989; Inalcik 1973; Zhelyazkova 1990a; Ihsanoglu 2004; Hupchick 1994; Lewis 1992; Ercan 1989).

This positive interpretation of the Ottoman Empire is absolutely unacceptable to the Bulgarian historiography. Generations of Bulgarian scholars have analysed the history of the Ottoman Empire, based on multiple sources, including the Ottoman ones, but always giving negative assessments and taking an attitude of utter rejection.

The lengthy period of Ottoman rule in Bulgaria is generally reviewed in a romantic-sentimental light, accompanied by twisting of historical facts of the day-to-day economic, social, and cultural life (Jirecek 1978; Snegarov 1958; Dimitrov 1983; Bozhilov et al. 1993; see also Bulgarian Academy of Sciences 1983; Yankov, Dimitrov, and Zagorov 1988). Such attitudes have strengthened stereotypes and perpetuated the social distances between Muslims and Orthodox Christians.

The prejudices embedded in the historical memory, culture, and education influence parts of the Bulgarian society, which continue to perceive the Muslim communities in negative terms. They see them as an alien body, incompatible with the Bulgarian nation, which belongs to the European Christian civilization. Such perceptions are persistent, despite the long tradition of sharing social and cultural spaces. Muslims have come to occupy a psychological niche in the national memory as the 'bad' heritage of the Ottoman Empire. A cliché for defining this period is: 'Bulgaria's five dark centuries'. Bulgarians believe that Ottoman rule made them suffer, arrested their economic and cultural development, resulted in Islamization of part of the nation (the Pomaks), and separated them for centuries from the European Christian civilization (Jirecek 1929; Snegarov 1958; Dimitrov 1983; Bozhilov et al. 1993).

In fact, this 'national victimization' places Bulgaria, as well as Greece and Serbia, in sharp contrast with other Balkan countries such as Bosnia and Herzegovina, Albania and Kosovo, where the attitudes towards the Ottoman period are more moderate and contain some positive connotations. Historical memories in Bosnia and Herzegovina, Albania and Kosovo are not so dramatic and these nations do not regard themselves as victims of a brutal Ottoman Empire.

To date, with few exceptions, Bulgarian historiography has made no comprehensive attempt to describe the Ottoman period of Bulgarian history in an objective and impartial manner. The efforts of some historians and textbook authors to offer an unbiased interpretation of historical events have met with significant public resistance—especially from the media and politicians, but also from fellow historians and textbook authors. These authors have tried to explain in an objective fact-based manner the socio-economic, demographic and cultural history of the Balkan provinces of the Ottoman Empire, finding not only negative but also positive aspects and trends in the period of Ottoman rule in Bulgaria (Zhelyazkova 1985, 1990a, 1990b; Georgieva 1994, 1999; Mutafchieva 1997; Mishkova 2006; Gruev and Kalyonski 2008).

The changed approach to the presentation of the Ottoman rule has been also reflected in some history textbooks (for example Delev et al. 1996). These textbooks review the period of Ottoman rule in a more moderate context. Positive social and economic trends in certain periods of the Ottoman rule are described—opportunities for cultural, religious, and educational self-government, for active participation in the economic life of the Empire and therefore for social prosperity.

As a result, sociological and anthropological studies of the attitudes and stereotypes related to ethnic and religious minorities in Bulgaria, carried out in recent years, have revealed that with only a few exceptions, most characteristics the Christian Bulgarians ascribe to Turks/Muslims are positive. The negative characteristics are 'Turkish slavery' and '(religious) fanatics' (Pamporov 2009). The first negative stereotype is persistent, having been reproduced and reinforced by the school system since the nineteenth century (Isov 2005). The stereotypes about '(religious) fanatics' is new. It was imported from abroad as a result of worldwide Islamophobia.

# Demography

All censuses conducted after the end of the Ottoman rule (from 1910 to 2011) show that the ethnic Bulgarians (predominantly Eastern Orthodox, and a small share of Catholics and Protestants) represent an overwhelming majority of Bulgarian population. Muslim minorities include Turks, Muslim Bulgarians (Pomaks), a proportion of Roma (roughly 40% of Roma are Muslims while the rest are Christians—Eastern Orthodox and Protestants), and a small number of immigrants and refugees. In addition, there are several other smaller indigenous ethnic and religious groups, as shown in Table 13.1.

Table 13.1 Population according to denomination and census years (1910–2011)

| Denomination | 1910 | 1920 | 1926 | 1934 | 1946 | 1992 | 2001 | 2011 |
|---|---|---|---|---|---|---|---|---|
| Number | | | | | | | | |
| Total population | 4,337,513 | 4,846,971 | 5,478,741 | 6,077,939 | 7,029,349 | 8,487,317 | 7,928,901 | 7,364,570 (5,758,301)** |
| Eastern Orthodox | 3,643,918 | 4,062,097 | 4,569,074 | 5,128,890 | 5,967,992 | 7,274,592 | 6,552,751 | 4,374,135 |
| Muslim | 602,078 | 690,734 | 789,296 | 821,298 | 938,418 | 1,110,295* | 966,978 | 577,139*** |
| Catholic | 32,150 | 34,072 | 40,347 | 45,704 | – | 53,074 | 43,811 | 48,945 |
| Protestant | 6,335 | 5,617 | 6,735 | 8,371 | – | 21,878 | 42,308 | 64,476 |
| Jewish | 40,067 | 43,232 | 46,431 | 48,398 | 43,338 | 2,580 | 653 | 706 |
| Armenian–Gregorian | 12,259 | 10,848 | 25,402 | 23,476 | – | 9,672 | 6,500 | 1,715 |
| Other and not indicated | 706 | 371 | 1 456 | 1,802 | 79,604 | 15,226 | 7,784 | 418,921 |
| Not affiliated to any | – | – | – | – | – | – | 308,116 | 272,264 |

| Structure in percentage | | | | | | | | |
|---|---|---|---|---|---|---|---|---|
| Eastern Orthodox | 84.0 | 83.8 | 83.4 | 84.4 | 84.9 | 85.7 | 82.6 | 76.0 |
| Muslim | 13.9 | 14.3 | 14.4 | 13.5 | 13.3 | 13.1 | 12.2 | 10.1 |
| Catholic | 0.7 | 0.7 | 0.7 | 0.8 | – | 0.6 | 0.6 | 0.8 |
| Protestant | 0.1 | 0.1 | 0.1 | 0.1 | – | 0.3 | 0.5 | 1.1 |
| Jewish | 0.9 | 0.9 | 0.8 | 0.8 | 0.6 | 0.0 | 0.0 | 0.0 |
| Armenian–Gregorian | 0.3 | 0.2 | 0.5 | 0.4 | – | 0.1 | 0.1 | 0.0 |
| Other and not indicated | 0.0 | 0.0 | 0.0 | 0.0 | 1.1 | 0.2 | 0.1 | 7.3 |
| Not affiliated to any | – | – | – | – | – | – | 3.9 | 4.7 |

Sources: The table represents author's interpretation of data from <http://www.nsi.bg/Census/StrReligion.htm>; 2011 census results: <http://www.nsi.bg/census2011/pageen2.php?p2=179>; Tomova 2005.
* This number includes 83,537 Muslims—*Alevi/Bektoshi/Kizilbasi*—who are entered in the census forms as Shi'ites.
** The figure 7,364,570 represents the entire population of Bulgaria. The figure 5,758,301 is the number of those who have answered the question about their religious affiliation. 1,606,269 (21.8%) have used the option not to answer. The methodology of the 2011 census has been criticized as presenting an unrealistic picture of the religious structure of the Bulgarian society (Ivanov 2011).
*** Muslims are distributed as follows: Sunni 546,004; Shi'ite 27,407; Other Muslims 3,728.

Most of the Muslims in Bulgaria are Sunni, but there is also a small Shi'a community. The national censuses, with a few exceptions (the 1992 census and to some extent the 2001 one), do not register the number of Muslim immigrants and refugees, or register these data only partially, i.e. only those who have acquired Bulgarian citizenship. For this reason, data on immigrants and refugees are shown outside the statistical tables in the section dealing with migrants' profile.

## Muslims' Social and Economic Status

The Bulgarian Muslim communities (Turks, Pomaks, Roma) have been profoundly affected by the difficult transition from planned to market economy. The hardest period was from 1989 to 1998, when numerous enterprises in the Muslim populated regions were closed down. The social and economic status of Muslims was further aggravated by the poor infrastructure in their settlements and their low level of education.

One of the first studies, dealing with the ethnicization of poverty in several post-communist states, was carried out by an international team of sociologists under the direction of Ivan Szelenyi from Yale University (Emigh, Fodor, and Szelenyi 2001; Szelenyi 2002). The texts included in the publication compared data collected in 1999–2000 in several countries to establish whether the post-communist period had brought on 'a new poverty' and the formation of 'a sub-class' during the 1990s in Central and Eastern Europe. Some of the texts analyse the degree of interaction between poverty and ethnic and religious affiliation, especially within the Roma group. A major finding of the Bulgarian sociologists in Szelenyi's team was that poverty and severe economic crisis, which accompanied the transition from communism to market economy, affected most disastrously the Muslim minorities and the Roma. During the research, the phrase 'to ethnicize poverty' became popular among the academic community. The term is based on sociological data explaining the remarkably high levels of unemployment among the Muslims and Roma, especially during the 1990s, as well as the higher levels of economic migration.

In the period 1999–2006, sociologists detected a permanent trend towards ethnicization of poverty, unemployment, access to education, and healthcare. The number of illiterate young Roma reached one-third of the community. About 40% of all the unemployed in Bulgaria are of minority origin. The share of Roma among the unemployed has more than doubled in a period of seven years. Sociologists warned that the perpetuation of such a condition carried serious risk for ethnic antagonism and social-economic conflicts. According to sociologists, even more troubling than the ethnicization of poverty itself was that the ethno-poverty had started to reproduce generationally, since poor families had more children in 2006 than in 1999 (Parvanov 2006).

Other issues attracting attention over the past ten years have been the relationships between education and poverty, social marginalization and demographic imbalances. A large number of studies survey the low levels of education among the Roma and especially the increasing number of school drop-outs, which has become a major social problem and has turned the Roma Muslim community into a group especially susceptible to being influenced by Salafi and Nursi activists. The data about their activities in the Roma ghettos are very hard to collect. Some information was obtained during the study of the IMIR research team, which included a Muslim Roma informant. The data were collected in the Roma neighbourhoods and the mosques in Pazardzhik and Plovdiv (Zhelyazkova, Grigorov, and Dimitrova 2005; Zhelyazkova, Angelova, and Vladimirov 2007). One of the Salafi preachers, active in the Pazardzhik Roma ghetto, was sentenced in 2005 for participation in radical groups and his effective imprisonment was conditionally postponed by the court. In 2010, the prosecution started a new investigation against him with the accusation that he was instigating religious hatred during his sermons.

Educational problems experienced by the minorities create social distances and new negative ethnic and religious stereotypes (Ivanov 2002, 2006; Pamporov 2009; Topalova and Pamporov 2007). According to the data from the 2011 census, 1.5% of the Bulgarian citizens aged 9 years or over are illiterate. The share of those who are illiterate is 0.5% among the ethnic Bulgarians, 4.7% among the Turks, and 11.8% among the Roma. All children between the ages of 7 and 16 years should attend school according to the law. However, 23.2% of the Roma children in this age group do not go to school. The share of such children in the Turkish community is 11.9%, while for Bulgarians it is 5.6% (see NSI 2011). The education level of the indigenous minorities is illustrated in Table 13.2.

Bulgaria does not have a consistent policy concerning the education of immigrants, despite the fact that the children of those who have legal status have the right to study in the municipal schools. Refugees' children receive more systematic treatment: initially they study Bulgarian in the integration centres and then are redirected to the municipal schools. Bulgaria formally applies the international standards on refugees without having its own concept of how to treat them. Some studies, like that of Elena

Table 13.2 Educational structure of larger ethnic communities in Bulgaria—persons over 20 (in %)

| Education | Bulgarians | Turks | Roma |
| --- | --- | --- | --- |
| University | 19.1 | 2.4 | 0.2 |
| High school | 47.7 | 21.9 | 6.5 |
| Secondary | 24.9 | 46.9 | 41.8 |
| Primary | 7.0 | 18.6 | 28.3 |
| Illiterate | 1.3 | 10.1 | 23.2 |

Source: The table represents author's interpretation of data from NSI 2003.

Sachkova (2000), suggest good practices of European countries with more experience in immigrants' integration. Sachkova's work depicts the educational policy, practical measures, and theoretical views on the education of migrant children in Switzerland, and discusses the issue of multicultural education. All these are very useful for the Bulgarian educational experts, but are for now regarded only as an agenda for the distant future.

# Ethnic Profiles of the Muslim Community in Bulgaria

## Turks

Turks are the largest Muslim community (Table 13.3). They are furthermore the most strongly consolidated community in the state with a very clear and unambiguous understanding of its ethnic identity. The only differences stem from affiliation to various Islamic movements. Some elements of in-group competition exist between Sunni Turks and *Alevi / Kızılbashi / Bektashi*. The *Kızılbashi*, a minority within a minority, have freely practised their specific rituals with no visible confrontation with the Sunni Turks since 1990 (Melikoff 1990; Norris 2006; Gramatikova 2011). Contradictions and objections between these two groups concern only some elements of lifestyle and religious practices.

Table 13.3 Number and percentage of Bulgaria's minority populations 1992/2001/2011

| Population | 1992 | 2001 | 2011 |
|---|---|---|---|
| Turks | 800,052 (9.4%) | 746,664 (9.5%) | 588,318 (8.8%) |
| Roma | 313,396 (3.4%) | 370,908 (4.6%) | 325,343 (4.9%) |
| Russians | 17,139 (0.2%) | 15,595 (0.2%) | 9,978 (0.1%) |
| Armenians | 13,677 (0.2%) | 10,832 (0.1%) | 6,552 (0.1%) |
| Jews | 3,461 (0.04%) | 1,363 (0.02%) | 1,162 (0.0%) |
| Macedonians | – | 5,071 (0.1%) | 1,654 (0.0%) |
| Greeks | 4,930 (0.1%) | 3,408 (0.04%) | 1,379 (0.0%) |
| Wallachians | 7,650 (0.1%) | 10,556 (0.1%) | 3,684 (0.1%) |
| Tartars | 4,515 (0.1%) | – | – |

*Sources*: The table represents author's interpretation of data from *Annual Book of Statistics of the Republic of Bulgaria* (Sofia, 1994, p. 51); <http://www.nsi.bg.> 2011; Census results: <http://www.nsi.bg/census2011/pageen2.php?p2=179>.

This has started to change in recent years. Anthropological researches carried out between 2008 and 2010 established increasing negative stereotypes against *Kızılbashi / Bektashi* among the Sunni and vice versa. The *Bektashi* were subjected to pressure to reduce their rituals, and their holy places were discreetly subjected to Sunnization (Kyurkchieva, Troeva-Grigorova et al. 2008; IMIR Archive 2010).[3]

Since the Bulgarian liberation in 1878, the government policy towards Turks as an ethnic and religious minority has been highly erratic, shifting from one extreme to another: from granting them a wide range of rights and freedoms to forcible change of their Turkish-Arab names, assimilation attempts, and periodical (since the beginning of the twentieth century) expulsions to Turkey. On numerous occasions, the state has used force against them and violated their human rights, resulting in deterioration of inter-confessional and inter-ethnic relations (Eminov 1997; Simsir 1988; Zhelyazkova 1998a, 2001a; Nazarska 1999a; Yalamov 2002; Ilieva 2010).

The first Bulgarian constitution (Tarnovo Constitution 1879) included articles safeguarding the rights of the Bulgarian citizens belonging to religious minorities, although none of its articles included terms like 'minority' or 'Muslims'. For example, article 40 guaranteed the right to free practice of religion to those citizens who were 'Christians of non-Orthodox denomination or other believers'. The constitution guaranteed the autonomy of minority religious communities and wide cultural rights for minority groups (the right to have their own places of worship, schools, newspapers and journals) (Tarnovo Constitution 1879; Nazarska 1999a).

The current Bulgarian constitution, adopted in 1991, also includes no reference to 'minorities'. The constitution only mentions the 'citizens whose mother tongue is not Bulgarian' (article 36) and adds that everyone has the right to 'develop their own culture in accordance with their ethnic affiliation, which is endorsed and guaranteed by the law' (article 54). While ethnic or religious groups are not recognized as collective bearers of rights, the constitution recognizes all citizens as equals and guarantees that they shall be treated equally regardless of their ethnicity or religion.

This principle is established in many other Bulgarian legal acts. Among the most important is the Law on Protection against Discrimination, which protects the distinctive culture and identity of minorities and underlines that they have an unalienable right to maintain and develop their culture, the right to practise their religion and use their language.

Both in the past (taking an indoctrinated approach) and in the post-1989 period, ethnologists, folklorists, and anthropologists in Bulgaria have intensely studied traditions and culture of the Turkish community. Anthropologists and ethnographers register and describe cultural and religious features of the Turks. Among the main findings of the more recent studies was that the process of modernization has led to greater freedom in practising of religious rituals.

---

[3] The IMIR archive consists of fieldwork logs, digital and other carriers of interviews made through a period including the last twenty years. All the information is available for secondary and tertiary analysis for any scholar interested.

Recent studies have also included regular surveys of their political commitments and activities. Studies note the massive electoral support of the Bulgarian Turks for the Movement for Rights and Freedoms (MRF; a party considered as representative of the interests of Turks and other Muslims in Bulgaria) and their reluctance to vote for other national parties (socialists, democrats, and centrists). The reason for this is the lack of trust in or even fear of the state policies.

The analyses and debates about Turkish participation in political life often boil down to the pros and cons of having a Turkish/Muslim political party in Bulgaria. The Movement for Rights and Freedoms, formed in 1990, has always been represented in parliament, and has been a member of three government coalitions (1993–4, 2001–5, 2005–9). The reaction of the majority population to the appearance of the MRF on the political scene was predominantly negative. The party has been criticized for tolerating corruption amidst its elite and for having too much influence over the economic life of the country.

Today, the Turks in Bulgaria to a significant extent perceive themselves as 'European Muslims'. An anthropological fieldwork study (Maeva 2006) analysing the economic migration patterns among the Turks has established that over the past ten years, Western Europe has become the main immigration destination for the Bulgarian Turks. In the 1990s, the most attractive destination was neighbouring Turkey, the language of which they speak and where they have relatives. Respondents stated that they felt culturally closer to the Western European communities than to employers, colleagues, and relatives in Turkey. The issues of religion and the way religious rituals are performed are important reasons for such perception. Bulgarian Turks consider themselves secular and as such, they were met with disapproval in Turkey, where they were deemed insufficiently devoted to religion.

Similar differences in identity perception between Bulgarian Turks and Turks from Turkey were noted also by M. Mancheva, who studied emigration of Bulgarian Turks to Germany (the survey conducted in 2008 covered the Berlin area). The study revealed that Bulgarian Turks most often search for employment among Turks and Kurds— long-term gastarbeiters (guest workers) from Turkey. Immigrants from Turkey perceive the Bulgarian Turks as barely religious, or even as infidels. Sometimes they refer to them as Christians, while the Bulgarian Turkish women, who are mostly secularized, educated, and employed, are considered as women of 'rotten morals'. While the Bulgarian Turks prefer to work for employers who are immigrants from Turkey due to their common language and ethnic origin, they at the same time define them as ignorant, backward, and as religious fanatics.

The identity of Bulgarian Turks in emigration consists of three major components: Bulgarian, Turkish, and European. The Turkish component is based on *ethnic origin* and *mother tongue*. The Bulgarian one involves *passport* (citizenship), *home country*, and *native place*. Bulgarian identity is also associated with *air* and *soil*. Being European entails a mentality that is *modern, open,* and *free* (Mancheva 2008).

The overwhelming majority of the Bulgarian Turks from younger and middle generations have a secular attitude. The Muslim tradition is maintained mainly by the elderly.

Young Turks dress in a secular manner, rarely attend mosques, and prefer visiting clubs and bars. They organize their weddings in a modern manner. Young Turks opt for secular schools and it is hard for the Muslim religious high schools to recruit students among them. Most of the mosque visitors in villages are elder men, and even they usually limit their attendance to Fridays and important holidays. Among the occasions when the young come to mosques in larger numbers are the iftar meals during Ramadan (Troeva 2012; Maeva 2006; Zhelyazkova 1998b).

Despite this, young Turks are strongly attached to their traditional culture and to the specific rituals inherited from their ancestors. In recent years, the Fethullah Gülen[4] movement has started to exercise considerable influence among them. No studies on Fethullah Gülen's influence in the country have been conducted in Bulgaria. The only study was done by a Turkish scholar, Kerem Öktem (2010). He examined the influence of Gülen's movement in the field of secular and religious education. The author concludes that the movement has replaced the influence of different Arab states.

## Pomaks (Muslim Bulgarians)

Pomaks are another important religious and cultural community in Bulgaria. (For an analysis of how Pomaks are presented in the works of Bulgarian social scientists, see Aleksiev 1997. For Pomaks in the communist period, see Gruev 2003; Gruev and Kalyonski 2008. On Pomak identity, see Konstantinov 1992; Karagiannis 1997; Neuburger 2004. On Pomaks in Bulgaria today, see Georgieva 2001; Kyurkchieva 2004; Aleksiev 2005.) They inhabit several regions of the Rhodope Mountains. The Bulgarian censuses do not include Pomaks as an ethnic identity option. As a result, their numbers are estimated based on a rather precarious calculation combining the data about persons who have registered as Muslims and at the same time have stated that their mother tongue is Bulgarian. Insulted by such an approach, many Pomaks have refused to be counted, while some declared themselves Turks. In 1992, the Bulgarian National Statistical Institute (NSI) estimated their numbers at approximately 160,000 and in 2001 at 130,000 (NSI 2001). Experts on minority issues believe that between 220,000 and 250,000 Pomaks lived in Bulgaria in 1992 (Zhelyazkova 2001a: 294).

The issue of Pomak identity is very complex. They have a borderline identity halfway between Bulgarians and Turks. They are Muslims, but their mother tongue is Bulgarian.

---

[4] Fethullah Gülen—a Turkish preacher, expert in Islam and leader of the *Gülen* movement. The movement consists of volunteer organizations united under Gülen's leadership. Gülen was born in Erzurum, Turkey in 1941. He gave his first sermon when he was 14. He became follower of Said Nursi before reaching the age of 18. Said Nursi encouraged Muslim and Christians to join efforts against aggressive atheism, pointing out that religions can cooperate to promote faith. In 2008, the *Foreign Policy* magazine selected Gülen the most influential living intellectual. Gülen never married. He lives in the USA. His personal website is available in twenty-two languages, including Bulgarian (<http://www.bg.fgulen.com>).

Pomaks do not have a uniform perception and identify themselves in various ways. They continue to search for their identity tracing back their historical genesis. Pomaks have endeavoured to affirm their identity through oral tradition, as recorded by the oldest representatives of the group, or have in some cases pinned their hopes on archaeological works to unveil written evidence of their pre-Ottoman Muslim origin (for various approaches to analysing the identity of the Muslim Bulgarians, see Balikci 1999; Velinov 2001; Eminov 2007; Gruev 2003).

Regardless of the fact that there are no official data, results from various studies (see Ivanova 2012) show that a large majority of Pomaks identify themselves either as Pomaks, as Muslim Bulgarians, or simply as Muslims, thus making religious affiliation overlap with the ethnic one. The latter have created their own theories of origin claiming to be the most ancient indigenous population of Bulgaria, converted to Islam long before the Ottoman incursion into the Bulgarian lands (Georgieva 1994; Stoyanov 1998; Balikci 1999; Telbizova-Sack 2000; Eminov 2007). Still, the majority share the common view that Pomaks adopted Islam during the time of the Ottoman Empire.

About 26% of Pomaks identify themselves as Bulgarians. Some from this group have converted to Christianity (mostly Orthodoxy, but in some cases also Protestantism). The tendency to identify as Bulgarians is most common in the Eastern Rhodopes, where Pomaks live among the Bulgarian Turks. In contrast, in the Western Rhodope municipalities like Goce Delchev and Yakoruda, where the population consists mostly of Pomaks and Christian Bulgarians, many Pomaks opt for Turkish self-identification, although they do not speak Turkish. Lastly, a small group claims Arab origin. They believe that they are descendants of pre-Ottoman Islamic missionaries to the Bulgarian lands.

A convincing analysis of the dynamics of the development of the Pomak identity is offered by Mihail Gruev who defines the Muslim Bulgarians as an ethnic–cultural group with multiple identities, the product of the dissolution of a formerly uniform and integral religious identity under the pressure of the Bulgarian state. Gruev supports Brunnbauer's thesis of a triple, horizontal classification of the Muslim Bulgarians' identity: Turkish, Bulgarian, and specifically Pomak (Muslim) (Gruev 2008; Brunnbauer 1998, 2001).

Pomaks practise a very syncretic form of Islam, i.e. Islam fused with local (Christian and pre-Christian) religious beliefs. Most of their religious rituals related to death, marriage, birth and seasonal holidays display deviations from the Qur'an rules and the way similar rituals are performed in Muslim countries. They perform specific rituals in memory of the deceased—the family donates money to the guests to redeem the sins of the deceased. Pomaks celebrate St George's Day (6 May—an important Christian holiday), calling it Hadarlez, donate sacred food for the souls of the deceased before and after the Ramadan lent, and perform many other rituals, which are not based on the Qur'an.

Pomaks are the most devout and actively practising religious community in Bulgaria. According to the study 'Attitudes of Muslims in Bulgaria', conducted by a team of sociologists and anthropologists in 2011, 32.2% of Pomaks declare themselves as 'deeply religious'. In comparison, the share of deeply religious among other communities is as follows: Turks—29.3%, Roma—23.3%, Christian Bulgarians—15.4% (Ivanova 2012).

Religion remains an important factor also among the younger generations of Pomaks. Parents enrol children in Qur'an reading classes and encourage them to study religion in municipal schools as an optional class. Pomak children are frequent winners in the annual national Qur'an reading contests in Sofia.

Although Pomaks themselves do not consider that the Islamic and Bulgarian components of their identity are in conflict, the wider society is growing increasingly suspicious towards the aspirations for acquiring knowledge of one's own religion (Islam), especially if this is done abroad. This is frequently interpreted as alienation from the Bulgarian nation. In addition to the negative public discourse, the people who have obtained their Islamic education abroad have attracted also the attention of security services.

In 2010, thirteen imams and Muftis (twelve Pomaks and one Roma) were investigated and accused of belonging to the Al Waqf al Islami organization, seated in Saudi Arabia. According to the prosecution, during the period 2008–10, the thirteen men preached radical ideology, based on Salafi elements during prayers in mosques, lectures, and conversations. A court trial against them started in the autumn of 2012—regardless of the fact that the accusations are poorly substantiated.

## Roma

Roma are the third largest ethnic community in Bulgaria after Bulgarians and Turks. They started to settle in the Bulgarian lands during the thirteenth century (Marushiakova and Popov 1993; Kenrick 1998). The Roma community is the most heterogeneous in the country. Roma differ according to religious beliefs and ethnic self-identification. While most self-identify as Roma, others do so as Bulgarians, and still others as Turks. There is a significant diversity related to mother tongue as well. Bulgarian, Turkish, and Roma with various dialects are spoken. There is also a division between 'settled' and 'nomadic' Roma. In addition to these, numerous subgroups exist in accordance with their typical craft and other features. As a result, the Roma are a 'community' mainly for the surrounding population. Roma themselves rarely have a sense of belonging to a 'Roma community'—differences, distances, and conflicts tend to be more pronounced among them than between Roma and other ethnic groups (Tomova 1995, 1998; Pamporov 2006; Tarnev and Grekova 2007; Topalova and Pamporov 2007; Grekova et al. 2008; Tilkidziev et al. 2009).

According to 2011 census data, one-third of Roma (34.5%) are not religious or did not want to declare their religion. Of those who stated which religion they belong to, 56% (or 36.6% of all Roma) are Orthodox Christians, 27.8% (or 18.2% of all) are Muslims, and 15.4% (10% of all) are Protestants. The number of Protestant Roma has been steadily rising over the past ten years as a growing number of evangelical churches have won followers among both Orthodox Christians and Muslim Roma. The Protestant churches attract Roma because they are among the very limited number of institutions that work systematically and directly with the Roma. They take care of children, providing them with education and shelter. The evangelical churches also have a positive influence on Roma morals and behaviour (Slavkova 2007).

In addition to converting to Protestantism, Muslim Roma are also open to joining movements which are not traditionally part of Bulgarian Islam such as Wahhabi,[5] Nursis,[6] Suleymanists,[7] and in recent years Fethullahci.[8] Roma can be easily accessed and influenced by such non-traditional religious movements due to their low social and educational status. As an underclass, facing negative attitudes and intolerance in the Bulgarian society, Roma are highly vulnerable and the proselytizing by non-traditional Islamic movements mentioned above in the Roma ghettos quickly attracts new followers.

## Bulgarian Muslims in Emigration

Since 1989, the population of Bulgaria has substantially decreased—from 8,992,000 (1989 estimate) to 7,364,570 (2011 census data). While some of this decrease can be attributed to low birth-rate, the most important factor is the intensity of the emigration waves. Emigration from Bulgaria has understandably attracted a significant interest of scholars from various fields: ethnology, anthropology, folklore, sociology, and history.

Emigration was not a matter of choice only for ethnic Bulgarians, but also for members of historical Muslim minorities. Furthermore, unlike the Bulgarians, for whom it was exceptionally difficult to leave the country under the communist regime, large numbers of Bulgarian Muslims and especially of Turks had emigrated in the 1945–89 period. This was on the one hand a result of their desire to escape from communist repression and forced assimilation. On the other hand, emigration was permitted or even encouraged by the communist authorities, who used it as a way to reduce the share of Muslims among the Bulgarian population.

---

[5] Wahhabi—another name for the *Hanbali*. The Hanbali school is one of the fundamental legal schools in Islam, mainly prevalent in Saudi Arabia. It dominated Baghdad during the twelfth and thirteenth centuries when the followers of other shariah schools were subjected to persecution. The supporters of the Hanbali school are considered by the other three schools as dogmatic interpreters of the religion and not as lawyers.

[6] Nursis (*nurciler*)—Islamic movement, which appeared in Turkey in the 1950s. It was founded by Badiuzzam Said Nursi with the objective of bringing society back to the norms of Islam.

[7] Suleymanists (*Suleymancilar*): followers of the late Suleyman Tunahan, a preacher in two important Istanbul mosques, who expanded his community through his then-illegal Qur'an study courses. The Suleymanists are now divided under the leadership of two brothers, both Suleyman's grandsons (see Jacob M. Landau, *Radical Politics in Modern Turkey*, Leiden: Brill, 1974; <http://www.tek1.net/suleymancilar-cemaati-kimdir.html>; and <http://tr.wikipedia.org/wiki/S%C3%BCleymanc%C4%B1lar>).

[8] Fethullahci—see footnote 3 on Fethullah Gülen, <http://istanbul.ffe-ps.org/2012/05/16/les-fethullahci-origines-et-objectifs/>, and <http://www.faz.net/aktuell/feuilleton/tuerkischer-islamismus-die-anhaenger-des-fethullah-guelen-1664740.html>.

Historians were the first (in the early 1990s) to describe the forced resettlement of 360,000 Turks from Bulgaria. Their attention focused on emigrants' accommodation and adaptation in Turkey, their experience of living in temporary refugee camps, and the economic niches where they managed to find employment. Half of the refugees had not managed to adapt to the new conditions, or suffered because of separated families or nostalgia. This was among the main reasons that caused mass return after the fall of the communist regime (Hoepken 1989; Vasileva 1992).

Despite the democratization, emigration of Turks continued after 1990. The main difference was that while before, the reasons for emigration were mostly political, after the fall of the communist regime the push factors were predominantly economic. The extremely difficult economic transition was characterized by the devaluation of the Bulgarian currency, which wiped out personal savings, a thwarted agrarian reform, and closing down of a large number of public enterprises. The price of tobacco, a traditional crop for majority of Turkish farmers, plummeted. This pushed many Bulgarian Turks towards Turkey, where many of them had relatives and friends, and the absence of the language barrier increased their chances of finding employment (Vasileva 1992).

Studies quoted already, as well as numerous others (for example, Zhelyazkova 1998b; Karamihova 2002) have focused on the emigrants, their migration models and motivations, the socio-cultural aspects of their integration, and their dual belonging. The findings of these surveys are that Bulgarian Turks, who migrate to Turkey, quickly find free spaces on the labour market and have good professional achievements, but find it harder to adapt to the cultural environment in Turkey. The reasons for the difficulties are that Bulgarian Turks are less religious and more secular, more modern, more educated. The attitude of the native Turks to the Bulgarian immigrants is burdened with specific prejudices: they are perceived as not sufficiently religious, as granting too large freedom to their wives and daughters. This makes adaptation in Turkey complicated and is one of the reasons for the shift in the emigration patterns in the late 1990s.

Another boom of emigration of Bulgarian Turks was registered in 1996–7. The severe financial and economic crisis, which struck Bulgaria in these years, had an especially strong impact on Muslims, as most of them lived in economically deprived and underdeveloped areas of the country. The state-owned enterprises in these regions were among the first to close their doors, and as no alternative employment was provided, the minority-populated regions were hit by exceptionally high unemployment levels (double the national average). However, in contrast to the early 1990s, this time the main destinations of the migrants became Western European countries like Germany, the Netherlands, Denmark, and Sweden (Georgieva 1998).

Emigration of a high number of Bulgarian Turks had both positive and negative effects for the community. Remittances sent by the emigrants became an indispensable source of income for many Bulgarian Turkish families, who traditionally reside in the most economically deprived parts of the country. On the other hand, large-scale emigration has negative social and psychological connotations. Families are separated and children are raised by a single parent or by other relatives. Migration thus created a substantial number of 'transnational families' in Bulgaria. A research conducted as part of the European

Commission funded project *Gender, Migration and Intercultural Interactions in the Mediterranean and South-East Europe: An Interdisciplinary Perspective* (2008–11) investigated also the issue of separation of families due to labour migration. It established that the consequences of transnational family life and above all of transnational parenthood were predominantly negative, and in most critical cases included elements of dissolution of families and alienation of children. However, the families endured the challenges out of financial and economic necessity and tried to compensate the negative changes by the sole benefit of emigration—economic gain (Nazarska and Hajdinjak 2011).

Numerous Bulgarian experts on minority and ethnic studies have turned their attention to the issue of migration of people of minority origin. Thus, scientific knowledge about minorities and methodological experience amassed in studies of ethnicity were employed in the newly developed field of migration studies. These developments can be observed in *From Ethnicity to Migration* (Krasteva 2004), an edited volume explaining the philosophy and theory of ethnic policies in Bulgaria, as well as the development of new researches on ethnic and religious minorities.

Two other publications review migration studies in Bulgaria after 1989. Elchinova (2009) presents a critical analysis of migration researches in the field of anthropology, while Ragaru (2008) offers an exhaustive review of migration studies.

According to a report of the National Statistical Institute (2002), Turks constituted 12% of the emigrating Bulgarian citizens. They were the group with the highest rate of emigrants. Most of the Turkish emigrants were men below 40 years old, and with only primary education. The main destinations were Germany, Spain, Greece, the UK, Canada, and the USA. While emigration to North America was almost exclusively for a long time or permanent, European countries attracted short-term migrants. After 2000, women also started to emigrate in increasing numbers. Most of them were with primary and secondary education, and emigrated for both seasonal work and long-term employment (Zhelyazkova 2003; Karamihova 2002).

Similar migration trends were observed among the Roma population. Roma constituted 6% of all emigrants. The age and education factors, as well as the destinations, coincided with those of Turks. In addition to the above-listed countries, many Roma sought employment in France, Sweden, and Finland (National Statistical Institute 2002: 25).

## Muslim Immigrants in Bulgaria

The opposite process—immigration into Bulgaria—is a new phenomenon, as the country has been primarily a transit zone, due to being economically unattractive compared to other European states. Not surprisingly, studies of immigration are fewer than those focused on emigration. Under the communist regime, this field of research was virtually non-existent despite the fact that the number of foreigners coming to communist Bulgaria was not negligible. However, young people from Africa or the Middle East, who came to study in universities or who stayed permanently in Bulgaria through mixed marriages, were not treated as immigrants.

Academic interest over the past twenty years has remained focused primarily on indigenous Muslims. A case in point are the Yearbooks on Muslims in Europe, published by Brill, which pay no attention to Muslim immigrants in Bulgaria, probably due to their small numbers (Maréchal et al. 2003; Nielsen, Akgonul et al. 2009, 2010). A quite comprehensive review of literature on Bulgarian emigration and immigration (Mancheva and Troeva 2011), funded under the EC Seventh Framework Programme, has also confirmed that studies dealing with immigration in Bulgaria are modest in number compared to those dealing with emigration. Nevertheless, the interest in immigration has developed since the late 1990s and relies on both quantitative and qualitative methods of research. Studies on immigration approach topics such as institutional, policy, and legislative frameworks, and critical assessment of the human rights aspect of immigrant reception and treatment.

There were 107,245 immigrants in Bulgaria in 2010, or 1.4% of the entire Bulgarian population (UN Department of Economic and Social Affairs—Population Division 2009). Since immigrants and refugees are not covered by censuses, there are no accurate data on the number or percentage of Muslims among them. Over two-thirds of foreigners living permanently in Bulgaria are from non-EU European countries (Russia, Ukraine, Moldova, Macedonia, and Turkey), while around 15% are from Asia and Middle East.[9]

Statistical data on immigrants, including Muslims, in Bulgaria are inaccurate and based on experts' estimates. Researchers put the number of Muslims among all immigrants in the range of 30,000. According to a study of the Bulgarian Helsinki Committee (BHC 2006), an average immigrant from a Muslim country is well educated: most immigrants (54%) have a high school degree, 37.1% have a university degree (Bachelor or Master), and 2.1% have higher academic achievements. The educational status of the immigrants is higher than that of the local population—largely due to the fact that the majority of immigrants came in order to study at university. Many of those who the Bulgarian public perceives as Arabs (immigrants from the Middle East and Maghreb) are employed in retail trade and restauranteurship. The majority of Arab immigrants inhabit large cities like Sofia, Plovdiv, Burgas, and Varna. They do not form compact communities (do not reside in the same neighbourhood), but live dispersed among the native population.

In contrast, their business activities are usually concentrated on specific streets. As a consequence, certain city areas have started to look like retail-trade immigrant areas. Part of the explanation for this arrangement is the influence of Bulgarian spouses in mixed marriages (a significant part of the Muslim immigrants have Bulgarian spouses).[10] While the Bulgarian wives prefer to live in the urban areas populated mainly

---

[9] See <http://www.nsi.bg/ORPDOCS/Pop_5.8_Migration_DR_EN.xls>.

[10] Marriages between male immigrants from Middle East and Bulgarian females are quite common, especially for the generations born in the 1960s and 1970s. Many Bulgarians born in that period studied with and formed friendships and relationships with students from Middle Eastern (but also Asian and African) countries, who used to come to study in Bulgaria before 1989 in quite considerable numbers. See Nazarska and Hajdinjak 2011.

by Bulgarian citizens and not in the communities of their husbands' fellow countrymen, they do not interfere in the businesses of their husbands, who prefer to locate their shops in specific streets or areas, where most of the businesses are managed by other immigrants from the Middle East (Zhelyazkova, Angelova, and Vladimirov 2007).

Many Muslim immigrants came to Bulgaria before 1989 as students and after graduation remained to live in the country permanently. Many came also in the 1990s, relying on the personal and professional networks of their relatives and friends, who used to be students in Bulgaria. In contrast, the majority of immigrants arriving in Bulgaria since 2001 are classical economic migrants or refugees fleeing from conflicts or political instability in their countries or region (Krasteva 2005). According to the data from the State Agency for Refugees, in the 1993–2012 period, 20,600 refugees have come to Bulgaria. Of this number, 28% came from Afghanistan, 25% from Iraq, and 5% from Iran.[11]

Most of the economic immigrants choose Bulgaria as an initial step, because it is the nearest and easiest European country to access. Considering the fact that Bulgaria is the poorest EU member state and that the State Agency for Refugees and Bulgarian Red Cross have at their disposal a very limited budget, it is not surprising that many immigrants consider the support they receive as insultingly insufficient. This is especially true for those who had higher status and prestigious professions in their countries of origin. That is why most of them take the logical step to continue their journey on to richer European countries, which are also known to be more generous to refugees and individuals with a humanitarian status (Zhelyazkova, Angelova, and Vladimirov 2007).

In recent years, as a result of Bulgarian EU membership and reforms undertaken in order to fulfil the Schengen criteria, it has become much more difficult to enter the country. The Bulgarian News Agency BTA quoted the Minister of the Interior on 15 March 2008 saying that some 10,000 individuals had been stopped in attempts to enter the country illegally in 2007. It is assumed that at least that many had managed to cross the border. During the same year, 317 ships were intercepted for various violations in the Black Sea, some of them for trafficking in human beings. At the time of writing of this chapter (2011–12) new immigration and refugee waves are expected from various Muslim countries experiencing revolutions and civil war (most notably Libya and Syria); however, data on the number of immigrants are not accessible to scholars as they are kept confidential by the Ministry of the Interior.

Compared with the large body of scholarly literature on the indigenous Muslim minorities in Bulgaria, the number of publications on the refugee and immigrant flows is rather small. The first studies on immigration were conducted in the late 1990s and were based on both quantitative and qualitative methods, examining the constitutional, legislative, and political background to access and accommodation of refugees and immigrants in Bulgaria. The studies (Vladinska 1998; Petkova 2002; Radeva 2003; Manfred Woerner Foundation 2003; Guentcheva et al. 2003; Drucke 2004; Jileva and Guiraudon 2006; Krasteva 2006; Hristova 2007) provide a comparative review of the policies towards refugees in some European countries, as well as critical analyses of the

---

[11] See <http://www.aref.government.bg/docs/Top%2010%20english1010.doc>.

level of harmonization with international human rights standards. The studies depict the institutional framework for refugees and immigrants in Bulgaria and the specific social problems they encounter. Understandably, these problems differ from those experienced by immigrants in Western Europe. The system providing asylum for the refugees, as well as the social and economic conditions to which they have to adapt, are unsatisfactory. There is no developed system to ensure refugees' inclusion in the labour market. The financial assistance for the refugees is insufficient to ensure normal existence and this forces them into the labour black market.

Some studies (Bulgarian Helsinki Committee 2006; Ilareva 2007) evaluate the perception and treatment of immigrants in Bulgaria in the context of respect for human rights, and more particularly, the ways in which society accepts them and how institutions treat them. Positive experience from other EU states is given as an example. The general conclusion is that the institutional structure dealing with refugees and immigrants in Bulgaria is inadequate. The necessary healthcare and social and financial support are missing, and there is shortage of lawyers and interpreters to provide legal and language assistance during the procedures for granting temporary or permanent status. Institutions have no practice in informing and educating society about the immigrants present in Bulgaria. Consequently, society has poor knowledge on the number of immigrants, countries of origin, models of immigrants' movement to and from Bulgaria, and of their social and educational status.

A comprehensive review of the refugee situation in Bulgaria can be found in *The Figures of the Refugee* (Krasteva 2006). The book studies different aspects of the refugee situation in the world, and provides analyses of the Palestinian, Afghani, and Iraqi refugee communities in Bulgaria. Different forms of adaptation of these communities to life in Bulgaria are examined, including their struggle with the complicated procedures for obtaining some form of legal status, their attempts to develop their own business or their inclusion in the labour black market. Being the oldest of the three immigrant communities studied here, the Palestinians are well organized and usually have a higher position on the labour market. Afghanis and Iraqis who come to Bulgaria often have a relatively good education and professional qualification, but have difficulties in finding adequate employment. Their social status in Bulgaria is often considerably lower than the one they had enjoyed in their homelands.

Some studies explore the gender features of the immigration waves to Bulgaria. They established that approximately two-thirds of the Muslim immigrants in Bulgaria are male. Most of the women have arrived together with their families. Single female immigrants are very rare.

The gender aspect plays a prominent part in the issue of religiosity of Muslim immigrants. A study of immigrants from the Middle East (Zhelyazkova, Grigorov, and Dimitrova 2005) established that about 8% of the Muslims (mainly from Jordan, Lebanon, and Syria) follow their religion strictly (many of them are followers of fundamentalist movements and schools). These are the same 8% cent of the respondents whose wives do not have a single Bulgarian female friend. Children of the most religious immigrants (4.3%) do not have Bulgarian friends. In the most extreme cases (1.2%

of the Muslim immigrants), children are not allowed to go to Bulgarian schools as the parents are afraid that the children may lose their Muslim virtues under the influence of the secular educational system. Instead, their children study at home. The research established that the number of atheists is similar to the number of those who are deeply religious. The highest share of atheists is among those who settled in Bulgaria during the 1990s—10%. Returning to the gender aspect of religiosity, it comes as no surprise that Muslim immigrants in Bulgaria brought with them highly patriarchal traditions from their home countries. Thus 41.2% of the Arabs believe that the most important thing for a woman is to raise her children, and only 16.2% are of the opinion that women should work on equal footing with men. The desire to preserve their identity and maintain its most important features is prominent. Over half (54.7%) of the Arab children systematically study the traditions, rituals, and history of Islam and their nation. Even more (62%) of the respondents take measures for their children to study their mother tongue. However, only 10% enrol their children in schools with larger groups of Arab/Muslim students (schools at various embassies and the three schools in Sofia where Arab language is taught).

Research teams consisting of sociologists and social anthropologists have examined also the attitudes of Bulgarians towards immigrants and refugees (Pamporov 2009, 2010). Despite the relatively small number of immigrants and refugees, there are some indications of racist attitudes and discrimination. The prejudices against Muslim or black immigrants are similarly strong as prejudices against the local Roma. For instance, only 27.5% of Bulgarians would invite Arabs into their homes, 25% would invite a black African, and 25.2% would invite a Bulgarian citizen of Roma origin. The question about the willingness to live in the same city also produced similar results: only 34.5% of Bulgarians accept the idea of living in the same city/town with Roma, 34.3% with Arabs, and 32.4% with Africans. The picture is similar with regard to the willingness of the Bulgarians to work for a company where managers are of a different ethnicity or race—while 44.5% would accept a boss from Western Europe, only 11.7% would work for an Arab, 10.7% for a Roma person, and 10.6% for a black African. The study also listed the most common social stereotypes and prejudices against Arab immigrants in Bulgaria. While a few are positive or at least neutral (Arabs are rich; Arabs have oil), most are highly negative. Arabs are described as lazy, dirty, and cunning, and as fanatics and terrorists.

Most of the research on immigrants conducted since 2007 has been done by Bulgarian think tanks and different state and private academic institutions under the European Commission's Fifth, Sixth, and Seventh Framework Programmes (Grekova, Kyurkchieva, and Kosseva 2010; Mancheva and Troeva 2011; Nazarska and Hajdinjak 2011). The surveys show that Muslim immigrants face numerous obstacles in Bulgaria. They include poor command of Bulgarian language; legislative shortcomings; difficulties in contacts with the administration (issuing of documents and permits; tax and revenue administration, municipal authorities, police and others); lack of knowledge of Bulgarian legislation; and limited opportunities for contacts with fellow nationals. In addition to the unfavourable social climate described in the previous paragraph, many immigrants believe that the institutional and administrative setting in Bulgaria is becoming increasingly unwelcoming. According to a 2005 survey, 27% of the respondent immigrants are of the opinion that Bulgarian immigration policy is becoming more restrictive and only 14% observe positive changes. According to 39% of the immigrants, the corruption level in Bulgaria is high. The immigrants from the Middle East and Africa complain of the hostile attitude of the media, aggressive behaviour of the police, and lack of access to free medical assistance. Only 34% of the immigrants consider themselves as successfully integrated in the Bulgarian society, 42% as partially integrated, and 24% see themselves as a marginalized community (Ivanov and Atanasov 2005).

## Islam in Public Space

Many Bulgarian studies on Islam in public space, Islamic institutions, and the relations with the state are one-sided, thematically limited, and ignore a significant part of the problems of both Islam and society as a whole. Researchers have focused mainly on the traditions, holidays, and cultural features of Muslims in Bulgaria. All this is viewed through the ethnicity perspective, while the issues of religion and Islam and its manifestations in public spaces are left aside. The scholars provide a detailed account of the everyday life and rituals of the Muslim communities, but it is extremely rare for them to analyse the specific features of Islam, the Muslim community's institutions, its educational needs, internal community problems, and their place in public space.

In short, the literature on the ethnic and religious communities in Bulgaria is thematically disproportionate with uncharted fields in the sphere of Islamic religious theory and practice and with emphasis on the ethno-cultural profile of the ethnic minorities in Bulgaria. As a result we have a vast body of literature dealing with Turks and their identity (Eminov 1997; Simsir 1988; Zhelyazkova 1998a, 1998b, 2001a; Yalamov 2002; Ilieva 2010; IMIR Archive 2010), with Pomaks and their complex multiple identity (Aleksiev 1997; Karagiannis 1997; Georgieva 2001; Gruev 2003; Neuburger 2004; Kyurkchieva 2004; Gruev and Kalyonski 2008; Troeva 2011), and with Roma whose integration is an ongoing difficult social and cultural problem (Tomova 1995, 1998; Pamporov 2006; Tarnev and Grekova 2007; Topalova and Pamporov 2007; Grekova et al. 2008; Tilkidzhiev, Milenkova et al. 2009).

A traditional grassroots system of cohabitation among various religious communities, which became known as the Bulgarian ethnic model in the 1990s, was described in detail in one of the first post-communist studies on Islam in Bulgaria—*Relations of Compatibility and Incompatibility between Christians and Muslims in Bulgaria* (Zhelyazkova, Nielsen, and Kepel 1995). The study was the result of a large-scale interdisciplinary research project financed under PHARE—Democracy.[12] The study established

---

[12] One of the first programmes of the European Community in support of the democratic changes in Poland and Hungary. Later PHARE extended funding to democracy development projects in all

that in the ethnically and religiously mixed regions where Muslims and Christians lived in cohabitation, calm and equilibrium prevailed and no threatening stereotypes existed. The research was based on a national representative survey, content analysis of printed media, and in-depth interviews including anthropological monitoring. A major conclusion was that the centuries-old model of cohabitation of people professing different religions could hardly be destroyed by unreasonable policies and tensions inflamed by political extremists. The mutual understanding between Christian and Muslims living in mixed settlements rested on factors such as respect and participation in the religious holidays of the other denomination, exchanges of gifts of ritual food, and participation in weddings, funerals, and births in the families of the neighbours who are of a different religion. The study has also ascertained that mixed marriages are rare in ethnically and religiously diverse regions and thus the arguments between communities over the religious identity of children born in such marriages are avoided. In most of the cases of marriages between Christians and Muslims, the couples leave their home settlements to live in the anonymity of the large cities.

The most extensive study on Islam in Bulgarian public space is most likely an eight-volume series entitled *The Fate of Muslim Communities in the Balkans* (1997–2001). While some of the volumes look at the wider Balkan region, volumes one, two, four, seven, and to some extent eight contain researches on Muslim communities in Bulgaria (Zhelyazkova, Alexiev, and Nazarska 1997; Gradeva and Ivanova 1998; Lozanova and Mikov 1999; Gradeva 2001; Zhelyazkova and Nielsen 2001). The perspective of these volumes is predominantly historical and includes topics such as: the Ottoman / Muslim written culture, Islamic cult buildings (as mosques, *turbes* and *tekkes*), centres of Islamic mysticism in some Bulgarian towns, Muslim urban and rural organization and architecture (neighbourhoods formed during the Ottoman period, bridges, libraries, clock towers), and epigraphic monuments. In general, the studies highlight different aspects of the presence of Islam in public space and in the Bulgarian national culture.

A study by Myumyun Isov (2005), a young Bulgarian scholar of Turkish background, offers a different perspective on the status of Turks in the Bulgarian history. He analyses how history was taught in the educational system of Bulgaria and how the historical textbooks have created negative stereotypes against the Muslims and Turks. Examining the ethnocentric historical narrative presented in Bulgarian schools, especially in relation to the Ottoman heritage, Isov arrived at the conclusion that the place of Muslims and Islam in the Bulgarian public space is still presented in predominantly negative terms, which reflects unfavourably on the children from the Turkish community.

Systemic studies covering the entire spectrum of knowledge on the presence of Muslims in the Bulgarian lands, their culture, education, and relations with the state and society are very rare. Scholars have worked in a sporadic and piecemeal manner, offering in-depth analyses of only individual aspects of the presence of Islam in Bulgaria.

---

countries of Central and Eastern Europe, following the fall of the Berlin Wall. The results of the research were published in a book of the same title in 1995 by the International Center for Minority Studies and Intercultural Relations (IMIR).

However, no attempt has ever been made to compiled these works in a single, comprehensive study. Random information on topics concerning Muslims in Bulgaria can be found on the site of the Chief Muftiate's office and the yearbooks which the High Islamic Institute (HII) has started to publish in recent years (High Islamic Institute 2009–11).

On the other hand, the *Yearbook of Muslims in Europe* issued by Brill has been, over the past years, a good source of information on the numerical strength of Muslims in every European country, their place in the public space, the status of the muftiates, and the number of mosques and Qur'an schools. Another multi-aspect interpretation of Islam in Europe is a study by Brigitte Maréchal (2003), which covers Bulgaria, too. She analyses the social tenets of Islam, the organization, spiritual leadership, and temple network. Maréchal organizes her findings in the context of comparative analysis with other European countries—mainly Greece and Romania.

Understandably, not all works dealing in such general terms with Islam in Bulgaria can be profoundly analytical. Their emphasis is on registration and description of facts. The value of such publications is that they describe the peculiar problems of Muslims in Bulgaria against the backdrop of the situation elsewhere in Europe. This comparative approach helps draw a comprehensive picture of the presence of Islam in the European space as a whole, presenting resolved and unresolved problems, and outlining specific national features.

## Legal Status of Muslims in Bulgaria

After the Bulgarian liberation in 1878 and the restoration of the Bulgarian state, the first constitution (known as Tarnovo Constitution) granted equal rights and freedoms to all religious and ethnic communities in Bulgaria. They included the right to have their own places of worship, schools, newspapers, and journals. Turkish schools, where the language of instruction was Turkish, were financially supported by the state. On the other hand, from a demographic point of view, after five centuries of Turkish rule, the confessional and ethnic perspective had turned upside down. Muslims had become a minority and were marginalized, while Orthodox Christians (and Bulgarians as an ethnic group) turned into the dominating group. This was reflected also in the constitution, where Muslims were not specifically mentioned. Instead, article 40 referred to those subjects of the Bulgarian Principality who were 'Christians of non-Orthodox denomination or other believers'.

This was the backdrop against which Muslim minorities in Bulgaria sought and found their niche in the social structure and political life. While enjoying significant cultural autonomy in the new Bulgarian state established in 1878, their status as a religious community was regulated only in 1919, with the rules of confessional governance of Muslims in the Kingdom of Bulgaria. This legal act codified the relations between the confession and the state in terms of each party's rights and duties. The Muslim community was headed by a Chief Mufti, elected among the Muftis in Bulgaria. The Chief Mufti served as a liaison with the Shaykh al-Islam in Istanbul on religious and civil matters (Zhelyazkova 2011).

Despite the principles enshrined in the Tarnovo Constitution, Bulgarians to this day find it difficult to accept Muslim minorities, especially the Turkish one, as an inseparable part of the nation. Muslims feel insecure and marginalized even though they have proved to be exceptionally loyal citizens who share the national objectives, have participated in all wars, and have done their share of duty and sacrifice for their country (Tahirov 1981; Yalamov 2002). The current Bulgarian constitution (1991)[13] has contributed to the Muslim feeling of insecurity. The frequently criticized article 13(3) states that 'Eastern Orthodox Christianity shall be considered the traditional religion in the Republic of Bulgaria'. Placing Orthodox Christianity above the other religions practised in the country automatically relegates all other religions to a disadvantaged position. In addition to a strong symbolic message that Muslim and other non-Orthodox Bulgarian citizens are of somewhat lesser status, this formulation has also practical consequences. These have been clearly outlined in the Denominations Act. The Denominations Act develops the constitutional provisions and states that the Bulgarian Orthodox Christian Church has a historic role for the Bulgarian state and actual significance for the state's life. The church is ex lege recognized as a legal person and has the right to govern itself in accordance with its own internal rules. In contrast, all other denominations in Bulgaria have to apply for registration at the Sofia City Court in order to acquire legal personality.[14]

The organizational structure of the Muslim confession in Bulgaria consists of several units, each with a specific place and functions (Figure 13.1). The highest authority is the National Conference, which has its Chairman and members.

Muslims in Bulgaria are organized in a Muslim Denomination in compliance with the Bulgarian Denominations Act. Their leader is the Chief Mufti, who heads the institution of the Chief Muftiate. The Chief Muftiate and the Muslim Denomination itself are officially registered by the Sofia City Court as a religious community under the Denominations Act. The Chief Muftiate represents all Muslims in Bulgaria, regardless of their ethnic origin and the Islamic movement they belong to. Thus, it is in charge not only of the Sunni from the Hanafi school, but also for the *Alevi / Kızılbashi / Bektashi*, who have representatives in the Senior Muslim Council (SMC).

The leaders of the heterodox Muslims (*Alevi / Kızılbashi / Bektashi*), called Baba,[15] are considered imams by the Chief Muftiate and receive salaries as the Sunni imams do. Any religious specificity or differences among Muslims remain indiscernible for the general public and politicians, who regard all of them simply as Muslims. This mistaken perception carries legal and financial consequences for the heterodox Muslim community, as their *waqfs* are merged with the Sunni ones, and the community is dependent on the governance of the Sunni majority (Merdjanova 2009, 2010).

---

[13] For the text of all Bulgarian constitutions, see <http://www.parliament.bg/en/const>.

[14] For the Denominations Act 2002 in English, see <http://cupandcross.com/bulgarian-law-on-religions-law-on-the-religious-confessions>.

[15] Baba—from Turkish language. Literally means 'father', an outdated form to respectfully address a sheikh, which is used in Bulgaria.

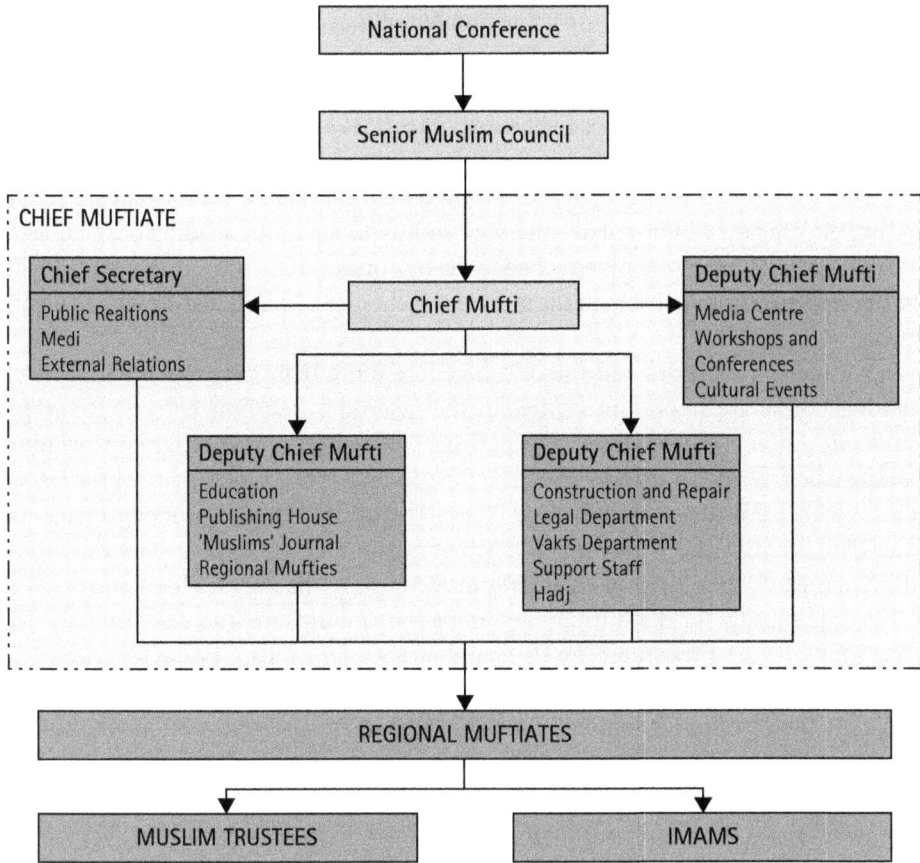

FIGURE 13.1 Organizational structure of the Muslim confession in Bulgaria

*Note*: The chart has been kindly provided by the Chief Muftiate in the Bulgarian language and translated by the author.

The Senior Muslim Council (SMC) is the highest administrative authority of the Muslim Denomination, empowered to convene Muslim Conferences for the election of the new Chief Mufti, his deputies, and a new Chairman of the SMC. In 2010, the Chief Muftiate supported eighteen regional muftiates in towns having larger Muslim communities. The number of the muftiates can vary according to the necessities of the confession (when the Muslim population in a given region decreases as a result of migration flows, the respective muftiate is closed and vice versa) and the decisions of the Chief Muftiate.

The number of imams is approximately 1,000: 285 young (below 40 years of age) and 635 elderly ones. This generational ratio is important since it is related to the education of the imams and the way they teach. A proportion of the young imams have been educated abroad and preach under dogmas closer to the Qur'an requirements, while the older ones have lower education received in Bulgaria and observe the local Muslim traditions. The number of imams is insufficient to cover all mosques and masjids (respectively 1,156 and 302 in 2010). The number of mosques built after 1989 is 165, and of the masjids—sixty-nine. Another fifty-two mosques and four masjids are under construction or unfinished due to shortage of funds.

There are 1,225 registered mosque boards of trustees according to 2011 data. Some of them run Qur'an classes, controlled by the Chief Muftiate, which also organizes summer Qur'an classes, as well as exams for children for the level they have reached in memorizing the Qur'an. Children have the opportunity to study the reading of the Qur'an and religion in Sunday schools attached to the mosques and they are also provided with the opportunity to study Islam in the municipal schools as an optional class up to eighth grade.

In addition to mosques and masjids, there are more than fofty *tekkes* and *turbes*.[16] Although these are important centres of the heterodox Muslims (*Alevi / Bektashi / Kızılbashi)*, some of them attract also persons belonging to other religions (including Christian believers). *Tekkes* have not been functioning as real sanctuaries for the last 60 years as there are no dervishes anymore. Most have turned into places for pilgrimage and rituals for *Bektashi* and *Kızılbashi*. The actual functioning ritual places are the *turbes*, which may exist separately, but are usually located within the *tekkes* (Mikov 2007).

The state subsidy for the Muslim denomination amounts to €100,000 annually. The Chief Muftiate uses these funds for the maintenance of the mosques and for remunerations of imams and regional Muftis. Other sources of funding include the real estate owned by the Muslim Denomination. Restitution of the property nationalized under the communist rule remains a huge problem. Due to slow and cumbersome procedures, in some parts of the country only 30% of the property has been returned. As the state subsidy and the revenues from the properties are insufficient, additional funds for imams' remuneration and mosque repair works are provided by donations from the congregation or from abroad.

## Religious Education

There are three secondary Islamic schools in Bulgaria and a *hafiz*[17] school financed by the Chief Muftiate. The schools are subject to inspections by the Ministry of Education's Regional Inspectorates to ensure that the education offered there meets the state education requirements. The schools teach Islam, Arabic, Turkish, and English languages in addition to all mandatory classes envisaged for the nationwide educational system. The textbooks are prepared by the Chief Muftiate and approved by the Ministry of Education. Most of them come from Turkey and are adapted to Bulgarian conditions. This is because there are no textbooks on Islam theology prepared by Bulgarian experts.

---

[16] *Tekke*—a dervish sanctuary. *Turbe*—a tomb of a Muslim saint. Both are worshipped and visited by the heterodox Muslims in Bulgaria—*Aliani / Kızılbashi / Bektashi*.

[17] *Hafiz, hafuz* (Arabic)—a person who memorizes the text of the Qur'an.

The 2010 *Yearbook of Muslims in Europe* contains an excellent article by Ahmet Alibashic—a comparative study of Muslim university education in the Balkans, which covers Bulgaria as well. A comprehensive historical and contemporary review of the traditions and present status of Muslim religious education in Bulgaria by Evstatiev and Makariev (2010) gives a detailed analysis of the complex heritage of the Muslim religious education in Bulgaria. Another comparative study on Islamic education in the Balkans is an Oxford University Press publication by Kerem Öktem (2010), tracing the sources of funding of scholarship programmes—namely, the Turkish Diyanet (Presidency of Religious Affairs to the Prime Minister of Turkey), as well as the informal influence of the Fethullah Gülen.

All these studies present a comprehensive picture of Muslim religious education in Bulgaria, from the mosque classes on reading the Qur'an, through the Muslim secondary schools to the highest level—the High Islamic Institute (HII).[18] The findings of the studies are that Bulgaria has a poorly developed system of religious education. The poor quality of the education makes it difficult to attract pupils for Muslim high schools (8–12 grades). The HII does not have academic accreditation either. Such a situation naturally creates interest in receiving scholarships and education abroad. Yet, the studies have established that scholarships programmes and support for schools provided by Turkey and various Islamic foundations from abroad are significantly lower than the opportunities granted by the municipal and state schools in Bulgaria.

The articles demonstrate that the Bulgarian state has a controlling power over Islamic religious education through the Ministry of Education and Science and its local inspectorates. The Ministry and its inspectorates have the authority to limit the external influences on the Muslim education in Bulgaria.

The High Islamic Institute is officially under the auspices of the Ministry of Education and Science. It does not have appropriate facilities and is forced to rely on official small-scale funding and on donations and financial support from Turkey and other Muslim countries. This, in turn, gives these donors ground to have a say on the preparation of the curriculum and selection of lecturers.

In 2012, the HII remains without academic accreditation, which means that the diplomas are not recognized in Bulgaria and the students cannot continue their education under Masters or other programmes in Bulgarian and European universities. Thus, many young Muslims, supported by the Chief Muftiate, leave Bulgaria to study in Islamic universities in Saudi Arabia, Turkey, Egypt, Syria, and Jordan.

There are no official data about the number of Bulgarian citizens who have obtained higher Islamic education abroad (Saudi Arabia, Jordan, Yemen, or Turkey, while among the older generations also in Soviet Republics—mainly Azerbaijan). Deputy Chief Mufti Birali Birali quoted a number of 300 persons with higher Islamic education in a

---

[18] The High Islamic Institute (HII) is a university preparing Islamic clerics and scholars. It was established in 1998 as a successor of the Clerical Islamic Institute. HII does not have official accreditation by the Bulgarian authorities.

September 2012 interview, but this number includes also the graduates of the Higher Islamic Institute in Sofia and not just those educated abroad (Lefedzhiev 2012). When young Muslims who have studied abroad return to Bulgaria as imams, they import into their communities Salafi influences and often preach that the traditional local rituals should be abandoned as they deviate from the sources of Islam.

On several occasions, young Pomaks who have finished their studies in Arab countries and returned home opposed the local imams from older generations. A study on relations between 'traditional' and 'new' Islam in Bulgaria (Troeva 2012), based on in-depth interviews with Pomaks, revealed the existence of substantial intergenerational tensions in the community. These tensions are mostly a result of the attempts of the young imams to do away with the traditional religious rituals and return to the 'correct' (as understood and practised in the Arab states) Islam.

Populist parties in Bulgaria reject any proposal for accommodating the HII in more adequate premises, or for the establishment's integration as a department of an existing university in order to ensure its normal functioning (Stoyanov 2011). At the same time, these same parties periodically create tensions, pointing explicitly to the fact that many imams study in Arab countries, thus making their education dependent on support from Turkey.

A futile debate takes place intermittently about the idea for the Muslims in Sofia to build an Islamic compound on land they own. The compound is envisaged to include a mosque, a library with a conference rooms, premises for the HII, and a dormitory (Nielsen, Akgonul et al. 2009). Local authorities and politicians fear this might provoke public unrest instigated by nationalist parties and movements.

Currently (as of 2012) the overall educational legislation is subject to a public debate on the issue of whether religion (Eastern Orthodox, Muslim, Catholic, Protestant, etc.) should be taught in Bulgaria as part of the school curriculum. It is not yet clear whether schoolchildren will have the opportunity to study their respective religions as theological systems. An alternative option is to introduce the subject Comparative History of Religion, to allow all pupils equal access to knowledge of various religions.

## Religious Practices

Unlike the political and social aspects of minorities' status, where most of the surveys were made during the post-communist period, the holiday and ritual systems of Muslim and other minorities in Bulgaria have been studied since the end of the nineteenth century.

There is ample bibliography of works on ethnic Turks written and published during the first half of the twentieth century (Bobchev 1929; Marinov 1941, 1956). A study with a strong emphasis on the religious aspect is that of G. Galabov (1924), who analyses the Muslim law with a special emphasis on the history and dogmas of Islam.

The studies written during the socialist period (1945–89) followed the rules of atheist propaganda and presented Muslim traditions and rituals in a negative way, accentuating the destructive role of Islam and singing praise to socialist ideas. The authors write that they have observed a decline of the religious consciousness among the Bulgarian Turks and the rise of a new secular (socialist) one (Mizov 1958, 1965; Dzambazov 1964; Aliev 1978, 1980).

There has been a boom of theological literature on Muslim religious practices since 1989: collections of sermons, interpretations of hadiths, leaflets with instructions on the appearance of the Muslim women, textbooks introducing the basics of Islam (usually translated and adapted from Turkish editions). The entire body of this type of literature is published, certified, and distributed among the Bulgarian Muslims by the Chief Muftiate and is not popular among the general public outside the Muslim community (Topbash 2005: Cheker 2009[19]).

Among the studies that deserve special attention are those examining different aspects of the religious attitudes of Pomaks (Muslim Bulgarians): the identity–religion relation (Krasteva-Blagoeva and Blagoev 2003; Kyurkchieva 2004; Troeva 2011), tales of Genesis (Lozanova 2008), and pilgrimage (Valchinova 1999, 2008). The researchers analyse the changes in the traditional ways of professing Islam (Georgieva 1999; Gruev 2003; Kyurkchieva 2004; Troeva 2011), in traditional clothes (Georgieva 1994; Kyurkchieva 2004; Ghodsee 2007, 2009), and in the construction of mosques as a new differentiating mark in a predominantly Christian environment (Georgieva 1994). The findings of these researches confirm that the Bulgarian speaking Muslims are strongly attached to their specific Muslim practices, and that they are a stable and relatively capsulated community that is very resistant to changes induced by external factors. They are the most devout Muslim believers in Bulgaria.

A small number of studies deal with the subject of the religious identity of Turks and Pomaks. These studies also indicate the probability of a current or future radicalization of this largely secular population (Zhelyazkova 1998a; Ragaru 2001; Maeva 2006).

Attempts to spread Wahhabism in Bulgaria have proved relatively futile for three reasons:

1. Turkish Muslims have secular attitudes; they are closer to influences from the West and Turkey and are not interested in the religious novelties offered by the Wahhabi representatives from the Arab countries.
2. Pomaks, who are the authentic and traditional carriers of Islam in Bulgaria, accept the missionaries with the appropriate hospitality, but assess their ideas as alien to the Pomak traditions and send them away.
3. The Movement for Rights and Freedoms, the political party influencing almost all Turks, a large part of the Pomaks, and part of the Roma, is secular and does not spread religious influences among its supporters, due to purely partisan interests, in order not to create a competitor amidst the Muslim community.

A very limited number of studies on the religious practices of immigrants and refugees have appeared in recent years. These studies (Manfred Woerner Foundation 2003;

---

[19] See also the list of books on the website of Chief Mufti office <http://genmuftibg.net/en/library/books.html>.

Krasteva 2005, 2006; Hajdinjak 2011) have found low levels of religiousness among immigrants.[20] Attending the mosques is not among their priorities either. To a certain extent, this is a result of the significant number of mixed marriages in Bulgaria (Zhelyazkova, Grigorov, and Dimitrova 2005; Nazarska and Hajdinjak 2011) and the influence of local extended families. After marriage, Muslim immigrants often live together or under the influence of their Bulgarian relatives, who accept them as new members of the family (sons-in-law). To these, one may add the influence of the old immigrants with left-wing political orientation and atheist attitudes, and also the willingness of the new immigrants to adapt to the spiritual environment in the host country.

As mentioned above, only between 2% and 8% of the Muslim immigrant community adhere strictly to religion and traditional rituals. They include followers of some Islamic movements and schools such as Salafi and Wahhabi (Krasteva 2005; Zhelyazkova, Angelova, and Vladimirov 2007). The attachment to Salafism or Wahhabism is assessed in these surveys based on observations and in-depth interviews. The followers of these movements usually do not allow their women to have contacts outside their homes, and teach their children at home to ensure that they do not break the strict religious rules.

There are no surveys dealing specifically with the Wahhabi influence among the Muslims in Bulgaria, save for the studies of ethnologists and anthropologists on the attempts of some young imams, who have graduated in Medina, to introduce more strict religious rules among the Muslims in Bulgaria.

## Gender and Religion

Some scholars focus on gender relations in the life of the Bulgarian Muslims (Neuburger 2004; Ghodsee 2007). Especially interesting are the policies of the Bulgarian communist regime for integrating and assimilating Pomaks by influencing Muslim women, including through prohibition of their traditional dress and their inclusion into the state education system. Ghodsee explores how gender relations among Pomaks had to be renegotiated after the collapse of communism and after the economic changes that led to the closure of the state-subsidized lead and zinc mines, which were an important source of livelihood for the male Muslim population. She shows how mosques have replaced the mines as the primary site for now jobless and underemployed men to express their masculinity, and how Muslim women have encouraged this as a way to combat alcoholism and domestic violence.

The survey *Migrations, Gender and Intercultural Interactions in Bulgaria* completed in 2010 under the Seventh Framework Programme of the European Commission revealed

---

[20] Scholars define the levels of religiousness mainly through qualitative methods: observation and in-depth interviews, relying mainly on self-evaluation by the respondents, as well as on the frequency of visits to the mosques, as declared by the respondents, participation or non-participation in the prayers, the observation or lack of such of the Ramadan fasting, the observation of prohibitions on certain foods and drinks, the way the women dress, and the viewpoints of the respondents on children's education.

the interesting fact that many immigrant Muslim women living in Sofia rarely visit the sole mosque in the city. The reason is that they find it to be extremely inconvenient: small and male-dominated, to the point that even the female section is used by men due to insufficient space. For these reasons, many of them prefer to attend Christian churches located near their homes, where they like to light candles. Christian churches also provide them with a feeling of security and anonymity (Troeva and Mancheva 2011).

An earlier study (Zhelyazkova, Grigorov, and Dimitrova 2005) on Muslim immigrants from the Middle East and Central Asia has revealed that some immigrants from Muslim countries had left their homeland not only for economic or political reasons, but also to escape the religious conservatism of their families and communities. Many of those who come from the Middle East, Central Asia, the Maghreb, and Africa say they feel more comfortable in Bulgaria than in their respective countries of origin. Male immigrants are free to communicate with women and do not have to observe rigid rules. The same is true for women—some of them feel more freedom, they have the opportunity to study or work, to have female friends and to have achievements outside home and family.

## Participation in Political Life

The minorities in Bulgaria rarely support the Socialist Party, since it is a successor of the former Communist Party, which carried out the assimilation policy against them. Regardless of the fact that their social status should direct them to the left, they overwhelmingly support the Movement for Rights and Freedoms (MRF), which is situated in the centre or the centre-right part of the political spectrum.

Scholars in Europe and the USA have displayed an increasing interest in the political representation of Muslims in Bulgaria. Bernd Rechel (2005) deserves attention for analysis of the rights of minorities in post-communist Bulgaria. It is a detailed study of the Muslim minorities, in which Turks are described as 'a success story', Pomaks as 'a minority at the margins', and Roma as 'the country's pariahs'.

A number of historical studies by Bulgarian scholars examine not only the dynamics of religious and ethnic identity of Turks and Pomaks, but also their political activities (Eminov 1997; Stoyanov 1998; Zhelyazkova 1998b, 2010; Ivanova 2002; Eldarov 2004; Daskalov 2005; Yalamov 2005; Gruev and Kalyonski 2008; A. Todorov 2010).

There are very few studies devoted to the political participation and orientations of the Bulgarian Turks and Muslims prior to 1944. The Constituent Assembly (parliament) convened after Bulgaria's liberation included sixteen representatives of the minorities: twelve Turks, two Greeks, one Jew and one Bulgarian Protestant or 6.9% of all members (Nazarska 1999b). With the exception of these first years, there were no Jewish and Greek MPs in the period until 1944. The political parties found it more prudent to seek support among the more compact Turkish and Pomak communities, which did not raise any specific demands in exchange for their support.

During the same period, the Roma were as a rule excluded from political processes. All other ethnic and religious groups (Jews, Armenians, Greeks, Wallachians, Russians, and others) had become integrated into the country's social and political life—a situation which continued through the communist and the post-communist periods (A. Todorov 2010).

Some studies are devoted to the political system, political parties, and Bulgarian society (including minorities) and its political practices during the six decades between the liberation (1878) and the onset of the Soviet influence (1944). Issues such as elections, electoral attitudes, government crises, or how Muslims were used, or rather, abused for the purpose of manipulating public opinion and drawing political dividends, have been thoroughly explored (Nikolova 2004; Daskalov 2005).

The establishment of communist rule in Bulgaria in 1944 led to intensive political changes, which were crowned by the creation of a Soviet-type regime similar to those in other countries in Central and Eastern Europe. This situation changed the nature of the political institutions and of the very election process. Paradoxically, the constitution of 1947 gave, for the first time, the right to vote to all citizens above the age of 18. These were in essence democratic provisions, but their introduction coincided with stripping elections of any content (A. Todorov 2010). Within the new political system, the Muslim community suffered spiritual and political stagnation on an equal footing with all other ethnic and religious groups. The repressive apparatus of the state security services and the political system controlled everyone, regardless of their ethnic and religious identity.

Research on the place of Muslims in the Bulgarian political system expanded intensively after the end of the communist regime. Separation of political ideology from science made possible a new approach to and understanding of past events—political and social. For the first time scholars had the opportunity to unveil the secrets of the political government in Bulgaria over the 1944–89 period. The research was further boosted by the opening of a significant part of the secret archives in recent years.

The MRF, the first political party representing Turks and other Muslim communities in Bulgaria, was founded in 1990. Since its establishment, the MRF has always been represented in parliament, in local government, and participated in three government coalitions. The MRF, which defines itself as a liberal party adhering to universal human rights values, believes that the state has to implement an active policy for the integration of minorities into all spheres of society. Although the party often raises issues that concern the Bulgarian Muslims, especially in election periods, and regularly looks for and receives the support of Muslim religious leaders, the MRF is clearly a secular party (Hajdinjak 2008; MRF n.d., 2006).

The support for the MRF among Turks has been steadily increasing from 44% in 1994 to 72% in 2005. In the local elections, the MRF has been constantly winning in more than thirty out of 264 Bulgarian municipalities (for election results see the Central Election Commission's website). This success is not surprising, given the fact that in the MRF, for the first time in Bulgarian history, Turks and Muslims have a party they can consider their own and through which they are represented on central and local level of government. This gives them a sense of security and a degree of pride. Although in recent years, political scientists and sociologies have detected a growing dissatisfaction in the Muslim community over the MRF (the main reasons are the corruption of the MRF elite and the authoritarian style in which the party is managed), when elections are due, Turks and Muslims vote for their 'own people'.

The considerable political power of the MRF and its related influence in economic life (in countries in transition like Bulgaria, the economy is closely linked with politics and often depends on clientelistic and nepotistic networks controlled by the political parties) has been the bone of contention in a heated political debate. Nationalist and populist parties claim that the MRF is unconstitutional in terms of article 11(4) of the Bulgarian constitution, which states: 'There shall be no political parties on ethnic, racial or religious lines, nor parties which seek the violent seizure of state power'. While being an entirely legitimate political organization, the MRF also expanded its influence among other religious and ethnic groups, thus turning into a real nationwide party.

# ISLAMOPHOBIA AS A RESULT OF THE 9/11 EVENTS

## Radicalization or Islamophobia?

Virtually no studies have been conducted on the issue of (real or hypothetical) Muslim radicalization in Bulgaria. Likewise, the existence of Islamophobia has yet to attract the attention of scholars. In contrast, both issues have been widely covered by the media, which often give the floor to various experts in Islam, the Middle East, and the Maghreb to provide analysis and discussion.

Fears and suspicions regarding the appearance and spread of radical Islam in Bulgaria are usually associated with the traditional Muslim communities in Bulgaria and not with immigrants. This fact confirms the marginal place of immigrants in public perception.

Radicalization and Islamophobia are interrelated because after 9/11 (and the later terrorist acts in Great Britain and Spain), there was a growing fear of possible radicalization of the Muslim population in Bulgaria under the influence of external factors. Nationalist parties and media found propitious soil to activate their followers using the language of hatred. As a result, media publications and broadcasts on the radicalization of Muslims have been, in their majority, manipulative, xenophobic, and Islamophobic. Radicalization is explained by these media, usually without arguments and in an Islamophobic vein, as being related to external influences and funding.

The media space is clearly divided, as is the Bulgarian society. On the one hand are the nationalists and Islamophobes (political parties like *Attack* and *Order, Law, Justice*, TV channels such as SKAT and Alpha, and newspapers such as *Nova Zora* (New Dawn) and *Ataka*), while on the other, are liberal-minded intellectuals, such as *Kultura* (Culture) newspaper, and journals *Tema* (Theme), *Sociologicheski Pregled* (Sociological Review), and *Liberalen Pregled* (Liberal Review).

Islamophobic media publications are usually structured upon unproven allegations that indigenous Muslims in Bulgaria are being increasingly radicalized, and that with the assistance of Arab foundations, they create 'sleeping terrorist cells', which can be activated on the spur of the moment. In support of such allegations, the authors point to the presence of 'Islam' as a free optional subject in school curricula. Teachers and mayors in Pomak towns and villages are accused of being Islamic fundamentalists, mosque reconstruction is passed off as a sign of radicalization, while neither those who write or speak, nor those who read or listen really comprehend the meaning of these words. Political lingo, media publications, and TV broadcasts of that sort have resulted in several police actions—arrests, searches in the houses of Muftis, and confiscation of computers, books, and phones.

The opposite side is represented by liberal intellectuals (Tz. Todorov 2010), scholars, and human rights organizations. They plead for common sense and normality in relation to Muslims, explaining that the use of force and hostile media attacks create the risk of disrupting the centuries-old equilibrium between Christians and Muslims in Bulgaria.

Tensions reached a climax in May 2011. In a drive to increase its popularity, the nationalist party *Ataka* (Attack) organized a rally in front of the Sofia Mosque, initiating clashes between its followers and the Muslim congregation. The Bulgarian society demonstrated exceptional maturity on the occasion and unanimously condemned this blatant act of racism and xenophobia. The parliament also reproached *Ataka*, while the Prosecutor's Office started a criminal investigation. Support for *Ataka* in opinion polls dropped drastically from 8% to under 4% and the local and presidential elections, which followed soon after these events, proved to be a failure for this party (Minchev 2011; Koleva and Krachunov 2011).

Growing suspicions towards Muslims have been influenced also by the recent publications by Oriana Fallaci[21] and Thilo Sarazzin,[22] on the one hand, and of Wolfgang Palaver[23] on the other, on the issues of the reformulations of the 'politically correct' approach to intolerance and xenophobia, and the ideas of 'the end of multiculturalism' and Islamophobia (Fallaci 2004, 2006; Sarazzin 2010; Assheuer 2010).

Although these new ideas, philosophical trends, and political concepts have reached Bulgaria with some delay, they are today accepted by part of the society. This is especially

---

[21] Oriana Fallaci (1930–2006)—one of the most famous Italian journalists who shocked the world with her fierce criticism of Islam after the terrorist attacks of 9/11.

[22] Thilo Sarazzin (1945) is a German politician (SPD) and a former member of the Executive Board of the Deutsche Bundesbank (until 30 September 2010). In his 2010 book *Deutschland schafft sich ab* ('Germany is Abolishing Itself'), the most popular book on politics by a German-language author in a decade, he denounces the failure of Germany's post-war immigration policy, sparking a nationwide controversy about the costs and benefits of the ideology of multiculturalism.

[23] Wolfgang Palaver—Univ.-Prof. Dr., Chair of the Institute of Systematic Theology, Innsbruck.

true for the nationalist and xenophobic parties, as well as for populist movements within traditionally democratic parties, and the people supporting them. There is, of course, an alternative—the liberal and multicultural point of view promoted by human rights activists and intellectuals, and by some media such as the *Kultura* newspaper. The academic and intellectual circles continue to approve of and support multiculturalism, tolerance, and the rights of the religious communities—the concepts and ideas born by the changes after 1989.

The new global trends of anti-Muslim sentiments have in the Bulgarian case reinforced old stereotypes of repudiating the heritage of the Ottoman Empire. The forced Islamization of Bulgarians and the destruction of the Bulgarian Christian culture are themes that are being constantly recalled. The radical political party *Ataka* is fond of slogans such as 'genocide of the Bulgarians under the Ottoman rule'. Using such rhetoric, the radical parties attract new followers. They come from the ranks of Bulgarians disillusioned for various reasons, the poor elderly people and high school students. As a result, in the 2005 and 2009 parliamentary elections *Ataka* received respectively 8.1% and 9.4% of the votes, thus passing the 4% threshold with a comfortable margin. However, support for the partly dropped sharply to 2% in early 2012 as a result of the extremist attack of its members on the Sofia Mosque and internal disagreements in the party.

*Ataka* and similar parties, as well as the media with nationalistic orientation, are usually responsible for producing and spreading theories that the radical Islamic propaganda is infiltrating Bulgarian Muslim communities. These accounts are as a rule poorly substantiated and produced by incompetent authors, unable to distinguish and understand terms as 'Salafism', 'Wahhabism', 'Radicalism', and 'Jihadism'. Such attitudes insult the local Muslims and they start to isolate themselves from the macro society as a result. The media are rarely interested in their point of view and they are therefore unable to defend themselves.

In recent years, these political and media discourses motivated the security service, which on a few occasions acted with investigations and arrests of Muslim clerics and Islamic religion teachers. For example, in March 2009 the mayor and the Muslim religious teacher in the village of Ribnovo, in the Rhodope Mountains, were arrested by the police on unfounded accusations of spreading radical Islam. The case turned out to be completely unsubstantiated and was clearly motivated by unjustified Islamophobia (Valkov 2009).

The fear of Jihadist influence is unfounded. The scientific surveys on this issue, albeit few in number, have detected no Jihadist moods among the Muslim minority in Bulgaria (Ivanova 2012; Troeva 2012).

Instead of being thoroughly researched, the new processes of emancipation and search for identity among Muslims in Bulgaria have been used for political purposes or to justify false accusations of fundamentalism and radicalism (Focus Agency 2009; Tsacheva 2011). Such superficial and sometimes openly Islamophobic approaches are typical for short articles and interviews in some electronic media and in politically biased newspapers like *Ataka*. Countering them are several notable works of Vladimir Chukov (2004), Tzvetan Teofanov (2004), and Simeon Evstatiev (2012). These experts in Islamic philosophy and culture, the Qur'an, and contemporary global trends take a stand against Islamophobia and denounce publications that equate Islam with some of its fundamentalist and radical movements more related to political extremism.

The most recent and very accurate study of the sentiments of Bulgarian Muslims (Turks and Pomaks) was carried out in 2011 by scholars from the New Bulgarian University and Alpha Research polling agency, who used quantitative methods and in-depth interviews. The findings show that political Islam is non-existent in Bulgaria and that the levels of religiousness among the Muslims are relatively low. This study (Ivanova 2012) reaffirms the results of preceding researches on the Muslim minority in Bulgaria, namely, that there is no visible radicalization of Muslims, although the local traditions and rituals tend to be replaced by doctrinal ones mastered by the new generation of imams who are university graduates (Dermendzhieva 2011).

Claims and theories about the presence of radical Islamic movements among the Bulgarian Muslims are usually presented by former or current security experts teaching in universities or research institutes, as for instance Velko Atanasoff (2009). The *Ataka* newspaper has carried dozens of articles portending the danger of Islamization, of Muslim/Turkish separatism, of attempts by Turkey to conquer Bulgaria through its neo-Ottoman doctrine. Current events are being exploited by relating them to the past and promoting the idea of putting Turkey to trial for having perpetrated genocide of the Bulgarian population during Ottoman rule (*Ataka* 2011).

The Chief Muftiate, as well as the regional muftiates, exercises strict control to prevent external influences and disruption of the Muslim community's local traditions. The Chief Mufti declared that imams returning after education in Saudi Arabia, Jordan, or Syria should work under the authority of the official Muslim Denomination in Bulgaria and the manner of their preaching is controlled on a monthly basis. The official magazine of the Chief Muftiate (*Muslumanlar*) publishes recommended Friday sermons. Thus the topics are not only provided to imams, but they also have the obligation to write monthly reports on what and where they have preached. The Chief Mufti believes that there is no danger of changes in the traditional understanding of Islam among the congregation (Moskov 2012).

## New Developments in External Influences among Bulgarian Muslims

The new trends among the Muslims in Bulgaria, including the external influences, are not understood in essence by society and the media. Terms as 'Salafism', 'Wahhabism', and 'Jihadism' are considered as something monolithic, which is coming from outside and represents a danger for the country. As a result, most publications do not attempt to provide explanation of the differences among the various Muslim movements, and describe them solely as radicalization.

Researcher Kerem Öktem thinks that the public debates on 'Islamic extremism in the Balkans' and the search for an 'Islamic diagonal' or 'Green axis' are unfounded. The author believes that Salafism, Wahhabism, takfiri Islamism, 'all used rather loosely as synonyms for allegedly growing Islamic radicalism, represent a predominantly marginal phenomenon, which is now waning'. Öktem's findings, based on field research carried out in 2010, conclude that the Salafi influence with regard to clothes, polygamy, and belief is limited to isolated cases in villages in Bosnia, Macedonia, Albania, and some Roma neighbourhoods in Bulgaria (Öktem 2010). To a certain extent, the author underestimates these influences, especially with regard to the evident Salafi and Wahhabi educational activity and funding, which brought the wearing of hijab and polygamy to the Sanjak region of Serbia (Zhelyazkova 2008).

On the other hand, Bulgarian experts and social anthropologists have confirmed, based on fieldwork, that the Salafi influence is hardly noticeable among Bulgarian Muslims (author's personal archive—fieldwork conducted between 2005 and 2010; Kyurkchieva et al. 2008). Imams who have graduated from the Al-Azhar University in Cairo, the Islamic University in Medina, or other Arab universities, return to Bulgaria with the intention to purify local Islam through strict adherence to Salafi teaching.[24] They, however, meet with stubborn reluctance on the part of their families and fellow citizens to accept changes in their traditional rituals. Usually, the imams educated abroad eventually embrace the local tradition (author's personal archive—fieldwork conducted between 2005 and 2010).

External Muslim impact in the Balkans and in Bulgaria, in as much as it exists, is influenced by a peculiar background—the conflict of interests between the Saudi Arabian (and other Persian Gulf states') influence on the one hand and Turkey's geopolitical ambitions on the other. This competition can be observed in temple architecture, education, and clothes (for instance the appearance of hijab first in Bosnia, then in Sanjak, Albania, Kosovo, Macedonia, and in isolated cases in Bulgaria) (Zhelyazkova 2004, 2008).

According to Öktem, the preachers and missionaries from the Arab Peninsula are often 'imbued with a purist and authoritarian spirit of Salafism'. This is an ideological disadvantage, which curtails their impact on the Balkan Muslims, despite the generous supply of charity and development aid. They 'approach the Muslims of the Balkans as godless people who have forgotten true Islam'. 'Ignorant of local conventions, religious syncretism and inter-faith traditions that flowered in the centuries of the Ottoman rule, unsympathetic to both the dominant Sunni school of Hanafism and the *Bektashi* and

---

[24] Twenty-five people obtained their religious education in Medina before 2009. Five more graduated (or were about to do so) in the 2009–13 period. In the same period, five more young Muslims from Bulgaria started their education in Medina. Less than half of the graduates of the Islamic University in Medina work as imams or Muftis after returning to Bulgaria (others work in professions unrelated to religion). The sources of this information are interviews of the author with respondents from the Chief Mufti Office in Sofia.

In autumn 2012, eight of the Medinah graduates were charged with preaching 'religious hatred and non-democratic ideology' and a trial against them started in the District Court in Pazardzhik. Five more people were defendants in the same trial—one had finished the Higher Islamic Institute in Sofia, while four had no theological education.

*Alevi* traditions, Arab missionaries' messages are perceived as too arrogant and too removed from the region's Muslim identities to make real inroads into the society at large' (Öktem 2010; see also Clayer and Bougarel 2001).

Öktem is correct in asserting that the Muslim communities in the Balkans are mostly under the control of the Muftis, mosques' boards of trustees, and imams, while their political elites support the local traditional practices. These practices do not create tensions and suspicions, and are perceived as 'European Islam', 'traditional Islam', or simply 'our Islam'. Öktem believes that these factors will prevent the introduction of hardline Salafism in the Balkans in the future (2010).

The new Turkish geopolitical agenda is usually referred to as the neo-Ottoman doctrine.[25] Serbian expert in Ottoman studies and diplomat Darko Tanaskovic (2010) believes that since the 1950s, an Islamic intellectual, administrative, and political elite has formed in Turkey. This elite was strongly influenced by the dervish orders, which were banned by Ataturk. After the military *coup d'état* in 1980, this elite became clearly organized. Some of the most active promoters of Islam on the Turkish political stage such as T. Özal, N. Erbakan, and Ismail Gem are closely related to the Ottoman mystic order of *Nakshibendi*, which is traditionally influential in politics (Tanaskovic 2010). The order wields power in other Balkan states as well (Maréchal, Allievi et al. 2003; Karpat 2010). Over the past twenty years and especially after 2002, the *Diyanet* and the Turkish Cooperation and Development Agency (TIKA), established by Turgut Özal in 1992, have been especially active. These institutions started to exercise influence in Bulgaria only about a decade ago. In Western Europe they were already active in the 1980s among the large immigrant diaspora (Nielsen 2004; Karpat 2010).

Both Tanaskovic and Öktem analyse the doctrine of Ahmet Davutoğlu,[26] relating its development to the Islamic philosophic circle called by Tanaskovic 'Malaysian Brotherhood'. This is a circle of university professors, who have attended the International Islamic University of Malaysia and who took high government or educational positions after returning to Turkey, especially after 2002, when Erdogan came to power.

It is generally accepted that Ahmet Davutoğlu gave a strong impetus to the liberal Islamic project in Turkey and in the Balkans, especially in Bosnia and to a lesser extent in Albania, Kosovo, and Macedonia. For the time being, this project cannot take root in the Turkish political organizations in Bulgaria, which remain strictly secular. The influence of organizations such as that of Fethullah Gülen can be felt among the Muslim clergy and the denomination in general (mainly through publishing and the educational

---

[25] The term is used by media and analysts for the concept developed by the Turkish Minister of Foreign Affairs Ahmet Davutoğlu for a policy of good neighbour relations and increased influence in territories that were part of the Ottoman Empire, as well as for taking care of Turkish-speaking and Muslim populations living in such territories.

[26] Professor Ahmet Davutoğlu has been the Foreign Minister of Turkey since 2009 and was formerly chief adviser to the Prime Minister. He is a political scientist by education. Davutoğlu is generally linked to the notion of Turkish neo-Ottomanism, which favours a commonwealth with its neighbours and old Ottoman connections.

activities—scholarships and teachers). Bulgarian society, including the media and the academic community, remains largely unfamiliar with these developments and to date, no serious studies have been conducted.

These forms of external influence and contacts with the Muslims abroad made the Muslims in Bulgaria feel for the first time that they belong to the Muslim *Ummah*, which gives them greater self-confidence and a feeling of belonging to a transborder community. The society interprets this as possible radicalization and the debate on this issue is reflected by the media (e.g. Ilchevski 2007; Todorova 2010; Yordanova 2004; Yovcheva 2010).

# Conclusion

The state of scholarly research on Islam and the Muslim communities in Bulgaria can be summarized in the following way.

The indigenous Muslims (Turks, Pomaks, part of Roma, and a small Tatar community) have been well studied over the past hundred years. The origin and formation of Muslim communities in Bulgaria have been widely and systematically examined by scholars from numerous fields: history, demography, anthropology, folklore studies, linguistics, and sociology. A specific topic arousing the continuous interest of Bulgarian scholars are the patterns and forms of the spread of Islam in Bulgaria during the Ottoman period. Another well-researched theme is the cohabitation of Christians and Muslims, and the means they employ to maintain mutual understanding and peaceful coexistence.

The state policies of various governments (from the liberation of Bulgaria in 1878 to date) with regard to the Muslim communities have ranged from periods of violent oppression to periods of protection of their culture and education. These policies have also been extensively studied by a wide variety of scholars. Quite often, the findings of these studies are contradictory. This is not a result only of applying different methods and approaches, but also because for decades, these studies were employed in the service of the dominant political ideology and were not always objective.

Although the bibliography on Islam in Bulgaria is in general quite extensive and rich, there are several fields that are insufficiently studied. There is an obvious lack of interdisciplinary studies that could accurately analyse contemporary external influences among the local Muslims. The academic community and the media remain largely unfamiliar with the religious debates inside the Muslim community. The political aspirations and activities of the Muslims and the parties that represent them rarely fall into the focus of scholars. The same is true of the most recent attitudes of the Muslims with regard to their own religious, ethnic, and civil identity. Finally, their relations with Muslims in neighbouring Balkan countries, in Western Europe, and in the Arab states have not been studied at all.

Since 2000, social scientists have turned their attention to the immigrants. Sociologists and anthropologists have produced demographic profiles of the main immigrant groups in Bulgaria. Scholars are mainly interested in their social-economic status, education, integration, and interactions with Bulgarian institutions and citizens. Two related issues attracting attention in recent years are the presence of illegal immigrants and their participation on the black labour market. The question of immigrants' religiousness has been studied only to a limited extent.

A number of important subject have yet to attract the attention of Bulgarian scholars. They include immigrants' associations and the internal communal life of immigrants; models and forms of adaptation in the host country; immigrants' integration in the educational system; and their participation in economic and political life.

A special challenge for the academic community are the migration attitudes of the immigrants; whether they intend to settle permanently in Bulgaria or plan to use the country as a temporary stop on their further migration to the West. Practically no research has been conducted on immigrants' relations with their fellow nationals and relatives who are immigrants in other European countries, or with their kin in the countries of origin.

## Bibliography

### Bulgarian Language Publications

Aleksiev, Bozhidar. 1997. Родопското население в българската хуманитаристика (Rhodope Population in Bulgarian Humanitarian Studies). In Мюсюлманските общности на Балканите и в България. Исторически ескизи (Muslim Communities in Balkans and Bulgaria. Historical Sketches). Sofia: IMIR, 57–112.

Aleksiev, Bozhidar. 2005. Фолклорни профили на мюсюлмански светци в България (Folklore Profiles of Muslim Saints in Bulgaria). Sofia: Prof. Marin Drinov Press.

Aliev, Ali. 1978. Задачи на атеистичната пропаганда сред мюсюлманското население (Objectives of the Atheist Propaganda among the Muslim Population). In Лекционна пропаганда (Propaganda Lectures) 4: 57–63.

Aliev, Ali. 1980. Формиране на научно-атеистичния мироглед у българските турци (Formation of Scientific-Atheist Worldview among the Bulgarian Turks). Sofia: n.p.

Arnaudov, Hristo (ed.) 1872–81. Пълно събрание на държавните закони, устави, наставления и високи заповеди на Османската империя, превод от турски (Complete Collection of State Laws, Rules, Guides and High Orders of the Ottoman Empire, Translation from Turkish). Istanbul-Ruse: Printed by Hristo Arnaudov.

Ataka. 2011. No. 1596-1636. <http://www.vestnikataka.com>.

BHC. 2006. Изследване на правата на мигрантите в България (Финален доклад) (Study of Migrants' Rights in Bulgaria (Final Report)). Sofia: Bulgarian Helsinki Committee.

Bobchev, Stefan. 1929. За делиорманските турци и за къзълбашите (принос към държавно-правната и културната история на България) (On Deliorman Turks and Kızılbashi (Contribution to the State-Legal and Cultural History of Bulgaria)). Sofia: BAS Collections, Vol. 24.

Bozhilov, Ivan, Vera Mutafchieva, Konstantin Kosev, Andrei Pantev, and Stoicho Grancharov. 1993. История на България (History of Bulgaria). Sofia: IK 'Hristo Botev'.

Bulgarian Academy of Sciences. 1983. *История на България в четиринадесет тома, т.4: Българският народ под османско владичество /от XV до началото на XVIII в./* (*History of Bulgaria in Fourteen Volumes. Vol. 4: Bulgarian Nation under the Ottoman Rule from the 15th to the Beginning of the 18th Century*). Sofia: BAS.

Cheker, Orhan. 2009. *Благоприличното облекло на жената според исляма* (*Decent Clothes for a Female According to Islam*). Sofia: Chief Muftiate of the Republic of Bulgaria.

Constitution of Bulgaria. 1991. <http://www.parliament.bg/en/const>.

Daskalov, Rumen. 2005. *Българското общество, т. 2: Население. Общество. Култура* (*Bulgarian Society, Vol. 2: Population. Society. Culture*). Sofia: IK Gutenberg.

Delev, Petar et al. 1996. *История на България за 11 клас* (*History of Bulgaria for 11th Grade*). Sofia: Izdatelstvo 'Otvoreno Obshtestvo'.

Dermendzhieva, Maria. 2011. Проф. Евгения Иванова: В България няма политически ислям (Prof. Evgenia Ivanova: There is No Political Islam in Bulgaria). In *Гласове (Glasove)*, 12 December. <http://www.glasove.com/prof-evgeniya-ivanova-v-bulgariya-nyama-politicheski-islyam-18037>.

Dimitrov, Ilcho (ed.) 1983. *Кратка история на България* (*Short History of Bulgaria*). Sofia: Nauka i Izkustvo.

Drucke, Luise. 2004. Бежански режими в пост-комунистическите страни (Refugee Regimes in the Post-Communist Countries). In Anna Krasteva (ed.), *От етничност към миграция* (*From Ethnicity to Migration*). Sofia: New Bulgarian University, 107–14.

Dzambazov, Ismail. 1964. *Религиозни празници и обреди в исляма* (*Religious Holidays and Rituals in Islam*). Sofia: n.p.

Elchinova, Magdalena. 2009. Миграция и трансформиране на локалната общност (сравнение между две рурални общности в България) (Migration and Transformation of Local Communities (Comparison of Two Ritual Communities in Bulgaria)). In *Български фолклор (Bulgarian Folklore)*, Vol. 2, 7–22.

Eldarov, Svetlozar. 2004. *Православието на война. Българската православна църква и войните на България 1877–1945* (*Orthodox Christianity at War: The Bulgarian Orthodox Church and the Wars of Bulgaria 1877–1945*). Sofia: Voenno izdatelstvo.

Evstatiev, Simeon. 2012. *Религия и политика в арабския свят: ислямът в обществото* (*Religion and Politics in the Arab World: Islam in the Society*). Sofia: Iztok-Zapad.

Focus Agency. 2009. *Радикалният ислям в пресата през последните години* (*Radical Islam in the Media during the Recent Years*). 17 March. <http://forum.clubpolitika.com/lofiversion/index.php/t8649.html>

Galabov, Galab. 1924. *Мюсюлманското право с кратък обзор върху историята на догмите на исляма* (*Muslim Law and a Short Review of the History of Islamic Dogmas*). Sofia: n.p.

Georgieva, Tsvetana. 1994. Съжителството като система във всекидневния живот на християните и мюсюлманите в България (Cohabitation as a System in the Everyday Life of Christians and Muslims in Bulgaria). In Antonina Zhelyazkova, Jørgen Nielsen, and Giles Kepel (eds.), *Връзки на съвместимост и несъвместимост между християни и мюсюлмани в България* (*Relations of Compatibility and Incompatibility between Christians and Muslims in Bulgaria*). Sofia: IMIR, 140–64.

Gradeva, Rossitsa (ed.) 2001. *Съдбата на мюсюлманските общности на Балканите. Т. 7. История на мюсюлманската култура по българските земи* (*The Fate of Muslim Communities in the Balkans. Vol. 7: History of Muslim Culture in the Bulgarian Lands*). Sofia: IMIR.

Gradeva, Rossitsa and Svetlana Ivanova (eds.) 1998. *Съдбата на мюсюлманските общности на Балканите. Т. 2. Мюсюлманската култура по българските земи* (*The Fate of Muslim Communities in the Balkans. Vol. 2: The Muslim Culture in the Bulgarian Lands*). Sofia: IMIR.

Gramatikova, Nevena. 2011. *Неортодоксалният ислям в България. Минало и съвременност* (*Unorthodox Islam in Bulgarian Lands. Past and Present*). Sofia: Gutenberg Publishing, IMIR.

Grekova, Maya et al. 2008. *Ромите в София: от изолация към интеграция?* (*The Roma in Sofia: From Isolation to Integration?*). Sofia: Iztok-Zapad.

Gruev, Mihail. 2003. *Между петолъчката и полумесеца. Българите мюсюлмани и политическият режим (1944–1959)* (*Between Red Star and Crescent: The Bulgarian Muslims and the Political Regime (1944–1959)*). Sofia: IK 'Kota'.

Gruev, Mihail. 2008. Българомюсюлманските (помашки) идентичности—опит за типологизация (Identities of Bulgarian Muslims (Pomaks)—A Typologization Attempt). In Svetlana Ivanova (ed.), *Етнически и културни пространства на Балканите. Ч. II. Съвременност—етноложки дискурси. Сборник в чест на проф. Цветана Георгиева* (*Ethnic and Cultural Spaces in the Balkans. Part II: Contemporary Times—Ethnologic Discourses. Contributions in Honour of Prof. Tsvetana Georgieva*). Sofia: St. Kliment Ohridski University Press, 335–54.

Gruev Mihail and Aleksei Kalyonski. 2008. *Възродителният процес. Мюсюлманските общности и комунистическия режим* (*The Revival Process: Muslim Communities and the Communist Regime*). Sofia: CIELA.

High Islamic Institute. 2009–11. *Годишник на Висшия ислямски институт* (*Yearbook of the High Islamic Institute*). Nos. 1–3. Sofia: High Islamic Institute.

Hristova, Nadezhda. 2007. *Режим на пребиваване на чужденците на територията на България* (*Regulation of Stay of Foreigners on the Territory of Bulgaria*). Sofia: Siena.

Ilchevski, Stefan. 2007. Мюсюлманската общност в България: избор между традиция, реислямизация, секуларизация и радикализация (The Muslim Community in Bulgaria: Choice Among Tradition, Re-Islamization, Secularization and Radicalization). In *Свобода за всеки* (*Freedom for Everyone*). October. <http://svobodazavseki.com/broj-13/37-myusyulmanskata-obshtnost-v-balgariya-13.html>.

Ilieva, Nadezhda. 2010. *Турската етническа група в България (1878–2001)* (*The Turkish Ethnic Group in Bulgaria (1878–2001)*).Sofia: National Institute of Geophysics, Geodesy and Geography—BAS.

Isov, Myumyun. 2005. *Най-различния съсед. Образът на османците (турците) и Османската империя (Турция) в българските учебници по история през втората половина на ХХ век* (*The Most Different Neighbour: The Image of the Ottomans (Turks) and the Ottoman Empire (Turkey) in the Bulgarian Textbooks in History during the Second Half of the Twentieth Century*). Sofia: IMIR.

Ivanov, Mihail. 2011. *Данните на НСИ замъгляват етническата картина* (*NSI Data Obscure the Ethnic Picture*). 25 July. <http://www.bghelsinki.org/bg/publikacii/obektiv/mikhail-ivanov/2011-07/dannite-na-nsi-zamglyavat-etnicheskata-kartina>.

Ivanov, Mihail and Atanas Atanasov. 2005. *Демографско развитие на Република България* (*Demographic Development of the Republic of Bulgaria*). Sofia: NCCEDI, BAS, NSI, United Nations Population Fund.

Ivanova, Evgenia. 2002. *Отхвърлените 'приобщени' или процеса, наречен 'възродителен' (1912–1989)* (*The Rejected 'Integrated' or the Process Called 'Revival' (1912–1989)*). Sofia: Eastern European Humanitarian Studies Institute.

Ivanova, Evgenia. 2012. *Идентичност и идентичности на помаците в България (Identity and Identities of Pomaks in Bulgaria)*. <http://www.librev.com/index.php/component/content/article/23-discussion-bulgaria/1516-2012-03-06-09-21-19>.

Jireček, Konstantin. 1978. *История на българите (History of the Bulgarians)*, ed. Petar Petrov. Sofia: Nauka i Izkustvo.

Koleva, Irena and Ivaylo Krachunov. 2011. 'Атака' нападна джамия заради тонколони ('Ataka' Attacks the Mosque Because of the Loudspeakers). In *Труд (Trud)*. 20 May. <http://www.trud.bg/Article.asp?ArticleId=898696>.

Krasteva, Anna (ed.) 2004. *От етничност към миграция (From Ethnicity to Migration)*. Sofia: New Bulgarian University.

Krasteva, Anna. 2005. *Имиграцията в България (Immigration in Bulgaria)*. Sofia: IMIR.

Krasteva, Anna. 2006. *Фигурите на бежанеца (The Figures of the Refugee)*. Sofia: New Bulgarian University.

Krasteva-Blagoeva, Evgenia and Goran Blagoev. 2003. Идентичност и религия: българите мюсюлмани (Identity and Religion: Bulgarian Muslims). In *Българска етнология (Bulgarian Ethnology)* 1: 44–55.

Kyurkchieva, Iva. 2004. *Светът на българите мюсюлмани от Тетевенско. Преход към модерност (The World of the Bulgarian Muslims in Teteven Region: Transition to Modernity)*. Sofia: IMIR.

Lefedzhievev, Nikolai. 2012. Заместник-главният мюфтия Бирали Бирали: Ако някой проповядва омраза, да си носи отговорността (Deputy Chief Mufti Birali Birali: Whoever Preaches Hate Will Be Held Responsible). *EkipNews.com*. 25 September. <http://www.ekipnews.com/news/mnenia/intervjuta/zamestnik_glavniqt_mjuftiq_birali_birali_ako_nqkoj_propovqdva_omraza_da_si_nosi_otgovornostta/139615/>.

Lozanova, Galina. 2008. *Сътворението в устната традиция на Българите мюсюлмани (Creation in the Oral Tradition of Bulgarian Muslims)*. Sofia: Prof. Marin Drinov Press.

Lozanova, Galina and Lubomir Mikov (eds.) 1999. *Съдбата на мюсюлманските общности на Балканите. Т. 4. Ислям и култура (The Fate of Muslim Communities in the Balkans. Vol. 4: Islam and Culture)*. Sofia: IMIR.

Maeva, Mila. 2006. *Българските турци-преселници в Република Турция. Култура и идентичност (Bulgarian Turks: Emigrants in the Republic of Turkey: Culture and Identity)*. Sofia: IMIR.

Marinov, Vasil. 1941. *Делиорман (южна част). Областно географско изучаване (Deliorman (Southern Part))*. Regional Geographic Study, Sofia.

Marinov, Vasil. 1956. *Принос към изучаване на бита и културата на турците и гагаузите в Североизточна България (Contribution to the Study of Way of Life and Culture of Turks and Gagauz in Northeastern Bulgaria)*. Sofia: n.p.

Marushiakova, Elena and Veselin Popov. 1993. *Циганите в България (Gypsies in Bulgaria)*. Sofia: Klub'90.

Mikov, Lyubomir. 2007. *Култова архитектура и изкуство на хетеродоксните мюсюлмани в България (XVI–XX век). Бекташи и къзълбаши/алевии (Cult Architecture and Art of Heterodox Muslims in Bulgaria (XVI–XX centuries). Bektashi and Kızılbashi/Alevi)*. Sofia: Prof. Marin Drinov Press.

Minchev, Ognian, 2011. *Нападението срещу джамията в София е позорен акт, който изисква наказание! (Attack on the Sofia Mosque is a Shameful Act That Has to Be Punished!)*. 21 May. <http://www.librev.com/index.php/--/1243-2011-05-21-15-51-19>.

Mishkova, Diana (ed.) 2006. *Балканският XIX век. Други прочити (The Balkan Nineteenth Century: Other Readings)*. Sofia: RIVA.

Mizov, Nikolai. 1958. *Антинаучната и реакционна същност на мюсюлманската религия (The Antiscientific and Reactionist Nature of Muslim Religion)*. Sofia: n.p.

Mizov, Nikolai. 1965. *Ислямът в България (Islam in Bulgaria)*. Sofia: n.p.

Moskov, Nikolai. 2012. Главният мюфтия Мустафа Хаджи: Щяхме да храним цял месец бедните в София, не ни разрешиха (Chief Mufti Mustafa Hadzhi: We Could Feed the Poor in Sofia for an Entire Month, But We Were Not Allowed To). In *24 часа (24 Hours)*. 22 August. <http://www.24chasa.bg/Article.asp?ArticleId=1514205>.

MRF. n.d. *Устав на Движението за права и свободи (Statute of the Movement for Rights and Freedoms)*. <http://www.dps.bg/about/regulations.aspx>.

MRF. 2006. *Програмна декларация, приета на VI Национална конференция на ДПС 2006 г. (Programme Declaration Adopted on the VI National Conference of MRF in 2006)*. <http://www.dps.bg/media/cms_content/programna-deklaraciaDPS2006.doc>.

Mutafchieva, Vera. 1997. Някои разсъждения относно разсъжденията на Бернар Лори върху историческия мит 'Пет века ни клаха' (*Some Thoughts on the Thoughts of Bernard Lory on the Historical Myth 'They Have Been Slaughtering Us for Five Centuries'*). <http://www.libsu.uni-sofia.bg/Statii/Mutafchieva.html>.

Nazarska, Zhorzheta. 1999a. *Българската държава и нейните малцинства 1879–1885 (Bulgarian State and its Minorities 1879–1885)*. Sofia: LIK.

Nazarska, Zhorzheta. 1999b. Етническите и религиозните малцинства в българския парламент (1879–1885) (Ethnic and Religious Minorities in the Bulgarian Parliament (1879–1885). In *Исторически преглед (Historical Review)* 1–2: 3–22.

Nikolova, Veska. 2004. *Между консерватизма и либерализма. Народната партия 1894–1920 (Between Conservatism and Liberalism: The People's Party 1894–1920)*. Sofia: Vital.

NSI. 2003. *Преброяване на населението, жилищния фонд и земеделските стопанства през 2001. Население, кн.1. Демографски и социални характеристики на населението (Population and Housing Census 2001. Population, Vol. 1. Demographic and Social Characteristics of Population)*. Sofia: National Statistical Institute.

NSI. 2011. *Преброяване 2011—основни резултати (Census 2011—Main Results)*. Sofia: National Statistical Institute. <http://www.nsi.bg/EPDOCS/Census2011final.pdf>.

Pamporov, Aleksei. 2006. *Ромското всекидневие в България (Roma Everyday Life in Bulgaria)*. Sofia: IMIR.

Pamporov, Aleksei. 2009. *Социални дистанции и етнически стереотипи за малцинствата в България (Social Distances and Ethnic Stereotypes on Minorities in Bulgaria)*. Sofia: Open Society Institute.

Pamporov, Aleksei. 2010. Социални дистанции към бежанците като съседи (Social Distances towards Refugees as Neighbours). In *Политики (Politics)* 4. <http://politiki.bg/?cy=174&lang=1&aoi=223525&aom=readInternal&aop_id=650>.

Parvanov, Kalin. 2006. Етнизация на бедността (Ethnicization of Poverty). In *Тема (Theme)* 42, 23–29 October. <http://www.temanews.com/index.php?p=tema&iid=190&aid=4835>.

Radeva, Marinela. 2003. *Промени в политиката и дейностите по интеграция на бежанците в Република България. Доклад (Changes in Policy and Activities on Integration of Refugees in the Republic of Bulgaria. Report)*. Sofia: State Agency for Refugees.

Sachkova, Elena. 2000. *Образованието на децата мигранти—швейцарският опит (Education of Migrant Children: The Swiss Experience)*. Sofia: St. Kliment Ohridski University Press.

Sadulov, Ahmed. 2000. *История на Османската империя (XIV-XX в.)* (*History of the Ottoman Empire (XIV–XX c.)*). Veliko Tarnovo: Faber.

Slavkova, Magdalena. 2007. *Циганите евангелисти в България* (*Evangelical Gypsies in Bulgaria*). Sofia: Paradigma.

Snegarov, Ivan. 1958. *Турското владичество—пречка за културното развитие на българския народ и на другите балкански народи* (*Turkish Rule—An Obstacle for the Cultural Development of the Bulgarian and Other Nations on the Balkans*). Sofia: BAS.

Stoyanov, Borislav. 2011. Фундаменталисти призоваха София да се превърне в ислямистки център на Балканите (Fundamentalists Call for Sofia to Become Islamist Centre in the Balkans). In *Атака (Attack Newspaper)*, No. 1574, 25 March.

Stoyanov, Valeri. 1998. *Турското население в България между полюсите на етническата политика* (*The Turkish Population in Bulgaria between the Poles of the Ethnic Policy*). Sofia: LIK.

Szelenyi, Ivan (ed.) 2002. *Бедността при посткомунизма* (*Poverty under Post-Communism*). Sofia: Iztok-Zapad.

Tahirov, Shukri. 1981. *Единението* (*Unity*). Sofia: Fatherland Front Press.

Tanaskovic, Darko. 2010. *Неоосманизмът—Турция се връща на Балканите* (*Neo-Ottomasnism—Turkey Returns to the Balkans*). Sofia: Iztok-Zapad.

Tarnev, Ivailo and Maya Grekova. 2007. *Социален и здравен профил на ромите в 16 населени места в България* (*Social and Health Profile of the Roma in 16 Bulgarian Settlements*). Sofia: Iztok-Zapad.

Teofanov, Tzvetan. 2004. *Арабската средновековна култура, т. 1–2* (*Arabic Culture in the Middle Ages. Vol. 1–2*). Sofia: St. Kliment Ohridski University Press.

Tilkidziev, Nikolai, Valentina Milenkova, Kamelia Petkova, and Natasha Mileva. 2009. *Отпадащите роми* (*The Relegated Roma*). Sofia: IOO.

Todorov, Antoni. 2010. *Граждани, партии, избори в България 1879–2009* (*Citizens, Parties, Elections in Bulgaria 1879–2009*). Sofia: Iztok-Zapad.

Todorova, Bogdana. 2010. Радикалният ислям в България—много спекулации и невежество (Radical Islam in Bulgaria—Many Speculations and Much Ignorance). In *в. Сега (Sega Newspaper)*, 18 October.

Tomova, Ilona. 1998. Роми (Roma). In Anna Krasteva (ed.), *Общности и идентичности в България* (*Communities and Identities in Bulgaria*). Sofia: Petekston, 329–55.

Topalova, Velina and Aleksei Pamporov (eds.) 2007. *Интеграцията на ромите в българското общество* (*Integration of the Roma in the Bulgarian Society*). Sofia: Institute of Sociology at BAS.

Topbash, Osman Nuri. 2005. *Ислямът—форма и дух* (*Islam—Spirit and Form*). Sofia: Chief Muftiate.

Troeva, Evgenia. 2011. *Религия, памет, идентичност: българите мюсюлмани* (*Religion, Memory, Identity: The Bulgarian Muslims*). Sofia: Prof. Marin Drinov Press.

Troeva, Evgenia. 2012. 'Традиционен' и 'нов' ислям в България ('Traditional' and 'New' Islam in Bulgaria). In *сп. Български фолклор (Bulgarian Folklore)* 3–4: 5–23.

Tsacheva, Boryana. 2011. Интервю с Алекс Алексиев (Interview with Aleks Aleksiev). In *24 часа (24 Hours)*, 16 February.

Valkov, Ilia. 2009. ДАНС задържа и пусна кмет и учител, заподозрени в 'ислямски радикализъм' (State Agency for National Security Detained and Then Released from Custody a Mayor and a Teacher Suspected of 'Islamic

Radicalism'). In *Дневник (Dnevnik)*, 16 March. <http://www.dnevnik.bg/bulgaria/2009/03/16/690695_dans_zadurja_i_pusna_kmet_i_uchitel_zapodozreni_v>.

Vasileva, Darina. 1992. Изселническият въпрос в българо-турските отношения (The Resettlement Issue in Bulgarian–Turkish Relations). In Valeri Rusanov (ed.), *Аспекти на етнокултурната ситуация в България (Aspects of the Ethnic-Cultural Situation in Bulgaria)*. Sofia: Center for the Study of Democracy, Friedrich Naumann Foundation, 58–67.

Vladinska, Neli. 1998. Роля на системите за социално подпомагане и социални услуги при прилагане на политики и стратегии за интеграция на мигранти и етнически групи (The Role of the Social Assistance and Social Services Systems in the Implementation of Policy and Strategies for Integration of Migrants and Ethnic Groups). In *Годишник на Варненския свободен университет (Varna Free University Yearbook)*, Year 4, No. 1.

Yalamov, Ibrahim. 2002. *История на турската общност в България (History of the Turkish Community in Bulgaria)*. Sofia: IMIR.

Yalamov, Ibrahim. 2005. *Кемализмът и отражението му в България (Kemalism and its Reflection in Bulgaria)*. Sofia: Avangard Prima.

Yankov, Georgi, Strashimir Dimitrov, and Orlin Zagorov (eds.) 1988. *Проблеми на развитието на българската народност и нация (Problems of Development of the Bulgarian Nation)*. Sofia: Bulgarian Academy of Sciences.

Yordanova, Yana. 2004. Кой плете мрежите на радикалния ислям в България (Who is Creating the Network of Radical Islam in Bulgaria?). In *Капитал (Capital)*, 14 August. <http://www.capital.bg/politika_i_ikonomika/bulgaria/2004/08/14/227487_koi_plete_mrejata_na_radikalniia_isliam_v_bulgariia/>.

Yovcheva, Yovka. 2010. На мюсюлманите им е нужен 'джихад', но в областта на образованието и науката—Интервю с ректора на Висшия ислямски институт доц. Ибрахим Ялъмов (Muslims Need 'Jihad', but in the Field of Education and Science—Interview with the Dean of High Islamic Institute Ibrahim Yalamov). In *Darik News*, 20 September. <http://dariknews.bg/print_article.php?article_id=590240>.

Zhelyazkova, Antonina. 1997. Формиране на мюсюлманските общности и комплексите на балканските историографии (Formation of Muslim Communities and the Complexes of the Balkan Historiographers). In *Мюсюлманските общности на Балканите и в България (Muslim Communities in the Balkans and in Bulgaria)*. Sofia: IMIR, 11–56.

Zhelyazkova, Antonina. 2004. Етнически кризи и спешна антропология (Ethnic Crises and Urgent Anthropology). In Anna Krasteva (ed.), *От етничност към миграция (From Ethnicity to Migration)*. Sofia: New Bulgarian University, 75–91.

Zhelyazkova, Antonina. 2008. Босна—новите измерения на враждата—толерантната непоносимост (май 2004 г.) (Bosnia—New Dimensions of Hostility—Tolerant Intolerance (May 2004)). In Svetlana Ivanova (ed.), *Етнически и културни пространства на Балканите. Ч. II. Съвременност—етноложки дискурси. Сборник в чест на проф. Цветана Георгиева (Ethnic and Cultural Spaces in the Balkans. Part II: Contemporary Times—Ethnologic Discourses. Contributions in Honour of Prof. Tsvetana Georgieva)*. Sofia: St. Kliment Ohridski University Press, 387–417.

Zhelyazkova, Antonina. 2011. Държавата, мюфтийската институция и обществото в България (State, Mufti Institution and Society in Bulgaria). In *Обектив (Obektiv)* 184. January. <http://www.bghelsinki.org/bg/publikacii/obektiv/antonina-zheliazkova/2011-01/drzhavata-miuftiiskata-institutsiia-i-obshchestvoto-v-blgariia>.

Zhelyazkova, Antonina, Valeri Grigorov, and Donka Dimitrova. 2005. Имигранти от Близкия и Средния изток (Immigrants from Near and Middle East). In Anna Krasteva (ed.), *Имиграцията в България (Immigration in Bulgaria)*. Sofia: IMIR, 19–73.

## Publications in Other Languages

Assheuer, Thomas. 2010. Blut, Schwerter, Barmherzigkeit—Wolfgang Palaver. *Die Zeit*, 8 November. <http://www.zeit.de/2010/42/Palaver-Interview>.
Attanassoff, Velko. 2009. *Alternative Islamic Structures in Bulgaria: Parallel, Independent, and 'Anti-Establishment' Groups*. Report at Conference in Sarajevo: Administration of Islamic Affairs in Secular States: Southeast European Experience.
Balikci, Asen. 1999. Pomak Identity: National Prescriptions and Native Assumptions. *Ethnologia Balkanica* 3: 51–7.
Bernd, Rechel. 2005. *Minority Rights in Post-Communist Bulgaria*. Birmingham: University of Birmingham.
Brunnbauer, Ulf. 1998. Histories and Identities: Nation-State and Minority Discourses. In *In and Out of the Collective: Papers on Former Soviet Bloc Rural Communities*, Vol. 1. Sofia: Bulgarian Society for Regional Cultural Studies, 1–10.
Brunnbauer, Ulf. 2001. The Dynamics of Ethnicity: Pomak Identities. *EthnoAnthropoZoom (Journal of the Insitute of Ethnology and Anthropology)*, Skopje.
Castellan, Georges. 1999. *Histoire des Balkans: XIVe–XXe siècle*. Paris: Fayard.
Chukov, Vladimir. 2004. *Islamic Fundamentalism*. Sofia: East West.
Clayer, Nathalie and Xavier Bougarel. 2001. *Le Nouvel Islam Balkanique: Les musulmas, acteurs du post-Communisme 1990–2000*. Paris: Maisonneuve et Larose.
Emigh, Rebecca Jean, Eva Fodor, and Ivan Szelenyi. 2001. The Racialization and Feminization of Poverty? In Rebecca Jean Emigh and Ivan Szelenyi (eds.), *Poverty, Ethnicity and Gender in Eastern Europe During the Market Transition*. Westport, CT: Greenwood Press, 1–32.
Eminov, Ali. 1997. *Turkish and Other Muslim Minorities of Bulgaria*. London: Hurst and Co.
Eminov, Ali. 2007. Social Construction of Identities: Pomaks in Bulgaria. *Journal of Ethnopolitics and Minority Issues in Europe (JEMIE)* 2: 1–22. <http://www.ecmi.de/fileadmin/downloads/publications/JEMIE/2007/2-2007-Eminov.pdf>.
Ercan, Yavuz. 1989. *Osmanli Imperatorlugunda Bulgar ve Voynuklar*. Ankara: TTK.
Evstatiev, Simeon and Plamen Makariev. 2010. Islam and Religious Education in Bulgaria: Local Tradition Vis-à-Vis Global Change. In Jørgen Nielsen (ed.), *Yearbook of Muslims in Europe*, Vol. 2. Leiden and Boston: Brill, 635–61.
Fallaci, Oriana. 2004. *Oriana Fallaci intervista se stessa*. Milan: L'Apocalisse.
Fallaci, Oriana. 2006. *The Force of Reason*. New York: Rizzoli International.
Gellner, Ernest. 1994. *Encounters with Nationalism*. Oxford: Blackwell.
Gellner, Ernest. 1996. *Conditions of Liberty: Civil Society and its Rivals*. Budapest: CEU Press.
Georgieva, Tsvetana. 1998. The Motivation for Emigration of the Bulgarian Turks. In Antonina Zhelyazkova (ed.), *Between Adaptation and Nostalgia: The Bulgarian Turks in Turkey*. Sofia: IMIR, 45–75.
Georgieva, Tsvetana. 1999. Coexistence as a System in the Everyday Life of Christians and Muslims in Bulgaria. *Ethnologia Bulgarica* 3: 59–84.
Georgieva, Tsvetana. 2001. Pomaks: Muslim Bulgarians. *Islam and Christian-Muslim Relations* 12(3): 303–16.
Ghodsee, Kristen. 2007. Religious Freedoms versus Gender Equality: Faith-Based Organisations, Muslim Minorities, and Islamic Headscarves in the New Europe. *Social Politics: International Studies in Gender, State and Society* 14(4): 526–61.
Ghodsee, Kristen. 2009. *Muslim Lives in Eastern Europe: Gender, Ethnicity, and the Transformation of Islam in Post-Socialist Bulgaria*. Princeton: Princeton University Press.

Grekova, Maya, Iva Kyurkchieva, Maya Kosseva, and Orlin Avramov. 2010. *Discrimination as a Social Practice: Bulgaria 2008–2010*. Sofia: IMIR.

Guentcheva, Rossitza, Petya Kabakchieva, and Plamen Kolarski. 2003. *Migration Trends in Selected EU Applicant Countries. Volume I—Bulgaria: The Social Impact of Seasonal Migration*. Vienna: International Organization for Migration. <http://www.pedz.uni-mannheim.de/daten/edz-k/gde/04/IOM_I_BG.pdf>.

Hajdinjak, Marko. 2008. Thou Shall Not Take the Names Ethnic or Minority, And I Will Bless Thee: Political Participation of Minorities in Bulgaria. In *Political Parties and Minority Participation*. Skopje: Friedrich Ebert Stiftung Office Macedonia. <http://www.fes.org.mk/pdf/Politicalpercent20Partiespercent20andpercent20Minoritypercent20Participation.pdf>.

Hajdinjak, Marko (ed.) 2011. *Migration, Gender and Intercultural Interactions in Bulgaria*. Sofia: IMIR.

Hoepken, Wolfgang. 1989. Zivkiv-Erklarung zu Unruhen unter der turkischen minderheit Bulgariens (Dokumentation). *SOE* 38(5): 327–32.

Hosch, Edgar. 1995. *Geschichte der Balkanländer. Von der Frühzeit bis zur Gegenwart*. Munich: C. H. Beck.

Hupchick, Dennis. 1994. *Nation or Millet? Contrasting Western European and Islamic Political Cultures in the Balkans*. Wilkes-Barre: Wilkes University Press.

Ihsanoglu, Ekmeleddin. 2004. *A Culture of Peaceful Coexistence: Early Islamic and Turkish Examples*. Istanbul: Research Centre for Islamic History, Art and Culture.

Ilareva, Valeria. 2007. Bulgaria`s Treatment of Asylum Seekers. *Forced Migration Review* 29: 60–1.

Inalcik, Halil. 1973. *The Ottoman Empire: The Classical Age, 1300–1600*. London: Phoenix Press.

Ivanov, Andrey (ed.) 2002. *Avoiding the Dependency Trap*. Bratislava: UNDP.

Ivanov, Andrey (ed.) 2006. *At Risk: Roma and Displaced in Southeast Europe*. Sofia: UNDP.

Jeliazkova, Antonina and Tzvetana Georgieva. 1994. L'Identité en periode de changement (observations sur certaines tendances du monde mixte des Rhodopes). *Cahiers internationaux de Sociologie* 96: 126–43.

Jileva, Elena and Virginie Guiraudon. 2006. Immigration and Asylum. In Paul M. Heywood, Erik Jones, Martin Rhodes, and Ulrich Sedelmeier (eds.), *Developments in European Politics*. Basingstoke: Palgrave Macmillan, 280–98.

Karagiannis, Evangelos. 1997. *Zur Ethnizitat der Pomaken Bulgariens*. Munster: Lit.

Karamihova, Margarita. 2002. *The Emigration Attitudes in the Rhodopes*. Sofia: IMIR.

Karpat, Kemal. 2010. *Elites and Religion: From Ottoman Empire to Turkish Republic*. Istanbul: Timas Publishing.

Kenrick, Donald. 1998. *Historical Dictionary of the Gypsies (Romanies)*. Lanham, MD: Scarecrow Press.

Konstantinov, Yulian. 1992. An Account of Pomak Conversions in Bulgaria. In Gerhard Seewan (ed.), *Minderheitenfragen in Sudosteuropa*. Munich: Südost-Institut, R. Oldenbourg Verlag, 343–59.

Kyurkchieva, Iva, Evgenia Troeva-Grigorova, Maya Kosseva, Tsvetanka Boncheva-Lucheva, and Bonka Dimitrova. 2008. *Minority Rights, Inter-Ethnic and Inter-Religious Relations in Municipalities with Diverse Population*. Sofia: IMIR.

Lewis, Bernard. 1992. Legal and Historical Reflections on the Position of Muslim Populations under Non-Muslim Rule. *Journal of Institute of Muslim Minority Affairs* 13(1): 1–16.

Mancheva, Mila. 2008. Practicing Identities across Borders: The Case of Bulgarian Turkish Labour Migrants in Germany. In Michael Peter Smith and John Eade (eds.), *Transnational Ties: Cities, Migrations and Identities*. New Brunswick: Transaction Publishers, 163–82.

Mancheva, Mila and Evgenia Troeva. 2011. Migrations to and from Bulgaria: The State of Research. In Marko Hajdinjak (ed.), *Migrations, Gender and Intercultural Interactions in Bulgaria*. Sofia: IMIR, 13–60.

Manfred Wörner Foundation. 2003. *Rights and Integration of Immigrants in Bulgaria*. Sofia.

Mantran, Robert (ed.) 1989. *Histoire de L'Empire Ottoman*. Paris: Librairie Arthème Fayard.

Maréchal, Brigitte, Stefano Allievi, Felice Dassetto, and Jørgen Nielsen (eds.) 2003. *Muslims in the Enlarged Europe: Religion and Society*. Leiden and Boston: Brill.

Melikoff, Iren. 1990. The Kızılbashi Issue. *Sovetskaya Tyurkologia* 5: 75–91.

Merdjanova, Ina. 2009. Bulgaria. In Jørgen Nielsen (ed.), *Yearbook of Muslims in Europe*, Vol. 1. Leiden and Boston: Brill, 61–7.

Merdjanova, Ina. 2010. Bulgaria. In Jørgen Nielsen (ed.), *Yearbook of Muslims in Europe*, Vol. 2. Leiden and Boston: Brill, 107–14.

Nazarska, Georgeta and Marko Hajdinjak. 2011. Mixed and Transnational Families in Bulgaria. In Marko Hajdinjak (ed.), *Migration, Gender and Intercultural Interactions in Bulgaria*. Sofia: IMIR, 111–53.

Neuburger, Mary. 2004. *The Orient Within: The Muslim Minorities and the Negotiation of Nationhood in Modern Bulgaria*. Ithaca and London: Cornell University Press.

Nielsen, Jørgen. 2004. *Muslims in Western Europe*, 3rd edn. Edinburgh: Edinburgh University Press.

Nielsen, Jørgen, Samim Akgonul, Ahmet Alibasic, Brigitte Maréchal, and Christian Moe (eds.) 2009. *Yearbook of Muslims in Europe*, Vol. 1. Leiden and Boston: Brill.

Nielsen, Jørgen, Samim Akgonul, Ahmet Alibasic, Brigitte Maréchal, and Christian Moe (eds.) 2010. *Yearbook of Muslims in Europe*, Vol. 2. Leiden and Boston: Brill.

Norris, Harry T. 2006. *Popular Sufism in Eastern Europe: Sufi Brotherhoods and the Dialogue with Christianity and 'Heterodoxy'*. London and New York: Routledge.

NSI. 2002. *The Contemporary Development of the Migration Policy in Bulgaria*. Sofia: National Statistical Institute.

NSI. 2011. *Population Census in the Republic of Bulgaria (Final Data)*. Sofia: National Statistical Institute. <http://www.nsi.bg/census2011/PDOCS2/Census2011final_en.pdf>.

Öktem, Kerem. 2010. *New Islamic Actors after the Wahhabi Intermezzo: Turkey's Return to the Muslim Balkans*. Oxford: European Studies Centre, University of Oxford. <http://www.balkanmuslims.com/pdf/Oktem-Balkan-Muslims.pdf>.

Petkova, Lilia. 2002. The Integration Process of the Turkish Minority in Bulgaria in the Post-Cold War Era: Parallel Trends in Minority Treatment in Greece and Turkey. *Kakanien Revisited* 27(06). <http://www.kakanien.ac.at/beitr/fallstudie/LPetkova1.pdf>.

Ragaru, Nadege. 2001. Islam in Post-Communist Bulgaria: An Aborted 'Crash of Civilization?' *National Papers* 29(2): 293–324.

Ragaru, Nadege. 2008. Introduction. In Patrick Michel, Enzo Pace, and Antonela Capelle-Pogacean (eds.), *Les recompositions des figures du religieux dans l'Europe d'aujourd'hui*. Paris: Presses de Sciences Po, 17–40.

Sarrazin, Thilo. 2010. *Deutschland schafft sich ab. Wie wir unser Land aufs Spiel setzen*. Munich: Deutsche Verlags-Anstalt.

Simsir, Bilal. 1988. *The Turks of Bulgaria (1878–1985)*. London: Rustem and Brother.

Sugar, Peter. 1977. *Southeastern Europe under Ottoman Rule, 1354-1804*. Washington: University of Washington Press.

Telbizova-Sack, Jordanka. 2000. Die Pomaken Bulgariens zwischen Identitätsverlust und Selbstbehauptung. In Cay Lienau and Ludwig Steindorff (eds.), *Ethnizitat, Identitat und Nationalitat in Sudosteuropa*. Munich: Sudosteuropa-Gesellschaft, 70-88.

Todorov, Tzvetan. 2010. *The Fear of Barbarians: Beyond the Clash of Civilizations*. Chicago: University of Chicago Press.

Tomova, Ilona. 1995. *The Gipsies in the Transition Period*. Sofia: IMIR.

Troeva, Evgenia and Mila Mancheva. 2011. Migration, Religion and Gender: Female Muslim Immigrants in Bulgaria. In Marko Hajdinjak (ed.), *Migration, Gender and Intercultural Interactions in Bulgaria*. Sofia: IMIR, 155-91.

United Nations Department of Economic and Social Affairs, Population Division. 2009. *Trends in International Migration Stock: The 2008 Revision*. <http://esa.un.org/migration/p2kodata.asp>.

Valtchinova, Galina. 2008. 'Jérusalem des Rhodopes' vs. 'La Mecque des Rhodopes': deux lieux de pèlerinage entre la Bulgarie, la Grèce et la Turquie. *Chronos. Revue d'Histoire de l'Université de Balamand* 18: 55-86.

Velinov, Aleksandar. 2001. Religiose Identitat im Zeitalter des Nationalismus. Die Pomakenfrage in Bulgarien. Dissertation. Koln.

Zhelyazkova, Antonina. 1985. Social Aspects of the Process of Islamization in the Balkan Territories of the Ottoman Empire. *Etudes Balkaniques* 3: 107-22.

Zhelyazkova, Antonina. 1990a. *The Spread of Islam in the Western Balkan Lands under the Ottoman Rule (15th-18th Centuries)*. Sofia: BAS.

Zhelyazkova, Antonina. 1990b. The Problem of Authenticity of Some Sources on the Islamization of the Rhodopes, Deeply Rooted in Bulgarian Historiography. *Etudes Balkaniques* 4: 105-11.

Zhelyazkova, Antonina. 1998a. Turks. In Anna Krasteva (ed.), *Communities and Identities in Bulgaria*. Ravenna: Longo Editore Ravenna, 287-306.

Zhelyazkova, Antonina (ed.) 1998b. *Between Adaptation and Nostalgia: The Bulgarian Turks in Turkey*. Sofia: IMIR.

Zhelyazkova, Antonina. 2001a. Bulgaria in Transition: The Muslim Minorities. *Islam and Christian-Muslim Relations* 12(3): 283-301.

Zhelyazkova, Antonina. 2001b. The Bulgarian Ethnic Model. *East European Constitutional Review* 10(4): 62-6.

Zhelyazkova, Antonina. 2003. *Urgent Anthropology Vol. 2: Albanian Prospects. Fieldwork*. Sofia: IMIR.

Zhelyazkova, Antonina, Bojidar Alexiev, and Georgeta Nazarska. 1997. *The Fate of Muslim Communities in the Balkans. Vol. 1: The Muslim Communities in the Balkans and in Bulgaria*. Sofia: IMIR.

Zhelyazkova, Antonina, Violeta Angelova, and Zhelyu Vladimirov. 2007. *Undocumented Workers: Bulgarian National Report*. Sofia: IMIR. <http://www.imir-bg.org/imir/reports/Undocumented%20workers%20Bulgaria%20report.pdf>.

Zhelyazkova, Antonina and Jørgen Nielsen. 2001. *The Fate of Muslim Communities in the Balkans. Vol. 8: Ethnology of Sufi Orders: Theory and Practice*. Sofia: IMIR.

Zhelyazkova, Antonina, Jørgen Nielsen, and Giles Kepel (eds.) 1995. Relations of Compatibility and Incompatibility between Christians and Muslims in Bulgaria. Sofia: IMIR.

# PART IV
# ISLAM AND EUROPEAN SECULARISM

CHAPTER 14

# THE INSTITUTIONALIZATION OF ISLAM IN EUROPE

SILVIO FERRARI AND ROSSELLA BOTTONI

## THE INSTITUTIONALIZATION OF ISLAM IN EUROPE: AN OVERVIEW

## Introduction

THE expression "institutionalization of Islam in Europe" holds two meanings that need to be properly distinguished (Rath et al. 2001: 6–8). First, it indicates the process of formation of organizations (associations, schools, mosques, and so on) that are designed to meet the needs of the Muslim population that lives in Europe. Normally it is a bottom-up process that starts from the initiatives of local Muslim communities, although it may be encouraged by their states of origin or residence. Second, the same expression is used to refer to the public recognition that these organizations can achieve: in this case, it is a top-down process that stems from the initiative of the public authorities which—at local, national, or supra-national level—acknowledge the social value of a Muslim organization and give it some kind of legal recognition. To give an example of these two dynamics, the creation of a Muslim school is only the first step in the process of institutionalization, which is completed when that school is recognized by the public authorities of a European country and included in its school system. It is obvious that these are two sides of the same coin: without the existence of Muslim organizations no public recognition is possible and without public recognition the existence of the Muslim organizations remains largely confined to the private sphere. It is also clear that this is a two-way process: the institutionalization not only involves the adjustment of Muslim communities to the European context in which they live, but also results in the change of this context as a consequence of their presence and public recognition (Tatari 2009: 283, 286). When these two processes do not walk at the same pace, tensions can easily emerge in the countries where the Muslim communities live: they can occur both when the legal recognition lags too long behind the emergence of Muslim organizations and when, on the contrary, it is given too soon, before they have acquired sufficient strength.

The first part of this chapter aims to provide a reading frame that allows to decrypt the process of institutionalization of Muslim immigrant communities in Europe in the second half of the last century, identifying its context, players, and dynamics.[1] The second part contains a critical survey of the writings devoted in the last few years to the concept of institutionalization of Islam and its main manifestations.

## The Context

The institutionalization of Islam in Europe does not take place inside an empty space. Muslims live in countries that have their own social organization, political structure, cultural identity: all these elements help to delineate the context within which the Muslim communities are to develop their own institutions. The importance of the context is so strong that one of the best comparative studies on the institutionalization of Islam in Europe concludes that "the outcome of the process of institutionalization is to a far greater degree determined by the societies in which Muslims settle, than by Muslims themselves" (Rath et al. 2001: 287).

At its deepest level this context is based on a number of cultural assumptions that are accepted as facts and most often remain implicit. The most important of them is the conviction that Islam is a religion that can be assimilated to Christianity and therefore can be regulated making use of the same principles that govern the relations between the states and the Christian churches. This is not new: Judaism underwent the same process of assimilation to Christianity and, starting from the Napoleonic era, it had to adopt an organizational model similar to that of the Christian churches.

The relations between states and religious communities in Europe are based on two principles: the distinction between politics and religion on the one hand and the cooperation between political and religious authorities on the other. Both principles derive from Christianity, but this origin has been obscured by the secularization of European public law that started after the wars of religion in the sixteenth and seventeenth centuries: at the end of an evolution that lasted for over two centuries, these two principles have been adopted even in the countries whose policy is inspired by secularism and the separation of church and state (Augsberg 2014; Ferrari 2014). They have therefore become a common heritage of Europe and apply to the relations between the states and all religious communities that reside in their territory, including those which do not give these two principles the same importance attributed to them in the Christian legal tradition.

The cultural context in which Muslims are placed requires, even in the most secular countries of Europe, the acceptance of these conditions: otherwise the Muslim

---

[1] In the first part of this chapter we shall not take into account the Muslim communities that have been permanently present in some parts of Europe since the days of Ottoman rule.

communities face significant difficulties in obtaining recognition by the public authorities and in completing their process of institutionalization.

The distinction between politics and religion, although operating in different and sometimes contradictory forms (as in the countries that still retain vestiges of a state church), lies beneath the public law of all European states: the principle that all citizens shall enjoy equal civil and political rights, regardless of their religious affiliation, is its most visible expression. This distinction is so important that its explicit acceptance is a precondition for the Muslim representative institutions that want to obtain the legal recognition by the state (Basdevant-Gaudemet 2004).

In Europe, the distinction between politics and religion goes hand in hand with the cooperation between political and religious authorities. This implies that the religious communities are to organize themselves in a way that makes possible their dialogue with state authorities. This requirement is the link that connects the cultural context, to which reference has been made so far, to the legal one.

All European countries support, albeit in different forms and degrees, the religious communities: almost all provide for the teaching of religion in public schools, and grant religious communities free access to public-owned media, many directly or indirectly finance religious organizations (Robbers 2005). This support is selective in the sense that it is not extended to all religious communities but only to those which fulfill some requirements. One of these is the ability of the religious group to set up—both at local and national level—representative institutions that can work as counterparts of state institutions in the management of the support the latter offer to religious communities. For example, in countries where a denominational teaching of religion is offered in public schools (as it is the case of Germany and Spain), it is impossible to teach any religion (including Islam) without the existence of a central religious authority, which prepares the list of the teachers who are authorized to teach that religion, cooperates with state agencies in training them, approves the curricula, and so on.

The creation of Islamic representative institutions at national level, however, is not enough to ensure effective cooperation with the state if there is no stable and clearly identifiable religious personnel that provide the link between the local entities and the central institutions of the Islamic community. For this reason the formation of a Muslim "clergy" has become another condition upon which the full inclusion of Islam in the system of relations between states and religions in Europe depends. Where these two conditions are met—for example in Austria—it has been possible to ensure the teaching of Islam in public schools, the building of mosques, and the public funding of Muslim communities (Aslan-Heinrich 2009); where they are not fulfilled, as in Italy, none of this has been done (Coglievina 2009).

Italy is not the only example of how slow and complicated is the process of institutionalization of Islam: similar difficulties affect many European countries. Part of the problem is the sudden acceleration of the process of institutionalization in the last few years. At the end of the last century, many scholars and politicians agreed that Muslim immigrants needed time to develop their own organizations and that it would have been a mistake to force upon their institutions a public role for which they were not yet ripe.

But September 11 radically altered the political context within which the process of institutionalization was placed.

The Twin Towers attack of September 2001 and what followed it have led most European governments, of whatever political color they were, to follow a strategy based on two priorities: (a) reducing the gap between the political and legal status enjoyed by the Muslim communities and by the other religious groups, in order to assuage the feeling of discrimination that could have fueled Islamic radicalism; (b) ensuring that the leadership of the Islamic organizations recognized by the state would fall into the hands of "moderate" Muslims. The first of these two priorities led some European states, France for example, to speed up the institutionalization of Islam by actively intervening in the process of formation of its representative institutions, even at the cost of heavily deviating from the separatist principles that had inspired the French church–state policy for over a century (Basdevant Gaudemet 2004; Bowen 2007: 1011–12); the second led other governments, that of Belgium for example, to exclude radical Muslims from the elections aimed at selecting the leadership of the Islamic organizations, even at the cost of deviating from the democratic principles that were intended to be affirmed (Foblets-Overbeeke 2004). In some European countries, therefore, the institutionalization of Islam has been pursued in a way that is doubly problematic: on one hand because it has empowered artificial and hardly representative Muslim institutions (Frégosi 2008) and on the other because it called into question principles—in particular the state respect of internal autonomy of religious communities—which were well established in the legal tradition of the European countries.

This last remark introduces a further element of complexity, showing that, while the Muslim communities have to accommodate to the cultural, legal, and political context within which they are placed, the context itself is modified by the presence of these communities. In fact, the European system of relations between states and religions is in transformation because it is no longer able to govern effectively the religious plurality of Europe, of which the increase of the Muslim population is one of the causes. It is not possible to analyze here the new characters that the relationship between states and religions is taking in Europe, but at least it should be noted that the institutionalization of Islam is at the same time a product of the context in which it takes place and a cause of its transformation (Rath et al. 2001: 12).

## The Players

Within the cultural, legal, and political context that has been described move the various players who, for different reasons, are involved in the process of institutionalization of Islam.

The first and most important of them are the Muslim communities which since the 1950s have settled in Europe. Their variety in terms of ethnic and national origins, political ideologies, and religious orientations fuels different strategies of institutionalization, but the latter have not yet been studied in the light of these background elements. As a consequence, the analysis of the institutionalization process is still framed within very broad and general categories.

The integration of Muslim communities in Europe has frequently been analyzed through the dialectic of individualization and institutionalization, in which a question of great political importance is implicit: will the integration of Islam in Europe happen through the individualization or the institutionalization of the Muslim religion? (Peter 2006: 105). Although this chapter focuses only on the second process, some brief reference to the first is helpful to provide the overall framework of the debate.

The term individualization refers to the emancipation of the young Muslim generations from traditional religious practices and doctrines, rooted in the social and ethnic heritage of their families: according to the analysis of some scholars, this process should result in a "liberated" Islam that, through the media of a global society, is able to take a critical distance from the cultural background inherited from the communities of origin (Kaya 2010: 47). This trend is contrasted to the process of institutionalization of Islam managed, in agreement with many European governments, by a group of Muslim "'religious brokers' who act as a buffer between their own religious communities and the state": their constituency is comprised by "faithful subjects who are ready to remain within the boundaries of the religious community without having the need to incorporate themselves in the mainstream society." Such a strategy is not without risks: it can result "in migrants not being perceived as full members of the receiving society" and can perpetuate their minority status (Kaya 2010: 51–60). But, others argue, the institutionalization of this "official" Islam is the only way to provide, in the name of the tradition, an alternative both to the reduction of Islam to a private affair and to the drift towards radical and fundamentalist positions.

The elements of weaknesses of these top-down processes of institutionalization of Islam are quite evident: in particular they are the scarce effectiveness of the "official" Muslim representative institutions, created more to meet the security needs of European governments than to respond to a real demand coming from the Muslim communities; their lack of any theological legitimacy and thus of the capacity to formulate and affirm a theological position susceptible to be accepted by the Muslim community at large; and their difficulty to free themselves from the conditionings placed on their actions by the states from which immigrant communities originate (see Frégosi 2008: 13).

These shortcomings have led some scholars to be wary of a process of institutionalization which excludes the younger and more dynamic Muslim generations and is in contrast with the loss of centrality of all religious institutions highlighted by the diffusion of new forms of belief at the edges of their boundaries (see Frégosi 2008: 13). Explicating the political fallout of this scientific analysis, other scholars have pointed out that "an excessive focus on organized forms of Islam [...] can be detrimental for an open democratic and Western political system" (Silvestri 2010: 55). The emphasis placed on its institutional profiles leads to understand Islam as a homogeneous entity based on some basic features which are common to all Muslims and make them capable to deliver univocal "Islamic answers" to the new challenges posed by the European context in which Muslim communities must find their place (Silvestri 2010: 54–5; see also Guolo 2007: 101–6): but this representation of Islam is far from reality.

However, the soundness of these findings does not mean that the theories based on individualization are exempted from criticism. To them it was opposed that the process of individualization is ambivalent: it can encourage the democratization of the religious sphere and the liberalization of doctrinal interpretations and religious practices but it can also favor the "predominance of fundamentalist interpretations" and the adoption of "strict doctrines that insist on personal responsibility and the duty of believers to follow Islamic prescriptions" (Cesari 2009: 152–3). From a different point of view it can also be noted that an approach focused on individualization of religious faith uncritically applies to Islam categories mainly derived from the transformation of European Christianity (Asad 1993).

These conflicting theories highlight the opportunity to overcome a rigid contraposition between individualization and institutionalization, as if one would necessarily exclude the other. As a consequence some scholars have suggested that the development of Muslim communities in Europe can escape the alternative between privatization of religious faith and revival of traditional religion and reconnect instead to the reformist currents which had developed in the Muslim world in the late nineteenth century. Although the soundness of this claim is yet to be demonstrated, it has the advantage of not conceiving the process of individualization "as something taking place in separation from institutionalized Islam" (Peter 2006: 110).

Along with Muslim communities, states and international organizations are another player to be taken into account. In this case a different dialectic has led the analysis of the scholars, that between national and international dimensions of the process of institutionalization of Islam in Europe. Koenig (2007) pointed out that the progress of European integration has paved the way for a transnational governance of the religious phenomenon, run by organizations like the Council of Europe and the European Court of Human Rights and based on the principles of religious freedom and equality: this new "post-national and multi-cultural paradigm of social order" tends to create "new legal frameworks, political opportunity structures and cultural repertoires for claims of religious recognition" (Koenig 2007: 913) and opens up new opportunities for the Muslim groups which are able to make use of this "transnational European platform of engagement with religion" (Silvestri 2009: 1229). At the same time, Koenig is aware of the uncertainties and limitations of this process, contrasted by the growing "re-interpretation of Church–State relations as symbols of national identity" (Koenig 2007: 928) and by the reaffirmation of the priority of domestic over international law in defining the context in which Islam must find its place. More than the birth of a "Euro-Islam," concludes Koenig, we should expect "the emergence of different institutional varieties of European Islam" (Koenig 2007: 929).

Koenig's contribution dates back to 2007 and the years that have passed since then have done nothing but confirm the "re-nationalization" of Europe. This trend supports Soper and Fetzer's (2007) call to focus the attention on the national systems of relations between states and religions, which influence and make different the way Islamic communities settle in each country. By analyzing the different models of institutionalization of Islam followed in three European countries, these authors "contend that the differences in how Britain, France and Germany have responded to Muslim religious needs are based on how those states have resolved Church–State issues in the past" (Soper and Fetzer 2007: 935). Although this observation is correct, church–state relations should not be considered as the only relevant factor, as rightly indicated by Tatari (2009): taken alone they cannot explain the process of institutionalization of Islam, which is the outcome of a complex interaction of different components (Laurence and Vaisse 2006).

If church–state relations were the key perspective to analyze and explain the process of institutionalization of Islam, one could wonder why countries with different systems—such as Italy, France, and Switzerland—face the same problems in dealing with issues like, for example, the building of mosques.

Considering the construction of mosques (but the same analysis can be applied to other profiles of the institutionalization of Islam), Maussen (2005) showed that the same event can acquire different meanings according to the political horizon in which it is placed: in one country the creation of a great center of Muslim prayer and teaching is considered as an element of integration of Islam in the European society, in another as an element of separation exploited by the fundamentalist fringes of Muslim communities to set up enclaves where norms and values antithetical to European culture are promoted and practiced.

These two views coexist and are interwoven in all European countries, whatever system of church–state relations is followed. They largely constitute the common ground on which—albeit with large fluctuations—takes shape the "Islamic politics" of most European States, oriented towards a "controlled institutionalization," in which the adjustment of the legal status of Islam to that of other religious communities is accompanied by requirements affecting the first but not the latter. The different church–state systems of the European countries explain how this political strategy is implemented but do not affect its contents and general direction. On closer inspection, there is nothing new: it is an updated version of the church–state policy that has been prevailing in Europe for a long time, based on the "control of religion by the state through selective recognition and support of religious institutions" (Bowen 2007: 1008).

Before closing the remarks devoted to the states and international organizations, it should be noted the lack of studies that examine in a comparative way the politics of the countries of origin of Muslim immigrants. Turkey, Morocco, and Algeria play an important role in promoting and controlling the institutionalization of Islam in Germany, France, Belgium, and other European countries: on the one hand they are keen to avoid that the leadership of the European Muslim communities falls in the hands of radicals who, expelled from their country of origin, migrated to Europe; and on the other they are interested in presenting themselves as interlocutors which European states should take into account when defining their immigration, security, and integration policies. The scarcity of researches aimed to comparing the strategies adopted by these states has so far prevented from giving the right emphasis, at European level, to this component of the institutionalization of Islam.

Finally, a last player has to be taken into account: the institutions of higher learning and their most prestigious leaders that are based outside of Europe but are capable through their decisions, of influencing the behavior of European Muslims (Bowen 2007: 1011). Their importance is due, in part, to the structural characteristics of the Muslim community, where a single center of authority does not exist, and partly to the weakness of the representative Muslim institutions created in Europe. But, once again, this situation is less exceptional than it may appear at first sight: for centuries English or French Catholics were accused of obeying a foreign authority, the pope, but this has not prevented in the long run their recognition as citizens as trustworthy and loyal as any other.

## The Dynamics

It has already been said that the institutionalization of Islam in Europe cannot be understood without examining, at the same time, the context in which it takes place: the presence of Muslim communities has changed the European system of relations between state and religion and the need to adjust to this system has changed the features of Muslim communities. The problem is further complicated by the fact that there is neither a single Islam nor a single system of religion–state relations in Europe: both terms—Islam and the European system of state–religions relations—are to be declined in the plural. Taking as an example the teaching of religion in public schools, the increasing number of Muslim students has raised the same question all over Europe: how to provide adequate information and knowledge about Islam. The answers have been different depending on the school system adopted by each state: some of them supply a non-denominational teaching of religion, aimed at providing a basic knowledge of the different religions practiced in a country; others offer classes where a specific religion is taught. In the first group of countries expanding the space dedicated to Islam in the school curricula has been relatively easy; in the latter group much more complex problems have arisen, mainly linked to the need to involve the Muslim community in the selection of teachers, the definition of textbooks, and so on. As a consequence, in the countries where a system of denominational teaching of religion is in place, the teaching of Islam is not always guaranteed.

Similar differences emerge when dealing with other issues, related to the creation and recognition of Muslim representative institutions, such as religious slaughter and the building of mosques (see the appendix table to this chapter). However, behind the wide range of arrangements that characterize the relations between European states and Muslim communities, it is possible to identify two dynamics that mark the entire process of institutionalization of Islam. Pluralism and neutrality are the best words to describe them.

It is quite evident that the progressive institutionalization of Muslim communities has forced all European legal systems to become internally more plural. A vigorous discussion about legal pluralism is taking place in many countries, led by "anthropologists, political scientists and legal specialists who consider how contemporary cultural and religious diversity challenges legal practice, how legal practice responds to that challenge and how practice is changing in the encounter with the cultural diversity occasioned by large-scale, post-war immigration" (Grillo et al. 2009: 1). This debate is still at an early stage and it is difficult to assess the impact it will have on the European legal systems. However, it is significant that the discussion is no longer confined to small academic circles: the 2008 speech of the Archbishop of Canterbury, Rowan Williams, advocating a system of "overlapping jurisdictions" in which "individuals retain the liberty to choose the jurisdiction under which they will seek" justice in certain specific areas (Williams 2008: 274), made the front page of all English newspapers.

This pluralistic drive has found different expressions from country to country: the debate on the recognition of Islamic law and the place that should be given to it in the state legal system is strong in Britain (Ahdar and Aroney 2010), but is almost nonexistent in Italy. However, in almost all European countries, the school system is open to the teaching of different faiths and the public funding of religions has been extended to religious groups that were previously excluded from it. In some cases Muslim communities are still deprived of the enjoyment of these rights, but it is probably only a matter of time before they are extended to them. All in all, the European public space is now much more plural than twenty or thirty years ago and this outcome is largely due to the institutionalization of Islam in Europe.

A more plural public space, however, is a less neutral public space. The neutrality of public space has been largely understood in Europe as the exclusion of religion from the public sphere and its confinement to the private life: the legal recognition of Islam, which represents the highest point of its process of institutionalization, runs counter this conception of neutrality. For example, a judicial system that enforces the "secular" state law upon all citizens regardless of their religious membership is functional to a neutral public space, not to a plural one (the compulsory civil marriage that is in force in some states is a good example of this system). On the contrary, a system that recognizes the validity of religious-based personal laws meets the demands of plurality (but not of neutrality) of the public space (think of those countries where it is possible to perform a state-valid marriage in different forms, secular and religious). This analysis explains why one of the institutions that have upheld with greater force the neutrality of the European legal and institutional systems, the European Court of Human Rights, has often rejected the Muslim request for a more plural structuring of the public space. The Court case-law on the Islamic headscarf is crystal clear on this point: the Court has always upheld the French and Turkish prohibition to wear the headscarf at school, considering this ban the best way to grant the neutrality of the public space (and implicitly discarding the possibility that neutrality can be granted through the inclusion in this space of different religious symbols) (Danchin 2011).

Islam is thus at the crossroads of tensions that affect the structure of the European public space, which some would like more plural and inclusive of different religions and others more neutral and less religiously characterized.

The integration of Islam in Europe through a process of institutionalization is in line with the first scenario, based on the plurality of the public space: the emphasis is on the Muslim communities and their organizations which, once legally recognized by the state, ensure the full inclusion of Islam in the European society. In this perspective, the public financing of Muslim communities, the introduction of shariah in the legal systems of the European states, and the teaching of Islamic religion in state schools play a central role. On the contrary, the integration of Islam in Europe through a process of individualization of the Muslim faith is more consistent with the other scenario, centered on the attainment of a neutral public space: in this case the accent falls on the protection of individual rights (even against the family, the group, the religious community to which a person belongs), in a context where the religious needs of every Muslim—exactly because they are expression of an individual interest—are answered in the private sphere. In this perspective the emphasis is placed on the right to change religion, to criticize the tenets of the Islamic doctrine, to have access to divorce on equal footing with the other spouse.

It is reasonable to assume that combining both dynamics—institutionalization and individualization—and scenarios—plurality and neutrality of the public space—is the most productive way to foster the integration of Muslims in Europe. However, it is by no means an easy matter. In this work the role of legal experts is of decisive importance, as they are trained to deal with the concrete problems that Muslims have to face—building of mosques, ritual slaughtering, creation of schools, and so on—through a case-by-case approach. This is the only way to overcome the ideological nature of the debates surrounding the presence of the Muslim communities in Europe.

# Literature Review on Institutionalization of Islam

## Introduction

As highlighted by Buijs and Rath (2006), there exists a vast body of literature on Islam, amounting to a few thousand books, essays, and reports, a significant part of which focus on the issue of institutionalization. This issue has been studied through different disciplinary approaches "that are in constant competition with each other. The fragmentation of the body of scholarly knowledge is contingent on disciplinary idiosyncrasies, on national research traditions and agendas, and on individual preferences for particular theoretical approaches. Anyone who wants to take part in Europe's research community must be aware of this heterogeneity" (Buijs and Rath 2006: 28). Because of the great variety of methodological approaches, research objectives, and examined issues, an exhaustive account of the existing literature would be merely descriptive. In order to offer an analytical and critical review, the second part of this chapter is more restricted in its scope.

In the first place, only books, edited volumes, and articles which have been published after 2006 will be examined in this chapter. Recent reviews of the contemporary literature on Muslims in Europe are contained in IMISCOE working papers by Buijs and Rath (2006) and Maussen (2007), and in the report prepared on behalf of the European Parliament by Dassetto, Ferrari and Maréchal (2007), where a number of issues—including the institutionalization of Islam and the accommodation of Islamic presence and practices—have been examined. It would be useless to repeat what is already contained in these reviews and bibliographies, which offer a solid starting point for our work.

In the second place, with very few exceptions, only scholarly works dealing with the institutionalization of Islam in a comparative perspective will be reviewed in these pages. This approach seems more helpful not only because this section follows the "national" chapters of this book that have focused on single-country studies, but also because of the intrinsic importance of comparative studies. As underlined by Cesari (2009), they provide a diachronic and synchronic interpretative key of the differences existing among European countries as regards the institutionalization of Islam, and they explain why different solutions have been adopted in different states and why such a process is more advanced in some countries and less in others. Not many scholars have taken up to this challenge, but those who have done so have produced an interesting corpus of literature.

## Notions and Uses of the Interpretative Category of "Institutionalization of Islam"

Before examining comparative studies on the institutionalization of Islam, it is useful to consider how this notion has been employed in contemporary literature, having regard to the lack of a single understanding of the expression "institutionalization of Islam."

Maussen (2005) has defined this process as the accommodation of Islamic practices, that is, the process of finding and making a place for Islam in Western European societies. Frégosi (2010) has adopted a similar definition, by identifying the specific areas where it is needed to find and make a place for Islam. Institutionalization of Islam is understood as the whole set of processes and legal and political mechanisms aimed to structure Muslim communities at local, national, and/or transnational level, to grant them the right to exercise religion in worship places, and to allow the development of Muslim associations and the recognition of certain practices within the framework of existing political and legal systems.

Whereas these definitions encompass a broader political and sociological dimension, other scholars have based their definition on a stricter legal ground. The institutionalization of Islam has been defined by Maréchal as "the official recognition by state agencies" of Islam (2003: 149) and by Rohe (2010) as the process of "recognition" of Muslim norms, for example in private international law, civil law, and social security law.

The different notions of the institutionalization of Islam result in different methodological approaches and study perspectives. Some scholars have identified the theoretical approaches through which this issue may be studied (Maussen 2005; Tatari 2009), whereas others have focused not so much on theory as on the thematic (Buijs and Rath 2006; Godard 2007; Silvestri 2007, 2010; Ferrari 2008; Rohe 2010) and geographical areas (Silvestri 2009) where this process takes place.

Maussen (2005) has regarded the institutionalization of Islam as an issue that can be approached through three different theoretical approaches, identified with reference to the theories on (a) resource mobilization, (b) national regimes of religious accommodation, and (c) political opportunity structures.

Resource mobilization theories focus on the attempts and ability of Muslim organizations and associations to mobilize and accomplish their objectives in the European countries, as in the case of the establishment of a mosque or a house of prayer. Religious accommodation approaches examine this issue from the perspective of the legal rules and administrative procedures regulating Islamic practices. Finally, the political opportunity structure is a dynamic conceptual model: "instead of analysing *either* the internal processes of mobilization of resources by Muslim organizations, *or* the legal framework and the regulation of Islam in different countries, this theory advocates the analysis of the *interactions* between the two" (Maussen 2005: 21). This third approach has been implicitly endorsed by Frégosi (2010). This author has highlighted that institutional dynamics aimed at making the presence of Islam visible and at officializing the permanent character of its inclusion are dependent not only on public regulation of Islam, but also on Muslim communities' strategies to take part in the political system in order to promote their "social normalization."

Tatari (2009) has noted that, besides the three theoretical approaches mentioned by Maussen, a fourth research perspective is commonly adopted by the social scientists who "contend that it is primarily national ideas about citizenship, nationhood and assimilation that determine the state response" to the accommodation of Muslim communities' religious needs (Tatari 2009: 279). The author has argued that a complex interpretative model is needed to understand the institutional framework of Islam (as well as of any other religion), which includes the Muslim minorities themselves as the fifth independent variable (besides the four already mentioned). Tatari has also underlined that Islam should not be regarded as a monolithic category, and studies on its institutionalization should take into account the diversities of local Muslim communities. This model, referred to as "dynamic-compound," aims at taking into account the interaction of these five components of the institutionalization of Islam. Their different combination explains the differences among European states in the accommodation of Muslims' religious practices.

A second group of scholars has not focused on theoretical approaches but has identified the thematic areas where the institutionalization of Islam takes places. The broadest approach is the one adopted by Buijs and Rath (2006), who have mentioned as many as seven (sometimes overlapping) spheres: religious (concerning the right to religious freedom of Muslim organizations, and the accommodation of issues such as religious leaders, festivals, practices, and places of worship); legal (legal recognition of religious practices and provisions, for example in family law); educational (religious education, training of religious leaders, diffusion of knowledge and values through the media); socio-economic (slaughterhouses, financial institutions, business associations, unions); socio-cultural (associations supporting women, children, old people; music, sports clubs; etc.); health and social care (circumcision, spiritual assistance in hospitals, prisons, and barracks); and political (creation of political organizations and parties, political participation).

Other scholars have considered the institutionalization of Islam mainly, but not exclusively, in the area of the creation of Muslim representative organizations and their legal recognition. The reading of two essays (Silvestri and Godard 2007) in an edited book on European Islam suggests that this process not only involves the creation of representative organizations, but also their emergence as political actors and the development of dynamic relations with other forces and subjects. Silvestri, in particular, has underlined that in the last two decades there have been attempts to create Islamic consultative bodies that have been the result not so much of Muslim communities' initiatives as of European governments' wish to establish representative institutions. This strategy was inspired by the need to react to such communities' "disorganization," on the one side, and to exclude external interlocutors like the governments of Muslim countries, on the other side. Such a policy has also sought to ensure that national/European forms of Islam are developed according to a "moderate" *Weltanschauung*. In this perspective, Laurence has studied institutionalization as a process of centralization, domestication, re-territorialization, and de-transnationalization. A state seeks an alliance "within its Islamic community in order to assert its *national* sovereignty" (2012: 133), as a form of "damage control in defense of national unity" (2012: 132). Because challenges are posed not only by political Islam and terrorism, but also by foreign government control (defined by the author as "Embassy Islam"), governments have recognized that integration of Muslims "require the reining in of certain transnational characteristics of religious communities" (2012: 155). Given these premises, it may be understood why the outcomes of the creation of Islam Councils in Europe (with a view to moderate political Islam and excluding Embassy Islam) are regarded as "imperfect institutionalization" (2012: chapter 6).

In the process of institutionalization meant as creation of Islamic consultative bodies, Silvestri has also noted that European states expect that "such institutions should be in place if Muslims want to 'earn' a place in the complex mechanisms of governance in EU institutions and member states" (2010: 48) and require that the Islamic communities develop structures similar to those of the Christian churches, in order to fit in the national systems of relations between state and religious denominations. Fuess (2007), too, has stressed that states relate to Muslim communities also on the basis of the existing institutional arrangements developed in the course of time in the interplay with Christian churches. In doing so, they do not take into account the organizational differences between Islam and other religions that are more hierarchically structured. This Eurocentric and "Christianocentric" approach is likely to raise a number of problems: for example, not all Muslim citizens or residents in the European countries are willing to identify themselves with such an artificial representative body (Silvestri 2010: 52).

When the institutionalization of Islam is understood as the creation and legal recognition of Muslim representative organizations, Ferrari (2008) has also warned of the danger that European states conceive this process as the precondition not only for the establishment of effective forms of cooperation with state authorities, but also for the exercise of the right to religious freedom and the respect of the internal autonomy of the Muslim communities, that is for the enjoyment of rights that should be available also to non-institutionalized religious groups.

Another thematic area has been explored by Rohe (2010), who has studied the institutionalization of Islam as the process of "recognition" of Muslim norms, by stressing that this dynamic should not be understood as "silent or even overt 'Islamization' of the legal system in force... It is simply the law of the land which itself opens the door to the application of 'foreign' norms within well-defined limits" (2010: 150).

Finally, the issue of the institutionalization of Islam has not been examined only by identifying either the related theoretical approaches or the thematic areas where this process takes place, but also by studying its "geography." The prevalent focus on the national context is justified by a number of considerations, among which are the relevance of European countries' specific cultural and historical tradition that has shaped state–religions relations, and their sovereign competence to manage such relations (Silvestri 2009). However, as a number of studies have highlighted, countries are not the exclusive place where the institutionalization of Islam takes place. According to Maussen, studies should not focus on the government's responses and on state accommodation of Islam only, but rather on "different units, modes and domains of governance" (2007: 62), including the government's different institutional levels (from municipal to federal), private actors, networks of organizations, and transnational movements. As regards public actors, at infra-national level, municipalities, regions, and (where it applies) federate states are important actors of this process. At supranational level, the same role may be played by the European Union (EU).

In another study (2009), Maussen has highlighted in particular the need that scholars studying national accommodation policies also take into account the relevance of municipal choices, which may interpret and apply national arrangements in a different way. This is especially true for the balancing of different—and sometimes opposing—interests raised by religious demands that can be effectively met only at local level, as is the case of the building of places of worship. For this reason, in his study on Islam's institutionalization in France and the Netherlands as regards the creation, development, and functioning of mosques, the author devotes two chapters to two municipal case studies (Marseilles and Rotterdam). Although he warns that these municipalities' patterns should not be regarded as representative for the two countries, he nonetheless highlights the importance of differences that can be identified not only between countries (France vs. the Netherlands) but also between local institutions (Marseille vs. Rotterdam) authorities.

Maussen's remark, according to which the study of the institutionalization of Islam at local level offers a wider and more accurate picture than the description of the national legislation and institutional framework, highlights the importance of works carrying out comparative studies not only between two or more different countries, but also within the same country. Ipgrave, Miller, and Hopkins have compared three English primary schools, "focusing on the approaches of teachers and school leaders to the faith backgrounds of their pupils, their constructions of Islam for these educational contexts, and their preparation of Muslim children for a religiously plural Britain" (2010: 73). Their research results will be examined below. What should be noted here is the fact that this comparative approach enables to take into account important variables in studies concerning the degree of Islam's institutionalization in a given country by stressing that not all Muslim communities within the same territory may present the same level of institutionalization. Soper and Fetzer (2007), too, have noted that the situation of Muslim communities in Germany varies according to the different *Länder*, because the same religious demands are accommodated by some and rejected by others. This is the case of the wearing of the Islamic headscarf by teachers in schools and, in some cases, by other categories of public officials, which is allowed in eight of the sixteen *Länder*, and prohibited in the other half.

Finally the EU should not be considered an uninterested and insignificant actor in religious affairs merely on the grounds of its official narrow competence in this field. More importantly, it should not be regarded as "a simple juxtaposition of individual countries in which religions are embedded and operate in relation to national interests and national history" (Silvestri 2009: 1213). In this perspective, a few studies have started to be carried out that highlight the EU's specific religious sensitivity, its supranational political dimension, its peculiar institutional arrangements with faith communities, including Islam, as well as informal policies towards them (Silvestri 2009: 1214ff.). At the same time, special care should be taken when including the EU in studies on the institutionalization of Islam: for purposes of brevity and for customary reasons, it is common to refer to the EU as a homogeneous entity, but in fact this is an organization composed of several institutions, which may have different preoccupations when dealing with faith communities and, in particular, with those that are perceived as more controversial, like Islam. These are especially the cases of the European Commission and the European Parliament: the first focuses on the diplomatic accommodation of tensions while the second, being naturally the venue of the democratic politics, represents the place where most (if not all) opinions concerning the (in)opportunity and the (un)desirability to institutionalize Islam are voiced (Silvestri 2009: 1228ff.).

## Comparative Studies on Islam's Institutionalization

In this section the different variables taken into consideration when studying the institutionalization of Islam are examined, and some specific topics—religious slaughter, the building of mosques, and education—are analyzed as test-cases for the application of these variables.

From the very beginning it should be stressed that a single model followed by all countries does not exist: each state has found or has to find the one more consistent with its own cultural and social reality. For example, as regards the issue of representation (directly linked, as mentioned above, to that of Islam's institutionalization), France and Belgium have supported the creation of a single institution representing all Muslims at the national level; Spain has opted for a federation of associations reflecting the theological, ethnic, and political variety existing in Spanish Islam; Sweden and the Netherlands are characterized instead by the pluralism of legal entities representing the interests of local Muslim communities (Ferrari 2008; Shadid and van Koningsveld 2008). Because of the variety of the national solutions, the studies that have examined the situation of Muslims in different European countries and within the same country in a comparative perspective are especially important.

Some are purposely descriptive (for example, Kreienbrink and Bodenstein 2010) but are no less significant. This is especially the case of the *Yearbook of Muslims in Europe* (Nielsen 2009–11), covering forty-six states, which represents the most updated instrument to obtain information in particular on countries such as Albania and Bosnia and Herzegovina, on which there were virtually no comprehensive data.

Other studies are more analytical and have identified a number of variables explaining the differences in the development and outcomes of the process of Islam's institutionalization. Variables may be grouped in two categories. The first focuses on characteristics peculiar to each country that, as such, may affect the institutionalization not only of Muslim communities but also of other religious minorities. Among them are religious demography (that is, the relatively religious homogeneity existing in European countries), religious traditions, legal systems to manage state–religions relations, socio-economic structure, political culture, notion of citizenship, and dynamics of immigrants' settlement. The second category includes some differentiating factors among Muslim communities themselves (be them in different countries or within the same state), for example their origin (some communities are historical, while others are the result of the immigration process and, in the latter case, their geographical origin matters, too); their will and/or ability to take advantage of the available opportunities; the concerns raised by their more or less pronounced radicalization.

## Country-Related Variables

A variable that is taken into account by virtually all studies directly or indirectly focused on Islam's institutionalization is the national system of state–religions relations (see among others Godard 2007; Maussen 2009; Fuess 2007). For example, in his comparative study of Portugal and Ireland, Pais Bernardo has stated that these states "share structural similarities at a socio-religious level—Catholicism is majoritarian—and politically—centralized political systems" (2009: 7). Nonetheless, the process of institutionalization of Islam has been achieved to a different extent and with different modalities in the two countries. According to the author, Ireland's soft separatism, compared to Portugal's concordatarian model, has made the accommodation of religious diversity and, thus, of Islam easier.

The church–state system variable is certainly useful to describe the framework where the process of Islam's institutionalization takes place, but it cannot explain alone its development and outcomes. As correctly noted by Maussen (2007), legal surveys and case studies should incorporate insight in the social context and applications of laws, regulations, and policies. Sakaranaho (2006) has chosen to compare Ireland and Finland because they are two religiously homogeneous countries (the majority of the population being Catholic in the former, and Evangelical Lutheran in the latter) that are gradually evolving into multicultural societies (inter alia) because of the increase of Muslim immigrants. This development, in turn, requires the elaboration and implementation of new policies concerning the integration of religious minorities. Both countries have a majority church enjoying a number of privileges (either from a legal or a social point of view) in comparison to other religious communities; at the same time, they have granted a part of such advantages to (some or all) minorities, according to a pattern which the author has called a "model of extended privileges." Despite these similarities, the accommodation of Muslim religious demands has not produced the same results. For example, in Finland there is no purpose-built mosque, whereas Ireland has two of them. This difference cannot be explained on the grounds of religious demography and the evolving system of state–religions relations, but by taking into account another variable, that is the diverse economic position of the Irish Muslim communities, which are generally more affluent than their Finnish counterparts.

An important country-related variable concerns the dynamics of immigrants' settlement, which undoubtedly influences the process of Islam's institutionalization. Rohe (2006) has described four patterns of the relationship between Islam's institutionalization and the more general dynamics through which immigrants (who still make up a sizeable percentage of Muslims in European countries) settle in the host state: (1) assimilation, which requires the immigrants' renunciation of their own identity and the adoption of the residents' ones; (2) overlap of different cultures, that is, the opposite of the first model; (3) segregation, which implies the lack of any contacts and exchanges between immigrants and residents; (4) acculturation, which enriches both components of the population through the acquisition of each other's cultural elements. For example, in his study of the mosques issue in France and the Netherlands, Maussen (2009) has considered French cultural assimilation and Dutch pluralism and multicultural integration, among other variables.

## Muslim Communities-Related Variables

Because the country-related variables determining the dynamics and outcomes of Islam's institutionalization (for example, the national system of state–religions relations or dynamics of immigrants' settlement) may be the same affecting similar processes for some of the other religious minorities, a different set of variables—concerning specifically Muslim communities and their own peculiar characteristics—needs to be taken into account.

In this perspective, an important factor is Muslims' historical origin. In a number of European countries, Muslims are a very small community but have been resident for centuries. This is the case, inter alia, of Baltic and Balkan states (Larsson 2009; Norris 2009). Some countries dealt with Muslim communities during their colonial or imperial past (France and the United Kingdom on the one hand, Austria on the other), while others (Italy, Spain, and Germany) have started hosting them as a result of more or less recent immigration waves (Godard 2007). How Muslims' varied historical origin has affected Islam's institutionalization has been explored by scholars in different ways.

Some scholarly works have studied Islam's institutionalization dynamics in the past (Cimbalo 2008; Clayer and Germain 2008) highlighting that what seems to be today a new problem was already tackled in the course of history by a number of European states, and dealt with successfully. Cimbalo in particular has noted that Balkan Islam is often overlooked or neglected, also (or maybe above all) because Muslim communities are integrated and largely share the same values that are prevalent in the societies where they reside. For this reason, they are not regarded as needing protection. According to the author, this lack of consideration is a mistake which reduces the European states' awareness of the existence of positive experiences of accommodation of both Western values and Muslim needs. Although such a synthesis has been the outcome of a long historical process, it proves that religious pluralism may be promoted without undermining contemporary democracies. Maussen (2009) has compared France and the Netherlands, two colonial powers that, before experiencing large waves of immigration from Muslim countries, ruled over Muslim populations. However, the French colonial regime pursued a civilization mission, whereas the Dutch were more interested in economic exploitation. Such differences (considered along with other variables) may explain the two countries' different notions of citizenship which, as noted above, contribute to develop dynamics of Islam's institutionalization in one way rather than another one.

History plays an important role not only as cultural legacy, but also in its stricter meaning of passing of time. Maussen (2009) has examined mosque-related policies in an historical perspective, because the development of public policy discussions, as defined by governing strategies and public opinion trends, changes over time. The author has highlighted that both national and local responses are not static, and differences can be identified not only between countries (France vs. the Netherlands) or local institutions (Marseille vs. Rotterdam), but also within the same country or municipality in the passing of time. As regards the issue of funding, at the beginning of the 1990s the Dutch government changed its policy. It decided that immigrants' worship houses would not be funded directly, but municipal authorities tried nonetheless to help Muslims by assisting them in the search for appropriate premises and locations or by using indirect ways of financial support. In France, the idea of a direct funding of mosques was inconceivable until the first half of the 1990s, and some cities like Marseilles further implemented policies to prevent Muslim communities from improving their worship conditions and building better houses of prayer or mosques. In the second half of the decade, the situation changed and several French municipalities not only became more supportive and accommodating, but in some cases they even ended up funding the building of worship places.

Muslims' geographical origin can be diverse, like in France, where there are communities coming from different African countries, or relatively homogeneous, like Turks in Germany (Godard 2007). Like other variables, this one alone cannot determine a high or low degree of Islam's institutionalization. In the French case, the contrasts among the different national communities have limited the effectiveness of Islam's representative body. In Germany, the Muslim Turk community's importance has favored the inclusion of the teaching of Islam in public schools but, because its recipients are Turks, this course is often taught in Turkish (and sometimes includes element of Turkish language and culture), which results in a lower institutionalization of non-Turk Muslim communities' educational needs.

Another variable that helps to explain the degree and the dynamics of Islam's institutionalization in a given country is the extent to which Muslim communities take advantage of the available opportunities. An example is offered by Sakaranaho (2006). In Finland, a number of rights are recognized to registered religious communities, but Muslims seem reluctant to use this option: in fact, out of approximately 30,000 Muslims only 3,000 belong to a registered Islamic community. At the same time, this does not seem to result necessarily in discrimination because, while registered members must attend Islamic religion as a compulsory course in public schools, those who are not have the choice between three options: the teaching of Islam, of Lutheran religion, or of ethics and philosophy of life. As for Irish Muslim communities, they have adopted the structure of charitable organizations, taking advantage of the fact that, differently from predominantly Protestant countries like Finland, Muslims are not required to become members of a registered religious community, and, unlike other predominantly Catholic countries, Ireland does not require the existence of a single representative body for the establishment of dialogue and cooperation with the Muslim communities.

The concern about Muslim communities' radicalization is a further factor taken into account by some scholars to assess the degree and the dynamics of Islam's institutionalization. Godard has maintained that these concerns have "certainly accelerated the processes of recognizing official bodies representing the Muslim faith" (2007: 184). According to the author, European countries, albeit to different degrees, have recognized Muslim communities in order to counteract the danger of religious fundamentalism. But accommodation of Muslims' religious demands occurs above all when these communities are not regarded as a threat to public order or national security, as is the case of Finland and Ireland. This may explain why neither country has experienced conflicts over the display of religious symbols comparable to those occurred in other Western European countries (Sakaranaho 2006). At the same time (and this remark highlights both the strict interconnection of several variables and the need to adopt a dynamic research perspective) an important role is played by time. Radicalization may occur over time. Likewise, Islam-related perceptions may change over time. As noted by Allievi (2009), as new generations take the place of the first waves of Muslim immigrants, Islam is perceived as less threatening; on the other hand, crises may also occur in contexts where its presence has been longer and more stable, producing negative effects on the process of institutionalization.

## *The Interplay Among Variables*

The more variables are taken into account, and the more the interaction between state and Muslim communities is examined in a dynamic and not in a static way—the more comprehensive and exhaustive research results can be attained. For example, Silvestri has focused on the "socio-economic structures, legal frameworks, past histories, political cultures, and opportunities available" (2011: 187). The dissimilarities produced by the different combination and impact of such factors can be relevant, like in the case of the United Kingdom and Italy, which are characterized by a significant gap. The British process of institutionalization of Islam is a dynamic one: grassroots Muslim mobilization is very strong, and communities have addressed successfully their religious and cultural needs and have multiplied initiatives of cooperation with state agencies. By contrast in Italy "concerns about Muslims are still primarily seen through the lenses of immigration and citizenship": therefore, "until this issue is resolved it is doubtful that Muslims will be able to participate fully in Italian society and politics" (2011: 186). However, "holistic" approaches are rare, and one should be aware that they cannot always be adopted because of the aforementioned variety of scientific backgrounds, theoretical and methodological approaches, and individual research preferences.

The way the different combination of variables influences the degree and the dynamics of the process of Islam's institutionalization can be better exemplified by studying the accommodation of specific religious demands. Religious slaughter, the building and funding of mosques, and the integration of Islamic religious education in European countries' school system can be taken into account as test-cases.

*(i) Religious slaughter.* Although these studies (Ferrari and Bottoni 2010, Lerner and Rabello 2006–7) have not directly addressed the issue of Islam's institutionalization, they are nonetheless worth mentioning because the accommodation of Muslims' religious practices—including the most hotly debated ones, like the right to slaughter animals according to the Islamic rite—is part of the process of institutionalization. The conclusion that can be drawn from the comparison of the legal regulations and practices on religious slaughter in European countries is that each country's policy is hardly determined by its system of state–religions relations. For example, France, where the principle of secularism requires that the public space remains religiously neutral, has been the most accommodating country in the management of the emergency situation that occurs every year on the occasion of the Aid el-Kebir festival, "when a great number of animals are slaughtered and slaughterhouses cannot meet the requests coming from local Muslim communities, for operational reasons or because of restrictions on the maximum number of animals that can be killed or yet other reasons. In such a context in the 90s, France's municipal authorities tried to meet such requests, by allowing 'exemption sites', that is, temporary structures outside slaughterhouses." This practice changed only after 1999, when France was called to order by the Veterinary Office of the European Union and warned that it would be heavily fined if it continued to breach the

European Directive, which requires that any slaughter of animals is carried out inside a slaughterhouse (Ferrari and Bottoni 2010: 15).

Nowadays, European countries regulate religious slaughter on the basis of a compromise between two principles, which are regarded as conflicting. The first is the increasing awareness of animal welfare, which grounds the prohibition to slaughter without previous stunning, because this practice is considered as inflicting unnecessary pain. The second one is the protection of the fundamental human right to religious freedom. When the first principle is regarded as overriding, then religious slaughter without previous stunning is forbidden (this is the case of a few countries including Switzerland, Norway, and Sweden). In contrast, when a state (and these are the majority in Europe) considers the carrying out of religious slaughter as one of the rights comprised by the concept of religious freedom, then it also allows a derogation from the requirement to stun animals before religious slaughter. Solutions, however, are not always clear-cut (prohibition vs. permission), which also explains the difficulty to assess the degree of Islam's institutionalization or accommodation of one specific religious practice. For example, Germany allows the carrying out of religious slaughter without previous stunning only for religious communities whose mandatory rules require slaughter without stunning or prohibit consumption of meat of animals not slaughtered in this way. Because this requirement is fully complied with only by Jewish communities (some Muslim communities in Germany accept pre-stunning provided that it does not cause the death of the animal to be slaughtered), a great number of courts have not granted exemption to perform religious slaughter to Muslim communities, on the grounds that no specific Islamic religious rule explicitly forbids the consumption of meat from animals stunned before slaughter.

*(ii) Building and funding of mosques.* The previous example highlights the importance of another variable, which should be taken into account by studies on Islam's institutionalization but instead is regrettably neglected: the degree of institutionalization of other religious minorities. The inclusion of this factor in the analysis would help to better assess the significance of the accommodation of Muslims' specific religious demands (and especially the most controversial ones, like the building and funding of mosques) within the whole process of Islam's institutionalization. Allievi has noted that in a number of European countries conflicts over mosques have taken place, albeit in different forms and frequency. Although no unequivocal answer can be given to the question of whether conflicts over mosques are increasing or decreasing, in France, the United Kingdom, and Belgium, their number seems to be declining or has remained small; the opposite is true as far as Germany, Austria, Italy, Spain, and Greece are concerned. In other countries, such as the Netherlands and Sweden, it is not so much the number of conflicts that has increased, but their intensity. Thus, local conflicts over mosques are less frequent and less intense where Islam is more institutionalized at national level. In fact, the real issue does not seem to be the building of mosques, but the presence of Islam; the conflict is focused on Islam's visible symbols, but actually revolves around its doctrine and practices. This means that "there are not many other ways available to bring the debate out into the public arena: that the conflict is an extraordinary way of

addressing an issue that is itself ordinary" (Allievi 2009: 86). Muslim communities have often seemed resigned to accept the hostility they face; further, the fact that only few of them have reported the attacks against their places of worship suggests that there is "a serious potential danger that is created not by the Islamic community but by movements of opinion and groups of activists mobilizing against them" (2009: 85).

Although this and other studies (Maussen 2009; Allievi 2010) are specifically focused on Islam's institutionalization in a particular field (the building and, in some cases, funding of Islamic places of worship), and do not purposely widen their research perspective, one should be careful to draw from them general conclusions on the *whole* process of institutionalization of Islam. In other words, its degree of success (or failure) should not be assessed in absolute terms, but should rather be compared with the degree of institutionalization of other religious minorities. In this way, what is sometimes perceived as the "Islamic exceptionalism" might prove to be a common problem experienced by other marginalized communities (Cesari 2007: 49ff.; Allievi 2009: 7): this is the case, for example, of the Witnesses of Jehovah and the obstacles they face in many countries (just like the Muslims) to build places of worship as well as to obtain the recognition of legal personality as a religious denomination (and not merely as a private association).

*(iii) Education.* Different strategies to integrate Islamic religious education in European countries' school systems result in differences as to the dynamics and outcomes of Islam's institutionalization. A first example is offered by the comparison of the regulations concerning the teaching of Islamic religion in public schools in France or Italy. Islam is taught in neither country. However, France forbids the teaching of any religion in public schools, whereas Italy stipulates that only the Catholic religion or the religions of the eleven denominations that have signed an agreement with the state (that is, eight Christian Churches, the Jewish Union, the Buddhist Union, and the Hindu Union) can be taught. This means that a comparable situation in two different countries (lack of the teaching of Islamic religion in public schools) does not necessarily allow drawing the same conclusions on the dynamics of the process of Islam's institutionalization. A second example is offered by Shadid and van Koningsveld in their comparative study on Islam in the Netherlands and Belgium (2008). Whereas there are approximately forty Dutch Islamic primary schools, only one is operational in Belgium. However, these differences should be evaluated in the light of the national provisions concerning the teaching of Islam in public schools: in Belgium there have been legal arrangements since the 1970s that have provided for the inclusion of Islamic religion in public schools' curricula; by contrast, the Dutch educational system has always favored the creation of ideologically or religiously-oriented private schools. The same context has been highlighted by Sakaranaho (2006). Islamic private schools are active in Ireland, whereas they are still at a planning stage in Finland. This difference has been explained by noting that Ireland tends to favor the establishment of denominational private schools much more than Finland (see the appendix table at the end of the chapter). Further, the teaching of Islam is offered as an optional course by Finnish public schools. Thus, in these cases, it would not be correct to draw the conclusion that Muslims' educational needs are not accommodated by Belgium and Finland because of the lack of available opportunities to

establish an Islamic private school, overlooking that these countries have arranged different institutional facilities (the teaching of Islam in public schools).

In fact, as studies on this issue reveal (see among others Pépin 2009; Schreiner et al. 2007), a number of countries meet the educational needs of Islamic religious communities by giving preference to either the inclusion of the teaching of Islamic religion in public schools' curricula or the establishment of Islamic private schools. The former is the case of Germany; the latter of the Netherlands and the United Kingdom (Niehaus 2009). Where Islam is included in the national curriculum, it is taught either as Islamic religious education (for example in Belgium, Austria, Spain, Finland) or within a non-denominational religious course (for instance in the United Kingdom, Sweden, Norway); the Dutch school system allows the teaching of Islam both in a non-denominational religious course or in a specific one devoted to Muslim religion, provided there is a request by a sufficient number of pupils or their parents (Fuess 2007). According to Jozsa (2007), countries may be divided not only according to whether the teaching of Islam is denominational or non-denominational: they may also be differentiated by looking to who is in charge for the organization of the religious classes. The author has identified three patterns as religious education may be "in the solely responsibility of religious communities, in the solely responsibility of the state and with shared responsibility between state and religious communities" (2007: 70). For example, in the Austrian public schools the teaching of Islam is managed and controlled by the Islamic Religious Community. On the one side, this reflects a high degree of institutionalization of Islam but, on the other, it may also produce negative effects on the social integration of a part of Austrian Muslims insofar as religious education is based on the Sunni doctrine and is carried out in cooperation with the Egyptian University of al-Azhar, neither of which represent the whole Muslim community in the country.

In some countries (like Switzerland) Islamic private schools do not exist and Islam is not taught in public schools; in others, Muslims enjoy both options (Fuess 2007). There are also solutions other than the teaching of Islam in public schools and the creation of Islamic private schools: the attendance of Qur'anic courses in the afternoons or during the weekends, where nonetheless pupils do not have the opportunity to become familiar with a multicultural environment and are taught by teachers whose qualifications may be dubious (Niehaus 2009); the teaching of Islam in non-Muslim denominational institutes, as is the case of some Catholic private schools in Austria (Fuess 2007).

The aforementioned situations mainly describe the impact of national school systems that, as such, generally concern the entire population, but the importance of variables regarding specifically Muslims and of their interplay with country-related variables must be equally assessed. The institutional facilities arranged by each state to meet specific educational needs are not made available to all religious communities. As far as Islamic private schools are concerned, Daun (2008) has noted that these schools are most numerous in Greece and the Netherlands and, after taking into account other European countries as well, he has concluded that immigration seems to be the most important factor that explains the increasing number of Muslim schools. There are nonetheless important exceptions to this pattern. As the author himself has admitted, "[a]lthough the percentage of immigrants in [the Netherlands] is not higher than in Belgium, England, France, and Germany, for example, the country has many more Muslim schools than any other country" (2008: 362). It should be added that Greece too does not fit smoothly into this interpretative model: Islamic private schools are not equally distributed on the national territory, but they are concentrated in Western Thrace. This region, in fact, enjoys a special status granted by the international treaties on the protection of minorities signed in the first half of the twentieth century, and Islamic communities residing there are entitled to a set of rights, which are not recognized to Muslims living in other regions of Greece.

The Greek example allows us to introduce two important remarks concerning the dynamics of Islam's institutionalization. The first one is the assessment of the importance of Muslim communities' historical origin in order to enjoy a number of rights or privileges (in this perspective, also see Nalborczyk 2011). The second one is the consideration that the outcomes of the process of Islam's institutionalization are different not only in different countries, but also within the same country. This issue, albeit in another context, has been explored by Ipgrave, Miller, and Hopkins (2010), who have compared the accommodation of Muslims' educational needs in three British primary schools. Like in other European countries, the great majority of Muslims in the United Kingdom are educated in public schools. Therefore, two of the three examined schools are non-denominational community schools that, like other public schools, have to find a balance between the parents' demands to promote their children's religious background and the need to ensure that the development of their religious identity does not result in the increase of current trends towards segregation and does not endanger their education to democratic citizenship. By contrast, the third institute is an Islamic school, which does not provide the typical education that most English Muslim pupils receive but offers nonetheless the schooling environment where, according to polls, almost half of Muslim parents would like their children to be educated. The results of this comparative study reveal that the different educational approaches are not two, but three—that is, as many as the examined schools. In one public school, Islam is "neutralized." Children receive a secular education, and religious difference is regarded as a potentially disturbing factor to social cohesion. The other public school regards Muslims' religious identity as a positive element in the educational process and allows public expressions of faith. Finally, the Islamic school obviously emphasizes all aspects related to Islam in life and learning but, at the same time, pays special attention to encourage the students' engagement in the wider society and to prevent inward-looking attitudes.

These remarks explain why, in the study where Islamic schools in the Netherlands and the United Kingdom are compared, Niehaus does not offer a definitive reply to the question as to whether they "promote processes of identity formation within a democratic society or whether they rather lead to disengagement from the wider society." As the author has noted, there exist considerable differences in "size, structure, management, academic results, and religious as well as pedagogical outlook" (2009: 113), and a high heterogeneity "in terms of internal regulations, educational approaches and Islamic practices" (2009: 116) among Muslim schools. An Islamic school as such does not necessarily convey a set of values which are incompatible with those inspiring the education philosophy in public schools. A number of Muslim institutes use the same textbooks and materials that are adopted in public schools, or teach the same national curriculum without any change: thus, they do not characterize themselves as "Islamic schools" (that is, as schools promoting Islamic identity) but rather as "schools for Muslims" (in other words, attended mainly by pupils of Islamic religion). Having in mind these preliminary remarks, Niehaus has highlighted the differences existing between the two countries. Muslims represent most of the staff members in British Islamic schools, but only up to a quarter in the Dutch ones. As a consequence, Dutch Muslim students are usually regarded as better equipped to engage in an inter-cultural and inter-religious dialogue with people professing a different religion or having a different *Weltanschauung*: this in turn, reduces (or is supposed to reduce) the risk of developing divisive and exclusionary patterns of behavior towards the wider society. A second difference lies in the strategies adopted to pursue social cohesion. In the United Kingdom, many Islamic schools (especially those that are funded by the state) are required to adapt their programs and curricula in order to actively promote democratic citizenship. In the Netherlands, this issue has been dealt with in a different way, by encouraging socio-economic integration: in other words, Islamic schools are treated as "black schools," whose students mostly come from marginalized families. Therefore, "a shift has occurred from focusing on identity formation to improving academic standards and quality of education" (Niehaus 2009: 123).

## Which Type of Comparison?

"We need"—Cesari writes (2009: 169)—"to compare Muslims with other contemporary religious groups and the present situation to past historical precedents in Western societies". In other words, to understand the current formation of Islamic identities in Europe "it is necessary to take into account how other immigrant groups from other religious traditions [...] integrate into a given society" and "how religious groups that are now settled [...] experienced this integration process in earlier historical periods."

Few scholars doubt that comparison is the best way to understand the integration of Muslim communities in Europe. Therefore Cesari's appeal must be carefully considered, particularly because it makes reference to both synchronic and diachronic comparison. From the first point of view, the current degree of institutionalization of Islam must be assessed contrasting it with the degree of institutionalization reached today by other comparable religious communities. The key word here is "comparable." There is little point in comparing the problems raised by the building of a mosque and those connected to the building of a Catholic church in Italy or Spain: such an analysis would confirm what we already know, that is the selective character of the church–state systems of the European countries. In contrast, it could make sense comparing a mosque and a place of worship of the Jehovah's Witnesses. Although the two religions and religious communities are completely different, they share the fact of being relatively new and (albeit for

Table 14.1 Comparative table on the institutionalization of Islam in Europe[1]

| Country | Legal recognition of Islam and/or Muslim communities[2] | Existence of a representative body | Places of worship | Legal rules on religious slaughter | Teaching of Islam in public schools | Private Islamic schools[3] |
|---|---|---|---|---|---|---|
| AUSTRIA | Islam has been one of the six recognized religious societies since 1912. | The *Islamische Glaubensgemeinschaft Österreich* is the main Islamic organization. It was recognized in 1979 as a corporation under public law and, as such, it enjoys a number of rights, but it is not regarded as the representative body for all Muslims in Austria. | There are five mosques with minarets, and approximately 260 prayer rooms. | Religious slaughter under certain conditions is allowed, but post-cut stunning is required. | Denominational teaching of a few religions is offered at public schools and Islam is included. The teaching of Islam started in 1982. As of 2010, Islam is taught in 2,700 schools to about 40,000 students by 350 teachers. | There are six Islamic private schools in Vienna. |
| BELGIUM | Islam has been one of the six recognized religious denominations since 1974 (a seventh religious denomination, Buddhism, is in the process of being recognized). | There are a number of organizations but none of them represent the entire Muslim community. For this reason the government tried to establish in 1998 a representative body, *Exécutif des Musulmans de Belgique*, whose activity is nonetheless paralysed by interferences by the government and foreign diplomatic authorities, and by competition among national Islamic groups. | There are 333 mosques and prayer houses. | Religious slaughter without previous stunning is allowed under certain conditions. | Denominational teaching of the six recognized religious denominations and a non-denominational ethics class are offered at public schools. Islam is included. As of 2011, it is taught to approximately 30,000 pupils in 800–900 primary and secondary schools. | There are two private Islamic schools in Brussels. Further, there are six schools run by the Gülen movement, which nonetheless refuse the label of "Islamic school." |

| | | | | |
|---|---|---|---|---|
| DENMARK | There are one national church, 11 recognized religious communities, and more than 100 religious communities acknowledged under the Marriage Act, whose representatives can be authorized by the Minister of Justice to celebrate marriages. Twenty-three of them are Muslim communities. | There are many different Muslim associations and organizations, some of which started to organize themselves in umbrella organizations. The main ones are the Danish Turkish Islamic Foundation, the Union of Muslim Immigrant Associations (regarded by some as linked to the Milli Görüş movement), Idara Minhaj-ul-Qur'an International Denmark (which is Sunni-oriented), and the Alevi Association in Denmark. | As of 2006, there were about 115 mosques and prayer houses, including three purpose-built mosques. | Religious slaughter without previous stunning is allowed under certain conditions for all animals with the exception of cattle. For cattle, Denmark prescribes post-cut stunning. | Only one religious course is taught in public schools. It is based on the Evangelical Lutheran denomination, but it also includes elements about Islam and other religions. | There are approximately 30 private Islamic schools. |
| FINLAND | The Evangelical Lutheran Church and the Orthodox Church have a special status according to the law. All other religions, including Islam, are on an equal footing. Muslim communities, like other religious communities, can register and obtain the legal personality under the 2003 Religious Freedom Act. As of 2010, there were 29 Muslim registered communities. | The main umbrella organization is the Islamic Council of Finland (<http://www.sine.fi>), established in 2006. The Finnish Islamic Party, founded in 2007 and representing Salafist Muslims, should also be mentioned (<http://www.suomenislamilainenpuolue.fi>). | There are about 40 mosques and prayer houses, including two purpose-built mosques. | The province of Åland forbids religious slaughter without previous stunning. In the other provinces, the law stipulates that stunning and slaughtering must be performed at the same time. | Islam can be taught, where at least three pupils in a municipality ask for it. Courses of Islamic religion have been well established in all larger cities since the 1990s. | There are no Islamic private schools, but it should be noted that all over Finland there are few private schools. |

(Continued)

Table 14.1 (Continued)

| Country | Legal recognition of Islam and/or Muslim communities[2] | Existence of a representative body | Places of worship | Legal rules on religious slaughter | Teaching of Islam in public schools | Private Islamic schools[3] |
|---|---|---|---|---|---|---|
| FRANCE | According to Art. 2 of the 1905 Separation Law, the Republic does not recognize any religion (*culte*). Muslim communities, like other religious communities, can obtain legal personality as worship associations (*associations cultuelles*) or cultural associations (*associations culturelles*). | There are a number of organizations but none of them represents the entire Muslim community. For this reason the government tried to establish in 2002 a representative body, *Conseil Français du Culte Musulman*, whose real capacity to represent French Islam has nonetheless often been questioned by Muslims themselves. | There are approximately 2,150 places of worship, including about 20 mosques with minarets. | Religious slaughter without previous stunning is allowed under certain conditions. | No religion is taught in schools. | In France, private schools can contract with the state (they receive public funding and have then to follow the public school curriculum) or can be without a contract (they do not receive financial assistance, but they are free to organize themselves as they wish). There is one Islamic private school with a contract in the Réunion overseas department, and six without a contract in the metropolitan territory. |

| | | | | |
|---|---|---|---|---|
| GERMANY | In each *Land* religious communities can obtain legal personality as a corporation under public law (which entails the enjoyment of a higher number of rights) or as an association under private law.<br><br>A number of Muslim communities have registered as associations under private law, but none of them has acquired the legal status of public law corporation yet. | There are many different Muslim associations and organizations, some of which started to organize themselves in umbrella organizations. The largest ones are the Turkish-Islamic Union of the Presidency for Religious Affairs, the Union of Islamic Cultural Centres, the Islamic Council for the Federal Republic of Germany, and the Central Council of Muslims in Germany. These four organizations cooperate in the Coordination Council of Muslims in Germany. Outside it, two more umbrella organizations should be mentioned: the Alevi Community of Germany, and the Islamic Community of the German Shi'i Communities. | There are approximately 2,600 mosques and prayer houses, including about 180 purpose-built mosques. The number of Alevi prayer houses is unknown. | Religious slaughter without previous stunning is allowed under certain conditions (the issue is too complex to be summarized here. See pp. 638–9 of the chapter for details). | Islam is taught in public schools of a number of *Länder*, including Berlin. However, in many cases, this teaching is provided for in classes of language organized for the immigrant children (usually Turkish, but also Arabic, Bosnian, and Albanian), which results in the exclusion of all Muslim students of a different mother tongue. | As of 2004, there were three private Islamic schools: one of primary level in Berlin, another one of secondary level in Munich, and the third one operating at both levels. |
| GREECE | The Greek constitution stipulates that the prevailing religion is that of the Eastern Orthodox Church. It also distinguishes between the so-called known religions, which enjoy a number of rights, and others.<br><br>Under international law treaties, the Islamic communities in Western Thrace have a special legal status and enjoy a number of rights. Those residing elsewhere do not. | Muslim communities in Western Thrace are administered by three Muftiates, which operate as public institutions under the supervision and with the funding of the government.<br><br>In the rest of the country, there are many Muslim associations and organizations. | There are about 300 mosques in Western Thrace, two on Kos, one on Rhodes, and about 80 places of worship in greater Athens and other major cities. | Religious slaughter without previous stunning is allowed under certain conditions. | Islam is taught at the five public schools of Western Thrace. In the rest of Greece, only the Orthodox religion is taught, with the occasional addition of elements about other religions including Islam. | As of 2009, there were numerous Islamic private schools in Western Thrace (188 elementary and two secondary schools), but none in the rest of Greece. |

(*Continued*)

Table 14.1 (Continued)

| Country | Legal recognition of Islam and/or Muslim communities[2] | Existence of a representative body | Places of worship | Legal rules on religious slaughter | Teaching of Islam in public schools | Private Islamic schools[3] |
|---|---|---|---|---|---|---|
| IRELAND | Ireland does not have an established church, and has not signed any agreements with religious denominations. Formally, all religious communities are on an equal footing. Muslim communities, like other religious communities, can obtain legal personality as charities. | There are a number of associations and institutions, but no central national organization. | There are three purpose-built mosques and a number of prayer houses. | Religious slaughter without previous stunning is allowed under certain conditions. | It does not apply. Primary and secondary education is essentially private, although it is funded by the state. | There are two Islamic private primary schools in Dublin. |
| ITALY | The Catholic Church and six religious denominations, with which the state has signed respectively a Concordat and six agreements (*intesa*), enjoy more rights than other religious communities, including the Islamic one. All religious communities can obtain legal personality as *ente morale*, which is the typical legal form through which a given association, organization, or institution is recognized as a religious denomination. However, only one Muslim organization has obtained legal personality as *ente morale*, while others seem to have preferred legal recognition as civil law associations or non-profit organizations. | There are a number of organizations, but none of them represents the entire Muslim community. | There are over 200 places of worship, including three purpose-built mosques. | Religious slaughter without previous stunning is allowed under certain conditions. | The curriculum of all public primary and secondary schools must include the teaching of the Catholic religion. The teaching of a different religion can be offered upon request, provided that the representative body of the concerned religious denomination has signed an agreement (*intesa*) with the state. Thus, no teaching of Islamic religion can be offered in public schools. | There are no private Islamic schools. |

| | | | | |
|---|---|---|---|---|
| NETHERLANDS | Religious denominations are not officially recognized. A religious community can obtain legal personality as a church, an association, or a foundation. Muslim communities are usually structured as associations or foundations. | There are a few organizations but none of them represents the entire Muslim community. For this reason the government has tried to establish a representative body. | There are over 450 mosques and prayer houses. | Religious slaughter without previous stunning is allowed under certain conditions. A bill has been presented to parliament to prohibit (both to Muslims and Jews) the carrying out of religious slaughter without previous stunning. | Parents may request that Islam be taught in a public school, but have made limited use of this possibility. | There are 41 Islamic private schools: 39 are primary and two are secondary schools. |
| NORWAY | The Lutheran Church has a special legal status. No other religious denomination, including Islam, is recognized. Religious communities, including Muslim ones, can obtain legal personality as registered organizations. | There is an umbrella organization called the Islamic Council of Norway, with which political authorities have established regular communication, but it does not represent all Muslim communities in the country. | There are a purpose-built mosque in Oslo and about 40 prayer houses. | Religious slaughter without previous stunning is forbidden. | Non-denominational teaching of religion is offered at public schools, which includes the teaching of some elements about Islam and other world religions. | There are no Islamic private schools, but it should be noted that in the whole country there are few private schools. |
| PORTUGAL | A special legal status is recognized to the "religious communities settled in the country." The Islamic Community of Lisbon has obtained such a status. The other Muslim communities, like any religious community, may obtain legal personality as a private association or as a registered religious community. | The Islamic Community of Lisbon acts informally as the representative body of all Sunni Muslims. | There are over 30 places of worship, including 4 mosques. | Religious slaughter without previous stunning is allowed under certain conditions. | Islam can be taught in public schools if there is a minimum number of 10 pupils. No public school currently offers such teaching. | There is an Islamic private secondary school in Palmela, near Lisbon. It has about 200 students, about 10% of whom are non-Muslims. In 2009, it ranked as the best secondary school in the country (among public and private schools altogether). |

(Continued)

Table 14.1 (Continued)

| Country | Legal recognition of Islam and/or Muslim communities[2] | Existence of a representative body | Places of worship | Legal rules on religious slaughter | Teaching of Islam in public schools | Private Islamic schools[3] |
|---|---|---|---|---|---|---|
| SPAIN | Like in Italy, there is a three-tier system of relations between the state and religious denominations: (1) the Catholic Church, which has signed a concordat, (2) three religious communities, which have signed an agreement, (3) the other religious communities, which do not have the same rights as those having bilateral relations with the state. Unlike Italy, Spain has signed an agreement with the Muslim community (a federation called Islamic Commission of Spain). | The Islamic Commission of Spain is recognized as the representative body of Muslims in Spain. | There are about 785 places of worship. | Religious slaughter without previous stunning is allowed under certain conditions. | Islam has been taught in some public schools since 2003 in Ceuta, Melilla, Madrid, and the autonomous communities of Valencia and Aragon. | There is one private Islamic school in Madrid, offering pre-school, primary, and secondary education to about 400 students |
| SWEDEN | The Lutheran Church has a special legal status. No other religious denomination, including Islam, is recognized. However, the Swedish Commission for Government Support to Religious Communities acknowledges some religious communities, which receive public funding. Six Muslim organizations have been acknowledged so far. | There are six umbrella organizations, representing approximately 75% of Sweden's Muslims. | There are 6 purpose-built mosques and a number of prayer houses. | Religious slaughter without previous stunning is forbidden. | Non-denominational teaching of religion is offered at public schools, which includes the teaching of some elements about Islam and other world religions. | There are 9 Islamic private schools. |

| | | | | | |
|---|---|---|---|---|---|
| UNITED KINGDOM | There are two established churches, the Church of England and the Church of Scotland. No other religious denomination, including Islam, is recognized. Muslim communities, like any other religious community, can obtain legal personality as charities. | There are a number of organizations, but none of them represents the entire Muslim community. The most important ones are the Muslim Council of Britain, the British Muslim Forum, the Sufi Muslim Forum, the Sunni organization named Minhaj ul-Quran, the Quilliam Foundation (presenting itself as the symbol of integrated British Islam), the Al-Khoei Foundation (representing Shi'a Muslims in Britain and overseas), and the Mosques and Imams National Advisory Board (launched as a collaboration platform between the main Muslim organizations). | There are approximately 2,000 mosques and prayer houses. | Religious slaughter without previous stunning is allowed under certain conditions. | Only one non-denominational religious class is offered at public schools, which includes the teaching of some elements about Islam and other world religions. | There are six primary and five secondary Islamic voluntary-aided schools. There are also over 50 Islamic independent schools. |

[1] *Sources*: Nielsen 2009–2011; Dassetto et al. 2007; Ferrari-Bottoni 2010; Kuyk et al. 2007. These data, may differ from those presented by other authors, whose works have been reviewed in the second part of this chapter. The data and the whole chapter are updated to 2012.

[2] The expression "legal recognition" should be understood as having three different (but not mutually exclusive) meanings:
(a) special consideration given to Islam as a religion, as a result of its historical presence in a country, as is the case in Austria and Belgium;
(b) special consideration given to the representative body of all Muslims, as is the case in Spain;
(c) conferral of legal personality to one or more Muslim organizations, regardless of their representativeness, as is the case in Italy and the United Kingdom.

[3] Only primary and secondary schools have been taken into account, with the exclusion of kindergartens, university teaching, Qur'anic courses offered by mosques and courses for the training of imams and religious personnel.

different reasons) controversial in Europe: therefore comparing the strategies they follow to overcome popular opposition and gain admission in European society can be helpful to understand the analogies and differences of their process of institutionalization.

Diachronic comparison raises different questions. Maussen (2007) has underlined that, in order to explain the differences in the accommodation of Islam in the European countries, it is advisable to strengthen an historical perspective. This invitation should be followed without reservation but *cum grano salis*, as what we learn from the past is not always helpful to understand the present and, even less, to predict the future. In the case of Islam, in particular, a new element has to be taken into account: the growing fear that Europe is entering a phase of demographic, economic, political, and military decline. Although it is not the first time that this doubt has made its way in the Old Continent (it had already happened after the First and, in terms even sharper, the Second World War, when the United States took the central place that previously had been occupied by the great European powers), the expectation that the center of gravity of the world will move eastward, beyond the borders of Western civilization, has made many Europeans unsecure, suspicious of any change and rather backward-looking. Migration, which was "a source of content" during the 1960s, has now become "a source of fear and instability in Western nation-states" (Kaya 2010: 48) and a "pluralism of fear" has replaced "a pluralism of hope" (Modood 2009). Consequently, what would have been easier a few decades ago is more difficult today and the integration of Islam in Europe meets obstacles that would have been less serious in times of economic expansion and widespread social welfare.

This change makes diachronic comparison much more complex. It is not possible to rely on patterns of institutionalization that were effective in the past and apply them to the present situation: without taking into account the new context, that could be useless or even counterproductive. Reality is always much more complex and unpredictable than the human mind can grasp: discovering analogies and differences between two social or legal phenomena is not equal to discovering the best way to govern them. This is a lesson that any scholar in comparative studies is bound to learn.

## Note

For this chapter, Silvio Ferrari has written the entire section "The Institutionalization of Islam in Europe: An Overview" and the sub-section "Which Type of Comparison?" in the section "Literature Review on the Institutionalization of Islam." Rossella Bottoni has written the remaining parts.

## Bibliography

Ahdar, R. and Aroney, N. (eds.) (2010). *Shari'a in the West*. Oxford: Oxford University Press.
Allievi, S. (ed.) (2009). *Conflicts over Mosques in Europe: Policy Issues and Trends*. Brussels: Network of European Foundations.

Allievi, S. (ed.) (2010). *Mosques in Europe: Why a Solution Has Become a Problem*. Brussels: Network of European Foundations.
Asad, T. (1993). *Genealogies of Religion: Discipline and Reasons of Power in Christianity and Islam*. Baltimore: Johns Hopkins University Press.
Aslan, E. and Heinrich, P. (2009). "Austria," in J. S. Nielsen (ed.), *Yearbook of Muslims in Europe*, Volume 1. Leiden: Brill, 25–34.
Augsberg, I. (2014 forthcoming). "Religious Freedom as 'Reflexive Law,'" in S. Lavi and R. Provost (eds.), *Religious Revival in a Post-Multicultural Age*. Oxford: Oxford University Press.
Basdevant-Gaudemet, B. (2004). "Islam in France," in R. Aluffi B.P. and G. Zincone (eds.), *The Legal Treatment of Islamic Minorities in Europe*. Leuven: Peeters, 59–81.
Bowen, J. (2007). "A View from France on the Internal Complexity of National Models," Journal of Ethnic and Migration Studies 33(6): 1003–16.
Buijs, F. J. and Rath, J. (2006). *Muslims in Europe: The State of Research*. IMISCOE Working Paper no. 7. <http://library.imiscoe.org/en/record/314221>.
Cesari, J. (2007). "Muslim Identities in Europe: The Snare of Exceptionalism," in A. Al-Azmeh and E. Fokas (eds.), *Islam in Europe: Diversity, Identity and Influence*. Cambridge: Cambridge University Press, 49–67.
Cesari, J. (2009). "Islam in the West: From Immigration to Global Islam," *Harvard Middle Eastern and Islamic Review* 8: 148–75.
Cimbalo, G. (2008). "L'esperienza dell'Islam dell'Est Europa come contributo ad una regolamentazione condivisa delle libertà religiose in Italia," in R. Aluffi Beck-Peccoz (ed.), *Identità europea e integrazione dei musulmani in Italia e in Europa. Omaggio alla memoria di Francesco Castro*. Turin: Giappichelli, 71–104.
Clayer, G. and Germain, E. (eds.) (2008). *Islam in Inter-War Europe*. New York: Columbia University Press.
Coglievina, S. (2009). "Italy," in J. S. Nielsen (ed.), *Yearbook of Muslims in Europe*, Volume 1. Leiden: Brill, 179–92.
Danchin, P. (2011). "Islam in the Secular Nomos of the European Court of Human Rights," *Michigan Journal of International Law* 32: 663–747.
Dassetto, F., Ferrari, S., and Maréchal, B. (2007). *Islam in the European Union: What's At Stake in the Future?* Brussels: European Parliament.
Daun, H. (2008). "Religious Education and Islam in Europe," in D. B. Holsinger and W. J. Jacob (eds.), *Inequality in Education: Comparative and International Perspectives*. Hong Kong: Comparative Education Research Centre, 348–68.
Ferrari, S. (2008). "Le comunità musulmane e i rapporti con lo Stato," in A. Pacini (ed.), *Chiesa e Islam in Italia. Esperienze e prospettive di dialogo*. Milan: Ed. Paoline, 45–56.
Ferrari, S. (2014 forthcoming). "The Christian Roots of the Secular State," in S. Lavi and R. Provost (eds.), *Religious Revival in a Post-Multicultural Age*. Oxford: Oxford University Press.
Ferrari, S. and Bottoni, R. (2010). *Report on Legislation on Religious Slaughter in the EU Member, Candidate and Associated Countries*. <http://www.dialrel.eu/dialrel-results>.
Foblets, M.-C. and Overbeeke, A. (2004). "Islam in Belgium: The Search for a Legal Status of a New Religious Minority," in R. Potz and W. Wieshaider (eds.), *Islam and the European Union*. Leuven: Peeters, 1–39.
Frégosi, F. (2008). *Dynamiques d'institutionnalisation de l'islam en Europe: tentative de décryptage*. <http://www.iep.univ-cezanne.fr/media/FREGOSI-Islam-Europe-2008.pdf>.

Frégosi, F. (2010). "Dynamiques d'institutionnalisation et de régulation publique de l'islam en Europe: état des lieux et perspectives d'évolution," in *Le statut juridique de l'Islam en Europe. Actes du colloque international organisé par le Conseil de la communauté marocaine à l'étranger. Fès, 14 et 15 Mars 2009*. Rabat: Marsam, 215–36.

Fuess, A. (2007). "Islamic Religious Education in Western Europe: Models of Integration and the German Approach," *Journal of Muslim Minority Affairs* 27(2): 215–39.

Godard, B. (2007). "Official Recognition of Islam," in *European Islam: Challenges for Public Policy and Society*. Brussels: Centre for European Policy Studies.

Grillo, R., Ballard, R., Ferrari, A., Hoekema, A. J., Maussen, M., and Shah, P. (2009). *Legal Practice and Cultural Diversity*. Farnham: Ashgate.

Guolo, R. (2007). *L'Islam è compatibile con la democrazia?* Bari: Laterza.

Ipgrave, J., Miller, J., and Hopkins, P. (2010). "Responses of Three Muslim Majority Primary Schools in England to the Islamic Faith of Their Pupils," *Journal of International Migration and Integration* 11(1): 73–89.

Jozsa, D.-P. (2007). "Islam and Education in Europe With Special Reference to Austria, England, France, Germany and the Netherlands," in R. Jackson, S. Miedema, W. Weisse, and J.-P. Willaime (eds.), *Religion and Education in Europe: Developments, Contexts and Debates*. Münster: Waxmann, 67–80.

Kaya, A. (2010). "Individualization and Institutionalization of Islam in Europe in the Age of Securitization," *Insight Turkey* 12(1): 47–63.

Koenig, M. (2007). "Europeanising the Governance of Religious Diversity: An Institutionalist Account of Muslim Struggles for Public Recognition," *Journal of Ethnic and Migration Studies* 33(6): 911–32.

Kreienbrink, A. and Bodenstein, M. (eds.) (2010). *Muslim Organisations and the State: European Perspectives*. Nürnberg: Federal Office for Migration and Refugees.

Larsson, G. (ed.) (2009). *Islam in the Nordic and Baltic Countries*. New York: Routledge.

Laurence, J. (2012). *The Emancipation of Europe's Muslims: The State's Role in Minority Integration*. Princeton: Princeton University Press.

Laurence, J. and Vaisse, J. (2006). *Integrating Islam: Political and Religious Challenges in Contemporary France*. Washington, DC: Brookings Institution Press.

Lerner, P. and Rabello, A. M. (2006–7). "The Prohibition of Ritual Slaughtering (Kosher Shechita and Halal) and Freedom of Religion of Minorities," *Journal of Law and Religion* 22(1): 1–62.

Maréchal, B. (2003). "Institutionalisation of Islam and Representative Organisations for Dealing with European States," in B. Maréchal, S. Allievi, F. Dassetto, and J. Nielsen (eds.), *Muslism in the Enlarged Europe*. Leiden: Brill, 150–82.

Maussen, M. (2005). *Making Muslim Presence Meaningful: Studies on Islam and Mosques in Western Europe*. Amsterdam School for Social Science Research Working Paper 05/03, May. <http://www.setav.org/ups/dosya/17082.pdf>.

Maussen, M. (2007). *The Governance of Islam in Western Europe: A State of the Art Report*. IMISCOE Working Paper no. 16, June. <http://library.imiscoe.org/en/record/234826>.

Maussen, M. (2009). *Constructing Mosques: The Governance of Islam in France and the Netherlands*. Amsterdam: Amsterdam School for Social Sciences Research.

Modood, T. (2009). "We Need a Multiculturalism of Hope," *The Guardian*, 24 September.

Nalborczyk, A. (2011). "Relations between Islam and the State in Poland: The Legal Position of Polish Muslims," *Islam and Christian–Muslim Relations* 22(3): 343–59.

Niehaus, I. (2009). "Emancipation or Disengagement? Islamic Schools in Britain and the Netherlands," in A. Alvarez Veinguer, G. Dietz, D.-P. Jozsa, and T. Knauth (eds.), *Islam in Education in European Countries: Pedagogical Concepts and Empirical Findings.* Münster: Waxmann, 113–27.

Nielsen, J. (ed.) (2009–11). *Yearbook of Muslims in Europe*, 3 vols. Leiden: Brill.

Norris, H. (2009). *Islam in the Baltic: Europe's Early Muslim Community*. London and New York: Tauris Academic Studies.

Pais Bernardo, L. A. (2009). "The Accommodation of Islam in Portugal and the Republic of Ireland: A Comparative Case Study," MA thesis. <http://lisboa.academia.edu/LuisBernardo/Papers>.

Pépin, L. (2009). *Teaching about Religions in European School Systems: Policy Issues and Trends*. Brussels: Network of European Foundations.

Peter, F. (2006). "Individualization and Religious Authority in Western European Islam," *Islam and Christian–Muslim Relations* 17(1): 105–18.

Rath, J., Penninx, R., Groenendijk, K., and Meyer, A. (2001). *Western Europe and its Islam*. Leiden: Brill.

Robbers, G. (ed.) (2005). *State and Church in the European Union*. Baden-Baden: Nomos.

Rohe, M. (2006). "The Migration and Settlement of Muslims: The Challenges for European Legal Systems," in P. Shah and W. Menski (eds.), *Migration, Diasporas and Legal Systems in Europe*. New York: Routledge, 57–72.

Rohe, M. (2010). "On the Recognition and Institutionalisation of Islam in Germany," in M.-C. Foblets, J.-F. Gaudreault-Desbiens, and A. Dundes Renteln (eds.), *Cultural Diversity and the Law*. Brussels: Bruylant, 145–94.

Sakaranaho, T. (2006). *Religious Freedom, Multiculturalism, Islam: Cross-Reading Finland and Ireland*. Leiden: Brill.

Schreiner, P., Kuyk, E., Jensen, R., and Manna, E. L. (2007). *Religious Education in Europe: Situation and Current Trends in Schools*. Oslo: IKO Publishing House.

Shadid, W. A. R. and van Koningsveld, P. S. (2008). *Islam in Nederland en België*. Leuven: Peeters.

Silvestri, S. (2007). "Muslim Institutions and Political Mobilisation," in *European Islam: Challenges for Public Policy and Society*. Brussels: Centre for European Policy Studies.

Silvestri, S. (2009). "Islam and Religion in the EU Political System," *West European Politics* 32(6): 1212–39.

Silvestri, S. (2010). "Public Policies Towards Muslims and the Institutionalization of 'Moderate Islam' in Europe. Some Critical Reflections," in A. Triandafyllidou (ed.), *Muslims in 21st-Century Europe*. London: Routledge, 45–58.

Silvestri, S. (2011). "Institutionalising British and Italian Islam: Attitudes and Policies," in H. Yilmaz and C. Aykaç (eds.), *Perceptions of Islam in Europe: Culture, Identity and the Muslim 'Other'*. London: I. B. Tauris, 159–94.

Soper, J. C. and Fetzer, J. S. (2007). "Religious Institutions, Church–State History and Muslim Mobilisation in Britain, France and Germany," *Journal of Ethnic and Migration Studies* 33(6): 933–44.

Tatari, E. (2009). "Theories of the State Accommodation of Islamic Religious Practices in Western Europe," *Journal of Ethnic and Migration Studies* 35(2): 271–88.

Tulkens, F. (2009). "The European Convention on Human Rights and Church–State Relations: Pluralism vs. Pluralism," *Cardozo Law Review* 30: 2575–91.

Williams, R. (2008). "Civil and Religious Law in England: A Religious Perspective," *Ecclesiastical Law Journal* 10: 262–82.

CHAPTER 15

# SHARIAH IN EUROPE*

MATHIAS ROHE

## THE EUROPEAN DEBATE

## Introduction

"MARIA statt Scharia" (Maria instead of Sharia) was one of the slogans of the right-wing, populist, and anti-Islamic Swiss People's Party (SVP) in the 2009 electoral campaign.[1] On the other extreme, "Sharia4Belgium"[2] and "Sharia4Holland"[3] are extremist Muslim groups explicitly rejecting the Belgian and Dutch democratic systems. But what are they exactly talking about when using the term "shariah"?

Shariah—in the narrow understanding as "Islamic law"—is often perceived to be the opposite of secular legal orders, both by most Islamists[4] and by large numbers of the European public. The heated reaction to the Archbishop of Canterbury's famous speech in February 2008[5] about a possible introduction of some parts of shariah law into the English legal system is but one example of a resistance to shariah defined in the narrow sense. In Germany, Chancellor Merkel has supported the view expressed by former president Wulff in 2010 that Islam along with Christianity and Judaism now belongs

---

* This chapter is in part based on research in the context of RELIGARE (see http://www.religareproject.eu>), a three-year project funded under the Socio-Economic Sciences & Humanities Programme of DG Research of the European Commission's Seventh Framework Research Programme. I am grateful to Preet Kaur Virdi from Queen Mary College/University of London for her most valuable remarks and language editing.

[1] Cf. <http://www.tagesanzeiger.ch/schweiz/standard/SVP-moechte-lieber-Maria-statt-Scharia/story/10749271>.

[2] Cf. the website <http://www.shariah4belgium.com/>.

[3] Cf. the report in Trouw, December 22, 2010, available at <http://www.trouw.nl/tr/nl/4324/Nieuws/article/detail/1798930/2010/12/22/Shariah4Holland-wil-vechten-voor-de-wetgeving-van-Allah.dhtml>.

[4] For European movements of political Islam cf. only Laurence 2012: 70–104.

[5] Cf. Rowan Williams, "Civil and Religious Law in England: A Religious Perspective," available at <http://www.archbishopofcanterbury.org/articles.php/1137/archbishops-lecture-civil-and-religious-law-in-england-a-religious-perspective>; John Milbank, "The Archbishop of Canterbury: The Man

to Germany.[6] She has similarly responded to widespread irritation in the German public by saying that "the measure for integration is the Basic Law (German constitution) rather than shariah, Islamic law."[7] According to representative polls conducted in Germany in 2012,[8] only 22% condoned Wulff's statement, whereas 64% objected. The public climate has become unfavorable even to academic debate on these issues. The author was repeatedly accused by the prominent feminist journalist Alice Schwarzer[9] and the Turkish author Necla Kelek[10] of promoting the replacement of German legal order by shariah, simply because he *informs* the public about the *existing* German legal order with respect to the treatment of Islamic norms.

Acceptance or rejection[11] of shariah has consequently become one of the most heated debates in European public discourse, involving not only non-Muslims, but also a considerable number of Muslims[12] including some Muslim activists and "ex-Muslims," like Magdi Allam[13] or Necla Kelek,[14] who are among the fiercest critics of any kind of visible

---

and the Theology Behind the Shari'a lecture," in Ahdar and Aroney 2010, 43–57; Jean-François Gaudreault-Desbiens, "Religious Courts' Recognition Claims: Two Qualitatively Distinct Narratives," in Ahdar and Aroney 2010, 59–69.

[6] Cf. "Wulff: Islam gehört zu Deutschland," *Der Tagesspiegel*, October 3, 2010.

[7] Cf. "Merkel verteidigt Wulff," *Sueddeutsche Zeitung*, October 6, 2010, p. 6.

[8] Cf. "Die Furcht vor dem Morgenland im Abendland," *Frankfurter Allgemeine Zeitung (FAZ)* November 11, 2012, p. 10 (polls conducted by the Institut für Demoskopie Allensbach for the newspaper).

[9] Cf. Patrick Bahners, *Die Panikmacher. Die deutsche Angst vor dem Islam* (München: C. H. Beck, 2011), 233–51, and the statement of the author, available at <http://www.zr2.jura.uni-erlangen.de/aktuelles/kanal.shtml>.

[10] Cf. "Das ist Kulturrelativismus," *FAZ*, February 15, 2011(available at <http://www.faz.net/aktuell/feuilleton/islam-debatte-das-ist-kulturrelativismus-1592162.html>) and the reaction of the author in "Das ist Rechtskulturrelativismus," *FAZ*, February 22, 2011 (available at <http://www.faz.net/aktuell/feuilleton/debatten/islam-debatte-das-ist-rechtskulturrelativismus-1595144.html>).

[11] Cf. Jocelyne Cesari, "Shari'a and the Future of Secular Europe," in Cesari (2010: 145): "shari'a law, perhaps more than any other aspect of Islam, is perceived as a threat to Western culture."

[12] For Germany cf. the representative study of the Ministry of the Interior from 2007, *Muslime in Deutschland* (by Katrin Brettfeld and Peter Wetzels), p. 389: 72.9% rejected the idea of shariah influence on the existing laws in Germany, and 64.9% rejected it regarding the laws of the country of origin. The study is available at <http://www.bmi.bund.de/cae/servlet/contentblob/139732/publicationFile/14975/Muslime%20in%20Deutschland.pdf>. Brigitte Schepelern Johansen and Riem Spielhaus rightly criticize the study (mapping a decade's production of surveys and polls among Muslims in Europe, in a paper presented at the workshop "Quantifying the Muslim," November 2–4, 2011 in Copenhagen, to be published in the *Journal of Muslims in Europe*), since the evaluation of the questions related to shariah follows a generally negative pre-understanding of shariah, reducing it to its critical legal parts.

[13] He is an Italian Muslim convert to Christianity from Egyptian origin who gained public attraction by the public baptism performed by Pope Benedikt XVI in 2008.

[14] She is a sociologist living in Germany. After initially having scientifically worked on Islamic religiosity in the daily life of pupils in Germany of Turkish origin, she has now shifted to strong emotional views against Islam and its culture, generalizing her personal negative experiences to an extent which is untenable from a scientific perspective (cf. Bahners, n. 10, pp. 131–74; Klaus Bade, *Kritik und Gewalt* (Schwalbach: Wochenschau Verlag 2013), pp. 147 ss. in particular). Thus, she has become an "authentic" chief witness for Islamophobic groups and politicians (cf. only the repeated reports on the fiercely Islamophobic German weblog "politically incorrect").

Muslim religious presence in the European public space. But what are people talking about when demanding or rejecting the application of shariah rules in Europe?

## What is Shariah?

Shariah, in the narrow understanding as "Islamic law," is broadly perceived in Europe not only among non-Muslims (cf. below) to be the opposite of secular legal orders. This is wrong for two reasons. First, this understanding does not capture the full scope of shariah rules. To a large extent, shariah contains religious norms regarding doctrine and rite, which fall under freedom of religion granted by European legal orders.

Second, even if perceived in a narrow legal sense, there are broad fields of shariah norms that are in full accordance with European legal convictions, in the fields of civil contract, tort, and economic law, for example. Moreover, in sensitive areas, like family law, where traditional shariah interpretations are in conflict with European legal requirements regarding gender equality, freedom of religion, and equality of religions and beliefs,[15] some modern interpretations (e.g. Tunisian family law since 1956) have overcome such obstacles to a vast extent. Thus, it is a primary objective to clarify the different perceptions of the term "shariah law" among Muslims themselves as well as within the broader European public.

In a literal sense, as well as according to the Qur'an Surah 45: 18, the term shariah means "the path which has been prepared, the divinely appointed path." Technically, there are two current definitions that are notably different and thus often cause misunderstanding. Broadly speaking, "shariah" refers to any religious and legal rule prescribed by Islam, including those that address fulfilling the duties of worship and charitable giving, as well as those that regulate contract, family, and penal law. It includes not only the field of norms (*furu '*, the "branches"), but also a system of finding and interpreting the shariah sources like the Qur'an, the Sunna of the prophet of Islam Muhammad, and the other "minor" sources developed by scholars over the centuries (*usul*, the "roots").[16] Irrespective of the claim to be a "God-given" set of norms, this broad interpretation of shariah provides a flexible system of norms, where the interpretation strongly relies on the circumstances of time and space. It remains the responsibility of human beings to interpret and apply these norms. Plural interpretations within and among the schools of "law" (*ikhtilaf al-madhahib*) are the backbone of Islamic normativity, supported by a Hadith saying that "Dispute in my community is a grace."[17] Thus, on the basis of shariah, legal work rooted in the Islamic tradition has resulted in interpretations fundamentally

---

[15] For details cf. Wael Hallaq, *Sharī'a: Theory, Practice, Transformations* (Cambridge: Cambridge University Press, 2009), 271–85; Rohe (2011: 351–68 in particular).

[16] Cf. only Hallaq (n. 15), 72–124 in particular; Rohe 2011: 9–18, 43–73 in particular.

[17] Cf. the article "Ikhtilaf," *Encyclopedia of Islam II*, vol. 3 (Leiden and London: Brill, 1986) (by J. Schacht), p. 1061 s. The hadith might be apocryphal, but it is constantly used in the normative debate on pluralism.

contradicting each other. For example, polygamy is allowed, often under certain restrictions, in most countries following shariah rules. In Tunisia, polygamy was abolished in 1956 according to a new interpretation of conflicting Qur'anic provisions. The key to this pluralism of interpretations is the principle of *ijtihad*, which means own individual or collective reasoning in dealing with the sources instead of simply adopting the views of scholars of the past (*taqlid*).

In Europe, however, most non-Muslims as well as many Muslims,[18] understand "shariah" in a narrower sense that is limited to legal norms that regulate personal status and family relations, inheritance, and sometimes corporal punishment. While the application of rules concerning the broader interpretation of shariah (prayer, fasting, etc.) usually does not conflict with secular European laws and norms, the application of shariah in the narrower sense can lead to conflict. In matters of personal status and inheritance, shariah law in its traditional interpretations maintained in many Islamic states, discriminates between the sexes and religions. The distribution of rights and duties between spouses and within the family follows patriarchal schemes often similar to European family norms until the recent past. Concerning inter-religious legal relations, Islamic law stipulates that it supersedes laws of other religions. It also prohibits inter-religious marriage to a certain extent.[19] Such provisions are in conflict with contemporary European laws following the human rights standards recognizing equality of sexes and religions. This can also be said regarding the draconic forms of corporal punishment of certain offenses that are practiced in a number of Muslim countries.[20] Despite the variety of interpretations, the perception of shariah law as in total contrast to European secular legal orders that respect and promote human rights is visible in the jurisprudence of the European Court of Human Rights (ECHR).[21] This becomes clear in the court's short statement in a decision dating from 2003,[22] which inter alia had to deal with the dissolution of the Turkish Refah partisi led by Necmettin Erbakan. This party was suspected of promoting the interests of political Islam relying on shariah principles against the constitutional principle of laïcism:

> The court concurs in the Chamber's view that sharia is incompatible with the fundamental principles of democracy [...]. Like the Constitutional Court (sc.: of Turkey), the court considers that sharia, which faithfully reflects the dogmas and divine

---

[18] This understanding can be found among Muslims of Turkish origin in particular, since the law reforms under Atatürk explicitly aimed at replacing the "outdated" shariah laws concerning these fields of law.

[19] Cf. e.g. Rohe (2011), pp. 82 s.

[20] Cf. e.g. Rudolph Peters, *Crime and Punishment in Islamic Law* (Cambridge: Cambridge University Press, 2005), pp. 53 ss., 142 ss.

[21] Cf. the arguing in Refah Partisi and others, "Turkey," February 13, 2003 (RJD 2003-II, p. 306) (an English version is available at <http://www.iilj.org/courses/documents/RefahPartisivTurkey.pdf>); this is a deficit recognized by some judges of the court as well in an informal exchange with the author.

[22] ECHR in Refah Partisi and others, "Turkey," February 13, 2003 (RJD 2003-II, p. 306 n. 15). Cf. Rex Ahdar and Nicholas Aroney, "The Topography of Shari'a in the Western Political Landscape," in Ahdar and Aroney 2010, pp. 1, 21–3.

rules laid down by religion, is stable and invariable. Principles such as pluralism in the political sphere or the constant evolution of public freedoms have no place in it. [...] It is difficult to declare one's respect for democracy and human rights while at the same time supporting a regime based on sharia, which clearly diverges from Convention values, particularly with regard to its criminal law and criminal procedure, its rules on the legal status of women and the way it intervenes in all spheres of private and public life [...].

This is not the place to decide whether the Turkish Refah Partisi had in fact promoted the implementation of traditional shariah law, which would indeed contradict the Convention. It is only problematic that no specific research was done on the concrete interpretation of shariah. Far beyond European courts, there is widespread fear in Europe—sometimes fueled by Islamophobic parties, organizations, individuals,[23] and media—that Muslims may introduce such norms within their own communities on the continent.

## European Perceptions of Shariah

Some Muslim groups and individuals[24] have repeatedly suggested or demanded the introduction of shariah into the European legal context.[25] Such debate first arose in Britain in the 1980s and subsequently spread to other European countries in recent years. In general, these discussions mostly lack clarity. If Muslims are simply asked about their opinion on "shariah in the West," it is unclear whether they consider the religious commands and rites (falling under freedom of religion), or whether they wish Islamic legal rules to be applied to an extent beyond the framework of the law of the land.[26] It is in the latter case where possible conflict arises. An example of such simplifying approaches is a poll taken of 500 British Muslims in 2006, in which 40% of respondents supported the introduction of shariah law there.[27] Given that some aspects of Islamic law contradict the principles of the prevailing secular legal order (see the previous section), the broader British public has roundly and soundly rejected the idea of implementing shariah norms in the British context without distinguishing between the aspects in conformity with the

---

[23] Cf. the contributions in the volume Thorsten Schneiders (ed.), *Islamfeindlichkeit. Wenn die Grenzen der Kritik verschwimmen*, 2nd edn. (Wiesbaden: VS Verlag für Sozialwissenschaften, 2010).

[24] Cf. e.g. the book of the Muslim extremist Sālim Ibn, *'Abd al-Ghanī al-Rāfi'ī, ahkām al-ahwāl al-šakhsīya li-l-muslimīn fī l-gharb* (Riyadh 2001).

[25] For the Union of Muslim Organisations of Britain and Eire cf. Sebastian Poulter, "The Claim to a Separate Islamic System of Personal Law for British Muslims," in Chibli Mallat and Jane Connors (eds.), *Islamic Family Law* (London: Graham and Trotman, reprint 1993), pp. 147 ss.

[26] For a variety of understandings and the possible distortion of results on generalizing poll questions cf. only John Esposito and Dalia Mogahed, *Who Speaks for Islam? What a Billion Muslims Really Think* (New York: Gallup Press, 2007), pp. 52–5.

[27] Available at <http://www.icmresearch.co.uk/pdfs/2006_february_sunday_telegraph_muslims_poll.pdf> (p. 14).

law of the land and otherwise. In fact, it is far from clear what the desire to apply shariah norms seeks to achieve: Is it practicing religious rites or establishing a religious infrastructure, which is protected under the principle of freedom of religion? Is it the replacement of the existing legal order, with respect to family issues, criminal cases, or state organization? Or is it something in between, where the law of the land prevails as long as individual choice is protected?

While a number of studies covering Islamic and Europe countries have been conducted in the last decade,[28] there is little concrete information available on the specific attitudes of Muslims towards the *legal aspects* of shariah in European continental countries.[29] Many polls and surveys were initiated from the angle of security interests and the perceived Muslim threat. In addition, the category of "Muslim" is far from being clear; religious aspects are combined with ethnicity or other factors concerning migration issues.[30] Moreover, it is mostly Muslims living in big cities who are interviewed and taken as representative of the whole Muslim population. Correlations in answers are sometimes simply equated to causation. Thus, little reliable data has been published.

Concerning state organization (secular democracy under the rule of law), there are polls indicating a high degree of confidence in state institutions among European Muslims.[31] Only in Austria were *concrete* questions on shariah law-related issues raised in fully published representative polls conducted by the Ministry of the Interior and a commercial enterprise conducting polls (Gfk Austria) in 2009. According to them, 50% of Turkish Muslims and those having Turkish family roots condoned the application of shariah rules in family and inheritance matters while 22% rejected that and 16% wanted

---

[28] Cf. the survey by the Pew Research Center on "The World's Muslims: Unity and Diversity," published on August 9, 2012 based on more than 38,000 face-to-face interviews with Muslims in 39 countries, available at <http://www.pewforum.org/uploadedFiles/Topics/Religious_Affiliation/Muslim/the-worlds-muslims-full-report.pdf>; no questions relating to legal provisions were implemented; 50,000 interviews have been conducted earlier by Gallup; cf. Esposito and Mogahed (n. 26). Cf. also the evaluation of 50 quantitative surveys and polls concerning Muslims taken in Europe since 2000 by Riem Spielhaus, "Measuring the Muslim: About Statistical Obsessions, Categorisations and the Quantification of Religion," *Yearbook of Muslims in Europe*, vol. 3 (2011): 695–715; cf. also Brigitte Johansen and Riem Spielhaus, "Counting Deviance: Revisiting a Decade's Production of Surveys among Muslims in Western Europe," *Journal of Muslims in Europe* 1 (2012): 81–112.

[29] According to Johansen and Spielhaus (n. 28), p. 104, the main themes covered integration, belonging and identity, radicalization and security, religiosity and religious practice, political and civil participation, gender and sexuality, but only a few questions related directly to shariah rules as a topic.

[30] Cf. only Stefano Allievi, "How the Immigrant has Become Muslim: Public Debates on Islam in Europe," *Revue européenne des migrations internationales* 21/2 (2005): 1–23; Riem Spielhaus (n. 29), pp. 698–702, 709–12 in particular; Johansen and Spielhaus (n. 29), pp. 87–103 in particular.

[31] According to a Gallup polling in 2006/2007 among more than 3,600 Muslims in Britain, France, and Germany, the confidence of Muslims in the democratic institutions of the respective country of residence equates or even overrides the average of the population, cf. the summary report "Muslims in Europe: Basis for Greater Understanding Already Exists" (April 30, 2007), available at <http://www.gallup.com/poll/27409/Muslims-Europe-Basis-Greater-Understanding-Already-Exists.aspx>. Cf. also Cesari (2010) (n. 11), p. 146.

to differentiate with regard to the respective rules of Islamic law. The "religious"[32] group among them supported the measure by 62%, but also within the "secular" group a relative majority of 42% was in favor of this, opposed by 32%.[33] The most decisive factor here was access to German language and education: the lower the language knowledge and educational level, the higher the support for Islamic law.[34] On the other hand, research among Muslim women in Europe indicates that a considerable number of them prefer the application of European family laws rather than shariah-inspired laws of their country of origin,[35] since the former alone grant equal rights in these matters. The application of the latter is thus perceived as an injustice.[36] Consequently, Moroccan attempts to enter into bilateral agreements on the applicability of family law in Dutch–Moroccan cases with the Netherlands failed, not least due to strong opposition among Moroccan women living in the Netherlands who feared losing access to the gender-neutral Dutch family law.[37] Further concrete quantitative research is more than desirable in this field.

While little specific information on Muslim attitudes towards concrete shariah law provisions is available, shariah in general is heavily rejected among the broad European public—including a considerable number of Muslims themselves. Since mistrust towards "Islam" in general is widespread in Europe, shariah as an integral part of it shares the same fate. Explicitly anti-Islamic political parties have gained considerable ground in several European countries within the last two decades, where they are represented in parliaments, such as the Fremskrittsparti in Norway, the Sverigedemokraterna in Sweden, the Dansk Folkeparti (DF) in Denmark, the Partij voor de Vrijheid (PvV) in the Netherlands, the Vlaams Belang in Belgium, the Mouvement National Républicain (MNR) in France, the Schweizer Volkspartei (SVP) in Switzerland, the Freiheitliche Partei Österreichs (FPÖ) in Austria, the Lega Nord in Italy, and the Jobbik Party in Hungary.[38] Some of these parties even have partly influenced governments. According to representative polls in several European states published in 2010, nearly half of the

---

[32] Cf. Peter A. Ulram, *Integration in Österreich. Einstellungen, Orientierungen, und Erfahrungen von MigrantInnen und Angehörigen der Mehrheitsbevölkerung* (2009), pp. 18, 45: the definition of "religious" covers Muslims for whom their religious norms are more important than Austrian law, whereas the "secular" Muslims prefer the latter. These definitions are not totally clear, since the two subgroups of "moderate religious political" Muslims, who put religious norms in the foreground, but do not want them to be implemented into state legislation, are mixed with the "religious-political integralists," who wish also the latter (p. 45). 508 Muslims were interviewed, a number which is taken to be representative for Austrian Muslims of Turkish origin (Ulram, n. 3, p. 12).

[33] Ulram (n. 32), p. 47.

[34] Ulram (n. 32), p. 44 in particular.

[35] Cf. Edwige Rude-Antoine, "La coexistence des systèmes juridiques différents en France: l'example du droit familial," in Kahn 2001, pp. 147, 159.

[36] Cf. Marie-Claire Foblets, "Le statut personnel musulman devant les tribunaux en Europe: une reconnaissance conditionelle," in Kahn 2001, pp. 33, 52.

[37] Cf. Leila Jordens-Cotran, "Application of the Law of Nationality and the Right to Respect the Identity of Minorities," in Austrian Association for the Middle East Hammer-Purgstall 2009, pp. 58 s.

[38] The policies of some of these parties are analyzed by Hans-Georg Betz and Susi Meret, "Revisiting Lepanto: The Political Mobilization against Islam in Contemporary Western Europe," in Maleiha Malik 2010, pp. 104–25.

population believes that there are too many Muslims in their country, and similar numbers consider Islam to be "a religion of intolerance" and support the idea that "Muslim views on women contradict our values."[39] Unequal treatment of the sexes[40] and religions/beliefs according to traditional shariah interpretations are the most criticized phenomena regarding shariah regulations; other interpretations are simply neglected. Furthermore, there is a widespread reluctance in European societies as a whole to accept religiously founded norms in secular states apart from those rooted in Christianity. According to representative polls in France in October 2012, 43% of the French regard Muslims as a threat to their national identity, whereas only 17% perceive the Muslim community as an enrichment. Sixty percent (as compared to 55% two years before) said that Islam is too important regarding its influence and visibility in the country.[41]

Muslim extremist groups, such as Sharia4UK[42], Hizb al-Tahrir,[43] or Khilavet Devleti[44]—many of them based in the UK—or individuals, such as Abdul Ghaffar El Almani alias Eric Breininger,[45] indeed propagate shariah to be the only valid normative order for Muslims anywhere in the world. This includes adherence to the draconian corporal punishments according to traditional Islamic penal law. According to these groups and individuals, shariah is indeed opposed to democratic principles under the rule of law. This is equally true for crude perceptions of shariah in Salafi youth culture. A former rapper called Deso Dogg (alias Mamadou Cuspert),[46] more recently known

---

[39] Cf. Friedrich Ebert Stiftung Forum Berlin (ed.) (authors Andreas Zick, Beate Küpper, and Andreas Hövermann), *Intolerance, Prejudice and Discrimination: A European Report* (Berlin 2011), p. 61, available at <http://library.fes.de/pdf-files/do/07908-20110311.pdf>.

[40] A thorough exemplary analysis of the contemporary legal and political developments in Iraq relating to gender issues in personal law is presented by Layla Al-Zubaidi, "The Struggle over Women's Rights and the Personal Status Law: A Test Case for Iraqi Citizenship?," *Orient (German Journal for Politics, Economics and Culture in the Middle East)* 2/2011: 39–52.

[41] Cf. the IFOP study *L'image de l'Islam en France. Résultats détailles Octobre 2012*, available at <http://www.ifop.com/media/poll/2028-1-study_file.pdf>, pp. 5, 18.

[42] A small group derived from the former extremist group "al-Muhajiroun" led by the extremist solicitor Anjem Choudary; cf. an interview with him from August 10, 2012, available at <http://www.cbn.com/cbnnews/world/2012/August/UK-Islamist-Leader-Islam-Will-Dominate-America/> (November 11, 2012).

[43] An extremist group acting worldwide, founded in Jerusalem in 1953 by the Muslim scholar Taqi al-Din Nabhani, aims at restoring the Islamic caliphate and rejecting democracy; cf. e.g. their British website <http://www.hizb.org.uk/> and Mathias Rohe, "Islamismus und Schari'a," in Bundesamt für Migration und Flüchtlinge (ed.), *Integration und Islam* (Nürnberg, 2005), pp. 120, 135 ss. in particular.

[44] Cf. Werner Schiffauer, *Die Gottesmänner—Türkische Islamisten in Deutschland* (Frankfurt am Main: Suhrkamp, 2000).

[45] Breininger was a German convert to Islam following a jihadist-Salafi ideology who was killed in Pakistan in 2010; he has published an autobiography titled *Mein Weg nach Jannah* (My way to Jannah, i.e. paradise); on shariah cf. p. 95 (a report on him and his ideology is available in Niedersächsisches Ministerium für Inneres und Sport—Verfassungsschutz, *Islamismus—Entwicklungen—Gefahren—Gegenmaßnahmen*, Hannover 4/2012, pp. 60–2).

[46] He is one of the most prominent German Salafi extremists; cf. Nina Wiedl, *The Making of a German Salafiyya: The Emergence, Development and Missionary Work of Salafi Movements in Germany* (Aarhus CIR, 2012), p. 48.

as Abou Maleeq, has written a *nasheed* (song of praise) with the title "Awake finally! *Allahu akbar*," calling Muslims to fight in *jihad*[47] and adding verses "*Mujahid, Mujahid, Scharia,* Somalia, *La ilaha illa Allah, Allahu Akbar, Allahu Akbar*; Emigrate, emigrate, Uzbekistan, Afghanistan, we are fighting in Chorassan, *Allahu Akbar, Allahu Akbar*."[48] "Sharia" here appears as a token of extremist self-definition including the appeal to jihad.

While such individuals and groups only represent a small minority of European Muslims, visible Islam as a part of shariah normativity has come under general pressure in a number of European countries. Currently, the building of mosques, with their characteristic minarets, has become the focus of debates on limiting religious freedom. In Switzerland, the right-wing SVP (Swiss People's Party) launched a successful campaign in 2009 against the building of any new mosques on Swiss soil.[49] In the Austrian state of Carinthia previously governed by the populist, right-wing party BZÖ (Prime Minister Jörg Haider), anti-mosque legislation was passed by parliament in 2008.[50] The text of the applicable laws refers to the "protection of the local view" in a seemingly neutral way. The newly established local commission has to examine whether a building fits into the existing architectural frame or not. In case of doubt, a certain legal procedure has to be brought forward within the municipality.[51] In practice, this amendment is specifically aimed at Muslim buildings of worship: in the draft law from January 31, 2008 mosques were mentioned as an example of the projects to be dealt with by the commissions. The Prime Minister of Carinthia (Kärnten), Jörg Haider, promised the voters during the electoral campaign in 2008 that his state would be "the first country with laws prohibiting the construction of mosque and minarets."[52] This clearly demonstrates the abuse of legislative power by Islamophobic political movements, since these laws obviously violate the neutrality of the state towards religions and the principle of equal treatment under the veil of only formal neutrality. In the same vein, a draft law brought into the Italian parliament in 2008 by the Lega Nord aimed at banning the establishment of mosques.[53] According to polls conducted in the Netherlands in 2008, between 56% and

---

[47] In this context, the term *jihad* has to be interpreted in the traditional sense as struggle/warfare aiming at enlarging the realm of Islam (cf. only Ruud Peters, *Jihad in Classical and Modern Islam* (Princeton: Markus Wiener, 1996), pp. 28 ss; Rohe 2011, pp. 149 ss). It is noteworthy that the vast majority of Muslims nowadays follows newer interpretations, reducing *jihad* to self-defense in case of aggression and to the necessity of combating the evil within everyone's personality.

[48] Translation from German by the author. The German text is published in Niedersächsisches Ministerium für Inneres und Sport—Verfassungsschutz (n. 45), p. 75 s.

[49] Cf. Vincenzo Pacillo, "'*Stopp Minarett*'? The Controversy over the Building of Minarets in Switzerland," in Ferrari and Pastorelli 2012, 337–52.

[50] Cf. Heine, Lohlker, and Potz 2012, p. 131.

[51] For details cf. Heine, Lohlker, and Potz 2012, p. 132; Farid Hafez and Richard Potz, "Moschee- und Minarettbauverbote in Kärnten und Vorarlberg," in John Bunzl and Farid Hafez (eds.), *Islamophobie in Österreich* (Innsbruck/Wien/Bozen: StudienVerlag, 2009), 144–56.

[52] Cf. Heine, Lohlker, and Potz 2012, p. 131.

[53] Cf. "Moschee, la legge-muro della Lega 'Non deve nascere una ogni 4 ore,'" *Corriere della sera*, August 22, 2008 (Alessandro Trocino).

87% of those who vote for major political parties support halting construction of large mosques that have characteristically Islamic architecture.[54]

In Cologne, Germany, the plans of DITIB (a major Muslim Turkish organization related to the Turkish state) to build a mosque with 55-meter minarets have triggered protests since 2007 not only by extreme right-wing nationalists. The mosque opponents have protested the "visible claim of power" that such mosques represent, also implying obvious distrust of those who wish to build them. At the same time, a broad political majority in Cologne supports the mosque-building plans, arguing that Muslim members of German society have a right to the visibility that comes with the mosques. German law would certainly support this view, provided that the building and environmental codes that apply to construction projects for religious purposes[55] are met. Obviously, visible symbols of Islam are still broadly perceived as foreign and even inimical. In sum, public attitudes towards Islam and Islamic norms differ considerably from the legal framework regulating freedom of religion and the applicability of religiously based norms, including those of shariah.

In the following section, the scope and limits drawn by European legal orders for the application of important religious and legal shariah rules will be explained.

# The Legal Situation: On the Scope and Limits for the Application of Shariah Rules[56]

## Introduction: Differentiation between Religious and Legal Rules

The starting point for the application of shariah norms in Europe and worldwide today is the principle of territoriality. Each country is ruled by its own legal order which decides whether and to what extent "foreign" norms might be applied. The legal system is not multicultural as far as it concerns the decisive exercise of legal power, despite the existence of normative pluralism within European societies.[57]

---

[54] Cf. "Twee derde wil stop op grote moskeeën," *Nederlands Dagblad*, June 5, 2008 (available at <http://www.nd.nl/Document.aspx?document=nd_artikel&id=115299>. Only among the voters of the left-ecologist (GroenLinks: 30%) and liberal (D66: 39%) parties supporters of such a stop are minorities.

[55] These are privileged at German law; cf. Rohe 2007, p. 83.

[56] This article relies in this part on relevant data collected within the RELIGARE project (n. 1). For the systems of coexistence of norms in Europe cf. Mathias Rohe, "Family and the Law in Europe: Bringing Together Secular Legal Orders and Religious Norms and Need", in Shah, Foblets, and Rohe (eds.) *Family, Religion and Law: Cultural Encounters in Europe* (Farnham: Ashgate, 2014).

[57] Cf. the most informative volume *Shari'a As Discourse* edited by Jørgen Nielsen and Lisbet Christoffersen (Farnham: Ashgate, 2010), namely the chapter on the British situation written by Prakash Shah, p. 117, and the models developed by Lorenzo Zucca, *A Secular Europe* (Oxford: Oxford University Press, 2012), pp. 194–6 in particular.

It is necessary to distinguish legal norms enforceable by official state measures from all sorts of norms and acts operating socially without the validation by the official legal system of enforcement. In the latter field, normative pluralism is indeed widespread. But in case of conflict, compulsory state rules will prevail over social or religious ones. However, the legal system maintains the flexibility to accommodate pluralism to a considerable extent.[58]

First, in applying shariah norms, the legal orders fundamentally differentiate between religious and legal issues. Religious issues are regulated by the European and national constitutional provisions including article 9 of the European Convention on Human Rights (ECHR), which grants freedom of religion including state neutrality towards religions. Thus, from a legal (certainly not a socio-cultural) point of view, there are no "foreign" religious norms as opposed to "domestic." In contrast, in legal issues the application of foreign legal rules is an exceptional case, broadly restricted to some areas of civil law (as opposed to public law).

Second, regarding religious norms, freedom of religion is not limited to private worship, but also grants an adequate (though not unlimited) protection of religious needs in various aspects of public life (from building mosques to social-security issues) and private labor law.[59] Nevertheless, European countries vary in their applications of these provisions due to differing interpretations regarding the desirable degree of distance between the state and religion.[60]

France and parts of Switzerland, for example, impose strict separation between state and religion through the principle of *laïcité*. In France, civil servants and even pupils cannot display ostensible religious symbols during work or school hours. In Britain, by contrast, Muslim women teachers (not to mention pupils) and officers and lawyers in court may wear veils. The European Court of Human Rights has accepted such differing national approaches under the "margin of appreciation" given to the national legislator in decisions from 2001 to 2005. The court effectively refused to rule that banning the wearing of headscarves in schools and universities by teachers[61] and students[62] violates article 9 of the ECHR. Thus the ECHR grants a minimum though considerable European standard of rights, whereas some national constitutions, as in Germany, open broader space for religion in public space.[63]

---

[58] For the scope and limits of such accommodation cf. the concise chapter of John Witte, "The Future of Muslim Family Law in Western Democracies," in Ahdar and Aroney 2010, p. 279.

[59] Cf. Rohe 2007, pp. 79, 82–8.

[60] For an overview cf. Richard Potz and Wolfgang Wieshaider (eds.), *Islam and the European Union* (Leuven: Peeters, 2004); European Parliament, Directorate General for Internal Policies of the Union, *Islam in the European Union: What's at Stake in the Future?*, May 2007 (PE 369.031); Mathias Rohe and Sebastian Elster, "Zur öffentlichrechtlichen Situation von Muslimen in ausgewählten europäischen Ländern," in Bundesministerium des Inneren Wien and Sicherheitsakademie, *Perspektiven und Herausforderungen in der Integration muslimischer MitbürgerInnen in Österreich* (Wien, May 2006).

[61] Dahlab, Switzerland, February 25, 2001, NVwZ 2001, p. 1389.

[62] Leyla Shahin, Turkey, November 20, 2005, NVwZ 2006, p. 1389.

[63] For details cf. Silvio Ferrari, "Religion in the European Public Spaces: A Legal Overview," in Ferrari and Pastorelli 2012, 139–56 and the other contributions on details in the same volume.

# The Application of Islamic Religious Rules

## Introduction

Conflicts regarding Islam mostly concern the appearance in the public space.[64] The aim of secularity and state neutrality has translated into severe restrictions on the expression of religion in institutional public space (e.g. concerning civil servants) in all European countries. In common public space (streets, etc.), religion can be expressed to a vast extent. Differences between countries can be explained by different perceptions of the role of state and religions. In a somewhat simplifying view, countries following the model of strict laïcism try to reduce the public visibility and influence of religions, since they are taken to challenge the supremacy of state power. Other countries recognize the potential of religions to positively contribute to society, reinforcing peace and stability in society, as well as common human rights values. Such basic elements of political culture certainly influence the scope of religious freedom in the public sphere. Nevertheless, in all European states a far-reaching minimum standard is granted by article 9 of the ECHR. In which legal fields can religious shariah norms be applied then?

## The Political Debate on Public Law

The secular state by definition has to treat religions equally and neutrally despite variations in implementing these principles. Muslims have established a religious infrastructure, such as mosques, organizations, education initiatives, and media, in the twentieth century in many European countries. While the visibility of the Islamic religion might trigger heated debates among the European public, the application of shariah provisions concerning religion is not so problematic from a legal point of view, since it simply requires the application of the legal rules of the land. Thus, there is no element of challenge with respect to the sovereignty of the law of the land. The latter alone decides on the protection of religious freedom.

On the other hand, an "internal" challenge arises if the state's own secular democratic principles, namely that of state neutrality concerning religion and belief and their equal treatment, are not applied. The treatment of Muslims in daily administrative and legal practice turns out to be a litmus test for the seriousness of European legal orders in implementing their basic principles. In Italy for example, there exist no clear regulations on establishing a religious infrastructure for religious minorities. This consequently makes the building of mosques difficult for Muslim communities.[65] In Germany, some

---

[64] Silvio Ferrari has developed a very helpful model by distinguishing between (open) common space, (free and plural) political space, and (neutral) institutional space (n. 63).Thus, it can make a difference to admit religious symbols for pupils in public schools for granting the freedom of expression and the plurality of experiences, whereas it can be problematic to shape this space by the compulsory display of a religious symbol like the crucifix.

[65] Cf. Regional administrative court of Emilia Romagna judgment no. 792 of November 26, 2009, confirmed by the judgment of the Council of State no. 683 of January 28, 2011; Regional administrative court of Lombardia judgment no. 6226 of December 28, 2009 concerning the establishment of mosques in buildings used for commercial purposes before.

states like Baden-Württemberg have introduced religious dress code restrictions for (female) teachers or state officers.[66] Seemingly neutral formulae are used, without mentioning dress, but parliamentary proceedings make clear that these regulations aim at prohibiting wearing the headscarf. Within the same law, Christian or occidental "cultural values" (including dress elements) are declared not to violate the duty to keep neutrality. Such laws most likely violate the constitutional principle of equal treatment of religions and beliefs:[67] the state may decide under its power of discretion (margin of appreciation accepted by the ECHR) whether religious symbols worn by public servants are handled more or less restrictively. In any case, the degree of restrictions has to apply equally. More generally, the more the Christian heritage of Europe is perceived to be *legally* (not only culturally) dominant by the public or in politics and administrations, the more likely deviations from the existing laws are.

To some extent, the confrontation with Muslim needs and creeds may help to clarify fundamental issues regarding the relation between constituent elements of European states: often, in debates among Muslims and non-Muslims alike, democracy and the rule of law are simply equated. In reality though, the two might be in conflict with each other. While a broad scope of political decisions has to be made in accordance with the will of the majority, human rights—including individual and collective freedom of religion and belief[68]—draw firm limits to this will for the sake of legitimate minority rights, the individual being the smallest minority in this sense. Efficient protection of these rights is necessary not only regarding dictatorial interference, but also towards democratic decisions. The Swiss minaret ban from November 2009 (amendment of the Swiss federal constitution by article 72 section 3[69]) is an example of a conflict between democracy and the rule of law. While the Swiss political elites except the Islamophobic right-populist SVP refused this ban, a majority of 57% voted in support of it. Nevertheless, according to a nearly unanimous conviction among European lawyers, this ban violates article 9 ECHR, which grants freedom of religion not only in private, but also in public space. The majority is not entitled to infringe basic rights of the minority. In case of conflict, the rule of law protecting everyone equally supersedes democratic majorities. It is interesting that a considerable number of those supporting the ban had no objections to minarets in particular. Instead, they used the vote to express their unspecific concern about Islam and immigration.[70]

---

[66] Cf. Ruben Seth Fogel, "Headscarves in German Public Schools: Religious Minorities are Welcome in Germany, Unless—God Forbid—They Are Religious," *New York Law School Law Review* 51 (2006/2007), pp. 620, 640 ss. in particular, available at <http://a.nyls.edu/user_files/1/3/4/17/49/NLR51-306.pdf>.

[67] Cf. the relevant decision of the German Constitutional Court from September 24, 2003 (available at <http://www.bundesverfassungsgericht.de/entscheidungen/rs20030924_2bvr143602.html>); a new case challenging the Baden-Württemberg law on schools will be decided in 2014.

[68] Cf. only art. 18 UNDHR, art. 9 ECHR.

[69] The text and legal references are available at <http://www.admin.ch/ch/d/sr/1/101.de.pdf>.

[70] Cf. the short, but very precise analysis in "Vier Gründe für das Minarettverbot," *Die Presse*, November 20, 2009 (Carola Schneider).

The Swiss example could not have occurred in other democratic European countries, since contrary to the Swiss system of so-called direct democracy, the rule of law is superior to democratic majority decisions. Nevertheless, on the political level the Swiss debates are far from being unique. In Austria, some states have tried to ban or restrict the establishment of mosques and minarets by law in a formally neutral shape but clearly aimed specifically at Muslims. In Germany, according to representative polls in 2010, 58.4% of the population condoned the idea of considerably restricting Muslims' right to practice their religion.[71] Information and education about constitutionally protected human rights is evidently a never ending task with respect to society as a whole rather than to single groups alone.

The most recent example of using the public appearance of Islam for mainly internal political reasons is legislation on the so-called *burqa*-ban in some European countries. While legislation was passed in France, Belgium, and some municipalities in Italy and Spain, in the Netherlands and Switzerland, parliamentarian initiatives have been stopped.[72] Interestingly, it is directed not against the *burqa* alone, an Afghan women's garment covering the whole face while leaving the eyes visible, which has virtually never appeared in a European context, but against various forms of niqab, a type of garment covering the whole face while the eyes are covered with mesh. This kind of garment is widespread, e.g. in Saudi-Arabia, and promoted by Islamist and Salafi Muslims. Apparently, besides tourists from the Gulf states it seems to be worn rarely in Europe.[73] Research in France reveals that among the few Muslim women who wear this garment, a considerable number are European converts to Islam.[74]

From a legal point of view, this kind of garment can be prohibited under the existing general rules regulating public security or education, concerning all situations of public life where visibility of the face as a whole is simply necessary for legitimate reasons.[75] It

---

[71] Oliver Decker et al., *Die Mitte in der Krise. Rechtsextreme Einstellungen in Deutschland 2010* (Berlin: Friedrich-Ebert-Stiftung, 2010), p. 134, available at <http://library.fes.de/pdf-files/do/07504.pdf>.

[72] For the European debate cf. Sara Silvestri, "Comparing Burqa Debates in Europe," in Ferrari and Pastorelli 2012, 275–92 and the forthcoming volume on the *burqa*-ban edited by Silvio Ferrari (to be published by Ashgate). For the Swiss developments in September 2012 cf. "Swiss parliamentarians reject burqa ban," *Al-Arabiya News*, September 28, 2012, available at <http://english.alarabiya.net/articles/2012/09/28/240687.html>. Cf. also Natasha Bakht, "Veiled Objections: Facing Public Oppositions to the Niqab," in Lori B. Beaman (ed.), *Reasonable Accommodation: Managing Religious Diversity* (Vancouver and Toronto: UBC Press, 2012), 70–108.

[73] According to a report in the French newspaper *Le Figaro* from September 9, 2009 ("Deux mille femmes portent la burqa en France"), the French Ministry of the Interior estimates that around 2,000 women in France are wearing this garment.

[74] Cf. the report "Qui sont les femmes qui portent la burqa en France?" in *Le Figaro* from June 19, 2009.

[75] Cf. the relevant judgments of the ECHR in *El Morsli* v. *France* (no. 15585/06 from April 4, 2008) concerning security checks at the entrance to consulates, *Dogru* v. *France* (no. 27058/05 from December 4, 2008), and *Kervanci* v. *France* (no. 31645/04 from December 4, 2008) concerning physical education in schools. In contrast, in *Ahmet Arslan and Others* v. *Turkey* (no. 41135/98 from February 23, 2010), the court held that previous Turkish laws prohibiting citizens to wear religious garments in public violated art. 9 ECHR.

might also make sense to specifically protect women against being forced to wear the niqab. *Burqa*-ban legislation goes far beyond these fields. In France, legislation came into force in April 2011[76] to ban garments preventing identification in public space as a whole, irrespective of the presence or absence of particular dangers for public interests, as far as it concerns women wearing such garments voluntarily.

Obviously, such legislation is at least in part deemed to broaden political support by proving the "defense of European values" in times when politicians are struggling with all sorts of highly disputed economic and social problems.[77] The necessity and the practicability of this legislation were only marginally taken into account in this debate. Nearly no difference was made between the restriction of self-determination by legal measures on one side and a societal debate on the garment indeed (and righteously) irritating civil society on the other side. Some supporters for the ban brought forward the argument that it is impossible to suppose a free decision of women to wear the niqab, since the simple presence of the niqab proves the woman wearing it to be forced to do so. This argument cannot convince for two reasons. First, according to inquiries by the French Ministry of the Interior, among the relatively few women wearing a niqab (around 2,000 in France as a whole), a considerable number are converts to Islam who freely decided on their dress.[78] Second, if the niqab is worn under pressure, from a rule of law perspective it would be bizarre to punish those who already suffer from being forced under the niqab by penalty payments. Given the fact that French lawyers, including the Conseil d'État,[79] advised against a general ban of the niqab in public beyond specific situations (security issues, public servants, etc.), the promulgation of the law obviously was driven much more by political aims (symbolic policy of demonstrative "cultural self-defense") than by "usual" legal-regulatory purposes.

Similarly, the Belgian parliament has renewed the ban of the dissimulation of the face in part or totally, aiming at the niqab, in public space in July 2011 with only one opposing vote.[80] This was a remarkable phenomenon at a time when the country was unable to build a government for more than one year, faced considerable problems with its state debt, and given the fact that there was only a small number of persons in the country wearing such a garment.[81] Meanwhile, the Belgian Constitutional Court has approved

---

[76] Loi no. 2010-1192 du 11. Octobre 2010 interdisant la dissimulation du visage dans l' espace public.

[77] Cf. e.g. the studies of John R. Bowen, *Why the French Don't Like Headscarves: Islam, the State, and Public Space* (Princeton: Princeton University Press, 2008).

[78] N. 74.

[79] Cf. the report of March 31, 2010 "Conseil d'État rejects proposed prohibition of burqa, niqab" available at <http://humanrightsinireland.wordpress.com/2010/03/31/conseil-d%E2%80%99etat-rejects-proposed-prohibition-of-burqa-niqab/>.

[80] Cf. "Burqa ban unites a politically divided Belgium," DW-world.de, July 23, 2011, available at <http://www.dw-world.de/dw/article/0,,15260969,00.html>.

[81] In other countries like Germany, there were short debates in parliaments and the media, ending up with the broadly accepted conviction that there is simply no need for a general ban on such garments under the legal principle of self-determination, and therefore no legitimate foundation for respective legislation; cf. e.g. the expert hearing in the Federal parliament (Committee for Human Rights and Humanitarian Aid) on October 27, 2010 to which the author has contributed; the official protocol of

the law,[82] except for the case of wearing the niqab within a mosque, which according to the decision falls under the freedom of religion.

## Civil Law

Another formal level where religious norms may have an impact are social relations governed by civil law, specifically (but not exclusively) employment law. In this field, possible conflicting interests of employers and employees have to be weighed with respect to the employee's religious needs on one hand and the employer's needs on the other.[83] In general, most Muslims do not face legal problems concerning their employment. For those who need to pray during work hours, acceptable solutions can be found. Many either pray during regular breaks or concentrate their prayers in the morning and evening. In Britain, a bus driver claiming the right to interrupt his work five times a day for prayer lost his case for obvious reasons.[84] On Fridays employers often allow breaks for Muslim employees to participate in communal prayer at mosques or allow employees to finish working earlier in the day. Muslim workers are also generally allowed to use vacation days during the feasts of Eid ul-Fitr at the end of Ramadan and the Eid al-Adha (Festival of Sacrifice) in the month of pilgrimage.[85]

If the need to be present for prayer or celebration of holidays conflicts with employment requirements, solutions seem to be found mainly outside the courts, since there is little relevant case law available. A rare case in Germany concerning a conflict between employment law and the requirements of Muslim prayer or Eid feasts dates from 1964,[86] indicating that mutually acceptable solutions to such potential conflicts are readily found. A new case in 2009[87] was decided in favor of a Muslim employee who wanted to perform the ritual pilgrimage to Mecca. Her interests[88] were taken to be of superior importance in comparison to the needs of her employer. In 2011, the German Federal Labor court decided in favor of a Muslim employee in a supermarket

---

the hearing is available at <http://www.bundestag.de/bundestag/ausschuesse17/a17/anhoerungen/Religionsfreiheit/Wortprotokoll.pdf>. The expert's written preparatory statements are available at <http://www.bundestag.de/bundestag/ausschuesse17/a17/anhoerungen/Religionsfreiheit/index.html>.

[82] Decision from December 7, 2012, report available at <http://www.deredactie.be/cm/vrtnieuws.english/news/121207_Burqa>. Three reasons were given to justify the ban: the niqab is taken to threaten public security; gender equality and individuality as necessary prerequisites for a democratic society.

[83] For details cf. Mathias Rohe, "Schutz vor Diskriminierung aus religiösen Gründen im Europäischen Arbeitsrecht—Segen oder Fluch?," in Rüdiger Krause, Winfried Veelken, and Klaus Vieweg (eds.), *Gedaechtnisschrift für Wolfgang Blomeyer* (Berlin: Duncker & Humblot, 2004), p. 217.

[84] Reported in Wasif Shadid and Pieter Van Koningsveld, *Religious Freedom and the Position of Islam in Western Europe* (Kampen: Kok Pharos, 1995), p. 102.

[85] Cf. Niloufar Hoevels, *Islam und Arbeitsrecht* (Köln: Carl Heymanns, 2003).

[86] LAG Duesseldorf JZ 1964, 258.

[87] ArbG Koeln (Az.17 Ca 51/08), BeckRS 2010, 73919.

[88] The 53-year-old woman was employed in the school administration. The next period of holidays coinciding with the time of the pilgrimage would have been thirteen years later, at which point, she would have reached the age of 64. This would be likely to render the pilgrimage during the hot summer time much more challenging or, due to possible health reasons, even impossible. Additionally, she feared that her mother, who was taking care of her disabled child, would not be able to continue this at that time.

who was ordered to refill shelves with bottles containing alcohol after having worked in other parts of the market before and was dismissed when refusing the new work.[89] According to the court, the employer had omitted to examine whether the employee could have reasonably been given other duties not bringing him in conflict with his religious convictions. A British labor tribunal dismissed a similar claim of an employee in 2008.[90] In this case the employer was obviously able to convince the tribunal that he had made every effort to find alternative work for the employee; in this case German jurisprudence would also uphold the dismissal. Interestingly, the broad media debates in both cases—which seem to be extremely rare in numbers in Europe—are in stark contrast to those surrounding the widespread problem of dismissals due to alcohol abuse.

Furthermore, there are decisions in favor of Muslim female employees wearing a headscarf in cases where no security reasons are at stake. The German Federal Labor court accepted the claim of the appellant who wore her headscarf to work at a warehouse.[91] Stressing the great importance of religious freedom, the court ruled that this freedom cannot be abrogated by mere suppositions of possible economic detriment to the employer. Even in case of proven economic detriment, the employer would first have to consider whether the employee could work in a less sensitive capacity before being entitled to terminate her contract. Since European legislation on protecting employees against discrimination on religious grounds has been introduced, the scope of protection will probably broaden even more. A case from Berlin in March 2012[92] might illustrate this. The application of a well-qualified Muslim woman from Iraq wearing a headscarf for a job in a dental surgery was rejected because the employer insisted on "religious neutrality" in his enterprise. The Berlin Labor Court argued in favor of the applicant, stressing that there is no right to unconditionally keep any sign of religion outside the (non-religious) enterprise.[93] The employer was ordered to pay €1,500 in damages to the claimant. This decision was regarded as a milestone by NGOs fighting discrimination.

*Penal Law*

In penal law, the application of religious norms of all kinds has to be restricted to marginal issues, since it is the aim of penal law to grant a common minimum of standards within society. The only case where Islamic (and Jewish) religious provisions are relevant

---

[89] Federal Labor Court, February 24, 2011, available at <http://juris.bundesarbeitsgericht.de/cgi-bin/rechtsprechung/document.py?Gericht=bag&Art=pm&Datum=2011&anz=16&pos=0&nr=15389&linked=urt>.

[90] Cf. the report available at <http://www.thisisderbyshire.co.uk/Muslim-worker-loses-Tesco-booze-bid/story-11581305-detail/story.html>.

[91] Federal Labor Court NJW 2003, 1685.

[92] Cf. Berlin Labor Court, March 28, 2012 (55 C1 2426/12).

[93] Cf. the report "German Dentist Fined for Anti-Hijab Bias" from October 20, 2012, available at <http://www.onislam.net/english/news/europe/459596-german-dentist-fined-for-anti-hijab-bias.html>.

is male circumcision performed according to the medical standards of care. This procedure may be well qualified to be a (minor) corporal harm, but nevertheless is taken to be justified on acceptable religious grounds.[94] It is relevant that this attitude, which was nearly unanimous for decades, is now disputed in recent legal literature.[95]

Until 2012, Sweden was the only country to introduce specific legislation on circumcision. In 2001, the Swedish parliament restricted permission for carrying out circumcision to physicians, only after the infant was more than two months old, and the procedure was performed in hospitals according to medical standards of care.[96] In May 2012, the German regional court of Cologne[97] held male circumcision, even if performed by medical standards of care, to be punishable under German penal law. This decision went against a unanimous opinion in the judiciary[98] so far, which held this procedure to be lawful. It was based on short and poorly balanced reasoning, simply stating that the parents cannot validly consent to the harm caused to the child. The court made no attempt whatsoever to weigh up the parent's motivation of integrating the child into a religious community according to their definition of the best welfare of the child with the (relatively minor) violation of the integrity of the child's body. This decision, given by one out of 116 regional courts, was not binding beyond the specific case before them, but nevertheless caused uproar in the Jewish and Muslim communities. It was rejected by most of the political parties and by leading politicians including the Chancellor who said that the country will certainly not turn into a "nation of comedians." Legislation aimed at clarifying the permission of male circumcision performed according to medical standards of care and without unnecessary harm has passed the German parliament on December 12, 2012.[99] The ongoing debate shows an increasingly aggressive secularist tone condemning any religious rites to be backward and irrelevant in a secular society.[100]

---

[94] Cf. e.g. the judgment of the Finnish Supreme Court in October 2008 (report available at <http://yle.fi/uutiset/supreme_court_male_circumcision_not_a_crime/6115572>). For Germany cf. Rohe 2011, p. 344. Certainly, major harms like female mutilation will never be justifiable or excusable on religious or cultural grounds whatsoever.

[95] Cf. Holm Putzke, "Die strafrechtliche Relevanz der Beschneidung von Knaben," in Putzke et al. (eds.), *Festschrift Herzberg* (Tübingen: Mohr Siebeck, 2008), pp. 669–709, in an unusually aggressive tone.

[96] Cf. a report available at <http://sverigesradio.se/sida/artikel.aspx?programid=1316&artikel=974694> (July 30, 2012); cf. also the new debate on a total ban in the report "Swedish docs in circumcision protest" from February 19, 2012, available at <http://www.holmputzke.de/images/stories/pdf/2008_fs_herzberg_beschneidung.pdf> (July 31, 2012).

[97] LG Köln decision of May 7, 2012 (151 Ns 169/11).

[98] According to German law of social welfare, the state even has to finance the costs of a decent celebration of the circumcision in case of need, cf. OVG Lüneburg FEVS 44, p. 465.

[99] Cf. Entwurf eines Gesetzes über den Umfang der Personensorge bei einer Beschneidung des männlichen Kindes from November 5, 2012, Bundestagsdrucksache 17/11295, available at <http://dipbt.bundestag.de/dip21/btd/17/112/1711295.pdf>.

[100] Cf. the lucid essay of Heiner Bielefeldt, UN special rapporteur for freedom of religion and belief teaching at the University of Erlangen-Nürnberg, "Marginalisierung der Religionsfreiheit?" available at <http://www.polwiss.uni-erlangen.de/professuren/menschenrechte/UN%20Sonderberichterstatter/bielefeldt_beschneidungsurteil_vorabfassung.pdf> (July 31, 2012), to be published.

In the aftermath of the German debate, in Norway[101] and Switzerland,[102] similar campaigns are underway to ban any kind of (male) circumcision of minors who are not capable to decide on their own.

Another field of possible tensions may arise from informal dispute resolution in criminal cases conflicting with the penal legal order. A relevant case involving Salafis was reported in Spain in 2009. A group of seven persons originating from North Africa had allegedly "sentenced" a woman having committed adultery to death in a "shariah court" condoned by the victim's family.[103] They were later set free because the woman had disappeared and thus could not identify the accused before the court. In 2011, a book appeared in Germany dealing with "shariah judges" settling criminal disputes among Muslims in the country.[104] It is based on sixteen case studies in the cities of Berlin, Bremen, and Essen, including interviews with so-called shariah justices of peace, lawyers, and attorneys. Allegedly, crime victims were pressed to accept financial compensation for "silence" while witnesses were intimidated. The cases referred to conflicts concerning members of huge Kurdish family clans (comprising several thousand members) who have indeed established legally unacceptable "parallel" structures challenging state authority in penal law matters. While forms of *voluntary* mediation between culprits and victims are established in penal issues under state supervision, the limits should be clear: exercising pressure on victims or witnesses cannot be tolerated by the state. But it is far from clear whether the decisions relied on shariah rules or, more probably, on cultural norms only bearing a religious surface.

## *Informal Application*

Finally, religious norms can be "applied" at an informal level, merely by practicing them. It is mainly in the sphere of religious rules—concerning the relations between God and human beings (*'ibadat*) and the non-legal aspects of relations between human beings (*mu'amalat*)—where a European shariah (in this context: Islamic "theology") is possibly developing.[105] In such cases, the opinions contained in religious rulings, or fatwas, would distinguish between legal validity of the transactions at stake and their religious acceptability. This is not a new development in Islam, but it may rely on the traditional distinction between the religious and the legal dimensions of human behavior (e.g. the

---

[101] The Norwegian Senterpartiet formulated demands on banning male circumcision; cf. the report available at <http://www.dagbladet.no/2012/06/19/kultur/debatt/omskjering/helse_bergen/bar_overkropp/22180612/> (July 30, 2012).

[102] Cf. the report "Keine Chance für Verbot von Beschneidungen" from July 24, 2012, available at <http://www.20min.ch/schweiz/news/story/Keine-Chance-fuer-Verbot-von-Beschneidungen-17282420>.

[103] Cf. "Juicio islàmico por adulterio a una mujer en Reus" (Salud Muñoz), Elmundo.es 06.12.09, available at <http://www.elmundo.es/elmundo/2009/12/06/espana/1260084030.html>.

[104] Joachim Wagner, *Richter ohne Gesetz. Islamische Paralleljustiz gefährdet unseren Rechtsstaat* (Berlin: Econ, 2011).

[105] Cf. Mathias Rohe, "The Formation of a European Shari'a," in Malik 2004, p. 161; studies of present developments are presented by Shadid and Van Koningsveld 2003, p. 149, and by Waardenburg 2003, pp. 241, 308, and 336.

distinction between the categories of what is considered to be forbidden (*haram*), and what is considered to be "invalid" (*batil*)).[106] Obviously, this reflects a broader trend among Muslims in Europe and other Western countries towards a de-territorialization and de-legislation of shariah developing it anew as a merely or primarily ethical/moral set of norms. This approach is developed by Muslim scholars under the heading of shariah provisions providing guidance rather than governance.[107] The scope of scholars ranges from rather traditionally oriented ones, represented by the European Council for Fatwas and Research, which differentiates between the legal and the religious/moral aspects of human acts[108] and other proponents of a "minority *fiqh*,"[109] to innovative approaches like those of Abdulaziz Sachedina,[110] Ahmad Moussalli,[111] Tareq Oubrou,[112] Amina Wadud,[113] or Mouhanad Khorchide.[114]

But it should be mentioned that there are some efforts by extremist Islamist groups and the Salafi movement that aim at the construction of an exclusive Muslim normative order opposing the governing rules of the land (cf. above). According to research done in the German state of Bavaria in 2012,[115] there are indeed some cases of shariah-inspired

---

[106] Cf. Rohe 2009, pp. 9–18.

[107] Cf. Abdullahi An-Na'im, "Islam and the Secular State," pp. 28–44 in particular; Abdulaziz Sachedina, "The Role of Islam in the Public Square: Guidance or Governance?," in Muqtedar Khan (ed.), *Islamic Democratic Discourse* (Lanham: Lexington Books, 2006), p. 173. This trend can be discerned also among Muslim teachers and students in Germany who are involved in establishing Islamic confessional instruction and university education according to the German legal system (cf. Mouhanad Korchide, *Islam ist Barmherzigkeit—Grundzüge einer modernen Religion* (Freiburg: Herder, 2012), and observations by the author who has been closely involved in the establishment of these projects for more than a decade. Cf. also Jocelyne Cesari, "Islam in France: The Shaping of a Religious Minority," in Yvonne Yazbeck Haddad (ed.), *Muslims in the West: From Sojourners to Citizens* (Oxford: Oxford University Press, 2002), pp. 36, 41 ss.

[108] Cf. Mathias Rohe, "The Formation of a European Shari'a," in Malik 2004, pp. 176, 179 in particular.

[109] Cf. e.g. Alexandre Caeiro, "Transnational 'Ulama', European Fatwas and Islamic Authority: A Case Study of the European Council for Fatwa and Research," in Martin van Bruinessen et al. (eds.), *Producing Islamic Knowledge: Transmission and Dissemination in Western Europe* (London: Routledge, 2011), 121–41; Sarah Albrecht, *Islamisches Minderheitenrecht. Yūsuf al-Qaraḍāwīs Konzept des fiqh al-aqallīyāt* (Würzburg: Ergon, 2010); Hellyer 2009, pp. 79–99.

[110] Abdulaziz Sachedina, "The Role of Islam in the Public Square: Guidance or Governance?", in Muqtedar Khan (ed.), *Islamic Democratic Discourse* (Lanham: Lexington Books, 2006), p. 173.

[111] Ahmad S. Moussalli, *The Islamic Quest for Democracy, Pluralism, and Human Rights* (Gainesville: University Press of Florida, 2003).

[112] Tareq Oubrou, "Introduction théorétique à la chari'a de minorité," *Islam de France* 2 (1998), p. 27; Tareq Oubrou, "La charia de minorité: contribution pour une integration légale de l'islam" (February 21, 2003), available at <http://www.islamlaicite.org/article24.html> (November 10, 2012); cf. also Manni Crone, "Shari'a and Secularism in France," in Nielsen and Christoffersen 2010, pp. 141, 145–8 in particular.

[113] Cf. her work *Inside the Gender Jihad: Women's Reform in Islam* (Oxford: Oneworld, 2006), pp. 92 ss.

[114] Cf. his work *Islam ist Barmherzigkeit. Grundzüge einer modernen Religion* (Freiburg/Breisgau: Herder, 2012), pp. 116 ss.

[115] The Bavarian Ministry of Justice implemented a research group of legal practitioners and social organizations working on preventive and repressive measures, the former led by the author. The results are as yet unpublished.

"parallel justice" in family matters, where undue pressure was exercised on women to refrain from their rights under German law.

## The Application of Islamic Legal Rules

### Introduction

When it comes to legal shariah provisions (in the form of modern state law), their application may cause more tensions. While the guarantee of freedom of religion is a part of European legal orders, foreign laws are possible "competitors" of these orders. In the course of a century-old development, personal law systems implementing a kind of legal pluralism have been replaced in Europe and large parts of the world by territorially unified laws granting internal pluralism, but reserving the right of last decision to state law in case of conflicting norms.[116] Thus, it is up to the law of the land alone to decide which legal norms are applicable and to what extent. While the secular state does not and cannot claim to provide spiritual guidance or a coherent system of morality, it claims indeed the right of last decision concerning the legally binding regulations of human interaction in this world.[117]

Certainly, religious convictions may play an important role in formulating and reforming the existing law. Nevertheless, such religious reasoning has to pass a "secular argumentative filter" as to its concrete contents.[118] God's (perceived) will cannot replace reasonable argumentation. For example, the prohibition of drinking alcohol might be derived from religious commands. Secular regulations on banning the consumption of alcohol in certain public spaces (e.g. schools, working places, traffic) cannot rely on such commands. They have to be based on a reasoning that addresses public welfare by weighing up security issues against individual freedom.[119]

What then are secular arguments for the application of Islamic legal rules in a European legal context? There are two different kinds of reasons here. The following examples will demonstrate that such reasons are "external" insofar as the law of the land simply prescribes the application of such norms in a given case more or less irrespective of the intention of the parties involved. "Internal" reasons are those rooted in the desires of the parties themselves. The latter may be differentiated into technical/institutional, cultural, and religious ones.

---

[116] For the problems of legal transplants concerning personal law systems into Western legal orders cf. only Jean-François Gaudreault-Desbiens, "Religious Courts, Personal Federalism, and Legal Transplants," in Ahdar and Aroney 2010, 159–80.

[117] Cf. Heiner Bielefeldt, *Muslime im säkularen Rechtsstaat* (Bielefeld transcript, 2003, pp. 32–6 in particular).

[118] Cf. only Jürgen Habermas, *Glauben und Wissen. Friedenspreis des Deutschen Buchhandels 2001* (Frankfurt am Main: Suhrkamp, 2001), p. 22; Jürgen Habermas, *Zwischen Rationalismus und Religion. Philosophische Ansätze* (Frankfurt am Main: Suhrkamp, 2005), p. 137.

[119] Cf. e.g. Silvio Ferrari, "Islam und Laizität," in Gian Enrico Rusconi (ed.), *Der säkularisierte Staat im postsäkularen Zeitalter* (Berlin: Duncker & Humblot, 2010), pp. 269, 273.

## External Reasons (Given By the State)

There are three fields of law where Islamic norms may be applicable or recognized for mainly external reasons. Firstly, private international law may lead to the application of Islamic law within the limits of public policy. Secondly, in some states Islamic norms were implemented into the existing law (UK, Spain) of the land or maintained under international treaty obligations (Greece) for historical reasons. Thirdly, given legal facts created under Islamic law may be recognized under Western laws for social reasons.

All these fields are part of civil law, as opposed to public and penal law. In matters of civil law, which primarily regulates private relations (from contract and tort up to family and inheritance issues), individual preferences are of prime importance. It is in this context that foreign legal norms may be applied or tolerated as far as possibly conflicting state interests are not concerned. But it is increasingly the case that modern "strong" states tend to interfere more intensely into fields perceived to be solely or mainly "private" in the past.

Family issues are particularly relevant. Whereas in some parts of the world, including many countries in the Islamic world,[120] there is a perception of the family being predominantly private and thus excluding any state intervention except in extreme cases of violence, European states have developed a dense system of state control and intervention to protect the welfare of the weaker members of the family. As a consequence, private interests in exercising private autonomy and being granted reliable relations according to their own decisions have to be weighed against possibly conflicting protective state interests under the auspices of public policy. The following examples will show the considerably different principles and outcomes in various European legal orders.

## Private International Law (State Law)

Private international law (PIL), which regulates conflicting laws pertaining to civil matters, is the most prominent level on which Islamic legal rules can be directly applied. Civil law essentially regulates the legal relations between private individuals, whose welfare is of prime importance. This includes the continuity of existing legal relationships (such as marriage) when crossing "legal borders" (so-called "theory of vested rights" developed by the eminent British and US lawyers Dicey and Beale). In such primarily private matters of an international dimension (e.g. caused by foreign citizenship or residence) it is desirable to apply the substantive law having the most significant relationship to the case to be decided. The revolutionary idea underlying this concept is the principal equality of all legal orders, which is why foreign law can be applied. The question as to whether foreign or national substantive law should be applied in particular cases must therefore be determined, and this is done by the provisions of PIL, which weigh up the relevant interests.

---

[120] This term is widespread, but rather inaccurate. It is used as a synonym for "countries with a Muslim majority population," but is not intended to express the (wrong) idea that these states and their societies are solely or even mainly ruled and driven by the religion of Islam.

Nevertheless, the legal community in every country may decide that in certain matters the same substantive law should be applicable to everyone resident there. This would be the case particularly in matters touching the roots of legal and societal common sense, like those regulated by mandatory family law. The PIL provisions on public order draw the necessary limit to maintain important common standards, such as human rights.

In shariah-based law, there are many provisions, e.g. concerning contracts, that do not contradict European laws. The main conflicts arise in family and inheritance matters over constitutional and human rights, such as gender equality and freedom of religion, including the right not to believe, and the protection of minors. Provisions reflecting classical Islamic law preserve strict separation between the sexes with respect to their social roles as well as far-reaching segregation of religions under the supremacy of Islam. Though child marriage is abolished in some Islamic countries, it is still practiced in others.[121] The different ways of reasoning within European legal orders shall be demonstrated using case law examples concerning repudiation (*talaq*, unilateral divorce) and polygamy.[122]

According to traditional Islamic law, which is still in force in many Islamic countries despite a number of internal reforms in favor of women,[123] only the husband is entitled to terminate the marriage by a unilateral declaration of repudiation without any reason being given. This has to be repeated two additional times, and attempts at reconciliation have to be made, but in case of their failure the marriage is dissolved. Such a procedure clearly contradicts the European legal principle of equality of sexes, since wives only have very limited rights to divorce,[124] in addition to the principle of life-long marriage, which does not allow the dissolution of the marriage by such easy procedures. According to

---

[121] Cf. e.g. a recent decision of the Court of Appeals (Kammergericht) of Berlin (FamRZ 2012, 1495): the marriage between a former Lebanese German Shi'i Muslim and a 14-year-old Lebanese Shi'i girl valid under Lebanese law (according to the still valid Ottoman family code) was not recognized due to a violation of German public order. A 14-year-old person is not considered to be able to freely and responsibly decide on a fundamental issue like marriage (the minimum age in Germany, dependent on the consent of the parents or the competent court, is 16).

[122] For studies concerning the application of Islamic legal provisions cf. Foblets (n. 36), pp. 33, 63 with numerous references, and Foblets, "The Admissibility of Repudiation: Recent Developments in Dutch, French and Belgian Private International Law," *Hawwa* 5(1) (2007): 10–32; Veronika Gärtner, *Die Privatscheidung im deutschen und gemeinschaftlichen Internationalen Privat- und Verfahrensrecht* (Tübingen: Mohr Siebeck, 2008); Rohe 2011, p. 353; Julia Koch, *Die Anwendung islamischen Scheidungs- und Scheidungsfolgenrechts im Internationalen Privatrecht der EU-Mitgliedstaaten* (Frankfurt am Main: Peter Lang, 2012).

[123] For new developments cf. Ziba Mir-Hosseini, "Islamic Family Law and Social Practice: Anthropological Reflections on the Terms of the Debate," in Austrian Association for the Middle East Hammer-Purgstall 2009, pp. 37–48 with numerous references; Rohe 2011, pp. 182 ss., 207 ss.; Maaike Voorhoeve (ed.), *Family Law in Islam: Divorce, Marriage and Women in the Muslim World* (London: I. B. Tauris, 2012).

[124] Cf. Rohe 2011, pp. 93 ss., 216 ss. Courts usually differentiate between these forms of divorce: foreign decisions are then recognized if the cases meet the prerequisites of a "equal rights" divorce, cf. only the French Court of Cassation, February 23, 2011, No. 10-14.760.

unanimous regulations in European legal orders, a *talaq* cannot be validly pronounced on European soil.[125] Furthermore, usually European legal orders refuse to recognize *talaq* procedures performed abroad when their citizens/domiciliaries or residents are involved.[126] Nevertheless, how should a European legal system address the case where the *talaq* has become valid abroad under another legal order?[127] Would European "public order" prevent its recognition in any case (as opposed to *khul'* or other forms of divorce for discord[128]) or only in those cases where the wife was not able to defend her rights and did not agree to the divorce? There is a remarkable shift within European legal orders within the last decade. The traditional PIL approach, where the *outcome* of applying the respective foreign law is addressed, is increasingly challenged in favor of examining the foreign norm itself.

German,[129] Italian,[130] and Spanish[131] courts still adhere to the traditional approach broadly.[132] Thus, the recognition of *talaq* would contradict public order in cases where the wife was not able to claim her legitimate interests or was not even informed about the divorce. In other cases, where the prerequisites for divorce according to the law of the land would be fulfilled in a comparable way or if the wife agrees, the legality of such a divorce according to Islamic tenets would be accepted by the controlling legal authority.

Belgium followed this way until 2005, when the courts started to handle recognition more strictly after the enactment of the new rules on PIL.[133] The same development can be found in court decisions in France since 2004[134] and the Netherlands, where in

---

[125] Cf. e.g. Civil Court Brussels, May 26, 1978; House of Lords, *R. v Secretary of State for the Home Department ex p. Fatima Ghulam*, [1986] AC 527 (HL).

[126] Cf. only art. 46 Family Law Act 1986 of England & Wales; art. 57 sections 2.2., 2.3. Belgian PIL code 2004.

[127] For an overview cf. Katajoun Alidadi, "The Western Judicial Answer to Islamic Talaq," *UCLA Journal of Islamic & Near Eastern Law* 5 (2005): 1–80; Foblets (n. 122).

[128] Cf. French Court of Cassation, February 23, 2011, no. 10-14.760, regarding a French-Moroccan case where the spouses had lived separately for three years and the divorce was not qualified as a unilateral divorce by the Moroccan court; Court of Appeals Versailles, March 25, 2010, no. 08/08808; Dutch Supreme Court, July 13, 2001, rechtspraak.nl LJN AB2623 (WPNR 2001 (6470)); Cour d'appel Antwerpen, June 30, 1982, J.D.I. 1982, 740 s.

[129] Cf. e.g. Court of Appeals Hamm, March 7, 2006, BeckRS 2007, 00423; Court of Appeals Frankfurt am Main, May 11, 2009, 5 WF 66/09, BeckRS 2009, 24414; Mathias Rohe, "Islamic Law in German Courts," *Hawwa* 1 (2003), pp. 46, 50.

[130] Cf. Court of Appeals Cagliari, May 16, 2008, No. 198.

[131] Cf. Supreme Court, ATS, April 21, 1998, RJ 3563.

[132] The Court of Appeals Stuttgart is stricter in its rules; cf. the decisions in IPRax 2000, 427; FamRZ 2004, 25.

[133] Court of Cassation, April 29, 2002; after 2005 cf. Court of Appeals Mons, December 20, 2007; Civil court Liège, June 26, 2009; Labor court Brussels, May 27, 2010; but also Labor court Brussels, January 12, 2011. Cf. Foblets (n. 123); Koch (n. 123), pp. 175–8.

[134] Older decisions by the Court of Cassation from 2001, 2002 were now overruled since a turn of the same court in 2004 (February 17, 2004, No. 01-11.549, and No. 02-11.618; Court of Cassation, January 3, 2006, No. 04-15.231; Court of Cassation, November 4, 2009, No. 08-20.574). The decisions of 2004 were implicitly approved by the ECHR in the decision of November 8, 2005 (Affaire D.D. c France, no. 3/02, available in the French version at the court's website <http://hudoc.echr.coe.int>), pointing at the relevant new French decisions.

the past the differentiation made by German courts equally applied.[135] In Austria, the Supreme Court[136] from the beginning refused to accept any kind of *talaq*. There is an emerging trend in PIL to follow a policy of legal symbolism, which means to abstractly defend principles as such instead of deliberating the particularities of a case before the court.

The crucial legal question is whether legislative bodies and the courts compare foreign legal norms categorically as with their normative domestic "counterpart" in an abstract way, or whether the results of the strict application of foreign norms must be controlled in specific cases. The abstract "human rights approach" leads to clear results—the rejection of *talaq* in any case. In addition, it can be used as a political instrument to demonstrate European "cultural self-defense" against Islamic law.

The concrete approach is less strict, but it might help the divorced wife, in cases when she wishes to remarry and therefore needs the recognition of the previous *talaq*, for example.[137] In case of non-recognition she would be forced to apply for divorce in European courts, which would often turn out to be equally time-consuming and expensive, particularly if the husband is living in a country which is not easily accessible for judicial correspondence, or if his address is unknown. If the residence permit for the woman is dependent on the new marriage, her need for having the *talaq* recognized is even more pressing. The abstract "human rights approach" would then turn itself against the person it intends to protect, and the woman is consequently punished twice.

The same differences are visible in dealing with polygamous marriages validly conducted under foreign laws. Polygamy fundamentally contradicts European legal standards; therefore it cannot be contracted legally in Europe and is even punishable under many European penal codes. Similarly, polygamous marriages by European citizens or domiciliaries that have been performed abroad are not recognized within the different European legislations.[138] The question arises in other cases (where neither citizens nor domiciliaries are involved) as to whether the second wife or other wives can be entitled to claim their rights to maintenance against their husband, rights to participate in the estate of the deceased husband under succession law or in social security claims he acquired during his time of employment.

In England, a court has rejected the claim to a widow's pension by a woman who was engaged in a polygamous marriage, resulting in none of the wives in the marriage

---

[135] The last decisions in this sense were Court of Cassation, July 3, 2001 (Rev. crit. int. privé 2002, 704 note Gannagé).

[136] OGH decision of August 31, 2006 (6Ob189/06), Zeitschrift für Rechtsvergleichung 2007, 35; OGH decision of June 28, 2007 (3Ob130/07z); both decisions available at <http://ris.bka.gv.at>.

[137] This was the case in the decisions of the German Supreme Court from 2004 (BGH FamRZ 2004, 1952) and from 2007 (NJW-RR 2007, pp. 145, 148 ss). The same policy seems to be followed in Denmark according to Peter Arnt Nielsen, *Internasjonal privat- og procesret* (Copenhagen: Gjellerup/Gad, 1997), pp. 69–70.

[138] Cf. the English Court of Appeal in *Hussain v. Hussain* [1982] 1 AllER 369.

receiving a payment.[139] A Dutch court rejected in 2009 the request of the second wife for divorce, because the marriage was not recognized either.[140] German social security laws treat polygamous marriages as legally valid, provided that the marriage contracts are valid under laws applicable to them at the time of their conclusion.[141] The legal reasoning is not to deprive women in polygamous marriages of their marital rights, including maintenance. Thus, according to German[142] and Spanish[143] social security laws widow's pensions are divided among widows who were living in polygamous marriages. In Belgium, widow's pensions have to be generally divided similarly to the German situation; nevertheless, there is dispute between courts[144] as to whether in cases where the first wife has the nationality of a country prohibiting polygamy, the second wife has to be excluded from widow pension claims. The underlying "principle of proximity," which aims at granting the first wife the full amount of rights in monogamous marriages, applies in France according to the jurisdiction of the Court of Cassation. In consequence, no share of a widow's pension was granted to the Algerian second wife of a deceased husband who was still married with a French wife.[145] In contrast, the same court held that a polygamous marriage valid under the domestic law of either spouse can be recognized.[146] Similarly, English courts[147] have granted a second wife dower payment agreed upon in the marriage contract under the law of contract, thus separating this particular provision from status issues.

The law differentiates between mainly private aspects of marriage and predominantly public ones, especially those relating to immigration law. Italian[148] or German[149] law for

---

[139] Court of Appeal in *Bibi v. Chief Adjudication Officer* [1998] 1 FLR 375: none of the widows is accepted to be one legally; cf. the critical remarks of David S. Pearl, *Islamic Family Law and Its Reception by the Courts in England*, Harvard Law School Islamic Legal Studies program, Occasional Publications, May 2000, p. 14.

[140] District Court Utrecht, January 21, 2009, LJN BH 3029.

[141] Cf. Regional Court Frankfurt am Main FamRZ 1976, p. 217; Regional Court Osnabrück NJW-RR 1998, p. 582; Local Court Bremen StAZ 1991, pp. 232, 233; Administrative Court of Appeals Kassel NVwZ-RR 1999, pp. 274, 275.

[142] Cf. para 34 sect. 2 Social Code I.

[143] Cf. Superior Court of Justice of Galicia (TSJ de Galicia, Sala de lo Social), April 2, 2002; Superior Court of Justice of Madid (TSJ de Madrid, Sala de lo Social), July 29, 2002; Superior Court of Justice of Andalusia (TSJ de Andalusia, Sala de lo Social), January 30, 2003; Superior Court of Justice of Catalonia (TSJ de Cataluña, Sala de lo Social), July 30, 2003.

[144] Cf. the Belgian Court of Cassation, December 3, 2007, and Constitutional Court, June 4, 2009. The latter equated the situation of simultaneous polygamy to the (well established Belgian) successive polygamy (re-marriage after divorce), which equally leads to shared claims in the public sector pension scheme. The same reasoning can be found in Spanish cases.

[145] Court of Cassation, July 6, 1988, No. 85-12.743.

[146] Court of Cassation, September 24, 2002, No. 00-15.789.

[147] Cf. *Shahnaz v. Rizwan* [1964] 2 All E.R. 993; *Qureshi v. Qureshi* [1971] 1 All E.R. 325.

[148] Cf. Regional Administrative Court of Emilia-Romagna, December 14, 1994, No. 926; Court of Appeals Turin, April 18, 2001.

[149] Cf. OVG Koblenz, March 12, 2004 (10 A 11717/03), available at <http://www.asyl.net/index.php?id=185&tx_ttnews[tt_news]=19684&cHash=e4a46e2d9a> (July 28, 2012).

instance, provides only the first wife in polygamous marriages with marital privileges within its scope of application, for example regarding residence permits. Alternatively, a Dutch judgment[150] from 2009 accepted such a marriage for immigration purposes, but (more consistently) another Dutch court[151] rejected in 2006 the possibility for the second wife to voluntarily participate in the social security scheme of her "husband."

Which are the main reasons for lawyers to decide in such different manners? From a legislative perspective, two types of goals must be considered. One goal would be to establish clear-cut legal norms in absolute accordance with prevailing social mores, in this context, the sole validity of monogamous marriages. This would lead to rejection of polygamous marriages that are legal in other parts of the world and would leave the weaker parties without legal protection, which could encourage the creation of a parallel system of social norms among the parties involved. Suppose the second wife claims maintenance from her husband, wants to participate in inheritance after his death, or wishes a divorce from him. None of these claims can be accommodated if she were to access European courts in cases of conflict. The only solution would then be to resort to informal, socially accepted bodies for granting appropriate remedies.

The other goal would be to render justice for individuals who legally enter polygamous marriages in other jurisdictions and who make claims in a jurisdiction that rejects such marriages. In these cases it has to be made clear that accommodation for individuals does not mean acceptance or approval of polygamy. Usually, courts following this approach would first stress in their decisions that polygamy is not accepted as a legal institution. They would then continue by saying that the claimant should not be deprived from her rights which she has reasonably relied on under the legal order which applied at the time of the marriage.

*Dispositive Substantive Law*

A second area for indirect application of foreign legal norms exists within the framework of so-called "optional" civil law. Here, the legislator opens space for private autonomy in creating legal relations. This includes the choice of rules within the given compulsory legal framework. For example, there are various methods of investment that do not violate the Islamic prohibition against usury (*riba*, which according to traditional interpretations means not accepting or paying interest).[152] To enable business financing, Islamic law permits the formation of types of companies (e.g. *mudaraba*) for this specific purpose.[153] In such companies gain and loss is shared among the partners according to the

---

[150] Rechtsbank Den Haag, November 23, 2009.

[151] District court Rotterdam, 20 July 2006, Rechtspraak.nl LJN AY5484 concerning the application of the Treaty regarding Social Security between the Netherlands and Morocco.

[152] Cf. Kilian Bälz, "Scharia Jet Set: Islamic Banking," *INAMO Berichte und Analysen* 57 (Spring 2009): 14–17 with rich factual background; Luqman Zakariyah, "Legal Maxims and Islamic Financial Transactions: A Case Study of Mortgage Contracts and the Dilemma for Muslims in Britain," *Arab Law Quarterly* 26 (2012): 255–85.

[153] Cf. Reinhard Klarmann, *Islamic Project Finance* (Zürich/Bâle/Genève: Schulthess, 2003); Kilian Bälz, "A Murbaha Transaction in an English Court," *ILAS* (2004), pp. 11, 117 ss.

success or failure of the company. None of the partners may thus profit on the expense of the others. In addition, traditional forms of complex sales contracts (e.g. *murabaha*) are used for the same purpose. This established form of subsequent contracts contains at least two sales contracts regarding one item (e.g. a machine for industrial production), where the margin of profit for the buyer/re-seller is determined as a part of the second contract. Thus, a bank financing the purchase of the machine by the entrepreneur would first buy the machine and then sell it to her customer. Functionally, the denominated margin of profit replaces the interest rate to be paid if the purchase would be financed by credit. None of these transactions would contradict European contract laws in general.[154]

European states started to use such instruments or facilitated them by legal amendments. Thus, in the UK a special vehicle for "Islamic mortgages" has been developed, enabling Muslims to purchase real estate while avoiding conflicts over *riba* on the basis of a *murabaha*. This combination of transactions was financially unattractive, since full stamp tax had to be paid for either of the transactions, while economically only one transaction was intended. Now, stamp tax has to be paid only once. In 2005, the German state of Sachsen-Anhalt offered "Islamic" bonds replacing interest payments by broadly accepted instruments of financial participation in the state's real estate property to attract Muslim investors. Similarly, investments prohibiting engagement in alcohol and pork production and pornography, for example, are now offered in many European countries by Islamic or other banks.[155] This is taken to be a kind of ethical economics which usually does not cause any legal problems in principle.

In the field of matrimonial law, introduction of Islamic norms into marriage contracts has also been addressed within several European legal systems. This field gains prime importance in the European states following the Rome III regulation on international divorce law from December 2010.[156] This regulation prefers the law of habitual residence as the prime connecting factor in international cases, adding the possibility to choose the law of nationality of either spouse. The same system applies in the new EU regulation on succession and wills from July 2012.[157] In all the European states which followed the principle of nationality in family matters until now, there will be a dramatic shift in numbers from "international" to "internal" cases in the future, since jurisdiction rules usually lead to the courts of habitual residence, which then will regularly apply the law of the land. Instead of controlling the application of foreign laws by international public order, the stricter principles of internal legal order ("good morals") will apply. Institutions of Islamic family law will now regularly be scrutinized by the principles of the established family law rules. This is

---

[154] Cf. e.g. Michael Mahlknecht, *Islamic Finance* (München: C. H. Beck, 2008); Hans-Georg Ebert and Friedrich Thießen, *Das islamkonforme Finanzgeschäft* (Stuttgart: Deutscher Sparkassenverlag, 2010); Michael Gassner and Philipp Wackerbeck, *Islamic Finance*, 2nd edn. (Köln: Bank-Verlag, 2010).

[155] Cf. Rohe 2011, pp. 368 ss. According to newspaper reports, there are such developments for example in the UK, in the Netherlands, Belgium, Germany, Switzerland, and Austria; no in depth-research results have been published yet on this issue.

[156] EU regulation no. 1259/2010.

[157] EU regulation no. 650/2012.

certainly a major challenge for European lawyers, since European family laws are certainly based on Christian perceptions of marriage, while being "secularized" during the last decades.[158] Reasonable accommodation has to be sought by clarifying misunderstandings and false conflicts in cases where legal institutions are in fact not contradictory, and to examine to what extent party autonomy opens space for private choice in arranging marriage, in cases such as matrimonial property, for example.[159]

Contractual conditions regulating the payment of dower (*mahr* or *sadaq*)[160] in Muslim marriages in particular, had to be judged.[161] It should be noted that such payments are due to the bride,[162] not to her father/family as is the case in other customary law practices among Kurds,[163] or in countries such as Yemen, Afghanistan, or Pakistan which are not recognizable under European laws,[164] including Turkey.[165] Such payments would be considered as a sales price for the bride, which would challenge her human dignity as well as her free will to decide whether or not to marry. To the contrary, *mahr* claims would only improve the legal situation of the bride, and thus cannot be considered to violate her rights.[166] On the other hand, taking the payment of *mahr* as an indispensable prerequisite for a valid marriage could violate European public policy, since this could contradict the principles of freedom of marriage and equality of the spouses.[167]

Often the dower payment is divided into two parts: the first one due at the time of the marriage is only symbolic, whereas the second part is due at the time of (unilateral) divorce by the husband or at his death. This regulation can be an effective instrument of protection for wives who, according to traditional Islamic law, can only claim post-marital maintenance for three months, or as a tool for bargaining over the post-marital custody for children, which is generally distributed according to patriarchal principles—the wife can then waive her claim for the deferred *mahr* in exchange for the husband's agreement on a favorable custody regulation. In Britain, according to

---

[158] Cf. Gerhard Dilcher and Ilse Staff (eds.), *Christentum und modernes Recht* (Frankfurt am Main: Suhrkamp, 1984), the contributions of Gerhard Dilcher ("Ehescheidung und Säkularisation," pp. 304–59) and Helmut Coing ("Die Auseinandersetzung um kirchliches und staatliches Eherecht im Deutschland des 19. Jahrhunderts," pp. 360–75) in particular.

[159] The results of the relevant RELIGARE research were published in 2013; cf. also the case law data available at the RELIGARE database (accessible at <http://religare-database.eu/>).

[160] For details cf. Rohe 2011, pp. 85 ss.

[161] Cf. the study of Pascale Fournier on the application of *mahr* provisions in Western courts (2010, pp. 35–100 in particular).

[162] This was stressed by the French Court of Cassation, November 22, 2005, No. 03-14.961: therefore, the *mahr* cannot be qualified as a "prix de vente."

[163] Cf. Christian Rumpf, *Einführung in das türkische Recht* (München: C. H. Beck, 2004), p. 118.

[164] Cf. e.g. Court of Appeals Hamm, January 13, 2011 (I-18 U 88/10).

[165] The Court of Cassation has rejected a başlık para claim due to a "breach of the law and ethical values" of the country; T.C. Yargıtay (19. Civ) no. 2009/6565; decision no. 2010/4421.

[166] The *mahr* was misinterpreted in this sense by Regional court Köln IPRspr. 1980 no. 83; Court of Appeals Lyon, December 2, 2002, reversed by Court of Cassation (1ère civ) November 22, 2005, no. 03-14.961.

[167] Cf. the relevant French decision by the Supreme Court (1ère civ) April 4, 1978 (Benziane), and the Belgian decision Court of Appeals Ghent, September 12, 1994 (the lack of dower alone is no proof for the

a court decision in 2010[168] such an agreement was accepted, whereas before they were taken to be void among British citizens or domiciliaries for violation of British public policy.[169] Dutch,[170] French,[171] and German[172] courts have similarly accepted these agreements in principle. On the other hand, a Danish court[173] has qualified such agreements as simple donation promises, which then usually are in need of specific forms of contracting often unknown to the parties. This does not necessarily meet the complexity of such agreements, which could become meaningful for the couple when leaving for a country governed by Islamic family law, and clearly indicates the need for more in-depth information about Islamic law institutions in European courts.[174] In some cases widespread prejudice concerning Muslims might be invoked by the parties themselves. In a German case from 1998, a Turkish wife having accepted a guarantee in favor of her husband claimed that, being married to a Turkish Muslim, she was not free to decide on the contract. By this argument she wanted to have the contract declared void for lack of free will. She did not provide concrete evidence for having been pressed or forced into this contract, but only argued on the basis of an abstract view on "suppressed Muslim wives." The German Supreme Court[175] rejected this claim and clearly stated that there is no room for the *presumption* of Turkish wives living in a "typical Muslim marriage" to be deprived from autonomous decision-making in daily life without any concrete evidence in the particular case.

On the other hand, such prejudice has to be rejected when used against Muslims. In a German case in 2010, an insurance company refused to pay damages to a Muslim pensioner who was hurt in a road accident for the time he was unable to care for the household (which he had done for years) while his wife was still working as an employee. The reason for the payment refusal was the alleged "fact" that Muslim men do not wash

lack of consent between the spouses); but see also Court of Appeals Bruxelles, February 1, 1994 (JLMB 1994, 599) and May 10, 1996 (RTDF 1998, 43), where the lack of dower was taken as an evidence for the lack of consent, but only among other elements indicating a sham marriage.

[168] *Radmacher v. Granatino* [2010] UKSC 42. The prior decision approving *mahr* (*Uddin v. Choudhury* [2009] EWCA Civ 1205) concerned a case of informal marriage.

[169] Information given to the author by Alberto Neidhardt from University of London/Queen Mary College in 2011.

[170] Rb Alkmaar, October 16, 2008; Rb Rotterdam, February 22, 2010.

[171] Court of Cassation, December 2, 1997, no. 95-20.026 and November 22, 2005, no. 03-14.961.

[172] Federal Supreme Court, NJW 1999, p. 574; OLG Celle FamRZ 1998, p. 374; OLG Saarbruecken NJW-RR 2005, p. 1306.

[173] Eastern High Court of Denmark, April 6, 2005; for possible functions of *mahr* in Denmark cf. Niels V. Vinding and Lisbet Christoffersen, *Danish Regulation of Religion, State of Affairs and Qualitative Reflections* (Copenhagen, August 2012), p. 38.

[174] In a seminar for European judges organized within the RELIGARE research framework in December 2011 the participants unanimously expressed the need to build up easily accessible information structures for courts and administrations. As an example for the necessity of detailed information cf. Werner Menski, "Life and Law: Advocacy and Expert Witnessing in the UK," in Holden 2011, pp. 151, 168 ss. in particular.

[175] BGH NJW 1999, 135.

dishes or care for the household in other ways according to the "traditional patriarchal male self-understanding in marriage." After media reports of the case were disseminated, the company decided to pay.[176] Both cases demonstrate how parties try to navigate by using prejudice to their respective advantage, and how critical it is for lawyers to carefully handle the facts.

*Introduction of Islamic Provisions into the Law of the Land*

Islamic norms were applied in the European territories under Islamic rule from the Middle Ages until the end of the Ottoman Empire. Today such norms are part of the legal system only in Greece regarding the Muslims of Turkish and Bulgarian origin in Thrace according to the Lausanne Treaty 1923 (see the chapter on Greece). They still live under shariah law based on Ottoman family law.[177] In fact, the legal "freeze" by the Lausanne Treaty is increasingly at odds with the family law reforms within Turkey in the course of the "secularization policy" under Mustafa Kemal Atatürk in the 1920s. They started in 1926, when the Swiss Civil Code provisions on family law, which were patriarchal in Christian-European style of the time, replaced the former shariah-inspired laws. The secularization policy was last amended in 2002 with a completely gender-neutral legislation. A paper on family law and the full implementation of gender equality drafted on behalf of the Ministry of Justice proposes the abolishment of the shariah regime introduced in Greece. Due to delicate political questions at stake, the Greek government does not seem to be inclined to present similar suggestions to the parliament.[178]

A few European states have introduced Islamic legal provisions concerning family matters that can be applied in Muslim communities on a voluntary basis. As to the celebration of marriages in Britain, Muslim institutions may apply to become entitled to register marriages under the Marriage Act 1949 section 46 with civil effects. In Spain, since 1992 Islamic legal norms regulating marriage contracts have been applied to Muslims[179] in tandem with compulsory secular state provisions for the registration of these marriages.[180] Furthermore, according to the Divorce (Religious Marriages) Act of 2002, courts can require the dissolution of a religious marriage before granting a civil divorce.[181] The Adoption and Children Act of 2002 amended the Children Act of 1989,

---

[176] Cf. the report "Ein Muslim spült nicht ab," September 25, 2010, available at <http://www.nw-news.de/lokale_news/guetersloh/guetersloh/3788789_Ein_Muslim_spuelt_nicht_ab.html> (July 30, 2012).

[177] Cf. Konstantinos Tsitselikis, "The Legal Status of Islam in Greece," in Rohe (guest ed.), *Shari'a in Europe, Die Welt des Islams* 3/44 (2004), 402, 417 ss.; Konstantinos Tsitselikis, *Old and New Islam in Greece: From Historical Minorities to Immigrant Newcomers* (Leiden: Martinus Nijhoff, 2012), pp. 367 ss.

[178] For a critical report on the current situation cf. Lina Papadopoulou, "Trapped in History: Greek Muslim Women Under the Sacred Islamic Law" (2010), available at <http://papers.ssrn.com/sol3/papers.cfm?abstract_id=1877048> (October 11, 2011).

[179] Cf. Joaquín Mantecón-Sancho, "L'Islam en Espagne," in Potz and Wieshaider (eds.) (n. 60), pp. 109, 130 ss.

[180] Cf. Article 59 Código Civil in conjunction with the administrative provision of the general directorate of the Civil Registry and the Notary from February 10, 1993.

[181] Cf. Lord Nazir Ahmad, "Notes on the Judicial Situation of Muslims in the United Kingdom," in Thorsten Schneiders and Lamya Kaddor (eds.), *Muslime im Rechtsstaat* (Münster: Lit Verlag, 2005), p. 72;

introducing "special guardianship" provisions to enable parental relationships by legal means other than adoption, which is forbidden by Islamic law.[182] This option is not formulated on the basis of religion and is thus open to all, irrespective of religion.

The formal incorporation of Islamic law is nevertheless an exceptional case relating to merely formal legal provisions like the procedural aspects of marriage contracts, and not the substantive ones. In contrast, potential substantive aspects like the minimum age of marriage, polygamy, or repudiation (*talaq*) pronounced on European soil, are not accepted under domestic substantive law.

In other European countries, such legislation has not been proposed. In Germany, most Muslims of Turkish and Bosnian origin would vehemently oppose the introduction of shariah legal norms: according to their understanding, traditional Islamic family and inheritance law, which was abolished in their home countries long ago, contains unacceptable patriarchal concepts and legal inequality of religions. Moreover, personal-status laws based on traditional mores of particular religious communities often conflict with modern law codes that secular European countries formulate and enforce for their populations as a whole.

European states maintain centralized control over the definition and enforcement of core rights and duties of the citizenry as a whole, irrespective of ethnic, religious, or other group affiliation. Thus when conflicts arise between commonly defined individual rights and collective claims, the former will prevail. This is why European family laws, which follow the principle of equal treatment of sexes, religions, and beliefs of all citizens and inhabitants, cannot accept the implementation of collective normative systems opposing these basic principles. The constitutions in force would not permit another solution, for example, the introduction of laws that would abolish gender-neutral equal rights in favor of a system of mere "equal dignity." Given the fact that European family laws to a large extent contain mandatory rules (e.g. regarding the prerequisites for valid marriages and divorces), personal and family matters cannot be seen as merely "private."

## Internal Reasons

### Technical/Institutional Reasons

In cases of intermarriage and transnational conduct of life, the persons involved may have a mere technical interest to create legal relations recognized in all the countries involved, irrespective of the concrete contents or the religious connotation of the law. Problems arise when some religiously-founded foreign state laws do not recognize decisions on marriage, divorce, or custody by secular states in matters of family law, while they would recognize informal acts by religious personnel or (ADR) decisions on the basis of the same religiously-orientated laws. According to verbal reports by many

---

Urfan Khaliq, "Islam and the European Union: Report on the United Kingdom," in Potz and Wieshaider (eds.) (n. 60), pp. 219, 246 ss.

[182] Cf. Qur'an surah 33, 4. s; art. "tabanni" in *wizarat al-awqaf, al-mawsu'at al-fiqhiya*, vol. 10 (Kuwait, 1987).

family lawyers, this seems to be the case in Morocco,[183] Iran, Pakistan,[184] and Tunisia, despite the fact that Tunisia went far in recognizing foreign decisions contrary to traditional Islamic family law.[185]

To give a practical example dealt with in the German local court of Siegburg in late 2011,[186] a couple living in Germany, married according to Iranian law in Iran, asked for a divorce in Germany. According to German PIL, Iranian family law had to be applied in this case. Both spouses agreed to the divorce. The wife intended to travel to Iran with her children for an urgent family visit, but then wanted to return with the children to Germany. According to information about the legal situation in Iran, the parties were aware that the husband could challenge the German divorce to be invalid under Iranian law because the German court's declaration of divorce would not be accepted to properly replace the husband's pronunciation of the Islamic *talaq* or his agreement to a *khul'*-divorce. In consequence, the husband was able to claim that the couple was still married, being able then to prevent the wife and the children from leaving the country without his consent. Thus, the court in a very exceptional manner decided to overcome the problem of recognition by making the husband sign the procedural files, declaring his consent to the divorce. A representative of the Iranian embassy and an imam were also invited to the procedure. Though this was not usual "German" procedure, an additional service was accommodated for the sake of the parties. Nevertheless, usually courts are either unaware or not inclined to assist parties in this way. Parties are then forced into informal procedures fulfilling the prerequisites of the legal order in the parties' country of origin.

In other cases known to the author, mere formal reasons such as the lack of documents required for marriages under the law of the land might draw immigrants, such as Iraqi refugees in Germany, to enter into informal religious marriages in order to create socially accepted fundamentals for living together.

*Cultural Reasons*

Many groups of Muslim immigrants maintain the structures of family life current in their countries of origin. Some of them are reluctant to use the legal remedies provided by the law of the state they are living in because they believe that they are bound to legal

---

[183] For Morocco (non-recognition of Belgian, Danish, and Dutch decisions) cf. also the references in L. Jordens-Cotran, *Nieuw Marokkaans Familierecht en Nederlands IPR* (Den Haag: Sdu uitgevers bv, 2007); Mohamed Loukili, "L'ordre public en droit international privé marocain de la famille," in Bernard-Maugiron and Dupret 2010, pp. 138–58 in particular.

[184] For Iran and Pakistan cf. also Kirsten Cherry, "Marriage and Divorce Law in Pakistan and Iran: The Problem of Recognition," *Tulsa Journal of Comparative & International Law* 8.2. & 9.1. (2001): 319–54.

[185] Cf. Monia Benjemia, Souhayma Ben Achour, and Meriem Bellamie, "L'ordre public en droit international public Tunisien de la famille," in Bernard-Maugiron and Dupret (2010), pp. 217–32 in particular (the article deals with *private* international law).

[186] Unpublished. Cf. the report "Scheidung mit Richter und Mullah, KStA," November 16, 2012, available at <http://www.ksta.de/region/amtsgericht-scheidung-mit-richter-und-mullah,15189102,12032204.html>.

orders different from the law of the land. Others are simply unaware of the fact that in certain matters, including those pertaining to family law, the formal legal rules of the state of residence have to be observed for creating legally enforceable relations.

There is evidence on that particularly regarding Muslims in Britain.[187] For three decades some dozen[188] informal "Islamic shariah councils" have been in operation in the country. The procedural formalities and the qualifications of the members are highly diverse.[189] They are mainly dealing with divorce issues regarding legally invalid, but religio-socially accepted Islamic marriages, or valid marriages in cases when the social environment does not accept the civil divorce alone for cultural or religious reasons, or if such procedures are necessary to obtain recognition in the country of origin. In this case, husbands are asked to agree to the Islamic divorce by pronouncing a *talaq* or by agreeing on a *khul'* or *mubarat* (cf. above). Since all kinds of solutions stay in the hands of the husband, he has the potential to exercise pressure on the wife regarding her claims to *mahr*, which then have to be waived in favor of the husband.[190] The decisions of such institutions are not legally binding,[191] but may gain considerable social relevance.

Here, accessible information about the rules of the law of the land for immigrants is needed. In addition, a lack of cultural sensitivity in some state institutions including courts may lead to distrust and reluctance. Evidence, e.g. from Canada,[192] supports this view. The author came across an example of a German family court to which a Turkish woman applied for divorce. She had been forced into her marriage, was severely abused and virtually imprisoned by her husband during the ten years of her stay in Germany. At last, she dared to apply for divorce. In the courtroom, one of the first questions the judge raised in a strict tone was why translation into German was needed, since the applicant

---

[187] Cf. Jørgen Nielsen, *Emerging Claims of Muslim Populations in Matters of Family Law in Europe*, CSIC-MR Birmingham, CSIC Paper no. 10, November 1993; Pearl and Menski 1998, pp. 51 ss., 73 ss.; Shah-Kazemi 2001; Prakash Shah, *In Pursuit of the Pagans: Muslim Law in the English Context*, RELIGARE working papers, March 2012, available at <http://www.religareproject.eu/system/files/Working%20Paper%209%20Prakash%20Shah.pdf> (July 30 2012).

[188] The number is unclear. Samia Bano has contacted 30 tribunals. The figures given range from 30 to 80 approximately. One of the biggest institutions is the London-based shariah council, which according to its own statistics has dealt with 3,000 cases from 1996–2002 and 2,000 cases from 2003–5, mainly concerning Muslim women's applications for Islamic divorce (cf. the Council's website, available at <http://www.islamic-sharia.org/about-us/about-us-9.html>); cf. also John Bowen (who did the broadest research on shariah councils in the UK so far), "How Could English Courts Recognize Sharia?," *University of St. Thomas Law Journal* 7(3), pp. 411, 418 ss., available at <http://anthropology.artsci.wustl.edu/files/anthropology/imce/How_Could_English_Courts.pdf>.

[189] Cf. Bano 2012a, pp. 19 ss.

[190] Cf. Bano 2007, pp. 2–26.

[191] Cf. the British decision in *Al-Midani* v. *Al-Midani* [1999] C.L.C. 904, regarding a decision of such a body in an inheritance dispute among Muslim sisters; the arbitration agreement pointing to an "Islamic judicial body" to be involved was not considered to be fulfilled, since the Islamic shariah council had no statutory authority.

[192] Cf. Anne Saris, Jean-Mathieu Potvin, Naïma Bendriss, Wendy Ayotte, and Samia Amor, *Étude de cas auprès de Canadiennes musulmanes et d'intervenants civils et religieux en résolution de conflits familiaux* (Monréal, March 2007), p. 44.

had lived a considerable time in the country. Such behavior certainly has the potential to deter potential applicants from resorting to state institutions.

A new phenomenon of Islamic marriages has emerged according to reports from several European countries. Some couples explicitly intend to avoid legal consequences under the law of the land (e.g. mutual claims to maintenance and rights to inheritance; costly procedures in case of divorce; loss of social benefits due to sufficient financial means of the spouse), but wish to give their relationship social legitimacy, particularly to placate their parents and families. In some reported cases,[193] couples who fall in love and want to marry against the will of their families can exercise pressure on them by the "fait accompli," which is a kind of revival of marriages agreed upon within the family after the groom has "abducted" the bride, leaving parental consent to this marriage as the sole option for keeping "family honor." Evidence from Denmark shows that such couples tend to marry validly under the law of the land when children are born or when they decide to purchase real estate property.[194] Apart from the religious legitimization aiming at the social environment, this behavior reflects common usage in present Western societies.[195]

*Religious Reasons*

As regards religious reasons, there are two attitudes which fundamentally differ regarding the law of the land. First, Islamic norms may be applied *within the existing framework of the law of the land* as far as this law is dispositive for the parties involved. This is the case in vast parts of contract law (cf. above). In addition, attempts to neutrally reconcile family members in case they are voluntarily seeking religious advice are possible under European legal orders and mostly welcomed.

The second case—fundamentally different from the one above—is the informal application of Islamic norms for reasons of religiously driven *rejection of "worldly" laws* given by "infidels." "Eternal God-given law" is then (wrongly) opposed to "weak man-made law."[196] For example, a former imam in a Berlin mosque (Masjid al-Nur) has published a book in 2001 in Riyadh under the (Arabic) title of *The Rules in Family Matters for Muslim Minorities in Germany*.[197] In this book, he constantly calls German laws and court decisions to be "norms of unbelief" (*ahkam al-kufr*)[198] and appeals to Muslims to

---

[193] Cf. Anika Liversage, "Secrets and Lies: When Ethnic Minority Youth Have a Nikah," in Prakash Shah et al. (eds.), *Family, Religion and Law: Cultural Encounters in Europe*, pp. 165–80.

[194] Cf. Liversage, "Secrets and Lies: When Ethnic Minority Youth Have a Nikah."

[195] This was the unanimous impression of the presenters in the RELIGARE conference held in London on September 3, 2012 (papers to be published in the volume mentioned in n. 194).

[196] Cf. only the appeal of an extremist Belgian group published in 2011, "Oh Moslims! Blijf weg bij hun rechtbanken," available at <http://www.shariah4belgium.com/index.php?option=com_content&view=article&id=87%3Aoh-moslims-blijf-weg-bij-hun-rechtbanken&catid=35%3Aboeken&Itemid=58&lang=en>.

[197] Sālim Ibn, 'Abd al-Ghanī al-Rāfi'ī, ahkām al-ahwāl al-šakhsīya li-l-muslimīn fī l-gharb.

[198] Sālim Ibn, 'Abd al-Ghanī al-Rāfi'ī, ahkām al-ahwāl al-šakhsīya li-l-muslimīn fī l-gharb, p. 618.

always obey shariah family law rules alone. This imam demands that traditional Islamic law punishment for illegitimate sexual relationship, called *zina*, which is stoning to death or lashing, should apply to Muslims in Germany. In his opinion this should even be extended to cases of marriage between a Muslim wife and a non-Muslim husband (which is void under Islamic law), and even in cases where the parties are unaware of the traditional Islamic rules. Furthermore, he describes the German system of social care as an evil, which enables women to disregard their marital duty of "obedience" (*ta'a*) to the husband because the social system removes that need for his maintenance payments.[199] Such attitudes towards the leading principles of gender equality, the equality of religions and beliefs, and human rights standards in penal law are certainly a challenge both for the existing secular legal orders as well as for the vast majority of Muslims who do not understand their religion in this extremist way. The same is certainly true regarding Salafi extremists who feel entitled to kill others when "protecting their religion," such as in cases of alleged blasphemy.[200]

Two points regarding the European legal framework and shariah norms should be made clear. First, the fundamental principles of European legal orders cannot be subject to reduction or abolition. Second, the vast majority of Muslims in Europe seemingly supports fundamental European principles rather than rejects them (cf. the sources mentioned above). In the field of private law, mainly in the UK[201] a broader discussion has emerged among Muslims on the (optional) introduction of a Muslim law of personal status and inheritance. Given the present status of legal developments and evidence from Islamic shariah councils in Britain, this would lead to forms of legal inequality of sexes and religions.[202] At a conference in Leiden in June 2011 on shariah in the West,[203] Shaykh Fayz Siddiqi, a leader in the field of shariah councils, explained the philosophy of the British Muslim Arbitration Tribunals (MAT) established since 2007 in London, Birmingham, Bradford, Manchester, and Nuneaton under the Arbitration Act (1996)[204] regarding their working practices and results. Contrary to the informally working

---

[199] Sālim Ibn, *'Abd al-Ghanī al-Rāfi'ī, ahkām al-ahwāl al-šakhsīya li-l-muslimīn fī l-gharb*, p. 79.

[200] A Turkish Salafi extremist (Murat K., 26 years old) severely hurt two police officers in Bonn, Germany, on May 5, 2012, during a protest by a right-wing organization (Pro NRW) against Muhammad cartoons. The culprit declared that he felt and still feels obliged to enforce the "values of Islam" violently, and that he does not accept freedom of expression if it contradicts Islam (according to his interpretation). He demonstrated his rejection of secular institutions by refusing to rise in the courtroom, cf. the report "Mit Gewalt für den Islam," *Süddeutsche Zeitung*, October 11, 2012, p. 6.

[201] Cf. the references in n. 187 and Klausen 2007, p. 190 s.

[202] Cf. Shah-Kazemi 2001; Richard Freeland and Martin Lau, "The Shari'a and English Law: Identity and Justice for British Muslims," in Asifa Quraishi and Frank E. Vogel (eds.), *The Islamic Marriage Contract: Case Studies in Islamic Family Law* (Cambridge, MA: Harvard University Press, 2008), pp. 331–47 (pp. 340 ss. in particular); Bano 2012a, 2012b; Maleiha Malik 2012.

[203] Information available at <http://hum.leidenuniv.nl/lucis/eerder-bij-lucis/lucis-conference-2011-sharia-in-the-west.html>.

[204] A broader report on religious laws and legal institutions in England and Wales including Islamic rules has been recently published by Douglas et al. 2011. Cf. also the website of the MAT, available at <http://www.matribunal.com/>.

shariah councils (cf. above), the MAT are entitled to issue formal awards under this Act, e.g. related to commercial disputes including economic issues arising from family disputes. In family status issues (most notably divorce and custody of children) they have no formal competence,[205] but aim at providing informal aid, e.g. in cases of social need for an Islamic divorce[206] equal to other shariah councils. Nevertheless, decisions of the MAT might gain additional legal effect in other countries, if they are recognized there. Thus, they have undeniable relevance in the field of law, while not directly under the law of England and Wales. Moreover, if they are issued in larger numbers, they may create a certain normative culture among those Muslims who attribute normative authority to them. Thus, the legal system of the law of the land is inevitably concerned by the normative basis of such decisions, if it differs from the law of the land.

In fact, at the conference mentioned above Siddiqi explained that a great number of cases are dealing with divorce, due to the need or wish of the (mostly female) applicant to obtain a document leading to social acceptance of the divorce and of a subsequent new marriage.[207] Being asked about gender-biased provisions of traditional Islamic divorce law, he downplayed the totally different legal positions of husband and wife in matters of repudiation by suggesting there was no significant difference between the two, the husband giving the declaration of divorce and the wife receiving it. The exclusive right of the husband to pronounce the repudiation (*talaq*) of the wife as well as other gender-biased regulations in favor of the husband and thus the dimension of legal-cultural conflicts between traditional shariah provisions and European family law was not even considered. This attitude does not necessarily reflect the work of these institutions as a whole. To the contrary, Samia Bano[208] has stated that the twenty-two shariah councils in the UK she contacted seek to avoid any conflict with civil law, e.g. by requiring the civil divorce of a registered marriage before issuing an Islamic divorce. Furthermore, John Bowen sheds light on the fact that the shariah councils are considerably diverse in their attitudes regarding gender relations.[209] Nevertheless, it is likely to trigger more resistance against them among the broader public, since it seems to verify the widespread prejudice against shariah law mentioned earlier.

The work of such councils and tribunals seems to serve persons seeking religious support, but also those living in considerable distance to the British legal institutions, who seek socially acceptable conflict regulations within the community. This is equally true for cases when divorces under British law are not fully accepted by the parties or the community unless the Islamic divorce (by *talaq* or *khul'*) has also taken place.[210] The

---

[205] Cf. Douglas et al. 2011, pp. 17, 22 s. Cf. also Robert Blacklett, "The Status of Religious 'Courts' in English Law," *Disputes and International Arbitration Newsletter* (2009), pp. 11, 13.

[206] Cf. the MAT website, available at <http://www.matribunal.com/cases_faimly.html> (December 9, 2012).

[207] Bano 2012b, p. 93, and elsewhere.

[208] Bano 2012a, p. 24.

[209] Bowen 2012, pp. 84 ss, reporting some concrete cases decided in favor of the wives.

[210] For details cf. Shah-Kazemi 2001; Bowen 2012, pp. 84 ss.

price to be paid then is a considerable lack of rights in comparison to the standards of the law of the land,[211] as far as the councils follow traditional divorce rules. In 2011, Lady Cox, a member of the House of Lords, introduced a bill proposal (Arbitration and Mediation Services (Equality) Bill) aimed at preventing Muslim tribunals from making decisions in family and criminal law and from using discriminatory practices like giving a woman's testimony less weight than a man's.[212] The second reading in the House of Lords took place on October 19, 2012. No decisions have been made so far. The British Academy Policy Centre has issued a briefing on this bill[213] which contains a possible viable solution:

> The preferred option is to apply cultural voluntarism and mainstreaming on a pragmatic basis. These build on current legal structures and allow minority groups to operate their legal order among themselves, without giving them the endorsement of state law,[214] but providing opportunities for individuals to access the state system where it applies to them or where their actions have legal consequences under the ordinary law [...]. The state retains the power to withhold such consequences from activities that conflict with "liberal constitutional norms" and some activities may be completely prohibited particularly if they cause harm [...]. This allows flexibility: for the state, to decide on a case-by-case basis whether to intervene, and to individuals, to move between groups, and between such groups and the state system.

For European countries, except the UK, there is little information about Muslim attitudes towards Muslim religious norms being applied in a binding way by imams or Muslim scholars. According to interviews conducted by Jytte Klausen among 300 European Muslim leaders from September 2003 to February 2005, a large majority of interviewees outside the UK (mostly more than 70%, as compared to only 20% in the UK) rejected the statement that secular civil law should respect religious law and allow imams and Islamic scholars to decide on legally binding decisions for Muslims living

---

[211] For details cf. Shah-Kazemi 2001; Maleiha Malik, "Feminism, Multiculturalism and Minority Women," in Alison Diduck and Katherine O'Donovan (eds.), *Feminist Perspectives on Family Law* (London: Routledge, 2006), 211–31; Rohe 2011, pp. 380 ss.

[212] Available at <http://www.publications.parliament.uk/pa/bills/lbill/2010-2012/0072/2012072.pdf>. For supportive and critical voices cf. the report "Bill limiting Sharia law is motivated by concern for Muslim women," *The Guardian*, June 8, 2011, available at <http://www.guardian.co.uk/law/2011/jun/08/sharia-bill-lords-muslim-women>. In June 2010 already the "One Law For All campaign" has been launched against the application of shariah law in Britain; cf. the website <http://www.onelawforall.org.uk/about/>.

[213] British Academy Policy Centre, "The Arbitration and Mediation Services (Equality) Bill," available at <https://www.britac.ac.uk/policy/Arbitration-and-mediation-services-bill.cfm> (November 11, 2012), p. 3, no. 11 s.

[214] Jean-François Gaudreault-Desbiens, "Religious Courts' Recognition Claims: Two Qualitatively Distinct Narratives," in Ahdar and Aroney 2010, 59–69, rightly points to the problems linked with religiously based claims of collective recognition of a parallel legal system. Cf. also his chapter on "Religious Courts, Personal Federalism, and Legal Transplants," in Ahdar and Aroney 2010, 159–80.

in the country.²¹⁵ European legal orders generally admit formal, legally binding ADR (adjudication) in commercial disputes,²¹⁶ but reject it regarding family status issues (e.g. marriage, divorce, custody), including England and Wales.²¹⁷ In the latter fields state protection and transparent procedures granted by state courts are taken to be of prime importance. Even for the UK it is not totally clear whether the MAT operating presently are entitled or willing to decide such cases.

## Concluding Observations

In many European countries there is a considerable gap between the legal attitude towards Islam and shariah norms on one hand and the public perception and debate on the other. Obviously, shariah is taken to be "the other" in political debates irrespective of its fields and interpretations, which are partly in accordance with the law of the land and in part contradict it. Generally, the diversity of shariah rules and interpretations covering mainly non-legal issues is vastly ignored in the European public. At the same time, there is a considerable lack of awareness in European societies as a whole regarding the legal framework of freedom of religion, equal treatment, and the true meaning of "secular" law.

The scope and limits of the application of Islamic norms are highly dependent on the respective national tradition regulating the relations between the state and religions. Nevertheless, a broad common standard of religious freedom is granted by article 9 of the ECHR. European legal systems seem to be well prepared in general to accommodate the religion of Muslims, granting far-reaching and equal rights. This attitude is in contrast to many political moves trying to formulate a European or national self-definition in sharp segregation from Islam and shariah in a very simplifying manner and in contradiction to hitherto liberal legal standards. This might have had some impact on restrictive legislation, as is the case in several European countries like Switzerland (e.g. the minaret ban), France, Belgium, the Netherlands (e.g. the *burqa*-ban), and Austria (the intention to prevent building mosques by only formally neutral state laws), and on the arguing in court decisions like those of the ECHR in the case of Refah Partisi.

---

²¹⁵ Klausen 2007, p. 192.

²¹⁶ Cf. e.g. cases from Britain concerning an award rendered by an Ahmadi Qdha Board tribunal in a dispute over the beneficial ownership of property (*Bhatti v. Bhatti* [2009] EWHC 3506 (Ch)); concerning a contractual requirement that disputes are to be resolved by an arbitrator drawn from a specific religious community (*Jivraj v. Hashwami* [2010] EWCA Civ 712).

²¹⁷ Cf. e.g. the Danish decision of Eastern High Court of Denmark, February 21, 2006 (OE2006.B-3980-05), rejecting a custody contract arranged by an imam and the Dutch case Supreme Court, January 20, 2006 (available at rechtsprak.nl: LJN: AU3724; RvdW 2006, 107) stressing that maintenance claims agreed upon in a mediation agreement cannot be enforced after one of the partners rejected to stick to the agreement; similarly the same court on April 10, 2009 (LJN BG9470, RvdW 2009, 512).

From a legal perspective, the normative system of shariah has to be discerned by its religious and legal parts. The former enjoy the full protection of religious freedom in all fields of the law formally and informally. The latter are restricted according to the law of the land to precisely defined fields like private international law, internal optional civil law, and some related issues mentioned already as far as they are formally applied or brought forward. On the informal level there are indications in various European countries, e.g. the UK, that some groups of Muslims resort to shariah rules for various reasons, including small numbers of Salafi or other extremist individuals and organizations openly opposing the governing legal system.

In general, legal pluralism as such usually does not endanger socio-legal cohesion in mere "international" cases with few links to the state of a temporary stay, which can be sufficiently tackled by appropriate rules of private international law, whereas "internal" cases involving residents do have such a potential. How then to properly differentiate between "international" and "internal"? In this regard, I would favor choosing habitual residence as the most significant connecting factor in family law issues, as immigration countries usually do for good reasons.

Concerning internal law, thorough studies of the scope and limits for dispositive law and ADR are necessary. In the field of family relations, state protection countering typical imbalances of power in family relations seems to be indispensable. Thus, most Western legal orders are restricting options especially with respect to basic legal institutions and ADR.[218] Nevertheless, such protection has to be based on sound information about the facts of the cases to be dealt with, and has to respect the broad scope of individual preferences in social life as long as they duly respect the rights of others. In this sense, the system of a uniform secular law for all must not be mistaken with demands for "one rule for all."[219] Instead, private autonomy being an important part of European legal orders has to be taken seriously. It is indispensable for reasonable accommodation of all societal groups including religious ones.

To overcome mere technical or institutional problems by applying the law of the land, international efforts to improve the mutual recognition of state decisions are needed. For the cases of lack of documents, administrations and courts should be ready to find creative solutions or make more use of hardship rules.

Immigrants from countries maintaining a personal law system should be reasonably informed about the legal situation of their new home country. This includes information about the role of state law and institutions in family-related issues: in the West, the state and its legal system have achieved a strong position during the last centuries.

Problems remain in cases where parties are reluctant to bring their cases to state courts for various reasons. If they refrain from doing so without any state-recognized alternative, the conflicts will remain and might even increase. Thus, if state court solutions are

---

[218] Cf. the impressive study of Bano (2012b) on shariah councils in the UK. According to her research, gender-related inequality of bargaining (and decision-making) power is widespread in these institutions.

[219] Cf. Zucca, *A Secular Europe*, p. 133; cf. also Jeremy Waldron, "Questions about the Reasonable Accommodation of Minorities," in Ahdar and Aroney 2010, 103–13.

to be maintained, it is absolutely necessary to react to those reasons for possible rejection which can be altered without touching the content of the law. One practical solution is to increase information and cultural sensitivity among judges and administrations.[220]

Secular legal orders in liberal societies have only limited instruments for implementation and self-perpetuation. They basically rely on the broad societal acceptance of their fundamental rules and convictions. But can such legal orders not only be obeyed, but be accepted by devout Muslims as being "theirs" as well? The overwhelming majority of Muslims living in the West seems to answer in favor of that. They recognize that these legal orders equally search for justice. Understanding the "*maqasid al-shari'a*," the deeper reasons for Islamic rules, in search for an overlapping consensus between them and the rules of secular states could be a viable solution on a contemporary intellectual level.

It is strongly recommended to support the development of Muslim research and the educational system driven by such thinking, dealing with the conditions of life in secular societies and their basic values. Muslims should take their fair part in the common debate about the future of our common laws. On the other hand, equal standards in granting reasonable accommodation by individual choice within this framework have to be defended—even against majorities—according to the rule of law. The secular democratic state under the rule of law can only succeed by visibility in daily practice.

Last but not least, research on shariah in Europe is still in its infancy, despite a considerable number of valuable studies mentioned in this chapter. First, the scope and density of research varies significantly between European countries. Whereas the UK, Belgium, the Netherlands, France, Germany, Austria, and Denmark are covered to a remarkable extent in general, there are lacunae regarding nearly all countries in Eastern and South-Eastern Europe. The same is true to a lesser extent for Spain, Italy, and Greece.

More concretely, there is a lack of representative research on how Muslims in Europe perceive the role of shariah in their lives. The main shortcoming up to now is the fact that often people are simply asked about "shariah" as such, without specifying the totally different aspects of religious-ethical beliefs, religious rites, and legal norms.

More information about Muslim religious conflict resolution mechanisms and the reasons for their coming into existence is needed. Whereas in the UK and in Nordic countries several studies address this issue, there is a dearth of research about the situation elsewhere, despite some indications that such mechanisms operate in other countries. Further information is required on the "customer" perspective,[221] where the impact of resorting to non-state conflict resolution on the parties involved is examined. In addition, we should know more about the possible interaction of debates on the relation between shariah, democracy, and the rule of law in Europe as well as the Middle East and other predominantly Muslim parts of the world.

---

[220] Cf. e.g. Connolly 2010 and the essays in Holden 2011.
[221] The importance of and the difficulties in obtaining data are demonstrated in the study of Samia Bano (2012b), p. 54 in particular.

To end optimistically: there is no danger for young scholars that they will face a lack of interesting issues in the future.

## Select Bibliography

Ahdar, Rex and Aroney, Nicholas (eds.) (2010). *Shari'a in the West*. Oxford: Oxford University Press.

Aldeeb Abu-Sahlieh, Sami and Aronovitz, Alberto (eds.) (1999). *Le droit musulman de la famille et des successions à l'épreuve des ordres juridiques occidentaux*. Zürich: Schulthess.

Al-Hamarneh, Ala and Thielmann, Jörn (eds.) (2008). *Islam and Muslims in Germany*. Leiden and Boston: Brill.

Aluffi Beck-Peccoz, Roberta and Zincone, Giovanna (eds.) (2004). *The Legal Treatment of Islamic Minorities in Europe*. Leuven: Peeters.

An-Na'im, Abdullah Ahmed (2008). *Islam and the Secular State: Negotiating the Future of Shari'a*. Cambridge, MA and London: Harvard University Press.

Asayyad, N. and Castells, M. (eds.) (2002). *Muslim Europe or Euro-Islam: Politics, Culture, and Citizenship in the Age of Globalization*. Lanham: Lexington Books.

Austrian Association for the Middle East Hammer-Purgstall (ed.) (2009). *Family, Law and Religion: Debates in the Muslim World and their Implications for Co-operation and Dialogue*. Vienna: Gröbner.

Bakht, Natasha (2005). *Arbitration, Religion and Family Law: Private Justice on the Backs of Women*. Ottawa: National Association of Women and the Law.

Bano, Samia (2007). "Islamic Family Arbitration, Justice and Human Rights in Britain," *Law, Social Justice & Global Development Journal* 1: 2–26. <http://www.go.warwick.ac.uk/elj/lgd/2007_1/bano>.

Bano, Samia (2012a). "An Exploratory Study of Shariah Councils in England with Respect to Family Law," University of Reading, October 2. <http://www.reading.ac.uk/web/FILES/law/An_exploratory_study_of_Shariah_councils_in_England_with_respect_to_family_law_.pdf>.

Bano, Samia (2012b). *Muslim Women and Shari'ah Councils: Transcending the Boundaries of Community and Law*. Basingstoke: Palgrave Macmillan.

Bar, Christian von (ed.) (1999). *Islamic Family Law and its Reception by the Courts in the West*. Köln: Heymanns.

Bernard-Maugiron, Nathalie and Dupret, Baudoin (eds.) (2010). *Ordre public et droit musulman de la famille en Europe et en Afrique du Nord*. Brussels: Bruylant.

Boele-Woelki, Katharina, Braat, Bente, and Sumner, Ian (2003). *European Family Law in Action*. Antwerp: Intersentia.

Bowen, John R. (2009). *Can Islam Be French? Pluralism and Pragmatism in a Secularist State*. Princeton: Princeton University Press.

Bowen, John R. (2012). *Blaming Islam*. Cambridge, MA: MIT Press.

Bramadat, P. and Koenig, M. (eds.) (2009). *International Migration and the Governance of Religious Diversity*. Montreal & Kingston: Metropolis.

Bretfeld, K. and Wetels, P. (2007). "Muslime in Deutschland". Berlin: Federal Ministry of the Interior.

Büchler, Andrea (2011). *Islamic Law in Europe? Legal Pluralism and its Limits in European Family Laws*. Farnham and Burlington: Ashgate.

Cadet, Fabien and Peruzzetto, Sylvaine (2005). *L'ordre public en droit international de la famille. Étude comparée France/Espagne*. Paris: L'Harmattan.

Cesari, Jocelyne (2010). *Muslims in the West After 9/11: Religion, Politics and Law*. Abingdon and New York: Routledge.

Charnay, J.-P. (2001). *La Charia et l'Occident*. Paris: L'Herne.

Cilardo, Agostino (2002). *Il diritto islamico e il sistema giuridico italiano*. Naples: Ed. Scientifice italiane.

Connolly, Anthony J. (2010). *Cultural Difference on Trial: The Nature and Limits of Judicial Understanding*. Farnham and Burlington: Ashgate.

Conseil de la communauté marocaine à l'étranger (ed.) (2010). *Le statut juridique de l'Islam en Europe. Acte du colloque international organisé par le Conseil de la communauté marocaine à l'étranger Fès, 14 et 15 Mars 2009*. Rabat: Marsam.

Douglas, Gillian et al. (2011). *Social Cohesion and Civil Law: Marriage, Divorce and Religious Courts*. Cardiff University, June. <http://papers.ssrn.com/sol3/papers.cfm?abstract_id=1940387>.

Ferrari, Silvio and Bradney, Anthony (eds.) (2000). *Islam and European Legal Systems*. Aldershot: Ashgate.

Ferrari, Silvio and Pastorelli, Sabrina (eds.) (2010). *Religion in Public Spaces: A European Perspective*. Farnham and Burlington: Ashgate.

Fetzer, Joel S. and Soper, C. Christopher (2005). *Muslims and the State in Britain, France, and Germany*. Cambridge: Cambridge University Press.

Foblets, Marie-Claire and Carlier, Jean-Yves (2005). *Le code marocain de la famille: Incidences au regard du droit international privé en Europe*. Brussels: Bruylant.

Foblets, Marie-Claire, Gaudreault-Desbiens, François, and Rentel, Alison Dundes (eds.) (2010). *Cultural Diversity and the Law*. Brussels: Bruylant.

Foblets, Marie-Claire, Graziadei, Michele, and Vanderlinden, Jacques (eds.) (2010). *Convictions Politiques et Religieuses et Droits Positifs*. Brussels: Bruylant.

Foblets, Marie-Claire, Maréchal, Brigitte, and Nielsen, Jørgen (eds.) (2001). *Convergences musulmanes. Aspects contemporains de l'islam dans l'Europe élargie*. Louvain la-Neuve: Bruylant.

Fournier, Pascale (2010). *Muslim Marriage in Western Courts: Lost in Transplantation*. Farnham: Ashgate.

Fulchiron, Hugues et al. (1999). *L'étranger face et au regard du droit. Rapport du recherché*. Université Jean-Moulin, Lyon III, April.

Gärtner, Verena (2998). *Die Privatscheidung im deutschen und gemeinschaftsrechtlichen Internationalen Privat- und Verfahrensrecht: außergerichtliche Ehescheidung im Spannungsfeld von kultureller Diversität und Integration*. Tübingen: Mohr Siebeck.

Grillo, Ralph (ed.) (2008). *The Family in Question: Immigrants and Minorities in Multicultural Europe*. Amsterdam: University of Amsterdam Press.

Grillo, Ralph, Ballard, Roger, Ferrari, Alessandro, Hoekema, André, Maussen, Marcel, and Shah, Prakash (eds.) (2009). *Legal Practice and Cultural Diversity*. Farnham and Burlington: Ashgate.

Heine, Susanne, Lohlker, Rüdiger, and Potz, Richard (2012). *Muslime in Österreich*. Innsbruck and Vienna: Tyrolia.

Hellyer, H. A. (2009). *Muslims of Europe: The "Other" Europeans*. Edinburgh: Edinburgh University Press.

Holden, Livia (ed.) (2011). *Cultural Expertise and Litigation: Patterns, Conflicts, Narratives*. Abingdon and New York: Routledge.

Jänterä-Jareborg, Maarit (2004). "Foreign Law in National Courts: A Comparative Perspective," in *Recueil des Cours*. Hague Academy of International Law. Leiden and Boston: Martinus Nijhoff Publishers, 185–385.

Jayme, Erik (ed.) (2003). *Kulturelle Identität und Internationales Privatrecht*. Heidelberg: C. F. Müller.

Jeldtoft, Nadia and Nielsen, Jørgen S. (eds.) (2012). *Methods and Contexts in the Study of Muslim Minorities*. Abingdon and New York: Routledge.

Kahn, Philippe (ed.) (2001). *L'étranger et le droit de la famille: pluralité ethnique, pluralisme juridique*. Paris: La Documentation française [Mission "Droit et Justice"].

King, Michael (ed.) (1995). *God's Law versus State Law: The Construction of an Islamic Identity in Western Europe*. London: Grey Seal.

Klausen, Jytte (2007). *The Islamic Challenge: Politics and Religion in Western Europe*. Oxford: Oxford University Press.

Laurence, Jonathan (2012). *The Emancipation of Europe's Muslims: The State's Role in Minority Integration*. Princeton and Oxford: Princeton University Press.

Levey, Geoffrey Brahm and Modood, Tariq (eds.) (2009). *Secularism, Religion and Multicultural Citizenship*. Cambridge: Cambridge University Press.

Malik, Jamal (ed.) (2004). *Muslims in Europe*. Münster: Lit.

Malik, Maleiha (2010). *Anti-Muslim Prejudice: Past and Present*. Abingdon and New York: Routledge.

Malik, Maleiha (2012). *Minority Legal Orders in the UK*. London: British Academy Policy Centre. Available for download at <http://www.britac.ac.uk/policy/Minority-legal-orders.cfm>.

Mehdi, Rubya and Nielsen, Jørgen S. (2011). *Embedding Mahr (Islamic Mahr) in the European Legal System*. Copenhagen: DJ Ø F.

Mehdi, Rubya, Petersen, Hanne, Reenberg Sand, Erik, and Woodman, Gordon (eds.) (2008). *Law and Religion in Multicultural Societies*. Copenhagen: DJ Ø F.

Meeusen, J., Pertegas, M., Straetmans, G., and Swennen, Fr. (eds.) (2007). *International Family Law for the European Union*. Antwerp and Oxford: Intersentia.

Murphy, John (ed.) (2000). *Ethnic Minorities, their Families and the Law*. Oxford: Hart Publishing.

Nichols, Joel A. (ed.) (2012). *Marriage and Divorce in a Multicultural Context*. Cambridge: Cambridge University Press.

Nielsen, Jørgen, Akgönül, Samim, Alibašić, Ahmet, Goddard, Hugh, and Maréchal, Brigitte (eds.) (2009). *Yearbook of Muslims in Europe*, vol. 1. Leiden and Boston: Brill.

Nielsen, Jørgen and Allievi, Stefano (eds.) (2002). *Muslim Networks and Transnational Communities In and Across Europe*. Leiden: Brill.

Nielsen, Jørgen and Christoffersen, Lisbeth (eds.) (2010). *Shari'a as Discourse: Legal Traditions and the Encounter with Europe*. Farnham: Ashgate.

Nolte, Georg, Keller, Helen, von Bogdandy, Armin, Mansel, Heinz-Peter, Büchler, Andrea, and Walter, Christian (eds.) (2007). *Pluralistische Gesellschaften und Internationales Recht*. Heidelberg: C. F. Müller.

Pahud de Mortanges, René and Tanner, Erwin (eds.) (2002). *Muslime und schweizerische Rechtsordnung. Les musulmans et l'ordre juridique suisse*. Freiburg: Universitätsverlag.

Panafit, Lionel (1999). *Quand le droit écrit l'islam*. Brussels: Bruylant.

Pearl, David and Menski, Werner (n.d. [1998]). *Muslim Family Law*. Lahore: Brite Books.

Potz, Richard and Wieshaider, Wolfgang (2004). *Islam and the European Union*. Leuven: Peeters.
Poulter, Sebastian (1998). *Ethnicity, Law and Human Rights*. Oxford: Clarendon Press.
Rohe, Mathias (guest ed.) (2004). *Sharī'a in Europe, Die Welt des Islams* Special Theme 44(3).
Rohe, Mathias (2007). *Muslim Minorities and the Law in Europe: Chances and Challenges*. New Delhi: Global Media Publications.
Rohe, Mathias (2011). *Das islamische Recht: Geschichte und Gegenwart*, 3rd edn. München: C. H. Beck [English translation: Rohe, Mathias (2014). *Islamic Law in Past and Present* (translated by Gwendolin Goldbloom). Leiden/Boston: Brill.]
Roy, Olivier (1999). *Vers un islam européen*. Paris: Éditions esprit.
Shachar, Ayalet (2001). *Multicultural Jurisdictions: Cultural Differences and Women's Rights*. Cambridge: Cambridge University Press.
Shadid, Wasif and van Koningsveld, Pieter (eds.) (2002). *Religious Freedom and the Neutrality of the State: The Position of Islam in the European Union*. Leuven: Peeters.
Shadid, Wasif and van Koningsveld, Pieter (eds.) (2003). *Intercultural Relations and Religious Authorities: Muslims in the European Union*. Leuven: Dudley.
Shah, Prakash and Menski, Werner (eds.) (2007). *Migration, Diasporas and Legal Systems in Europe*. London: Routledge Cavendish.
Shah, Prakash, Foblets, Marie-Clare, and Rohe, Mathias (2014). *Family, Religion and Law: Cultural Encounters in Europe*. Farnham: Ashgate.
Shah-Kazemi, S. N. (2001). *Untying the Knot: Muslim Women, Divorce and the Shariah*. London: Nuffield Foundation.
Silvestri, Sara (2008). *Europe's Muslim Women: Potentials, Aspirations and Challenges*. Brussels: King Baudouin Foundation.
Tsitselikis, Konstantinos (2012). *Old and New Islam in Greece: From Historical Minorities to Immigrant Newcomers*. Leiden: Martinus Nijhoff Publishers.
Van Bruinessen, Martin et al. (eds.) (2011). *Producing Islamic Knowledge: Transmission and Dissemination in Western Europe*. London: Routledge.
Van der Ven, Johannes A. (ed.) (2012). *Empirical Research in Religion and Human Rights*. Leiden and Boston: Brill.
Yazbeck Haddad, Yvonne (ed.) (2002). *Muslims in the West: From Sojourners to Citizens*. Oxford: Oxford University Press.
Waardenburg, Jacques (2003). *Muslims and Others: Relations in Context*. Berlin: de Gruyter.
Zucca, Lorenzo (2012). *Law and Religion in the European Constitutional Landscape*. Oxford: Oxford University Press.

CHAPTER 16

# HIJAB

JENNIFER A. SELBY

HEADCOVERINGS worn by some Muslim women have been differently understood and debated across Europe.[1] This chapter focuses on veiling practices in ten Western European countries. In addition to theologically-framed expressions of modesty and piety, headscarves have been the foci of innumerable public discussions, including debates about immigration and cultural integration, the governance of religious difference and visible religiosity, as well as gender equality. These debates are widespread, but there is little consensus regarding how the public presence of hijabs is articulated and legislated. The European Commission and the European Parliament adopted the Charter of Fundamental Rights of the European Union on December 7, 2000 but it remains non-binding in law and appears to have little impact on unifying the outcomes of individual cases (McGoldrick 2006: 30). The European Court of Human Rights (ECHR) secured by the Convention for the Protection of Human Rights and Fundamental Freedoms is a central arbiter in the adjudication of several of the cases described here.[2] Generally speaking, the ECHR has not articulated religious

---

[1] Not all women who consider themselves Muslim wear headcoverings and some women may cover intermittently. Some may not cover in their daily lives but may veil depending on the context: for instance when attending a mosque, praying, or visiting a Muslim-majority country (e.g. Shadid and von Koningsveld 2005: 38). Not only contextually-based, these choices also depend on life stage and factors including piety, social status, class, and political affiliation.

[2] The Strasbourg-based European Court of Human Rights (ECHR), established in 1958 and secured in 1998, has been praised and critiqued for its role in the deliberation of headscarf cases. Peter Cumper and Tom Lewis call the ECHR one of the world's most successful human rights bodies, but also critique its failure to develop the parameters of article 9, which guarantees freedom of thought, conscience, and religion for minority groups (2009: 599). Jane Freedman (2007) analyzes the universalist assumptions of the court, which she argues ignore context and structural inequalities, while Antje Pedain (2004: 539) notes that the ECHR tends to stress public dimensions of belief to the detriment of private ones (i.e. where motivations are "acts of faith"). With reference to a number of high profile cases, Carolyn Evans argues that the Court typically defines the wearing of headscarves as a "practice" and not as a "belief," which positions their protection under article 9 (2006: 3). In this way, the ECHR has demonstrated a relatively narrow approach to religions in public spaces, more confined than common interpretations in the UK, for instance.

freedom as absolute: headscarves can be restricted if they do not fit into its broad understanding of public freedoms and security (Amiraux 2003: 135). The Court's decisions are often grounded in the contexts of nation-states where significant legislative variances exist. As we shall see, a number of countries have issued bans on the wearing of headscarves in public institutions and/or in the public sphere, others have no prohibitive regulations and little public debate, while a last group falls somewhere in between.

To consider this range, I outline the ways veiling is commonly expressed sartorially, theologically, and politically in the next section. I then briefly chart recent literature, studies, court cases, and polling on hijabs in Austria, Belgium, France, Germany, Italy, the Netherlands, Spain, Sweden, Switzerland, and the United Kingdom. The chapter subsequently reviews scholarly literature on hijabs in Western Europe and the prevalent nation-state and cultural diversity frameworks often used to explain their differing acceptances and refusals. While there are a variety of explanations, and while some restrictions cannot be understood at the national level, discourses on headscarves reveal a great deal about the parameters of national identity or how being, for instance, German, Swedish, or Austrian is imagined. Three influential factors that shape national debates include securitization and immigration policies, secular politics, and gender equality critiques. I conclude by considering how the public visibility of headscarves has become emblematic of broader polemical debates about Islam in Europe.

## Defining the "Hijab"

"Hijab" is a commonly used but imprecise term. Best translated as "modesty," it can also signify a curtain or barrier. Generally, a woman wearing Islamically-understood modest dress is considered to "wear hijab" (Shadid and van Koningsveld 2005: 36). Veiling can thus include concealing all or some parts of the body. This range of meanings explains why veiling is sometimes described as a mobile form of *purdah* (seclusion) that offers a visible separation to women while allowing movement in the public sphere (see, for example, Werbner 2007: 175, who describes girls of Pakistani origin in the UK whose veiling as purdah allows for freedom of movement). The more precise Arabic term for that which only covers the head is the rarely used *khimar*.

To capture these broad usages and definitions, in this chapter I use the terms "hijab," "veil," and "headscarf" interchangeably to refer to a cloth that partially covers the hair and neck and the body to a lesser degree. I use "full-face-covering veil" to refer to the niqab and burqa that cover the face, with the niqab exposing the eyes and the burqa concealing the entire face. Despite the fact that veiling is practiced across a number of cultural and religious traditions among both men and women, I refer solely to the practice of veiling in Islam.

Typically conceptualized as a female religious expression of modesty, veiling has been characterized as pious, illusory, deceptive, concealing, safeguarding, apocalyptic, propagandizing, fashionable, oppressive to women, an indication of an unwillingness to integrate, a sign of protest, as repressive, and as liberating (Heath 2008; Werbner 2007: 175; Shadid and van Koningsveld 2005; Mernissi 1994: 182). Hijabs have multitudinous and at times contradictory meanings, many of which are influenced by variations in the cultural and social statuses of women and common dress codes in historical periods. Motivations for veiling are similarly multiple, overlapping, and changing. In Western social scientific writing these include invocations of religious, social, and sexual modesty, piety, femininity, and fashion (Bouhdiba 1975; Mernissi 1994; Gaspard and Khosrokhavar 1995; Khosrokhavar 1997; Venel 1999; Lorcerie 2005; Tersigni 2005; Keaton 2006). Natasha Bakht (2012) aptly calls the hijab a "shifting signifier" in that it cannot be understood as a symbol with a singular meaning. Debates on these meanings and motivations abound both within and outside Muslim communities. For instance, Asma Barlas argues that, "In the Qur'an, there are two sets of verses that deal with aspects of veiling, but without explicit mention of 'the veil'" (2006: 267). She suggests that veiling is no longer mandated in contemporary society and that it reflects concerns from a former context (2004: 102). Some interpreters therefore read a specific injunction for veiling in the Qur'an while others see a less formalized call for modesty. This range of readings and intentions underscores the difficulty in interpreting their meanings (Scott 2005: 118).

Headscarves vary in fabrics, colors, and the extent to which they cover. Beyond the way I describe the hijab as commonly shielding the hair and neck, other forms include *bandannas*, that cover some of the hair while referencing hip hop and youth cultures; *chadors*, long draping coverings which extend from the head below the knees keeping the face visible, and most common in Iran; *dupattas*, generally worn by Pakistani and Asian women and typically a light chiffon scarf that is loosely draped around the neck; niqabs, a piece of cloth attached at either side of the forehead, fully covering the body and the face except for the eyes; and burqas which cover the entire face and body, often including gloves to cover the hands, with a mesh screen to shield the eyes. The *jilbab*, or "outergarment," is related to these coverings in loosely draping over the body, sometimes reflecting a desire to be more conservative in appearance. It is a long loose tunic-like or coat-like garment that covers the entire body except for the face and hands (Werbner 2007: 166; Winter 2006: 280).

These sartorial manifestations of modesty are theologically supported through reference to and interpretation of Islamic texts and *fiqh* (Islamic jurisprudence). Understood as a revealed text, the Qur'an is given the most credence in supporting modest dress, even if it describes a wide range of topics related to law and theology and does not focus on clothing. Aforementioned, there are competing interpretations of modesty based on Qur'anic passages that generate interpretative debates amongst theologians, legal experts, and practitioners, as well as in Western courts and commissions (Barlas 2006; McGoldrick 2006; Fournier 2010). There are a number of Qur'anic passages that are commonly referenced in these discussions, like a verse calling for women and men to dress and behave modestly (Qur'an 24: 30–1). Another passage (24: 60) suggests that older women who are not married "incur no sin if they discard their garments, provided that they do not aim at a showy display." Surah 34 further recommends modest behavior from women so as not to excite men, "drawing a veil across their chests." Other passages like 53: 33 call upon the Prophet's wives or the "mothers of the believers" to "lengthen their garments" to avoid insult. To protect women's modesty, men should address them from behind a barrier or curtain (i.e. a "hijab"). Altogether there are nine references to the hijab in the Qur'an that are interpreted and varyingly translated into Islamic law, practice, and belief.

The other central textual source of appellation for modest dress and social comportment in Islam stems from the *hadīth*, a vast collection of sayings about the exemplary life of the Prophet Muhammad. A number of *hadīth* describe veiling as an integral practice for the wives of the Prophet. A range of interpretations exists in this body of literature, as well. Ghassan Ascha (1995) notes that like the Qur'anic verses treating modesty, the mothers of the believers can be differently interpreted as both perfect modest exemplars of their sex and as reflecting the social constraints of the Prophet's context. Again, these readings are open to interpretation and ignite questions of religious authority. They explain in part why some hijab-wearing women and legal authorities believe veiling is an integral part of their practice, why others do not, and why different styles and types of headscarves and coverings exist based on theological understandings.

Beyond these theological concerns, hijab-related debates and controversies in Western European nation-states have important political histories related to colonialism and immigration. While the ten Western countries under discussion have varying colonial histories (if at all), Orientalist discourses have shaped the exoticization and fears related to women's headcoverings. Edward Said's now-classic analysis of Western colonial perspectives of the Orient in *Orientalism* (1978) does not focus on gender-representativity or Muslim women's dress, but he remarks that, particularly in prevalent French and British literature and artwork, the "Oriental" and headscarved woman is uniformly portrayed as distant, passive, exotic, subservient, veiled, and reacting to events; she is never a participant. Later scholars have similarly noted how Orientalist perspectives were integral to rationalizing European colonialism in the eighteenth and nineteenth centuries (Appadurai 1996; Dobie 2001). In the French case, Neil Macmaster and Toni Lewis (1998) argue that the end of French colonialism in Algeria meant a shift from a sexualized imagery of headscarves to more terrorism-related and politicized descriptions. These fears of visible markers of Islam continue in Europe in the postcolonial era with images of dark chadors following the Iranian Revolution, headscarved women with the Gulf War, and a supposed rise in Islamically-inspired international terrorist activities in the post-9/11 period, including attacks in Madrid in 2004 and London in 2005. These incidents have meant that some hijab-wearing women have experienced Islamophobia related to their public visibility. They have also been generative of political outcomes.[3]

---

[3] In the United States, for instance, anthropologists have pointed to how interest in "freeing" women in Afghanistan from their burqas may rightly underline atrocities occurring under the Taliban, but effectively maintains silence about the role of the West in creating these situations (Hirschkind and Mahmood 2002: 342; Abu-Lughod 2002: 784–5).

Scholars of Islam and gender studies have pointed to how continuing imperialist politics in postcolonial times pejoratively position headscarves through feminist critiques (Abu-Lughod 2002; Mahmood 2005, 2008; Razack 2008). We may therefore conclude that hijabs take on various theological, sartorial, and political meanings dependent on their context and sources of authority.

# HEADSCARVES IN WESTERN EUROPEAN NATION-STATES

Hijabs are differently interpreted among Muslims and academics but also by individuals, organizations, schools, courts, and other public institutions. I aim to highlight how, on the one hand, these ten countries differ in their social and legal treatments of veils while, on the other hand, recent public opinion data unilaterally depict disdain for full-face headscarves. Firstly, I examine nationally-based responses to hijabs. On one end of the spectrum are those nation-states that take a non-restrictive approach toward the wearing of partial head and body coverings like Austria, the Netherlands, and the United Kingdom. Birgit Sauer (2009) suggests that these countries display greater "tolerance" than their neighbors; I prefer the qualifier of "lesser restriction" as discourses of religious tolerance do not necessarily explain these decisions. Countries like Italy, Spain, Sweden, and Switzerland fall somewhere in the middle as they have been more selective in how they apply prohibitions. On the other end of the spectrum are those that take a decidedly prohibitive approach toward Muslim coverings, including France, Belgium, and some German federal states. For the sake of brevity, I focus on headscarf debates in public schools. Secondly, I turn to recent survey data that depict a broad-based Western European rejection of niqabs and burqas in the public sphere. I ask why this commonality in treatments of these garments is so marked.

## Headscarf Regulations

This section begins with three countries that have been more liberal in their interpretations of hijabs: Austria, the Netherlands, and the United Kingdom. As we will see, these countries cannot be grouped together in their positions on full-face-covering hijabs.

### Less Formally Restrictive

Austria is unique among the nation-states under examination in terms of its formalized articulations of religious diversity and its official encouragement of Islamic schools. Heated public debates regarding headscarves have not taken place and no formal bans exist in public schools or institutions. Of course, on-the-ground Austrian positions toward hijabs are more complex as they combine both restrictive and nonrestrictive elements. On the one hand, Austria does not purport to be a multicultural society. A 2008 report from the Austrian civil anti-racism institution ZARA suggested that the number of verbal abuses against Muslims wearing headscarves was on the rise. Yet, on the other hand, despite its immigration policies based on the *jus sanguinis* citizenship model (where citizenship is determined by parentage and not by place of birth) and support for anti-immigration right-wing political parties, Austria maintains lenient regulations concerning the expression of religious beliefs and practices in the public realm in Europe (Gresch et al. 2008: 411). There are no official restrictions against wearing headscarves and Islamic public schools are publicly funded.

Related to schools, a 2001 headscarf case in the town of Traun gained attention when a headscarf-wearing student was denied enrollment in a secondary school. The ban was eventually lifted on the grounds of religious freedom (Sauer 2009). In 2004, a school in the city of Linz similarly ordered a ban on "headgear," which included scarves and caps. Following the formal legal complaint of a parent, local authorities overturned the ban citing Austria's constitutional provisions for the freedom of religion (Holzleithener and Strasser 2006: 11–12). In the wake of this 2004 case, the Ministry of Education, Science and Culture went further to issue a decree stating that as a religious sign, the headscarf is protected by the Basic State Law as well as by the European Convention on Human Rights (Gresch et al. 2008). The current political climate in Austria generally indicates that Muslim women may wear their headscarves in schools, public offices, and in photos for public documents as long as their faces are clearly identifiable. A full-face hijab ban in Austria appears unlikely given that hijabs are generally perceived and protected as religious signs. Nevertheless, other indicators suggest that the Austrian socio-political climate may not be entirely welcoming to non-Christian religious signs in the public sphere. For that reason, in general Austria is relatively open to visible religious symbols.

Like the United Kingdom, the Netherlands has been typically characterized as multicultural in its approach to religious and cultural diversity. Headscarves are generally accepted in the Dutch public sphere and typically not positioned as barriers to women's rights, like in pervasive legal discourses in France and Spain. Debates on cultural diversity and gender in the Netherlands tend instead to focus on so-called issues of "immigrant women" including honor killing, female genital mutilation, and domestic violence. Some scholars (Lettinga and Saharso 2008) have suggested that this climate toward headscarves may be shifting, and that if between 1999 and 2006 religious identity claims including those for headscarves were generally accommodated, this spirit of "neutrality" has changed. The acceptability of full-face-covering veils has been questioned and conservative political parties have gained force.

Inquiries and cases involving hijabs are typically brought before the Commission on Equal Treatment (also translated as the Dutch Equal Opportunities Commission), created in 1994. The Commission has historically not restricted religious expression in its decisions, seeing it as a fundamental right (see: <http://www.cgb.nl/English>). It has reviewed a broad range of cases. In an October 2005 case, for instance, a woman was refused a job as an Arabic teacher at the Islamic College of Amsterdam because she refused to wear a hijab. The Dutch Equal Opportunities Commission ruled that her dismissal was wrongful. Yet, as noted in the next section, this common stance may be shifting. The rise of right-wing political parties like Geert Wilders's Dutch Freedom Party and pervasive public concerns with full-face veils appear to be transforming a once pervasive liberal position toward a more conservative vision.

Lastly, also grouped among the less restrictive nation-states, the United Kingdom differs in its discourse on hijabs from most European nation-states under examination here because of its liberal multiculturalism.[4] There are no formal restrictions on headscarves in the UK, including in public schools. While the Churches of England and Scotland are established religious institutions, basic curricula in public schools include the teaching of non-Christian traditions. What follows examines a number of cases that have emerged in public schools as well as data on Islamophobia.

The highest profile hijab-related debates in the United Kingdom have focused on public schools. There are only five Muslim schools amid England and Wales's 25,000 schools (McGoldrick 2006: 176), so most Muslim children attend state or faith-based schools where parents may elect to have their children opt out of Christian collective worship. There are some commonly-held guidelines on school uniforms but the parameters are largely left to the schools themselves. In 1989, the same year as the first of France's "Headscarf Affairs," 14- and 15-year-old sisters Aisha and Fatima Alvi refused to remove their headscarves at a girls' grammar school in Manchester (a position which was eventually accepted). This 1989 incident was among the first significant mediatized public debates on hijabs in the UK.

While there have been many more cases, including the January 2004 case of a teacher who forcibly removed a student's headscarf in Peterborough and was prosecuted for assault, and the 2003 banning of all headgear at Icknield High in Luton, Bedfordshire that was later overturned (Werbner 2007: 173), the "Shabina Begum case" remains precedent-setting in the UK. Two other developments should be noted that framed the context of this specific public school case: in 1997 the Department of Education approved funding of the Islamia Primary School in London and a Human Rights Act in 1998 ensured that school uniform policies did not interfere with religious freedom (Kiliç 2008: 444).

The "Begum case" centered on a Buckinghamshire girls' grammar school's uniform policy and the acceptability of the jilbab (and not the headscarf). At the time of the case, 71% of students at the school categorized themselves as of Bangladeshi or Pakistani origin and 79% identified themselves as Muslim; 60% of these female Muslim students wore hijabs, which were accepted in the dress code so long as they were in keeping with the school's colors (Kiliç 2008). A 14-year-old student at the Denbigh High School in Luton, Ms. Shabina Begum, sought to wear a jilbab, arguing that the accepted shalwar kameeze (a loose Indian pantsuit garment) was not acceptable according to her sense of

---

[4] The tenor of this position is debated as some scholars have charted an assimilationist turn, wherein notions of "civic Britishness" threaten to replace "multiculturalism" as the UK's primary political discourse (Squires 2007: 539; Kiliç 2008: 449).

religiously-informed modesty. In the initial proceedings against the school in December 2002, both Begum and the school found sources and experts who confirmed that the school's uniform both was and was not in keeping with a normative Islamic dress code. In September 2004, after having not attended school for more than two years, Begum found a local school, Burnham Grammar, which permitted her to wear the jilbab (Kiliç 2008: 446). Nevertheless, with reference to article 9 (the right to manifest religious practices and beliefs) and article 2 (the right to education) of the European Convention on Human Rights, Ms. Begum went to court in order to seek a declaration that she had been unlawfully excluded from her former Luton school and should be entitled to a home tutor sponsored by the state. The Luton school's principal, herself a Muslim woman of Bengali origin, stood by the importance of the school's uniform so that the jilbab was not allowed.

While Ms. Begum initially won her case on appeal in March 2005 in the Court of Appeal, the verdict was later overturned by the House of Lords in March 2006, denying her the right to wear her jilbab at school and for it to pay for a tutor. The judges at the House of Lords explained that the school had made great efforts to maintain a uniform policy that respected Muslim beliefs and that the dress code (that allowed for color coordinated hijabs and the shalwar kameeze) was in accordance with mainstream Muslim opinion on modesty (BBC News 2004a). Moreover, the judge determined that Begum was excluded from school because of her "failure to abide by the school uniform policy rather than her religious beliefs as such" (McGoldrick 2006: 182). The final outcome of the Begum case reflects engagement with the ECHR and the continued allowance of hijabs and Muslim dress in public schools in the UK, while at the same time it demonstrates that limits on public school dress exist.

The Begum case remains important in the chronology of the acceptability of headscarves in the UK, but, arguably, hijab debates gained velocity and changed focus after the 2006 pronouncement by Foreign Minister Jack Straw that full-face-covering hijabs signal "separation and difference." The vociferous debate that followed has not extended to hijabs. Indeed in contrast to more restrictive measures in other nation-states, widespread disapproval emerged in Britain following the French 2004 ban on conspicuous religious signs in public schools. A 2005 Pew Global Attitudes study found that 62% of British citizens believed that banning the headscarf in public schools was *not* a good idea (Menasce-Horowitz and Morin 2006). In response to the French situation and hijab restrictions in parts of Germany, the International Network Assembly for the Protection of the Hijab was formed with the goal of reversing current bans, preventing new ones, and creating awareness of the "negative stereotypical image of the hijab which lies at the root of this discrimination" (Dear 2004; Tarlo 2007: 133). The campaign received support from a number of MPs and the mayor of London who, in his speech to the Assembly noted, "I am determined London's Muslims should never face similar restrictions [to those in France]," adding that the law reflected religious intolerance on par with extreme religious intolerance like the Holocaust (cited in Werbner 2007: 177).

Despite these political initiatives to protect against headscarf restrictions, there is continued evidence of Islamophobia directed against hijab-wearing women in the

United Kingdom. The 1997 Runnymede Trust Report found that Muslims in Britain experienced significant Islamophobia and recommended that the Race Relations Act be amended to include religious discrimination. These concerns were heightened following September 11, 2001 and the London bombings of July 7, 2005. Based on the responses of 1,200 Muslims in a nation-wide survey, before September 11, 2001 60.8% of women experienced being treated condescendingly. After September 11, 68.5% reported experiencing discrimination (Ameli and Merali 2006: 1). Numerous aggressive individual incidents have also been reported, like that of a 21-year-old male who pleaded guilty to racially aggravated common assault and a public order offence when he tore off the hijab of a 23-year-old woman in the street (BBC News 2007). These incidents and numerous ones like them suggest continued fear and discrimination toward hijabs in the UK.

## More Restrictive Headscarf Policies and Cases

This section turns to Italy, Spain, Sweden, and Switzerland as countries that have been more selective in how they apply prohibitions toward hijabs.

Hijab debates in Italy have taken place within a political and historical context that has held an explicitly privileged role for the Catholic Church. While there is no formal separation of religion and state articulated in the 1946 Italian constitution, the government has sought to foster a tolerant position toward non-Catholic faiths. Related to Islam, this means that mosques may receive funding from foreign governments and that multicultural discourse is increasingly prevalent in the public sphere (Pojmann 2010: 234). Hijab debates have been relatively muted in Italy, particularly when compared to those described in Belgium and France. Given the Catholic bases of the country's national identity, most major public debates about religiosity in the public sphere have focused on whether crucifixes should hang in non-confessional state schools. Nevertheless, in the post-9/11 period, Italy's military engagement in Iraq and Prime Minister Silvio Berlusconi's statement that Western civilizations are "superior" to Islamic ones (Alvanou 2008: 123) have stirred some Islamophobic responses. What follows overviews a number of key cases and Italian public opinion on the visibility of hijabs.

In March 2004 as international attention turned to France's legislation against conspicuous religious signs in public schools, a woman of Moroccan origin was dismissed from a daycare center in the northern Italian city of Samone because of her hijab (BBC News 2004b). After some public outcry, however, the Interior Minister insisted that the decision be reversed and stated that "the Islamic veil, worn with dignity, without ostentation, is an innocuous symbol of a cultural and religious identity which deserves all our respect" (cited in McGoldrick 2006: 208). This position appears to have been broadly shared across the country. A 2004 Caritas/Migrantes survey suggests that 70% of Italians disagreed with enacting a law similar to that in France banning conspicuous religious symbols in schools (Caritas/Migrantes 2004).

While the Muslim population in Italy remains relatively small and debates limited, the hijab appears to be readily accepted in the public sphere. There have been few school hijab-related controversies, as most have focused on the public visibility of Catholicism. General acceptance is perhaps also reflected in the example of a headscarf-wearing

Italian Muslim woman who ran for Perugia's communal council for the *Sinistra e Liberta* (Left Ecology Freedom) coalition. She indicated to the press that she had received positive responses from most Italians (ADNKronos International 2009). In short, while Italy's strong Catholic history and culture have made it the focus of debates in schools, more recent legislation suggests a publicly-supported legal turn against full-face veils.

Like in Italy, debates on hijabs in the public sphere in Spain have become more heated recently related to full-face-covering veils. Spain's history differs from most other European nation-states as it was under Muslim rule for more than 500 years, from the eighth to the thirteenth centuries. There are no clear national guidelines concerning the public visibility of hijabs. The country's highest profile hijab-related case took place in 2002 when 13-year-old Fatima Elidrisi was told by Catholic nuns running a state-funded private school near Madrid that she was not allowed to wear her headscarf (McGoldrick 2006: 206). This Catholic school had been assigned to her by the Regional Ministry of Education. Ms. Elidrisi did not attend school for months and was reported to the Inspectorate of the Regional Ministry of Education for absenteeism. The regional Ministry overruled the decision and eventually allowed her hijab because, "a person cannot be deprived of the right to an education just because she is wearing a scarf" (Bedmar and Palma 2010: 67). Despite this local accommodation, the case sparked national debate. For example, the Conservative Social Affairs Minister, Juan Carlos Aparicio, called headscarves "not a religious sign but a form of discrimination against women" (Henley 2004; Bedmar and Palma 2010: 67). In the wake of this case, there remains little national uniformity on the admissibility of wearing hijabs in public schools. In 2007 an 8-year-old girl was suspended from a Girona school after refusing to remove her hijab. The Department of Education overruled the school's decision and ordered that the girl be allowed to return. It insisted that the Spanish state respect all religious traditions (Islam Online 2007).

Despite these more recent governmental protections of hijabs in public schools two studies suggest that most Spaniards oppose their presence. A December 2009 survey found that 61% of Spaniards opposed the presence of hijabs in schools, compared with 18% in favor (of note, these views extended to the visibility of yarmulkes and crosses, as well; Estudio Fundacion BBVA 2010: 35). Martin-Muñoz and López-Sala (2005) also note a rise in Islamophobia following the 2004 Madrid bombings that focused on hijabs. Both of these studies suggest an increasingly hostile public response. While Spain does not have a nation-wide legal position regarding hijabs, like in Germany and Switzerland individual provinces are able to legislate restrictions that have focused on niqabs and burqas.

Public debates surrounding headscarves have also taken a more moderate tone in Sweden. As in most contexts discussed in this chapter, there are no accurate numbers as to how many women in Sweden wear hijabs. There are, however, a number of social scientific studies that have charted an increasing number of first-generation women who have chosen to wear headscarves as adults post-migration, claiming it is a way for them to relate to their tradition and strengthen their identity as minorities (Folkesson 2011: 126; see also McGinty 2006 on converts who take up headscarves as part of their practice). The Swedish government has made no formal calls for a ban in the public or educational spheres, although the opposition Liberal party has called for a ban for girls up to age 15 in public schools, arguing for the equal rights of the child (Hellgren and Hobson 2008: 395).

Despite assertions that Sweden restricts immigration and cultural diversity, a number of recent cases suggest that there are protections for public expressions of religiosity including the hijab. Even if members of the minority Christian Democratic Party have sought restrictions without success (Euro-Islam 2010), Swedish Prime Minister Frank Reindfeldt has stated that he is against such legislation for it "shouldn't lead to certain women being isolated even more from Swedish society" (cited in *The Local* 2010). A January 2010 case of a woman in Malmo, Sweden who was asked to leave a bus after she refused to remove her covering received media attention. The driver said he needed to see her face even though her bus pass did not call for photo identification. The transit company eventually paid a $4,203 settlement to the woman (Simpson 2008; United Press International 2008). Still, cases of Islamophobia toward hijabs have been charted. While unscientific, a Swedish radio program conducted an informal study which concluded that of the two women with very similar CVs who applied for the same jobs with 200 employers in Sweden, the woman without a hijab was contacted by thirty-five employers while the woman with a hijab was called by eight employers (Allah.eu 2010). Thus, there may not be outright legislation against them, but concern with the physical presence of headscarves remains. Sweden therefore falls in the middle range of hijab treatments in Western Europe. Despite restrictions in its immigration and cultural diversity policies and concerns with full-face coverings, polling data suggest that Swedes are open to the visibility of the more common hijab.

Like its neighbors, Switzerland has experienced a number of mediatized hijab debates that may be partially explained by its articulation of secularism and by its comparatively strict citizenship rules. Of the country's 311,000 Muslims, only approximately 10% have Swiss nationality (McGoldrick 2006: 120). In addition, the Swiss recognize Catholicism and Protestantism as official religions. As a federation of states, all matters of religion fall under the cantons within the limits of federal constitutional law and are typically determined on a case-by-case basis. The cantons of Geneva and Neuchatel have the most clearly articulated separations of state and religion; unsurprisingly, these cantons are also those that have been the sites of legal cases involving hijabs.

The country's precedent-setting headscarf case—known as the 1996 Dahlab case—began when the General Directorate for Primary Education prohibited a school teacher who had converted from Catholicism to Islam from wearing her headscarf when teaching. The Geneva cantonal government determined that teachers must "endorse both the objectives of the state school system and the obligations incumbent on the education authorities, including the strict obligation of denominational neutrality" (cited in McGoldrick 2006: 121; Cavanaugh 2007: 15). Ms. Dahlab was asked to stop wearing her headscarf under section 6 of the Public Education Act. Court documents note that Dahlab had not received complaints related to her headcovering from her colleagues, parents, or teachers. She appears to have been sensitive to allegations of proselytism and allegedly told her students she covered her head to keep her ears warm (Evans 2006: 6). Nevertheless, the court characterized her headscarf as a "powerful external symbol" that was "imposed on women by a [religious] precept" and "hard to square with the principle of gender equality" (Cavanaugh 2007: 15).

Like headscarf-wearing plaintiffs in other European nation-states, in her appeal to the Federal Court, Ms. Dahlab alleged a violation of her freedom of religious expression. However, in November 1997 the Federal Court upheld the Geneva cantonal decision based on the domestic courts' articulation of rights and of the neutrality of the state, determining that Ms. Dahlab was a civil servant in a secular state and that "the wearing of a headscarf and loose-fitting clothes remains an outward manifestation which, as such, is not part of the inviolable core of freedom of religion" (cited in McGoldrick 2006: 123). The European Court of Human Rights concurred with this decision noting that in the context of Swiss law and with the possibility of influencing young children, the decision should stand. In this ECHR case the Swiss legal and social context shaped the final decision.

## Most Restrictive

In comparisons across European nation-states about the status of full-face and partial hijabs, France is often positioned as a key restrictive example given its Republican understanding of church and state (known as *laïcité*), its nationally-based legislation against hijabs in government offices and schools in September 2004, and its banning of full-face-covering veils in the public sphere in April 2011. Hijab debates in the Republic have been under intense public and governmental scrutiny for more than thirty years. As Chouki El Hamel aptly summarizes, "no subject about Islam and Muslims [has] received more attention, aggravated attitudes, provoked more fear and anger and more broadened the divide that separates France from its five million Muslim residents than the controversy of the hijab" (2002: 297).

The separation of church and state guaranteed by *laïcité* (French secularism) situates the visibility of headscarves in the public sphere as problematic. With the exception of the Alsace-Moselle region that was then under German occupation (and which today has a sizeable Muslim population of Turkish origin), the 1905 law concretized a strict separation between private and public spheres. While some scholars have argued that secularism has become a religion in its own right (Roman 1991), the 1905 law aimed to place all religious institutions on an equal plane (Scott 2005). Since the 1970s, with the waning socio-political influence of Catholicism and the significant immigration of Muslims from France's former North African colonies, debates about French secularism in the Republic have emphasized Islamic practices, particularly the visibility of hijabs.

Debates peaked in October 1989 with what is now known as the "Headscarf Affair" in a junior high school (Brulard 1997; Venel 1999; Dayan-Herzbrun 2000; Bowen 2004a; Killian 2006). As "laboratories of the future" (Gauchet 1998), questions about secularism have arisen for more than 200 years in the country's public schools (Poulat 1987; Stock-Morton 1988; Baubérot 1998; Laborde 2005; Bowen 2007). In a public junior high school in Creil, a northern suburb of Paris, the school's headmaster informed three young women they would be expelled if they continued wearing their *foulards* (headscarves) on school property, calling their defiance an "insidious jihad" (Poulter 1997: 57; Scott 2005: 106). By wearing religious signs deemed conspicuous in a public Republican space, the young women were, according to the school's administration, explicitly rejecting *laïcité*. Vocal members of the local French Muslim community argued that it was customary for Muslim women to veil themselves in the presence of men and that doing so was an affirmation of their religious identities and should be respected in a democratic, pluralistic state (Bloul 1996). Conversely, school spokespersons maintained that the symbolic nature of the headscarf was in breach of France's secular principles. The case was eventually brought to the *Cour de cassation* (French Supreme Court) which ruled that religious symbols were permissible so long as they were not "conspicuous" or "militant," leaving the interpretation of these terms to individual schools (Brulard 1997: 179). This 1989 Affair was significant in that for the first time Islam and hijabs were formally characterized as problematic for the French public school system.[5]

Post-1989, *laïque* formulations in the public education system have continued to stress the maintenance of a religious and gender-neutral space related to headcoverings. While there have been innumerable veil-related controversies in France, I focus here on three defining moments in 1994, 2004, and 2011. In 1994, as local school administrators sought clearer guidelines on religious symbols, the government responded with the *Circulaire Bayrou* (or Bayrou Decree) issued by Education Minister François Bayrou. It introduced a distinction between "discreet" signs, which "express a personal attachment to (someone's) convictions" and "ostentatious signs" that "constitute *in themselves* elements of proselytism or of discrimination" (Joppke 2007a: 323). The *Circulaire* was received with some criticism by nine Muslim associations, including the *Union des organisations islamiques* (Union of Islamic Organizations) and the *Fédération nationale des musulmans de France* (National Federation of French Muslims), who said the decree would encourage girls to leave school (El Hamel 2002). From 1994 to 2003 a number of expulsions, student protests, and judicial decisions both confirmed and overturned the school expulsions of headscarf-wearing girls from the ages of 9 to 18 (Winter 2006). The Conseil d'État rejected Bayrou's claim that certain signs could be separated from the intentions of those who carried them and left it to teachers and administrators to interpret the actions of their students. In the wake of this ruling, the Minister of Education appointed Hanifa Chérifi as official mediator for problems linked to the wearing of the veil.

As teachers called for more stringent guidelines and with renewed discussions of *laïcité* surrounding the centenary year of the 1905 law, in July 2003 President Jacques Chirac requested a commission to be led by Bernard Stasi to examine religious signs in public schools. The four-chaptered *Commission de réflexion sur l'application du*

---

[5] Following the Headscarf Affair the French Prime Minister also established the *Haut conseil à l'intégration* (High Council for Integration). The Council considers integration issues and makes proposals, but has no regulatory or legal powers (McGoldrick 2006: 50).

*principe de laïcité dans la République*, or Stasi Commission Report, was released on December 11, 2003. Led by Stasi and a group of nineteen notable scholars, government officials, and other experts, and following forums and selective interviews across the country, the Commission made twenty-six recommendations to protect secularism (Weil 2009; Laurence and Vaisse 2006). Only one of these, a recommendation to ban "conspicuous" religious symbols—notably the Islamic veil, the Jewish *kippah*, and large Christian crosses—in public elementary and high schools was translated into law with the beginning of the 2004 academic year. The Stasi Report deemed more discreet signs acceptable, like medallions, small crosses, Stars of David, Hands of Fatimah, or little Qur'ans (Stasi Commission Report 2003: 23). Lawmakers voted on a bill to ban conspicuous religious signs (Law 2004: 228) in public schools and government on February 10, 2004. It received strong support and passed almost unanimously a month later on March 15, 2004 (Gerin Commission Report 2003; Lyon and Spini 2004; Weil 2009: 2701). Despite international attention and controversy when the law was passed, like from Human Rights Watch who suggested it violated the European Convention on Human Rights and was Islamophobic in focus (Human Rights Watch 2004), the actual enforcement of the law in September 2004 was relatively uneventful (Selby 2011b). Nevertheless, France has the most restrictive national legal regulations against headscarves in Western Europe.

Belgium's positions on hijabs are shaped by its cultural split. Its French and Dutch communities have traditionally had different approaches toward religious diversity: its French communities lean more toward the previous *laïque* French model while the Flemish tend to operate under more Dutch-inspired pluralist ideals (Severs 2010). Until recent attention on the regulation of full-face veils, public debates on headscarves in Belgium have emphasized hijabs in public schools. Despite a number of significant restrictions in the public sphere, religion is not excluded from public education in Belgium. Public school students have the option of participating in either non-denominational ethics classes or religious instruction from among the state's recognized religions. With governmental financial support, the Muslim community provides teachers with some of this religious instruction.

Yet, despite this seeming openness toward Islam in public schools, the country's interpretations of hijabs have become increasingly restrictive in recent years. In the 1990s, public schools began implementing hijab bans through by-laws that allowed individual schools to determine their own dress codes for teachers and students. In considering these school restrictions, comparison with France is useful. In 2002, the Belgian government's position was similar to that in France in 1989: the decision was left to individual schools as to what they would restrict and allow (McGoldrick 2006: 210). Most recorded disputes took place at a local level. Since then, restricting the presence of headscarves has become more prevalent. By late 2005, approximately 70% of secondary schools under French community authority had banned hijabs, up from 41% in 2000. As of 2008, only eight of 111 public schools in Brussels allow students to wear headscarves (Islamic Human Rights Commission 2008). Aforementioned, the Flemish side has taken a more pluralistic approach.

The religious freedoms of teachers are differently perceived than those of students. The Belgian Federal Council of Education banned headscarves for teachers in 2007, with the exception of religious education teachers who teach Islam (Islamic Human Rights Commission 2008). Like in France, private Islamic schools and Catholic schools are exempt from these rules. The country's first Islamic school—the Avicenna Islamic school in Molenbeek—opened in the fall of 2007. Hijab debates in Belgium were revived in 2009 with the oath-taking of a veiled representative for the Christian-Democrat party in the Brussels parliament and with the decision of two school principals to ban hijabs in their schools in Hoboken and Antwerp (these schools had been two of the eight that still accepted veiled girls (Severs 2010: 7)).

Beyond public schools, governmental regulation of hijabs in Belgium has shifted. While in January 2001, Belgium's high court ruled that a Muslim woman wearing a headscarf could not be denied an identification card (US Department of State 2002), by December 2004, the government announced it was considering a ban on conspicuous religious symbols including hijabs for civil servants. Since the early 2000s, wearing religious symbols of all kinds has been prohibited for selected public service officials, such as judges, police, and other uniformed officials (Severs 2010). Polling data suggest reluctance toward the visibility of headscarves. A 2007 study conducted by the Center for Psychology at Catholic University of Louvain-la-Neuve noted that one in three native Belgians were bothered by women wearing headscarves in public and that half would like to see them banned in certain places (Expatica News 2007; Université catholique de Louvain 2007). Belgium is the second country in Europe to institute a legal ban on full-face-covering hijabs. Despite its two models of religious diversity, Belgium has more recently leaned toward the restrictive *laïque* interpretation of public schools and spaces.

As the last more restrictive country under examination, German hijab debates have differed from the French veil affairs in that they have drawn national and international attention almost a decade later—in 1998—and have primarily been determined by the country's sixteen states or *Länder* which hold substantial legislative and judicial autonomy. Unlike in France and Belgium, there is no unified national policy position on headcoverings in Germany. Generally speaking, hijab debates have focused on schools and government offices where the reigning view in German courts has been that public school teachers and government officials should not wear headscarves to ensure "precautionary neutrality" (Saharso 2007: 525). Two factors shape its hijab debates: citizenship rights and religion/state relations.

In the first place, reformed in 2000, the country's ethno-cultural citizenship model has played a significant role in headscarf debates insofar as it has historically not encouraged immigration and multicultural difference.[6] The disenfranchised citizenship status of many Turkish-origin Muslims in Germany impacts how hijabs are perceived for,

---

[6] These ethno-cultural notions of nationalism may also bolster conservatism toward Muslim headscarves in German public institutions. This trend became apparent after reunification as an attempt to redefine German national identity (Sauer 2009: 88).

as Beverly Weber (2004) notes, headscarves have become pejorative markers of social status, depicted as worn by uneducated immigrant women whose visibility is further predicated on their presumed lack of agency and their cultural difference (Ewing 2000, 2008; Rottman and Ferree 2008). At the same time, in response to these pejorative representations, new scholarship suggests that an increasing number of young Muslim women in German urban centers wear headscarves as a response to this stigma (Weber 2004: 40–1).

In the second place, in contrast to other European nation-states described here, Germany does not have an official or established church. Article 137 in its 1919 constitution provided that "there is no state church," a position which has been incorporated into its contemporary Basic Law (cited in McGoldrick 2006: 108). This seeming legal neutrality toward religious traditions has been called into question by some scholars who claim that it is not uncommon for Christian symbols to be regarded as cultural symbols, while Muslim symbols are depicted as religious or political signs (Joppke 2007a: 328; Weber 2004: 48). In other words, pervasive Christian culture is commonly portrayed as tolerant, open, and changing, while Islam is static and specific. Headscarves in particular symbolize this Islam-based cultural exclusion. This bias against Islam and headscarves distinctively emerged in December 2003 when Johannes Rau, then-president of Germany, called for greater religious neutrality so that if headscarves were banned in public schools then monks' habits or crucifixes should be similarly restricted. In response to Rau's call, Bavarian Minister-President Edmund Stoiber was most vocal and noted that the hijab alone entailed "a political symbol incompatible with our democracy" and that the president should not cast doubt on "our national identity distinguished by the Christian religion" (cited in McGoldrick 2006: 118).

In the midst of this complex citizenship and Christian-focused church–state context, a number of hijab cases emerged in the 1980s primarily related to passport and identification pictures. In most cases women were permitted to wear their headscarves and received little political or media attention. Beginning in the early 1990s headscarf debates in Germany began emerging in public schools. While there are numerous examples of these cases, the Ferestha Ludin case is emblematic. Its outcomes had an unexpected and profound effect on the country's fractured positions on hijabs.

In 1998, Ms. Ferestha Ludin, a school teacher of Afghan origin, sued the province of Baden-Württemberg claiming that she was not hired because she wore a hijab, a decision she alleged violated her freedom of religious expression (Sauer 2009: 81; McGoldrick 2006: 111–14; Mahlmann 2003; Saharso 2007). Prior to looking for work, Ms. Ludin had worn her hijab as part of her teacher training without issue. The school board in Baden-Württemberg considered that young children were easily influenced and that her hijab would produce a negative influence because, while Ludin claimed she wore her hijab as a religious obligation, the *Oberschulamt Stuttgart* (Supervisory School Authority of Stuttgart) saw it as a political symbol incompatible with public neutrality and the separation of church and state outlined in German Basic Law (Cavanaugh 2007: 16). The case remained in the German courts for five years as Ludin appealed to the Upper Administrative Court, the Federal Administrative Court, and the Federal

Constitutional Court (Saharso 2007: 524). Of note, in comparison to a number of other European nation-states, none of these courts referenced Article 3.2 of the Basic Law guaranteeing the equality of men and women as a reason for banning the headscarf in schools (Mahlmann 2003: 1111).

The case's final 5 to 3 decision in September 2003 in Germany's Constitutional Federal Court determined that Ludin could not be excluded from teaching because of her hijab. The court noted that the decision in her favor was in accordance with the European Court of Human Rights and that the presence of a headscarf would not necessarily impede teaching the values of the German constitution (Mahlmann 2003: 1104). The decision did, however, leave future interpretation of the "outward appearance" of instructors open to reinterpretation, which opened possibilities for locally-based legislation (Cavanaugh 2007: 17).

Thus, while the Constitutional Court ruled in Ms. Ludin's favor, in general, Germans had a very different perspective on the 2003 decision. As Matthias Mahlmann notes, the final judgment in the Ludin case surprised most German citizens, as most held one among a variety of positions against the hijab in public schools. These ranged from pro-Christian/anti-Islam views, to a desire to discourage any visible religiosity, to hopes of "emancipating" Muslim women, to concerns with immigration and outright xenophobia (2003: 1109). Most Germans saw the allowance of hijabs for public school teachers as problematic in maintaining the pedagogical neutrality of the state (Sauer 2009: 82; Amiraux 2003: 129). Public opinion in the wake of the Ludin case thus provoked an important counter result as ten German federal states dominated by the Christian Democratic party quickly passed laws banning headscarves for teachers (McGoldrick 2006: 115). Indeed, with the exceptions of Berlin, which has called for the exclusion of all religious signs and the city of Stuttgart which declared the ban for headscarf-wearing Muslim teachers as unlawful because Catholic nuns can teach in their habits (Sauer 2009: 82), following the Ludin case, the states of Hamburg and Brandenburg that have had no legal restrictions passed anti-veiling legislation, as did Baden-Württemberg, Bavaria, Hesse, Lower Saxony, Saarland, Bremen, and North Rhine-Westphalia, which exempted Christian and Jewish religious symbols from its reach (Joppke 2007a: 331).

Germany's restrictive citizenship laws and Christian presence in public schools and culturally familiar symbols have affected public perceptions of headscarves. Yet, despite this restrictive perspective, most Germans accept the visibility of students' headscarves in public schools and few support an outright ban on full-face hijabs.

## Full-Face-Covering Headscarf Regulations and Public Opinion

Despite significant differences in how headscarves are perceived and legislated across these ten European nation-states, recent public opinion polls and government discourse and legislation reveal an emerging and significant common reluctance toward niqabs and burqas. While multiple and overlapping, I submit that the following five concerns recur in these public and governmental discussions: (1) that full-face hijabs reflect a patriarchal oppression of women; (2) that they reveal a rejection of pervasive cultural values, particularly the secularization of the public sphere; (3) that their presence entails a safety or security threat; (4) that they impede social relationships or "neighborliness"; and lastly, (5) that they cannot be defended from an Islamic theological perspective (i.e. that there is insufficient support for full-face covering within Islamic legal sources like the Qur'an). As we shall see, legislative and governmental discourses in these ten countries draw on these arguments differently.

Aforementioned, the UK saw public debate on niqabs and burqas escalate in October 2006 when then-Foreign Minister Jack Straw commented that they signaled "separation and difference," impeded communication, and obstructed community relations (*The Guardian* 2006). Straw was responding to the case of a young niqab-wearing teaching assistant who was suspended from her position (Werbner 2007: 164). Straw's response to the case drew international attention. In a riposte in *The Times*, the Archbishop of Canterbury Rowan Williams defended the teacher in question's right to wear religious symbols like the niqab in the workplace on the grounds that the state is "not the source of morality" and that "the ideal of a society where no visible public signs of religion would be seen—no crosses around necks, no side locks, turbans or veils—is a politically dangerous one" (cited in Werbner 2007: 164). Straw later apologized for the statement, but the pronouncement revealed tensions on the acceptability of full-face veils in multicultural Britain that other smaller school council-level disputes on hijabs did not garner.

There are currently no bans or restrictions on burqas and niqabs in the United Kingdom. British Tory MP Philip Hollobone has pushed to launch a bill that would ban face-covering garments in the public sphere similarly to France and Belgium, but it has been overruled by the Home Secretary, Theresa May (Morris and Morrison 2011). The UKIP (the United Kingdom Independence Party) is the first British party to call for a ban on full-face hijabs in the public sphere. UKIP leader Nigel Farage has said they are a symbol of an "increasingly divided Britain," that they "oppress women" and are a potential security threat (BBC News 2011). The British National Party has also called for the veil to be banned in Britain's schools (BBC News 2011). Most Britons appear to support a public ban of full-face hijabs. When asked in a March 2010 poll conducted by the *Financial Times* whether they would like to see a full-face hijab ban in their country, 55% supported the ban, 25% did not, and 20% were unsure (Blitz 2010). As we saw in the previous section, the more common hijab has been more widely accepted.

There is similarly no official ban on full-face-covering veils in Austria, where the niqab and burqa are exempt from the security-based prohibitions on disguises at public gatherings and demonstrations with reference to legal protections for religious signs. Nevertheless, appealing to concerns for gender equality, Gabriele Heinisch-Hosek, Social Democrat Minister for Women and Public Services, stated in 2009 that, "I consider the burka a sign of the submission of women" and that a burqa ban would be considered if the number of women wearing the garment increases significantly (*Austrian Times* 2009). In addition, even if there appears to be little threat, other indicators suggest that the Austrian socio-political climate may not be entirely welcoming to all non-Christian religious signs in the public sphere.

Mirroring most of the countries under examination here, a relative openness toward hijabs in Sweden becomes more restrictive in discussions of full-face-covering hijabs. Mandatory directives were issued in 2003 by the National Education Agency to prohibit girls from wearing the burqa and niqab in public schools to ensure "the common values of the sexes and respect for the democratic principle on which the education system is based" (McGoldrick 2006: 215). Swedes appear to share this position. A study done by *Uppsala Universitet- Sociologiska Institutionen* suggests that 60% of Swedes believe it is acceptable to wear religious headcoverings like the hijab to work as long as it does not cover the face. The study concludes that only 2.8% of Swedes deem full-face veils acceptable (Islam in Europe 2010).

There are no formal burqa or hijab prohibitions in Switzerland. Like in Austria, in 2009, Justice Minister Eveline Widmer-Schlumpf stated that a ban on full-face coverings would be considered if the proportion of women wearing the burqa increased significantly. Far-right Swiss Democrat Rene Kunz stated that the burqa is "a symbol of the domination of men over women" (News.com.au 2010). There appears to be grassroots support for this position. Echoing the country's November 2009 minaret ban, in May 2011 a petition in the canton of Ticino collected more than eleven thousand signatures to attempt to force a referendum on the prohibition of full-face hijabs (*The Local* 2011). The canton of Aargau's parliament similarly introduced a motion to the Council of States. The motion was approved with a vote of 89 to 33. There is popular support in Switzerland for the restriction of niqabs and burqas: 57.6% support a ban, 26.5% are against, and 15.9% are undecided (News 24 2010).

Public debates on Islam in Italy have also focused on full-face-coverings. At the time of writing, formal restrictions were in place in the north with a national ban in development. On August 2, 2011, an Italian parliamentary commission approved a draft law that would ban women from wearing face-covering veils in public. Following an argument that they impede cultural integration, the law was sponsored by Souad Sbai, a Moroccan-born member of the Italian Freedom People Party. Sbai indicated that she felt that legislation would decrease the number of women who are "forced" to cover their faces, while helping them to better integrate into Italian society (Farris 2011). The proposal recommended that women found wearing the veil in public would face fines ranging from €100 to €300. Persons found forcing a woman to cover her face in public would be more severely reprimanded with a charge of €30,000 and up to twelve months in prison (*Huffington Post* 2011; *The Guardian* 2011).

Several northern regions of Italy passed legislation banning the niqab and burqa in public places in October 2010, drawing upon a 1974 law that prohibits clothing or coverings that hinder identification. Briefly noting that the burqa and niqab do not have Qur'anic legitimacy, an Italian Interior Ministry report asserted that full-face-covering veils would be banned for "security reasons" (Walker 2010). Novara is an example of a city that passed a rule against all veils in the public sphere in 2010. In one case, Amel Marmouri was fined €500 for wearing her burqa to the post office. Media reports suggest that her husband refused to let police see Ms. Marmouri unveiled (*Daily Mail* 2010; Walker 2010). Similarly, media reports in the north have focused on the burkini (a fully-covering female bathing suit). In one case a woman was asked to leave a public pool on the grounds that her bathing suit was unhygienic (*Daily Mail* 2010). Niqabs have had little public support in Italy according to a *Financial Times* poll. When asked whether they would support a ban on full-face hijabs like that in France, 63% of Italians supported the possibility of a ban, 23% did not, and 14% were undecided (Blitz 2010).

In Spain, a nation-wide ban curtailing full-face veils was considered in the summer of 2010 on the grounds of female oppression, but was ultimately rejected by parliament (Tremlett 2010). Nevertheless, certain regions have enforced legal restrictions on clothing that covers the face in public, arguably to limit full-face-covering veils. Some areas in the provinces of Catalonia and Andalusia, where Muslim populations are more significant, have enforced bans on wearing the full-face veil in public. The Catalonian city of Lleida, for instance, has enforced a law so that a woman found wearing one in public is first warned and then fined between €300 and €600. Its mayor Ángel Ros appealed to concerns about women's equality and a rise in religious radicalism, saying, "This is about equality between men and women. The burqa and the niqab are symbols of the political use of a religious dogmatism that had begun to appear in Lleida" (Tremlett 2010). The city of Barcelona passed similar legislation in 2010 that prohibits the full-face veil in all municipal buildings. In general, Spaniards appear to support this legislation. With figures similar to those in Italy, a 2011 *Financial Times* survey suggests that 65% supported a possible ban, 21% did not support the ban, and 14% were unsure (Blitz 2010).

In keeping with the escalation of debates treating face-covering headscarves across Europe, niqabs and burqas have also come under recent scrutiny in Germany. At the time of writing, the state of Hesse is the only *länder* that has imposed a ban on the full-face veil for public sector workers, implemented in February 2011 (BBC News 2011). Support for a law on full-face veils like that in Belgium and France has received less support across Germany. A 2010 *Financial Times* survey found that 50% of Germans supported a formal ban of full-face veils, 32% did not support the ban, and 18% were unsure. Of note, when asked whether they would support a burqa ban alongside a wider prohibition of religious icons in the public sphere, only 10% of respondents supported the ban (Blitz 2010).

In the Netherlands there is general acceptance toward headscarves that emerges as more restrictive with niqabs. In 2003 the Commission on Equal Treatment approved the prohibition of the niqab in public schools and universities on the basis that it hinders communication (Shadid and Van Koningsveld 2005). This case led the Minister of Education to create a guideline on clothing in public schools that allowed for the hijab but not for full-face coverings. By 2005, the Netherlands was the first European country where a potential burqa ban came to the forefront. Although the Dutch cabinet refused the controversial bill from Geert Wilders's rightist Dutch Freedom Party (*Partij voor de Vrijheid*), the issue remains on the agenda alongside Wilders's push to impede so-called Muslim immigration (Lettinga and Saharso 2008; Erlanger 2011). In response to Wilders's bill against full-face-covering hijabs, the Minister of Integration,

Rita Verdonk, created a commission to study the implications of a general ban, which were published as a report in 2006 (Vink 2007). The report concluded that a public ban on full-face hijabs infringed the Netherlands' nondiscrimination principle and the right to freedom of religion and of choice.

Anti-full-face hijab rhetoric emphasizes securitization (Saharso 2007; Lettinga and Saharso 2008). By January 2012, the Dutch minority government inched toward banning forms of clothing that cover the face including balaclavas and motorcycle helmets. The Interior Affairs Ministry commented, "people should be able to look at each other's faces and recognize each other when they meet" (Reuters 2012). Like neighboring Belgium, the Dutch government cited security concerns as a reason for the ban and framed it as a move to safeguard public order and allow all members to fully participate in society. Prime Minister Maxime Verhagen said the ban was intended to ensure that a Dutch tradition of open communication was upheld, as well as to ensure public safety (Reuters 2012). While the most recent governmental position is clear, public opinion polls suggest that the Dutch are divided. A July 2005 poll states that 51% of those surveyed supported a ban on headscarves, and 46% opposed it (Horowitz and Morin 2006).

These common public attitudes toward niqabs and burqas have translated into legislation in Belgium, which is the second country in Europe to institute a formal ban on full-face-covering hijabs. After much governmental debate, and while strongly critiqued by Belgium's Muslim Council and by Amnesty International, on April 28, 2011, the government approved a law banning full-face veiling in the public sphere. Rationale for the law emphasized how veils prevent accurate identification of the individual, thereby threatening public safety. The law went into effect on July 22, 2011. Those caught with their faces covered in public can face fines (€137.50) and/or up to seven days' imprisonment (BBC News 2011). At the time of writing, the full-face veil ban was challenged by two burqa-wearing women who claimed the law is discriminatory (BBC News 2011).

Seven years after the 2004 ban on conspicuous religious signs in public schools, France became the first European country to pass a law banning face-covering veils. It is estimated that there are between 367 and 2,000 women in France who wear niqabs (*Le Figaro* 2009; Gerin 2010: 24–9). The "burqa ban" was preceded by a commission and a report, the "Fact-finding mission on the practice of wearing the full veil on the national territory" (or the *Rapport d'information fait en application de l'article 145 du règlement au nom de la mission d'information sur la pratique du port du voile intégral sur le territoire national*). This "Gerin Report" was instigated at the request of André Gerin, a communist member of the National Assembly and former mayor of Vénissieux. In early 2009, Gerin noted to the French National Assembly what he saw as an alarming rise in the number of women donning the *voile intégral* or full-face hijab in his constituency. He cautioned that to be "politically correct" and ignore the problem was tantamount to accepting it and that rising fundamentalist Islamism would promote sexist practices and fracture national identity. His position had broad political support, including from then-president Sarkozy.

Legislating a ban on full-face veils in France also had strong popular support prior to its adoption. An opinion poll conducted by Taylor Nelson Sofres for *Europe 1* in

April 2010 suggested that 63% of the French population fully supported an outright ban (Étude TNS Sofres-Logica 2010). A similar February 2010 survey conducted by the *Financial Times* indicated that 70% of French citizens supported the ban (Blitz 2010). The law restricting niqabs and burqas in the public sphere was put into practice on April 11, 2011. It entails €150 fines or citizenship classes (or both) for a woman caught covering her face. It carries far greater penalties for husbands, fathers, or brothers convicted of "forcing" the veil on a woman. A €30,000 fine and a year in prison would be doubled if the victim is a minor (*La Depeche* 2011).[7] Within the first nine months of the ban's enforcement, 237 women were cited by police and six women had been convicted; none of the women had been sent to a citizenship class (*Arab News* 2012).

# INTERPRETING DIVERSE HEADSCARF REGIMES

This overview of the current statuses of hijabs makes evident the wide range of interpretations and legislation across these ten Western European nation-states. With this broad topography of more liberal allowance in the UK to more overt restriction in France in mind, this third section charts these three broad approaches comparatively: first, I turn to the citizenship and immigration models within these ten nation-states to see how they have affected the public acceptability of headscarves; second, I consider conceptualizations of cultural diversity and religiosity in public schools related to hijabs; and lastly, I examine commonly articulated concerns about headscarves in Western Europe related to their supposed expression of radical Islamism and patriarchy. While useful in offering points of comparison, I conclude by critiquing the limitations of these models.

## Citizenship and Immigration Models

One way the varying positions on headscarves across these nation-states can be conceptualized is by examining the ways in which they, in part, reflect immigration policies and citizenship regimes. A number of social scientists have analyzed how cultural diversity is negotiated in European nation-states (Castles 1995; Joppke 2007b; Lettinga and Saharso 2008). While these perspectives on cultural diversity often problematically position Muslims in Europe as immigrants, turning to common elements within citizenship/nationhood models nevertheless offers a useful window to address how

---

[7] The July 2008 case of "Mme. M." is cited in the Gerin Report as an occasion where a woman had been forced to wear a niqab. Mme. M. was denied French citizenship due to her deemed adoption of radical Islam incompatible with French values; court documents released to the press reported that her husband had required her to cover her entire face. The Conseil d'État (State Council) interpreted her full-face veil as solely a political sign and pointed to how the garment reflected her anti-Republican beliefs and comportment (*Le Monde* 2008; Gerin 2010: 164; Selby 2011a: 390).

national identity can be bolstered relative to hijabs, both by excluding or including them (Bowen 2012). Recall, for instance, how concerns with hijabs in Germany were heightened as a unifying national concern following reunification. Following the conceptualizations of Sauer (2009) and Castles (1995), I situate these ten nation-states into three broad categories.

The first model captures the French case, unique among those discussed here for its civic-assimilationist (Sauer 2009: 79) or simply assimilationist (Castles 1995: 298) perspective. This assimilationist context remains open to new Muslim immigrants as citizens but does not generally promote religious or cultural difference. Instead, a common point of allegiance for all citizens—public sphere secularity—ideally grants equal rights and responsibilities in matters of education and political participation regardless of the confessional loyalties of its citizens. Arguably, this context allows for the fostering of religious diversity among the Muslim minority for, as Cécile Laborde notes, "it is precisely because religious freedom is important that no religious group should be granted recognition" (2005: 314). In other words, the French citizenship paradigm purports that the public sphere must be free from potentially exclusionary religious references. At the same time, its expectation that immigrants become culturally indistinguishable from the majority population means that difference, apparent in the public visibility of partial or full headscarves, is problematic (Scott 2005: 110). This concern is articulated in the two government-commissioned reports that bolstered the 2004 and 2011 laws banning hijabs in public schools and full-face hijabs in public spaces. Both reports problematize multicultural politics for promoting *communautarisme* (communitarianism), which, contrary to shared nationhood, is understood to promote ghettoized segregation and unequal minority communities. Hijabs are thus positioned as threats to cohesive national unity.

Six of the ten countries examined in this chapter fall into a second model, an ethno-cultural (Sauer 2009: 85) or differential exclusion (Castles 1995) approach: Austria, Belgium (which, on the French side, could fall under the first *laïque* category and on the Flemish side espouses a slightly more pluralistic perspective), and some federal states of Germany, Italy, Spain, and Switzerland. Compared to the first model, the German model has not defined itself in Republican universalistic terms. Rather, Germany has emphasized "Christian-Occidental values" (Joppke 2007a: 335). This ethno-cultural perspective is based on *descent* rather than the third model examined in the next section that emphasizes *consent* to common values and principles. This ethno-cultural or differential model typically imposes the strictest citizenship requirements for immigrants. Austria, for instance, requires cultural and social integration as a precondition for naturalization (Sauer 2009: 85), and it and a number of countries including Germany, Switzerland, and Belgium have historically recruited guest workers for more transitory labor demands or as refugees for temporary protection who do not later receive citizenship rights (Castles 1995: 294). I have grouped Italy and Spain under this category because of their historical (and arguably, in Italy, contemporary) affiliation with Catholicism as an unspoken condition of national identity. At the same time, these nation-states do not endorse complete prohibition of religious signs sometimes because of the value accorded to religiosity (read: the so-called cultural visibility of Christianity).

The last model encompasses a more pluralistic (Castles 1995: 301) or multicultural (Sauer 2009: 89) approach and includes the Netherlands, Sweden (arguably), and the United Kingdom.[8] Compared to the second paradigm, the multicultural model promotes diversity by granting relatively easy access to citizenship and generally recognizes cultural differences. Particularly in contrast with the civic-assimilationalist model in France, the pluralist version implies that minority communities are granted equal rights without demanding the prohibition of visible elements of cultural difference. With reference to Western European hijab debates, this means that there are relatively few restrictions in these nation-states against their visibility in the public sphere.

These three citizenship paradigms are useful in recasting articulations of shared nationhood alongside the headscarf perspectives of these countries. However, the grouping of the larger second group is problematic in its explicatory capabilities because, as Sauer (2009: 89) explains, the ethno-cultural-based citizenship regime can lead to both greater accommodation toward non-Christian religious signs, like in the case of Austria, and to more prohibitive regulations, like in Germany. Considering common factors in the religio-social and legal landscapes of these countries, to which I now turn, is a second useful lens with which to consider headscarf regimes across Western Europe.

## Islam in Public Schools

Another way that these national perspectives on headscarves can be understood is vis-à-vis their articulation of cultural diversity or religiosity in public schools. As Antje Pedain notes, "there are few countries in Europe whose courts have not yet had occasion to rule on the presence of headscarfs in educational institutions, whether worn by pupils or by teachers" (2004: 537). These cases question the role of religion and the parameters of religious freedom in public education. Examination of the historical situation of religion in the public spheres of these countries falls outside the parameters of this chapter, so for the sake of brevity, I consider mediatized cases in public schools in France, Germany, Italy, Austria, and Britain.

In keeping with its assimilationist Republican context, public schools in France are generally understood as microcosms of its political society where children learn about citizenship and participate in a shared public identity that transcends their personal, local, cultural, and religious affiliations. Headscarf debates in 1989, 1994, and 2004 (where hijabs were grouped with other "conspicuous religious signs" like yarmulkes and rarely seen large crosses) emphasized the inadmissibility of visible and distinguishing religiosity among students in this shared Republican space. Indeed, *laïcité* has an institutional doctrine of separation but also a principle of conscience that "prescribes norms of conduct both for religious organizations and for individual citizens" (Laborde

---

[8] Cavanaugh (2007: 1) qualifies this branch as a "*limited* pluralist European model."

2005: 307). Schools in France may be characterized as religiously neutral, but they are not politically neutral, particularly amidst concerns about whether female students are able to choose their religious garments free from familial expectations, or peer group or neighborhood pressures (Poulter 1997: 71). Debates have generally not extended to teachers who are expected to uphold and represent the neutrality of the state and cannot publicly express their religious beliefs (Laborde 2005: 325).

In contrast to these hijab-free public schools promoting *laïque* civic values, schools in Britain are more broadly responsive to the needs and demands of individuals in local communities, and tend to see public education as a meeting place of private and public spheres. Unlike in France, in Britain religion is typically taught in schools with the pedagogical aim that instruction of the major religious traditions of the world relativizes them for students (Dwyer 1999: 174; Werbner 2007: 176). In general, public schools are conceptualized as arenas in which difference should be taught and discussed from a position of neutrality in order to educate citizens toward mutual tolerance and respect for difference. This typical position has meant that, until Jack Straw's far-reaching comments on the niqab, most of the hijab cases examined in Britain have been resolved at the institutional level and have involved the violation of school uniforms and not headscarves. Many public schools encourage hijabs.

Germany differs from France and Britain insofar as federal states determine whether hijabs are deemed acceptable in schools.[9] Moreover, headscarf-related controversies affect students in France and teachers in Germany. As Christian Joppke explains, "in Germany it was never in question that students were free to wear religious dress as they see fit, while in France it was ever in question that teachers, the proverbial *instituteurs* of secular Republican morality, were to remain neutral in their personal attire" (2007a: 326). Students in Germany are typically allowed to wear hijabs provided they do not cause disruption and are deemed inoffensive. The outcome of the 1998 Ludin case shows how teachers are not granted the same liberty because, as representatives of the state, their religiously-informed dress might conflict with the school's commitment to "neutrality."

The more concordatory models of religion in Germany, Italy, and Austria thus allow for greater visibility of hijabs in public schools among students, even if Christian values and practices typically underscore instruction. Public school debates in Italy, for instance, have focused on whether visible crucifixes are appropriate. Austria does not presume a secular position in its educational system and Catholicism remains present. However, Birgit Sauer points out that, ironically, given the strength of right-wing populist parties and the difficulties of achieving citizenship, the public dominance of the Catholic Church in Austria explains the country's moderate public hijab debates: "A ban on headscarves might result in a similar prohibition of Christian symbols" (Sauer 2009: 88). In sum, the relative acceptability or not of hijabs in public schools is another

---

[9] On a national level, Islam is not officially recognized, few Muslim organizations are funded, and solely Christianity is taught in public schools (Sauer 2009: 85).

way to think about how these nation-states have framed these garments in one among many public institutions. A range of interpretations is evident, from the highly restrictive understanding of religious diversity in French public schools, to the allowance for students and not teachers in Germany, to the more liberal tolerance of visible religious signs in Britain.

## Concerns for a "Fundamentalist" Islam

A third way in which to consider these nationally-based Western European headscarf debates is to examine whether or not two prevalent arguments against their public presence are invoked: that they are symbols of patriarchy and/or that they reflect radical political Islamism. These themes have emerged as arguments to prevent hijabs in some nation-state contexts and not in others. Indeed, in some representations, Muslim women who wear a hijab are deemed as symbols of patriarchy (and sometimes misogyny), fundamentalism, or terrorism and as therefore dangerous and inassimilable within "European culture."[10] These two points are separated in this section arbitrarily. My aim is not to determine whether hijabs are inherently patriarchal or necessarily political, but to point to when these arguments have emerged in different nation-state contexts particularly in relation to full-face-covering veils.

### Headscarves as Signs of Patriarchy

Concerns for women's equal rights have been central to recent discussions on the acceptability of hijabs in the public sphere. Gender equality advocates have expressed concerns that they symbolize a lesser treatment of women and hinder parity by denying Muslim women full access to the public sphere as equal citizens. There is also dispute about patriarchal calls for modest covering within the Qur'an. As described in the first section, part of this contention stems from Orientalist and colonialist characterizations of headscarf-wearing Muslim women as eroticized and passive, later shifting to postcolonial terrorism-related representations. Other concerns point to the theologically-explained passivity and lesser rights accorded to women under interpretations of shariah in some contexts. Like the representation of the niqab-wearing woman in the anti-minaret campaign in Switzerland (see Figure 16.1), these characterizations are not benign. Concern to cover and uncover parts of women's bodies in the public sphere—ensuring normativity related to social sexual behavior—have contributed to a "feminization" of debates on Islam in Europe.

These arguments related to patriarchy can be multifaceted. A number of scholars have noted how both defenders and opponents of headscarf restrictions refer to principles of non-discrimination and women's equal rights (Severs 2010: 2; Sauer 2009; Werbner

---

[10] The 2010 French Gerin Report that preceded the ban on niqabs and burqas, for example, deems invocations for their existence as Salafi and as Taliban-inspired (Gerin 2010: 48–61).

FIGURE 16.1 Poster of the SVP with woman wearing niqab, 2009.

Source: © Schweizerzeit Verlags AG.

2007: 163; Winter 2006: 282). They note how those who seek to restrict headscarves in the public sphere argue that in so doing, they liberate women from patriarchal oppression and assert their rights of freedom of expression and equality. This desire to protect women's rights against "patriarchal control" has been particularly important in arguments to enforce limitations on hijabs in France, Germany, Spain, and Sweden. French feminist philosopher Elisabeth Badinter's statements exemplify a commonly articulated linkage between the "liberation" of women, especially with reference to the Afghan situation, and the freeing of Muslim women in Europe from patriarchal religiosity embedded in hijabs. Badinter argues that European feminists should draw a lesson from the 2004 French legislation against hijabs in schools: "Soon feminists in the rest of Europe will realise the headscarf is a terrible symbol of submission. You cannot denounce what has been going on in Afghanistan while tolerating the veil in Europe—even if women claim they are wearing it voluntarily" (cited in Freedman 2007: 37–8). On this point, as Bronwyn Winter (2006) points out, feminist groups often find themselves in unlikely alliances with the anti-immigration platforms of the political right (see also Selby 2011a: 380).

A more complex situation appears in the Netherlands where the Dutch women's movement is more divided on the acceptability of headscarves (Sauer 2009: 87). Sawitri Saharso and Doutje Lettinga (2008) argue that less emphasis is placed on the veil as signifying traditional gender roles in the Netherlands than in some countries, but that Somali refugee and prominent author Ayaan Hirsi Ali has gained contested recognition as a spokesperson for the liberation of women in Islam (and from headscarves) based on her life experiences told in two bestselling autobiographies. At the same time, a number of Dutch headscarved women began the "Islamic Women's Manifesto" to push for recognition and an alternative voice. This group differs from the French highly politicized suburban-focused (where most Muslims in France live) *Ni Putes Ni Soumises* (NPNS, Neither Whores Nor Submissives) who, to the surprise of some, supported the 2004 ban in France on headscarves in public schools based on their interpretation of feminist principles (Fernando 2009). In this way, like other feminist organizations in France, NPNS played an active role in promoting secularism (in this case, the removal of visible religious signs) to ensure women's rights (Scott 2005, 2007; Selby 2011b). Despite the pervasiveness of these rights-driven critiques, Western European nation-states are not uniform on this point. In the German context for one, Saharso (2007) claims that hijab debates are generally not constructed around issues of gender and are generally understood as relating more to integration and citizenship (Rottman and Ferree 2008).

## *Headscarves as Signs of Terrorism*

In addition to concerns for their embedded patriarchal influences, hijabs have also been restricted in Western European nation-states because they are seen as terror-ridden signs. The acceptance of full-face-covering veils is sometimes equated with enabling conservative terrorist regimes. In this correlation restrictions against them act to safeguard Western nation-states from fundamentalism and concomitant violence. Much of this discourse became vocalized following September 11, 2001 and later attacks in Madrid and London.

These events have been generative of a number of effects for Muslim minorities in the West, including a heightened gaze on headscarves (Bowen 2009; Shryock 2010). As visible signs of a vilified Islam, hijabs thus become symbolically positioned as contrary to shared unifying values and cause for heightened security. A number of studies and sites support this suggestion. The European Monitoring Centre on Racism and Xenophobia identified such a rise, specifically noting the headscarf as the "visible identifier as a target of hatred" (2001).

A closer look at the 2009 campaign prior to a referendum on the construction of minarets in Switzerland also exemplifies these anxieties (see Figure 16.1). Three elements in the Swiss no campaign's poster are worth noting: the woman figured is obscured and dark-skinned, evoking racial difference from the majority Caucasian Swiss population; second, the woman wears a rarely-seen niqab, suggesting that the visibility of minarets will promote more niqab-wearing women; and third, situated behind the niqab-wearing woman are missile-shaped minarets, effectively associating full-face-covering hijabs with fear and undesirable militarization. The advertisement thus links minarets and niqabs and equates them with war and terrorism. In the case of the Swiss minaret referendum, a number of pundits suggested that this powerfully-charged racialized anti-minaret campaign had a decisive impact on the resulting ban on minarets (Soukup 2009). That there are few women wearing these full-face coverings in Switzerland and even fewer minarets in the Swiss landscape are obscured in this image. It conveniently taps into racism, discrimination, and xenophobia associated with niqabs and burqas.

Similar security concerns emerged against full-face veils in the defense of the April 2011 French ban against burqas and niqabs. They have also been articulated in Belgium, Italy, the Netherlands, and in Switzerland. In these nation-state contexts, beyond ensuring accurate identification, there is fear that full-face veils will obscure the identifying characteristics of a potential criminal. Recall in Italy how a rarely invoked law against the wearing of masks was reformed to include full-face hijabs. Arguments for their removal to ensure security sometimes invoke theological interpretation of their illegitimacy, in part to try to demonstrate that the rationale to censor them is not Islamophobic or against the practices and beliefs of most Muslims. The 2010 Gerin Report in France that preceded the 2011 law carefully referenced theologians and prominent French Muslims who concluded that full-face veils are "un-Islamic" (Gerin 2010: 38, 431). There are thus a number of examples of how headscarves are read as problematic political signs that reflect potential danger.

This third section has examined three ways to analyze the similarities and differences in headscarf regimes. One way to understand differences across Western Europe is through approaches toward cultural diversity, whether they be assimilationist, ethno-culturalist, or multicultural-pluralist. The Republican assimilationist perspective in France means that while there is a desire to be inclusive and grant membership rights to immigrants, citizens are encouraged to accept a commonly-shared public sphere devoid of religious differences. A second way cultural elements of difference are articulated vis-à-vis headscarves is in how they mirror "church–state" relations. Again with reference to the French case, a similar notion of sameness is evident in how *laïcité* has emerged in public schools as foundational for citizenship. Hijabs appear as impediments to this sameness. Thirdly, we can note how some countries have emphasized feminism and securitization to a greater or lesser extent.

## Comparative Issues

While these rubrics offer frameworks with which to consider headscarf regimes across Europe, these comparative categories are problematic for a number of reasons. First, they ignore how veiled women are often excluded from these legal and policy discussions. Even if not obvious in the ten-country overview, many of the policies and laws that regulate hijabs are formalized without consultation with the women who wear them. This silencing can have a negative effect on women who may already be marginalized by citizenship, social class, and education. On this point, Valérie Amiraux aptly notes a double discrimination in Europe, that in "wearing the headscarf, women become visible twice, first as members of a religious minority (the Muslim believers), second as gendered social actors (women)" (2003: 137). They can be similarly doubly silenced.

Second, the way that these laws and public discussions are reported often give the impression that there are far more women wearing hijabs, niqabs, and burqas than there may be in actual fact. I again turn to the French context to make this point. A 2003 IFOP study suggests that 26% of Muslim women who call themselves *pratiquantes* (practicing) wear the hijab, of whom only 8% are under 35 years old and 30% are 50 years or older (IFOP 2011: 28). Yet, 2003–4 publicized discussions in France on the acceptability of hijabs in public schools gave the impression that the number was far higher. More generally, full-face-covering hijabs are ubiquitous in photography and news stories in ways that do not reflect the diverse ways women do and do not wear hijabs. A personal anecdote exemplifies this point. In July 2011 I searched through thousands of stock photography and internet and news images for a photograph of a group of French Muslim women who both wore and did not wear headscarves. I had taken numerous similar photos of a variety of coverings among the women with whom I lived and interviewed while conducting ethnographic fieldwork in a Parisian suburb (Selby 2012). To protect their anonymity and given concerns of modesty articulated by some of the women, my own photographs were not appropriate for publication, particularly for a book cover. After an exhaustive search for a similar image to those I had easily and often taken, I came up empty handed. Of course, there are millions of images available of Muslim women, but the multitude of burqa- and niqab-wearing images available do not reflect their prevalence in Western Europe. In the Parisian suburban housing project area that was the location of my research, where most of the area's 8,200 inhabitants were Muslim, only two women wore full-face veils. These two women were Caucasian converts, a second element not often featured in images of niqab-wearing women in the European Union.

The last issue worth noting in the comparative frameworks I have presented here is how they presuppose a common pattern within nation-states that obscures internal divisions on the regulation of hijabs. The porousness between internal national borders extends to blurred distinctions between private and public spheres (Amiraux 2003: 143).[11] In Germany, Italy, Switzerland, and Spain, provincial states and local cities are able to decide how they wish to regulate headscarves in the public sphere; these policies are not reflective of decisions of other provinces or states within their national boundaries. Thus, solely focusing on nation-state positions as I do in this chapter presupposes a homogeneity that may not reflect the countries' internal diversity.

## Conclusion: Whither Headscarves?

This chapter has examined the multiplicity of ways ten Western European nation-states have negotiated the public visibility of hijabs in recent years. While their socio-legal

---

[11] As Valérie Amiraux explains, liberal secularism (more radical in France, more flexible in the United Kingdom) is based on a notion of confessional freedom, wherein religious practice is framed as reducible to preferences and choices, so that religiosity is solely relegated to the private sphere (2007: 133).

treatment toward the more common headscarf differs, a trend toward the banning the full-face hijabs in the public sphere and/or in public institutions is noteworthy. Rather than restating common and differing positions across nation-states in this conclusion, I ask more broadly, why have headscarves become emblematic of contestation about Islam in Europe?

As the cases and debates in this chapter make clear, as "shifting signifiers" these cloth coverings reflect concerns with immigration, integration, and securitization heightened in the post-9/11 period, are visibly religious in an age of secularization, and appear to counter commonly held gender and feminist politics (see also Göle 2005: 109). Predictions about the future of these debates are not useful. As "European Islams" communicate and rearticulate Islamic law for contemporary times and contexts, and as Western European nation-states continue debating the acceptability of these garments, these examples across these ten nation-states make clear that the significance of hijabs remains multitudinous and changing.

# Acknowledgments

I thank Emily Worsley for her assistance in putting together sources for this chapter. Some sections are drawn from *Questioning French Secularism* (Palgrave Macmillan, 2012).

# Bibliography

Abide, L. J. 2006. "Muslims in Austria: Integration through Participation in Austrian Society," *Journal of Muslim Minority Affairs* 26(2): 263–78.

Abu-Lughod, L. 2002. "Do Muslim Women Really Need Saving? Anthropological Reflections on Cultural Relativism and its Others," *American Anthropologist* 104(3): 783–90.

ADNKronos International. 2009. "Italy: First Veiled Italian Muslim Woman Runs for Local Elections" [online] May 28 <http://www.adnkronos.com/AKI/English/Politics/?id=3.0.3369783904> [Accessed July 13, 2011].

Ahmed, L. 1992. *Women and Gender in Islam: Historical Roots of a Modern Debate.* New Haven: Yale University Press.

Allah.eu, 2010. "Sweden: Hijab a Problem for Getting a Job." September 2 <http://www.allah.eu/about-islam/sweden-hijab-a-problem-for-getting-a-job.html> [Accessed July 11, 2011].

Alvanou, M. 2008. "Muslim Communities in Italy and Social Stress Minority Issues," in M. Finklestein and K. Dent-Brown (eds.), *Psychosocial Stress in Members of Minority Groups as a Factor of Terrorist Behaviour.* Amsterdam: IOS Press, 122–7.

Ameli, S. R. and Merali, A. 2006. "Hijab, Meaning, Identity, Otherization and Politicas: British Muslim Women," *British Muslims' Expectations Series,* January 26 <http://www.ihrc.org.uk/file/BMEG_VOL4.pdf> [Accessed July 20, 2011].

Amiraux, V. 2003. "CFCM: A French Touch?," *ISIM Newsletter,* 12, June: 24–5.

Amiraux, V. 2007. "The Headscarf Question: What Is Really the Issue?," in S. Amghar, A. Boubekeur, and M. Emerson (eds.), *European Islam: Challenges for Public Policy and Society*. Brussels: Centre for European Policy Studies, 124–43.

Andezian, S. 1988. "Migrant Muslim Women in France," in T. Gerholm and Y. Lithman (eds.), *The New Islamic Presence in Western Europe*. London: Mansell Publishing, 196–205.

Appadurai, A. 1996. *Modernity at Large: Cultural Dimensions of Globalization*. Minneapolis: University of Minnesota Press.

*Arab News*. 2012. "France Fines Six Muslim Women for Wearing Niqab." January 3 <http://arab-news.com/world/article558351.ece>.

Asaad Buaras, E. 2010. "Swiss Court Upholds Basketball Hijab Ban," *Muslim News*, February 26 <http://www.muslimnews.co.uk/paper/index.php?article=4517> [Accessed July 25, 2011].

Ascha, G. 1995. "The 'Mothers of the Believers': Stereotypes of the Prophet Muhammad's Wives," in R. Kloppenborg and W. J. Hanegraaff (eds.), *Female Stereotypes in Religious Traditions*. Leiden: Brill, 89–108.

Assemblée Nationale. 1905. Projet de loi relative à la séparation des Églises et de l'État, February 9 <http://www.assemblee-nationale.fr/histoire/eglise-etat/1905-projet.pdf>.

*Austrian Times*. 2009. "Disputes around Austrian Women's Minister's Demand for Burka Ban," December 30 <http://www.euro-islam.info/2009/12/30/disputes-around-austrian-womens-ministers-demand-for-burka-ban> [Accessed July 26, 2011].

*Austrian Times*. 2011. "Muslim Women Often Victimised, report says" [online] March 22 <http://www.austriantimes.at/news/General_News/2011-03-22/31642/Muslim_women_often_victimised,_report_says>.

Bakht, N. 2012. "Veiled Objections: Facing Public Opposition to the Niqab," in L. G. Beaman (ed.), *Defining Reasonable Accommodation: Managing Religious Diversity*. Vancouver: UBC Press, 70–108.

Barlas, A. 2004. "Amina Wadud's Hermeneutics of the Qur'an," in S. Taji-Farouki (ed.), *Modern Muslim Intellectuals and the Qur'an*. Oxford: Oxford University Press, 97–123.

Barlas, A. 2006. "Women's Reading of the Qur'an," in J. D. McAuliffe (ed.), *The Cambridge Companion to the Qur'an*. Cambridge: Cambridge University Press, 255–72.

Baubérot, J. 1998. "La laïcité française et ses mutations," *Social Compass* 45(1): 175–87.

BBC News. 2004a. "Schoolgirl loses Muslim gown case." June 15 <http://news.bbc.co.uk/2/hi/uk_news/education/3808073.stm> [Accessed July 20, 2011].

BBC News. 2004b. "Italian Minister Joins Veil Row." March 24 <http://news.bbc.co.uk/2/hi/europe/3564483.stm> [Accessed July 20, 2011].

BBC News. 2006. "Dutch Muslims Condemn Burqa Ban" [online] November 18 <http://news.bbc.co.uk/2/hi/6160620.stm> [Accessed May 28, 2011].

BBC News. 2007. "Man Admits He 'Pulled Off' Hijab" [online] August 30 <http://news.bbc.co.uk/2/hi/uk_news/wales/6970761.stm> [Accessed July 15, 2011].

BBC News. 2011. "The Islamic Veil across Europe" [online] April 11 <http://www.bbc.co.uk/news/world-europe-13038095> [Accessed July 29, 2011].

Blitz, J. 2010. "Poll Shows Support in Europe for Burka Ban," *The Financial Times* [online] March 1 <http://www.ft.com/intl/cms/s/0/e0c0e732-254d-11df-9cdb-00144feab49a.html#axzz1R8ZEUn6q> [Accessed July 4, 2011].

Bloul, R. 1996. "Engendering Muslim Identities: Deterritorialization and the Ethnicization Process in France," in B. D. Metcalf (ed.), *Making Muslim Space in North America and Europe*. Berkeley: University of California Press, 234–50.

Bouamama, S. 2004. *L'affaire du foulard islamique: la production d'un racisme respectable*. Roubaix: Le Geai Bleu.
Bouhdiba, A. 1975. *La sexualité en islam*. Paris: PUF.
Bouzar, D. 2004. "Françaises et musulmanes, entre réappropriation et remise en question des norms," in C. Nordmann (ed.), *Le foulard islamique en question*. Paris: Éditions Amsterdam, 54–64.
Bouzar, D. and Bouzar, L. 2010. *La République ou la burqa: les services publiques face à l'islam manipulé*. Paris: Albin Michel.
Bowen, J. R. 2004. "Muslims and Citizens: France's Headscarf Controversy," *Boston Review: A Political and Literary Forum* (February/March).
Bowen, J. R. 2007. *Why the French Don't Like Headscarves: Islam, the State, and Public Space*. Princeton: Princeton University Press.
Bowen, J. R. 2009. "Recognizing Islam in France after 9/11," *Journal of Ethnic and Migration Studies* 35(3): 439–52.
Bowen, J. R. 2012. *Blaming Islam*. Cambridge, MA: MIT Press.
Brulard, I. 1997. "Laïcité and Islam," in S. Perry (ed.), *Aspects of Contemporary France*. London: Routledge, 175–90.
Caritas/Migrantes. 2004. *Immigration Statistical Dossier 2004. 14th Report on Immigration: Open Society, Dynamic and Safe Society* [online] <http://www.dossierimmigrazione.it/schede/book-dossier2004-eng.pdf> [Accessed July 13, 2011].
Castles, S. 1995. "How Nation States Respond to Immigration and Ethnic Diversity," *Journal of Ethnic and Migration Studies* 21(3): 293–308.
Cavanaugh, K. 2007. "Islam and the European Project," *Muslim World Journal of Human Rights* 4(1): 1–20.
Cesari, J. 1998. *Musulmans et républicains: les jeunes, l'islam et la France*. Paris: Éditions Complexe.
Clendenning, A. and Heckle, H. 2010. "Spain Parliament Rejects Burka Ban—For Now," *Associated Press* [online] July 21 <http://www.msnbc.msn.com/id/38332675/ns/world_news-europe/t/spain-parliament-rejects-burqa-ban-now/> [Accessed May 29, 2010].
Council of Europe. n.d. *Dahlab v. Switzerland*—Admissibility Decision [online] <http://strasbourgconsortium.org/document.php?DocumentID=1136> [Accessed July 26, 2011].
Cumper, P. and Lewis, T. 2009. "Taking Religion Seriously? Human Rights and the Hijab in Europe: Some Problems of Adjudication," *Journal of Law and Religion* 24(2): 599–627.
*Daily Mail*. 2010. "'I Have To Keep Her Indoors Now': Muslim Husband's Shocking Response as Wife is First to be Fined £430 for Wearing a Burka," May 5 <http://www.dailymail.co.uk/news/article-1271848/Woman-Italy-fined-430-wearing-burqa.html>.
Dayan-Herzbrun, S. 2000. "The Issue of the Islamic Headscarf," in J. Freedman and C. Tarr (eds.), *Women, Immigration and Identities in France*. Oxford: Berg, 69–84.
Dear, P. 2004. "Women Vow to Protect Muslim Hijab," *BBC News*, June 14 <http://news.bbc.co.uk/2/hi/uk_news/3805733.stm>.
Dilas-Rocherieux, Y. 2005. "Tradition, religion, émancipation: La question du voile chez les jeunes musulmanes," *Débat* 136 (September–October): 108–16.
Dobie, M. 2001. *Foreign Bodies: Gender, Language, and Culture in French Orientalism*. Stanford, CA: Stanford University Press.
Dolezal, M., Helbling, M., and Hutter, S. 2010. "Debating Islam in Austria, Germany and Switzerland: Ethnic Citizenship, Church–State Relations and Right-Wing Populism," *Western European Politics* 33(2): 171–90.

Duits, L. and van Zoonen, L. 2006. "Headscarves and Porno-Chic: Disciplining Girls' Bodies in the European Multicultural Society," *European Journal of Women's Studies* 13(2): 103–17.

Dwyer, C. 1999. "Veiled Meanings: Young British Muslim Women and the Negotiation of Difference," *Gender, Place and Culture* 6(1): 5–26.

El Hamel, C. 2002. "Muslim Diasporas in Western Europe : The Islamic Headscarf (Hijab), the Media and Muslims' Integration in France," *Citizenship Studies* 6(3): 293–308.

Erlanger, S. 2011. "Amid Rise of Multiculturalism, Dutch Confront Their Questions of Identity," *New York Times*, August 13 <http://www.nytimes.com/2011/08/14/world/europe/14dutch.html?pagewanted=all> [Accessed May 30, 2011].

Estudio Fundacion BBVA European Mindset. 2010. [online] April <http://www.elpais.com/elpaismedia/ultimahora/media/201004/27/sociedad/20100427elpepusoc_1_Pes_PDF.pdf> [Accessed July 18, 2011].

Euro-Islam. 2010. "Burqa Ban in Sweden?" January 28. <http://www.euro-islam.info/2010/01/28/burqa-ban-in-sweden/> [Accessed July 11, 2011].

European Freedom Initiative. n.d. "Belgian Burqa Ban Set to Become Law" [online] <http://www.european-freedom-initiative.org/index.php?option=com_content&view=article&id=77%3Abelgian-burqa-ban-set-to-become-law&lang=en>.

*European Jewish Post*. 2011. "Swiss Canton Voters Could Ban the Burqa" [online] May 21 http://www.eip-news.com/2011/05/swiss-canton-voters-could-ban-the-burqa/> [Accessed May 30, 2011]. **Page no longer available.

European Monitoring Centre on Racism and Xenophobia. 2001. *Anti-Islamic Reactions in the EU after the Terrorist Acts Against the USA, 12 September to 31 December 2001*. European Union <http://fra.europa.eu/fraWebsite/attachments/Spain.pdf>.

Evans, C. 2006. "The 'Islamic Scarf' in the European Court of Human Rights," *Melbourne Journal of International Law* 7(1) <http://www.austlii.com/au/journals/MelbJIL/2006/4.html>.

Ewing, K. P. 2008. *Stolen Honor: Stigmatizing Muslim Men in Berlin*. Stanford, CA: Stanford University Press.

*Expatica News*. 2007. "Fifty Percent of Belgians Want Headscarf Ban," May 25 <http://www.euro-islam.info/2007/05/25/fifty-percent-of-belgians-want-headscarf-ban/>.

Ezekiel, J. 2006. "French Dressing: Race, Gender, and the Hijab Story," *Feminist Studies* 32(2) (Summer): 256–78.

Fadil, N. 2005. "Individualizing Faith, Individualizing Identity: Islam and Young Muslim Women in Belgium," in J. Cesari and S. McLoughlin (eds.), *European Muslims and the Secular State*. Aldershot: Ashgate, 143–54.

Falconi, M. 2011. "Swiss Canton Voters Could Ban the Burqa," *The Local* [online] May 20 http://www.thelocal.ch/national/20110520_217.html> [Accessed July 26, 2011].

Farris, S. 2011. "In the Burqa Ban, Italy's Left and Right Find Something to Agree On," *Time* [online] August 4 <http://www.time.com/time/world/article/0,8599,2086879,00.html> [Accessed August 7, 2011].

Fautré, W. n.d. "Full Veil, Burqa, Niqab, Hijab…a Challenge to 'European' Values?" *Religious Freedom* <http://neurope.eu/religiousfreedom/full-veil-burqa-niqab-hijab%E2%80%A6-a-challenge-to-%E2%80%98european%E2%80%99-values/> [Accessed May 28, 2011].

Fernando, M. L. 2009. "Review of *Breaking the Silence: French Women's Voices from the Ghetto* (2006)," *Journal of Middle East Women's Studies* 5(1): 97–100.

Foblets, M. C. 1996. *Familles, Islam, Europe: le droit confronté au changement*. Paris: L'Harmattan.

Folkesson, K. 2011. "Invisible Activity: The Case of Muslim Women Migrants in Fittja, Sweden," in F. Eckardt and J. Eade (eds.), *Ethnically Diverse City: Future Urban Research in Europe 4*. Berlin: BWV, 115–40.
Fournier, P. 2010. *Islamic Marriage in Western Courts: Lost in Transplantation*. Farnham: Ashgate.
Freedman, J. 2007. "Women, Islam and Rights in Europe: Beyond a Universal/Culturalist Dichotomy," *Review of International Studies* 33(1): 29–44.
Galindo, E. and Alonso, E. 1996. "Les relations entre musulmans et chrétiens en Espagne," *Islamochristiana* 22: 161–91.
Gaspard, F. and Khosrokhavar, F. 1995. *Le foulard et la République*. Paris: La Découverte.
Gauchet, M. 1998. *La religion dans la démocratie: parcours de la laïcité*. Paris: Éditions Gallimard.
Gerin Commission Report. 2010. <http://www.assemblee-nationale.fr/13/pdf/rap-info/i2262.pdf>.
Göle, N. 2005. *Interpénétrations: L'Islam et l'Europe*. Paris: Galaade.
Govan, F. 2010. "Spain Considers Burka Ban," *The Telegraph* [online] July 20 <http://www.telegraph.co.uk/news/worldnews/europe/spain/7898629/Spain-considers-burka-ban.html> [Accessed May 28, 2011].
Gresch, N., Hadj-Abdou, L., Rosenberger, S., and Sauer, B. 2008. "Tu felix Austria? The Headscarf and the Politics of 'Non-issues,'" *Social Politics* 15(4): 411–32.
Gressgård, R. 2006. "The Veiled Muslim, the Anorexic and the Transsexual: What Do They Have in Common?," *European Journal of Women's Studies* 13(4): 325–41.
*The Guardian*. 2006. "I Felt Uneasy Talking to Someone I Couldn't See" [online] October 6 <http://www.guardian.co.uk/commentisfree/2006/oct/06/politics.uk> [Accessed July 21, 2011].
*The Guardian*. 2011. "Italy Approves Draft Law to Ban Burqa" [online] August 3 <http://www.guardian.co.uk/world/2011/aug/03/italy-draft-law-burqa> [Accessed August 16, 2011].
Hadj-Abdou, L., Seiglinde, R., Sawitri, S., and Birte, S. 2011. "The Limits of Populism: Accommodative Headscarf Policies in Austria, Denmark, and the Netherlands," in R. Sieglinde and B. Sauer (eds.), *Politics, Religion and Gender: Framing and Regulating the Veil*. London: Routledge, 132–49.
Hancock, C. 2008. "Spatialities of the Secular: Geographies of the Veil in France and Turkey," *European Journal of Women's Studies* 15(3): 165–79.
Heath, J. (ed.) 2008. *The Veil: Women Writers on its History, Lore, and Politics*. Berkeley: University of California Press.
Helbling, M. 2008. "Islamophobia in Switzerland: A New Phenomenon or a New Name for Xenophobia?" Paper prepared for Annual Conference of the Midwest Political Science Association <http://www.unil.ch/webdav/site/issrc/shared/8._Telechargement/Colloque_de_Recherche/Helbling_2010_Islamophobia.pdf>.
Hellgren, Z. and Hobson, B. 2008. "Cultural Dialogues in the Good Society: The Case of Honour Killings in Sweden," *Ethnicities* 8(3): 385–404.
Henley, J. 2004. "Europe Faces Up To Islam and the Veil," *The Guardian* [online] February 4 <http://www.guardian.co.uk/world/2004/feb/04/schools.schoolsworldwide> [Accessed July 13, 2011].
Hirschkind, C. and Mahmood, S. 2002. "Feminism, the Taliban, and the Politics of Counter-Insurgency," *Anthropological Quarterly* 75(2): 337–54.
Holzleithener, E. and Strasser, S. 2006. "Gender Equality, Cultural Diversity: The Austrian Experience" [online] Presented: June 7–8 <http://www.lse.ac.uk/genderInstitute/whosWho/profiles/NuffieldReport-final.pdf> [Accessed July 26, 2011].

Huffpost. 2011. "Italy Burqa Ban: Muslim Veil Law Passes Parliamentary Commission" [online] August 2 <http://www.huffingtonpost.com/2011/08/02/italy-muslim-burqa-ban_n_916104.html> [Accessed August 7, 2011].

Human Rights Watch. 2004. "France: Headscarf Ban Violates Religious Freedom" [online] February 26 <http://www.hrw.org/en/news/2004/02/26/france-headscarf-ban-violates-religious-freedom>.

Hunt, R. 2002. "Islam in Austria," *Muslim World* 92(1): 115–28.

IFOP. 2011. *IFOP Study on French Muslims* <http://www.la-croix.com/Religion/S-informer/Actualite/Tous-les-resultats-de-l-etude-Ifop-La-Croix-sur-les-musulmans-francais-_NG_-2011-08-01-694857>.

Iqbal, C. 2007. "The Understanding of Cultural Symbols such as the Veil and Hijab in Britain and France," *International Journal of the Humanities* 5(3): 131–40.

Islam in Europe. 2010. "Sweden: Majority Think Wearing the Hijab is Acceptable," August 6 <http://islamineurope.blogspot.com/2010/08/sweden-majority-think-wearing-hijab-is.html>.

Islam Online. 2007. "Schoolgirl Wins Spain Hijab Battle" [online] October 2 <http://www.islamonline.net/i3/ContentServer?pagename=IslamOnline/i3Layout&c=OldArticle&cid=1190886068942> [Accessed July 12, 2011].

Islamic Human Rights Commission (IHRC). 2008. *Freedom of Religion in Belgium and the Hijab*. February 1 <http://www.ihrc.org.uk/publications/briefings/5142-briefing-freedom-of-religion-in-belgium-and-the-hijab> [Accessed July 18, 2011].

Joppke, C. 2007a. "State Neutrality and Islamic Headscarf Laws in France and Germany," *Theory and Society* 36(4): 313–42.

Joppke, C. 2007b. "Beyond National Models: Civic Integration Policies for Immigrants in Western Europe," *West European Politics* 30(1) (January): 1–22.

Joppke, C. 2009. *Veil: Mirror of Identity*. Cambridge: Polity Press.

Kandiyoti, D. 1991. "Introduction: Women, Islam and the State," in D. Kandiyoti (ed.), *Women, Islam and the State*. Philadelphia: Temple University Press, 1–21.

Kastoryano, R. 2004. "Religion and Incorporation: Islam in France and Germany," *International Migration Review* 38(3): 1234–55.

Keaton, T. D. 2006. *Muslim Girls and the Other France: Race, Identity Politics and Social Exclusion*. Bloomington: Indiana University Press.

Khosrokhavar, F. 1997. *L'islam des jeunes*. Paris: Flammarion.

Kiliç, S. 2008. "The British Veil Wars," *Social Politics* 15(4): 433–54.

Killian, C. 2003. "The Other Side of the Veil: North African Women in France Respond to the Headscarf Affair," *Gender and Society* 17(4) (August): 567–90.

Killian, C. 2006. *North African Women in France: Gender, Culture, and Identity*. Stanford, CA: Stanford University Press.

Köker, L. 1996. "Political Toleration or Politics of Recognition: The Headscarves Affair Revisited," *Political Theory* 24(2) (May): 315–20.

Koopmans, R., Statham, P., Giugni, M. and Passy, F. 2005. *Contested Citizenship: Immigration and Cultural Diversity in Europe*. Minneapolis: University of Minnesota Press.

Kumar, K. 2002. "The Nation-State, the European Union, and Transnational Identities," in N. AlSayyad and M. Castells (eds.), *Muslim Europe or Euro-Islam: Politics, Culture, and Citizenship in the Age of Globalization*. Lanham, MD: Rowman & Littlefield, 53–68.

Laborde, C. 2002. "On Republican Toleration," *Constellations* 9: 167–83.

Laborde, C. 2005. "Secular Philosophy and Muslim Headscarves in Schools," *Journal of Political Philosophy* 13(3): 305–29.
Laborde, C. 2008. *Critical Republicanism: The Hijab Controversy and Political Philosophy*. New York: Oxford University Press.
La Depeche. 2011. "Le voile intégral dans les lieux publics mis à l'amende dès aujourd'hui," April 11 <http://www.ladepeche.fr/article/2011/04/11/1056533-le-voile-integral-dans-les-lieux-publics-mis-a-l-amende-des-aujourd-hui.html>.
Lathion, S. 2008. "Muslims in Switzerland: Is Citizenship Really Incompatible with Muslim Identity?," *Journal of Muslim Minority Affairs* 28(1): 53–60.
Laurence, J. and Vaisse, J. 2006. *Integrating Islam: Political and Religious Challenges in Contemporary France*. Washington, DC: Brookings Institution Press.
Le Figaro. 2009. "367 femmes portent la burqa en France" [online] July 29 <http://www.lefigaro.fr/flash-actu/2009/07/29/01011-20090729FILWWW00467-367-femmes-portent-la-burqa-en-france.php>.
Le Monde. 2008. "Une Marocaine trop religieuse pour être française," July 12 <http://www.lemonde.fr/web/recherche_breve/1,13-0,37-1043780,0.html>.
Le Monde. 2010. "Le Parlement vote l'interdiction du voile intégral" [online] September 14 <http://www.lemonde.fr/politique/article/2010/09/14/le-parlement-vote-l-interdiction-du-voile-integral_1411203_823448.html>.
Lettinga, D. and Saharso, S. 2008. "Contentious Citizenship: Policies and Debates on the Veil in the Netherlands," *Social Politics* 15(4): 455–80.
Llorent Bedmar, V. and Cabano-Delgado Palma, V. 2010. "The Muslim Veil Controversy in French and Spanish Schools," *Islam and Christian–Muslim Relations* 21(1): 61–73.
The Local. 2010. "Reinfeldt: no burqa ban in Sweden" [online] January 28 <http://www.thelocal.se/24654/20100128/> [Accessed July 11, 2011].
The Local. 2011. "Swiss Canton Voters Could Ban the Burqa" [online] May 20 <http://www.thelocal.ch/national/20110520_217.html>.
London Progressive Journal. 2008. "Does the Burka Stand up in Court?" [online] March 28 <http://londonprogressivejournal.com/article/91/veiled-sentiments:-does-the-burka-stand-up-in-court> [Accessed July 14, 2011].
Lorcerie, F. 2005. *La politisation du voile: l'affaire en France, en Europe et dans le monde arabe*. Paris: L'Harmattan.
Lyon, D. and Spini, D. 2004. "Unveiling the Headscarf Debate," *Feminist Legal Studies* 12: 333–45.
McGinty, A. M. 2006. *Becoming Muslim: Western Women's Conversions to Islam*. New York: Palgrave Macmillan.
McGoldrick, D. 2006. *Human Rights and Religion: The Islamic Headscarf Debate in Europe*. Oxford: Hart Publishing.
Macmaster, N. and Lewis, T. 1998. "Orientalism: From Unveiling to Hyperveiling," *European Studies Journal* 28: 121–35.
Mahlmann, M. 2003. "Religious Tolerance, Pluralist Society and the Neutrality of the State: The Federal Constitutional Court's Decision in the Headscarf Case," *German Law Journal* 4(11): 1099–116 <http://www.germanlawjournal.com/pdfs/Vol04No11/PDF_Vol_04_No_11_1099-1116_Public_Mahlmann.pdf>.
Mahmood, S. 2005. *Politics of Piety: The Islamic Revival and the Feminist Subject*. Princeton: Princeton University Press.
Mahmood, S. 2008. "Feminism, Democracy, and Empire: Islam and the War of Terror', in J. W. Scott (ed.), *Women's Studies on the Edge*. Durham: Duke University Press, 81–114.

Mandel, R. 1989. "Turkish Headscarves and the 'Foreigner Problem': Constructing Difference through Emblems of Identity," *New German Critique* 46 (Winter): 27–46.

Martín-Muñoz, G. and López-Sala, A. 2005. 'Migration and the Religiosity of Muslim Women in Spain," in J. Cesari and S. McLoughlin (eds.), *European Muslims and the Secular State*. Aldershot: Ashgate, 129–42.

Menasce Horowitz, J. and Morin, R. 2006. "Europeans Debate the Scarf and the Veil," *PEW Global Attitudes Project* [online] November 20 <http://pewresearch.org/pubs/95/europeans-debate-the-scarf-and-the-veil> [Accessed July 4, 2011].

Mernissi, F. 1994. *Le Harem Politique*. Paris: Albin Michel.

Mohamed, N. B. n.d. *Les femmes musulmanes voilées d'origine marocaine sur le marché de l'emploi* [online] <http://www.ulb.ac.be/socio/germe/documentsenligne/femmesmusulmanes_nadia.pdf>.

Morris, N. and Morrison, S. 2011. "May Rules Out Burka Ban in Britain," *The Independent* [online] April 11 <http://www.independent.co.uk/news/uk/politics/may-rules-out-burka-ban-in-britain-2266055.html> [Accessed May 29, 2011].

Moruzzi, N. C. 1994. "A Problem with Headscarves: Contemporary Complexities of Political and Social Identity," *Political Theory* 22(4) (November): 653–72.

Mushaben, J. 2005. "More Than Just a Bad Hair Day: The Muslim Head-Scarf Debate as a Challenge to European Identities," in H. Holger (ed.), *Crossing Over: Comparing Recent Immigration in Europe and the United States*. Lanham, MD: Lexington Books, 182–222.

News 24. 2010. "Swiss Want to Ban Burqa" [online] May 23 <http://www.news24.com/World/News/Swiss-want-to-ban-burqa-20100523> [Accessed July 26, 2011].

News Agencies. 2010. "Burqa Ban in Sweden?" [online] January 28 <http://www.euro-islam.info/2010/01/28/burqa-ban-in-sweden/> [Accessed July 11, 2011].

News.com. 2010. "Swiss Region Wants Burqa Ban" [online] May 6 <http://www.news.com.au/breaking-news/swiss-region-wants-burqa-ban-story-e6frfkuo-1225862840937> [Accessed July 26, 2011].

Page F30. 2010. "No Burka or Nikab Ban for Norway" [online] May 28 <http://www.pagef30.com/2010/05/no-burka-and-nikab-ban-for-norway.html> [Accessed May 28, 2011].

Pedain, A. 2004. "Do Headscarfs Bite?," *The Cambridge Law Journal* 63(3) (November): 537–40.

Pfister, G. 2000. "Doing Sport in a Headscarf? German Sport and Turkish Females," *Journal of Sport History* [online] <http://www.aafla.org/SportsLibrary/JSH/JSH2000/JSH2703/JSH2703h.pdf>.

Piza, N. 2010. "Italy to Become Next European Country to Ban Burka after Government Report Recommends Forbidding It in Public." *Mail Online* [online] October 7 <http://www.dailymail.co.uk/news/article-1318498/Italy-European-country-ban-burka-government-recommendation.html> [Accessed May 30, 2011].

Pojmann, W. 2010. "Muslim Women's Organizing in France and Italy: Political Culture, Activism, and Performativity in the Public Sphere," *Feminist Formations* 22(3) (Fall): 229–51.

Poulat, E. 1987. *Liberté-laïcité: les guerres des deux France et le principe de la modernité*. Paris: Cujas-Le Cerf.

Poulter, S. 1997. "Muslim Headscarves in School: Contrasting Legal Approaches in England and France," *Oxford Journal of Legal Studies* 17(1) (Spring): 43–74.

Poulter, S. 2000. "Legislating Religious Freedom: Muslim Challenges to the Relationship between 'Church' and 'State' in Germany and France," *Daedalus* 129(4): 31–54.

Predelli, L. N. 2004. "Interpreting Gender in Islam: A Case Study of Immigrant Muslim Women in Oslo, Norway," *Gender and Society* 18(4) (August): 473–93.

Razack, S. 2008. *Casting Out: The Eviction of Muslims from Western Law and Politics*. Toronto: University of Toronto Press.
Read, J. G. 2007. "Introduction: The Politics of Veiling in Comparative Perspective," *Sociology of Religion* 68(3): 231–6.
Reuters. 2012. "Dutch Plan Ban on Muslim Face Veils Next Year," January 29. <http://tribune.com.pk/story/328853/dutch-plan-ban-on-muslim-face-veils-next-year/>.
Roald, A. S. 2006. "The Shaping of a Scandinavian 'Islam': Converts and Gender Equal Opportunity," in K. van Nieuwkerk (ed.), *Women Embracing Islam: Gender and Conversion in the West*. Austin: University of Texas Press.
Roman, J. 1991. "La laïcité comme religion civile," *Esprit* 175: 108–15.
Rottman, S. B. and Marx Ferree, M. 2008. "Citizenship and Intersectionality: German Feminist Debates about Headscarf and Antidiscrimination Laws," *Social Politics* 15(4): 481–513.
Saharso, S. 2007. "Headscarves: A Comparison of Public Thought and Public Policy in Germany and the Netherlands," *Critical Review of International Social and Political Philosophy* 10(4): 513–30. <http://www.essex.ac.uk/ECPR/events/generalconference/budapest/papers/4/8/saharso.pdf>.
Said, E. 1978. *Orientalism*. New York: Vintage Books.
Salih, R. 2001. "Moroccan Migrant Women: Transnationalism, Nation-States and Gender," *Journal of Ethnic and Migration Studies* 27(4): 655–71.
Sauer, B. 2009. "Headscarf Regimes in Europe: Diversity Policies at the Intersection of Gender, Culture and Religion," *Comparative European Politics* 7(1): 75–94.
Scott, J. W. 2005. "Symptomatic Politics: The Banning of Islamic Head Scarves in French Public Schools," *French Politics, Culture & Society* 23(3): 106–27.
Scott, J. W. 2007. *The Politics of the Veil*. Princeton: Princeton University Press.
Sebian, E. n.d. "Islam in Belgium" [online] <http://www.euro-islam.info/country-profiles/belgium/> [Accessed July 26, 2011].
Selby, J. A. 2011a. "Islam in France Reconfigured: Republican Islam in the 2010 Gerin Report," *Journal of Muslim Minority Affairs* 31(3) (September): 383–98.
Selby, J. A. 2011b. "French Secularism as a Guarantor of Women's Rights? Islam and Gender Politics in a Parisian *Banlieue*," *Culture and Religion* 12(4) (December): 441–62.
Selby, J. A. 2012. *Questioning French Secularism: Gender Politics and Islam in a Parisian Suburb*. New York: Palgrave Macmillan.
Severs, E. 2010. "The Headscarf Debate in Belgium: Responsiveness and the Substantive Representation of Women." Paper presented as a poster at the APSA Annual Meeting Conference in Washington, DC (September 2) [online] <http://www.ecprnet.eu/databases/conferences/papers/913.pdf>.
Sevgi, K. 2008. "The British Veil Wars," *Social Politics* 15(4): 433–54.
Shadid, W. and van Koningsveld, P. S. 2005. "Muslim Dress in Europe: Debates on the Headscarf," *Journal of Islamic Studies* 16(1): 35–61.
Shryock, A. 2010. "Introduction: Islam as an Object of Fear and Affection," in A. Shryock (ed.), *Islamophobia/Islamophilia: Beyond the Politics of Enemy and Friend*. Bloomington: Indiana University Press, 1–28.
Silverstein, P. 2004. "Headscarves and the French Tricolor," *Middle East Report Online* [online] January 30 <http://www.merip.org>.
Silvestri, S. 2008. *Europe's Muslim Women: Potential, Aspirations and Challenges*. Brussels, King Baudouin Foundation <http://www.kbs-frb.be/uploadedFiles/KBS-FRB/3)_Publications/PUB_1846_MuslimWomen_03.pdf>.

Simonsson, L. 2010. "Sweden Education Minister Moves against Burqa," *M&C News* [online] August 4 <http://www.monstersandcritics.com/news/europe/features/article_1575444.php/Swedish-education-minister-moves-against-burqa> [Accessed May 30, 2011].

Stasi Commission Report. 2003. Published in full in *Le Monde*, December 12, 18–24 <http://medias.lemonde.fr/medias/pdf_obj/rapport_stasi_111203.pdf>.

Stock-Morton, P. 1988. *Moral Education for a Secular Society: The Development of "Morale Laïque" in 19th Century France*. Albany: State University of New York Press.

Tarlo, E. 2007. "Hijab in London," *Journal of Material Culture* 12(2): 131–56.

Tersigni, S. 2005. "La pratique du hijab en France: Prescription, transmission horizontale et dissidence," in F. Lorcerie (ed.), *La politisation du voile en France, en Europe et dans le monde arabe*. Paris: L'Harmattan, 37–52.

Timmerman, C. 2000. "Muslim Women and Nationalism: The Power of the Image," *Current Sociology* 48 (October): 15–27.

Tremlett, G. 2010. "Burqa Bans Spread across Catalonia," *The Guardian* [online] July 2 <http://www.guardian.co.uk/world/2010/jul/02/lleida-burqa-ban-spain?INTCMP=SRCH> [Accessed July 13, 2011].

United Press International. 2008. "Muslim Woman Wins Discrimination Case," April 13 <http://www.upi.com/Top_News/2008/04/13/Muslim_woman_wins_discrimination_case/UPI-23851208105979/> [Accessed July 11, 2011].

Université catholique de Louvain. 2007. "Belgian Attitudes Toward the Veil," May 25.

US Department of State. 2006. "Belgium: International Religious Freedom Report 2006," Bureau of Democracy, Human Rights, and Labor, Department of State Website [online] <http://www.state.gov/g/drl/rls/irf/2006/71371.htm>.

Van Sickle, A. 2008. "Veiled Sentiments: Does the Burqa Stand Up in Court?" *London Progressive Journal* [online] March 28 <http://londonprogressivejournal.com/article/91/veiled-sentiments:-does-the-burka-stand-up-in-court> [Accessed July 14, 2011].

VEIL (Values, Equality and Difference in Liberal Democracies) (UK). 2008 [online] October 29 <http://www.univie.ac.at/veil/Home3/index.php?id=7,52,0,0,1,0> [Accessed July 20, 2011].

Venel, N. 1999. *Musulmanes françaises: des pratiquantes voilées à l'université*. Paris: L'Harmattan.

Vink, M. P. 2007. "Dutch 'Multiculturalism' Beyond the Pillarisation Myth," *Political Studies Review* 5: 337–50.

Vinthagen Simpson, P. 2008. "Muslim Woman Receives Damages for Headscarf Slight," *The Local* [online] April 12 <http://www.thelocal.se/11070/20080412> [Accessed July 28, 2011].

Walker, P. 2010. "Muslim Woman Fined for Wearing Burqa in Northern Italy," *The Guardian* [online] May 5 <http://www.guardian.co.uk/world/2010/may/05/woman-fined-burqa-italy?INTCMP=SRCH> [Accessed July 13, 2011].

Warner, C. M. and Wenner, M. W. 2006. "Religion and the Political Organization of Muslims in Europe," *Perspectives on Politics* 4(3): 457–79.

Watson, H. 1994. "Women and the Veil: Personal Responses to Global Process," in A. S. Ahmed and H. Donnan (eds.), *Islam, Globalization, and Postmodernity*. London: Routledge, 141–59.

Weber, B. 2004. "Cloth on Her Head, Constitution in Hand: Germany's Headscarf Debates and the Cultural Politics of Difference," *German Politics and Society* 22: 33–64.

Weil, P. 2009. "Why the French Laïcité is Liberal," *Cardozo Law Review* 30(6): 2699–714.

Werbner, P. 2007. "Veiled Interventions in Pure Space," *Theory, Culture and Society* 24(2): 161–86.

Westerfield, J. M. 2006. "Behind the Veil: An American Legal Perspective on the European Headscarf Debate," *American Journal of Comparative Law* 55(2): 637–78.

Williams, R. 2006. "A Society that Does Not Allow Crosses or Veils in Public is a Dangerous One," *The Times* [online] October 27 <http://www.timesonline.co.uk/tol/comment/columnists/guest_contributors/article614933.ece>.

Winter, B. 2006. "Secularism Aboard the Titanic: Feminists and the Debate over the Hijab in France," *Feminist Studies* 32(2): 279–98.

World Radio Switzerland. 2009. "Justice Minister Revises Anti-Burqa Statement" [online] November 10 <http://worldradio.ch/wrs/news/wrsnews/justice-minister-revises-anti-burqa-statement.shtml> [Accessed May 30, 2011].

ZARA. 2008. "Racism Report 2008: Case Report on Racist Incidents and Structures in Austria" [online] <http://www.zara.or.at/materialien/rassismus-report/Racism_Report_2008.pdf>.

# PART V
# ISLAM AND EUROPEAN POLITICS

# CHAPTER 17

# ISLAMOPHOBIA

## AYHAN KAYA

## ISLAMOPHOBIA: A HISTORY OF THE TERM

IN a report submitted to the European Commission by Jocelyne Cesari et al. (2006: 5), it is stated that although negative perceptions of Islam in Europe can be traced back to the Crusades in many ways, Islamophobia is rather 'a modern and secular anti-Islamic discourse and practice appearing in the public sphere with the integration of Muslim immigrant communities and intensifying after 9/11'.[1] Islamophobia is a much used but little understood term, which is believed to have become popular after the report of Runnymede Trust's Commission on British Muslims and Islamophobia (CBMI) entitled *Islamophobia: A Challenge for Us All* (Runnymede 1997). In this report it is asserted that the first usage of the term was by an American newspaper reporter in 1991. 'Islamophobia' was defined by the CBMI as 'an unfounded hostility towards Islam, and therefore fear or dislike of all or most Muslims', and further elaborated by the proposal of eight possible Islamophobic mindsets. The eight statements are: (1) Islam is seen as a monolithic bloc, static and unresponsive to change; (2) Islam is seen as separate and 'other'. It does not have values in common with other cultures, is not affected by them and does not influence them; (3) Islam is seen as inferior to the West. It is seen as barbaric, irrational, primitive and sexist; (4) Islam is seen as violent, aggressive, threatening, and supportive of terrorism, and engaged in a 'clash of civilizations'; (5) Islam is seen as a political ideology and is used for political or military advantage; (6) Criticisms made of the West by Islam are rejected out of hand; (7) Hostility towards Islam is used to justify discriminatory practices towards Muslims and exclusion of Muslims from mainstream society; and (8) Anti-Muslim hostility is seen as natural or normal.

---

[1] The website <http://www.euro-islam.info> offers a very detailed map of the news and analysis on Islam in Europe and North America. The site is sponsored by GSRL Paris/CNRS Paris and consists of over forty researchers.

The term Islamophobia has become popular since the Runnymede Trust report's publication in describing the phenomenon. There is currently no legally agreed definition of Islamophobia; and the social sciences have not developed a common definition, policy, or action to combat it either. Besides, there are a number of other possible terms to refer to negative feelings and attitudes towards Islam and Muslims, such as 'anti-Muslimism', 'anti-Muslim racism', 'intolerance against Muslims', 'anti-Muslim prejudice', 'anti-Muslim bigotry', 'hatred of Muslims', 'anti-Islamism', 'anti-Muslimism', 'Muslimophobia', 'demonisation of Islam', and 'demonisation of Muslims' (Richardson 2012). Probably the most commonly used term in today's world is Islamophobia. Richardson (2012) also reminds us of the fact that there is a similar range of contested terms in other languages as well, not only in English. For instance, in German there is a contest between *Islamophobie* (fear) and *Islamfeindlichkeit* (hostility). In French, the contest is in part between *islamophobie* and *racisme anti-arabe*, or *racisme anti-maghrébin*, the latter two phrases indicating that the phenomenon is mainly seen as a form of anti-immigrant racism without having theological and cultural connotations. The Scandinavian term *Muslimhat* literally means 'hatred of Muslims'. Such terminological differences may reflect a set of differences of understanding and focus. These different terms may be used to distinguish between various manifestations of the phenomena under discussion. For instance, as Sivanandan rightly states, the term *anti-Muslim racism* is used to refer to hate crimes and to harassment, rudeness, and verbal abuse in public spaces, whereas the term *Islamophobia* refers to discourse and mindsets in the media, including the broadsheets as well as the tabloids (Sivanandan 2010).

Since Fred Halliday put 'Islamophobia' in inverted commas in the title of his article '"Islamophobia" Reconsidered', written in 1999, the term Islamophobia has also been discussed by scholars. Some criticisms refer to the unintended consequences of the term, or its possible political and ideological exploitation. Halliday himself furnishes an example. Halliday (1999: 898) argues that the term 'reproduces the distortion...that there is one Islam' and that this serves to 'play into the hands' of individuals, or groups in Muslim communities who seek to promote a more conservative agenda and to arrogate to themselves the authority to speak for the tradition and culture, whether on the status of women, rights to free speech, or violence. Halliday (1999: 898) also posits an objection on the grounds that the term is a misnomer. According to him, once upon a time, 'the enemy' was the religion of Islam, which was attacked by the Crusades and the Reconquista. But today the target has changed. The attack now is not against Islam as a faith, but Muslims as a people. This is why he prefers the term 'anti-Muslimism'.[2]

Similarly, delineating the rationale employed by words such as 'anti-Muslim prejudice' and 'anti-Muslim racism', which demonstrate hostile attitudes towards Muslims, Maleiha Malik (2010) prefers the term 'anti-Muslim prejudice' to Islamophobia, rejecting the pathos and seeming irrationality of the use of the term 'phobia' to describe hostility towards Muslims in favour of a calculated prejudiced orientation. In this regard,

---

[2] See also Halliday (1996: chapter 6), where he introduces the term 'anti-Muslimism'.

paraphrasing Edward Said, Semati also eloquently relates Islamophobia to both racism and Orientalism:

> Islamophobia is a cultural-ideological outlook that seeks to explain ills of the (global) social order by attributing them to Islam. It is a way of thinking that conflates histories, politics, societies and cultures of the Middle East into a single unified and negative conception of Islam. It is an ideology in which the 'backwardness' of the other is established through an essentialized Islam. It is, as a form of racism, an essentialist view of peoples whose culture it deems 'different' in an eternal, fixed, and immutable fashion. It is a way of conceptualizing (international) politics that explains political acts and political violence not in terms of geopolitical calculations, motives, and actors, but in terms of religion. Islamophobia posits 'Islam' as a conception of the world that is incompatible with modernity, with civilization, and, more important, with Euro-Americanness. Islamophobia, on the one hand, creates difference (the 'other') and, on the other hand, erases difference (all of 'them' are the 'same'). (Semati, 2010: 266–77)[3]

Other scholars define Islamophobia as cultural racism (Meer and Modood 2009; Schiffer and Wagner 2011), the roots of which could be traced back to the writings of Arthur de Gobineau (1816–82), who was a French nobleman. The main concern of de Gobineau (1999) was to offer an answer to the ever-fascinating question of why civilizations rise and fall. De Gobineau argued that history is composed of continuous struggle among the 'white', 'yellow', and 'negroid' races. He underlined the superiority of the 'white race'. The lesson of history is, according to de Gobineau (1999: 56) as argued in 1853, that 'all civilisations derive from the white race, that none can exist without its help, and that a society is great and brilliant only so far as it preserves the blood of the noble group that created it, provided that this group itself belongs to the most illustrious branch of our species'. He always complained about the mixture of the races (miscegenation), which, he believed, led to the crisis of civilization. The racist thoughts in de Gobineau's works spring from his fear of the 'Oriental' attacks on the 'Occidental' lands, which would cause miscegenation and the fall of civilizations. His line of thinking resembles closely the contemporary debate regarding the alleged invasion of the West by Islam expressed by Theo van Gogh, Pim Fortuyn, Oriana Fallaci, and George Bush, a point to which I shall return shortly.

As Andrew O'Hagan (2008) has observed very well, Islamophobia is one of the big questions of our day, presenting a problem that is most often answered 'with ignorance or with common hysteria, and almost never with fresh thinking'. The damage this brings to bear on the European public is 'making a monster where it shouldn't exist, a monster made from the mania of our own fear' (Evans 2010: 3). The 'monster made from the

---

[3] Similarly, one could also argue that the contemporary European identity is partly built upon what I call *Islamophobism*, or anti-Muslim racism, in a fashion similar to the late nineteenth and early twentieth centuries when European identity was partly built upon anti-Semitism.

mania of our own fear' presumably derives from a *glocal* (global + local) context shaped by a growing feeling of insecurity making individuals more and more heteronomous in a way that essentializes communal, ethnic, cultural, linguistic, and religious boundaries. It is this kind of feeling of insecurity that makes individuals lean on what is cultural, religious, and communal in an age of prudentialism. Nostalgia, the past, ethnicity, culture, and religion turn out to be a kind of lighthouse beckoning even the members of the majority societies back to the shore—the one point on the landscape that gives hope of direction in a time characterized by prudentialism, the post-social state, insecurity, fear, loneliness, distrustfulness, and aimlessness (Stewart 2000; Miller and Rose 2008). This is actually the way the neo-liberal state operates: through securitizing and stigmatizing those who are ethno-culturally and religiously different from the majority societies, a point which will be discussed soon.

Neither should one underestimate the impact of the major international organizations on the changing definition of Islamophobia in the aftermath of 9/11. The United Nations,[4] the Council of Europe,[5] the Organization for Security and Co-operation in Europe,[6] and the European Union (EUMC 2006) have lately discussed the term within the broad concepts of racism and racial discrimination. Therefore, they base their approaches to identifying the phenomenon and its manifestations on internationally accepted standards on racism. In 2005 a Council of Europe publication 'Islamophobia and its Consequences on Young People' referred to Islamophobia as 'the fear of or prejudiced viewpoint towards Islam, Muslims and matters pertaining to them. Whether it takes the shape of daily forms of racism and discrimination or more violent forms, Islamophobia is a violation of human rights and a threat to social cohesion' (Council of Europe 2004).

---

[4] For the definition of racial discrimination by the UN, see the International Convention on the Elimination of All Forms of Racial Discrimination adopted and opened for signature and ratification by General Assembly resolution 2106 (XX) of 21 December 1965, entry into force 4 January 1969.

[5] See European Commission against Racism and Intolerance (ECRI)'s general policy recommendation No. 7 on national legislation to combat racism and racial discrimination, adopted on 13 December 2002. Since then, noting that intolerance, discrimination, and radicalization have recently seized control of the European public discourse, the Council of Europe decided to create a Group of Eminent Persons in order to prepare a report within the context of the Pan-European project *Living together in 21st century Europe* to be submitted to the Committee of Ministers prior to the Istanbul Ministerial of 11 May 2011. The group consists of nine high-ranking individuals with a specific expertise and a particular interest in the subject. Former German Foreign Minister Joschka Fischer is the Chairman, and British journalist Edward Mortimer became the *rapporteur* responsible for preparing the draft report. The other members of the Group are Timothy Garton Ash, Emma Bonino, Martin Hirsch, Danuta Hubner, Ayşe Kadioglu, Sonja Licht, Vladimir Lukin, and Javier Solana Madariaga. The Group of Eminent Persons is expected to help the Council of Europe to deal with new challenges to the security and stability of European citizens. For further information see the report of the Group of Eminent Persons, <https://wcd.coe.int/wcd/ViewDoc.jsp?Ref=GroupEminentPersons&Language=lanEnglish&Ver=original&Site=CM&BackColorInternet=C3C3C3&BackColorIntranet=EDB021&BackColorLogged=F5D383> (accessed 23 June 2013).

[6] See OSCE Meeting on the Relationship Between Racist, Xenophobic and Anti-Semitic Propaganda on the Internet and Hate Crimes, Conference in Paris, 16 and 17 June 2004, available at <http://www.osce.org/cio/37720> (accessed 22 March 2013).

Despite this lack of consensus, several scholars use the term, such as Richardson (2012), Esposito (2011), Schiffer and Wagner (2011), Allen (2010), Geisser (2010), Laitin (2010), Semati (2010), Meer and Modood (2009), Werbner (2005), Vertovec (2002), and Modood (2002). Against this background, the term Islamophobia is used in this chapter to define the overarching narrative which informs the manifestations of both anti-Muslim prejudice and anti-Muslim racism. In other words, I will use the term to refer to a set of particular discourses and mindsets formed by the politicians, security forces, bureaucracy, media, and some civil society organizations and academics. Apart from this scholarly debate, the term has also gained a political signification with European politics, which has negatively conditioned public opinion by means of securitizing migration and stigmatizing multiculturalism, a point which will be delineated further in the following pages.

## Political Relevance of the Term: Discriminatory Public Opinion Vis-à-Vis Islamic Practices

Islamophobic discourse has become mainstream in the West since 9/11. It seems that social groups belonging to the majority nation in a given territory are more inclined to express the distress resulting from insecurity and social-economic deprivation through the language of Islamophobia, even in those cases which are not related to the actual threat of Islam or Muslims. Islamophobic discourse has certainly resonated a great deal in the last decade. It has made the users of this discourse heard by both the local and the international community, although their distress did not really result from anything related to Muslims in general. In other words, Muslims have become the most popular scapegoats in many parts of the world, to be blamed for any troubled situation. For more than a decade, Muslim-origin migrants and their descendants are primarily seen by the European societies as a financial burden, and virtually never as an opportunity for the country. They tend to be associated with illegality, crime, violence, drugs, radicalism, fundamentalism, and conflict, and in many other respects are represented in negative ways.

A Pew survey held in 2006 indicated that opinions of Muslims in almost all of the Western European countries are quite negative. While one in four in the USA and the UK displayed Islamophobic sentiments, more than half of Spaniards and half of Germans said that they did not like Muslims, and the figures for Poland and France were 46% and 38% for those holding unfavourable opinions of Muslims. The survey revealed that prejudice was marked mainly among older generations and appeared to be class-based. People over 50 and of low education were more likely to be prejudiced.[7] Similarly, the Gallup Organization Survey of

---

[7] For the dataset of the surveys on Islamophobia see <http://pewresearch.org/>; <http://people-press.org>; and for an elaborate analysis of these findings see <http://www.guardian.co.uk/world/2008/sep/18/islam.religion>. One can also visit the website of *Islamophobia Watch* to follow the record of racist

Population Perceptions and Attitudes held for the World Economic Forum in 2007 indicated that three in four US residents believe that the Muslim world is not committed to improving relations with the West. The same survey found that half of respondents in Italy (58%), Denmark (52%), and Spain (50%) agree that the Muslim world is not committed to improving relations. Israelis, on the other hand, represent a remarkable exception with almost two-thirds (64%) believing that the Muslim world is committed to improving relations. The picture on the other side of the coin is not very different either. Among the majority-Muslim nations surveyed, it was deciphered that majorities in every Middle Eastern country believe that the West is not committed to better relations with the Muslim world, while respondents in majority-Muslim Asian countries are about evenly split (WEF 2008: 21).

Another poll made by the Pew research institute in the United States in August 2010 reveals that the favourable opinions of Islam among the American public have declined since 2005; 35% of the public say that Islam encourages violence more than other religions.[8] Similarly, the British Social Attitudes Survey held in 2009 shows that 45% of the British do not like Muslims much, and do not really believe in free speech at all. It has been revealed that dislike of Muslims is related to the belief that Britain is too diverse, and that religious diversity is harming Britain, as was also recently expressed by the British Prime Minister David Cameron in February 2011.[9] Islamophobia has also become visible in those countries which are known to be non-religious and very secular, such as Sweden. Sweden received harsh criticisms from the Swedish UN association in 2009 for failing to abide by a number of UN conventions. It was stated in the report that hate crimes increased in Sweden as a result of Islamophobia, anti-Semitism, and homophobic sentiments.[10]

---

incidences in each country: <http://www.islamophobia-watch.com/islamophobia-watch/category/anti-muslim-violence> (accessed 22 March 2013). The European Commission has also recently funded several FP7 projects focusing on the legal, political, and social discrimination of religious minorities, particularly Muslims, in the European Union. The projects RELIGARE and ACCEPT PLURALISM are two examples. RELIGARE (Religious Diversity and Secular Models in Europe, 2010–13) is about religions, belonging, beliefs, and secularism. It examines the current realities, including the legal rules protecting or limiting (constraining) the experiences of religious or other belief-based communities. Where the practices of communities or individuals do not conform to state law requirements, or where communities turn to their own legal regimes or tribunals, the reasons behind these developments need to be understood. See <http://www.religareproject.eu/>. ACCEPT PLURALISM (Tolerance, Pluralism and Social Cohesion: Responding to the Challenges of the 21st Century in Europe, 2010–13) investigates whether European societies have become more or less tolerant during the past twenty years. In particular, the project aims to clarify: (a) how tolerance is defined conceptually, (b) how it is codified in norms, institutional arrangements, public policies, and social practices, (c) how tolerance can be measured (whose tolerance, who is tolerated, and whether degrees of tolerance vary with reference to different minority groups). This was a project I was also involved in. See <http://accept-pluralism.eu/>.

[8] For more detail see <http://people-press.org/files/legacy-pdf/647.pdf>.

[9] For the British Social Attitudes Survey see <http://www.natcen.ac.uk/study/british-social-attitudes-26th-report/our-findings#hotlink5> (accessed 20 April 2013). For the speech of David Cameron dated February 2011 see <http://www.bbc.co.uk/news/uk-politics-12415597> (accessed 16 August 2013).

[10] See 'Sweden slammed for UN rights failures' (9 November 2009), available at <http://www.thelocal.se/23150/20091109/> (accessed 23April 2013).

The growing distance between the lifeworlds of the majority societies and their allochthonous Muslim-origin minorities has also become evident. Detlef Pollack, a sociologist from Münster, conducted an extensive survey in Germany, France, Denmark, Portugal, and the Netherlands in late 2010. The study reveals that the German society, in comparison to the French, Dutch, and Danish, has recently generated a more intolerant perspective towards Islam. His findings also disprove the statement of the German President Christian Wulff on 19 October 2010, saying that 'Islam is part of Germany'.[11] The findings actually reaffirm that Germans *perceive* Islam as not belonging in Germany. The study also reveals that fewer than 5% of Germans, compared with more than 20% of Danes, French, and Dutch, consider Islam to be a tolerant religion, according to the study. These findings are also confirmed by another survey, which the German Marshall Fund conducted in 2010. The respondents in several different countries were asked about their perception of the level of integration of Muslim immigrants and their descendants into their societies. Canadians were split evenly, with 45% believing Muslim immigrants were integrating well and 44% thinking they were integrating poorly. Americans were the most optimistic about Muslim integration, 45% of whom thought these immigrants were integrating well, while 40% said that they were not. A further 14% claimed that they did not know, probably because of comparatively low numbers of Muslim immigrants residing in the United States, whereas in Europe, Spanish and German respondents were remarkably pessimistic about the integration level of Muslim origin immigrants and their descendants, where large majorities said that Muslims were integrating poorly (70% and 67%, respectively). They were followed by the Dutch (56%), the British (53%), the French (51%), and a plurality of Italians (49%) who also thought that Muslim immigrants were integrating poorly (GMF 2010).

A survey conducted by the Friedrich Ebert Foundation in various EU countries in 2011 revealed that in most of the countries a majority believe that Islam is a religion of intolerance, with agreement just below 50% only in Great Britain and the Netherlands (Table 17.1). In almost all the countries, more than half of the respondents said that Muslims make too many demands; Portugal was the only exception, with about one-third. The statement that there are too many Muslims in the country is affirmed by just over one-quarter in Portugal and by about one-third in France. In Germany, Great Britain, Italy, and the Netherlands more than 40% of respondents complain that there are too many Muslims in their country, in Hungary about 60%. The figures for those who say that Muslim culture is compatible with their own, range from 17% in Poland and 19% in Germany to about half the population in Portugal and France. A majority of more than 70% of European respondents find that Muslim attitudes towards women are incompatible with their own values. One-third of the surveyed countries think that Muslims treat Islamist terrorists as heroes, although somewhat fewer believe that terrorism finds moral support in the Muslim community (ranging from under 20% in Germany and the Netherlands to nearly 30% in Hungary). It is obvious that Europeans

---

[11] For the President's speech see <http://www.bbc.co.uk/news/world-europe-11578657> (accessed 26 April 2013).

Table 17.1 Anti-Muslim statements (agreement in %)

| Item | Germany | UK | France | Netherlands | Italy | Portugal | Poland | Hungary |
|---|---|---|---|---|---|---|---|---|
| There are too many Muslims in [country]. | 46.1 | 44.7 | 36.2 | 41.5 | 49.7 | 27.1 | 47.1 | 60.7 |
| Muslims are too demanding. | 54.1 | 50.0 | 52.8 | 51.8 | 64.7 | 34.4 | 62.3 | 60.0 |
| Islam is a religion of intolerance. [France: Islam is a religion of tolerance.] | 52.5 | 47.2 | 52.3 | 46.7 | 60.4 | 62.2 | 61.5 | 53.4 |
| The Muslim culture fits well into [country/Europe]. | 16.6 | 39.0 | 49.8 | 38.7 | 27.4 | 50.1 | 19.0 | 30.2 |
| Muslims' attitudes towards women contradict our values. | 76.1 | 81.5 | 78.8 | 78.2 | 82.2 | 72.1 | 72.1 | 76.8 |
| Many Muslims perceive terrorists as heroes. [France: question not asked.] | 27.9 | 37.6 | – | 29.2 | 28.5 | 30.3 | 30.2 | 39.3 |
| The majority of Muslims find terrorism justifiable. [France: not justifiable.] | 17.1 | 26.3 | 23.3 | 19.9 | 21.5 | 22.4 | 26.0 | 29.6 |

Source: FES 2011.

are largely united in their rejection of Muslims and Islam. The significantly most widespread anti-Muslim attitudes are found in Germany, Hungary, Italy, and Poland, closely followed by France,[12] Great Britain, and the Netherlands. The extent of anti-Muslim attitudes is lowest in Portugal (FES 2011: 60–3).

On the other side of the picture, Muslim-origin migrants and their descendants are highly concerned about the ways in which they are being treated by the majority societies in the West. For instance, a survey conducted by the European Monitoring Centre

---

[12] Vincent Geisser (2010) argues that French Islamophobia often intermingles with 'hijabophobia' (rejection of the Islamic veil). He claims that there is a French republican form of Islamophobia, which is partly different from other forms of Islamophobia: according to the French republican form, 'a perfect Muslim is one who has given up a part of his faith, beliefs and "outdated" religious practices. A beautiful mosque is a quiet one without minaret, practically invisible, in harmony with the republican context. An emancipated Muslim woman is one who has escaped from her tribe, being freed of an "Islamic male's" supervision' (Geisser 2010: 45).

on Racism and Xenophobia (EUMC 2006) reveals that Islamophobia, discrimination, and socio-economic marginalization have a primary role in generating disaffection and alienation among Muslim-origin migrants and their descendants residing in the European Union countries. Muslims feel that acceptance by society is increasingly premised on 'assimilation' and the assumption that they should lose their Muslim identity. This sense of exclusion is of particular relevance in the face of the challenges posed by terrorism, particularly in the aftermath of 9/11, which has put them under a general suspicion of terrorism (Cesari 2009).

The increase of negative attitudes towards Muslims in Europe is confirmed by opinion polls carried out by different researchers as detailed above. In some European countries, the percentage of those interviewed who have either a 'somewhat unfavourable' or a 'very unfavourable' opinion of Muslims has substantially increased between 2005 and 2010 or, in specific cases, has remained at a high level, sometimes close to 50%. Islam is even perceived as a major threat to Europe by many Europeans because they feel that the minority is growing and that Islam is incompatible with 'modern European life'. All the public surveys in Europe and the USA confirm the prevalence of negative opinions about Islam. It is likely that the negative perception of Islam in the European countries mainly springs from the Muslim-origin migrants and their descendants residing in the respective countries, while in the USA this negative perception is more likely to be coming from the foreign policy challenges posed by Islam in general.

One could describe a few recent events to demonstrate the indirect or direct ascendancy of the Islamophobic perception of Western societies: the assassination of Pim Fortuyn in the Netherlands on 6 May 2002, the Danish Cartoon crisis in 2006, the Swiss minaret debate in 2009, and the burning of the Qur'an by an American pastor in Florida in 2011. Pim Fortuyn was a former university professor of sociology, a political columnist, and a gay activist in the Netherlands. He was well known for his extravagant and luxurious lifestyle. He was unable to find a place for himself within the established political parties, and he founded his own party, List Pim Fortuyn (LPF) in 2001. He was in favour of lower taxes, less government, abortion rights, and euthanasia. His views on immigration and Islam made him even more popular. He called Islam a 'backward culture', and he openly stated that 'there were too many immigrants in the Netherlands'. Immediately before the elections he was assassinated by an animal-rights activist. This was the first political assassination in the Netherlands in 400 years. Pim Fortuyn's Islamophobia apparently paid off for the LPF in the general elections held on 15 May 2002, as they received 17% of the vote and twenty-six seats in parliament (Andeweg and Irwin 2005: 16–17).

When *Jyllands-Posten* published twelve cartoons depicting the Prophet Muhammad in September 2006, they could not have predicted the far-reaching and devastating consequences it would have for a small country of 5.4 million people. What started as a trivial attempt to provoke debate in defence of free speech would go on to cause an unforeseen inter-cultural clash on a global scale. Some consider it Denmark's biggest international crisis since 1945. Damaging not only the Danish economy (a loss of $1 billion in exports), the 'Cartoon crisis' destroyed Denmark's reputation as an open and tolerant society. Many Muslims forbid any visual depictions of the Prophet Muhammad altogether, though others allow it as long as the images are respectful (Laegaard 2007; Kaya 2009). Harmless by most secular standards, the cartoons in this case satirized the Prophet Mohammad—this was their intended purpose in general. While some found the drawings mildly offensive, others experienced sheer outrage and saw the cartoons as an attempt to humiliate them. The reactions ranged from peaceful demonstrations to violent riots, embassy protests, and flag burnings all around the word, and even resulted in a significant number of deaths worldwide. In a country where Muslim immigrants remain fairly geographically segregated (Mouritsen 2006: 74), the media's influence worked as a stronger force to affect people's perceptions about Muslims, since the contact between the groups remains limited. *Jyllands-Posten* facilitated a common stereotype that perceives all Muslims as terrorists.

Similarly, in Switzerland, a country where the contact between the majority society and Muslim-origin immigrants remains very limited in everyday life, the negative perception about Muslims was explicitly articulated by the majority society through the debate on minarets. The requests by Muslim-origin immigrants to erect mosques and minarets aroused significant public opposition in various European cities (Baumann 2009; Nielsen et al. 2009; Geisser 2010; Allievi 2010). The Swiss majority vote in the 2009 referendum to ban the building of minarets is not a single and exceptional result. Rather, it is a dramatized culmination of Swiss politics shifting from long-practised equilibrium to populist polarization and aggressive exclusion of minorities. But what was really interesting in the Minaret Referendum was that those Swiss citizens who did not have any interaction with the Muslims in their everyday life were more inclined to oppose the erection of minarets (Pfaff-Czarnecka 2009). On the other hand, those interacting with the Muslims in everyday life either did not go to the polls, or expressed their indifference to the issue. The reaction of the majority of the Swiss citizens to the minaret issue was probably the reflection of their unrest originating from the global financial crisis, increasing immigration of highly skilled Germans, and domestic political problems. Public expression of ongoing structural problems by means of a kind of hate-speech against Muslims has become a popular discourse in Switzerland as well as in other European countries.

Another event demonstrating the growing negative perceptions of Islam and the Muslims in the West is the burning of the Qur'an by a pastor in Gainesville, Florida on 20 March 2011. A controversial evangelical preacher oversaw the burning of a copy of the Qur'an in a small church after finding the Muslim holy book 'guilty' of crimes committed against humanity, especially since 9/11.The burning was carried out by pastor Wayne Sapp under the supervision of pastor Terry Jones, who in September 2010 drew sweeping condemnation over his plan to ignite a pile of Qur'ans on the anniversary of the 9/11 attacks. The event was presented as a trial of the book in which the Qur'an was found 'guilty' and 'executed'. Although the event was open to the public, fewer than thirty people attended.[13] However, it caused several different uproars in different parts

---

[13] See the website of *International Herald Tribune*, 21 March 2011, <http://tribune.com.pk/story/135836/quran-burnt-in-florida-church> (accessed 13 September 2013).

of the world, especially among Muslims, in a way that has further exacerbated the divide between the two worlds.

Despite these very visible and mediatized crises, practices of discrimination against Islam or Muslims *per se* are more difficult to measure. Firstly, this is because most European countries do not count population by religion. Secondly, these acts of discrimination are most of the time underreported, or misreported; that is to say that discriminatory practices against Muslims may have other causes like discrimination against immigrants, or discrimination against a segregated population. In any case, when religious practices or dress codes are at stake, it is indeed possible to define them as Islamophobic.

The highest levels of discrimination were found in employment and in services provided by the private sector. For instance, the European Union Minorities and Discrimination Survey (EU-MIDIS) held in 2009 very clearly depicts that Muslim-origin individuals residing in the European space complain primarily about discrimination in the labour market. For instance, the Pew Global Attitudes Survey of 2006 found that unemployment registered as a worry (very or somewhat) for 78% of Muslims in Great Britain, 84% in France, 81% in Germany, and 83% in Spain. Other surveys discussed above also show increasing numbers of attacks and instances of discrimination against Muslims, as well as rallies and public gatherings with anti-Muslim messages. But how can we explain the fact that Islamophobic attitudes are more visible in places where there are almost no Muslims, as seen in the Swiss minaret debate in the late 2000s?[14] The answer to be given in what follows to this question will show that Islamophobia operates as a form of governmentality that is constructed by conservative politicians, intellectuals, media experts, and public figures.

## ISLAMOPHOBIA AS FORM OF GOVERNMENTALITY

Islamophobia could be interpreted as a distinctive feature of what Michel Foucault calls modern governmentality, because it operates as a discourse, travelling between state, civil society, and citizens in a way that produces, organizes, and governs subjects. Today, political power is exercised through a set of multiple agencies and techniques, some of which are only loosely associated with the executives and bureaucracies of the state (Miller and Rose 2008: 26). The state is not the source, or agent, of all governing power, nor does it monopolize political power; rather, the powers and rationalities governing individual subjects and the population as a whole operate through a range of formally non-political knowledge and institutions such as Islamophobia, or anti-Muslim

---

[14] An FES Report (2011: 161) also revealed that anti-Muslim attitudes exist without Muslims. For instance, in the Eastern European countries, where the number of Muslims is negligible, prejudice against Muslims is quite prevalent due to the power of prejudice. Prejudice exists in the absence of contact with the group against which it is directed. See Table 17.1.

prejudices. The ensemble of legal and non-legal, pedagogical, cultural, religious, nationalist, and social discourses of Islamophobia together produce what Foucault understands as the signature of modern governmentality.

Contemporary states are more inclined to use multiple forms of governmentality to control and rule the masses. These multiple forms range from the processes of securitization of migration (Doty 2000; Huysmans 2006; Walters 2006; Kaya 2009) to the growing political discourse of tolerance (Brown, 2006), or from multiculturalism (Povinelli 2002) to Islamophobia. The ways in which these multiple forms of governmentality are performed by the states reveals a very important aspect of modern governmentality. It is a form of discourse: the government defines a discursive field such as prevention of migration or 'combating Islamic terrorism' in which the exercise of power is rationalized. This occurs by the reformulation of citizenship and naturalization regimes, the introduction of citizenship tests and integration tests, the overemphasis on secularism and laicism as opposed to religious forms of life, the specification of objects and borders, and the provision of fears, arguments, and justifications. In this manner, government defines, frames, and sometimes even fabricates a problem to be addressed, and then offers certain strategies for handling it. As will be elaborated shortly, the securitization and stigmatization of migration and Islam by contemporary Western states also operates as a form of governmentality along the same lines.

Islamophobia as a form of governmentality is being manufactured in parallel with the growing stream of ethnicization, racialization, and culturalization of what is social and political in the West since the early 1990s (Brown 2006). This stream is advocated by several politicians, public servants, bureaucracy, judiciary, police, and the media in order to hold socio-economically and politically deprived migrants and their descendants responsible for their isolation, exclusion, poverty, unemployment, unschooling, and any kind of failure in everyday life (Balibar 2004: 37–8). The European context is different from the American context where Islam was predominantly portrayed by the Bush regime as a challenge coming from outside the 'nation under siege'. European politics has rather used Islam as an 'enemy within' to be the pretext for a certain type of politics discriminating against those whose values are different from the Europeans'. The introduction of citizenship tests and integration tests in several European countries has become a popular debate as both kinds of tests are explicitly designed on the basis of cultural criteria. The rationale of these tests is to restrict the immigration of unqualified candidates. Citizenship reforms in most of the European countries have become more restrictive in the last decade due to fears about terrorism, violence, and the alleged rejection of Western values by Muslim-origin immigrants.

The introduction of the 'attitude test' (*Gesinnungstest*) by the state of Baden-Württemberg in 2006 was the first step towards a more restrictive regime of citizenship towards Muslim-origin migrants and their descendants in Germany, who are asked for their views on issues like domestic violence, arranged marriages, religious freedom, and terrorism.[15] The citizenship test became a national exercise in Germany in August 2007

---

[15] See <http://www.integration-in-deutschland.de/> (accessed 10 August 2013).

as the amended Nationality Act came into effect. It was stated by the Federal Ministry of the Interior that knowledge of German civic values will now be required for naturalization. The definition of civic values includes having basic knowledge of the legal and social order and the way of life in Germany as well as competency in the national language (Federal Ministry of the Interior 2007). The 2007 amendments mark a backward step from the 2000 Citizenship Law in the sense that this new civic-based citizenship has now turned the pre-2000 blood-based restriction on citizenship into a restriction based on 'values'. The so-called civic integration seems to be discriminatory to Muslims, who are negatively targeted as an ethnic group in Europe under the guise of liberalism (Joppke 2007). Such tests have also recently been introduced in Austria, Denmark, Greece, the Netherlands, and the United Kingdom. What is polemical and controversial about the tests is not only limited to its content: there is also a debate about who is required to take the test. For instance, the test is only required for 'non-Western' peoples in the Dutch case.[16] While the test is required for all 'non-Westerners', analysis reveals that the test is oriented particularly towards applicants of Muslim origin, who are often perceived and narrated by many politicians and public figures as a threat to the political, social, and cultural security of the prescribed nation (Bauböck and Joppke 2010).

## Politics of Fear: Securitization of Islam

Muslims are increasingly represented by the advocates of Islamophobia as members of a 'precarious transnational society', in which people only want to 'stone women', 'cut throats', 'be suicide bombers', 'beat their wives', and 'commit honour crimes'. These prejudiced perceptions about Islam have been reinforced by the impact of the previously stated events, ranging from the Iranian Revolution to the official ban on the *burqa* in France in 2011. Recently, quite a number of people in the West have felt the urge to defend Western civilization against this 'enemy within' that is culturally and religiously dissimilar to the 'civilized' Western subject. Samuel Huntington interpreted the Islamic resurgence as an attempt to counter the threat of Western cultural advance. He noted

---

[16] The Dutch Ministry of Justice states that the following groups of people are exempted from taking the Basic Civic Integration Examination (Dutch Language test and Knowledge of Dutch Society test) (Section 17(1) of the Aliens Act 2000 (Vreemdelingenwet 2000): (a) persons of Australian, Belgian, Canadian, Cypriot, German, Danish, Estonian, Finnish, French, Greek, British, Hungarian, Irish, Icelandic, Italian, Japanese, Latvian, Liechtenstein, Lithuanian, Luxemburg, Maltese, Monegasque, New Zealand, Norwegian, Austrian, Polish, Portuguese, Slovakian, Slovenian, Spanish, Czech, Vatican, American, Swedish, or Swiss nationality; (b) persons of Surinamese nationality who have completed a minimum of primary education in the Dutch language in Suriname or the Netherlands, and can show this by means of written proof (certificate, testimonial) issued and authenticated by the Surinamese Ministry of Education and Public Development; (c) persons who are coming to the Netherlands for a temporary period, such as study, au pair work, exchange or medical treatment; (d) persons with a work permit, self-employed persons, and knowledge migrants; and (e) family members of a person in possession of an asylum residence permit. See <http://english.justitie.nl/themes/immigration-and-integration/integration/the-act.aspx> (accessed 14 August 2013).

that the resurgence is a broad global movement that represents an effort to find solutions not in Western ideologies, but in Islam (Huntington 1996: 110).[17] Silvio Berlusconi, then the Italian Prime Minister, is one of those to have felt this urge:

> We are proud bearers of the supremacy of western civilisation, which has brought us democratic institutions, respect for the human, civil, religious and political rights of our citizens, openness to diversity and tolerance of everything... Europe must revive on the basis of common Christian roots. (*The Guardian*, London, 27 September 2001: 15)

Then American President George Bush's speech regarding the 'Axis of Evil' (29 January 2002) was also perceived by the American public in particular as an attempt to demonize 'Islamic fundamentalism' and the 'enemies of freedom' (Asad 2003: 7). Although Bush, as well as some European leaders like Tony Blair and Jacques Chirac, repeatedly stated that the war did not represent a fight against Islam, many people across the world were highly engaged in deepening the Islam-bashing displayed very explicitly in the following speech of George Bush:

> Our military has put the terror training camps of Afghanistan out of business, yet camps still exist in at least a dozen countries. A terrorist underworld—including groups like Hamas, Hezbollah, Islamic Jihad, and Jaish-i-Mohammed—operates in remote jungles and deserts, and hides in the centers of large cities... First, we will shut down terrorist camps, disrupt terrorist plans, and bring terrorists to justice... While the most visible military action is in Afghanistan, America is acting elsewhere... Our second goal is to prevent regimes that sponsor terror from threatening America or our friends and allies with weapons of mass destruction. Some of these regimes have been pretty quiet since September the 11th... (George Bush, 29 January 2002)[18]

Similarly, Italian journalist and novelist Oriana Fallaci is another figure who generated a very contested discourse in the aftermath of 11 September vis-à-vis Muslims:

> I say: Wake up, people, wake up!... You don't understand, or don't want to understand, that what is under way here is a reverse crusade. Do you want to understand or do you not want to understand that what is under way here is a religious war? A war that they call *Jihad*. A Holy War. A war that doesn't want to conquest of our territories, perhaps, but certainly wants to conquer our souls... They will feel authorized to kill you and your children because you drink wine or beer, because you don't wear a long beard or a chador, because you go to the theatre and cinemas, because you listen to music and sing songs... (Cited in Marranci 2004: 108)

---

[17] For a detailed account of the ways in which the 'clash of civilizations' paradigm was revitalized in the aftermath of 11 September, see Sussex (2004).

[18] 'President Delivers State of the Union Address', Press Release of the Office of the Press Secretary (29 January 2002), available at <http://www.whitehouse.gov/news/releases/2002/01/20020129-11.html> (accessed 25 February 2013).

This right-wing stream of reactions was also echoed in other parts of the Western world. Dutch media presenter and politician Pim Fortuyn (2001) published a book entitled *Against the Islamization of Our Culture*, in which he claimed Islam was a threat to Western civilization in a way that contributes to the othering of migrant-origin individuals residing in the West. Islam-bashing has become a popular sport practised by ministers, politicians, media specialists, and even prime ministers in the European Union as well as in the other parts of the world. Today, hostile language, offensive language, racist statements, and anti-immigrant policy propositions or real measures take place every day in the news. Conversely, aggressive language and threats directed against politicians who are perceived to be at fault, for whatever reason, have spread as well. The language of hatred replaces the language of dialogue.

After the strikes against the United States on 11 September, the 'Muslim' became reified as the enemy of the state, as a regressive, violent, bloodthirsty, and menacing fanatic: the typical terrorist. Corey Robin (2004) explicated very well the ways in which the Muslims and the Middle Easterners, especially Iraqis, were stigmatized by the Bush administration as 'typical terrorists' with reference to the anthrax scare in the wake of 9/11. Between October and November 2001, when the story broke, five people were killed by anthrax, and eighteen others were infected with it. Government officials immediately hunted for signs that the attack originated in the Middle East, particularly Iraq. This incident provided the Bush administration with a good excuse to go after Iraq. However, no one could find any evidence linking the anthrax attack to the Middle East. Later it was revealed that the perpetrator of the attack was an American citizen, with likely connections to the US military (Robin 2004: 16–17). Similarly, this kind of politics of fear has also had a deep impact on the Muslim residents of the USA, who are considered to be guilty until proven innocent, a reversal of the classic American legal maxim. For instance, it is reported that in 2005 the FBI admitted that it had yet to identify a single Al-Qaeda sleeper cell in the United States (Esposito 2011: 12–13).

Mehdi Semati (2010) also finds a correlation between the rise of the Islamophobic discourse prevailing in the West and the ongoing political crisis in the Middle East. With a special focus on the United States, he claims that the current discourse of Islam and Muslims is inextricably bound with the issues of the protection of national security and of terrorism, which tend to shape all other issues concerning the Middle East. The present-day notion of terrorism, however, has a relatively short history. The origin of today's terrorism discourse is located in the American foreign policy of the 1980s, during the presidency of Ronald Reagan. This era has been characterized as the era of aggressive militarism and a ruthless foreign policy as a response to the perceived erosion of American power and standing in the international political arena. The preceding presidency of Jimmy Carter witnessed events and policies that contributed to a real and perceived decline in America's credibility as a superpower due to the loss of Nicaragua, Iran, and Afghanistan. The failure in American foreign policy vis-à-vis such events led to a call for a renewal of the projection of American power around the globe. A central tool of the foreign policy of the Reagan regime was 'resurgent America' (Prince 1993). The idea of projecting American power in this era brought about aggressive intervention policies around the globe: the invasion of Grenada, supporting the Contra's war in Nicaragua, and the bombing of Libya were some of these actions. This aggressive jingoist militarism, which culminated in the military operation in the Persian Gulf in 1991, was part of a renewed Cold War by the Reagan administration in the New World Order to reassert American leadership after a period of perceived decline. The major thrust of foreign policy in the 1980s was formulated in response to (perceived) Soviet Union aggression. The threat of terrorism, as 'Russia's secret weapon', became a major theme in the new Cold War. American foreign policy during the Bush administration became more engaged in the war against the Axis of Evil, mainly symbolized by the (perceived) 'terrorist' Islamic countries (Semati 2010: 259–60).

As demonstrated already, right-wing politicians and public intellectuals, in their speeches, often present themselves as tolerant and understanding, but more often they subtly or blatantly convey the idea that Muslims are not welcome in Europe. The same is true for debates about minority groups residing within the country. Except for a few notable anti-racist voices, the discourse of the political elites thus confirms and reformulates the broader anti-foreigner and anti-Muslim sentiments in Europe and the United States since 9/11 (Cesari 2013: chapter 5). Hence, Islam is seen as an existential threat to European and American political and security interests and extraordinary measures against it are justified by the state (Cesari 2013: xvii). The securitization and stigmatization of religious objects and activities like mosques, praying, headscarves, and Islamic vocabulary has also prompted states to invest more in the protection of their national borders against the 'intrusion of immigrants and Muslims' (Doty 2000; Bigo 2002; Walters 2006; Huysmans 2006; Cesari 2006; Kaya 2009; Bahners 2011). States have invested in an impressive array of policing technologies—personnel (border patrol agents), material structures (fences and lights), and surveillance devices (helicopters, ground sensors, TV cameras, and infrared night vision scopes)—at the borders in order to keep the so-called undocumented immigrants out of the country.

As Chris Allen (2007a, 2010) very eloquently revealed, Islamophobia is not really a 'phobia', it is rather a form of governmentality, or an ideology, 'similar in theory, function and purpose to racism and other similar phenomena, that sustains and perpetuates negatively evaluated meaning about Muslims and Islam in the contemporary setting in similar ways...that inform and construct thinking about Muslims and Islam as Other' (2010: 195). The aim of Islamophobia as a form of governmentality is to make the majorities believe that Muslims and Islam constitute an 'enemy within' in the European context, and an 'outside enemy' in the American context so that the unity of the nation can be protected against the national, societal, and cultural security challenges coming from inside or outside (Doty 2000; Huysmans 2006; Kaya 2009; and Allen 2010). However, in both contexts what is challenged by the Islamophobic form of governmentality is the multicultural status of Western societies.

## Crisis of Multiculturalism

More specifically, states are unlikely to accord powers and resources to minorities that they view as potential collaborators with neighbouring enemies. Today, this is not an issue throughout the established Western democracies with respect to authocthonous national minorities, although it remains an issue with respect to certain immigrant-origin groups, particularly Muslim-origin groups after 11 September. As stated earlier, ethno-cultural and religious relations become securitized under these conditions. Relations between states and minorities are seen, not as a matter of normal democratic debate and negotiation, but as a matter of state security, in which the state has to limit the democratic processes of political participation, negotiation, and compromise to protect itself. The state of securitization of minorities is likely to lead to the rejection of minority political mobilization by the larger society and the state. Hence, the securitization of ethno-cultural relations both erodes the democratic space to voice minority demands, and decreases the likelihood that those demands will be accepted.

The situation with respect to immigrant groups is more complex. In the European context, the same factors that push for multiculturalism in relation to historic minorities have also generated a willingness to contemplate multiculturalism for immigrant groups (Kymlicka 2010). However, immigrant multiculturalism has run into difficulties where it is perceived as carrying high risks with regard to the national, societal, and cultural security of the majority society. Where immigrants are coupled with violence, honour crimes, drug use, drug trafficking and human trafficking, and are seen as predominantly illegal, as potential carriers of illiberal practices or movements, and as net burdens on the welfare state, then multiculturalism also poses perceived risks to the shared moral principles of the nation, and this perception can reverse the forces that support multiculturalism. Accordingly, multiculturalism bashing is also inclined to become a popular sport often revisited in times of social, political, and economic turmoil.[19] In moments of societal crisis, the critique of multiculturalism turns out to be a form of governmentality employed mostly by Christian Democratic parties to mobilize those segments of the society who have an inclination towards right-wing extremism due to growing feelings of anomie, insecurity, and ambiguity.[20]

---

[19] For a similar debate in Germany in the 1990s, see Heitmeyer et al. (1997). Wilhelm Heitmeyer et al. (1997) concluded that it is the Turks who are not tempted to integrate and incorporate themselves into the German society. Their main criterion in declaring the self-isolationist tendency of the Turkish-origin youths was their perceived contentment to live with Islam and Turkishness. This polemical debate around the work of Heitmeyer et al. (1997) is in close parallel to the debate revolving around Thilo Sarrazin's (2010) book, engaging high-level politicians including the Chancellor and the President of Germany.

[20] One should not underestimate the destructive effects of such nationalist anti-multiculturalist rhetoric on Western societies such as Norway and the UK. For instance, the myths that Muslim immigrants are taking over Europe and that multiculturalism is harmful contributed to the murder of seventy-nine individuals by right-wing extremist Anders Behring Breivik in Norway on 22 July 2011 (see BBC website, 23 July 2011, <http://www.bbc.co.uk/news/world-europe-14259356> accessed 15 August 2013). In a similar vein, British PM David Cameron had also criticized the multiculturalist rhetoric in February 2011, a few months before the London riots in August 2011. In boroughs where more than half the youth centres have closed, youth unemployment is rising, and negative experience with police is repeated through the generations, many children and young adults feel that neither the state nor the community has anything to offer them. For further detail on the notorious speech of David Cameron on multiculturalism, see <http://www.bbc.co.uk/news/uk-politics-12415597> (accessed 16 August 2013); and for more detail on the London riots, see <http://www.bbc.co.uk/news/uk-14436499> (accessed 16 August 2013).

Securitization and stigmatization of migration and Islam has brought about the ascendancy of a political discourse known as *the end of multiculturalism*—a discourse which has often been revisited in the last two decades since the war in Bosnia in 1992, leading to the birth of the Huntingtonian clash of civilizations paradigm. The discourse of the end of multiculturalism is often built upon the assumption that the homogeneity of the nation is at stake, and thus it has to be restored at the expense of alienating those who are not ethno-culturally and religiously part of the prescribed community of 'us'. It should be kept in mind that migration was a source of content in Western Europe during the 1960s. More recently, however, migration has been framed as a source of discontent, fear, and instability for nation-states in the West. What has happened since the 1960s? Why has there been this shift in the framing of migration? The answers to such questions lie at the very heart of the changing global social-political context.

Undoubtedly, many different reasons, such as deindustrialization, unemployment, poverty, exclusion, violence, and neo-liberal political economy turning the uneducated and unqualified masses into the new 'wretched of the earth' to use Frantz Fanon's (1965) terminology, can be enumerated to answer such critical questions. After the relative prominence of multiculturalism debates in both the political and scholarly arenas, we witness today a change in the direction of debates and policies about how to accommodate cultural diversity. Diminishing belief in the possibility of a flourishing multicultural society has changed the nature of the debates about the integration of migrant-origin groups. Initially, the idea of multiculturalism connoted compromise, tolerance, respect, interdependence, and universalism, and was expected to bring about an 'intercultural community'. Over time, it began to be perceived as a way of institutionalizing difference through autonomous cultural discourses and cultural archipelagos (Cesari et al. 2006). Europe and the other parts of the world including the USA have experienced increasing tensions between national majorities and ethno-religious minorities, more particularly with marginalized Muslim communities.[21]

It seems that the declaration of the 'failure of multiculturalism' has become a catchphrase of not only extreme-right-wing political parties but also of centrist political parties all across the continent, although it is not clear that each attributes the same meaning to the term.[22] Angela Merkel for the first time publicly dismissed the policy of multiculturalism as having 'failed, failed utterly' in October 2010, and this was followed swiftly by David Cameron's call for a 'more active, more muscular liberalism' and Nicolas Sarkozy's statement that multiculturalism is a 'failed concept'. Geert Wilders, leader of the Freedom Party in the Netherlands, has made no apologies for arguing that

---

[21] Similarly, Koopmans et al. (2005), and Sniderman and Hagendoorn (2007) suggested that immigrant multiculturalism in the Netherlands as well as in the other European countries produced adverse effects.

[22] Multiculturalism was also criticized by several left-wing scholars with the claim that multiculturalism became a neo-liberal and neo-colonial form of governmentality, imprisoning ethno-cultural and religious minorities, migrants, and their children in their own ghettos. For a more detailed account of the critique of multiculturalism, see Rosaldo (1989); Rath (1993); Radtke (1994); Russon (1995); Koopmans et al. (2005); Sniderman and Hogendoorn (2007); Kaya (2001, 2009).

Christians 'should be proud that our culture is better than Islamic culture' (*Der Spiegel*, 11 September 2010). Thilo Sarrazin (2010), a politician from the Social Democratic Party who sat on the Bundesbank board and is the former Finance Senator for Berlin, has argued in his bestselling book that Germany is becoming 'naturally more stupid on average' as a result of immigration from Muslim countries. In his critique of Thilo Sarrazin's highly polemical book *Germany Does Away With Itself* (*Deutschland schafft sich ab*, 2010), Jürgen Habermas states that German *Leitkultur* (leading culture) is currently being defined not by 'German culture' but by religion: 'With an arrogant appropriation of Judaism—and an incredible disregard for the fate the Jews suffered in Germany—the apologists of the *Leitkultur* now appeal to the "Judeo-Christian tradition", which distinguishes "us" from foreigners' (Habermas 2010).

Referring to genetic arguments, Sarrazin claims in his book that the future of multicultural Germany is threatened by the wrong kind of immigrants, coming especially from Muslim countries. Although his arguments are based on a conventional racist rhetoric, he is highly credited by German society for securitizing the policies of citizenship (Habermas 2010; Widmann 2010). His racist arguments were later followed by those of the German Chancellor Angela Merkel, who denounced multicultural rhetoric, as well as by the Bavarian Prime Minister Horst Seehofer's hate speech against the migrants coming from Turkey and Arab countries (Habermas 2010). The German experience also reveals that the European form of multiculturalism is not yet equipped to accommodate Islam, which has recently become very visible in the public space (Laitin 2010). Interestingly, the German practice, as well as other practices in France, Belgium, the Netherlands, Denmark, and the UK, has ended up with a kind of holy alliance between the secular left and Christian right against Islam (Roy 2007: xii).

These populist outbreaks contribute to the securitization and stigmatization of migration in general and Islam in particular. In the meantime, such interventions also deflect attention from constructive solutions and policies widely thought to promote integration, including programmes for language acquisition and increased labour market access, which are already suffering because of austerity measures all across Europe including Germany, Belgium, the UK, and the Netherlands. The 2007 Human Rights first report on Islamophobia states that such an anti-Islamic political discourse blames Muslims as a group for the marginalization they feel, even while the discriminatory policies and practices that exclude them from the mainstream are reinforced' (HRF 2007: 2). Furthermore, critics of the failure of at least some parts of the Muslim population in Europe to fully integrate often become advocates of measures that would further isolate and stigmatize these minorities.

The debate is not restricted to the critique of multiculturalism. Difference-blind Republicanism, which is the other model of managing ethno-cultural and religious diversity, has also failed. The Republican French model has largely collapsed in the last decade. Although France set out to create politically equal citizens without regard to religion, language, race, ethnicity, and gender, it no longer recognizes the politics of recognition generated especially by migrants of Muslim background, ignores the cultural, religious, and ethnic differences emphasized by minorities, and adopts an assimilation policy, all of which serve to show that the Republican project and its values are under threat. These demands, voiced by migrants and minorities and left unresolved by the Republic, clearly show that the Republic at hand needs to be democratized. In other words, Republicanism needs to be reformed by incorporating the egalitarian claims of migrant origin people who are affiliated with a true Republican rhetoric underlining equality, justice, and rights in all spheres of life including politics, education, labour market, and culture (Kaya 2009). Not only does France fail to provide migrants and their children with equal access opportunity to political space and the labour market, but it also cannot provide them with a venue where they can convert their cultural capital to economic capital upon graduation. As such, it can be said that France, much like many other Western nations, discriminates against Muslim-origin migrants and their descendants at work. As Michèle Tribalat (2003) put it very eloquently, what is the point in working hard for success at school if you are going to be discriminated against?[23] She reports that the presence of discrimination raises the problem of coherence between Republican principles and the reality of French society. One should remember that the unemployment rate among university graduates of French ethnic origin is 5%, but 27% among those of North African origin.[24] This ratio is much higher than it is in Germany (4% and 12%), Belgium (5% and 15%), and the Netherlands (3% and 12%) (Crul and Vermeulen 2003).

# Conclusion

Migration has recently been framed as a source of fear and instability for the nation-states in the West. In the 1960s and 1970s, it was rather a source of contentment and happiness. Several different factors, such as deindustrialization, economic crisis, changing technology, unemployment, poverty, neo-liberal political economy, Islamophobia, and cultural racism, can serve to explicate the reasons for such discontent. Furthermore, this period of social-economic and political change in the West went in tandem with the rise of discourses like the 'clash of civilizations', 'culture wars', and Islamophobia that presented societal heterogeneity in an unfavourable light. The intensification of Islamophobia made easier by Al-Qaeda-type violence and the radicalization of some segments of Muslim-origin immigrant communities in several countries reinforced the societal unrest resulting from immigration. The result was the

---

[23] The data collected by the work of Kaya and Kentel (2005) affirm Tribalat's findings concerning the discrimination faced by immigrant populations and those of foreign origin. French-Turks, when asked, address mostly the problem of discrimination in France (17%).

[24] In order to cope with institutional racism in the labour market as well as in other spheres of life, migrant origin people tend to give traditional French first names to newborn children. Gérard Noiriel (1988: 233) indicates that this is an old practice among migrants: in a Polish community in northern France, 44% in 1935, 73% in 1945, 82% in 1955, and 98% in 1960.

introduction of restrictive migration policies and increased territorial border security vis-à-vis the nationals of third countries who originated from outside the European continent.

Unemployment, poverty, exclusion, institutional discrimination, and Islamophobia have become the main reasons for the Muslim-origin immigrants and their descendants to question the political and legal structure of their countries of settlement in a way that has made them hesitate to integrate into those countries. Instead they have tended to find refuge in the comfort of certain communities of sentiment, such as religious, ethnic, cultural, and fellowship communities. Such communities of sentiment provide immigrants and their children with a safe haven that protects them against uncertainty, insecurity, ambiguity, poverty, unemployment, and exclusion. In this sense, religiosity becomes one of the most resourceful tactics for migrants to come to terms with the existing structural problems.

Furthermore, the supremacy of cultural-religious discourse in the West is likely to frame many of the social, political, and economic conflicts within the range of religious differences. Many of the ills of migrants and their descendants, such as poverty, exclusion, unemployment, illiteracy, lack of political participation, and lack of will to integrate, are attributed to their Islamic background, which is stereotypically believed to be clash with Western secular norms and values. Culturalization of political, social, and economic conflicts has become a popular sport in a way that reduces all sorts of structural problems to cultural and religious factors.

However, one should not underestimate the fact that European Muslims have become even more politically mobile after the rise of Islamophobic tendencies in the aftermath of 9/11. The growing interest and success of Muslim-origin candidates in local, general, and European elections (see national chapters in this Handbook) indicates that the time of crisis characterized by Islamophobia has brought its own window of opportunity for the European public in general. Ultimately, the Breivik incident in Norway on 22 July 2011 demonstrated that Islamophobia as a form of governmentality is not sustainable anymore. And let us not forget that the *failures of one form of governmentality* result in opportunities for the formulation of another.

# Acknowledgements

I would like to express my gratitude to Jocelyne Cesari, Senem Aydin Düzgit, Peter Widmann, and Ayşe Tecmen for their invaluable comments and suggestions.

# Bibliography

Allen, Christopher (2007a). 'Islamophobia and Its Discontents', in Samir Amghar, Amel Boubekeur, and Michael Emerson (eds.), *European Islam*. Brussels: CEPS, 144–68.

Allen, Christopher (2007b). 'The "First" Decade of Islamophobia: 10 Years of the Runnymede Trust Report: *Islamophobia: A Challenge for Us All'*. West Midlands, UK. <http://www.euromedalex.org/sites/default/files/Decade_of_Islamophobia.pdf>.
Allen, Christopher (2010). *Islamophobia*. Farnham: Ashgate.
Allievi, Stefano (ed.) (2010). *Mosques in Europe: Why a Solution Has Become a Problem*. London: Alliance Publishing Trust.
Andeweg, Rudy B. and Gallen A. Irwin (2005). *Government and Politics of the Netherlands*. Basingstoke: Palgrave Macmillan.
Asad, Talal (2003). *Formations of the Secular: Christianity, Islam, Modernity*. Stanford, CA: Stanford University Press.
Bahners, Patrick (2011). *Die Panikmacher. Die deutsche Angst vor dem Islam* (The Scaremongers: The German Fear of Islam). Munich: C. H. Beck.
Balibar, Étienne (2004). *We, the People of Europe: Reflections on Transnational Citizenship*. Princeton and Oxford: Princeton University Press.
Bauböck, Reiner and Christian Joppke (eds.) (2010). 'How Liberal are Citizenship Tests?' *EUI Working Papers 41*. Robert Schuman Centre for Advanced Studies, European University Institute, Florence.
Baumann, Martin (2009). 'Temples, Cupolas, Minarets: Public Space as Contested Terrain in Contemporary Switzerland', *Religio: Revue pro religionistiku* 4: 141–53.
Bigo, Didier (2002). 'To Reassure and Protect after September 11th', *Social Science Research Council Essays* 2. <http://www.ssrc.org/sept11/essays/bigo.htm>.
Brown, Wendy (2006). *Regulating Aversion: Tolerance in the Age of Identity and Empire*. Princeton: Princeton University Press.
Cesari, Joselyne (2003). 'Muslim Minorities in Europe: The Silent Revolution', in J. Esposito and F. Burgat (eds.), *Modernizing Islam: Religion in the Public Sphere in the Middle East and in Europe*. New Brunswick, NJ, Rutgers University Press, 251–69.
Cesari, Jocelyne (2006). *Securitization and Religious Divides in Europe: Muslims in Western Europe after 9/11*. Paris: Challenge.
Cesari, Jocelyne (ed.) (2009). *Muslims in the West after 9/11: Religion, Politics and Law*. London: Routledge.
Cesari, Jocelyne (2013). *Why the West Fears Islam: An Exploration of Muslims in Liberal Societies*. Basingstoke: Palgrave Macmillan.
Cesari, Jocelyne et al. (2006). 'Securitization and Religious Divides in Europe: Muslims in Western Europe after 9/11'. Report submitted to the Changing Landscape of Citizenship and Security 6th PCRD of European Commission, Paris.
Council of Europe (2004). 'Islamophobia' and its Consequences on Young People'. Report by Ingrid Ramberg, European Youth Centre Budapest (1–6 June), Budapest.
Crul, Maurice and Hans Vermeulen (eds.) (2003). 'The Future of the Second Generation: The Integration of Migrant Youth in Six European Countries', Special issue of *International Migration Review* 37(4) (Winter): 965–86.
De Gobineau, Arthur (1999). *The Inequality of Human Races*, trans.Adrian Collins. New York: Howard Fertig Publications.
Doty, Roxanne L. (2000). 'Immigration and the Politics of Security', *Security Studies* 8(2–3): 71–93.
Esposito, John (2011). 'Introduction', in John Esposito and Ibrahim Kalın (eds.), *Islamophobia: The Challenge of Pluralism in the 21st Century*. Oxford: Oxford University Press, 9–17.
EUMC (European Monitoring Centre on Racism and Xenophobia) (2006). *Muslims in the European Union: Discrimination and Islamophobia*. Austria: Printer MANZ CROSSMEDIA GmbH & Co KG.

Evans, Tony (2010). 'The Limits of Tolerance: Islam as Counter-Hegemony?' *Review of International Studies*. <http://www.rairo-ita.org/action/displayAbstract?fromPage=online&aid=7780256&fulltextType=RA&fileId=S0260210510000185>.

Fanon, Frantz (1965). *The Wretched of the Earth*. New York: Grove Weidenfeld. Reprint of *Les damnés de la terre*. Paris, 1961.

Federal Ministry of Interior (2007). 'Was hat sich durch Artikel 5 des Gesetzes zur Umsetzung von aufenthalts- und asylrechtlichen Richtlinien der Europäischen Union vom 19. August 2007 geändert?' <http://www.bmi.bund.de/cln_028/nn_164892/Internet/Content/Themen/Staatsangehoerigkeit/DatenundFakten/Was__aendert__sich__durch__das__Richtlinienumsetzungsgesetz.html> [Accessed 1 November 2010].

FES (Fredrich Ebert Stiftung) (2011). 'Intolerance, Prejudice and Discrimination'. A European Report prepared by Andreas Zick, Beate Küpper, and Andreas Hövermann. Berlin. <http://www.fes-gegen-rechtsextremismus.de>.

Fortuyn, Pim (2001). *De islamisering van onze cultuur*. Uitharn: Karakter Uitgeners.

Foucault, Michel (1979). 'Governmentality', *Ideology and Consciousness* 6: 5–21.

Geisser, Vincent (2010). 'Islamophobia: A French Specificity in Europe?', *Human Architecture: Journal of the Sociology of Self and Knowledge* 8(2): 39–46.

GMF (German Marshall Fund) (2010). 'Transatlantic Trends: Immigration 2010', *Key Findings* 3. Washington: GMF.

Habermas, Jürgen (2010). 'Leadership and *Leitkultur*', *New York Times* (28 October). <http://www.nytimes.com/2010/10/29/opinion/29Habermas.html>.

Halliday, Fred (1996). *Islam and the Myth of Confrontation*. London: I. B. Tauris.

Halliday, Fred (1999). 'Islamophobia Reconsidered', *Ethnic and Racial Studies* 22(5) (September): 892–902.

Heitmeyer, Wilhelm, Joachim Müller, and Helmut Schröder (1997). *Verlockender Fundamentalismus (Enticing Multiculturalism)*. Frankfurt am Main: Suhrkamp Verlag.

HRF (Human Rights First) (2007). *Islamophobia: 2007 Hate Crimes Survey*. New York: Human Rights First.

Huntington, Samuel (1996). *The Clash of Civilisations and the Remaking of the World Order*. New York: Simon & Schuster.

Huysmans, Jef (2006). *The Politics of Insecurity*. London: Routledge.

Joppke, Christian (2007). 'Transformation of Immigrant Integration in Western Europe: Civic Integration and Antidiscrimination Policies in the Netherlands, France, and Germany', *World Politics* 59(2) (January): 243–73.

Kaya, Ayhan (2001). *'Sicher in Kreuzberg': Constructing Diasporas, Turkish Hip-Hop Youth in Berlin*. Bielefeld: Transcript Verlag.

Kaya, Ayhan (2009). *Islam, Migration and Integration: The Age of Securitization*. Basingstoke: Palgrave Macmillan.

Kaya, Ayhan and Ferhat Kentel (2005). *Euro-Turks: A Bridge, or a Breach, between Turkey and the EU*. Brussels: CEPS Publication.

Kaya, Ayhan and Ferhat Kentel (2007). *Belgian-Turks: A Bridge, or a Breach, between Turkey and the European Union?* Brussels: CEPS Publication.

Koopmans, Ruud, Paul Statham, Marco Guigni, and Florence Passy (2005). *Contested Citizenship: Immigration and Cultural Diversity in Europe*. Minneapolis: University of Minnesota Press.

Kymlicka, Will (2010). 'The Rise and Fall of Multiculturalism? New Debates on Inclusion and Accommodation in Diverse Societies', in Steven Vertovec and Susanne Wessendorf (eds.), *The Multiculturalism Backlash: European Discourses, Policies and Practices*. London: Routledge, 32–49.

Laegaard, Sune (2007). 'The Cartoon Controversy as a Case of Multicultural Recognition', *Contemporary Politics* 13(2): 147–64.

Laitin, David (2010). 'Rational Islamophobia in Europe', *European Journal of Sociology* 51: 429–47.

Malik, Maleiha (ed.) (2010). *Anti-Muslim Prejudice in the West, Past and Present*. London: Routledge.

Marranci, Gabrielle (2004). 'Multiculturalism, Islam and the Clash of Civilisations Theory: Rethinking Islamophobia', *Culture and Religion* 5(1): 105–17.

Meer, Nasar and Tariq Modood (2009). 'Refutations of Racism in the "Muslim Question"', *Patterns of Prejudice* 43(3–4): 335–54.

Miller, Peter and Nikolas Rose (2008). *Governing the Present*. Cambridge: Polity Press.

Modood, Tariq (2002). 'The Place of Muslims in British Secular Multiculturalism', in Nezar Alsayyad and Manuel Castells (eds.), *Muslim Europe or Euro-Islam: Politics, Culture and Citizenship in the Age of Globalization*. Lanham, MD: Lexington Books, 113–30.

Modood, Tariq (2007). *Multiculturalism: A Civic Idea*. Cambridge: Polity Press.

Mouritsen, Per (2006). 'The Particular Universalism of a Nordic Civic Nation: Common Values, State Religion, and Islam in Danish Political Culture', in Tariq Modood, Anna Triandafyllidou, and Ricard Zapata-Barrero (eds.), *Multiculturalism, Muslims and Citizenship*. New York: Routledge, 70–93.

Nielsen, Jørgen S., Samim Akgönül, Ahmet Alibašić, Brigitte Maréchal, and Christian Moe (eds.) (2009). *Yearbook of Muslims in Europe*. Leiden: Brill.

Noiriel, Gérard (1988). *Le creuset français: Historie de l'immigration XIXe–XXe siècle*. Paris: Seuil.

O'Hagan, Andrew (2008). 'Fear of Islam is Ruining Our Chance for Peace', *The Telegraph* (8 April). <http://www.telegraph.co.uk/comment/columnists/andrewo_hagan/3557031/Fear-of-Islam-is-ruining-our-chance-for-peace.html> [Accessed 2 May 2011].

Pfaff-Czarnecka, Johanna (2009). 'Accommodating Religious Diversity in Switzerland', in P. Bramadat and M. Koenig (eds.), *International Migration and the Governance of Religious Diversity*. Montreal and Kingston: McGill-Queen's University Press.

Povinelli, Elizabeth A. (2002). *The Cunning of Recognition: Indigenous Alterities and the Making of Australian Multiculturalism*. Durham: Duke University Press.

Prince, Stephen R. (1993). 'Celluloid Heroes and Smart Bombs: Hollywood at War in the Middle East', in R. Denton (ed.), *The Media and the Persian Gulf War*. New York: Praeger, 235–56.

Radtke, Frantz O. (1994). 'The Formation of Ethnic Minorities and the Transformation of Social into Ethnic Conflicts in a So-Called Multi-Cultural Society: The Case of Germany', in J. Rex and B. Drury (eds.), *Ethnic Mobilisation in a Multi-Cultural Europe*. Farnham: Avebury.

Rath, Jan (1993). 'The Ideological Representation of Migrant Workers in Europe: A Matter of Racialisation?', in J. Solomos and J. Wrench (eds.), *Racism and Migration in Western Europe*. Oxford: Berg Publishers, 215–32.

Richardson, Robin (2012). *Countering Islamophobia through Education: International Guidelines*. Paris: UNESCO. <http://www.insted.co.uk/countering-intolerance.pdf>.

Rosaldo, Renato (1989). *Culture and Truth: The Remaking of Social Analysis*. London: Routledge.

Roy, Olivier (2007). *Secularism Confronts Islam*, trans. George Holoch. New York: Columbia University Press.

Runnymede Trust (1997). *Islamophobia: A Challenge for Us All*. London: Runnymede Trust.

Russon, John (1995). 'Heidegger, Hegel, and Ethnicity: The Ritual Basis of Self-Identity', *The Southern Journal of Philosophy* 33: 509–32.

Said, Edward (1978). *Orientalism*. New York: Vintage.

Sarrazin, Thilo (2010). *Deutschland schafft sich ab: Wie wir unser Land aufs Spiel setzen*. Munich: DVA Verlag.

Schiffer, Sabine and Constantin Wagner (2011). 'Anti-Semitism and Islamophobia: New Enemies, Old Patterns', *Race and Class* 52(3): 77–84.

Semati, Mehdi (2010). 'Islamophobia, Culture and Race in the Age of Empire', *Cultural Studies* 24(2): 256–75.

Sivanandan, Ambalavaner (2010). 'Fighting Anti-Muslim Racism: An Interview with A. Sivanandan', London: Institute of Race Relations (15 March). <http://www.irr.org.uk/2010/march/ha000031.html>.

Sniderman, Paul M. and Louk Hagendoorn (2007). *When Ways of Life Collide*. Princeton: Princeton University Press.

Stewart, Kathleen (2000). 'Nostalgia: A Polemic', in George E. Marcus (ed.), *Reading Cultural Anthropology*. Durham: Duke University Press, 252–66.

Sussex, Matthew (2004). 'Cultures in Conflict? Re-evaluating the "Clash of Civilisations" Thesis After 9/11', in Peter Sherman and Mathew Sussex (eds.), *European Security After 9/11*. Aldershot: Ashgate, 28–50.

Tribalat, Michèle (1995). *Faire France: Une enquête sur les immigrês et leurs enfants*. Paris: Éditions La Dêcouverte.

Tribalat, Michèle (2003). 'The French "Melting Pot": Outdated—or in Need of Reinvention?' in S. Milner and N. Parsons (eds.), *Reinventing France: State and Society in the Twenty-First Century*. Basingstoke: Palgrave Macmillan, 127–42.

Vertovec, Steven (2002). 'Islamophobia and Muslim Recognition in Britain', in Y. Yazbek Haddad (ed.), *Muslims in the West: From Sojourners to Citizens*. Oxford and New York: Oxford University Press, 19–35.

Vertovec, Steven and Susanne Wessendorf (eds.) (2010). *The Multiculturalism Backlash: European Discourses, Policies and Practices*. London: Routledge.

Walters, William (2006). 'Security, Territory, Metagovernance: Critical Notes on Anti-illegal Immigration Programmes in the European Union'. Paper presented at Istanbul Bilgi University (7 December).

WEF (World Economic Forum) (2008). 'Islam and the West: Annual Report on the State of Dialogue'. Gallup Survey Report, World Economic Forum, Geneva (January).

Werbner, Pnina (2005). 'Islamophobia, Incitement to Religious Hatred: Legislating for a New Fear?' *Anthropology Today* 21(1): 5–9.

Widmann, Peter (2010). 'Merchants of Fear: Sarrazin vs. Muezzin', *Germany Brief*, Istanbul Bilgi University. <http://eu.bilgi.edu.tr/docs/Sarrazin_Muezzine_Karsi_English.pdf>.

# CHAPTER 18

# RADICALIZATION

## DANIELA PISOIU

RADICALIZATION, in particular in connection to 'Muslims in Europe' has become increasingly present as a matter of empirical investigation and theoretical conceptualization in the European research landscape and political discourse in recent years. As Silke (2011: 20) notes, 'In the 1970s and 1980s, there were no claims of Irish Republican Army (IRA) members being "radicalized", and there was no reference to a "radicalization process". Such a terminology and framework has primarily been a post 9/11 phenomenon and it has been developed in regard to al-Qa'ida and its disparate affiliates.' What are the reasons for this development? The same reasons why the European Union and its member states have afforded radicalization special attention in their security and social policies: the assumed connection to Islamist terrorism—in itself a relatively novel development on the continent, and the subsequent securitization of migration and integration of Muslim minorities in Europe. In the words of Vidino (2009: 61): 'The 2004 Madrid and 2005 London attacks, as well as the arrest of hundreds of European Muslims who had been involved in a variety of terrorist activities, have clearly shown that radicalization is a problem in Europe.' Necessary or exclusive associations between radicalization on the one side, and terrorism, Islamism. and 'Muslims' on the other, should to be treated with caution. Radicalization is a cognitive and behavioural process that may or may not lead to or include the use of violence and the latter may or may not concretize in acts of terrorism. Further, radicalization is not ideology-specific, i.e. one might speak of left-wing or right-wing radicalization for instance. As Al-Azmeh (2006: 1, original emphasis) argues:

> If one were therefore to approach Islamist radicalization in a manner that renders it comprehensible, one must eschew the altogether common perspective of exoticization which regards Islamism as a phenomenon *sui generis*, to be comprehended only in its own terms. One would need to take it as an instance of radicalization overall, subject like other movements that one may describe generically as radical to the conditions that give rise to radicalization overall.

Finally, it should not be associated with a particular group, in this case the 'Muslims in Europe' or the 'Muslim immigrants to Europe'. Whether or not community or religious aspects play a role in this particular variant of the radicalization process is a different question dealt with at a later point in this chapter; what for now is important to remember is that radicalization is a highly individual and individualized process, to which features such as belonging to a particular religious or ethnic community are not inherent. 'Radicals' and 'radicalizing' are individuals and small groups with a high degree of background heterogeneity, including converts. It would therefore be misleading to speak about 'the radicalization of Muslims in Europe'. The following will deal with the definition of radicalization, empirical developments, and main theoretical approaches to its explanation, as well as main elements of debate surrounding 'home-grown' radicalization, the role of the internet, radicalization hubs, religion, and deradicalization.

# WHAT IS RADICALIZATION?

Definitional problems surrounding 'radicalization' mirror to some extent the case of 'terrorism', with no generally agreed definition, a fluid meaning, and security-loaded negative connotations. Critical assessments have unpacked the constructed nature of the term, pointing out for instance the mediated connotations of danger, vulnerability, and risk (Hoskins and O'Loughlin 2009), or its various meanings depending on the various contexts of usage—security, integration, and foreign policy—and argue for a relative rather than absolute conceptualization (Sedgwick 2010). There are several approaches to the definition of radicalization: some focus on the cognitive aspect: 'Radicalization refers to the process of coming to adopt militant Islamist ideology' (Mullins 2012: 111), while yet others associate it with the use of violence: 'It is a personal (and at times, interpersonal) process in which individuals adopt extreme political, social, and/or religious ideals and aspirations, and in which the attainment of particular goals justifies the use of indiscriminate violence. Radicalization is both a mental and emotional process that can prepare and motivate an individual to pursue violent behaviour' (Wilner and Dubouloz 2011: 418). This definition also illustrates a recent trend in both scholarship (Ongering 2007; Neumann and Rogers 2008) and policy: the superimposition of terminology related to 'extremism', in the understanding that radicalization is a process leading to extremism, or that extreme ideas (in the sense of opposing democracy and pluralism) are symptoms of early engagement in the process. This has occurred against the background of an increasing use of the term 'extremism' in reference to violent illegal action during the last decades and of attempts to situate the new wave of Islamist radicalism within the existing European terminological complex, at the same time underlining its political rather than religious-fundamentalist character. A useful definition is that provided by Dalgaard-Nielsen (2010), who starts from the meaning of the root word 'radical'. It reflects the unspecific ideological character of the radicalization process and focuses on its essential content rather than manifestations:

> radical is understood as a person harbouring a deep-felt desire for fundamental socio-political changes and radicalization is understood as a growing readiness to pursue and support far-reaching changes in society that conflict with, or pose a direct threat to, the existing order... *violent* radicalization—[is] a process in which radical ideas are accompanied by the development of a willingness to directly support or engage in violent acts. (Dalgaard-Nielsen 2010: 798, original emphasis)

Her further differentiation of 'violent radicalization' has the merit of outlining the fact that violence is not a necessary component of radicalization. At the same time it suggests that there are two different radicalization processes, one violent and one non-violent, which is something that has not been proven empirically and is highly unlikely. Ordinarily, violence emerges at some point during the radicalization process in the case of both individuals and organizations, and the trajectory towards it is not necessarily unidirectional.

# The Geography of Islamist Radicalization in Europe

When speaking about Islamist radicalization in Europe, one usually means Islamist radicalization in Western Europe. By looking at the statistics of suicide attack incidents between 2001 and 2012 for instance—twenty in Russia and twelve in Western Europe (GTD 2014)—a more inclusive approach would seem appropriate. That this is not necessarily recognized is due not only to a biased scholarship interest, but also to the conceptualization of the term as it applies to the European space. Radicalization ordinarily refers to the ideological adherence and behavioural involvement of certain individuals and groups in global jihadism. The development in Russia that comes closest to this understanding is the Chechen jihad, whereby this is rather a case of Islamization of an existing nationalist/separatist conflict (for an elaborated account of how this conflict has been integrated in the international jihadi movement and further spread to other republics in the North Caucasus, see Garner 2013; Campana and Ratelle 2014). Also often to be found under the labels of radicalization and radical Islam are the increasing predominance of Salafism and Salafist organizations, both indigenous and coming from abroad, and the frictions and competition with traditional forms of Islam in Northern Caucasus and to some extent Tatarstan (Yemelianova 2010). The last two approaches are also present to a certain extent in the context of the radicalization of Muslim communities in Western Europe; they are, however, not a core component of the problematic. Beyond the significance of the developments in the Northern Caucasus as such, the situation there, similar to previous conflicts in Bosnia Herzegovina and Kosovo, has had an operational and ideological impact on radicalization processes in the West, too. These conflicts have functioned as initial radicalization trigger points for individuals originally travelling there on charity missions and Chechnya has been a preferred destination for jihadi warriors, along with Waziristan and Syria more recently. Additionally, these conflicts have played, along with those in Afghanistan and Iraq, an important role in the construction of the jihadi narrative of oppression exercised by Western powers on Muslims around the world. At the same time, recent developments indicate a shift of focus, whereby scores of Chechen fighters from at home and abroad are joining the Syrian conflict, which might show again the global nature of the jihadi movement, as well as the completion of the 'jihadization' of the Chechen struggle.

Islamist radicalization in Western Europe is ideologically, in terms of membership and, some would argue, the background contributory factors, related but not confined to colonial histories, work and post-conflict immigration to, and the situation of immigrant Muslim minorities in Europe. In Bakker's (2008: 79) sample of jihadis associated with the thirty-one terrorist incidents since 2001, the dominant nationalities were Moroccan, Algerian, and British, whereas the majority was found to have roots in North Africa and Pakistan. It would be inaccurate, however, to derive from this an exclusively community or ethnic-related explanatory framework. In the 1980s and 1990s one could speak of 'imported conflicts', through the spill-over effect of the Islamist movement in Algeria and the arrival of 'activists, leaders, ideologues involved in local insurgencies, separatist and anti-occupation struggles' in Arab countries, Afghanistan, Pakistan, Chechnya, and Bosnia (Nesser 2011: 176). The phenomenon is currently global, both in terms of objectives and membership. Networks spread across countries and operational cells display an increasingly mixed composition, with first-, second-, and third-generation immigrants and converts and focus on conflicts partly not related to the countries of origin.

Looking at the form and degree of penetration of Islamist terrorism in Europe mapped in empirical studies (Jordan and Horsburgh 2005; Reinares 2006; Grignard 2008; Nesser 2008; Mullins 2010; Nesser 2014), several stages can be differentiated. In the 1980s, Europe played the role of a marginal basis of operations, while the 1990s saw two concomitant developments: the establishment of resident international networks such as GIA (Armed Islamic Group), GSPC (Salafist Group for Call and Combat), Hamas, Ansar al Islam, Salafia Yihadia, Hizbollah, GICM (Moroccan Islamic Combatant Group), and the Tunisian Combat Group, in several countries (Spain, France, Germany, Netherlands, UK, Italy and Belgium) and their emerging interrelatedness; and members of certain organizations such as the GIA participating in the Afghanistan war and their subsequent refuge in Europe as veterans along with other 'Arab-Afghans'. This in effect then also marked the link between classical nationalistic struggle and the global jihad and initiated the wave of radicalization through the returning *mujahideen*. In operational terms, Europe still was primarily a basis of procurement, financing, and propaganda rather than a target. In some accounts, though, already then Al-Qaeda-directed cells commenced the plotting of attacks on the continent, while operatives would travel to the Pakistani–Afghani area (Coolsaet and de Swielande 2007). Also exceptionally, GIA affiliates carried out the series of bombings in France in 1995. These would be the two phases of classical jihad outside Europe and in Europe respectively, whereby classical jihad is 'armed struggle to overthrow Muslim world regimes and establish Islamic states, and...armed struggle against non-Muslims occupying Islamic territories' (Nesser 2011: 175). With the turn of the century, the wave of terror plots targeting various countries in Europe commenced and peaked with the infamous Madrid and London bombings in 2004 and 2005. Again in Nesser's account (2011), this corresponds to the phase of global jihad inside Europe, against all enemies of Islam, whereby Europe had become a legitimate target due to the involvement in the war in Iraq and controversies such as the headscarf and the Cartoons affair. In a subsequent assessment, Nesser concludes on an overall increase of the number of jihadi plots in Europe, and on the multiplication of targets beyond the 'usual suspects' France and the UK, the two countries with, in his assessment, a history of involvement in Muslim affairs (Nesser 2014). The broad trends at the moment are an increasingly decentralized, international, and highly mobile jihadi network, undertaking training and combat travel to conflict areas—Pakistan, Afghanistan, Iraq, Chechnya, Somalia, Syria; the 'boomerang effect' (Ranstorp 2010)—these individuals returning to Europe, indoctrinating, recruiting, and plotting attacks there; and sporadic, mostly failed low-scale attacks perpetrated by relatively autonomous and unprofessional cells. The Syrian conflict seems to attract an unusually high number of European foreign fighters, yet the impact of their presence there as well as their possible trajectories once back home have not been so far captured in analysis. The operational structure in the North Caucasus is somewhat different. Jamaats (communities) are the 'basic structure of radicalism' (Yarlykapov 2010: 141), originally a traditional form of organization, some of which then shifted orientation from traditional structures to separatism and from ethnic separatism to religious separatism and jihadism, currently with international and multiethnic, religious, and intellectual membership, and partly educated leadership (Yarlykapov 2010: 142–5). More recent analyses observe a geographical expansion of the jihad in Russia beyond the Chechen borders, through the establishment of a network of 'combat jamaats' throughout the North Caucasus, under the leadership of the Caucasus Emirate (Garner 2013: 428–9). The latter is not only responsible for several attacks on the Russian territory, but is also assumed to support plots in Western Europe (Garner 2013: 429). Ideologically, the jihadi discourse has crossed the borders of individual countries to be integrated in that of the global jihad—as a sort of melting pot where European political protest ideas also found a point of entry, while operatives of various origins and ethnicities mix within the same cell, associate temporarily with others for particular operations, and travel from one conflict zone to another. Grignard (2008: 92) named this an 'internationalist' project, marked by a global ideology and an operational fusion having occurred in Afghanistan and Londonistan—the latter labelled as such due to the high concentration of radical veterans and preachers. In this context, conditions existent in Europe, European policies, and the fact that some of the jihadis are European citizens and radicalized within Europe are, as will be seen below, not necessarily relevant in themselves (except perhaps in operational and counterterrorism terms, given the financial and mobility advantage of having a European passport), but only to the extent that they integrate into the global jihadi narrative and movement. Also in the case of the North Caucasus, analysts observe an alignment of the jihadi discourse to that of Al-Qaeda, with little reference to the Chechen history (Garner 2013: 429).

# Theoretical Approaches to Explaining Islamist Radicalization

Mapping out the area of Islamist radicalization in Europe, the issues considered of interest, and the types of explanations proposed is a rather complex undertaking, given the somewhat schizophrenic approach to its research. Radicalization has established itself as an independent object of study, yet there is neither an overarching theory to deal with it, nor a theoretical tradition into which it could naturally be placed. In some accounts, such a theory would be neither necessary nor possible (McCauley and Moskalenko 2008). To make matters worse, there is also no general agreement on what exactly should be studied: individuals, groups, or communities, in Europe, in the Middle East, or perhaps Northern Africa, behaviour or ideas. This has to do with the fact that the way in which radicalization is researched depends on the respective discipline, theories, and methods scholars associate their expertise with; and there are quite a few disciplines that have something to say in matters of radicalization: religious studies, psychology, political science, sociology, criminology, communication and cultural studies, and the special fields of terrorism studies and social movements. For the purposes of simplicity, three paradigms can be delineated in terms of unit of analysis: one is to look at Islamist radicalization as a type of social movement, seen either as endogenous or in the tradition of the Middle Eastern ones; this sometimes overlaps with the social movements *theoretical* approach, also sporadically used in the second paradigm, which is essentially socio-psychological and looks at individuals; the third, the macro-approach, focuses on communities, Diasporas, cultural and religious specificities, issues related to identity, political Islam, Salafism, and jihadism.

With the exception of 'rational choice' approaches, the underlying rationale of all of these paradigms is that of 'grievance'. This concept permeates most of the assessments on the causes of radicalization at all levels of analysis and seems particularly problematic in the case of individuals. While it might be relatively easy to point to various levels of insufficiency, frustration, and anger among Muslim communities in Europe and especially abroad, it is not always straightforward to show that the individuals involved have also experienced these or if not how they came to share this sense of grievance. What occurs therefore is the formulation of hypotheses that try to combine the two levels of analysis: in some opinions, the individual adopts group grievances on the basis of common identity (national or religious), in others, there is correspondence between group grievance and one's own, be it literal or under the more general label of 'oppression by the West' (Khosrokhavar 2005; Waldmann 2010). On the reverse and with application to group radicalization, personal grievance would be framed and interpreted as group grievance in order for it to account for group sacrifice (McCauley and Moskalenko 2008).

## The Jihadi Social Movement

In a first approach, Islamist radicalization refers to a jihadi endogenous or exogenous social movement of global orientation, based on fundamentalist Islamic tenets but more deeply rooted in socio-political and cultural conditions existent in Europe and the Middle East, respectively. Olivier Roy (2004, 2008b) postulated the existence of an endogenous—in terms of membership and underlying conditions—neo-fundamentalist and anti-imperialistic social movement, in the tradition of the European radical left. His argument builds on the observation that the Al-Qaeda ideology and aims are de-culturalized and de-territorialized and that European radicals perceive themselves as belonging to a virtual *ummah*, rather than the host or the original community and culture. Evidence for this would be the fact that recruits fight in other countries than those of origin and embrace an extreme variation of Salafism in a quasi-born-again fashion. Quintan Wiktorowicz (2005) looked at the Islamist organization Al Muhajiroun in the UK from the perspective of an Islamist activist social movement framework of analysis and employed some of the precepts of social movement theory, such as the role of social networks, selective incentives, and framing. The two authors' outlooks on motivation and involvement mechanisms are examined in more detail in the following two sections, since they *de facto* focus on communities and individuals respectively.

The second approach here inscribes Islamist radicalization in Europe within a broader social movement traceable to the socio-economic and cultural conditions specific to the Arab world and based on a series of grievances: perception of hostility between the Arab and the Western world, frustration with underdevelopment, double standards, colonialism, humiliation, powerlessness, economic disadvantage, the poor–rich gap, the educated unemployed, corruption, and doctrinal openness to exclusivist interpretations, all leading young people to protest. The concurrent phenomena of Islamization, politicization, and demonization of the 'Other' would then create an explosive mix concretized in acts of terrorism (Al-Azmeh 2006: 7, 8). In a further theoretical development, this sense of grievance would find its way to Europe not necessarily in a direct genealogy, but rather through the intermediary of discourse: 'a minority within these communities [in the West] has cultivated a mindset and sense of grievance that has its foundations in the anti-Western discourse that permeates the Islamic world, including Pakistan' (Pargeter 2008: 145).

Beyond the theoretical advantages warranted by seeing radicalization as a social movement, which incidentally Al-Qaeda is also at times labelled as, the question needs to be raised whether we are indeed speaking about a social movement in the classical sense. Roy's (2008b: 112) characterization rather plays the role of making the differentiation between the concept of a hierarchical, central organization and that of 'bottom-up networks'. It might in fact be that precisely this type of loose structure and indeed ideological and programmatic division of the jihadi 'movement' prevent the various networks, cells, and groups from constituting a genuine social movement in the sense of 'distinct social process, consisting of the mechanisms through which actors engaged in collective action: are involved in conflictual relations with clearly identified opponents; are linked by dense informal networks; share a distinct collective identity' (Della Porta and Diani 2006: 20).

## The Individual

Works on individual Islamist radicalization can be broadly classified in two categories: one descriptive, dealing with psychological and socio-economic profiles (Taarnby 2007; Leiken and Brooke 2006; Reinares 2006; Bakker 2008), at times linked to specific radicalization paths and motivations (Nesser 2006a), and the other analytical, in the sense that one is given explanations as to the 'why' and the 'how' of individual and group radicalization. The first approach has proved rather unhelpful beyond mere statistical description, due to the empirical heterogeneity of backgrounds on the one hand, and on the other, the gradual nature of socialization processes into terrorism, the incidence of 'supportive qualities' or 'lures', and the 'migration between roles' (Horgan 2008b: 84). The analytical approach can be again split into two—one is deterministic, in the tradition of the root causes of terrorism explanation and looking at individual or composite factors and triggers; and one developmental, based on the psychological and criminological concept of social learning and on social movement mechanisms of mobilization.

### *Deterministic Approaches*

Whereas psychological abnormality has been largely rejected as characteristic or cause of radicalization (Bakker 2006; Sageman 2008), various personal and structural specificities have been proposed as explanation instead. For the particular case of the Chechen Black Widows, Speckhard (2008: 1017) emphasized the role and consequences of psychological trauma in a conflict situation, associated with cultural and social conditionalities. Other commonly mentioned factors within this approach are marginalization, deprivation, alienation, discrimination, foreign policy, and overall being 'worse-off' than the majority population (Dittrich 2006; Nesser 2006b; Choudhury 2007; COT 2008). Not surprisingly, the list of structural strains has increased in recent years and with every new case. Ranstorp (2010: 4) speaks in the meantime about a 'kaleidoscope' of contributing factors, split into personal and global grievances that interact: internal— lack of public Muslim debate about the justification of violence, polarization, identity crisis, alienation, radical imams, the glorification of jihad and martyrdom, discrimination, stigmatization and criminalization of youths; and external—perceived injustice against Muslims abroad and Western double-standards, military intervention, and the 'changing role of global media and cyberspace', to which are added 'almost inexhaustible lists of precipitating factors'. It is apparent from this list that several levels of analysis have been gathered together: assumed causes, together with elements of discourse and facilitating factors. Taking these apart is not simply a matter of academic pedantry, but makes a difference in that certain elements may be considered as motivating factors, or, on the contrary, a matter of opportunity or chance, and therefore requesting different types of intervention. Special attention to the analysis of discourse is warranted from two points of view: first, in order to discern whether certain assertions are reflective of a previous state of things unleashing streams of thought and decision-making, or rather means to create certain frames of interpretation, readings of the reality and motivations; and second, to ascertain whether claims are the natural reflection of ideological discourse or indeed personal concerns.

But there are bigger problems with this approach than the question of how to organize and group contributory factors. One is clearly the ever increasing number of factors to the point of 'everything can lead to radicalization'. A second fundamental problem is the difficulty of showing causal relationships between the various determining factors and individual processes of radicalization. Taylor and Horgan (2001: 52, original emphasis) noted in relation to involvement in terrorism that

> whilst behaviour may well be determined by the contemporary and historical environment in which it occurs, analyses of this form overemphasize the *inevitability* of particular circumstances, giving a false sense of predictability and inevitability...whilst many people experience circumstances that may be correlated with induction into a terrorist lifestyle, relatively few people actually become violent terrorists.

While hypothesising that radicalization might occur against the background of political, spiritual, and social needs—search for meaning, injustice against Muslims and social belonging—Slootman and Tillie (2006: 5) admit that 'radicalization is dependent on accidents and coincidences in the surroundings of the individual personality'. Looking at the actual profiles of radicals, it becomes apparent that their socio-economic and educational profile is either above the average of their respective communities or reflects it. As Cesari (2008: 97) notes, 'the conventional image of the single, disenfranchised young man is not an accurate representation of reality'. In fact, attempts to identify a jihadi profile have failed so far. Nesser (2006a: 11) noted that

> uncovered jihadi cells in Europe have usually consisted of a diversified group of individuals, encompassing multiple different nationalities and ethnic backgrounds, ages, professions, family backgrounds and personalities. Because of this diversity, it is hard to establish the degree to which, or whether, social background variables matter in the recruitment process.

This should raise serious questions as to whether focusing on individual or structural characteristics is helpful at all in finding explanations for radicalization.

Another major issue has to do with methodology, in particular the ways to operationalize and measure contributory factors, such as applying minority or community statistics to individuals, mixing the individual with the organizational unit of analysis, or ignoring initial phases of the radicalization process. Mullins (2012: 117) for instance makes an argument that conditions in the West might play a role, among others because the Austrian alleged GIMF (Global Islamic Media Front) members mentioned the issue of student fees in their requests, ignoring the previous engagement in student politics of one of the individuals and the effects of the various stages of politicization on his development. Nesser (2006b: 337–8) developed a series of proxies to measure the impact of the Iraq war on the Madrid and van Gogh incidents, concluding that

> In the Madrid case, the Iraq link scored significantly on all proxies of analysis, indicating massive motivational spill-over from Iraq. In the Dutch case, the motivational landscape appeared to be more complex... the members of the Hofstad Network were mainly driven by grievances related to the domestic Dutch context, but there were indicators that the terrorists also were influenced by Al Qaeda's ideology of global *jihad* and the invasion and occupation of Iraq.

Methodologically, there are a series of issues connected to the way in which indicators were created and in particular what they are supposed to measure. Elements such as the modus operandi of the terrorist attack or the ideological profile of the terrorist networks are rather suited to explain organizational strategic behaviour rather than individual motivation, and that mostly in relation to objectives rather than causes. In other analyses, the Iraq war did not have any impact on the Madrid incident (Alonso 2010).

An aspect that should be taken into account when discussing the possible impact of macro-level variables, personal experiences, and events, especially when they relate to situations and individuals outside Europe, is that of perception and interpretation. In other words, the question to be asked should be not necessarily what their impact as such is, but rather how and to which extent certain circumstances and events, in themselves perhaps little significant, might be so formulated as to create a strong case for injustice, identifiable sources thereof and the dire need for action. Further, instead of conceptualizing events such as the war in Iraq or the Cartoons incident as 'causes' of radicalization, one might think about how they have been included in the broader narrative. Authors have constantly noticed the way in which recruiters play upon elements of discontent, at times of existential and personal nature, having to do with certain circumstances such as transition to adulthood, imprisonment, or conflict of generations (Wiktorowicz 2005; Neumann 2008). In this sense, external events are open to manipulation: 'These resources [Islamist media] have helped jihadists to use major issues—for example the war in Iraq—to radicalize and recruit young French and European Muslims' (Beyler 2006: 93). A more promising way therefore seems to be a focus on the mechanisms through which organizational and individual actors frame issues for purposes of resonance with a certain public, such as with the help of framing theory, as will be discussed.

## *Developmental Approaches: Process*

The second approach can be traced to the conceptual and theoretical evolution from 'root causes' to 'pathways', from 'determining' or 'contributing factors' to ways of involvement, personal histories, and processes (Horgan 2008b: 82); in a word, the 'how' rather than the 'why'. The concept of pathways can solve some of the problems associated with 'contributory factors', but arguably only in the understanding of 'mechanisms' which are liable to generalization. Indeed, some of the conceptualizations are in essence the same with those of contributory factors; Ranstorp (2010: 4) argues, for instance that there are: 'multiple pathways and speeds of progression, devotion and functions within groups'. This is in effect nothing else than postulating that pathways are as individual and potentially infinite in numbers as previously factors. Consistently, this leads to the unsatisfactory result of absence of theory:

> it seems unlikely that any single theory can integrate all the influences that bring individuals to radical political action, although a conceptual framework in which to view these influences may be possible... In every individual trajectory to terrorism of which we are aware, multiple mechanisms can be identified... there are multiple and diverse pathways leading individuals and groups to radicalization and terrorism. (McCauley and Moskalenko 2008: 429)

What basically occurs is an evolution from a search for commonalities at the level of features—psychological or socio-economic—through the realization of the high heterogeneity of backgrounds, to the adoption of idiosyncrasy at the level of pathways as a whole. The problem here is confusion between mechanisms and factors and between motivating mechanisms and concrete motivations. While there arguably are a multitude of concrete individual motivations and circumstances along the radicalization process, there is no apparent reason why common mechanisms and motivational variables might not constitute a general explanatory framework, such as the one proposed by Taylor and Horgan (2001).

Another aspect relates to the nature and incidence of various radicalization factors and mechanisms along the radicalization process. While most accounts conceptualize them as 'reactive' (McCauley and Moskalenko 2008: 430), some speak about gains, 'lures', or positive incentives (Horgan 2005). Taylor and Quayle (1994: 21, 28) identified several 'rewards' for engagement in terrorist attacks and general involvement: meeting cultural stereotypes and gaining kudos, status, endorsement by peers and family, and the continuity of behaviour with the past. In more recent analyses and specifically for radical Islamists, selective incentives such as 'being a hero' or reaching 'glory' were found (Roy 2007; Sageman 2007). The way such incentives might function was explained by using the social learning theory in criminology, which postulates the adoption of rules and values based on the feedback of the social environment—the observation of models and rewards and punishments received (Bandura 1973), and conceptualized as behavioural reinforcers (Taylor and Horgan 2001) and as occupational motivational variables (Pisoiu 2011).

Related to this and along the idea of process rather than multiple pathways, it is of relevance to think about the ways in which various mechanisms can be identified within the process, at which level and with which function. In other words, mechanisms might not necessarily be individual or path-specific, but simply occurring at different stages of the process. As Horgan (2008b: 81) noted, 'answering questions about why people may wish to initially become involved in terrorism may have little bearing on what they do (or are permitted to do) as terrorists or how they actually become engaged in specific terrorist operations'. Taking for instance the set of radicalization mechanisms proposed by McCauley and Moskalenko (2008) and grouped by individual, group, and mass radicalization, several observations can be made. First, it needs to be noticed that group mechanisms intervene in individual radicalization as well, whereas lone-wolf phenomena are virtually non-existent (Kaplan et al. 2014). Further, some of the mechanisms presented as individual pathways (personal victimization, political grievance, joining a radical group: slippery slope towards more extreme behaviour, and the power of love: network of friends, lovers, and family) might and usually do combine in actual biographies. In fact, the role of social networks in joining (Sageman 2004) is one of the few generally acknowledged constant ingredients of radicalization processes. Mechanisms such as the slippery slope were already found to occur as a matter of common evolution within terrorist groups (Brown 1986). In the few holistic theoretical attempts (Horgan 2008b; Pisoiu 2011), a series of mechanisms were found along the radicalization process, such as status, the community feedback, the gradual isolation from the previous social environment into exclusive milieux and the decrease in relevance of alternatives, and including two of the ones proposed by the two authors: 'extreme cohesion under isolation and threat' and the dehumanization of the enemy. Others, such as competition for the same basis of support, competition with state power, and within-group competition, could be elements of a more elaborated model which would also include interactions of the organization with the state and other organizations. These types of developments might of course also be studied at the level of sheer organizational behaviour, with the observation that what one would explain at that point would be 'radicalization' in the sense of use or increase of use of violence, and/or the group ideology becoming more extreme.

One of the more complex questions is that of the relationship between the cognitive and the behavioural level. In other words, how does an individual evolve from particular ideas to actual actions and, further, how do individuals come to adopt new ideas in the first place, especially if in contradiction with existent ones? A relatively high quantity of scholarship has been produced on the content and rooting of the Al-Qaeda ideology, or what has been labelled Global Salafi Jihad or jihadism (Sageman 2004; Wiktorowicz 2005, 2006). Attempts to situate it within Wahhabism and Salafism were criticized by Hellmich (2008), with the argument that 'Wahhabism has evolved from its traditional beginnings, and its standards have moderated to a certain degree over the past century' (2008: 114), and given the diversity and inconsistencies within the Salafi movement (2008: 118). Wesley (2008) argues along similar lines, noting that movements with the same ideology will promote different messages, which would render the focus on Salafism in general relatively useless, and that many recruits joined without having a full understanding of the jihadist ideology. Some other authors focused on individual features of the jihadist discourse, such as parallels with the Western non-liberal schools of thought (Jones and Smith 2010), the multitude of aims, values, rationales, and identities (Michelsen 2009), the evolution towards common goals in the form of the global war against the West (Nesser 2011), or the narrative elements of the jihadi rhetoric: persecution, precedent, piety, and perseverance, similar to the IRA case (Ryan 2007). The relevance of studying ideological contents needs to be relativized in light of the critique advanced by Taylor and Horgan (2001: 48), who outline the 'fundamental distinction between ideology as a *process* (structuring and influencing behaviour) and the content of *particular* ideologies. The extent to which ideology controls and influences our behaviour may be seen as something apart from particular ideological prescriptions, which contain as it were the content of a particular ideology.'

The more appropriate question therefore is: what are the mechanisms through which ideological discourse has an effect on behaviour? How are radical ideas adopted in the first place and how do they influence behaviour? Two approaches have been developed to answer this question: one psychological revolving around the concept of 'cognitive opening' and one sourced in social movement theory based on the concept of 'frame resonance'.

## Cognitive Openings

The concept of 'cognitive opening' was first proposed by Wiktorowicz (2005) in a three-stage model of engagement in Islamist activism. In the first stage an interest for the radical movement develops which is triggered by a cognitive opening which 'shakes certitude in previously accepted beliefs' and creates a willingness of exposure to 'new ways of thinking and worldviews'. 'Religious seeking', the second stage, is one of coping with the state of cognitive crisis, where 'religious meaning' helps in finding answers. The final stage is engagement in risky activism (Wiktorowicz 2005: 5–6). The crises determining the cognitive openings are either independent or induced by movement activists and can be economic (losing a job, blocked mobility), social or cultural (cultural weakness, racism, humiliation), political (repression, torture, political discrimination), and personal crises such as death or victimization by crime (Wiktorowicz 2005: 20). Grievances like conflict between the mores in the West and the Islamic law, assimilation vs. maintenance of cultural identity, Islamophobia, racism, exclusion, unemployment, and relative deprivation determine in their turn these crises (Wiktorowicz 2005: 89–91). Horgan's (2008b) model revolves around an element similar to that of cognitive opening determined by a set of exceptional circumstances. He argues that an 'openness to socialization into terrorism' is determined by certain 'predisposing risk factors' (2008b: 84), in the form of: emotional vulnerability—anger, alienation, disenfranchisement, dissatisfaction with the current activity and seeing terrorism as necessary, identification with victims, sense of reward, kinship or other social ties (2008b: 84–5). Common to both models are the role of social networks and the rational choice aspect of 'selective incentives', placed at the end of the process where salvation or 'paradise' is conditioned by engagement in violence (Wiktorowicz 2005: 175–8), and among the other predisposing factors, respectively.

The model developed by Wilner and Dubouloz (2011) rests on the transformative learning theory from education and rehabilitation science and looks at the psycho-cognitive processes associated with radicalization, the 'psycho-cognitive construction of new definitions of self', 'ideological learning': the 'internalizing [of] the rationales that legitimize violent behavior' (Wilner and Dubouloz 2011: 419). Their model is also based on an initial moment of 'crisis', or 'trigger phase', determining a cognitive opening for new sets of beliefs and values which are adopted, then cemented through confirmation from the social environment and which eventually legitimize violence. Triggers determining the initial crisis are both structural and personal, in a sense the same as the original 'contributing factors': socio-political alienation, foreign policy, crisis events and dilemmas that 'lead to critical reflection and reassessment of one's life, current social position, future ambitions, and personal relationships that can restructure an individual's meaning perspective' (Wilner and Dubouloz 2011: 423). Subsequent to the moment of crisis, existing ways of interpreting experiences are challenged by the 'Islam–West dichotomy' and replaced with the new reality. Finally, by 'socializing with like-minded individuals, the new identity is strengthened. With peer-based validation, the transformation is reinforced' (Wilner and Dubouloz 2011: 423). Violence is a result of the individual's newly acquired value system: 'Changes in behaviour (including violent behaviour) is one product of the outcome phase and is a reflection of the solidification and empowerment of the individual's new meaning perspective, belief system, and identity' (Wilner and Dubouloz 2011: 423).

There are a series of difficulties associated with certain aspects of these models: first, of course, the necessary existence of one or several moments of crisis; related to this, the incidence of meta-level variables as triggers for crises, such as alienation or foreign policy, which brings us back to the specificity argument. Further, it might be indeed difficult to pin down such a sudden cognitive shift, given that the nature of the crises considered for radicalization do not have the quality of existential threat encountered in health science for instance. Apart from that, the general development of the radicalization process has been found to occur in an incremental manner, of 'small steps', rather than sudden transformation or breach. A second point of critique relates to the actual assimilation of new sets of values and beliefs. The models do not offer a deeper account of how this might occur, beyond a simplistic assessment of initial replacement and subsequent validation by the social environment. It should be safe to assume that learning would occur on the basis of previously acquired schemata, rather than on a 'tabula rasa' basis, and that the social environment has a role to play along the entire process of learning, and not just towards its end. A third relates to the incidence of precisely religious tenets as reservoirs of new meaning perspectives. There seems to be an assumption that religion or a particular religious-ideological discourse would be the only resource for this redefinition of views, or that a certain causal connection would exist between crisis and religious seeking. Whereas it might be accurate to assume that deep existential crises might lead to an increase in or search for spirituality, it is debatable whether this scheme could be superposed on a process of, essentially, politicization and increasing militant engagement.

There are, however, also significant findings in these models: the role of social validation in the process of adopting new ideas and the fact that behaviour, including violence, becomes legitimated by the existence of new values and rules. The latter is consistent with the findings of other models analysing discourse (see the Discourse sub-section).

*Discourse*

Another way to look at the relationship between ideas and behaviour is at the level of discourse and its persuasion potential. The role of narratives has been acknowledged in the literature, yet usually in a descriptive manner, without going more into the details of how certain interpretations are internalized and further influence behaviour. Payne (2009) compares the Al-Qaeda with the UK and US propaganda narratives, the elements of conflict between the West and Islam, self-defence, and the legitimacy of jihad on the one hand, and the dichotomy moderates–extremists, terror as illegitimate, and the idea of Britishness as open, liberal, and inclusive, on the other. Some work has been done based on framing theory in social movements, particularly the description of two elements of frame resonance: empirical resonance and the credibility of the frame articulators. Lia (2008: 4) explained the attractiveness of the Al-Qaeda narrative through three elements of resonance: foreign occupation, religious desecration, and economic imperialism. Wiktorowicz (2005) elaborates at length on the various elements of credibility of the frame articulators: reputation, authenticity, sacred authority, knowledge, character, and personality. Other explored mechanisms of persuasion pertaining to the jihadi narrative and discourse are that of building a differential and strong collective identity around the ideas of vanguard, exceptionality of piety, and the value of dying for the cause of jihad (Cheong and Halverson 2010), the generation of collective action frames by social actors such as Al-Qaeda around a sense of injustice (Hellmich 2010), frame alignment between the beliefs of potential recruits and the movement's narrative (Neumann 2008), or rhetorical mechanisms of moral justification to neutralize inhumane behaviour (Cottee 2010). The exploration of the role of discourse and framing for the understanding of processes of ideological adherence and behavioural change is still in an initial stage. The approaches are largely descriptive—they identify relevant elements of discourse and acknowledge the interplay of mechanisms such as frame alignment, yet fail to go deeper into how these mechanisms might in fact work at the individual and group level. More importantly, an analytical differentiation needs to be made concerning the mere correspondence between parts of the message and recipients' opinions, and the actual creation of new frames of interpretation, whose resonance with the recipient would rely on deeper levels of meaning—beliefs and values. Finally, apart from the unidirectional production of meaningful frames—from the organization to the public or from the recruiter to the recruitee, the emergence of frames within social interaction also needs to be explored.

## Communities, Culture, Identity

Apart from individuals and social movements, communities or 'Muslims in Europe' also come up as being radicalized in various ways. The meaning of the term here is not only in the sense of radical political activism with the potential of eventual engagement in terrorism, but a broader variety of manifestations: violent and non-violent, political and non-political, religious and non-religious. Labels vary from legal protest to radical Islam, Islamism, non-integration, nationalist struggle, Salafism or Jihadism, the common denominator being that they involve individuals who are Muslim. This is then associated with particular characteristics assumed specific to the 'Muslim community'—socio-economic and educational underperformance, discrimination and marginalization, structural and cultural challenges facing traditional communities, as well as affective and narrative continuity with countries of origin and the respective situations of grievance and conflict. While all these indicators might be true (though one could argue, in differentiated ways for different generations and ethnic groups), this type of causal relationship is highly problematic as there is no reason why these particular characteristics, or at least in this composition should lead to radicalization. In other words, the protests against the war in Iraq might have been pushed by a sense of cultural relatedness and injustice, and not necessarily by the socio-economic situation; on the reverse, the 2005 riots in Paris could be safely classified within socio-economic protest rather than caused by cultural disintegration, for instance. A highly problematic assumption stands at the basis of this association: that Islamist radicalization in Europe would be a sui generis phenomenon and having to do with the quality of being Muslim or Muslim in Europe. We speak therefore not about Islamist radicalization as a variation of radicalization in general, but rather of the *radicalization of Muslims*. Consequently, the types of explanations are also drawn from the assumed particularities of the Muslim community, inherent or circumstantial. The argument goes: terrorist or violent radicals are naturally a minority, which however emerges from a broader community and due to conditions affecting this broader community and not others. The focus of the research is therefore to discern these specificities.

The approach to community radicalization is usually placed within historical and cultural accounts by country experts (Beyler 2006; Abbas 2007; Amghar 2009; Belarouci 2009; Briggs and Birdwell 2009; Veldhuis and Bakker 2009). For the countries with colonial and work immigration, the attitude of the receiving majority towards immigrants appears to have evolved from initial ignorance to panic at the shock of a 'dangerous otherness'. At the arrival of 'guest workers' from various Muslim countries to Western Europe there was a perception on both sides that this would be temporary, so that there was little incentive to integrate, physically or culturally, in the host society or for the latter to acknowledge their presence for that matter, a situation which surprisingly perpetuated even after the waves of family reunification, where it became *de facto* clear that these people were going to stay. In a second phase, a series of historical events, like the Palestinian intifada in 1987, Salman Rushdie's *Satanic Verses* in 1988, the Gulf War, and the progression of radical Islam in Algeria, gradually 'radicalized' these communities—which is an umbrella term for the rising of political awareness, interest, and position-taking towards events occurring in the Muslim world and episodes of violence. Several types of violence are included here, from demonstrations to riots to assassinations and terror attacks, and also included are the influence of Islamist ideologies and groups, such as with the appearance in the 1980s of dissidents from the Middle East, the Maghreb, and Pakistan, in Barnes's (2006: 2) words, 'a polyglot group of intellectuals, preachers, financiers, arms traders, technology specialists, forgers, travel organizers and foot soldiers'. Vidino (2005: 20) argues that 'The mosques and networks established by them [asylum-seekers] went on to radicalize thousands of immigrant or European-born Muslims.' The 1990s brought an additional layer: the awareness of the existence of various Islamist groups and organizations and their proselytizing activities, such as Milli Görüs, the Tabligh, Salafis, and neo-Salafis like Hizbut-Tahrir and Al Muhajiroun, in a constellation of religious or religious-political orientation, national and international focus. A recent development is the emergence of the debates around the issues of marginalization and stigmatization of Muslims in Europe, integration and parallel societies.

Explanations of community radicalization in Western Europe occur along four dimensions: one is through the establishment of a relationship with conditions and developments existing in the Middle East, including ideological influences. Roy (2008a) calls this a 'vertical approach', one which basically follows the history of Islamic fundamentalism, political Islam, and political conflicts with Western powers up to the present date and further focuses on a loose association of Muslims and violence, from ethno-cultural to delinquency and terrorism. Muslim communities in Europe either find themselves in identical situations of strain as those abroad, or brought these along to the continent. Abbas (2007) paints the picture of a historical Muslim sufferance and resistance against Western colonial and capitalistic powers—the 'radicalization of Islam', a context in which the marginalization of Muslims in Western Europe is then inscribed. Kilcullen (2007: 649) argues that European Muslims have brought 'grievances and political divisions from their countries of origin'. Finally, Speckhard (2009: 151) differentiates between the first generation of immigrants, having family and tribal ties with the countries of origin, and therefore being concerned about what occurs there, and the indoctrinated second and third generations. This occurs through the exploitation of marginalization, frustration, and prejudice, and the virtual 'bringing home' of conflicts 'by showing videos, graphic pictures and giving descriptions of how Muslims in Palestine, Kashmir, Chechnya, Iraq and Afghanistan suffer under what they claim is direct or indirect Western oppression'.

The second approach looks at the frictions arising from the condition of being a minority, in a different cultural environment: the erosion of traditions and moral codes, the conflict of cultures and generations, disintegration and identity issues as being in-between. The third and usually added on the second is the specific condition of the Muslim minority which suffers from assumed Muslim specific grievances: marginalization and discrimination. Finally, a broader crisis dimension is that of post-modernity, with excessive individualism and loss of meaning, which supposedly affects Muslim minorities to a greater extent, given their propensity towards communitarianism. The four dimensions are at times treated in a conglomerate with emphases on certain aspects. Common to all is the apprehension of the added-value jihadism is supposed to bring—that of a surrogate, strong identity, meaning and mission in life.

Roy's (2004) explanatory framework is a good example of the second and third approach. He emphasizes the element of marginalization and loss of identity, in a situation of break with pristine cultures:

> All of these preachers and organizations target second-generation Muslims, explicitly playing on their sense of being victims of racism, exclusion and loneliness in the West, and hence are very successful among Blacks or non-Muslim members of the underclass, as well as gaoled petty criminals. They offer a valorising substitute identity: members of the vanguard of internationalist jihadists who fight the global superpower and the international system. (Roy 2004: 309)

Different to the first approach, Roy dismisses the idea of a continuity with the countries of origin, and thus, *de facto*, the concept of a Muslim Diaspora: 'Relations between militants and their country of origin are weak or non-existent; we are facing not a diaspora but a truly deterritorialised population. Almost none of the militants fought in his own country, or in his family's country of origin (except some Pakistanis)' (Roy 2004: 305). Khosrokhavar (2005: 155) finds that the cultural identity issue is not so much one of lost identity but rather of being in-between cultures which leads to 'existential rupture', triggering a rejection of the West. Second, he reintroduces the initial link to communities at home, through the concept of 'humiliation by proxy'. Humiliation is a central concept of his explanatory framework and concretizes in three variations:

> First, there is the humiliation they experience in everyday life because they feel that they have been economically marginalized and made feel socially inferior, as is the case with the excluded Maghrebin youth in France, or young West Indians and Pakistanis in Great Britain. Second, thanks to the media, they experience the humiliation of the Muslim world in Bosnia, Afghanistan, Iraq or Palestine. Mechanisms of identification then lead to the internalization of that feeling. Finally, there is sometimes a feeling that their immersion in the Western world has defiled them... Taking part in the operations of a group that is fighting Western hegemony and arrogance inside the West gives the individual a new sense of pride and restores his lost dignity. (Khosrokhavar 2005: 152)

An additional dimension of identity crisis is that of the post-modern society (Khosrokhavar 2005; Belarouci 2009), with a particular effect on Muslims: the multicultural city is 'lonely and insular' especially for 'people from the Islamic world, where the quest for a community or *umma* is part of their imaginary' (Khosrokhavar 2005: 158). Anonymity and individualism are destabilizing, disintegrating and threaten the traditional social and family links, thus opening the door to virtual identities.

There are a series of problems associated with this approach. First, again, the specificity argument—the difficulty of explaining why, if presumably these aspects affect an entire community or parts of it, only a few individuals actually radicalize. As Dalgaard-Nielsen (2010: 801) rightly notes:

> Why is it that only a small minority of the individuals exposed to the same structural influences eventually turn to violent groups? What accounts for the difference between the minority, which reacts to the overall socioeconomic, political, and cultural context, with violence and those who instead chose to become engaged in constitutional politics, those who remain apolitical, and those who seek meaning in an introspective religious movement?

Difficulties also arise regarding the incidence of economic grievances. Thus, Roy (2004: 324) asserts that the motivation to join Al-Qaeda is not born out of a 'depressed social or economic' situation, yet the parallel to the leftist movements as well as the underlying logic of working-class protest 'in depressed housing estates and degraded inner cities' seem to speak to the contrary. The very assumption of causality between individual radicalization and involvement in terrorism—since in the end this is the level at which radicalization becomes visible—and the situation of particular communities needs to be treated with caution. Problematic are arguments such that the fact that European individuals fought in various conflicts abroad is a proof of 'extensive radicalization of large segments of the European Muslim population' (Vidino 2005: 20). On the reverse, the fact that certain communities might display features of marginalization or discrimination does not automatically lead to the conclusion that precisely these features are drivers of individual radicalization. In other words, while the socio-economic and cultural diagnoses might be correct, the causal connection to radicalization is highly questionable.

An obvious contradiction within this approach marks the existence of a link with the countries of origin, i.e. whether there is a Diaspora or rather a deterritorialized, uprooted, global, virtual community. Reference to the radicalization of specific ethnic communities is complicated by the fact that groups and cells display more and more a mixed national and ethnic background, not to speak of the presence of converts. The concept of a Muslim community is weakened by the still prominent ethnic identification and separation of the various communities. A concept such as that of 'humiliation by proxy' presupposes the existence of a community link which religion as such can hardly provide. Something of the sort of a 'fictive kin' emergent in religious communities (Speckhard and Ahkmedova 2006) or the type of group identity subordinating that of the individual specific to protest movements would by definition need the respective contact and group mechanisms. In fact, some authors argue that the 'Muslim community' or the (only) existence of a Muslim identity is in fact constructed. Roy (2004: 132–3) explains this through the creation of 'Muslim' as a neo-ethnic category understood in anthropological terms and Islam as the culture of a neo-ethnic group which 'creates a common conceptual ground between Western categories and the strategy of would-be community leaders to reconstruct a "Muslim" community on a basis that can fit Western cultural and legal categories of identities'. Barnes (2006: 17–18) argues against the forcing into one identity, that of Muslim (and this explanation assumes that there is a Muslim identity) by faith schools and census questions, because one has multiple identities and should be allowed to choose what one wants to be or be most. Taking this further, Al-Azmeh (2006: 10) speaks about the creation of 'virtual communities' with 'imagined origins, confirming alienation', the creation of extra-territoriality through special laws and increased authorities to the imams, based on the assumption that 'Arab countries being predominantly Muslim, it is somehow natural that their inhabitants would gravitate towards Islamist political creeds.' What these arguments in fact imply is that precisely the elements of uprootedness, difference, and propensity to protest might in fact become a self-fulfilling prophecy and something that the community approach, with the assumed specifics associated with the 'Muslims', would actually create rather than combat. As some authors have noted, policies aimed at countering violent extremism and targeting entire Muslim communities entail the danger of constructing 'suspect communities' and thus negatively impacting community cohesion, or even acting as triggers of radicalization (Vermeulen 2014).

The scholarship on radicalization in Russia could be partly situated within the second and third approach, in particular the arguments relating to the collapse or the challenging of traditional social and religious structures and to situations of socio-economic and political grievance. On the reverse, the socio-economic prosperity in Tartarstan is for instance considered as one of the reasons why the radical threat here is 'at the political margins' (Khurmatullin 2010: 118). With regard to the factors leading to an increase in preponderance of the 'new religiosity' or new Islamic fundamentalism, a series of parallels can be drawn between Russia and Western Europe. These are the Salafi penetration from Saudi Arabia and Central Asia, the proselytizing of organizations such as Hizb ut-Tahrir and Jamaat e-Tabligh, and in the North Caucasus the targeted actions of Salafis challenging clan and ethnic structures, addressing social problems and promoting individual access to the content of the Qur'an (Khurmatullin 2010; Malashenko 2006; Yemelianova 2010). Interestingly and different from some of the Western European analyses, these elements are supposed to explain just that, the phenomenon of increasing Islamization, and not jihadism or engagement in violence. The latter is related to enduring political and economic grievances and the appropriation of the separatist struggle by the mujahideen:

> In Chechnya, war conditions predetermined a constituent prevalence of the jihadist form of Islamic activism. The major agents of radical Islam there were foreign *mujahidin* (Islamic fighters), who came to assist their Islamic brethren in fighting the jihad against the Russian invasion; and radical Dagestani Wahhabis, who fled to Chechnya in the late 1990s. (Yemelianova 2010: 131, original emphasis)

Clearly, in this case there is no need for mechanisms such as that of 'humiliation by proxy'. The few analyses of individual motivations in fact relate to actual experiences of psychological trauma combined with an ideology more nationalistic in nature than jihadi *per se* (Speckhard and Ahkmedova 2006).

# Main Debates Around Islamist Radicalization

## Home-Grown Radicalization

Subsequent to the 7 July bombings in London and the realization that the perpetrators were 'born and bred' in Europe, the topic of 'home-grown radicalization' took an important place in the academic and policy debates. Apart from the difficulty of placing motivation within the usual oppression/frustration complex specific to environments outside Europe, security considerations also came into play. A threat coming from the inside is more intensely perceived, not only because it 'comes from our midst' but also because it is more difficult to recognize and control. Making matters worse, one of the trends in the following years was the presence not only of 'born and bred' individuals, but also of those without specific religious or migration backgrounds—the convert phenomenon. This clearly had implications for the conceptualization of the entire radicalization phenomenon—as movement, network, or part of the global jihad or indeed European.

The meaning of 'home-grown' evolves broadly around two dimensions: linkage to the West, and to a terrorist organization abroad. Crone and Harrow (2010: 4, original emphasis) call these '*belonging* in the West' and '*autonomy* from terrorist groups abroad', with several indicators for each. While operational autonomy is relatively easy to assess, belonging to the West involves more complex aspects; indicators may be nationality or country of origin, the amount of time spent in Europe, whereby it is also not straightforward what for instance 'formative years' would mean, or the place of radicalization as mentioned by Mullins (2012: 111), whereby the geographical location might have little to do with the social environment, especially if we think about isolated communities. One could of course stretch the discussion to other levels, such as root causes or ideology. In this sense, the question would become: are the driving forces behind radicalization endogenous or exogenous to the European socio-political space? And is ideology based on European concepts and principles or rather external? As discussed already, approaches differ: authors speak about a jihadi 'movement' in the tradition of the European protest movements, completely separated from the socio-political realities of the Muslim world, a de-territorialized, virtual community. Some others see, on the contrary, a clear continuity of both ideology and grievance between political Islam and the current jihadism. Given these difficulties and the continuously changing nature of radicalization and recruitment, it is difficult to produce an accurate and especially durable assessment. What can in any case safely be argued is that an entirely home-grown radicalization is not probable, given the global nature of ideology and networks. Operationally, Crone and Harrow (2010: 5) noted that 'More recent cases indicate that individuals increasingly seek out accessible terrorist communities abroad in countries, such as Pakistan, Yemen, Chechnya, or Somalia.' Similarly, Kilcullen (2007: 649) finds that 'most terrorist incidents on European soil since 9/11 have *not* been purely home-grown, but have drawn on sponsorship, support or guidance from AQ [Al-Qaeda]'. Finally, the prime example, 7 July and the 2006 airline bombing plot, eventually showed 'clear links to senior Al Qaeda commanders operating in Pakistan's lawless frontier border area with Afghanistan' (Hoffman 2009: 1100; see also Barbieri and Klausen 2012 for a similar assessment of the London-based jihadi movement up to 2008).

## Internet

Apprehensions of the role of the internet in the radicalization process vary from a type of use which is in no way specific to Islamist radicals—namely that of communication, source of knowledge, and social networking—to specific functions replacing real-life situations, such as in the case of training (Kohlmann 2008). Paz (2009: 116) calls the internet 'the Open University for Militant Jihadi Studies' and argues that 'militant jihadi movements, groups, clerics, and scholars, turned the Internet into their main, and sometimes only, vehicle for propaganda, indoctrination, publicity, and teaching of their messages. Their "soft power" is the Internet.' More differentiated views see it not as a unidirectional communication channel, but rather as a platform of discussion where various types of information and interpretations interact and compete: 'Thanks to the perpetual beta, everything, whether a product of states or militants, is open to challenge on the Internet' (Ryan 2010: 678). Through the intermediary mechanisms of social networking and previous involvement in support activities, Bowman-Grieve (2010: 83) finds virtual community involvement as a 'potential pathway towards radicalization'. Neumann (2008: 55) goes further to argue that the internet has become a social environment where certain views and behaviours are 'normalized' and more extreme ones even encouraged—a phenomenon of 'hyper-radicalization'. This would be an equivalent of the 'real world' video-watching conspiratorial apartments and group mechanisms of intensification of opinions. Finally, in spite of the availability, in the meantime, of significant amounts of operational information online, empirical evidence shows that Al-Qaeda has not pursued online jihadi training (Stenersen 2008), that cells aim at and usually go through 'real' training (Nesser 2008; Stenersen 2008), and that the latter is in a direct relationship with operational effectiveness (Gohel 2009). Kenney (2010) explains this through the differentiation between *techne* (abstract technical knowledge) and *metis* (experiential knowledge) and argues that the internet cannot provide *mētis*. This could be also a plausible argument why one could not speak of an overall 'online radicalization', since, while social networking, information, perhaps to some extent also group pressure can develop virtually, for operational skills and resources resort to the real world would be necessary.

## Prisons and Universities

Prisons and universities as hubs of radicalization slid into focus after the observation that high numbers of violent radicals had higher education and/or criminal backgrounds and that in some cases the process of radicalization occurred or deepened in these locations (Reinares 2006; Gutiérrez et al. 2008; Brandon 2009, 2011; Alonso 2012). While accounts of university radicalization usually focus on the role of radicalizing agents, in the case of prisons several explanations were proposed having to do with the particular condition of the environment and that of the individual in this environment, i.e. vulnerability in a situation of stress and alienation, an existential crisis of finding a new path after failure (Neumann 2008), or indeed an ideology that expresses anger and anti-establishment attitudes (Beyler 2006). These aspects need to be treated with caution in view of several considerations. One has to do with the assumed automatic link between certain experiences and radical Islam—similarly to the argument of identity crisis in general. As Olsen (2008: 4) notes, 'for some inmates, conversion processes lead to radical Islam, while for other inmates they represent a movement away from radicalization—representing instead a way of obtaining a more nuanced and inclusive understanding of Islam'. And indeed such transformations have the potential of reversibility, if one thinks about the general reinsertion mechanisms involved: 'many of those who adopt radical ideologies in prison, whether out of conviction or for more pragmatic reasons, often discard their extremist beliefs on their return to mainstream society' (Brandon 2009: 4). On a broader level, it appears difficult to show that the actual radicalization process—and not just conversion or the Salafization of student societies for that matter—and the conditions conducive to it pertain to these environments or (also) have to do with previous experiences. A more promising avenue seems to be the consideration of prisons and universities as forums, platforms for the exchange of ideas and social networking, much like mosques or cafés for instance, where it might or might not come to the presence and influence of certain individuals and messages or the effect of group mechanisms.

## Role of Religion

That the religion Islam cannot be considered as a cause of radicalization has become a generally acknowledged fact. A series of religion-related aspects, however, have made their way into discussions, such as religiosity and Islamic fundamentalism. In the conceptualization of radicalization as a reaction to post-modernity, religiosity is the *de facto* state of being radical. Khosrokhavar (2005: 156) argues that the fight against Evil becomes an 'existential project' and is similar to modern cultist mechanisms: 'The Manichaeism of this religiosity overcomes the discontent of our late modernity, which offers us no more than quasi-convictions and imperfect motives, a mental landscape painted in half-tones, and a vision of self and other that oscillates between narcissism and rejection.' Similarly, Belarouci (2009: 11) argues that 'the return to religion appears as a response to the profound unease present in most societies. Indeed, religion seems to be designed to supply the answer to the question "who am I?" It promotes the construction of a personal identity for the individual and a cultural identity for the group', and she cites studies showing that there is a link between exclusion, discrimination, and ostentatious display of religion. The problem here of course is that, while the case might be made that new religiosity emerges as a reaction to post-modern anxiety, it is not clear that this is indeed applicable to the type of political radicalization we are looking at. Individual biographies of violent radicals for instance suggest that motivations are usually mundane, political, and unlikely to be inscribed in this type of intellectualized existential crisis. An interesting hypothesis was proposed by Aly and Striegher (2012), who differentiate between a pre-radicalization phase, where religion might offer answers to personal issues, and a radicalization phase, when violent behaviour is triggered by factors of another nature, such as group mechanisms and personal benefits.

With regard to Islamic fundamentalism, Slootman and Tillie's, by their own assessment, most important conclusion from their research is that 'the religious and political dimensions are *independent* of each other. This means that orthodoxy does not lead automatically to political discontent (and from there to potential radicalization), and vice versa. It is important to recognize this. Someone who is orthodox is not *per se* radical, nor will this person automatically become radical' (2006: 4, original emphasis). Others, however, do focus on strands such as the Salafis or the Tabligh as possible factors of pre-radicalization. This has not only an analytical relevance, but also at the level of policy, since one of the questions posed in counter-radicalization decision-making processes is whether to engage in partnerships with organizations which voice fundamentalist messages or not. In other words, the question is: are they 'conveyor belts' or 'firewalls'?

From the point of view of the discursive commonalities between the Islamist messages and that of Al-Qaeda, several pro and con arguments have been proposed. Neumann (2008: 32) finds that organizations such as Hizb-ut Tahrir, the Tabligh, and al-Muhajiroun are gateway organizations which play three roles: socialization in milieux that can include violent extremists, indoctrination into a mindset that legitimizes the use of violence for political and religious purposes, and subversion—the promotion of ideas coming against democracy and social cohesion. Vidino (2009) advances the hypothesis that such organizations might play the role of arsonists, pushing a message that plays on the separate identity of Muslims as well as the alleged persecution to which Muslims are subjected in Europe and which taken to its logical end justifies violence. In the words of a former activist, non-violent Islamists 'advocate separatist, confrontational ideas that, followed to their logical conclusion, lead to violence. At the very least, the rhetoric of radicals provides the mood music to which suicide bombers dance' (Vidino 2009: 72). On the reverse, precisely this commonality of message has been considered as a plus in the attempt to limit the influence of violent radical ideas. Moskalenko and McCauley (2009: 240) argue that such organizations are in fact a competitor for Al-Qaeda, given the similarity of goals. Amghar (2009: 38) states that 'this form of religious radicalism and the anti-French tirades of its militants act as a sort of "safety valve" that diverts the militants from direct action'. The problem might be of course the fact that there is no a priori reason why individuals should choose a pacifist rather than a violent way to live out their ideology. In fact, in some accounts (Husain 2007), precisely the militancy of some organizations made them more attractive for potential recruits. In pragmatic policy terms, however, the case could be made that targeted deradicalization could have something to gain from this ideological interrelatedness. Lambert in Jackson (2008: 298) makes the point that 'Salafi and Islamist community groups in London often have the best tools with which to undermine al-Qaida propaganda within their own youth communities.' Lambert (2009: 69–70) also argues that because Al-Qaeda distorts these ideologies, they are the best suited to combat it; additionally, they are the best placed to recognize radicalization and recruitment processes where they occur. Still along the ideological component coupled with policy considerations, a different aspect is, beyond the priority of combating jihadism, the potential anti-democratic and anti-community cohesion implications such a world-view might entail (Paris 2007). Belarouci (2009: 17) argues that non-violent organizations are in fact more dangerous because they promote non-integration.

Apart from the strict ideological level and considering a developmental approach to radicalization, one needs to consider the potential social networking role of such organizations, in the sense of facilitators of contacts and meeting places. This is a promising way to understand jihadis' previous associations with non-violent organizations such as Hizbut-Tahrir or Tabligh, as listed by Barnes (2006) and Hoffman (2009). Beyler (2006: 95) argues that 'selected *tabligh* believers are indeed sent to attend Pakistani madrassas—known by the intelligence community to be safe havens for terrorists—in order to deepen their religious knowledge'. Briggs and Birdwell (2009: 110) note that 'these organisations can find themselves being used as convenient spaces for individuals to convene—often in the margins—where the culpability of the organization is due more to its poor visibility and governance than a commitment to violence'.

## Deradicalization

The scholarship on Islamist deradicalization in Europe has developed to a lesser extent than the one on radicalization and has generally focused either on individual processes, or the assessment of deradicalization programmes. To a greater extent than within the radicalization scholarship, parallels have been noted to involvement in other types of political violence, gangs, criminal lifestyle, religious movements, racist and right-wing extremism: 'although the political and ideological content may be different, the social and psychological processes involved may well be rather similar, or at least comparable' (Bjørgo and Horgan 2009: 2–3). An important and perhaps counterintuitive finding is that deradicalization should not be understood simply as the reverse of the radicalization process. Horgan (2008a: 3) noted that 'answering questions about what keeps people involved with a terrorist movement may have surprisingly little, if any, bearing on what subsequently causes them to disengage from terrorist operations or from the organization (and/or broader network or movement) altogether'. Finally, different to most accounts on radicalization, it would appear that behavioural change does not necessarily follow cognitive change and may in some cases not occur at all—thus the differentiation between deradicalization and disengagement:

> When they leave terrorist or other extremist groups and behaviours, some individuals are stripped of their radical views as a *consequence* of having left the group rather than being a cause for leaving. Thus, people often re-adjust their value system in order to make it in accordance with their new patterns of behaviour. However, there are also some individuals who distance themselves from the extremist group and its violent means, but retain their extremist views on society. (Bjørgo and Horgan 2009a: 3)

This has clear application in deradicalization programmes and concerning the question of which one is more efficient and more realistic to aim for. Silke (2011: 18) argues for instance that 'deradicalising prisoners—which requires changing their mindset and ideological beliefs—is exceedingly difficult'. Furthermore, given that the immediate policy priority is to reduce violence, attempting to change behaviour appears more reasonable in this respect and would concretize in the provision of incentives for reinsertion (2011: 20). One might of course argue, and here we are back at the issue of definitions, that disengagement from radical activities or leaving a terrorist organization might not be sufficient, if identification with a radical ideology or the refusal to participate in the democratic process is considered a threat.

## Conclusion

Islamist radicalization in Europe is a research child born prematurely, marked by substantial political pressure, social change, and global unrest. At the dawn of the jihadi campaigns on European soil and increasingly targeting it, insecurity, insufficient knowledge of the 'other', and a wish for quick fixes had an impact on the research agenda. It is therefore little surprising that the development of theoretical tools for its study and the availability of grounded analyses still leave much to be desired. There are nevertheless some elements of progress which have brought us closer to the understanding of why and especially how individuals and groups come to nurture ideas of radical political and social change and possibly act on them in violent ways. That Muslim minorities in Europe tend to display lower income, educational, and housing indicators than the mainstream, along with experiences of discrimination and marginalization has become in the meantime not so easily associated with a certain vulnerability or openness to jihadism. Simplistic constructions of 'cause–effect' have been slowly overtaken by concepts such as 'pathways', 'process', and 'selective incentives', looking at developments through time, although concepts such as 'factors' and 'crises' still maintain a certain amount of attractiveness. Rather than attempting to establish causal relationships with qualities and structural factors, some of the more promising analyses have concentrated on the ways in which individuals might come to adopt new values and norms in interaction with the social environment. Rather than descriptively displaying and unpacking elements of ideological content, advances have been made in understanding the mechanisms through which a world-view permeated by a sense of injustice against Muslims might be adopted and further legitimize violent behaviour.

Islamist radicalization is an individual process, occurring in interaction with various levels of social environments and at the intersection of various types of discourse. More importantly, it is not something specific or derived from the quality of being Muslim. Developments at the macro-level, be it discrimination, the collapse of original social structures, external conflicts, or foreign policy need to be understood not as direct causes or contributing factors, but as elements of discourse purposefully created and further developed within social interaction. While further studies are necessary to explore the mechanisms of radicalization and especially those of deradicalization and disengagement, we are nevertheless at a healthy distance from initial ideas implying that there is something 'wrong' with European Muslims.

## References

Abbas, T. 2007. Introduction: Islamic Political Radicalism in Western Europe. In T. Abbas (ed.), *Islamic Political Radicalism: A European Comparative Perspective*. Edinburgh: Edinburgh University Press, 3–14.

Al-Azmeh, A. 2006. *Making Governance Work against Radicalisation*. Copenhagen: Danish Institute for International Studies.

Alonso, R. 2010. Radicalisation and Recruitment among Jihadist Terrorists in Spain: Main Patterns and Subsequent Counter-Terrorist Measures. In M. Ranstorp (ed.), *Understanding Violent Radicalisation: Terrorist and Jihadist Prison Movements in Europe*. London and New York: Routledge, 207–30.

Alonso, R. 2012. The Spread of Radical Islam in Spain: Challenges Ahead. *Studies in Conflict & Terrorism* 35: 471–91.

Aly, A. and Striegher, J.-L. 2012. Examining the Role of Religion in Radicalization to Violent Extremism. *Studies in Conflict & Terrorism* 35: 849–62.

Amghar, S. 2009. Ideological and Theological Foundations of Muslim Radicalism in France. In M. Emerson (ed.), *Ethno-Religious Conflict in Europe: Typologies of Radicalisation in Europe's Muslim Communities*. Brussels: Centre for European Policy Studies, 27–50.

Bakker, E. 2005. *Jihadi Terrorists in Europe. Their Characteristics and the Circumstances in Which They Joined the Jihad: An Exploratory Study*. The Hague: Netherlands Institute of International Relations Clingendael.

Bakker, E. 2008. Jihadi Terrorists in Europe and Global Salafi Jihadis. In R. Coolsaet (ed.), *Jihadi Terrorism and the Radicalisation Challenge in Europe*. Aldershot: Ashgate, 69–84.
Bandura, A. 1973. *Aggression: A Social Learning Analysis*. Englewood Cliffs, NJ: Prentice-Hall.
Barbieri, E. T. and Klausen, J. 2012. Al Qaeda's London Branch: Patterns of Domestic and Transnational Network Integration. *Studies in Conflict & Terrorism* 35: 411–31.
Barnes, H. 2006. *Born in the UK: Young Muslims in Britain*. London: Foreign Policy Centre.
Belarouci, L. 2009. Islamism: The Process of Identity Formation. In T. M. Pick, A. Speckhard, and B. Jacuch (eds.), *Home-Grown Terrorism: Understanding and Addressing the Root Causes of Radicalisation among Groups with an Immigrant Heritage in Europe*. Amsterdam: IOS Press, 3–17.
Beyler, C. 2006. The Jihadist Threat in France. In H. Fradkin, H. Haqqani, and E. Brown (eds.), *Current Trends in Islamist Ideology*. Washington: Hudson Institute, 89–113..
Bjørgo, T. and Horgan, J. 2009. *Leaving Terrorism Behind: Individual and Collective Disengagement*. Abingdon and New York: Routledge.
Bowman-Grieve, L. 2010. The Internet and Terrorism: Pathways towards Terrorism and Counter-Terrorism. In A. Silke (ed.), *The Psychology of Counter-Terrorism*. London: Routledge, 76–88.
Brandon, J. 2009. The Danger of Prison Radicalization in the West. *CTC Sentinel* 2: 1–4.
Brandon, J. 2011. British Universities Continue to Breed Extremists. *CTC Sentinel* 4: 6–8.
Briggs, R. and Birdwell, J. 2009. Radicalisation Among the Muslims in the UK. In M. Emerson (ed.), *Ethno-Religious Conflict in Europe: Typologies of Radicalisation in Europe's Muslim Communities*. Brussels: Centre for European Policy Studies, 109–35.
Brown, R. 1986. *Social Psychology*, 2nd edn. New York: Free Press.
Campana, A. and Ratelle, J.-F. 2014. A Political Sociology Approach to the Diffusion of Conflict from Chechnya to Dagestan and Igushetia. *Studies in Conflict & Terrorism* 37: 115–34.
Cesari, J. 2008. Muslims in Europe and the Risk of Radicalism. In R. Coolsaet (ed.), *Jihadi Terrorism and the Radicalisation Challenge in Europe*. Aldershot: Ashgate, 97–108.
Cheong, P. H. and Halverson, J. R. 2010. Youths in Violent Extremist Discourse: Mediated Identifications and Interventions. *Studies in Conflict & Terrorism* 33: 1104–23.
Choudhury, T. 2007. *The Role of Muslim Identity Politics in Radicalisation (A Study in Progress)*. London: Department for Communities and Local Government.
Coolsaet, R. and De Swielande, T. S. 2007. *Belgium and Counterterrorism Policy in the Jihadi Era (1986–2007)*. Madrid: Real Instituto Elcano.
COT. 2008. *Causal Factors of Radicalization*. The Hague: Institute for Safety, Security and Crisis Management.
Cottee, S. 2010. Mind Slaughter: The Neutralizations of Jihadi Salafism. *Studies in Conflict & Terrorism* 33: 330–352.
Crone, M. and Harrow, M. 2010. *Homegrown Terrorism in the West, 1989–2008*. Copenhagen: Danish Institute for International Studies.
Dalgaard-Nielsen, A. 2010. Violent Radicalization in Europe: What We Know and What We Do Not Know. *Studies in Conflict & Terrorism* 33: 797–814.
Della Porta, D. and Diani, M. 2006. *Social Movements: An Introduction*. Malden, MA and Oxford: Blackwell Publishing.
Dittrich, M. 2006. *Muslims in Europe: Addressing the Challenges of Radicalization*. Brussels: European Policy Centre.
Garner, G. 2013. Chechnya and Kashmir: The Jihadist Evolution of Nationalism to Jihad and Beyond. *Terrorism and Political Violence* 25: 419–32.

Gohel, S. M. 2009. The Internet and its Role in Terrorist Recruitment and Operational Planning. *CTC Sentinel* 2: 12–15.

Grignard, A. 2008. The Islamist Networks in Belgium: Between Nationalism and Globalisation. In R. Coolsaet (ed.), *Jihadi Terrorism and the Radicalisation Challenge in Europe*. Aldershot: Ashgate, 85–94.

GTD. 2014. Global Terrorism Database. <http://www.start.umd.edu/gtd/> [Accessed 25 April 2014].

Gutiérrez, J. A., Jordan, J., and Trujillo, H. 2008. Prevention of Jihadist Radicalization in Spanish Prisons: Current Situation, Challenges and Dysfunctions of the Penitentiary System. *Athena Intelligence Journal* 3: 1–9.

Hellmich, C. 2008. Creating the Ideology of Al Qaeda: From Hypocrites to Salafi-Jihadists. *Studies in Conflict & Terrorism* 31: 111–24.

Hellmich, C. 2010. The Physiology of Al-Qaeda: From Ideology to Participation. In M. Ranstorp (ed.), *Understanding Violent Radicalisation: Terrorist and Jihadist Movements in Europe*. London and New York: Routledge, 68–83.

Hoffman, B. 2009. Radicalization and Subversion: Al Qaeda and the 7 July 2005 Bombings and the 2006 Airline Bombing Plot. *Studies in Conflict & Terrorism* 32: 1100–16.

Horgan, J. 2005. *The Psychology of Terrorism*. New York: Routledge.

Horgan, J. 2008a. Deradicalization or Disengagement. *Perspectives on Terrorism* 2, 3–8 <http://www.terrorismanalysts.com/pt/index.php/pot/article/view/32> [Accessed 26 April 2014].

Horgan, J. 2008b. From Profiles to Pathways and Roots to Routes: Perspectives from Psychology on Radicalization into Terrorism. *The Annals of the American Academy of Political and Social Science* 618: 80–94.

Hoskins, A. and O'Loughlin, B. 2009. Pre-Mediating Guilt: Radicalisation and Mediality in British News. *Critical Studies on Terrorism* 2: 81–93.

Husain, E. 2007. *The Islamist: Why I Joined Radical Islam in Britain, What I Saw Inside and Why I Left*. London: Penguin.

Jackson, R. 2008. Counter-Terrorism and Communities: An Interview with Robert Lambert. *Critical Studies on Terrorism* 1: 293–308.

Jones, D. M. and Smith, M. L. R. 2010. Beyond Belief: Islamist Strategic Thinking and International Relations Theory. *Terrorism and Political Violence* 22: 242–66.

Jordan, J. and Horsburgh, N. 2005. Mapping Jihadist Terrorism in Spain. *Studies in Conflict & Terrorism* 28: 169–91.

Kaplan, J., Lööw, H., and Malkki, L. 2014. Introduction to the Special Issue on Lone Wolf and Autonomous Cell Terrorism. *Terrorism and Political Violence* 26(1): 1–12.

Kenney, M. 2010. Beyond the Internet: Mētis, Techne, and the Limitations of Online Artifacts for Islamist Terrorists. *Terrorism and Political Violence* 22: 177–97.

Khosrokhavar, F. 2005. *Suicide Bombers: Allah's New Martyrs*. London: Pluto Press.

Khurmatullin, A. 2010. Tatarstan: Islam Entwined with Nationalism. In R. Dannreuther and L. March (eds.), *Russia and Islam: State, Society and Radicalism*. London: Routledge, 103–21.

Kilcullen, D. J. 2007. Subversion and Countersubversion in the Campaign against Terrorism in Europe. *Studies in Conflict & Terrorism* 30: 647–66.

Kohlmann, E. F. 2008. Al-Qa'ida's 'MySpace': Terrorist Recruitment on the Internet. *CTC Sentinel* 1: 8–9.

Leiken, R. S. and Brooke, S. 2006. The Quantitative Analysis of Terrorism and Immigration: An Initial Exploration. *Terrorism and Political Violence* 18: 503–21.

Lambert, R. 2009. Police and Muslim Communities in London. In T. M. Pick, A. Speckhard, and B. Jacuch (eds.), *Home-Grown Terrorism: Understanding and Addressing the Root Causes of Radicalisation among Groups with an Immigrant Heritage in Europe*. Amsterdam: IOS Press, 51–73.

Lia, B. 2008. Al-Qaida's Appeal: Understanding its Unique Selling Points. *Perspectives on Terrorism* 2: 3–10 <http://www.terrorismanalysts.com/pt/index.php/pot/article/view/44/91> [Accessed 26 April 2014].

McCauley, C. and Moskalenko, S. 2008. Mechanisms of Political Radicalization: Pathways Toward Terrorism. *Terrorism and Political Violence* 20: 415–33.

Malashenko, A. 2006. Islam in Russia in 2020. In *Between Suicide Bombing and the Burning Banlieues: The Multiple Crises of Europe's Parallel Societies*. ESF Working Paper No. 22, June.

Michelsen, N. 2009. Addressing the Schizophrenia of Global Jihad. *Critical Studies on Terrorism* 2: 453–71.

Moskalenko, S. and McCauley, C. 2009. Measuring Political Mobilization: The Distinction Between Activism and Radicalism. *Terrorism and Political Violence* 21: 239–60.

Mullins, S. 2012. Iraq Versus Lack of Integration: Understanding the Motivations of Contemporary Islamist Terrorists in Western Countries. *Behavioral Sciences of Terrorism and Political Aggression* 4: 110–13.

Nesser, P. 2006a. Jihad in Europe: Recruitment for Terrorist Cells in Europe. In L. Bokhari, T. Hegghammer, B. Lia, P. Nesser, and T. H. Tonnessen (eds.), *Paths to Global Jihad Radicalization and Recruitment to Terror Networks*. Proceedings from an FFI seminar, Norwegian Defence Research Establishment, OMS Seminar, 15 March, Oslo.

Nesser, P. 2006b. Jihadism in Western Europe After the Invasion of Iraq: Tracing Motivational Influences from the Iraq War on Jihadist Terrorism in Western Europe. *Studies in Conflict & Terrorism* 29: 323–42.

Nesser, P. 2008. How did Europe's Global Jihadis Obtain Training for their Militant Causes? *Terrorism and Political Violence* 20: 234–56.

Nesser, P. 2011. Ideologies of Jihad in Europe. *Terrorism and Political Violence* 23: 173–200.

Nesser, P. 2014. Toward an Increasingly Heterogeneous Threat: A Chronology of Jihadist Terrorism in Europe 2008–2013. *Studies in Conflict & Terrorism* 37: 440–56.

Neumann, P. 2008. *Joining Al-Qaeda: Jihadist Recruitment in Europe*. London: International Institute for Strategic Studies.

Neumann, P. R. and Rogers, B. 2008. *Recruitment and Mobilisation for the Islamist Militant Movement in Europe*. London: International Centre for the Study of Radicalisation and Political Violence. <http://icsr.info/wp-content/uploads/2012/10/1234516791ICSREUResearchReport_Proof1.pdf> [Accessed 26 April 2014].

Olsen, J. A. 2008. *Radicalisation in Danish Prisons: What is Happening, and What Can We Do About It?* DIIS brief. Copenhagen: Danish Institute for International Studies.

Ongering, L. 2007. *Home-Grown Terrorism and Radicalisation in the Netherlands: Experiences, Explanations and Approaches*. Testimony before the U.S. Senate Homeland Security and Governmental Affairs Committee. <http://www.investigativeproject.org/documents/testimony/292.pdf> [Accessed 22 November 2010].

Pargeter, A. 2008. *The New Frontiers of Jihad: Radical Islam in Europe*. Philadelphia, PA: University of Pennsylvania Press.

Paris, J. 2007. A Framework for Understanding Radical Islam's Challenge to European Governments. *Transatlantic Issues*. Hudson Institute.

Payne, K. 2009. Winning the Battle of Ideas: Propaganda, Ideology, and Terror. *Studies in Conflict & Terrorism* 32: 109–28.

Paz, R. 2009. Reading Their Lips: The Credibility of Militant Jihadi Web Sites as 'Soft Power' in the War of the Minds. In T. M. Pick, A. Speckhard, and B. Jacuch (eds.), *Home-Grown Terrorism: Understanding and Addressing the Root Causes of Radicalisation among Groups with an Immigrant Heritage in Europe*. Amsterdam: IOS Press, 114–26.

Pisoiu, D. 2011. *Islamist Radicalization in Europe: An Occupational Change Model*. London and New York: Routledge.

Ranstorp, M. 2010. Introduction. In M. Ranstorp (ed.), *Understanding Violent Radicalisation: Terrorist and Jihadist Movements in Europe*. London: Routledge, 1–18.

Reinares, F. 2006. Towards a Social Characterisation of Jihadist Terrorism in Spain: Implications for Domestic Security and Action Abroad. *ARI Real Instituto Elcano* 34.

Roy, O. 2004. *Globalised Islam: The Search for a New Ummah*. London: Hurst & Company.

Roy, O. 2007. *The Future of Radical Islam in Europe*. A roundtable discussion at the Council on Foreign Relations, New York, 6 November. <http://www.cfr.org/radicalization-and-extremism/roundtable-series-global-islamic-politics-future-radical-islam-europe-rush-transcript-federal-news-service/p14743> [Accessed 26 April 2014].

Roy, O. 2008a. Al Qaeda in the West as a Youth Movement: The Power of a Narrative. *CEPS Policy Briefs*. Centre for European Policy Studies.

Roy, O. 2008b. Al-Qaeda: A True Global Movement. In R. Coolsaet (ed.) *Jihadi Terrorism and the Radicalisation Challenge in Europe*. Aldershot: Ashgate, 109–14.

Ryan, J. 2007. The Four P-Words of Militant Islamist Radicalization and Recruitment: Persecution, Precedent, Piety, and Perseverance. *Studies in Conflict & Terrorism* 30: 985–1011.

Ryan, J. 2010. The Internet, the Perpetual Beta, and the State: The Long View of the New Medium. *Studies in Conflict and Terrorism* 33: 673–81.

Sageman, M. 2004. *Understanding Terror Networks*. Philadelphia, PA: University of Pennsylvania Press.

Sageman, M. 2007. *Radicalization of Global Islamist Terrorists*. Testimony to the U.S. Senate Homeland Security and Governmental Affairs Committee, 27 June. <http://hsgac.senate.gov/public/index.cfm?FuseAction=Hearings.Hearing&Hearing_ID=9c8ef805-75c8-48c2-810d-d778af31cca6>.

Sageman, M. 2008. *Leaderless Jihad: Terror Networks in the Twenty-First Century*. Philadelphia, PA: University of Pennsylvania Press.

Sedgwick, M. 2010. The Concept of Radicalization as a Source of Confusion. *Terrorism and Political Violence* 22: 479–94.

Silke, A. 2011. Disengagement or Deradicalization: A Look at Prison Programs for Jailed Terrorists. *CTC Sentinel* 4: 18–21.

Slootman, M. and Tillie, M. 2006. *Processes of Radicalisation: Why Some Amsterdam Muslims Become Radicals*. Amsterdam: Institute for Migration and Ethnic Studies, Universiteit van Amsterdam.

Speckhard, A. 2008. The Emergence of Female Suicide Terrorists. *Studies in Conflict and Terrorism* 31: 995–1023.

Speckhard, A. 2009. The Militant Jihad in Europe: Fighting Home-Grown Terrorism. In T. M. Pick, A. Speckhard, and B. Jacuch (eds.), *Home-Grown Terrorism: Understanding and Addressing the Root Causes of Radicalisation among Groups with an Immigrant Heritage in Europe*. Amsterdam: IOS Press, 143–60.

Speckhard, A. and Ahkmedova, K. 2006. The Making of a Martyr: Chechen Suicide Terrorism. *Studies in Conflict & Terrorism* 29: 429–92.

Stenersen, A. 2008. The Internet: A Virtual Training Camp? *Terrorism and Political Violence* 20: 215–33.

Taarnby, M. 2007. Understanding Recruitment of Islamist Terrorists in Europe. In M. Ranstorp (ed.), *Mapping Terrorism Research: State of the Art, Gaps and Future Directions*. London: Routledge, 164–84.

Taylor, M. and Horgan, J. (2001). The Psychological and Behavioural Bases of Islamic Fundamentalism. *Terrorism and Political Violence* 13: 37–71.

Taylor, M. and Quayle, E. 1994. *Terrorist Lives*. London: Brassey's.

Veldhuis, T. and Bakker, E. 2009. Muslims in the Netherlands: Tensions and Violent Conflict. In M. Emerson (ed.), *Ethno-Religious Conflict in Europe: Typologies of Radicalisation in Europe's Muslim Communities*. Brussels: Centre for European Policy Studies, 81–108.

Vermeulen, F. 2014. Suspect Communities: Targeting Violent Extremism at the Local Level—Policies of Engagement in Amsterdam, Berlin and London. *Terrorism and Political Violence* 26: 286–306.

Vidino, L. 2005. Jihad from Europe. *Journal of International Security Affairs* 9: 19–25.

Vidino, L. 2009. Europe's New Security Dilemma. *The Washington Quarterly* 32: 61–75.

Waldmann, P. K. 2010. *Radicalisation in the Diaspora: Why Muslims in the West Attack their Host Countries*. Madrid: Real Instituto Elcano. <http://www.realinstitutoelcano.org/wps/portal/web/rielcano_en/contenido?WCM_GLOBAL_CONTEXT=/elcano/Elcano_in/Zonas_in/DT9-2010 > [Accessed 26 April 2014].

Wesley, R. 2008. Combating Terrorism Through a Counter-Framing Strategy. *CTC Sentinel* 1: 10–12.

Wilner, A. S. and Dubouloz, C.-J. 2011. Transformative Radicalization: Applying Learning Theory to Islamist Radicalization. *Studies in Conflict & Terrorism* 34: 418–38.

Wiktorowicz, Q. 2005. A Genealogy of Radical Islam. *Studies in Conflict & Terrorism* 28: 75–97.

Wiktorowicz, Q. 2006. Anatomy of the Salafi Movement. *Studies in Conflict & Terrorism* 29: 207–39.

Yarlykapov, A. 2010. The Radicalization of North Caucasian Muslims. In R. Dannreuther and L. March (eds.), *Russia and Islam: State, Society and Radicalism*. London: Routledge, 137–54.

Yemelianova, G. M. 2010. Divergent Trends of Islamic Radicalization in Muslim Russia. In R. Dannreuther and L. March (eds.), *Russia and Islam: State, Society and Radicalism*. London: Routledge, 122–36.

# CONCLUSION: IS THERE A EUROPEAN ISLAM?

## JOCELYNE CESARI

In coining the term Euro-Islam, Bassam Tibi[1] advocated for the adaptation of Muslims to the civic and political contracts of their countries of residence and for the necessity to adjust Islam to the liberal values of the West. In his words, Islam should be reformed to comply to Europe's post-Enlightenment values and norms such as human rights, rule of law, democracy, and gender equality. Since Bassam Tibi's initial contribution, the concept of Euro-Islam has been hotly debated and alternative definitions have been advanced. For example, Tariq Ramadan has distinguished between the customs and ethnicities of different Muslim countries and the religious principles of Islam, arguing that the latter can be (or are already part) of European cultures.[2] According to his approach, Islamic principles *per se* do not require reform, but an acculturation process is needed in order to separate these principles from the different countries of origin of Muslim immigrants and adapt them to different European cultures.

Interestingly, according to this Handbook the advocates of Euro-Islam who assume that the values of Islam and the values of Europe are inherently incompatible, and are at odds with the reality of the vast majority of Muslims across Europe. For example, the country chapters analyse the increasing number of surveys that show the loyalty of Muslims to their countries of residence. At the same time, they describe the persistence of the suspicions or doubts of the 'host' societies about the integration of Islam into European cultures. In fact, all the chapters in this volume attest to an increase in the concerns about Muslims' loyalty to their national communities. They also show that the persistence of patriarchal cultures and the growing influence of some anti-Western religious interpretations among Muslims actually reinforce the dominant perception that Islam clashes with European liberal values and lifestyles.

In this regard, the visibility of Salafism, which has monopolized the debate on the 'true' Islam not only among Muslims but also in the eyes of the general population across Europe, reinforces the antinomy between the West and Islam. In Salafi thinking,

---

[1] Bassam Tibi (ed.), *Political Islam, World Politics and Europe* (New York: Routledge, 2008).
[2] Tariq Ramadan, *To Be a European Muslim* (Leicester: The Islamic Foundation, 1999).

good Muslims are religiously conservative, wear the hijab, follow strict gender separation, avoid promiscuity, and limit their relations with non-Muslims or Muslims who do not behave like them. In contrast, bad Muslims have been 'contaminated' by the Western lifestyle and values and, therefore, are in need of purification. As attested to in the different contributions of the Handbook, this discourse fails to reflect the malleability and flexibility of Muslim religious practices. Nevertheless, it still operates as an authoritative interpretation of Islamic orthodoxy and influences Muslims' identification to their religious tradition. Thus, the 'good' Muslim becomes an ontological category based on total acceptance without critique of divine law, which is defined as immutable. As an inverted image, the 'good' Muslims in the eyes of Europeans are secular and Westernized while the bad Muslims are doctrinal, anti-modern, and virulent.[3] In other words, a distinction between radical, 'bad' Islam and moderate, 'good' Islam has become a common political framing across European democracies.[4]

In this sense, the clash is not between civilizations but between essentialized and inverted perceptions of Islam and Muslims that reinforce each other. Therefore, any claim about Euro-Islam contains the risk of reinforcing this clash of essentialisms. Additionally, cultural, social, and ethnic diversity among Muslims in Europe within and across countries constitutes another challenge to the realization of Euro-Islam. For example, the Handbook sheds light on the cultural gap between Eastern and Western Muslims in Europe who do not share the same historical and political experience and for whom Islam is part and parcel of ethnic or national identities.

Another reason why 'Euro-Islam' is problematic is that it prioritizes symbolic integration over social or political integration and tends to culturalize debates on the social mobility or economic advancement of Muslim groups. Symbolic integration refers to the inclusion of a particular group into the history and shared memory of a national community. These shared cultural practices divide the world into those who are 'citizens' or 'friends', and those who are 'enemies'.[5] Symbolic boundaries are thereby constructed around the 'national community' both inter-nationally and intra-nationally. For example, 'enemies' do not only reside outside of the territorial confines of the nation-state, but may also lie within, reflecting the 'internal structure of social divisions', as well as particular national myths, narratives, and traditions.[6] Symbolic boundaries within any

---

[3] Mahmood Mamdani, *Good Muslim, Bad Muslim: America, the Cold War, and the Roots of Terror* (New York: Three Leaves Press, 2005), 24.

[4] Interestingly, some Muslim spokespeople are the most active advocates of this dichotomy. As members of the incriminated minority, they can voice criticisms that would seem unduly harsh or politically incorrect coming from the majority groups. Probably the most representative figure of the good Muslims is Ayaan Hirsi Ali, who is mentioned in several chapters of this book.

[5] J. C. Alexander, 'Citizen and Enemy as Symbolic Classification: On the Polarizing Discourse of Civil Society', in M. Fournier and M. Lamont (eds.), *Cultivating Differences: Symbolic Boundaries and the Making of Inequality* (Chicago: University of Chicago Press, 1993), 289–308. Zygmunt Bauman, 'Modernity and Ambivalence', *Theory, Culture and Society* 7 (1990): 143–69. Philip Schlesinger, *Media, State and Nation: Political Violence and Collective Identities* (London: Sage, 1991).

[6] Schlesinger, *Media, State and Nation*.

given national community operate on a two-dimensional typology: friends/enemies and internal/external.[7] Some groups are internal enemies (territorial/linguistic/ethnic minorities); others are external (hostile foreign countries).

Across the countries described in this volume, it appears that Muslims have become both internal and external enemies.[8] They are internal enemies because they seem to endanger the core liberal values of European societies as well as adding a burden to social problems like unemployment or ghettoization of some urban areas.

They are also the external enemies because of the war on terror and the rise of violent Islamic activism. Under these conditions, any expression of Islamic identity or practice, from head covering to dietary rules, is seen as a political act and therefore deemed illegitimate. This double process of estrangement and externalization from the national community has deeply influenced the integration policies in Western Europe by questioning citizenship acquisition and undermining the recognition of cultural diversity. In the eastern part of Europe, Muslim minorities were in some cases already built in as the 'others' or the internal enemies. The rise of external threats has reinforced the internal one, leading in countries like Greece or Russia to a dichotomy between the internal historical Muslims and the external ones (immigrants from Muslim countries).

Even more disconcerting, the externalization of Islam puts the 'burden of proof' on Muslims alone; making symbolic integration a unilateral process of assimilation to European values with a strong emphasis on European secularism presented as a universal norm.

## Conclusion: Relativizing Secularism

The European experience of separation of church and state, privatization of religious activities, and the decline of religious practices has served as the universal standard to define secularism. Therefore, when citizens contradict this standard by adopting dress code, dietary rules, or other religious obligations with social implications, the secular political cultures of the West are in crisis. Muslims are troublesome because they express their individuality through religious postures that for most Europeans are not compatible with the idealized secular civism.

These tensions have the consequence of relativizing European secularism by showing that it is a way to discipline all religions when they include prescriptions and

---

[7] This approach builds on Georg Simmel's structural approach of the stranger, which examines an individual's twofold position as an outsider and an insider when entering into a new group.

[8] See Jocelyne Cesari, *Why the West Fears Islam: Exploration of Muslims in Liberal Democracies* (New York: Palgrave Macmillan, 2013).

commitments that do not conform to this neat private–public division.[9] They also reveal how secularism can turn into an ideology or counter-religion aimed against any forms of religion in public space.[10] The French version of secularism, or *laïcité*, is an illustration of this extreme ideological interpretation of secular principles.

In sum, to avoid a unilateral symbolic integration of Muslims within national communities would require a dramatic change in the current liberal and secularist narratives. It is a daunting task, but it can be done. Then, instead of being a disciplinization of the bad Muslims, Euro-Islam could mean symbolic integration of the Islamic heritage and cultural practices within different European national cultures without endangering the basic principle of equality between citizens.

## Select Bibliography

Amir-Moazami, Shirin (2007). 'Euro-Islam, Islam in Europe, or Europe Revised through Islam? Versions of Muslim Solidarity within European Borders', in Nathalie Karagiannis (ed.), *European Solidarity and Solidarity Beyond Europe*. Liverpool: Liverpool University Press, 186–213.

Asad, Talal (1993). *Genealogies of Religion: Discipline and Reasons of Power in Christianity and Islam*. Baltimore: Johns Hopkins University Press.

Batnitzky, Leora Faye (2011). *How Judaism Became a Religion: An Introduction to Modern Jewish Thought*. Princeton: Princeton University Press.

Bauman, Zygmunt (1990). 'Modernity and Ambivalence', *Theory, Culture and Society* 7: 143–69.

BBC News (2011). 'State Multiculturalism Has Failed, Says David Cameron', 5 February. <http://www.bbc.co.uk/news/uk-politics-12371994> [Accessed 27 July 2012].

Beider, Harris (2012). *Race, Housing, & Community: Perspectives on Policy and Practice*. Hoboken, NJ: Wiley-Blackwell.

Biggs, Stephen (2012). 'The Monist', *Liberalism, Feminism, and Group Rights*. <http://www.readperiodicals.com/201201/2600287491.html#b> [Accessed 25 July 2012].

Buruma, Ian (2012). 'Europe's Turn to the Right', *The Nation*, 10 August. <http://www.thenation.com/article/162698/europes-turn-right> [Accessed 27 July 2012].

Celermajer, Danielle (2007). 'If Islam Is Our Other, Who Are "We"?' *Australian Journal of Social Issues* 42(1): 103–23.

Cesari, Jocelyne (2006). 'Securitization and Religious Divides in Europe: Muslims in Western Europe After 9/11', GSRL-Paris and Harvard University, 1 June.

Goldberg, David Theo (2006). 'Racial Europeanization', *Ethnic and Racial Studies* 29(2): 331–64.

Islamopedia Online. 'Missed Opportunity for a Greater Inclusion of Islam in the United States'. Last modified 17 March 2011. <http://islamopediaonline.org/blog/missed-opportunity-greater-inclusion-islam-united-states> [Accessed 25 July 2012].

---

[9] For an analysis of the disciplinization of Islam in the European context, see Cesari, *Why the West Fears Islam*; for Judaism see Leora Faye Batnitzky, *How Judaism Became a Religion: An Introduction to Modern Jewish Thought* (Princeton: Princeton University Press, 2011).

[10] Cesari, *Why the West Fears Islam*, 113.

Kundnani, Arun (2009). *Spooked: How Not To Prevent Violent Extremism*. London: Institute of Race Relations.

Kundnani, Arun (2012). 'Multiculturalism and Its Discontents: Left, Right and Liberal', *European Journal of Cultural Studies* 15(2): 155–66.

Lentin, Alana and Gavin Titley (2012). 'The Crisis of "Multiculturalism" in Europe: Mediated Minarets, Intolerable Subjects', *European Journal of Cultural Studies* 15(2) (April): 123–38.

Mamdani, Mahmood (2005). *Good Muslim, Bad Muslim: America, the Cold War, and the Roots of Terror*. New York: Three Leaves Press.

Schlesinger, Philip (1991). *Media, State and Nation: Political Violence and Collective Identities*. London: Sage.

Tibi, Bassam (ed.) (2008). *Political Islam, World Politics and Europe*. New York: Routledge.

Toynbee, Polly (2004). 'Why Trevor Is Right', *The Guardian*, 7 April. <http://www.guardian.co.uk/politics/2004/apr/07/society.immigration> [Accessed 8 April 2004].

US Office of Immigration Statistics (2004). *2004 Yearbook of Immigration Statistics*. Last modified January 2006. <http://www.dhs.gov/xlibrary/assets/statistics/yearbook/2004/Yearbook2004.pdf> [Accessed 27 October 2012].

Young, Hugo (2001). 'A Corrosive National Danger in Our Multicultural Model', *The Guardian*, 6 November. <http://www.guardian.co.uk/world/2001/nov/06/september11.politics> [Accessed 20 November 2001].

Zine, Jasmin (2006). 'Between Orientalism and Fundamentalism: The Politics of Muslim Women's Feminist Engagement', *Muslim World Journal of Human Rights* Special Issue: Post-September 11th Developments in Human Rights in the Muslim World 3(1).

# Names Index

Aarbakke, V  358
Abbas, T  786
Abbattecola, E  268
Abduh, Muhammad  453
Abdulwahab, Taimour  411
Abu-Dhar (Oleg Marushkin)  550
Accoyer, Bernard  47
Adam, Ilke  241
Ad-Darsh, Syed  91
Adida, Claire  29
Afandi of Chirkey, Sa'id  540–1, 547–8
Al-Ahdal, Abdallah  226
Al-Alawi, Irfan  506
Al-Albani, Muhammad Nasiruddin  14
al-Albani, Nasir al Din  483–4
Ali ibn Abi Ṭalib  393, 480
Alibashic, Ahmet  593
Alidadi, Katayoun  241
Allam, Magdi  657–8
Allen, Christopher  749, 760
Allievi, Silvestre  265, 274, 279, 286, 299, 637, 639
Almani, Abdul Ghaffar El (Eric Breininger)  663
Alvi, Aisha  707
Alvi, Fatima  707
Aly, A  793
Amato, Giuliano  282
Ambrosini, M  268, 276, 291
Amghar, Samir  37, 48, 794
Amiraux, Valérie  729
Amir-Moazami, Schirin  108, 132
Amirpur, Katajun  139
Anagnostou, D  364, 370
Anas, Imam Malik ibn  447
Anderson, M  412
Andersson, P  401
Andreassen, R  413
*Andrić, ivo*  432

An-Na'im, Abdullahi A  448
Antoniou, D  356, 376–7, 382
Anwar, Muhammad  74, 87–8, 90
Aparicio, Juan Carlos  710
Arigita Maza, E  343
Arkoun, Mohamed  448
Armstrong, Karen  448
Arnauti, Shuayyib Muharrem  484
Ascha, Ghassan  704
al-Assad, Bashir  509
Astor, A  325
Atanasoff, Velko  602
Atatürk, Mustafa Kemal  604, 686
Attanassof, Velko  445
Ayuso Guixot, MA  292
Al-Azhar, sheikh of  12
Al-Azmeh, A  770, 789

Baaz, Abdul Aziz Ibn  14
Badić, Murat  468
Badinter, Eliabeth  727
Bakht, Natasha  703
Bakker, E  773
Baleta, Abdi  502
Baltsiotis, L  357
Bamba, Ahmadu  287–8
al-Banna, Hassan  36
Bano, Samia  692
Bardot, Brigitte  41
Barlas, Asma  703
Barnard, Benno  248
Barnes, H  786, 789, 794
Barrios Baudor, GL  317
Barton, Stephen  75–6, 87–8, 90
Bastenier, Albert  229, 249–50
Bat Ye'or  415
Baubérot, Jean  31
Bausani, A  265
al-Bayhaqi, Abu Bakr  447

Bayramova, Fawziya  540, 543
Bayrou, François  32, 34, 713
Begum, Shabina  707–8
Bektovic, S  412
Belarouci, L  793, 794
Belkacem, Fouad  248
Benn, T  45
Berglund, J  412
Berlusconi, Silvio  275, 709, 758
Bernardo, Pais  634
Bershia, Sali  502
Bevelander, P  401, 413, 414
Beyler, C  794
Biffi, Giacomo  274
Bilalli, Idriz  496
Birali Birali  593–4
Birdwell, J  794
Blair, Tony  758
Bobrovnikov, Vladimir  532
Boenders, W  179
Boja, Rexhep  487–8, 495
Bolkestein, Frits  199
Bonne, Karijn  245
Borou, C  360
Borell, K  413
Børresen, S  401
Bosman, André  198
Boubakeur, Dalil  36, 37
Bourdieu, Pierre  412
Bousetta, Hassan  238–9
Bouyeri, Mohamed  165–6, 192
Bowen, John  692
Bowman-Grieve, L  791
Bracke, Sarah  251–2
Branković, Vuk  432
Breininger, Eric (Abdul Ghaffar El Almani)  663
Breivik, Anders Behring  141, 765
Brems, Eva  242
Brettfeld, K  133
Brezhnev, Leonid  522
Briggs, R  794
Brion, Fabienne  242
Brubaker, Rogers  109, 144
Bugari, Sulejman  448, 450
al-Buhairi, Salem  226
Buijs, FJ  628–30
Al-Bukhari, Imam  447

Bunar, N  401
al-Burhani, Al-Hajj Nooh Said  483
Bush, George W  747, 756, 758–9

Caetani, L  265
Čajlaković, Zenica Imam Husein  448
Cameron, David  86, 750, 762
Caneva, E  291
Carlbom, A  410
Carter, Jimmy  759
Castells, M  78
Castles, S  723
Catherine II, queen of Russia (Catherine the Great)  517
Čaušević, Džemaludin  454
Čavić, Dragan  468
Cerić, Mustafa  418, 455
Cesari, Jocelyne  28, 45, 112, 629, 643, 745, 778
Chaouki, Khalid  295
Chérifi, Hanifa  713
Chiesi, AM  273
Chirac, Jacques  32, 44, 46–7, 713, 758
Christopoulos, D  357
Chukov, Vladimir  601
Cimbalo, G  636
Clycq, Noël  233, 251–2
Cohen, Job  188
Colom González, F  321
Contreras Ortega, V  328
Corbin, Henry  448, 546
Courtens, G  292
Cox, Caroline  693
Crone, M  790–1
Cuspert, Mamadou (Deso Dogg/Abou Maleeq)  663–4

Dahlab, Lucia  711–12
Dahmane, Abdessattar  248
Dalgaard-Nielsen, A  771–2, 788
Dassetto, Felice  222, 229, 249–50, 265, 629
Daun, H  641
Davie, Grace  298
Davutoglu, Ahmet  464, 604
Dawud, Imam Abu  447
de Gobineau, Arthur  747
De Stoop, Chris  249
Debeer, Jonathan  237
Decimo, F  273

Degauge, Muriel 249
Demetriou, O 355
Deso Dogg (Mamadou Cuspert/Abou Maleeq) 663–4
Didero, Maike 136–7
al-Din, Taj 539
Dornhof, Sarah 134
Đozo, Husein 453–4
Drider, Kenza (Kendra) 45
Dronkers, Jaap 231
Dubouloz, C-J 783
Dudayev, Jokhar 542, 549
Duquet, Nils 230–1
Durić, Meliha 468

El Aroud, Malika (Umm Obeyda) 248
El Asri, Farid 229, 247
El Bachiri, Lila 246
El Battiui, Mohamed 235
El Fadl, Khaled Abou 448
El-Ghandour, Naim 377
El Hamel, Chouki 712
Elchinova, Magdalena 582
Elidrisi, Fatima 710
Erbakan, Necmettin 604, 659–60
Erdoğan, Recep Tayyip 604
Errichiello, G 273
Esati, Lulëzim 496
Esposito, John L 448, 749
Evergeti, V 362, 366, 375, 377, 379–80, 382
Evers Rosander, E 328
Evstatiev, Simeon 593, 601–2
Eydi, Akbar 448

Fadil, Nadia 242, 245
Fahd bin ʿAbd al-ʿAzīz Al Saud, king of Saudi Arabia 14–15, 225
Fallaci, Oriana 265, 274–5, 295, 600, 747, 758
Fanon, Frantz 762
Farage, Nigel 718
Färber, Alexa 129
Fatima, daughter of Prophet 450–1, 480
Fava, T 284
Fayzov, Ildus 517
Ferrari, Silvio 281, 629, 631
Fetzer, Joel S 25, 624, 633
Field, Clive 84
Filandra, Šaćir 433, 467

Fjordman (Peder Jensen) 416
Fleischmann, Fenella 232
Foblets, Marie-Claire 240–1
Fortuyn, Pim 192, 199, 747, 753, 759
Foucault, Michel 245, 412, 755–6
Fourest, Caroline 36
Fraihi, Hind 249
Franco, Francisco 312–14
Frégosi, F 629 30
Frindte, W 135
Frings, Dorothee 117
Frisina, A 294–6
Fuess, Albrecht 138, 631

Galal, LP 412
Gardell, M 413
Gazidede, Bashkim 502
Geaves, Ron 79–80, 87–9, 93
Geisser, Vincent 36, 46, 749
Gellner, Ernest 568
Gem, Ismail 604
Gerin, André 33–4, 37, 43, 721, 729
Gest, Justin 329–30
al-Ghazali, Abu Hamid 447
Ghazy, Randa 295
Ghirighelli, B 293
Gilliat-Ray, Sophie 77, 92
Girardi, D 297
Giscard d'Estaing, Valéry 25, 30
Godard, B 637
Gogonas, N 370, 380
Gol, Jean 224–5
Goli, M 414
González Enríquez, C 330
Gorbachev, Mikhail 523
Gradaščević, Husein-kapetan 433
Graham, Bill 463
Grignard, Alain 249, 774
Gropas, R 364, 370
Gruev, Mihail 578
Guéant, Claude 38–9
Gülen, Fetullah 482–3, 577, 593, 604–5
Güngör, Derya 243
Guolo, R 282, 286, 292
Gustafsson, K 412

Habermas, Jürgen 763
Hadžibajrić, Fejzulah 449

Hafizović, Rešid 454
Hagherty, MJ 325
Haider, Jörg 664
Hajatpour, Reza 139
Hakimov, Raphael 537
Halilović, Safvet 448
Halliday, Fred 746
Hamed, Hajd 392
Hamid, S 89
Hamiti, Xhabir 495, 496
Handžić, Mehmed 454
Hanifa, Imam Abu 447
Harrow, M 790–1
Hasan ibn Ali 480
Hatziprokopiou, P 362, 366, 375, 377, 379–80, 382
Heinisch-Hosek, Gabriele 718–19
Hellmich, C 781
Helqvist, I 407
Hervik, P 413
Hewlett, Nick 44
Hirshi Ali, Ayaan 170–1, 200, 727–8
Hirschon, Renee 353
Hitler, Adolf 107
Hoare, Marko Attila 466
Hoffman, B 794
Hollande, François 44
Hollobone, Philip 718
Hopkins, P 633, 642
Horgan, J 778, 781–2, 795
Horsti, K 413
Hoxha, Enver 481
Huntington, Samuel 508, 757–8, 762
Husayn ibn Ali 480
Hüseyinoglu, A 353
Hussain, Dilwar 87
Hussian, M 413
Hussain, Serena 71

Ihle, Annette H 408
Imhoff, R 141–2
Immig, N 353
Introvigne, M 281
Ioannidou, N 359
Ipgrave, J 633, 642
Isov, Myumyun 588
Izetbegović, Alija 452

Jackson, R 794
Jacobsen, Brian Arly 395, 398, 408, 411
Jacobsen, CM 412
Janmaat, Hans 200
Jansen, Hans 199
Jawad, H 45
al-Jawziyya, Ibn Qayyim 447
Jeldtof, Nadia 267, 412
Jemal, Heydar 535, 547
Jensen, Peder (Fjordman) 416
Jensen, T 412
Jiménez-Aybar, I 317
John Paul II, pope 457
Joly, D 81–2
Jones, Terry 750
Jonker, Gerdien 125
Joppke, Christian 725
Jouili, Jeanette 108
Jover, José María 340
Jozsa, D-P 641

Kadare, Ismail 507
Kanmaz, Meryem 235, 239
Karadžić, Radovan 432
Karadžić, Vuk 432
Karčić, Fikret 435, 444, 454
Karić, Enes 444, 453–4
Karakasidou, A 356
Karlsson Minganti, P 412
Kassimeris, G 375, 378
Kathir, Ibn 447, 462
Katsikas, S 353
Kavazovic, Hussein 418
Kaya, Ayhan 9, 223
Kelek, Necla 657–8
Kendra (Kenza Drider) 45
Kenney, M 791–2
Kentel, Ferhat 233
Khaldun, Ibn 447
Khalid, Amr 447
Khatami, M 448
Khomeini, Ruhollah 225, 546
Khorchide, Mouhanad 139, 675
Khosrokhavar, F 787, 793
Kilcullen, DJ 786, 791
Klausen, Jytte 112, 693
Klinkhammer, Gritt 135
Koçi, Hafiz Sabri 481, 483

Koenig, Matthias 130, 624
Koutroubas, Theodoros 250
Krasniqi, Shefqet 494–5, 496
Kreienbrink, A 119
Kruschchev, Nikita 521, 523
Kühle, Lene 407–8, 412
Kunz, Rene 719
Kuppinger, Petra 128
Kurban, D 359
Kurdić, Šefik 448

Laborde, Cécile 723
Laitin, David 29, 749
Lakshman-Lepain, Rajwantee 480
Lambert, Robert 794
Lamghari, Younous 241
Larcher, Gérard 47
Larsson, G 405, 412, 413
Latas, Omer Pasha 433
Latrèche, Mohamed Ennacer 37
Laurence, J 34, 43, 631
Le Pen, Jean-Marie 25, 49
Le Pen, Marine 38, 47–8
Lechkar, Iman 247
Legert, Alfred C 445
Leggewie, Claus 140
Leghari, IU 378
Leirvik, O 398, 411
Lesthaeghe, Ron 242–3
Lettinge, Doutje 727
Leveau, R 44
Lewis, Philip 79
Lewis, Toni 704
Lia, B 784
Liengaard, I 412
Little, Kenneth 67
Ljevaković, Enes 455
Longman, Chia 242
López Barrios, F 325
López García, Bernabé 329
López-Sala, A 710
Ludin, Ferestha 716–17, 725
Lunkin, Roman 551
Luqman, S 371

Machelon, Jean-Pierre 41
MacMaster, Neil 704
Maddanu, S 296

Mahlmann, Matthias 717
Makariev, Plamen 593
Maleeq, Abou (Mamadou Cuspert/Deso Dogg) 663–4
al-Malik, Amir 'And (Aleksei Pashintev) 547
Malik, Maleiha 746–7
Malm, A 413
Mamdani, M 45
Mancheva, M 576
Mantovan, C 284–5
Maréchal, Brigitte 36, 229, 246, 250, 589, 629
Marjani, Shihab al-Din 537
Markussen, HI 413
Marmouri, Amel 719–20
Marushkin, Oleg (Abu-Dhar) 550
Maroni, Roberto 282
Martens, Albert 224, 228, 229–31
Martín-Muñoz, G 710
Martini, Carlo Maria 292
Marx, Karl 532–3
Masood, Ahmad Shah 248
Maududi, Maulana 88–9
Maussen, Marcel 47–8, 625, 629–30, 632–3, 635–6, 652
Mavromatis, G 357
Máxima, princess (now queen) of Netherlands 175
Maxwell, Rahsaan 43
May, Theresa 717
Mazllami, Mazllam 496
McCauley, C 781, 794
McLoughlin, Seán 77, 89, 92
Medina, sheikh of 12
Meer, Nasar 749
Merah, Mohamed 47–8
Merkel, Angela 12, 656–7, 762–3
Michail, D 355
Miller, J 633, 642
Milošević, Slobodan 465, 487, 489
al-Misri, Imad 451
Mitsotakis, Konstantinos 358
Mitterand, François 39
Mladić, Ratko 466–7
Modood, Tariq 74, 749
Moe, Christian 439
Mohamad, Ben Ali 392
Moniquet, Claude 249
Moors, A 184

Moreras, J 324
Moroz, E 546
Moskalenko, S 781, 794
Moulaert, Frank 230
Moussalli, Ahmad 675
Moussaoui, Mohammed 34, 36–7, 39
Mucchielli, Laurent 48
Muckel, Stefan 129
Muhammad (the Prophet) 13, 81, 372, 379, 414, 416, 450–1, 457, 460–1, 658, 704, 753–4
Mullins, S 779, 790
Musa, Sanin 448
Muslim, Imam 447
Musliu, Osman 495–6
Mustafa, Mohamed Kamal 327
al-Mustansir, Muhammad I 392
Mutahhari, Morteza 448

Naik, Zakir 506
Naqshbandi-Mahmudi, Avar 540
al-Nasa'I, Imam 447
Naso, Paolo 281–2
Natvig, RJ 413
Al-Nawawi 447
Negri, A 292–3
Nesser, P 774, 778–9
Neumann, PR 791, 793
Niehaus, I 642–3
Nielsen, Jørgen 76–7
Njegos, Petar II Petrovic 432
al-Nur, Masjid 690–1
Nusri, Said 464–5

Obama, Barack 550
Offa, king of Mercia 67
O'Hagan, Andrew 747–8
Oktem, Kerem 577, 593, 602–4
Olsen, JA 792
Omar, Abu 298
Omel'chenko, Elena 528–9, 531
Oran, B 353
Orsi, Robert 45
Osmani, Mullah 496
Østberg, Sissel 412
Østergaard, K 412
Otterbeck, J 412. 413, 414, 416
Oubrou, Tareq 675

Ouis, P 412
Ozal, Turgut 604
Özsoy, Ömer 139

Pacini, A 282
Palaver, Wolfgang 600
Panafit, Lionel 237
Papadopoulou, Dora 381
Papagaroufali, E 370
Papanastasiou, A 380–1
Papantoniou, A 370
Pashintev, Aleksei (Amir 'And al-Malik) 547
Payne, K 794
Paz, R 791
Pedain, Antje 724
Pedersen, Marianne Holm 408, 412
Pedziwiatr, Konrad 240, 244
Pérez-Agote Poveda, A 317
Perocco, F 275, 287
Peter, Frank 131–2, 141
Petronoti, M 370
Peucker, Mario 117, 120
Pezo, Adnan 451
Phalet, Karen 232
Pisanu, Giuseppe 282
*Plant Contreras, Ana i* 313, 338, 343
Podvorica, Armend 495
Pollack, Detlef 751
Purdam, K 86
Putin, Vladimir 517, 523–4, 534–5, 537, 539–40, 542, 547–8, 550–1

Qaddafi, Muammar 225
Qader, Abdel 295
Qadïrov, Ahmad 535, 551
Qadïrov, Ramzan 535
Al-Qaradawi, Yusuf 448
al-Qarni, 'A'id 447
Quayle, E 780
Quilliam, Abdullah 68
Qursawi, Abd al-Nasir Abu'l-Nasr 537
al-Qurtubi, Abu Abdullah 447

Ragaru, Nadege 582
Ramadan, Tariq 36, 174, 188, 802
Ramić, Šukrija 455
Ranstorp, M 777, 780

Rasmussen, Poul Nyrup 399
Rath, J 628–30
Rau, Johannes 716
Rea, Andrea 241
Reagan, Ronald 759–60
Rechel, Bernd 597
Recker, J 141–2
Reetz, Dietrich 127
Reindfeldt, Frank 711
Rex, John 73–4
Rexhepi, Sulejman 488, 490
Rezaei, S 414
Rhazzali, Mohammed Khalid 290
Riccio, Bruno 273, 288
Richardson, Robin 746, 749
Roald, AS 412
Robin, Corey 759
Rohe, Mathias 8, 118, 632, 635
Ros, Ángel 720
Rose, Flemming 414
Rosenow-Williams, Kerstin 126–7
Roy, Olivier 403, 776–7, 786–8
Royal, Ségolène 44
Ruiz Vieytez, E 328
Rushdie, Salman 10, 47, 81–2, 84, 226, 786
al-Rusi, Haran (Vadim Sidorov) 546–7

Sabirova, Guzel 528–9, 531
Sachedina, Abdulaziz 675
Sachkova, Elena 573–4
Sagitova, Liliya 538–9
Saharso, Elisabeth 727–8
Said, Edward 45, 252, 413, 704, 747
Sa'id the Buryat (Aleksandr Tikhomirov) 547
Saint-Blancat, Chantal 268, 279, 284, 287
Sakaranaho, T 635, 637, 640
Salgado, O 326
Salih, R 273
Salvanou, E 375
Salvarini, B 281
Samouris, A 375, 378
Sander, Åke 396, 405, 412
Sapp, Wayne 754
Sarazzin, Thilo 600, 763
Sarkozy, Nicolas 33, 35–6, 44, 47, 49–50, 721, 762
Saroglou, Vassilis 252

Sartori, Giovanni 265, 274–5
Satarov, Fayz al-Rahman 517–18
Sauer, Birgit 705, 723–5
Sbai, Souad 719
Scaranari Introvigne, S 292
Schäuble, Wolfgang 131–2
Scheffer, Paul 231
Schiffauer, Werner 125, 127–8
Schiffer, Sabine 749
Schiller, Nina Glick 475
Schimmel, Annemarie 448
Schmidt, Garbi 144, 407–8, 412
Schmidt di Friedberg, Ottavia 268, 279, 284–5, 288
Schwarzer, Alice 657
Sciortino, G 268, 274–5
Seehofer, Horst 762
Selimoski, Jakub 491
Sells, Michael 431–2
Selmer, B 412
Semati, Mehdi 749, 759
Šeta, Djermana 448
Shadid, Wasif 640
Shaimiev, Mintimer 537, 539–40
Al-Shawkani, Muhammad 447
Shehu, Xhemali 484–5
Siddiqui, Ataullah 78–9
Siddiqui, Fayz 691–2
Sidorov, Vadim (Haran al-Rusi) 546–7
Silajdžić, Haris 452
Silke, A 770, 795
Silvestri, Sara 282, 284, 631, 638
Simonsen, JB 407, 412
Sinani, Avni 496
Sivanandan, Ambalavaner 746
Skoulariki, A 372, 375
Slootman, M 778, 793
Sloth, Line Vikkelsø 399
Smajić, Aid 461
Smajlović, Ahmed 449
Solzhenitsyn, Alexander 523
Soper, J Christopher 25, 624, 633
Sorabji, Cornelia 444
Speckhard, A 777, 786
Stalin, Josef 477, 521, 532, 554
Stasi, Bernard 32, 713–14
Stichs, A 119

Stoiber, Edmund 716
Straw, Jack 73, 708, 718, 725
Striegher, J–L 793
Sultan Sjöqvist, M 412
Sultanov, Kamil 546
Sultanov, Shamil 546
al-Suyuti, Jalal al-Din
Svanberg, I 412
Szelenyi, Ivan 572

Tabatabai, Muhammad H 448
al-Tabligh, Jamaat 37
al-Tahawi 447
Tanaskovic, Darko 604
Tarrés, S 326–7, 339
Tatari, E 625, 630
Taylor, M 778, 780
Teofanov, Tzvetan 601
Teresa, Mother 503
Tërnava, Naim
Tezcan, Levent 132, 143
Thielmann, Jörn 142–4
Tibi, Bassam 448, 802
Tikhomirov, Aleksandr (Sa'id the Buryat) 547
Tillie, M 778, 793
Al-Tirmidhi, Imam 447
Torrekens, Corinne 239
Touag, Hanifa 247
Trabelsi, Nizar 248
Triandafyllidou, A 275, 382
Tribalat, Michèle 764
Trubeta, S 382
Tsitselikis, K 357, 359, 372–3
Turajanzada, Ishan Nur al-Din Jan 526

Ukaj, Arid 508
'Umarov, Ayyub 549–50
Umarov, Dokku 543
Umm Obeyda (Malika El Aroud) 248

Vaisse, J 34, 43
Valfort, Marie-Anne 29
Van Amerongen, Arthur 249
Van den Branden, Stef 244–5
van Gogh, Theo 10, 108–9, 165–6, 173, 192, 196, 747, 779
van Koningsveld, Peter 640
Van Robaeys, Bea 230

Van San, Marion 232
Vandermeersch, Anke 248
Vanderwaeren, Els 244
Verbeke, Wim 245
Vercellin, G 265
Verdonk, Rita 721
Verhagen, Maxime 721
Vernet, Juan 340
Vertovec, Steven 749
Vidino, L 770, 786, 793–4
Vilks, Lars 416
Villiers, Philippe de 50
Vincentini, A 284
Vogt, Kari 398, 411, 412
Vrielink, Jogchum 242

Wadud, Amina 675
Wagner, Constantin 749
Wahab, Muhammed Ibn Abdel 13
Wanche, SI 380
Warsi, Saeeda 86
Weber, Beverly 716
Werbner, Pnina 68, 76, 81, 87–8, 90, 749
Wesley, R 781–2
Westerlund, D 412
Wetzels, P 133
Widmer-Schlumpf, Eveline 719
Wiegers, Gerard 91
Wihtol de Wenden, C 44
Wiktorowicz, Quintan 776, 782, 784
Wilders, Geert 197, 199–201, 706, 720–1, 762
Williams, Rowan 7, 85, 627, 656, 718
Wilner, AS 783
Wimmer, Andreas 475
Winter, Bronwyn 727
Winter, TJ 89–90
Wulff, Christian 656–7, 750

Ya'qupov, Wali-Allah 517–18, 540, 548
Yeltsin, Boris 517, 528, 544
Yiakoumaki, V 358

Zanfrini, L 297
Zatti, G 292
Zayd, Nasr Hamid Abu 448
Zibouh, Fatima 238
Zilio-Grandi, I 293
Zoccatelli, PL 281

# Subject Index

**Abdullah Quilliam Society** 68
**accommodation**
 education and schools 640–3
 family law 684
 institutions/organizations 620, 630, 635
 radicalism/radicalization 637
 shariah law 694–6
**acculturation** 3, 16, 635, 802
**Afghanistan**
 burqas 704 n. 3
 corporal punishment and stoning 7
 dower 684
 jihadis 773–4
 *mujahideen* 517, 773, 789
 Pakistan 791
**Ahmadiyya movements** 107, 108 n.2, 125–7, 140, 319, 377, 393, 407–8, 418
**Aid el-Kebir festival** 282, 638
**Al-Qaeda** 47, 250, 509
 foreign occupation 779, 784
 Internet 791
 Islamophobia 759, 764
 Madrid bombings 2004 779
 motivation to join, reasons for 785, 788
 propaganda 784
 radicalism/radicalization 773, 775–6, 779, 781, 784, 788, 791, 793–4
 Salafism 781
 social movement, as 776
 training 791
 transnationalism 776
**Albâch** 48
**Albanian Muslims** 475–511 *see also* **Kosovo**; **Macedonia**
 agreements between states and religious communities 499
 Albanian Democratic Party 491
 atheist state, as 477
 Balkan wars 477
 believing, behaving, and belonging 477–84, 492–4
 Bektashi 480–2, 485, 490, 499–501
 BRDIA 484–5
 Catholic Church 477–80, 482–3, 486, 488, 499, 501–3, 510
 census data 480
 clash of civilizations 477, 506–7, 508
 Christianity and Christians 478–83, 506
  Catholic Church 477–80, 482–3, 486, 488, 499, 501–3, 510
  persecution 477
  Protestantism 483, 499
 communism 476–8, 481–3, 486, 492–4, 498–9, 502, 506–7, 509–10
 Constitution 499, 502
 conversions, forced 478
 culture and cultural heritage 478–80, 484, 487, 494, 497, 502, 508, 510–11
 democracy and democratic principles 477, 492, 507
 demographics 478
 diaspora 475, 491, 496
 discrimination and equal treatment 485, 493–4, 496–7
  gender relations/women 492, 496–7
  Islamophobia 477, 496, 507–8
 diversity 477, 478–87
 education and schools
  foreign donors and influence 498
  higher education 482, 498, 500
  public schools 500, 504, 510
  radicalism/radicalization 482–3
  religious education 482–3, 491, 494, 497–8, 500, 503, 506
  segregation 498
 employment 497, 500

**Albanian Muslims** *(Cont.)*
  equality amongst religions  480, 499
  ethno-nationalism  476, 478
  European Union  507
  Evangelical Brotherhood of Albania
    (VUSH)  499
  forced migration  478
  foreign donors and influences  482–3, 487,
    491, 496, 498, 506, 509–10, 603
  freedom of religion  480, 499
  gender relations/women  492, 496–7
  generational differences  494, 509
  government policy  492, 499
  Greece  477–9, 480–1
  Gülen movement  482–3
  Hanafi school  483
  hijab/headscarves  488, 496, 497, 603
  history/historical perspective  2, 4, 476–91,
    508–11
  identity  476, 478–9, 481, 490, 499, 507–8,
    510
  imams, Muftis and clerics
    foreign donors and influence  483
    Grand Mufti  481
    radicalism/radicalization  495
    training  483, 500
  immigration/migrants  478, 480–1, 502
  institutions/organizations  480, 483–6, 490,
    493, 495–502, 507, 509, 634
  international constraints  506–9
  Internet  496–7, 506
  Islamic schools  500, 503
  Islamophobia  477, 496, 507–8
  Italy  268–9, 272, 291, 481
  Jews/Judaism  501, 506
  labour migrants/guest workers  481
  languages  476, 482, 492
  legal status  499–502
  majority Muslim population  2, 4, 475, 477,
    486, 489, 503
  media  476–7, 492, 506–8
  minorities in other countries, Albanian
    Muslims as  475, 477
  mixed communities  479
  moderates  488, 491
  Montenegro  475, 485
  mosques
    building/establishment  487, 501, 502, 506,
      508
    mosque war  495
    radicalism/radicalization  491
    Salafism  495–6
  Muslim Community of Albania
    (MCA)  481–3, 499–500, 502, 507
  national identity  507–8
  nationalism  475–6, 478, 485, 489–90
  nationalization of religion  480
  naturalization  475
  neutrality of state  499, 509
  Organization of the Islamic Conference
    (OIC)  502
  Orthodox Church  478–82, 489, 499
  Ottoman Empire  476–7, 478–80, 492,
    506–7, 509, 569
  persecution by state  477–8, 479 n.3, 481,
    485
  political identity  476, 507
  political participation/representation  491,
    498
  population shifts  481
  prayers  488
  propaganda and promotion  506
  Protestantism  483, 499
  publications  483–4, 487–8, 506
  public sphere/visibility  493, 498–506, 508
  race and ethnicity  476–7, 478–9, 484–5,
    489, 491–2, 496, 499, 510
  radicalism/radicalization  482–3, 491–2,
    495–6, 506, 508–10
  recognition  480, 499
  registration or licensing  499–500
  religious authorities  483–4, 486–8, 496,
    508–9
  religious education  482–3, 491, 494, 497–8,
    500, 503, 506
  religious identity  478, 481, 499, 507–8, 510
  religiosity  480, 492–4
  repatriation after WW1  479
  representative bodies  500
  restitution of religious property  501, 502
  revival of religion  482, 492–4, 498–9
  rituals, festivals and holidays  488
  role of religion in society  502–6
  rural areas  485, 494, 497–8, 503, 506

Salafism 480 n. 4, 483–4, 487–8, 491, 494–8, 510, 603
Saudi Arabia 478, 482–3, 488, 497, 506, 603
scholarship 476–84, 487, 499, 507
Second World War 480–1
secularism/secularization 480, 492, 497, 499, 500, 502, 508–9
sectarianism 476, 479–80, 487, 499, 502, 509–10
security/securitization 477
segregation 477, 496–8
September 2011, terrorist attacks on United States 477, 493–4, 506–8, 510
Serbia 475, 489–90
shariah law 501–2
Shi'a Muslims 478, 506
social dynamics 492–8
social media 496–7, 506
socio-economic status 477, 492, 494
Sufism 478, 480–1, 483–8, 490, 494
Sunni Muslims 480–2, 484–6, 490, 506
theology 483–4, 488, 492
traditionalists/conservatives 482, 488, 494–8, 508–11
traditions, competing 482
transnationalism 508–9
Turkey 478, 480, 482, 495
uniqueness of Islam among Albanians 478–9
war on terror 477
youth 481, 494–5, 507
Yugoslavia 476–9, 484–6, 490, 496, 498–9, 501, 509–10
Alevis 115–17, 122–3, 574–5, 590, 592, 603–4
Alevitische Community Germany (AABF) 125
Algeria
 Algerian Islamic Salvation Front 48
 Algerian War 24, 29–30, 47
 France 24, 26–7, 29–30, 37, 39, 47, 625, 681, 704
 radicalism/radicalization 47–8, 773, 786
 Spain 315–16, 330, 336, 341
 terrorism 47
Alids 393
Al-Qaeda 509, 759, 770, 773, 775–7, 781, 784, 788, 791, 793–4

anti-Islamic attitudes *see* Islamophobia
anti-Semitism 127, 201, 747 n.3, 750
Arab Spring 268, 540, 584
Armed Islamic Group (GIA) 47–8, 773
assimilation 4–6
 Euro-Islam 804
 hijab/headscarves 729
 institutions/organizations 620, 630, 635
 Islamophobia 653
 radicalism/radicalization 782–3
asylum seekers 4, 9, 363, 786
Austria
 Austro-Hungary 429–30, 433, 436, 440–1
 Catholicism 725
 citizenship 706, 756
 education and schools 641, 644, 662, 705–6, 724–5
 freedom of religion 706
 full-face covering 718–19
 halal/religious slaughter 644
 hijab/headscarves 705–6, 718–19, 723–4
 immigration/migrants 706
 Islamic Religious Community 641
 Islamophobia 757
 language 662
 mosques, building/establishment of 639, 644
 naturalization 723
 neutrality 669
 public opinion/perceptions 661–2
 recognition 644
 religious education 641, 644
 representative bodies 644
 right-wing populist parties 662, 706, 725
 security/securitization 718–19
 shariah law 662, 664, 669, 680, 694
 Sunni Muslims 641
 *talaq*, recognition of 680
 Turks 661–2
 xenophobia and racism 706
Austro-Hungary 429–30, 433, 436, 440–1
Avars 523, 541
'Axis of Evil' 758, 760

bad Islam and good Islam, distinction between 803
Balkan wars 429, 434, 438, 445–8, 450–2, 461–8

**Barelvi movement** 88, 377
**Bashkortostan** 520, 524, 543, 552
**Bektashi mystical order** 356, 480–2, 485, 490, 499–501, 574–5, 590, 592, 603
**Belgium** 222–54
  accommodation 240–2
  Al Qaeda 250
  allochthons, Muslims as 228
  assimilation 228, 233
  attachment to countries of origin 225
  believing, behaving, and belonging 242–6, 253
  Brussels 222, 238, 243
  burquas 242, 721
  Catholics 235–6
  chaplains 235
  Christianity and Christians 235–6, 244
  citizenship 223, 225, 229, 240, 253
  civil and political actors, Muslims as 238–40
  comparative approach 239, 243
  crime 232
  culture and cultural heritage 228, 231–4, 243, 253
  democracy and democratic principles 241, 250
  demographics 222, 224, 238–9
  demonstrations and protests 225–6, 247–8, 249–50
  discrimination and equality 233, 241, 253
    gender relations/women 240–2, 244, 246, 248, 251–2
    Islamophobia 223, 251–3
    xenophobia and racism 233, 248, 251
  diversity 241
  dual identity 234
  education and schools 229, 231–2, 238, 251, 640, 642
    higher education 230–1
    hijab/headscarves 251, 714–15
    public schools 235–6, 715
    religious education 235, 243, 640–1, 644
    segregation 231
    symbols 234
  employment 224–5, 230–1, 234, 241–2, 252
  Equal Opportunities and Opposition to Racism (CEOOR) 227
  euthanasia and process of dying 244–5
  Executive of Muslims of Belgium (EMB) 236–7
  family law 240–1
  family reunification 224
  fear, emergence of expertise of 248–9
  Flemings/Flanders
    hijab/headscarves 714
    integration 226, 234, 253
    Islamophobia 251
    language 223, 234
    mosques 235
    pluralism 714, 723
    political parties 226–7
    regional fractures 223, 235
  Francophones/Wallonia 222–3, 225–8, 238, 249–50, 252–3
    hijab/headscarves 714
    integration 226
    mosques 235
    regional fractures 223, 235
  freedom of religion 235, 252, 671, 715
  funding 235, 237
  gender relations/women 240–2, 244, 246, 248, 251–2
  generational differences 230, 233–4, 239, 243–6
  government policy 224, 226–7, 231–2, 236–7, 241, 253
  halal/religious slaughter 228, 245, 644
  healing practices 247
  health and healthcare 235, 245
  hijab/headscarves 226, 229, 233, 240, 705, 714–15, 723
    ban 241–2, 669, 671, 705, 714–15, 721
    burquas 242, 721
    education and schools 251
    employment 252
    full-face covering 242, 671, 721
    Islamophobia 252
    niqabs 671, 721
    public opinion/perceptions 714–15
    public space/visibility 721
    security/securitization 721, 729
    shariah law 669, 670–1, 694
    symbols, ban on conspicuous religious 715

historical perspectives 223–7
homosexuality 248
identity 225, 233–4, 238, 240, 243–7, 251
*ijtihad* 244
imams, Muftis and clerics 235, 249
immigration/migrants 224–8, 231–2, 251–2
individuals and individualization 229, 242–5, 253
institutions/organizations 6, 223, 234–42, 246–53, 634
integration 223, 226–34, 237–9, 253–4
international context 247–51
Internet 248
interventionism 237–8
Islamic Cultural Centre (ICC) 225–6, 237
Islamophobia 223, 251–3
language 222–3, 225–6, 234–5
legal aspects 240–2
marriage and divorce 244, 252, 681
media 222, 225–6, 234–5, 238, 248–50
moderates 226, 232
Moroccans 224–5, 230–4, 238, 240, 242–9
mosques 242–3
 building/establishment 639, 644
 funding 235, 237
 number 235
 public sphere 238–9
multiculturalism 231–2, 241
musical genres 247
Muslim Brotherhood 246–7
nationalist reforms of state apparatus 226
nationality identity 234
naturalization 230
neutrality model 234, 237, 241, 253
niqabs 671, 721
Other, Muslims as ethnic and religious 227–9, 252
personal law 240–1
pillarization, principle of 235
pluralism 241–2
political participation/representation 223, 226–8, 235, 237–40, 250–1
polygamy 681–2
poverty 229–30
prisoners 235–6, 248
Protestantism 235
public opinion/perceptions 222, 714–15

public space/visibility 222, 223–4, 228–9, 233–4, 238–40, 721
publications 248–9
race and ethnicity 227–33, 236, 238, 243, 252–3
radicalism/radicalization 223, 225–9, 237, 247–52, 622
Ramadan 236, 241, 243
recognition 224, 226, 233–8, 644
regional fractures 223, 235
religious education 235, 243, 640–1, 644
religious identity 225, 238, 240, 243–7, 251
religiosity 232–3, 242–6, 253
renewed engagements with Muslim tradition, examining 246–7
representative bodies 6, 226–7, 229, 236–9, 253, 644
residential pattern 222
return 224, 233
right-wing populist parties 226–7, 251, 662
Salafism 246–7
Saudi Arabia 225, 236
scholarship 222–4, 227–8, 232, 234, 238, 240, 244, 246, 252–4
secularism/secularization 223–5, 228–9, 242–5, 250, 253–4
security/securitization 222, 249, 721, 729
separation of church and state 235, 244
September 11, 2001, terrorist attacks on United States 222, 248
shariah law 240–1, 656, 662, 681–2
Shi'a Muslims 247
socio-economic status 223–4, 228–34, 253
state and religion relations 234–5
stereotyping 252
Sunni Muslims 244, 247
symbols, ban on conspicuous religious 234, 715
terrorism 222
theology 236, 244–5
traditionalists/conservatives 239, 244
transnationalism 225
Turks 224–5, 230–1, 233–4, 238, 242–4
unemployment 229–30
xenophobia and racism 233, 248, 251
youth 232–3, 238–40, 244, 246
**Bektashi** 356, 480–2, 485, 490, 499–501, 574–5, 590, 592, 603–4

## SUBJECT INDEX

**believing, behaving, and belonging** 11–12 *see also* **religiosity**
**Beth Din** 85
**Beurs movement** 24–5, 30, 34, 44
**Bosnia and Herzegovina** 429–69
  abroad, studying 444, 446, 452, 453, 459
  Active Islamic Youth (AIY) 451
  aid 461–2
  arms 461–2, 463
  associationism 457, 459
  Austro-Hungarian rule 429–30, 433, 436, 440–1
  Balkan wars 429, 434, 438, 445–8, 450–2, 461–8
  believing, behaving, and belonging 430, 444–65
  Bogumils 431
  Bosniaks 429–31, 433–41, 451, 465–9, 477
  burial and cemeteries 455, 457, 458
  Catholics and Catholic Church 431–2, 437, 457
  census data 468, 469
  chaplains 437
  Chetniks (extremists) 434
  Christianity and Christians 431–2, 437, 457, 463
  communism 429–30, 434–5, 444, 446–8, 453, 465
  concerts, organization of 449
  conversion 430–2, 448, 464
  Croatia/Croats 430, 432–4, 438, 442, 451, 465–7
  culture and cultural heritage 432, 436, 439, 458, 462–4, 467, 469
  Dayton Peace Accords 429, 452, 467
  democracy and democratic principles 437, 452
  demographics 429, 469
  desecularization 444
  diaspora 469
  discrimination and equal treatment 430, 437, 448, 452, 468, 496
    gender relations/women 448–51, 455, 456, 687
    Islamophobia 430, 496
  donors 446–8, 450–53
  education and schools 440–4, 469
    abroad, studying 444, 446, 452, 453, 459
    Faculty of Islamic Studies 442, 444, 446, 455–7, 459
    foreign donors and influence 446
    Gazi Husrev Bey Madarasah 442, 444, 446, 456
    gender relations/women 456
    higher 438, 444, 446, 458–9
    hijab/headscarves 456
    Iran 463–4
    public schools 437, 446, 459
    religious education 436, 441–2, 444–6, 448, 452, 459
    Saudi Arabia 462–3
    Turkey 464–5
  employment 456, 458–9
  ethnic cleansing 430, 433, 466–9
  Euro-Islam 439
  European Union 430
  Faculty of Islamic Studies 442, 444, 446, 455–7, 459
  family law 438, 448–9, 456, 460
  fatwas 443, 453–5, 457–9
  foreign donors and influence 418, 444–8, 450–2, 459–65, 469, 603
  freedom of religion 437, 445
  Gazi Husrev Bey Madarasah 442, 444, 446, 456
  gender relations/women 448–51, 455, 456, 687
    Kewser organization 450–1
    Nahla organization 450
    representative bodies 450–1
  generational differences 438, 444, 454, 456
  genocide 430, 433, 466–9
  Germany 105–6, 687
  government policy 429, 477–8
  Grand Mufti 418, 440, 442–3, 485
  Hanafi school 435, 441, 451
  health and healthcare 437, 435
  hijab/headscarves 444, 448, 456, 603
  history/historical perspective 2, 4, 429–49, 453–4, 465–9
  historiography 430–2
  identity
    national 429, 434, 439, 444, 468–9
    religious 429, 431, 439

*ijtihad* 435
imams, Muftis and clerics 440–3
  appointment 440
  education and schools 459
  foreign donors and influence 418, 459
  Grand Mufti 418, 440, 442–3, 485
  Islamic Community (IC) 441–2, 459
  organization 441–3
  revival 452
  training 440, 443, 446, 459
independence 465
indigenous Muslim community 429
institutions/organizations 429–30, 432, 436, 440–6, 449–52, 455–6, 634
International Court of Justice 467
International Criminal Tribunal for the former Yugoslavia (ICTY) 465 n. 135, 466–7
Internet 469
interpretation 439, 446–8, 451, 453–4, 459
inter-religious relations 455, 456–8
Iran 463–4
Islamic Community (IC) 436–60, 463–4
Islamized pre-Islamic Bosnian culture 435
Islamophobia 430, 496
Jews/Judaism 434, 457
Kosovo 432, 445, 448–9, 460, 483
language 432, 436, 447–8, 452, 459, 462, 464–5
Law on Freedom of Religion and the Legal Position of Churches and Religious Communities 437
  main characteristics of Bosnian Islam 436–40
  majority Muslim population 2, 4, 430, 452
  marriage and divorce 438, 448–9, 456
  Maturidi, Sunni Islam tradition of 435
  media 444–5, 461, 465, 468
  *mektebs* 445–6
  minority, as part of 429
  modernity 430, 432–4, 439
  mosques 457–8, 460–1
    building/establishment/reconstruction 444–7, 450, 457, 461, 462–3, 468
    destruction 436, 442, 446–7, 465, 468
    operation 440, 443

mystical Islam, attitudes to 455, 458–9
national identity 429, 434, 439, 444, 468–9
nationalism 433
niqabs 448, 456
Orthodox Church 431–2, 437, 468
Ottoman Empire 429–35, 440, 467, 569
personal law 438, 448–9, 456, 460
pluralism 438–9, 448
political participation/representation 461
popular Islam, attitudes to 455, 458–9
prayers 435, 443, 457–9, 461
prisoners 431, 436, 467
public opinion/perceptions 440, 455
public sphere/visibility 435, 444, 446, 449–50
publications 443, 445–9, 453–4, 462–5
Qur'an 441, 460–1, 462–4
  interpretation 446, 448, 453–4
  recitation 449, 458, 461
radicalization 438–40, 443–5, 451–2, 773
reformism 435–6
refugees and displaced persons 4, 105–6, 429, 434, 462–4, 467
reintegration into wider Muslim community 435–6
religious authorities 436, 447, 453–9, 485–6
religious education 436, 441–2, 444–6, 448, 452, 459
religious identity 429, 431, 439
religious revival 430, 444–65
religiosity 430, 444, 460–1
representative bodies 429–30, 449–52, 460
revival of religion 444–5, 451–2
rituals, festivals and holidays 432, 435, 437, 441, 457–8, 460–1
*Saff* 451, 455–8
Salafism 438–40, 445, 447–8, 451–2, 454–9, 462–5, 603
Saudi Arabia 438, 446–7, 462–3, 603
scholarship 431, 434–6, 443, 447–9, 453–8, 464, 468–9
  alternative and mainstream, difference between 455–8
  growth of mainstream 453–5
  revival 447–9
Second World War 429, 434, 453
secularism 436, 439–40, 444, 446

**Bosnia and Herzegovina** *(Cont.)*
  security  440, 445, 453, 469
  separation of church and state  437–8
  September 2011, terrorist attacks on United States  430, 451, 452, 463, 469
  Serbia/Serbs  430–4, 437–8, 442, 451, 465–7
  shariah courts  436, 437–8, 460
  shariah law  436–9, 448–9, 456, 460, 464
  Shi'a Muslims  448, 450, 454, 458–9, 464
  socio-economic status  431, 469
  Srebrenica massacre  466
  Srpska, Republic of  437, 442, 447, 466–8
  state-religion relations  437
  stereotyping  448
  Sufis  434–6, 438–9, 443, 445, 448–50, 452, 454, 457–9, 464
  Sunni Muslims  435, 448, 451–2
  symbols  444
  *tariqas*  449–50, 460
  terrorism and violence  439–40, 451, 468
  theology  434–5, 438–9, 450–4, 459, 464, 469
  traditionalists/conservatives  433–6, 438, 442, 445–51, 454, 459–61
  transnationalism  443
  Turks/Turkey  464–5, 604
  Ustasha (Croat extremists)  434
  war crimes  434, 438 n.35, 465, 467
  youth  449, 451, 456
  Yugoslavia
    as part of  429, 434, 437, 440, 444, 446, 465
    dissolution  429–30, 435, 436, 464, 465–8
    liberalization  453
**Britain** *see* **United Kingdom**
**Bulgaria**  4, 565–606
  abroad, studying  593–4, 602–3
  age  576–7, 591–2
  assimilation  575, 580, 596–7
  *Alevi/Kizilbashi/Bektashi*  574–5, 590, 592, 603–4
  *Ataka* nationalist party  600–2
  believing, behaving, and belonging  594–6
  Bulgarian Turks for the Movement for Rights and Freedoms (MRF)  576
  burial and cemeteries  578, 588
  Catholics  569, 594
  census data  570–1, 577, 579, 583
  Chief Mufti  589–92, 592–3, 602
  Christianity and Christians  566–9, 576–9, 588, 594–5, 597, 600–1, 605
    Catholics  569, 594
    Orthodox Church  568–9, 579, 589–90
    Protestants  569, 578–80, 594, 597
  citizenship  576
  communism  565–6, 572, 580–2, 592, 594–8
  comparative approach  584, 589, 593–4
  constitutions  575, 589–90
  culture and cultural heritage  4, 566–9, 575–7, 581, 587–9, 605
  demographics  569–73, 605–6
  demonstrations and protests  600–1
  Denominations Act  590
  diaspora  604
  discrimination and equal treatment  572, 575, 581, 586, 589, 600
    gender relations/women  576, 581–6, 595–7
    Islamophobia  566, 567, 569, 599–605
  Eastern Orthodox Church  568–9, 579, 589–90
  economic migration  572
  education and schools  568, 572–4, 582–3, 585–8
    abroad, studying  593–4, 602–3
    curriculum, debates on inclusion of study of religion in  594
    foreign donors and influence  593, 602–3, 605
    gender relations/women  596
    higher education  565, 583, 593–4
    illiteracy  572–3
  imams, Muftis and clerics  592–3
  immigration/migrants  573–4, 606
  languages  592
  mosques  592–3
  Pomaks  579
  poverty  572–3
  religious education  589, 592–4
  Roma  572–3, 580
  textbooks  592–3
  Turks  577
  employment  572, 576, 581–2, 585–6, 596, 606
  European Muslims  576

European Union 4, 584
Fethullahci 580
forced resettlement 581
foreign donors and influence 566, 599–605
freedom of religion 567–8, 575
fundamentalism 600, 602
gender relations/women 576, 581–6, 595–7, 603
generational differences 576–7, 579, 591, 593–4, 602
government policy 573–4, 583, 587, 597–8, 605
Greece 354–5, 358–9, 686
Gülen movement 577, 593
Hanafi school 590, 603
health and healthcare 572, 585
High Islamic Institute (HII) 593–4
hijab/headscarves 603
historiography 568–9
history/historical perspective 2, 567–9, 588, 597
human rights 575, 583, 585, 598, 600
identity 568, 576–80, 587, 595, 597, 601, 605
illiteracy 572–3
imams, Muftis and clerics
  abroad, studying 594, 602–3
  age 591–2
  Chief Mufti 589–92, 592–3, 602
  education and schools 592–3
  legal status 589
  literature, certification of 595
  number of imams 591–2
  radicalism/radicalization 579, 594, 600–2, 604
  Salafism 579, 594, 596, 604
  Thrace, Muftis in 359
  training 591–2
immigration/migrants 4, 567, 569, 572–4, 580–7, 591, 599, 604–6
  education and schools 573–4, 606
  emigration 580–3
  gender relations/women 597
  illegal 584, 606
  immigrants in Bulgaria 582–7
  new migrants 567
  religiosity 595–6
  traditionalism/conservatism 597
  Turkey, to 576
institutions/organizations 565–6, 583, 586–7, 598, 604–6
integration 573–4, 581, 587, 596, 598
interpretation 569, 589, 595
Islamic schools 592–4
Islamophobia 566, 567, 569, 599–605
Jews/Judaism 574, 597–8
Kurds 576
labour migrants/guest workers 576, 581–2, 606
language 576, 577, 579, 581, 585–6, 589, 592
legal status 589–92
marriage and divorce 582, 583–4, 588, 596
masculinity 596
media 587, 599–602, 604–5
*millet* system under Ottoman Empire 568
mixed marriages 582, 583–4, 588, 596
moderates 569
mosques 579, 589, 594–6
  building/establishment 592, 594–5, 600
  demonstrations and protests 600–1
  education 592–3
  gender relations/women 596–7
  Turks 577
Movement for Rights and Freedoms (MRF) 576, 595, 597–9
multiculturalism 574, 600–1
Muslim Conferences 591
National Conference 590
national identity 568
national victimization 569
nationalism 599–602
neo-Ottoman doctrine 602, 604
number of Muslims 572, 583
Nursi activists 573, 580
organizational structure 590–2
Orthodox Church 568–9, 579, 589–90
Ottoman Empire 566–9, 575, 578, 588, 601–5
political participation/representation 566, 576, 594–602, 604
polygamy 603
Pomaks (Muslim Bulgarians) 477, 568–9, 577–9, 594–7, 600, 602, 605
poverty 572–3
prayers 579

**Bulgaria** *(Cont.)*
  Protestants  569, 578–80, 597
  public opinion/perceptions  579, 586–7, 590, 594, 598–600
  public sphere/visibility  566–7, 587–97
  publications  588–9, 595, 599–602, 604–5
  Qur'an  578, 591–3
  race and ethnicity  567, 569, 572, 574–88, 597–9, 605
  radicalism/radicalization  567, 569, 579, 594–5, 599–605
  Ramadan  578
  refugees  567, 569, 572–4, 581, 583–5
  regions  567
  registration  590
  religious authorities  598
  religious education  589, 592–4
  religious identity  576–80, 595, 597, 605
  religiosity  578–9, 581, 585–6, 594–6
  representative bodies  595
  repression  580, 605
  resettlement, forced  581
  residence patterns  583–4
  restitution of property  592
  return  581
  rituals, festivals and holidays  574–5, 578–9, 586–8, 592, 594–6, 602–3
  Roma  569, 572–3, 579–82, 586, 597–8, 603, 605
  Salafis  573, 579–80, 594–6, 601–4
  Saudi Arabia  579, 602–3
  Schengen criteria  584
  scholarship  565–9, 588–9, 594, 597, 605
  secularism/secularization  576–7, 581, 595, 598, 604
  security services  579, 598, 601
  segregation  573, 580, 601
  Senior Muslim Council (SMC)  591
  September 2011, terrorist attacks on United States  567, 599–605
  shariah courts  568
  Shi'a Muslims  572
  socio-economic status  569, 572, 580–2
  state subsidy  592
  stereotyping  556–8, 573–5, 586, 588, 601
  Suleymanists  580
  Sunni Muslims  572, 574–5, 590, 603
  *tekkes* and *turbes*  592
  terrorism and violence  600
  theology  567, 592, 595
  Thrace, Muftis in  359
  traditionalism/conservatism  567–8, 577, 586–7, 590–7, 599, 602–4
  transnationalism  581–2, 605
  Turks/Turkey  569, 573, 574–82, 587–99, 602–5
  unemployment  572, 581, 596
  xenophobia and racism  599–601
  youth  576–7
**burqas**  702, 705, 710, 717–22, 729–30, 757

**Canada**  190, 241, 582, 751
**Catholics**  3, 6, 626, 634–5, 637, 640–3
**Ceuta and Melilla**  313, 327, 332, 338
**chadors**  703–4, 758
**Charter of Fundamental Rights of the EU**  701
**Chechnya**  534–6, 540–2
  Black Widows  777
  combat jamaats  774
  diaspora  555
  discrimination  526
  elections  542
  public opinion/perceptions  551–2
  radicalism/radicalization  535–6, 541–2, 549, 551, 772–5, 789
  Salafism  536
  separatism  519, 536, 772
  solidarity structures  540
  suicide bombers  546 n. 72, 777
  wars  520, 529, 534, 536, 540, 548–9, 552–5
**children, protection of**  678
**China**  518, 543, 545
**Christianity and Christians**  11, 620, 631–2 *see also* **Catholics**
**Circassia**  529, 554
**citizenship**
  citizen and Muslim, being a  11–12
  culture and cultural heritage  5
  Euro-Islam  804
  hijab/headscarves  722–4
  institutions/organizations  630, 638, 642
  'Islamic problem'  5
**clash of civilizations**  745, 757–8, 762, 764

civil law 671–2, 677–86, 693–4, 695
Cold War 358, 477, 519, 521, 760
colonialism 79 n.13, 223, 636, 704–5, 773 *see also* postcolonialism
commercial disputes, ADR in 694
communist era 3–4, 5, 532, 666
communitarianism 9, 723, 787
comparative approach 2, 5, 9, 634–43
   hijab/headscarves 729–30
   institutions/organizations 620, 625, 629, 633–52
   tables 644–51
   types of comparison 643–52
conception of religion *see* definition of Islam and Islamic conception of religion
conflict of laws 190, 321, 629–30, 677–82, 695
*Conseil Français du Culte Musulman* (CFCM) 34–6, 37, 39, 41, 47–8
conservatives *see* traditionalists/conservatives
Convention on the Rights of the Child 1989 372
converts 669–70, 710–11, 730, 764, 771, 773–4, 788, 790
corporal punishment 7, 659, 663
Council of Europe (CoE) 518, 624, 748
Crimean War 517
criminal law 7–8, 672–4, 677, 691
criminology 105–6, 109, 133, 775, 777, 780
Croatia/Croats 430, 432–4, 438, 442, 451, 465–7, 499
Crusades 745–6
culture and cultural heritage
   acculturation 3, 16, 635, 802
   believing, behaving, and belonging 11–12
   citizenship 4, 5
   culturally sentimental Muslims 10
   discrimination and equality 805
   diversity 702, 722–4, 729, 803–4
   education and schools 724
   Euro-Islam 802–4
   family law 688–9
   hijab/headscarves 702–3, 717, 722–3, 729
   identity 8, 793, 803
   institutions/organizations 620–2, 624–7, 632, 634–5, 638, 643
   Islamophobia 756

   judges and administrations, sensitivity of 696
   marriage and divorce 690
   race and ethnicity 747
   radicalism/radicalization 775–7, 782, 785–90
   security/securitization 3
   shariah law 8, 676, 688–90
   values, rejection of European 717
   Western superiority 753, 757, 759–65
Cyprus 358, 529

Da'awat-e Islami 127, 378
Dagestan 521–4, 526, 529, 531, 535–6, 540–7, 552–4
Danish Cartoon controversy 189, 753–4
   demonstrations and riots 414, 754
   freedom of expression 1, 342, 414, 753
   Greece 362
   Islamophobia 84, 753
   *Jyllands-Posten* 414, 416, 753–4
   Norway 416
   public opinion/perceptions 10, 334, 416
   radicalism/radicalization 774, 779
   Sweden 411
   terrorism 754
Darqawa tariqa 324–5
Dayton Peace Accords 429, 452, 467
defensive Muslims 10
definition of Islam and Islamic conception of religion 9–16
   believing, behaving, and belonging 11–12
   citizen and Muslim, being a 11–12
   identity building 11–12
   Muslim, definition of 10
   public opinion/perceptions 10
   religiosity of individuals 10–13, 15
   Salafism, growth of influence of global 12–16
   social media 10, 15
   transnationalism 10, 12
democracy and democratic values
   Euro-Islam 802
   individuals and individualization 624
   institutions/organizations 622, 633, 636, 642
   radicalism/radicalization 793
   shariah law 663, 668–9, 696

**Denmark**  *see also* **Danish Cartoon controversy**
  assimilation  399–400
  asylum seekers and refugees  394
  Catholics  402
  census data  392
  Christianity and Christians  400, 402
  citizenship  400, 757
  citizenship test  757
  converts  395
  Copenhagen  400–1, 403, 407–8
  crime  404
  culture and cultural heritage  403, 409, 414
  Danish People's Party (DPP)  399–400
  demographics  403–4
  discrimination and equality  393, 400, 404, 413–14, 750–1, 753, 763
  dower  684
  education and schools  404, 407–8, 645
  employment  404
  family reunification  394, 400
  freedom of expression  414
  government policy  413–14
  halal/religious slaughter  409, 645
  hijab/headscarves  400, 404
  historical perspective  392
  identity  403, 408
  immigration/migrants  392, 394–5, 402–4, 413–14
  institutions/organizations  407
  integration  403, 409–10
  international constraints  413–14
  Internet  409, 416
  Jews/Judaism  408
  Islamophobia  393, 400, 414, 750–1, 753, 763
  language  404
  marriage and divorce  684, 690
  media  407–8
  mosques, building/establishment of  393, 407–8, 645
  national identity  408
  number of Muslims  395
  Pakistanis  391, 393–5
  parliamentary debates  408
  public opinion/perceptions  400, 408–9, 413
  public space/visibility  407–9
  radicalism/radicalization  414
  recognition  645
  religious education  645
  religious identity  403
  religiosity  402–3
  representative bodies  407, 645
  right-wing populist parties  399–400, 662
  September 11, 2001, terrorist attacks on United States  413
  shariah law  662, 690
  Shi'a Muslims  407–8
  socio-economic status  403–4
  Sunni Muslims  407
  terrorism  413–14
  youth  402–3, 407–8
**Deobandi 'school of thought'**  79–80, 88, 90, 377, 393 *see also* **Tablighi movement**
**diaspora**  775, 787–8
**discrimination and equality**  *see also* **gender relations/women; Islamophobia; xenophobia and racism**
  culture and cultural heritage  805
  double discrimination 729
  education and schools  637
  employment  755, 763
  European Convention on Human Rights  624
  hijab/headscarves  708, 729
  institutions/organizations  624
  radicalism/radicalization  6, 622
  rituals, festivals and holidays  84
  shariah law  658–9, 663, 667–8
  stereotyping  708, 754, 765, 780
  underclass  5
**diversity**
  culture and cultural heritage  702, 722–3, 729, 803–4
  Euro-Islam  803–4
  family law  8
  institutions/organizations  622, 627, 635, 637
  race and ethnicity  803
  shariah law  694
**divorce**  *see* **marriage and divorce**
**dower**  684–5, 689
**dupattas**  703

Eastern Europe 3–9
  communist era 3–5, 532, 666
  ethnic or folklore studies 3–4, 5, 352, 566
  immigration studies 3–4
  'Islamic problem' 5
  Ottoman Empire 3–4, 5
  religious studies 3–4
education and schools
  accommodation 640–3
  Catholics 6
  comparative tables 644–52
  culture and cultural heritage 724
  discrimination and equality 637
  foreign donors and influence 14, 626
  higher education 626, 792
  hijab/headscarves 705–30
    public schools 705–30
    shariah law 669–70
    teachers 706–7, 711, 714–18, 724–6
  identity 642–3
  immigration/migrants 641
  institutions/organizations 621, 626–8, 631, 633–4, 637, 640–52
  Islamic schools 14, 642–52, 705, 715
  Jews/Judaism 640
  public opinion/perceptions 642
  public schools 621, 627, 637, 640–3, 705–30
  radicalism/radicalization 12, 792
  religiosity 724
  religious education 621, 626, 628, 631, 633–4, 637, 640–52
  Salafism 12
  Saudi Arabia 14
  segregation 642
  shariah law 669–70
  Tablighi movement 784
  teachers 706–7, 711, 714–18, 724–6
  training 6, 621
  universities, radicalization in 792
Egypt/Egyptians
  Bosnia and Herzegovina 438, 446–8, 451, 453
  Greece 362, 364–8, 370, 377, 379–81
  Italy 265, 268, 271–4, 284, 289, 292, 294–5, 298
  Muslim Brotherhood 36
  Netherlands 159, 189
  United Kingdom 70
Eid al-Adha 41, 379, 671
Eid al-Fitr 84, 86, 379–80, 671
enemies, Muslims as external and internal 803–4
employment and labour market
  discrimination 755, 763
  globalization 5
  hijab/headscarves 672, 706–7, 711, 714–18, 724–6
  immigration/migrants 4, 5 n.3, 761–5
  Islamophobia 755, 763
  prayers 39, 50, 90, 381, 671
  rituals, festivals and holidays 671–2
  shariah law 671–2
  unemployment 763–5
Enlightenment 339, 802
equality see discrimination and equality
essentialism 9, 747–8, 803
ethnicity see race and ethnicity; xenophobia and racism
Eurabia thesis 415–16
Eurocentricism 631–2
Euro-Islam 537, 539, 624, 802–5
European Convention on Human Rights (ECHR)
  discrimination and equality 624
  hijab/headscarves 701–2
  institutions/organizations 624
  public space/visibility 627
  shariah law 659–60, 666–7, 694
  thought, conscience and religion, freedom of 666–7, 694
  transnationalism 624
  Turkish Refah Partisi 659–60, 694
European Union (EU)
  Charter of Fundamental Rights of the EU 701
  halal/religious slaughter 639
  institutions/organizations 629, 631–3
  Islamophobia 745, 748, 753, 755, 759
  radicalism/radicalization 770
  Regulation on Succession and Wills 683
  Rome III Regulation on international divorce law 683
  Schengen criteria 584
  xenophobia and racism 748 n. 5

ex-Muslims 10, 657–8
external influence *see* **foreign donors and influence**

**family law** *see also* **marriage and divorce**
  accommodation 684
  culture and cultural heritage 688–9
  diversity 8
  dower (*mahr* or *sadaq*) 684–5, 689
  equality of religion and beliefs 658
  freedom of religion 658
  gender relations/women 658, 662, 687, 691
  information to immigrants, provision of 695
  optional civil law 683–4
  public policy 677, 684–5
  recognition of foreign decisions, lack of 687–8
  shariah law 413, 658–9, 661–2, 676, 677, 683–5, 687–8, 691, 694–5
**family reunification** 785–6
**fatwas** 14, 674–5
**female genital mutilation (FGM)** 168–71, 177
**feminism** 241 n.28, 244, 246, 251–2, 456, 657, 727–9
**festivals** *see* **rituals, festivals and holidays**
**Fethullah Gülen movement** 125, 393, 418, 463–4, 482–3, 577, 593, 604–5
**finance** 682–3
**Finland**
  education and schools 637, 640–1, 645
  halal/religious slaughter 645
  integration 635
  Ireland 635, 640–1
  mosques, building/establishment of 635, 645
  multiculturalism 635
  number of Muslims 637
  recognition 645
  registration 637
  representative bodies 645
  socio-economic status 635
  symbols, display of religious 637
*Fitna* (film) 189
**foreign donors and influence** *see also* **Salafism; transnationalism and transnational**
  networks
  education and schools 14, 626
  institutions/organizations 626, 631–2
  Internet 14
  mosques, building/establishment of 14, 709
  publications and literature, distribution of 14
  radicalism/radicalization 599, 774
  shariah law 665–6, 676–7, 679–80, 682–3, 687–8
**folklore and folklore studies** 4–5, 531, 566, 580, 605
**foreign policy** 753, 759–60, 771, 777, 783, 796
**former Muslims** 10, 657–8
**forum shopping** 85
**framing** 131, 196, 414, 762, 776, 779, 784, 803
**France** 23–51 *see also* **France and headscarf affairs**
  Al-Qaeda 47–8
  Algeria 26–7, 37, 39, 625, 681, 704
    Algerian War 24, 29–30, 47
    radicalism/radicalization 47–8
    terrorism 47
  assimilation 23, 27, 41, 635, 763–4
  *banlieues* 24–5, 28–9, 45, 49–50
  believing, behaving, and belonging 41–2
  Beur movement 24–5, 30, 34
  *beurgeoisie* 29–30
  burials and cemeteries 34, 39–40
  *catholaïcité* 31
  Catholicism 31, 34–5, 39, 709, 712, 715
  CFCM and other groups 34–7, 39, 41, 47–8
  Charles de Gaulle Roissy airport, security at 49–50
  Christian crosses, restrictions on large 32
  Christianity and Christians 29, 31–2, 34–6, 39, 709, 712, 715
  citizenship 43
  civilization mission 626
  *Collectif Contre L'Islamophobie en France (CCIF)* 30, 46, 48
  colonialism 636
  Constitution 31
  converts (*Français de Souche*) 24, 26, 28, 43
  culture and cultural heritage 24, 27, 31–2, 37, 39–41, 47
  demographics 26–7, 30, 51
  demonstrations and protests 24–5

deportation 49
discrimination and equality 25–9, 30–9, 45–51
  gender relations/women 26, 28, 30–7, 41–2, 44 n.8, 46, 51
  Islamophobia 29, 38, 45–51, 746, 749, 751–2, 755, 763–4
  xenophobia and racism 25, 34, 45, 50
diversity 637
DNA testing 49
dower 684
education and schools
  *beurgeoisie* 29
  culture 31
  discrimination and equality 764
  foreign donors and influence 35
  funding 31, 34–5
  institutions/organizations 640, 642
  Islamic schools 34–5
  Islamophobia 764
  language 31
  levels 29–30
  public schools 31–4, 46, 709, 712–15, 721–6, 728–30
  religious education 14, 34–5, 640, 646
  religiosity 31
  Stasi Commission 32, 713–14
employment 24–31, 34, 45–6, 49–51, 755
European Convention on Human Rights 627, 666
family law 51
family reunification 25, 30, 49
feminization of immigration policy 30–1
foreign donors and influence 35, 626
*Front National* (FN) 25, 38, 47–9
gender relations/women 26, 28, 30–7, 41–2, 44 n.8, 46, 51
generational differences 25, 27, 29, 31, 34, 37, 41–52, 44–5, 51
government policy 25, 30–1, 48–9, 622
halal/ritual slaughter 29, 34, 38, 40–1, 638–9, 646
historical perspective 23–7, 38–9, 626
identity building 25, 31
imams, Muftis and clerics 34, 37–8, 41
immigration/migrants 23–30, 38–9, 47–50, 763–4

individuals and individualization 36, 41
industrialization 24–5, 30
institutions/organizations 34–41, 51, 625–6, 634
integration 29, 35–7, 49–50
Internet 40
invisibility, equality through 27
Islamic schools 34–5
Islamism 38, 47
Islamophobia 29, 38, 45–51, 746, 749, 751–2, 755, 763–4
Jews/Judaism 32, 34–6, 39–40, 47, 714
*laïcité* 6, 23, 27, 31, 34, 39–40, 42, 51, 622, 666, 805
language 31, 38, 49
Machelon Report 38
Maghreb origins 24–6, 43–4
marriage and divorce 679
media 40–1, 43
Mohamed Merah incident 47–8
Moroccans 26–7, 36, 625
mosques 38–9, 42
  building/establishment of 24, 36, 38–9, 50, 625, 635–7, 639, 646
  illegal 50
  imams, training of 38
  Marseillle, Mosque of 39
  Paris Mosque 24, 36, 38
nationality discrimination 28
neutrality 627
North African immigrants 24–6, 28–31, 50
number of Muslims 23–7, 42–3
pan-Islamic globalized Islam 34
police, discrimination by 45, 49–50
political participation and representation 23, 25, 38, 43–5, 47–9, 51
polygamy 46–7
postcolonialism 2, 3
poverty 28, 45
prayers 34, 38–42, 50
Protestants 32, 34–6, 39
public perception/opinion 24–6, 48–50, 663
public space, religion in 23, 33–4, 38–42
publications 43
race and ethnicity 31, 45–6, 49
radicalism/radicalization 37, 47–50, 51, 774

France *(Cont.)*
  recognition  646
  regionalisms  31
  religiosity  30–1, 34, 41–5, 51
  religious education  14, 34–5, 640, 646
  repatriation  25
  representative bodies  6, 34–9, 41, 47–8, 637, 646
  Republicanism  23, 763–4
  research  23–4, 31, 34, 41, 44, 48
  right-wing populist parties  25, 38, 47–9, 662
  riots  24, 45, 46–50, 785
  rituals, festivals and holidays  39, 41–2
  Salafism  37, 48
  Saudi Arabia  37
  scholarship  23, 29–33, 36–7, 45, 47–9, 51
  security/securitization  48–9
  segregation  28
  separation of state and religion  6, 23, 27, 31, 34, 39–40, 42, 51, 622, 666, 805
  September 11, 2001, terrorist attacks on United States  45–6, 47–9
  shariah law  40, 51, 662–3, 666, 679
  social housing projects (*banlieues*)  24–5, 28–9, 45, 49–50
  social mobility  29–30
  social movements  25, 30
  socio-economic status  24, 26, 27–30, 43–7, 51
  state-religion relations  31
  Stasi Commission  32, 713–14
  statistical studies  23–30
  stereotyping  41
  stigma  46
  stop and search of vehicles  49
  street prayers  38–9, 42
  symbols, ban on religious  32–4, 666
  *talaq*, recognition of  679
  terrorism and violence  47, 49, 773–4
  traditionalism/conservatism  37
  Turks/Turkey  26–7, 625
  unemployment  25, 27–30, 45–6
  xenophobia and racism  25, 34, 45, 50
  youth  24, 27–9, 32, 34, 42, 47–8, 50
France and headscarf affairs  23, 30–5
  age  43, 730
  assimilation  723, 724
  ban  32–4, 37, 43, 669–70, 705, 708–9, 712–14, 721–2, 727–9, 757
  Bayrou Decree  32, 713
  burquas  33, 43, 669–70, 722, 730, 757
  Catholicism  712
  citizenship  723, 729
  colonialism  704
  converts  669–70, 730
  discrimination and equality  29, 33, 46, 50, 727, 752 n.12
  diversity  723
  education and schools  31–5, 44, 46, 627, 712–15, 723–6, 729
  employment  29
  European Convention on Human Rights  627, 666, 714
  freedom of religion  723
  full-face covering  33, 37, 43, 669–70, 721–2, 730, 757
  gender relations/women  30–4
  Gerin Report  33–4, 37, 729
  hijabophobia  46, 50, 752 n.12
  identity  724
  immigration/migrants  30–1, 712, 723
  Internet  730
  Islamic schools  34–5
  Islamism  33, 44
  Islamophobia  46, 50, 714, 752 n.12
  Jewish *kippa*, restrictions on  32
  *laïcité*  23, 31–2, 712–14, 723–5, 729
  media  43
  neutrality  725
  niqabs  33, 37, 43, 721–2
  patriarchy  727
  penalties  33
  political history  704
  political participation/representation  45, 50, 723
  public opinion/perceptions  31, 33 n.5, 712, 721–2
  public space/visibility  30–3, 722–3
  religiosity  42–3
  representative bodies  713
  Salafism  37
  schools  31–3, 46
  security/securitization  33, 729

segregation 723
shariah law 669–70, 694
Stasi Commission 32, 713–14
stigma 34
symbols and signs, ban on
    conspicuous 714, 724
teachers 32, 34, 713–15, 725
thought, conscience and religion, freedom
    of 666
unemployment 29
**freedom of expression** 1, 252, 342, 414, 416,
    727, 753, 691 n.200
**freedom of religion**
    family law 658
    halal/religious slaughter 639
    hijab/headscarves 701–2
    institutions/organizations 624, 629, 632
    mosques, building/establishment of 664
    private international law 678
    shariah law 658, 661, 664–8, 676, 695
    thought, conscience and religion, freedom
        of 666–7, 694
**Freedom Party (PVV) (Netherlands)** 169,
    172, 176, 197–9, 201, 707, 720, 762–3
*Front National* **(FN) (France)** 25, 38, 47–9
**fundamentalism**
    hijab/headscarves 726–9
    institutions/organizations 625
    interpretation 624
    Islamism 726
    Islamophobia 758
    patriarchy 726–8
    radicalism/radicalization 624, 637, 771, 776,
        789, 792–3
    Salafism 783
    terrorism 726, 728–9

**gender relations/women** *see also* **hijab/
    headscarves**
    Euro-Islam 802–3
    family law 658, 662, 687, 691
    feminism 241 n. 28, 244, 246, 251–2, 456,
        657, 727–9
    honour crimes 168–71, 411, 757, 761
    Islamophobia 751
    patriarchy 717, 726–8, 731, 802
    private international law 678–9

Salafism 803
segregation 496–8
shariah law 658–9, 662–3
**generational differences**
    believing, behaving, and belonging 11
    hijab/headscarves 710
    individualization 623, 637–8
    Islamophobia 749–50
    radicalism/radicalization 773, 785–7
**Gerin Report** 33–4, 37, 43
**Germany** 104–45 *see also* **Germany and
    hijab/headscarves**
    1945, after 107–8
    accommodation 104, 129–30
    age 107, 114, 122, 134–5
    arbitration 130
    asylum seekers 117–18
    attitude test 756–7
    believing, behaving, and belonging 105,
        108, 110–14, 131
    Bosnians 105–6, 687
    burials and cemeteries 130
    Catholics 109, 717, 723
    census data 109–10
    Christianity and Christians 111, 115, 123–4,
        128–30, 143
        Catholics 109, 717, 723
        Protestants 109, 137
    citizenship 109, 115, 756–7
    constitutional law 129–30, 657, 666, 668–9
    converts 105, 107–8
    criminal cases, informal dispute resolution
        in 674
    culture and cultural heritage 106–8, 128,
        135, 140, 689–90
    democracy and democratic principles 106,
        133–4, 139
    denominations 115–16, 124
    demonstrations and protests 140
    dialogue initiatives 135–6
    diaspora 127
    discrimination and equality 117, 120–2, 129,
        134–5, 139–44
        gender relations/women 105–8, 118–24,
            128, 132, 135, 139, 676, 685–7, 691
        Islamophobia 140–3, 746, 749, 751–2,
            755–7, 763–4

**Germany** *(Cont.)*
    Islamoprejudice 141–2
    xenophobia and racism 142
  dower 684–5
  diversity 105–7, 123
  double citizenship 109
  education and schools 105–6, 114, 118–20, 122, 137, 140, 637
    higher 118, 138
    institutions/organizations 637, 642
    public schools 6, 105–6, 118, 130, 137–8, 716–17, 725–6
    radicalism/radicalization 133–4
    religious education 105, 130, 137–8, 641, 647
    university chairs 106, 130, 138–9
  employment 117–22, 128, 140, 671–2
    access to labour market 117–20
    asylum seekers, ban on 117–18
    conditions 105
    discrimination 117–20, 140
    gender relations/women 118–19, 132, 139, 685–6
    Islamophobia 755
    labour migrants/guest workers 105–6, 114, 137
    presumptions 685–6
    radicalism/radicalization 121
    unemployment 119
  equality of religions 669
  European Union 128
  family law 690–1
  family reunion 105, 137
  federal government 104
  finance 683
  foreign donors and influence 106, 130, 138–9
  former Muslims, movements of 10
  framing 131
  freedom of religion 669, 672
  gender relations/women 105–8, 118–24, 128, 132, 135, 139, 676, 685–7, 691
  generational differences 105, 114, 117, 119
  German Islam Conference (DIK) 104, 110, 122–4, 126, 131–2
  governmental policy 104–6, 126–7, 130–8, 145, 715, 762
  guest workers 105–6, 114, 137
  halal/religious slaughter 639, 647
  hate speech 763
  historical perspectives 105–25, 143
  home-grown extremists 133
  housing 120
  identity 116–17, 127–8, 135
  imams, Muftis and clerics 107, 121, 122–3, 138
  immigration/migrant backgrounds 105–15, 120, 124, 131–2, 136, 144–5, 763
  individuals and individualization 108, 144–5
  inner-Muslim debates 105
  institutions/organizations 6, 105–7, 110, 116–17, 124–31, 136–7, 140, 625, 667–8
  integration 104, 106, 110–11, 121, 131–5, 138, 144–5
  Internet 128–9, 140–1
  Islamic Studies 105–6, 138–9
  Islamism 134
  Islamophobia 140–3, 746, 749, 751–2, 755–7, 763–4
  Islamoprejudice 141–2
  Jews/Judaism 107, 111, 131, 134, 137, 142, 717, 763
  jihadis 133, 139
  journals 139
  knowledge production 3, 105, 108–9, 138–9, 142–5
  Kurds 674
  labour migrants/guest workers 105–6, 114, 137
  *Länder* 104, 131, 633
  language 111, 119, 122–4, 129, 143
  legal issues 105, 129–30
  male circumcision 672–3
  marriage and divorce 679, 681–2, 688
  media 105–6, 109, 134 n.26, 141, 686
  mosques 106–8, 121, 122–4, 138, 143
    associations 122–3, 128–9, 131
    building/establishment 104, 108, 128, 140–1, 647, 665
    conflicts 140–1
  multiculturalism 600 n. 22, 763
  national identity 104
  nationality 109, 112
  Nazi regime 38, 107

networking 128, 143
numbers and characteristics of Muslim
    populations 109–16
Pakistanis 112, 133
Palestinians 105–6, 112
political participation, activism and
    representation 124, 135–7, 140–2, 665
polygamy 681–2
prayers 123–4, 128–30
Protestants 109, 137
public opinion/perceptions 105–6, 139–44,
    669
public space/visibility 105–6, 122, 128–30,
    139–44, 666
publications 104–5, 124, 138–9
race and ethnicity 111, 121, 124, 129, 141 n.30,
    142–3
radicalism/radicalization 106, 110, 132–5,
    139, 141, 145
  age 134–5
  discrimination and equality 121, 134–5
  education 133–4
  home-grown extremists 133
  jihadis 133, 139
  security 132–3, 135
  surveillance 132–5
  terrorism and violence 133–5, 141
recognition 126–7, 647
refugees 105–6
religious education 105, 130, 137–8, 641, 647
religious identity 116–17, 128
*Religion Monitor* 110, 116
religiosity 105, 108, 110, 114, 116–17, 122, 135,
    143–4
representative bodies 6, 105, 108, 647
residence patterns/concentrations 104,
    106–7, 114
return 105
right-wing movements and parties 142
rituals, festivals and holidays 124, 134
scholarship 109, 131, 134, 138–9, 141–2
security/securitization 104, 132–3, 135, 763
separation of church and state 129–30
September 11, 2001, terrorist attacks on
    United States 104, 108–9
shariah law 130, 656–7, 667–9, 675–6,
    681–2, 687–91

Shi'a Muslims 115–16, 125, 143
socio-demographic category, Muslims as
    a 105, 108–9, 144
socio-economic status 120–1
stereotyping 141, 144
Sufism 116 n. 7
Sunni Muslims 115–16, 143
surveillance 132–5
*talaq*, recognition of 679
terrorism and violence 106, 108, 127–8,
    133–5, 141
theology and pedagogies 137–9, 141
traditionalists/conservatives 135
transnationalism 116, 124, 127–8
Turks/Turkey 110–17, 120–8, 142–3, 715–16
  dower 684–5
  education and schools 137, 637
  gender relations/women 687
  institutionalization of Islam 125–6, 625
  Islamophobia 142
  political participation and
    representation 135–7
  religiosity 108, 114
  shariah law 687
unemployment 119
university chairs 106, 130, 138–9
xenophobia and racism 142
youth 105, 107, 114, 133
**Germany and hijab/headscarves** 107, 121–2,
    130, 135–6
assaults 120
ban 705, 708, 710, 717, 720
burquas 710
Christianity and Christians 716, 723
citizenship 715–16, 723–4, 728
Constitution 716–17
discrimination and equality 120, 122
education and schools 118, 130, 140, 633,
    666, 715–17, 725–6
employment 118–19, 121–2, 672
freedom of religion 716–17
full-face covering 710, 720
government policy 715
immigration/migrants 715–16
institutions/organizations 633
integration 728
*Lander* 705, 710, 715–17, 720, 725, 730–1

Germany and hijab/headscarves *(Cont.)*
    male members of family, influence of 122
    media 716
    motives for wearing 122
    multiculturalism 715–16
    neutrality 715–16, 725
    niqabs 710
    patriarchy 727
    political participation/representation 137
    public opinion/perceptions 717, 720
    public space/visibility 717
    race and ethnicity 723
    religiosity 122
    reunification 723
    separation of religion and state 716
    shariah law 668
    state-religion relations 715
    stigma 716
    teachers 118, 130, 140, 633, 666, 717, 725–6
    Turks 121, 715–16
GIA (Armed Islamic Group) 47–8, 773
globalization 1, 5, 12–13, 34, 623
Golden Dawn (Chrisi Avgi) (Greece) 371
Global Salafi Jihad 781–2, 790
good Islam and bad Islam, distinction between 803
government policy
    halal/religious slaughter 638
    hijab/headscarves 715, 729
    institutions/organizations 631, 636, 638
    Islamophobia 759, 762–3
    multiculturalism 9
    radicalism/radicalization 793–5
Great Britain *see* United Kingdom
Greece 350–82 *see also* Thrace, Muslim minority of
    Albania 352, 363–6, 368, 477–9, 481
    asylum seekers 363, 368
    Athens 352, 355–7, 368–9, 371, 375–9, 381
        central mosque 351–2, 362–3, 369, 372–3, 377, 379
        internal migration 355–6, 362
    believing, behaving, and belonging 354–7, 379–81
    Bulgarians 354–5, 358–9, 686
    burial and cemeteries 372, 376
    census data 352, 364
    Christianity and Christians 361–2, 366, 380–1
    citizenship 363, 366, 368–9, 757
        Code 366 n. 13
        test 747
    comparative approach 362, 382
    Constitution 357–8, 372
    contentious issues 369–72
    conversions 366, 377, 381
    culture and cultural heritage 353, 355, 358, 361, 370, 378
    Cyprus 358
    democracy and democratic principles 371
    demographics 366
    demonstrations/protests 371–2
    diaspora 380–1
    discrimination and equal treatment 352, 357–8, 362, 370–2, 380–1
    diversity 380
    Eastern Europe and former Soviet Union 363–4
    economic migration 364, 368–9
    education and schools 351, 360–1, 641–2
        higher education 361
        mosques 376
        Programme for the Education of Muslim Children (PEM) 361
        religious education 357, 361, 372, 380–1, 641, 647
        Roma 357
        socio-economic status 361
    Egyptians 362, 364–8, 370, 377, 379–81
    enemies, Muslims as internal and external 804
    employment 356–7, 363–4, 366–9, 380–1
    European Convention on Human Rights 357, 360, 372
    European Union 358, 364
    exclusion 355, 357
    family law 359, 373, 686
    freedom of religion 358, 360, 372–3
    gender relations/women 359, 366–7, 370–1, 686
    generational differences 363
    Golden Dawn (Chrisi Avgi) 371
    government policy 357–9, 363, 368–9
    Greco-Turkish War 352

Greek-Arabic Cultural Centre  377
Greek civil war  354–5, 366 n.13
Greek nation-state  351–3
Greek War of Independence  351
halal/religious slaughter  370, 378, 647
hijab/headscarves  370
history/historical perspective  350–61
housing  368, 380
human rights  368
identity  350–1, 357–8, 361, 363, 369–71, 380–1, 599
immigration/migrants  350, 361–82
institutions/organizations  352, 362, 375, 376–9
integration  361, 363, 382
international law  372
Internet  377
Iraqis  380
Islamophobia  370–1, 757
Kemalists  354, 356, 358
labour migrants/guest workers  363–4, 366–9
language  352–7, 360–1, 375–7, 380
Lausanne, Treaty of  352–4, 357, 360, 373, 686
legal disputes  372–3
living conditions  367
Macedonia  352, 359
marriage and divorce  359, 370, 381
media  358, 362, 379
Middle East  364
millet system  350, 354, 359
mixed couples  370, 381
moderates  369
mosques
  Athens, central mosque in  351–2, 362–3, 369, 372–3, 377, 379
  building/establishment  351–2, 362–3, 372–6, 377, 379, 639, 647
  education  376
  informal  374–6, 378
  recognition  357
Mufti courts  359
multiculturalism  351, 369
Muslim Association of Greece (MAG)  377, 379
national identity  350–1, 363, 369–71, 380–1

nationalism  350–2, 369–71
networks  362
new Islam (recent immigrants)  4, 350, 361–82
New Lands, annexation of  351–2
number of Muslims  351–3, 361, 364–6
old Islam  350–61
Orthodox Church  351, 366, 369, 372
Other  350, 354, 358
Ottoman Empire  350–1, 354, 359, 569, 686
Pakistanis  362, 364–8, 371, 375–81
Palestinians  362, 365, 380–1
Piraeus  368, 379
plural identity  357
police, Islamophobia and racism amongst the  371
political participation/representation  358, 369, 371
Pomaks  355–6, 357, 360–1
population exchange  352–4
prayers  366, 373–5, 377, 379, 381
public opinion/perceptions  362–3, 369–72
public sphere/visibility  379–81
publications  362
race and ethnicity  4, 351–3, 357–8, 362–3, 366, 370–1, 375
radicalization  371–2
Ramadan  370, 379
recognition  357, 372, 380, 647
refugees  362, 368, 376–7
religious education  357, 361, 372, 380–1, 641, 647
religious identity  369, 380, 599
religiosity  355–7, 362, 366, 370, 375, 379–81
representative bodies  352, 362, 375, 376–9, 647
residence patterns  352–3, 355–6, 368–9
return  364
right-wing parties  369, 371
riots  371
rituals, festivals and holidays  362–3, 370, 378–81, 647
Roma (gypsies/Athiganoi)  355–7
scholarship  353, 359, 365, 376, 381
Second World War  353–4
secularism/secularization  356, 371
security  477

**Greece** *(Cont.)*
  segregation  354, 368, 375
  shariah law  359, 373, 686
  Shi'a Muslims  375–6, 377, 379
  socio-economic status  361
  South Asia  362, 364, 367–8, 375, 377–8, 381
  special celebrations and everyday religious practice  379–81
  stereotyping  351, 357, 370
  stigma  357
  Sufis  377–8
  Sunni Muslims  375–6
  terrorism  370–1
  theology  377
  thought, conscience and religion, freedom of  360, 372
  traditionalists/conservatives  355–6, 358, 369, 374, 376, 380
  transnationalism  356, 362, 377, 379–81
  Turkey/Turks  351–61, 366, 369–70, 381
  unemployment  357, 368
  xenophobia and racism  363, 370–1
  youth  364
**Grenada, invasion of**  759–60
**Group for Call and Combat/Al-Qaeda of the Islamic Maghreb) (GSPC)**  48, 773
**Gülen movement**  125, 393, 418, 463–4, 482–3, 577, 593, 604–5
**Gulf War 1991**  135, 334, 704, 786

**Habashi movement**  418
**hadith**  13–14, 446, 463, 483–4, 501, 595, 658
**Hajj**  41, 90–2, 440–1
**halal/religious slaughter**
  Aid el-Kebir festival  282, 638
  animal welfare  639
  comparative tables  644–52
  Eid al-Adha  41
  Euro-Islam  804
  European Union  639
  freedom of religion  639
  government policy  638
  institutions/organizations  626, 628, 631, 633, 638–9, 644–52
  Jews/Judaism  639
  state-religion relations  638
**Hanafi school**  375, 435, 441, 451, 480 n.4, 490, 532, 540, 590, 603–4

**Hanbali school**  532, 580 n.5
**headscarves**  *see* **hijab/headscarves**
**healthcare**  631
**hijab/headscarves**  2, 7, 701–31
  assimilation  729
  bandannas  703
  bans  708, 731
  burqas  702, 705, 710, 717–22, 729–30, 757
  chadors  703–4, 758
  Charter of Fundamental Rights of the EU  701
  citizenship model  722–4
  colonialism  704–5
  comparative approach  729–30
  culture and cultural heritage  702–3, 722–3, 729
  definition  702–5
  discrimination  708, 729
  dupattas  703
  education and schools  669–70, 705–30
  employment  672, 706–7, 711, 714–18, 724–6
  Euro-Islam  804
  European Convention on Human Rights  701–2
  feminism  705, 726–9
  freedom of religion  701–2
  full-face covering  669–71, 702–3, 706–8, 710–12, 714–23, 728–30, 757
  fundamentalism  726–9
  generational differences  710
  government policy  715, 729
  historical perspective  704–5
  identity  702, 723
  immigration/migrants  704, 722–4, 731
  interpretation  703–5, 722–30
  Islamism  721–2, 726
  Islamophobia  704
  jilbabs  703, 707–9
  less formally restrictive regulation  705–9, 717–22
  London bombings 2005  704, 709, 728
  Madrid bombings 2004  704, 710, 728, 774
  media  729–30
  modesty  701–4, 707–8
  more restrictive policies and cases  705, 709–12, 719–20
  most restrictive regulation  705, 712–17, 720–1

multiculturalism 724
niqabs 669–71, 702, 703, 705, 710, 717–22, 729–30
Qur'an 703–4, 719
patriarchy 717, 726–8, 731
pluralism 724
political meanings 704–5
postcolonialism 704
public opinion/perceptions 10, 701, 705, 717–22, 729–30
public schools 705–30
public space/visibility 702, 704
radicalism/radicalization 774
reasons for wearing hijab 701–2, 710–11
regulations 705–17
religious authorities 704
Salafism 15, 669, 803
sartorial meaning 702–3, 705
scholarship 705
seclusion, as mobile form of 702
security/securitization 702, 717, 731
September 11, 2001, terrorist attacks on United States 704
shariah law 669–71, 694
social relationships, impeding 717
state-religion relations 729
stereotyping 708
teachers 706–7, 711, 714–18, 724–6
terrorism 704, 709–10, 726, 728–9, 731, 774
theological meaning 703–5, 717
traditionalists/conservatives 702–3, 707, 710, 716, 727–8, 803
xenophobia and racism 706, 717, 728–9
**historical lands of Muslims in Europe** 2, 4
**historical perspective** 2–3, 7, 11, 13, 704–5, 773–5, 785–6
**Hizb al-Tahrir al-Islamiyya** 12 n.19, 407, 536, 540, 555, 663, 786, 789, 793–4
**Hofstad group** 190, 192–3, 779
**holidays** *see* rituals, festivals and holidays
**homogenization** 16, 623, 633–5, 637, 730, 762
**homosexuality** 177, 189, 248, 295
**honour crimes** 168–71, 411, 757, 761
**human rights** *see also* **European Convention on Human Rights (ECHR); freedom of religion**
Charter of Fundamental Rights of the EU 701

cultural identity, right to 8
Euro-Islam 802
International Covenant on Civil and Political Rights (ICCPR) 372
private international law 678
shariah law 7, 659, 667–8
**humiliation** 754, 776, 782, 787–8, 790
**Hungary**
Austro-Hungary 429–30, 433, 436, 440–1
Islamophobia 751–2
right-wing populist parties 662

**Ibadis** 115, 117
**identity**
building 11–12
culture and cultural heritage 793, 803
education and schools 642–3
Euro-Islam 803–4
hijab/headscarves 702, 723
institutions/organizations 635, 643
national identity 702, 723, 803
postcolonialism 4
race and ethnicity 11–12
radicalism/radicalization 775, 777, 785–90, 792–3
religious identity 643, 804
residence 11–12, 635
socio-economic status 11–12
transnationalism 10, 12
*ijtihad* 96, 244, 290, 296, 299, 435–6, 438, 537, 659
**imams, Muftis and clerics**
binding decisions 693–4
institutions/organizations 621, 632
radicalism/radicalization 789
Salafism 14
training 631
**immigration/migrants** 2–5
culturalization 5
cycles 3
Danish Cartoon controversy 754
Eastern Europe 4
education and schools 641
employment 4, 5 n.3, 761–5
Euro-Islam 802
family law, provision of information on 695
family reunification 785–6
hijab/headscarves 704, 722–4, 731

**immigration/migrants** (*Cont.*)
  illegal/irregular immigrants 760
  immigration studies 3–5
  institutions/organizations 620–7, 634–8, 643, 652
  integration 4–5
  'Islamic problem' 5
  Islamophobia 751–3, 756, 759–65
  labour, source of low-skilled 4, 5 n.3
  multiculturalism 761–2
  new immigration countries 4
  postcolonialism 3
  radicalism/radicalization 773, 785–6
  refugees 4
  security/securitization 3, 749, 756, 760–2
  socio-economic status 4–5
  stigma 756, 762
**individuals and individualization**
  analytical approach 777
  assimilation 782–3
  cognitive openings 782–4
  criminology 777, 780
  culture and cultural heritage 777, 782
  definition of individualization 623
  democracy and democratic values 624
  deradicalization 794–5
  descriptive works 777
  deterministic approaches 777–9
  development approaches 780–2
  discourse 784
  foreign policy 777
  frame resonance 782
  framing theory 779, 784
  generational differences 623, 637–8
  globalization 623
  identity 777, 792
  institutions/organizations 623–4, 628
  Internet 777–8, 781
  interpretation, liberalization of 624
  Islamophobia 782
  jihadis 778, 784
  mobilization 777
  pathways 780–1, 796
  personal issues 793
  political, spiritual and social needs 778
  prisons 792
  private affair, religion as a 11, 623, 627–8
  processes 780–2, 794, 796
  psychology 777–8, 782
  radicalism/radicalization 623–4, 771–96
  secularism/secularization 804
  shariah law 668, 676–7, 687
  social conditionalities 777
  social learning theory 777, 780, 783
  social networks 781
  social validation 784
  socio-economic status 777
  terrorism and violence 777–84, 793
**institutionalization/organizations** 619–52
  *see also* **representative bodies**
  acculturation 635
  accommodation 629–31, 635–52
  assimilation 620, 630, 635
  bottom-down process 619
  Christianity and Christians 620, 626, 631–2, 634–5, 637, 640–3
  citizenship 630, 638, 642
  colonialism 636
  comparative approach 620, 625, 629, 633–52
  context 620–3, 626, 632, 635
  controlled institutionalization 625
  cooperation between political and religious authorities 620–1
  country-related variables 634–5, 641
  culture and cultural heritage 620–2, 624–7, 632, 634–5, 638, 643
  definition 619, 629–33
  democracy and democratic principles 622, 633, 636, 642
  demographics 634
  discrimination and equality 624
  diversity 622, 627, 635, 637
  dynamics 626–8, 630, 635–6, 638, 640
  education and schools 621, 626–8, 633–4, 637, 640–52
  Eurocentricism 631–2
  Euro-Islam 624
  European Union 629, 631–3
  foreign donors and influence 626, 631–2
  freedom of religion 624, 629, 632
  fundamentalism 625
  funding 621, 628
  geography 632, 637

governance, modes of 632
government policy 631, 636, 638
halal/religious slaughter 626, 628, 631, 633, 638–9, 644–52
historical perspective 636–7, 643, 652
homogeneity 623, 634
identity 635, 643
imams, Muftis and clerics 621, 631
immigration/migrants 620–7, 634–8, 643, 652
imperfect institutionalization 631
individuals and individualization 623–4, 628
institutionalization of Islam 619–52
integration 623–5, 628, 635–6, 643, 652
international law 624
interpretation 619, 629–33
Islam Councils, creation of 631
literature review 628–53
local level, at 632–3
marriage and divorce 628
media 621, 631
moderates 622
mosques, building/establishment of 621, 626, 628, 630, 633, 635–40, 643–52
  comparative tables 644–52
  funding 636–7
  public opinion/perceptions 636
multiculturalism 635
Muslim communities, initiative of 619–22, 632, 638
Muslim Communities-related variables 635–8
nationality 622
nationhood 630
neutrality 626–8
official institutionalization 623
players 622–6
pluralism 626–8, 635–6
political and legal status of Muslims 622
political opportunity structures 630
political participation and representation 631, 638
politics and religion, distinction between 620–1
politics of countries of origin 625
prayers 625, 631, 637

prisoners 631
privatization of faith 624, 627
public authorities, initiative of 619
public opinion/perceptions 637–8
public schools 621, 627, 637, 640–3
public space/visibility 6, 626–30
publications 628–53
race and ethnicity 622
radicalism/radicalization 622, 624–5, 634, 637, 772, 786
recognition 619, 621, 624–6, 629, 631–2, 637, 644–52
reform 624
registration 637
religious authorities 621–3, 630–1
representative bodies 621–3, 626, 629, 631–2, 637, 644–52
resource mobilization 630
revival of traditional religion 624
rituals, festivals and holidays 631, 638
secularization/secularism 620–1, 627
security/securitization 625
segregation 625, 635
separation of church and state 6, 620, 622
September 11, 2001, terrorist attacks on United States 622
shariah law 626–8, 632, 661, 667–8, 676, 687–8, 695
socio-economic status 631, 638
state-religion relations 624, 626, 632, 635, 638, 643
strategies 622–3
supra-nationalism 632
terrorism and violence 631, 773
thematic approach 630–2
theoretical approaches 630–2
top-down processes 619, 623
traditionalists/conservatives 623–4, 632
transnationalism 7, 12, 624, 629, 631–2
variables 634–43
  country-related 634–5, 641
  interplay between 638–43
  Muslim Communities-related 635–8
youth 623
**integration**
  Euro-Islam 803–4
  hijab/headscarves 731

840    SUBJECT INDEX

integration *(Cont.)*
   immigration/migrants 4–5
   institutions/organizations 623–5, 628, 635–6, 643, 652
   Islamophobia 751, 756, 763–5
   lawyers, role of 628
   political agendas 3, 4–9
   public space/visibility 6, 7
   radicalism/radicalization 785–6, 794
   representative bodies 7
   secularism/secularization 805
   symbolic integration 803–4
intergenerational differences *see* generational differences
international constraints 2, 9, 413–17, 506–9
International Court of Justice (ICJ) 467
International Covenant on Civil and Political Rights (ICCPR) 372
International Criminal Tribunal for the former Yugoslavia (ICTY) 465 n.135, 466–7
international law 186, 190, 466, 624 *see also* private international law
Internet
   hyper-radicalization 791
   radicalism/radicalization 771, 777–8, 781, 791–3
   Salafism 12, 14–16
   social network 791
   training 791
interpretation
   fundamentalism 624
   hijab/headscarves 703–5, 722–30
   *ijtihad* 96, 244, 290, 296, 299, 435–6, 438, 537, 659
   individuals and individualization 624
   institutions/organizations 619, 629–33
   literal interpretation 13–14, 37, 483, 553
   pluralism 658–9
   Qur'an 13, 37, 483, 553
   Salafism 803
   shariah law 658–9, 666, 694
'intolerable subjects' 5
investments 682–3
IRA (Irish Republican Army) 770, 782
Iran
   Bosnia and Herzegovina 463–4
   chadors 703
   Iranian Revolution 1979 444, 704, 757
   recognition of foreign decisions 688
   Sweden 397
Iraq
   Greece 380
   Gulf War 1991 135, 334, 704, 786
   invasion (2$^{nd}$ Gulf War) 84, 334, 709, 759, 773–4, 779, 785–7
   jihadis 773
   Kurds 362
   Norway 393
   refugees 4, 112, 159, 398, 498, 584–5, 688
   Sweden 397, 405
Ireland
   accommodation 635
   Catholics 634–5, 637
   diversity 635
   education and schools 640–1, 648
   Finland 635, 640–1
   halal/religious slaughter 648
   institutions/organizations 634–5, 637
   IRA 770, 782
   model of extended privileges 635
   mosques, building/establishment of 635, 648
   multiculturalism 635
   recognition 648
   representative bodies 637, 648
   socio-economic status 635
   symbols, display of religious 637
ISIS (Islamic State of Iraq and al-Sham) 509
Islamic conception of religion *see* definition of Islam and Islamic conception of religion
Islamic law *see* shariah law
Islamic marriages 178, 190, 195, 689–90
Islamic Movement Millî *Görüş* 125, 126–7, 133, 786
Islamic schools 14, 642–52, 705, 715
Islamism
   hijab/headscarves 721–2, 726
   Islamophobia 746, 751
   neo pan-Islamism 12
   radicalism/radicalization 770–7, 779–80, 782, 785–6, 789–91, 793–6
   shariah law 656, 669, 675

**Islamophobia** 2, 9, 745–65
  anti-Muslim racism and prejudice 746–9
  anti-Muslimism 746
  assimilation 753
  citizenship 756–7
  clash of civilizations 745, 757–8, 762, 764
  Council of Europe 748
  Crusades 745–6
  culture and cultural heritage 756–7, 759–65
  Danish cartoon crisis 84, 753–4
  definition 745–7
  demonstrations and protests 755
  employment 755, 763–5
  essentialism 748
  European Union 745, 748, 753, 755, 759
  fundamentalism 758
  gender relations/women 704, 751
  generational differences 749–50
  government policy 759, 762–3
  governmentality, as form of 755–64, 765
  hijab/headscarves 704
  immigration/migrants 751–3, 756, 759–65
  integration 751, 756, 763–5
  invasion of the West 747
  *Islamophobia Watch* 749 n.7
  Israel 750
  Italy 750, 752
  Jews/Judaism 763
  language 763
  media 746, 755
  Middle East, crisis in 759
  mosques, building/establishment of 664
  multiculturalism 749, 756, 760–4
  natural and normal, as being 745
  Orientalism 747
  Other 745, 759–60
  political ideology, Islam as 745
  political participation/representation 765
  political relevance of the term 749–55
  public opinion/perceptions 749–56, 762–4
  Qur'an by American pastor, burning of 753, 754–5
  race and ethnicity 747, 756
  radicalism/radicalization 782
  right-wing populist parties 759–63
  Runnymede Trust 84, 709, 745–6
  scapegoating 749
  scholarship 746, 749
  security/securitization 748–9, 756–64
  segregation 755
  September 11, 2001, terrorist attacks 9, 745, 748–9, 753–4, 759–61, 765
  shariah law 660, 664
  socio-economic status 749, 753
  stereotyping 754, 765
  stigma 748, 756, 762–3
  terrorism and violence 751–4, 756, 759
  traditionalists/conservatives 746, 755
  transnationalism 757
  United Nations 748
  Western superiority, idea of 753, 757, 759–65

**Israel**
  Islamophobia 750
  Israel/Palestine conflict 250, 786

**Italy** 265–99
  activism 273–4, 285, 288, 294–7
  Albanians 268–9, 272, 291
  believing, behaving, and belonging 289–90
  bilateral agreements between state and confession ('intesa') 281–4
  Bossi-Fini Law 271
  burials and cemeteries 282
  Catholic Church 266, 274, 277–84, 291–3, 643, 709–10, 723, 725
  census data 267
  chaplains 282
  Christianity and Christians 268, 270, 296, 709–10
    Catholic Church 266, 274, 277–84, 291–3, 643, 709–10, 723, 725
    crucifixes/crosses 277, 709, 725
    Protestants 279, 292–3
  Christmas 277
  citizenship 272–3, 275, 291, 293, 296–7, 638
  Committee for Italian Islam 282
  comparative approach 278
  crucifixes/crosses 277, 283 n.2, 709, 725
  culture and cultural heritage 265, 274–7, 279–80, 284–5, 289, 295–9
  democracy and democratic principles 279
  demographics 270, 279
  demonstrations and protests 277, 288, 296
  deportations 297–8

Italy *(Cont.)*
  diaspora 268, 288, 299
  discrimination and equal treatment 275–80, 281, 284
    gender relations/women 268, 270, 272–3, 275, 289–90, 294–6, 299
    homosexuality 275, 295
    Islamophobia 267, 274–80, 298, 709, 750, 752
    xenophobia and racism 274–7, 291
  diversity 268, 274, 280–1
  dual citizenship 273
  education and schools 276–7, 289
    agreements with state 640
    crucifixes 277
    higher education 294, 297
    hijab/headscarves 709
    Islam of Europe masters 297
    language 292
    public schools 277, 282, 710, 724
    religious education 282, 289, 291–3, 640, 648
  Egyptians 265, 268, 271–4, 284, 289, 292, 294–5, 298
  employment 268, 270–1, 273, 285, 296–7
  entrepreneurship 273
  Eritreans 268
  ethnography 273, 290, 299
  exclusion 283, 298
  family reunification 268, 270, 285
  foreign donors and influence 284
  freedom of religion 277
  full-face covering 719–20
  gender relations/women 268, 270, 272–3, 275, 289–90, 294–6, 299
    gender roles 273, 299
    hijab/headscarves 266, 295–6, 669, 705, 709–10, 719–20, 723, 725, 730
  generational differences 272–4, 285, 288, 290–1, 294–8
  GMI association 294–7
  government policy 265–80, 298
  halal/religious slaughter 273, 289, 290, 299, 648
  health and healthcare 276
  hijab/headscarves 266, 295–6, 669, 705, 709–10, 719–20, 723, 725, 730
  historical perspective 265–6, 286
  homosexuality 275, 295
  human rights 277
  identity 265, 275–6, 281, 283, 288, 290–1, 295–6, 709
  *ijtihad* 290, 296, 299
  imams, Muftis and clerics 282, 287–8, 296, 294
  immigration/migrants 265–80, 284, 293, 295–9, 638
    Bossi-Fini Law 271
    irregular 265–6, 270, 276–7
    Martelli Law 271
    policy 266, 267–80
    regularization 271
    sending countries, cooperation with 268
    Sicily 268
    Turco-Napolitano Law 271
    youth 293–7
  individuals and individualization 267–8, 293, 299
  institutions/organizations 6, 266, 274, 281–2, 284–8, 293, 294–5, 298, 621, 667
  integration 267, 270–3, 284, 291, 298
  inter-faith dialogue 291, 292–3, 295–6
  'intesa' 281–4
  Islam of Europe masters 297
  Islamic Council 282
  Islamic Cultural Centre of Italy 285
  Islamophobia 267, 274–80, 298, 709, 750, 752
  Jews/Judaism 268, 279, 281, 292, 295–6
  jihadis 297–8
  labour migrants/guest workers 268, 270–1, 285
  Lampedusa, arrivals on 268
  language 292
  Libyans 268
  local policies, heterogeneity of 276–80
  Lodi mosque conflict 2000 265, 279
  Maghreb, Muslims from the 268–9, 271, 273–4, 290, 294
  marriage and divorce 272, 292–3
  mixed marriages 292–3
    polygamy 681–2
    *talaq*, recognition of 679
  Martelli Law 271

media 266–7, 275, 277, 279, 294–5, 719–20
Middle Eastern Muslims 268–9, 271, 273–4
mixed marriages 292–3
moderates 282, 285
Moroccans 268–9, 271–4, 276, 285–91, 294, 297
mosques 285–6, 289–90
building/establishment 266, 278, 280, 282, 625, 639, 648, 665, 667
conflicts 276, 277–80
funding 709
Lodi mosque conflict 2000 265, 279
radicalism/radicalization 297
recognition 278, 293
multiculturalism 266, 285 n.3, 709
multiple identity 290–1
Muslim, definition of 267
Muslim exception 265
national identity 265, 275–6, 283, 295–6, 709
naturalization 272, 297
neutrality 281
new Islam (recent immigrants) 2, 4, 265, 268–75, 298–9
Northern League (*Legal Nord*) 274–5, 277, 283–4, 291, 662, 664
number of Muslims 267–70, 294
Orientalist tradition 265
origins, diversity of 289–90
Other 274–5, 294
Pakistanis 268, 270, 276, 284, 290, 299
Palestinians 294–5
pluralism 266, 268, 270, 277, 279, 281, 284, 287–93, 298–9
political participation/representation 274, 277, 279, 283–4, 295–7
Northern League (*Legal Nord*) 274–5, 277, 283–4, 291, 662, 664
political parties 270, 274–5, 277, 279, 283–4, 291, 295, 297, 662, 664
polygamy 681–2
postcolonial immigration 268
practices, diversity of 289–90
prayers 278, 289
prisoners 290–1
Protestants 279, 292–3

public opinion/perceptions 265–7, 274–5, 283, 298, 709, 719–20
public space/visibility 267, 276–88, 293–7
crucifixes/crosses 277, 283 n.2, 709, 725
hijab/headscarves 709–10
publications 265, 268
race and ethnicity 266–7, 273–9, 284, 295
radicalism/radicalization 267, 295, 297–8
Ramadan 282, 289–91, 295
recognition 266, 278, 280–3, 288, 293, 296, 648
refugees 270
regions 265–6, 275–8, 281, 284–5, 288–91, 297, 299
religiosity 289–90, 294, 296, 709
religious authorities 295–5
religious education 282, 289, 291–3, 640, 648
representative bodies 274, 282, 284, 290, 293, 294–5, 648
residence patterns 268, 270
residence permits 271
right-wing populist parties 270, 274–5, 277, 279, 283–4, 291, 295, 297, 662, 664
rituals, festivals and holidays 277–8, 282, 289–91, 293, 295
Salafis 293, 297–8
scapegoat, Islam as 265
scholarship 294, 299
secularism/secularization 265–6, 276, 279–80, 283, 292–3, 296–7, 299
security/securitization 275, 297–8, 719, 729
segregation/ghettoization 270
Senegalese 268–9, 273, 284–5, 287–90
September 11, 2001, terrorist attacks on United States 265, 293, 294, 297
shariah law 293, 627, 662, 667, 679, 681–2
Shi'a Muslims 268, 270
Sicily 265, 268, 284–5
socio-economic status 266, 270–4, 279
Somalians 265, 268–70, 273, 284
South-East Asians 268–9, 271, 276, 285
special treatment 281–3
state-religion relations 280–3
stereotyping 266–7, 293, 295
Sufism 287–8
Sunni Muslims 270

Italy *(Cont.)*
   symbols, bans on religious  277, 283 n.2, 709, 725
   *talaq*, recognition of  679
   tax advantages  282
   terrorism  266, 297–8
   theology  265, 296
   traditionalists/conservatives  273, 295
   transnationalism  273, 288, 295, 299
   Tunisians  268–9, 271–3, 284, 289–90
   Turco-Napolitano Law  271
   UCOII (Union of Islamic Organizations and Communities in Italy)  285–7, 294
   Veneto region  284, 289, 297
   xenophobia and racism  274–7, 291
   youth  267–8, 272, 274, 282, 285, 290, 293–9

**Jabhat al-Nusra**  509
**Jadidism**  521–2, 537
**Jamaat-i-Islami movement**  88
**Jamaat at-Tabligh** *see* **Tablighi movement**
**Jews and Judaism**
   anti-Semitism  127, 201, 747 n.3, 750
   Beth Din  85
   Christianity and Christians  620
   education and schools  640
   halal/religious slaughter  639
   Islamophobia  763
   male circumcision  672–3
   organizational model  620
   ritual slaughter  639
   sociology of religion  3
**jihadis**  772–5, 784–5, 787, 794–5
   classical jihad  774
   converts  773–4
   definition  664 n. 47
   Global Salafi Jihad  781–2, 790
   home-grown jihadis  790–1
   identity  777
   individualization  778, 784
   Internet  791
   networks  773–4, 777
   oppression narrative  773
   social movement  776–7
   terrorism and violence  48, 89, 297–8, 343, 773, 789–91
**jilbabs**  703, 707–9
**juridical schools** (*madhab*)  13, 36

*Jyllands-Posten*  414, 416, 753–4
**Kaplan movement**  125
**Khilavet Devleti**  663
**Kizilbashi**  574–5, 590, 592
**Kosovo**  475, 478, 483, 485–8
   Bosnia and Herzegovina  432, 445, 448–9, 460, 483
   census data  486 n. 11
   Circassian national movement  529
   constitution  499, 500, 502
   demonstrations  503–4
   discrimination  503–4
   donations from Gulf states  487
   education  488, 497–8, 500–2, 504
     higher  500–1, 504
     hijab/headscarves  504
     religious  497, 500–1, 504, 506, 510
   European Union  494, 507, 510
   foreign donors and influence  495–7, 506, 509–10
   freedom of religion  499, 500
   fundamentalism  503
   gender relations/women  497
   Grand Mufti  487, 485
   hijab/headscarves  497, 504, 603
   identity  502, 510
   imams, Muftis and clerics  487–8, 495
   Islamic Community of Kosovo (ICK)  487–8, 495–6, 497–8, 500, 503, 510
   Islamophobia  494, 496, 507–8, 510
   language  502
   legal status  499–501
   media  506
   mosques, building/establishment of  503, 510
   nationalism  499
   Orthodox Church of Serbia  500
   Ottoman Empire  569
   political parties  504, 510
   public opinion/perceptions  502–3
   publications  506
   race and ethnicity  502–3, 510
   radicalism/radicalization  494–5, 506, 508–10
   registration  500
   religiosity  492–3
   religious education  497, 500–1, 504, 506, 510
   religious identity  502, 510
   restitution of religious property  501

revival of religion 506
rural areas 485–8, 494, 498, 503
Salafism 487, 494–6, 497, 506, 510
Saudi Arabia 487–8, 495, 498, 506, 603
secularism/secularization 496, 509
segregation of women 497
Serbians 489–90, 497, 502–3
shariah law 501–2
socio-economic status 494
Sufis 485–8, 494, 506
Turks/Turkey 604
UN resolution 487
United States 494
UNMIK 494–5
war 503, 510

**Kumyks** 523, 541
**Kurds/Kurdistan** 70, 112, 161, 362, 366, 393, 397, 576, 674, 684

**language** 14–15, 637, 662, 746, 757, 763
*Legal Nord* (**Northern League**) (**Italy**) 274–5, 277, 283–4, 291, 662, 664
**Libya, US interventions in** 225, 247–50, 760
**London bombings 2005**
foreign donors and influence 9
hijab/headscarves 704, 709, 728
home-grown jihadis 790
Islamophobia 9, 599
public opinion/perceptions 334
radicalism/radicalization 9, 770, 774, 790
security/securitization 371–2
September 11, 2001, terrorist attacks on United States 9
social cohesion 82
socio-demographics 108–9
**lone-wolves** 781
**loyalty to countries of residence** 802

**Macedonia** 475, 478, 486, 488–91
Bektashi Community 501
Catholic Church 501
census data 489
Christianity and Christians 501, 505
citizenship 489
communism, end of 504
Constitution 489, 499, 502, 504–5

discrimination and equality 498, 504, 508, 510
diversity 490
education and schools 498, 501, 505
European Union 507
Evangelical Methodist Church 501
foreign donors and influence 603
freedom of religion 499, 501
fundamentalism 488–9
gender relations/women 498
Greece 352, 359
hijab/headscarves 603
identity 504, 508
imams, Muftis and clerics 359, 490
institutions/organizations 501, 505, 507
Islamic Religious Community (IRC) 490–1, 501, 504–5
Jewish community 501
legal status 499, 501
Millennium Cross 505
mosques, building/establishment of 505
Muslim Religious Community (MRC) 491, 504
national identity 504
nationalism 488, 499, 508
number of Muslims 489
Orthodox church 489, 501, 504–5
public space/visibility 504–6
race and ethnicity 505
radicalism 491, 510
recognition 504–5
registration 501
religionization of landscape 505
religiosity 492–3
religious education 498, 501, 505
religious identity 508
restitution of religious property 501
revival of religion 504
Salafism 491, 603
Saudi Arabia 603
secularism/secularization 499, 509
segregation of girls 498
shariah law 501–2
Skopje 2014 urban revitalization project 505
Sufism 501
Thrace, Muftis in 359
Turks/Turkey 604
war on terror 508

**Madrid bombings 2004**
  foreign donors and influence 9, 248
  hijab/headscarves 704, 710, 728, 774
  Islamophobia 9, 341
  public opinion/perceptions 341
  radicalism/radicalization 248, 342–3, 770, 774, 779
  September 11, 2001, terrorist attacks on United States 9
  socio-demographics 108
**Machelon Report** 38
**male circumcision** 672–3
**marriage and divorce**
  dower 689
  gender relations/women 678–80
  human rights 680
  institutions/organizations 628
  Islamic marriages 690
  minimum age 678, 687
  polygamy 659, 680–2, 687
  repudiation, termination by 190, 321, 359, 678–80, 687–9, 692
  Rome III Regulation on international divorce law 683
  shariah law 8, 627, 678–80, 687
  *talaq* 190, 321, 359, 678–80, 687–9, 692
**Maturidi, Sunni Islam tradition of** 435
*media*
  free access 6, 294, 621
  *hijab/headscarves* 729–30
  *institutions/organizations* 631
  'Islamic problem' 5
  Islamophobia 746, 755
  radicalism/radicalization 771
  Salafism 14–15
**Melilla and Ceuta** 313, 327, 332, 338
  *migrants* see **immigration/migrants**
**military service** 175, 321, 352, 410
*Millî Görüş* 125, 126–7, 133, 786
**moderates** 89, 622, 631, 781, 784, 803
**'Mohamed Merah' incident** 47
**Moluccans** 159–60
**Montenegro** 475, 485
**Morocco/Moroccans**
  Belgium 224–5, 230–4, 238, 240, 242–9
  diaspora 288
  family law 662
  France 625
  Italy 268–9, 271–4, 276, 285–91, 294, 297
  jihadis 773
  Netherlands 159–65, 168–72, 179–81, 184–5, 191, 197–8, 200, 202, 662
  recognition of foreign decisions 688
  Spain 313, 315, 322, 324, 326–31, 335–43
**mosques, building/establishment of**
  comparative tables 644–52
  foreign donors and influence 14, 709
  freedom of religion 664
  funding 636–7
  institutions/organizations 621, 626, 628, 630, 633, 635–40, 643–52
  Islamophobia 664
  public opinion/perceptions 636
  public policy 636
  radicalism/radicalization 86
  shariah law 644–5
**Al Muhajiroun** 776, 786, 793
*mujahideen* 444–5, 451–2, 517, 549, 773, 789
**multiculturalism**
  communitarianism, state response to 9
  crisis 760–4
  failure of multiculturalism 762–3
  *hijab/headscarves* 724
  *immigration/migrants* 761–2
  *institutions/organizations* 635
  'Islamic problem' 5
  Islamophobia 749, 756, 760–4
  neo-liberal and neo-colonial, as 762 n. 22
  public opinion/perceptions 763
  radicalism/radicalization 9, 787
  representative organizations, creation of 9
**Muslim Brotherhood (MB)** 13, 36, 133, 246–7, 250, 287, 393, 418
**Muslim, definition of** 10

**national identity** 702, 723, 803
**Nazi regime** 38, 107
**neoliberalism** 5, 9, 410, 748, 762, 764
**neo-pan-Islamism** 12–13
**Netherlands** 158–204
  1970s onwards 158
  age 177, 185
  AIVD (Dutch Intelligence Agency) 193–5
  allochthones/autochthones, definition of 162
  Amsterdam 159, 172–4, 183, 187–8

arts, research into the 203
asylum seekers and refugees 159, 185
believing, behaving, and belonging 176–85, 202
burial and cemeteries 177, 186
burquas 183–5
Catholics 180, 187, 189, 195
chaplains 189
Christianity and Christians 162, 176, 178, 184–9, 197
　Catholics 180, 187, 189, 195
　Protestants 179–80, 189, 195, 197
citizenship 174, 187–8, 757
citizenship test 757
CMO ('contact body Muslims-government') 189–90
colonialism 636
Commission on Equal Treatment 706–7, 720
commitment to Dutch society 173
Constitution 185
converts 159–60
crime 168–71, 173
culture and cultural heritage 158, 160, 162–77, 180, 184, 191, 195, 201–2, 706
discrimination and equality 165, 168, 184, 185–7
　Constitution, equal treatment provisions in 185
　freedom of opinion 200–1
　gender relations/women 158, 168, 186, 190–2, 202–3, 706, 727–8
　hijab/headscarves 184
　radicalism/radicalization 194
　xenophobia and racism 168, 196
diversity 162, 164, 168, 173, 188–9
domestic violence 168–71
double identity 175, 190
dower 684
education and schools 158, 165, 166–7, 172–3, 176, 178, 195, 201
　gender relations/women 186, 202–3
　higher education 182–3, 203
　hijab/headscarves 184–5, 189, 706–7, 720
　history test 175
　institutions/organizations 640, 642–3
　mosques 182, 186
　multiculturalism 163
　public schools 182, 720
　religious education 158, 182–4, 204, 640–1, 649
　segregation 166–7
employment 165–9, 199, 203
　discrimination 168, 184
　diversity 168
　dress 176, 184, 189
　gender relations/women 168, 203
　hijab/headscarves 184, 189
　labour/guest workers 159–60, 163–4, 166, 172, 179, 201–2
　unemployment 167–9
　youth 167
empowerment 164, 183, 186–7, 195
entrepreneurship 203
ethnography 176–7
European Convention on Human Rights 201
family law 190–1, 662
family reunification 159–60, 191 n.55
female genital mutilation 168–71, 177
finance 192
forced marriages 191–2
foreign donors and influence 179, 203
freedom of opinion 199, 200–1
freedom of religion 185–6, 200, 721
Freedom Party (PVV) 169, 172, 176, 197–9, 201, 707, 720, 762–3
gender relations/women 158, 168, 186, 190–2, 202–3, 706, 727–8
generational differences 165–7, 171–2, 177–81, 183, 191, 194, 199–204
government policy 160, 162–5, 172–5, 185–91, 193–6, 202, 636
halal/religious slaughter 186, 649
health and healthcare 162, 166, 168, 196
hijab/headscarves 177, 189, 669, 705, 706–7
　burquas 183–5
　Commission on Equal Treatment 706–7, 720
　cultural diversity 706
　discrimination and equality 184
　education and schools 184–5, 189, 706–7, 720
　employment 176, 184, 189
　freedom of religion 721
　full-face covering 183–5, 720–1

**Netherlands** *(Cont.)*
    gender relations/women 706
    immigration/migrants 706
    multiculturalism 706
    niqabs 184–5
    patriarchy 727–8
    pluralism 724
    political parties 706–7
    public opinion/perceptions 706–7, 721
    right-wing populist parties 706–7, 720–1
    security/securitization 721, 729
    shariah law 669, 694
    teachers 184, 189, 706–7
  history/historical perspective 158, 159–60, 163–4, 174–5, 201
  history test 175
  homosexuality 177, 189
  honour crimes 168–71
  housing 172
  human rights 193
  identity 174–8
    culture 164, 175
    national 196
    plural 175
    radicalism/radicalization 194
    religious 177–9, 188, 200
    shared values 176
  imams, Muftis and clerics 179–80, 186
    chaplains 189
    foreign donors and influence 179
    home-grown 183
    radicalism/radicalization 179–80, 183, 203
    recruitment 160
    training 183
  immigration/migrants 159–65, 171, 188, 191, 197, 201, 706–720–1
  *inburgering* 173, 175, 183
  incitement of hatred 200–1
  individuals and individualization 178, 188
  Indonesians 158, 159, 172
  infrastructure, research into religious 204
  institutions/organizations 6, 158, 180–3, 186, 189–90, 192, 195, 204, 634
  integration 158, 160, 162, 164–77, 186–8, 191–6, 198–9, 204, 643
  international law obligations 185
  Internet 179, 203
  Islamic marriages 190–1, 195
  Islamic schools 158, 183–4
  Islamic studies 176
  Islamophobia 196–201, 751–2, 762–3
  Jews/Judaism 176, 178, 180, 189, 201
  jihadis 193
  labour/guest workers 159–60, 163–4, 166, 172, 179, 201–2
  language 160, 163, 166–7, 180, 195, 757 n.16
  legal matters 158, 201
  living environment 172–3
  loyalty to country 175, 177
  marriage and divorce 171, 177, 178, 190–2
    forced marriage 191–2
    gender relations/women 203
    import marriages 191
    Islamic marriages 178, 190–1, 195
    polygamy 681–2
    shariah law 190–2, 679–82
  media 164, 177, 179–81, 188, 198–200
  moderates 197–8
  Moluccans 159–60
  Moroccans 159–65, 168–72, 179–81, 184–5, 191, 197–8, 200, 202, 662
  mosques 177–8, 181
    building/establishment 159–60, 187–8, 635–6, 649, 664–5
    education and schools 182, 186
    funding 187
  multiculturalism 158, 162–6, 171, 173–4, 200, 635, 706, 762–3
  municipalities and social cohesion 173–4, 194, 202
  national allegiance 173
  national identity 196
  National Minorities Conference 180
  nationality 161–2, 175, 177, 190
  naturalization 161–2
  Netherlands Coordinator for Combating Terrorism (NCTb) 194
  neutrality 185–7
  new immigrants 159
  niqabs 184–5
  number of Muslims 162, 189, 199
  Other, Muslims and Islam as the 198–9
  patriarchy 727–8
  personal freedom 176

pluralism 635, 724
political participation/representation 169, 172, 176, 180–2, 188–9, 197–202, 706–7, 720, 762–3
postcolonial migrants 159–60, 163, 172
prayers 178
prisoners 169, 186, 189, 195
private domain 178
private welfare support, state support for 186
profiling 193
Protestants 179–80, 189, 195, 197
psychological factors 168, 177, 191
public opinion/perceptions 164, 174, 182–4, 195–200, 706–7, 721
public sphere/visibility 158, 178, 183, 203
race and ethnicity 161–9, 177–81, 187–8, 197–8, 201–2
radicalism/radicalization 158, 177, 190, 193–6, 202
    AIVD (Dutch Intelligence Agency) 193–5
    discrimination 194
    foreign donors and influence 203
    imams, Muftis and clerics 179–80, 183, 203
    integration 192, 194–6, 204
    Islamophobia 199
    profiling 193
    salafism 194
    securitization 195–6
    segregation and parallel societies 193–5, 204
    socio-economic status 165–6
    terrorism 193–4
    youth 193–4
recognition 649
religious authorities 178–80, 183, 189, 203
religious education 158, 182–4, 204, 640–1, 649
religious identity 177–9, 188, 200
religiosity 177–80, 202
representative bodies 180–1, 189–90, 649
research 158, 165, 167–84, 188, 191, 196, 198–204
residence patterns 159, 172, 198
return 160, 163
right-wing populist parties 169, 172, 176, 197–201, 662, 706–7, 720–1, 762–3

rituals, festivals and holidays 158, 163, 176, 178, 190–1
Rotterdam 159, 172–4, 181, 183, 186, 188
Salafism 194
scholarship 158, 163–4, 175–6, 179, 193, 201–3
secularism/secularization 158, 179–80, 182, 202
security/securitization 192–6, 721, 729
segregation 166–7, 172, 193–5, 203–4
separation of church and state 185–7, 190
September 11, 2001, terrorist attacks on United States 178, 182, 196–7
shared values 173, 176, 662
shariah courts/tribunals 178, 192, 204
shariah law 178, 190–2, 204, 656, 669, 679–82, 694
social bonding and isolation 203–4
social cohesion 173–6, 187–9, 194
social welfare system, burdens on 171–2
socio-cultural status 165–6, 173–5, 198
socio-economic status 163, 165–73, 177, 179, 199, 643
Somalians 159, 170–1, 198
state, relations with 185–92, 195
Surinamese 159–60, 162, 165, 168–9, 172, 179–80
surveillance 193
*talaq*, recognition of 679–80
terrorism 179–80, 190, 192–6
theology 158, 177, 179, 182–3, 189, 201–2
traditionalists/conservatives 170, 178, 191, 203
transnationalism 203
Turks 159–65, 168–72, 175, 179–81, 184, 191, 197–8, 200, 202–3
unemployment 167–9
upbringing 177
white flight 172
xenophobia and racism 168, 196
youth 158, 167–70, 173, 177, 179, 190, 193–4
**networks** *see* **transnationalism and transnational networks**
**neutrality** 6, 626–8, 667–9
**Nicaragua, Contra's war in** 760
**niqabs** 702, 703, 705, 710, 717–22, 729–30
**Northern League** (*Legal Nord*) **(Italy)** 274–5, 277, 283–4, 291, 662, 664

**Norway**
  Danish Cartoon controversy 416
  discrimination and equality 406, 411, 413, 416
  education and schools 649
  employment 406, 411
  Eurabia thesis 416
  freedom of expression 416
  gender relations/women 406
  halal/religious slaughter 649
  historical perspective 392
  immigration/migrants 397–8, 405–6
  institutions/organizations 398, 411
  international constraints 416–17
  Internet 416
  Iraq 393
  Islamic Council of Norway 411
  Islamophobia 411, 413, 416
  male circumcision 674
  media 411
  mosques, building/establishment of 411, 649
  multiculturalism 761 n. 20
  number of Muslims 397–8
  Oslo and Utøya atrocities of 22 July 2011 141, 413, 761 n.20, 765
  Pakistan 393
  Progress Party 400
  public opinion/perceptions 411
  public space/visibility 411
  recognition 649
  registration 398
  religious education 649
  representative bodies 411, 649
  right-wing populist parties 400, 662
  scholarship 392
  shariah law 662
  Somalians 397–8
  socio-economic status 405–6
  state church, registered members of 392
  terrorism/violence 141, 411, 413, 761 n.20, 765
  Tunisians 392
  unemployment 406
**Nursis** 465, 573, 580

**Observatorio Andalusí** 313–15, 332
**oil crisis** 224 n.6, 225, 391
**oppression narrative** 773, 775–6, 786

**Organization of the Islamic Conference (OIC)** 225, 315, 502
**Orientalism** 223, 252–3, 371, 704, 726, 747
**orthodoxy, evolution of** 10, 16, 196, 505, 538
**Oslo and Utøya atrocities of 22 July 2011** 141, 413, 761 n.20, 765
**Other** 745, 759–60, 776, 804
**Ottoman Empire**
  Eastern Europe 3–4, 5
  millet system 350, 354, 359, 433, 568
  Orientalism 223

**Pakistan/Pakistanis**
  Afghanistan 791
  Denmark 391, 393–5
  dower 684
  dupattas 703
  hijab/headscarves 702–3, 707
  Germany 112, 133
  Greece 362, 364–8, 371, 375–81
  Italy 268, 270, 276, 284, 290, 299
  nationalist associations 10
  Norway 393, 398
  radicalism/radicalization 773–4, 776, 786–7, 791, 794
  recognition of foreign decisions 688
  Scandinavia 391, 393–8, 402, 406
  shariah law 684, 688
  Spain 313, 315–16, 324, 326, 336
  Tablighi movement 794
  United Kingdom 68–70, 72, 74, 76, 81, 86, 99, 702, 707, 773–4
  Waziristan 773
**Palestine/Palestinians**
  Germany 105–6, 112
  Greece 362, 365, 380–1
  intifada 786
  Israel/Palestine conflict 250, 786
  Italy 294–5
  radicalism/radicalization 250, 786–7
**pan-Islamism** 12–13, 34, 36, 468, 529
**Paris Mosque (GMP)** 24, 36–7, 38–9
**patriarchy**
  colonialism 726
  discrimination and equality 726–7
  Euro-Islam 802
  feminism 727–8, 731

fundamentalism 726-8
hijab/headscarves 717, 726-8
Orientalism 726
postcolonialism 726
public opinion/perceptions 726
public space/visibility 727
**penal law** 672-4, 677, 691
**perennialists** 454 n.100
**personal law** 627, 676, 683, 691, 695 *see also* family law
**pilgrimage** 41, 90-2, 339, 410, 440-1, 462, 540, 592, 595, 671
**Pious Forefathers** (*al-salaf al-salih*) 13-14
**political ideology, Islam as** 197-8, 415, 745
**political participation/representation** 2, 631, 638, 662, 706-7, 723, 753, 761-2, 765
**polygamy** 659, 680-2, 687
**Pomaks (Muslim Bulgarians)** 594-7, 605
  abroad, studying 579, 594
  Bektashi mystical order 356
  Christianity and Christians 578
  education and schools 579, 594, 600
  gender relations/women 596
  Greece 355-6, 357, 360-1
  identity 577-9, 587, 594-5, 597
  numbers 577
  oral tradition 578
  Ottoman Empire 477, 568-9
  persecution 477
  political participation and representation 597
  race and ethnicity 577-8, 597
  radicalism/radicalization 579, 595, 600, 602
  religiosity 578-9, 595
  rituals, festivals and holidays 578
  Salafism 579
  social and economic status 582
  Thrace, Muslim majority in 355-6, 357, 360-1
  Turks 577-8
**Portugal** 634-5, 649, 751-2
**postcolonialism** 3, 4, 13 n.22, 704, 726
**Preventing Violent Extremism (PVE)** 83
**prison and prisoners** 631, 792
**private international law** 190, 321, 629-30, 677-82, 695
**privatization of religion** 34, 229, 541-2, 554, 623-4, 627, 804
**prayers**

employment 39, 50, 90, 381, 671
institutionalization of Islam 625, 631, 637
**Protestantism** 3, 43 n.3, 179, 637
**psychology** 777-8, 782
**public international law** 186, 190, 466, 624
**public opinion/perceptions** *see also* Islamophobia
  Danish Cartoon controversy 10, 334, 416
  education and schools 642
  full-face coverings 717-22
  hijab/headscarves 10, 701, 705, 717-22, 726, 729-30
  institutions/organizations 637-8
  mosques, building/establishment of 636
  multiculturalism 763
  Orientalism 371
  Salafism 802-3
  shariah law 657-65, 694
  social media 10
  special pleading 10
  terrorism and violence 10
**public schools** 621, 627, 637, 640-3, 705-30
**public space/visibility** 5-8
  assimilation 6
  cooperation between state and religious institutions, methods of 6
  European Convention on Human Rights 627
  hijab/headscarves 702, 704, 717, 727
  illegitimacy of role of religion 7
  institutions/organizations 626-30
  integration 6, 7
  neutrality 626-8
  pluralism 626-8
  politics and religion, differentiation of 6
  Salafism 802-3
  secularism/secularization 6, 805
  shariah law 7-8, 667
**Pussy Riot** 548

**Qurʾan**
  burning by American pastor 753, 754-5
  hijab/headscarves 703-4, 719
  literal interpretation 13-14, 37, 483, 553
  Pious Forefathers (al-salaf al-salih) 13-14
  production of copies 15
  Salafism 13-14
  shariah law 658-9

**Quilliam Foundation (UK)** 83

**race and ethnicity** *see also* **xenophobia and racism**
  Eastern Europe 4
  Euro-Islam 803
  identity building 11–12
  institutions/organizations 622
  'Islamic problem' 5
  Islamophobia 756
  new immigrants 4
**radicalism/radicalization** 2, 3, 770–96 *see also* **jihadis**
  accommodation 637
  al-Qaeda 773, 775–6, 779, 781, 784, 788, 791, 793–4
  assimilation 782–3
  asylum seekers 9
  bringing home conflicts 786
  cognitive openings 782–4
  colonialism 773
  communitarianism 787
  community radicalism/radicalization 785–90
  criminology 777, 780
  culture and cultural heritage 775–7, 782, 785–90, 793
  Danish cartoons controversy 774, 779
  definition 770, 771–2
  democracy and democratic values 793
  demonstrations and protests 786
  deradicalization 771, 794–5, 796
  deterministic approaches 777–9
  development approaches 780–2
  diaspora 775, 787–8
  discrimination and equality 6, 622, 785–8, 796
  economic grievances 788
  European Union 770
  family reunification 785–6
  foreign donors and influence 599, 774
  foreign policy 777
  framing theory 779, 784
  freedom of movement 9
  fundamentalism 624, 637, 771, 776, 789, 792–3
  generational differences 773, 785–6
  geography 772–5
  government policy 793–5
  group grievances 775–6
  hijab/headscarves 774
  historical perspective 773–5, 785–6
  home-grown radicals 771, 790–1
  hubs 771
  humiliation 787–8, 790
    proxy, by 788, 790
  hyper-radicalization 791
  identity 775, 777, 785–90, 792–3
  imams, Muftis and clerics 789
  immigration/migrants 773, 785–6
  individuals and individualization 623–4, 771–96
    analytical approach 777
    cognitive openings 782–4
    deterministic approaches 777–9
    development approaches 780–2
    discourse 784
    frame resonance 782
    framing theory 779, 784
    identity 777, 792
    pathways 780–1, 796
    processes 780–2, 794, 796
    social conditionalities 777
    social learning theory 777, 780, 783
    terrorism and violence 777–84, 793
  institutions/organizations 622, 624–5, 634, 637, 773
  integration 785–6, 794
  Internet 771, 777–8, 781, 791–3
  IRA 770, 782
  Iraq war 779, 785
  Islamism 770–7, 779–80, 782, 785–6, 789–91, 793–6
  Islamophobia 782
  left-wing radicalization 770
  lone-wolves 781
  London bombings 2005 770, 774
  Madrid bombings 2004 248, 342–3, 770, 774, 779
  Middle East 786
  mosques 786
  media 771
  mobilization 777
  *mujahideen* 444–5, 451–2, 517, 549, 773, 789

multiculturalism 9, 787
networks 786
non-integration, promotion of 794
North Caucasus 772, 774-5
number of Muslims 9
oppression narrative 773, 775-6, 786, 790, 793
organizations 772, 786
Other 776
political, spiritual and social needs 778
pre-radicalization 793
prisons 792
processes 780-2, 794, 796
psychology 777-8, 782
rational choice theory 775, 782
religiosity 789, 792-3
representative bodies 6, 637
right-wing radicalization 770
role of religion 792-4
Salafism 772, 775-6, 785, 789, 792-4
security/securitization 637, 770, 790
September 11, 2001, terrorist attacks on United States 770, 791
shariah law 691, 695
social conditionalities 777
social learning theory 777, 780, 783
social movements 775, 785
social networks 781, 791, 794
socio-economic status 777, 788-9, 795-6
stereotyping 780
stigma 786
suicide attacks 770, 772, 794
Tablighi movement 48, 88, 786, 793
terrorism and violence 5, 9, 770-91, 793-6
theoretical approaches 775-90
traditionalists/conservatives 772, 774-5, 785-7, 789
training 791
universities 792
virtual communities 789-91
xenophobia and racism 782, 787
**Ramadan** 92, 295, 339
diversity 530
Eid al-Fitr 84, 86, 379-80, 671
employment 241, 671
Pomaks 578
religiosity 42, 232 n.16, 241, 243, 289, 379, 460-1, 577, 596 n.20

representative bodies 236
xenophobia and racism 291, 370
**rational choice theory** 775, 782
**recognition**
comparative tables 644-52
family law 687-8
foreign law 8
institutions/organizations 619, 624, 626, 629, 631-2, 637, 644-52
norms, of 632
selective recognition 625
shariah law 626-7, 677, 679-81, 684, 687-9, 692, 695
**refugees and asylum seekers** 4, 9, 363, 786
**Regulation on Succession and Wills (EU)** 683
**religion, freedom of** *see* **freedom of religion**
**religiosity** 10-13 *see also* **believing, behaving, and belonging**
culturally sentimental Muslims 10
defensive Muslims 10
education and schools 724
generational differences 11
hijab/headscarves 724
minimally believing/practising Muslims 10
pious Muslims unconcerned with public affairs 10
radicalism/radicalization 789, 792-3
Ramadan 42, 232 n.16, 241, 243, 289, 379, 460-1, 577, 596 n.20
residence, area of 11
rise in religiosity, social conservatism and apoliticism 9
social media 15
socio-economic status 11
sociologically Muslim 10
strict observance 10
**religious authorities** 620-3, 630-1, 704 *see also* **imams, Muftis and clerics**
**religious slaughter** *see* **halal/religious slaughter**
**representative bodies**
comparative tables 644-52
discrimination and equality 6
institutions/organizations 621-3, 626, 629, 631-2, 637, 644-52
integration 7

**representative bodies** *(Cont.)*
  moderates 6, 622, 631
  multiculturalism 9
  radicalism/radicalization 6, 637
  secularism/secularization 7
  state, reshaping of Islam by the 7
**research agendas** 3–9
  Eastern Europe 3–9
  ideological influences 3–4
  immigration studies 3–5
  international constraints 9
  political influences 3–4
  public space, religion in 5–8
  religious dimension 3
  sociology of religion 3
  Western Europe 3–9
**resource mobilization** 630
**right-wing populist parties** 656, 662–5, 727, 759–63
**riots** 24, 45, 46–50, 72, 371, 414, 754, 761 n.20, 785
**rituals, festivals and holidays** *see also* **burials and cemeteries; halal/religious slaughter;**
  **prayers; Ramadan**
  Aid el-Kebir festival 282, 638
  Christmas 277
  discrimination 84
  Eid al-Adha 41, 379, 671
  Eid al-Fitr 84, 86, 379–80, 671
  employment 671–2
  female genital mutilation (FGM) 168–71, 177
  institutions/organizations 631, 638
  male circumcision 672–3
  pilgrimage 41, 90–2, 339, 410, 440–1, 462, 540, 592, 595, 671
  shariah law 658, 660–1, 671, 673–4, 696
**Roma**
  Bulgaria 569, 572–3, 579–82, 586, 597–8, 603, 605
  census data 579–80
  discrimination and equality 357, 586
  education and schools 357, 360, 572–3, 580, 582
  employment 356–7, 572, 582
  exclusion and marginalization 357, 598
  ghettos 573
  Greece (gypsies/Athiganoi) 355–7
  identity 579
  immigration/migrants 582
  integration 587
  language 360, 579
  non-traditional movements, influence of 580
  number of Roma 574
  Orthodox Christians 579–80
  political participation and representation 598
  Protestants 579–80
  race and ethnicity 357, 579
  radicalism/radicalization 573
  religiosity 357
  Salafism 573, 580, 603
  segregation 573, 580
  socio-economic status 572
  stereotyping 357
  stigma 357
**Rome III Regulation on international divorce law** 683
**Runnymede Trust's Commission on British Muslims and Islamophobia (CBMI)** 84, 709, 745–6
**Rushdie affair** 10, 47, 81–2, 84, 226, 786
**Russia** 517–56 *see also* **Chechnya**
  Afghan *mujahideen* resistance 517
  antagonism or accommodation 519–20
  Avar model 523
  Azerbaijan 526
  Bashkortostan 520, 524, 543, 552
  believing, behaving, and belonging 518, 521–3, 530
  Beslan attack 551 n. 85
  blogosphere 546
  Caucasus 518, 521, 525–9, 532, 540–3, 546–7, 551, 553–5
  censorship 545
  census data 524–5
  Central Asia 518, 521, 525–7, 543, 547–8, 554–5
  China 518, 543, 545
  Christianity and Christians 527, 548
  Circassia 529, 554
  civil and criminal procedures 533
  Cold War 358, 477, 519, 521, 760
  comparative approach 530–1, 554–5
  constitution 538

converts 545–50
Council of Europe 518
culture and cultural heritage 519, 521–2, 530, 534, 538–9, 545, 555
Dagestan 521–4, 526, 529, 531, 535–6, 540–7, 552–4
democracy and democratic principles 540, 547
demographics 518, 520, 523–5, 528–9, 547
demonstrations and protests 522, 543
deportations 541–2
dialectics 519–20, 521–2, 533
diaspora 555
discrimination and equal treatment 526, 528, 530
  gender relations/women 520, 528–9, 531–2, 537, 547
  Islamophobia 9, 520, 548, 551–5
diversity 519, 527–9, 533–4, 536, 544
DUMRT (Muslim Spiritual Board of Tatarstan) 539–40
education and schools 543–5, 548–9, 553–5
  higher education 544–5
  language 529
  mosques 545
  political issue, as 543–4
  religious education 520, 522, 526, 529, 532, 539, 543–4, 549
  textbooks 534
employment 525–7, 539
enemies, Muslims as internal and external 804
essentialism 520
ethnography 532–3, 549, 553, 556
Euro-Islam project 537, 539
family in transmission of knowledge, role of family 528–9, 539, 549, 554
fluidity of the religious field 532–8
foreign donors and influence 534–5, 539–40, 548, 554
freedom of religion 534
fundamentalism 535, 537–8, 551
gender relations/women 520, 528–9, 531–2, 537, 547
generational differences 528–30, 539, 542, 545–6, 549–50, 555
government policy 530, 538, 545, 548, 551, 553, 555

Greece 363–4
halal/religious slaughter 530
hijab/headscarves 528, 531–2
history/historical perspective 2, 4, 517–23, 537–8, 543–4
human rights 553
identity 524–5, 527–9, 534–6, 553–4
*ijtihad* 537
imams, Muftis and clerics
  foreign donors and influence 554
  funding 533, 543
  multiplication of muftiates 539, 541, 543
  radicalism/radicalization 517, 536, 540, 548, 552
  Sufism 540–1
immigration/migrants 518, 523–8, 538, 543, 548, 555–6
institutions/organizations 522, 526, 534, 538–9, 542–3, 548–9
integration 518, 523–32, 555
inter-faith relations 528
Internet 526, 530, 543, 546, 550
interpretation 522, 537, 553
Islamic Revival Party of the USSR (IRP) 535, 542, 547, 555
Islamophiles 518, 551–4
Islamophobia 9, 520, 548, 551–5
Jadidism 521–2, 537
Jews 534
jihadis 525, 529, 541–2, 547, 550
kolkhoz system 522, 541
Kremlin-approved extremism 547–9
Kumyks 523, 541
labour migrants/guest workers 525–7, 539
language 522, 529–32, 552
marriage and divorce 526, 531
media 517–18, 521, 526, 530, 535, 546, 548–52
mixed marriages 526, 531
moderates 518, 534
mosques 526, 536, 539, 545, 548–9
*mujahideen* 517, 549
Muscovy 519
National Organization of Russian Muslims (NORM) 546
nationalism 546, 554–5
number of Muslims 524
Organisation of the Islamic Conference (OIC) 517

**Russia** *(Cont.)*
  Orient, relationship to  519
  Oriental studies  519, 521–3, 532, 553, 556
  Orthodox Church  520, 528, 532, 534, 538, 544–9, 555
  Ottoman Empire  517, 529
  political participation/representation  518, 527, 535, 542–3
  politicization, barriers against Islam's  549–50
  prayers  526
  privatization of religion  541–2
  protest organizations  543
  Protestants  527
  public opinion/perceptions  518, 536, 551–2
  public sphere/visibility  518, 524, 538–43
  publications  533, 535, 545–6, 552
  qualitative parameters  528–9
  quantitative approaches of religious affiliations and practices  527–8
  Qur'an  532, 545, 553
  race and ethnicity  519, 522–9, 531, 534–40, 548, 553–5
  radicalism/radicalization  517–18, 528–9, 534–7, 553, 789
    converts  545–50
    jihadis  525, 529, 541–2, 547, 550
    Kremlin-approved extremism  547–9
    hijab/headscarves  528
    imams, Muftis and clerics  517, 536, 540, 548, 552
    Internet  546
    Islamophobia  552
    jihadis  525, 529, 541–2, 547, 550
    securitization  550–2
    terrorism and violence  546–8, 550–1
    traditionalism/conservatism  545–7
  Ramadan  530
  reform  521–2, 536–40
  regions  520
  religious authorities  520, 533, 538–41, 545, 551
  religious education  520, 522, 526, 529, 532, 539, 543–4, 549
  religious identity  524–5, 527, 534–6
  religiosity  522, 524–7, 532, 555
  representative bodies  543
  repression  518, 522, 540, 552–3
  resettlements, impact of mass  522–3, 541
  retraditionalization  531
  return  529
  rituals, festivals and holidays  520, 527, 530–1, 532–3, 540
  Salafis  522–3, 525, 527, 534, 535–8, 540–1, 555
  Saudi Arabia  517, 529, 540
  scholarship  519–21, 526, 532–4, 538, 545, 552
  Second World War  520
  secularism/secularization  518, 521–2, 533–42
  security/securitization  519, 534, 550–3
  segregation  528, 538–9, 541, 548
  separation of church and state  545
  September 2011, terrorist attacks on United States  543, 550
  Shafii theology  532
  Shanghai Five  518
  Shi'a Muslims  546
  Siberia  532
  social sciences  532–8, 551, 553, 555
  socio-economic status  518, 528
  sociology of religion  518, 521, 523–4, 528–32, 540
  Soviet Union  9, 363, 417, 517–29, 532–41, 545–8, 553, 556, 760
  stagnation period  522
  stereotyping  522, 531
  Sufism  523, 540–3, 546–9, 555
  suicide bombers  531, 547, 772
  Sunni Muslims  540, 546, 550
  Tablighi movement  555
  Tajikstan  525–6, 535, 543, 555
  Tatarstan  520, 524, 526, 528–32, 536–40, 542, 549, 551–2, 555
  terrorism and violence  518–19, 546–53, 772
  theology  522, 532–3, 544
  traditionalists/conservatives  519, 521, 525, 529–40, 543–51, 555
  transnationalism  518, 522, 525, 534–6, 543, 545, 549–53, 555
  Tsarist Russia  517–20, 524, 532, 536–8, 543–4, 553, 556
  violence  536, 540–1, 548, 550–3
  Volga region  520–1, 524 n.18, 528, 530, 536–7, 542–3, 554

xenophobia and racism 526
youth 528-9, 542, 545-7, 549-51, 555

**Salafism/Wahhabism** 772, 775-6, 785, 789
Al Qaeda 781
deradicalization 794
dress code 15
Euro-Islam 802-3
fundamentalism 793
gender relations/women 803
Global Salafi Jihad 781-2, 790
growth of influence of global
  Salafism 12-16
hijab/headscarves 15, 669, 803
imams, Muftis and clerics 14
Internet 12, 14-16
Islamic centres, building of 14
Islamization of societies 13
juridical schools (*madhab*) 13
literal interpretation of Qur'an 13-14, 803
literature, distribution of 14
media 14-15
neo pan-Islamism 12-13
Pious Forefathers (al-salaf al-salih) 13-14
postcolonialism 13 n. 22
pre-radicalization 793
proselytization (dawa) 14-16
public education programmes 12
public opinion/perceptions 802-3
public space/visibility 802-3
Qur'an 12-15
revivalism 13-14
Roma 573, 580, 603
Saudi Arabia 13-15
schools, financing of 14
shariah law 663-4, 675-6, 691, 695
social problems, dealing with 793
Sunni Islam 14
transnationalism 12
universities 14, 792
West, attitudes to 13 n. 22
youth 663-4

**Saudi Arabia**
Albania 478, 482-3, 488, 497, 506, 603
Bosnia and Herzegovina 438, 446-7, 462-3, 603
Bulgaria 579, 602-3

education and schools 14, 462, 483, 497-8, 593
fatwas 14
foreign donors and influence 13-15, 225-6, 360, 482-3, 495-8
  Bosnia and Herzegovina 446-7, 462-3
  Bulgaria 579, 602-3
  Kosovo 487-8, 506
France 37
imams, Muftis and clerics 14, 360, 488, 496, 602
Internet 14, 16
Kosovo 487-8, 495, 498, 506, 603
Macedonia 603
niqabs 669
oil crisis 225
Qur'an, production and distribution of 15, 462
Russia 517, 529, 540
Salafism 13-15, 37, 462-3, 789
segregation of women 497
Spain 315, 326

**Scandinavian countries** 391-419
arts, involvement in the 418
assimilation 398-401
Christianity and Christians 402
citizenship 392, 394
converts 391
culture and cultural heritage 391, 399-400, 412
demographics 391-2
discrimination and equal treatment 394, 417
employment 401, 417
essentialism 407
family law 413
gender relations/women 417, 418
history/historical perspective 392, 412
homosexuality 418
housing 417
identity 399, 406-7
immigration/migrants 391-412, 417-18
individuals and individualization 412-13, 418
institutions/organizations 406, 412, 417-19
integration 398-401, 419
international obligations 413-17

**Russia** *(Cont.)*
  Internet 418
  interpretation of Islam 412, 417–18
  Iraqis 393
  Islamophobia 413, 417, 746
  knowledge production 391
  language 393
  masculinity 418
  media 391, 393, 398–9, 413, 417
  moderates 417
  mosques 393, 406, 417–18
  multiculturalism 413
  Muslim Brotherhood 418
  Muslim, definition of 393–4
  nationality 402
  number of Muslims 392–8, 401–2
  Pakistanis 391, 393–8, 402, 406
  political participation/representation 394, 401, 417–19
  prayers 403, 417
  prisoners 410
  public opinion/perceptions 391–2, 400, 417
  public sphere/visibility 6, 406–11
  publications 396, 399, 413
  qualitative perspectives on individuals and groups 412–13
  race and ethnicity 392–3, 402, 407
  radicalization 417
  regions 393
  religious authorities 412
  religious identity 399, 406–7
  religiosity 418
  representative bodies 406, 417–19
  right-wing populist groups 417
  rituals, festivals and holidays 401, 411–12
  Salafis 393, 418
  security 417
  segregation 401, 417
  shariah law 412–13
  Shi'a Muslims 393
  socio-economic status 394, 401–6
  Somalians 394–5, 397–8, 402, 406
  South-East Asia 391
  stereotyping 413, 415, 418
  Sufis 393, 418
  Sunni Muslims 393
  terrorism and violence 394, 417
  traditionalists/conservatives 417
  transnationalism 418
  Turks 391
  unemployment 401
**scapegoating** 265, 550, 749
**scholars of the past** (*taqlid*) 659
**schools** *see* **education and schools**
**secularism/secularization** 2, 804–5
  education and schools 642
  Euro-Islam 803–5
  halal/religious slaughter 638
  immigration/migrants 756
  individuals and individualization 804
  institutions/organizations 620–1, 627
  Islamophobia 748–9, 756–64
  neutrality 6
  public space/visibility 805
  radicalism/radicalization 770
  relativization 804–5
  representative bodies 7
  shariah law 656, 658–63, 667, 676, 691, 693–6
**security/securitization**
  culture and cultural heritage 3
  hijab/headscarves 702, 717, 731
  immigration/migrants 3, 749, 756, 760–2
  institutions/organizations 625
  Islamophobia 748–9, 756–44
  radicalism/radicalization 637, 790
  September 11, 2001, terrorist attacks on United States 3
  shariah law 661, 676
**segregation/seclusion** 625, 635, 642, 702, 754–5
**Senegalese/Senegal**
  France 29
  Italy 268–9, 273, 284–5, 287–90
  Spain 315–16, 324, 328, 336–7
**separation of church and state** 6, 620, 622, 666
**September 11, 2001, terrorist attacks on United States**
  hijab/headscarves 704, 728
  institutions/organizations 622
  Islamophobia 9, 745, 748–9, 753, 759–61, 765

links between Western Muslims, radical
  Islam and terrorism  9
Qur'an by American pastor, burning of  754
radicalism/radicalization  770, 791
security/securitization  3
suspect Muslim communities  5
**Serbians/Serbia**
  Albania  475, 489–90
  Bosnia and Herzegovina  430–4, 437–8,
    442, 451, 465–7
  Chetniks (extremists)  434
  fundamentalism  503
  hijab/headscarves  603
  Islamophobia  496, 603
  Kosovo  489–90, 497, 502–3
  national identity  499
  nationalism  489–90
  Ottoman Empire  569
  religious authorities  485
  Salafism  603
**Shah Jahan Mosque, Woking (UK)**  68
**Shanghai Cooperation Organisation
  (SCO)**  518, 543, 545
shariah law  2, 656–96
  accommodation  684, 694–6
  application of Islamic legal rules  676–94
    external reasons given by the state  676,
      677–87
    internal reasons  676, 687–94
  application of Islamic religious
    rules  667–76
  arbitration  8
  children, protection of  678
  civil law  671–2, 677–86, 693–4, 695
  commercial disputes, ADR in  694
  constitutions, inclusion in  8
  construct to oppose Islam, as  7
  contract  8, 658, 677–8, 680–1, 683–7, 690
  corporal punishment  659, 663
  criminal law  7–8, 674
  cultural identity  8
  cultural reasons for application  676,
    687–95
  cultural sensitivity of judges and
    administrations  696
  decontextualization  7–8
  definition  656–60

democracy and democratic principles  663,
  668–9, 696
differentiation between religious and legal
  rules  665–7
dispositive substantive law  682–6, 695
diversity  8, 694
dower (*mahr* or *sadaq*)  684–5, 689
ECtHR, case law of  659–60
education and schools  662, 669–70
employment  671–2
enforcement, official system of  666, 687
equality of religion and beliefs  658–9, 663,
  667–8
European Convention on Human
  Rights  659–60, 666–7, 694
ex-Muslims  657–8
external reasons for application given by the
  state  676, 677–87
  dispositive substantive law  682–6, 695
  introduction of Islamic provisions into
    law  686–7
  private international law  677–82
family law  7–8, 658–9, 661–2, 676, 677,
  684–92, 694–5
*fatwas*  674
finance  682–3
fixed medieval set of laws, construct as  7
foreign donors and influence  665–6, 676–7,
  679–80, 682–3, 687–8
foreign law, recognition of  8
freedom of religion  658, 661, 664–8, 672,
  676, 678, 695
gender relations/women  658–9, 662–3,
  678–80, 692–3
hadith  658–9
hijab/headscarves  669–72, 694
human rights  7, 659, 667–8, 678
*ijtihad*  659
imams, Muftis and clerics, binding
  decisions from  693–4
individuals and individualization  668,
  676–7, 687
informal application  674–6
institutions/organizations  626–8, 632, 661,
  667–8, 676, 687–8, 695
internal reasons for application  676, 687–95
  cultural reasons  676, 688–90

**shariah law** *(Cont.)*
   religious reasons 676, 690–4
   technical/institutional reasons 676, 687–8, 695
   interpretation 658–9, 666, 694
   introduction of Islamic provisions into law 686–7
   investments 682–3
   Islamism 656, 669, 675
   Islamophobia 660, 664
   language 662
   legal situation 665–94
   male circumcision 672–4
   marriage and divorce 8, 190, 321, 359, 627, 678–80, 687–90, 692–3
   mosques, building/establishment of 664–5
   Muslim-majority countries 7
   mutual recognition 677, 679–81, 684, 687–9, 692, 695
   national identity 663
   neutrality 667–9
   not to believe, right 678
   optional civil law 682–6, 695
   overlapping jurisdictions 627
   penal law 672–4, 677, 691
   personal law 627, 691
   pluralism 8, 658–9, 665–6, 695
   polygamy 659, 680–2
   polygamy 687
   private international law 677–82, 695
   public law 667–71, 677
   public opinion/perceptions 657–65, 694
   public policy 684–5
   public space/visibility 7–8, 667
   Qur'an 658–9
   radicalism/radicalization 691, 695
   recognition 7–8, 626–7
   religious reasons for application 690–4
   repudiation, termination of marriage by 190, 321, 359, 678–80, 687–9, 692
   right-wing populist parties 656, 662–5
   rituals, festivals and holidays 658, 660–1, 671–4, 696
   Salafism 663–4, 675–6, 691, 695
   scholars of the past (*taqlid*) 659
   scope and limits of application 665–94
   secularism/secularization 656, 658–63, 667, 676, 691, 693–6
   security/securitization 661, 676
   state-religion relations 666–7
   Sunna 658
   *talaq* 190, 321, 359, 678–80, 687–9, 692
   technical/institutional reasons for application 676, 687–8, 695
   territoriality, principle of 665
   thought, conscience and religion, freedom of 666–7, 694
   traditionalists/conservatives 658–60, 663, 674–5, 678–9, 682–8, 691–3
   transnationalism 687
   youth 663–4
**Sharia4Belgium** 248, 656
**Sharia4Holland** 656
**Sharia4UK** 663
**Siddiqui Report** 78–9
**slaughter** *see* **halal/religious slaughter**
**social learning theory** 777, 780, 783
**social media** 10, 15
**social networks** 781, 784, 791
**social security** 680–1
**sociologically Muslims, individuals who are** 10
**sociology of religion** 3, 158, 267, 518, 527
**socio-economic status** 2, 11–12
   discrimination and equality 5
   identity building 11–12
   immigration/migrants 4–5
   institutions/organizations 631, 638
   'Islamic problem' 5
   Islamophobia 749, 753
   radicalism/radicalization 777, 788–9, 795–6
   underclass 5, 580, 787
**Somalians/Somalia**
   Italy 265, 268–70, 273, 284
   Netherlands 159, 170–1, 198
   Norway 397–8
   Scandinavia 394–5, 397–8, 402, 406
   refugees and asylum seekers 4, 70, 159
   United Kingdom 66–7, 70
*SOS Racisme* **(France)** 25, 30
**Soviet Union** 9, 363, 417, 517–29, 532–41, 545–8, 553, 556, 760
**Spain** 311–44 *see also* **Madrid bombings 2004**

# SUBJECT INDEX

Algeria 315–16, 330, 336, 341
Andalusia 313, 322–3, 325–7, 332, 339, 341
Aragon 322, 330–2
Association of Muslims in Spain (AME) 318
autonomous regions 322–31
Basque country 322, 328–9, 332
believing, behaving, and belonging 335–42
burials and cemeteries 327
Canary Islands 328, 332
Catalonia 322–8, 333
Catholics 312, 314, 317–18, 321, 330, 337, 340, 643, 723–4
census data 312
Ceuta and Melilla 313, 327, 332, 338
Christianity and Christians 334, 337, 340, 643
  Catholics 312, 314, 317–18, 321, 330, 337, 340, 643, 723–4
  Protestants 323, 328
clash of civilizations 311, 342
colonialism 340
comparative approach 334–5
Constitution 312, 318
converts 313–15, 318, 325, 329
cooperation agreements 318–19, 321, 323, 330–2
criminal cases, informal dispute resolution in 674
culture and cultural heritage 312, 322–3, 326, 328–9, 333, 341–2
democracy and democratic principles 338
demographics 312, 343
demonstrations and protests 325
discrimination and equality 327–9, 331–2, 336, 341–3, 720, 727
diversity 312, 322–31
education and schools 312–13, 323–4, 330–3
  gender relations/women 328–9, 331–2
  higher education 313, 326, 329
  hijab/headscarves 331–3, 342, 710
  public schools 6, 330–2
  religious education 321, 329–33, 335, 650
employment 315–17, 327–8, 336, 755
essentialism 341
family law 321
family reunification 322, 330

freedom of expression 342
freedom of religion 317, 318, 342
gender relations/women 327–9, 331–2, 341–3, 720, 727
generational differences 314–15, 329, 336
halal/religious slaughter 321, 650
health and healthcare 336
hijab/headscarves 331–3, 705, 709, 710, 723, 730
  Catalonia 333
  Catholicism 723–4
  education and schools 331–3, 342, 710
  full-face coverings 333, 720
  Islamophobia 710
  Madrid bombings 710
  Muslim rule 710
  patriarchy 727
  public opinion/perceptions 710, 720
  radicalism/radicalization 720
  shariah law 669
historical perspective 311–12, 317, 322, 326, 339–44
homosexuality 335
housing 336
human rights 338
identity 313, 335, 338
imams, Muftis and clerics 321, 324, 327, 338
immigration/migrants 311–17, 322–44
indigenous Islam 312
individuals and individualization 318
institutions/organizations 6, 312–14, 318–30, 333–6, 342–3, 634
integration 322–4, 338, 341
Internet 343
Islamic centres 324–5
Islamic Commission of Spain (CIE) 318–21, 331–2
Islamic Council of Spain 319
Islamophobia 312, 339–42, 710, 749–51, 755
Jews/Judaism 323, 334, 340
jihadis 343
Junta Islámica 326
language 312, 329, 332–3
legal framework 312, 317–18, 344
loyalty to country 338
Madrid 319, 322, 325, 327, 329–30, 335
marriage and divorce 318, 321–2, 681

**Spain** *(Cont.)*
  Moro, use of term 340–1
  Moroccans 313, 315, 322, 324, 326–31, 335–43
  mosques 321–9, 336, 338
    Andalusia 325–7
    buildings/establishment 324–5, 639, 650
    Catalonia 324–5
    gender relations/women 327
    Madrid 329
  Muslim rule 339–40, 710
  new Islam (recent immigrants) 2, 4
  niqabs 333
  North Africans 313, 322, 325–31, 335
  number of Muslims 312, 328, 330
  Observatorio Andalusí 313–15, 332
  Pakistanis 313, 315–16, 324, 326, 336
  pluralism 311–12, 317–23, 328, 330–1
  political participation/representation 312, 338–9
  polygamy 681
  prayers 317, 323–4, 335
  prisoners 321, 327, 343
  private international law 321–2
  Protestants 323, 328
  public opinion/perceptions 312, 334–5, 339–42, 710, 720
  public space/visibility 317–31, 335
  publications 311, 314, 327, 334
  race and ethnicity 341–2
  radicalization 334–5, 342–3, 720
  Ramadan 339
  recognition 313, 317–19, 323, 331–3, 650
  regions 312, 314, 322–31, 344
  religious authorities 6, 315, 338
  religious education 321, 329–33, 335, 650
  religious identity 335, 338
  religiosity 313, 317–18, 333–42
  representative bodies 6, 313–14, 318–30, 333, 335–6, 342–3, 650
  riots 327
  rituals, festivals and holidays 321, 332, 335, 338–9, 650
  Saudi Arabia 315, 326
  scholarship 314–15, 322
  secularism/secularization 317, 335
  segregation 328, 335, 341
  Senegalese 315–16, 324, 328, 336–7
  September 11, 2001, terrorist attacks on United States 342–4
  shariah law 321, 669, 681
  socio-economic status 312–17
  Spanish Federation of Islamic Religious Entities (FEERI) 318–21
  state-religion relations 335, 338
  stereotyping 341–2
  Sufism 323, 324–5
  theology 324
  transnationalism 312, 324, 327–8, 339, 344
  unemployment 315, 336
  Union of Islamic Communities in Spain (UCIDE) 318–21
  Valencia 313, 319, 322–3, 327, 330
  war on terror 344
  youth 329, 339
**Srebrenica massacre** 466
**Srpska, Republic of** 437, 442, 447, 466–8
**Stasi Commission** 32, 713–14
**state-religion relations** 624, 626, 632, 635, 638, 643, 666–7, 729
**stereotyping** 708, 754, 765, 780
**stigma** 34, 46, 83, 274, 357, 748–9, 756, 759–63, 777, 786
**stoning** 7, 691
**succession and wills** 683
**Sufism** 13, 324–5, 328 n.5, 356, 480–2, 485, 490, 499–501, 574–5, 590, 592, 603
**suicide attacks** 248–9, 411, 416, 531, 546 n.72, 547, 772, 777, 794
**Sülemanci movement** 125
**Suleymanists** 418, 580
**Sunna** 13–14, 319, 331, 658
**Sunni Muslims** 14, 641
**Surinamese** 159–60, 162, 165, 168–9, 172, 179–80
**Sweden**
  age 396
  Christian Council of Sweden 401
  Christian Social Democrats (Brotherhood Movement) 409
  Christianity and Christians 392, 401, 409
  citizenship 395–7, 409
  converts 710–11
  crime 400
  culture and cultural heritage 411, 711

Danish Cartoon controversy 416
democracy and democratic principles 409
demographics 396
diaconal work 410
discrimination and equality 405, 413
diversity 711
education and schools
  hijab/headscarves 710–11, 719
  public schools 711, 719
  religious 410–11, 650
employment 401, 405, 410, 414–15
entrepreneurs 410
Eurabia thesis 415
freedom of religion 711
gender relations/women 409–20, 415, 705, 709, 710–11, 719, 727
halal/religious slaughter 410, 650
hate crimes 750
health and healthcare 409–10
hijab/headscarves 410, 705, 709, 710–11, 719, 727
historical perspective 392, 395
honour killings 411
housing 401, 405, 414–15
immigration/migrants 395–7, 400–1, 711
institutions/organizations 396–7, 409–10, 634
international constraints 414–16
Internet 410, 416
Iranians 397
Iraqis 397, 405
Islamic Centre 396–7
Islamism 410–11
Islamophobia 413–15, 711, 750
male circumcision 673
Malmö 400–1
media 410–11, 415, 711
moderates 410
mosques, building/establishment of 393, 396–7, 410–11, 639, 650
multiculturalism 410
number of Muslims 395–7
patriarchy 727
pluralism 724
police registers 392
political participation/representation 400–1, 409–11, 415, 662

popular culture 411
private issue, religion as a 411
public opinion/perceptions 400, 410–11, 413, 415, 710–11, 719
public space/visibility 409–11
publications 396
race and ethnicity 397, 403
radicalism/radicalization 410–11, 414–16
recognition 650
registration 392–3
religiosity 392, 403, 711
religious education 410–11, 650
representative bodies 650
residence patterns 401
resident permits 396
right-wing populist parties 400, 410, 415, 662
rituals, festivals and holidays 321, 332, 335, 411
security/securitization 410–11, 415–16
segregation 405
shariah law 662
Social Democrats for Faith and Democracy 409
socio-economic status 405
SST (Commission for State Grants to Religious Communities) 396, 409
Stockholm 405
suicide bombers 416
Swedish Democrats (SD) 400
Tatars 395
terrorism 410–11, 415–16
Turks 392
unemployment 405
Union of Islamic Congregations in Sweden (FIFS) 409
violence 400
youth 396, 401, 403, 410–11, 415
**Switzerland**
cantons 711
citizenship 711
education and schools 711–12, 641
European Convention on Human Rights 712
freedom of religion 712
gender relations/women 719
hate speech 754

Sweden *(Cont.)*
  hijab/headscarves 669, 705, 709, 711–12, 719, 723, 728–30
  Islamophobia 753, 754–5
  male circumcision 674
  media 711
  mosques/minarets, building/establishment of 39, 625, 664
    hate speech 754
    Islamophobia 753, 754–5
    no campaign poster 726–7, 728–9
    referendum 754
    shariah law 668–9, 694
  neutrality 712
  official religions 711
  public opinion/perceptions 719, 754
  religious education 641
  right-wing populist parties 656, 662, 664, 668
  secularism/secularization 711
  security/securitization 729
  separation of state and religion 666, 711
  shariah law 656, 662, 664, 668–9
  Swiss People's Party 656, 664, 668
  xenophobia and racism 729
**symbols** 7, 803–5 *see also* **hijab/headscarves**
  boundaries 803–4
  institutionalization of Islam 627, 637, 639
  shariah law 665–6, 668, 680
**Syria, conflict in** 509, 547, 584, 773–4

**Tablighi movement** 293, 393, 540, 555
  fundamentalism 793
  gateway organization, as 793
  globalization 37
  jihadis 794
  Muslim Brotherhood 13
  Pakistan 794
  pre-radicalization 793
  proselytising 15 n. 30, 326 n.4, 377–8
  radicalism/radicalization 48, 88, 786, 793
  religious education 794
  Russia 555
  Salafism 13
  terrorism and violence 297
  transnational networks 127, 326–7, 339, 418
**Tajikstan** 525–6, 535, 543, 555

**takfiri Islamism** 541, 603
*talaq* 190, 321, 359, 678–80, 687–9, 692
*tariqas* 324–5, 328 n.5, 443
**Tatars/Tatarstan**
  radicalism/radicalization 772, 789
  Russia 520, 524, 526, 528–32, 536–42, 549, 551–2, 555
  Sweden 395
**territoriality, principle of** 665
**terrorism and violence** *see also* London bombings 2005; Madrid bombings 2004;
**September 11, 2001, terrorist attacks on United States**
  Danish Cartoon controversy 754
  deradicalization 795, 796
  Euro-Islam 804
  fundamentalism 726, 728–9
  hijab/headscarves 704, 726, 728–9, 731
  institutions/organizations 631, 773
  IRA 770, 782
  Islamophobia 728, 751–4, 756, 759
  jihadis 48, 89, 297–8, 343, 773, 789–91
  legitimatizing role of religion 793
  lone-wolves 781
  multiculturalism 761 n. 20
  Oslo and Utøya atrocities of 22 July 2011 141, 413, 761 n.20, 765
  public opinion/perceptions 10
  radicalism/radicalization 5, 9, 770–91, 794–6
  stereotyping 754
  suicide bombers 248–9, 411, 416, 531, 546 n.72, 547, 772, 777, 794
  war on terror 5, 222, 468, 477, 508, 804
**thought, conscience and religion, freedom of** 666–7, 694
**Thrace, Muslim minority of** 350–61, 381–2
  burials and cemeteries 376
  Citizenship Code 366 n. 13
  demographic description 354–7
  discrimination and equal treatment 352, 357–8
  education 360–1, 372
  employment 355–7, 369
  ethnic composition 354–7
  family law 686

gender relations/women 359
government policy 357–9, 369
imams, Muftis and clerics 357, 359–60, 376
judicial system 358, 359
language 352–8, 360
legal status 357–9
marriage and divorce 372
migration to urban areas 355–6, 368–9
mosques 359–60, 373
Muftis 357, 359–60, 376
  courts 359
  election versus appointment 359–60
  pseudo Muftis 360
  recognition 357, 360
nationality, loss of 358
new immigrants 366
political participation/representation 358
Pomaks 355–6, 357, 360–1
recognition 357, 360
religiosity 354–5, 357
Roma (gypsies/Athiganoi) 355–7
Sunni Muslims 356
Turks 350–61, 686

**traditionalists/conservatives** *see also* **right-wing populist parties; Salafism**
hijab/headscarves 702–3, 707, 710, 716, 727–8, 803
institutions/organizations 623–4, 632
Islamophobia 746, 755
literalism 13–14, 37, 483, 553
moralization, trend towards 9
orthodoxy, redefinition of 10, 16
radicalism/radicalization 772, 774–5, 785–7, 789
religiosity, rise in 9
shariah law 658–60, 663, 674–5, 678–9, 682–8, 691–3
social conservatism, rise in 9

**transnationalism and transnational networks** *see also* **foreign donors and influence**
Council of Europe 624
European Convention on Human Rights 624
identity 10, 12
institutions/organizations 7, 12, 624, 629, 631–2

'intolerable subjects' 5
Islamophobia 757
orthodoxy, redefinition of 10, 12, 16
Salafism 12
shariah law 687

**Tunisians/Tunisia**
France 26
Italy 268–9, 271–3, 284, 289–90
Norway 392
polygamy 659
recognition of foreign decisions 688
shariah law 659, 688

**Turks/Turkey**
Albania 478, 480, 482, 495
Austria 661–2
Belgium 224–5, 230–1, 233–4, 238, 242–4
Bosnia and Herzegovina 464–5, 604
Bulgaria 569, 573, 574–82, 587–99, 602–5
Cyprus 358
diaspora 127
discrimination and equality 122
dower 684–5
education and schools 137, 577, 627, 637
employment 120, 128, 576
European Convention on Human Rights 659–60, 694
France 26–7, 625
gender relations/women 121, 627, 687, 715–16
Germany 110–17, 120–8, 142–3, 715–16
  dower 684–5
  education and schools 137, 637
  gender relations/women 687
  hijab/headscarves 121, 715–16
  institutionalization of Islam 125–6, 625
  Islamophobia 142
  political participation and representation 135–7
  religiosity 108, 114
  shariah law 687
Greece 351–61, 366, 369–70, 381
  Greco-Turkish War 352
  Kemalists 354, 356, 358
  population exchange 352–4
  Thrace, Muftis in 360
  Turkification 358, 360
Gülen movement 482

**Turks/Turkey** *(Cont.)*
  hijab/headscarves 121, 627, 715–16
  identity 597
  imams, Muftis and clerics 360
  institutionalization of Islam 125–6, 625
  Islamophobia 142
  Kemalists 354, 356, 358
  Kosovo 604
  Kurds 161, 362, 366
  Macedonia 604
  military service 175, 352
  mosques 123
  Netherlands 159–65, 168–72, 175, 179–81, 184, 191, 197–8, 200, 202–3
  neutrality 627
  political participation and representation 135–7
  Pomaks 577–8
  religiosity 108, 114
  Scandinavia 391–2
  secularism/secularization 356, 686
  shariah law 687
  Sweden 392
  Thrace, Muslim minority of 350–61, 686
  Turkish Refah Partisi 659–60, 694
**underclass** 5, 580, 787
**United Kingdom** 63–93 *see also* **London bombings 2005**
  8th century to 1945 65–8
  1945 to present day 68–70, 80–1, 89–90
  age 71
  assimilation 81
  asylum seekers 70, 74
  Bangladeshi settlers 70, 72
  banking and finance 73
  believing, behaving, and belonging 68, 74–5, 87–92
  Birmingham Central Mosque, shariah council of 85
  British Muslim Arbitration Tribunals (MAT) 691–4
  British Muslim Studies 73, 93
  buildings 68
  burials and cemeteries 74, 75–6
  burquas 718–20
  Cardiff
    mosque in 1860, establishment of 68
  Yemeni and Somali seafaring communities 66–7
  Catholics 626
  census data 63, 70–4, 81
  Centre for Research in Ethnic Relations (CRER) 73–5, 77, 79
  Centre for Research on Islam and Christian-Muslim Relations (CSIC) 76–7, 79
  chaplains, 78, 82
  charities 92
  children, special guardianship of 686–7
  Christianity and Christians 66, 76, 85, 626
  cities, settlements in particular 63–4, 66–8
  citizenship test 757
  colleges 63
  communal networking 74
  community cohesion 82
  Community Religions Project (CRP) 74–5, 77
  comparative approach 66
  culture and cultural heritage 73–4, 689
  demobilized servicemen, settlement of 68
  demographic change 70–3
  diaspora 79, 89
  discrimination and racism 72–4, 81–5
    employment 84–5
    Equality Act 2010 85
    hijab/headscarves 708–9
    Islamophobia 9, 83–4, 707, 708–9, 745–6, 749–52, 758, 763
    xenophobia and racism 72–4
  diversity 70, 75, 87–92, 750
  dower 684–5, 689
  dress in workplace 84
  economic activity 71–3
  economic migration 69–70
  education and schools 71, 73–4, 76, 86, 90–2
    funding 81–2
    hijab/headscarves 91, 666, 707–9, 725–6
    Islamic Studies in Britain 76, 78–90
    public schools 642, 707–8, 724
    religious education 74, 78, 81–2, 84, 87, 90–1, 633, 642–3, 651
    seminaries 79
    universities 78–9

employment 71–3, 84–5, 671–2, 755
entrepreneurship, wealth-creation and achievement 73
Equality Act 2010 85
Equality and Human Rights Commission (EHRC) 85
European Convention on Human Rights 666, 708
family law 85, 684–5, 689, 692, 694
far-right extremism 84
fasting 92
fatwas 91, 226
foreign donors and influence 79–80, 626
framing 81
freedom of religion 707–8
funding 73–4, 81–2
gender relations/women 69–71, 76, 82, 86, 91–2, 662, 692–3
generational differences 69, 88–9
government policy 66, 71, 74, 76–7, 80–7, 92
halal/religious slaughter 73, 76, 91 651
health and healthcare 71–2
hijab/headscarves 705, 707–9, 720–1
  ban, debate on 708, 718
  burquas and niqabs 718–20, 725
  discrimination 708–9
  education and schools 91, 666, 707–9
  European Convention on Human Rights 708
  full-face coverings 708, 717–20, 725
  freedom of religion 707–8
  institutions/organizations 725–6
  Islamophobia 707, 708–9
  London bombings 709
  media 707
  multiculturalism 707, 718
  pluralism 724
  public opinion/perceptions 708, 718
  right-wing populist parties 718
  September 11, 2001, terrorist attacks on United States 709
  thought, conscience and religion, freedom of 708
historical perspective 65–73, 80–1, 626
housing 71–2, 86
identity 73–4, 78, 81–2, 84, 87–8, 93
*ijtihad* (interpretive effort) 78

imams, Muftis and clerics 75, 79–80, 92
immigration and settlement 64, 65–75, 82, 86
individuals and individualization 78, 83–4
institutions/organizations 82, 86–92, 624–6, 725–6
integration 64, 87–92
inter-disciplinary perspectives 73–80
Internet 76–8, 91
IRA 770, 782
Islamic centres 74
Islamic Studies in Britain 76, 78–80
Islamisation of space 90
Islamophobia 9, 83–4, 707, 708–9, 745–6, 749–52, 758, 763
Jewish courts 85
Jews/Judaism 84–5
jihadis 773–4, 776
language 71
leadership 76, 79–81
life-cycle rites 74, 75–6
literary works 66
Londistan 774
margin of appreciation 666
marriage and divorce
  dissolution of religious marriages 686
  gender relations/women 692–3
  polygamy 680–1
  register marriages, places entitled to 686
  shariah law 689, 692–3
  *talaq* 689, 692–3
media 67, 83, 85, 707
mobilization 82–3
mortgages 683
mosques
  building/establishing 68–9, 75–6, 87, 90, 639, 651
  leadership 81
  networking 74–5
  religious education 78, 90–1
  Yemeni and Somali seafaring communities 66–7
multiculturalism 64, 74, 81–2, 93, 266, 707, 718, 761 n.20
Muslim Council of Britain (MCB) 81–2
myth of return 69, 70, 81, 89–90
networking and community 74–6, 81–2

**United Kingdom** *(Cont.)*
  newer migrants 70, 82
  niqabs 718–20, 725
  number of Muslims 70
  official religion, in 6
  Pakistanis 68–70, 72, 74, 76, 81, 86, 99, 702, 707, 773–4
  pluralism 85, 724
  policing 83
  political participation and representation 72, 81–7, 638, 718
  polygamy 680–1
  postcolonialism 2, 3
  poverty and deprivation 72–3
  prayers 90, 92
  'Prevent' projects 87
  Preventing Violent Extremism (PVE) agenda 83
  prisoners 90
  private space of homes 76
  professionalization of welfare and pastoral services Muslim communities 77–8
  protest and lobbying 81–2
  public opinion/perception 83–4, 708, 718
  public space/visibility 6, 84, 90
  publications 70, 80, 84, 87, 92
  Qur'an, recitation of 78
  race and ethnicity 69–75, 81–2
  radicalism/radicalization 80, 83, 93, 784
  Ramadan 92
  recognition 651
  reform movements 87–8
  religious education 74, 78, 81–2, 84, 87, 90–1, 633, 642–3, 651
  religious identity 73–4, 81–2, 84
  representative bodies 81–2, 86, 651
  research 63–80, 83, 86–7, 91–3
  residence patterns 66–8, 71–3, 76, 85–6
  return 69, 70, 74–5, 81, 89–90
  right-wing populist parties 718
  riots/urban disturbances 72, 761 n.20
  rituals, festivals and holidays 75, 84, 92
  Runnymede Trust 84, 709, 745–6
  Rushdie affair 10, 47, 81–2, 84, 226, 786
  Salafis 89
  scholarship 66, 75, 77, 79, 91, 93
  schools of thought 88, 91, 93
  seafaring communities 66–7, 69
  segregation 67, 72–4, 82
  seminaries 79
  September 11, 2001, terrorist attacks on United States 77, 84, 86, 709
  shariah councils 85, 91, 689, 691–3
  shariah law 78, 84–5, 91, 627, 660, 680–1, 689, 691–4, 695–6
  Shi'a Muslims 93
  social cohesion 82, 87, 643
  social media 66
  social policy 64, 80–7
  social welfare 86
  socio-economic status 71–2, 81
  Somalians 66–7, 70
  South Asia, settlers from 68–76, 81, 88, 92
  state-church relations 625
  stereotyping 84
  Sufis 68, 75
  symbols 666
  *talaq* 692–3
  terrorism 83–4, 93, 770, 782
  thought, conscience and religion, freedom of 708
  traditionalists/conservatives 78, 91
  transnationalism 68, 75, 93
  UKIP 718
  universities 78–9
  xenophobia and racism 72–4
  Yemeni and Somali seafarer communities 66–7
  youth 64, 71, 79–80, 82, 89, 93

**United Nations (UN)** 748
**United States** *see also* **September 11, 2001, terrorist attacks on United States**
  Al-Qaeda 759
  anthrax attacks 759
  Cold War 358, 477, 519, 521, 760
  foreign policy 753, 759–60
  Grenada, invasion of 759–60
  Gulf War 1991 135, 334, 704, 786
  immigration/migrants 5 n. 3
  Iraq, invasion of 84, 334, 709, 759, 773–4, 779, 785–7
  Islamophobia 749–50, 753, 756, 758–60, 762
  Kosovo 494

Libya, bombing of 225, 247–50, 760
Nicaragua, Contra's war in 760
radicalism/radicalization 784
Salafism 14
Soviet Union aggression 760
terrorism and violence 759–60
university chairs, financing of 14
**universities, radicalization in** 792
UOIF (*Union des organizations islamiques de France*) 35–6, 41

violence *see* terrorism and violence
virtual communities 789–91
visibility *see* public space/visibility
Vlaams Bloks 226–7, 251

Wahhabism *see* Salafism/Wahhabism
Al Waqf al Islami 579
war on terror 5, 222, 468, 477, 508, 804
Waziristan 773
Western superiority, idea of 753, 757, 759–65
women and girls *see* gender relations/women; hijab/headscarves
World Muslim League (WML) 225

xenophobia and racism
   anti-Semitism 127, 201, 747 n.3, 750
   European Union 748 n. 5
   hijab/headscarves 706, 717, 728–9

radicalism/radicalization 782, 787

*Yearbook of Muslims in Europe* 589, 593, 634
**Yugoslavia**
   Albania 477–9, 484–6, 490, 498–9, 501, 509–10
   Bosnia and Herzegovina
      as part of 429, 434, 437, 440, 444, 446, 465
      dissolution 429–30, 435, 436, 464, 465–8
      liberalization 453
   dissolution
      Albania 486, 498–9, 510
      Bosnia and Herzegovina 429–30, 435, 436, 464, 465–8
   diversity 484–6
   identity 490
   International Criminal Tribunal for the former Yugoslavia (ICTY) 465 n. 135, 466–7
   inter-war period, experience during 478
   Islamophobia 496
   Jews/Judaism 434
   liberalization 453, 476
   persecution 478–9
   public space/visibility 498
   restitution of religious property 501
   Salafism 663–4
   security 477
   socialism, experience under 478